SOCIOLOGY

Concepts and Applications in a Diverse World

FOURTH EDITION

Thomas J. Sullivan
NORTHERN MICHIGAN UNIVERSITY

ALLYN AND BACON

Boston ■ London ■ Toronto ■ Sydney ■ Tokyo ■ Singapore

Editor-in-Chief, Social Sciences: Karen Hanson
Marketing Manager: Karon Bowers
Composition and Prepress Buyer: Linda Cox
Manufacturing Buyer: Megan Cochran
Cover Administrator: Linda Knowles
Text Design: Melinda Grosser for *silk*
Photo Researcher: Laurie Frankenthaler
Production Administrator: Deborah Brown
Editorial-Production Service: P. M. Gordon Associates

Library of Congress Cataloging-in-Publication Data
Sullivan, Thomas J., 1944–
    Sociology : concepts and applications in a diverse world / Thomas
J. Sullivan. — 4th ed.
        p.   cm.
    Includes bibliographical references and index.
    ISBN 0-205-26488-3
    1. Sociology.   I. Title.
HM51.S948   1997
 301—dc21   97-3622
                                                  CIP

Photo credits appear on page 605, which constitutes a continuation of the copyright page.

Printed in the United States of America

10   9   8   7   6   5   4   3   2   1   01   00   99   98   97

FOR NANCY

Brief Contents

Contents

CHAPTER THREE

Socialization 74

CHAPTER FOUR

Groups and Organizations 106

CHAPTER SEVEN

Social Inequality: Race and Ethnicity   216

CHAPTER EIGHT

Social Inequality: Gender   252

CHAPTER ELEVEN

Religion   368

CHAPTER TWELVE

Education and the Mass Media   402

CHAPTER THIRTEEN

Political and Economic Institutions 438

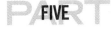

PART FIVE — *Human Ecology and Social Change* 475

CHAPTER FOURTEEN

Human Ecology: Population and Community 476

CHAPTER FIFTEEN

Collective Behavior, Social Change, and Modernization   514

Featured Inserts

 OTHER WORLDS,
Other Ways

APPLYING SOCIOLOGY

Sociology and the Mass Media

Preface

As the twentieth century draws to a close, the world has been changing in dramatic ways. The Soviet Union has collapsed, the Berlin Wall has fallen, and Germany has been reunited. Communications satellites and computer technology have produced some wondrous advances, such as the Internet, that hold the potential for uniting peoples around the globe. At the same time, ethnic antagonisms rage with tragic consequences in places like Bosnia and Herzegovina, Rwanda, and Burundi. The racial and ethnic diversity of the U.S. population means that such events might occur here if social conditions change. The nations of the world exhibit growing levels of interdependence; well-paying manufacturing jobs in the United States disappear as employers seek cheaper labor in Mexico, Korea, and other Third-World nations. The scourge of cocaine, heroin, alcohol, and other drugs continues to increase health and crime problems in the United States. Greater gender equality has been achieved in the United States and some other nations than could have been imagined one hundred years ago; yet further progress on this front seems to be stalled, and women in many nations still struggle against highly inequitable social institutions.

Sociology emerged as a field of study in the nineteenth century because people found that the sociological perspective provided useful insight into the problems societies faced as they industrialized. Against the backdrop of late-twentieth-century progress and problems alluded to in the preceding paragraph, the discipline of sociology has continued to develop and make contributions to society. Most importantly, sociology has continued to expand our understanding of how societies work and how human behavior is shaped by cultural, structural, and institutional forces. This understanding is especially important today because of the persistence of beliefs among many people that human behavior can be understood on purely individualistic and voluntaristic grounds—that people's personal characteristics, qualities, and motivations determine their actions and that their behavior is a consequence of their own free choices. This individualistic approach can be misleading because it ignores the power of social and cultural structures in shaping people's behavior.

Another important development in sociology in the late twentieth century has been the reemergence of an interest in applying sociological knowledge to make positive changes in social institutions, social structures, and people's everyday lives. This application goes beyond the goal of understanding how societies operate or what determines human behavior. Using the well-developed foundation of basic sociological theory and research, many contemporary sociologists focus their work on suggesting and evaluating solutions to social problems or helping people to improve their lives. Today, sociological work is as likely to culminate in recommendations for changes in social policy or suggestions for restructuring people's personal lives as it is to stop with an understanding of why people do what they do. In fact, I believe that these efforts to apply sociology have been as exciting, innovative, and important as the more basic research that is still being done by many sociologists.

This fourth edition of *Sociology: Concepts and Applications in a Diverse World* has been prepared to reflect these changes in both the world at large and the discipline of sociology. It retains the features from earlier editions, and adds some significant new features that assist in achieving that goal. This edition provides a solid introduction to the discipline of sociology while developing these themes: the excitement and contribution of *applied sociology*, the value of taking a *global perspective* that recognizes the interdependence of all cultures and societies, the growing importance of *diversity and difference* in the United States and the world, and the central role that *modern technologies of communication and the mass media* have in shaping society and people's daily lives.

New Features in the Fourth Edition

In order to develop these themes, address the changes that are occurring in the world, and assist the student in gaining sociological insight into today's world, I have added three significant new features to the fourth edition.

1. **Mass Media and Modern Communications Technology** In the high-tech, global environment of the twenty-first century, the mass media and modern communications technologies will become far more pervasive and important than many people imagined thirty or fifty years ago. They influence values, norms, and behavior as well as help to shape social institutions and contribute to patterns of dominance and inequality. Whereas earlier editions of this book addressed issues of the mass media, a significant amount of new material, including some discussions of the Internet (for example, Chapters 4 and 12), has been added to the fourth edition, and some of the earlier material has been expanded and highlighted. Twelve of the fifteen chapters now have a special section devoted to the sociological analysis of the mass media and modern communications technologies; one-quarter of Chapter 12 is devoted to discussing the media as a social institution. The titles of these sections are listed, by chapter, on pp. xvi–xvii, and this special icon (M) is used to highlight the media discussion in each chapter.

2. **Sociology on the Internet** Extending the focus of the fourth edition on modern communications technologies, an Appendix has been added to this edition that teaches the student to explore sociological issues on the Internet. It begins with a brief introduction to the Internet and then offers exercises for finding sociological materials related to every chapter in the book. The exercises are designed to encourage the students to gain insight into the sociological significance of what they find on the Internet and to use it as a vehicle for deepening their understanding of the sociological imagination. The results that students obtain from these exercises could be used by the student as a part of a term paper project or by the instructor as a focus for classroom discussions.

3. **Study and Review** At the end of each chapter, a new *Study and Review* section has been added to give students an opportunity to test how well they have grasped the material in the chapter. Each section contains a list of key terms, multiple-choice questions, true-false questions, fill-in questions, matching questions, and essay questions. Correct answers are also provided. These various testing formats offer an assess-

ment of the different kinds of information found in each chapter and will assist students in organizing their study. Students will thereby have a good measure of how much they have learned and a comprehensive review of the content in the chapter, as well as help in preparing for exams.

Continuing Features

A number of features from the third edition were effective in developing the themes of this book and assisting students in exploring the world as sociologists. These features have been retained:

1. **Theoretical Perspectives** The presentation of the discipline of sociology continues to be organized around the three core theoretical perspectives: functionalism, conflict theory, and interactionism. These perspectives, which serve as a foundation on which to build a framework of understanding of the sociological approach, are introduced in the first chapter and then used throughout the book. This approach provides students with a sound understanding of the perspectives by the end of the semester, and the perspectives can then be used to analyze any sociological issue.

2. **Applied Sociology** Throughout the book, sociology is applied to the understanding, evaluation, and solution of problems in the United States and the world. In addition, each chapter contains at least one boxed section titled *Applying Sociology* that addresses issues of applied research, social policy development, clinical sociology, and personal applications of sociological principles in the student's life and work. This feature addresses the discipline's growing focus on applied sociology and shows how sociological theory and research can guide the search for solutions to societal and personal problems. In addition, Chapter 1 includes a major section describing the field of applied sociology. The titles of the Applying Sociology inserts are listed, by chapter, on p. xvi.

3. **Globalization, Cross-Culturalism, and Diversity** An important theme running through this book is globalization: the trend toward increasing interdependence among the nations and peoples

of the world. Nations can no longer be studied as independent entities because the political, economic, and social forces that shape people's lives now operate on a worldwide level. This makes a global perspective essential to preparing students to live and work in the modern world. A part of this global view is a *cross-cultural perspective* that helps students to understand the social and cultural nature of human societies and to see how cultures and peoples are similar to and different from one another. In addition, an emphasis on *diversity* is important because diversities of race, ethnicity, gender, or cultural heritage are often at the core of discrimination, differential opportunities, and social conflict. Issues of globalization, cross-culturalism, and diversity are addressed in this book in four ways:

A. The book begins with an extensive discussion of the importance of diversity, a global perspective, and the sociological imagination in Chapter 1.

B. Practically every chapter has a section that explores a global perspective on the topic of that chapter. This assists the student in exploring issues of, say, gender inequality or changes in family structure not only in the United States but also in societies around the world.

C. Boxed sections called *Other Worlds, Other Ways* illustrate sociological concepts and issues in the context of societies and cultures around the world. Two such sections are included in each chapter; their titles are listed, by chapter, on pp. xv–xvi.

D. Each chapter opens with an in-depth discussion of the issues in that chapter as they apply to a culture different from the contemporary, mainstream culture of the United States.

All these features discuss cultures and nations from all parts of the world, although they take a repeated look at some nations that are especially important to the United States or the world, such as China, Mexico, and Japan. In addition to these specific features, issues of globalization, cross-culturalism, and diversity are incorporated throughout the book.

4. **Myth–Fact Feature**   This feature encourages students to recognize that social reality is complex and that our commonsense knowledge of the world can be either wrong or so overly simplified that it seriously distorts our understanding of the social world. This feature encourages students to distinguish beliefs that have no scientific foundation from sociological facts that have been substantiated through systematic research. It highlights the central role of research in understanding social issues. This feature is introduced in Chapter 1 in the first *Applying Sociology* section; thereafter, it appears as a boxed section at the beginning of each chapter.

5. **Further Readings**   Each chapter concludes with a short list of books relevant to topics in that chapter. These books should be available in college or community libraries or bookstores. They include books that further the themes of cross-culturalism, diversity, and applied sociology that are central to this textbook. Students whose imaginations have been stimulated by this introduction to sociology can continue to sharpen their sociological eye by looking at some of these suggested readings.

6. **Thorough Updates**   This fourth edition has been thoroughly updated with new theories, research, and data where appropriate. To assist the instructor in making the transition to the new edition, I have listed the significant changes in each chapter in the Instructor's Manual that accompanies this book.

7. **Pedagogical Aids**   A number of elements are designed into the text to assist the student in learning the material. The *Study and Review* section and the *Summary* at the end of each chapter give the student the opportunity to review the material in a variety of different ways. A *Learning Objective* has been placed, in color, below every major heading in the text; this cues students to the broad points to learn and remember as they read each section.

8. **Ancillaries**   To assist the instructor, I have prepared an *Instructor's Manual and Test Bank* for use with this textbook. It includes a large test bank of essay questions, multiple-choice questions, and true/false questions. It also contains, for each chapter, suggestions for teaching and discussion, a list of films to be used, and a list of the changes in the fourth edition. A *Computerized Test Bank* is also available.

A variety of video options are available with this textbook; please contact your local Allyn and Bacon representative for more information. And finally, be sure and check out the Allyn and Bacon website at http://www.abacon.com for a variety of resources related to this text.

Organization

The sequence of chapters remains the same in the fourth edition. The chapters are grouped according to sociological themes. Consequently, the book is organized into five parts: Part One has one chapter that introduces the student to the *sociological perspective,* including a discussion of theoretical perspectives and research methods. Part Two contains four chapters that focus on the major links between *the individual and society,* including culture, social structure, socialization, groups and organizations, and deviance and social control. Part Three consists of three chapters whose focus is *social stratification and social inequality,* including analyses of class, race, ethnicity, and gender. Part Four includes five chapters that cover the major *social institutions:* the family, health care, religion, education, politics and the economy. Part Five contains two chapters whose theme is *human ecology and social change,* including population issues, urbanization, collective behavior, social change, and modernization.

Acknowledgments

Many people have contributed to the completion of this new edition. At Allyn and Bacon Publishing Company, Karen Hanson coaxed the project with tenacity and insight, and the book has benefited immensely from her support. I am especially thankful for the research assistance that I received from some special students at Northern Michigan University over the years: Susan Phillips, Suzie Touchton, Erica Shorkey, and Jason Maki. I also received some excellent advice and assistance from a number of colleagues at one point or another in the development of this book: Lynda

Ann Ewen, West Virginia Institute of Technology; Tonya Hilligoss, Sacramento City College, Sacramento, California; Roger W. Little, University of Illinois at Chicago Circle; Ann Lencyk Pawliczko, Fordham University, Bronx, New York; Jim Phillips, Kings River Community College, Reedley, California; Kathleen H. Powell, Frostburg State University, Frostburg, Maryland; William F. Powers, Suffolk County Community College, Selden, New York; Steven Schada, Oakton Community College, Des Plaines, Illinois; J. Carroll Sims, Virginia State University, Petersburg, Virginia; Shirley Strom, Henry Ford Community College, Dearborn, Michigan; and Theodore C. Wagenaar, Miami University, Oxford, Ohio. I am grateful also to the following reviewers of this edition: David Neal, Texas Women's University, Denton, Texas; Alton M. Okinawa, University of Hawaii, Hilo; Brenda Phillips, Texas Women's University, Denton, Texas; and Joseph Ventimiglia, University of Memphis, Memphis, Tennessee.

For me, sociology continues to be one of the most exciting, fast-paced, and demanding disciplines because it presents a continual challenge to traditional and established ways of thinking about the world. Over the years that I have been a sociologist, I have engaged in sociological research and practice in many diverse settings. I have evaluated programs to help schoolchildren in need and programs for services targeted at pregnant teenagers; I have advised administrators who run programs for homeless teens as well as those providing services to women recovering from drug addictions; I have conducted research on people's responses to life-threatening illnesses. Through all of this, my passion for the sociological enterprise has grown stronger. Sociology engenders an openness, an eagerness, and an intense desire to learn more about all aspects of the human condition. By knowing other people, their lives, and their society, we can better understand ourselves. My hope is that this book will generate the same passion in the students who read it; as a result, a few may start down the exciting road to becoming the next generation of sociologists.

Thomas J. Sullivan
Marquette, Michigan

PART ONE

The Sociological Perspective

Part One introduces the sociological perspective and includes a discussion of the three theoretical perspectives in sociology, the scientific method as used in sociology, and the specific research methods that are used for making observations.

CHAPTER 1:   WHAT IS SOCIOLOGY?

ONE CHAPTER *What Is Sociology?*

Bonerate is one of the many islands that make up the nation of Indonesia (Broch, 1990). Located a few hundred miles north of Australia, near Java, it has about 5,000 inhabitants, many of whom live in small villages of a few hundred people. Residents of Bonerate survive by gathering naturally growing foods, engaging in limited agriculture, fishing, and taking part in the copra and spice trade between the Moluccas and Java. Bonerate does not, however, provide an easy or plentiful existence. The soil is poor, and many of the fields have coral limestones in them that cannot be removed and make working the fields difficult. Water is scarce on the island, especially during the dry season, when the island becomes arid. This scarcity means that the growing season for various fruits and vegetables is short. Agriculture is also difficult because of the lack of irrigation and fertilizers, and both agriculture and fishing are hampered by the rather primitive level of technology used on the island.

Life is hard on Bonerate, and the people would be considered poor by the standards of many around the world. The islanders must work hard to earn a living. In common with other Indonesian peasants, they see life as difficult and to an extent bad, fraught with adversities and dangers (Koentjaraningrat, 1988). Consequently, they focus their attention on the present, not the future, and feel compelled to do their best. If they work hard, they believe, difficulties caused by bad fate, accidents, or disasters can be overcome. Despite this worldview, however, they are not necessarily unhappy with their situation. An anthropologist described one small village on Bonerate this way:

> Miang Tuu is a small village where all of the residents know each other well. It is a dense community where few secrets can be kept from fellow villagers. This setting provides a good feeling of unity, but also at times "a feeling of being watched and having to conform," the villagers say. Most Miang Tuuans express love for their home village. (Broch, 1990, p. 10)

Basically the islanders' sense of security in the face of adversity arises from the existence of the *gotong royong*, or mutual self-help system. If they have difficulties, family members and fellow villagers will come to their aid. In other words, a community network of support helps the residents of Bonerate get through life. People will provide food if someone's crops are attacked by insects and help rebuild a house if it is destroyed by bad weather. And it is assumed that people will help their neighbors in turn when they confront adversity. The people of Bonerate are very aware that their lives depend on others, and they work hard at maintaining good relationships with one another. Bonerate culture emphasizes the importance of getting along with others and maintaining cooperative and agreeable relationships. To this end the islanders are adept at controlling their emotions and not angering or alienating others. The purpose of such behavior is to maintain the community, which is the ultimate support for the people on Bonerate.

If we shift our attention from Bonerate to the United States, we see a remarkable contrast. Compared to Bonerate, the United States is a much more individualistic—some would say self-centered—culture. In fact, the sociologist Robert Bellah and his colleagues, concluding an in-depth investigation of cultural values in the United States, stated that individualism "lies at the very core of American culture" (1985, p. 142). Individualism places personal desires and achievements ahead of collective accomplishments and goals. Bellah and colleagues argue that individualism in the United States goes to such an extreme that "anything that would violate our right to think for ourselves, judge for ourselves, make our own decisions, live our lives as we see fit, is not only morally wrong, it is sacrilegious" (1985, p. 142). In the United States, people say things like "Watch out for Number One" and "What's in it for me," and they assume that others recognize, if not agree with, the sentiment implied, namely, that individual desires are as important as, if not more important than, collective or community needs. In the late-twentieth-century United States, enjoyment and personal pleasure seem to challenge duty or obligation to the group as preeminent forces in life. People divorce their spouse, leave their family, move across the country to find a job or a place in the sun—all in search of the elusive goal of *self*-fulfillment.

How different from the people of Bonerate and their practice of *gotong royong!* They make efforts to get along with one another. Although people in the United States certainly cooperate at times, they are much more likely than the islanders to compete openly and display overt disdain, anger, or hostility toward others. In fact, Bellah and his colleagues identified this tendency as a serious problem in the United States: "We have committed what to the republican founders of our nation was the cardinal sin: we have put our own good, as individuals, . . . ahead of the common good" (1985, pp. 284–285).

A principle that is so supportive and sustaining in Bonerate—community—seems disturbingly absent in the United States. To suggest the central importance of community in social life, the sociologist Amitai Etzioni comments as follows:

> Communities are not merely environments to which an actor adjusts as he or she would to a new climate, but they also influence to a great extent the person's most inner desires, preferences, and moral commitments. This is not to suggest that there is no free will or choice but to recognize that individuality is honed out of social, collective (communal) backgrounds. (1991, p. 125)

What has been said so far should not be taken as an indictment of culture in the United States or as an affirmation of Bonerate life. What is being emphasized, first of all, is the importance of *community* in the many forms that it can take. Bellah and Etzioni express a theme that is central to the discipline of sociology: that human beings are social creatures sustained by community. Not all sociologists will agree with Bellah's critical assessment of the condition of community in the United States. In fact, evidence of community in the United States can be found in the impressive assistance that people often give their neighbors during floods, fires, earthquakes, and other natural disasters. But all sociologists would agree that community in the United States is different from community on Bonerate, and they would agree with Etzioni's judgment that some type of community is vital to human social life and constitutive of human nature.

The second point this comparison is intended to emphasize is the cultural diversity found among human groups, as illustrated by the contrast between Bonerate and the United States. Only by observing and comprehending that diversity can we fully grasp what it means to be human and social. The approach this book will take is to look at many different cultures and societies. If we limit our vision to the United States, we will see only part of the picture. Only the broadest cultural reach will provide us with the most accurate assessment of how societies work and how human behavior is shaped. This book will encourage you, as it reviews the values and social practices in many cultures, to assess critically what works and why and then to apply that knowledge to your own culture.

Sociology is a scientific discipline that strives to understand human beings and human social behavior. This chapter will introduce the subject matter of sociology, including its unique perspective. It will also describe how sociology uses the scientific method to gain systematic knowledge about human behavior.

What Is Sociology?

You should be able to discuss the sociological perspective and describe the main characteristics of the other social sciences and science in general.

Sociology is *the scientific study of societies and human social behavior.* The basic premise of sociology is that human behavior is largely determined by the groups to which people belong and by the societies in which they live. Human groups can range from small collections of friends to larger configurations such as football teams or concert audiences. Among the things that interest sociologists regarding such groups are the following: How do they develop? How are new members incorporated into groups? How does face-to-face contact between group members affect each person's behavior? How does the group respond when confronted by another, possibly hostile, group?

When a number of groups coordinate their actions, another level of social activity emerges in the form of organizations such as corporations, hospitals, or schools, and sociologists also study these types of human affiliations. Finally, groups and organizations combine to form societies, the most encompassing of human social forms. Societies can range from small bands of fifty people who survive by hunting game and gathering fruits and berries to enormous industrial societies with millions of people. Sociologists are interested in how these societies function and also how they differ from one another on such matters as the distribution of resources and the role of family and kinship in people's lives. At the core of all sociological investigations is a particular perspective that sets sociology apart from other approaches to human behavior.

The Sociological Perspective

A perspective is a point of view or a distinctive way of viewing something. Sociology offers a unique perspective on human beings, recognizing that human behavior consists of far more than individuals acting independently of one another. The **sociological perspective** emphasizes *the powerful role that group membership and social forces play in shaping behavior.* Sociologists focus on social interaction and social relationships rather than on individuals. Each person is born into a particular group in a given society, and life becomes a progression from one set of groups to another. Most of us begin our lives in a family, which provides us with social standing in a community and makes available certain fundamental opportunities in life—to learn, mature, and become independent.

As we grow older, we develop friendships and enter school. Aspirations and desires that will shape our choices later in life are nurtured by each of these very important groups. As adults, we may develop our own families or establish intimate ties with other adults. In a sense, we are never really alone because we constantly remember, reflect on, and imagine how others have responded to us. The sociological perspective, then, concentrates on human groups and their multiple influences on human behavior.

The Diversity of Social Reality A key insight of the sociological perspective is that beliefs, values, and behaviors are *relative* to particular groups or societies and can be understood only in the context of those affiliations. The members of a group or society share a view of reality that determines what they believe to be right and wrong, proper or reprehensible. This means that tremendous diversity exists in human behavior from one society to another. Among the Tuareg in Saharan Africa, for example, it is customary for men to wear veils over their faces at virtually all times. They do so despite the fact that the practice is physically uncomfortable and inconvenient when eating or smoking (Murphy, 1968). Basuto women in southern Africa, as evidence of their undying love, rub their beloved's sweat, blood, or hair into open wounds on their bodies. The resulting scars are symbols of their affection (Ashton, 1967). Many people in the United States might view these social practices as silly, degrading, or repulsive. Yet the Tuareg and the Basuto would think it stupid for a man in the United States to confine his feet in uncomfortable and smelly shoes on a hot day and would laugh at U.S. women who have their earlobes pierced to accommodate shiny baubles they think are attractive. The point is that none of these social practices can be completely understood unless it is viewed in the context of the shared view of reality found in a particular culture.

Within any society, there is also considerable variation in beliefs, values, and behaviors from one group to another. Marijuana and cocaine, for instance, are accepted among some rock musicians, entertainers, affluent singles, and college students in the United States. Many others, by contrast, disdain these drugs but consume alcohol freely. At the other extreme, Baptists are strongly opposed to the use of any alcohol or drugs, and Mormons reject the use of tea or coffee containing caffeine, which they consider a drug. This tremendous diversity, both within U.S. society and across cultures, has led sociologists to realize that beliefs, values, and behaviors can be fully understood only within the social context where they occur.

Cross-Cultural and Global Perspectives In the late twentieth century, one can easily overlook diversity. After all, people drive cars and drink Coke in Caracas and Bangkok while McDonald's restaurants open in Moscow and Beijing; at the same time, movies, music, and MTV from the United States are a hit with young people in more and more nations. It seems that everyone is grasping for what is characteristic of the United States in aspirations, lifestyle, and economic relations. There is a danger, however, of overemphasizing superficial realities and ignoring more fundamental differences between peoples. Eating at McDonald's or drinking Coke does not mean that a person has adopted U.S. culture. Culture is much more pervasive than these food preferences, involving many complex and subtle beliefs, values, and aspirations. Much of the convergence we see in the world today involves material technology rather than beliefs, values, and aspirations. The United States, Saudi Arabia, and Japan are much alike in technological development but worlds apart in terms of religious beliefs or the value placed on the individual. If we overemphasize what people share in common, we miss something very significant: the extent of cultural diversity and an understanding of the substantial impact that culture has on our perceptions, values, desires, and behaviors. People of different cultures do truly live in a different world. Recognizing and understanding the importance of this diversity is one of the keys to developing a true sociological perspective.

To begin understanding the importance of differences between people it is helpful to look at something familiar. Most of us have had the experience of misunderstandings between generations. For example, as an adolescent, you may have felt that your parents did not understand what was important to you or why certain musical styles, clothing styles, or hairstyles were in vogue or out. Or some older students with adolescent offspring of their own may have difficulty understanding why their offspring are so immersed in certain fashions or do not behave more responsibly or politely. Two things are sociologically significant for understanding this parent–adolescent misunderstanding. The first is that adolescents and their parents are at different stages in their lives. Adolescents are very much concerned with proving their self-worth among their peers and establishing their sexual identity. One of the ways they do these things is by being in style or hip (or whatever it is called at a given point). Adults in their thirties or forties, on the other hand, have different concerns: Their sexual identities are more established, and things such as paying a home mortgage or saving for their children's college tuition may be more important than being "cool" or in style. For both groups, their location in the life span influences what they value and what takes on importance for them. The important point for sociologists is not which viewpoint is "correct" but rather the insight that everyone's viewpoint is a product of his or her social situation (in this case, the stage in the lifespan).

The second thing that is sociologically significant is that adolescents and their adult parents grew up at different points in history. Research shows that people's experiences in their teens and early twenties, while they are coming of age, have a powerful impact on their overall viewpoint and what they value and perceive as important (Alwin, Cohen, and Newcomb, 1991). Many parents of adolescents today came to maturity in the 1960s, when many people considered civil rights, civil disobedience, and social awareness to be important. It was a time of optimism and hope for a better future. Adolescents today are coming of age during a time that has been described as more self-centered, when there is much talk of reduced job opportunities and many people believe that this generation may have less than their parents had. So, adolescents and their adult parents have different viewpoints because they came of age at different points in history. Again, the sociological insight is that their viewpoints are socially situated, in this case influenced by the historical situations they experienced in their youth.

Based on these ideas, the sociologist C. Wright Mills (1959) argued that the sociological perspective offers the ability to understand that our own behavior and viewpoints are shaped by the intersection of biography and history: the point we are at in our own lives (biography) and the point in history in which we live. The adolescent and adult who have just been mentioned differ from each other in both biography and history. Yet, they are also very similar: Because they are parent and child, they share the same racial or ethnic character, social class setting, neighborhood, and possibly the same gender. Despite these similarities, they have difficulty understanding each other. This difficulty demonstrates the impact that small differences in biography and history can produce.

Now imagine much vaster differences. Compare a wealthy white European with a poor Haitian of African descent. Or imagine how biography and history would shape the viewpoint of a Comanche Indian of the seventeenth century when encountering white Europeans, who would call themselves "settlers" but would likely be seen as "invaders" by the Comanche. To go further afield, would the biographical and historical experiences of an Australian Aborigine of 500 years ago produce behavior, values, or viewpoints that late-twentieth-century Anglo Americans could comprehend? This is the challenge of sociology: to understand the role of this diversity in shaping our own and others' lives and societies. The sociological task is not to assess which values, viewpoints, or behaviors are right or proper but rather to achieve the insight that every set of values, viewpoints, and behaviors is a product of a particular intersection of biography and history.

Every chapter of this book includes many illustrations of this diversity, within both modern U.S. society and societies around the world and through history. In some examples, the discussion of diversity is incorporated in the text; in others, special sections titled *Other Worlds, Other Ways* highlight some especially important issues. Where appropriate, a major section of the chapter is devoted to a global view of the topic of the chapter.

The issue of diversity is important because it is central to grasping the sociological perspective. It is also important because diversity often produces, or is the justification for, social inequality, discrimination, mistreatment, differential opportunities, and social conflict. Efforts to reform society and change these conditions require an accurate understanding of the nature, extent, and

The sociological perspective emphasizes that human beings are social creatures who derive joy and sustenance from other people. It stresses the powerful role of groups and social forces in shaping people's behavior. This perspective can both emancipate and empower people.

importance of diversity. Sociology offers this understanding. In fact, from sociology's inception in the last century, many sociologists have viewed their discipline as a key tool for accomplishing such reform. Finally, comprehending the diverse nature of human life is critical for a nation such as the United States if it is to act effectively in an increasingly global, interdependent world. There is a tendency today to believe that interdependence among peoples is something new to the twentieth century, when in fact trade and wars between peoples are as old as history. For example, during the Crusades, legions of soldiers from Europe went to

the Middle East centuries before the Persian Gulf War. The plight of seventeenth-century farmers in New England was affected by the decisions of merchants and politicians in London and Paris, just as the livelihood of modern-day autoworkers is affected by decisions made in Tokyo or Seoul. There is, however, a difference today in the intensity, complexity, pervasiveness, and immediacy of global interdependence. Although some people might have ignored it or been unaware of it in earlier eras, such ignorance is impossible today. What is also different today is that we have sciences such as sociology and anthropology to help guide us through the thicket of cross-cultural misunderstanding that can arise when people from very different cultures come together at work, in school, or in other settings.

The sociological perspective, then, is a unique and remarkable view; it is a form of consciousness that recognizes that human behavior consists of far more than individuals acting independently of one another. Group memberships, social interaction, and social relationships are at the center of sociologists' attention. The sociological perspective offers a special awareness of the world that enables people to approach their own lives with introspection and insight. Peter Berger (1963) referred to the sociological perspective as an "emancipated vista" that can free people from blind submission to social forces that they do not understand. C. Wright Mills (1959) coined the term **sociological imagination** in referring to *the ability to understand the relationship between what is happening in people's personal lives and the social forces that surround them.* For both Berger and Mills, the more people learn about society and social processes, the better equipped they will be to understand their own lives and the impact of society on them. To be emancipated, of course, is not always pleasant because we often learn that social forces hinder us from achieving sought-after goals. A poverty-stricken mother, for example, may not like the realization that her children will be penalized by the inequities in the U.S. educational system, which have adverse effects on the poor. Nevertheless, it is precisely a better understanding of the role of such inequities that can lead to improvements in the educational process. In providing this insight, sociology offers not only emancipation but also *empowerment:* It assists people in taking control of their own circumstances and lives.

Sociology as a Science

Traditional and religious sources of knowledge rest on untested or unquestioned assumptions. Sociology, by contrast, uses a scientific approach to studying people, which distinguishes it from other means of understanding human behavior. Some people are leery of studying human beings scientifically because they believe human behavior is so spontaneous and unpredictable that objective procedures are of little use. Other people maintain that a scientific approach reduces people to "statistics," human emotions to numerical equivalents, and in so doing ignores that undefinable kernel that makes us "human." In reality, people are quite predictable, as will be shown throughout this book. Where hesitation to study people scientifically exists, it usually rests on a misunderstanding of science—its possibilities as well as its limitations.

Science is *a method of obtaining objective and systematic knowledge through observation.* Science has certain characteristics that distinguish it from nonscientific sources of knowledge (Sullivan, 1992).

First, science is *empirical,* which means that it is based on observation. Scientists must be able to demonstrate that what they claim to be true can actually be observed in reality. Commonsense reasoning and traditional or intuitive knowledge cannot take the place of this observation.

Second, science is *systematic;* it follows methodical and generally accepted procedures. Consequently, scientific research is always open to critical review and assessment by other scientists in order to determine whether errors or biases have influenced the conclusions. As part of this assessment, scientific investigations are often repeated, a process that scientists term *replication.* Replication helps prevent unreliable or selective interpretations by determining whether other scientists reach the same conclusions using the same procedures. Replication provides further verification for scientific findings.

Third, science focuses on *causation.* Scientists assume that all events are caused, or determined, by something else. A major feature of scientific research is the search for these causes. For two or more phenomena to be causally related, there must be an association between them. For example, when water is heated to 212 degrees Fahrenheit (100 degrees Celsius) at an air pressure of one atmosphere, it will change from a liquid to a gas. As far as we know, there are no exceptions to this association. In other cases, the association between two or more phenomena is probabilistic. This means that the occurrence of one event increases the likelihood, or probability, that the other will occur, but the relationship does not necessarily occur in every case. It will be shown that most associations involving social phenomena are probabilistic.

APPLYING SOCIOLOGY
Untangling Myths and Facts: Sociology and Common Sense

Sociologists take the position that scientific research provides the most accurate and useful knowledge with which to understand human social behavior. Science, of course, is not the only way to gain an understanding of the world. For example, people often use tradition as a source of guidance. Tradition might take the form of religious teachings about sex and marriage or proverbs such as "Birds of a feather flock together" and "Two heads are better than one." People also turn to their own personal experience for direction. If we visit a prison and see that most inmates are nonwhite, this experience can lead us to believe that most crimes are committed by nonwhites. Knowledge based on tradition and experience often accumulates and blends together to form what people call common sense: practical wisdom that people believe is sound but with no special training or expertise to support it. Every generation adds to the store of commonsense knowledge, and we routinely rely on it in our everyday lives when assessing situations or making decisions.

In fact, sociology has been called "the science of common sense" by critics who assume that it merely "proves" what everybody else already knows. Of course, sociology sometimes does confirm what many people already accept. We should not be surprised that scientific research shows that some commonsense beliefs are true, because people need some accurate commonsense knowledge of human behavior to interact with others and function effectively in society. However, sociological research also shows that many commonsense beliefs about human behavior are false or at least vastly oversimplified. Consider these statements:

1. If the poor were willing to work, there would be little need for welfare.
2. Divorce was relatively unheard of in societies before this century, but it has been increasing dramatically in the United States in recent years.
3. Because of the civil rights movement and affirmative-action legislation, the gap in income between African Americans and white Americans

has narrowed substantially in the past three decades.
4. Teenagers are too young to be mature and responsible, and this is why societies encourage them to stay in school until they are eighteen years old rather than work for a living or begin raising a family.

At one time or another, each of us has probably believed that at least some of these statements are true. Yet, sociological research has shown each one to be false, or at least to be far too simple to provide a complete understanding of a complex social reality.

1. This statement is false because it is not an unwillingness to work that puts most people on welfare. Most people receiving public assistance are children, single mothers who cannot afford the day care that would free them for work, the aged, and the disabled. In addition, many poor people, including many receiving public assistance, do work—at low-paying jobs that they use to supplement their assistance. The need for welfare arises from a complex mixture of social conditions: a shortage of jobs and a lack of training for the jobs available, among others.
2. This statement is partly true and partly false. In many premodern societies, married couples had the option of dissolving their union. In some hunting-and-gathering bands, in fact, divorce was easier to accomplish and much more common than it is in the United States today: Marriage ended when a couple decided to stop living together. It is true, however, that the divorce rate in the United States has increased, from 8.8 per thousand married women in 1940 to more than 20 per thousand today. The reasons for this increase will be discussed in Chapter 9. However, the divorce rate may not continue to increase in the future. In fact, it has held fairly steady since the mid-1970s.
3. Unfortunately, research shows that the gap has not narrowed at all (see Chapter 7). Although

many African Americans have benefited from such developments, the poverty of the black "underclass" seems to be especially intransigent to change. Overall, average black income was 55 percent of average white income in 1965; it is still 55 percent in the 1990s—no change.

4. This, again, is a myth. Teenagers are quite capable of mature, responsible behavior. In fact, in preindustrial societies, most people have joined the adult world of work by their teen years and may have even begun raising a family. Industrial societies, by contrast, have created a new stage in the life cycle called *adolescence,* consisting of people who are biologically mature but considered by society to be dependent and immature. Having such a stage in the life cycle fulfills certain needs for industrial societies: It makes possible an extended period of education during which young people learn what they need to know in order to become contributing adults. Society expects teens to be immature and irresponsible because this expectation makes it easier to keep them in a dependent status (see Chapter 3).

What is wrong with common sense in these realms? Basically, common sense does not normally involve an empirical and systematic effort to distinguish fact from fiction. Rather, it tends to accept untested and unquestioned assumptions because "everyone knows" they are true, and to reject contradictory information. In other words, some commonsense knowledge is a "myth" in that there is little evidence of its truth, although some people still accept it as true. Commonsense knowledge is also very slow to change—even when change seems called for—because the change may threaten cherished values or social patterns. In addition, common sense often explains everything, even when those explanations contradict one another. When we see two people with similar personalities become friends, we say, "Birds of a feather flock together." Yet when we see an athletic woman dating a bookish, cerebral man, we say, "Opposites attract." But which assertion is true?

Scientific research does far more than merely document what we already know. Sometimes it does just that, but at other times it directly contradicts common sense. Most of the time, however, the truth is vastly more complicated than common sense suggests. Sociological research incorporates procedures that advance our knowledge by establishing facts through observation and by using procedures that reduce bias. Common sense is important and should not be ignored, but an unthinking and unverified acceptance of commonsense beliefs can blind people to social realities. This fact has important implications for social policy. The recognition, for example, that most people receiving welfare need it desperately to survive is a strong argument against cutting back on public assistance programs. It is only through the development of an accurate, scientifically verified understanding of such social problems that we can hope to overcome them—even if it means relinquishing some of our most cherished commonsense preconceptions.

Each of the remaining chapters includes two features that emphasize these points. At the beginning of each chapter, a "Myths and Facts" section will contrast some inaccurate or misleading commonsense beliefs about the topics in that chapter with the facts as they have been established through research. This comparison will encourage students to distinguish beliefs that have no empirical foundation and may in fact be myths from facts that have been substantiated through observation. Each chapter also includes at least one "Applying Sociology" section, which illustrates the use of sociological research in solving problems or evaluating how effective solutions are. This section emphasizes the theme of applying sociological research to solve human problems. The hope is to instill an awareness that solutions to problems should rest, at least in part, on research and testing to see what works.

Fourth, science is *provisional*. The results of scientific investigations are considered tentative, and they are always open to question and possible repudiation. There are no ultimate, sacred, or unchangeable truths in science. In the early part of the twentieth century, for example, many social scientists accepted the findings of the Italian criminologist Cesare Lombroso (1911) that some people are "born criminals," genetically inferior human beings who are throwbacks to a more primitive human type. Lombroso had empirical data, although not very systematically collected, to prove his point. But acceptance by scientists is always provisional and never unquestioned, so continued testing of Lombroso's ideas showed them to be false. Today, social scientists recognize that crime is a product mostly of learning and social conditions rather than genetics.

Finally, science is *objective*. Scientists strive to prevent their personal values from affecting their investigations. This impersonality does not mean that scientists have no values or emotional passions. Many are intensely concerned about social issues such as crime, divorce, environmental pollution, nuclear power, strategic arms control, and equal rights. At the same time, scientists realize that personal values can, and probably will, bias their findings. They have therefore introduced checks such as replication and provisionality to guard against the influence of personal bias on the body of scientific knowledge.

Science is not foolproof, but it is the most effective means of acquiring systematic, verifiable knowledge about the world. Science, of course, has its limitations, and it is crucial to understand which issues it cannot resolve. Science is the preferred source of knowledge on issues that can be resolved *through observation*. Some issues are not amenable to such resolution. For example, science cannot verify the existence of a supreme deity or say which religious beliefs are correct, because these are not issues that can be settled through observation. They are matters of faith, choice or revelation, not of science. Likewise, science cannot tell us which personal values are right or preferable because these are again matters of personal judgment. Science may help show us how to live up to our values or the consequences of following particular values, but it cannot tell us which values we should live by. This choice may

best be served by religious teachings or traditional knowledge. The Applying Sociology section (on pp. 10–11) provides some further comparisons of the scientific approach of sociology with the commonsense approach on which people often rely.

The Social Sciences

There are many scientific disciplines, each investigating a particular sphere of the world. The *natural sciences* study nature and the physical universe. They include the physical sciences, such as chemistry and geology, and the biological sciences, such as biology and zoology. The *social sciences* are the disciplines that use the scientific method to study human behavior, groups, and society. Sociology is one of the major social sciences; there are a number of others.

Anthropology, the social science most similar to sociology, is the study of the cultures, customs, origins, evolution, and physical characteristics of human beings. Sociology places more emphasis on group structures, processes within cultures, and the impact of face-to-face social interaction than does anthropology.

Psychology focuses on the mental processes of individuals, dealing with phenomena such as memory, perception, motivation, and emotions. Although sociologists are also interested in explaining the behavior of individuals, they do so by studying the social environment that surrounds people. Sociology and psychology overlap in the subdiscipline of *social psychology*, which is the study of how people's thoughts, feelings, and behaviors are influenced by their interactions with others.

Economics, one of the oldest of the social sciences, is concerned with the production, distribution, and consumption of goods and services and with people's behavior as economic consumers. Sociology is concerned with economics as a form of social behavior, and economists draw heavily on the findings of sociologists in explaining economic behavior.

Political science has traditionally been most involved with political philosophy and the study of governmental forms. In the twentieth century, however, there has been a shift toward a more systematic study of political processes. This shift has been influenced in part by the development of *political sociology,* which is the study of social behavior and social processes in political or governmental contexts.

Although the other social sciences narrow their focus to a particular realm of human social behavior, sociology is more general and encompassing. Sociologists deal with *all* forms of human social behavior, whether they occur in an economic, a political, a religious, or another context.

Theoretical Perspectives in Sociology

You should be able to explain the roles of theories and hypotheses in sociological research and to discuss the major theoretical perspectives in sociology and explain how they are used.

To this point, sociology has been defined in terms of its unique perspective and its use of the scientific method. The practice of sociology actually involves the continual interplay of two key elements: *theories,* which embody the sociological perspective, and *research,* which is based on the scientific method. The goal of a science like sociology is to shape our knowledge into theories (Collins, 1989). Theories provide ideas that can be investigated through research, whereas the research, in turn, provides evidence on the accuracy or veracity of the theories. First, theories and their role in the scientific process will be discussed; then an outline of the major theories in contemporary sociology will be presented; finally, there will be a brief overview of how sociologists conduct research.

Theories and Hypotheses

A **theory** is *a set of statements that explains the relationship among phenomena.* Students occasionally approach theories as if they were mysterious, unusual, or possibly superfluous. In fact, people use theories frequently in their daily lives. Law enforcement officials investigating crimes, for example, rely on them heavily.

> The stereotype of the detective who asks for "just the facts" is inaccurate, for detectives are always working with and testing theory. . . . For instance, in homicide cases, the first people generally

contacted by detectives are friends, relatives, or acquaintances of the victim. Behind such investigative procedures is the theory that most homicides are committed by people who are socially close to the victim. (Sanders, 1974, p. 3)

The theories used by detectives and other laypeople are less systematic than those used by scientists, but they serve the same purpose: to relate phenomena in a causal framework and thereby explain and predict behavior. One sociological theory, for example, explains the relationship between family life and juvenile delinquency (Agnew, 1991; Hirschi, 1969). Referred to as *control theory,* this explanation maintains that juvenile delinquency increases when the attachment of young people to their families decreases. *Attachment* refers to such things as maintaining open channels of communication with parents, along with love, respect, and affection for them. According to control theory, communication reduces delinquency because it affords youth the chance to express their problems to parents before these difficulties explode into delinquency. Love and respect for parents play an important role because young people who have these feelings are more likely to avoid actions that might bring disapproval from their parents.

An important ingredient of theories is variables. A **variable** is *a property or characteristic of something that can take on different values.* Age, for example, is an important sociological variable, and its value ranges over all of those ages that people can possibly be. Ethnicity is another sociological variable, with its values being the various ethnicities people can have, such as Hispanic, Jewish, Italian, and Polish. Juvenile delinquency and family attachment are two of the variables that make up control theory. In terms of delinquency, a youngster may have engaged in no delinquent acts at all, a few such actions, or many of them. Family attachment, likewise, could range from virtually no attachment whatsoever to intimate involvement.

In the investigation of causal relationships, theories contain two different types of variables. **Independent variables** are *those that bring about changes in other variables.* **Dependent variables** are *those that are changed.* In control theory, family attachment is the independent variable that brings about the changes in delinquency, which is the dependent variable in this case. Of course, a dependent variable in one situation may serve as an independent variable in another, or vice versa. In a different setting, for example, juvenile delinquency could be the independent variable that affects how well a person does in school or the likelihood of a person's becoming an adult criminal. The important point here is that independent and dependent variables both play unique roles in the causal process.

Scientific theories are linked to scientific research through **hypotheses,** which are *tentative statements that can be tested regarding relationships between two or more variables.* The following hypothesis, for example, could be derived from control theory: Children who engage in delinquent acts such as vandalism will be less likely than nondelinquents to feel that they can confide in their parents. This is a statement whose accuracy can be assessed through observation. In cases such as this, a hypothesis is deduced from an existing theory; if the hypothesis is confirmed through research, it provides further support for that theory. In other cases, where no theory exists relating to a particular phenomenon, hypotheses are developed from intuition or "hunches" that often derive from earlier research. If these are confirmed, then a start can be made in building a theory to explain the findings. In this fashion, all scientific theories are subject to *verification:* Continued investigations determine whether the relationships specified by hypotheses derived from a theory do, in fact, exist. Confidence in any theory rests on

this verification process. If hypotheses derived from a theory are verified, then we have greater confidence in the theory; if they are not, our confidence is reduced (see Figure 1.1).

Some sociological theories focus on specific features of social life, such as learning the causes of juvenile delinquency or the sources of marital satisfaction. Quite a few of these theories will be discussed throughout this book. In addition to these highly specialized theories, however, there are a number of broader explanations of social reality called **theoretical perspectives.** These perspectives *provide some fundamental assumptions about the nature and operation of society and commonly serve as sources of the more specific theories.* In the 150 years since sociology was established as a scientific discipline, a heated debate has continued about the nature of the fundamental processes that underlie the operation of society. In approaching this question, most sociologists today are guided by one or more of the following theoretical perspectives: functionalism, conflict theory, or interactionism. The functionalist and conflict approaches are frequently referred to as *macrosociology* because they focus on large groups and social institutions and on society as a whole. The interactionist perspective falls under the category of *microsociology* because it concentrates on the intimate level of everyday interactions between people. This section will first summarize the perspectives and then suggest how to use them in analyzing social behavior.

FIGURE 1.1 The Process of Theory Verification

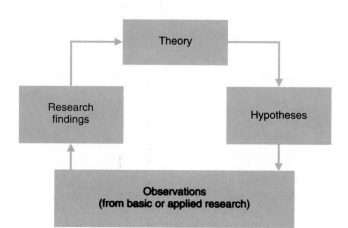

The Functionalist Perspective

The functionalist perspective grew out of the similarities early sociologists observed between society and biological organisms. The human body, for example, is composed of many different parts—the heart, the eyes, and the kidneys, to name but three—each of which performs a particular function. The heart pumps blood to the other organs of the body, the eyes transmit information about the external world to the brain, and the kidneys remove waste materials from the blood. These parts of the body do not exist in isolation, however, but are interrelated and interdependent. If one of them ceases to perform its function—if the heart stops, the eyes go blind, or the kidneys fail—the effective operation of the whole body is threatened, and survival itself may be in doubt.

Society, functionalists argue, operates in a way somewhat analogous to that of a biological organism. According to the **functionalist perspective,** *society is a system made up of a number of interrelated and interdependent elements, each performing a function that contributes to the operation of the whole* (Merton, 1968; Parsons, 1951; Turner & Maryanski, 1979). The elements of society include, for example, institutions such as the family, education, and the economy. The family provides for the bearing and rearing of children until they can live on their own. Educational institutions provide training in the various skills needed to fill jobs in society. The economy is responsible for producing food, clothing, and other necessities needed by families to survive as well as providing the books and other supplies needed for education. The family and the schools could not survive without the goods provided by the economy, and economic organizations need workers who have been socialized by the family and trained by the schools to work industriously. In addition to institutions, society is also made up of many social roles, social groups, and subcultures, and all these parts fit together into a reasonably well-integrated whole. For functionalists, then, all parts of society are interdependent and function together to provide the things that are essential to maintain society. In addition, there needs to be considerable agreement among the members of society regarding the content of important values and norms.

In a system with all the parts so tightly interdependent, a change in one element of society will probably lead to changes in other parts. For example, the establishment of compulsory education in the United States caused significant alterations in the economic sphere by removing children and eventually adolescents from the labor force, which made more jobs available for adults. Compulsory education also affected the family—with young people no longer working, the financial burden on parents was increased. When children could no longer help support the family financially, a gradual shift to smaller families began. Thus, changes in the educational sphere had important ramifications for the family and economic structures. Small changes can usually be absorbed with relative ease, but large or sudden changes can cause major social disruption. Therefore, functionalists argue, social systems are characterized by **stability** and a tendency toward *equilibrium*—a state of balance in which the relationships among the various parts of the system remain the same.

A central concern of the functionalist approach is the determination of just what functions each element in society performs. Such determination is not always easy because some functions are not as obvious as those in the preceding example. In fact, the sociologist Robert K. Merton (1968) suggests that there are two different types of functions: manifest and latent. *Manifest functions* are intended consequences of some action or social process and refer to what most people expect to result. *Latent functions* are consequences that are unexpected or unintended. For example, one of the manifest functions of colleges and universities is to provide people with specialized training. However, institutions of higher learning perform a number of latent functions. For instance, they serve as a marriage market, and they reduce unemployment by keeping some adults out of the job market. These latent functions are just as much a part of the system of higher education as its manifest purposes. In addition, some social practices may be *dysfunctional;* that is, they may disrupt social equilibrium rather than contribute to it. For example, encouraging large families in a society that is already overpopulated would be dysfunctional.

One major criticism of the functionalist perspective is that it overemphasizes the extent of stability and order in society. Because of this emphasis, it is argued, functionalism is a conservative approach that supports existing social conditions,

The conflict perspective makes us aware that people vary substantially in terms of the social and economic resources available to them. The social and economic policies that would benefit the well-off tennis player in this Asian nation would, undoubtedly, be quite different from those that would benefit the poorer residents of the nation.

even though these may be inequitable or oppressive. Functionalism tends to downplay the fact that social practices that are beneficial to one group in society may be dysfunctional to another. The functionalist perspective also ignores the fact that conflict and disharmony may be inherent features of society. The conflict perspective provides an alternative approach with respect to these shortcomings.

The Conflict Perspective

Conflict theorists emphasize the inevitability of coercion, domination, conflict, and change in so-ciety. The **conflict perspective** is based on *the idea that society consists of different groups who struggle with one another to attain the scarce societal resources that are considered valuable, be they money, power, prestige, or the authority to impose one's values on society.* In the nineteenth century Karl Marx provided the foundation for the conflict perspective when he viewed society as consisting of different social classes (1867–1895/1967). The two key social classes of his era were the workers and those who owned businesses and factories. Marx saw these classes as being in constant struggle with each other to improve their respective positions in society. The workers tried to gain more income and control over their work; the owners tried to make more profits by lowering labor costs and getting workers to work harder. For Marx, this conflict was irreconcilable because what benefits one group necessarily works to the disadvantage of the other. Furthermore, if one group can gain an advantage in this struggle, it will dominate and oppress the other group and enhance its own position. It might, for example, gain control of the government and pass legislation that limits the ways the subordinate groups could otherwise compete. In the nineteenth-century United States, for example, it was illegal for workers to organize for the purpose of collective bargaining. This law benefited factory owners because workers were unable to use their strength of numbers to gain higher wages or better working conditions.

Although Marx limited his focus to class struggle, modern versions of conflict theory in sociology hold that domination, coercion, and the exercise of power occur to some degree in all groups and societies because they are the basic social mechanisms for regulating behavior and allocating resources (Collins, 1975; Coser, 1956; Dahrendorf, 1959; Duke, 1976). In any society, there are dominant groups whose members will exert power over others to ensure that their interests are served. For example, because lucrative and rewarding occupational positions tend to be in short supply, dominant groups will try to preserve them for their own members. Whites might bar nonwhites from such jobs, or affluent groups might ensure that only their members have access to the education needed for certain jobs. In fact, Chapter 12 will show that controlling access to education is an important mechanism in modern societies for allocating desirable resources.

In the conflict view, groups exert what power they possess over others when it serves their interests, and society consists of a wide array of interest groups struggling to acquire a share of societal resources. An *interest group* is a group whose members share distinct and common concerns. Members of an interest group all tend to benefit from the same policies, practices, or distribution of resources, and those policies and practices probably work to the disadvantage of other interest groups. Some interest groups are formal organizations, such as the National Rifle Association, the Sierra Club, the National Manufacturers Association, or the American Civil Liberties Union. Others are informal, and people may not fully recognize that they are members of them. For example, college students constitute an informal interest group because all college students benefit from such things as lower tuition and increased government funding for student loans. Taxpayers without children of college age are another interest group, and they might oppose such policies because the policies would raise their taxes.

In the conflict view, social change involves redistributing scarce resources among various interest groups. The inevitable clash of interests ensures that any existing social arrangements will eventually be rearranged. Out of the resulting struggle, new winners will emerge and uneasy truces will be established. These truces, however, will be temporary, because new conflicts will develop that will lead to further struggle and change.

The conflict perspective can be criticized for overemphasizing the importance of conflict and disregarding the prevalence of stability. In addition, whereas functionalists are often accused of being too conservative, some conflict theorists can be criticized for having a radical view that places too much emphasis on changing society rather than trying to understand how order and stability can be maintained. Nevertheless, the conflict perspective helps us to understand the many ways in which conflict and the exercise of power are critical elements in social life.

The Interactionist Perspective

Although the functionalist and conflict perspectives offer competing views of social life, the interactionist perspective strikes out in a different direction by showing how the social processes described in those perspectives enter into people's daily lives and shape their behavior. The **interactionist perspective** *focuses on everyday social interaction among individuals rather than on large societal structures such as politics and education* (Blumer, 1962; Hewitt, 1994; Stryker, 1990). For interactionists, society consists of people interacting with one another; to understand society we must understand social interaction. It is through such interactions that groups, organizations, and society as a whole are created, maintained, and changed. The operation of educational institutions can be observed, for example, through students interacting with teachers and school administrators making decisions. It is these day-to-day interactions that lend education its shape and substance.

A central assumption of the interactionist perspective can be summarized by a paraphrase of a statement by the sociologists William and Dorothy Thomas (1928): If people define situations as real, the situations are real in their consequences. In other words, human action involves a period of examination and deliberation before people decide to act, and then they act on the basis of their beliefs and perceptions about situations. The term **definition of the situation** refers to *people's perceptions and interpretations of what is important in a situation and what actions are possible or appropriate.* A central part of social interaction is people's interpretations or definitions of others' behavior.

This process of definition or interpretation rests on the ability of human beings to use symbols. It is our symbol-using capabilities that enable us to attach complex social meanings to objects, events, or people. A *symbol* is something that stands for, represents, or takes the place of something else. Anything—any object, event, or word—can serve as a symbol. A crucifix, for example, symbolizes Roman Catholicism whether it is made from wood, metal, or plastic; the Star of David likewise symbolizes Judaism. The meaning attached to a symbol is derived from social consensus. We simply agree that a particular object will represent something. During World War II, for example, Winston Churchill used two fingers extended into the air and spread apart to symbolize victory in battle, and others agreed on the meaning of this gesture. During the 1960s, people used the same gesture to indicate support for the peace movement. Figure 1.2 illustrates some other

SYMBOL:

MEANINGS:

    1. Victory in battle (England, 1940s)
    2. Peace (United States, 1960s)
    3. Up yours (England, 1980s, with palm facing inward and upward jerk of hand)

SYMBOL:

MEANINGS:

    1. A-OK or all right (United States, 1990s)
    2. A scatological insult (Latin America, 1950s)
    3. Zero or worthless (south of France, 1990s)
    4. Money (Japan, 1990s)

FIGURE 1.2 Some Symbols and the Various Meanings That Have Been Attached to Them

symbols and suggests how important it is in a global world to be aware of how the meanings of symbols and gestures can change from one setting to another.

Because of our ability to use symbols, we live in a world that we create ourselves, through the meanings we attach to phenomena. In other words, we respond to symbolic or social meanings rather than to actual physical objects or actions, and what we do is the result of how we define and interpret those meanings. If someone shoves you at a football game, for example, you will probably assess or "interpret" the situation before responding. What was the person's intent and what did she mean by shoving me? Was it a hostile action or an accident, or was she trying to avoid being crushed by the crowd? On the basis of this interpretation, you will decide what response is appropriate.

Another example of how humans attach social meanings to objects or phenomena is through the use of labels that we give to people. When we label someone as a mother, a politician, or a bureaucrat, certain meanings that we have learned go along with the label. For some, *mother* is seen as virtuous, *politician* as untrustworthy, and *bureaucrat* as rigid and unthinking. Labels of deviants, such as *whore, crook,* or *nutcase,* typically carry some stigma and influence how we relate to these people. Moreover, when people have been labeled, we come to expect them to behave in certain ways. A central tenet of the interactionist perspective is that such social expectations, or norms, tend to influence the behavior of people who have been labeled, especially when the people themselves accept the meaning of the label attached to them. The prostitute, for example, who internalizes the social meaning implied by the label *cheap whore* may not aspire toward any other way of life. Her world and behavior are shaped by the fact that she accepts the stigmatizing label, whether it is true or not. This fact points to another important assertion of the interactionist perspective: What is important is not whether a particular definition of the situation is actually true but rather whether people believe the definition to be true.

For interactionists, social life rests on the development of consensus about expected behavior. Such shared expectations guide our activities and make cooperative actions possible. If this consensus breaks down, some sort of change must occur. Thus, for interactionists, social change involves developing some new consensus with different meanings and expectations. Some Roman Catholic groups, for example, have redefined what is appropriate behavior in church. Where they once expected quiet and reserved hymn singing, some now accept shouting, clapping, and guitar music.

The individual looms larger in the interactionist perspective than in the first two approaches. The interactionist perspective, however, also has its limitations. Because of the emphasis on face-to-face interaction in shaping social reality, there is a tendency to ignore the part that social institutions such as the family, religion, and the economy play in molding human behavior. Interactionism also tends to ignore large-scale social forces, such as industrialization, that are beyond the face-to-face setting but that greatly influence

People attach social meanings to objects, events, and gestures. This boy watching a pro-democracy demonstration in China is using two fingers spread apart and raised in the air as a symbol for victory. During the Vietnam conflict, the same gesture was used in the United States as a symbol for peace.

both the amount of stability and the extent of change in society.

Applying the Sociological Perspectives: Mass Media and Global Communications

Within the past twenty-four hours, most students reading this book have probably watched television; rented a movie on video; listened to music on a radio, tape, or compact disc; or read a mass circulation magazine such as *Time, People,* or *Sports Illustrated.* Some readers may have done all of these. If you performed any of these activities, then you were engulfed in the modern media of mass communications. The **mass media** are *the channels of communication in modern societies that can reach large numbers of people, sometimes instantaneously.* They consist of print media, such as books, magazines, and newspapers, as well as electronic media in the form of television and radios. This communications network, now global in nature, has become a central element of modern social life. It is so important that special attention will be devoted to it in this textbook. We will be explor-

ing its role in shaping society, social life, and human social behavior. In this chapter, the mass media will be used as a way of applying the three sociological perspectives to a particular realm of social life. Many of the following chapters will contain a special discussion of the mass media and global communications networks as they apply to the content of a particular chapter.

Recall that a central question for the *functionalist perspective* is what functions are performed by a particular part of society. If something exists, it must be performing some social functions. In the case of the mass media, a number of functions are being performed—some quite obvious, others less so. Most clearly, the modern mass media are one of the major mechanisms of communicating and exchanging information and ideas in the modern world. We learn about what products are for sale, what our political leaders have to say, and who is being traded by the New York Yankees or the Chicago Cubs by seeing it on television or reading it in newspapers or magazines. Certainly, we could learn about these things in other ways; earlier societies relied largely on word of mouth to communicate most such information. But word of mouth is considerably slower and less efficient and unnecessary now that technology makes possible rapid, almost instantaneous, and global information exchanges.

A less obvious function of the mass media is that the media make possible higher levels of social integration and social uniformity than are possible without this connective "tissue." This occurs because, with the media, vast numbers of people—whole nations or even the global population—can be exposed to major beliefs, values, and guidelines for behavior. Role models in the media encourage people to accept certain language or clothing styles or particular moral guidelines. This modeling has always occurred, of course, but on a much narrower scale. Because of the global reach of communications today, the media reduce regional variations in language, clothing styles, moral standards, and other social forms.

From the *conflict perspective,* the modern mass media are instruments of social control that can assist one group in the domination of other groups. Those who control the media have an advantage over other groups in that the controllers can shape what information and ideas are available to others. The more powerful groups who monopolize the media are in a position to influence others to purchase their products or accept their ideas and values. Modern media technologies are especially effective at this because they have such an alluring and irresistible appeal. Advertising, for example, can be so colorful and engaging that it influences people even though they are unaware of the influence. Political leaders can also use the media to propagate some ideas and suppress others. This selective presentation of information gives a significant advantage to those who control the media.

From the conflict perspective, the mass media are also big business. Considerable profits are to be made by convincing the public to watch the television programs, rent the movies, and buy the monogrammed shirts that will make the media elite wealthy. This represents a shift in resources from the less-well-off to the well-to-do. From the conflict perspective, there is a tendency for the mass media, and the wealth it produces, to become concentrated in the hands of a smaller and smaller group of people at the top of society.

Later chapters will explore the nature and extent of this concentration.

From the *interactionist perspective,* the key characteristic of the mass media is the power to shape definitions of a given situation through the ability to create, manipulate, and distribute symbols. By selecting what is presented and how it is presented, the media shape what people see as important and the meanings that are attached to people and events. As will be seen in Chapters 8 and 9, for example, people's definitions of what is proper behavior for men and women are influenced by how certain behaviors are portrayed in the media. In the 1950s, television shows such as *Father Knows Best, Ozzie and Harriet,* and *The Honeymooners* portrayed men as the intelligent, strong workers who earned money to support their families while the women stayed at home and did housework and raised children. Although this portrayal was a reflection of reality to an extent, it was also a distortion of reality because many women with children worked, and single mothers were not uncommon (although they were less common than today). Even though distorted, however, this portrayal of family life on television influenced the social meanings that people attached to the institution of the family: People tended to see the normal or desired family as consisting of a working father, a stay-at-home mother, and two children. The media rendition of the family became the symbol against which people tended to compare and assess their own personal circumstances. In the 1990s, different portrayals, such as successful single mothers on *Murphy Brown,* offer different symbols of the family. In these many ways, the mass media shape definitions of reality.

Using the Theoretical Perspectives

The preceding discussion of the sociological perspectives is brief and simplified, and there will be more detail in the remaining chapters. The major elements of each perspective have been outlined in Table 1.1. The three perspectives should not be viewed as either right or wrong, nor should one select a favorite and ignore the others. Instead, the perspectives should be seen as three different tools, each of which is useful in analyzing particular social phenomena. The three perspectives are not equally useful for examining every social topic,

TABLE 1.1 An outline of the sociological perspectives

	Functionalism	Conflict Theory	Interactionism
View of society	A system of interrelated and interdependent parts	Made up of groups struggling with one another over scarce resources	Individuals in face-to-face interaction create social consensus
View of the individual	Little concern with personality; people are shaped by society to perform important functions for society	Little concern with personality; people are shaped by social institutions and the position of their groups in society	People are symbol manipulators; the self (personality) arises from communication and social interaction
View of social change	The social system tends to resist change as disruptive	Change is inevitable and continuous	Change occurs when there is no shared consensus about expected behavior; change involves developing a newly found consensus
Key concepts	Integration, interdependence, stability, equilibrium	Interest, power, dominance, conflict, coercion	Interpretation, consensus, symbols, shared expectations, socially created reality

nor can any single perspective explain all aspects of human behavior and society. Furthermore, to gain a full understanding of any particular topic, the use of more than one approach may be required. In a sense, the perspectives are similar to a physician's instruments. Because of the human body's complexity, a doctor needs many devices to keep tabs on a person's health. Social phenomena are also very complex, and the theoretical perspectives are the instruments that sociologists have developed over the years to help them understand human behavior and society.

Conducting Sociological Research

You should be able to describe the three most commonly used research methods in sociology and discuss the problems of reactivity, objectivity, and ethics that all researchers confront.

It was pointed out earlier that science rests on systematic observation to determine how the world works. This section gives a brief introduction to how this observation is made in sociology so that you can better appreciate the contribution sociology makes to our understanding of the world.

Sociological research can have three distinct goals. Some research focuses on *description,* the search for factual information about some event, condition, or behavior. Descriptive research is typically used with a new topic about which we know little. Although description is an important part of research, most sociologists would also hope to explain and predict what they observe. *Explanation* is the goal of telling why or how something happened, whereas *prediction* refers to using known facts and explanations to forecast what will happen in the future or in different settings. In actuality, a single research project might involve description, explanation, and prediction.

Research Methods

Once hypotheses have been constructed, sociologists develop *a detailed plan that specifies how observations will be made in order to test the hypotheses.* Such plans are called **research methods.** The three methods most commonly used by sociologists are observational techniques, surveys, and experiments.

Observational Techniques   One of the fundamental research techniques used by sociologists involves looking, listening, and recording what they have observed. **Observational techniques** refer to *the direct observation of behavior by sociologists, either by seeing or hearing what people do.* These techniques can be used in many different settings. Observations are sometimes made in the artificial setting of a laboratory, where people are observed through a one-way window or their behavior is videotaped. In one study, for example, people were asked to report to a room in order to participate in a study of group activity. When they arrived, however, there was no one in the room and no hints were provided about what they should do. The investigator, Sandra Ball-Rokeach (1973), then observed through a one-way mirror how the people dealt with this very ambiguous situation. Her findings provided valuable information about how people react to confusing or ambiguous experiences, such as earthquakes or the bewildering aftermath of a war. She found, for example, that smaller groups of people are more cooperative and more effective at developing a plan of action for dealing with ambiguous situations than larger groups. She also observed that group activities fluctuated between those that focused on obtaining information to use in coping with the situation and those that enabled people to release the tension generated by the ambiguity.

Observations are also made in natural settings. This process is called **participant observation,** in which *the investigators take part in the activities of the people being studied.* Participant observation gives sociologists access to the everyday routines of people in a natural setting. Proponents of participant observation maintain that it is the most effective way to understand behavior from the perspective of the people under investigation and to learn about their beliefs, values, and views of their lives (Berg, 1989; Lofland & Lofland, 1995). An illustration of participant observation is the study of a slum community in Chicago by the sociologist Gerald Suttles (1968). This community, called the Addams area, was home for a number of racial and ethnic groups, including African Americans, Italians, Puerto Ricans, and Latinos. Suttles lived in the Addams area for about three years, beginning in the summer of 1963. Some participant observers make known their identity as researchers, but Suttles chose not to. Instead, he claimed to be a research assistant in a program sponsored by a local boys'

club aimed at fighting juvenile delinquency. This "cover story" enabled him to gain the trust and confidence that are essential for participant observers to obtain reliable information.

After three years of intensive observation, Suttles recognized that there is considerable social order in slum communities that outsiders cannot see. People tend to stereotype slums as dangerous and violent places, with marauding gangs adding to the chaos, but Suttles found that youth gangs actually protected the neighborhood from the aggression of others. In fact, he referred to such gangs as "vigilante peer groups," because they kept outsiders from preying on residents of the community. Many residents in the Addams area recognized that the gangs offered them a degree of protection while realizing that the gangs themselves could be a source of concern. Through his observations, then, Suttles was able to develop hypotheses regarding the role of gangs in maintaining order.

Not all gangs serve this protective function. More recently, the sociologist Ruth Horowitz (1987) conducted participant observation research on a Latino gang. She lived in the community where the gang members lived and went to their dances, parties, and homes. She did not conceal her research role as Suttles did because her identity did not pose a threat to the collection of valid data. In this community, residents disapproved of gang violence, but they also recognized that such violence was the youths' response to a distortion of the value of "honor" common in Latin American communities. Honor includes the idea that a man should command respect in his contacts with others. For the youths, toughness and violence (often alluded to as *machismo*) become a prime way of maintaining honor. Adults reject the violence but recognize the importance of protecting honor, so they have a negative but ambivalent attitude toward gang violence. Suttles's and Horowitz's participant observations have provided us with rich insight into the complexity that underlies gang activities among young people. Other research methods could not have provided this intimate view of the workings of a community or a juvenile gang.

Observational studies are valuable in that they focus on behavior in real-life situations where people are neither coaxed nor coached by the investigator. People behave much as they would if they were not being studied. Observational techniques also have certain drawbacks, however. The data gathered are often difficult to analyze, and the investigator's interpretation of the data often cannot be evaluated effectively by someone who was not at the scene. Thus, it is difficult to detect whether the investigator may have overemphasized some events and ignored others. In addition, participant observers sometimes find themselves under considerable pressure to join in the ways of those they are studying, so there is the danger that they may "go native" and become so identified with the group being studied that they lose objectivity (Shupe & Bromley, 1980).

Surveys **Surveys** involve *the collection of data by asking people questions about their behavior or attitudes.* Surveys can take the form of interviews or questionnaires.

In *interviews,* the investigator or an assistant asks questions and records answers. Some interviews are highly structured, with an interviewer asking the same questions of each person in the same order. Less structured interviews allow the investigator to deviate from a specified list of questions in order to make the inquiry more clear or to pursue some novel issue that may arise.

A *questionnaire* is a survey based on printed questions that people answer directly on a prepared form without the aid of an interviewer. Some questionnaires are administered directly to people, and others are mailed with instructions on how to complete and return them.

An interesting example of an ongoing survey is one conducted on first-year college students every year by the Higher Education Research Institute at the University of California at Los Angeles. The survey is given each fall to a nationally representative sample of first-time students at two-year and four-year colleges and universities. The surveys ask, among other things, about the students' values and goals in life. One question is the following:

Indicate the importance to you personally of each of the following:

a. helping others who are in difficulty
b. raising a family
c. being very well-off financially
d. developing a meaningful philosophy of life

For each alternative, the students can choose from these response choices: essential, very important, somewhat important, and not important. Students' responses to these questions during the period 1966 to 1989 are presented in Figure 1.3. (on p. 24) The most dramatic trends over this period are an increase in materialistic values, with many more students by 1989 placing importance in being financially well-off, and a dramatic decline in students who place value in a meaningful philosophy of life. During the same period, family issues seem to have grown in importance.

When doing surveys, sociologists are often interested in the responses of a large group of people, such as all college students, all Roman Catholics, or all Democrats. Obviously, it would be very expensive to survey such large groups, so instead researchers select a *sample,* a portion of the large group of interest, and the survey is then given to the sample. A critical consideration is to ensure that the sample is representative of the whole group. A *representative sample* is one that accurately reflects the characteristics of the population under study. The problems created when samples are not representative were illustrated in early investigations of homosexuality. During the 1940s and 1950s, studies of gay men by psychologists and psychiatrists using samples of people who had received psychological counseling led to the conclusion that homosexuality was the result of a personality disturbance that stemmed from disordered relationships with parents during childhood (Bieber et al., 1962). Virtually all of the homosexuals in the samples had such relationships with their parents—a strong association, indeed. The problem in the sampling technique employed is fairly obvious, however. Gay men who seek psychological or psychiatric counseling *are not representative* of all gay men. People who seek therapy, whether they be homosexual or heterosexual, do so because they *already* have personal problems. Gay men who did not have problems did not seek counseling in the first place, so they were not in the population from which the samples were chosen. Thus, these early studies contained a built-in bias toward the finding that gay men were psychologically disturbed. More recent surveys that included gays who were not receiving counseling have concluded that gay men and lesbians are no more likely than heterosexuals to

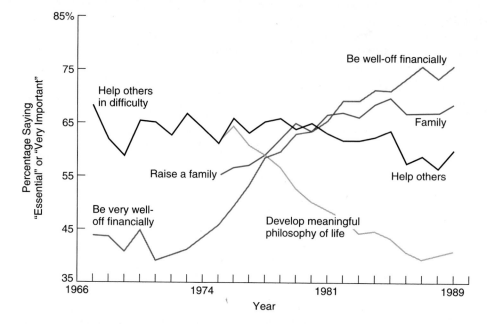

FIGURE 1.3 Values and Goals of First-Year College Students, 1966–1989 *Note:* From "Private materialism, personal self-fulfillment, family life, and public interest: The nature, effects, and causes of recent changes in the values of American youth," by Richard E. Easterlin and Eileen M. Crimmins, 1991, *Public Opinion Quarterly, 55,* p. 508.

have personality disturbances (Ross, Paulsen, & Stalstrom, 1988; Savin-Williams, 1990).

Surveys permit scientists to gather data inexpensively from a large number of people. They also enable sociologists to gather data about events that occurred in the past, such as how people voted in the last presidential election. In addition, surveys are used in tracing changes in behavior over time by replicating the survey at suitable intervals. But like all research techniques, surveys have their shortcomings. Because surveys are based on people's reports of their attitudes and behaviors, the resulting data may be inaccurate if people forget or misrepresent their views. In addition, surveys do not afford the rich data that are often obtained through other, more "natural" research designs, such as participant observation.

Experiments An **experiment** is *a controlled method of observation in which independent variables are manipulated in order to assess their effects on a dependent vari-*

able. In a common type of experiment, an *experimental group* is exposed to some factor, the independent variable, while a *control group,* which is like the experimental group in all other respects, is not exposed to that factor (see Figure 1.4). If a change occurs in the dependent variable within the experimental group but not the control group, then the change can be attributed to the independent variable. The key to an experiment is to make sure that the experimental and control groups are as similar as possible (in terms, for example, of age, gender, education, or social class background) so that variations in these factors can be ruled out as causes of differences between the two groups on the dependent variable.

An example of a sociological experiment was a study of how to reduce *recidivism,* or crimes committed by people after their release from prison (Rossi, Berk, & Lenihan, 1980). On the assumption that ex-prisoners commit crimes because they cannot support themselves, these sociologists hypothesized that ex-prisoners would be less likely

A. A Simplified Experimental Design

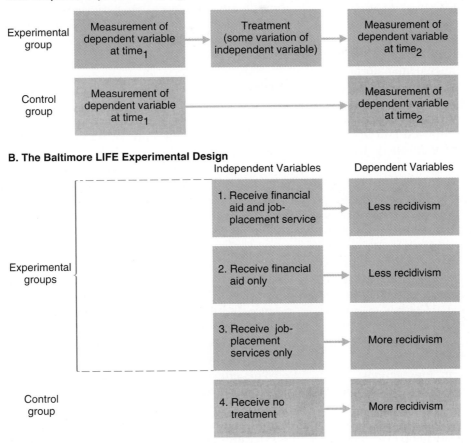

B. The Baltimore LIFE Experimental Design

FIGURE 1.4 A Diagram of Experimental Designs

to commit future crimes if their financial situation was improved upon release from prison.

The focus of the Baltimore LIFE (Living Insurance For Ex-prisoners) Project was inmates in Maryland state prisons who, on the basis of prior studies of released prisoners, were judged likely to commit another felony after release. These "high-risk" inmates were young males with multiple convictions, little financial security, and at least one property-related arrest. Two independent variables were used in this study: the provision of financial aid and job-placement services to these men upon release from prison (see Figure 1.4). There were three experimental groups. One received financial aid and job-placement services; a second received financial aid but no job-placement services; and the third

received job-placement services but no financial aid. The fourth group, a control group, received neither job-placement services nor financial aid. Inmates were randomly assigned to one of these four groups. The dependent variables were whether the ex-prisoners committed crimes after release and whether they were returned to prison.

The results of the study suggested that financial aid helped to reduce recidivism. The two groups who received financial aid had considerably lower rates of property-related crimes after being released than the other groups, a longer period of time passed before they were arrested again, and they were less likely ever to return to prison. However, financial aid did not affect the likelihood of these ex-prisoners committing *nonproperty* crimes. Job-placement counseling did not appear to help reduce recidivism: The two groups receiving financial aid had lower rates of recidivism whether or not they received job-placement counseling.

The Baltimore LIFE Project exemplifies *field experiments,* which are conducted in natural settings as people go about their everyday affairs. In *laboratory experiments,* artificial environments are constructed in which selected elements of the natural environment can be simulated and features of the investigation can be controlled. In one classic laboratory experiment, for example, authority relationships were simulated through an experimenter issuing orders to those participating in the study to administer strong electrical shocks to others. Although no one actually received electrical shocks, those who participated thought they were giving shocks and were surprisingly willing to obey the orders (Milgram, 1973). Through such simulations, we can learn about other authority relationships, such as soldiers obeying the commands of their superiors.

The major advantage of experiments is the ability to control extraneous variables and to determine whether changes in independent variables are the cause of changes in the dependent variable. Experiments can have drawbacks, however. The artificial setting of laboratory experiments, for example, may lead people to behave differently from the way they would if exposed to similar influences in a natural setting. In addition, in both field and laboratory experiments, the experiment and the experimenter may influence people's behavior in ways that cannot be predicted. This possibility is sometimes called the *experimenter effect.* The subjects in experiments may consciously or unconsciously pick up cues from the researcher about how they should respond. If they do, then changes in the dependent variable may be due to these influences rather than to the effects of the independent variable. Finally, many experiments, especially those conducted in laboratory settings, are limited to rather small samples, which makes generalizations to larger groups somewhat hazardous.

Issues in Conducting Sociological Research

Scientists studying human social behavior face some difficulties that are quite different from those that confront natural scientists. People, after all, are self-aware; they have opinions, emotions, and personalities that can make the sociologist's task more difficult, and in some cases very frustrating.

Reactivity The term *reactivity* refers to the fact that people react to being studied and may behave differently from the way they do when they don't think they are being studied. Suppose you are a parent and a sociologist enters your home to observe your relationships with your children. Videotaping equipment is set up to record your every word and move. Would you behave in the same way you would if the observer were not present? You might, but most people would feel strong pressures to be on their toes and present themselves as good parents. You might be tempted to be more permissive with and tolerant of your child than usual, giving fewer negative sanctions and being more forgiving. In other words, people *react* to being observed, and sociologists must take this tendency into account when conducting their research.

The effects of reactivity on sociological research were well illustrated in a study of worker productivity conducted at the Hawthorne Plant of the Western Electric Company near Chicago several decades ago (Jones, 1990; Roethlisberger & Dickson, 1939). The investigators began by introducing a number of improvements in the working environment, such as better lighting, more rest periods, and shorter workdays. Following each of these changes, worker productivity increased, which was what the investigators expected to happen. Had they stopped at this point, however, their conclusions would have been inaccurate, as the next phase in the investigation demonstrated. The experimenters then *reversed* the improvements by dimming the lighting, shortening the rest periods, and lengthening the workday. To the investigators' surprise, productivity continued to increase! After careful assessment, it became clear what had happened. The attention that the workers received as a consequence of being subjects in the study, rather than the specific changes in working conditions, led to the observed alterations in their performance. The workers viewed themselves as a special group who had been "chosen" to receive personal treatment by the company, and they responded by working harder. This type of reactivity is now referred to as the *Hawthorne effect:* The attention that people receive because they are involved in a scientific inquiry may alter their behavior. The experimenter effects discussed under the topic of experimental research designs are another form of reactivity.

Values and Objectivity   An issue that is especially important and quite controversial regarding research in sociology is that of scientific objectivity, or the attempt by scientists to prevent their personal values from affecting the outcome of their research. This effort does not mean that scientists are without values or passions. Many are intensely concerned about social problems such as crime, divorce, family violence, and nuclear war. At the same time, scientists realize that their personal values can, and probably will, bias their research. Early in the twentieth century, the sociologist Max Weber laid out one position on this issue when he argued that sociology should remain as *value-free* as possible because human values can distort sound scientific investigation (1919/1958). Weber thought that sociologists should suspend their personal and political values when engaging in scientific research. Present-day advocates of Weber's position would concede that such suspension is difficult to accomplish but that abandoning the effort would be disastrous: There would be no means of acquiring an accurate body of knowledge about human social behavior (Gordon, 1988).

Karl Marx (1848/1964) eloquently stated a position opposite to that of Weber's on this controversy. Marx was a strong champion of the cause of the poor and the downtrodden, and he wanted to use science to improve their plight. He thought that social scientists should bring strong moral commitments to their work and use science to change inequitable or immoral social conditions. Likewise, some sociologists today believe that social research should be guided by personal and political values and directed toward alleviating social ills (Fay, 1987; Harding, 1986).

The sociologist Alvin Gouldner (1976) has suggested a reasonable middle ground between these two positions. He agreed that scientists have values and that the influence of those values on research, which is often very subtle, can never be totally eliminated. But he proposed that we should deny neither our values nor the negative impact they can have on research. He urged that scientists should be explicit about what their values are. In this way, other scientists are forewarned and are thus better able to spot ways in which research findings may be influenced by personal bias.

Of course, science has built-in checks against the influence of personal bias. For example, because science is provisional and studies are often repeated, a particular area of inquiry is likely to be investigated by many scientists holding different values. If these diverse scientists reach similar conclusions, we can be reasonably confident that the conclusions are not biased by personal values. Checks such as these, although they are not foolproof, do enable the scientific method to advance toward establishing an objective body of knowledge about human social behavior.

Ethics   Sociological research is not an abstract affair carried out in the confines of musty academic halls. Quite the contrary, research brings sociologists in direct contact with people in all realms of their lives, and research can change those people's lives. Therefore, sociologists must consider whether research they conduct is ethical. Ethics has to do with what is proper or improper behavior, with moral duty and obligation. Basically, ethical research avoids violating the rights of the people being studied or harming them in any fashion. One ethical standard that sociologists follow is to protect people's right to *privacy,* or their ability to control when and under what conditions researchers will have access to their beliefs, thoughts, or behaviors. A related ethical standard is *confidentiality,* or ensuring that information or responses that people give a sociologist are not made public in a way that others could identify whose responses they are.

Problems of violating these ethical standards were dramatically raised in a very controversial research project conducted by Laud Humphreys (1970). Humphreys made observations of men having quick and impersonal sex in public restrooms. This research was participant observation, in which Humphreys acted as the "watch-queen," who warned of the approach of the police or of straight males while two other men had sex.

Humphreys did not tell the other participants that he was a researcher making scientific observations. He also noted the license plate numbers of the men's cars and was able to learn their addresses through public motor vehicle records. He then interviewed the men in their homes, gathering details about their personal lives but never letting on that he was doing research on their sexual behavior.

Many sociologists heavily criticized Humphreys's procedures on the grounds that he violated the subjects' right to privacy. Even though the men were clearly trying to hide their behavior from prying eyes, Humphreys made his observations without seeking their approval. One way of protecting privacy is through *informed consent:* telling research participants of all aspects of the research that might reasonably be expected to influence their decision about whether to participate. Issues of privacy, confidentiality, and informed consent are especially important in Humphreys's research because the men observed were engaging in highly stigmatized behavior. If the behavior became public knowledge, it might have changed their lives, since many of the men were married and had children. Many sociologists fault Humphreys for violating the men's privacy and failing to obtain informed consent.

Humphreys and his defenders argue that no ethical violations occurred because the men were in a public place and thus their behavior was legitimately accessible to Humphreys or anyone else who had a right to be in that place. In addition, Humphreys went to great lengths to protect the confidentiality of the information he collected. He took steps to ensure that the men's identities could not be discovered by anyone other than himself, and he destroyed anything that could identify them once he was done with his research project. In fact, none of the men's identities ever did become known to anyone but Humphreys.

Humphreys's research illustrates how ethical problems can be controversial and difficult to resolve. They can also require as much attention from the sociologist as does the actual conduct of the research itself. Humphreys spent much of his career debating and justifying his research. In recent years, some sociologists have actually spent time in jail in order to protect the privacy or confidentiality of their research subjects. For exam-

ple, the sociologist Rik Scarce conducted research on activists in the animal liberation movement in the early 1990s (Monaghan, 1993). A federal grand jury was investigating break-ins by such activists at university laboratories, and some of the activists the grand jury was interested in had been interviewed by Scarce as part of his research. He refused to answer certain questions about these activists put to him by the grand jury because he thought that it would violate the confidentiality he had extended to the people he interviewed. He was jailed for four months on contempt-of-court charges, suggesting how important the ethical issue of confidentiality was to Scarce. Generally, the courts have held that confidential communication between a researcher and research participant is not privileged, that is, protected from intrusion by the courts.

So, the consequences of research can be profound, and sociologists are very careful about what research they do and how they do it in order to avoid making ethical breaches. In fact, the American Sociological Association (ASA), the Society for Applied Sociology (SAS), and the Sociological Practice Association (SPA) all publish a Code of Ethics that assists sociologists in dealing with these issues. However, these issues are inherently complicated, and they are made more complex when sociologists do research in cultures different from their own, as the Other Worlds, Other Ways sections illustrate.

Putting Sociology to Use

You should be able to distinguish between basic and applied sociology, describe the different types of sociological practice, and show how sociology can be used in your everyday life.

The Development of Sociology

Sociology emerged in the 1800s and early 1900s as an instrument of both understanding and social reform (Lazarsfeld & Reitz, 1989). The nineteenth-century French philosopher Auguste Comte is considered the father of sociology because he was the first to use the term *sociology*. He argued strongly that society should be studied according to the same scientific methods that were used to understand the natural world. At about the same time, Harriet Martineau set the tone for a reformist sociology with her sociological work in England. She did research and writing on issues of slavery, colonialism, and the impact of industrialization on women (Hoecker-Drysdale, 1992). Early sociologists in the United States were also strongly motivated by a desire to reform society and make life better for people. In the early 1900s, for example, Albion Small focused his sociological analysis on problems of corruption and poverty in the United States, while Jane Addams concentrated her sociological work on the problems of poor women in the slums of Chicago. W.E.B. Du Bois, an African American sociologist, used sociological insight to attack the racism and exploitation that African Americans experienced at the hands of whites in the United States and elsewhere. Another African American sociologist, E. Franklin Frazier, conducted a groundbreaking study of a race riot in Harlem in 1935 that was a considerable advance over the understanding of such riots at the time (Deegan, 1988; Platt, 1991).

While this reform tradition has continued in sociology, another important trend emerged by the 1930s: the attempt to establish sociology as a legitimate and respected field of study in the eyes of laypeople, especially influential people who had money and other resources that the new discipline needed to support its research and develop new theoretical and methodological tools. For many sociologists, the discipline could best gain legitimacy and respectability by emphasizing the scientific, quantitative, and objective nature of the discipline. The best way to carve a societal niche, many thought, was to emphasize sociology's objective quest for knowledge and stress its independence from any special interests in society. To achieve this objectivity, many sociologists downplayed the reform emphasis of the discipline, and the pursuit of knowledge for the sake of knowledge rather than social change became the overriding thrust of many sociologists' work for a number of decades.

By the 1960s and 1970s, sociology had secured its position in society, and many sociologists were ready to give renewed emphasis to issues of reform and the practical uses of sociology. Today the discipline exhibits more of a balance between what have come to be called basic and applied sociology. In addition, sociologists remain as diverse a group as they were in earlier years in terms of racial or ethnic background and gender. Small, Martineau, and Du Bois have been replaced by black, Asian, and Hispanic male and female sociologists in the United States and around the world. As pointed out in Other Worlds, Other Ways: South Africa, this diversity is important to the ability of the discipline to understand diverse ways of life.

Basic and Applied Sociology

All sciences, including sociology, make a distinction between basic (or pure) science and applied science. The primary focus of basic science is to advance our understanding of some phenomenon, whereas applied science focuses on solving some real-world problem. Both basic and applied sociology are based on observation, but what they do with these observations is quite different.

The primary focus of basic sociology is on developing theories of human social behavior and testing hypotheses derived from those theories. **Basic sociology** refers to *sociological research whose purpose is to advance our knowledge about human social behavior with little concern for any immediate practical benefits that might result.* Basic sociology is an attempt to develop theories that explain how societies work and why people behave the way they do; the goal of basic sociology is to subject theories to the process of theory verification described earlier in this chapter.

Applied sociology consists of *research and other activities designed to focus sociological knowledge or research tools on a particular problem identified by some client with some practical outcome in mind* (Larson, 1995; Sullivan, 1992). The primary focus of applied sociology is on policy or changes in behavior: making recommendations about social programs or policies that might be implemented or about how to change behaviors. Applied sociology uses sociological theories and research tools to tackle some particular problem that somebody wants solved. It addresses questions like these: How well does some program or practice work? Does it achieve its goals? What consequences does it have? The overall focus is to direct existing knowledge and research tools toward the end of

OTHER WORLDS, *Other Ways*

SOUTH AFRICA: SOCIOLOGICAL RESEARCH IN DIVERSE CULTURES

Conducting sound sociological research can be a challenge in a culturally diverse world because the social and cultural context in which research is carried out can influence what kind of research can be done, how it can be done, and the validity of the results. In other words, sociologists need to know a lot about the culture in which they will be conducting research.

Certain political and social values are widely held in the United States. For example, most Americans believe that people should have autonomy and a right to self-determination—a right to control their life and what happens to them. Another widely held value is individualism, the belief that the individual's desires and achievements are more important than society's advancement or goals. Congruent with these values, the United States incorporates into its legal system many protections for individuals against the arbitrary exercise of power by the state or by powerful groups over the less powerful. In the realm of sociological research, these values imply that participation in such research should be voluntary and considered; people should never be tricked or coerced into participating. In line with these values, as has been shown, sociologists are

expected to obtain informed consent in which the people participating in the research are told what the research is about; what they will be expected to do as participants; any discomfort, harm, or stress they might experience; and who will benefit from the research. This expectation works well in most situations in the United States where most people are well educated and tend to be knowledgeable about the rights and protections that are available to them. In this cultural context, the ASA Code of Ethics can be implemented in a straightforward fashion: People are asked to sign a consent form on which is written all they need to know in deciding whether they will agree to participate.

If the research project is shifted from North America to black South Africa during the period of *apartheid,* when black South Africans were rigidly oppressed and had few social, political, or economic rights or opportunities, the situation is entirely different. For example, the sociologist Ivy Goduka conducted research on black schoolchildren in South Africa in the 1980s, before the end of *apartheid.* As Goduka put it at that time:

> South Africa is an authoritarian society that gives little or no state protection of individual rights, particularly for blacks. . . . [The apartheid laws] deny blacks in South Africa the right to vote and serve to keep them landless, powerless, and lacking in all the basic resources necessary for survival. Because they lack basic resources, blacks

social intervention. We may learn something new about human behavior along the way, but that is not the main point.

Sociologists who do basic research are typically employed at colleges or universities where their professional duties include doing research as well as teaching. Some applied sociologists are employed by universities, but many work for federal, state, or local government, private industry, or nonprofit organizations. In recent decades, at least one-quarter of sociologists with a doctoral degree have been employed in such nonuniversity settings (Lyson & Squires, 1993).

Sociological Practice

Applied sociologists do a number of specific kinds of jobs (Iutcovich & Iutcovich, 1987; Rebach & Bruhn, 1991). Some are *applied researchers* who collect and analyze data in order to recommend solutions to a particular problem faced by a client or organization. Some applied researchers, for

SOUTH AFRICA
0   miles   2000

Johannesburg

Cape Town

are not only illiterate and poverty-stricken, but also ignorant, vulnerable, and powerless to make decisions and choices directly affecting their own lives. (1990, pp. 329–330)

At that time, black South Africans could be told where to live, moved arbitrarily by the government, and even have their homes demolished if the government deemed it necessary. In all these circumstances, individuals had little say. The implications for informed consent in research are straightforward, according to Goduka: "Informed consent has no meaning to subjects who cannot even choose where they are to live, much less consent through elections to the government that makes those decisions for them" (1990, p. 333). The parents of the children Goduka studied lacked the education to read and understand the consent form. Established institutions such as school or government were so authoritarian that these black South Africans did not feel they had any choice in signing a consent form their child brought home from school. They agreed to participate in Goduka's research, but for most it was not a free and considered decision. Rather, they agreed so that no troubles would come to their children or as a submissive response to what were seen as all-powerful institutions. Some probably consented because they looked up to well-educated black South Africans (such as Goduka) who, they

hoped, might be able to bring some positive change to their lives.

So, the world looked very different to these South Africans, and the informed consent form had a meaning for them that was very different from the meaning it had for most people in North America or Europe. In fact, Goduka approached families in Michigan with the same consent form and encountered substantial resistance from both teachers and parents to the use of their students and children in research. People in the United States may not have understood the intricacies of sociological research, but they could read and understand the consent form, and more importantly, they accepted the belief that they could refuse participation even if that meant challenging institutional sources of power such as schools or the government. However, the South African experience cautions sociologists to recognize that some people in the United States may not be in a position to give truly informed consent either. Any subordinate group—prison inmates, the poor, racial minorities, in some cases even women—may feel strong pressures to agree to participate in research, especially when those requesting consent are the people or organizations that exercise some control over them. Once again, diversity both between and within societies provides some insight into social life.

example, have collected and analyzed data for the government to assess how well welfare reform policies achieve their goals. Others work for private corporations analyzing the best markets for new products.

A second type of applied sociologists are *sociological consultants*, sometimes called *social engineers*. They make recommendations to clients for changes in policies, programs, or practices based on the existing body of sociological knowledge about human groups and human social behavior.

Unlike applied researchers, consultants do not collect and analyze data themselves but rather rely on the sociological knowledge distilled from the research, both basic and applied, of others. Using this knowledge, sociological consultants offer solutions to problems for clients or offer a general understanding of the sociocultural environment relevant to a client. For example, a sociological consultant might use past research on the link between socioeconomic status and attitudes toward crime to help a lawyer pick a jury that would be most fair in its treatment of the lawyer's client. In other situations sociological consultants might make recommendations to a government agency or Congress regarding social policies that would achieve particular political goals.

A third category of applied sociologists is *clinical sociologists,* who attempt a sociological diagnosis of group problems and the behavior of people in groups and develop a planned program of change. Some clinical sociologists, for example, conduct family counseling directed toward helping families overcome problems, whereas others help people change undesired behaviors such as overeating or alcohol abuse (Fritz, 1991; Roberts, 1991). As with sociological consultants, sociological clinicians use existing sociological knowledge without conducting research themselves.

Sometimes the terms *applied sociology* or *sociological practice* are used to refer to these three spheres taken together (applied research, sociological consulting, and clinical sociology). The lines between the different spheres are not sharp: A sociologist might engage in all three activities as a part of a single project.

Using Sociology in Everyday Life

Most people who work as professional sociologists have either a master's degree or a doctorate in sociology. However, it is not necessary to achieve this level of education in order to put sociology to use. People with a bachelor's degree in sociology work in corrections, social service agencies, private business, journalism, urban planning, and many other job settings. In these jobs, sociological training is valuable because it informs the workers about the social sources of crime, poverty, and worker motivation, as well as about how cities work and organizations function. In fact, because virtually all jobs involve working with people and their social behaviors at some level, training in sociology can provide valuable knowledge for many jobs. In addition to teaching about social behavior, sociological training also imparts specific skills that employers are looking for: skills in research (including statistical and computer analysis training), critical thinking and problem solving, and interpersonal communication.

Of course, not everyone will major in sociology, because there are other useful majors. Nevertheless, students who major in economics, public relations, social work, business, or related fields can gain valuable support in their future work by choosing a minor in sociology or taking sociology courses as electives. The sociological insight gained will serve as a valuable adjunct to training in another major.

Beyond its utility in the workplace, sociology also has applications to our everyday lives as we make our way as social creatures through a world filled with other social creatures. The understanding of human behavior that sociology imparts can provide insight into the daily actions and choices of ourselves and others around us. Sociology tells us about why people marry and divorce, what functions religion performs, and how racism and sexism can affect the self-esteem and accomplishments of those against whom they are directed. Because practically all of us have some experience with these issues in our lives, sociology can provide us with the insight to make more informed choices. Sociology cannot tell us which choices to make, because nonsociological considerations, including religious and personal values, are a part of such choices. Sociology does, however, provide information about the social forces that shape our behavior. It also offers a valuable perspective, the sociological imagination, which makes us aware of how much our lives and behavior are shaped by social factors rather than biological or psychological ones. After all, students read books and take courses on health and medical care, even though they do not plan to be a doctor or a nurse; they merely want to learn enough to lead a more healthy life, recognize symptoms that need attending to, and be able to treat minor ailments that do not require medical intervention. In a similar fashion, even though you may not become a professional sociologist, you can learn enough about social structure and social process in this and other sociology courses so that you can more effectively navigate the social waters in which you will swim throughout your life.

Summary

1. Sociology is the scientific study of societies and human social behavior. The sociological perspective emphasizes the powerful role that group membership and social forces play in shaping

human behavior. A key element of the sociological perspective is the recognition that beliefs, values, and behaviors can be understood only in the context of the view of reality shared by a particular group or society.

2. Sociology is a science, which means that it is based on objective and systematic knowledge gained through empirical observation. Science, as a source of knowledge, is empirical, systematic, focused on causation, provisional, and objective.

3. In order to explain social phenomena, sociologists develop theories, which are linked to sociological research through hypotheses, or tentative statements that can be tested regarding the relationships between two or more variables.

4. Three theoretical perspectives guide most sociological research. The functionalist perspective views society as a system made up of interrelated and interdependent parts, each performing a function that contributes to the operation of the whole. The conflict perspective views society as consisting of numerous interest groups who struggle with one another in order to obtain scarce resources. The interactionist perspective focuses on everyday social interaction that is shaped by social meanings and shared expectations.

5. Research methods are the detailed plans that sociologists develop regarding how they will make observations to test hypotheses. The three most-used research methods are observational techniques, surveys, and experiments.

6. In studying human behavior, sociologists confront some special difficulties. One problem has to do with the phenomenon of reactivity: knowing that they are being observed, people may behave in ways they ordinarily would not. A second problem has to do with values and objectivity. There is considerable debate over whether sociology should be value-free or whether its purpose should be to change unfair and inequitable conditions. A third problem has to do with conducting ethical research, in which sociologists protect the privacy and confidentiality of those they study and follow procedures for informed consent.

7. The primary goal of basic sociology is to test theories and advance our knowledge of human social behavior; applied sociology focuses on social intervention, solving problems, and practical outcomes. Sociological practice can involve applied research, sociological consulting, and clinical sociology.

STUDY *Review*

Key Terms

applied sociology

basic sociology

conflict perspective

definition of the situation

dependent variable

experiment

functionalist perspective

hypothesis

independent variable

interactionist perspective

mass media

observational techniques

participant observation

research methods

science

sociological imagination

sociological perspective

sociology

survey

theoretical perspective

theory

variable

Multiple-Choice Questions

1. Which of the following statements would *not* be considered a part of the definition of the discipline of sociology?
   a. It is a scientific study.
   b. It studies societies.
   c. It studies human social behavior.
   d. It studies human genetic predispositions.
   e. All of the above are part of the definition.

2. Which of the following is *not* one of the distinguishing characteristics of science?
   a. Causation.
   b. Provisional.
   c. Objective.
   d. All of the above are distinguishing characteristics.
   e. Only a and c are distinguishing characteristics.

3. According to the chapter, commonsense knowledge
   a. is often superior to scientific knowledge.
   b. is based on systematic observation.
   c. usually involves representative samples.
   d. tends to accept untested and unquestioned assumptions.

4. The term *macrosociology* refers to theoretical perspectives in sociology that
   a. focus on large groups and social institutions and on society as a whole.
   b. derive from the functionalist perspective.
   c. focus on the intimate level of everyday interactions between people.
   d. focus on people's ability to use symbols and to interpret social meanings in social interaction.

5. Which sociological perspective grew out of the similarities that early sociologists observed between society and biological organisms?
   a. The functionalist perspective.
   b. The conflict perspective.
   c. The commonsense perspective.
   d. The interactionist perspective.

6. Which sociological perspective has at its core the idea that coercion and the exercise of power are basic social mechanisms for regulating behavior and allocating resources?
   a. The functionalist perspective.
   b. The conflict perspective.
   c. The sociological imagination.
   d. The interactionist perspective.

7. Which of the following statements would be most consistent with the interactionist perspective?
   a. Society is made up of groups struggling with one another over scarce resources.
   b. People are symbol manipulators who create their own world.
   c. Social problems arise when some element in society becomes dysfunctional.
   d. Society is a system made up of interrelated and interdependent parts.

8. Which sociological research method involves the collection of data by asking people questions about their behavior or attitudes?
   a. Observational techniques.
   b. Experiments.
   c. Surveys.
   d. Reactivity.
   e. Participant observation.

9. In conducting research in sociology, the best kind of sample to use is one that
   a. focuses only on people who are suffering from the problem being studied.
   b. will confirm the hypotheses of the research.
   c. is consistent with the values of the researcher.
   d. represents the whole group that is being studied.

10. Which of the following statements best characterizes basic and applied sociology today?
   a. Basic sociology has been dispensed with and applied sociology now dominates.
   b. Applied sociology has been dispensed with and basic sociology now dominates.
   c. There is a balance between basic and applied sociology.
   d. Both basic and applied sociology have been dispensed with in favor of scientific sociology.

True/False Questions

1. In comparing the contrasting viewpoints of adolescents and adults, the key task that a sociological analysis would focus on is to determine which viewpoint is correct.

2. Sociologists do not conduct research on commonsense beliefs because they mostly turn out to be true.

3. Sociology, economics, and anthropology are all considered to be social sciences.

4. Independent variables are variables that are presumed to bring about changes in other variables.

5. One of the main criticisms of the conflict perspective is that it overemphasizes the extent of social stability in society.

6. One of the core ideas of the interactionist perspective is that society consists of parts that are interrelated and interdependent.

7. The major advantage of surveys is that, compared to other research methods, they best enable researchers to determine if changes in an independent variable are the cause of changes in a dependent variable.

8. Max Weber is the sociologist who argued that sociology should remain as value-free as possible.

9. One of the ethical standards that sociologists attempt to adhere to in conducting research is reactivity.

10. Sociological consulting is one of the forms of applied sociology.

Fill-In Questions

1. In discussing social life on Bonerate, an Indonesian island, the beginning of the chapter was stressing the importance of _____.

2. The ability to understand the relationship between what is happening in people's personal lives and the social forces that surround them is what C. Wright Mills called _____.

3. When we say that science is *empirical*, we mean that science is based on _____.

4. Scientific theories are linked to scientific research through _____, which are tentative statements that can be tested regarding relationships between factors.

5. According to the functionalist perspective, social practices that disrupt social equilibrium rather than contribute to it are called _____.

6. Two key concepts of the conflict perspective are _____ and _____.

7. The concept of _____, attributed to sociologists William and Dorothy Thomas, is a key concept of the interactionist perspective.

8. When research is conducted by making direct observations in natural settings where the investigator takes part in the activities of the people being studied, the research method being used is called _____.

9. When sociologists conduct experiments in natural settings where people are going about their everyday affairs, these experiments are called _____.

10. _____ are applied sociologists who are sometimes called *social engineers*.

Matching Questions

_____ 1. interactionist perspective
_____ 2. Karl Marx
_____ 3. causation
_____ 4. goal of science
_____ 5. integration and interdependence
_____ 6. a type of observational technique
_____ 7. a type of survey
_____ 8. laboratory experiment
_____ 9. Hawthorne effect
_____ 10. Jane Addams

A. microsociology
B. developing theories
C. participant observation
D. reactivity
E. conflict perspective
F. early U.S. sociologist
G. a characteristic of science
H. an interview
I. artificially constructed environment
J. key concepts of the functionalist perspective

Essay Questions

1. Define sociology and the sociological perspective. What is the sociological view of diversity, and why is a cross-cultural perspective so important for sociology?

2. List and describe the characteristics of science.

3. What is commonsense knowledge? What are its weaknesses? How does scientific knowledge differ from common sense? How does science overcome the weaknesses associated with commonsense knowledge?

4. Define the terms *theory, variable,* and *hypothesis.* What different kinds of variables are used in scientific work? How do all of these work together in the process of science?

5. What are the basic assumptions of the functionalist perspective regarding the nature and operation of society?

6. Describe the conflict and interactionist theories in sociology and show how they differ from one another.

7. Define two of the three research methods described in the chapter and give an example. What are the advantages and drawbacks of each?

8. Describe the various positions that sociologists have taken on the issue of scientific objectivity. Include in your answer a discussion of the role of values in the scientific process.

9. With what kind of ethical issues do sociologists grapple? How do sociologists attempt to resolve these issues? Illustrate your answer with a discussion of how this point related to research done in South Africa.

10. Define and clearly distinguish between basic sociology and applied sociology. What are the different forms in which sociological practice can be carried out?

Answers

Multiple-Choice

1. D; **2.** D; **3.** D; **4.** A; **5.** A; **6.** B; **7.** B;
8. C; **9.** D; **10.** C

True/False

1. F; **2.** F; **3.** T; **4.** T; **5.** F; **6.** F; **7.** F;
8. T; **9.** F; **10.** T

Fill-In

1. community
2. sociological imagination
3. observation
4. hypotheses
5. dysfunctions
6. interest, power, dominance, conflict, coercion
7. definition of the situation
8. participant observation
9. field experiments
10. sociological consultants

Matching

1. A; **2.** E; **3.** G; **4.** B; **5.** J; **6.** C; **7.** H;
8. I; **9.** D; **10.** F

For Further Reading

Bannister, Robert C. (1991). *Jessie Bernard: The making of a feminist.* New Brunswick, NJ: Rutgers University Press. This is an intriguing biography of a woman who became a sociologist at a time when few women did so. It shows that gender affects women's lives among professional sociologists as well as others.

Barber, Bernard. (1987). *Effective social science: Eight cases in economics, political science, and sociology.* New York: Russell Sage Foundation. This book contains interviews with eight social scientists who describe some of the ins and outs of their applied research. It is an informal way to see how social science research is done and what the practitioners think of it.

Bart, Pauline, & Frankel, Linda. (1986). *The student sociologist's handbook* (4th ed.). New York: McGraw Hill. This is an invaluable resource for college students, in both sociology and other academic majors. The authors summarize the major approaches to sociology, as well as show how to locate sociology resource materials in the library and how to write a term paper.

Berger, Bennett M. (1990). *Authors of their own lives: Intellectual autobiographies by twenty American sociologists.* Berkeley: University of California Press. This book gives an inside peek at what led twenty well-known sociologists to choose that field of study. It conveys some of the excitement and promise of the field.

Berger, Peter. (1963). *Invitation to sociology: A humanist perspective.* New York: Doubleday/Anchor. This is a lively and informal look at the sociological perspective and the kinds of insights that it can offer to professional sociologists as well as nonsociologists.

Collins, Randall. (1992). *Sociological insight* (2nd ed.). New York: Oxford University Press. This book, in the vein of Mills's sociological imagination, tries to impart the power and insight of the general perspective of sociology.

Freeman, Howard E., Dynes, Russell R., Rossi, Peter H., & Whyte, William Foote. (Eds.). (1983). *Applied sociology: Roles and activities of sociologists in diverse settings.* San Francisco: Jossey-Bass. This book contains twenty-seven articles covering the complete range of applied research methods and applied settings in which sociologists can be found working on various social problems.

Mills, C. Wright. (1959). *The sociological imagination.* New York: Oxford University Press. An excellent book by an irreverent iconoclast who takes critical aim at his fellow sociologists. This is the work in which Mills develops the notion that each person's behavior is produced by the intersection of biography and history.

Nathan, Richard P. (1988). *Social science in government: Uses and misuses.* New York: Basic Books. Nathan, a political scientist, discusses some major applied research projects that have been sponsored by the government and points out the benefits as well as the drawbacks. He discusses research on welfare reform, job-training programs, revenue-sharing programs, and others.

Rebach, Howard M., & Bruhn, John G. (Eds.). (1991). *Handbook of clinical sociology.* New York: Plenum Press. A detailed overview of the fields of consulting and clinical sociology, the book provides many illustrations of the specific kinds of work that applied sociologists do.

Sullivan, Thomas J. (1992). *Applied sociology: Research and critical thinking.* New York: Macmillan. This book provides a brief introduction, easily understandable by the undergraduate, to applied sociological research. It describes the many ways in which sociological research is used to shape social policy and alleviate social problems.

Williams, Terry. (1989). *The cocaine kids: The inside story of a teenage drug ring.* Reading, MA: Addison-Wesley. This work is an excellent example of participant observation research. Williams spent much time over a period of five years with a group of teenage drug dealers in New York's Spanish Harlem. His is a fascinating account with some startling revelations.

PART TWO

The Individual in Society

Part Two covers the basic ways in which individuals are linked to society by learning shared meanings and patterns of behavior that make cooperative involvement with others possible. The chapters cover such topics as culture, social structure, socialization, groups and organizations, deviance, and social control.

TWO *Culture, Society, and Diversity*

The Comanche people roamed the southern Great Plains in the 1700s and 1800s, hunting buffalo from Wyoming and Nebraska south to Texas (Foster, 1991; Thurman, 1982; Wallace & Hoebel, 1952). The Comanches had a reputation among the early European settlers in the Great Plains as a fierce, combative people. In fact, the Comanches were a puzzle to the Euro-American traders and soldiers who began to fill the Great Plains in the 1800s because they seemed both disorganized and dishonest. The soldiers found it difficult to determine who led the Comanches, and deals made with a chief would not be adhered to by other Comanches. One Comanche might promise safe passage to merchants only to have another Comanche attack and plunder the group. The apparent disorganization even led some Euro-Americans to question whether the Comanches were a single people at all.

The confusion of these early settlers was due to the fact that they expected Comanche social life to be organized much like other societies they were familiar with, where a clearly identifiable leader (a president or king) existed and all other people and social units were subordinate to that person. Comanche social organization was quite different from this pattern; it consisted of five levels to which each Comanche belonged. The first was the *family,* which comprised all relatives who lived in the same camp together year round and shared in game and agricultural surplus. The second level was the *residence band,* which was a number of families that were linked with a particular leader or headman. Sometimes a residence band contained only one family and might be as small as twenty people, but usually it contained a number of families because they provided a larger and more productive economic unit that was less threatened by variations in the food supply.

The third level of Comanche social organization was the *division,* which consisted of a group of residence bands that farmed, traded, and hunted in the same geographic territory. A popular leader or brave warrior might exercise some control over a division, but this domination was more evanescent and temporary than leadership that Euro-Americans were used to. Such leaders might or might not exist for a particular division, and they might change rapidly. In addition, their leadership was incomplete, applying to some realms of social life but not others. In Comanche divisions, there was neither the organization nor the institutionalization of authority and leadership that the Euro-Americans were used to in terms of permanent leadership and ongoing structures, such as elections, to replace leaders. Also, the division performed largely ceremonial functions rather than served as a focus for food gathering or other practical tasks. Divisional gatherings, which might draw more than a thousand Comanches together, were a time to perform rituals, renew relationships, and possibly recruit others for a raiding party. When the divisional gathering was over, Comanche families and residence bands went their own way.

The fourth level of Comanche social organization was the *focused-activity group,* which formed for a particular purpose and dissolved once the objective had been achieved. So, for example, a few male warriors who wished to raid a settlers' camp would form a focused-activity group (the Comanches didn't use that name for it, of course) to do so. The group was not organized or sanctioned by a chief or leader and was not under the control of the head of a family, residence band, or division. Such unsanctioned activity was perfectly acceptable for Comanches, and most males engaged in it periodically. These focused-activity groups might be organized to seize more horses, exact revenge for an insult, or enhance a warrior's reputation. They were not a part of family or residence-band life but rather emerged from more personal goals or interpersonal conflicts.

These focused-activity groups point to the highly individualistic nature of Comanche society. Comanches acted more as individuals than as representatives of a family, residence band, or division. A raiding party, for example, might be formed by men from a number of different divisions who saw the raid as a vehicle for them to enhance their own personal reputation as warriors. Euro-Americans found this individualism hard to understand, even though individualism was important in their own culture. Anyone who understood what it meant to "be Comanche" could comprehend the motivation of these warriors.

"Being Comanche" brings us to the most expansive, and at the same time most amorphous, fifth level of Comanche social organization—the *Comanche community.* The community was a sense of common heritage and ancestry shared by all Comanches, and it was based on a shared sense of what it meant to "be Comanche." Being Comanche was more than just speaking the Comanche language; it also meant valuing the things other Comanches valued and seeing the world the way they did. Being Comanche meant understanding that men should display bravery as well as generosity in public and that kinship compelled a person to support other Comanches, no matter which residence band or division they belonged to. The divisional gatherings provided the periodic context in which Comanche values and personal relationships could be publicly enacted and reaffirmed. The Comanche community was important because it provided a common identity for the different Comanche divisions and residence bands that might never all gather together at one time. However, the Comanche community had no single, identifiable leader, a fact that many Euro-Americans

Myths FACTS

ABOUT CULTURE AND SOCIETY

Myth Standard English is the correct form of the English language.

FACT There is nothing inherently *correct* about Standard English; rather it is the linguistic form that is most acceptable to the dominant groups in society. Linguists have shown that Black English is an extremely flexible variant on the English language, and for those who understand it, this form can communicate as well as Standard English and may even avoid some of the rigidity of Standard English.

Myth Slang language is more commonly used among the less educated.

FACT Slang is an informal language or argot that is peculiar to a particular group. All subcultures show some development of argot because this special language performs important functions for groups.

Myth The role of working women with young children is a stressful one and these women experience high levels of psychological distress because of all the demands on their time.

FACT This statement is true if the women do not have assistance in carrying out their competing roles. If society provides some help, however, in the form of a husband who helps with the children or easy availability of child care, the stress and depression levels of working mothers are as low as those of working women with no children.

Myth The individualism found in advanced industrial societies such as the United States in the late twentieth century is unique. Few other industrial societies and no preindustrial societies give such free rein to individual actions.

FACT Individualism as a cultural value can be found in other societies, including preindustrial ones. The Comanche Indians of the southern Great Plains, for example, valued individualism, especially for males. In fact, European settlers were confused by this individualism because they could not fathom that the actions of individual Comanches were not controlled by their chief.

Myth People naturally seek to better themselves, a tendency that makes it impossible for human societies to avoid disparities in wealth, prestige, and power.

FACT Disparities in wealth and power are the product of certain kinds of societies. Small hunting-and-gathering bands have little surplus of food or material goods, so people are mostly equal in terms of wealth, prestige, and power.

---

failed to comprehend. They searched for a clear-cut leader or an identifiable institutional structure that would tie all Comanches together, without realizing that it did not exist.

You can begin to see the difficulty the Euro-American settlers confronted in dealing with the Comanches. Comanche "leaders" represented, at best, divisions and in some cases only residence bands. Even at the divisional level, their authority was limited to specific issues, and they were considered intermediaries who should report back to the residence band or division before concluding any negotiations. Comanche leaders might call themselves chiefs, but they were not paramount leaders in the way the Euro-Americans understood leadership. Add to that the individualism and the focused-activity undertakings of Comanches, and the Euro-Americans' conclusions about the disorganized nature of Comanche social life become more understandable.

Chapter 1 pointed out that sociology is the scientific study of societies and human social behavior. One reason for discussing Comanche society at some length is to illustrate the great diversity that exists in how societies are organized and what social behaviors are considered appropriate. Another reason for focusing on the Comanches is to reiterate the point that it can be a challenge to comprehend societies that are very different from one's own because of the natural tendency to see others through one's own lenses. Sociologists approach this diversity by discovering and analyzing the social elements that are common to *all* societies. Sociologists define **society** as *a group of people who are relatively self-sufficient and who share a common territory and culture.*

The fundamental elements that can be found in all societies fall under the headings of *culture* and *social structure.* These two terms are keys to understanding the sociological perspective because the basic components of culture and social structure are the building blocks of the sociological analysis of society. This chapter introduces these basic elements, which will then serve as the foundation for the sociological analysis in the rest of this book.

What Is Culture?

You should be able to define culture *and differentiate material and nonmaterial culture.*

The term *culture* has a number of different meanings, all of them valid for some uses. To examine the idea scientifically, however, requires distinguishing these meanings. People often use the term to refer to rather high-toned pastimes such as reading great literature, listening to classical music, or dining on gourmet foods. This meaning is implied when we speak of someone as being "cultured," and it has something of a judgmental air about it. It intimates that some people have culture and some people don't.

Sociologists take a much broader view of the term. For them, **culture** refers to *the total lifestyle of a people, including all of the ideas, values, knowledge, behaviors, and material objects that they share* (Geertz, 1973; Kroeber & Kluckhohn, 1952). This meaning seems to be what the anthropologist Sir E. B. Tylor had in mind more than a century ago when he defined culture as "that complex whole which includes knowledge, belief, art, morals, law, custom and any other capabilities and habits acquired by man as a member of society" (1871/1958, p. 1). According to the sociological view, then, all people have culture, for it is the learned social heritage that people accumulate

through time and pass on from generation to generation. Moreover, it provides people with a blueprint for how to lead their lives. It is from their culture that people learn what is good or bad, what is right or wrong, what they should or should not do, and even what they desire and what they dislike.

Often the terms *culture* and *society* are used interchangeably. This practice, although common, is somewhat imprecise sociologically. In the strictest sense, *society* refers to a *group of people* who are relatively self-sufficient and who share a common territory and culture; *culture* refers to that people's *traditions, customs, and behaviors.*

Material Culture and Nonmaterial Culture

The various elements of culture fall into two general categories: material culture and nonmaterial culture. **Material culture** consists of *all the physical objects, or artifacts, made or used by people, such as canoes, stone clubs, jet airplanes, and skyscrapers.* **Nonmaterial culture** consists of *those things that have no physical existence, such as language, ideas, knowledge, and behaviors.*

Material and nonmaterial culture are closely interrelated. Consider, for example, the many modern appliances, such as telephones, refrigerators, and televisions, that are found in most homes in the United States. These products are part of the material culture. They are things that only a society with advanced technological knowledge could produce, a point underlined when we consider that none of them existed, at least as we know them today, as recently as one hundred years ago. Moreover, these products have themselves shaped the nonmaterial culture. Television, for instance, delivers vast amounts of information to previously unheard-of numbers of people. In fact, in the relatively short time it has been around, television has become one of the major means for the transmission of nonmaterial culture in modern societies.

Sociologists and anthropologists rely heavily on the interrelations between material and nonmaterial culture in studying societies that no longer exist. Many earlier peoples left behind no written records, but from such artifacts as cave paintings, pottery, arrowheads, and burial mounds, investigators have been able to piece together some conception of the nonmaterial cultures of many of these societies.

The Components of Culture

You should be able to discuss the different elements of culture, including beliefs, values, norms, and language.

Culture is a complex phenomenon that can be expressed in an infinite number of ways. Consider, for instance, the foods people from different cultures eat. Common foods in the United States are such things as hamburgers, hot dogs, and french fries. Somewhere in the world there are people who consider octopus, locusts, and ants to be delicacies. The BaMbuti Pygmies in the Ituri rain forest in Zaire consider termites to be a delicacy (Turnbull, 1961). In some parts of Asia, the hot dog that is served is, in fact, canine. These foods would probably nauseate many people in the United States.

Attitudes toward parenthood are another example of the variety in human cultures. Western societies find it natural for children to come from the union of husband and wife. In fact, some groups in the United States consider birth under any other circumstances to be immoral. The Banaro of New Guinea, however, would be horrified to learn that firstborn children in the United States are normally fathered by the husband. Their traditions hold that a married couple's first child should be the offspring of a close friend selected by the wife's father (Goodman, 1967).

Obviously, it would be impossible to describe all of the variation that exists among cultures or, for that matter, all the facets of any single culture. It is possible, however, to isolate certain components that are common to all cultures, and understanding these components is an important first step in grasping how cultures and societies work. These components include beliefs, values, norms, and language.

Beliefs and Values

The most basic component of culture is **beliefs,** which are *the conceptions people have about what is true in the world.* Beliefs include ideas about what things exist in the world, how they work, and how they are related to one another. Some beliefs can be verified by observation. For example, we can measure how long it takes a plane to fly from Boston to San Francisco or how far it is from the Earth to the moon. Other beliefs, however, cannot be proven or disproven. For example, people around the world believe in any number of deities and devils. Many hold that there is some form of life after death, whereas others disagree.

These cultural beliefs help people understand the world and their place in it. However, people are seldom content simply to believe in something. They also tend to imbue their beliefs with moral significance. When that happens, beliefs become **values,** which are *people's ideas about what is good or bad, right or wrong.* People then use these values as guidelines for choosing goals and judging behaviors. Values, however, tend to be general and abstract rather than specific. For example, many people in the United States place considerable value on individualism, but individualism can be expressed in many different ways. A hard-driving executive may work so much that she has little personal life, whereas a political activist might organize demonstrations against nuclear power and an artist might spend long, solitary months creating a painting that departs from current artistic standards. In spite of their different pursuits, each of these people is expressing a version of the value of individualism.

U.S. Values Because values serve as guidelines for choosing goals and judging behaviors, the cultural values of a society must be considered in any study of that society. To begin, what can we say about values in the United States? A little thought will reveal that the development of a definitive list of U.S. values would be an impossible task. U.S. society is characterized by diversity. There are, for instance, many different racial, ethnic, and religious groups, and each has its own distinctive set of values. Certain mainstream values have a long tradition in the United States, however. They have played a significant role in shaping U.S. society, and they are still widely held by powerful groups (Parsons, 1971; Parsons & White, 1964; Williams, 1970). Some of the more prominent of these values will be discussed here, keeping in mind that the coverage is by no means exhaustive.

One of the key cultural values in the United States is the importance placed on *success*. Most often defined in terms of career achievement, success is taken as a sign that a person is worthy. In fact, stories of people who maximize their abilities and, in spite of almost overwhelming odds, make their mark on the world provide a theme that runs through much of our literature. Political candidates from humble backgrounds are quick to take advantage of our reverence for success by pointing out how hard they had to struggle to make it on their own. The emphasis on the value of success seems to be growing, at least among college students. In the 1960s, as noted in Chapter 1, fewer than 45 percent of first-year college students believed that being well-off financially was "very important" or "essential" to them (see Figure 1.3). By the 1990s, this figure had grown to 75 percent. Also, college women have become much more like college men in the emphasis they place on success as being essential to one's life and happiness.

Work and *activity* are also highly valued by many people in the United States. Indeed, some people place so much emphasis on work that they often define their own self-worth in terms of their jobs, and they tend to judge others in terms of the work they do. One of the first things people in the United States usually want to know about people they meet is what those people do for a living. Even in their leisure, they tend to view inactivity as undesirable, if not downright immoral. As a result, people in the United States always seem to be doing something—taking a trip, improving their tennis game, or pursuing a hobby like carpentry or needlepoint.

Another cluster of mainstream values in the United States consists of *progress, efficiency,* and *practicality.* People in the United States value striving to make things better, to improve the future in comparison to the present, and to do so in the most practical and efficient way. This value brings with it an acceptance of change, at least in material things and technology. Furthermore, people think developments and changes should be effected as quickly and as economically as possible so that nothing is wasted. One embodiment of this cluster of values is the emergence of the assembly line as a rapid and inexpensive mode of production that made mass quantities of consumer goods

available. However, it also changed the work experience for many workers. Taking pride in work and investing personal meaning in what is produced became more difficult for assembly-line workers. Goods were produced quickly and cheaply, but workers were less involved in their work and more alienated from it.

A value that some sociologists say "lies at the very core of American culture" is *individualism* (Bellah, Madsen, Sullivan, Swidler, & Tipton, 1985; p. 142). This is the belief that individual desires, achievements, and self-worth are more important than collective accomplishments and goals. Individual rights should not be interfered with by other needs of society, such as political, economic, or family needs. In other words, people should be free to pursue whatever they like without undue hindrance. The Bill of Rights of the U.S. Constitution spells out these individual rights, and the courts have generally striven to protect them. This individualism is expressed in many ways: the mythical cowboy/hero/loner portrayed in fiction; the mobility of people who leave home and family to find a job, get an education, or just travel; and the adulation some people in the United States give to individual sports stars. Individualism sometimes produces practices that foreigners find hard to comprehend, such as the widespread, personal ownership of firearms, a practice unheard of in many other nations. Individualism in the United States can go to such an extreme that "anything that would violate our right to think for ourselves, judge for ourselves, make our own decisions, live our lives as we see fit, is not only morally wrong, it is sacrilegious" (Bellah et al). A corollary of this value of individualism is *freedom:* to be free from demands by society, family, friends, or strangers that a person conform to their desired mode of conduct.

People in the United States also tend to place high value on *materialism* and *material comfort.* They expect to have nice cars, big houses, fine clothes, televisions, compact disc players, and the like. A high standard of living and the possession of numerous material goods have become almost synonymous with the U.S. way of life for many people, both in the United States and abroad. In a sense, people define their self-worth in terms of their ownership of such things. They feel proud to own a fine, new car rather than a battered car fifteen years old—even if both run well. In fact, the automobile may be the epitome of this materialism in the sense that much of the culture revolves around the automobile in the same way the culture of the Plains Indians revolved around the buffalo. Many people in the United States spend a good portion of their income supporting their cars; they wash them and ride around in them; they go to auto shows and races; they even went to war in the Persian Gulf in 1991 in part to protect the flow of cheap oil that fuels their cars.

The final mainstream value to be mentioned is *equality*. Many people in the United States believe that everyone should be treated with dignity and respect and should not be denied opportunities because he or she belongs to a particular gender or religious or racial or ethnic group. Furthermore, people in the United States tend to be antielitist, believing that there are few inherent differences between people and that a person's birthright does not bestow any special qualities or privileges.

These mainstream U.S. values are not, of course, exclusive to the United States. You read in the opening to this chapter, for example, that the Comanche Indians also valued individualism. There can be much variation, however, in the way cultures act on these values. Based on the same general value, a person in the United States might leave his family and climb the corporate career ladder, whereas the Comanche might join a focused-activity group to raid a settler's abode.

Japanese Values   We can gain a better comprehension of U.S. cultural values and their importance in people's lives by comparing them to a different set of values. Japan is like the United States in some ways: It is a modern, industrial nation, highly urbanized, with a fairly affluent standard of living. Its history and traditions, however, have produced a set of cultural values very different from those found in the United States. In reviewing Japanese cultural values, it is important not to see them as simply the reverse of U.S. values; they need to be understood on their own terms, as a unique blend of history and tradition (Burks, 1984; Kerbo & McKinstry, 1995; Reischauer, 1988).

Japanese culture stresses the importance of the *collectivity*, or community, and places high value on the group or the family. Individual Japa-

nese feel a strong obligation to their family, their work group, and their nation, and groups feel a strong sense of responsibility for their members. Each group member bears a share of the responsibility for preserving and protecting the group and avoiding bringing disgrace to it. People try to do well in business or education in part because success brings honor to the group. This point of view is very different from the emphasis on individualism in the United States. Of course, Japanese have a sense of their own individuality and self-worth, but it derives much more directly and completely from belonging to a group. A person expresses himself or herself by working for and supporting the collectivity and is rewarded with social approval.

The Japanese also value *harmony*, or getting along with people—what they call *wa*. They avoid contention and confrontation, and they are taught to help others and control the expression of their own desires. People are supposed to act politely and recognize and understand the feelings of others. Japan is racially and ethnically much more homogeneous than many other nations, certainly more so than the United States, and its people have achieved a high degree of cultural homogeneity. These conditions make harmony easier to achieve. Much more so than the United States, Japan exhibits a high degree of consensus regarding basic values. To say that the Japanese value harmony is not to say that aggression and competition are absent. They are also important elements of Japanese culture, but they are directed into arenas that are supportive of cooperation and the achievement of group goals.

The Japanese also value *tradition* and *authority*. They exhibit a strong respect for laws, rules, and customs. This attitude undoubtedly derives in part from Confucian teachings about uprightness, duty, and obligation (see Chapter 11). People obey the law and follow rules not out of fear of punishment but because it is a citizen's obligation. This does not mean that the Japanese never adopt new ways; they certainly do. The new ways, however, are incorporated into preexisting traditions, including the importance of community and harmony.

The differing value systems of Japan and the United States derive from profoundly different historical and societal developments. Japanese

As this collective barn building in an Amish community in Pennsylvania shows, the Amish place great value on group solidarity and use community ties to assist people in need.

religious history involves Shintoism, Buddhism, and Confucianism; the United States is heavily Judeo-Christian. The Japanese have historically lived on a small, crowded island where cooperation and harmony were essential to social stability, whereas the United States had a huge continent that was sparsely populated for much of its development. The cultivation of rice in Japan, the major crop, required cooperation among people because of the irrigation and other requirements of that subsistence system; farmers and ranchers in the United States could cultivate large plots of land with less need for the assistance of others.

Diversity and Change in Value Systems Although the values just described are important influences in

the United States and Japan, diverse groups in both societies hold strongly to values that are quite different from these mainstream values. Other Worlds, Other Ways: The Amish describes one such value system in the United States. All these different, and sometimes conflicting, values contribute to the pluralistic mosaic that is the United States in the late twentieth century.

Values also change over time in response to new societal developments. For example, in the United States since the 1970s, the traditional materialism may have taken a turn toward *private materialism,* including a decline in interest in public goals and service to community. In other words, the weakness of community, bemoaned by Robert Bellah in the beginning of Chapter 1,

OTHER WORLDS, *Other Ways*

THE AMISH OF PENNSYLVANIA: DIVERSE VALUES WITHIN A CULTURE

The Old Order Amish descend from sixteenth-century Swiss Anabaptists, sometimes called Mennonites because of Menno Simons, an early leader of the group (Hostetler, 1993; Kephart & Zellner, 1994). Simons was originally a Roman Catholic priest in the Netherlands, but he formed his own denomination in the 1500s because of some deeply held differences with the Roman church. For example, he believed in the separation of church and state and the right to refuse to bear arms or take oaths—positions strongly opposed by the church of that era. The Amish broke with the Mennonites in 1693 over a theological dispute, and some Amish began migrating to the New World in the early seventeenth century, originally settling in Pennsylvania.

The Old Order Amish have prospered in the United States. They have maintained their own separate existence and their distinct lifestyle over the span of almost three centuries of rapid cultural and technological change. Most people are familiar with images of the Amish people's small, horse-drawn carriages; their wide-brimmed hats; and their dark, simple coats and dresses. They seem to have achieved an almost impossible resistance to the booming culture around them. Indeed, their value system is as distinct as their clothing and their carriages. Some values they share with the larger, mainstream culture, such as their belief in the importance of hard work. For the Amish, however, work has a deeply religious meaning, whereas for many other people in the United States work is considered a secular, although still important, activity. Other Amish values are quite different from mainstream U.S. values. For example, the Amish reject the materialism that surrounds them. Their main concern is what God, not their fellow humans, thinks of them, and God, they believe, focuses on inner qualities, not outward appearances. The austerity in their clothing and general lifestyle is a product of this belief. Instead of materialism, the Amish value *humility* and *self-denial*. Pride and self-aggrandizement are considered sins, and one should never set oneself above one's fellows. So traits that are common in many societies—such as bragging or boasting—are rarely encountered among the Amish. In fact, cameras are forbidden, and it is considered wrong to have one's picture taken because that implies that there is something special about one's looks. Each person is important not as an individual but as a hard worker for the community.

This view leads to another important Amish value: *group solidarity.* The Amish believe that family and community (and a faith in God) will give people all the support they need to get through life. The Amish take care of one another; they do not accept welfare or Medicare or most Social Security benefits. If a person needs a barn raised, hundreds of neighbors will show up to do it; if someone is aged and infirm, the family will look after him or her. The community takes care of individuals and thus is more important than individuals—a direct contradiction to the individualism of the mainstream culture.

The final set of Amish values is *obedience* and *submission.* Each individual submits to and obeys family, community, and God, an attitude that is alien to individualism. The freedom that characterizes the larger culture is severely truncated among the Amish. They have the freedom to vote for the politician of their choice, but they are not free when it comes to matters of obeying the community or the church. People who exercise their freedom in these realms suffer severe disapproval and possibly even ostracism.

The Amish lifestyle seems to many in the United States to be uncompromisingly severe and restricted. Yet it is probably the unrelieved rejection of non-Amish ways—along with rural isolation—that has enabled the Amish to survive and thrive. They have problems, of course. Government regulation sometimes threatens to interfere with their way of life; young people are sometimes attracted by the materialism around them; and some Amish communities have left the fold in pursuit of a less severe lifestyle. Yet, overall, they have maintained a thriving existence, and they represent one of the many sets of diverse cultural values that give direction to the lives of various groups in the United States. With a society as large and complex as that of the United States, this diversity in value systems will undoubtedly continue.

seems even more severe in the 1990s. This trend is especially noticeable among high school and college students, who have placed increasing emphasis on making money as a major goal in life (see Figure 1.3). Reflecting this trend, they express growing interest in jobs in business, and especially large corporations, and less desire for public interest or social service jobs. Young people have also retreated from the ideas of political activism and government involvement in social change (Easterlin & Crimmins, 1991). Whereas this growing focus on private life over public concerns undoubtedly has numerous causes, one especially important one has been the weak state of the economy in the United States since the 1970s. Real wages have actually declined during the past two decades, even though people's aspirations regarding economic achievement have continued to grow. As the gap between aspirations and actual material accomplishments grew larger for many families, they tried to close the gap by having mothers work more and deferring having children. And they seemed to shift their values by emphasizing the private over the public.

Some people would argue that the traditional emphasis placed on materialism in the United States has also been changing toward *consumerism* and *commodification*. People seem to have become obsessed with things, or commodities, and how much people can purchase has become a defining aspect of their worth. Some have called this trend the *mallification* of society, referring to the central importance that shopping malls now play in social life, as shopping and consumerism become primary leisure-time activities. This trend is the product of the emerging subsistence pattern of advanced industrial capitalism, which is based on continued economic growth. Large corporations survive by producing goods and expanding markets. They need a mass of consumers to purchase these goods, and advertising encourages people to desire the products produced. These two trends—toward private life and consumerism—illustrate how cultural values are dynamic rather than static; they change as social conditions evolve.

Norms

A people's culture is such an ingrained part of their lives that most take it for granted. Further-

more, its effects are frequently so subtle that people are rarely aware of how strongly or in how many areas it influences them. For example, the distance at which people feel comfortable when talking to one another is strongly influenced by culture (Hall, 1966). Most people in the United States regard the area from six to eighteen inches around them as an intimate zone. The only people they normally allow within this zone are very close friends or lovers. Should a stranger invade it, they are likely to feel uncomfortable and anxious. Among Arabs, however, practically all social interaction takes place within this zone. In fact, Arabs may be insulted if someone tries to converse with them from outside it.

The example of personal distance brings us to *norms*, the third component of culture. **Norms** are *rules of conduct that guide people's behavior in particular situations.* They are the expectations that people in a society share about how they ought to behave. Unlike values, which involve general preferences, norms are specific guidelines for behavior. In the United States, for instance, people usually dress appropriately for wherever they are going, they avoid spitting in public places, they acknowledge people they know when they meet them, and they try to show up on time for appointments. Norms, then, are an integral part of day-to-day lives. They provide a script for personal behavior, and they allow people, to some extent, to predict the behavior of others. By so doing, they provide the order and stability necessary for a society to exist.

A society teaches its members the types of behavior that are expected through **sanctions,** which are *rewards or punishments for conforming to or violating norms.* Sanctions can take many forms, depending on the type of behavior and the type of norm involved. They can be weak or strong, formal or informal, and positive or negative. The smile and "thank you" that a person receives for opening a door for another is a weak, informal, positive sanction. The frown the person gets for not opening it is a weak, informal, negative sanction. Chapter 5 will analyze this process of social control at greater length.

Norms that are customary, popular, and widely performed, but not required, are called **folkways** (Sumner, 1906). Examples of folkways in the United States include shaking hands, bathing frequently, and being quiet in church. There is some pressure to conform to folkways; violating them usually results in weak, informal, negative sanctions. Such violations occur frequently, however, and they are normally not taken very seriously, although a person who repeatedly ignores folkways may be viewed as strange or eccentric. Still, when we observe the social scene around us, we see that most people comply with most folkways most of the time.

Mores are *norms that are associated with strong feelings of right and wrong, the violation of which usually results in sanctions.* They are the social rules that deal with such things as murder, incest, theft, and public nudity, and they are taken very seriously. People who violate folkways are usually tolerated, but people who violate mores are usually punished. The sanctions applied tend to be strong, formal, and negative. Violators may be ostracized, banished, flogged, put in prison, or put to death. These strong reactions are one reason people adhere to mores. More important, however, is the fact that people are taught to adhere to their cultural mores almost from the time they are born. As a result, people incorporate the mores into their own personal codes of conduct. This process, called **internalization,** *causes people to view the violation of most mores with antipathy such that they would not even consider committing such a violation. As a result, they control their own behavior.* Most people, for example, are so horrified at the thought of incest that they never even consider it. This example illustrates an important point about culture: Much of it is so ingrained that we are unaware that we have learned it and don't feel that the beliefs, values, and norms are an imposition. We learn to *want* what our culture *demands* of us. Chapter 3 will analyze this learning process in more detail.

Laws are *norms that have been formally codified by political authority.* Many laws are based on mores, for people usually strive to give legal status to norms they believe in strongly. Familiar examples would include laws against murder, incest, and theft. Not all laws, however, are based on mores. Some, such as "blue laws" that prohibit stores from selling alcohol on Sunday morning, are based on folkways. Others, such as parking restrictions, are basically administrative and reflect no norms at all. Some laws even run counter to generally accepted

norms. The prohibition of alcohol during the 1920s in the United States, for example, was followed one decade later by its repeal because many people ignored the law and continued to use alcohol. Similarly, 34 percent of adults in the United States have used marijuana and 12 percent have used cocaine—both against the law (U.S. Bureau of the Census, 1995, p. 142). Fifteen percent of people between eighteen and twenty-five years of age have used some illegal drug in the last thirty days. So, the generally accepted norms in some groups make the use of marijuana, cocaine, and other drugs acceptable, even though use of them violates the law. These examples illustrate that laws can be established that go against strongly held custom, but there is also pressure in such cases to change or drop the laws.

Language

The final component of culture that will be discussed here is language. *Language* is a set of written or verbal symbols that people use in an agreed-upon way to communicate with one another (Lindesmith, Strauss, & Denzin, 1991; Miller, 1963). As discussed in Chapter 1, *symbols* are things that stand for and convey the meaning of other things. Language is a particularly important component of culture because it is through language that the other components—beliefs, values, and norms—are stored, communicated, and absorbed.

Our ability to use language lets us do many things that other animals cannot. We are not limited, as they are, by our physical environment or by barriers of time and space. Language permitted our primitive ancestors to store knowledge and transmit it to new generations. The invention of the written word vastly expanded this ability by freeing us from the limitations of human memory. Today, the mushrooming technologies of computerization, miniaturization, and microprocessing promise a virtual explosion in the amount of information that is available to us. Symbols and language also let us contemplate and use abstract ideas like *justice, equality,* and the *perfect person.* Our social and legal machinery is based on our notions of justice and equality, and our personal behavior is often guided by our ideal of what it is to be "perfect."

Linguistic Relativity   To understand fully the role of language in our lives, it is important to recognize that language is not solely a mechanism for communication. It can also shape our perceptions of the world. This insight originated with the anthropologist Edward Sapir (1929) and the linguist Benjamin Whorf (1956). After studying many different languages, they developed what has come to be called the *Sapir-Whorf hypothesis* or the *linguistic-relativity hypothesis*. Simply stated, this hypothesis proposes that the language we speak shapes how we think about and perceive the world. Far from being a passive means of communication, language actually influences what that world is like for each of us. Using language is like looking at the world through tinted glasses—we see what the filter presents to us.

One way that language filters reality is through the categories that it provides. Inuit (Eskimos), for example, have more than twenty different words for snow. Obviously, Inuit culture has developed and passed on this elaborate category system because making fine distinctions between types of snow is important to survival in the environment in which Inuit live. Sapir and Whorf's point is, though, that when Inuit children learn their language, they also learn to perceive and identify aspects of snow that would be imperceptible to speakers of a language such as English. (At the other extreme, the Aztecs of pre-Columbian Mexico, for whom snow was a rare event, used a single word for "ice," "snow," and "cold.") As another example, the Zuni, a Pueblo people of the American Southwest, had one word to indicate the colors orange and yellow—colors that speakers of English clearly distinguish. When confronted with an array of colors, speakers of Zuni are considerably less likely than speakers of English to separate the oranges and yellows as distinct colors. Other research shows that remembering colors is enhanced if a person's language has a name for the color (Kelling, 1975; Lucy & Shweder, 1979).

Language may also influence our understanding of nature. For example, the Hopi language of the Southwest made no distinctions among past, present, and future. The Hopi had no verb tenses and no nouns indicating times, days, or years. The Hopi language classified nature in terms of duration and considered time to be a continuous process, without breaks or stops. English, by contrast, has tenses and an elaborate set of words for dividing up time periods (*day, week, year,* etc.). In addition, English has a bipolar view of the world: It divides nature into nouns (people, objects, or events) and verbs (activities). In English, *lightning* and *eddy* are nouns; in Hopi, however, they are verbs because of their short duration. So, speakers of these two languages will perceive the world somewhat differently. Certainly, time will have a much more precise, measured, and quantifiable meaning for speakers of English than it will for speakers of Hopi, who have difficulty distinguishing, in language, past from future and precisely measuring time periods.

Sapir and Whorf have been criticized for arguing that language is all-powerful. Research done in linguistics, anthropology, and cognitive psychology since the Sapir-Whorf hypothesis was first proposed have established universals in languages: cognitive processes and tendencies in language that are found in all cultures. Sapir and Whorf, however, were aware of the limits of language's impact: They recognized that reality shapes languages in the sense that each language is an adaptation to a particular physical and cultural environment. Once language exists, however, it takes on a life of its own and shapes and reinforces the culture from which it arose. Language and culture, then, are mutually reinforcing (Gumperz & Levinson, 1991; Hoffman, Lau, & Johnson, 1986).

Language Reproduces Society   Language not only reflects the social practices of a culture; it also helps to maintain and reinforce them by reproducing the structure of society. This fact is strikingly illustrated by the use of language in Java (Hoebel, 1972).

In Javanese, there are four forms of speech. Which form is used in a particular situation depends on the relationship between the people involved. Individuals low on the social ladder address those higher up in one form and are themselves addressed in a second form. The socially elite have a third distinct form exclusive to their group, and the more common people have yet a fourth form. Thus the people of Java are constantly reminded of their relative positions in society when they conform to the proper language form. Furthermore, by following these language conventions, the Javanese continually reaffirm their acceptance of the existing social hierarchy.

The way people speak also has important social implications in the United States. *Standard English* is the form of English that is taught in the schools, and it is the form used in this textbook. However, some groups in the United States do not automatically learn Standard English. In many African American communities, for instance, people speak *Black English,* or black street speech (DeBose, 1992; Edwards & Winford, 1991; Speicher & McMahon, 1992). Black English is a variant of Standard English that developed from the languages of the west coast of Africa and the pidgin languages that served the maritime trade of the eighteenth and nineteenth centuries. The isolation of blacks in the United States, first on plantations and later in ghettos, along with centuries of servitude, slavery, and oppression, provided fertile ground for the development of a distinct dialect among blacks in the United States (Smitherman, 1986). Some of the reasons why dialects emerge under these conditions are discussed later in this chapter in Applying Sociology: Argot.

Black English is a distinct dialect having its own phonology, grammar, and syntax. For instance, consider the following phrases:

> It be kind of complicated.
> They be doing.
> If you be talking.
> We do be out.

In these examples, the word *be* is used in a way that is not found in Standard English. *They be doing* does not mean *they are doing* or *they were doing* or *they will be doing.* Rather, it is a tenseless use of the verb *be* that refers to doing something intermittently over a period of time without any particular reference to past, present, or future.

Neither Black English nor Standard English is inherently correct. Languages are, after all, merely systems for combining words that users have agreed on. Both languages can be used to communicate quite effectively by those who understand the rules of the language. Yet the dominant groups in the United States speak Standard English and assume that it is a superior language. These people presume that those who speak Black English, or any other version of English, do not know how to speak the language "correctly." This assumption can make it more difficult for speakers of Black English in school or on the job. Students, for example, may receive a lower grade for speaking or writing English "incorrectly," and workers may not be hired if they do not speak "proper" English. So, success can hinge on the ability to speak Standard English, and those who speak another dialect may be at a distinct disadvantage in terms of educational and occupational opportunities. This fact illustrates the powerful contribution of language in reproducing and reinforcing existing social hierarchies in the United States.

This section has reviewed the four basic components of culture. These concepts will be at the center of the analysis of society throughout this book. You need to recognize at this point, however, that these components are linked with one another in intricate ways. The next section will consider these components in operation in society, as they combine to coordinate social behavior and to promote as well as resist cultural change.

Cultural Consensus and Diversity

You should be able to describe cultural integration as well as the various types of cultural change, including the sources from which change may arise.

People are seldom aware of the dynamic nature of culture. In fact, the components of culture just discussed are often taken as givens, as conditions that are imposed on people and over which they have virtually no control. But in reality, beliefs, values, norms, and language are changing constantly in response to developments that arise either inside or outside society. Change takes place because the elements of culture are actually mechanisms that enable societies to adapt to their environment and survive. The purpose of this section is to offer a better appreciation of the dynamic nature of culture by looking at some of the forces that promote cultural changes as well as some of those that resist it.

Cultural Integration

Any culture includes countless beliefs, values, norms, and artifacts. Consider, for instance, some of the cultural elements that exist in the late-twentieth-century United States. It has schools, televisions, polluted rivers, communications satellites, factories, pornographic movies, football games, automobiles, the gay liberation movement, personal computers, Popsicles, and handguns. Such a list could obviously go on and on. Indeed, listing all the elements of any culture would be an impossible task. There are simply too many of them.

The elements of a culture, in spite of their wide diversity, are linked together in many intricate and sometimes subtle ways. Frequently, various elements are in conflict. The massive quantities of consumer goods that people in the United States desire and have become used to, for example, are in many instances at odds with their desire for a pollution-free environment. More often, however, the different elements of a culture complement one another. They are more or less integrated into reasonably well-organized patterns.

The extent to which cultures are integrated can sometimes be more easily seen in societies other than one's own. The Kapauku Papuans, a group of people who live in New Guinea and who were studied by the anthropologist Leopold Pospisil (1963), provide an especially vivid illustration. Among the Kapauku, pigs are the major source of wealth and power. The pigs are fed on sweet potatoes, which makes agriculture an important part of Kapaukun culture. Custom, however, dictates that only women can cultivate sweet potatoes and raise pigs, making women vital to the production of wealth. This fact is reflected in the Kapaukun family structure. The Kapauku are polygynous, which means that a man can have more than one wife. Needless to say, the more wives a man has, the more wealth they can produce for him. To ensure that there are enough wives to go around, there must be more women than men. This necessity has, in turn, affected the Kapaukun view of warfare and the war-related roles of men and women. Intertribal wars are a regular occurrence, but killing women in these wars is considered highly immoral, simply because they are so valuable. A number of males, though, are killed off in war regularly, which guarantees that the necessary surplus of females is maintained.

Cultural Change

Cultural integration has a major impact on the changes that occur in cultures. As noted in Chapter 1, any system made up of interrelated parts tends to develop a state of equilibrium. As a result, change in one part of the system causes changes in other parts. This process is particularly evident in cultures, which makes cultural change a very important topic in sociology. This chapter looks at some of the sources of cultural change. Chapter 15 investigates this topic more fully.

Changes in a society's culture can come from the outside or can develop internally. A major external source of change is *diffusion,* which is the spread of cultural elements from one culture to another. Diffusion is likely whenever two cultures come into contact. For example, the first people to smoke tobacco were American Indians. In the 1500s, however, English and Spanish explorers of the New World carried tobacco with them when they returned home, and its use soon spread throughout Europe, northern Africa, and the Middle East. With modern communications technologies and the global mass media, the process of cultural diffusion around the world has become rapid, extensive, and continuous. Cultural beliefs, values, and other items are spread (for example, through the Internet) such that the traditional boundaries between cultures have become much more vague. In fact, a global cyberculture may be emerging from this process of cultural diffusion.

As noted at the beginning of this discussion, the introduction of new elements into a culture is likely to cause changes in other elements. For instance, the Spanish brought to the New World a type of wheat that could be grown during the winter. Cultivation of this new wheat allowed tribes that had been nomadic hunters and gatherers during the winter, such as Pimas and Papagos of what is now Arizona, to stay in one place all year round. This permanence, in itself, was a significant change in their lifestyle, but it, in turn, led to further changes. The Pimas and Papagos soon became prey to roaming bands of Apaches, who lived by stealing from more sedentary peoples. The Pimas and Papagos were therefore forced to develop a more centralized political organization so that they could defend themselves from the Apache marauders (Plog & Bates, 1980).

An important internal source of change is *innovation,* which is the development of new ideas, behaviors, or material products. Although

Modern communications technologies and the mass media make for rapid, extensive, and continuous cultural diffusion around the globe.

innovations have occurred throughout human history, the twentieth century has witnessed unbelievably rapid innovations with far-reaching effects on people's lives. Automobiles, computers, nuclear bombs, airplanes, television, and fiber optic cables have made people's lives in the late twentieth century very different from life at any other time in human history. Today, people live longer and more comfortable lives with more and better food and housing. These discoveries and inventions demand that workers have more knowledge and skills than in the past, a requirement that has transformed educational structures from informal learning into a highly formal, lengthy, and complex educational process (see Chapter 12). The result has been a highly literate and educated workforce and populace. These technological discoveries and inventions have also brought about a more elaborate occupational structure, with thousands upon thousands of different jobs for people to fill. Healing has been transformed into a technologically sophisticated process that can cure many diseases and repair many injuries that would have maimed or killed people in the past (see Chapter 10). This transformation affects the family because women and children are less likely to have a spouse die before old age (see Chapter 9).

Discoveries and inventions can also produce negative outcomes. Technological change has created weapons of mass destruction that are capable of killing millions of people in a short period of time. Airplanes and missiles can rain death from the sky. One nuclear bomb exploding over a major city would probably kill three million people almost instantaneously. So, cultural change

OTHER WORLDS, *Other Ways*

Sometimes the divergence between ideal and real cultures makes it impossible for people to live out the ideal culture in their lives no matter how much they might wish to. This impossibility is well illustrated by changes currently affecting the family in Mexico (Fowler-Salamini & Vaughan, 1994; LeVine, 1993; Riding, 1989). Mexico is a relatively poor nation that is substantially less industrialized than is the United States. Although it has large cities, such as Mexico City and Guadalajara, many Mexicans still live in rural areas. The population is growing at three times the rate of the population of the United States.

As is true in many developing nations, the ideal culture in Mexico emphasizes the value of the extended family, which has combined financial resources and an elaborate network of support for people who do not have much of their own. The ideal Mexican family is also patriarchal, with males having most of the power and decision-making authority. As Mexico has experienced some economic development in the twentieth century, some of these patterns have changed, such as nuclear families becoming more common. But the culture still emphasizes the value of strong extended family networks and male dominance. This emphasis on family has been supported by the persisting importance of *machismo* in Mexican culture. *Machismo* refers to dominant manliness as personified by the Spanish conquistador—the aggressive, action-oriented, virile man.

For many Mexicans, this ideal culture is becoming increasingly difficult to realize as economic realities intrude on their lives. Poverty, especially in rural areas, forces many Mexicans to migrate in search of jobs, and this population dispersion puts substantial pressure on both the value of the family and male dominance in the family (Brydon & Chant, 1989; Massey, 1987). Tens of thousands of Mexicans, most of them men, migrate out of Mexico each year in search of work. Most of them go to the United States looking for work as farmhands or low-skilled laborers, and the work is difficult and low-paying. More important, migration removes the men from their families for long periods, sometimes permanently. Their absence seriously erodes the control and authority they can exercise in the family. When they are away,

has become pervasive and constant, with both positive and negative outcomes.

Ideal Culture Versus Real Culture

Another important internal source of change for many societies is the difference between ideal culture and real culture (Schusky & Culbert, 1967). **Ideal culture** refers to *the beliefs, values, and norms that people claim to follow*. **Real culture** refers to their *actual behavior in relation to these professed beliefs, values, and norms*. In the United States, for example, people place value on such ideals as equality, honesty, and obeying the law. Despite the ideal of equality, however, there has always been considerable discrimination, particularly against minority groups and women. Moreover, even though most people in the United States consider themselves to be honest and law-abiding, lying, cheating, and stealing are common occurrences.

That there is a gap between what people claim is proper and the way they actually behave does not mean that people are by nature two-faced. Rather, it indicates that many factors influence people's behavior. Honesty, for example, is a praiseworthy ideal, but some individuals may feel that cutting a few corners is necessary just to make a decent living. They see themselves as honest

women run the household and raise the children, and the essential nature of male support for the family is called into question.

The low wages that poor Mexican men can command are often not enough to support a family. In addition, the *machismo* complex, along with the migratory lifestyle, can lead Mexican men to father children with a number of women, which spreads the man's meager resources over a number of families. For these reasons, poor Mexican women often work to support their families. Whereas some Mexican women go to the United States, they more commonly migrate within Mexico itself looking for work (Fernandez-Kelly, 1983a). Most often, they move from a rural area to a large city where jobs can be found working as a domestic or a laborer in a factory. Many U.S. companies have opened manufacturing plants near the Mexican border to take advantage of this low-skilled, cheap labor supply. The women often leave their extended families and their husbands, who may not be able to find work in the same city or may have gone to the United States looking for work. The women set up their own household with their children. Although they maintain ties with their families, the bonds inevitably grow weaker as time and distance separate family members. So, whether they like it or not, these women gain more independence and autonomy from both males and their families. However, life is still a difficult struggle as they try to raise their children with poverty-level wages.

These migration patterns are produced by basic changes in the structure of the Mexican economy: the automation of agriculture, which means fewer jobs in rural areas; the growth of low-paying jobs in the industrial sector, fueled by economic demand in other nations; and a weak labor union movement, whose development has been discouraged by both business people and politicians in Mexico. The result has been growing unemployment and low wage levels for many workers. The consequence for many Mexicans is increasing difficulty in maintaining the ideal culture of extended family and male dominance. The reality for many poor Mexican women is that they cannot rely on a male for support for their family. This situation shows the power that culture and social structure have over people's lives. As more Mexicans face these same dilemmas, the ideal culture may begin to change to take into account the realities of modern life.

people confronted with situations that prevent them from behaving honestly. Furthermore, there is inconsistency in the ideal culture itself. For instance, though honesty is highly valued in the United States, so is success. Often, then, people are faced with choosing which aspects of the ideal culture should come first.

As the gap between the ideal culture and the real culture widens, the contradictions in people's lives begin to create tensions. If the gaps become sufficiently large, pressures to reduce them often lead to cultural change. In recent decades, this process has been especially evident in the area of discrimination in the United States. The discrepancy between the ideal of equality and the practice of denying opportunities to African Americans, women, and other minorities became too great for many people to accept. As a result, the last couple of decades have seen major efforts to reduce such inequities. Other Worlds, Other Ways: Mexico describes how a similar gap between the ideal culture and the real culture may produce some cultural change in Mexico.

Ethnocentrism and Cultural Relativity

Many people in the United States find it difficult to imagine living in another culture, and people from other cultures feel much the same way about living in the United States. Indeed, just about everyone thinks that his or her way of life is the one "right" way. *This tendency to view one's own culture as the best and to judge other cultures in comparison to it* is called **ethnocentrism.**

Ethnocentrism is a natural result of the fact that a society creates its own beliefs, values, and norms. It also promotes the sense of "we-ness" that holds societies together. Ethnocentrism, however, can get out of control and become destructive. Especially when one group feels threatened by another, those under threat tend to become more ethnocentric, developing increasing dislike for the threatening group and establishing more social distance from them (Grant, 1991). Too often, a group's belief in its own superiority leads to racism, persecution, exploitation, and even genocide. The Nazi treatment of Jews and the treatment of American Indians by European colonists of the New World are but two haunting examples.

Ethnocentrism can also undermine our efforts to understand ways of life different from our own. Being too quick to judge a social practice or belief of another culture as wrong or absurd can blind us to the meaning it has for the people involved and the way it fits into their lives. Social scientists therefore promote the idea of **cultural relativity,** which holds that *the lifestyles of various peoples should be viewed in terms of their own culture rather than that of the observer.* Basically, it involves suspending judgment and realizing that each culture reflects a particular society's adaptation to its environment. This objectivity in no way means that we should unquestioningly accept the beliefs and social practices of other cultures. For example, few people in the United States today would accept the Trobriand Islanders' belief that pregnancy is caused by the spirit of a dead ancestor entering a woman's body (Malinowski, 1954). However, by applying the idea of cultural relativity, we can understand that this belief is central to the Trobriand Islanders' view of the world and is therefore a valid part of their lives.

Subcultures

Although it is possible to describe some of the aspects of U.S. culture and list a few of its main-

stream values, it is not possible to develop a truly comprehensive picture of culture in the United States. The society is simply too diverse. The norms of the ghetto are light-years away from those of the middle-class suburb, the values of the young have little meaning for the elderly, and the beliefs of the well-to-do are largely foreign to the poor. One result of all this diversity is the formation of subcultures. A **subculture** is *a group within a culture that shares some of the beliefs, values, and norms of the larger culture but also has some that are distinctly its own.* As is true of most large societies, particularly those that have industrialized, the United States has a large number of subcultures. There are, for example, the Amish in Pennsylvania, the Cubans in Miami, the gays in most large cities, the punk set, and the drug set. There are even a few hippies left over from the 1960s.

Actually, everyone in the United States could belong to a wide array of subcultures based on such characteristics as age, gender, social standing, job, religion, or leisure pastimes. However, membership in a subculture is not simply a matter of fitting into a particular category. Instead, it is based on accepting the beliefs, values, and norms of the subculture and identifying with other members of it (Fine & Kleinman, 1979; Widdicombe & Wooffitt, 1995). A person can, for instance, be a prison inmate without belonging to the prison subculture or a sports fan without belonging to a sports subculture if that person does not identify with the subculture and share its ideas.

Subcultures tend to develop when members of a segment of society become aware of the fact that they share interests—beliefs, practices, or characteristics—that differ from those of the larger culture. This tendency is especially strong when the people in that segment of society are denied participation in some dimensions of the larger culture. By seeking out their own kind and banding together, they are able to create their own support system. Often it allows them to develop sufficient strength not only to preserve their own interests but also to improve their social lot. Consider, for example, the recent increases in the subcultural consciousness of African Americans and many other racial and ethnic minorities as well as gay men and lesbians. Applying Sociology: Argot (on pp. 58–59) adds further insight into these ideas by showing how the special languages used in subcultures can enhance their solidarity and make them more effective support systems.

Social Structure

You should be able to describe the functions of statuses, roles, groups, and institutions in maintaining social structure.

Now that some of the more important aspects of culture have been examined, it is time to look at the other general category of characteristics common to all societies—social structure. **Social structure** refers to *the organized patterns of social interaction and social relationships that exist in a group or society.* Although we may not be aware of it, we deal with such patterns almost constantly, at school, at work, even at home with friends or family. Without these organized patterns of behavior, social life as we know it would be impossible, for social structure provides the order and stability necessary for any group or society to function. An understanding of social structure is therefore a fundamental building block of the science of sociology. Indeed, much of this book is a detailed examination of concepts and ideas introduced in this section.

The section will begin by examining *status* and *role,* two concepts that underlie any type of interaction among people. Then it will look at *groups* and *social institutions,* two of the most important manifestations of social structure.

Status

Status, like *culture,* is a term that has more than one meaning, even among sociologists. People often talk about high-status jobs such as doctor, lawyer, or government official and low-status jobs such as janitor, stripper, or prostitute. They also talk about status symbols—expensive foreign cars, designer clothes, or memberships in exclusive clubs—which are things people buy to show how well-off they are. Used in these ways, status equates with prestige and implies judgments that rank people in comparison to one another. Although this meaning is somewhat similar to the way sociologists use the term, it is defined here without referring to rank-

ings or value judgments because differences in status do not always imply that one person is higher or lower in prestige than another person. Here, then, **status** will refer to *a designated position in a group or society* (Biddle & Thomas, 1966).

Virtually any identifiable aspect of a person, such as gender, age, job, race, religion, or social class, can be a status. Each status is imbedded in a network of statuses, and every individual has many statuses. People using this book, for instance, probably have some of the following social positions: student, young person, adult, middle-aged person, male, female, black, Latino, Baptist, Roman Catholic, Buddhist, agnostic, American, or Canadian. These positions locate them in relation to other people who have specific statuses. If one is female, for example, one has a somewhat different relationship with other males and females than if one is male.

Statuses can be either ascribed or achieved. **Ascribed statuses** *are assigned to people and represent social positions over which people have little say about occupying.* For example, each of us is born either male or female and as a member of some race. In addition, we may become cancer sufferers or crime victims, also ascribed statuses. **Achieved statuses,** by contrast, *are based on people's accomplishments or activities and reflect social positions people gain through their own efforts.* Someone who earns a college degree, for example, achieves the status of *college graduate.* Other achieved statuses are occupation, marital state, parenthood, check forger, and bank robber.

Sometimes, *a particular status becomes central to the way people view themselves or are viewed by others.* Such a social position is called a **master status** (Karp & Yoels, 1979). In the United States, as in many other societies, gender, race, and age are frequently master statuses. For example, people often react differently to male rather than female secretaries or to older rather than younger entertainers. Many times, however, the way people see others differs from the way others see themselves. For instance, employees may see their supervisor in the master status of *boss,* but the supervisor may see herself as *low person on the executive totem pole.*

Whether or not a particular social position is a master status depends in part on the situation. For

APPLYING SOCIOLOGY
Argot: The Special Language of Subcultures

There are thousands of subcultures in the United States and everyone belongs to some. People often take for granted their participation in subcultures without realizing the important social functions subcultures perform. When we apply sociological insights to our own personal life, we begin to recognize that subcultures help to reinforce feelings of group solidarity and identification and feelings of self-worth and importance. Subcultures create a distinctive social environment that reflects the special values, goals, and unique qualities of the members of the subculture. Even the way members of a subculture speak contributes to achieving these functions (Widdicombe & Wooffit, 1995). As you review language usage in a few subcultures in the United States, you should think about subcultures to which you belong and their special languages.

The specialized language of a subculture is known as an *argot.* There are almost as many argots as there are subcultures. Reports have been published on the argots of musicians, teenagers, prostitutes, beauticians, lumberjacks, convicts, furniture salespeople, miners, sailors, undertakers, and even sugar-beet workers, to mention just a few (Mencken, 1957). That the use of argot is so widespread suggests that it serves important social functions, but in understanding argot several factors should be kept in mind. First, the groups that develop argots are almost endlessly diverse, and in many cases the terms they devise are unique to their situations. The term *gun,* for example, would be used to mean "syringe" only in a drug subculture. Second, argot changes constantly. Some of the terms cited here will almost certainly have gone out-of-date by the time you read this. Indeed, an argot may die out altogether if the subculture that uses it disappears, as happened with the vaudeville and hobo subcultures earlier in the twentieth century. Nevertheless, it is possible to identify some of argot's general social functions.

Probably the most important is that it separates group members from nonmembers. A group's argot may function in much the same way as a password. Those who know it are the "ins"; those who do not are the "outs." In a way, argot serves this purpose even better than a password—you could bribe someone to tell you a password, but an argot can be learned only by intimate association with the group that uses it. Among teenage drug gang members in Michigan, for example, a *skeezer* is a woman of low status, *def* means "first rate" or "desirable," and *diss* means "to show disrespect for" (Taylor, 1993). Anyone ill-advised enough to try to learn such an argot from a book would be bound to make mistakes, and there are few things more embarrassing than using a term incorrectly when you are trying to show that you are one of the "ins."

A related function of argot is that of reinforcing group identity. One of the ways groups define themselves is by excluding those who lack certain characteristics. By signifying that some do not belong, the use of argot draws together those who do. Indeed, some words in the argots of certain subcultures may be used precisely because they are unintelligible to others. Teenagers, for example, might use the words *airhead* (meaning "slow" or "stupid," or among some teens, "a blond") or *slime bucket* (meaning "males" from a female's point of view) in part because such words set them apart from their parents, teachers, and others of a different generation. What better way to develop a separate identity than to devise a language that the uninitiated have trouble understanding?

In the same way, argot can reflect and reinforce a subculture's own values and priorities. A survey of the argot of some residents of Michigan's Upper Peninsula reveals such terms as *chook, swampers, choppers,* and *artics* (see Table 2.1 for these and more argot). That many terms concern winter and inclement weather suggests that such climatic conditions play an important role for people living in that part of Michigan. Indeed, this is true, for cold, inclement weather is characteristic of the "U.P." for at least six months of every year.

Argot also often contains special words to describe those who belong and those who don't, as a further way of separating insiders from outsiders. Prison inmates in Michigan, for example, call white female correctional officers *sweat hogs,* whereas young prisoners are *bloods* (see Table 2.1). Female drug gang members in Michigan call the police *the hook.* Residents of Michigan's Upper Peninsula refer to themselves as *U.P.ers* or *Yoopers,* whereas those in the rest of the state are known as *apple knockers* (because apples were historically grown in the Lower Peninsula of Michigan), or more derogatorily, *trolls* (because they live "below," or south of, the bridge that connects the two peninsulas of the state).

Finally, an argot may offer concise ways to refer to roles and statuses not generally found in the mainstream of society. A survey of terms used in Michigan prisons uncovered these terms in the inmate subculture (Kalinich & Pitcher, 1987): *jocker* for an aggressive partner in a homosexual relationship; *daddy* for one who controls a homosexual, similar to a pimp; and *kid* for a young, passive homosexual. Although many prison inmates do not participate in homosexual activities, it is clear that homosexuality is a salient element of the inmate subculture, and virtually all inmates need to be familiar with the associated argot.

Argot often serves these functions without the speaker or listener being aware of it. Applying sociology in this fashion to your own life can offer insight into some of the functions of the argots you speak at work, in school, in church, or among your friends and family. Without your being aware of it, the language you speak every day helps maintain and reinforce group boundaries and impart a sense of belonging and identity.

TABLE 2.1 Subcultural argot

Argot of Michigan Prison Inmates, 1986		Argot of Michigan's Upper Peninsula Residents	
Blood	Young inmate	Yooper	A person who lives in the Upper Peninsula (U.P.er)
Break bad	Your wife or girlfriend leaves you		
Do whopper	A young, loud inmate	Chook	A knitted stocking cap worn in winter
Doing all day	Serving a life sentence	Wuh!	Expression of surprise (as in, "Oh my gosh!")
Hang it up	Commit suicide		
Ride out	Transfer to another prison	yah	Yes
		Yous	Plural of you, as in "yous guys"
Short	Cigarette butt		
Sweat hogs	White female correctional officers	Down below	Referring to the Lower Peninsula of Michigan
What it be?	How's it going with you?	Puck	A male who plays hockey
Kite	An inmate's letter to a prison official about an official matter	Swampers	Tall green boots used for hiking in wet or muddy places
Skating	Being in an unauthorized place	Pank	Pat or smash down, as in "pank it down good" or "your hair gets panked down when you sleep"
Works	Needle and syringe used for injecting drugs		
Be cool pills	Authorized psychotropic medication	Choppers	Lined leather mittens worn with chooks and swampers
Bogart	Flush drugs down toilet		
		Artics	Black rubber galoshes or overboots

example, at work the master status of a female college professor is most likely to be *professor*. The fact that she is also *female* will probably be less relevant. By contrast, a woman who works as a stevedore, as a jockey, or in some other job where women are still relatively uncommon may be viewed by her coworkers in the master status of *woman*.

Master statuses can also play a part in prejudice and discrimination. Frequently, people judge others according to characteristics they automatically associate with a particular master status without ever looking at the individuals themselves. Women as well as blacks and members of other minority groups run into this often, but it can happen to anyone. The English, for instance, often view red-haired people with suspicion.

Roles

Roles are, in a sense, *clusters of norms; they are the behaviors expected of a person who occupies a certain status.* Every status has a number of roles associated with it. For example, a person with a status of soldier is expected to be neat, appear patriotic, follow the orders of superiors, and serve as a good example for subordinates. Similarly, a college professor is expected to teach, write, give and grade tests, and counsel students. *All the roles associated with a particular status* are called the **role set** (Mer-

ton, 1968). A schematic diagram indicating roles and role sets for the statuses of university professor, police officer, and mother is presented in Figure 2.1. Because the terms are so closely related, people sometimes have a tendency to confuse the words *status* and *role*. Keeping them separate is easy, however, if one simply remembers that a person occupies a status and performs a role.

Social Roles and Social Interaction   In playing various roles, people are guided by *role expectations,* which are norms based on custom and tradition that outline how a particular role should be performed. Role expectations are a major source of order and stability in society and make cooperative activities possible. People are usually aware of the expectations associated with their own roles as well as those of people with whom they are likely to interact. Thus they can anticipate how others will probably behave toward them and can coordinate their own behavior accordingly. Social interaction thereby can become reasonably predictable.

For instance, consider the common interchange that occurs between a customer and a cashier in a grocery store. Both are usually aware of what each expects. Customers are supposed to select the items they want, take them to the cashier, and pay the amount rung up. The cashier, in turn, is supposed to check the items, charge the

FIGURE 2.1 A Schematic Presentation of the Relationship Among Status, Role, and Role Set

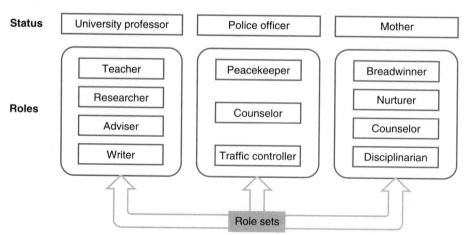

proper amount, give the correct change, and provide a sales receipt. If these expectations are not met, some sort of trouble may ensue. For example, if customers try to leave a store without paying, they run the risk of being arrested. Or, if the cashier tries to charge too much, a heated argument is likely to occur.

Of course, people do not always behave according to role expectations. We see violations every day. If these violations become too widespread, however, the fabric of social order would be seriously threatened.

The expectations of a particular role are influenced by the statuses of the people with whom one interacts. For example, students are normally expected to be respectful and somewhat deferential when dealing with professors. With other students, however, they are expected to behave as equals. Furthermore, role expectations are colored by the situation. Students, for instance, would normally be more casual with their professors at a student–faculty ball game than they would be in the classroom.

Although role expectations provide general guidelines for how a role should be played, we should not assume that they are rigid. In fact, *role performance,* the actual behavior of people in particular roles, can vary tremendously. Unmarried college students, for example, may be expected to date, but dating can take many forms. Students may go out with one person or with many. They may prefer quiet strolls through museums or crowded parties. They may go out almost every night or only on weekends. And some, in the interest of their studies, may rarely date at all.

One of the most obvious reasons for differences in role performance is personality. Some people are outgoing, some are reserved, some tend to dominate, and some tend to be submissive. Personal characteristics such as these play a big part in the way people behave. So do the other statuses they occupy. For instance, the behavior of a married college student who is also a mother or father will probably be quite different from that of a student who is still dating. Similarly, the concerns of students who are middle-aged or older will differ from those of students just out of high school, and these concerns will normally affect the ways they perform their student roles.

The variation in the way people behave means that social interaction is a creative process. To help explain how it occurs, the sociologist Erving Goffman (1959) developed a "dramaturgical" analogy. People, said Goffman, can be viewed as similar to actors in a play. They begin with a basic script in the form of role expectations. Then, using their imagination and ingenuity, they create their own special performance of their roles. An important part of this process is **impression management,** which is *an individual's effort to control the meanings that others attach to his or her performance.*

One example of impression management is the clothing and hairstyles people select for themselves. Business people in many settings wear neat suits and ties in order to communicate respectability and conservatism to other business people and customers. College students, by contrast, may wear jeans, slacks, or sweatpants, depending on what they want to communicate to those around them. These same students may raise their hand and ask many questions in class in order to convince the professor and other students that they are bright and interested. Or some students may never raise their hand in class because they believe that such an expression of nterest in academic or intellectual matters will make them appear "uncool." This flexibility makes for interesting and versatile role performances, but it also makes predicting people's behavior more difficult and complex. *Predicting how others will behave, or how they think and feel,* is a process that sociologists call **role-taking,** and it is central to social interaction. When role-taking, we try to imagine how others perceive a situation. We imaginatively put ourselves in their place and try to figure out what meanings they attach to people or events. Role-taking occurs in everyday situations, such as when someone tries to imagine how another will react to a request for a date, and it occurs in momentous situations, such as when President Bush and his advisers tried to imagine how Saddam Hussein would react to the build-up of allied troops in the Persian Gulf in 1990. This process of role-taking, then, shapes people's behavior as they use these predictions of others' likely actions in deciding how to behave. (People don't ask for dates because they predict rejection, whereas President Bush proceeded with the troop build-up after predicting that Hussein would not voluntarily leave Kuwait.)

Role Strain and Role Conflict   Most of the time, role expectations make life more manageable. As has been noted, they help to create social order and stability by providing us with a general idea of what will happen in interactions with others. However, role expectations can also create problems. In certain instances, they can lead to role strain and role conflict. **Role strain** *develops when people have difficulty performing a role* (Goode, 1960). Sometimes a person does not have the skills or qualities required to perform a particular role. For example, a promotion may place a person who has inadequate business training and is not very adept at handling people in the role of manager. Similarly, students may enter medical or law school only to find that they do not have the desire or dedication necessary to bear the tremendous workload. Role strain can also occur when a person simply does not like some aspects of a role. College professors, for instance, are often expected to write articles or books in their fields of professional expertise. In fact, being published is sometimes a criterion for receiving tenure. Some professors, however, love teaching but find writing difficult. Many students run into similar problems when they take courses that require term papers.

Another form of role strain is called **role conflict.** Role conflict occurs *when two or more roles a person must play are incompatible or inconsistent.* Sometimes the conflict involves roles associated with different statuses. Consider the problem faced by a police officer who goes to a party thrown by a college friend who offers his guests marijuana. As a police officer, the person is expected to enforce the law. As a friend, however, she is expected to bring no harm to her friend. Thus, no matter what she does, she will violate the expectations of at least one of her roles.

Roles associated with the same status can also be in conflict. Nurses, for example, are expected to care about their patients. At the same time, they are expected to maintain objectivity and a degree of professional distance. Similarly, mothers and fathers are expected to provide their children with affection, but they are also expected to discipline them when they misbehave.

Unfortunately, role conflict and role strain are inevitable, particularly in a society as complex as that of the United States where individuals occupy many different statuses that require them to perform many different roles. As a result, role conflicts are problems everyone must face. Often people simply accept the fact that some of the expectations of their roles will create conflict or strain. Nurses and parents, for example, usually feel that the pleasure and satisfaction they receive from their roles outweigh the difficulties. Role strain that is not resolved, however, can be detrimental to people's physical and mental health. It can lead to feelings of frustration, anxiety, and failure. Role strain is also associated with ulcers, heart disease, and many other physical and mental ailments (Krantz, Grunberg, & Baum, 1985). The negative impact of role strain in people and institutions is spelled out in more detail in Applying Sociology: Role Strain and the Social Structure (on pp. 64–65).

Instead of ignoring role strain, one might do something to resolve the problem. In fact, people often view role strain as providing a challenge. The new manager, for instance, might take courses at night to improve his business and managerial skills. The Applying Sociology section suggests some ways that sociological practitioners work to alleviate role strain. Sometimes, however, people simply cannot handle certain role expectations and therefore abandon the role. The police officer, for instance, might stop seeing her buddy, and some medical and law students decide to drop out of school.

Groups and Social Institutions

Although status and role are concepts that apply to individuals, they actually come into operation only when two or more people interact. A mother, for instance, can only play the role of nurturer when she has a child to take care of, and a college professor must have students in order to play the role of teacher. Furthermore, interaction among people usually takes place in some sort of group context—a family, a class, a clique, and so on. Indeed, sociology could be considered the study of groups, for virtually all the areas of interest normally investigated by sociologists pertain to groups either directly or indirectly. Because groups are so important, Chapter 4 will discuss this subject in detail. For now, **groups** may be defined as *collections of people who interact with one another on the basis of interrelated statuses and roles and who feel some awareness that they share something in common.*

Social institutions are *relatively stable clusters of statuses, roles, and groups that work together to fulfill some need that all societies must satisfy.* For instance, societies must ensure the physical survival of their members by providing food, clothing, shelter, and health care. They must maintain social order and provide for defense. They must replenish their population through reproduction or recruitment and then train these new members so that these individuals fit into the society productively. Finally, they must develop some sort of belief system to provide meanings and goals that can be shared by most, if not all, of their members. These needs, though few in number, are vital and are filled by political, economic, educational, family, health-care, and religious institutions. Indeed, no society can hope to survive unless it develops enduring ways of meeting these needs effectively. Chapters 9 through 13 will examine, in considerable depth, the major institutions found in all societies.

A Comparative View of Societies

You should be able to describe the five basic subsistence patterns and explain how societies change as they make the transition to industrialism, postindustrialism, and global interdependence.

Our comprehension of the world today is strongly shaped by the prevalence of industrial societies. To be sure, there are still a few scattered primitive groups such as the Indians of the western Amazon forests of Brazil. There are also some countries that are still largely agricultural, particularly in Asia, Africa, and South America. All these societies, however, are rapidly giving way to industrial technologies and lifestyles. Nevertheless, one of the best ways to understand one's own society is to view it in comparison to other types of societies. By looking at the variety of means people have used in adapting to their particular environments and technologies, people can better appreciate the forces influential in their own society, both now

and in the past. Therefore, this chapter will close with a brief look at the social structure of several different types of societies.

These societies may be classified by their subsistence patterns, or how they solve the problem of securing the basic necessities of food, clothing, and shelter. Five subsistence patterns emerge—hunting and gathering, pastoralism, horticulturalism, agriculturalism, and industrialism (see Gregg, 1991; Johnson & Earle, 1987; Lenski, Lenski, & Nolan, 1991).

Preindustrial Societies

The oldest and simplest social structure is that found in *hunting-and-gathering societies,* which are most often nomadic groups that number no more than sixty or so individuals. In these societies, everyone who is able must participate in the search for food. Furthermore, there is seldom a surplus of food, so no one is able to amass any wealth. Thus, hunting-and-gathering societies are essentially egalitarian. The only statuses are normally those based on gender and age. The men usually hunt, fish, and make or repair weapons. The women gather nuts and berries, make clothes, and tend to the cooking. Children take on adult tasks as soon as they are physically able. There are no specialized leadership roles, and decisions about such things as where to hunt or whether it is time to move to a new territory are usually made by common consensus. Similarly, whatever social control is needed is administered by the entire group through gossip and ridicule or, in cases of serious infractions, through ostracism. The family is a key institution in hunting-and-gathering societies, and most societal needs are accomplished in the family. Thus, economic, political, and even religious tasks are performed by family members, and there are no separate institutions that fulfill these needs. Families are usually loosely organized, and the responsibility for raising children is frequently shared by all the adults.

Social structure becomes somewhat more complex in pastoral and horticultural societies, both of which first emerged some twelve thousand years ago. *Pastoralism* involves raising herds of domesticated animals, and *horticulturalism* is based on cultivating plants such as wheat, rice, and other grains using a few simple tools. These patterns of

APPLYING SOCIOLOGY

Role Strain and the Social Structure: Its Impact on People and Their Lives

Role expectations need to be clear, compatible, and achievable; otherwise, role strain can occur. Role strain is a problem for society because it can make it more difficult for people to perform their roles adequately and make a contribution to society. One major application of sociological research over the years has been to assess precisely what the consequences of role strain are for people and organizations, and how the social structure might be changed to alleviate role strain and its negative impact.

Role strain often arises during periods of transition and change, as one part of society changes while another part has not adequately adapted to that change. In terms of recent changes in role structure in the United States and many other societies, a major development has been the changing roles of women and men. Not too many years ago, the norms of marriage led men to be employed in a paying job and women to take care of the home and child rearing. With the growth of equality between the sexes, women have been given more occupational opportunities and have been encouraged to pursue employment outside the home. However, women still take most responsibility for child care. For many women, the result is role strain: difficulty in performing the overload of tasks that results from their participation in both employment and domestic arenas.

Role strain can have a detrimental impact on people's psychological well-being. People react to it with feelings of anxiety, depression, or unhappiness. They feel overworked and unfulfilled. The sociologists Catherine Ross and John Mirowsky (1988) found that two factors in the social structure had a major impact on working women's psychological well-being: the easy availability of child care and a husband who shares in the child-care responsibilities. Women who had these two advantages had relatively low levels of depression because these arrangements reduced the extent of role strain the women experienced. In fact, these women had the same low levels of depression as working women who did not have children. Working women who had difficulty arranging child care for their children had much higher levels of depression. And, if their husbands did not help with child care, they had extremely high levels of depression. Ross and Mirowsky conclude, "It is not children per se who create stress for employed mothers, but the absence of supportive arrangements." (p. 135)

The solution is not necessarily for women to quit work and become full-time child rearers. Despite the economic problems that might arise if Mom quits work, nonworking mothers have considerably higher depression levels than working women with easy availability to child care.

> Nothing offsets the stress of young children for the nonemployed. The women who are at home all day with the children may feel . . . that the children are making constant demands on them, that they have no privacy, that they are isolated from other adults, and that they are stuck in the house. (Ross & Mirowsky, 1988, p. 135)

This situation does not mean that some women are not happy as full-time mothers. Some clearly are. For many women, however, full-time motherhood is not the best alternative. These women gain gratification from both their child-rearing roles and their work outside the home with other adults. For the psychological

---

subsistence are far more productive than hunting and gathering. As a result, pastoral and horticultural societies not only are assured of a steady supply of food, but they also can manage surpluses in the form of food or livestock. As a result, they tend to be much larger than hunting-and-gathering societies, numbering in the hundreds and in some cases the thousands. The food surplus also frees some people from the necessity of food production, and more specialized statuses emerge. Such activities as providing political and economic leadership, performing religious rituals, and healing the sick become special statuses that are distinct from people's positions in the family. In addition, the increased size and complexity of these societies make specialized statuses essential. Furthermore, some individuals or families manage to accumulate more wealth and, as a result, more power than others. This power often becomes hereditary (i.e., passed on through generations), which leads to the development of some social class distinctions. For the most part, however,

well-being of these women, society needs to provide the institutional and family supports that would enable them to do both without experiencing high levels of role strain.

Role strain is also often found in occupational settings where too much is asked of people or they are asked to do conflicting things. For example, studies of social workers have found role strain in the form of incompatible expectations (Harrison, 1980). These can occur when a social worker is expected to act as an advocate for a client, such as a youthful offender, but also to serve as a representative of the law or the courts. Studies of nurses have also found high levels of role strain resulting in part from heavy work schedules that do not permit nurses to give the kind of personal care to patients that they were trained to give, and shift work that disrupts nurses' social life (Stamps & Piedmonte, 1986). The same thing has been found among correctional officers in prisons. George Gross and his colleagues (1991) found that certain structural conditions produced stress among correctional officers: having too few officers to provide adequate security, having unclear departmental policies about what correctional officers can do, and having unclear policies regarding what is appropriate behavior in dealing with inmates. Correctional officers who work under such conditions of role strain suffer high levels of physical and emotional distress as well as interpersonal problems.

When professionals such as these experience role strain, it sometimes results in *burnout:* an emotional disengagement from clients, dissatisfaction on the job, feelings of worthlessness, and physical and interpersonal problems. Because of these personal problems, burnout creates high levels of employee turnover as people quit their jobs in response to this role strain. Turnover is costly for organizations like hospitals and social service agencies because skilled workers leave and new workers must be trained.

Applied sociological research, then, can help isolate some of the sources of role strain and point to ways to alleviate that strain. Such research also illustrates the point made in Chapter 1: that sociologists identify personal problems, such as depression or burnout, as *structural* problems—arising out of characteristics of the social structure such as role expectations and role strain. Sociological research and analysis also point to solutions to stress-related problems. At the structural level, sociologists advise organizations to change the workplace to give nurses or correctional officers a lighter workload or more control over the flow of their work. In other cases, sociologists suggest social policies, such as more widely available day-care services, that would alleviate the stress of women who work and have children. When changing the social structure is not possible or does not entirely alleviate the problem, clinical sociologists, psychologists, and other counselors develop stress-reduction programs or suggest alternate occupational goals that make it possible to avoid stressful situations (Church, 1991). Gross and his colleagues (1991), for example, recommended the establishment of support groups that would enable the families of correctional officers to help relieve their stress. Some clinical sociologists work with families to rearrange the norms of family life in situations where mothers work so that a more equitable distribution of responsibilities can be achieved.

statuses and roles are still determined by gender and age. The men usually farm, herd livestock, collect fuel for fires, and prepare leather for clothes. The women tend small gardens, prepare food, and make clothing and utensils.

Some six thousand years ago, the invention of the plow led to the development of *agricultural societies*. The plow, which brings nutrients to the surface of the soil, greatly increases the productivity of the land and allows it to be farmed almost continuously. This development, in turn, gave rise to much larger societies with much greater food surpluses and significantly reduced the number of people needed in the actual production of food.

Agricultural societies have very complex social structures, mainly because they need so much coordination, management, and support. For instance, they require centralized political and economic organizations to coordinate the production and distribution of food, set up trade relations with other societies, and maintain social order. One consequence of this centralization is the appearance of cities. Another is a tremendous increase in the number and variety of statuses, which include merchants, artists, metalworkers, physicians, traders, religious figures, and bureaucrats. Furthermore, wealth and power tend to become concentrated in the hands of a few people. Economic differences among people become more pronounced, and a fairly rigid class structure emerges. In fact, extensive inequality is an inherent feature of virtually all agricultural societies. Thus, although age and gender are still important statuses, people's social positions become increasingly determined by other statuses such as occupation, ethnicity, family background, and wealth.

Industrial Societies

The most complex social structure is found in industrial societies, which, as mentioned at the beginning of this section, have become the most pervasive type of society in the world today. Industrialism is an extremely productive subsistence pattern in which machines and power tools, run by new sources of energy such as fossil fuels, accomplish tasks that were previously done by hand.

As a result, a relatively small number of people can feed the rest of the population.

There is a virtual explosion in the number and variety of economic activities in industrial societies. In addition, most tasks are broken down into small, specialized segments, each of which is performed by a different person. Consequently, industrial societies have an elaborate system of statuses and roles. Although gender and age are still important in some contexts, occupation is the chief determinant of a person's social position. Moreover, extreme wealth and power become harder to hold onto in industrial societies, so there is a decrease in the overall amount of social inequality. Thus achievement replaces ascription, and such statuses as race and family background begin to decline in importance.

The most dramatic shift in societal evolution has been between the four preindustrial societies and industrial society (see Table 2.2). Industrial societies have social structures that stand in stark contrast to all the others. The German sociologist Ferdinand Tönnies described the difference in terms of *gemeinschaft* versus *gesellschaft* types of societies (1887/1963).

Gemeinschaft, which translates roughly as *"community," refers to social life that is governed by*

TABLE 2.2 The transition from preindustrial to industrial societies

	Preindustrial	Industrial
Social relations	More personal and intimate	Very impersonal
Social structure	Few statuses and roles; ascription is important	Complex array of statuses and roles; achievement overshadows ascription
Institutions	May be some specialized institutions, but family tends to be most important	Specialized institutions emerge in political, educational, and other realms; family overshadowed by other institutions
Social control	Largely informal	Formal means, such as the police, become ever more important
Division of labor	Simple, based most often on age and sex	Complex, based on many characteristics, but occupation is especially important; age and gender are secondary
Culture	Homogeneous, with value consensus and few subcultures	Diverse, with many subcultures and numerous conflicting values

personal, informal considerations, with tradition and custom prevailing. People place the welfare of the community before personal interest, are strongly bound to the other members of their community, and value these community ties very highly. In the gemeinschaft, people relate to one another because of liking, sympathy, or enjoyment—because the relationship itself provides many positive feelings and personal fulfillments. Gemeinschaft-like social relationships tend to predominate in preindustrial societies.

Gesellschaft, meaning *"society" or "association," refers to social relations characterized by specialization, individualism, and rationality.* Specialization emerges in the form of separate social roles and social institutions that are developed to accomplish specific tasks and to achieve certain goals. Individualism and a concern with personal interest predominate and come to replace loyalty to a group or society. The ends or goals that people seek in social relationships are more specific and limited, such as making money or exchanging products. Calculation, impersonality, and formality come to dominate social relationships. Increasingly, relationships become contractual rather than personal. Gesellschaft-like social relationships tend to predominate in industrial societies. Chapters 4 and 14 will consider the distinction between gemeinschaft and gesellschaft social relationships in more detail.

A Global Perspective: Postindustrialism and Global Interdependence

With the emergence of industrial societies, societal development has not stopped. What appears to be emerging is an advanced industrial or **postindustrial society.** *Such societies are dominated by a highly technological form of production and devote more attention to service industries, information production, and economic consumption than they do to industrial production and manufacturing* (Bell, 1973; Beniger, 1993). Fewer people work in factories producing goods. Subsistence shifts its focus to producing information, organizing people, and providing services. The key resources are no longer physical skills and strength; instead, education, intellectual skills, the ability to manipulate information, and skills at organizing people become important. The positions in the social structure that receive high rewards are those of writers, teachers, scientists, managers, and the designers of products. These people work with their brains rather than their brawn; they manipulate people, information, and knowledge rather than manufacture goods or products. Increasingly, people are employed in transportation, research, government, recreation, and banking—all occupations that provide services. As information and knowledge become more important, the result is further innovations—robotics, computers, cybernetics, fiber optics—that lead to a further shift toward an information-based, service-oriented economy. Today, about 70 percent of the jobs in the United States are white-collar or service jobs. The emergence of a postindustrial society is explored at a number of points in this book, especially in Chapter 15.

Not all societies today are advancing into a postindustrial era. The societies that have made the most progress toward postindustrialism are the United States and Canada, most of Europe, Japan, Australia, and New Zealand. These are sometimes called *First-World countries.* The term *Third-World countries,* also called *less developed countries,* refers to the many nations around the world that lag substantially behind the First-World nations in terms of economic development and affluence. Some of these nations, such as Somalia and Bangladesh, are very poor; others, such as Panama and Algeria, are much better off economically, although still far behind the First-World nations. (The term *Second-World countries* refers to the former Soviet Union, Eastern Europe, and mainland China, but it is not used much since the collapse of the Soviet Union and the end of the Cold War.) There is much diversity among these Third-World nations; some are still largely agricultural and rural, such as Ethiopia, whereas others are making strides toward urbanizing and industrializing, such as South Korea. The reasons for this diversity among nations and the implications of it will be explored at a number of points in subsequent chapters.

Societies today, much more so than in the past, live in an interdependent global community. The linkages between First-World and Third-World countries, for example, are extensive and irreversible. This situation has wide ramifications for the social structure in the United States in terms of the jobs and opportunities that are available. Increasingly, assembly-line and production jobs are going to less developed nations while the

The mass media of television and advertising present images that reflect the mainstream values of the elites who control the media. This advertisement projects a positive image of material wealth, youth, and physical beauty.

design and information jobs remain in the advanced industrial nations. Things such as economic growth, crime, and drug use in the United States are now affected by developments in many places around the globe. This theme will be addressed at numerous points in this book, as it looks at the social mechanisms that shape and direct that global interdependence.

Mass Media and the Production of Culture

You should be able to describe the contribution of the mass media to the production and dissemination of cultural values and norms.

For most of human history, culture was produced and transmitted largely through personal, face-to-face contacts between people. By watching the behaviors and hearing the words of relatives or neighbors with whom they were familiar, people learned what values were most desired, what norms were acceptable, and which social role performances would be received positively. With the emergence of the modern mass media and technologies of communication, people can now learn about cultural values, norms, and social roles through the far more impersonal contact of television, movies, magazines, rock videos, or the Internet. This means that family, friends, and neighbors become less influential in the production and transmission of culture (Real, 1977).

In comparison to other modes of transmitting culture, the media presentation of culture is impersonal; it is directed at a large and heterogeneous audience rather than shaped and focused for consumption by particular individuals. Mass-media culture is also carefully crafted and orchestrated rather than spontaneous. Finally, mass-media culture in most cases involves a one-way transmission of information rather than an interaction between the source and the recipient. Because of these characteristics, the culture transmitted through the mass media tends to be less spontaneous and more standardized and simplified. It tends to encourage reaction and acceptance on the part of the recipient rather than reflection, choice, and involvement in the production of culture.

Since the elites in society tend to control the media, the images that the mass media present tend to reflect and support the mainstream values of those elites. In the United States, for example, the media stress the value of material consumption, reflecting one of the central mainstream values discussed earlier in this chapter. Through advertising and other images, people are told that the way to fulfillment is through owning shiny new cars, handsome (and expensive) clothing, and an endless array of other material products. The images presented on television and in the movies indicate that the average person in the United States is far wealthier and much more comfortable materially than is actually the case; this can make viewers wonder how "successful" they have been if they possess less than they see in the media.

Another common theme in the media in the United States is the importance of youth and physical beauty. A study of magazines devoted to teenagers (mostly females), for example, found that about half the space in these magazines is devoted to advertising (Evans, Rutberg, Sather, & Turner, 1991). In addition, the articles and advertisements in magazines such as *Seventeen, Young Miss,* and *Sassy* overwhelmingly stressed the importance of fashion and physical beauty. One-half of the advertisements in these magazines were for clothing, beauty products, fashion products, and other appearance-enhancing items. The message communicated is that self-improvement through proper use of makeup and hairstyles is the road to success, especially for young women. According to these portrayals, the goal in life for women should be the attraction of males; little space is devoted to political issues, social responsibility to community, or advancement of one's education or career. The magazines that young men are likely to read, such as *Sports Illustrated, Field and Stream,* or *Road and Track,* stress athletic prowess, daring, and competition.

Rock music and rock videos also stress the importance of youth, physical beauty, and physical strength. MTV, for example, portrays youth and physical beauty in an appealing way. It also portrays violence as a common, if not integral, part of sexuality and gender relationships. In fact, heavy viewers of MTV are more likely to accept sexual violence as a part of relationships and to believe that women cannot or should not defend themselves from aggression on the part of males (Basow, 1992; Lindsey, 1997).

The stress on physical beauty is also a manifestation of the value of individualism in U.S. culture: the road to success is through individual, rather than collective, actions. The mythical lone hero is pervasive in the media, whether it be Clint Eastwood in the "Dirty Harry" movie series, Arnold Schwarzenegger as the Terminator, or Superman. The theme presented is that real, positive heroes act alone, often against the resistance of others. Especially for men, the image presented is that the strong individual acting alone can right wrongs, save society from evil, and accomplish other social goods. Collective involvement and cooperative actions are not given nearly the same stress.

So, in the modern world, the mass media play an integral role in producing and transmitting cultural values and norms. These media portrayals of cultural values are, of course, highly functional in a capitalist, consumer-oriented society because they encourage people to buy the many products produced and they encourage behaviors, such as individualism, that are congruent with capitalist economic arrangements. However, the impact of the media is complicated. Whereas media influence does have a tendency to homogenize culture—spread a common culture over widely diverse groups—the technology also makes it possible for a variety of subcultures to emerge and maintain themselves through magazines, music, and the Internet. The possibilities for communication are vastly greater because of modern communications technology. Some of these subcultures will have or develop values and norms that are at variance with the mainstream cultural values. So, the modern mass media do play an important part in producing and transmitting culture, but this effect is complicated, with tendencies toward both homogenizing culture and diversifying it.

Summary

1. Societies vary greatly in development, size, and social practices. To study them effectively, sociologists look at a few fundamental characteristics common to all societies. These characteristics pertain to culture and social structure.

2. Culture refers to the total lifestyle of a people. Cultural elements can be divided into material culture, which refers to physical products, and nonmaterial culture, which refers to elements that have no physical existence. Material and nonmaterial culture are closely interrelated, and each greatly affects the other.

3. Beliefs, values, norms, and language are components that are common to all cultures. Beliefs are people's conceptions about what is true in the world. Values are very general guidelines for behavior. Whereas mainstream values can be found in all cultures, there is also a diversity of values, and values change over time as social conditions change. Norms are more specific guidelines for behavior. Language not only makes possible communication but also shapes our view of reality and reinforces social practices.

4. There are forces in cultures that both promote and resist change. Because the elements of a culture are usually fairly well integrated, change in one aspect usually results in change in another. Change can come either from outside or from within a culture. A major source of external change is diffusion. Sources of internal change include innovation and the gap between ideal culture and real culture.

5. Ethnocentrism promotes a feeling of "we-ness," but it can undermine our efforts to understand other cultures. Social scientists therefore promote the idea of cultural relativity, which holds that the lifestyles of various peoples can be understood only in terms of their own culture rather than that of the observer.

6. The United States and most other advanced nations are too diverse to have one common culture. They have a number of subcultures. Membership in a subculture requires sharing its values and identifying with its members.

7. Social structure helps to make social interaction orderly and predictable. The foundation of social structure lies in the concepts of status and role.

8. Role expectations, which are based on custom and tradition, provide general guidelines for people to use in devising their performance of their roles. Most of the time, they help to make life more manageable, but they sometimes cause people trouble in the form of role strain and role conflict.

9. Two important manifestations of social structure are groups and institutions. Most social interaction occurs in some sort of group context. Institutions are relatively stable clusters of statuses, roles, and groups that work together to meet the basic needs of a society.

10. Five different types of subsistence patterns have been identified among human societies, and they involve movement toward more extensive and more elaborate social structures. Societies are also distinguished in terms of whether they are preindustrial, industrial, or postindustrial in nature, and twentieth-century societies can also be characterized as either First-, Second-, or Third-World nations. In the modern world, the mass media and technologies of global communication are playing an increasingly important part in the production and transmission of culture around the world.

STUDY AND *Review*

Key Terms

achieved status	culture	gesellschaft	internalization
ascribed status	ethnocentrism	group	laws
beliefs	folkways	ideal culture	master status
cultural relativity	gemeinschaft	impression management	material culture

mores

nonmaterial culture

norms

postindustrial society

real culture

role conflict

role set

role strain

roles

role-taking

sanctions

social institution

social structure

society

status

subculture

values

Multiple-Choice Questions

1. All of the following would be considered a part of material culture *except*
    a. physical objects.
    b. physical artifacts.
    c. language.
    d. television sets.
    e. home appliances.

2. "Conceptions that people have about what is true in the world" is known as which component of culture?
    a. Beliefs.
    b. Values.
    c. Language.
    d. Ideal culture.
    e. Real culture.

3. All of the following were listed as Japanese cultural values *except*
    a. harmony.
    b. material success.
    c. collectivism.
    d. authority.
    e. tradition.

4. The austere clothing of the Amish of Pennsylvania is a reflection of which of their cultural values?
    a. Individualism.
    b. Collectivism.
    c. Equality.
    d. Humility.
    e. Harmony.

5. In most societies, the prohibitions against murder and incest would be considered to be
    a. folkways.
    b. mores.
    c. material culture.
    d. social roles.

6. The ideal culture in Mexico would be best characterized as
    a. matriarchal.
    b. individualistic.
    c. socialistic.
    d. patriarchal.

7. Which of the following would be the best example of an ascribed status?
    a. Being born male.
    b. Graduating from college.
    c. Getting married.
    d. Selling drugs.

8. Research has found that role strain tends to produce all of the following *except*
    a. feelings of depression and unhappiness.
    b. difficulty in performing roles.
    c. feelings of empowerment.
    d. burnout.

9. Specialized statuses, such as political leaders and healers, first emerge in which type of society?
    a. Hunting and gathering.
    b. Horticultural and pastoral.
    c. Agricultural.
    d. Industrial.

10. In a gemeinschaft type of society, in comparison to a gesellschaft society, which of the following would most likely be true?
    a. Social relations are more personal.
    b. Social control is more formal.
    c. The division of labor is more complex.
    d. The family is more overshadowed by other institutions.

True/False Questions

1. The Comanche Indian society of the nineteenth century stressed individualism as did the Euro-American culture of the time.

2. One of the mainstream cultural values in the United States, according to this chapter, is tradition.

3. Cultural norms are more specific guidelines for behavior than are cultural values.

4. Based on the linguistic-relativity hypothesis, the chapter concludes that language is a powerful force shaping culture, whereas culture has little impact on language.

5. *Diffusion* refers to a source of cultural change that is internal to a society rather than external.

6. In the study of other cultures, social scientists promote ethnocentrism, rather than cultural relativism, as the more useful way to understand a culture.

7. What is important about a master status is that it is central to the way in which people view themselves or are viewed by others.

8. Role conflict is one form of role strain.

9. Industrial societies place more stress on gemeinschaft than do preindustrial societies.

10. Canada, Germany, and Japan would be considered Second-World countries.

Fill-In Questions

1. The term _____ refers to the total lifestyle of a people, including all of the ideas, values, knowledge, behaviors, and material objects that they share.

2. The various elements of culture fall into two general categories: _____ and _____.

3. The fact that people in the United States strive to make things better and to improve the future in comparison to the present reflects the cultural value of _____.

4. _____ refers to the process by which people incorporate social norms into their own personal codes of conduct.

5. When two cultures come into contact, cultural change is likely to occur through a process of _____.

6. Argot is the specialized language of a(n) _____.

7. What distinguishes the concepts of *status* and *role* is that a person _____ a status and _____ a role.

8. _____ refers to imaginatively putting yourself in another's place and trying to figure out what meanings that person attaches to situations and in what behaviors he or she will engage.

9. The oldest and simplest type of social structure is found in _____ societies.

10. Societies that stress service industries and information production rather than industrial production and manufacturing are called _____.

Matching Questions

_____ 1. Sapir-Whorf hypothesis
_____ 2. ethnocentrism
_____ 3. machismo
_____ 4. social institutions
_____ 5. success
_____ 6. residence band
_____ 7. rewards or punishments
_____ 8. Somalia and Bangladesh
_____ 9. gesellschaft
_____ 10. all roles associated with a particular status

A. dominant manliness
B. linguistic relativity
C. role set
D. Third-World countries
E. level of Comanche social organization
F. promotes a sense of "we-ness"
G. U.S. mainstream value
H. sanctions
I. association
J. family and religion

Essay Questions

1. Describe the kind of social organization found among the Comanche people of the Great Plains. Why did it confuse the early Euro-American settlers in the plains?

2. Define the four components of culture discussed in this chapter. Give two examples of each: one example from the United States and one from another culture.

3. Compare and contrast mainstream cultural values in the United States with those in Japan.

4. Who are the Amish? Describe their beliefs and values.

5. What is the linguistic-relativity hypothesis? What is the evidence for and against it?

6. Discuss the notions of cultural integration and cultural change. Why are these important? How do they help us understand how cultures work?

7. What functions does a specialized argot perform for a subculture?

8. What part do roles play in the process of social interaction? Include in your answer the various concepts, such as role-taking and impression management, that were discussed in this chapter.

9. What problems can role strain create for people and society? Give some examples. What can be done about these problems?

10. Compare and contrast social life in preindustrial and industrial societies in terms of culture, social structure, social institutions, and social control.

Answers

Multiple-Choice
1. C;   **2.** A;   **3.** B;   **4.** D;   **5.** B;   **6.** D;   **7.** A;   **8.** C;
9. B;   **10.** A

True/False
1. T;   **2.** F;   **3.** T;   **4.** F;   **5.** F;   **6.** F;   **7.** T;   **8.** T;
9. F;   **10.** F

Fill-In
1. culture
2. material culture, nonmaterial culture
3. progress, efficiency, practicality
4. internalization
5. diffusion
6. subculture
7. occupies, performs
8. role-taking
9. hunting-and-gathering
10. postindustrial societies

Matching
1. B;   **2.** F;   **3.** A;   **4.** J;   **5.** G;   **6.** E;   **7.** H;   **8.** D;
9. I;   **10.** C

For Further Reading

Bellah, Robert N., Madsen, Richard, Sullivan, William M., Swidler, Ann, & Tipton, Steven M. (1991). *The good society.* New York: Knopf. This thought-provoking book is about the shaken confidence of people in the United States over their ability to achieve community. It suggests some ways to revitalize and transform institutions such as the family, politics, and the economy.

Callaghan, Karen A. (Ed.). (1994). *Ideals of feminine beauty.* Westport, CT: Greenwood. This book explores the extent to which standards of feminine beauty involve values and norms that are an integral part of a cultural heritage. It provides some excellent cross-cultural comparisons regarding ideals of feminine beauty.

Coakley, Jay J. (1994). *Sport in society* (5th ed.). St. Louis: Mosby. Sports is a key institution in cultures and societies, and this book explores the many aspects of the impact of sports: how it affects and is affected by race, ethnicity, politics, the economy, gender, religion, the media, and so on.

DeVita, Philip R., & Armstrong, James D. (1993). *Distant mirrors: America as a foreign culture.* Belmont, CA: Wadsworth. This is an intriguing view of U.S. culture from the perspective of foreigners who have settled in the United States. It gives a glimpse of what the country looks like to others.

Etzioni, Amitai. (1993). *The spirit of community: Rights, responsibilities, and the communitarian agenda.* New York: Crown. Recognizing the decline of community in the United States, and clearly disturbed by it, Etzioni proposes a new political agenda, called *communitarianism*, that suggests ways of infusing more public interest into the lives of people in the United States.

Fine, Gary Alan. (1987). *With the boys: Little league baseball and preadolescent culture.* Chicago: University of Chicago Press. An insightful analysis of one dimension of the culture of young people in the United States today, the book discusses the male sex role, socialization, cultural values, status hierarchies, and argot as they exist in this U.S. subculture.

Giacalone, Robert A., & Rosenfeld, Paul. (Eds.). *Applied impression management: How image-making affects managerial decisions.* Newbury Park, CA: Sage. This book of readings provides many illustrations and applications of Erving Goffman's notion of impression management to the world of work and organizations.

Goffman, Erving. (1959). *The presentation of self in everyday life.* New York: Doubleday. This is still the classic statement on role expectations and role performance from a dramaturgical perspective. Goffman, now deceased, was a master at unveiling some of the hidden ways we shape our social world.

Harris, Marvin. (1985). *Good to eat: Riddles of food and culture.* (1985). New York: Simon & Schuster, This book shows the diversity of human cultures by explaining some of the variations in what, when, and how people eat.

Harris, Marvin. (1974). *Cows, pigs, wars, and witches: The riddles of culture.* New York: Vintage. A noted anthropologist takes a fascinating look at unique and often bizarre social practices in other cultures. He offers interesting ideas regarding their origin and meaning, suggesting that what seems puzzling to us is usually explicable in the context of its own culture.

Mead, Margaret. (1935). *Sex and temperament in three primitive societies.* New York: Morrow. This is a first-rate ethnography by a classical anthropologist that documents the diversity possible in human cultures.

Miller, Timothy. (1991). *The hippies and American values.* Knoxville: University of Tennessee Press. This book documents the persisting impact of a subculture, the hippies of the 1960s, on U.S. society and also shows the evolution of cultural values.

Wolf, Daniel R. (1991). *The rebels: A brotherhood of outlaw bikers.* Toronto: University of Toronto Press. This is an ethnography of a motorcycle gang illustrating many of the points made in the chapter regarding subcultures.

THREE *Socialization*

The Samoan Islands include more than 1,200 Pacific islands between Hawaii and Australia. They were originally settled, possibly as long as three thousand years ago, by voyagers in canoes coming from the west. Traditionally, Samoans survived by gathering wild food such as coconuts as well as by fishing and raising pigs and chickens. The basic social unit was the *aiga,* or extended family group, and Samoan cultural values emphasized deference and respect for those older than oneself. Samoan social structure was hierarchical, with some *aiga* having more status and prestige than others. Whereas the Samoan culture has been heavily influenced by the intrusion of industrialism and a market economy in the past century, many traditional values and practices persist, including the central role of the *aiga* and respect for age.

Early in the twentieth century, leading anthropologists, including Margaret Mead, observed Samoan and other traditional cultures around the world and interpreted what they saw as support for a position called **cultural determinism,** which posits that *cultural influences determine the behaviors and personalities of people.* In other words, human beings are infinitely malleable and are molded by the culture in which they are raised. Mead (1961) described the Samoans as a gentle and harmonious people who were respectful to others, especially their elders. They were moderate in their behavior and controlled in the expression of their feelings. They were also compassionate and considerate and showed generosity to others. For Mead, these characteristics were the Samoan personality, stamped in by the socialization experiences of Samoans as children.

More recent research, however, describes a more complicated socialization process in which Samoans are molded by their culture but also resist some of the pressures and demands that are put on them. The result is more variation in personality and behavior than Mead and other early anthropologists believed existed (Freeman, 1983; Mageo, 1991; Ritchie & Ritchie, 1989). For example, Samoan culture does discourage open displays of strong emotion and affection between people, as Mead suggested. In old Samoa, husbands and wives never touched or showed affection toward each other in public. In fact, there is no Samoan equivalent of the English phrase *being in love* with someone. Children begin to learn this emotional distancing at a young age. Early in life, parents begin to distance themselves emotionally from their children. For example, by the time children are about six months old, parents stop picking them up and attending to their crying. This behavior is to discourage children from focusing on their own needs and to encourage them to take their proper place in the family or larger communal group. Further parental distancing is achieved by shifting most child-rearing tasks from parents to older children.

Both parents and children, however, resist this cultural pressure toward emotional distance: When children are sick, parents become very emotional and hold and attend to their children constantly. Children for their part throw tantrums when parents distance themselves. And Samoan culture makes adaptations by providing a substitute or compensation: the ethos of *alofa,* or a love for all people. This love imparts a general warmth to Samoan social life and is reflected in the exchange of goods in traditional ceremonies. It focuses attention away from the individual relationship and directs it toward the communal. What is important is not the bond between individuals but the linkage of the individual to the whole group. In addition, despite the cultural socialization, some people are expressively emotional. In fact, Samoans call people with a tendency toward excessive emotional displays *lotovaivai,* or having a weakness as far as emotions go. Such emotional outbursts are especially common when someone dies or departs on a journey. So, *alofa* and *lotovaivai* are, in a sense, cultural concessions that recognize that socialization is not perfect; not everyone will at all times display the moderate and controlled emotions that are the Samoan ideal.

Respect for and deference to one's elders is also taught to Samoan children at a young age. For example, one elder will tell a child to take an object to another elder some distance away, and the latter will thank the child for the object. This procedure will be repeated many times until the obedience becomes habitual, at which point the "thank you" is omitted. Then the child is expected to respond automatically to the orders of an older person. Evidence shows that these socialization practices do instill a tendency toward deference among Samoans that can be detected even in adulthood. Yet, some children resist this pressure to obey elders and become *failoto,* or stubborn, rather than deferential. In addition, though it is frowned on, some Samoans will negotiate status deference by refusing to respond to an elder. Other Samoans will refuse to demand the deference that is rightfully theirs because of age or family position or will deemphasize status issues when interacting with others.

Socialization is *the process by which people develop personal identities and learn the ways of a particular group or society.* The Samoan experience illustrates the power of the socialization process: It produces a Samoan personality that is, on the whole, clearly different from the personalities of people in the United States or people from many other cultures. Samoans do tend to be more gentle, considerate, and respectful of their elders. However, the Samoan experience also shows that cultures are not perfect in imparting attitudes, personalities, or behaviors. Situational differences as well as

Myths & FACTS

ABOUT SOCIALIZATION

Myth The most positive psychological and social development of children occurs when they are raised in families by their mothers and fathers.

FACT There has been much research on this issue, and so far the conclusion is that removal from the family, at least for a time, may not be detrimental to children. For example, children who are sent to day-care settings seem to develop as well as children raised totally within their families. Day care may have a more negative impact on very young children, and poor-quality day care is certainly undesirable. However, children seem to be able to adapt to many different settings for socialization.

Myth Entertaining television shows and movies that contain some violence, such as *Terminator* or *Lethal Weapon,* do not harm young people who watch them as long as the shows are clearly fictional and fanciful.

FACT Television can be a powerful socializing agent, teaching the young norms for acceptable behavior. Overwhelming research evidence concludes that young people who watch violent shows on television are more likely to behave aggressively or violently themselves, especially in situations that are conducive to violence. This likelihood is especially true for boys between the ages of eight and twelve and for those who are more aggressive to begin with.

Myth Socialization and development occur while people are growing to biological maturity and are accomplished by the time people reach adulthood. By the 1990s, adulthood for men and women had become quite similar.

FACT Socialization and development continue throughout people's lives, and adulthood is a time of periodic changes in life tasks and goals for most people. Adulthood for many women is still quite different from adulthood for many men because society places different demands on women. For example, the decision to have children has more serious implications for the possibilities and accomplishments of adult women than it does for men.

Myth The stages of the life cycle, such as infancy, adolescence, and adulthood, are shaped largely by biological considerations, particularly by what people are capable of doing at a given chronological age.

FACT Actually, the reality of the life cycle is far more complicated than this. Although biological limitations play a part in what society allows us to do, particularly among the very young and very old, the social structure is more important than biology in shaping the life cycle from childhood through adulthood. In fact, one stage in the life span—adolescence—does not even exist in most preindustrial societies. Adolescence is a social creation to meet the unique demands of industrial societies and has virtually nothing to do with biological maturation or capabilities.

---

variations in individual temperament lead some Samoans to be less gentle, considerate, and respectful than other Samoans. Culture is important in socialization, but it is not the only influence. The Samoan personality that Mead described is more the ideal or model behavior and attitude among Samoans. As with all ideals, people approach it to varying degrees, and some people diverge significantly from it. The rigid cultural determinism of Mead and other early anthropologists is too simplified to describe a socialization process that is actually a two-way street: Culture pressures and demands while individuals react and resist. The outcome, in terms of identities and behaviors, is a product of both forces.

So, through the socialization process, society exerts considerable power over its members by teaching them what they should be like and how they ought to behave. As the sociologist Peter Berger (1963) points out, however, this power is not usually seen as harsh or domineering.

For most of us the yoke of society seems easy to bear . . . because most of the time we ourselves desire just that which society expects of us. We want to obey the rules. We want the parts that society has assigned to us. (p. 93)

In other words, many of the beliefs, values, and norms of a culture become so internalized by its members that adherence to them seems self-directed. This chapter analyzes how the socialization process achieves this end and which social groups play a part in it.

Heredity and the Environment

You should be able to assess the different approaches to the roles of heredity and the environment in the socialization process and compare the contributions of each.

Before looking at the socialization process, this chapter will consider the relative importance of heredity and the environment in shaping human behavior. The question of which has more influence, usually referred to as the *nature versus nurture* issue, has been, and still is, the source of much debate.

On the one hand, the *nature* position holds that human behavior is the product of a person's heredity, which is determined at birth and is thus beyond human control. According to this view, many of our characteristics, abilities, and personality traits are dictated by our biological equipment, innate intelligence, and hormonal makeup.

On the other hand, the *nurture* position argues that human beings are flexible and adaptable and that human behavior is determined by the learning and social contact that people experience as they mature. The philosopher John Locke, for example, argued that human beings are born *tabula rasa,* which means "with a clean slate." He believed that people have few biologically imposed limitations and that their behaviors and abilities are largely the result of learning during the socialization process.

Biology and Human Behavior

To assess the nature versus nurture debate, we must first look at the role of biology in human behavior. **Biological determinism,** in contrast to Mead's cultural determinism, posits that *human behavior and many elements of social structure are a product of the genetic and physiological characteristics of people.* Certainly, our biological makeup does have implications for our social behavior. For one thing, human beings have *biological reflexes,* such as sucking or coughing. But these reflexes are relatively simple physiological responses, and they operate only briefly in terms of our whole life span. Moreover, they can be shaped by learning. For example, human infants are born with an automatic reflex to suck when objects are placed in the mouth. However, this reflex is quickly replaced through learning as children begin to choose what they will suck on.

Human beings also have certain *biological drives,* such as hunger, thirst, and the desire for sex. These are generalized urges that can motivate behavior. There are no biologically based cues, however, that tell people how to act on these drives. We must therefore learn how to satisfy them. With regard to hunger, for instance, we learn what to eat (fruits and vegetables rather than insect larvae), when to eat (three times a day rather than one or five), and how to eat (usually with a knife and fork rather than with our hands).

Finally, human beings have certain *biological characteristics* that shape both our abilities and our behavior. For example, children with Down Syndrome, a genetic disorder that is sometimes called *mongolism,* are severely limited in their capacity for learning. In addition, some people have greater manual dexterity, more athletic prowess, a more active disposition, or a more cheerful temperament than do others. But these things are also influenced by learning and social experience. The person with great athletic prowess will become an athlete only if given certain opportunities, and the naturally cheerful person can become morose if negative events happen in her life.

So, human behavior is a result of both biological and social forces. But do human beings have *instincts,* meaning complex patterns of behavior that are inborn and largely beyond their control? After all, the behavior of many other animals is controlled by instincts. For instance, if we isolate a male rat at birth and place it, as an adult, in the company of a sexually receptive female rat, the completely inexperienced rat will be able to perform sexually with an expertise equal to that of far more experienced male rats.

Most scientists today conclude that human behavior is not under such rigid biological control. Yet, evidence can be found for a strong, if less rigid, biological control over complex social behavior in humans and many other animals. Recent applications of these ideas have been labeled **sociobiology,** *a field based on the idea that the genetic makeup of humans and other animals plays a powerful role in shaping their social behavior* (Nielson, 1994; van der Dennen & Falger, 1990). Sociobiologists maintain that there are many parallels between human and animal behavior. A male stickleback fish, for example, will protect against all intruders a nest containing fertilized eggs deposited by the female stickleback. Anything approaching the nest that resembles another stickleback will be viciously attacked (Tinbergen, 1955). Such protection of territory can be found in many species, and it is clearly a biologically produced behavior in these species rather than a product of learning. Robert Ardrey (1967) popularized such behavior as the *territorial imperative,* suggesting that such protection is necessary for some species to survive. Human parallels of such territoriality would include such things as protecting territory from other human groups through warfare or other means.

As another example, animals of a number of species exhibit *altruism,* which refers to doing things that benefit others of one's species even though it may be dangerous or deadly to oneself. Kamikaze bees will die defending their hive, soldier termites will end their lives in order to spray a deadly liquid at their enemies, and human beings will place their own lives in danger to protect their children. Other behavioral tendencies that are common in both humans and animals include aggressiveness, selfishness, and the formation of dominance hierarchies.

Sociobiologists argue that these tendencies are common in species because they are inborn traits determined by genes. These various traits exist because they enhance the chances of survival for the species. The stronger, more powerful, and more aggressive members of a species are more likely to survive, mate, and pass on their genes to the next generation. A mother who dies to save her children enhances the likelihood that her genes will survive in the gene pool even though she herself dies. Sociobiologists reason that aggressiveness and altruism are a part of our genetic makeup because people who behave aggressively or altruistically increase the chances for the survival of their genes. Over many eons, those aggressive and altruistic genes come to predominate in the gene pool of the species. This happens, sociobiologists argue, in humans as well as in other animals.

These biological explanations of human behavior have been controversial because they can be interpreted to mean that people have little control over their actions and that society has little influence over people's behavior in these realms. In fact, the biological explanations are currently being used by some to explain such complex social behaviors as crime, warfare, and homosexuality. Are these social behaviors programmed into our genes as sociobiologists suggest? For a number of reasons, both sociologists and sociobiologists recognize that reality is more complex than this biological determinism (Maryanski & Turner, 1992; Wolfe, 1993).

First, few human traits or behaviors are universal among human beings. The prevalence of behaviors such as altruism or aggressiveness varies widely from person to person, situation to situation, and culture to culture. Although every kamikaze bee will die protecting its hive, some human beings protect their children whereas others abuse, abandon, or even kill them. In fact, infanticide has at times been an accepted social practice among some human groups. If altruism and aggressiveness were completely instinctive, this variation would not occur.

Second, a vast body of evidence from social science research, some of it presented throughout this book, documents the extent to which people's behavior is a function of learning and social influence. The further up the evolutionary chain we look toward human beings with a highly developed cerebral cortex, the more powerful a role learning and culture play in shaping behavior.

Finally, sociobiologists recognize that genetically determined behavioral tendencies create only general tendencies to behave in certain ways. Whether people actually behave aggressively or altruistically depends on numerous social and cultural influences. In fact, sociobiologists recognize that these genetic tendencies in human beings can be altered or in some cases even overcome by learning and other social forces.

Most experts today agree that both biological determinism and cultural determinism are incomplete answers to the nature versus nurture debate. Both biological and sociocultural factors are important parts of the explanation of human social behavior. Whereas Locke's *tabula rasa* notion may not be entirely accurate, the images on the slate at birth are vague and undeveloped and are given shape and form through learning and experiences after birth.

Children Raised in Isolation

Whatever the influences of heredity may be, contact with others is important throughout our lives, and it is especially vital during our early years. Infants are incapable of taking care of themselves, so they are totally dependent on others for survival. Furthermore, social interaction is essential during this period if biological, psychological, and social development is to proceed normally. This point is poignantly illustrated by studies of children who have been raised in isolation from human contact.

In 1938, a six-year-old girl named Anna was discovered in the attic of a farmhouse (Davis, 1940). She had been strapped to a chair, with her hands tied above her head. Anna was born to an unmarried woman, and her grandfather, being ashamed of this, insisted that she be kept out of sight. As a result, she spent her first six years in isolated, dreary surroundings, receiving only the minimal attention necessary to keep her alive. When finally discovered, Anna was unable to walk, talk, feed herself, or keep herself clean. She was apathetic, expressionless, and indifferent to other people.

At about the same time, a young girl named Isabelle, whose history was remarkably like Anna's, was also found (Davis, 1947). Isabelle, too, had been hidden away because she was born out of wedlock. She spent most of her first six years in a dark room with her mother, who was a deaf mute. When she was discovered, Isabelle had developed intellectually only to about the level of a six-month-old infant. Although she made strange croaking sounds, she could not speak. She was able to communicate with her mother through gestures, however. Isabelle was also afraid of strangers, especially men, and acted something like a wild animal around them.

In 1970, yet another girl, Genie, was discovered living in isolation (Curtiss, 1977). Genie had spent almost all of her first thirteen years locked in a room by herself. She had had little contact with other people and had only rarely even heard a human voice. During the day, Genie was strapped to a potty in such a way that she could hardly move. At night, she was sometimes dressed in a kind of straitjacket and was placed in a crib covered with wire mesh. When she was found, Genie could not speak. She was also disruptive and disgusting. For instance, she would blow her nose onto anything available and, when excited, would urinate wherever she happened to be.

What was the fate of these three unfortunate youngsters? When Anna died four years after being found, she had made some progress, but her level of development was still far from appropriate for her age. She could speak some words and phrases, but she could not construct sentences. She was able to follow the directions of her caretakers, however, and she could call them by name. She was also able to participate in some group activities, such as playing ball, but she was never able to take leadership roles.

Isabelle was placed in an institution where she received expert training. She quickly learned to speak, to walk and run without difficulty, and even to sing in musical harmony. In fact, by the time she was eight and a half, her level of development appeared to be comparable to that expected of others in her age group. Isabelle's good fortune probably stems from the skill of her trainers and the fact that she had intimate contact with her deaf-mute mother during her isolation. This interaction, limited though it was, was something that Anna did not experience, and it probably accounts for some of the differences in the subsequent development of the two girls.

Genie, who had also had virtually no contact with other humans when she was isolated, did not fare as well as Isabelle, either. After five years of training, she had developed some language skills and was able to form relationships with people, but she still lagged behind her age group in these areas.

These three tragic cases demonstrate the critical importance of human contact and affection in infancy. Without them, a child cannot learn even the basic rudiments of human behavior. Personality and social behavior do not arise from biological maturation alone; they also require social contact and social experience. Furthermore, if social deprivation is extensive and prolonged, as was true for Anna and Genie, development may be permanently stunted. Recognizing the importance of social interaction to human development, this chapter now considers how the process of socialization occurs.

The Process of Socialization

You should be able to describe the contributions made by Cooley, Mead, and Erikson to our understanding of the socialization process and discuss the functioning of the agencies of socialization and the different types of socialization.

Socialization is a complex process. It begins at birth and continues throughout people's lives as they learn the ways of their society and of the various groups to which they belong. This section will look at some of the more important aspects of the socialization process. It will begin with a discussion of the development of personality and self-concept, which provide the foundation for all later socialization. It will then examine the groups and institutions through which socialization is accomplished as well as the different types of socialization. It will close with a discussion of socialization as a lifelong experience.

The Development of Self:
The Interactionist Perspective

Human beings are unique among animals in part because we can say "I." We have, in other words, an awareness of ourselves as individuals. We can also think about ourselves in various circumstances. We can imagine, for instance, what it would be like to be somebody else, or how another person might view us. We are not born with this ability, however. Human infants have no sense of themselves as something separate from their surroundings. According to the interactionist perspective, we develop this awareness of self, this

sense of our own identity, through interaction with other people.

An important aspect of our identity is our **personality**, which is *a constellation of attitudes, needs, traits, feelings, and ways of behaving.* Our personality develops over time, but once formed it usually remains fairly constant throughout our life. Another important aspect of our identity is our **self-concept**, which is *the conception that we all have about who we are—our unique characteristics and attributes—as well as about our nature and worth as human beings.* Personality and self-concept are closely interrelated, but self-concept is less constant than personality. It tends to change periodically throughout people's lives, especially when their position in the social structure changes.

The initial development of personality and self-concept occurs during infancy and childhood. Indeed, these two aspects of self form the foundation of the socialization process and strongly influence the nature and success of other aspects of socialization. Thus, infancy and childhood are critical times for all of us in the socialization process. People who do not develop an adequate self as children will have difficulty fitting well into society. For these reasons, any examination of the socialization process must begin with a look at how personality and self-concept emerge.

Cooley Charles Horton Cooley was one of the founders of the interactionist perspective. In Cooley's view (1902), we are not born with a self, nor does the self emerge merely because we mature biologically. Instead, the self is a social product. It develops through our interactions with other people. According to Cooley, an important ingredient of these interactions is people's ideas of how others view them or their behavior. He coined the term **looking-glass self** to refer to *the process through which we develop our sense of self based on the reactions of other people to us or to our actions.* There are, Cooley maintained, three basic steps in the *looking-glass* process. First, we imagine how we, or our behavior, appear to other people. For example, we may think that someone sees our appearance as neat and attractive or as disheveled and ugly. Second, we imagine how these people evaluate us or our behavior. We decide, for instance, that they judge our appearance as good or bad. Third, we experience some feeling because of this

The act of seeing ourselves reflected in a "looking glass" is the analogy Charles H. Cooley used to describe the social process of learning who we are by seeing ourselves reflected in the reactions of other people to us.

judgment. We may feel pride if we imagine a good evaluation or shame if we think that it is bad. We engage in this process continuously. Thus, every time we are aware of someone reacting to us in any way—as smart or dumb, nice or mean—that person either reinforces or contradicts our concept of ourselves. In this way, our self-concepts are developed and then maintained or changed.

To see better how the looking-glass self operates, consider your own gender identity, the sense you have of yourself as male or female. Of critical importance in the development of gender identity are other people's reactions to us. Normally, others treat us consistently as having a particular gen-

der. In fact, these reactions are what initially form our sense of who we are sexually, and they reinforce it all the time. Try to imagine, though, how you might feel if everyone suddenly began to treat you as a member of the opposite sex. Surprise and amusement might quickly turn into anger and then, possibly, into confusion and doubt. Although such an occurrence is highly unlikely, thinking about it should illustrate the extent to which we all depend on the reactions of others for a sense of who we are.

Other people's reactions also influence our behavior because we normally strive to behave in ways that are consistent with our conceptions of ourselves. If, for instance, you view yourself as a friendly person, you will usually behave toward others in a fashion consistent with that self-concept; that is, you will probably be friendly. Similarly, if you think of yourself as intelligent, you will probably do things, such as read, study hard, and pay attention in class, that are consistent with that self-concept. Furthermore, by doing these things, you are likely to improve your performance in school and thereby reinforce your conception of yourself as intelligent. Thus, the looking-glass process can be self-reinforcing. The looking-glass process is diagrammed in Figure 3.1. It shows that a person's behavior is influenced by his or her self-concept, although other factors also shape behavior. Then, others around the person assess and react to that person's behavior. The person, in turn, perceives and interprets those reactions, and this interpretation influences the person's self-concept.

Cooley reasoned that some elements of our self-concepts, such as our identity and our sense of self-worth, are formed during childhood and remain fairly stable throughout life. For such elements, the development of self is more important in childhood than at other times in our lives. Nevertheless, Cooley and other interactionists emphasize that the looking-glass process functions throughout the life span. Every time we enter a new social situation, develop new social relationships, or take on new statuses, the reactions of others influence our self-concepts.

Mead George Herbert Mead is generally credited with having expanded on Cooley's ideas and with

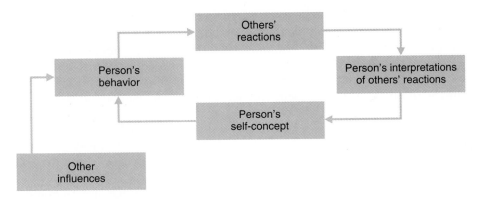

FIGURE 3.1 The Looking-Glass Self

having provided the theoretical basis for the interactionist approach to sociology. Mead (1934) viewed society as an arena of interaction in which people relate to each other and exchange information, attitudes, reactions, and meanings. Like Cooley, Mead stressed that people not only react to each other, but also interpret each other's actions. Integral to this interpretation is the use of symbols, which are things that represent other things (see Chapter 1). Mead used the term **significant symbols** to refer to *those symbols that many people recognize and understand in the same way.* For example, the traffic signal is a significant symbol in modern societies. All drivers attach the same meaning to the colors red (stop), yellow (caution), and green (go). From the time of our birth, we begin to acquire an array of significant symbols. One of the most important sets of significant symbols we acquire is language (see Chapter 2).

Mead viewed the socialization process as a sequence of stages through which people develop the social skills that enable them to coordinate their behavior with that of others (Lindesmith, Strauss, & Denzin, 1991). Early in the socialization process, human infants are capable only of simple *imitation.* They mimic other people because doing so brings rewards such as food or attention. For example, one-year-olds are often coaxed by their parents to wave when someone leaves the house. Although the infant may learn to wave at the appropriate time, waving is not a significant symbol for the infant because it does not have the same meaning for the infant as it does for the parents.

As the child matures, imitation gives way to pretending. During the *play stage,* children begin to act out the roles of other people. For example, they move toy trucks around a "construction site," play at being cowboys or police officers, or use dirt and water to make mud "pies." According to Mead, this pretend behavior is critical to human development. When they take the roles of other people, even if only pretending, children behave as though they were that other person and thereby learn how to view the world from different perspectives. At this point in the socialization process, according to Mead, children take the roles of **significant others:** *specific people, such as a parent or sibling, whose opinions the children care about.*

During the play stage, role-taking is compartmentalized. Children usually play only one role at a time. In addition, because it is a pretend situation, they need not take the actual reactions of other people into account. In Mead's next stage, the *game stage,* children perform roles that require them to coordinate their actions with those of real people. This requirement calls for them to assess situations from different perspectives. Role-taking becomes more complex because children must ask themselves how others will react to what they do and how they should react to what others do. Through this role-taking and coordination of behavior, what Mead called the *generalized other* begins to emerge. The **generalized other** refers to *the organized attitudes, rules, and judgments of an entire group.* This general viewpoint becomes internalized, providing guidelines for behavior and criteria for assessing self-worth. Mead used baseball as an analogy in explaining the game stage. In a baseball game, each player must assess the actions of all the other players and coordinate his or her behaviors accordingly. In other words, each person's behavior is contingent on everyone else's behavior. The rules of baseball are analogous to Mead's generalized other, in that both provide explicit guides for behavior.

Mead viewed the self as consisting of two interrelated parts: the *me* and the *I*. The *me* is the part of the self that reflects our perceptions of what other people think of us. It is the part that permits evaluation and enables us to control our behavior. But if the *me* were the only aspect of the self, human behavior would be mechanical, repetitive, and frankly, quite boring. Mead was not content with the idea that human beings are merely social puppets, however. Human interaction is both symbolic and interpretive. Although we respond to others, we also manipulate symbols ourselves and interpret different situations according to what we have learned through our own socialization. Hence, Mead proposed another part of the self, the *I*. The *I* is the independent, spontaneous, and unpredictable side of the self. Thus our behavior is shaped not by the *me* alone but by the ongoing interaction between the *me* and the *I*. The *I* is the subjective, internal part of the self; the *me* is more external and objective. Imagine yourself interacting with a friend. The *I* is more spontaneous: "I want to tell this person what I'm thinking." The *me* is more controlled: "She will probably get angry, and I don't want her mad at me, so I won't say it."

Erikson Cooley and Mead focus on describing and analyzing the general process of social interaction that occurs throughout childhood and shapes personality and self-concept. Socialization does not end with childhood, however, or even with adolescence, and the psychologist Erik Erikson (1950, 1982) developed a theory of socialization that recognized this fact. His theory describes eight distinct stages of development and provides more detail on how social interaction at each stage can affect a person's self-concept. The general interactional processes described by Cooley and Mead are the mechanisms by which many of the developments Erikson proposes actually

occur. Each of Erikson's stages involves a challenge or crisis that must be confronted regarding how one views oneself and one's relationships with others. How the conflict is resolved determines how the person thinks about himself or herself and whether he or she develops a stable, positive personal identity and social maturity. Furthermore, Erikson viewed the stages as sequential: positive resolution of one stage cannot be achieved until the challenges of the previous stages have been satisfactorily resolved.

Infancy is Erikson's first stage of development, and the challenge of this stage is *trust versus mistrust*. The infant is thoroughly dependent on others for care, affection, and even survival. If the support is there, and if it is provided in a loving and stable fashion, then the infant develops a sense of security and trust about the world in general and other people in particular. If neglected or treated poorly, the infant learns to mistrust others. These feelings of trust or mistrust then extend into later life and influence the resolution of later stages and the development of social relationships.

In the stage of *early childhood*, children two and three years old face the crisis of *autonomy versus shame or doubt*. They begin to explore their environment, and the challenge they confront is to develop a sense that they can deal effectively with their surroundings. When children are encouraged to try new things and are supported in doing so, they can become self-confident and develop feelings of autonomy, responsibility, and independence. If they are overprotected, criticized, or rejected, then shame and self-doubt are likely to emerge.

Children in *late childhood*, ages four and five, are confronted with *initiative versus guilt*. They begin to do more exploration independent of their parents, such as developing new friends to play with, and their social worlds expand considerably. This stage includes Mead's play stage, and playing with peers is a way of trying out different roles. If they are supported in this activity by their parents and are accepted by peers, they develop a sense of initiative, purpose, and direction. If they are discouraged or rejected, a sense of guilt develops because they have done something on which both adults and peers frown.

Children of *school age*, between six and twelve years old, confront the crisis of *industry versus*

As this four-generation family in the United States symbolizes, socialization and development are lifelong endeavors, with distinct challenges or crises to be confronted at various points along the way.

inferiority. School challenges them with the impersonal world of adult social institutions and expectations. Children are expected to develop new skills and compete with others. If successful, they develop a sense of industry, or mastery, because they have accomplished tasks that are viewed as important by society and that transcend the world of children. A sense of inferiority and failure results if the child has difficulty at these tasks or is constantly criticized for each misstep along the way.

The challenge of *adolescence* is *identity versus role confusion.* Adolescents are coming close to taking their place in the adult world, and they need to develop a sense of who they are, what their capabilities are, and how they will relate to other people. Especially important at this stage is the development of close intimacy with peers of both sexes. Erikson recognized that adolescents' preoccupation with what others think of them reflects the basic challenge of the adolescent stage. Even fleeting adolescent infatuations are a reflection of this struggle for identity—finding out who one is by seeing oneself reflected in peers' reactions. If adolescents have supportive adults and positive relationships with peers, they come through this stage with a clear and positive personal identity. Without such supports, they can develop low self-

regard and confusion as to who they are and what they might become.

The challenge of *young adulthood* is *intimacy versus isolation.* The major life task at this stage is to establish an enduring intimate relationship and pursue a career or adult vocation. For many people, the intimacy takes the form of marriage and family, but other forms of intimacy, such as close companionship, are also possible. When such intimacy does not develop, feelings of isolation appear.

The challenge of *adulthood into middle age* is *generativity versus stagnation.* As people move through adulthood, they attempt to avoid stagnation and self-absorption by making renewed efforts to contribute to community welfare and future generations. The opposite is stagnation into undemanding, unrewarding, unexciting routines.

The final stage is *old age*, where the challenge is one of *integrity versus despair.* As they confront the end of their lives, people review and reflect on the past. If this assessment brings a sense of accomplishment, completeness, and fulfillment, then people can feel a sense of integrity, or acceptance of their life as positive and significant. If the reflection is heavy with failure and lost opportunities, then the result is despair and the feeling that one's life has been wasted or unimportant.

Erikson's developmental theory has been very influential because it captures important challenges that people confront at different stages in the life span. Furthermore, research supports Erikson's contention that there is a definite sequencing to the stages and that resolution of the challenges at one stage is important to positive resolution of challenges at later stages (Whitbourne, Zuschlag, Elliot, & Waterman, 1992). This sequencing, however, is not rigid, in the sense, for example, that identity is an issue only during adolescence. The identity issue can arise at numerous points in the life span as people move into new jobs, marry, or make other role transitions. These later identity crises, however, tend to be of less magnitude and less centrality than identity issues during adolescence. Identity crises in adulthood occur against a backdrop of already having resolved identity issues in adolescence. The person who has successfully resolved the challenge of adolescence and emerged with a positive and coherent sense of identity will be better equipped to handle identity crises in adulthood than the person who experienced role confusion in adolescence.

Although Erikson was a psychologist, his theory of socialization was thoroughly sociological and consistent with the interactionist perspective. After all, the center of his attention was the development of people's self-concepts through social interaction. He recognized that the self consists of social meanings communicated during social interaction and that the self develops as a result of challenges from the social environment and changes in the person's role structure. Going into school (school age), gaining independence from the family (adolescence), and developing a career (young adulthood) are all changes in status that require some reorganization of roles and selves. So, it is ultimately social challenges that precipitate the development of the self.

Agencies of Socialization

Socialization occurs in various settings in which a variety of individuals and groups leave their imprints on children as they mature and on adults as they move through life. In some cases, this process involves direct, face-to-face contact, as when a parent scolds a child or friends congratulate a person for landing a new job. In other cases, it occurs indirectly, as when educators shape school policies that determine what children will learn in the classroom. **Agencies of socialization** are *the people, groups, and institutions that play a part in the socialization process.* Here four of the most important agencies of socialization—the family, peer groups, schools, and the media—will be discussed.

The Family   The most important agency of socialization for most human beings is undoubtedly the family. The sensitive and malleable early years of life, when we are defenseless and dependent, have traditionally been spent almost exclusively within the family context. It is there that we first learn about intimacy, emotions, power, and other elements of human relationships as we experience our initial interactions with other human beings. It is there, also, that we begin to learn the components of culture and social structure, including language, norms, and values. In short, it is in the family that we learn to be human. The learning that occurs during this period is effective and influential because the family usually protects us and provides us with nourishment and affection. This dependence makes us especially receptive to the influence, both formal and informal, of family members.

Another reason for the pervasive influence of family in the socialization process is that it provides us with our social positions in society. The family determines such ascribed statuses as racial and ethnic background and influences other statuses, such as religion and social class. These statuses strongly shape our contacts with others and our opportunities in the world. They also determine how we are brought up. For instance, parents from different backgrounds raise their children in different ways and expect different things from them. Working-class parents tend to encourage obedience, conformity, respect, cleanliness, and neatness. Middle-class parents are more likely to encourage curiosity, self-direction, and expressiveness and to place more emphasis on egalitarian relationships (Ellis & Petersen, 1992; Kohn & Slomczynski, 1990).

Although the impact of later experiences is very important, the first few years of life in the family context provide people with a crucial foundation in terms of the development of personality, self-concept, and a distinct system of values. Subsequent experiences tend to build on this foundation rather than replace it. Applying Sociology: Day Care (on pp. 88–89) addresses the issue of whether children suffer in some way when they are raised in nonfamily settings such as day-care centers. Other Worlds, Other Ways: Israel (on pp. 90–91) also addresses this issue by investigating the impact of communal child-rearing practices on the Israeli kibbutz, which is quite different from socialization in the nuclear family in the United States.

The Peer Group The agency of socialization that is probably second in importance to the family is the peer group, which is a group of friends who are approximately the same age and have similar social positions. The family is a hierarchal group, with parents in a position of authority and dominance over the children. In a peer group, however, children find more egalitarian relationships because no one child in the group is normally dominant in all respects. There is therefore more give-and-take, which gives children the opportunity to learn how to relate to others in a cooperative framework (Kohlberg, 1981; Youniss, 1985).

Eventually, the family is supplanted by the peer group as the main social relationship for young people. Especially after entering school, young people begin to spend more time with their peers than with members of their families, with the possible exception of siblings who are very close to each other in age. Furthermore, virtually all children have to live apart from their families sooner or later, and in a world that is somewhat different from that of their parents. Children usually confront different values and technologies and have different experiences. The peer group helps substantially in the transition that is required. It provides young people with a subculture that gives them a set of norms, values, and beliefs that offers an alternative to those of their parents.

Peer groups offer young people an identity that supports some independence from their families. This offer is especially important in industrial societies where young people are typically isolated from the statuses and rewards of the adult world. The peer group offers an alternative status and reward system. It might take the form of familiarity with contemporary music, proficiency in athletics,

or outstanding academic achievement. Chapter 2 noted that a distinctive language, or argot, can play an important role for teenagers by encapsulating the values of their subculture. In their many forms, then, peer group subcultures offer young people ways to feel important and worthwhile. Moreover, they give young people a sense of contributing to society or, at least, to their peer group.

The School In the family and in peer groups, children are involved in intimate personal relationships that are normally based on love or some other type of attachment. When they enter school, however, they begin to experience the impersonality of the world, usually for the first time. Parents tend to accept and respect their children regardless of their performance in reading, writing, or other tasks. But teachers, who replace the parents as authority figures in schools, are more demanding. They judge performance on the basis of impersonal criteria, and poor performance brings low grades, rebukes, and possibly the failure to advance to the next grade. In school, then, children begin to learn the value placed on performance in an industrial society, and they become acquainted with the costs that accompany failure.

Schools teach children the basic literacy skills, particularly reading and writing, that are necessary in an industrial society, and they provide training in the more complicated skills that will be used later in the adult world of work. In addition, schools supplement the family in transmitting the components of culture and social structure. For example, U.S. schools teach children patriotic values through such subjects as history and such rituals as reciting the Pledge of Allegiance. They also communicate to students values of the larger society. Furthermore, children in schools learn about new statuses and roles that do not exist in the family. For instance, they learn about the school hierarchy, which consists of the assistant principals and principals above the teachers and the janitors and kitchen staff below the teachers. Young people become aware that they too occupy a position—as students—in the school hierarchy. They also learn that the school has a rhythm of its own. They must be on time even though they might wish to be late, and they must switch from one subject to another, say, from art to math, as directed by the clock rather than personal whim. In

APPLYING SOCIOLOGY
Day Care: Problem or Solution?

In the 1970s, one-quarter of women with children under six years of age were working; by the 1990s, this figure had grown to 58 percent (Veum & Gleason, 1991). In some cases, both parents work in order to pursue a career or provide adequate income for their families; in other cases, a single mother must work in order to support her family. In either case, someone must care for these children while the parents work (see Figure 3.2). When relatives or friends are not available to provide these child-rearing services, increasing numbers of parents turn to day care. Day care has been controversial because it seems to violate the traditional notion that children should be raised by their parents, and for some, this is a symptom of the erosion of the modern family. A key question is whether day care can do as good a job at socializing children as the parents do. As has been stated, the family is probably the most important agency of socialization, especially for young children. Thus, the widespread use of day care represents a significant departure from traditional child-rearing practices and has aroused considerable debate.

Critics of day care, such as the psychoanalyst Selma Fraiberg (1977), argue that children need much love and understanding in their early years if they are to become emotionally healthy adults. Day-care workers, she argues, are often overburdened—with high children-to-staff ratios and substantial turnover among employees—and cannot provide the intimate involvement and sense of attachment that children need. Another critic, Dr. Burton White

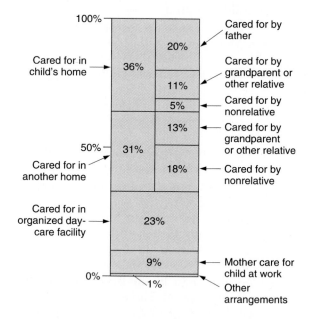

FIGURE 3.2 Child-Care Arrangements Used by Employed Mothers for Children Under Five Years of Age in the United States, 1991. *Note:* From *Statistical Abstract of the United States, 1995* (p. 390) by U.S. Bureau of the Census, 1995, Washington, DC: U.S. Government Printing Office.

(1984), director of Boston's Center for Parent Education, comments: "A child needs large doses of

short, children in school learn that there are pressures and demands in the real world over which they have little control but to which they must adapt.

Finally, school brings some independence from the family. In fact, school may be the child's first major contact with the world outside the family. In school, children are largely isolated from adults, which encourages the formation of peer group associations. Moreover, schools offer children a wide range of peers with whom they can become involved. Thus, schools enhance the so-

cializing impact of peer groups and further reduce the influence of the family.

The Mass Media   During the twentieth century, the widespread increase in literacy and the tremendous advances in technology have brought about enormous growth in the mass media. Mass media are forms of communication that reach large numbers of people without direct, face-to-face contact. They include television, radio, films, magazines, newspapers, and so on. Although socialization is not a manifest function of the media, it has

custom-made love, [and] you can't expect hired help to provide that. I see the trend toward increasing use of day care as a disaster" ("What Price Day Care?" 1984: 16).

Child rearing is a sensitive topic because our attitudes about it are so strongly influenced by traditional values relating to the family. In the United States, we see the family as very important and also value the privacy of the family unit. Tradition considers the family, and especially maternal care, as the primary and essential element of good child rearing. Given these strong values, opinions about child rearing may be subject to considerable ethnocentrism, in which traditional ways of raising children are seen as the only proper ways of doing so. In such situations, research by applied sociologists and other social scientists can help to alleviate the danger that one's values will lead to biased and inaccurate conclusions about which child-rearing approaches will be effective. Decades of such research have now accumulated, comparing children who attended various types of day-care centers with children raised in the home by parents, relatives, or others. Virtually all this research shows that children exposed to day care do at least as well as, and often better than, children raised exclusively in the home by their parents (Clarke-Stewart, 1993). Day-care children do as well in verbal and cognitive abilities, creativity, cooperation, and social competence as do home-raised children. Children placed in day care do at least as well as children raised at home in intelligence and psychosocial development and in sociabil-

ity and academic achievement. Further, economically disadvantaged children in day care show less decline in IQ scores than is typically found among such children (Caughey, DiPietro, & Strobino, 1994; Ispa, Thornburg, & Gray, 1990; Wasik, Ramey, Bryant, & Sparling, 1990). Day-care children are also as much attached to their parents as are children cared for in the home (Kagan, Kearsley, & Zelazo, 1978).

Research does suggest a few situations in which day care may not be best for children. For example, children enrolled in day care for extended periods or at a very young age may become more aggressive and less cooperative, and economically disadvantaged children are often sent to poor-quality day-care centers, which may adversely affect their emotional development (Honig & Park, 1993; Kahn & Kamerman, 1987; Mott, 1991). But this mass of research leaves us fairly confident that good day care can do at least as well in raising children as the parents can. Actually, this conclusion should not be surprising, because day-care centers have the resources to offer children much more—in terms of people to interact with, adults trained in child development and education, and such physical resources as games and educational materials—than does the average home. The typical nuclear family offers a child a much more limited range of social contacts and educational experiences.

become one of its latent functions (see Chapter 1). Television, in particular, has become a pervasive socializer, especially for young children. In the process, it has further diluted the role of the family by competing with parents for their children's time and attention.

Media such as television provide children with an "eye on the world" that enables them to learn a great deal. For example, they can learn verbal and mathematical skills from public television programs such as *Sesame Street*. Similarly, they are encouraged in their self-development by pro-

grams like *Mr. Rogers' Neighborhood* and *Barney*, which teach them to view themselves positively and to value their own and others' individuality. However, the primary impact of the media in socialization is in enabling children to view role models such as sports figures, movie stars, or cartoon characters. Television also allows children to observe a wide range of occupations, such as those of waitress, taxi driver, or police officer, and to gain some sense of what tasks and duties are associated with them. In spite of the fact that much of what children see on television is distorted and

THER WORLDS, *Other Ways*

ISRAEL: COMMUNAL CHILD REARING ON A KIBBUTZ

The word *kibbutz* is derived from the Hebrew word for "group," and it means "a large community group." Approximately 3 percent of Israelis live on a kibbutz, and Israeli kibbutzim range in size from fifty to two thousand people. The kibbutz movement rose out of the Eastern European Jews' experience of persecution. The sense of alienation and loss of community the persecution produced led them to search for ways to create a supportive community for themselves. The kibbutz ideology that resulted focused on creating a community based on economic cooperation, democratic assemblies, dispersed leadership, the importance of work, a concern for all members of the community, and a denial of individual property. The first kibbutz was established by immigrants to Israel in 1909.

Child-rearing practices in the kibbutz are quite different from those in most industrial societies such as the United States (Blasi, 1986; Rabin & Beit-Hallahmi, 1982). In the latter societies, parents in the nuclear family have primary responsibility for raising their children, which is done largely in isolation from others. In the kibbutz, child rearing is seen as the responsibility of the whole community. There are infants' houses for children up to two years old and toddlers' houses for those between two and four years of age. The children put together as infants in the infants' house will form a children's group that is kept together for many activities until the beginning of high school. In the past in some communes, children even slept in the children's houses, and this separation from parents was considered an integral part of the children's development. Today, however, almost all communes allow children to sleep in their parents' home at night, although they spend most of their days under the tutelage of the kibbutz child-care workers.

A specially trained child-care worker called a *metapelet* is assigned to a children's group and may continue to work with the same children as they develop. The *metapelet* supervises the children in toilet training as well as in learning to eat and dress, and other routine activities. The kibbutz devotes considerable resources to raising children and ensuring that the child-care workers are well trained and attuned to the needs of children at different stages of development. The *metapelet* is not, however, a surrogate parent but rather acts as a child-care professional. The kibbutz and the *metapelet* are seen as supports to the parents in their efforts to be both parents and workers in the commune. Parents visit their children often and do many things with them. The kibbutz tries to assist the parents in having relaxed and pleasurable time to

---

unrealistic, it is one of their major sources of information about culture and social structure in the United States.

In 1950, only 9 percent of households in the U.S. had a television set. Today virtually all have at least one (see Figure 3.3 on p. 92). Nevertheless, despite the pervasiveness of television and the fact that children spend more time watching television than they do in school or talking to their parents, we know relatively little about its impact on socialization. One area that has been studied extensively is the relationship between viewing violence on TV and violent or aggressive behavior. There is growing evidence that a link exists, although it is a complex one that is influenced by numerous factors such as the other socialization experiences of the child. Recent reviews of scientific investigations of this link have concluded that watching violence on television and in the movies does increase the likelihood that children and youth will act aggressively or violently themselves, especially in situations that are conducive to violence (see the extended discussion of this subject in Chapter 12). The impact is greater on males than

spend with their children and to avoid situations where the children must compete with the parents' work for attention and affection.

The more fragmented system of child rearing in the United States places considerable demands on parents as individuals since they have exclusive responsibility for raising their children. One consequence of this situation was noted in the Applying Sociology in Chapter 2: Women who have difficulty getting child-care support are at risk of high levels of psychological distress. Because a kibbutz has more supports, it may offer children more consistently positive and predictable parenting. Furthermore, the children's houses are designed especially for children, which means that situations that might create child-rearing difficulties can be avoided. Adult objects like books or knives, for example, can be kept out of the children's house, and thus a source of conflict between adult and child is removed. In addition, the children do not compete with adults for the use of various parts of the house, so this tension is avoided. Through all this training, individualism is deemphasized while working for the good of the community is held in high regard. In this way, the kibbutz passes on to the new generation the values that serve as the community's foundation.

Day care in the United States and communal child rearing on the kibbutz both give a primary role in bringing up children to nonfamily members. But the two systems are really more different than they are alike. Most important, day care is really just substitute care rather than being integrated into a community network of child rearing. Day care is an isolated institutional response, whereas the kibbutz integrates child-rearing supports from many institutional sectors to help parents and children. If we look at societies throughout history, something resembling the communal child rearing of the kibbutz is far more common than the isolation of child rearing in the nuclear family in the United States.

There have been studies of the effectiveness of child rearing on the kibbutz in terms of personality development and adjustment. In general, they show that kibbutz child-rearing practices are probably no less effective and no more detrimental than familial child rearing (Rabin & Beit-Hallahmi, 1982). People raised in a kibbutz are as strongly attached to their parents and as socially competent as people raised in families, and they show the same variations in personality that are found among other groups. Kibbutz-raised adults may experience slightly more psychological distress and may have slightly more difficulty in developing attachments and intimacy with another person, but the differences are relatively minor.

on females, and it is more substantial on children who are more aggressive to begin with. Children between the ages of eight and twelve seem to be especially vulnerable to the effects of watching violence on television.

Types of Socialization

Socialization can take a number of forms. Three of the most important forms are primary socialization, anticipatory socialization, and resocialization.

Primary Socialization **Primary socialization** occurs in childhood. It is *the process that transforms infants into truly social human beings by teaching them basic values, skills, and language.* It also accounts for the initial development of personality and self-concept. A major debate among social scientists involves the extent to which primary socialization influences other socialization experiences occurring in later stages of the life span. Sigmund Freud and some present-day psychologists have argued that early life experiences largely, though not exclusively, determine people's personalities and

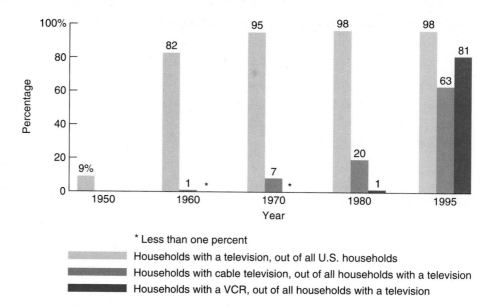

FIGURE 3.3 Use of the Mass Media in the United States, 1950–1995. *Note:* From *Trends in Television* by Television Bureau of Advertising, Inc., annual; A. C. Nielson.

behaviors throughout their lives. These scholars maintain that the resolution of early childhood conflicts, such as those between societal demands and a child's impulses, establishes personality tendencies that are fairly impervious to change.

Sociologists view self-concept and personal identity as somewhat more malleable than this deterministic view, with people going through periodic transitions throughout their lives during which their self-concept must adapt. People can even change radically in later life. Nonetheless, sociologists recognize that primary socialization in early childhood certainly influences the development of adult self-esteem and personal identity. For example, what children learn from their parents about racial identity influences their adult behavior. Studies of African Americans show that when parents teach their children racial pride and the value of their African heritage, as adults those children are more committed to African culture and identify more closely with the African American community (Demo & Hughes, 1990). In addition, black children who are raised to keep their distance from whites and to be cautious or fearful of them have less contact with whites as adults. So, primary socialization has a continuing effect on

people's lives, with important implications for the way people feel about themselves as adults and the way they relate to other people. Other Worlds, Other Ways: Japan (on pp. 94–95) documents how primary socialization contributes to the learning of basic cultural values and norms.

Anticipatory Socialization **Anticipatory socialization** *involves learning the values, beliefs, and behaviors of a group that a person does not presently belong to but plans to join in the future.* It allows people to begin to make the changes in their attitudes and actions that will be necessary once they enter the new group. For example, students in medical, nursing, or law school experience anticipatory socialization when they are encouraged to think like doctors, nurses, and lawyers although they do not yet occupy those statuses. Similarly, a pregnant woman may read all she can about raising children and may even begin to plan how she will treat her own child before she actually becomes a mother.

The primary purpose of anticipatory socialization is to ease the transition into a new status or group. Research on army recruits, for example, shows that soldiers who adopt the beliefs and values of army officers, which are quite distinct from the beliefs and values of enlisted personnel, are more likely than other soldiers to be promoted, are more readily accepted by the new group, and make more rapid adjustments to their new status (Merton, 1968). Other research shows that expectant parents can benefit from anticipatory socialization to the parental role. Socialization experiences such as baby-sitting someone else's child or attending parenting classes make for better adjustment to the parental role with less stress (Gage & Christensen, 1991).

Although anticipatory socialization is beneficial in helping people make the transition to a new status or group, it is not always functional for the group that a person plans to leave. For example, an office worker who hopes to move into a supervisory position may begin adopting the values and attitudes of his supervisors. He may begin to frown on fellow workers who do things supervisors dislike, such as take coffee breaks that are longer than allowed, pilfer small quantities of office supplies, or refuse to work as hard as they might. Because his attitudes go against the interests of the other office workers, tension, difficulties with cooperation, and even a reduction in productivity may result.

Resocialization When infants begin to learn about the world, they have a clean slate with little to "unlearn." When a twenty-seven-year-old woman becomes a mother, however, she has had twenty-seven years of learning experience. Some of this experience may help her make the transition to motherhood, but other parts of it may hinder her adaptation. In any event, this new mother will have to undergo **resocialization,** which refers to *learning new sets of values, beliefs, and behaviors that are different from those previously held.* A person experiencing resocialization must unlearn the old as well as learn the new.

All of us experience resocialization throughout our lives as we move from one status to another and one group to another. In some situations, this process is rather mild, as when we take a new job or become parents. In other situations, it requires dramatic changes, as when a person enters prison. One example of resocialization is the transition from a high school to a college or university environment. Expectations in high school are quite different from those that confront a college student. Those who begin or return to college after engaging in other life experiences, such as working or raising children, also undergo resocialization, if only in having to learn how to relate to younger adults. Applying Sociology: Changing Personal Troubles (on p. 96) points to some ways that applied sociologists use the resocialization process to assist people with personal difficulties.

Socialization Through the Life Span

The concepts of anticipatory socialization and resocialization make us aware that socialization is a lifelong process. It continues throughout our lives as we take on new roles and make role transitions that take us from infancy through adulthood to old age. Children give up their dependency on parents and devote more attention to peers, young adults leave their families to establish their own relationships, and older adults must confront the certainty of their mortality. Society, however, does not leave people alone to struggle with these transitions. Through socialization, people are provided with new roles and relationships to replace the old.

Societies carve out people's lives into a series of stages. These stages constitute the **life span** or **life cycle,** which is *a succession of statuses and roles that people in a particular society experience in a fairly predictable pattern as they grow older* (Neugarten & Datan, 1973). Biology plays an important role in the life cycle, particularly at the beginning and the end. In infancy, each of us is dependent on others for our survival, and thus the statuses open to us are limited. In old age, physiological degeneration may limit our capabilities and again make us dependent on others. Society cannot rely on any of us during these periods to the extent that it can during the other stages of the life cycle. Between infancy and old age, however, the social structure of a society is more important than biology in shaping our lives. Thus, although biology does play a role, we should be cautious about viewing the life cycle as a biologically created sequence. Rather, it is a socially approved sequence of stages, adjusted for certain biological limitations, that guides people's behavior as they live their lives.

OTHER WORLDS, *Other Ways*

JAPAN: LEARNING CULTURAL VALUES THROUGH PRIMARY SOCIALIZATION

Chapter 2 presents terms such as *cultural values* and *social structure,* which can seem abstract and removed from people's everyday lives. According to the interactionist perspective, socialization is one of the key vehicles for translating these elements of society into daily thoughts and behavior. As children interact with parents and others, they learn what things are valued and how to perform roles properly. Some of this information is communicated by the way parents talk to their children. To understand more fully how this communication occurs, sociologists study the routine interactions between parents and children to see what in language varies from one culture to another.

Some aspects of parents' talk with their children are found in all cultures. For example, parents everywhere speak to their young children in shorter and more simplified speech than they use with adults because parents recognize that young children are not capable of the sophisticated communications of adults. Beyond these basics, however, culture plays a powerful role in shaping parent–infant talk. In Japan, for example, mothers make more extensive use of baby talk, or nonsense words, with their children and use it for a longer period of time than do mothers in the United States (Fernald & Morikawa, 1993). Japanese mothers also use a more simplified speech with their children—fewer words and less complex sentences. In addition, they use more frequent backchannel vocalizations with their children (White, 1989). *Backchannel* is a term used by linguists to refer to verbal and nonverbal communications that send information to a speaker without claiming the floor. For example, head nods and utterances like *uh-huh* and *yeah* tell a person who is speaking that the silent person is listening but without actually interrupting and taking over as the main speaker.

These differences reflect and support some important cultural values in Japan. One such value is *omoiyari,* or maintaining harmony in the relationships between people. Another value is *amae,* or mutual dependence, especially between mother and infant. When Japanese mothers use baby talk and simple

In some societies, the stages of the life cycle are based strictly on age considerations, and all people of a particular age group have similar statuses and roles (Foner & Kertzer, 1978). Among the Latuka of Sudan, for example, the life cycle has five stages: children, youths, rulers of the village, retired elders, and the very old. People in a particular stage are viewed as a single body in terms of their rights and obligations, and they make the transition to the next stage as a group. In industrial societies, chronological age is only one determinant of the rights and privileges of individuals. Many other factors, such as social class, ethnicity, and personal achievement, also play important roles. Early research on the adult life cycle in industrial societies such as the United States tended to describe a single sequence of stages that most adults were presumed to experience. Erikson's theory of socialization, for example, included three stages during the adult years. Other research was based on interviews, mostly with men, at different points in their lives to see if any common experiences emerged. Based on this research, the following six stages of adult development were described (Hudson, 1991; Levinson, 1978):

1. *Leaving the Family.* The first major transition involves gaining independence from the family, usually in the late teens or early twenties. The transition is gradual for many people, as when they begin college but come home for vacations or get jobs and become financially independent

speech, they are treating their child gently and emphasizing the supportiveness of the relationship between mother and child; they are trying to make it easy for the child to speak to the mother. In other words, Japanese mothers place importance on establishing a positive emotional bond with their children. When mothers in the United States speak to their children, they emphasize teaching to increase the child's linguistic competence and to encourage independence. The use of backchannel communication indicates harmony in social interaction and also places the other person, the speaker, rather than oneself, the listener, at the center of attention. So, even in the ways that mothers talk to their children, the children are learning not only language but also cultural values. In Japan, they learn of the importance of mutual dependence between people and harmony in social relations.

Examples of this process can be seen when mothers play with toys with their children. Mothers in the United States tend repeatedly to tell the child the name of the toy ("That's a car. See the car?"), whereas Japanese mothers talk about exchanging the toy with the child ("I give it to you. Now give this to me. Yes! Thank you.") and actually name the toy much less frequently. In the Japanese approach, the emphasis is on giving as a way of maintaining a relationship. The point of playing with the toy with a child is not to teach the child the name of it but to communicate the value of polite exchanges between people. Other research shows that Japanese mothers place more stress on showing empathy and positive feelings for toys that children are playing with or for other people (Clancy, 1986). They also more explicitly teach their children the cultural norms for polite speech and rehearse them in the social routines that will be expected of them as adults. They teach their children to be polite to others and to consider the thoughts and feelings of others. They expect their children to master polite expressions at a younger age. All of this socialization places great emphasis on the child's role as a member of the social group and community.

Parents may not be consciously aware of all that goes on as they talk with their children. Nevertheless, language learning during primary socialization plays a part in introducing the child to basic cultural values and norms.

while still living at home. In some cases, however, the transition can be very abrupt, as when a man marries in his late teens. Eventually, most adults establish living arrangements independent from their families.

2. *Getting into the Adult World.* During their twenties, men create the foundations for their life structures by developing the groundwork for their future plans. A decision about whether to go to college is often made during this stage. Some people drift through this period without developing a firm foundation. At about age thirty, however, such people often have a crisis in which they must confront their lives and develop some solid life structure.

3. *Settling Down.* During their thirties, men typically make their places in the world. They solidify occupational gains, nurture family relationships, and develop visions of what they hope their future will be like.

4. *Becoming One's Own Person.* By their late thirties, men are trying to gain autonomy and recognition. This is a time when men make crucial moves, such as entering new lines of work that seem more promising than the old.

5. *The Midlife Transition.* During their early forties, men often experience a period of self-examination during which they assess their values and accomplishments. Successful men may regret the

People confront personal troubles of one sort or another periodically throughout their lives: A loved one dies, a relationship ends, a job is lost. People respond with feelings of unhappiness, depression, despair, anxiety, or some other negative emotion. One striking thing about these personal troubles and people's reaction to them is that their source is rooted squarely in what sociologists call the social structure and socialization (Mirowsky & Ross, 1989). The second Applying Sociology section in Chapter 2 began to address this issue by pointing out that women's psychological distress sometimes arises from the role conflict they experience when society does not provide the supports they need to act effectively as both mothers and breadwinners. Likewise, many other personal problems are rooted in role conflict, ambiguous or incompatible norms, unachievable values or goals, or difficulties in communication between people of different statuses or roles.

Socialization also plays a part in these troubles because as children we learn characteristic ways of responding to problems and develop resources, such as a positive self-concept and high self-esteem, that help us cope with difficulties. All of us confront personal troubles, but some respond to them in a more mature, constructive way. All of us have experienced failed relationships, for example, but for some it is a highly depressing and debilitating experience, whereas others snap back quickly and begin to reorganize their life.

As noted in Chapter 2, applied sociology helps alleviate these problems by explaining how the social structure contributes to the problems and how it can be rearranged to reduce them. Sociologists also recognize that socialization and resocialization are impor-

tant mechanisms in this process (Fein, 1990; Rebach, 1991). Sociologists do not see personal problems as personal defects or individual inadequacies but rather as rooted in roles and relationships. During the socialization process, dysfunctional roles can be created. If people are going to change their lives, they must relinquish these dysfunctional roles and reconstruct new, more healthy role sets. This relinquishment and reconstruction comprise the resocialization process. For example, children raised by an alcoholic parent often take on responsibilities in the family that the parent shirks. As a result, the child is shouldering responsibilities normally handled by someone older and is often without adult guidance and support. As adults, these children may persist in these patterns of taking excessive responsibility for the actions of others. Children raised by alcoholics also often work hard to please their parent, who they believe might stop drinking if the child were better. Such people can become perfectionists as adults. Resocialization involves changing people's definition of the situation in terms of what they consider to be appropriate and acceptable role behavior by themselves and various role partners. For the person raised by an alcoholic parent, such change can mean first recognizing the extent to which adult patterns of behavior are produced by early socialization experiences, and then relinquishing the feelings of responsibility for the actions of others and the perfectionism that can produce a workaholic or threaten relationships. Clinical sociologists assist people in this process by helping them identify the dysfunctional roles and relationships in their lives and guiding them as they rearrange these roles and relationships in more positive ways.

---

things bypassed for the sake of achievement. Those who have not achieved what they hoped may bitterly realize that their chances are gone forever.

6. *Restabilization.* During their mid-forties, men create a new life structure based on the soul searching that took place during the midlife transition. This serves as the foundation for later adult

life. Whether or not a person grows and enjoys later life depends to a large extent on this new life structure.

These stages are sometimes called the *male model* of adult development because they seem most relevant to the experiences of middle-class and affluent men who value work as an important part of their identity and are encouraged to pursue lifelong careers. They are able to do so, in part, because their wives are given prime responsibility for child rearing and housework, which frees the men to devote attention to their careers. Women, by contrast, often have a different trajectory, based on the expectation that they will bear and rear children (Blumstein & Schwartz, 1983; Levinson, 1996; Schlossberg, 1985). Essentially, women, especially in recent decades, experience a significant tension between following the traditional mother/homemaker role and the nontraditional career role. A choice between these two roles is a decision that men, for the most part, do not have to make. Some women resolve the dilemma by choosing the homemaker role, but this often creates midlife anxieties over whether their lives have been unnecessarily limited and they have become too dependent on others.

The women who choose the career path also confront tension because most do not abandon the mother/homemaker role and must decide the relative weight to give to each. This can create anxieties over whether they are performing satisfactorily in either role (an example of role strain discussed in Chapter 2). In addition, pursuing these dual roles can actually make it more difficult for women to do as well as men in their careers. After all, in families where women work and pursue a career, they also do most of the cooking, shopping, baby-sitting, and cleaning. These dual responsibilities can interfere with the ability of women to achieve occupational goals. In their twenties and thirties, when men are establishing themselves in the world of work, women spend precious energy on these homemaking and child-rearing duties. If they take time off work to raise their children, their career advancement may be set back. Even women who pursue a career are more constrained in their career choices by family considerations than are men. For example, women who receive doctoral degrees and seek university teaching positions often choose their teaching jobs on the basis of where their husbands can find work (Gallagher, Johnson, Van Valey, & Malaret, 1992). Men, by contrast, are more free to choose jobs on the basis of what will most advance their career. As a consequence, women tend to teach at lower-status universities than do men and are more likely to experience downward mobility in their careers. Thus, even career women experience more de-

mands to accommodate their career to family needs and to the husbands' career advancement. Women who enter the career world after bearing and rearing children must do in their late thirties and forties what men did in their twenties and early thirties. These women will be competing against younger and more recently educated workers, and their potential career span and earning time are shorter by ten to twenty years in comparison to that of men. This difference can put women at a considerable competitive disadvantage. It can also mean disrupting established family patterns in order to accommodate the mother's new career.

Because of these difficulties and anxieties associated with adult development in women, women often express more uncertainty and ambivalence about their lives. In many ways, their adult lives are more difficult, and they are less happy with what they have done (Hudson, 1991; Kaufman & Richardson, 1982; Levinson, 1996). In addition, research suggests that, during the socialization process in childhood, men and women learn fundamentally different ways of relating to the world and that this difference has implications for adult development. Men learn to be separate, autonomous, self-reliant, independent, self-sufficient, and aggressive. Women learn to be connected, caring, nurturant of others, attached, and interdependent. This difference influences adult development because the characteristics of men seem more associated with advancement and success in the work world, whereas the characteristics of women give them more advantage in family and nurturant roles. In fact, the psychologist Carol Gilligan (1983) points out that the description of adult development has "focused on the progress of the solitary self—wandering through stages with a focus on achievement and work." Whereas the male model has people marching predictably through a sequence of stages, Gilligan argues that women are confronted with a series of "renegotiations" of interdependence and caring about other people during their life cycles. So when women enter the work world, they experience some degree of tension because it reduces their ability to maintain their nurturant and caring roles with family and others. Men do not experience the same tension because their socialization equips them to accept more readily independence and separateness from others.

Current research on the adult life span in modern societies suggests that it is ethnocentric to assume that the middle-class, male model is somehow "normal." Instead, we now realize that people can experience a diversity of sequences. Some women choose not to work at all outside the home and devote their energies to their family. Other people face social structural barriers, such as poverty, that prevent them from following the male model. Still other people, because of divorce or losing a job, may have to make a dramatic life transition that does not fit into this sequence of stages. In some subcultures, adults are expected to live with or near their parents and to maintain strong ties of affiliation with and support for them. For these people, "leaving the family" may be an irrelevant stage in adulthood. So, although role transitions and the accompanying socialization continue through the adult years, the diversity of modern life makes it impossible to specify one sequence of adult stages that is experienced by all, or even most, people.

Additional Perspectives on Socialization

You should be able to explain and contrast the functionalist and conflict perspectives on socialization.

This chapter has tried to impart a sense of what socialization is all about. Future chapters will cover a lot more about this process as they examine more closely the groups, institutions, and social forces that interact to make society what it is. We must remember, however, that not only is the topic of socialization incredibly vast, but also there are a number of ways of looking at it. The interactionist view of socialization has already been discussed through the work of Cooley, Mead, and Erikson. Therefore, this chapter will close with a brief consideration of some of the concerns of the two other major theoretical approaches to socialization.

The Functionalist Perspective

From the functionalist perspective, socialization is the essential mechanism for integrating human beings into society. It therefore plays a critical role in maintaining societal equilibrium and in enabling society to achieve its goals:

> Socialization is . . . training . . . for participation in society, a participation that is seen as occurring on terms set "by society" rather than on the individual's own terms. The emphasis is on the social purpose of socialization, a process conceived of as designed to achieve conformity of individuals to social norms and rules. (LeVine, 1969, p. 507)

The process of molding human beings into individuals who are able to function coherently and productively within society begins during infancy. It continues as people move into new social positions and new social relationships. Throughout their lives, then, people must become acquainted with new values, attitudes, and skills. Most develop the personal qualities that enable them to function in society. However, if people are not appropriately socialized at each stage in the life span, the equilibrium and stability of society are threatened.

One important element in lifelong socialization, according to the functionalist perspective, is the *rite of passage,* a ceremony that marks and celebrates a person's transition from one status to another (Brown, 1969; Van Gennep, 1960). Rites of passage symbolize and publicly proclaim the adoption of new statuses. Furthermore, these rites encourage people to identify with their new statuses and to internalize the values and norms that go with them. Puberty rites, which mark the transition from childhood to a more adult status, are common in many societies, for instance. Often, youngsters must fast, wear different kinds of clothing, or kill particular animals as a part of the puberty rites. Some societies call for circumcision of males to mark their ascent to manhood and clitoridectomy, or removal of the clitoris, to mark the sexual maturity of females (Bodley, 1994). Examples of puberty rites in the United States include religious ceremonies such as the Jewish bar mitzvah and the Roman Catholic confirmation. Graduation from high school or college, marriage, and retirement are other transitions that involve the assumption of new rights and responsibilities and are therefore often marked by ceremonies. For some people, however, there may not be many clear-cut rites of passage. A person who graduates from high school and then drifts along with no permanent job, for example, often dwells in a sort of marginal state between adolescence and adulthood because he or she is not completely accepted in either status. For functionalists, clear and dramatic rites of passage are important because they demonstrate the acceptance of people occupying new positions in society.

Functionalists also argue that the stages of the life span are intimately related to the needs of particular societies. For this reason, the stages that occur in industrial societies differ substantially from those in preindustrial societies (Ariès, 1962; Flacks, 1971). In preindustrial societies, people usually learn how to fill adult positions fairly early in life. The technology is relatively simple, so little training or education is required. In addition, most people need not be literate in order to be productive. Therefore, the transition from childhood to adulthood generally takes place by the midteens, and sometimes it occurs as early as age eight. Only among select groups in society, such as a ruling elite or priesthood, are inactivity and nonproductivity prolonged.

In industrial societies, by contrast, the complex technology and elaborate division of labor demand a highly educated and literate populace. Thus training and education must be more extensive than in preindustrial societies. Furthermore, the abundance of goods and services provided by industrial technology makes it possible for a small number of people to supply everything that society needs. As a consequence, it is not necessary for all physically mature people to participate in the workforce.

These two factors contribute to two major differences between life stages in preindustrial and industrial societies. First, the age at which people in industrial societies are allowed to enter the adult world is postponed (Côté & Allahar, 1996; Kett, 1977). Childhood continues into the early teens and is followed by a new stage, adolescence, which runs from roughly thirteen to eighteen years of age. Adolescence is viewed as a time of preparation for adulthood, in terms of both education and psychological maturation. People in this age category are not considered adults. They are not expected to assume adult obligations such as supporting a family, and they are not accorded certain adult privileges, such as being able to vote or to drink alcohol.

The second difference between the life stages in preindustrial and industrial societies involves old age. In preindustrial societies, people normally work until they die. In industrial societies, however, many men and women retire from work long before death. This difference exists because industrial societies require fewer workers and because people tend to live longer in industrial societies.

The Conflict Perspective

Most approaches to socialization have a distinctly functionalist emphasis. However, socialization can also be seen from the conflict perspective. From this point of view, socialization seems to be a coercive process that advances the interest of one group while working to the disadvantage of others. It reflects and supports the existing social structure of a society, including the predominant power relationships. In hunting-and-gathering societies, where there are few distinctions on the basis of wealth and power, there are also few groups with competing interests. Thus the socialization process is usually not terribly coercive. In more complex societies, however, there are great disparities in wealth and power, and many competing groups exist. In these societies, socialization becomes a tool that the more powerful use to maintain their upper hand.

The coercive dimension of socialization may be most dramatically illustrated in **total institutions,** which are *organizations isolated from the rest of society in which the behavior of the members is tightly controlled and regimented* (Goffman, 1961). Mental institutions and prisons are examples of total institutions. Some other organizations, such as the military and primary and secondary schools, have some of the characteristics of total institutions. Total institutions can be seen as microcosms of society. They therefore face many of the same problems as a society, including the need to integrate new members in a nondisruptive fashion. Entrance into prison, for example, is marked by a jarring resocialization process during which the prior values, roles, and identities of the inmates are stripped away and replaced with new ones that are compatible with their place in the prison hierarchy. Prisoners are forced to accept a thoroughly powerless and dependent position.

U.S. Marine basic training and the behavior of this drill sergeant epitomize the isolation from other groups and the coercive socialization that can be a part of entrance into total institutions.

Even such mundane personal matters as eating, sleeping, and bathing occur at a pace and in a manner dictated by organizational rhythms rather than individual needs. Through these procedures, inmates learn their position in the prison social structure, which is a degrading and humiliating one, and their identity in the organization, which is based primarily on dependence and ineffectuality.

The socialization process in the larger society can also frustrate human needs and desires. For example, some conflict theorists argue that children born into lower-class families are "socialized to fail." It is in the family that children acquire their aspirations for the future, their psychological orientation toward those in authority, and their assessment of the characteristics of their own social group. Lower-class youngsters, however, are less likely than more affluent youngsters to be taught to aspire to desirable and powerful occupations, to see authority figures as equals who can be manipulated, or to view themselves as powerful and positive individuals who can gain mastery over their environment. Instead, they are more likely to learn to be content with low-prestige jobs; to take a submissive and, indeed, almost fearful posture toward people in authority; and to view themselves as shackled by social forces beyond their control.

Lower-class youngsters also learn to seek immediate gratification of their desires rather than to delay gratification in order to pursue long-term goals. Hence, they are more likely to reject advanced education, even if available, in favor of leisure pursuits or a lower-paying job that promises immediate returns. Lower-class children who develop these characteristics are unlikely, as adults, to strive for desirable or rewarding positions, which reduces the amount of competition that those in the middle class must face. Moreover, they become a malleable group that poses little threat to those in positions of power (Knottnerus, 1987; MacLeod, 1987; Smith, 1981).

From the conflict perspective, then, the socialization process is not a mechanism for fitting human cogs into the wheels of society. Instead, it is a means of ensuring that the unequal division of the social pie will continue and that the large share that the dominant groups receive will not be threatened. Ultimately, it is a coercive and divisive process that places groups in opposition to one another.

Summary

1. Culture and social structure are transmitted through socialization. Socialization begins during infancy and continues throughout life.

2. Both heredity and the environment play a necessary role in shaping human behavior. Instincts control much of the behavior of lower animals, but most scientists today agree that human behavior is not dictated by instincts.

3. Through social interaction, people develop a self, or identity, which includes a personality and a self-concept. The interactionist approach to personality and self-concept places more importance on the role of face-to-face social interaction and downplays the importance of biological drives and the assumption that the individual and society are in conflict. Charles Horton Cooley coined the phrase the *looking-glass self* to refer to the process by which we develop our sense of self through the reactions of other people to ourselves or our behavior.

4. George Herbert Mead saw human interaction as a process of reacting to each other and interpreting each other's actions through the use of symbols. The socialization process, according to Mead, begins with imitation. It then moves through the play stage to the game stage. In this process, each of us learns to take the roles of other people, which ultimately allows us to see ourselves playing a variety of roles in society. Mead also saw the self as having two parts: the *I* and the *me*. Erik Erikson identified eight stages in the socialization process, from infancy to old age.

5. Socialization occurs in various settings as individuals move through their lives. Agencies of socialization are the people, groups, and institutions that play a part in socialization. Four of the most important are the family, peer groups, schools, and the media.

6. There are three major types of socialization: primary socialization, anticipatory socialization, and resocialization.

7. Societies tend to divide people's lives into a series of stages. These stages constitute the life span or life cycle, which is a succession of statuses and roles that people in a particular society experience in a fairly predictable pattern as they age.

8. For functionalists, socialization plays a critical role in maintaining societal equilibrium and in enabling society to achieve its goals. It is the essential mechanism for integrating human beings into society.

9. From the conflict perspective, socialization can be seen as a coercive process that advances the interests of one group while working to the disadvantage of others. The coercive dimension of socialization is most dramatically illustrated in total institutions.

STUDY and Review

Key Terms

agencies of socialization

anticipatory socialization

biological determinism

cultural determinism

generalized other

life cycle

life span

looking-glass self

personality

primary socialization

resocialization

self-concept

significant others

significant symbols

socialization

sociobiology

total institutions

Multiple-Choice Questions

1. Which of these positions would be most consistent with that of sociobiology?
   a. Cultural determinism.
   b. Biological determinism.
   c. The *nurture* position on human behavior.
   d. The *tabula rasa* position on human behavior.

2. Which of the following is most consistent with this book's position on the relationship between biology and human social behavior?
   a. Learning and other social forces can alter inborn genetic tendencies.
   b. Specific genes that cause particular forms of human behavior have been identified.
   c. Sociologists have concluded that biology plays little, if any, role in human behavior.
   d. Altruism and aggression have been shown to result mostly from biological factors.

3. The looking-glass-self process most clearly derives from which sociological perspective?
   a. The functionalist perspective.
   b. The conflict perspective.
   c. The interactionist perspective.
   d. The biological-determinism perspective.
   e. The significant-other perspective.

4. According to Erik Erikson, the key challenge that people confront during adolescence is
   a. trust.
   b. identity.
   c. industry.
   d. generativity.

5. Which of the following is *not* a conclusion of the research regarding the impact of day care cited in this chapter? In comparison to children raised at home,
   a. day-care children are as attached to their parents.
   b. day-care children do as well in intelligence and psychosocial development.
   c. day-care children are as sociable.
   d. children enrolled in day care for extended periods may become more aggressive.
   e. all of the above were conclusions cited.

6. Child rearing in the Israeli kibbutz is different from child rearing in most other industrial societies in that in the kibbutz child rearing is seen as the responsibility of
   a. the whole community.
   b. the nuclear family.
   c. the government.
   d. the grandparents.
   e. the extended family.

7. Which of the following statements is true regarding the peer group as an agency of socialization?
   a. It is more important than the family for young children.
   b. It provides children with their first exposure to self-concept development.
   c. It offers young people an identity that supports some independence from the family.
   d. It exposes children to more hierarchical relationships than does the family.

8. Students in medical school would be most clearly going through
   a. primary socialization.
   b. anticipatory socialization.
   c. sociobiology.
   d. biological determinism.
   e. total institutionalization.

9. The movement of adult women in the United States through their life span could be best characterized as
   a. a predictable march through a clear-cut sequence of stages.
   b. almost identical to the male experience.
   c. a series of renegotiations based on interdependence and caring about others.
   d. a stress on autonomy, independence, and self-sufficiency.

10. From the conflict perspective, the socialization process could be best characterized as
    a. playing a critical role in maintaining the equilibrium of society.
    b. a mechanism for integrating people into productive positions in society.
    c. serving the needs of the whole society rather than some special interest group.
    d. a coercive and divisive process that places groups in opposition to one another.

True/False Questions

1. This chapter concludes that the biological makeup of human beings does have implications for human social behavior.

2. The experiences of the young girls Anna and Genie demonstrate that, even in the absence of human contact during infancy and young childhood, human beings readily learn language and other social skills.

3. Personality tends to be less constant during a person's life than does self-concept.

4. During the game stage, according to George Herbert Mead, children develop social skills by simply mimicking or imitating what other people do.

5. Erik Erikson views the stages in his theory of socialization as sequential.

6. One reason that the family is such an important influence in socializing young children is that the children are dependent on the family.

7. Seeing violence in the mass media increases the likelihood that children will act aggressively or violently themselves.

8. Biology plays a more important role in shaping behavior in the middle of the life span than it does at the beginning or the end.

9. Current research on the adult life span suggests that the middle-class, male model of life-span development should be the norm for all men and women.

10. The point at which people are allowed to enter the adult world generally occurs at an older age in industrial societies than it does in preindustrial societies.

Fill-In Questions

1. When the philosopher John Locke argued that human beings are born *tabula rasa*, he meant that they are born with _____ .

2. _____ is a field based on the idea that the genetic makeup of humans and other animals plays a powerful role in shaping their social behavior.

3. Two stages in the socialization process described by George Herbert Mead were the _____ and the _____ .

4. According to Mead, the two interrelated parts of the self are the _____ and the _____ .

5. According to Erik Erikson, the challenge that infants confront during the first stage of development is _____ .

6. The agency of socialization that is probably second in importance to the family is _____ .

7. The primary impact of the media in the socialization of children is enabling them to _____ .

8. Two important cultural values that Japanese children learn during the socialization process are _____ and _____ .

9. Learning new sets of values, beliefs, and behaviors that are different from those previously held is called _____ .

10. _____ is a ceremony that marks and celebrates a person's transition from one status to another.

Matching Questions

_____ 1. looking-glass self
_____ 2. cultural determinism
_____ 3. sociobiology
_____ 4. agencies of socialization
_____ 5. life cycle
_____ 6. rite of passage
_____ 7. total institutions
_____ 8. *lotovaivai*
_____ 9. Isabelle
_____ 10. generativity versus stagnation

A. biological determinism
B. transition from one status to another
C. coercive socialization
D. life span
E. child raised in isolation
F. developmental stage of Erik Erikson
G. Charles Horton Cooley
H. Margaret Mead
I. schools and mass media
J. Samoan emotional weakness

Essay Questions

1. Make arguments both for and against the position of biological determinism. Include in your answer an assessment of sociobiology.

2. Describe the experiences of the three children described in this chapter who had been raised in some degree of isolation from human contact. What do their experiences teach us about learning and socialization?

3. According to Cooley and Mead, how does socialization during childhood occur?

4. Describe how Erikson's theory of socialization is different from Cooley's and Mead's. Describe the stages in Erikson's theory.

5. Assess the issue of whether children sent to day care are reared as effectively as children raised in the home. Summarize the research on both sides of the issue.

6. Describe the four agencies of socialization discussed in the chapter in terms of the special contributions that each makes to the socialization of the young.

7. Describe the three most important forms that socialization can take. State what each accomplishes and give an example of each.

8. How does the primary socialization of children in Japan and the United States differ?

9. Describe the "male model" of adult development. How does the adult development of women tend to differ from this?

10. Compare and contrast the functionalist and conflict perspectives on the process of socialization.

Answers

Multiple-Choice
1. B; 2. A; 3. C; 4. B; 5. E; 6. A; 7. C; 8. B;
9. C; 10. D

True/False
1. T; 2. F; 3. F; 4. F; 5. T; 6. T; 7. T; 8. F;
9. F; 10. T

Fill-In
1. a clean slate
2. sociobiology
3. imitation, play stage, game stage
4. I, me
5. trust versus mistrust
6. peer group
7. view role models
8. harmony, mutual dependence
9. resocialization
10. a rite of passage

Matching
1. G; 2. H; 3. A; 4. I; 5. D; 6. B; 7. C; 8. J;
9. E; 10. F

For Further Reading

Ariès, Philippe. (1965). *Centuries of childhood: A social history of family life.* New York: Vintage. This book is an eye-opening look at what childhood was like and how children were viewed in some preindustrial European societies.

Clausen, John A. (1993). *American lives: Looking back at the children of the Great Depression.* New York: Free Press. This book is an insightful, longitudinal study of more than three hundred people born in the 1920s. By looking at their lives and accomplishments, Clausen concludes that developing competence, dependability, and intellectual curiosity by the end of adolescence is very important in adult success and achievement.

Elkin, Frederick, & Handel, Gerald. (1988). *The child and society* (5th ed.). New York: Random House. This classic work provides a comprehensive overview of sociological research on the socialization process during childhood.

Fein, Melvyn. (1993). *Integration anger management: A common-sense guide to coping with anger.* New York: Praeger. This applied sociologist shows how personal troubles, such as the anger that can destroy personal relationships, can arise from social structure and socialization and how sociological principles relating to socialization and resocialization can help to alleviate these troubles.

Gilligan, Carol, Lyons, Nona P., and Hammer, Trudy J., eds. (1990). *Making connections.* Cambridge, MA: Harvard University Press. This in-depth study of growing up among adolescent females in the United States suggests that U.S. culture inculcates in them a lack of confidence and feelings of uncertainty.

Lewontin, R. C. (1984). *Not in our genes.* New York: Pantheon. This book is about biological and sociobiological explanations of socialization and human development. As the title suggests, the author is a critic of such approaches, but his analysis is complete and fair.

Mead, Margaret. (1961). *Coming of age in Samoa.* New York: Dell. (Original work published 1928.) Although Mead's work has been unfavorably criticized, it is still a classic analysis of the adolescent period in a society quite different from American society.

Postman, Neil. (1982). *The disappearance of childhood.* New York: Delacore. This book presents a critical view of the impact of television on children's development. The author argues that television exposes all secrets (about sex, death, etc.) to children and robs them of childhood, which should be a time of innocence and hope.

Rymer, Russ. (1993). *Genie: An abused child's flight from silence.* New York: HarperCollins. This is a truly fascinating book about Genie, the girl discussed in the chapter who suffered severe isolation in childhood. The author discusses controversies regarding language socialization as well as describes how the scientific community treated Genie and the abilities she developed in early adulthood.

CHAPTER FOUR
Groups and Organizations

It has been five hundred years since European explorers first made landfall in the Western Hemisphere. For most of those years, it made little difference to the Yanomamo Indians, as the Europeans gradually transformed the Americas. However, the good fortune of the Yanomamo (also called Yanomama) in avoiding the encroachment of the newcomers could not last forever.

The Yanomamo people live in remote portions of southern Venezuela and northern Brazil, scattered in 125 villages that contain between 40 and 250 people each (Chagnon, 1992; Smole, 1976). Their territory is so remote that most of these villages had little or no contact with outsiders until the 1970s. The Yanomamo territory is heavily forested, its rolling hills covered with palm, hardwood trees, scrub brush, and vines. The Indians live in huts made from the poles, vines, and leaves of the tropical rain forest. They subsist by hunting monkeys, pigs, and wild turkeys and gathering wild fruits, nuts, and tubers. They also have gardens, where they cultivate plantain, banana, sweet manioc, and maize. Although rain forests seem lush to those unfamiliar with them, wild game and flora are sparse and the soil is shallow. Therefore, the Yanomamo must periodically find new hunting areas and move their gardens as the topsoil is depleted. In the terms used in Chapter 2, the Yanomamo have a mixed hunting-and-gathering and horticultural subsistence pattern.

Yanomamo daily life in these small villages is casual and personal. Everyone knows everyone else. Some people wake before dawn to build up the fire, and then they visit others to make plans for the day or maybe go back to sleep. When it is light, men or women prepare breakfast, and the men who will hunt that day leave the village. Other men go out to work in their garden, transplanting banana cuttings or felling trees and clearing brush. Women collect firewood and help with planting and weeding. By midmorning, it is too hot and humid to continue working, so everyone retires to bathe in a stream, eat a meal, and rest in their hammocks. Children play close to the adults all day and learn what they need to know to be good Yanomamo by watching the adults hunt, cultivate, or rest. In late afternoon, as the weather cools, some men and women go back to working in the gardens or gathering firewood, while others relax in the shadows and take hallucinogenic drugs. The large evening meal is a time to relax and socialize with others. Successful hunters show their solidarity with others in the group by giving away much of the meat they caught that day. Both men and women participate in food preparation, although women do the larger share. After dusk, fires are prepared for the night; if a person's fire has gone out, he or she simply borrows a few glowing sticks from a neighbor to restart it. Daily routines in one Yanomamo village are described thus:

> Life is public both within and without the village-house. People know how one another's children behave and how a man treats his wife. They know what food others eat, what game a hunter captures, and what game was not successfully retrieved. Yanomama may respond to the activity of others with indifference, vocal anger, casual interest, or laughter. (Early & Peters, 1990, p. 5)

In Yanomamo society, no one would have to fend for himself or herself; the community ties dis-

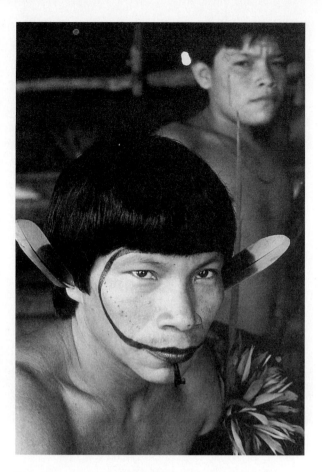

This Yanomamo group lives in a remote region of Brazil and has managed to retain much of its traditional culture and way of life into the 1990s, Their way of life is vastly different from that of most peoples today where large groups and formal organizations predominate.

cussed in Chapter 1 are elaborate and comprehensive. The daily routines just described are repeated from one season to the next, and there are not great variations in wealth and poverty. There are distinctions: Men have higher status than women. Someone not born in a particular village is considered an "outsider" and discouraged from participating in some Yanomamo activities. A headman in a village has some privileges that others do not have. Yet, for the most part, life for the Yanomamo is highly egalitarian and personal.

Lest this picture seem idealized, the Yanomamo are also known as "the fierce people" because they can be aggressive and violent. Men

Myths & FACTS

ABOUT GROUPS AND ORGANIZATIONS

Myth Individual decision making is clearly superior to group decision making: "If you want something fouled up, just depend on a committee to decide what to do."

FACT Research has demonstrated that group decisions are more reasoned and reliable than individual decisions. In this case, the old commonsense saying, "Two heads are better than one," is supported by empirical evidence.

Myth Groups are cautious and reserved in making decisions. That explains why it takes so long for groups to reach a decision.

FACT Group decisions tend to be more extreme—sometimes more daring, other times more cautious—than those made by individuals. This tendency has been referred to as the *risky shift* phenomenon and described as *group polarization.*

Myth Bureaucracies are slow and inefficient.

FACT Although bureaucracies can be legitimately criticized for being inflexible and rigid, they are extremely efficient in accomplishing well-structured and straightforward tasks that involve a uniform sequence of events.

Myth Patriotism is the most important thing that motivates soldiers to fight and die in combat.

FACT Whereas patriotism may play a part, of much greater importance is group cohesiveness and camaraderie among the members of a military squad or platoon. Heroism in battle probably owes more to supporting one's buddies in combat than to patriotism.

Myth Computer technology is decentralizing the workplace by allowing more people to be their own boss and run their business from their home.

FACT The impact of computers on the workplace is more complicated than this. Although some workers do benefit, others who work at home are isolated employees with little power to influence the conditions of their work or to bargain for health benefits or other advantages.

---

settle disputes by battling one another with clubs, and elders proudly flaunt their scars as signs of their bravery over the years. Women can be cruelly beaten by their husbands or kidnapped by raiders from another Yanomamo village. Feuds between Yanomamo villages can last for many years and result in mutual ambushes and killings. Yet, the Yanomamo social structure, as with all social structures at their level of subsistence, is relatively small, simple, and personal. Everyone knows everyone else and his or her place in the social order.

As the Europeanization and bureaucratization of the Western Hemisphere proceeded, it finally affected Yanomamo life and social structure. In the 1950s, missionaries made contact with some Yanomamo villages, bringing them the Bible and "civilized" life. Over the following two decades, farmers in Brazil and Venezuela gradually encroached on Yanomamo lands, clearing forests for cropland. In the 1980s, gold was discovered in Yanomamo territory, bringing prospectors and miners looking for wealth. In 1987, a violent clash erupted between Brazilian miners and some Yanomamo in which three Yanomamo and five miners were killed. In 1993, Brazilian gold miners were blamed for the massacre of forty Yanomamo men, women, and children and the burning of their village. The mining companies have also been accused of wreaking havoc on the Yanomamo environment and introducing deadly diseases such as tuberculosis and malaria. After centuries of isolation, the Yanomamo are being unwillingly drawn into a very different type of social organization, characterized by large, impersonal, formal organizations quite alien to their traditional way of life. They must deal with strangers from faraway places on a daily basis. Impersonal organizations and decisions made by people they are unfamiliar with change their lives in ways over which they have little control; corporations and bureaucracies, often located in foreign lands, now shape their fate.

Traditional Yanomamo life and the new world they now confront represent the extremes of the types of groups that humans create in order to survive. As described in Chapter 2, social structure is one of the fundamental elements that is found in all societies, and groups and organizations are two important manifestations of social structure. A *social group* was defined as a collection of people who are aware of their membership, have common goals and interests, share statuses and roles, and interact with one another. People live out their lives in a vast network of such groups. A Yanomamo male is born into and socialized by a family, goes out to hunt with a small group of other men, and sits around the fire in a casual group in the evening to exchange stories. In modern industrial societies, similar small groups can be found, but large and impersonal groups such as business, educational, and government organizations—unknown in traditional Yanomamo society—have become much more prominent. In an almost infinite variety of ways, groups and organizations shape our relationships with others and guide our behavior. This chapter will analyze the most important types of groups and organizations in terms of their structures and how they function to influence behavior.

Types of Groups

You should be able to describe the major types of social groups and discuss their functions.

Primary and Secondary Groups

There are many different types of social groups, and each plays a different part in our lives. The study of groups and group processes begins by distinguishing among the groups that perform different functions for people and for society. One central distinction between groups is that between those in which we have close personal ties with people and those in which we do not. Along these lines, sociological analysis makes an important distinction between primary and secondary groups.

Primary groups are *small in size and characterized by personal, intimate, and nonspecialized relationships between their members.* A family, a friendship group, an athletic team, and a pair of lovers are examples of primary groups. Primary groups usually involve face-to-face contact; generate strong feelings of group loyalty and identification; and provide warm, supportive, and emotionally gratifying ties with others. In fact, one of the major functions of primary groups in society is to provide people with a relatively secure refuge in which they can be themselves without fear of rejection or ridicule. In addition, primary groups function as mediators between the individual and other parts of society (Dunphy, 1972). The family, for example, provides socialization in the values and norms of society. Likewise, peer groups serve as buffers that help us cope with the impersonal or alienating elements of school or work. We can tolerate some degree of such impersonality because of the support that we receive in primary groups. Finally, primary groups play a central role in shaping our personalities and self-concepts. It is typically from family and friends that we gain a sense of who we are and of our value and worth. However, even when primary groups perform the same function in two different cultures, cultural values and traditions still stamp some distinct patterns and meanings on how people in primary groups relate to one another. Other Worlds, Other Ways: Japan shows how this cultural difference affects friendship in Japan and the United States.

In preindustrial societies, much of social life revolved around primary groups. As noted in Chapter 2, family and kinship played an important role in hunting-and-gathering societies. In most horticultural and agricultural societies, like the Yanomamo, people also lived in small villages among people they knew well. With the coming of industrialization, this situation changed. The German sociologist Ferdinand Tönnies (1887/1963) observed the impact of increasing impersonality on the lives of rural peasants in nineteenth-century Germany and distinguished between gemeinschaft and gesellschaft types of societies (see Chapter 2). The type of group that dominates in gesellschaft (industrial) societies is the secondary group.

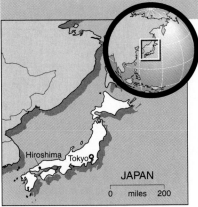

THER WORLDS, *Other Ways*

JAPAN: CULTURAL VARIATION IN FRIENDSHIPS

Friendships are significant social matters. Friends help us feel good about ourselves and maintain a positive sense of self-worth. By virtue of the fact that they want to spend time with us, our friends communicate that we are worthwhile people. Friends are also an important support network that we can call on when we are in need. We turn to friends when we are feeling low or need a ride to school or other assistance. In small, preindustrial societies like the Yanomamo, much of this assistance was provided by an extended kinship network. In industrial societies, where families are smaller and kinship is less important, friendships expand to fill in the gap.

Friendships are primary groups that fulfill many of the functions of primary groups mentioned in the text, and they perform some similar functions in all cultures. Yet, there are some significant differences, especially in the social meanings attached to friendships and how friends relate to one another (Barnlund, 1989). In Japan, for example, friendship is surrounded by obligation and responsibility. To take on a friend means to take seriously the obligation to assist that person in any difficulties he or she might have. In fact, this obligation is taken so seriously that Japanese are more reluctant than people in the United States to take on new friendships. They seem more aware of and sensitive to the burden that friendship creates, while in the United States people tend to think in terms of "the more friends the better." As a part of the burden of friendship, Japanese see friendships as more permanent than do people in the United States, as lifelong connections and responsibilities. The ending of a friendship is seen very negatively in Japan, whereas in the United States it is viewed as common and sometimes necessary—not good, but something that happens because people move, change, or become interested in new things.

Even when separated by some geographic distance, Japanese friends are reluctant to say their friendship has ended. Such reluctance is also found, to an extent, in the United States, but friends are usually more willing to let friendships go in the United States.

Friends in Japan avoid arguments, disagreements, and other sorts of conflict as much as possible (Halloran, 1969; Ozaki, 1978). Japanese are surprised at the amount of explicit conflict that can occur between friends in the United States. With the strong emphasis placed on individualism in the United States, people consider open conflict to be an honest display of one's feelings and may feel that Japanese are being dishonest or insincere when they don't tell friends what they truly think. The Japanese approach, however, is not a matter of dishonesty but of maintaining harmonious social relations (see the discussion of Japanese cultural values in Chapter 2). For the Japanese, harmony is more important than what they might consider a selfish display of emotion. In addition, the Japanese identity is more firmly grounded in social relationships, like friendships, whereas people in the United States tend to idealize the isolated self. In the United States, people will break off friendships over some conflict or other and then become reconciled and resume the friendship at a later date. Japanese avoid letting conflict build to the point that it threatens a relationship. There is conflict in Japan and friendships do break up; reconciliations, however, are rare.

Thus, although the status of "friend" can be found in all cultures, the social meaning of that status is quite variable and shaped by cultural values. This variability illustrates the emphasis of the interactionist perspective on the emergence of social meanings through social interaction. Sociological categories, such as primary group, secondary group, and reference group, help us identify some common processes across cultures. However, cultures then suffuse those categories with special and unique meanings that represent the diversity in human societies.

Secondary groups are *based on task-oriented, impersonal, and specialized ties with people; they may be small but are often large.* Business organizations, universities, the U.S. Army, and hospitals are all examples of secondary groups. Consider the last time that you dealt with people who work in the registrar's office or other unit in your school. Unless these people were close friends, your relationship with them was probably secondary in nature. In your role as a student, for example, the people who work in the registrar's office interact with you in a contractual way, rather than a personal, primary fashion. Despite their impersonality, secondary groups are very important in an industrial society because they enable us to achieve specified goals. By treating you in an impersonal way, the registrar's office at your school can process hundreds of students each day. Were the relationship unspecialized—if you decided to chat with the clerk about football because you were both interested in the topic—the major goal of the registrar's office, to register students in classes, would not be achieved as quickly or completely, or perhaps at all.

The distinction between primary and secondary groups is one of degree. Some primary relationships may involve certain secondary elements, and some of the interchanges in a secondary group may be warm and personal (see Figure 4.1). Likewise, over time, one type of group can change into the other. The important point is to understand the extent to which a particular group has primary or secondary characteristics and thus serves different functions in social life.

In-Groups and Out-Groups

In addition to noting the distinction between primary and secondary groups, sociologists also call attention to how people view their own and other groups. William Graham Sumner (1906) coined the terms *in-group* and *out-group* to distinguish between groups that generate quite different feelings. An **in-group** is *one that we feel positively toward and identify with, and that produces a sense of loyalty or "we" feeling.* **Out-groups** are *those to which we do not belong and that we view in a neutral or possibly hostile fashion.* We view out-groups as "they," as different from and less desirable than ourselves. In-groups

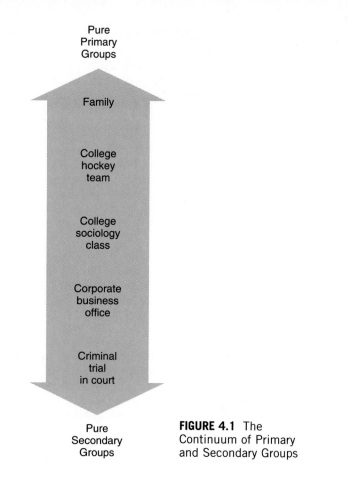

Pure Primary Groups

Family

College hockey team

College sociology class

Corporate business office

Criminal trial in court

Pure Secondary Groups

FIGURE 4.1 The Continuum of Primary and Secondary Groups

might include your family, your friends, the church you attend, or the bowling team to which you belong. Out-groups might include bowling teams that compete with yours, those who hold different religious beliefs, your supervisors at work, or the administrators and faculty at your university. In-groups and out-groups depend on a person's perspective: One person's in-group is another's out-group. In addition, in-groups and out-groups may be primary or secondary, large or small. Your baseball team, which may be a primary group, may be an in-group for you but an out-group for opposing teams. Likewise, a high school, which is a secondary group, can serve as an in-group for its members but an out-group for people attending other high schools.

All groups have boundaries to distinguish those who belong from those who do not, and boundaries help to distinguish in-groups from out-groups. In some groups, the boundaries are clearly demarcated by formal entrance rituals. People join a religion by undergoing a formal ritual such as baptism; one becomes a physician by graduating from medical school and passing the required examinations; a person enters a fraternity by successfully enduring "hell" week or other hazing ceremonies. In other groups, boundaries are defined by certain visible signs: wedding rings may define a married pair; clothing styles can signify one's allegiance to particular groups; skin color identifies one as a member of a particular racial group. For many groups, however, there are no rituals or visible signs to demarcate boundaries. For these groups, identification and we-feelings are important elements in defining boundaries and maintaining membership. Among friends, for example, membership is defined by one's loyalty to the group as measured by how much time is spent with them or what one is willing to do for them. Although we-feelings are important in many groups, they are especially important in groups that possess few other mechanisms for defining group boundaries. (Chapter 2 discussed the role of argot, or a group's special language, in helping identify group boundaries.)

In-groups and out-groups are important because of the roles they play in social life. The loyalty generated among members of an in-group, for example, can motivate people to endure many hardships together. People will give, sacrifice, or suffer a great deal to help members of their families, whereas the needs of an acquaintance or stranger would be ignored. In addition, we often stereotype members of an out-group, and those stereotypes influence the way we treat the members of that group. The elderly, for example, are often stereotyped as being frail and senile, and younger people's treatment of them often reflects this view—sometimes to the point of being condescending and insulting. As will be discussed in Chapters 7 and 8, discrimination against a group can arise from such stereotypes. Finally, threats from an out-group can increase loyalty and cohesion among in-group members. The most obvious example is warfare, in which nations view each other as threatening and people on both sides rally together to overcome the foe.

Reference Groups

A **reference group** is *a group that people use as a standard in evaluating or understanding themselves, their attitudes, and their behavior.* A person in college, for example, may adopt the attitudes, clothing styles, and leisure interests of other college students. One need not be enrolled in college, however, to use college students as a reference group. Some high school students may identify with their college counterparts, attend college athletic events, and adopt the clothing styles of college students as a standard of fashion. Thus people are not necessarily *members* of the reference groups they use as standards.

Reference groups can be very powerful and pervasive elements in our lives, serving as sources of values, attitudes, and standards of conduct. Because we regard membership in or acceptance by these groups as important, we adopt their perspective on many things, often without being aware that we have done so. This process is illustrated by a classic study of political attitudes among college students. Theodore Newcomb (1943, 1958) initiated his study in the 1930s at Bennington College, an exclusive women's college in Vermont. At the time, Bennington had a young and very liberal faculty, whereas the students came from families that were generally conservative. When students first enrolled at Bennington, they tended to hold the conservative views of their parents. That did not last, however. Newcomb found that there was a strong likelihood that the students' political attitudes would become more liberal the longer they attended Bennington. The reason was that the prestige of a student at Bennington depended in part on her political stance. To be accepted by other students, to gain entrance to sororities, to be elected to student office—all were easier if one had liberal political attitudes. Many of the students adjusted their attitudes accordingly. In short, the reference group for the students in relationship to political and social attitudes gradually changed from their parents to the faculty and other students. This liberalizing influence of college was further documented in the 1970s in a study that found that college students' sex-role attitudes and religious beliefs became less traditional over time, especially for those who eventually graduated (Funk & Willits, 1987). A restudy of the original Bennington women in the 1980s offers yet further support for the importance of reference groups in shaping attitudes (Alwin, Cohen, & Newcomb, 1991). Throughout their lives, the impact of college experiences on the political attitudes of these women persisted. Of course, some of their attitudes did change over time, but change was most likely to occur because of the impact of other reference groups, especially their spouses, their friends, and their children. When change occurred, it was typically to bring their attitudes closer into alignment with post-college reference groups to which they were exposed.

A few Bennington students maintained their conservative views, retaining their parents as a reference group for their political attitudes. Newcomb found that these students maintained closer contacts with their families, telephoned their parents more frequently, and made numerous trips back to their home community. They were also less likely to participate in campus politics or the major sororities and clubs. Instead, they joined groups on campus that were isolated from the mainstream of campus events. It was easier to maintain their parents as a reference group if they kept closer ties with them and reduced ties with liberal students and other similar groups.

Reference groups, then, serve as standards against which we assess ourselves and the validity of our beliefs and values. They also serve as sources of aspiration. When people attend college, for example, they learn the goals other college students aspire to and may come to value those goals themselves. As we move from one group to another, such situations can create difficulties, of course. Friends who do not attend college, for example, may not understand why your attitudes are changing as you attend college because they do not use college as a reference group as you do. They may view your pulling away from them as insensitivity, but you are actually beginning to assess yourself by the standards of a different group.

Social Collectivities

Some collections of people that are commonly called groups do not qualify as such under the restricted way that sociologists use the term. The term *social category* refers to people who share some characteristic in common, such as Italians, Muslims, rock fans, golfers, or racquetball players. The term *aggregate* refers to people who happen to be in the same place at the same time, even though they may not interact with one another. Examples would include people riding the same bus or people in an elevator together. Such collectivities do not qualify as a social group in the sociological sense because they do not have interrelated statuses and roles or an awareness of sharing something in common. Such social collectivities are important, however, because social categories, and especially aggregates, can transform themselves into a group if the members begin interacting and other group characteristics develop.

Group Structure and Process

You should be able to describe the social structure of groups and explain the processes involved in group decision making and ensuring group conformity.

In the previous section, groups were distinguished in terms of the functions they perform. Sociologists also distinguish between groups in terms of their size, ranging from small groups, where people engage in face-to-face interaction, to large, impersonal organizations. Much social life is lived out in small groups. Even in large organizations, much social activity occurs in small groups, as when, for example, people in a corporation meet to make business decisions or teachers in schools counsel students. These small-group settings are sufficiently important to understanding social life that sociology devotes considerable attention to studying their structure and the process of social interaction that takes place within them (Hare, 1976).

Status and Role

As indicated in Chapter 2, statuses and roles are two central elements of social structure, and they can be found in all groups—large or small, primary or secondary—because all groups have a social structure. These statuses and roles organize and coordinate the behavior of group members in relation to one another and indicate what behaviors are appropriate for each group member. In this fashion, they contribute to stable and orderly social interaction in groups. This phenomenon can be illustrated by examining the group structure of one friendship group that undoubtedly parallels structures found in many friendship groups, including your own.

During the height of the Depression in the 1930s, the sociologist William F. Whyte (1965) journeyed to an Italian slum area of Boston that he called *Cornerville*. He lived there for a few years, getting to know a group of young men he called the *Norton Street Gang*. (Whyte's research, by the way, is a form of participant observation as discussed in Chapter 1.) They were financially destitute men, as were many people then, and periodically unemployed. Although the precise membership of the group shifted over time, Whyte was able to identify the major characters in the group (see Figure 4.2). He was also able to observe a system of statuses and roles that helped define the rights and obligations of each member.

Chapter 2 said that differences in status do not always imply differences in ranking or prestige between people. In many groups, however, different statuses are ranked in terms of prestige or importance, and this ranking influences the behavior of people in those statuses. For example, a young man called Doc was recognized as the leader of the gang. For these young men, physical prowess was highly valued, and the leader was expected to be physically strong and tough. Doc became the group's leader by beating up the previous leader. In addition, the gang members expected their leader to lend money to other gang members but generally not to borrow from them. If he did borrow, he was expected to pay it back quickly. The leader was also responsible for establishing and maintaining links with other groups. It was Doc, for example, who established a bowling night with a women's social club. It was also Doc's responsibility to settle disputes between members of the group, to make decisions when members disagreed, and to suggest new activities for the gang.

The status structure of the group also influenced the expectations for conformity to group

FIGURE 4.2 Social Organization of the Norton Street Gang. *Note:* From *Street Corner Society* by William F. Whyte, 1995, Chicago: University of Chicago Press. Copyright 1955 by The University of Chicago Press. Reprinted by permission of the publisher.

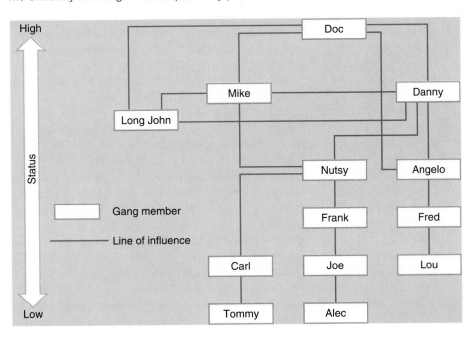

norms and roles, with high-status people under greater pressure to conform. For example, at one point Doc made an effort, with the backing of the Norton Street Gang, to enter a political race. When he withdrew his candidacy without consulting others in the group, they were disappointed and began to question whether he really possessed the qualities necessary to be a leader. People with lower status in the group, by contrast, could violate many norms without seriously threatening their position.

The impact of social status on behavior seemed, oddly enough, even to affect the bowling scores of the members. Whyte found that bowling scores tended to parallel the status positions in the group. Although some members with low status in the group bowled well in competition with people outside the gang, they invariably lost to Doc when the gang went bowling. Whyte attributed this difference to the informal mechanisms of control used on low-status members, such as verbal taunting, when they scored better than high-status members. Such taunting made the low-status members sufficiently nervous that they would not bowl as well as they might have, or they may have bowled poorly intentionally. Interestingly, Whyte had the highest bowling scores of the group, but this success was permitted, apparently, because he was regarded as an outsider.

As mentioned, membership in the Norton Street Gang shifted over time; this drifting into and out of such groups is common. Sociologists have studied the group dynamics involved in joining and leaving such groups. One influential factor is how many social connections a person has in the group (McPherson, Popielarz, & Drobnic, 1992). The more connections, such as friendships or obligations to individuals in the group, people have, the less likely they are to leave the group. This fact is especially true when those connections involve people who are similar to one another in terms of gender, race, or some other important characteristic. Generally, high-status individuals in a group have a greater network of connections than those of less status, partly because they are likely to have been in the group longer. Knowledge of such group dynamics is helpful to group leaders, who can work to increase the connections of new members in the group as a way of reducing the likelihood they will drift away.

So, studies by Whyte and other sociologists illustrate how group structure—statuses and roles—shapes behavior by defining which behaviors are appropriate for each position in the group. You probably belong to at least one informal group of friends such as that described by Whyte. Certainly the status and role structure of your group will not mirror exactly the Norton Street Gang, but you should be sensitive to the statuses and roles that do exist. Which people have higher status? Who has influence over whom? Who initiates activities, makes decisions, or settles disputes? Who can get away with nonconformity? Who has the greatest impact in determining whether a new person will be permitted to join the group? The precise form of a particular group's social structure depends on many factors. One such factor is leadership, which will be used to illustrate some further dimensions of group structure and process.

Leadership

One of the most important, and more thoroughly investigated, statuses in groups is that of leader. **Leadership** refers to *the exercise of influence over a group such that group behavior is directed toward particular outcomes or goals* (Hollander, 1985). In some groups, leadership is a formal position, as with a teacher in the classroom. In other settings, leadership is informal, shifting, and sometimes difficult to determine clearly. In peer groups, athletic teams, or a crowd at a homecoming party, it is often difficult to predict who will guide the actions of the group, and leadership may shift from one person to another over time.

Two important roles that leaders perform and that need to be performed in all groups are *task* and *socioemotional roles* (Bales, 1953; Fiedler, 1981). **Task roles** (also called **instrumental roles**) are *the actions of leaders that move the group toward achieving its goals.* Examples of task leadership would include a teacher directing students, a manager overseeing the activities of a group of employees, or a mother working to support her family. **Socioemotional roles** (also known as **expressive** or **relationship-oriented roles**) are those in which *leaders work to produce harmony, enjoyment, relaxation, or high morale among group members.* A surgeon who jokes to ease tension, an employer who hosts a party for his or her employees, or a friend who listens to the complaints of a buddy—all would be performing socioemotional roles.

These two leadership roles can be performed by the same person or by different people. It is sometimes difficult for the same person to accomplish both because they are, to a degree, inconsistent with each other. In a family, for example, a mother who works outside the home may have to insist that her children mow the lawn while she is away when they would prefer to play. Her exercise of authority and her absence—both called for by her position as instrumental leader—may, in fact, increase tension or disharmony in the family. Socioemotional leadership, by contrast, would call for listening, understanding, and sympathy—all of which may make it more difficult to get the lawn mowed. Furthermore, the two roles sometimes call for different skills. The task role may require skills in coordination and command, whereas the socioemotional role may require patience and understanding. Although some people possess all these skills, many do not.

In addition to variations in how they perform their task and socioemotional roles, leaders differ in their degree of *directiveness*. Different levels of directiveness can influence the attitudes and behaviors of group members (Lewin, Lippitt, & White, 1939; White & Lippitt, 1960). *Autocratic leaders* are thoroughly directive, dictating all actions and techniques to be used in achieving group goals. *Democratic leaders* allow group members to take part in shaping the policies of the group and choosing procedures for accomplishing group goals. Group members are allowed more freedom in deciding what their own actions will be. *Laissez-faire leaders* withdraw from participation in the group and give group members almost complete freedom to make decisions and choose alternative actions.

There are more tension and conflict with directive leaders than with less directive types. In autocratic groups, for example, more hostility and aggression are generated and scapegoating is common with a single individual often serving as the target of the group's hostility. In addition, group members are more positive toward groups with nondirective leaders, and less directive leadership creates more satisfaction among group members, greater interest in the group, and

more friendly and enjoyable relationships among group members. Directive leaders, however, appear to encourage more productivity. Although some studies find no differences in productivity as a result of leadership, few studies conclude that nondirective leadership is more productive (Fiedler, 1967; Shaw, 1976; Whitcomb & Williams, 1978).

With an understanding of the impact of leader directiveness on group behavior, it can be seen that having a directive leader is sometimes beneficial and sometimes not. In battle or in surgery, for example, there is neither the time nor the luxury for debate, freedom, or choice. In a work group, directive leadership may be less satisfying to group members but still preferable because it enhances productivity. Evidence shows, however, that democratic rather than authoritarian directiveness in leaders is more influential and results in higher employee productivity and commitment (Tjosvald, Andrews, & Struthers, 1992). In groups where membership and participation depend on people's satisfaction and interest, however, nondirective leadership may be necessary to hold the group together. Among friends or in charity drives where participation is voluntary, nondirective leaders may be essential to avoid the disintegration of the group. In other words, the best style of leadership depends on the type of group involved and the goals of the group (Fiedler, 1981). It also depends on the environment in which the group carries out its work. In a stressful environment where the group experiences hindrances to its work, a less structured group without clear-cut leadership seems to do better; in a quiet, stable, positive environment, groups with structured leadership outperform less structured groups at the same tasks (Worchel & Shackelford, 1991). It can be seen, therefore, that many factors come into play to influence leadership in groups, and sociologists need a lot of information (about group goals, environment, membership characteristics, and so on) before making recommendations about the most effective leadership for a particular group.

Finally in regard to leadership, considerable research and controversy over the years have been generated over the role of gender. Popular wisdom, which is supported by some research, suggests that men are more natural leaders and women more natural followers (Eagly, 1983). In group settings, it is held, men are more influential and women are more likely to be influenced. Certainly, the traditional sex-role stereotype of women as the weaker and more passive of the two sexes is consistent with this view. Research also suggests, however, that much or all of this difference in leadership capacity may result from the fact that, in a society where gender differences still persist, men have more formal opportunities to hold leadership positions, thus gaining experience at and demonstrating a capacity for leadership. There may be a self-fulfilling prophecy at work: The cultural stereotype of men as leaders results in men being pressured to take such positions, and the experience they gain in those positions imparts more leadership abilities to them than to women. Nevertheless, it is not gender, per se, that affects leadership but rather the opportunities made differentially available on the basis of gender. As women gain more opportunities in leadership and management roles, things should begin to change, and recent research reports a less clear-cut gender effect on leadership (Gurman & Long, 1992; Hegstrom & Griffith, 1992; Sapp, Harrod, & Zhao, 1996).

Decision Making in Groups

This discussion of the social structure of groups has considered issues related to social interaction among group members, such as the degree of directiveness in the interaction between leaders and members. Another area of social interaction among group members that has been extensively studied is decision making in groups.

Some people believe that "two heads are better than one"—that group decisions are superior to those made by individuals. Others believe that decision making by groups is inherently inefficient and faulty. What is the reality behind these contradictory commonsense notions? Actually, it depends on whether the group is solving a problem or exercising judgment and making choices. Research has demonstrated that groups are clearly superior to individuals in everything except speed when it comes to solving problems. Groups come up with a wider range of solutions to problems, and the solutions are better and more accurate (Shaw & Costanzo, 1982). There are a

number of probable reasons for the superiority of group performance in problem solving: More individual effort and creativity are brought to bear in a group; groups are more likely to recognize and reject errors; the ablest and most confident group members strongly influence the group decision; and greater interest in the problem is aroused in a group and people are more highly motivated to seek a solution (Phillips & Wood, 1984; Watson, Michaelsen, & Sharp, 1991).

Many decisions that groups make are not related to problem solving but rather involve judgment, assessment, and choice among a number of alternatives. And no alternative is necessarily correct. For example, deciding how to spend a weekend has this judgmental character. Group decisions on judgmental issues are characterized by a phenomenon known as **group polarization:** *The decisions tend to be more extreme than those made by individuals* (Kogan & Wallach, 1964; Myers & Lamm, 1976). This phenomenon was originally identified as a *risky shift:* People in groups tend to make more daring and bold choices than they would if acting individually. To some extent, this tendency contradicts the commonsense notion that groups are cautious and reserved. Continuing research has shown, however, that although group discussion *does* bring about a shift in the decisions of individuals, the shift *need not* be in the direction of more risk. If the group's position is cautious and conservative, then individuals tend to shift their decisions in that direction. In short, group decisions tend to be more extreme—either more daring *or* more cautious—than decisions made individually by the same people. This phenomenon has been found to occur in many diverse settings, including people making business decisions as well as burglars deciding whether a location is an appropriate target (Cromwell, Marks, Olson, & Avary, 1991; Williams & Taormina, 1992).

There are several possible reasons for the group polarization phenomenon (Hong, 1978; Mackie & Cooper, 1984). First, it may be that during group discussions, people shift their decisions in directions that appear to be more highly valued by the group. In other words, people tend to adopt the values of the group in making decisions. Another reason for group polarization may be that people shift their opinions because they have been persuaded by the information and arguments emerging from group discussion. Group members who hold extreme positions may feel more strongly about their position, argue more persuasively, and thus have greater influence on the group's decisions. Finally, especially in groups exhibiting a risky shift, people in groups probably feel less responsibility for the decisions and thus less inhibited in making risky ones.

Group Conformity

Although groups can provide support and security, they can also be controlling and coercive. They can be powerful instruments for getting people to conform to group norms. An early experiment by the social psychologist Muzafer Sherif (1936) documented that in ambiguous situations people tend to conform to the expectations of those around them. When we find it difficult to judge on our own what are proper actions to take, we turn to others to help us make the judgment. And, Sherif found, people denied that the group had influenced their behavior. A particularly nightmarish illustration of such conformity occurred in March 1968 in the Vietnamese village of My Lai. On orders from their superiors, American soldiers shot and killed hundreds of Vietnamese men, women, and children, even though they offered no resistance and may not have been Vietcong soldiers or supporters (Hersch, 1970). Why was there such conformity, with a horrendous outcome, at My Lai? Although any such incident is extremely complicated, we can identify a few factors that contributed to its occurrence.

One element, obviously, that influenced the soldiers' behavior was fear. As one reporter who was in Vietnam put it: "You're scared to death out there. We just wanted to go home" (quoted in Hersch, 1970, p. 48). Fear alone, however, is an insufficient explanation, because some people react to fear with bravery, some by withdrawal, and others by committing inhumane acts. There was another important dimension at My Lai that day: The solders were a part of a group in the army with an established authority structure and leadership. Military officers were in command, and their authority over enlisted men was understood and recognized by all. Some of the soldiers prob-

ably assumed that officers in positions of authority had good reason for giving the order to shoot. For other soldiers, their reluctance to defy authority was probably more overpowering than the atrocities they were ordered to commit. Few things are more deeply ingrained in a soldier's awareness than the necessity to obey the commands of superior officers. In battle, prompt obedience to orders can save lives, and the punishment for disobedience can be severe. Confronted with the dilemma of either conforming or perhaps being severely disciplined for refusal, some of the soldiers—with little time to think over the issues—chose to conform because it probably seemed to be the less risky path in the long run.

There was yet another factor in operation at My Lai: The ambiguity of clearly defining who the enemy was and where battle lines were drawn. Vietnam was a guerrilla war, and "the enemy"—the Vietcong—was elusive. They wore no uniforms to distinguish them from civilians; they often lived in areas where they fought and thus could melt back into the population after battle; and civilians—young and old, men and women—were often used to carry weapons and supplies and to participate in battles or in terrorist activities. In just such ambiguous situations, Sherif has shown us, there is a strong tendency to conform to the expectations and actions of others around you. For many of the soldiers at My Lai on that day, conformity meant joining in the shooting.

The massacre at My Lai was a complicated, chaotic, and bewildering event. Those who were involved were not necessarily cruel or demented personalities. They were normal people doing a rather unusual job in the most bizarre circumstances. It should make us aware that none of us is immune to powerful and pervasive group processes. All of us have found ourselves in ambiguous situations, and we probably tended to conform in those settings. In fact, every time we make a judgmental decision we are in an ambiguous situation, because the choice between alternatives is to a degree unclear. Irving Janis (1982) has found that when groups make decisions, there are pressures to avoid controversy that might cast doubt on the wisdom of the group's decision. This process, which Janis dubbed **groupthink,** *involves pressuring group members to make decisions unanimously, sometimes at the expense of critical thinking and* *the realistic appraisal of alternatives.* The pressure is especially strong in highly cohesive groups (Turner, Pratkanis, Probasco, & Leve, 1992). Dissenters might be ridiculed or ignored, or group members might withhold their doubts about a decision rather than threaten the camaraderie that accompanies group consensus. Janis even concludes from his research that some historical fiascoes resulted in part from groupthink. He attributes the lack of preparedness at Pearl Harbor in 1941, for example, to the unwillingness of high government officials to challenge the existing consensus that the Japanese would not attack. More recent researchers have suggested that groupthink influenced the decision to launch the space shuttle *Challenger* in 1986, which exploded a minute after launch, killing all seven astronauts onboard. After analyzing events leading up to the disaster, researchers concluded that problems with the shuttle might not have been ignored had groupthink not played a part (Moorhead, Ference, & Neck, 1991). Social cohesion influences groupthink and many other aspects of group dynamics and social interaction. Applying Sociology: Group Cohesion and Combat Effectiveness in Wartime describes the efforts of sociological practitioners who have worked over the years with the U.S. military to organize a more effective, combat-ready force by enhancing cohesion in groups.

This discussion has barely touched on the myriad ways in which small groups influence human behavior. This topic will be discussed again at numerous points in the remainder of this book. For now, however, we need to recognize that the small groups that we belong to are frequently parts of larger organizations. It is to these organizations that we now direct our attention.

Organizations

You should be able to compare Weber's analysis of bureaucracies with the human relations approach and explain the functioning of informal structures in organizations.

As pointed out earlier, primary groups play a central role in our lives. Today, however, we spend much of our time in secondary groups such as schools, factories, government offices, or banks.

Sociologists refer to these types of secondary groups as **formal organizations:** *large, specialpurpose groups that are explicitly designed to achieve specific goals* (Haas & Drabek, 1973). Like other groups, formal organizations are characterized by sets of interrelated statuses, roles, and norms, although these features are more complex in organizations than in smaller groups. Formal organizations also involve clearly established rules, regulations, and standards of conduct that are designed to coordinate people's behavior to achieve specific organizational goals. There are many different types of formal organizations (see Table 4.1 on p. 122).

There has been considerable debate among sociologists over the central features of formal organizations. This chapter will present two major models of formal organizations—the bureaucratic and the human relations models—and then assess them using the theoretical perspectives. As it does so, try to evaluate the models from your own experiences in formal organizations—the schools you have attended, the places you have worked, and the religious groups to which you have belonged.

Bureaucracy

The sociologist Max Weber (1925/1947) characterized those formal organizations that dominate modern societies as **bureaucracies:** *rationally created formal organizations that are based on hierarchical authority and explicit rules of procedure.* Weber recognized that bureaucracies existed in preindustrial societies as well, such as ancient Egypt and China and in the Roman and Byzantine empires. Not until the past few centuries, however, with the emergence of large societies based on complex technologies, have bureaucracies come to permeate people's daily lives. The reason is simple. Spontaneous, casual, and personal relationships—such as those found in primary groups—are inefficient when it comes to coordinating the activities of many people working toward specific goals. Imagine trying to build a library with no hierarchical authority among the workers or explicit rules of procedure. If no workers felt like mixing cement, the walls could not be built. If the electricians decided to spend the day at the beach, the drywallers could not construct the walls. To cope with these problems, the trend

APPLYING SOCIOLOGY
Group Cohesion and Combat Effectiveness in Wartime

Central to the sociological imagination is the recognition that group structures and processes affect people's behaviors. One of the more important group characteristics is **group cohesion,** or *the degree to which groups stick together and members feel committed to one another and attracted to the group.* In other words, cohesive groups tend to stick together, even under adversity, whereas less cohesive groups more easily disintegrate under pressure or competing demands. More cohesive groups have higher levels of morale and less difficulty retaining members and are often more persistent and effective in achieving their goals.

The military services in the United States have had a continuing interest in this subject since at least World War II because they want their soldiers to continue fighting as a cohesive group even under the most adverse conditions—combat, where deprivation, injury, and death are routine. Applied sociologists have been conducting research and helping the military services establish policies that will result in the most cohesive fighting force. The focus of much of this research has been on the role of primary groups in motivating soldiers to fight. Studies of the German army by sociologists during World War II, for example, showed that many units continued to fight well even when they were badly outnumbered and had probably lost the war. It was not a belief in the Nazi cause that produced this tenacity in battle, because many German soldiers showed little commitment to the Nazi ideology. Instead, sociologists discovered that it was the solidarity and loyalty that soldiers felt toward others in their squad or platoon that motivated their effective combat action under adverse conditions. They did not want to let their buddies down or feel their buddies' wrath should they not pull their weight. Based on their research, two sociologists concluded that "a soldier's ability to resist is a function of the capacity of his immediate primary group (his squad or section) to avoid social disintegration" (Shils & Janowitz, 1948, p. 281). Surveys by sociologists during World War II showed the same thing among U.S. soldiers: Group solidarity was the most frequently mentioned factor that kept soldiers going in combat (Stouffer et al., 1949).

During the Korean War, sociologists experimented with having four-person teams of soldiers trained together and transferred to new units together as a way of enhancing primary-group ties and group cohesion. In comparison to training and transferring soldiers individually, this approach did produce higher levels of both morale and performance (Segal, Schubert, & Li, 1991). In fact, all the sociological research of the 1940s and 1950s pointed to the efficacy of training and rotating soldiers in groups rather than individually, and this practice was a major recommendation to the military services by applied sociologists. Despite this advice, the U.S. Army went back to the individual rotation system during the Vietnam buildup of the 1960s. It did so largely for political reasons, but the consequence, argued some critics, was lower unit cohesiveness and poorer combat performance (Faris, 1977; Moskos, 1970). By contrast, some Vietcong units, one of the major opponents of the United States in Vietnam, were organized into cells of three to five soldiers who endured danger and severely difficult living conditions together. That experience built up strong ties of loyalty and made them tenacious combatants (Karnow, 1981).

With the all-volunteer military of the 1980s and 1990s, interest in and research on the effects of unit cohesion have continued (Segal, Schubert, & Li, 1991). Sociologists such as Morris Janowitz and David Segal have continued to work with the military services to determine when and under what conditions unit morale is higher and has positive consequences on performance. They are still trying to determine, for example, at what group level—the squad, platoon, company, or battalion—changing policies can have most impact on morale. Since World War II, sociologists have learned that the impact of primary-group ties on cohesion and behavior is more complex than originally thought. Applied sociologists have also learned that their recommendations are only one factor that shapes social policy and that they are sometimes ignored (as they were in Vietnam when they argued strongly against the individual rotation plan). Nonetheless, unit cohesion represents one area in which sociological practitioners have had a continuing impact on people's lives.

TABLE 4.1 Types of formal organizations

Type	Membership	Benefits	Examples
Voluntary	People join of their own volition and receive no financial compensation	Members gain some personal gratification from pursuing a hobby or goal	New York Road Runners Association, the United Way, U.S. Olympic Committee
Coercive	People are required to join for either their own benefit or societal good	Society or some groups benefit from the membership of some in these organizations	Schools with compulsory education, prisons, the military when there is a compulsory draft
Utilitarian	People are not forced to join a particular organization but feel compelled to join some organization	People join because it would otherwise be difficult or impossible to achieve personal goals	Organizations from which we make a living
Mutual benefit	Membership could be either voluntary or coercive	Members of the organization are the main recipients of its benefits	Schools, churches, labor unions
Service	Membership could be either voluntary or coercive	Clients of the organization are the main beneficiaries	Stores, social service agencies, community mental health centers, auto repair shops
Commonweal	Membership could be either voluntary or coercive	It provides a service to the general public rather than to specific clients	Environmental Protection Agency, the Rockefeller Foundation

Note: From *Formal Organizations: A Comparative Approach* by Peter M. Blau and W. Richard Scott, 1962 (San Francisco: Chandler); *A Comparative Analysis of Complex Organizations* by Amitai Etzioni, 1975 (Glencoe, IL: Free Press).

in modern societies has been toward *rationalization*—the replacement of spontaneous, shifting, and ambiguous rules of procedure with explicit rules that are based on the most efficient means to achieve practical goals. This growing rationalization has resulted in the development of bureaucracies.

Characteristics of Bureaucracies   Weber's analysis of bureaucracy was based on an *ideal type,* which is an abstract description based on many observations of actual bureaucracies. An ideal type highlights the essential features of such organizations. Although no single bureaucracy fits this ideal type exactly, Weber identified six characteristics that make bureaucracies distinctive.

First, bureaucracies are characterized by a *division of labor*—each person is responsible for a specific, specialized set of tasks at which that person is to become proficient. In a university, for example, we turn to the campus police rather than the physics department for traffic control and to the food service rather than the registrar to prepare a luncheon.

Second, bureaucracies also have a *hierarchy of authority* that specifies the chain of command—who must answer to whom (see Figure 4.3). This hierarchy is typically pyramidal, with each person responsible to a particular person above and responsible for the activities of particular people below. Without a hierarchy of authority, there would be little centralized control. In most universities, faculty members have authority over students in that they can require the students to write papers and take examinations to pass a course. In turn, the faculty are accountable to the chairpersons of their departments and the deans of their college or school.

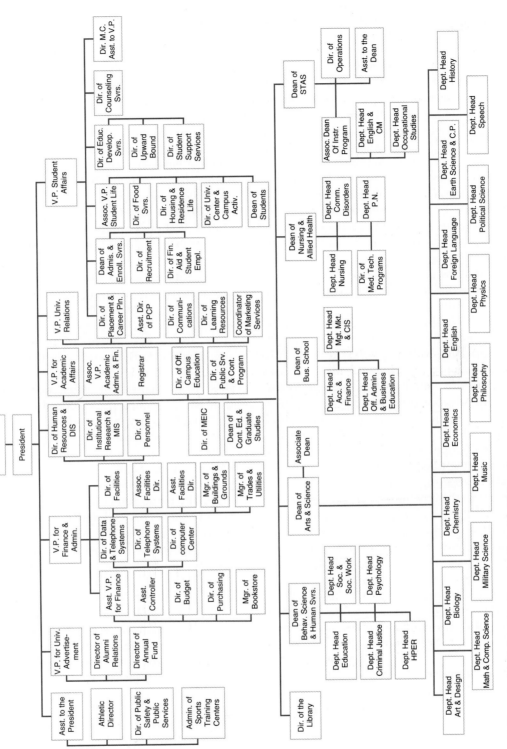

FIGURE 4.3 Administrative Organization of a University

Third, people's conduct and job responsibilities in a bureaucracy are governed by *formal rules and procedures* that typically appear in written form. In a university, for example, the university bulletin is a set of rules that specifies what each student must do to earn a degree. One university bulletin, for example, specifies that a sociology major must complete 124 course credits, including 38 credits in sociology course work, in order to receive his or her college degree.

Fourth, *specialized skills and knowledge* are established as criteria for occupying a position in the bureaucracy. In a university, faculty positions require a certain educational background and research experience, usually including a Ph.D. The steam plant engineer, responsible for maintaining the heating system, may have been trained through experience and promoted from apprentice positions in the university.

Fifth, many positions in the bureaucracy are full-time occupations, with *career ladders and advancement* occurring within the organization. This aspect of bureaucracies enhances their stability over time and the commitment of people to the organization. Advancement is usually determined by merit, seniority, or both. Other criteria, such as friendship or family ties, are generally not considered, at least not openly, because they might result in positions being filled by unqualified people.

Finally, relationships in bureaucracies are ideally characterized by *impartiality and impersonality*. People relate to one another as positions in the bureaucracy rather than as individuals with special needs and qualities, because personal considerations might interfere with efficiency and fairness. College professors assign grades on the basis of students' performance, not on the basis of how friendly, interested, or enthusiastic they appear to be. To do otherwise might result in unqualified people receiving college degrees.

A Critique of Bureaucratic Organization With these characteristics, bureaucracies clearly have certain advantages, at least with respect to some tasks (Champion, 1975; Gross & Etzioni, 1985; Zand, 1974). Bureaucracies are orderly and stable, and the people in them know who can do what and when they will do it. They are also speedy and efficient organizations for accomplishing certain kinds of things, especially well-structured and

straightforward tasks that involve a uniform sequence of events. Automobile or breakfast cereal factories, for example, benefit from bureaucratic organization, as do military organizations and prisons. College students, however, who are no strangers to bureaucracy because virtually all institutions of higher education today are bureaucratic, may disagree that bureaucracies are speedy and efficient. You are undoubtedly familiar with the laments—sometimes cynical, sometimes resigned—that are directed at bureaucracies: "You can't beat the system," "We're drowning in red tape," or "It's the old (name your institution here) shuffle." These comments point to the fact that, despite their advantages, bureaucracies have shortcomings.

One of the major shortcomings of bureaucracies is that their strong emphasis on following established rules and regulations can lead to rigidity and inflexibility. The rules become ends in themselves rather than means of achieving organizational goals. Early in this century, Thorsten B. Veblen (1912) coined the term *trained incapacity* to refer to a situation in which people have been trained so completely to follow the rules that they are unable to act independently or innovatively. They develop bureaucratic "tunnel vision." For example, in preparation for travel to a professional meeting, I personally encountered trained incapacity while making reservations at a hotel. I had originally made reservations for a seven-day stay, but my plans changed and I attempted to cancel the reservations for the last two days but to keep the reservations for the other five days. I was quickly informed by the reservations clerk that, according to the computer, the hotel was completely booked for those five days so a reservation could not be made. Of course, this was true, because the seven-day reservation included those five days. Repeated attempts to persuade the clerk that this change in reservations would not add any additional booking, but would actually open up a room for two days, were to no avail. Patience soon gave way to a heated exchange. When tempers on both sides were at the breaking point, a supervisor intervened and settled the issue satisfactorily. The reservations clerk was blindly sticking to the rule that prohibited him from taking any further reservations when the computer indicated that the hotel was full. Such behavior arises when participants forget the overall goal of the organization and become totally preoccupied with the means of obtaining that goal.

The normal operation of bureaucracies, then, can have the effect of stifling creativity. Bureaucratic rules and regulations are designed to apply to standard situations; they become inefficient and sometimes useless when applied to the novel or unusual. Bureaucracies tend to reward obedience to rules rather than the creation of new ways to achieve goals. The sociologist Robert Merton (1968) has even argued that a *bureaucratic personality* develops, which emphasizes conformity, rigidity, and timidity. Along similar lines, C. Wright Mills (1959, p. 171) feared "the ascendency of the cheerful robot"—the person who willingly accepts and obeys authority in bureaucratic settings rather than questioning, challenging, and innovating.

Another shortcoming of bureaucratic organization is widely known as the Peter Principle. It can be stated succinctly: In a hierarchy, employees tend to rise to their level of incompetence (Peter & Hull, 1969). To illustrate, suppose that Carl has just taken an entry-level position in a large company. He finds his work stimulating and is eager to advance, so he works diligently. After a year or two, he is singled out for his excellent performance and promoted to manager of his department. This job gives him more responsibility, and he finds the adjustment difficult, but within a few months he has mastered it and is again being praised by his superiors. A few years later he is offered a job in middle management. He accepts, but this time the job proves to be too much for him. His strength has always been dealing with people, but his new job involves working with numbers and doing long-range planning. The praise from above stops, and so does his rise through the corporation. In his rise through the ranks, he left behind him two levels of employees less competent than himself. He has now become their incompetent leader.

Will Carl be fired? Probably not. By the time most bureaucrats have reached what the Peter Principle calls *Final Placement,* they are difficult to remove or demote. Often they have been working at a company for a number of years and have the power and resources to conceal their incompetence and protect their positions. They may have competent secretaries and underlings, for example, to help them muddle through their work, or they may be able to delegate work to other bureaucrats.

One critic pointed to a final shortcoming of bureaucracies by arguing that bureaucrats are like crabgrass in that both proliferate rapidly and resist efforts to cut back their number (Joyner, 1978). That critic might have been thinking of Parkinson's Law, which states that work in a bureaucracy tends to occupy the number of workers assigned to it and fill the time available for its completion, regardless of the actual amount of work involved (Parkinson, 1962). Bureaucrats must *appear* to be busy or they may be considered expendable. If a task can be finished in less than the time available for it, they may actually create work to fill the remaining time. Eventually, they come to regard this "make-work" as very important, and they feel burdened under the load. Assistants may be hired to help out, but that means even more work because the assistants must be trained and supervised. As workers are added, the amount of paperwork necessarily increases, filling the time of even more bureaucrats. Thus, according to Parkinson, bureaucracies tend to grow even when the work they do does not. Parkinson's Law may be behind the tendency of governments at every level to expand.

Although this list of the shortcomings of bureaucracies may paint a rather grim picture of incompetence and inertia, reality in most organizations is not quite that bleak. Most bureaucracies perform reasonably well, and most bureaucrats are conscientious and reasonably competent. Nevertheless, bureaucratic organizations do have the tendencies described here, and efforts must be made to structure them in ways that reduce the negative impacts. Applied sociologists have played an important role in this effort, through research and consultation on how to organize bureaucracies and other organizations most effectively. Applying Sociology: Organizational Diagnosis describes the role of sociologists in detecting and reducing groupthink in organizations.

The Human Relations Approach

Anyone who has experienced bureaucratic life can recognize that Weber's characterization of bureaucracies ignores several important considerations.

In the 1980s, the Beech-Nut Corporation admitted that it had produced and sold millions of jars of fake apple juice (Welles, 1988). The second largest baby-food producer in the United States had labeled as apple juice a product that had no natural apple juice in it. Its actions were clearly unethical and illegal; yet this corporation, which had prided itself on its pure and natural products for many decades, went ahead and made millions of dollars on the deal. What apparently happened is that groupthink played a part in this corporate decision (Sims, 1992). The company was under strong financial pressure, and it believed that other companies were selling artificial juice as natural. Individuals involved in the decision had strong loyalties to the company and were willing to close their eyes to any ethical lapses. Company executives also showed a degree of arrogance that led them to feel some degree of invulnerability to the negative consequences of their decisions. These conditions provide fertile ground for the emergence of groupthink. The outcome was a poor decision to produce the fake juice, and ultimately the corporation paid dearly in criminal charges.

Beech-Nut could have benefited from a service that some sociological practitioners offer: *organizational diagnosis.* This term refers to using the theories, methods, and research findings from sociology and other social sciences to assess how well an organization operates and how its performance can be improved (Harrison, 1991). Organizations turn to social scientists when organizations believe they have a problem with people, groups, interpersonal relationships, or organizational culture. These are not purely business or economic concerns, although they have implications for how well a business does economically. Groupthink is one type of sociological problem that organizations might face; other problems would include low morale among workers or interpersonal conflicts between employees in an office. All these problems have to do with how groups are organized and how people interact with one another in organizations.

In conducting an organizational diagnosis related to groupthink, sociologists rely on past research that shows what social conditions are conducive to groupthink and how groups can be changed to reduce it. They may also collect data on how the organization operates, possibly through direct observation or with surveys. Armed with this information, the sociologist recommends changes that would reduce the likelihood of groupthink. Depending on the particular organization, the following might be included among the recommendations:

1. Organizational managers should encourage the open airing of doubts and objections to any decision.
2. Outsiders should participate in the decision-making process to challenge the positions of group members.
3. Several independent groups should be set up to study the issues.
4. Other groups should be brought into the decision-making process to avoid being isolated from competing viewpoints.
5. Conflict should be built into the decision-making process. This can be done either by assigning each group member to be a devil's advocate and criticize the group decision or by structuring the decision making into a debate where both sides of the issue are fully aired.

These sociological recommendations focus on the group process by which a decision is made rather than on telling the business which decision to make.

In particular, Weber's view says little about *people* and their hopes and needs. To incorporate these elements into the operation of organizations, the human relations model of organizations has emerged. The *human relations approach* is based on the assumption that the social, psychological, and physical needs of people who work in organizations must be considered if the organizations are to be productive and efficient (Haas & Drabek, 1973). The human relations model rose to prominence in the 1920s and 1930s following investigations in a number of industrial settings. Elton

Mayo (1933), for example, was called in to a textile mill near Philadelphia to find reasons for an astonishingly high turnover rate of 250 percent a year among employees. Various incentive schemes had failed to resolve this problem, and Mayo experimented with a number of changes. He gave the workers a rest period, let workers on each group of machines decide when they would stop, and made a nurse available to them for injuries. Following these changes, a sense of group cohesion and unity emerged, and productivity increased while turnovers declined. In part to extend Mayo's work, a series of investigations were conducted between 1927 and 1932 in the Hawthorne plant of the Western Electric Company near Chicago, where telephone equipment was assembled (Roethlisberger & Dickson, 1939). Various improvements were made in the work conditions, such as the provision of rest breaks and a shorter workday. As a consequence, the productivity of the workers improved. Today we recognize that the link between these environmental factors and work performance is complicated, but these early investigations laid the foundation for the human relations approach to formal organizations.

Proponents of the human relations approach argue that the feelings, desires, and aspirations of workers must be satisfied, at least to a degree, if organizations are to be efficient (Argyris, 1964; Likert, 1967). The desire for companionship or creativity, for example, cannot be "turned off" once employees cross the factory gate or the office door. Rather, these personal elements—an anathema to Weber's bureaucratic model—should be considered in the structure of a formal organization. For example, satisfying social contacts in the work environment could be provided by organizing the work flow and rest breaks so that people have opportunities for relaxed conversation with other workers. Alternatively, work groups can be made smaller so that primary-group relations and cohesiveness are more likely to develop.

Proponents of the human relations approach to organizations argue against a rigid hierarchy or authority structure. Within the framework of this approach, supervision should be supportive and personal rather than dictatorial or exploitive. In addition, workers should play a role in the decision-making process whenever possible, and supervisors should be accountable to the people under them. Although supervisors have greater authority than their subordinates, the former should be attentive to the latter's concerns or complaints, especially if identifiable grounds exist for the dissatisfaction. In fact, the relationship between supervisors and their subordinates can be viewed as having many of the qualities of a primary group. The bond between supervisor and worker should not be solely utilitarian—it should be a broader tie that involves many more personal elements.

The major elements of the bureaucratic and human relations models are presented in Figure 4.4 (on p. 128). The human relations approach does not reject every element of Weber's bureaucratic model. Clearly, a division of labor, a hierarchy of authority, rules and procedures, and special qualifications to hold positions are necessary. The impersonality of Weber's approach is explicitly rejected, however, and adherence to rules is viewed flexibly rather than rigidly. In addition, whereas Weber conceived of authority flowing down the hierarchy, the human relations model offers employees some input into the decisions made by those above them. This approach seems most suitable for organizations in which extreme discipline is not necessary, tasks are not rigidly uniform, or employee motivation or morale is important. Thus a university, a hospital, or an advertising firm might benefit from this type of organization (Champion, 1975; Litwak, 1961).

The Informal Structure

All organizations develop some type of informal structure. This structure involves personal relationships guided by norms and rituals that emerge separately from the formal rules and regulations of the organization. Informal structures perform a number of functions. First, they provide people with personal ties that the formal structure lacks. We all enjoy being with people who like and respect us, whether at work or at play, and organizational rules on such matters are likely to be ineffective. Even in organizations modeled on the human relations approach, concern about the personal needs of the organization's members is to a degree utilitarian: The purpose is to increase

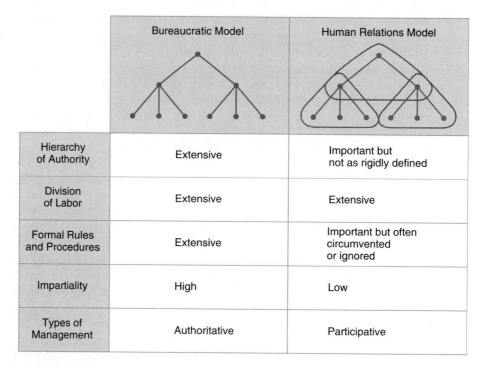

	Bureaucratic Model	Human Relations Model
Hierarchy of Authority	Extensive	Important but not as rigidly defined
Division of Labor	Extensive	Extensive
Formal Rules and Procedures	Extensive	Important but often circumvented or ignored
Impartiality	High	Low
Types of Management	Authoritative	Participative

FIGURE 4.4 Approaches to Formal Organizations

productivity. People seek primary relationships, as has been noted, because such relationships are pleasurable and help reduce stress. So people in organizations become friends, fall in love, and develop close ties with one another—all largely independent of organizational dictates.

The informal structure does more, however, than simply provide for personal relationships. It also helps people protect themselves against what they perceive as unreasonable or dangerous demands of the organization. The workers at the Hawthorne plant mentioned earlier, for example, informally regulated the speed at which they worked so that they did not have to work too fast. Sarcasm and ridicule were used to control those who were inclined to work harder. They were castigated as *rate busters* and singled out for a *binging*, being hit on the arm. These actions, although mild, expressed the displeasure of the group and encouraged conformity to informal group norms.

In addition, the informal structure permits adaptations to situations or demands that are not provided for in the formal structure. In some cases, adaptation may involve violating official rules to help achieve organizational goals. During

the Korean War, for example, the sociologist Roger Little (1970) lived with an army rifle company in Korea and observed an informal practice called *scrounging,* which involved collecting all the supplies abandoned by other companies upon leaving an area. Officially, discarded supplies must be turned in to a central supply depot, but the supply sergeants usually kept the equipment as a barter bank. If their company developed a supply shortage because of carelessness or a slowdown in official supply channels, items in the barter bank could be traded for the scarce supplies. Although officially illegal, scrounging was tolerated and sometimes encouraged by company commanders because it was an efficient way to keep their units fully supplied. In fact, supply sergeants who were highly skilled at scrounging were in great demand among the units.

Finally, the informal structure in organizations makes it possible to adjust to individual variations in skills, resources, and characteristics. We are not, after all, mindless, emotionless automatons, waiting to do the bureaucracy's bidding. Some people are faster than others, some more intelligent, some more outgoing. Although bureau-

In an ideal bureaucracy, people should be treated on the basis of the skills and expertise they bring to the organization. However, characteristics such as gender can lead people to be treated differently, especially when few people in the organization possess that characteristic.

cratic rules may consider all people in a given position to be the same, people take these differences into account informally.

Gender in Organizations

Gender is one difference that often shapes how people are treated by the informal structure of organizations. Sociologist Rosabeth Moss Kanter (1993) found this in one large corporation that she has studied at length. One characteristic of organizations that she found to be important is *relative numbers,* or the ratio of people with a particular characteristic in an organization to those who do not have that characteristic. In the case of gender, men substantially outnumber women in the upper-management ranks. Or to put it more colloquially, women in management are often "tokens." Kanter found that this characteristic of corporations substantially influenced the opportunities for women and their behavior. For one thing, it made these women highly visible; they be-

came symbols for "what women can accomplish." Because of this, they felt tremendous pressures to work harder, to avoid making mistakes, and to perform better than the men. They also sometimes felt lonely because they were different from other members of the work group; when a group has token status, it is easy for the majority group to exaggerate the differences between tokens and the others, and this may lead to feelings of isolation and exclusion on the part of the token.

Of course, the visibility of token women in corporations has positive benefits for some; for example, it can lead to getting more attention and this can sometimes enhance possibilities for advancement in the corporation. However, Kanter's point is to show how a person's position in the structure of an organization—in this case, a group's relative numbers—shapes opportunities and behavior. Presumably, any tokens in an organization, such as men in a largely female corporation, would have similar experiences. Kanter argued that women's experiences in corporations would change when their numbers grew and they were no longer tokens. However, as Chapter 8 shows, that may not be happening. As the number of women in corporations grows, it appears that male managers feel their positions threatened and sometimes respond by discrimination in wages or promotions—women get paid less and are less likely to be promoted to the top ranks (Glass Ceiling Commission, 1995; Yoder, 1991). There is often a "glass ceiling" beyond which women find it difficult to be promoted. So, even though corporations may claim that gender is irrelevant to how they operate, Kanter's and others' research on the informal structure of organizations documents that gender is very influential in terms of opportunities and behavior.

Sociological Perspectives on Organizations

You should be able to compare and contrast the functionalist, conflict, and interactionist perspectives on formal organizations.

The sociological approaches to the study of formal organizations just presented are either explicitly or implicitly functionalist in orientation. To round out an understanding of organizations, it would be useful to make this functionalist emphasis explicit and then contrast it with the conflict and interactionist approaches to organizations.

The Functionalist Perspective

Functionalists view organizations as systems of interrelated parts that are organized to achieve goals in a way that enhances efficiency and productivity (Parsons, 1956). An elaborate division of labor, for example, is viewed as beneficial because each worker becomes highly proficient at a small task that can be learned quickly. Efficiency is enhanced as the work process is broken into units that can be rapidly accomplished by individual workers. Consensus regarding the overall goal of the organization, whether it involves assembling a product or providing a service, is assumed to be widespread. The nature of the tasks necessary to accomplish goals is important in determining whether the organization takes a bureaucratic or human relations form. Some organizations combine elements of more than one of these models, having some divisions organized according to one model and some based on the other. A pharmaceutical company might organize its production and distribution divisions on the basis of bureaucratic organization and its marketing departments on the basis of the human relations approach. The different tasks of each division dictate the structure most suited to it.

Conflict is recognized as an element of organizational life, arising as individuals adapt to organizational demands or as the organization responds to internal or external events. Functionalists, however, view this conflict as either an unwanted organizational element that needs to be kept within reasonable limits or as a catalyst for organizational changes that will result in greater efficiency and productivity.

The functionalist perspective also views organizations as one of many parts of larger social and cultural systems. As in all systems, these parts must be reasonably well integrated, and this connectedness means that the workings of one part of the system may be affected by elements of other parts of the broader social and cultural system. Other Worlds, Other Ways: China (on pp. 132–133) illustrates this fact by showing how cultural values can affect how well people in organizations work and thus how well organizations achieve their goals.

The Conflict Perspective

Despite the overwhelming functionalist bent of sociologists studying organizations, there have been efforts to assess organizations and bureaucracies from the conflict perspective (Goldman & Van Houten, 1977; Heydebrand, 1977; Zey-Ferrell, 1981). From this perspective, organizations are viewed as mechanisms of social control within the context of a struggle between interest groups. Power relations and a class struggle exist *before* an organization develops, and organizational properties reflect those underlying power and class relations. The goals of the organization, the technology used, the division of labor—all reflect the interests of dominant groups and support their interests, giving them an advantage over subordinate groups. The division of labor, for example, places the worker at a substantial disadvantage in relationship to the owners. When the work process is broken down into simple units, individual workers become expendable because others can quickly learn their jobs, which involve few skills. This procedure is highly coercive because workers who can be replaced easily are likely to make few demands on management. This is not to say that these organizations are not also efficient and productive. It has been shown, however, that bureaucracies have weaknesses that reduce their efficiency but that these inefficiencies are insufficient motivation for organizational change. Inefficiencies are tolerated because bureaucratic organization still coerces and controls subordinates effectively, and these coercive purposes are as important in determining organizational structure as the productivity that the structure offers.

Although the human relations model diverges in many ways from the bureaucratic model, organizations of this sort are nonetheless mechanisms of domination. From the conflict perspective, the human relations approach simply offers management new ways of controlling through subtle manipulation (Carey, 1967; Rice, 1982). It points to ways of inducing workers to increase their productivity voluntarily, irrespective of increases in economic return to workers. In other words, subtle manipulation of a worker's environment replaces direct coercion through a hierarchy of authority, but the goal is still the same: to further the interests of management by getting more productivity from workers.

In the 1980s and 1990s, many corporations in the United States tried to introduce elements of the human relations model into work settings (Waldman, 1987). They hired consultants to run programs to provide attitudinal training and changes in values among their employees. The idea was to change the corporate culture from a highly bureaucratic one to one that emphasized partnership between management and employee, cooperation, teamwork, and company loyalty. This *transformation work* presumably represented a new ideology of management. However, Harley Shaiken, a professor of work and technology, is skeptical that anything substantially new has developed: "Unfortunately, most of the so-called transformation work today is really just a sub-stitute for giving workers real autonomy and responsibility" (quoted in Waldman, 1987, p. 1). At one insurance company, a training program was followed by a 20 percent increase in work quotas, and employees who objected were fired. The goal of most of these programs is simple: to increase corporate productivity by changing worker apathy into complaisance or corporate loyalty.

The Interactionist Perspective

Interactionists tend to shift the focus from formal structure and hierarchy in organizations to informal structure (Day & Day, 1977; Fine, 1984; Strauss, Fagerhaugh, Suczek, & Wiener, 1985). From this perspective, formal organizations are not rigid, static structures emphasizing only rationality and efficiency. Rather, they constitute a *negotiated order*, which is created out of the formal structure through the social interaction prescribed by the informal structure. The formal structure is important, but it comes to life only as people interact with one another. People with varying amounts of power and resources and with various characteristics "negotiate" with one another regarding what is acceptable and appropriate organizational behavior. Models of formal organizations would include this informal structure because it is an essential element in understanding how effectively an organization achieves its goals. The interactionist perspective, when taken in conjunction with the functional and conflict views, rounds out an understanding of formal organizations.

The Future of Bureaucracy

You should be able to explain the potential dangers of the bureaucratic tendency toward oligarchy and discuss possible future trends in bureaucracy.

Bureaucracy and Oligarchy

What lies in store for the future? It seems reasonable to assume that large bureaucratic organizations are here to stay and will continue to flood our lives with secondary relationships. Industrial societies are sufficiently large and technologically complex that such organizations appear to be

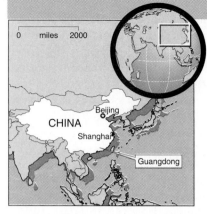

THER WORLDS, *Other Ways*

CHINA: CULTURAL VALUES AND GROUP BEHAVIOR—SOCIAL LOAFING IN ORGANIZATIONS

The value system of China has traditionally emphasized a collectivist orientation, which still persists today (Hofstede, 1980; Li, 1978). Collectivism is a set of values that places more emphasis on the group and group goals than on the individual. It discourages individual achievement and the advancement of self-interest, especially when these come in conflict with group needs. Chinese society focuses on collective action and social interests rather than personal goals. Although the coming of communism to China in 1949 may have given additional emphasis to this value orientation, collectivism predates the Communist Revolution and finds expression in Confucian beliefs about uprightness, duty, and obligation that go back thousands of years. It leads people to act on the basis of what best serves their in-group and to condemn those who pursue their own personal interests. In a collectivist environment, a major force is cooperation rather than competition.

This collectivist orientation in China is quite at odds with the individualistic, competitive values of the United States, where people emphasize self-sufficiency, control, and pursuit of personal goals that may clash with group goals. With these widely varying cultural orientations, it should not be surprising that people in China and the United States respond quite differently to some of the group and organizational processes discussed in this chapter. One impact these values have is on how well people work in groups—whether they work hard to achieve the goals of the group or take it easy and let others do the work. The term *social loafing* refers to the tendency for people in groups to put out less effort to achieve goals than when working alone (Latane, Williams, & Harkins, 1979). When in a group, the social-loafing attitude is: "I can coast and others will take up the slack and do the work."

Social loafing is more likely to occur in large groups and situations where people are not held accountable for their individual tasks. Cultural orientation also affects social loafing. A study was done of the work of managerial trainees in a variety of manu-

inevitable. Need we be concerned about this trend? There appear to be some potential dangers associated with bureaucracies that are especially chilling in democratic societies. In 1915, Robert Michels pointed out that bureaucracies display a tendency toward **oligarchy:** *Power tends to become concentrated in the hands of a few people at the top of organizations.* Michels referred to this tendency as the *iron law of oligarchy.* As Michels put it: "Who says organization, says oligarchy" (Michels, 1915/1966, p. 256). As such organizations become more powerful, people are in danger of losing more and more control over events in their daily lives, of finding themselves powerless and dominated by a few individuals they do not even know.

For Michels, the iron law of oligarchy derives from three elements of organizations. First, to operate effectively, any large organization must develop mechanisms for coping with administrative and decision-making problems, and it is more efficient if only a few people are responsible for this function. Spreading authority over a large number of people can cause uncertainties about who is empowered to do what and conflicts over incompatible decisions. Second, those who emerge as leaders in organizations tend to be adept at influencing and controlling members, and they can use the resources of the organization to maintain their position. They can, for example, place loyal followers into strategic positions in organizational

facturing and service organizations in Guangzhou, China, and in the United States (Earley, 1989). Social loafing was found among the workers in the United States but not among the Chinese workers. In the United States, workers put out more effort when working alone toward a goal than when working in a group. In China, it was the reverse. The collective ethic in China leads workers to place group goals ahead of their own personal interests. They value the group goals and are at least as willing to work toward the group goals as toward their own personal goals. They seem to gain satisfaction from group accomplishments. In addition, Chinese workers expect other workers to make contributions rather than to loaf, and they are willing to work without worrying that others will take advantage of them by loafing. By contrast, workers in the United States place more value on individual accomplishments and rewards. When placed in a group, they loaf when someone else will take up the slack and work to achieve the group goals. And workers in the United States, unlike those in China, assume that other workers will loaf, and thus they will be taken advantage of if they do not loaf.

The collective orientation in Chinese culture has other implications for group processes. There is evidence, for example, that Chinese internalize stronger conformist values than do people in the United States and that they are socialized to place greater value on unity and cooperation in groups and to avoid anger and hostility toward group members. The Chinese also seem to place more value on strong leadership in groups and to see that leadership as legitimate and essential to group accomplishments (Hofstede, 1980; Wilson, 1977).

These cultural differences have important implications for the policies of organizations and agencies. For example, work groups that depend on cooperation and that do not provide rewards for individual accomplishments may enhance performance in collectivist cultures such as China and Japan. The same programs, however, may reduce productivity because of social loafing if implemented unchanged in the United States. The way people respond to the same group structures, such as leadership, and the same group processes, such as work groups, depends on the cultural orientation of the people involved.

administration. Finally, in many organizations, most rank-and-file members do not have the time, energy, resources, or desire to contest the power of the leadership.

In many ways, Michels's argument is persuasive. We can plainly see that, in many large U.S. organizations, such as Exxon or IBM, control and decision making are concentrated among a few people at the top. In addition, political decisions are concentrated in the hands of a relatively few powerful politicians at the state and national levels. Because democracy presumably rests on the consent of the governed, and because individual freedom and autonomy are basic values in the United States, oligarchical organizations and gov-

ernments pose a potential threat. Yet, the conflict perspective informs us that there are social mechanisms that can counter the tendency toward oligarchy. Namely, people can form interest groups and join organizations that can serve as countervailing forces to the leaders of political or organizational hierarchies. Such civic engagement involves average citizens being active in groups that connect people with the social and political life of their communities and that help shape the economic, political, and legal structures of those communities. This has been done effectively by the civil rights movement a few decades ago and by the environmental movement today. Both groups have been able to change the direction of some of the policies of oligarchical organizations in dramatic ways.

It is also important to remember that in a democracy, authority and power require the consent, or at least the acquiescence, of the governed. Leaders can maintain their power only if the membership accedes to their leadership. Thus even oligarchical leaders must be somewhat responsive to the members of a particular organization. For example, even though power and control are concentrated in the hands of a few within many large organizations in the United States, many stockholders are involved, and if all of them decide to take their money elsewhere, the leadership structure will crumble.

Finally, bureaucratic organizations can be designed to reduce oligarchical tendencies. Power and control can be dispersed among a number of semiautonomous groups to keep one from gaining total dominance over the others (Olsen, 1978). This *balancing of power* can be seen in the structure of many colleges and universities. Although the administration has a great deal of decision-making authority, this power is balanced by a board of trustees or board of control (which is typically composed of community members) and faculty groups (such as an academic senate) that maintain some control over curriculum-related decisions.

Predictably, there is no ultimate solution to the problem of oligarchy. Bureaucracies present a formidable test of democratic principles, most of which were formed in an era of small communities and town hall meetings, long before the appearance of the huge organizations so common today. At the same time, as Michels pointed out, bureaucracies are beneficial in structuring an enormous social organization, and modern societies would be hard-pressed to maintain their current lifestyle without them. The challenge, then, is to ensure that the balance of power does not slip too far toward oligarchy. In this quest, sociological knowledge of groups and organizations can be extremely helpful in seeking and achieving the proper balance. These issues will be explored in more depth in Chapter 13.

Limits to Bureaucracy

Although large organizational and bureaucratic structures are likely to be central features of mod-ern life in the future, are there limits to how far their reach will extend? Are there trends in the opposite direction? Answers to these questions are both controversial and speculative, but some thoughts can be offered (Bartos, 1996). First of all, the U.S. economy is shifting from an industrial economy based on the production of goods to an economy that emphasizes service, information, and consumption. (See Chapters 2 and 15.) Along with this change has come a shift from manual labor jobs that require little more than muscle power to more professional occupations that require intellectual skills and high levels of education. Such occupations, including those of doctors, teachers, scientists, lawyers, and social workers, are less likely to involve complete dependence on highly bureaucratic organization. These professionals do at least some of their work in what are called *professional organizations* or *postentrepreneurial organizations,* which are smaller, are less hierarchical, and have fewer rules and procedures (Champion, 1975; Kanter, 1989). Professionals have more autonomy in when, where, and how they do their work and are more likely to treat coworkers as equals. In professional organizations, supervisors are more likely to serve as coordinators who make materials and resources available for other professionals to do their work. Organizations in a service economy are still bureaucratic to a degree, but the nature of the work being done by some of them benefits from a more professional, less hierarchical emphasis. That is not true of all of them, however. Even in the service and educational industries, workers who are doing manual labor work still tend to be in highly bureaucratic environments. So, the shift to a service and information economy may produce changes in some employees' lives, but those whose jobs involve well-structured and repetitive tasks that can be rationalized will likely continue to work in highly bureaucratic settings.

Another development that may have implications for bureaucratization and centralization is the revolution in computer technology and communications. The growing availability of personal computers, facsimile machines, modems, and communications satellites points to the possibility of decentralizing the workplace and removing people from some of the bureaucratic structures. In 1980 the futurist Alvin Toffler coined the phrase *electronic cottage* to describe the workplace that such technologies would make possible. People could work in their homes, linked to other people and work settings through fiber optic cables and radio signals. Professors' lectures could be projected to many distant settings, and secretaries could work at home and send their products out over telephone lines or through the mail on computer disc. Today, business executives in many locations hold meetings through televised conference calls. Toffler believed that technology would enable many more people to become self-employed and allow others to work much more independently of bureaucratic organizations.

Some of Toffler's projections have come true, with 39 million Americans working at home (Calem, 1993). Electronic technology has been a boon, especially for people who can do their work alone (for example, writers or other creative people) and for those who are independently employed and do not need a large office in which to meet and work with clients. Of those who work at home, 60 percent are self-employed. Another one-fifth are people who take work home from the office after hours, and 16 percent are *telecommuters,* employees whose bosses allow them to work at home instead of the office at least one day of the week.

These numbers, along with other research, tell us a couple of things about Toffler's vision of the impact of computer and telecommunications technology on work (Volti, 1988; Wellman et al., 1996). First, although many people do work at home, a good number of them are still part of a bureaucratic organization. Although physically separated from others in the bureaucracy, these home workers must still interact with office people and are constrained by the rules of the bureaucracy. Second, the people who benefit most from this trend are professionals and creative people because their tasks can best be done in non-bureaucratic settings. These workers are least likely to be in highly bureaucratic settings anyway. Third, some home workers gain little advantage, other than convenience, from working at home: They still do low-paying, boring, repetitive work for large corporations. Some such workers, for example, input information from insurance policies and claims reports into computer files for insurance companies. Many such workers are women

with young children at home. They often work on a piece-rate basis and are deprived of the opportunity for unionization and company-supplied health and retirement benefits. The irony in their situation is that such home-based work was banned in many industries, such as textiles, early in the twentieth century because it promoted the exploitation of workers. Computer technology seems to be expanding such exploitive workplace environments again. In fact, many labor unions have pushed for extending bans on such work. As one union spokesperson put it: "If history is any guide, we can say with certainty that abuse of electronic homeworkers is inevitable. . . . An early ban would try to prevent a repeat of past experiences in a new guise" (quoted in Volti, p. 127).

As with so many things, the impact of these new technologies will be complicated. Some groups will benefit while others will definitely be hurt. Groups that benefit will be those with the educational credentials or other resources that will enable them to take advantage of changing conditions. Groups without significant resources could find themselves worse off. Furthermore, these changes may not produce a significant overall limitation on bureaucracies in modern societies as a whole, although they will have an impact on which people will be affected by bureaucracies and in what form these people will be affected.

Mass Media: Impact on Groups and Organizations

Much of this chapter is about how people interact with one another in groups and organizations. The modern technologies of communication have pervasive and profound impacts on these groups and organizations and people's social interaction in them. This is true of television, radio, and the print media as well as the emerging forms of the Internet and the World Wide Web (the Net).

One impact of such technologies is that they can increase tendencies for people to withdraw from many group involvements into the more private realms of home and family. The preceding discussion of oligarchy suggests that the impact of oligarchy on organizations and on society could be reduced by people joining interest groups and forming organizations that enhance civic participation—citizens actively shaping the social and political lives of their communities. Yet, evidence has emerged in the past few decades that the extent of such civic engagement is declining in the United States (Putnam, 1996). Since the 1950s, the amount of time that people spend visiting neighbors and engaging in informal socializing has declined significantly. In addition, memberships in clubs and voluntary organizations, such as the PTA, the League of Women Voters, or a labor union, have dropped by one-half. Between 1900 and 1950, the United States was a nation of "joiners"; since then, people have fled to more personal and familial pursuits.

One of the causes of this transition has probably been television: As the number of households with a television has steadily increased from less than 10 percent in 1950 to virtually all households today (see Figure 3.3), people have steadily withdrawn from civic involvement outside the home, and leisure time has become primarily private. Today, one need not go outside and be with others in order to be entertained. In fact, since most households have multiple television sets, family members need not even interact with one another; they can be entertained separately. In addition, research shows that people who watch more television join fewer groups and engage in less civic involvement than do those who watch less television (Putnam, 1996). Such privatization of social life comes at the expense of nearly every other type of group activity outside the home. The disturbing element of this trend is that it is through "joining"—coming together with others in various groups and organizations—that people can resist and change the direction of political and economic oligarchies. Such joining is one of the key elements of democratic expression, and the ability of citizens to influence oligarchies suffers in its absence.

Another impact of modern communications technologies on social interaction in groups is that people's contacts with others become more passive and secondary in nature. Television and radio audiences passively receive messages. Social interaction on the Internet or the World Wide Web is more active but still secondary in nature: People's interaction is often specialized and narrowly focused, revolving around particular hobbies, personal interests, or job-related needs on various newsnets, lists, or chat rooms (Wellman et al., 1996). In addition, interaction on the Net involves less "social presence" than does face-to-face social interaction: Many of the social cues that guide our interactions with others, such as facial expressions, vocal intonations, or body postures, are missing. This may make it more difficult for people to develop full primary relationships until they have a face-to-face meeting (which, of course, does sometimes follow the development of a relationship on the Net). On the other hand, less social presence may free people from being treated badly or unequally because of their gender, race, or physical characteristics. This may produce more egalitarian social contacts than occur when people are aware of all these social characteristics in face-to-face contact (Wellman et al.).

Some significant differences can be found between the conventional media of television and print and the emerging communications technology of the Net. As determined by the technology involved, the sender of messages in conventional media is typically a large formal organization, such as a commercial business or a government agency. This is so because only such large organizations have the resources to afford the equipment required to communicate through these media. The audiences for messages are anonymous to one another, and the communication is largely unidirectional, with a passive audience who can shape media content only indirectly. Furthermore, the message is not tailored to particular individuals and their reactions; the mass audience receives one standardized message. With this format, conventional media technologies enable those who control them, such as large corporations or powerful political groups, an opportunity to manipulate the attitudes, perceptions, and behaviors of the audience.

The rapidly emerging Net, on the other hand, has some strikingly different characteristics. For one thing, large corporations and organizations do not control the messages sent over the Net; in fact, there is no passive audience, since the technology of the Net is inherently interactive. Thus, a true culture emerges on the Net, with the development of norms to guide behavior and a specialized argot to enhance communication. Some of the argot has developed to describe behaviors on the Net, such as *spam* (indiscriminately sending messages to many addresses on the Net) and *flame* (a hostile and aggressive response to someone on the Net); some of the argot describes the computer and telecommunications technology on which the Net rests, such as *baud rates* or *nodes*. Life on the Net involves a true subculture, as described in Chapter 2: a group that shares some of the values and norms of the larger culture of which it is a part, such as U.S. culture, while having some values and norms that are distinctly its own. Such subcultural emergence does not occur with conventional media because the audience cannot participate directly in the interaction out of which subcultures emerge.

Because the Net is so accessible and interactive, some commentators see it as an empowering technology, possibly overcoming the privatizing tendencies of conventional media and reversing the decline in civic engagement and group involvement. Individuals can come into contact with a wide array of groups and organizations, or they can use the technology of the Net to form new organizations and attract and communicate directly with a large audience of people with similar interests. If this occurs, then the technology of the Net may erode the monopoly of communications that those at the top of oligarchies have previously had. In the past, most people depended on television, newspapers, and magazines for information about events and opinions, and those same people had limited opportunities to communicate their opinions and positions with others. The technology of the Net means that thousands of sources of information and opinion are instantaneously available, and each recipient of messages can also create and send messages to those thousands of people.

Developments in the field of computers and telecommunications are so new that sociologists cannot be sure that what has just been said about the impact of the Net will continue to hold true. In addition, changes occur so rapidly that it is almost foolhardy to attempt to predict the future. One technology consultant, for example, predicts that such modern technologies as the television and the telephone are already obsolete and will soon be replaced by *telecomputers* that perform the functions of these old instruments and much more (Gilder, 1993). In fact, he predicts that the terms *telephone* and *television* will soon sound as quaint and old-fashioned as *icebox* and *horseless carriage*. The technology is now available to transmit huge amounts of information and to send it interactively; we also have computers that can store and process masses of data. The television, on the other hand, is a passive receptacle into which networks send programs at prearranged times. The telecomputer of the future will be an interactive instrument that will connect its user with thousands of telecomputers in a web of information exchange around the world. The user would be able to connect with the computer of a coworker in another part of the city or nation, or with the computer of a library, movie storage center, art museum, or university to access a book, movie, art exhibit, or university lecture—to be viewed at leisure or stored for later viewing. No longer will it be necessary to follow a television schedule or go to the prearranged, 7:00 showing of a new movie release. In fact, television channels may become a thing of the past, as people will access thousands of databases rather than turn the channel. In addition, the telecomputers of the future not only will receive, but also will send: completed work to a coworker, thoughts and ideas to a global chat room on the Internet, or a creative work of art or fiction to those who request it. The same instrument will also be used to pay bills, order airline tickets, and regulate the furnace in the home. Some people may still choose at times to do things the old way, but no longer will it be necessitated by the technology of the passive television appliance. What is still uncertain is how groups, organizations, and tendencies toward oligarchy will be affected in this world of global telecommunications. We cannot be sure that the decentralized, interactive Net of the 1990s will have the same character in the decades to come.

Summary

1. Five types of groups are of frequent interest to sociologists: primary groups, secondary groups, in-groups, out-groups, and reference groups. Social groups are distinct from collectivities, such as social categories and aggregates.

2. Statuses and roles provide the basis for the social structure and help coordinate the behavior of group members. Structure and coordination contribute to the stability of social interaction in groups. One of the most important statuses in groups is that of leader.

3. Group decisions on judgmental issues are characterized by a phenomenon known as *group polarization*—originally identified as a *risky shift*. The term *groupthink* refers to tendencies in highly cohesive groups toward encouraging unanimity of opinion and consensus at the expense of critical abilities and the realistic appraisal of alternatives.

4. Certain types of secondary groups are known as *formal organizations*, which are large special purpose groups that are explicitly designed to achieve specific goals. The formal organizations that dominate modern societies are called *bureaucracies*.

5. Bureaucracies have been criticized for their impersonality, and out of this critique has emerged the human relations approach, which is based on the assumption that the social, psychological, and physical needs of people who work in organizations must be considered in order for organizations to be productive and efficient.

6. All organizations develop some type of informal structure, referring to personal relationships that are guided by norms and rituals that emerge separately from the formal rules and regulations of the organization.

7. Each sociological perspective offers some special insight into organizations and how they operate. Functionalists stress how organizations operate to coordinate people's behavior and help them achieve complex and difficult goals efficiently. The conflict perspective sees organizations as mechanisms of social control and coercion. Interactionists stress the importance of the informal structure and a negotiated order in organizations.

8. Bureaucracies display a tendency toward oligarchy. Yet there are also forces in modern societies that counter this tendency and work toward democratization and the decentralization of power in societies and organizations. The mass media and modern technologies of communication also have wide ramifications for groups and organizations, displaying tendencies toward the concentration of control but also toward decentralization and the empowerment of the average citizen.

STUDY *and* Review

Key Terms

bureaucracy

expressive roles

formal organization

group cohesion

group polarization

groupthink

in-group

instrumental roles

leadership

oligarchy

out-group

primary group

reference group

relationship-oriented roles

secondary group

socioemotional roles

task roles

Multiple-Choice Questions

1. Which of the following types of groups has a major function of providing people with a secure refuge in which they can act without fear of ridicule or rejection?
   a. Secondary groups.
   b. Primary groups.
   c. Reference groups.
   d. Social categories.

2. Reference groups most clearly do which of the following?
   a. Produce a sense of loyalty or "we" feeling.
   b. Make for task-oriented, impersonal exchanges between people.

c. Involve personal, intimate, and nonspecialized relationships between people.

d. Serve as standards for people to evaluate their own attitudes and behaviors.

3. Which of the following statements is true about leadership in groups?

a. Nondirective leaders produce more positive feelings toward the group among group members than do directive leaders.

b. Nondirective leaders produce more tension in the group than do directive leaders.

c. Nondirective leaders encourage higher group productivity than do directive leaders.

d. Laissez-faire leaders are more directive than are autocratic leaders.

4. Groups are superior to individuals in making decisions in all of the following ways *except*

a. groups make speedier decisions.

b. groups come up with a wider range of solutions to problems.

c. groups come up with better solutions to problems.

d. groups come up with more accurate solutions to problems.

5. According to research, the pressure toward groupthink is especially strong in

a. social collectivities.

b. out-groups.

c. highly cohesive groups.

d. groups with laissez-faire leaders.

e. groups during group polarization.

6. Research by sociologists during World War II has concluded that German soldiers fought well under adverse conditions because

a. the Germans had superior equipment.

b. the Germans felt loyalty toward others in their military unit.

c. the Germans were strongly committed to the Nazi ideology.

d. the Germans had strong ties to their families.

7. Which of the following is true of bureaucratic organizations?

a. They are highly flexible and adaptive.

b. They tend to encourage creativity and innovation.

c. They are efficient at doing well-structured tasks.

d. They are unstable organizations.

8. In contrast with organizations based on the bureaucratic model, organizations based on the human relations model tend to

a. place more stress on impartiality.

b. have a more rigid and extensive hierarchy of authority.

c. stress authoritative management.

d. stress more participative management.

9. Which of the following perspectives would be most likely to view conflict as an unwanted element in an organization?

a. The functionalist perspective.

b. The conflict perspective.

c. The interactionist perspective.

d. The negotiated order perspective.

10. According to Robert Michels, bureaucracies display a tendency toward

a. informality.

b. oligarchy.

c. cohesiveness.

d. groupthink.

e. social loafing.

True/False Questions

1. A corporate business office would be more likely to be a secondary group than would a college hockey team.

2. People in the United States see friendships as being more permanent than do people in Japan.

3. Sociologists would consider *all Japanese Americans* to constitute a social category.

4. A professor lecturing on U.S. history to a class of students would be performing an instrumental role rather than an expressive role.

5. Research has found that, on the whole, people in groups tend to make less risky and daring choices than they would if acting individually.

6. Bureaucracies first emerged in the industrial societies of the nineteenth century.

7. Parkinson's Law refers to the fact that groupthink tends to occur in cohesive groups.

8. The informal structure of organizations helps people protect themselves against what they perceive as unreasonable demands of the organization.

9. The collective orientation in China results in less social loafing than in the United States.

10. From the interactionist perspective, formal organizations can be considered a *negotiated order*.

Fill-In Questions

1. Groups that focus on task-oriented, impersonal, and specialized ties between people are called _____ groups.

2. Sociologists would call all of the people riding on the same subway train one morning _____ .

3. A store manager who throws a party for her employees so that they can relax and enjoy themselves is performing a(n) _____ role.

4. Leaders who are thoroughly directive, dictating all actions and techniques to be used in achieving group goals, are called _____ leaders.

5. _____ refers to a situation in which people have been trained so completely to follow bureaucratic rules that they are unable to act independently or innovatively.

6. The _____ states that, in a bureaucracy, people tend to rise to their level of incompetence.

7. In a(n) _____ , sociologists use their theories and methods to assess how well an organization operates and how its performance can be improved.

8. The _____ perspective argues that organizations are systems of interrelated parts designed to achieve goals efficiently and productively.

9. _____ refers to a tendency for people in groups to put out less effort to achieve goals than when working alone.

10. Robert Michels is quoted as saying, "Who says organization, says _____ ."

Matching Questions

_____ 1. group polarization
_____ 2. aggregate
_____ 3. task roles
_____ 4. Max Weber
_____ 5. *binging* and *scrounging*
_____ 6. group cohesion
_____ 7. Robert Michels
_____ 8. standard for evaluation
_____ 9. primary group
_____ 10. laissez-faire leader

A. bureaucracy
B. people riding in the same subway car
C. risky shift
D. oligarchy
E. behaviors that are part of the informal structure of organizations
F. reference group
G. "staying together" power
H. nondirective leader
I. instrumental roles
J. family

Essay Questions

1. This chapter discusses five different types of social groups. Define each one and describe what functions it performs. Give an example of each.

2. What are social collectivities and how do they differ from social groups? Define two types of social collectivities and give an example of each.

3. Describe the social meanings associated with friendship in the United States and Japan. How are they similar and how do they differ?

4. Describe the social structure of groups, including in your answer a discussion of status and role.

5. What is groupthink? When is it likely to occur? What are its consequences?

6. What are the characteristics of the bureaucratic model of organizations as described by Max Weber?

7. What are the advantages and disadvantages of a bureaucratic form of organization?

8. Describe the human relations approach to formal organizations. How does it differ from the bureaucratic approach?

9. Briefly discuss the functionalist, conflict, and interactionist perspectives on organizations. Show how they differ from one another.

10. Will there be more bureaucracy in our lives in the future or less? Describe the trends that point in each direction.

Answers

Multiple-Choice
1. B; **2.** D; **3.** A; **4.** A; **5.** C; **6.** B; **7.** C; **8.** D;
9. A; **10.** B

True/False
1. T; **2.** F; **3.** T; **4.** T; **5.** F; **6.** F; **7.** F; **8.** T;
9. T; **10.** T

Fill-In
1. secondary
2. an aggregate
3. socioemotional, expressive, relationship-oriented
4. autocratic
5. trained incapacity
6. Peter Principle
7. organizational diagnosis
8. functionalist
9. social loafing
10. oligarchy

Matching
1. C; **2.** B; **3.** I; **4.** A; **5.** E; **6.** G; **7.** D; **8.** F;
9. J; **10.** H

For Further Reading

Benveniste, Guy. (1987). *Professionalizing the organization: Reducing bureaucracy to enhance effectiveness.* San Francisco: Jossey-Bass. This book deals with the problems that the bureaucratic model poses for contemporary organizations. It will be especially helpful to students who are interested in learning more about alternatives to the bureaucratic model of governance in complex organizations.

Berger, Peter, Berger, Brigitte, & Kellner, Hansfried. (1979). *The homeless mind: Modernization and consciousness.* New York: Vintage. This enjoyable little book describes how living in a bureaucratic society affects our consciousness and our way of thinking—often in ways we would not imagine.

Bernhard, Gary J., & Glantz, Kalman. (1992). *Staying human in the organization: Our biological heritage and the workplace.* Westport, CT: Praeger. This is a stimulating and entertaining book that argues that humans by nature work better in small groups than in large organizations. The authors propose some ways workers in organizations can adapt.

Goffman, Erving. (1961). *Asylums.* Garden City, NY: Anchor/Doubleday. Although three decades old, this book remains one of the seminal investigations of the impact of formal organizations on behavior and identity. Goffman, now deceased, was probably one of the most sensitive sociological observers of the human scene.

Jankowski, Martin Sanchez. (1991). *Islands in the street: Gangs and American urban society.* Berkeley: University of California Press. This book is an interesting study of gangs, but it also involves an analysis of the organizational aspects of gang life. It provides another view on group organization like the one Whyte offered of the Norton Street Gang.

Johnson, David W., & Johnson, Frank P. (1997). *Joining together* (6th ed.). Boston: Allyn & Bacon. This book is a good summary of the theory and research on how groups work effectively. It is a good review of group structure and process.

Lorsch, Jay W. (ed.). (1987). *Handbook of organizational behavior.* Englewood Cliffs, NJ: Prentice Hall. This handbook is designed to provide the reader with a concise overview of what is known in the field of organizational behavior. The focus is on how people actually behave in organizations and why.

Martin, Joanne. (1992). *Cultures in organizations: Three perspectives.* New York: Oxford University Press. This book recognizes that culture—in the form of values, norms, ritual, language, and the like—exists in organizations. The author shows how to do a cultural analysis of organizations and what some of the implications of such analysis are.

Rawlins, William K. (1992). *Friendship matters: Communication, dialectics, and the life course.* New York: Aldine de Gruyter. This fascinating book summarizes research on how friendships—a key primary group in most people's lives—develop and change from childhood into old age. Gender differences are discussed throughout.

Sieber, Timothy, & Gordon, Andrew J. (eds.). (1981). *Children and their organizations: Investigations in American culture.* Boston: G. K. Hall. Combining the analysis in Chapters 3 and 4, this book analyzes the formal organizations that serve and socialize children: elementary and junior high schools, summer camps, 4-H Clubs, drug abuse programs, pediatric clinics, and so on. The authors show how these organizations teach children about U.S. culture, sometimes including aspects of it that their parents may not want them to learn.

Sklar, Leslie. (1991). *Sociology of the global system.* London: Harvester Wheatsheaf. This book analyzes how transnational corporations are transforming the world and some of its implications. These are the forces affecting the Yanomamo in Brazil.

FIVE *Deviance, Crime, and Social Control*

CHAPTER

Singapore is a tiny nation of about three million people at the southern tip of the Malay Peninsula (Milne & Mauzy, 1990). It is a former British colony that gained full independence in 1965. Most of its citizens are ethnic Chinese, but 15 percent are Malay and 7 percent are Indian. It is capitalist, urban, industrialized, and quite affluent, with a per capita annual income about equal to that in the United States. Although Singapore is economically similar to the United States, it is socially and politically quite different. In fact, socially and politically, it has been referred to as a *soft authoritarianism* because of the extensive efforts its leaders make to control people's personal and political behavior (Branegan, 1993).

Singaporean officials would like to see their people become more courteous, industrious, and healthier as well as more patriotic (Wilkinson, 1988). They hope to achieve this improvement through a combination of education, suggestion, and encouragement along with the iron fist of the law when necessary. For example, the government has strong powers to stifle political dissent, including a law that enables authorities to detain people without trial. Before they are released, political dissenters must make a public confession. The government also sharply restricts statements that might cause religious or racial tension and allows only token political opposition, with the government owning television stations and indirectly controlling the press. Radio, television, and newspapers are considered propaganda outlets for the government, and censorship of and outright bans on some magazines are common.

The government also has some ideas about how proper breeding can create a superior people in Singapore, so they encourage well-educated and successful people to have many children. Such people receive tax credits if they have more than three children, and some people receive a tax cut if they acquire more education. Through such policies, the Singaporean government actively encourages achievement and initiative in its citizens. The government also sponsors many educational programs focused on encouraging cohesiveness among different social and ethnic groups and discouraging antisocial behaviors, such as littering or spitting on the street.

The social-control efforts extend into realms that leave many people shaking their heads and wondering about the reasonableness of it all. There are stiff penalties for "antisocial" behaviors such as littering ($625 fine), failing to flush a public toilet ($94), and eating on a subway ($312). Chewing gum has been outlawed, and smoking in many public places is illegal. Some drug traffickers are hanged, and criminals can be subject to a severe whipping with a cane. In general, the police and judiciary have extensive powers over suspects and criminals in terms of detention. In the past, males with long hair below their collars have been detained and given haircuts.

How do Singaporeans react to the soft authoritarianism of their rulers? Many think that a lot of it is silly or heavy-handed, but most acquiesce and many believe it to be beneficial. Their view becomes more understandable when we look more closely at Singaporean society and culture. Singapore is a nation of immigrants coming mostly from poor and unstable countries. With this history, the residents place great value on stability and affluence. There may be too many controls in Singapore, but people also have a comfortable life without political and social chaos. In light of this immigrant background, some of the social-control efforts are focused on engendering a sense of common nationhood among Singaporeans. Officials are concerned that some immigrants are mostly devoted to seeking their fortune in Singapore rather than to the nation itself. Officials blame a lot of what they perceive as problems on what they call "Western values," such as individualism, permissiveness, and decadence. They wish to encourage "Asian values," which center on honesty, respect for elders and authority, and devotion to family and nation. These Asian values derive from traditional Chinese values, especially the Confucian teachings regarding obedience to established authority.

This description of Singapore centers around the core issues of this chapter: deviance, crime, and social control. Sociologists define **deviance** as *behaviors or characteristics that violate important group norms and as a consequence are reacted to with social disapproval.* Much of the focus in earlier chapters was on the degree to which people conform to cultural values and group norms that are approved by a particular group. Sociologists also recognize, however, that deviance, or socially *disapproved* behavior, is common in society. Sociology tries to understand and explain deviant behavior as well as conforming behavior. Sociology also investigates the mechanisms of social control that groups and society use to bring deviants into line. A key element of the sociological approach to deviance is that deviance is a function of the judgments of particular groups. Behaviors are deviant *because they are so defined by a particular group.* Authorities in Singapore defined having long hair or failing to flush a toilet as deviant, whereas the same actions in another society might be socially acceptable. This difference points once again to the diversity in human societies and to the relative nature of deviance.

Myths & FACTS

ABOUT DEVIANCE AND CRIME

Myth There is a clear line between the "criminal element" in society and the law-abiding and respectable people. If we could put that criminal element behind bars, the crime problem would be solved.

FACT Once again, social reality is far more complex than many commonsense beliefs would have it. It turns out that many crimes are committed by people who are otherwise considered quite respectable. For example, who commits vandalism? Teenage punks? Hostile and alienated losers? The social psychologist Philip Zimbardo conducted an intriguing study of people who vandalize automobiles in New York (Zimbardo, 1973). After seeing many stripped and battered automobiles on his way to work, he decided to observe who the vandals were. He bought an old car, left it on a street near New York University, and watched from a hidden location. Within ten minutes, the first vandals appeared: a father, mother, and their

eight-year-old son! The mother served as lookout while the father and son removed the battery and radiator. Later, another vandal was pushing an infant in a baby carriage. There followed a virtual parade of people who removed everything of value from the car and then began battering what was left. These vandals were often well dressed and chatted amiably with passersby as they toiled. Zimbardo's research leads to the conclusion that many criminals not only appear quite respectable but also probably consider themselves quite law-abiding.

Myth The most serious drug problem that confronts the United States is the flow of heroin, cocaine, and marijuana across its borders and into its cities.

FACT In terms of the number of people affected and the economic costs to society, most specialists on drug problems consider alcohol abuse to be the most severe drug problem in the United States.

The Relativity of Deviance

You should be able to describe the sociological perspective on deviance and explain how it differs from the absolute and statistical views.

Some people approach deviance in an *absolute* way, judging certain behaviors and characteristics to be good or bad and right or wrong by comparing them to some fixed standards. Religious views of deviance, for example, often reflect this approach, with some divinely revealed truths representing the standard. Others adopt a *statistical* view of deviance: Deviance involves a departure from an established average. Thus, a man who is seven feet tall could be considered deviant from this perspective, because the average height of most males is closer to five feet ten inches. Likewise, a heroin addict would be deviant because most people are not heroin addicts.

Sociologists, however, find neither the absolute nor the statistical views to be very useful because they cannot explain the enormous variety in people's definitions of deviance. In part, what is considered deviant depends on the culture in which it occurs. For example, in societies such as the Inuit (Eskimo) in the Arctic or the Murngin in Australia, a form of geronticide, or killing the elderly, was once practiced. If food was scarce and the band needed to move quickly to a new territory, the group would abandon older people to starvation, especially if they were sick and a burden on the others in the group (Harris, 1977). Although acceptable to the Inuit or Murngin, such practices would be considered highly deviant in most modern cultures.

Even within a single culture, there is considerable variation from one group to another in what is considered deviant. Some people in the United States, for example, view homosexuality as an acceptable form of sexual expression, whereas others are repelled by it. In addition to differences between cultures and subcultures, definitions of deviance also vary from one situation to another. It is acceptable, for example, to remove one's clothing in a physician's examination room, but the same action in a college classroom would be considered highly deviant.

To explain this variety, sociologists maintain that deviance is *relative,* or based on the social definitions of some group. Behaviors or characteristics can be considered deviant only within the context of the norms and values of a particular culture, subculture, or group. In fact, deviance is not inherent in *any* behavior or characteristic; rather, it arises from the relationship between a behavior and the social definition of that behavior by some group. As one sociologist put it, "Deviance, like beauty, is in the eyes of the beholder" (Simmons, 1969, p. 4). Most human actions have been defined as deviant by some group at some time, and most of us have engaged in some of these deviant actions, although we may not have defined them as deviant ourselves. But deviance refers not only to violating some rules or norms; in addition, there must be some *stigma,* or mark of disgrace, attached to the violation that sets the deviant apart from others (Goffman, 1963; Jones et al., 1984).

The following section will briefly review some nonsociological explanations of deviance and then present the major sociological approaches to deviance. Underlying these sociological explanations is the idea that deviance is relative.

Explanations of Deviance

You should be able to discuss the major explanations of deviance, including biological and psychological perspectives, as well as the three sociological perspectives on deviance.

Like all behavior, deviance is complex, and many people find it hard to understand. In fact, because deviance is often viewed as threatening or repugnant, it may be one of the more difficult forms of human behavior for people to comprehend, and people are often tempted to settle for overly simple explanations. To appreciate the complexity of deviance and crime, familiarity with nonsociological as well as sociological approaches to the issue is essential.

Nonsociological Approaches

Over the years, a variety of *biological approaches* to deviance have both gained and lost popularity, and most have proven of little value in explaining deviance. Biological approaches view deviance as arising, at least in part, from people's physical or biological makeup (Fishbein, 1990). For example, Cesare Lombroso (1911), an Italian army doctor and criminologist, argued that some people are born criminals, throwbacks to a more primitive stage of human evolution. Using male prison inmates as subjects, Lombroso defined and measured physical characteristics such as abnormally large jaws, high cheekbones, good eyesight, and an insensibility to pain. These people were, he claimed, more like apes than men, and their primitive development made it difficult for them to conform to conventional norms. Although popular in the early 1900s, Lombroso's biological explanation of crime has now been thoroughly rejected. Subsequent research has failed to establish any link between Lombroso's physical characteristics and criminality (Sykes & Cullen, 1992).

Since Lombroso's time, there have been numerous efforts to link such diverse forms of deviance as mental illness, alcoholism, and crime to purely biological causes. Most of these efforts have failed. One major criticism of these studies is that they typically are based on unrepresentative samples of people, such as criminals in prison. Recall the discussion in Chapter 1 about the importance of representative samples. Furthermore, in studies suggesting that biology does play a role, it appears to be but one contributing factor rather than the sole cause of deviance. For example, biological factors may play a part in a particularly severe form of mental illness known as schizophrenia (Cockerham, 1996). Some schizophrenics, although certainly not all, appear to inherit a tendency to develop this mental disorder. However, this inherited tendency alone does not bring about schizophrenic behavior. Such behavior emerges only if personal and social stress factors are also present. In addition, with some schizophrenics, there appears to be no genetic element involved. Purely biological theories of deviance, then, have been discredited, and sociologists have concluded that much deviance has nothing to do with biology (Chambliss, 1991; Gottfredson & Hirschi, 1990).

Psychological approaches to deviance, however, still receive considerable support. From this perspective, deviance is believed to result from some personality disorder or maladjustment that develops, often during childhood. For example, alcoholism has been explained in terms of excessive dependency needs and aggressiveness that can result from faulty childhood socialization. If children receive contradictory treatment from parents—loving indulgence some of the time, but threat and rejection at other times—they may grow up with a compulsive need for love and strong feelings of dependence on other people. The anxiety created when their disproportionate needs are not met, it is maintained, can lead to the excessive use of alcohol as a way of relieving these tensions (Light, 1986).

Although sociologists recognize the importance of personality and psychological processes in people's lives, such explanations offer only a partial understanding of deviance. In many cases, people who manifest various forms of deviance are free from the personality problems and psychological disorders that presumably cause them, and people with those disorders often do not establish particular patterns of deviant behavior. Many alcoholics, for example, are not excessively dependent on others. Even when psychological disturbances are associated with deviance, the causal direction is unclear: Do personality factors cause deviance, or does engaging in deviance, along with the stigma that often results, lead people to develop unique personality characteristics (Jeffrey, 1967)?

Sociologists have emphasized the role of culture, social structure, and social interaction in bringing about deviance. This chapter will discuss the major sociological approaches to deviance and crime: the functional, conflict and interactionist perspectives.

The Functionalist Perspective

An early functionalist, Emile Durkheim, provided one of the explanations for high levels of deviance and crime in industrial societies. One of the key features of industrial societies, he argued, is the weakening of many of the social bonds important in preindustrial societies. Ties to family, community, and church become less important in indus-

trial societies as families become smaller and workers more mobile and independent of their families (see Chapter 9). People are more free to pursue their own needs and fulfill their own desires; they are less constrained by the need to please relatives or account to a priest or minister. But this freedom has its costs. The reduction in social constraints also results in a degree of social disorganization as people pursue needs and goals that may be detrimental to the overall good of society. After all, bonds to family and church were one of the key mechanisms constraining people from committing crimes or engaging in other socially disapproved activities. When those bonds are weakened or removed, a certain amount of crime and social disorder will result. For Durkheim, then, deviance is one of the costs that we must pay to live in the type of society that we do, and recent research comparing many different societies supports his theory (Leavitt, 1992). More recently, Durkheim's views have been applied to juvenile delinquency in the form of a *social-control* theory of delinquency. The basic idea is that the chances of delinquency occurring can be reduced if youngsters maintain attachments and commitments to the conventional world of their parents, schools, and peers (Agnew, 1991; Hirschi, 1969).

Another influential functionalist approach to deviance and crime is Robert K. Merton's **anomie theory** (1968), which *posits that inconsistencies and contradictions in the social system precipitate many forms of deviance and crime.* Merton observed that *people in the United States are taught to strive for certain goals but are not always provided with the culturally approved means necessary to attain these goals.* Merton referred to *such inconsistencies and the confusion they can cause in people* as **anomie.** In the United States, for example, an important cultural goal is success, which is defined largely in material terms. One culturally approved way to become successful is to gain an education and work in some legitimate occupation. Some people, however, are prevented from succeeding in this fashion because of poverty, discrimination, or some other social condition. When people are thus hindered from achieving desired goals, deviance in one of its many forms may result. Deviance is the person's *mode of adaptation* to the anomie, although the person may not think of it this way

TABLE 5.1 Modes of individual adaptation to anomie

Modes of Adaptation	Accepts Culturally Approved Goals	Accepts Culturally Approved Means
I. Conformity	+	+
II. Innovation	+	−
III. Ritualism	−	+
IV. Retreatism	−	−
V. Rebellion	±	±

+ Signifies acceptance
− Signifies rejection
± Signifies rejection of prevailing goals and means and the substitution of new goals and means
Note: From *Social Theory and Social Structure* by Robert K. Merton, 1968 (revised and enlarged edition), Free Press, a division of Simon & Schuster. Copyright 1967, 1968 by Robert K. Merton. Reprinted by permission.

(see Table 5.1). Most people, of course, accept the culturally approved goals and use the culturally approved means of achieving them. According to Merton, this *conformity* provides stability for society. Most college students fall into this category, because they are using educational paths, which are socially approved means toward respectable and legitimate occupations.

The four modes of adaptation other than conformity may involve some deviant or criminal behaviors. The most common of these Merton called *innovation,* in which people pursue the cultural goals through illegal or other socially disapproved means. Innovation is likely to occur when people feel that legitimate routes to success are closed and that their only option is to turn to illegitimate ones. People who are unemployed or underemployed, for example, can provide for their families and themselves through robbery or burglary. Likewise, a person running a marginal business concern can survive by cheating on taxes or using deceptive advertising practices.

Another response to anomie is *ritualism,* which occurs when an individual almost compulsively accepts the culturally approved means but does not use them to achieve cultural goals. Merton uses as

an example of a ritualist the minor bureaucrat who has no hopes of improving his or her position yet follows closely all the rules and routines of the bureaucracy. Except in extreme cases, such ritualism would not be considered deviant by most groups.

People can also respond to anomie through *retreatism,* rejecting both the culturally approved goals and the legitimate means for achieving them. Unlike innovators, who feel that they lack access to the means, retreatists have often attempted to obtain these goals through legitimate means but have failed. Their adaptation to anomie, as illustrated by drug addicts or alcoholics, is to drop out and "escape."

Finally, *rebellion* occurs when people reject both the socially approved goals and the socially approved means and then seek to replace them with alternative goals and means. In many communes, for example, the conventional U.S. value of material success is rejected, as are the traditional means of achieving this success. Yet instead of simply dropping out, communards work to establish their own social order based on new cultural goals, such as the common ownership of goods, and new means, such as cooperative rather than competitive social relationships. A more radical example of rebellion is found in revolutionary groups such as the Palestine Liberation Organization in the Middle East, who try to destroy the existing social order while attempting to establish a new one.

Recent research on crime supports anomie theory. For example, crime rates, especially for property crimes, are higher in communities with greater economic inequality or with a larger disparity between incomes among groups. In such cities, the less fortunate can readily see the affluence around them, and some turn to crime to improve their own circumstances (Simons & Gray, 1989). Crime also goes up when there is an economic recession (Devine, Sheley, & Smith, 1988). Crime rates are high among the unemployed and low among the employed (Allan & Steffensmeier, 1989; Lafree, Drass, & O'Day, 1992).

The importance of anomie theory for understanding crime as a form of deviant behavior should be clear: Much criminal activity derives from the social and economic conditions of U.S. society. With high unemployment, high inflation, and reduced government spending on social services, economic disparities are exacerbated. In fact, the criminologist Elliott Currie (1985) has argued that the low crime rate in industrial societies such as Japan results in part from their programs promoting high employment and the fact that income disparities are much smaller than in the United States.

The functionalist perspective also emphasizes the interrelatedness of the various parts of the social system. Changes in one part bring about changes in other seemingly unrelated parts. Certain social trends and changes in the U.S. lifestyle over the past few decades have increased the opportunities for committing certain kinds of crime, particularly burglary, larceny, and theft (Cohen & Felson, 1979; Cohen, Felson, & Land, 1980; Miller & Ohlin, 1985). For example, the number of women working has increased dramatically since the 1960s; there has been an increase in the number of households with only one adult member; and people take more vacations now than in the past. The result of these three trends is that homes are much more likely to be left unattended for a part of the day and therefore become tempting targets for burglars. There has also been tremendous growth in consumer spending for items such as televisions and automobiles that are likely objects for theft. In short, the rise in crime results in part from increasing opportunities made available by trends that many people in the United States view as desirable. Unless alternative means of controlling such crimes are found, we may have to settle for the realization that some crimes represent an unfortunate by-product of the affluent and leisured U.S. lifestyle.

Merton's theory of deviance has some shortcomings (Nettler, 1974; Thio, 1994). Some sociologists question whether different groups within a society aspire toward the same cultural goals. Given the heterogeneous nature of industrial societies, for example, striving for success is highly valued by some people but certainly not by all. In addition, Merton's theory does not tell us why people adopt one response to anomie rather than another. Why do some people respond by becoming criminals whereas others become retreatists and still others rebel? Despite these criticisms, Merton's theory has been very influential and has helped explain many forms of deviance. Other approaches to deviance can help us in the areas where Merton's theory is weak.

The Conflict Perspective

In reviewing the functionalist argument, conflict theorists observe that the analysis of the "crime and deviance problem" tends to focus heavily on behavior that is more likely to occur among the less powerful groups in society: the young, the poor, and the nonwhite. In fact, the Federal Bureau of Investigation's Crime Index, the most widely publicized statistic on the amount of crime, emphasizes crimes such as assault, which the less well-to-do are more likely to commit, rather than embezzlement, gambling, or tax evasion, which are committed more by middle-class and respectable people. The so-called deviance and crime problem, then, as it is defined by the police, the courts, and the public, results from the activities of the less fortunate in society.

From the conflict perspective, the legal and criminal justice systems are geared to benefit the dominant groups in society (Kennedy, 1990; Quinney, 1974). Laws, after all, are mechanisms whereby some groups exercise control over the activities of other groups. Generally, it is the powerful who establish legislation defining what activities will be considered criminal and who decide what the penalties will be for those crimes. Thus, removing a television from a store is regarded as criminal, whereas polluting a stream may not be. Armed robbery can bring a fifteen-year prison sentence, whereas price-fixing that costs the public millions of dollars in excess expenditures may be punished with a light prison sentence or a fine.

It is also the powerful who can get the police to enforce the laws against some crimes while ignoring other infractions of the law. There are, for example, periodic and highly publicized drives against robbery, prostitution, and drug offenses. In 1989, the Bush administration declared "war" on illegal drugs, proclaiming that this problem is the United States' number-one crime issue. One does not, however, often see a politician launch such a campaign against corporate crime. From the conflict perspective, then, the social problem of deviance and crime is not simply a matter of social disorganization; it is also influenced by the preferences, predilections, and interests of various groups in society (Caringella-Macdonald, 1990).

Conflict theorists who have been influenced by the writings of Karl Marx view the causes of crime very differently from the way functionalists do. These conflict theorists blame certain characteristics of capitalism as an economic system (Headley, 1991). Capitalism is characterized by a constant search for greater profits, or at least a struggle against falling profits. This process can be especially fierce in a worldwide economy such as we have today where countries at many different levels of development compete with one another. In the process, capitalists search for ways to enhance profits by reducing costs through mechanization or automation of work or through relocation to areas where resources and labor are cheaper. Both mechanization and relocation put people out of work or force people into competition for lower-wage jobs. Because this process is a continual one, capitalism inevitably contains recurring cycles in which people are thrown out of work and communities are decimated by the loss of jobs. These inherent features of capitalism, then, mean that certain levels of poverty and the crime associated with it will always be with us, although which groups or communities are affected may shift over time.

In addition, capitalists need to sell their goods to make a profit, so they must instill in people a desire for the many products that capitalism can produce. At the same time, capitalists attempt to keep wages low to reduce the costs of production. A mass of unemployed people also benefits a capitalist economy by serving as a cheap labor force when new workers are needed. The unemployed also serve as a lesson to employed workers: Do not demand too high a salary or you, too, may be among the unemployed. The result, according to William Chambliss (1975), is a contradiction: "Capitalism creates both the desire to consume and—for a large mass of people—an inability to earn the money necessary to purchase the items they have been taught to want" (p. 51). For these people, crime is one way of resolving this dilemma. Unlike anomie theory, however, Marxian conflict theory does not assume that the problem can be alleviated through full employment;

rather, it sees these contradictions as inherent in a capitalist economy.

The Interactionist Perspective

Interactionist approaches do not dispute the sources of deviance and crime pointed to by the functionalist and conflict views. But interactionists see these views as incomplete because they do not explain how a person becomes deviant or why one person responds to anomie through crime or drug use and another does not. To find answers to these questions, we need to look at the socialization and interaction processes that influence people's daily lives.

Cultural transmission theories posit that *deviance is a learned behavior that is culturally transmitted through socialization.* The most influential of these theories is the **differential association theory,** developed by the criminologist Edwin Sutherland during the 1920s and the 1930s, which draws on the interactionist concern with social meaning arising from social interaction. According to Sutherland, *deviant behavior is learned in interaction with other people, for the most part within intimate primary groups such as families and peer groups* (Sutherland & Cressey, 1978). There are two elements of this learning process. First, people learn the specific techniques for engaging in deviance. For example, to use illicit drugs, a person needs to know how to obtain and take drugs such as heroin or cocaine. Second, one must learn to value deviant behavior more than nondeviant behavior. By associating with other deviants, people are more likely to learn to value their deviant activities and learn a rationale for why deviance is preferable to a more conventional way of life. Some people who use cocaine or other drugs, for example, claim that drugs make them feel more relaxed, sociable, and perceptive than they feel when not using drugs. Whether people become deviant depends on the extent and intensity of contact with groups that value a particular form of deviance and can train them in deviant techniques. It also depends on whether a person identifies with and takes the role of those deviants. Association with deviants without such identification is not likely to result in deviance.

According to cultural transmission theories, then, learning to be deviant involves mechanisms of socialization similar to those associated with learning any social status (see Chapter 3). If people have primary group ties with nondeviants, then they are likely to learn to value that lifestyle. Others who associate with deviants are more likely to become deviant.

Another interactionist approach to deviance is *labeling theory,* which shifts attention away from the individual deviant and toward the ways that others react to the deviant (Cavender, 1991). It also shifts attention from isolated or sporadic occurrences of deviance and toward deviance that is engaged in repeatedly and becomes a part of a person's lifestyle. **Labeling theory** suggests that *whether other people define or label a person as deviant is a critical determinant in the development of a pattern of deviant behavior.* According to this theory, many people engage in activities that could be defined as deviant, at least occasionally. In all likelihood, you have engaged in actions that have been so defined. Few of us, however, are caught and labeled—either by our friends or by official agencies—as deviants or criminals. Labeling theorists refer to this *violation of social norms in which a person is not caught or is excused rather than labeled deviant* as **primary deviance.** But labeling theory does not attempt to explain this type of deviance. Labeling theory concentrates on **secondary** or **career deviance**—*the deviant behavior that a person adopts in response to the reaction of others to their primary deviance.* Consider how such a response could happen (Matsueda, 1992).

We know that shoplifting among teenagers, at least of small items, is not uncommon. Imagine that a teenager, possibly out of curiosity or on a dare from peers, engages in a single act of shoplifting. This act would constitute primary deviance, because there has been no labeling and no change in the teenager's or the community's image of him or her. If, however, the young person's shoplifting is brought to the attention of the police, they may begin the labeling process by notifying the offender's parents. If this label becomes "public," it is quite likely that some stigma will attach to this teenager's reputation—perhaps a criminal record.

One key consequence of this labeling process is its effect on a person's self-concept. Because the teenage years are formative ones in terms of personal identity, the person may respond to others' reactions, at least in part, by accepting their judgment. After all, the stigma associated with deviant labels such as "criminal" and "delinquent" implies something negative about people who behave in that fashion. The terms *murderer, thug, robber,* and *thief* suggest the strong emotions that underlie these labels of deviants, and such labels can affect the way people view themselves. To the extent that labeling produces changes in a person's self-concept, this is an example of the looking-glass-self process discussed in Chapter 3.

A second key consequence of labeling involves the effect that labeling has on people's social relationships. After all, labels of deviants typically denote *master statuses* that powerfully shape how others define and relate to the deviant (see Chapter 2). If the criminal activity becomes publicly known, some of the person's conventional friends may shun him or her out of fear for their own reputations. The person may also find it difficult to develop new friends, at least among conventional peers, finding acceptance, instead, among youngsters who are already engaging in delinquent or criminal actions on a large scale.

As a result of these changes in self-concept and social contacts, labeling theorists argue, the likelihood of a deviant career developing is increased. Thus, labeling can perpetuate deviance and crime because, once people have been labeled, they have fewer alternatives, and the deviance becomes a part of their social identity. This situation represents secondary deviance because it results from a person's efforts to cope with the responses of others to primary deviation. It also represents, in a sense, a *self-fulfilling prophecy* in that the label of deviant helps to bring about the pattern of career deviance that people thought they were merely identifying when they first attached the label (Heimer & Matsueda, 1994).

One must be cautious in being overly deterministic about the influence of labeling. Labeling can and does have the effects that have been described, but such outcomes are not inevitable. People with strong and stable self-concepts may be able to avoid the negative influence of pejorative labels. They may also choose to associate with others who are unaware of the label, as when someone does not reveal to a new circle of friends that he is an "ex-con." Furthermore, labeling theory fails to account for the existence of primary deviance. A few early labeling theorists claimed that labeling could cause people to become deviant in the first place, but there is little evidence for this statement. The effects of the label usually arise *after* a person commits a deviant act and has been recognized and labeled.

Now that the major sociological theories of deviance have been described, you should understand better why sociologists take the position that deviance is *relative*. According to anomie theory, what is defined as deviant depends on what are considered socially approved means and goals in a particular society. Conflict theory sees deviance within a framework of definitions and judgments that are formulated and enforced by those in positions of power. For cultural transmission theory, deviance is a result of socialization, and people are capable of learning a wide variety of things. Finally, labeling theory makes us aware that being identified as a deviant depends, among other things, on the resources a person possesses and on his or her ability to avoid the negative aspects of being labeled. You should keep in mind in reviewing some different types of deviance that the line between deviance and nondeviance is shifting and vague rather than clear and obvious.

Extent of Deviance and Crime

You should be able to describe the major forms of deviance and crime found in the United States and explain why they occur.

It is important to distinguish between crime and deviance. A **crime** is *an act that violates a criminal code that has been enacted by an officially constituted political authority.* Some crimes are commonly perceived as deviant (see Figure 5.1); acts of this sort may be referred to as *mala in se*, or "bad in and of themselves." Rape, homicide, robbery, assault, and burglary are all acts that fall into this category because they represent violations of important group norms. Some behaviors, however, are criminal but not necessarily viewed as deviant. These acts fall under the category *mala prohibita*, or "bad because they are prohibited." Parking violations and minor tax evasion, for example, are not considered deviant by most people, and little stigma usually attaches to them even though they are violations of a criminal code. In addition, some behaviors and characteristics may be perceived as deviant but not classified as criminal. Extreme obesity and some forms of mental illness, for example, would, by the judgments of some groups, fall into this category. This chapter will review some types of deviance that are crimes and others that are not.

FIGURE 5.1 The Relationship Between Deviance and Crime

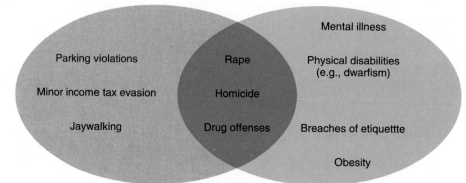

Sexual Deviance

The varieties of human sexual expression are almost endless, and most of them have been condemned, at one time or another, as deviant. Many people believe that there is a "natural" or "instinctive" expression of sexuality that people are aware of largely or completely without learning. Reflecting this belief, some people refer to variant sexual acts as "violations of nature." So for many people in the United States, "natural" sex is sex between men and women who are married. Some would even extend this "naturalness" to the sexual position assumed: genital contact in the "missionary" position (face-to-face with the male on top). Yet studies of other cultures indicate that socially acceptable sex takes far more forms than this. Consider one such culture:

> Sex—sex for pleasure and sex for procreation—is a principal concern of the Polynesian people on tiny Mangaia, the southernmost of the Cook Islands near the geographical center of Polynesia in the South Pacific.... They demonstrate that concern in the startling number of children born to unmarried parents, and in the statistics on frequency of orgasm and numbers of sexual partners. But that concern is simple fact-of-life—not morbid preoccupation.... There is great directness about sex, but the approach to sex is correspondingly indirect. Among the young, there is no dating, no tentative necking in the American sense. A flick of the eye, a raised eyebrow in a crowd, can lead to copulation—without a word. There is no social contact between the sexes, no rendezvous that does not lead directly to coitus—copulation is the only imaginable outcome of heterosexual contact. The sexual intimacy of copulation precedes personal affection. (Marshall, 1974, pp. 26–27)

Thus Mangaians have what people in the United States would call an extremely permissive attitude toward sexual behavior. Although sexual intercourse among unmarried persons is accepted by many people in the United States, multiple partners and casual sex tend to be frowned on, especially for women. If there is a natural or instinctive form of sexual expression, what are we to make of the Mangaians?

Consider some examples from other cultures. In Tahiti, young people were encouraged to masturbate (Bullough, 1976; Davenport, 1977). In the Truk Islands of the Pacific, sexual gratification is associated with pain and frustration, and sexual foreplay involves lovers inflicting pain on each other. Among most human groups, the female breasts are considered erotic organs, but that is not universal. Among the Mangaians, the breasts are not involved in foreplay and sexual arousal. Kissing is also a part of sexual expression in most human societies, but there are people among whom sexual intercourse occurs completely without kissing. The Siriono of Bolivia find kissing to be a disgusting act.

Sexual norms, then, are like other societal rules: They vary widely from one context to another, and people learn to accept what is socially approved in their group or culture. For many in the United States, prostitution is considered a deviant form of sexual behavior, even though it is widespread there and is considered acceptable in many other societies. Prostitution has been called the "world's oldest profession," for it has been present throughout recorded history. *Prostitution* refers to sexual activity in exchange for money or goods in which the primary motivation for the prostitute is neither sexual nor affectional (James, 1977). Estimates place the number of prostitutes in the United States at between 100,000 and 500,000 and the money generated each year at between $1 billion and $10 billion (Thio, 1994). The trade is clearly thriving, and the explanation is primarily economic: There are people willing to pay for the services and others who are willing to supply them for a price. Although prostitution is usually associated with women, almost one-third of those arrested for prostitution in the United States are males.

Drug and Alcohol Abuse

The use of drugs is another realm of human behavior where there is much disagreement about where normality leaves off and deviance begins. Some drugs, such as alcohol, are legal; others, such as heroin and marijuana, are not. Still other drugs are "controlled." For example, cocaine is illegal on the street, but it is used regularly in the practice of medicine. During the twentieth century, attitudes in the United States have changed considerably about whether certain drugs should be legal or illegal. Between 1920 and 1933, alcohol was illegal but marijuana was legal in most

Prostitution is considered deviant by many people. Yet, as these prostitutes in Cambodia illustrate, it persists for economic reasons: Some people are willing to pay for the service, and others benefit by supplying it for a price.

states. Today the reverse is true. When it comes to deviance, most of the attention surrounding drugs involves their abuse.

The abuse of alcohol, or *alcoholism,* is defined as a dependence on the substance by people who drink more than is socially acceptable in their group, or whose drinking has damaged their health, social relationships, or job performance. People in the United States are simultaneously enamored by the use of alcohol and concerned about its abuse. It is by far the most widely used, and abused, mood-altering drug in the United States. Estimates of the number of alcoholics in the United States vary, but most authorities agree that there are at least 10 million problem drinkers, or approximately 4 percent of the population.

Following alcohol, marijuana is probably the most widely used drug. Although it is still illegal in most places, many people have come to view the use of marijuana as the equivalent of the use of alcohol: For some, its occasional use is accepted, although excessive use is frowned on. It is estimated that about one-half of young adults between eighteen and twenty-five and about one-third of those older than twenty-five have used marijuana. Among high school seniors, 19 percent used marijuana at least once during a thirty-day period. However, rates of use of marijuana have declined considerably in the past twenty years (Johnston, O'Malley, & Bachman, 1996; U.S. Bureau of the Census, 1995, p. 142).

Cocaine, a stimulant derived from coca leaves, has become a popular psychoactive drug (Johnston, O'Malley, & Bachman, 1996; U.S. Bureau of the Census, 1995, p. 142). By the 1990s, 12 percent of all adults aged twenty-six and older in the United States had tried cocaine, compared with about 1 percent in the mid-1970s. Among young people aged eighteen to twenty-five years old, an identical 12 percent had tried it in the mid-1990s compared with 12 percent in 1974. The number of current users seems to be declining, however: Fewer than 2 percent of eighteen- to twenty-five-year-olds used cocaine in the last month in the mid-1990s compared with 3.1 percent in 1974. In fact, cocaine use seems to have peaked between 1980 and 1985 and has shown a substantial decline since then. Nevertheless, there is evidence that the decline is among casual users rather than heavy users or addicts. In addition, although equal proportions of whites, African Americans, and Hispanic Americans have tried cocaine, whites are less likely to be current users than are the other two groups. Cocaine use among whites tends to be more short-lived and probably more experimental.

Cocaine used to be an expensive drug, a fact that limited its use. Drug entrepreneurs, however, discovered ways to produce cheap and potent drugs from cocaine (Lerner & Raczynski, 1988; Witkin, 1991). One method uses heat and baking soda to turn the cocaine powder into smokable *crack* cocaine. (The term *crack* comes from the cracking sound cocaine makes when heated.) Crack (called *rock cocaine* or *hubbas*) gives an intense high—almost instantaneously because it is smoked—and is extremely addictive. It is also cheap enough to be available even to poor people with a few extra dollars in their pocket. Cocaine powder costs $75 a gram, whereas one hit of crack is as little as $5. Because of its cheapness, crack has been an especially cruel plague for many poor communities. Even mothers receiving welfare can afford crack if they neglect their personal needs and those of their families. Consequently, some poor women have become addicted to crack, given birth to children who are addicted, and then neglected and even abandoned their children as their crack habits spun out of control. Applying Sociology: Controlling Youth Gang and Drug Involvement (on p. 156) discusses some of the contributions that sociological practitioners have made to the drug problem in the United States.

Mental Illness

Mental illness is stigmatized in many societies, even though millions of people are considered to have serious mental disorders, such as schizophrenia, that severely impair their ability to function (Cockerham, 1996). Far more people suffer from milder mental disorders, such as anxieties and obsessions, but most are able to function in their daily lives. The stigma associated with mental illness probably arises from the belief that mentally disturbed people are prone to be disruptive or violent. Added to this belief is the fact that the symptoms of mental disorders are often social behaviors that violate group norms, such as inappropriate dress, foul and abusive language, or difficulty in maintaining normal social intercourse.

Many people, including some psychologists and psychiatrists, view mental illness as much like physical illness in that there is some malfunction in the person that, when corrected, will cure the mental disorder. Sociologists recognize that some of the symptoms of mental disorders are caused by problems or stresses in people's social lives. In some cases, mental disorders arise, or are made worse, because a person is labeled as mentally ill and then responds to that label. Thomas Scheff (1984), for example, argues that mental illness is a social role with certain expectations associated with it. Once we label a person as mentally ill, the person's behavior is shaped by the expectations associated with the label. As discussed earlier under labeling theory, the tag *mental illness* can become a self-fulfilling prophecy. In other words, secondary deviance arises as the person begins to behave in a way that he or she thinks a mentally ill person should. In fact, some have gone so far as to argue that who is labeled mentally ill is to a degree arbitrary. In a disturbing and now classic study, the psychologist D.L. Rosenhan (1973) managed to have himself and seven other people admitted to mental institutions as schizophrenics by saying that they were hearing voices that said things like "thud" and "hollow." All these people performed normally on various psychological tests and acted perfectly normal once admitted to the institutions. Yet all hospital personnel, including psychiatrists and nurses, accepted the label *schizophrenia* and treated them accordingly. In fact, the staff tended to interpret the patients' normal behavior as symptomatic of their mental illness. Note-taking, for example, or questions regarding when they would be released were considered abnormal.

The positions of people like Scheff and Rosenhan do not mean that there are not people with psychological disturbances that can have

Youth gangs have been a concern of sociologists ever since the 1920s. Over the years, sociologists have learned a lot about why gangs form, who joins them, how they are organized, and about their functions and dysfunctions. Researchers have also learned how youth gangs, sometimes organized on a regional or national level, have played an important part in the drug trade. The sociologist Daniel J. Monti (1991) became interested in gangs through his work on urban redevelopment in St. Louis. He learned of gangs in some of the neighborhoods he had studied and wanted to learn more of their impact on the neighborhoods undergoing redevelopment.

Working through the police department, he interviewed many gang members and presented his findings to police and city officials. The findings were not well received because many officials did not want to admit to the existence of an extensive gang problem. Later, Monti was appointed to the Missouri State Advisory Committee to the U.S. Commission on Civil Rights. In this position he was able to use his sociological analysis of gangs to organize testimony regarding the impact of proposed legislation on the problem of gangs and drugs. The testimony showed how school desegregation had an impact on gangs by helping to move gang activity to new areas. It also showed that some white gangs emerged in response to what they saw as a threat of minority students, and possibly

gangs, moving into previously white schools. Through his sociological insights, then, Monti was able to demonstrate links between educational policies and gang activities. He was also able to show that legislation proposed to control the gang and drug problems would affect mostly minority gang members, not whites. The reason was that the legislation would allow for the identification of gang members through the wearing of certain clothing styles or sporting tattoos. These styles were common among minority youth—both those who joined gangs and those who didn't—but uncommon among white youth. So, Monti's knowledge of gangs enabled him to detect how these policies would be ineffective by tagging some minority youth as gang members who were not and failing to detect gang members among white youth.

In part because of his work on gangs and on the civil rights commission, Monti was invited to survey gang activity in a number of school districts. The results of this research were submitted to school officials in each district, who then could use the findings to formulate community programs to address the problems created by gangs. Monti's work illustrates how sociological research becomes a significant part of the social-policy process and helps to develop programs to attack important social problems.

---

agonizing effects on their lives. The point is that mental illness is a complex type of deviance and involves social behaviors that require interpretation. What is normal behavior in one setting may be viewed as quite abnormal in another. Sociologists don't view mental illness as something inside a person's head but rather as a social role whose content can vary from one setting to another or one culture to another.

Violent Crimes

Violent crimes such as murder, assault, robbery, and rape are clear violations of group norms and the law. More than 23,000 murders were committed in 1994, along with more than one million ag-

gravated assaults (Federal Bureau of Investigation, 1995). Murders tend to be situational, in that they often occur as a result of some dispute, frequently trivial, over money or some element of personal demeanor; they are only rarely planned in advance. The victim is usually a relative, friend, or acquaintance of the assailant. In 1994, one-third of all homicides arose from an argument, whereas only 20 percent occurred during the commission of a felony. Assaults are much more likely to involve strangers than are murders. In addition to these offenses, there are more than a half million robberies every year, some of which involve personal injury to the victims.

Forcible rape, another violent criminal offense, occurs when an assailant sexually assaults another person. In 1994, there were more than 100,000 rapes known to the police in the United States, but many estimates place the actual number much higher because victims may be reluctant to report the crime. According to survey results, rape is the crime that women, especially those under thirty-five years of age, fear the most. Especially in urban areas, this fear affects their daily lives as they avoid going out alone, refuse to enter certain neighborhoods, and install deadbolt locks in their homes (Stanko, 1995). In addition to the physical danger and degradation experienced by rape victims, the act also has a political element in that it symbolizes and reinforces the power and domination of the assailant over the victim. As one social scientist put it regarding female rape victims: "Rape is to women as lynching was to blacks: the ultimate physical threat" (Brownmiller, 1975, p. 254). Only in recent decades, because of pressure from women's groups, have states begun to make raping one's wife a crime (Russell, 1990). Yet, not all states have done so. In eight states in 1990, men could not be charged with raping their wives as long as they were living together and the wife had not filed for divorce or protection. Twenty-six other states allowed charges of marital rape but with exemptions. Depending on the state, for example, a man could not be charged with raping his wife unless he had kidnapped her or threatened her with a weapon; some of these states did not permit rape charges if the wife was unable to consent to sex because she was drugged or unconscious. Only sixteen states accorded wives the same protection as other women by treating marital rape like any other rape. So some states still seem to believe that a wife is, to a degree, the "property" of her husband, at least for sexual access, a view that outrages many women and men. Sociologists have devoted much attention to understanding problems of rape and spouse abuse. Applying Sociology: How to Stop Men from Battering Women (on pp. 158–159) discusses research that culminated in direct social interventions to alleviate these problems.

Organized Crime

Much of the crime so far described is sporadic and individualized, such as the lone mugger or the small group of juveniles who robs homes. There are, however, forms of criminal activity that bene-fit from large-scale organization. For example, gambling and prostitution can be highly profitable to those who organize them. Other crimes, such as drug smuggling, involve large overhead costs (front money to purchase the drugs, for instance) that are difficult to fund without some organization. This leads to organized crime, or *syndicates:* criminal operations in which several criminal groups coordinate their illegal activities.

Although a great deal of criminal activity in U.S. society is organized to some degree, there is considerable debate about the structure and extent of this kind of crime in the United States. One view is illustrated by the image of the Mafia, consisting of a nationwide alliance of families, based on kinship and ethnic solidarity, that coordinate their criminal actions and control large areas of criminal activity. Whether the Mafia, or La Cosa Nostra, was ever as powerful and consolidated as its portrayal in the media suggests is subject to debate, but it is probably not nearly that large, cohesive, or controlling today (Abadinsky, 1994). Organized crime today also includes many other racially or ethnically based criminal gangs, including Asian organized crime, Colombian drug-trafficking organizations, and Hispanic street gangs. Many of these gangs operate in local or regional criminal markets, although some gain a national reach (Delattre, 1990).

In addition to illegal activities, organized crime also develops interests in legitimate business, such as real estate, trucking, and food processing, at least in part as mechanisms to launder the vast sums earned through their illegal activities (Santino, 1988). The amount of money that flows into the coffers of organized crime is difficult to determine because of its hidden nature, but one government estimate placed it at between $26 billion and $67 billion annually, which is probably a conservative figure (Zawitz et al., 1988).

The social context of organized crime must be kept in perspective. Organized crime does perform functions for society. After all, if there were no demand for the services it provides, it would perish. In addition, organized criminals may well have alliances with government and law enforcement groups in order to operate as freely as they do. What is perhaps even more unsettling is that the benefits of organized crime stretch far beyond the core criminal elements. Some legitimate business interests, political figures, labor

Domestic violence is a particularly tragic social problem, with its jarring intrusion of injury and cruelty into the intimacy of the family. It is also a difficult problem for police officers, who are often first on the scene of such violence and whose job it is to make complex and troubling decisions about how to handle the alleged perpetrator of the violence. Should they mediate the dispute between the couple, in an effort to resolve the conflict? Or should they aggressively pursue arrest? Or is there some other effective option, such as sending the abuser away in the hope that a period of separation will calm the passions that led to the violence?

In the past, this decision was left to the judgment of the individual officer at the scene. Those judgments were shaped in part by the experiences of the officers but also by each officer's personal feelings about spouse abuse and the relationship between men and women, and by many other social and cultural factors. Some officers had their favorite approach that they believed worked, but no one had any systematic knowledge about which strategy was really most likely to stop future outbreaks of domestic violence. In the early 1980s, the criminologist Lawrence Sherman and the sociologist Richard Berk (1984) developed an innovative program to collect systematic observations to begin resolving this problem. They based their approach on two competing theories of the effect of punishment in controlling crime. One theory, the specific deterrence doctrine, posits that

punishment, such as an arrest, tends to stop people from committing future crimes because they fear further punishment. The opposite approach, labeling theory, argues that punishment by an official law enforcement agency increases the likelihood of future crimes because it starts the person down the path of becoming a career criminal.

The police in Minneapolis cooperated with Sherman and Berk, who designed a field experiment to test their ideas (this type of research design was discussed in Chapter 1). They gave each officer a pad of police report forms that were in three different colors, each representing a type of intervention—separation, mediation, and arrest. The different-colored forms were ordered randomly in each officer's pad, and the officer took whatever action was called for by the color of the uppermost form. Thus each type of intervention was used an equal number of times and was chosen without the judgment of the officers coming into play. Sherman and Berk then looked to see which perpetrators of spouse abuse were most likely to be involved in repeat offenses over the next six months. (For ethical reasons, these procedures were followed only in cases of simple, or misdemeanor, assault where there was no severe injury or life-threatening situation.)

This was a complex piece of applied research, but basically Sherman and Berk discovered that arrest was the most effective form of intervention: Those who were arrested were less likely to be involved in

---

leaders, and other respectable citizens undoubtedly share in the profits of organized crime, sometimes unknowingly, thus contributing to its ongoing activities (Fijnaut, 1990).

White-Collar Crime

White-collar crimes are offenses committed by people in positions of respect and responsibility during the ordinary course of their business (Coleman, 1989; Sutherland, 1949). One such offense is antitrust violations, or attempts by businesses to monopolize a segment of the economy.

White-collar crime can also take the form of price-fixing, in which competitors agree to sell their products for a price higher than they would be able to in a truly competitive market. In the mid-1970s, for example, a price-fixing scheme involving the four major breakfast cereal makers in the United States is estimated to have cost the public some $128 million. Another type of white-collar crime is the fraudulent use of funds. In 1985, E. F. Hutton, one of the nation's largest investment firms, was convicted of an elaborate fraud in which it shuffled millions of dollars among numerous banks and bank accounts, making the

another domestic assault over the next six months than were those who experienced mediation or separation. This fact was true even though those arrested were released quickly and thus were free to commit further abuse. And this research made a difference in the lives of many women and men because the findings were used as the justification for changing social policies. In the past, police in many cities would rarely arrest suspected abusers. As a result of Sherman and Berk's findings, police officers in many cities were ordered by their superiors to consider arrest the preferred intervention in dealing with domestic assault cases. In some states today, police are given authorization to arrest in such cases even if the victim does not make a complaint—a vast improvement over the past policy of neglect.

Because social behavior is complicated, sociologists recognize that one research study is not likely to tell us all we need to know. To see if the Sherman and Berk findings would hold up in other places and at other times, variations on their study have been done in a number of cities, including Milwaukee, Atlanta, Omaha, and Charlotte, North Carolina (Dunford, Huizinga, & Elliott, 1989; Hirschel, Hutchison, & Dean, 1992; Pate & Hamilton, 1992). These replications have not provided as strong support for the efficacy of arrest as did the Sherman and Berk study. It may be that Sherman and Berk inadvertently studied a select group of abusers for whom arrest was particularly effective. The later studies have included a broader sampling of abusers. Nevertheless, sociologists are now beginning to narrow down their understanding of which batterers of women are deterred by arrest. For example, arrest seems to work well among people whose reputations would be affected by an arrest, such as the affluent and those with middle-class jobs. However, among those for whom conformity to conventional norms is less important to maintaining their lifestyle, such as those who are unemployed, arrest does not seem to have the desired effect.

These studies illustrate some of the central features of applied sociological research:

1. Applied research rests on an existing body of knowledge about human behavior (in this case, theories about the effect of punishment on people's future involvement in crime).
2. Applied research is founded on systematic observations (such as randomly assigning interventions on each domestic dispute call and carefully following up to see who becomes a repeat offender).
3. Applied research uses replication (such as repeating the study in a number of different communities).
4. Applied research culminates in policy recommendations (such as establishing standing orders for the police to use the arrest intervention).
5. Applied research is often interdisciplinary in nature (in this case, involving a sociologist and a criminologist).

funds appear to be in more than one bank account at a time. Hutton collected $8 million in interest on the same money from more than one bank. Finally, white-collar crime can take the form of fraudulent insurance claims, which amount to an $11 billion loss each year.

As these illustrations should make clear, white-collar crime can be very costly to society and may actually hurt more people than does street crime (Reiman, 1996). Despite this cost, the Federal Bureau of Investigation classifies most white-collar crimes as less serious offenses. The public in both the United States and Canada also seems to view most white-collar crimes as less serious than other crimes (Cullen, Link, & Polanzi, 1982; Goff & Nason-Clark, 1989). Occasionally, corporate criminals go to jail. During the past decade, a chairman of LTV Corporation was sentenced to four years for insider stock trading, and a Tennessee financier was given twenty years for financial irregularities. Between 1987 and 1990, Michael Milken, Ivan Boesky, and a number of other influential and wealthy stock traders were sent to prison for securities fraud, illegal insider trading in stocks, and various other violations of the securities laws (Stewart, 1991). But critics argue that these tend to be the exception rather than the rule and that the law is lenient on white-collar criminals, especially influential ones. Some of this leniency may come from the fact that white-collar criminals often cooperate with prosecutors in exposing other participants in illegal activities. In fact, both Boesky and Milken cooperated, and they spent relatively little time behind bars and left prison as fairly wealthy men.

It should be clear that deviance is widespread and varied, especially in heterogeneous industrial societies. In all likelihood, you have engaged in actions that have been defined by some groups as deviant. Table 5.2 lists some activities that are illegal in the state of Michigan and likely to be considered deviant by some groups. Few college students can honestly claim to have never committed some of these offenses. I personally

TABLE 5.2 Criminal activities under the state of Michigan penal code

1. You attempt to strike another person physically, but do not succeed.
(Sec. 750–81/750.92: Attempted Assault and Battery)
2. During a fight, you break your opponent's nose.
(Sec. 750.81a: Assault and Battery with Bodily Harm)
3. You set a fire in a wastebasket located in a public rest room.
(Sec. 750.73–.81: Arson)
4. You intentionally damage somebody else's property.
(Sec. 750.377a: Malicious Destruction of Property)
5. You knowingly trespass on another person's property.
(Sec. 750.552: Trespass)
6. You write a check, knowing that it exceeds the amount you have in your account.
(Sec. 750.218: False Pretenses)
7. You shoplift minor articles (candy bar, cigarettes, magazines).
(Sec. 750.356: Larceny)
8. You purchase a compact disc player that you know or believe is stolen.
(Sec. 750.535: Receiving Stolen Property)
9. You hide in the trunk of a friend's car in order to gain entrance to a drive-in movie without paying the admission fee.
(Sec. 750.292–93: Failure to Pay)
10. You participate in sexual activity with an animal.
(Sec. 750.158: Crime Against Nature)

11. You are married, and you have voluntary sexual intercourse with a person other than your spouse.
(Sec. 750.29: Felonious Adultery)
12. You engage in an act of sexual intercourse for money.
(Sec. 750.44: Soliciting and Accosting)
13. You participate in procuring a prostitute for another person or direct that person to a place of prostitution.
(Sec. 750.450: Aiders and Abettors)
14. You engage in sexual intercourse with any female under the age of 16 years.
(Sec. 750.13: Enticing Away Female Under Age 16)
15. You are involved in a fight involving two or more persons in a public establishment.
(Sec. 750.167: Disorderly Conduct)
16. You use obscene, profane language in the presence of women and children.
(Sec. 750.337: Improper Language)
17. You throw an empty can of soda out the window of your car.
(Sec. 752.901: Littering)
18. You play poker for money at a friend's home.
(Sec. 750.301: Accepting Money or Valuable Thing Contingent on an Uncertain Event)
19. You hide a firearm or knife with a blade exceeding three inches on your person while outside of your home.
(Sec. 750.227: Concealed Weapons, Carrying)

Note: From *Michigan Compiled Laws* (vols. 38–39), 1987, St. Paul, MN: West.

asked students in my college classes whether they had committed one or more of these offenses, and most said they had. Yet the students did not regard themselves as either criminals or deviants.

Deviance: Its Consequences for Society

You should be able to explain the functional and dysfunctional consequences of deviance for society.

It has been shown that deviance is widespread. The consequences of deviance are also broadly felt, ultimately affecting all parts of society. However, although many people tend to view deviance as "bad," sociologists recognize that deviance can be functional as well as dysfunctional.

The Dysfunctions of Deviance

One of the negative consequences of deviance is its cost. In sheer economic terms, crime costs U.S. society billions of dollars every year, through the maintenance of police forces, court systems, and prisons to house offenders. It costs $74,000 yearly to keep one offender in a maximum security prison. Other forms of deviance, such as alcoholism, also result in financial losses in the form of absenteeism from work, shoddy work from people who go to work while under the influence of alcohol, and the deterioration of personal relationships. These costs affect not only employers and employees but also the taxpayer, who is eventually touched by these behaviors.

Deviance has a number of other personal costs. One of these is the fear of crime felt by many urban residents, who barricade themselves in their homes each night and use double-bolt locks, burglar alarms, and watchdogs to put their minds at ease. Another personal cost of deviance is the tension created when people with conflicting lifestyles live side by side. For example, people who insist on "respectability" in their neighborhood may feel personally threatened if prostitutes begin to move in.

Another dysfunction of deviance is that some people may become disillusioned with conformity and choose to become deviant themselves. For example, when others are not penalized for cheating in business or selling illegal drugs, those who have previously conformed in these realms may begin to question the wisdom of their conformity. In addition, widespread deviance can lead people to lose faith and trust in societal institutions. Following the Watergate incident in the 1970s, for example, confidence in the U.S. government and its officials declined considerably.

In addition to the previous dysfunctions, there are usually negative consequences for the people who are regarded as deviant. For one thing, those recognized as deviant are denied key opportunities in society. Former prison inmates, the mentally ill, or the obese, for example, may be denied job opportunities that would probably be available to them had they not acquired a deviant status. Furthermore, the stigma associated with many forms of deviance can impair a person's self-concept, leading him or her to ignore opportunities or abandon efforts toward achieving socially valued goals, such as a respected occupation. A prostitute, for example, may internalize the social reaction that she is just a "cheap whore" and never aspire toward another way of making a living.

The Functions of Deviance

Deviance can have destructive consequences, but some forms of deviance can actually contribute to the maintenance of society. As one sociologist put it, a deviant "is not a bit of debris spun out by faulty social machinery, but a relevant figure in the community's overall division of labor" (Erikson, 1966, p. 19). How is this figure "relevant" to the community? In other words, what part does deviance play in the functioning of society? To begin with, the identification and sanctioning of deviants provides a lesson in what behaviors and characteristics society will tolerate. When people deride alcoholics as "drunks" or "winos," they are warning others about the denigration and ostracism they would suffer should they behave in a similar fashion. Emile Durkheim argued that deviance is actually a normal and quite necessary part of society because it helps identify the boundaries of acceptability.

Second, the punishment of deviance is a collective reaffirmation of those values that the deviant has violated, and this reaffirmation enhances group solidarity. When Germans stoned Jews in the streets in the 1930s, Germans were reinforcing their perception that they were a superior racial group and promoting a strong in-group feeling (see Chapter 4).

Third, deviance can act as a warning signal that there is a serious inconsistency or defect in society. High rates of alcoholism, for example, suggest that the social structure has failed to provide meaningful or satisfying positions for some in society.

Fourth, deviance can serve as a safety valve to prevent social discontent from being directed at basic societal values and institutions. The poor and the unemployed, for example, may turn to alcohol or drugs rather than supporting radical political groups advocating changes in the economic system and a redistribution of wealth. In this way, deviance contributes to the stability of society.

Finally, deviance can contribute to social change. In the 1950s, for example, cohabitation among young adults was highly stigmatized and rather uncommon, being limited largely to marginal groups such as "beatniks" or the poor. Since the 1960s, cohabitation has grown in acceptability and now provides an acceptable alternative for some adults who wish to carry on a sexual and emotional relationship openly but prefer not to marry. In short, what is deviant and stigmatized in one era may become normal in another era.

Deviance and Social Control

You should be able to explain the functioning of internal and external social controls and differentiate formal and informal social controls.

Despite the many types and causes of deviance, social order predominates, and society is surprisingly stable and predictable. We have little fear that the bureaucrat will appear at his desk in the nude, that the bank teller will assault us, or that a college professor will exhibit schizophrenic behavior. We are highly dependent on this social stability in our daily lives. It is achieved through various means of social control. **Social control** refers to *the set of mechanisms societies use to encourage people to conform to the norms of society* (Black, 1993).

Internal Sources of Social Control

There are many forms of deviant behavior—from prostitution to armed robbery to striptease dancing—but most would probably have no particular appeal for you even if there were no possibility of detection and punishment. These feelings on your part are largely the result of socialization, through which each of us internalizes sets of norms that guide our behavior. Conformity to internalized norms is an *internal* source of social control. The norms internalized are those of society or of some group to which we belong, and they can be so powerful that the very thought of violating them generates anxiety and guilt. As noted in Chapter 3, "most of the time we ourselves desire just that which society expects of us. We *want* to obey the rules. We *want* the parts that society has assigned to us" (Berger, 1963, p. 93). Most of us, for example, are so horrified at the thought of eating human flesh that the possibility would not even enter our minds unless faced with imminent starvation. Even then, many people have refused to do so and have died. Through socialization, then, *social* control can become *self*-control. From society's point of view, self-control is the most effective means of social control because it requires little surveillance and few active efforts to punish wrongdoers. People conform because they want to, not because they fear punishment.

External Sources of Social Control

The socialization process is pervasive but not completely effective. There are a host of psychological, sociological, biological, and situational influences that can channel people's behavior in socially disapproved directions. In addition, some deviance is inherently pleasurable and enticing. Thus socialization is not, by itself, sufficient to ensure conformity, and all societies develop external techniques of social control. These external techniques can be either informal or formal in nature.

Informal social controls are the various types of social pressures exerted by people in face-to-face settings to ensure the general observance of norms. Through these techniques, people express disapproval and thereby exert pressure on others to modify their behavior. There are many forms of informal social control. Criticism and ridicule, for example, can be effective means of exerting social pressure. Wearing a bathing suit to church or the opera, for instance, may draw a raised eyebrow, a hostile stare, or possibly a verbal reprimand. If the opinion of the congregation or the opera crowd is important to that person, such criticism will probably lead him or her to think twice about his or her dress.

Among the Kapauku Papuans of New Guinea, the public reprimand was one of the most important techniques of social control (Pospisil, 1958). For violations of important norms, members of the tribe would subject the offender to angry reproaches, sometimes continuing intermittently for many days. This experience was considered deeply humiliating for the offender, because people in such small societies must be concerned about everyone's opinion of him or her. This sanction caused so much shame among the Kapaukans that it was considered second only to death in its severity.

Gossip can also be an effective informal mechanism of social control. People tend to pass on accounts about the social "misbehavior" of others. Because most people are concerned about their reputations, gossip, or the threat of it, might motivate a person to forgo an adulterous affair or to conduct it in such a way that detection is less likely.

Social pressure can also be exerted through shunning or ostracism. Among the Mzab of southern Algeria, for example, a woman who has violated community rules, especially sexual mores, can be ostracized, a condition known as *tebreya,* for up to two years. During this period, other women are forbidden to have any conversations with her, and she is excluded from public ceremonies and religious rituals (Farrag, 1971). Such experiences can be painful and even terrifying. Because our self-concepts and sense of self-worth are largely derived from membership in groups, terminating or curtailing those memberships can affect our perceptions of our worth.

Formal social controls are the techniques that have been codified by a society and are applied by specifically designated agents, such as law enforcement bodies or the courts. In heterogeneous, industrial societies, formal social control becomes especially important because informal means are often inadequate. Informal social control through shunning or gossip is effective only if the people affected care about the opinions of others, and in modern societies where secondary relationships abound, that is frequently untrue. Ostracism can be exercised only if the deviant belongs to a group from which he or she can be isolated. Many deviants are strangers over whom we do not have such control, however. Thus we use formal agents of social control, such as the police and the courts, that have the power to control behavior through levying fines or imprisoning people. In the United States, these formal agents of social control tend to focus on deviance that is dangerous, such as crime. Other forms of deviance, which may be repugnant to some but not threatening to person or property, are less likely to come under the purview of formal agents of control. In some societies, however, such as Singapore and China, many different types of deviance are the focus of formal social-control efforts. Singapore was discussed in the beginning of this chapter; Other Worlds, Other Ways: China (on pp. 164–165) discusses how China uses a combination of both informal and formal controls to prevent deviance and crime.

Crime in the United States

You should be able to describe and explain the high crime rate in the United States and explain proposals for reducing crime.

Crime rates have risen rapidly in the United States in the past few decades. Many prisons house far more inmates than they can handle, and the public and politicians clamor for funds to build yet more prisons. Unlike noncriminal deviance, there is considerable consensus that something needs to be done about crime. But what? This chapter will close with an assessment of the crime problem, focusing especially on the role of recent social developments in changes in the crime rate.

The High Crime Rate

The Federal Bureau of Investigation (FBI) publishes an annual document called the Uniform Crime Reports (UCR). The report summarizes crime statistics collected by the FBI each month from law enforcement authorities in more than

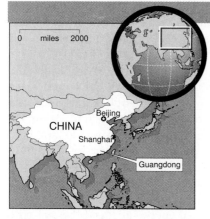

THER WORLDS, *Other Ways*

CHINA: A GRADUAL APPLICATION OF FORMAL SOCIAL CONTROL

People in the United States sometimes view Chinese history as if it began in 1949 with the Communist Revolution and the triumph of Mao Zedong. Certainly, the rise of communism has been significant for China, but what has happened since 1949 has been an accommodation with earlier history rather than an overthrow of it. After all, China is a country that has been populated for thousands of years by the same people with the same culture. This long-term stability has permitted the evolution of some strong and persistent cultural traditions. Sociologists have been particularly interested in the systems of law and social control that have evolved in China because they rely more heavily on informal procedures to control behavior than the U.S. system does (Li, 1977; Lubman, 1969).

In China, anything that disrupts the work setting, the neighborhood, or the nation as a whole is the focus of law and social control. As a consequence, not all "laws" in China have been passed by a legislature and appear in formalized criminal codes. Some guidelines for permissible behavior appear in government newspapers such as the *People's Daily,* where the consequences of noncompliance are also spelled out. In addition to things like murder and rape, Chinese authorities are also interested in whether somebody cheats on a spouse, loses a job, or drops out of school. These shortcomings might not be considered matters of official concern in the West, but in China they are the focus of significant social-control efforts.

Thus, what is against the "law" tends to be more ambiguous and shifting in China.

In China, people are urged to join study groups in their workplace or neighborhood, and these groups are a key element of social control. Through frequent meetings, the groups serve as a significant source of social pressure to conform and as a mechanism for detecting and dealing with those who do not. For example, the Chinese devote considerable effort to making sure that everyone understands what is permissible and what is not. They do this by making the rules for permissible behavior available to people, such as through admonitions in the *People's Daily* and by periodic discussion and analysis of laws and strictures in the study groups. These groups apply the laws to the practical circumstances of their members to create a clear awareness of the boundaries of the acceptable. In this way, these informal groups constantly reinforce society's version of what is acceptable and what is deviant.

The Chinese system of law also emphasizes early intervention in problem behaviors. The Chinese believe that serious problems do not arise without warning; the problems first appear as unhappiness, dissatisfaction, or minor transgressions of norms. In some cases, this early appearance may only take the form of "improper" thoughts, such as political dissent. For the Chinese, such dissent is indicative that the person is having difficulty conforming to society's rules. So, the study groups not only educate members but also serve to detect these early and relatively minor deviations. Since the group consists of people who live and work together on a daily basis, they are especially attuned to small deviations from normal ways of thinking and behaving. Members also find it

---

12,000 cities and towns. In the UCR, the FBI distinguishes between what are called Part I, or more serious, criminal offenses, and Part II, or less serious offenses (see Table 5.3 on p. 166). Part I offenses are considered more serious because many believe they pose the greatest and most direct threat to personal safety and property. The FBI also

presents a Crime Index, which is the official crime rate typically reported in the media. The Crime Index comprises the number of Part I offenses known to the police for every 100,000 people.

Between 1970 and 1980, according to the FBI, the rate of Crime Index offenses rose by a startling 49 percent. The 1980s, however, were another

difficult to hide illegal behaviors, such as stealing, from their intimates. The goal of these early interventions is to solve problems before they get out of control.

Group members also have a social duty to assist one another to overcome their shortcomings. Criticism of another person's lifestyle or work is considered proper because it is an extension of one's social duty to help other citizens. Since crimes or other transgressions hurt not only the victim but society as a whole, everyone has a stake in and a responsibility for preventing or detecting transgressors. What in the United States might be considered libelous or an invasion of privacy is considered a social obligation in China. The group has some responsibility for detecting the underlying causes of a person's transgressions, such as an unhappy marriage or conflict with a sibling, and trying to resolve it. Failings in the family are seen as root causes of many forms of juvenile deviance (Curran & Cook, 1993).

If a person continues to deviate, informal group pressure and public criticism increase as more and more people become involved. Only when these means fail or the violations become serious does the formal public security or state enforcement system intervene. This gradual effort to control behavior is quite different from the way the criminal process tends to work in the United States, where people who engage in minor forms of deviance are often left on their own. If the person does something more serious that the law cannot ignore, then the formal system intervenes, often with strong punishment.

China also places part of the blame for crime and deviance on external conditions rather than on character flaws of the individual. Crime might be the result of poverty or "capitalist tendencies," for example. Since the individual has not been rejected, this explanation opens the door for reform and rehabilitation. In fact, the Chinese believe that, when given the chance, most people will choose to do the right thing, and so most people are reformable.

Systems of law and criminal justice are cultural and historical products. The current Chinese system grew out of a long tradition of Confucian beliefs in the importance of order, harmony, and obligation (which, as noted, also plays a role in Singapore). Also China has a history of imperial authority that long predates the Communist Revolution and that gave emperors complete authority over citizens. These and other factors have shaped the Chinese legal system of today (Fairbanks, 1989). At the same time, the United States has a Judeo-Christian heritage that emphasizes individualism. The legal system is also influenced by the fact that the United States emerged when European colonists overthrew the power of the British monarchy. Whereas the Chinese system accepts the authority of the state over individuals, the United States legal system has focused on how to protect the individual from the unwanted exercise of power by the state. People in the United States tend to use highly charged phrases, such as *thought reform* or *thought control,* to describe what goes on in China. Yet, these phrases reflect, in part, a use of Western values to impose meaning on Chinese social institutions. It misses the extent to which Chinese criminal justice institutions are an outgrowth of Chinese Confucian heritage and historical development.

story: Crime Index offenses actually dropped by 2 percent between 1980 and 1990. Most of this drop was accounted for by the drop in property crimes. During the 1980s, violent crimes rose by 22 percent, but this was less of an increase than the 64 percent rise in the 1970s (see Figure 5.2 on p. 167). So far in the 1990s, the crime rate has stayed level or declined slightly. Yet, the crime rate is still far higher than it was in previous decades. If crimes were evenly spaced throughout the day, in 1994, there would have been one serious crime about every two seconds of each day and one violent crime approximately every seventeen seconds (Federal Bureau of Investigation, 1995).

TABLE 5.3 Classification of criminal offenses by the Federal Bureau of Investigation

Part I Offenses		Part II Offenses
Murder and nonnegligent manslaughter		Other assaults
Forcible rape		Forgery and counterfeiting
Robbery	} Violent crimes	Fraud
Aggravated assault		Stolen property; buying, receiving, possessing
Burglary		Vandalism
Larceny-theft		Weapons; carrying, possessing, etc.
Motor vehicle theft	} Property crimes	Prostitution and commercialized vice
Arson		Sex offenses (except forcible rape and prostitution)
		Drug abuse violations
		Gambling
		Offenses against family and children
		Driving under the influence
		Liquor laws
		Drunkenness
		Disorderly conduct
		Vagrancy
		All other offenses (except traffic)
		Suspicion
		Curfew and loitering law violations

Some of these increases, however, need to be placed in perspective. They may in part reflect changes in the likelihood of reporting crimes rather than actual increases in crime. Rape, for example, has traditionally been a vastly underreported crime. With more public discussion of rape in the 1970s and 1980s and strong pressure from feminist groups, both the police and the public have become more sensitive to the problems of rape victims. Many hospitals provide counseling for rape victims, and many states have rules that limit the use of information about a victim's previous sexual activities as evidence in court. These changes have encouraged more women to report rapes, and this encouragement undoubtedly accounts for some, although not all, of the increase in reported rapes.

Another reason for caution about UCR crime statistics is that they are based on crimes known to the police, and considerable crime is not brought to the attention of the police. Such unreported crime is not reflected in these statistics, which are conservative indicators of the nation's crime problem. It is estimated, for example, that only 45 percent of the violent crimes are reported to the police and as few as 28 percent of the thefts (Maguire & Flanagan, 1991, p. 254). When the reported and unreported crimes are put together, it is clear that the United States has a considerable crime problem, and people are concerned about it.

Reducing Crime

The question of how to reduce crime is highly controversial. However, the analysis of the sociological sources of deviance and crime earlier in the chapter points to a number of promising reforms. Given the role of poverty and economic inequities in fostering crime, it is plausible that reducing poverty and the economic disparity

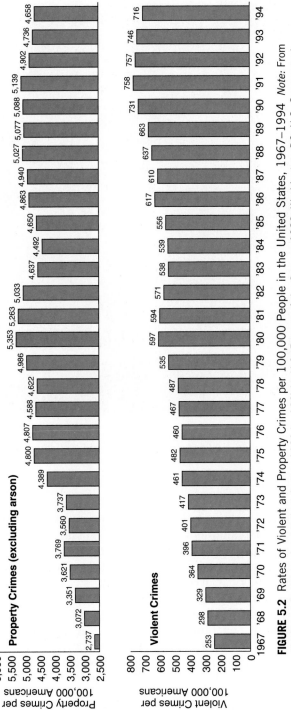

FIGURE 5.2 Rates of Violent and Property Crimes per 100,000 People in the United States, 1967–1994 *Note:* From *Statistical Abstract of the United States, 1980* (p. 182) by U.S. Bureau of the Census, 1980, Washington, DC: U.S. Government Printing Office; *Uniform Crime Reports: Crime in the United States, 1994* (p. 58) by Federal Bureau of Investigation, 1995, Washington, DC: U.S. Government Printing Office.

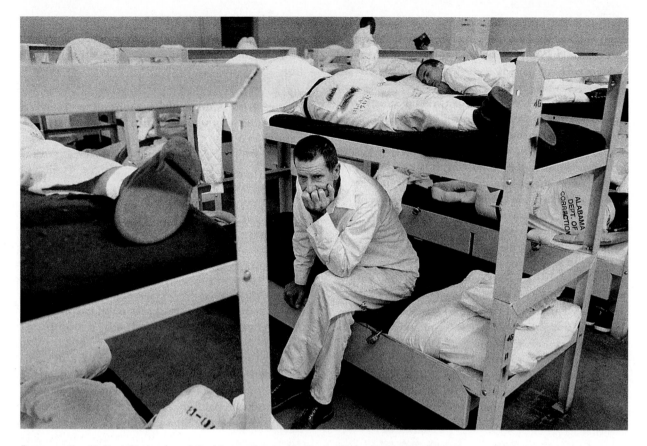

Because the United States has failed to confront effectively the social and economic conditions that produce crime, it has relied heavily on punishment, with one consequence being growing and crowded prison populations.

between the affluent and the poor would help reduce some forms of crime and delinquency. Especially important along these lines would be to provide equal educational and occupational opportunities for all people. Given Elliott Currie's (1985) analysis of crime in Japan discussed earlier, it may be possible to reduce poverty and economic disparity through programs that encourage fuller employment—government and private-sector programs to create new jobs and to provide job training to those without adequate job skills. In addition, the jobs people get must pay a living wage so that people can support their families. Furthermore, the sociologist Mark Colvin (1991) recommends that we fight crime by investing in the institutions that prepare people for productive roles in society: families and schools (see Chapters 9 and 12). Failures in the educational in-

stitutions and families have contributed to the inability of many young people to find and make use of legitimate avenues to opportunity. These calls for social reform are an attempt to attack the social and structural conditions that have created much, although not all, of the crime problem. Other Worlds, Other Ways: Japan (on pp. 170–172) explores in more depth the differences between Japan and the United States in this regard.

Beyond this social reform, a number of measures could be taken to reduce crime in the United States.

1. Legalize many victimless crimes, such as gambling, prostitution, and some drug violations. This would reduce the secondary crime associated with victimless offenses and free the criminal justice system to work with more serious crimes.

2. Focus judicial reform on providing swift, certain, and fair punishment rather than overly long and counterproductive prison terms.

3. Make punishment equitable, whether the crime occurs on a slum street or in a corporate boardroom. Disparities in punishment resulting from the racial, sexual, or socioeconomic characteristics of the offender should be carefully monitored and controlled.

4. Narrow the discretionary options of police officers, prosecutors, and judges and develop procedures to hold them accountable to the public for the fairness and reasonableness of their decisions and actions.

5. Provide all criminal defendants with truly equal legal counsel in order to reduce the inequities in convictions and sentences.

6. Develop correctional programs that promote rather than undermine personal responsibility and that provide offenders with real opportunities to succeed in legitimate occupations. These might include increased occupational training and counseling while imprisoned and work release and other alternatives to incarceration.

7. Make efforts to reduce the environmental opportunities for committing crime. These can take the form of better physical security, such as burglar-proof locks; better detection of crime through such mechanisms as burglar alarms and antishoplifting tags in stores; and improved surveillance, such as better street lighting.

Certainly other reforms can be considered. Which reforms will have a beneficial effect on the crime problem and on inadequacies in the criminal justice system can be determined only after programs have been initiated and evaluated. What should be clear is that only a broad-based and coordinated attack is likely to have a significant impact.

Crime, the Criminal Justice System, and the Mass Media

Earlier in this chapter, the interactionist perspective was used to explain why some people might engage in deviant behavior or commit crimes. This perspective also provides insight into the process whereby things like deviance and crime come to be defined as important public issues toward which individuals and policy makers should direct their attention. In modern societies, the mass media play an important role in this process of defining the situation or reality construction, because many people gain much of their information on and attitudes about crime by what they read in newspapers or magazines or watch on television (Cuklanz, 1996; Sacco, 1995). Overall, crime coverage consumes anywhere from 5 to 25 percent of all news coverage, depending on the particular type of media. The media devote more attention to covering crime than to reporting on the U.S. Congress or the President.

In terms of shaping the public's definition of reality, the picture of crime portrayed in the media is in some ways a significant distortion of reality. Comparing the media portrayals with the statistics and research on crime that social scientists have accumulated, one difference is that the volume of crime portrayed in the media has little relationship to the number of crimes actually committed. Furthermore, the media reports suggest that violent crime is more common than nonviolent crime, whereas crime statistics clearly indicate the reverse is true. The vast majority of crimes reported in the media are crimes committed by individuals, such as homicide or robbery, rather than crimes committed by organizations or corporations, such as price-fixing, securities violations, or the violation of environmental regulations.

In regard to the criminal justice system, the media present the police as more effective in solving crimes and apprehending criminals than the statistics suggest they actually are. The media also tend to feature the police quite prominently in news reports, but other facets of the criminal justice system (the courts, prisons, probation officers, and so on) are given less attention than their role in controlling crime would seem to warrant. Finally, the media often present a distorted image of crime victims, portraying all citizens as equally likely to be affected. In reality, poor minorities in inner-city communities are most likely to be victims. The chance that an affluent suburbanite will become a victim of, say, drug violence is actually quite small. Yet portraying victimization as randomly spread through the community is more likely to generate general concern about crime and lead people to see it as an important public issue.

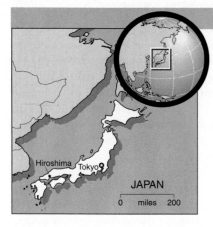

OTHER WORLDS, *Other Ways*

JAPAN: SOCIAL AND CULTURAL UNDERPINNINGS OF CRIME

It is sad to admit, but the United States is a disturbingly crime-ridden society when compared to most societies around the world. Figure 5.3 compares the homicide rate in the United States with the rate in various nations around the world. The U.S. rate is far higher than the rate in all European nations except for the Russian federation—a nation in considerable economic, social, and cultural collapse. The U.S. homicide rate is also much higher than in most Asian and Middle Eastern nations. Even a poor nation such as Egypt has a far lower rate. Some struggling nations in Latin America have higher homicide rates, but other poor nations in that region, such as

FIGURE 5.3
Homicide Rates in Various Nations
Note: From *Demographic Yearbook, 1993* (pp. 484–505) by the United Nations, 1995, New York: United Nations.

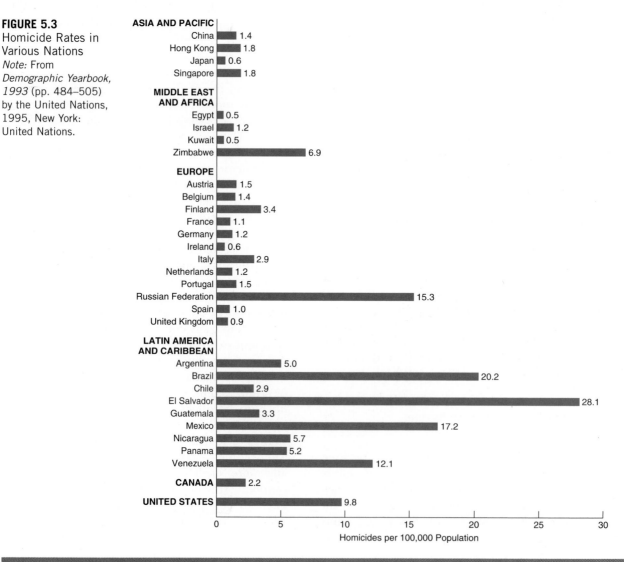

	Homicides per 100,000 Population
ASIA AND PACIFIC	
China	1.4
Hong Kong	1.8
Japan	0.6
Singapore	1.8
MIDDLE EAST AND AFRICA	
Egypt	0.5
Israel	1.2
Kuwait	0.5
Zimbabwe	6.9
EUROPE	
Austria	1.5
Belgium	1.4
Finland	3.4
France	1.1
Germany	1.2
Ireland	0.6
Italy	2.9
Netherlands	1.2
Portugal	1.5
Russian Federation	15.3
Spain	1.0
United Kingdom	0.9
LATIN AMERICA AND CARIBBEAN	
Argentina	5.0
Brazil	20.2
Chile	2.9
El Salvador	28.1
Guatemala	3.3
Mexico	17.2
Nicaragua	5.7
Panama	5.2
Venezuela	12.1
CANADA	2.2
UNITED STATES	9.8

Nicaragua and Panama, have homicide rates that are half that of the United States. Compared with Japan, another affluent, industrial nation, the United States comes off rather poorly (Currie, 1985; Hendry, 1995; Thornton & Endo, 1992). The United States has eighteen times more rapes, sixteen times more homicides, six times more burglaries, and nine times more drug-related offenses.

What accounts for this dramatic contrast with Japan? The unavailability of handguns in Japan plays a part, as does the much narrower gap between the affluent and the poor, as mentioned earlier in this chapter. Chapter 2 also noted that Japan and the United States have some dramatically contrasting cultural values, which undoubtedly play a part. One widely recognized difference is that Japanese society places much higher value on the group and family, whereas the United States emphasizes individualism and personal autonomy. Individual Japanese feel a strong obligation to their family and society, and families feel a strong sense of responsibility for the behavior of their members. Each family member bears a share of the responsibility for preserving the reputation of the family and avoiding bringing disgrace to it by doing something that might be socially disapproved such as committing a crime. Consequently, informal mechanisms of social control, such as threatened exclusion from the group, can control crime more effectively in Japan than in the United States.

Another difference is that Japanese culture instills a strong sense of respect for laws, rules, and customs. Such respect is seen as part of a citizen's social obligation, probably deriving from Confucian teachings about uprightness, duty, and obligation. In Japan, people obey the law because of this obligation, not just out of fear of authority or punishment; in the United States, people are more inclined toward cynical violation of the law if they think they can get away with it.

(continued)

These members of a *yakuza* (syndicate) in Japan are attending the funeral of one of their leaders. While engaging in illegal activities themselves, the *yakuza* also serves as an important source of social control in Japanese society.

OTHER WORLDS, *Other Ways*

JAPAN: SOCIAL AND CULTURAL UNDERPINNINGS OF CRIME *(continued)*

A third difference is that Japan is a much more racially and culturally homogeneous society where there is considerable consensus regarding desirable values and appropriate behaviors. Homogeneity removes one important source of misunderstanding, tension, and conflict that exists in the United States. Without these social fault lines, Japan offers its citizens a much more cohesive and supportive neighborhood and community environment.

A final difference is that Japanese society is much more *supportive* of individuals and their families than is U.S. society. Through economic and social policies, Japan strives toward full employment of its workers and tries to create a stable connection of workers to the workplace. As a consequence, the income distribution in Japan is much more equitable than in the United States, and no severely deprived and permanently disadvantaged underclass exists. These supportive policies create the foundation for the emergence of strong and stable family and neighborhood ties, which in turn exert strong social controls over misbehavior. In addition, Japan, along with many Western European industrial nations, has social policies that cushion the disruptions and hardships that can accompany the loss of work. These nations, for example, allow more generous unemployment benefits and give them to more unemployed workers than does the United States. Because of this generosity, less disruption of family and communal roles accompanies unemployment. This continuity is important because

it is not just economic circumstances that motivate crime; the destruction of family and communal supports that can accompany unemployment also reduce controls over misbehavior (Currie, 1985).

Thus, different cultural values account for some of the differences in crime between the two societies. Reality, however, is still more complicated. Many other factors contribute to Japan's low crime rate, but just one will be mentioned here (Kersten, 1993). Japan has very active and extensive criminal organizations, called *yakuza,* with hierarchies of bosses and an extensive corporate structure. They engage in illegal and semilegal as well as legal enterprises, and they have links to important politicians. They have extensive networks going into many Japanese neighborhoods, and their activities may actually serve to reduce crime overall. For example, they settle civil disputes, such as those arising over traffic accidents, and collect overdue loans. They also have tight control over Japan's illegal drug market, which helps to prevent a lot of the crime and violence that surround the wide-open market in illegal drugs in the United States. In addition, the *yakuza* probably deter small-scale robbery and theft in the neighborhoods where they have a considerable presence.

When considered separately, each of these elements of Japanese culture may make only a small contribution to the low Japanese crime rate; in combination, however, they advance a good way toward understanding the yawning gulf between crime in the United States and crime in Japan. They also emphasize the sociological perspective on crime, namely, that crime emerges from particular social and cultural conditions and can be reduced by changing these conditions.

The reasons the media present this image of crime and criminal justice have a lot to do with the organizational processes of news production and the position of the media in the political and economic institutions of society. First of all, the media are mostly private companies motivated by profit, and they devote attention to crimes they see as profitable—crimes that increase the sales of newspapers and magazines and the audience of television shows. To attract large numbers of viewers, they prefer stories that are short, simple, and personal. Crimes committed by individuals, especially street crimes like homicide or drug dealing, tend to be much simpler and can be focused on individuals such as the victim and the offender. Organizational and corporate crimes tend to be more complex and harder to explain to an audience unfamiliar with the complicated legalities of antitrust laws or securities violations. Uncomplicated crime stories are also easier for news organizations to write and produce, and this is important when shows or stories must be produced under rigid, daily deadlines. It also helps, especially for television, if the crime can be captured in a short, dramatic video segment that will appeal to audiences. This is why television is so fond of portraying drug raids: It is dramatic to see police officers with shotguns and combat dress bash in doors of apartments and apprehend startled suspects. Stories presented in the media about crimes against children also tend to be the most frightening and dramatic crimes, because they draw in audiences and readers, even though they do not represent most crimes against children. Nonviolent crime or corporate crime often cannot be captured in such visually appealing images, nor do they have the same drama as some individual crimes.

Another aspect of news organizations that influences the reporting of crime is that journalists and newsmakers sometimes try to organize individual stories around a broader news "theme" in order to legitimize the presentation of particular stories. After all, one reason for reporting about a particular crime, which may seem of little significance by itself, is that it is a part of a "crime wave." That is, this crime is symptomatic of a broader news issue that the public needs to be aware of. One study in New York, for example, found journalists reporting increasing numbers of crimes against the elderly as a part of a growing crime wave in the city (Fishman, 1978). Yet reviews of actual crime statistics and criminal victimization of the elderly could detect no actual increases in these types of crimes. The process of competitive journalism also contributes to this trend. Once one news source reports such a crime wave, other newspapers or television news organizations feel some pressure to follow suit in the competition for audiences (Orcutt & Turner, 1993).

Given these considerations, it is not surprising that the media present a distorted image of crime.

This view, once presented, is a powerful force in shaping the public's definition of the "crime problem." The police and other criminal justice authorities play an important part in creating this definition, because the media are heavily dependent on the police for access to news about crime. The police are typically the people who have most information about crimes and access to offenders, victims, and crime scenes; the police are also credible sources of information, which is important for the media. In giving information to the media, the police tend to portray themselves in the most positive light, by dwelling on cases they have successfully solved. One social scientist concluded that "the police role as the dominant gatekeeper means that crime news is often police news and that the advancement of a police perspective on crime and its solution is facilitated" (Sacco, 1995, p. 146). Police and government experts make themselves available to the media for comment on crime and criminal justice issues, and this places these authorities in a better position to communicate their perspectives because other groups with different views do not have such easy access. Since only one set of authorities is presented and these authorities tend to agree with one another, the impression is one of agreement among knowledgeable experts about the scope and causes of a problem—even though there is substantial debate and controversy over the nature of the crime problem today. The authorities with access to the media are in the best position to shape people's definition of the situation in regard to crime and thus to contribute to the process of reality construction.

Summary

1. Deviance consists of behaviors or characteristics that violate important group norms and that as a consequence are reacted to with disapproval. Behaviors and characteristics are deviant because they are so defined by a particular group.

2. Sociologists view deviance as relative to the norms and values of a particular culture, subculture, or group. Deviance is not inherent in any behavior or characteristic but rather arises from the relationship between a behavior and the social definition of the behavior by some group.

3. Two prominent nonsociological explanations of deviance are those resting on biological and psychological grounds. Purely biological theories of deviance have been discredited. In a few cases, biology may play a limited role in bringing about deviance, but most deviance has nothing to do with biology.

4. Although psychological approaches to deviance may shed some light on some forms of deviance, the role of psychological disturbances is limited, and it is often the deviance, and the public's reaction to it, that results in changes in personality.

5. Sociologists have emphasized the role of culture, social structure, and social interaction in bringing about deviant behavior. Functionalist theories of deviance focus on such things as social bonds, anomie, and opportunities for deviance or crime created by changes in the social system. The conflict perspective emphasizes the point that powerful groups have the resources to define what will be considered crime or deviance and against which behaviors social control will be exercised. This perspective also emphasizes that the structure of some economic systems may force some groups into criminal or deviant patterns of behavior. The interactionist perspective explains deviance and crime through processes of cultural transmission, differential association, and labeling.

6. Crime and deviance overlap, but they are not the same. Some crimes are considered deviant and others are not. Likewise, some forms of deviance are not crimes. There are many types of deviance, both criminal and noncriminal. In fact, deviance can take such a variety of forms that virtually everyone has engaged in activities that some groups have defined as deviant.

7. Deviance can be dysfunctional for society in a number of ways: It creates personal and economic costs, leads to disillusionment among conventional people, and results in reduced opportunities and possibly negative self-concepts for those who are stigmatized as deviant. However, deviance can also be functional: Punishing deviants helps clarify the limits of acceptable behavior and reaffirms important values. Deviance also points to defects in society, can serve as a safety valve for easing discontent, and can contribute to social change.

8. Social control refers to societal mechanisms for encouraging people to conform. Some norms are internalized sufficiently that social control becomes self-control. There are also external mechanisms of social control, some of which are informal, such as gossip or ostracism, and others of which are formal, such as the police or the courts.

9. The crime rate in the United States is at a very high level. Proposals to reduce crime derive from the sociological perspectives. The modern mass media play an important part in shaping people's definitions of reality regarding the nature and extent of crime and what should be done about it.

STUDY and Review

Key Terms

anomie

anomie theory

career deviance

crime

cultural transmission theories

deviance

differential association theory

labeling theory

primary deviance

secondary deviance

social control

Multiple-Choice Questions

1. Sociologists have concluded that
   a. biology explains a substantial amount of deviance.
   b. biology plays no role in causing deviance.
   c. when biology does play a role, it is but one contributing factor rather than the sole cause of deviance.
   d. biological explanations are more important than psychological ones in understanding deviance.

2. The concept of *anomie* is linked with which theoretical perspective in sociology?
   a. The functionalist perspective.
   b. The conflict perspective.
   c. The interactionist perspective.
   d. The biological perspective.
   e. The psychological perspective.

3. Conflict theorists argue that the causes of crime and deviance can be found in
   a. the labeling process.
   b. certain characteristics of capitalism.
   c. biological inadequacies of individuals.
   d. weakened social bonds in industrial societies.

4. Violations of social norms in which a person is not caught, or is excused rather than labeled deviant, are referred to as
   a. relative deviance.
   b. secondary deviance.
   c. tertiary deviance.
   d. career deviance.
   e. primary deviance.

5. The most widely used mood-altering drug in the United States is
   a. marijuana.
   b. alcohol.
   c. cocaine.
   d. heroin.
   e. nicotine.

6. Which of the following is true of homicides?
   a. They are rarely planned in advance.
   b. The majority occur during the commission of a felony.
   c. The majority of homicide victims are strangers to their assailants.
   d. The majority are committed as a part of organized crime activities.

7. The audience at a political rally boos at and heckles a speaker for expressing opinions the audience does not like. As a control over the behavior of the speaker, the response would be best called
   a. formal, internal social control.
   b. formal, external social control.
   c. informal, internal social control.
   d. informal, external social control.

8. Systems of law and criminal justice in China have been most clearly influenced by which of the following?
   a. Judeo-Christian heritage.
   b. Confucian beliefs.
   c. Buddhist teachings.
   d. Social scientists.
   e. All of the above.

9. One of the problems with the crime statistics provided by the FBI is that
   a. they are conservative indicators of the extent of crime.
   b. they overestimate the amount of crime that occurs.
   c. they have shown declines in crime in recent decades when crime has actually increased.
   d. they are available only once a decade.

10. The text recommends all of the following to help in the fight against crime and delinquency *except*
    a. reduce poverty.
    b. give longer prison sentences for most crimes.
    c. legalize some victimless crimes.
    d. promote personal responsibility among prison inmates.

True/False Questions

1. For sociologists, a behavior can be inherently deviant, without regard to people's interpretation or judgment of the behavior.

2. Anomie theory can lead to the conclusion that large disparities between income groups can cause crime.

3. According to anomie theory, most deviant behavior is produced by the mode of adaptation called *ritualism*.

4. Cultural transmission theories posit that crime can be blamed on certain characteristics of capitalism as an economic system.

5. Sexual norms are like other societal rules: They vary widely from one social context to another.

6. The studies of policies to reduce domestic violence illustrate that applied sociological research is only rarely interdisciplinary in nature.

7. People in the United States view most white-collar crimes as less serious than other crimes.

8. In China, the range of behaviors that are against the law tends to be much more ambiguous in nature and broader in scope than in the United States.

9. Even though handguns are largely unavailable in Japan, crime rates in Japan are at the same level as in the United States.

10. The text recommends making punishments swift and certain rather than overly lengthy.

Fill-In Questions

1. According to _____ approaches to deviance, deviance is linked to personality disorders or maladjustments.

2. Inconsistencies and contradictions in the social system and the confusion they can cause in people are referred to as _____ .

3. The most common mode of adaptation, according to Robert Merton, and the one that might take the form of deviant or criminal behavior, is called _____ .

4. The differential association theory of crime is one example of a(n) _____ theory.

5. If a drug user is discovered and responds to the discovery by becoming more closely involved with other drug users, this would be an example of _____ deviance.

6. Syndicates are associated with _____ crime.

7. Antitrust violations are one type of _____ crime.

8. _____ are the techniques for ensuring conformity to norms that are codified by society and applied by specifically designated agents.

9. Japanese citizens' sense of respect for law and social obligation probably derives from _____ teachings.

10. The text recommends that the United States fight crime by investing in the social institutions primarily responsible for preparing people for productive roles in society: _____ and _____ .

Matching Questions

_____ 1. Emile Durkheim
_____ 2. forcible rape
_____ 3. fraudulent insurance claims
_____ 4. differential association theory
_____ 5. mark of disgrace
_____ 6. Cesare Lombroso
_____ 7. sexual deviance
_____ 8. ostracism
_____ 9. a mode of adaptation to anomie
_____ 10. secondary deviance

    A. functionalist perspective
    B. interactionist perspective
    C. stigma
    D. career deviance
    E. a white-collar crime
    F. rebellion
    G. prostitution
    H. informal social control
    I. biological approach to deviance
    J. a Part I offense

Essay Questions

1. Describe the psychological approaches to deviance. How do sociologists assess them as explanations of deviance?

2. Describe the functionalist explanation of deviance and crime. Include in your answer a discussion of all of the modes of adaptation to anomie.

3. Explain deviance and crime from the conflict perspective. Show how it differs from the functionalist approach.

4. According to the differential association theory, what is the explanation for why some people commit crimes or engage in deviance whereas others do not?

5. Describe the functions that deviant behavior performs for society.

6. Describe how deviance is dysfunctional for society.

7. Define social control. Describe the forms it can take and give an example of each form.

8. Describe the legal and criminal justice systems in China. From what traditions does the Chinese approach derive? How is it different from that of the United States?

9. Why is the crime rate in Japan so much lower than it is in the United States?

10. What policies are suggested in the text to help reduce the crime rate in the United States?

Answers

Multiple-Choice
1. C; 2. A; 3. B; 4. E; 5. B; 6. A; 7. D;
8. B; 9. A; 10. B

True/False
1. F; 2. T; 3. F; 4. F; 5. T; 6. F; 7. T;
8. T; 9. F; 10. T

Fill-In
1. psychological
2. anomie
3. innovation
4. cultural transmission
5. secondary, career
6. organized
7. white-collar
8. formal social controls
9. Confucian
10. families, schools

Matching
1. A; 2. J; 3. E; 4. B; 5. C; 6. I; 7. G;
8. H; 9. F; 10. D

For Further Reading

Bursik, Robert J., Jr., & Grasmick, Harold G. (1993). *Neighborhoods and crime: The dimensions of effective community control.* New York: Lexington Books. This book looks at the causes of crime and suggests some programs for changing communities to help reduce the amount of crime.

Chin, Ko-lin. (1990). *Chinese subculture and criminality: Non-traditional crime groups in America.* New York: Greenwood Press. Although Chinese Americans do not usually come to mind as a high-crime group, this book analyzes the historical and cultural roots that make for a significant contribution by Chinese to the problem of organized crime in the United States.

Croall, Hazel. (1992). *White-collar crime: Criminal justice and criminology.* Buckingham, UK: Open University Press. This recent analysis of white-collar crime, written from a British perspective, offers a look at the problem in a different culture from that of the United States. It discusses the range, extent, regulation, detection, and punishment of these crimes.

Currie, Elliott. (1993). *Reckoning: Drugs, the cities, and the American future.* New York: Hill & Wang. This excellent overview of the drug problem in the United States covers some of the causes of deviance discussed in this chapter and presents a variety of policy initiatives that would be needed to reduce the problem significantly.

Erikson, Kai T. (1966). *Wayward puritans.* New York: Wiley. This classic sociological work on deviant behavior uses the experiences of the Puritans to demonstrate that deviance is relative and performs important functions in U.S. society.

Friedman, Lawrence M. (1993). *Crime and punishment in American history.* New York: Basic Books. This is a comprehensive look at how American culture has affected what were considered crimes and the punishments that were meted out for them.

Jenness, Valerie. (1993). *Making it work: The prostitutes' rights movement in perspective.* Hawthorne, NY: Aldine de Gruyter. This book analyzes why many consider prostitution to be deviant and describes a social movement that has attempted to reduce the stigma associated with the activity and "normalize" it.

Sherman, Lawrence. (1992). *Policing domestic violence: Experiments and dilemmas.* New York: The Free Press. This work summarizes the field experiments that have been done on the most effective police responses in dealing with spouse abuse. It is a good exercise in applied research on a complex social issue.

Simon, David R., & Eitzen, D. Stanley. (1993). *Elite deviance* (4th ed.). Boston: Allyn & Bacon. An excellent antidote to the myth that deviance occurs mostly among poor and disreputable people, this book chronicles the deviant activities of the rich and powerful.

Snow, David A., & Anderson, Leon. (1993). *Down on their luck: A study of homeless street people.* Berkeley: University of California Press. This valuable book develops a typology of street people based on why they became homeless and the conditions of their life on the street. It also provides an insightful description of that life.

Spradley, James P. (1970). *You owe yourself a drunk: An ethnography of urban nomads.* Boston: Little, Brown. Spradley uses an anthropological approach to deviant subcultures in a heterogeneous society—in this case, focusing on hoboes and street people whom some might consider deviant.

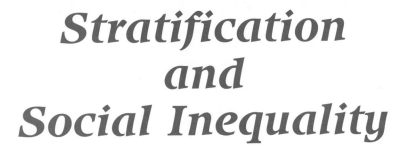

PART THREE

Stratification and Social Inequality

The chapters in Part Three analyze the hierarchical nature of human societies, discussing the tendency for social stratification and social inequality to characterize societies. In particular, the chapters assess inequality that is based on social class, race, ethnicity, and gender.

SIX *Social Stratification and Social Inequality*

In small hunting-and-gathering bands, there is little differentiation between or ranking of people. As described in Chapter 2, however, when societies become larger and a surplus of food and other resources accumulates, distinctions between people in terms of their social worth become common. The Natchez (pronounced "nachay") Indians developed an elaborate, rigid, and somewhat unusual ranking system (Swanton, 1911; White, Murdock, & Scaglion, 1971). At the time of first contact with Europeans in the mid-1500s, the Natchez were a tribe of about four thousand in the territory that is today the border between the states of Louisiana and Mississippi. They lived a sedentary village life that revolved around food production, mostly of maize. The Natchez worshiped the sun, and they were ruled by a group of nobles called Suns, with the chief being called the Great Sun. The Suns were treated with great deference and respect by other Natchez. The Great Sun was carried from one place to another on a litter lifted by eight men, and he had the authority to distribute food and other resources as well as to tell people when to work in the fields or when to hunt or fish. When the Great Sun died, his wives, guards, and retainers were also expected to die, and it is said that they considered such death a great honor.

Below the Suns in Natchez ranking were two more noble groups, called the Nobles and the Honored People; at the bottom were the lowly Stinkards. The Natchez reckoned descent through the mother's line, so at birth people were placed in the group of their mother. In most highly differentiated societies, people tend to marry those of approximately the same rank as themselves; the Natchez were unusual in that every member of the three noble classes were required to marry a Stinkard. Since social position is determined through the woman's lineage, this rule meant that a Stinkard male who married a Sun or a Noble experienced a rise in social status to the noble rank of his wife, or what sociologists call upward mobility. It also meant that a male Sun who married a Stinkard woman was downwardly mobile, although only by one step in the hierarchy. In other words, the Natchez ranking system and marriage customs were such that they forced a certain amount of circulation of people among the different ranks in society (Farb, 1978). Such circulation, or social mobility, is found as well in modern industrial societies such as the United States. As will be shown, however, it occurs in those societies not because of custom, as among the Natchez, but because of other aspects of the social structure.

There were other routes to social mobility among the Natchez. One common method was through warfare. If a Stinkard performed great deeds in war, he might become one of the Honored People, and his wife and children would move into the new position with him. They would even be given a new name to symbolize their new social position. So, even though heredity played an important part in determining people's social position among the Natchez, their ranking system was complicated, and there was more movement among the ranks than is found in many other societies. Another thing of note about the Natchez ranking system is that, although differences in prestige and resources existed among the different groups, the vast disparity between the wealthy and the poor that is found in many societies today did not exist. With control over the distribution of resources, the Great Sun could make sure that everyone was provided for. And since all in the noble classes would marry a Stinkard, they had some interest in the well-being of those people.

Unlike the Natchez, modern societies exhibit vast differences in wealth and poverty, even in the United States. In most societies around the world today, some people live in grinding and unrelieved poverty while a privileged few have unimaginable wealth. The purpose of this chapter is to explain this ranking and differentiation in human societies, whether it be among the Natchez Indians or in the modern United States. Sociologists use the term **social stratification** to refer to *the ranking of people into a hierarchy in which the resources considered valuable by society are unequally distributed.*

This chapter and the next two will focus on the origins and dimensions of stratification systems and how they regulate inequalities in the distribution of resources. In addition, they will consider the extent of inequality in the United States, especially as it is influenced by such factors as race, ethnicity, and gender. They will also consider the extent to which social opportunities are truly "equal" in the United States. They will note that stratification is one of the most important dimensions of society, affecting our lives from birth to death. It influences the jobs we seek, the diseases that afflict us, whom we associate with, the crimes we commit (or do not commit), and the clothes we wear. It plays a role in wars, revolutions, conflict, and changes in society. Social stratification is an element of society that will be considered in each of the remaining chapters of this book.

Dimensions of Stratification

You should be able to discuss Weber's interpretation of the stratification system, define socioeconomic status, and list the major characteristics of the caste, estate, and class stratification systems.

Weber's Analysis

Like most people, you have probably compared your own social position with that of others around you—students, laborers, lawyers, million-

Myths & FACTS

ABOUT THE STRATIFICATION SYSTEM

Myth The United States is moving toward an egalitarian society in which social classes will be largely eliminated and there will be no poverty.

FACT Looking at the historical and cross-cultural record, most sociologists argue that some stratification and inequality are probably inevitable in society because they perform positive functions for the social order. There is controversy over this view, however, in that inequality may not be inevitable but rather benefits those with wealth and power. Stratification might exist without poverty if the well-to-do were willing to share a larger part of their wealth with the poor.

Myth The United States is the only society in the world with a truly open class system where people's positions in the stratification hierarchy are determined largely by their own accomplishments.

FACT Characteristics that are unrelated to one's accomplishments—race, sex, and family background come to mind—exert a strong influence on what a person can achieve in the United States, so the U.S. stratification system is by no means completely open. Furthermore, there is only slightly greater opportunity for upward mobility in the United States when compared to other industrial nations.

Myth The poor are a drain on the public treasury that affluent citizens have to support out of their hard-earned dollars.

FACT Both the poor and the affluent in the United States are a drain on the public treasury, and both pay to support it. The affluent receive government handouts such as loans for college students, price-support payments to farmers, and tax deductions for meals and entertainment expenses connected with business. If we consider tax deductions for home mortgage interest to be a government housing subsidy, then families earning more than $50,000 per year receive more than half of all such federal subsidies. In addition, when we consider all taxes—on income, sales, investments, and so on—there is considerable debate over whether the affluent or the working poor pay a larger percentage of their income in taxes. So, the similarity is that both the affluent and the poor receive public assistance in the United States; the difference is that poor are labeled disreputable and stigmatized for doing so.

Myth The impoverished nations of the Third World can be blamed for the plight of their own people because of their political instability and their failure to inculcate an ethic of industriousness and hard work in their citizens.

FACT Although the nations themselves are not blameless, reality is more complicated. Over the centuries, and continuing today, some of these nations have suffered through invasions by Western colonial powers as well as Western economic interests. The exploitation they experienced as a result—in terms of the export of goods, natural resources, and profits—has contributed to the difficulties they confront today in building viable economies and reducing poverty.

---

aire baseball players, or the unemployed. What criteria do you use to locate yourself in relation to these people? The sociologist Max Weber argued that there are three major dimensions of stratification systems: wealth, prestige, and power (Weber, 1919/1958).

Wealth refers to *people's economic assets,* and it exists in many forms, depending on the characteristics of a particular society. Among the Swazi of South Africa, for example, a person's wealth is determined by the number of cows possessed (Kuper, 1963). In medieval Europe, wealth depended on the hereditary possession of land, without which it was difficult to gain a respected position in society. In the United States, wealth is often equated with *income:* the wages and salaries people earn for the work they do. For most people in the United States, income is the primary economic resource. There are many other sources of wealth, however, including property, equity in a home, stocks, bonds, trusts, and other resources that can be converted into money. According to Weber, *differences due to wealth or economic position create social strata, which he called* **social classes.** People in a given class *share similar life chances or opportunities to accumulate wealth and material possessions.* For example, you probably regard yourself as similar to certain other people economically, such as friends who appear to have about the same amount of economic resources. In contrast, those who have far more material things than you do may be seen as being in a different "class."

Chapter 2 defined a social status as a location or position in a group or society and said that everyone occupies many different statuses. Some statuses are hierarchical in nature, such that people who occupy particular positions are regarded as more deserving or honorable than others. Weber called this kind of regard *status honor.* It is now more commonly termed **prestige,** which means *the social esteem or honor that is accorded to particular people by others;* for Weber it was the second key dimension of stratification systems. As with wealth, sources of prestige vary from one society to another. Among the Plains Indians of North America, for example, warriors on horseback were accorded great prestige. They were critical to the survival of the tribe because there was considerable raiding and warfare among the various groups of Plains Indians (Oliver, 1968). One major determinant of prestige in the United States today is a person's occupation. Table 6.1 shows the results of a study that assessed how much prestige people in the United States accord to a variety of occupations. It can readily be seen that people give a higher prestige score to occupations that require more educational preparation, receive higher incomes, and involve more responsibility or supervision over people. A person's prestige in society does not, however, derive from occupation alone; it can also stem from the neighborhood in which one lives, the car one drives, or the club to which one belongs. According to Weber, *people who occupy similar prestige levels and share a common lifestyle* form **status groups.**

Weber argued that *power* is a third dimension of the stratification system, along with wealth and prestige. **Power** refers to *a social relationship in which people are able to realize their will, even against the resistance of others.* Power, of course, can arise from wealth or status, but it also has other sources. In some situations, power can emerge through the exertion of pure physical force, as when a large person coerces a smaller one. In other situations, *power becomes legitimized,* and we refer to it as **authority.** Professors, for example, have a form of power with respect to a student's college career, because they possess the authority to determine the grades the student receives. Weber used the term **parties** to refer to *the social strata resulting from differences in power.* Parties can take the form of political parties or any kind of political blocs or factions that attempt to influence the power structure of a group or society.

Socioeconomic Status

Weber recognized that the three dimensions of stratification are frequently interrelated, but they can also be independent of one another. Sometimes, for example, people possess considerable prestige but have very little power or influence. A well-known artist may be accorded esteem based on her work but have little opportunity to affect the actions of others. In other cases, people with immense and unquestionable power, such as organized crime leaders, are accorded little prestige. It is also possible to have wealth but possess little power or prestige. A few prostitutes, for example, can earn considerably more than the average citizen, but their lifestyle is viewed with disdain by most people and they are unlikely to possess any real power.

Sociologists use the term **socioeconomic status** (SES) *to describe a person's social location based on all three dimensions of the stratification system.* SES is one of the critical factors shaping our lives. Consider why you attend college, socialize with one group of friends rather than another, read certain magazines, or enjoy particular leisure-time activities. Although many factors influence such behaviors, SES is one of the most important. In fact, two sociologists summed up the results of decades of research on stratification by concluding that "the best single predictor of lifestyle is SES" (Zablocki & Kanter, 1976, p. 272). Later this chapter will assess the dimensions of stratification in the United States and their consequences for people's lives, but first it is helpful to examine some of the

TABLE 6.1 Occupational prestige in the United States

Occupation Title	Prestige Score	Occupation Title	Prestige Score
Physician	86	Computer operator	50
Lawyer	75	Funeral director	49
College professor	74	Enlisted person, army	49
Architect	73	Trained machinist	47
Chemist	73	Stenographer	47
Aerospace engineer	72	Plumber	45
Dentist	72	Insurance agent	45
Judge	71	Keypunch operator	41
Chief executive and general administrator public administration	70	Locomotive engineer	41
Member of the clergy	69	Farm operator or manager	40
Pharmacist	68	Automobile mechanic	40
High school teacher	66	Carpenter	39
Athlete	65	TV repair person	38
Public grade school teacher	64	Automobile dealer	34
Veterinarian	62	Hand-working occupations	32
Computer programmer	61	Cook in restaurant	31
Physician's assistant	61	Precision worker	30
Pilot	61	Trailer truck driver	30
Police officer	60	Cashier	29
Reporter	60	Coal miner	29
Announcer	55	Shoe salesperson	28
Construction foreman	54	Waitress	28
Personnel and labor relations manager	54	Garbage collector	28
Firefighter	53	Bartender	25
Social worker	52	Laborer	24
Electrician	51	Farm worker	23
Manager and administrator, business	51	Maid	20
		News vendor	19
		Food prep, restaurant	17

Note: From *General Social Surveys, 1972–1991 Supplement* by James Allan Davis & Tom W. Smith, 1992, Chicago: National Opinion Research Center, producer; Storrs, CT: The Roper Center for Public Opinion Research, University of Connecticut, distributor.

different types of stratification systems that can be found in societies.

Types of Stratification Systems

Stratification systems differ in the degree to which the movement of people from one level to another is permitted or encouraged. At one extreme are **closed stratification systems,** *which have well-defined ranks and rather rigid boundaries that are difficult or impossible for people to cross.* Ascribed statuses, such as those based on race or ancestry, play important roles in determining people's social position in closed stratification systems, and people usually remain in the same social position throughout their lives. At the other extreme are

open stratification systems, *having ranks with less well-defined boundaries that may be crossed more readily.* There are fewer barriers to advancement, and social position is determined more by individual achievement and merit. Achieved statuses that are based on factors like educational attainment are important in open systems. Stratification systems are never fully closed or fully open but vary widely between these two extremes. A sense of the variation possible in different stratification systems can be gained by looking at three types of systems: the relatively closed caste and estate systems and the more open class system.

Caste Systems   A **caste system** is *a stratification system in which membership in social ranks is hereditary, people in different ranks are rigidly segregated from one another, and marriage between ranks is strictly forbidden* (Berreman, 1987). The stratification system in India is an illustration of a caste system. Although no longer sanctioned by India's government, the caste system is justified by the Hindu religion and still has important influences on people's lives. At the foundation of this caste system is the Hindu belief in reincarnation, the notion that a person's soul is reborn, time and time again, in either human or nonhuman form. Furthermore, the quality of future reincarnations is determined by how well people live their present lives. The caste into which one is born is, in a sense, one's assignment for this incarnation. If a person fails to live according to the prescriptions and proscriptions of his or her caste, that person may be reincarnated in a lower caste position or in some nonhuman form. Thus the caste system in India is based on powerful religious beliefs that are backed by custom and ritual. By restricting marriage to members of the same caste, the homogeneity of each group is maintained and the possibilities for social interaction across caste boundaries are limited. Also, members of different castes are not permitted to eat in the company of one another, and other forms of social interchange are limited. Through such restrictions, the likelihood that caste barriers will be informally breached is reduced.

Some sociologists argue that there is a caste-like quality to parts of the stratification system in the United States in that certain racial, ethnic, and gender characteristics powerfully influence people's opportunities and social patterns (Hurst, 1992). White males, for example, find it much easier to achieve wealth, status, and power. They experience less discrimination in areas such as employment and housing than do females and some nonwhites (see Chapter 7). Some of the customs and rituals governing caste behavior in India also seem to have parallels in the United States, albeit with less force and rigidity. Marriage across racial lines, for example, is still somewhat uncommon in the United States. Only one-half of 1 percent of all marriages involve a black-white couple (U.S. Bureau of the Census, 1995). In addition, segregated residential patterns and schools mean that social contact between people of different races is also limited. So, although the United States is not a true caste stratification system, it contains social barriers to movement and interaction that have some similarities to castes.

Estate Systems   In an **estate system** of social stratification, *social position is still strongly influenced by heredity, but unlike in the caste system, land ownership and political or military power can also be important.* In estate systems, people's rights and duties are spelled out in laws rather than authorized solely by religious or social custom. Estate systems are still rigidly stratified societies, but one's hereditary characteristics are not the exclusive determinants of one's position in society. The feudal societies of medieval Europe were examples of estate stratification systems.

Developing in a time of weak or nonexistent central government, the feudal system was characterized by a lord–vassal relationship in which the lord exercised authority over some land by virtue of his birth or by conquest and allotted use of some land to vassals or serfs in exchange for loyalty and military service. Lords depended on the labor of serfs. Traditionally the serfs had a right to work a particular parcel of land because generations of them had worked it. They were "bound" to the land. They had obligations to the lord of the manor in the form of working part of the time in his fields or kitchens or stables and paying him some of their produce. The lord, in turn, provided them with military and civil protection, settled disputes, and gave assistance during floods or other difficulties. So there was a reciprocal relationship between lord and serf.

One major difference between caste and estate systems is that the former relies more on acceptance of the underlying value system that supports the prestige rankings. In the Indian caste system, for example, if people accept the religious beliefs that justify it, then they are likely to accept the legitimacy of the stratification system and their place in it. Estate systems rely more on the authority of monarchs or the exercise of military power to enforce acceptance of the system.

Another major difference is that estate systems permit more mobility than do caste systems. In some estate systems, for example, military or religious service stands as one institutionalized route to changing one's position in society. A serf in medieval Europe could gain some power, prestige, and possibly even ownership of land by loyal service to a lord in a military capacity, although such advancement was uncommon. He would thus rise out of his inherited estate. This change would be especially likely if the person showed extraordinary loyalty and talent and the lord wished to reward him. Military strength would be another way to gain land. A person who could get together a warring party and wrest some territory from others could, over time, claim a legal, hereditary right to the land. So, although heredity is important, it is not the sole way of placing people in the stratification hierarchy in estate systems. During the 1700s and 1800s the estate system of Europe evolved into a class stratification system, which will be discussed next. Estate systems, however, have persisted until more recent times in some parts of the world. Other Worlds, Other Ways: El Salvador (on pp. 188–189) describes the estate system that persisted in El Salvador well into the twentieth century and indicates some of the implications of its shift toward a class system.

Class Systems In **class systems,** *the boundaries between classes are more permeable, a person's socioeconomic position depends more on achievement, and there are fairly frequent opportunities to change social positions.* There are few legal or formally sanctioned inequalities between people, and social mobility is based on accomplishments and achieved characteristics, but inequalities still exist. Social contact and marriage are not officially restricted, although there may be considerable informal restrictions, such as a parent's admonition to a son or daughter: "I can't *stop* you from seeing that person, but I would *prefer* that you didn't." The informal mechanisms of social control described in Chapter 5 can be effective deterrents to contact and socializing between people at different levels of a class system. Because there is no single criterion for determining one's position in an open stratification system and because movement between ranks does occur, class systems do not exhibit clear and distinct boundaries between different social strata. Class lines tend to blur and considerable overlap exists.

Although the United States has many elements of a class system, it is not completely open because numerous ascribed characteristics still influence a person's social position. Some people, for example, are born to families with considerable wealth, which affords them an educational background that increases their likelihood of success. Having upper-middle-class parents and attending elite schools expose a person to social contacts that make advancement more likely. Likewise, people who live in a neighborhood with a superior educational system have an advantage that is unavailable to those residing in poor communities or in rural areas where the schools are likely to be of lower quality. In short, hereditary and other ascribed differences among people in U.S. society play important roles in the stratification system.

Now that the dimensions of stratification and the types of stratification systems have been presented, it is time to pose the question, Why does stratification exist?

Theories of Stratification

You should be able to describe the functionalist, conflict, and evolutionary theories of stratification as well as discuss the global dimensions of stratification.

The controversy regarding the origins and persistence of social stratification has been ongoing and frequently emotional. This controversy is understandable, because the issue of "haves" versus "have nots" has always elicited passionate debate. The central debate in sociology has been whether stratification exists because it is necessary

OTHER WORLDS, *Other Ways*

EL SALVADOR: CHANGING FROM AN ESTATE TO A CLASS STRATIFICATION SYSTEM

El Salvador is a small, Spanish-speaking nation of six million people in Central America. It is one of the poorest and most densely populated nations in the Western Hemisphere. For much of its history, El Salvador was a simple society organized as an estate system. Its chief economic activity was subsistence farming carried out on large tracts of land. In El Salvador, as in a number of countries in Latin America, the Spanish crown had rewarded *conquistadores* such as Cortes and Pizarro with large grants of land. Eventually agriculture centered in haciendas (large, self-sufficient estates). They were labor-intensive and provided for most of their own needs. Each one was headed by a landowner called a *patron,* and many peasants worked the fields. Given these origins, this landowning elite tended to be of European descent and the workers on the land of native descent. The relations between them were similar to those between the lord of a medieval manor and his serfs—relations were reciprocal but the system was still one of structured inferiority, because the ruling class dominated the shape of the exchange, and the peasants had no access to ownership of the land. They were also isolated, because there were no central transportation, postal, or educational systems. The rudimentary central government provided only a few services such as military protection (Dalton, 1972).

In the twentieth century, U.S. and other foreign corporations established footholds in El Salvador, bringing in new products and services and orienting existing agriculture away from subsistence foods and toward products that were profitable on the world market (Baloyra, 1982; Ebel, 1982). As agricultural products became more profitable, the hacienda became a business, and profit making replaced the more traditional obligations that had motivated people's behavior. The profitability of crops meant that the value of land increased and landowners adopted new labor-saving technology in order to produce crops more cheaply. They imported seed and machinery and grew mostly cash crops that were in demand in foreign markets, such as coffee and cotton. The peasants had little share in the landlords' profit. In fact, the labor-saving technology left many peasants without work,

---

for society or because its existence benefits powerful groups.

The Functionalist Perspective

Functionalists argue that stratification exists because it makes some contribution to the ongoing maintenance of society. According to Kingsley Davis and Wilbert Moore (1945), for instance, all societies must ensure that people fill essential positions and perform important tasks. Somebody must produce food, build shelter, heal the sick, and bury the dead. Otherwise, society cannot survive. Some of these positions, however, are considered more important than others. For example, physicians are more crucial than janitors.

Some positions are inherently more pleasant to perform. Most people would rather be a teacher than a garbage collector. Further, some positions call for natural abilities possessed by only a few. Not many among us, for example, could play professional tennis or football. Finally, some positions require extensive and difficult training for their proper performance.

According to Davis and Moore, the major problem that confronts any society concerns *motivation:* How can people be persuaded to occupy important positions and to perform the tasks associated with them adequately? Their answer is that rewards must be distributed such that people will want to fill the positions that need to be occupied, however difficult or unpleasant they may

and they lost their traditional right to the land. Some remained as wage laborers, but there was little else for the others to do. No surplus land and few factory jobs were available, because El Salvador did not have much industry. The peasants became underemployed or unemployed, creating a problem of surplus labor.

Over time, as the land and other resources became even more concentrated in the hands of a few, the courts, controlled by the landowners, defined the *patron*'s ownership of the hacienda to be primary and absolute. The peasants' traditional rights to the land were considered secondary, effectively disconnecting them from the land in law as well as in fact. For too many peasants, unemployment, malnutrition, illiteracy, and sometimes torture as a means of social control were the consequences of the socioeconomic changes (North, 1986).

As El Salvador changed from a subsistence, labor-intensive farming economy to a profit-motivated, export-oriented, machine-intensive capitalist economy, the central government also changed. It grew larger and more powerful, partly because of the need to build and maintain the roads, bridges, and ports that are the essential infrastructure of economic expansion. The government, however, remained securely in the hands of the ruling classes—chiefly the large landowners and urban business and professional elite.

Thus a class stratification system has emerged in El Salvador. It consists of very wealthy landowners, merchants, and other business people at the top. Below them is a middle class of government workers, farm managers, professionals, and small business people, mostly in urban areas, who provide essential services to the elite. Government workers, for example, help ensure political and economic stability through the courts and police powers. At the bottom are the idled peasantry, crowded into cities or squatter slums.

In traditional El Salvador, people were not rich, but peasants' traditional connection to the land offered them solace and security; they could support their families. In addition, others around them were in similar circumstances. In modern capitalist El Salvador, many poor have no way to support themselves, and they see others living comfortably and sometimes accumulating substantial wealth. This incendiary situation led to a destructive civil war in the 1970s and 1980s. There have been peasant rebellions in many nations where similar transitions have occurred (Montgomery, 1982; Wolf, 1969).

be. Higher rewards should go to the positions that are judged more important or less pleasant. Likewise, positions for which there is a scarcity of talent or which require extensive training should receive higher rewards. Social stratification, then, is a mechanism for allocating those differential rewards and motivating people to fill key positions in society.

Talcott Parsons (1951), also taking a functionalist view toward stratification, pointed out that the values of society tend to be integrated with, and supportive of, the stratification system. It is in part through the value system that tasks and positions are defined as important and useful to society. In the United States, for example, people place considerable value on economic achievement and material success (see Chapter 2), and those who succeed in those realms are usually accorded high positions on the three dimensions of the stratification system. People in the United States also value youth and physical beauty, and those who possess these characteristics, such as movie stars or athletes, are also awarded top positions in the stratification system.

Davis and Moore's functional approach has led to an ongoing debate concerning the degree to which rewards are actually related to the importance of a position or the scarcity of qualified personnel to fill it. One study found that the importance of positions was unrelated to rewards (Wanner & Lewis, 1978). In addition, a study of public school teachers over a forty-year span showed little support for the functionalist prediction that incomes would be higher when the supply of teachers was scarce (Betz, Davis, & Miller, 1978). At the same time, other research has provided support for Davis and Moore's basic propositions (Cullen & Novick, 1979). Thus there is still considerable controversy among sociologists regarding the extent to which stratification systems in modern societies perform the functions suggested by Davis and Moore. In fact, some have viewed the functionalist theory of stratification as merely a rationalization for the status quo (Tumin, 1953).

The Conflict Perspective

Karl Marx's (1867–1895/1967) conflict approach to stratification contrasts sharply with the functionalist view. Marx believed that economic forces are the central factors shaping both society and individual consciousness. Economic systems, he argued, influence the beliefs, values, norms, and social institutions of a society. In contrast to Weber, Marx maintained that prestige and power flow from one's economic position rather than being independent dimensions of stratification. For Marx, *a social class* consists of all those people who share a common economic position. In nineteenth-century England, Marx considered two social classes to be especially important. The *bourgeoisie*, or middle class, were those who owned the means of economic production such as the factories, the trading companies, and the banks. The *proletariat* were the working people, who owned little and sold their labor to the bourgeoisie in return for wages.

Marx viewed society as involving a constant struggle between social classes over scarce resources, with some managing to capture more of these resources than others. Thus stratification systems involve the unequal distribution of resources, which has little to do with rewarding talent or filling important positions. People gain desirable positions in the stratification system through coercion, exploitation, or possibly inheritance, and then they work toward protecting their resources against inroads by less fortunate groups. One way for powerful groups to protect their positions is to convince subordinate groups that the existing distribution of resources is "natural" or preferable. Through schools and the media, for example, people may be convinced to believe that everyone will be successful if he or she works sufficiently hard. The implication, of course, is that a lack of success is due to one's not having worked hard enough. One blames oneself rather than recognizing the role of coercion by powerful groups in limiting the opportunities of the less powerful. Marx called this failure to recognize what is in one's best interests *false class consciousness*. Eventually, Marx believed, the proletariat would develop *class consciousness,* or an awareness that their interests would be served by struggling with the bourgeoisie in order to change existing social arrangements. This struggle, said Marx, would culminate in a revolution that would replace capitalism with communism. These economic systems will be discussed in more detail in Chapter 13, but at this point, it should be recognized that under communism, according to Marx, scarcity would be eliminated; there would be no social classes and thus no inequality. Unlike most sociologists, then, Marx did not believe that social stratification is inevitable.

Many of Marx's predictions did not materialize. His forecast, for example, about the demise of capitalism, the emergence of communism, and the withering away of stratification and inequality has not proven accurate. Many of his observations are insightful, however, and modern conflict theorists have worked to modify and broaden his approach. C. Wright Mills (1956), for example, argued that Marx's emphasis on the ownership of economic resources as the basis for stratification oversimplifies today's class system. In reality, ownership in a corporate economy is spread over a large number of stockholders, most of whom have little actual control over the corporations. In the United States today, for example, power and authority rest with those who hold high-level positions in business, industry, or government where important decisions are made. Mills also viewed stratification as inevitable because huge economic institutions, whether capitalist or not, are controlled by people at the top of a society's hierarchy who possess considerable power.

Ralf Dahrendorf (1959) has broadened Marx's approach to stratification by shifting the focus of attention from economic relationships to authority relationships. In order to ensure conformity to role expectations in any group, argues Dahrendorf, someone must impose sanctions for nonconformity, and that person must have the power to do so. When the powerful are given the legitimate right to dominate others, then their power is transformed into authority. In Dahrendorf's view, then, stratification is a coercive system in which power and authority are used to control behavior, and some degree of stratification is probably inevitable in order to maintain social order in any group and in society as a whole.

Synthesis: An Evolutionary View

The controversy between functionalist and conflict views of stratification has raged for decades. To help resolve the debate, Gerhard Lenski (1966) has proposed a synthesis of the two views. Lenski begins by recognizing that people are basically selfish and interested in their own survival and that of those who are close to them. Socialization may dampen these tendencies in some people, but self-centeredness is still a part of human life. How, then, are goods and resources distributed? Do people simply hoard all that they can acquire? Such actions would be counterproductive as a sole distribution mechanism because we often need help from others. Lenski suggests that people share their resources with others in order to receive needed goods in return. In societies with little material surplus, such as hunting-and-gathering groups or some horticultural and pastoral societies, this type of sharing is essential for people to survive. When people share what they produce, there is little inequality. *Need*, rather than *power*, determines the distribution of resources in such societies.

As societies become more advanced, however, surpluses of food and material resources begin to accumulate, and the means for distributing them change radically. According to Lenski, "power will determine the distribution of nearly all of the *surplus* of goods" (Lenski, 1966, p. 44, italics added). In the power struggle for surplus resources, some people will be more competitive, some stronger, some faster, and some more crafty. The outcome, as suggested by the conflict approach, is the inequitable distribution of resources, with the inequities being substantial in agricultural and early industrial societies. Lenski recognizes that some inequalities may be functional for society, but he also argues that most societies are far more stratified than they need to be in order to survive. When power comes into play in distributing goods, those who have power accumulate all that they can. Furthermore, once inequities have been established, they tend to persist long after they serve any useful purpose. So, although functionalism might explain the necessity of some inequalities, it cannot explain *all* the inequity in stratification systems.

Lenski's approach is sometimes referred to as *evolutionary* because it assumes that societies move through a sequence of development that influences their stratification systems. As the type of economic production changes, so does the amount of inequality found in society (see Figure 6.1). Unlike Marx, however, Lenski is not an economic determinist. He recognizes that many factors, such as the natural resources available, the

FIGURE 6.1 Marx's and Lenski's Views on the Relationship Between Industrialization and Inequality

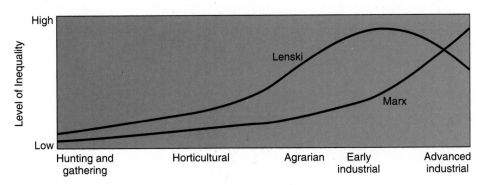

characteristics of leaders, and external military threats, play a role in generating inequalities. He also disputes Marx's contention that inequality would be greatest in industrial societies. In fact, Lenski argues that the level of inequality will decline in advanced industrial societies such as the United States and Western Europe because the new jobs created will make it possible for people to improve their lives, and the great wealth that industrialism provides will make more resources available to people. This situation is accompanied by income redistribution policies such as welfare and unemployment benefits and progressive income taxes. Table 6.2 is a summary of the major theoretical approaches to social stratification.

A Global Perspective on Stratification

The perspectives on social stratification discussed thus far view stratification systems as a property of one society that can be analyzed separately from stratification systems in other societies. In today's world, however, we need to go beyond this position, because an interdependent world system seems to be emerging. **World-system theory,** pioneered by the sociologist Immanuel Wallerstein (1979, 1984), *posits that the world's nations have become increasingly interdependent, both economically and politically, and are now linked in a worldwide stratification system, with some nations having more power and resources than others.* The major force in this world system is capitalism and its emphasis on market forces, profit making, and surplus accumulation. This world system will be described in more detail in Chapter 13, but it is relevant here because capitalism's drive to expand and find new markets creates a pressure to seek out new territories in which to invest. In fact, one of the unique characteristics of capitalism is its commitment to economic growth and expansion. The world expansion of capitalism began in the fifteenth century with the European voyages to the New World to find natural resources and trade that would be profitable for the European colonial nations, and

TABLE 6.2 A summary of the major sociological approaches to social stratification

	Conflict			Functionalist		Synthesis
	Marx	Dahrendorf	Mills	Parsons	Davis/Moore	Lenski
Basis of stratification	Economic relations resulting from *ownership* of resources	Authority relations	Economic relations resulting from *control* of resources	Evaluation of tasks as useful and important to society	Motivation to perform essential tasks	Distributive relations
Key processes	Scarcity and the division of labor	Role differentiation and the imposition of sanctions	Control of key decision-making positions	Ranking of positions a reflection of commonly held values	Unequal distribution of rewards to positions that are more important, etc.	With no surplus, *need* the determinant of distribution of resources; with surplus, *power* the determinant of distribution of resources
Is stratification inevitable?	No	Yes	Yes	Yes	Yes	Yes

it continues today as corporations seek new markets in a global economy.

The key to this world system is trade, with some nations being exporters of goods while others serve primarily as a labor pool and provider of natural resources. Whereas Marx saw the owners and the workers as the significant classes in the stratification of industrial societies, world-system theory views nations as the significant actors in a worldwide stratification system. One consequence of this world system is its impact on the stratification systems in the nations that are affected. In the case of El Salvador, as Other Worlds, Other Ways: El Salvador showed, the impact was a transition from an estate to a class stratification system. A second consequence is that an international stratification system emerges, with a hierarchy of nations divided roughly into *core nations* (capitalist, technologically advanced nations searching for opportunities to expand investment) and *peripheral nations* (less developed nations that provide cheap labor and produce food and raw materials). There are also *semiperipheral nations* that are large or have some special resources; they are therefore less dependent on the core nations and sometimes act as core nations themselves (Apter, 1986; Chase-Dunn & Grimes, 1995; Chirot, 1986).

In this international stratification system, the core nations dominate and exploit the peripheral nations. In fact, some world-system theorists argue that the nature of capitalism is such that it creates social inequalities through its tendency to distribute resources unequally. Such inequalities occur within nations, which have both rich and poor people, and at the international level, where the policies of core nations help keep peripheral nations less developed. The core nations extract natural resources from the peripheral nations and use these countries as cheap labor pools to produce agricultural and industrial goods that are then exported for profit. Through political, economic, and sometimes military intervention, the core nations encourage the emergence of political and economic elites in the peripheral nations that will support and assist in economic expansion of the core. This elite group in the peripheral nations benefits from the world system and supports policies that will maintain its role in the world capitalist system. For example, the political elites in some less developed nations in Latin America

have discouraged labor unions that would work to increase the pay and improve the working conditions of citizens of those nations, because unions might discourage investment by corporations from core nations that are looking for a cheap and passive labor force. Whereas elites in the peripheral nations may benefit from this policy, it tends overall to result in a shift of wealth from the periphery to the core as the corporations of the core nations drain profits from the periphery.

At the height of European imperial expansion, from the 1600s to the 1900s, the core nations often dominated through military conquest and occupation. In the twentieth century, domination is more often through free markets, trade agreements with elites in peripheral nations, and loans and investments that create a dependent relationship. In fact, world-system theory is sometimes called *dependency theory* because of the dependence of the peripheral nations on economic assistance, and sometimes military assistance, from the core nations. The international stratification system, then, rests on economic superiority within a worldwide division of labor. Figure 6.2 (on p. 194) shows the nations of the world based on their wealth as measured by their gross national product (GNP) per person. The GNP is the total of all the goods and services produced by a nation. In general, the high-income nations can be considered the core nations, the middle-income nations the semi-peripheral nations, and the low-income nations the peripheral nations. However, a nation may shift from one category to another over time and because of special circumstances. In addition, as with any stratification system, the world system is complicated and influenced by special traditions, historical circumstances, and geographic considerations. Other Worlds, Other Ways: Brazil and Venezuela (on pp. 196–198) looks at some of the implications of the world system for people living in peripheral nations.

It should be clear by now that social stratification is a complex phenomenon that can be understood only by analyzing it from a number of different perspectives. You should now have a number of possible answers to the question of why hierarchies, rankings, stratification, superiority, and subordination exist in societies. With this basic knowledge in hand, we can now shift our attention to a discussion of stratification in the United States.

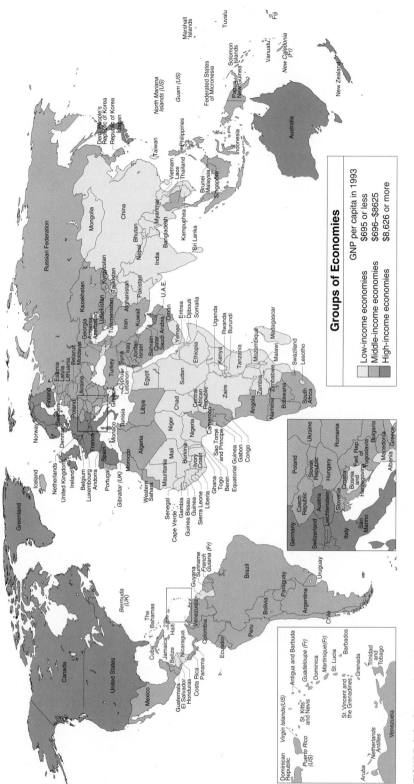

FIGURE 6.2 Global Stratification System: Nations Classified by Gross National Product (GNP) per Capita *Note:* From *World Development Report 1995: Workers in an Integrated World.* Copyright by The International Bank for Reconstruction and Development/The World Bank. Reprinted by permission of Oxford University Press, Inc.

Groups of Economies

	GNP per capita in 1993
Low-income economies	$695 or less
Middle-income economies	$696–$8625
High-income economies	$8,626 or more

Social Class in the United States

You should be able to explain how socioeconomic status is measured, describe the major social classes found in the United States, and discuss the extent and causes of inequality in societies.

Relying on Weber's three-dimensional model of stratification systems, this chapter will analyze the class structure in the United States in terms of wealth, prestige, and power. It will review the distribution of wealth and prestige, particularly the prestige associated with occupations. Chapters 7 and 8 will assess how such ascribed statuses as race, ethnicity, and gender shape the stratification system. Then, Chapter 13 will analyze the distribution of power in the United States while discussing political and economic institutions. First, however, the way sociologists measure stratification must be discussed, because people often mean different things when they use the terms *class* or *socioeconomic status.*

Measuring Socioeconomic Status

A common approach to measuring SES a few decades ago was the *reputational approach,* in which class structure was determined by the assessments of community "judges" of their fellow citizens. In other words, a person's reputation in the community was assessed by other community members who were familiar with large numbers of people. The reputational approach has fallen into disuse, however, because it cannot be used in large communities or at the national level, where "judges" could not be expected to make accurate assessments of the class position of many individuals. Another approach to measuring SES, still used sometimes today, is the *subjective approach,* also called the *self-placement approach.* With this technique, people are asked where they believe they fit into the class hierarchy. A 1994 survey, for example, found people in the United States placing themselves in the following way: upper class, 3 percent; middle class, 46 percent; working class, 45 percent; and lower class, 5 percent (Davis & Smith, 1994). One of the major disadvantages of the subjective approach is that it assumes that people can accurately place themselves in the stratification hierarchy. People, for example, may place themselves where they wish to be rather than where they are actually located.

Because of the limitations of these two approaches, sociologists today rely heavily on an *objective approach* to measuring SES. In the objective approach, people are placed in the class hierarchy through the use of "objective" criteria that the investigator determines are relevant to class placement and that do not depend on the judgments of members of the community under study. The following objective criteria have been used individually and in various combinations in studies of social class: occupation, income, source of income, educational attainment, racial or ethnic background, and lifestyle. The most widely used objective criterion of social class is occupation, because it combines in some fashion Weber's three dimensions of stratification. It reflects social prestige, it is related to one's income or wealth, and it is associated with the amount of power or authority possessed. Occupation has been used in two major ways. One approach is for the sociologist to rank occupations into a specified number of classes. The second approach has been to establish a prestige score for each occupation, based on the judgments of a sample of people from the community (see Table 6.1). These prestige rankings differ significantly from the reputational approach because occupations rather than individuals are being judged. One major weakness of the objective approach is that it simplifies a complex social reality by reducing many dimensions of stratification to a few. For example, occupations that are quite different in terms of income and educational requirements may be placed into the same social class, based largely on prestige. Nevertheless, the objective approach is subject to the least error and provides the investigator with the most information.

Class Structure in the United States

Because of the complexity of class structure in the United States, there are many ways to describe it. One useful approach is to consider five major classes: upper, upper-middle, lower-middle, working, and lower (Gilbert & Kahl, 1993; Rossides, 1990; Vanneman & Cannon, 1987).

THER WORLDS, *Other Ways*

BRAZIL AND VENEZUELA: THE THIRD-WORLD POOR IN THE GLOBAL STRATIFICATION SYSTEM

Brazil is a nation of 160 million people on territory about the same size as the United States. Brazil was colonized by Portugal, which makes it unique in Latin America in having Portuguese, rather than Spanish, as its national language. Brazil today gives some appearances of doing quite well. The United Nations Conference for Trade and Development (UNCTAD) classifies Brazil as a developing country that is a major exporter of manufactured goods; the World Bank calls Brazil a developing country with an economy that is in the upper range of the middle-income economies. Rich Brazilians live in high-rise condominiums along the beach in Rio de Janeiro; shiny glass office buildings tower over the downtowns of Rio, São Paulo, and other Brazilian cities; well-dressed office workers eat in posh restaurants and talk over cellular phones in their cars.

Yet there is another side to Brazil that shows the vast inequities of its stratification system (Jeffrey, 1993). Thousands of Brazilian children live in the streets, supporting themselves however they can, legally or illegally. Their plight came to light in a gruesome way in 1993 when about a dozen were shot to death as they slept in the middle of the night in alleys and doorways. Such killings of street children are not rare events in Brazil. No one is sure who killed them, although some suspect it may have been off-duty police hired by business people to clean up the streets and sidewalks of commercial areas. Such shootings have happened in the past, and there is even a name in Brazil for these assassins of children: *justicieros,* or "people who do justice." The children are considered a nuisance by many merchants when the children shine shoes, clean windshields, sell gum, or beg around stores and shopping areas. Some of the children also steal merchandise, rob tourists, and sell drugs. In the mean streets in which they live, they must do these things to survive.

Brazil had a strong economy in the 1970s and 1980s, but it seems to have benefited the few at the expense of the many (Maddison et al., 1992). The wealthiest 10 percent of Brazilians possessed 45 percent of the nation's wealth in 1980, and this disparity had grown to 53 percent by 1990. (For a contrast, the equivalent figure in the United States is 48 percent [Oliver & Shapiro, 1990]). Fifty percent of all Brazilians receive only 3.5 percent of national income while the remaining 50 percent receive 96.5 percent of all income. For many Brazilians, this disparity produces grinding poverty with little hope of improvement in the teeming *favelas,* or "slums," that surround the sparkling business centers and affluent residential areas of Brazil's cities.

Venezuela is classified as a semiperipheral nation by some world-system theorists. The UNCTAD calls it a major petroleum exporter among the developing countries, and it has a per capita income almost twice that of Brazil. Yet, in 1989, four days of bloody rioting occurred, with people protesting government policies and looting supermarkets and stores (Silverstein, 1993). Called the *27-F riots* because they began on February 27, they were put down brutally by police and security forces. Demonstrators and looters were slaughtered in the streets. People found in their homes with goods thought by police to have been looted were shot to death, and others died when security forces opened fire into slum shanty towns. In the end, the government reluctantly admitted that hundreds of people, mostly poor, had been killed. The military conceded that 2,500 victims may have been killed; human-rights activists put the figure at 4,000 or more. Like Brazil, Venezuela also exhibits a vast chasm between the well-to-do and the poor. Because of its oil wealth, Caracas is a modern, sophisticated city with many skyscrapers, theaters, and trendy restaurants. At the same time, 41 percent of Venezuela's people live below the poverty line.

World-system theorists argue that both Brazil and Venezuela reflect the current conditions in the world capitalist system (Braun, 1991). Land is owned by a small elite, and the masses of people are dispossessed. Those who cannot find work in the agricultural sector flock to teeming cities because there is nowhere else to go. Foreign corporations invest in agriculture and manufacturing in ways that emphasize maximization of profits. This policy often results in capital-intensive ventures that employ relatively few people and focus on export to affluent countries. Many people benefit from this arrangement: the multinational corporations, the political and economic elites in Brazil and Venezuela who invest in those corporations, and the limited number of workers who can find jobs in these enterprises. The core nations encourage these developments on the periphery by providing billions of dollars in loans directly or through such organizations as the International Monetary Fund and the World Bank. These loans are typically for capital-intensive, export-oriented, high-profit economic developments. Such developments certainly benefit multinational corporations in the core nations, but world-system theorists question whether the poor in peripheral nations see much benefit. And these loans become burdensome during

(continued)

These youngsters march at the funeral of poor Brazilian children massacred in the streets of Rio de Janeiro in 1993. The social class position of such poor children means that they have few opportunities and are very vulnerable to exploitation.

OTHER WORLDS, *Other Ways*

economic downturns, which is what happened in both Brazil and Venezuela in the 1980s. In bad times, both governments have slashed programs for the poor, often at the demand of the core-nation lending institutions, in order to keep up payments on the loans.

So, some social classes in Brazil and Venezuela benefit from these policies, especially the agricultural and industrial elites, merchants, and some skilled workers. For the lower social classes, however, which constitute a good percentage of both nations, they have meant abject poverty interspersed with brief periods of slight improvement. World-system theorists thus argue that the international stratification system based on world capitalism is a powerful influence on the distribution of socioeconomic resources in these two nations.

The Upper Class   The upper class, which constitutes less than 4 percent of the population, consists of those people with great wealth who play a large part in the political and economic institutions in the United States. Actually, there are a number of different groups in the upper class. For some, their positions are based on "old" wealth that has been passed on through a number of generations. Some of the more familiar names are Rockefeller, duPont, and Vanderbilt. Another group in the upper class is the *nouveau riche,* people who have recently amassed large fortunes through investments in oil, computers, telecommunications, real estate, or other money-making endeavors. Although most people would not notice the difference, members of the old wealth tend to view the nouveau riche as "upstarts" who lack the proper cultivation and sophistication to be fully accepted into the highest circles. A third group in the upper class—actually just on the doorstep—consists of those at the top of the federal bureaucracy and in elite managerial positions in large corporations. Because of their positions, they have considerable power over political and economic decisions, although their wealth may not be nearly as substantial as that of others in the upper class. Former President Ronald Reagan and some of his key advisers could be classified in this group. Their hold on an upper-class position is more tenuous than it is in the other two groups because it rests on their political position, which can be lost.

The Upper-Middle Class   The upper-middle class, constituting between 10 and 15 percent of the populace, consists of the business, professional, and managerial people who have relatively high incomes and a limited amount of wealth accumulated, primarily in the form of property and savings. Members of this class commonly have a college education, which is often supplemented by graduate training. Some self-employed people without college degrees, however, have gained entrance into this class through success in business. In addition, some upper-middle-class people, such as college professors, gain entrance to this class through the prestige of their occupations rather than large incomes.

The Lower-Middle Class   About one third of the U.S. population would be considered lower-middle class. This class is made up of people with modest incomes and comfortable lifestyles who must work hard to maintain their standard of living. Because they accumulate little wealth beyond small savings, their existence is somewhat more precarious than that of those above them in the stratification hierarchy. Examples of the lower-middle class are people who run small businesses, teachers, insurance agents, police officers, salespeople, lower-level management personnel, and clerical workers. This class, along with the upper-middle class, dominates U.S. society in terms of values, attitudes, and lifestyles.

The Working Class The working class, about 45 percent of the population, consists of skilled and unskilled blue-collar workers whose jobs generally involve manual labor. This category includes factory workers, construction workers, repair people, and so on. Working-class people may earn modest but comfortable incomes; sometimes their salaries are considerably greater than those of certain lower-middle class groups of people, such as public school teachers. However, their jobs are accorded little prestige by most people in the United States. They nonetheless consider themselves to be respectable and hardworking, the "solid core" that supports society.

The Lower Class At the bottom of the stratification hierarchy are people with poverty-level incomes or with no jobs, and those receiving welfare and other public assistance. The lower class includes the "working poor": 60 percent of the families that live below the poverty level have at least one member who earns wages for work. The lower class also includes people such as welfare recipients, migrant farm workers, derelicts, and many mentally ill and mentally retarded people who have been released from institutions into the community. One major question regarding the lower class is what societal mechanisms, if any, should be established to assist them in coping with their meager financial resources. Another major question that has been raised regarding the lower class is whether poverty is inevitable in a society like the United States. Is it possible to have stratification without poverty?

Inequality and Poverty

Extent of Inequality How unequal is the distribution of income and wealth in the United States? Two beliefs regarding U.S. economic inequality are widely held but demonstrably untrue. The first is that economic resources were widely distributed prior to industrialization, with few rich people and few poor. One estimate of the wealth in the country prior to the American Revolution, however, places about 45 percent of the total wealth in the hands of about 10 percent of the populace (Pessen, 1971). This figure has remained true up to today, with 10 percent of the people in the United States possessing close to 50 percent of the wealth. The second fallacious belief regarding economic inequality in the United States is that, since the Great Depression of the

1930s, government programs have reduced inequality by redistributing the existing wealth among larger numbers of people. In 1928, just prior to the Depression, 1 percent of the population possessed 36 percent of the total wealth. This figure declined to about 20 percent in 1949—the lowest amount ever in U.S. history—and since then has fluctuated between 20 and 30 percent.

Figure 6.3 (on p. 200) shows the extent of inequality in the past thirty years. Today, the poorest 20 percent of the population receives less than 5 percent of the total income in the United States while the wealthiest 20 percent receives more than 46 percent. Furthermore, these differences have increased slightly over the past three decades. In fact, the percentage of total income going to the poorest families is less today than it was in 1965 or 1980; the only group who saw their share of the total income increase since 1965 is the wealthiest 20 percent of families.

The maldistribution of resources in the United States is even greater when one looks at wealth (earned income, stocks, savings, equity in a home, and other economic resources) rather than just income. The top 20 percent of U.S. households possess 80 percent of the total wealth, whereas the bottom 20 percent have a negative net worth because they have more debts than assets (Wolff, 1995). This topic has been hotly debated, but most analysts agree with what Figure 6.3 suggests: In the last 30 years in the United States, the rich have gotten richer and the poor have gotten poorer (Danziger & Gottschalk, 1993). Also, poverty seems to have become more chronic, with people who fall into poverty today remaining poor for longer periods of time than was true in the 1960s and 1970s (Devine, Plunkett, & Wright, 1992).

The official poverty level in the United States is established by the Social Security Administration (Ruggles, 1990). The level is based on how much it costs to purchase a nutritionally adequate diet. Once the amount of money necessary for that purpose has been established, this amount is multiplied by three to arrive at the poverty income, based on the fact that the average family spends one-third of its income on food. Thus, three times the cost of food is assumed to provide adequate income for food, housing, medical care, and the other necessities of life. The poverty income cutoff is adjusted for family size and the cost of living in the region where a family lives, and it changes each

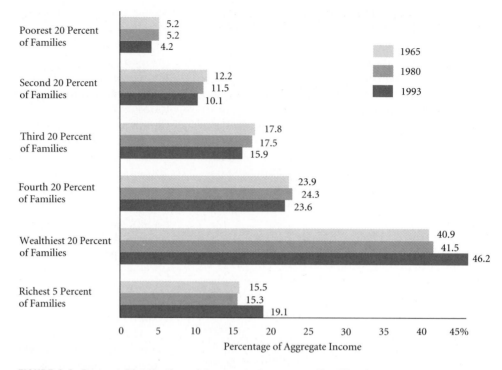

FIGURE 6.3 Percent Distribution of Aggregate Income to Families from the Poorest 20 Percent to the Richest 5 Percent, 1965–1993 *Note: From Statistical Abstract of the United States, 1978* (p. 455) by U.S. Bureau of the Census, 1978, Washington, DC: U.S. Government Printing Office; *Statistical Abstract of the United States, 1995* (p. 475) by U.S. Bureau of the Census, 1995, Washington, DC: U.S. Government Printing Office.

year to take inflation into account. Using this fixed-dollar cutoff point to define poverty is an *absolute* approach because it assumes that we can define poverty without making reference to the standard of living of other people in society.

According to this absolute definition of poverty, then, a nonfarm family of four people with an annual income of approximately $15,000 is considered by the government to be poor (see Table 6.3), which means that 39 million people in the United States—one out of every seven—were living in poverty in 1993. Throughout the 1980s, the poverty rate remained considerably higher than it had been in the 1970s. In 1993, the poverty rate was 15.1 percent—one of the highest rates since the mid-1960s—and more people were poor in 1993 than in any year since 1960. Furthermore, the gap between the nonpoor and the poor has been growing as the median family income has increased at a faster rate than has the poverty cutoff.

Certain groups in the United States are far more likely to be poor than are others (see Figure 6.4 on p. 202 and Figure 6.5 on page 203). Contrary to what many believe, two-thirds of the poor are white. Nonwhites are poor, however, at levels disproportionate to their numbers in the population. African Americans, for example, make up 28 percent of those below the poverty line. Forty percent of the nation's poor are children under eighteen, and 10 percent of the impoverished are elderly. These figures, which show that many of the nation's poor are very young or very old, suggest how misleading it is to say that most people are poor because they refuse to work. Finally, many poor people are working poor in that they do work, although for very low wages, or would work if jobs were available. In fact, less than 2 percent of the families in poverty have male heads of household who are simultaneously able to work, unemployed, and not looking for work.

A development that has been viewed with some alarm in recent years is the "feminization" of poverty. Despite increasing pressures toward eliminating inequities due to gender, some women—

TABLE 6.3 People below the poverty level in the United States: 1960–1993

Year	People Below Poverty Level		Average Poverty Income Cutoffs for Nonfarm Family of Four	Median Family Income of all Families
	Number (millions)	Percentage of Total Population		
1960	39.9	22.2	$ 3,022	$ 5,620
1966	28.2	17.3	3,223	6,957
1970	25.4	12.6	3,968	9,867
1975	25.9	12.3	5,500	13,719
1980	29.3	13.0	8,414	21,023
1981	31.8	14.0	9,287	22,388
1982	34.4	15.0	9,862	23,433
1983	35.5	15.3	10,178	24,549
1984	33.7	14.4	10,609	26,433
1985	33.1	14.0	10,989	27,735
1986	32.4	13.6	11,203	29,458
1987	32.5	13.5	11,611	30,853
1988	31.7	13.0	12,092	32,191
1989	31.5	12.8	12,675	34,213
1990	33.6	13.5	13,359	35,353
1993	39.3	15.1	14,763	36,959

Note: From *Statistical Abstract of the United States, 1995* (pp. 474, 480) by U.S. Bureau of the Census, 1995, Washington, DC: U.S. Government Printing Office.

especially female heads of households—seem to be losing ground. In the early 1990s, for example, 10.7 percent of all families in the United States lived below the poverty level, but the rate among female-headed families was 38 percent. And things may actually be getting worse. In 1959, 23 percent of all families living in poverty were headed by women; by the 1990s, this figure had grown to 53 percent (U.S. Bureau of the Census, 1993). As Figure 6.5 shows, children living in single-parent, female-headed families are especially likely to be living in poverty. (Issues of gender inequality will be discussed in more detail in Chapter 8.)

A Global View of Poverty By the standards of many nations around the world, many poor people in the United States would be considered reasonably well-off. Some people in other nations live in absolute poverty that is so stark and dehumanizing that it is difficult for people in the United States

to imagine. For these people, survival itself is a struggle. Few, if any, of the poor in the United States would fall into this category. In nations such as Haiti and Guatamala, as many as 70 percent of the people may live in absolute poverty; in El Salvador, the figure is 27 percent; in Indonesia and Nicaragua, 20 percent (United Nations, 1995). Compared to these nations, the United States is well-off. However, as Figure 6.6 (on p. 204) demonstrates, it is not so well-off when compared to other industrial nations. In that comparison, U.S. poverty rates tend to be significantly higher, especially among children.

Figure 6.3 shows a lopsided distribution of wealth in the United States. Are we out of line in this regard in comparison to other nations? It depends on whom we compare ourselves to (United Nations, 1995; Wolff, 1995). In many less developed countries around the world—such as Kenya, Peru, Brazil, and Panama—the wealthiest

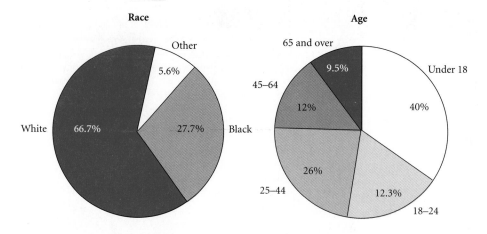

FIGURE 6.4 People Living Below the Poverty Level in the United States, by Race and Age, as a Percentage of All Poor People, 1993 *Note: From Statistical Abstract of the United States, 1995* (pp. 480–481) by U.S. Bureau of the Census, 1995, Washington, DC: U.S. Government Printing Office.

20 percent of the families earn 60 percent or more of the family income. In Brazil and Panama, the poorest 20 percent of the families receive only 2 percent of annual income—a small share indeed! So, the United States has a more equitable distribution of wealth than do these nations. In comparison to other wealthy nations in the world, however, the U.S. income distribution is lopsided. In only three of the twenty wealthiest nations do the top 20 percent of the families receive as large a share of income as in the United States; in none of these twenty nations does the bottom fifth receive as small a share as in the United States. For example, the wealthiest 1 percent of households in the United States possess nearly 40 percent of the nation's wealth. By contrast, the wealthiest 1 percent of households in Britain possess only 18 percent of that nation's wealth. In addition, trends of the past century have produced higher levels of inequality in the United States while the trend in Britain has been toward reducing levels of inequality.

Causes of Poverty   Why is there so much poverty in the United States? Many people believe it is because poor people are too lazy to work. People in the United States believe strongly in the work ethic and in the notion that their country is a land of opportunity where those who are willing to work can get ahead (Smith & Stone, 1989). Sociological research, however, shows that reality is more complicated than this picture. Research finds, for example, that poor people, especially the youth, want to work and are willing to work. It is not desire or ambition that they lack, but rather the opportunity to find jobs that pay enough to enable them to support their families in a respectable fashion (Freeman & Holzer, 1986). Also, as has been noted, many poor do work, and many of those who do not work are children, the elderly, the disabled, and mothers with young children.

So, the reason for high rates of poverty in the United States lies elsewhere than failed ambition. Part of the explanation is that there are many single-parent and female-headed families, which are at greater risk of falling into poverty. In addition, there are too few low-skill but adequately paying jobs that will enable people to support themselves and their families. Between 1963 and 1973, almost 50 percent of the new jobs created by the economy were high-wage jobs, whereas less than 20 percent paid poverty-level wages. Between 1979 and 1985, 44 percent of the new jobs created paid poverty-level wages, and only 10 percent were high-wage jobs. In fact, by the 1990s, more workers were stuck in low-paying jobs than had been true a decade earlier (Serrin, 1989; U.S. Bureau of the Census, 1992). People without access to education or job-training programs are likely to be stuck with these low-paying jobs, if they can find a job at all.

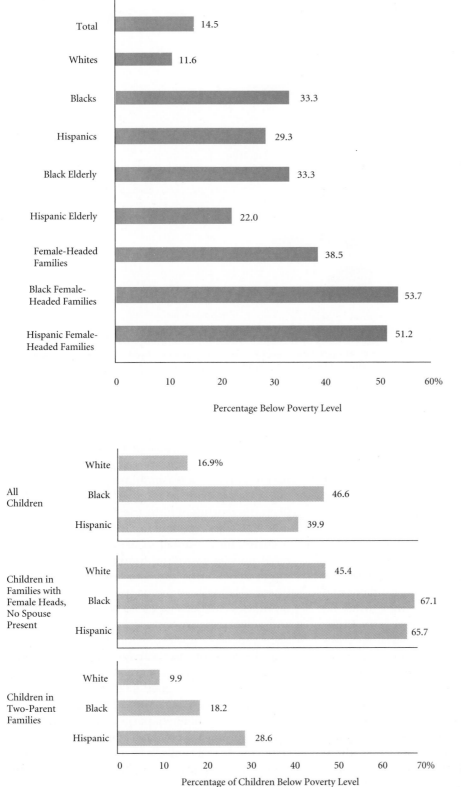

FIGURE 6.5 Percentage of People in Various Groups Below the Poverty Level in the United States, 1992
Note: From *Poverty in the United States: 1992* (Current Population Reports, Series P-60, No. 185) (pp. 1–14) by U.S. Bureau of the Census, 1993, Washington, DC: U.S. Government Printing Office.

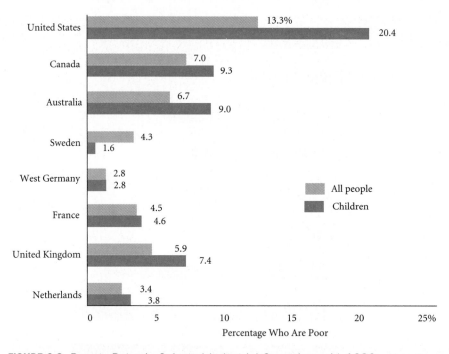

FIGURE 6.6 Poverty Rates in Selected Industrial Countries, mid–1980s *Note:* From *Challenge*, January/February 1992. Reprinted with permission of M.E. Sharpe, Inc., publisher, 80 Business Park Drive, Armonk, NY 10504.

Much concern about poverty in the United States has focused on the entrenched poor, sometimes called the *truly disadvantaged* or the *underclass,* who are isolated from the mainstream of society and remain poor for a long period of time (Devine & Wright, 1993; Marks, 1991). Both the functionalist and conflict perspectives point to some economic and political structures that contribute to the circumstances of this desperate group. William Wilson (1987, 1996) attributes the emergence of the underclass to some fundamental structural changes in the U.S. economy over the past several decades. One such change is the evolving labor market in modern industrial societies that are shifting from a product-based manufacturing economy to an information-based service economy. People in the underclass are without the skills and work experience useful in the latter-type economy, which places more emphasis on verbal talent and educational qualifications than on physical brawn and manual labor. At one time, there were ample jobs for people with strong backs and a willingness to work. By contrast, most well-paying

jobs today call for at least high school education and often post-high-school training. People who lack these credentials are relegated to the lowest-paying jobs or, increasingly, no jobs at all.

Another basic change in the economy has been the moving of industries away from the communities where poor people live. Relocation has occurred for a number of reasons, such as government policies providing funds to build new housing in the suburbs and freeways to get there (see Chapter 14). The outcome has been that factories, businesses, and jobs have fled poor neighborhoods and relocated in nonpoor areas. This trend has been especially disastrous for African Americans, who, because of discrimination in housing, have been forced to live in segregated neighborhoods where there are few good jobs (Massey, 1990).

Christopher Jencks (1992) points to some additional things that help perpetuate the underclass: because of stereotyping and racism, employers are reluctant to hire blacks, especially young black males. After all, even though jobs have left a community, ghetto residents can seek jobs outside their

This homeless mother and her children, camping under a freeway bridge in Oregon, had a home until the mother lost her job. Many poor in the United States are children living in single-parent families headed by women who can't find work to support their families.

neighborhood, even in the suburbs. But Jencks points to research showing that employers direct hiring efforts toward white neighborhoods and prefer not to recruit inner-city blacks, especially males (Neckerman & Kirschenman, 1991). Employers may perceive young black males as less skilled, educated, or trustworthy than white workers.

Is poverty inevitable? This is not the same question as the earlier one about whether social stratification is inevitable, because society could have stratification, or a hierarchical ranking of people with an inequitable distribution of resources, without poverty. Many functionalists would argue that some level of poverty is probably inevitable because it performs important functions, especially motivating people to seek and perform well at the jobs that society needs done. Functionalists would also argue, however, that poverty can be reduced through programs to provide people with the education and skills necessary to find jobs in an advanced industrial economy. These programs should teach people basic literacy skills and enable them to earn a high school diploma or other credentials they need to gain entry into the modern, service-based economy.

Conflict theorists, especially non-Marxians, would agree that stratification is inevitable but not poverty. Rather poverty results from the greed of elites who pursue a massively unbalanced distribution of resources. In this view, poverty could be ended by a redistribution of wealth, although that would not eliminate stratification; a more just distribution of wealth would leave some quite a bit better off than others but without the extremes of wealth and poverty that are found in many nations today. Economic forces, however, may make such a redistribution of wealth unlikely. Since the United States is part of the world capitalist system,

Sociological research documents that most poor people in the United States who are able to work would like to work and support themselves and their families. The problem is more a lack of jobs than failed ambition.

companies with high-paying jobs in this country may continue to seek low-priced laborers in other countries, leaving U.S. workers with fewer good jobs. As has been shown, stratification systems are now international in nature, and it is helpful to think of the various social classes as transcending national boundaries. So the corporate elites in the United States, Brazil, and Venezuela all benefit from certain practices, such as the movement of jobs around the globe to find the cheapest labor. Likewise, the poor in these three nations are relatively powerless and at the mercy of the decisions these elites make.

The question of poverty and its alleviation is important because, as Brazil, Venezuela, and El Salvador demonstrate, extreme maldistributions of wealth tend to produce hopelessness and despair among the poor, lead to drug trafficking and other crimes, and are fertile grounds for social and political unrest. It should be recalled, however, that in class stratification systems, people can and do change their positions in the hierarchy. The next section will analyze how much of

this social mobility occurs and why. Applying Sociology: Creating and Evaluating Programs That Assist the Poor describes the role that sociologists have played in increasing the chances for upward mobility among the poor in the United States.

Social Mobility

You should be able to describe the nature and extent of social mobility in industrial societies.

Ronald Reagan was born in a small town in Illinois and lived in a small apartment above a store as a child. He went on to gain considerable wealth as an actor and spokesman for corporations, and, of course, was elected to the highest public office in the United States. His life, along with the lives of people such as Abraham Lincoln, John D. Rockefeller, Andrew Carnegie, and H. L. Hunt, supports the belief that opportunity awaits those who are willing to work and persevere. Yet, how true is this belief?

Creating and Evaluating Programs That Assist the Poor

Chapter 1 noted that sociology has a significant history of interest in social reform, and one focus of that interest has been the plight of the poor. Although sociologists do not necessarily believe that poverty can be eliminated, they do believe that many poor people suffer unfair disadvantages because of the structural conditions that limit their opportunities. To change these conditions, much sociological work has focused on discovering the causes of poverty in order to develop social policies that will assist the poor. One important barrier that the poor confront is that their school and home lives do not give them adequate preparation for finding and keeping good jobs. This sociological wisdom was translated into social policy in the 1960s in the form of the Head Start program, which provides preschool children with enrichment and early learning experiences that middle-class children are more likely to receive at home (Zigler & Muenchow, 1992). These experiences are intended to instill in the children a desire for achievement, useful reading and writing skills, and a more positive self-concept that will help them in school and in life.

Sociological practitioners have played a part in the ongoing evaluation of Head Start. In a type of research called *program evaluation,* sociologists collect data to assess whether a program or policy is actually achieving the goals that have been set for it. This evaluation begins by translating the general objectives of a program into measurable goals. In the case of Head Start, the program's immediate goals are such measurable achievements as better grades in school, reduced need for remedial education, and lower rates of being held back a grade in school. More long-range goals might be higher rates of graduation from high school or entrance into college. This evaluation has involved comparing youngsters who have been through Head Start with equally poor youngsters who have not in order to see which group has higher grades in school or is more likely to graduate from high school. Such comparison provides objective, observable, and measurable information with which to evaluate social policy programs.

The results of this sociological and other social scientific research have provided strong evidence that Head Start gives poor children some significant advantages (Besharov, 1992; Lee, Brooks-Gunn, Schnur, & Liaw, 1990; Parker, Piotrkowski, & Peay, 1987). For example, research has shown that Head Start children, when compared to other poor children, are less likely to be assigned to special education classes or to be kept back a grade in school, and they do better on mathematics achievement tests and show more improvement in IQ scores. Head Start children are also less likely to get in trouble with the law or become teenage mothers. In addition, they have a better family life and a more positive self-concept. Finally, as young adults, Head Start children are more likely to go to college and hold a steady job requiring a skill. With benefits such as these, Head Start children should be better equipped to support themselves and their families as adults.

During the budget-cutting years of the Reagan and Bush administrations, Head Start retained considerable support from politicians and protection from cuts, in part because research demonstrated the clear benefits that derive from the program. Head Start is thus a good example of the role that sociologists play in the policymaking process, as they provide objective and accurate information with which to evaluate various policy alternatives. By helping to keep Head Start operating, sociologists are improving the lives of many among the poor. It may not be possible to eliminate poverty, but some of the inequities in the stratification system can be reduced by making opportunities more widely available.

Social mobility refers to *the movement of people from one social position to another in the stratification hierarchy.* There are two types of social mobility: horizontal and vertical. *Horizontal mobility* refers to a change in position that does not involve a corresponding change in social status. The son of a physician who becomes a lawyer or the store clerk who becomes a restaurant cook are examples of horizontal mobility, which is quite widespread in most societies. *Vertical mobility* refers to a change in position that involves an upward or downward shift in social status. The clerk who obtains a business degree in night school, a coal miner's daughter who becomes a physician, and a business executive who becomes an alcoholic and loses his job are all examples of vertical mobility.

Extent of Social Mobility

There are two primary types of vertical mobility. *Intergenerational mobility,* also called *generational mobility,* involves a change between the parents' position in the occupational hierarchy and that of their offspring. *Intragenerational mobility,* also called *career mobility,* is a change from an individual's first job and the occupation that becomes his or her major career position. Intergenerational mobility is especially important because it enables us to assess the extent to which inequities are built into society. If one's social position at birth determines later chances for achievement, then there will be little intergenerational mobility. Because of this fact, sociologists have been most interested in this type of mobility.

Social mobility is widespread in the United States and has increased since World War II. In 1945 less than one-third of males in the United States experienced intergenerational upward mobility; by the 1970s, this figure was about 50 percent (Featherman & Hauser, 1978). However, most of this mobility is short-range—the offspring of a blue-collar employee advances to a somewhat more prestigious blue-collar job, while that of a white-collar worker attains a slightly improved white-collar position. Thus, the stratification system in the United States is characterized by considerable stability with a high degree of occupational inheritance. That is, most children tend to take jobs that are quite similar in SES to those of their parents. Long-distance social mobility, such as from a low blue-collar to a high white-collar position, is relatively rare, although it does occur.

There are racial and regional variations in mobility rates (Matras, 1984). African Americans have considerably lower rates of upward mobility and higher rates of downward mobility than do whites, even when their family backgrounds and parents' educational levels are similar. However, these racial disparities are not as large as they once were. Southerners have lower rates of mobility than do people from other regions. In addition, family disruptions, such as one's parents'

divorce, experienced during childhood, reduce a person's likelihood of experiencing upward social mobility (Biblarz & Raftery, 1993). It seems that single-parent families and step-parent families, among other things, do less supervision and monitoring of schoolwork and provide fewer influential role models. These differences mean that children in families with both biological parents present have a better platform from which to compete in school and in the occupational world.

There also appear to be slightly more opportunities for upward mobility in the United States than in other industrialized countries, but the differences are not great (Fox & Miller, 1965; Lipset & Bendix, 1959; Wong, 1990). Working-class people in the United States have a better chance of moving into professional occupations than do their counterparts in other countries. Their chances for upward mobility, however, are still rather small, and there is a tendency for elite positions in the United States and other industrial nations to be inherited. What comes through most strongly in this cross-national research are the basic similarities of the stratification systems in industrialized societies.

Sources of Social Mobility

Some traditional beliefs in the United States posit that high rates of social mobility are due to the antielitist and antiaristocratic ideology that pervades U.S. culture. According to this view, advantages of birth or accident are less important in determining a person's position in society than are individual skills and initiative. However, such individual characteristics would not result in mobility unless there were opportunities in society for mobility. After all, the idea that people can improve their social position through individual accomplishments can be traced back many centuries, long before today's high levels of mobility existed. Furthermore, other industrial nations, including those with a historical aristocracy such as Britain and France, also have high rates of mobility. It would appear, then, that the critical factor associated with high rates of social mobility today is not a grass-roots belief about equality and achievement, but rather industrialization.

In fact, much of the social mobility that has occurred in the twentieth century is referred to as *structural social mobility,* indicating that it is the result of basic changes in the occupational and social structures of societies as they industrialize (Blau & Duncan, 1967; Hauser & Featherman, 1973). As societies industrialize, the number of low-status jobs declines, and the number of high-status jobs increases (DiPrete, 1993; Wright & Martin, 1987). Agricultural occupations, for example, have declined from about 37 percent of the workforce in 1900 to less than 3 percent today (see Chapter 13). In addition, there has been a decline in the number of unskilled manual-labor jobs with a consequent increase in the number of skilled-labor jobs. Finally, there are fewer blue-collar occupations and more white-collar managerial positions. The two occupational designations that have shown the largest increase since 1940 are salaried professionals and managers. As a consequence of these changes, a surplus of workers develops in lower-status jobs and a scarcity of people in the higher-status ones. Social mobility occurs as workers move up the occupational scale to fill the positions for which there is a scarcity of workers.

A related development involves the different fertility rates found in families at various occupational levels. Families in occupations at the lower end of the scale, such as farmworkers and unskilled laborers, generally have larger numbers of children, whereas those at the higher end, such as professionals and managers, tend to have fewer offspring. Consequently, families in occupational categories where there are fewer jobs are having more children, and families in expanding occupational categories are producing an insufficient number of children to fill those jobs. The result is a "push" on people at the lower end of the scale to move up in the occupational hierarchy in order to secure jobs. This push brings about social mobility, although we have seen that it tends to be short-range.

For most of the twentieth century, then, and especially between World War II and the 1970s, there has been considerable upward mobility in the United States, largely accounted for by opportunities created by these structural changes in the economy. There are reasons to believe, however, that significantly less upward mobility will be possible in the future. First of all, as the economy approaches a mature industrial phase, the occupational structure is stabilizing, with little growth in the higher-status or better-paying jobs (Hout, 1988; Krymkowski & Krauze, 1992). The Bureau of Labor Statistics projects a considerable slowdown in the growth of executive, administrative, and managerial jobs in the United States through the year 2000, while low-status jobs, such as service workers, will not decline nearly as much. In addition, corporations today use more "contingent" workers—part-time, temporary, or contract workers who are paid less, receive fewer benefits, and can be released more easily. The result will probably be fewer opportunities for mobility in the future, or at least stiffer competition for the good jobs.

Second, the United States now competes in a world economy, and many better-paying jobs from the United States have moved overseas where labor costs are lower. As this worldwide economic competition grows, the United States, with its high standard of living in comparison to most of the world, may lose more good jobs, and U.S. workers may face reduced opportunities for upward mobility because of it.

Third, social mobility may also decrease if people do not leave the workforce at a pace sufficiently rapid to create openings for all those entering it (Tepperman, 1975). As the U.S. population becomes older, top positions will be held by men and women who will neither die nor retire for many years, and young people entering the workforce will find it more difficult to locate jobs and achieve upward mobility. This problem may have been exacerbated when mandatory retirement was eliminated for most workers in 1986. Unless many new jobs open up, which few economists predict, the prospects are now somewhat dim for those who are entering the workforce. Taking all these factors into account, sociologists have made projections about rates of mobility through the year 2000, and the picture is bleak: a growing trend toward no mobility or even downward mobility during a person's working life, especially for men (Krymkowski & Krauze, 1992; Newman, 1993).

A lower overall mobility rate could create problems if people from various levels of the occupational hierarchy find themselves competing for the same desirable jobs. There could be tensions including increased discrimination and unrest. For example, families in desirable social positions might try to increase the likelihood that their own children, rather than young people from lower occupational rankings, would replace them in their desirable jobs.

Consequences of Stratification

You should be able to explain how people's positions in the stratification system affect various aspects of their lives.

Max Weber argued that economic differences between people translate into differences in *life chances,* or what people can accomplish during their lives. In addition, status differences lead to variations in lifestyles among people. In other words, a person's SES correlates with that individual's beliefs, choices, and behaviors. This chapter concludes with a review of some of the consequences of stratification for society.

Educational Achievement

The belief in equality in the United States rests heavily on the assumption that all people have equal access to an education, which they believe serves as a stepping-stone toward improving one's lot in life. Although the doors of schools in the United States are generally open to people irrespective of social background, the chances of advancing in the educational world are powerfully affected by SES (McClendon, 1976; Treiman & Terrell, 1975). In 1957, William Sewell (1971) began an ambitious study of the career plans of nine thousand high school seniors in Wisconsin. Dividing them into four socioeconomic groups, he followed their educational experiences for fourteen years. The differences among the groups were dramatic. Those with the highest SES were four times more likely than those with the lowest status to attend college. They were nine times more likely to receive some graduate or professional training. In other words, the higher the educational attainment, the greater the divergence between the achievement of people at different levels in the stratification system. Furthermore, these differences were not entirely a function of ability. Among high-income students with high abilities, only 10 percent chose not to attend col-

lege, whereas 25 percent of the low-income students of similar ability failed to go to college (Jencks et al., 1972). Some of these differences are undoubtedly due to economic opportunities, with low-income people less able to afford college. Yet in many cases, parents and teachers fail to develop the desire for higher education in students of low SES. Furthermore, inequalities in educational experience affect people throughout their lives, because those with better educations tend to have more desirable jobs and higher lifetime earnings. Even in retirement, the more educated among the elderly receive much higher pensions and other retirement income, showing how advantages established early in life can produce substantial stratification later in life (Crystal, Shea, & Krishnaswami, 1992). Although this link between SES and occupational achievement still exists, recent investigations have concluded that it is weaker today than it was forty years ago, primarily because of the wider availability of college educations to people at all levels of the socioeconomic scale (Baker & Vélez, 1996).

Health

Although physical and mental illnesses can be found at all class levels, socioeconomic position strongly influences an individual's health status (Freund & McGuire, 1995). For example, infants born to families of lower SES are more likely to die during the first year of life than are those born into more affluent families. People of lower status are also more likely to contract a wide range of illnesses, including arthritis, high blood pressure, visual problems, heart disease, diabetes, and cancer. In addition, lower-class people are more likely to suffer from severe mental disorders than are more affluent people (Williams, Takeuchi, & Adair, 1992).

There are a number of reasons for these differences. First, the poor cannot afford the level of health care available to more affluent people and are therefore more likely to let their health deteriorate before seeking care. Although the United States has made considerable strides in seeing that health care is available to all citizens, there are still costs, such as transportation or time lost at work, that can hinder one's ability to obtain medical care. Second, the poor often live in unsanitary conditions and have a nutritionally poor diet, and these increase one's susceptibility to disease. Third, the poor are less likely to recognize that they are ill and are more inclined to delay seeking medical care. This delay greatly increases the chances that an illness will become more severe or incapacitating. The affluent, by contrast, are more likely to seek care quickly. Finally, lower-class people are less likely to engage in preventive health care. They visit dentists and doctors less frequently, especially if there is nothing apparently wrong with them (Andersen & Anderson, 1979).

Status Inconsistency

Stratification can result in a situation that sociologists call *status inconsistency*, especially when people experience social mobility related to one dimension of stratification, such as wealth, but not to others, such as education or prestige. **Status inconsistency** occurs when *a person ranks high on one dimension of stratification but low on another.* The self-made millionaire, for example, can have substantial wealth and an affluent lifestyle but may not receive the social prestige that comes from high levels of education or from "old wealth." Likewise, the highly educated member of a racial minority holds statuses that are inconsistent with each other.

Status inconsistency can create difficulties for people because it is often unclear which status is relevant in a particular setting. People normally expect others to relate to them on the basis of their higher status, but that may not always happen. This condition can also lead people to become disenchanted with the status quo, because it does not provide them with the rewards they feel they deserve. As a result, status inconsistency can lead to tension and unhappiness that might have a number of outlets. For example, people whose income level is low and whose educational and occupational statuses are higher are more supportive of making changes in society than are those whose statuses are consistent (Wilson & Zurcher, 1976). In addition, men who have an occupational status that is inconsistently low for their level of education are at greater risk of abusing their wives than are men who are free of such status inconsistency (Hornung, McCullough, &

Sugimoto, 1981). These examples illustrate the complexity of modern stratification systems.

Self-Esteem

Those who occupy high positions in the stratification system are accorded substantial honor and privilege, whereas people below them receive less, in some cases very little. This differential distribution of honor and privilege would seem to imply a judgment about people's worth. Chapters 2 and 3 emphasize that people are shaped by the positions they hold in the social structure. Societal beliefs say that the successful, intelligent, hard-working, worthy people rise to the top. What does that say about those on the bottom of the hierarchy? Placement in the lower reaches of the hierarchy seems to imply a collective societal judgment that a person is less worthy. In other words, placement in the stratification system may influence people's self-concepts.

Self-esteem refers to the judgment that people make regarding their own overall worth; it is anchored in social circumstances and social relationships. Children born into families of low SES are likely to have lower self-esteem than do children in well-to-do families (Rosenberg & Pearlin, 1978; Wiltfang & Scarbecz, 1990). Furthermore, low self-esteem can have detrimental effects in many areas of people's lives. It can discourage children from applying themselves in school and deter adults from seeking higher-paying and more prestigious jobs. However, the link between stratification and self-esteem, although measurable, is not that strong. One reason for this is that many social conditions and social relationships influence one's self-concept, as was discussed in Chapter 3, and these can dilute the impact of the stratification system. A second reason for the weak relationship has to do with the *reference groups* discussed in Chapter 4. Reference groups are groups that we use as standards in evaluating ourselves. The reference groups that are chosen in making such comparisons depend in part on one's class position. If poor people compare themselves with the wealthy, they will not fare well in the comparison. But people can choose other standards or criteria than wealth in assessing their self-worth. People might claim that decency, morality, or religiosity are more important than wealth or education or fame. So, through choosing reference groups with which one compares favorably, the threat of degradation that can accompany low social standing may be eased.

Summary

1. Social stratification is the ranking of people into a hierarchy in which the resources considered valuable by society are unequally distributed. Max Weber argued that there are three interrelated dimensions of stratification systems: wealth, prestige, and power.

2. Caste systems of stratification are those in which membership in social ranks is hereditary, with people in different ranks being rigidly separated from one another. Estate stratification systems are those in which inheritance still strongly influences social position but landownership and political or military power are also determinants. In class systems, the boundaries between classes are more permeable, a person's socioeconomic position depends more on achievement, and there are fairly frequent opportunities to change social positions.

3. There are different theories of stratification. Functionalists argue that stratification exists because it makes some contribution to the ongoing maintenance of society. Conflict theorists argue that society involves a constant struggle between social classes over scarce resources. Gerhard Lenski has tried to synthesize the functional and conflict views using an evolutionary approach, in which it is assumed that, as the type of economic production changes, so does the amount of inequality found in society. World-system theory recognizes that stratification systems are now global in scope.

4. Social scientists have employed numerous techniques in measuring socioeconomic status (SES). In the past these included the reputational approach and the subjective, or self-placement, approach. Sociologists today rely heavily on the objective approach.

5. Most sociologists view the American class structure in terms of five levels: upper, upper-middle, lower-middle, working, and lower class. Poverty exists in the United States, and it is fairly extensive. It results primarily from the lack of sufficient jobs that pay a good wage.

6. Social mobility refers to the movement of people from one social position to another in the stratification hierarchy. There are two types of mobility: horizontal and vertical. A critical factor associated with mobility is industrialization, and much of the upward social mobility that has occurred in the twentieth century is referred to as structural, indicating that it is due to basic changes in the occupational and social structures as societies industrialize.

7. Stratification systems have multiple consequences for people, and economic differences among people translate into differences in life chances, or what people can accomplish during their lives. Among the things affected by stratification are educational achievement, health, status inconsistency, and self-esteem.

STUDY AND Review

Key Terms

authority

caste systems

class systems

closed stratification
    systems

estate systems

open stratification
    systems

parties

power

prestige

social class

social mobility

social stratification

socioeconomic status
    (SES)

status group

status inconsistency

wealth

world-system theory

Multiple-Choice Questions

1. The stratification system in the United States today could be best characterized as a (an) _____ system.
   a. caste
   b. estate
   c. closed
   d. class
   e. structured

2. Estate stratification systems differ from caste stratification systems in that estate systems
   a. permit more social mobility.
   b. rely more on religious values to enforce acceptance of the system.
   c. rely less on military power to enforce acceptance of the system.
   d. permit no social mobility between ranks in the system.

3. Which of the following theorists argued that stratification systems are not inevitable in societies?
   a. C. Wright Mills
   b. Gerhard Lenski
   c. Karl Marx
   d. Talcott Parsons
   e. Kingsley Davis and Wilbert Moore

4. World-system theory views _____ as the significant actors in a worldwide stratification system.
   a. nations
   b. owners and workers
   c. politicians
   d. proletariat

5. One of the weaknesses of the objective approach to measuring SES is that
   a. it cannot be used in large communities.
   b. people may place themselves where they wish to be in the stratification hierarchy rather than where they are.
   c. it simplifies a complex social reality.
   d. it is based on the subjective assessment of community judges.

6. Which of the following statements is true about poverty and wealth in the United States?
   a. Prior to industrialization, economic resources were equitably distributed, with few rich and few poor people.
   b. In the past thirty years, the rich have gotten richer and the poor have gotten poorer.
   c. The poverty rate is lower now than it was in the 1970s.
   d. Two-thirds of the poor are nonwhites.

7. The daughter of a truck driver graduates from medical school and becomes a physician. This is most clearly an example of
   a. structured social mobility.
   b. intergenerational social mobility.
   c. horizontal mobility.
   d. career mobility.

8. According to the text, the most critical factor producing high rates of social mobility in the United States today is
   a. U.S. beliefs about equality and achievement.
   b. the estate nature of the stratification system.
   c. industrialization.
   d. the U.S. educational system.

9. Which of the following is true regarding educational achievement and SES in the United States?
   a. The link between the two is weaker today than forty years ago.
   b. The link between the two is stronger today than forty years ago.
   c. The link between the two is about the same today as forty years ago.
   d. There is no longer any link between the two.

10. If a person experiences upward social mobility related to one dimension of the stratification system, such as wealth, but not the others, such as education or prestige, what can result is called
    a. generational mobility.
    b. structured mobility.
    c. horizontal mobility.
    d. status inconsistency.

True/False Questions

1. According to Max Weber, differences due to wealth or economic position create social strata called *parties*.

2. In the United States, people give higher prestige rankings to occupations that require more educational preparation as compared to those requiring less education.

3. Because some of Karl Marx's predictions have not come true, modern sociologists have rejected his approach to social stratification.

4. Gerhard Lenski's evolutionary theory of stratification posits that societies move through a sequence of development that influences the type of stratification system they have.

5. World-system theory is also sometimes called *dependency theory*.

6. Taken together, the upper class and the upper-middle class in the United States constitute about one-half of the total population.

7. Rates of poverty in the United States are significantly lower than they are in other industrial nations.

8. Program evaluations conducted on the Head Start program have concluded that the program gives poor children a significant advantage over comparably poor children not in Head Start.

9. African Americans have higher rates of both upward mobility and downward mobility than do white Americans.

10. The link between a person's position in the stratification system and that person's level of self-esteem is weak because many other social conditions influence self-esteem.

Fill-In Questions

1. The social strata that are produced by differences due to wealth or economic position are called _____ .

2. _____ refers to a person's social location based on wealth, prestige, and power.

3. According to the functionalist perspective, social stratification is a mechanism for _____ people to fill key positions in society.

4. Karl Marx argued that some people have _____ , which means that they fail to recognize what is in their own best interests.

5. According to world-system theory, the key to the operation of the world system is _____ .

6. The _____ approach to measuring SES asks people to state where they believe they fit into the class hierarchy.

7. The term _____ refers to the entrenched poor in the United States who are isolated from the mainstream of society and remain poor for a long period of time.

8. _____ is a type of research in which sociologists collect data to assess whether a program or policy is actually achieving the goals that have been set for it.

9. _____ is social mobility that is due to basic changes in the occupational and social structures of societies as they industrialize.

10. When a person ranks high on one dimension of the stratification system but low on another, the person is experiencing _____ .

Matching Questions

_____ 1. prestige dimension of stratification
_____ 2. stratification system of India
_____ 3. Kingsley Davis and Wilbert Moore
_____ 4. Venezuela
_____ 5. *nouveau riche*
_____ 6. preschool educational experience
_____ 7. class system
_____ 8. Gerhard Lenski
_____ 9. authority
_____ 10. Ralf Dahrendorf

A. functionalist approach to stratification
B. upper class
C. status groups
D. Head Start
E. legitimate power
F. caste system
G. conflict approach to stratification
H. semiperipheral nation
I. evolutionary theory
J. open stratification system

Essay Questions

1. Describe the nature of stratification systems as analyzed by Max Weber. Include in your answer an assessment of the three major dimensions of stratification systems.

2. Describe the different kinds of stratification systems that are found in societies based on the degree to which people are permitted to move from one level of the stratification hierarchy to another.

3. Describe the stratification systems of El Salvador, Brazil, and Venezuela. In your answer, use the sociological concepts that were used to describe them in the text.

4. Compare and contrast the functionalist, conflict, and evolutionary theories of stratification. Show clearly how they differ from one another.

5. What is world-system theory as it relates to social stratification? How does it differ from the other theories of stratification?

6. Describe the class structure in the United States as it was presented in the text. Describe how large each class is and who is a member of it.

7. How does the text answer the question of why there is so much poverty in the United States?

8. How extensive has social mobility been in the United States during this century? What have been the sources of this mobility?

9. What consequences do people's positions in the stratification system have for their educational achievement and their health?

10. What consequences do people's positions in the stratification system have for their self-esteem? What are the consequences of status inconsistency?

Answers

Multiple-Choice
1. D;　**2.** A;　**3.** C;　**4.** A;　**5.** C;　**6.** B;　**7.** B;　**8.** C;
9. A;　**10.** D

True/False
1. F;　**2.** T;　**3.** F;　**4.** T;　**5.** T;　**6.** F;　**7.** F;　**8.** T;
9. F;　**10.** T

Fill-In
1. social classes
2. socioeconomic status (SES)
3. motivating
4. false class consciousness
5. trade
6. subjective, self-placement
7. truly disadvantaged, underclass
8. program evaluation
9. structural social mobility
10. status inconsistency

Matching
1. C;　**2.** F;　**3.** A;　**4.** H;　**5.** B;　**6.** D;　**7.** J;　**8.** I;
9. E;　**10.** G

For Further Reading

DeMott, Benjamin. (1990). *The imperial middle: Why Americans can't think straight about class.* New York: William Morrow. This is a very readable book about the myth that many accept in the United States that social class is unimportant or irrelevant. The author describes many ways in which this belief leads us astray and can be destructive.

Gans, Herbert J. (1995). *The war against the poor: The underclass and antipoverty policy.* New York: BasicBooks. This book on social policy relating to poverty in the United States focuses on the tendency to stereotype and stigmatize the poor and to treat them as moral inferiors who are at least partially responsible for their circumstances. The author documents the many ways in which this tendency is highly negative and destructive as well as quite inaccurate.

Kerbo, H. R. (1991). *Social stratification and inequality: Class conflict in historical and comparative perspective* (2nd ed.). New York: McGraw-Hill. This thorough textbook on social stratification provides more coverage than is possible in this chapter and also offers some important cross-cultural and international comparisons.

Kotlowitz, Alex. (1991). *There are no children here: The story of two boys growing up in the other America.* New York: Doubleday. This realistic and wrenching description of what it is like to grow up poor and black in Chicago helps the reader see what poverty is like through the eyes of the poor.

Liebow, Elliott. (1993). *Tell them who I am: The lives of homeless women.* New York: Free Press. This enlightening and compassionate look at the lives of women who are homeless tells how they got that way and how they cope with it. Liebow is an anthropologist who did participant observation research to uncover this aspect of life in the United States.

Newman, Katherine. (1993). *Declining fortunes: The withering of the American dream.* New York: BasicBooks. In class stratification systems where social mobility occurs, some of that mobility is downward rather than upward. This anthropologist explores the nature, extent, and experience of downward mobility among middle-class, suburban families in the United States.

Phillips, Kevin. (1990). *The politics of rich and poor: Wealth and the American electorate in the Reagan aftermath.* New York: Random House. Phillips argues strongly that the 1970s and 1980s were a period of income redistribution in the United States, with funds flowing away from the lower and middle classes and into the hands of the well-to-do.

Ropers, Richard H. (1992). *Persistent poverty: The American dream turned nightmare.* New York: Plenum. This is a good analysis of how poverty results from long-term economic, social, and political policies and trends rather than from the inadequacies or shortcomings of the poor themselves. It documents the inconsistencies in government policies that contribute to the problem.

Scase, Richard. (1992). *Class.* Minneapolis: University of Minnesota Press. This short introduction to social stratification emphasizes that social class is still an important concept for understanding societies. Because it is written by a British sociologist, many of the illustrations are of the class systems in Britain and Europe.

SEVEN *CHAPTER* *Social Inequality: Race and Ethnicity*

Portuguese explorers heading for passage to India through the Cape of Good Hope in April 1500 were blown off course to the west and made the first European sighting of what would later become Brazil. Their ship anchored offshore, a few hundred miles north of modern-day Rio de Janeiro, and a small party of twenty or so Indians, completely naked and carrying bows and arrows, quickly gathered on the beach. The Portuguese sailors landed for the first meeting between Europeans and this new race of people in the Western Hemisphere. The contact was entirely peaceful, and the Indians were fascinated with the sailors' iron tools and their celebration of the Christian mass on the beach. The Portuguese, in turn, were fascinated by the unembarrassed nakedness of the Indians, both men and women. In these early contacts, the Portuguese found the Indians to be generous and innocent and to exhibit an extraordinary sense of freedom. Enchantment and fascination quickly turned to a sense of offense, however, because the Portuguese had been taught that nudity was immoral. Before this first contact was over, the Portuguese were giving the Indians clothing and trying to convince them to wear their new possessions (Hemming, 1978).

Some Europeans were much impressed with the newly discovered peoples of Brazil, seeing them as "noble savages." Roman Catholic missionaries saw them as innocents in the forest who needed to be protected and, of course, converted to Christianity. Thus began a horrendous episode of conquest, displacement, and enslavement for Brazilian Indians. In 1511, the Portuguese ship *Bertoa* made landfall near where Rio de Janeiro would later rise; she departed for Portugal a short time later with a cargo of brazilwood, parrots, jaguar skins—and thirty-five Indian slaves. Thus, a decade after discovery, the Indians were seen by some Europeans as an inferior race who could be treated like property, their human dignity and rights ignored. Some Indians went willingly to Europe, believing that they and their children were being taken to a promised land; many others were simply enslaved and forced to do the bidding of their European masters.

Gradually, many Europeans came to believe that the Indians—because of culture, temperament, and physical constitution—were not suited to slave labor. This change of heart, however, did not make things better for the Indians. Since the European colonizers and their heirs in the new land were driven by the dual engines of conquest and exploitation, the Indians came to be seen as worthless—or, worse yet, as obstacles to progress. As the colonizers and their descendants expanded away from the coast, they drove these "obstacles" from their lands and massacred the Indians when they resisted. Some Europeans protested the decimation of the Indians, but Brazil was far away and very large, and it seemed to many that there should be room for all. Also the colonial expansion enriched many in the Old World as well as the New. So, the pressures and the horrors continued unrelentingly over the centuries.

There was resistance to the displacement, enslavement, and slaughter of the Brazilian Indians. Jesuit missionaries, for example, organized some Indians into quasi-military missions that were independent of colonial government control and offered some protection against attacks by slavers. But the Jesuits were expelled from Brazil in 1760

Centuries ago, the ancestors of these Kayapo Indians of Brazil fought against the invasion of European explorers and capitalists into their tribal lands. Today, they are trying to make accommodations to the modern world while preserving as much of their traditional culture and way of life as they can.

(Hemming, 1987). Some Indians retreated into the impenetrable forests of interior Brazil and fought ferociously to protect their lands, killing anyone who intruded. But each of these forest strongholds was breached eventually by the Europeans. The Europeans who were on the front lines of this assault against the Indians were the *bandeirantes,* or "frontiersmen," and they are portrayed as mythic heroes by some present-day Brazilians—like the cowboys of the American West—but the Indians see them as slavers and killers of their ancestors. Some Indian tribes, such as the Botocudos, the Kayapos, and the Kaingangs, defended themselves admirably and effectively for some time, but their success only resulted in the mounting of major military expeditions to defeat them. In 1835, there was even a massive revolt on the part of the Indians and *mestizos* (people of mixed Indian and European ancestry) that spread along much of

Myths & FACTS

ABOUT RACE AND ETHNICITY

Myth The Civil Rights Act, affirmative action, and other social policies have eliminated racism in the United States.

FACT Although the amount of overt prejudice and discrimination against racial minorities has declined in the past few decades, research still finds considerable racism and discriminatory practices. Recent studies, for example, document discrimination against African Americans still occurring in housing and employment (Glass Ceiling Commission, 1995; Munnell, Tootell, Browne, & McEneaney, 1996; Yinger, 1995).

Myth If people insist on retaining a strong racial or ethnic identity, then ethnocentric tendencies make conflict, and sometimes violence, an inevitable development in such multiracial or multiethnic societies.

FACT Although such conflict and violence are all too common, political and social structures can be created that minimize the likelihood of it. Switzerland, for example, is made up of three distinct ethnic groups. Yet, they have overcome conflicts and worked together peacefully and cooperatively because of a political system that ensures the participation and influence of minorities.

Myth American Indians live comfortably with the benefits they receive from the government for being Indian and with the proceeds from the gambling casinos that are now permitted on some reservation land.

FACT Of all U.S. minorities, American Indians remain among the poorest. As a group, they suffer very high unemployment rates and have a median income that is less than half the national average. More than one-third of all Indian families live below the official poverty level. American Indians living on reservations tend to be worse off than their nonreservation counterparts, with large families often living in small, dilapidated homes.

Myth Nonwhites in the United States continue to lag behind whites in education, income, and occupational status in the 1990s.

FACT Contemporary reality is more complicated than this statement. African Americans, for example, have made considerable improvement, and their educational levels are coming very close to those of whites. Cuban Americans, Chinese Americans, and Japanese Americans are among the best educated groups in the United States. Some inequities persist, however. For example, African Americans and Hispanic Americans still lag considerably behind whites in average family income.

---

the Amazon River, but it was violently suppressed after four years. In the end, the Europeans proved too well organized and powerful, with their centralized authority that could coordinate and direct massive resources around the globe. The small, nomadic, unorganized, Stone Age tribes were simply no match for them. (The Yanomamo, discussed in the beginning of Chapter 4, are an example of a group continuing this battle today.)

This remarkable story of the Indians of Brazil contains within it many of the themes that sociologists find when people of different racial and ethnic groups come together: Racial or ethnic identity becomes the context for discrimination, exploitation, violence, and resistance. The United States, of course, has its own history of displacing Indian peoples and enslaving those of a different, nonwhite race. In a diverse world, these are important issues to understand if we are to comprehend how societies persist, develop, and change. Much of our attention on this topic is directed toward issues of social inequality—the extent to which opportunities and access to resources are differentially allocated on the basis of race or ethnicity. Such inequality is a central concern in the United States today since the populace is becoming increasingly diverse in racial and ethnic composition and since the country is far from eliminating hostility, prejudice, and discrimination based on racial and ethnic identity. If this fact needs documentation, the highly destructive riot in south central Los Angeles in 1992 offers stark testimony that race and ethnic relations in the United States today remain a problem to be addressed.

The preceding chapter discussed social stratification in societies in general. This chapter and the following chapter continue that analysis by discussing how characteristics such as racial and ethnic identity and gender shape the system of stratification in society. Characteristics such as race and ethnicity are *ascribed statuses* because they are assigned to people and represent social position that people have little or no say about occupying. Such statuses can serve as the basis for unequal treatment of groups, functioning as criteria for allocating resources and determining life chances and lifestyles. Sociologists refer to such groups as *minority groups,* and a discussion of what constitutes a minority group is the first topic in this chapter.

Minority Groups

You should be able to define minority group *and* racism *and identify what constitutes a racial and an ethnic group.*

A **minority group** is *a group whose members share distinct physical and cultural characteristics, who are denied access to power and resources available to other groups, and who are accorded fewer rights, privileges, and opportunities* (Marden, Meyer, & Engel, 1992). In the United States, black, Hispanic, Vietnamese, and some white ethnic groups such as rural Appalachians are considered minority groups because each has lower levels of educational and occupational attainment than other groups, and each has fewer opportunities. Chapter 8 will show that despite the numerical majority of women in the population, women are also considered a minority group because they have been denied equal access to education, jobs, and important positions that men have controlled for some time. This chapter, however, will focus only on minorities whose disadvantaged status arises from their racial or ethnic group membership.

The term *minority group,* then, refers not to numerical size but to a position in the stratification system of society. A rather extreme case of a numerically large group of people being dominated by a much smaller group can be found in South Africa's traditional system of *apartheid,* which persisted until it was dismantled in the early 1990s (Adam & Moodley, 1986). About 85 percent of South Africa's population is made up of black Africans. Under apartheid, these people had virtually no power, and a system of legal segregation maintained a rigid separation between the social worlds of blacks and whites. Blacks could not vote, they received limited educations, they were restricted to certain occupations, their travel in their own country was rigidly controlled, and they could live only in certain designated areas. The dominant group in South Africa under apartheid was the white Afrikaaners, a small group of descendants of early Dutch or Huguenot immigrants, who possessed virtually complete control over the political, economic, and social life of South Africa. Under apartheid, black South Africans could not vote for central government candidates, residential and school segregation existed, and legislation placed 87 percent of South African land in white hands. These arrangements made South Africa one of the most rigidly stratified societies in the world. As explained in Chapter 6, *social stratification* refers to the ranking of people into a hierarchy in which the resources considered valuable by society are unequally distributed. Ascribed characteristics such as race and ethnicity often determine a person's position in the stratification system. But the terms *race* and *ethnicity* can be easily misunderstood.

Race and Ethnicity

Scientists use the term *race* as a biological concept to identify a population that differs from others in terms of certain key genetic, hereditary traits. There is much controversy among anthropologists and biologists, however, over whether any traits are unique to particular races in the world today. Certainly some traits are more common in some races than others. But with extensive interbreeding among racial groups throughout human history, genetic traits and characteristics have tended to spread around the world. Indeed, if we were to take a representative group of people from two different racial groups in the United States, it would be difficult to determine, based on visible physical characteristics, where one group left off and the other began. However, although the biological reality of race may be hazy, its social reality is not. In fact, sociologists' definition of race is based on people's *belief* in racial differences: A **race** is *a group of people who are believed to be a biological group sharing genetically transmitted traits that are defined as important.* Thus, race is a social category because in U.S. society, as in others, people make important distinctions between people on the basis of such presumed biological differences, even when these variations are actually vague or nonexistent.

An **ethnic group** is *a people who share a common historical and cultural heritage and sense of group identity and belongingness.* Groups that share distinctive cultural traits such as a common language, national origin, religion, or a sense of historical heritage have been a major source of diversity that has enriched life in many societies. Hispanic Americans, Polish Americans, Gypsies, the Amish, and the Jews are but a few of the many ethnic groups in the United States that have made significant contributions to this nation's way of life. Nevertheless, much of the tension, conflict, and violence that have been part and parcel of U.S. history and still characterize social life today have focused on ethnic differences.

Racism

The subordination and oppression of minority groups is commonly supported by an ideology that assumes that members of the minority are innately inferior and thus deserving of their subordinate status. **Racism** is *the view that certain racial or ethnic groups are biologically inferior and that practices involving their domination and exploitation are therefore justified.* Racist ideologies in Nazi Germany justified genocidal attacks on the Jews, just as racism in the United States has been at the core of discrimination against African Americans, Asians, and other racial groups. For example, in 1979, five social activists, mostly black, were killed in Greensboro, North Carolina, by a group of Nazis and Ku Klux Klan members, motivated in part by racist beliefs, who were later acquitted of murder charges in the slayings (Wheaton, 1987). In 1989, a group of whites in New York killed a black teenager because they thought that he was dating a white girl from their neighborhood.

Despite the highest hopes of many people about equality, racism still persists in some parts of the United States. At this point in the discussion, it is helpful to understand how this kind of ideology arises and, in particular, how prejudice and discrimination develop and affect minority groups.

Sources of Prejudice and Discrimination

You should be able to explain the social and social psychological sources of prejudice and discrimination and describe the consequences that discrimination has for individuals and society.

Prejudice and discrimination are closely intertwined, so much so that people are likely to view them as the same thing. In reality, they are quite distinct. A **prejudice** is *an irrational attitude toward certain people based solely on their membership in a particular group* (Levin & Levin, 1994). Individuals are prejudged on the basis of whatever undesirable characteristics the whole group is presumed to possess. Prejudices can be positive, but they are often negative.

Discrimination, by contrast, refers to *behavior, particularly unequal treatment of people because they are members of a particular group.* The type of discrimination with which this chapter is most concerned is the denial of equal access to resources, privileges, or opportunities, practices that are often based on illogical and irrational grounds.

The relationship between prejudice and discrimination is complex. Although they are likely to go together, Robert K. Merton (1949) has demonstrated that sometimes they do not. In fact, people may combine prejudice and discrimination in four different ways. The most desirable combination, from the point of view of political and social values in the United States, is the *unprejudiced nondiscriminator,* who accepts other racial or ethnic groups in both belief and practice. The *prejudiced discriminator* has negative feelings toward a particular group and translates these sentiments into unequal treatment of people in that group. Members of the Ku Klux Klan, for example, have a strong prejudice against blacks and members of other racial groups; they advocate segregated schools and neighborhoods. These first two possibilities involve a consistency between belief and practice, but there are other possibilities. The *prejudiced nondiscriminator* is a kind of "closet bigot" who is prejudiced against members of some groups but does not translate these attitudes into discriminatory practices. A landlord, for example, may be prejudiced against Asian Americans yet still rent apartments to them because of laws forbidding housing discrimination. Because there are now many laws against discrimination that are strictly enforced, the incidence of this kind of relationship between prejudice and discrimination is likely to increase. The *unprejudiced discriminator* treats the members of some groups unequally because it is convenient or advantageous to do so rather than out of personal antipathy toward them. Salespeople in a real estate agency, for example, may have no personal prejudices but still decline to show houses in certain neighborhoods to African Americans because of the prejudices of people who already live in those neighborhoods.

Next, this chapter will review the major sources of prejudice and discrimination and then look at some of their consequences—the factors that lead them to be viewed as social problems.

Social Sources

Prejudice and discrimination can be understood in part through the theoretical explanations of social stratification presented in Chapter 6: the functionalist, conflict, and evolutionary perspectives. That discussion will not be repeated here. Instead the text will discuss some additional elements of the perspectives that apply especially well to problems of prejudice and discrimination.

Ethnocentrism   Chapters 2 and 4 discussed how important it is that people feel positive about their society and the groups to which they belong. **Ethnocentrism** is *the tendency to view one's own group or culture as an in-group that follows the best and the only proper way to live.* Feeling positive about one's own group, of course, is good because it gives one a sense of belonging and self-worth. For functionalists, ethnocentrism is functional because it produces loyalty, cohesiveness, and strong group ties. All these characteristics help groups stick together and achieve their goals. Ethnocentrism can, however, lead one to believe that other groups— especially those that are very different—have unfavorable characteristics. If one's own way of life is the only proper way to live, an individual may conclude that other lifestyles are improper. This conclusion can be used to justify unfair, hostile, and even genocidal attacks on other groups. Under Adolf Hitler, for example, the Nazis were so thoroughly convinced of the superiority of the alleged

Aryan race that the Jews became a despised out-group. Likewise, many Europeans who came to the Americas as colonists believed that their heritage contained all that was wise and desirable, and these racist beliefs fueled their treatment of Indians in the New World. Thus, if ethnocentrism gets out of hand, it can become dysfunctional and create social disorganization in the form of hostility, conflict, and discrimination, which can threaten the social order. Although ethnocentrism can have these negative consequences, according to functionalists, such outcomes are not inevitable if people are aware of and guard against them.

Competition   According to the conflict perspective, prejudice and discrimination arise when two groups find themselves in competition. This competition is often economic, for jobs or land, but it can also be based on noneconomic valued resources, such as access to attractive marriage partners or the right to practice a preferred religion. The more intensely groups compete, the more threatening each group becomes to the other and the more likely negative and hostile views are to emerge. When there are obvious differences between the groups, such as in skin color or religious practices, these differences can become the focus of prejudice. Discriminatory practices may emerge, sanctioned by law or custom, as a way to limit the access of the less powerful group to the scarce resources. Prejudice and discrimination can arise from competitive situations in a number of specific ways (Olzak, 1992).

Sociologist Edna Bonacich (1972) called one type of competitive situation a split labor market. A **split labor market** is *one in which two groups of workers are willing to do the same work, but for different wages.* In a split labor market, lower-priced laborers have a competitive advantage because employers prefer to hire them. Higher-priced workers find their position threatened by those willing to work more cheaply. In such a situation, the higher-priced workers will be inclined to discriminate against the inexpensive laborers in an effort to exclude them from certain occupations. Bonacich argues that this discrimination is a key factor in much racial, ethnic, and sexual antagonism because the presumed biological differences between the two groups can serve as the focus of discrimination that can be justified on racist grounds. If people believe that members of a particular racial group are lazy or untrustworthy, then this belief is a rationale for excluding that group from jobs that demand hard work and trustworthiness. Likewise, if people believe that women are best suited for clerical and secretarial positions, then this belief can be used to discriminate against women when they try to obtain more lucrative jobs in construction or other professions (Boswell, 1986).

Another type of economic competition is one in which a powerful group exploits a weaker one for its own gain. A clear example would be the relationship between the slaveholder and the slave in which the former gains substantially from the relationship, to the detriment of the latter. Slavery in the United States was clearly a form of economic exploitation supported by racist beliefs about the inferiority of blacks. Many of the poor today suffer a similar kind of exploitation because their work at low-paying and demeaning jobs benefits the more affluent in society (see Chapter 6). A variant of this type of exploitation is **internal colonialism,** in which *a subordinate group provides cheap labor that benefits the dominant group and is then further exploited by having to purchase expensive goods and services from the dominant group* (Doob, 1993). For example, the poor in the United States not only provide cheap labor but also purchase expensive health care, televisions, food, and other products that provide substantial profit to dominant groups.

Socialization and Conformity   Once patterns of prejudice and discrimination arise, they become incorporated into the values and norms of the group. Prejudice and discrimination toward particular groups then become legitimated, transmitted to new members through the socialization process, and frequently internalized (Blalock, 1982). A study of regional differences in prejudice toward African Americans during the 1960s, for example, found, not surprisingly, that there was greater prejudice in the South, especially within the states of the old Confederacy (Middleton, 1976). It also found, however, that people who lived in the South as children and then moved to other regions were less prejudiced than those who remained in the South. In the same way, people

who grew up outside the South and then moved there were more prejudiced than those who remained outside the South. In other words, people tend to conform to the prejudiced beliefs, values, and norms that are considered appropriate in the groups to which they belong.

Institutionalized Discrimination   Prejudice and discrimination sometimes become incorporated into social policies and practices, which can result in the perpetuation of prejudice and discrimination through **institutionalized discrimination** or **institutionalized racism:** *the inequitable treatment of a group resulting from practices or policies that are incorporated into social, political, or economic institutions and that operate independently from the prejudices of individuals.* One form of institutionalized discrimination is the use of physical size requirements as qualifications for certain jobs. Many police departments, for example, set minimum height requirements for police officers. Asian Americans have protested against this requirement because Asians are, on the average, shorter than whites and many therefore cannot qualify for police work. Discrimination in this form may not be direct; people may not be excluded from jobs because of their racial group. Rather, it is the minimum entrance requirements that effectively bar most members of a particular minority group from the jobs while serving as a barrier to only a few people in the dominant group. Through institutionalized discrimination, social inequality can persist long after prejudicial attitudes may have changed. In fact, much of the civil rights effort in the United States over the past thirty years has concentrated on eliminating this kind of discrimination.

Social Psychological Sources

A number of social psychological factors can play a part in the emergence of prejudice and discrimination. One involves the human tendency to categorize. The physical and social world is sufficiently complex that we need to simplify it by thinking in terms of general categories or by lumping together the elements that have something in common. Categories, however, can become *stereotypes*—rigid and oversimplified images in which each element or person in a category is assumed to possess all the characteristics associated with that category. Because some Jews work in banking, for example, some people might assume that all Jews are proficient in financial matters. Thus, stereotyping can contribute to prejudice and discrimination.

Prejudice and discrimination can arise when people become frustrated by their inability to achieve sought-after goals. Social psychologists have shown that frustration can lead to aggression in both overt and covert forms (Baron & Richardson, 1994; Berkowitz, 1971). Aggression can be expressed by direct physical assaults or through prejudice or discrimination. One form this aggression can take is *scapegoating,* or placing the blame for one's troubles on an individual or group incapable of offering effective resistance. This happened, for example, in the southern United States between 1880 and 1930 when thousands of blacks were lynched by angry mobs of whites, many of whom were unemployed or experiencing other economic problems. People experiencing severe difficulties or frustrations in their own lives sometimes lash out with racial hatred against others because such actions deflect their attention from their own disappointments or failings. Blame for the difficulties is diverted toward the out-group (Olzak, 1992).

The sources of prejudice and discrimination are complex, resulting from the intertwining of numerous sociological and social psychological factors. Most sociological research concludes that social factors such as ethnocentrism, competition, socialization, and institutionalized discrimination play the most important roles in that they set the stage for the operation of social psychological mechanisms. Without this social underpinning, prejudice and discrimination resulting from the social psychological mechanisms alone would likely be sporadic and unorganized. This finding is exemplified in the just-mentioned example of the lynchings of blacks by whites. Research makes clear that the frustration that helped create such horrid aggression was produced in part by the economic competition that existed in some communities in the South between whites and blacks. In locales where there was less such competition, lynchings were substantially less common, although they did occur (Soule, 1992). Unfortunately, the social sources of prejudice and discrimination are all too often present, and the consequences can be devastating to both society and individuals.

Consequences of Discrimination

Prejudice by itself can be relatively harmless, but it can become destructive when it fuels discrimination. Discrimination marks the spot where the social problems surrounding race and ethnic relations begin. In modern societies, discrimination against minorities has had a detrimental impact, although some groups benefit in the short run. First and most important, discrimination forces some groups into a disadvantageous position in the stratification system and adversely affects their life chances. Chapter 10 shows that discrimination results in higher rates of illness, injury, and death for minorities. This chapter discusses the fact that many minorities in the United States enjoy fewer socioeconomic resources and opportunities than do members of dominant white groups. Because the society's ideology holds out the promise that all can share in the American dream, being deprived of these opportunities can produce simmering resentments that periodically erupt in destructive violence.

A second consequence of discrimination is its effects on people's views of themselves. Those who feel the brunt of discrimination may come to accept the devalued and stigmatized view of themselves that is implied by their being powerless and on the bottom of society. Minority youth, for example, often have more negative self-concepts and a poorer sense of self-worth than do nonminority youth. Such negativity does not always occur, and the negative consequences can be overcome by supportive families, high-quality schools, and a minority culture that insulates people from the negativism implied by low social standing. Yet the research is clear that racism can and does result in lower self-esteem among minorities in some contexts (Martinez & Dukes, 1991; Pallas, Entwisle, Alexander, & Weinstein, 1990). And people with negative views of themselves and their worth may contribute less to society and may exacerbate existing social problems through criminal behavior, long-term poverty, domestic violence, child neglect, and the like.

A third consequence of discrimination is that it creates tense, hostile, and sometimes violent encounters between dominant and minority group members, thus destroying trust, communication, and cooperation. In settings such as school or the workplace where members of different groups interact, discrimination makes it difficult for people to work together. For example, racial clashes have at times plagued the U.S. military, and these conflicts make it more difficult to develop a cohesive, coordinated, and effective military organization. Other Worlds, Other Ways: Britain, Germany, Yugoslavia (on pp. 226–227) explores the all too common hostility and violence at many points around the globe today and suggests some of the social conditions that produce it.

A final consequence of discrimination is that it can undermine social and political values and institutions. Because the United States professes to value equality and human dignity, the violation of these values because of racism and discrimination can generate cynicism regarding U.S. political and economic institutions. It can also threaten the legitimacy of those institutions if people see them merely as tools to benefit those fortunate enough to have acquired some power in society. From the functionalist perspective, such undermining may represent the most serious of trends to combat—when people begin to lose faith in the system's core values and foundation, that system's survival may be in jeopardy.

Patterns of Intergroup Relations

You should be able to describe the patterns of intergroup relations that emerge between dominant and minority groups and the minority reactions to such domination as well as discuss the possibilities for cooperation in a multiracial or multiethnic society.

When different racial and ethnic groups live together in one society, racial and ethnic differences are sometimes ignored and play no part in how people relate to one another. In many situations, however, prejudice and discrimination produce some specific patterns of intergroup relations based on dominance and subordination. The sociologists George Simpson and J. Milton Yinger (1985) have identified six distinct relationships, each founded in the subordination of one group by another.

Forms of Domination

At one extreme, a dominant group might engage in **genocide,** or *the attempt to exterminate an entire minority group.* Genocide is, unfortunately, all too common

These Bosnians were imprisoned in the early 1990s in the ethnic conflict that erupted when communist rule collapsed in the former Yugoslavia. Their treatment is grim testimony to the tragic consequences that can result from ethnic differences and hatred.

THER WORLDS, *Other Ways*

BRITAIN, GERMANY, YUGOSLAVIA: THE SOCIAL AND ECONOMIC SOURCES OF RACIAL HATRED AND CONFLICT

In too many places around the globe, we can see the social sources of prejudice and discrimination producing intense racial hatred and conflict. The details change, in terms of the racial or ethnic identity of the antagonists and the epithets hurled, but the underlying conditions that produce it are distressingly similar and familiar.

In London in 1993, for example, an avowed racist from a neo-Nazi political party was elected to Parliament on a platform calling for deportation of all nonwhites from Britain (Stevenson, 1993). His supporters at a victory rally chanted "We hate Pakis" and "There ain't no black in the Union Jack." In this case, the hatred was directed against immigrants from former British colonies of Pakistan, India, and some islands in the Caribbean. Racially motivated attacks on Asians and blacks by whites have been on the increase in Britain in the late 1980s and 1990s. Often, they consist of a small group of attackers descending on one individual, but there have also been extensive street brawls. Large groups of minority youth have attacked the police, whom the youth often view as highly racist themselves rather than as the defenders of minorities. Mobs of neo-Nazi skinheads have rampaged through minority neighborhoods breaking shop windows, stealing from stores, and menacing local residents. In some cases, the police do little to stop them. Fueling this hostility are high levels of unem-

ployment in Britain—the neo-Nazi elected to Parliament was himself unemployed.

In recent years, Germany has also experienced one of the largest waves of racial violence since World War II (Levin & McDevitt, 1993). Neo-Nazi and skinhead youth have openly attacked Vietnamese, Mozambicans, and Turks on the street, in one case killing an African by pushing him off a train. They have firebombed homes, hotels, and apartment buildings where immigrant foreigners live. In some cases, these attacks have involved mobs of hundreds of youths in terrifying descents on relatively helpless immigrants and their families. In Germany, as in Britain, the violence is attributed to a relatively small number of neo-Nazis and racist skinheads, but public opinion polls point to substantial support for the attitudes these youth espouse, especially for "racial purity" in Germany and the removal of foreign workers.

In Germany, these episodes have been influenced by the end of the Cold War, the collapse of the Soviet Union, and the resulting reunification of Germany. Germany has had to absorb the devastated economy of the former East Germany. This problem has meant dealing with highly inefficient factories, undertrained workers, and environmental disasters. The result for Germany has been soaring unemployment and growing expenditures for social services such as welfare and health care. Germany also faces a shortage of housing and fairly deplorable living conditions for some of its citizens. Apparently, neo-Nazi activism is proving to be a persuasive and attractive force as a source of authority for young Germans attempting to navigate the largely uncharted waters of their new post–Cold War

---

in history. The Nazis attempted to exterminate the Jews and other groups during World War II, and the Serbs in the former Yugoslavia in the early 1990s were accused of the wholesale slaughter of Muslims in an attempt at "ethnic cleansing." The policies and practices of the European immigrants to the New World during and after the 1500s came very close to genocide of the native peoples. For instance, the Portuguese decimated the Brazilian Indians discussed in the beginning of this chapter.

The Natchez people discussed in the beginning of Chapter 6 were almost completely wiped out by the French after the Natchez, upset with French encroachment on their territory, attacked a trading post. The few Natchez remaining after the brutal massacre were sold into slavery in the West Indies (Farb, 1978). Estimates are that at least two-thirds of the Indian population in the United States was annihilated by the direct and indirect actions of the white Europeans.

world. The irony in this situation is that immigrant workers—the source of the young Germans' fury—may play a big role in repairing the German economy because they provide a source of cheap labor to rebuild competitive industries and attract investment. In addition, Germany is an aging society with a fairly low birthrate and may not be able to supply an adequate labor force from indigenous sources. Nonetheless, the immigrants offer a ready scapegoat for the anger of the youth.

The collapse of the Soviet Union also unleashed intense ethnic and religious hostilities in the former Yugoslavia (Kressel, 1996). Centuries-old hostilities among Orthodox Christian Serbs, Roman Catholic Croats, and Muslims have led to a horrific struggle in which each group has tried to grab a piece of territory for itself. This intense and protracted war has produced tens of thousands of deaths, concentration camps where inmates are starved and brutalized, rapes of thousands of women and girls, and masses of refugees without homes. The authoritarian rule of communism was able to stifle these hostilities for many decades, although it obviously did not eliminate them. Once the central government was weakened and the struggle for the control of post-communist Yugoslavia began, these ethnic and religious connections became the organizational focus for those who wished to gain power. Some groups attempted to organize a multiethnic, multireligious Yugoslavia that would accept and tolerate differences, but they have been overwhelmed by more powerful forces seeking "ethnically cleansed" territories for their people.

These and other examples of racial and ethnic conflict around the world point to the role of social forces in bringing them about or in making them much more extensive than they might otherwise be. Ethnocentrism by itself can produce some mix of racism and xenophobia. That is certainly true in the former Yugoslavia, where ethnic and religious traditions go back hundreds of years and are an important source of identity and community authority. Likewise, whites in Germany and Britain trace their ancestry to what they understand as white forefathers, and some find the imposition of foreign ways on their heritage to be offensive. Beyond ethnocentrism, competition has also been an important fuel to these hatreds. In Germany and Britain, for example, people are clearly responding to economic difficulties and unemployment by trying to drive out those they feel are unfairly competing for what they see as rightfully their jobs. To this extent, they are part of the capitalist world system described in Chapter 6. The movement of immigrants from one part of the globe to another makes available a supply of cheap labor that can be used by capitalists to develop new markets and industries. Such movement is not a new phenomenon—the transportation of slaves from Africa to the Western Hemisphere in the 1600s was part of the global movement of labor fueled by the needs of capitalism. The immigrants in Germany and Britain are an extension of that same process. The global fluidity of labor helps to keep costs down and profits up, but it also produces conflict and hatred when those immigrants are perceived to threaten the opportunities of indigenous labor.

A more common relationship between dominant and minority groups is **segregation,** *an arrangement in which the social lives of the two groups are kept separate.* In many nations, members of dominant and minority groups go to different schools and churches and live in different neighborhoods. South Africa's apartheid was a very rigid form of segregation, and the separation of African Americans and whites in the United States was almost as rigid until a few decades ago. Even today, contin-

uing discrimination, along with social norms and informal pressures, have produced a high level of residential segregation and a minimal level of social contact between blacks and whites in the United States (Gillmor & Doig, 1992; Massey & Denton, 1992; Sigelman, Bledsoe, Welch, & Combs, 1996). In Chicago, for example, 71 percent of African Americans live on a block where 90 percent of the residents are also African American. Among Asian Americans, Vietnamese are the most highly segregated group, and Asian Americans as a whole live in communities that are highly segregated from African Americans. All this segregation persists despite the fact that the Civil Rights Act of 1964 outlawed racial discrimination in housing.

Most minorities experience some degree of **continued subjugation,** in which *the dominant group uses a variety of practices to maintain subordination and exploitation.* Subjugation can be achieved through laws that prohibit minorities from holding certain occupations or going to certain schools. These practices of subjugation are designed to protect the position of the dominant group from any possible inroads by the minority. In most cases where racial or ethnic identity is relevant to intergroup relations, continued subjugation is pervasive.

In some situations, dominant groups control minorities through **population transfer,** *the voluntary or involuntary movement of minorities to particular geographic areas.* South Africa forcibly moved many black South Africans to new residential communities. White European settlers in the United States used the strategy to gain control of native lands: They relocated Indians to reservations. In such population transfers, the dominant group usually reserves the most desirable, productive, and profitable lands for itself while relegating the minority to lands that are limited or marginal. Population transfer also occurred recently in the former Yugoslavia as Serbs forced Muslims out of Serb-dominated communities.

Assimilation is *the process by which a racial or ethnic minority loses its distinctive identity and way of life and becomes absorbed into the dominant group* (Alba, 1995). In some situations, especially when a minority group is small and powerless, assimilation occurs with few changes in the lifestyle of the dominant group. The Inuit in Alaska, for example, have had little impact on the dominant society of white European immigrants to the United States. The Inuit, however, have had to adapt by forgoing their traditional subsistence activities of fishing and hunting and by taking jobs in the cash economy that the Europeans brought to the Western Hemisphere. By contrast, when minorities are large or cohesive, or have some power, their members may change the dominant culture in the process of assimilating. Italian Americans, for instance, have become largely assimilated yet have left their distinctive mark on U.S. culture in the form of such foods as pizza and spaghetti.

Assimilation is neither a rapid nor a simple process, and people can assimilate in some realms and not others. People are reluctant to change deeply held values or practices, but they will more readily change things they see as less important or more practical. In addition, dominant groups may permit particular racial or ethnic groups to assimilate in some realms but discourage it in others. As a consequence, sociologists identify a number of different ways in which people can assimilate (Gordon, 1978b). *Cultural assimilation* refers to adopting the cultural patterns of dominant groups, such as their religious beliefs or their social values. It is often the first, and sometimes the only, type of assimilation to occur. *Structural assimilation* refers to joining the important social groups and organizations of the dominant group, such as their schools, churches, or clubs. Jewish Americans, for example, have achieved cultural assimilation along with some structural assimilation, but they are still excluded from some groups and organizations of non-Jewish Anglos.

Pluralism, the sixth pattern of intergroup relations, is one in which *a number of racial and ethnic groups live side by side, each retaining a distinct identity and lifestyle while also sharing in some aspects of the larger culture* (Simpson, 1995). In other words, to use a term introduced in Chapter 2, pluralism involves the persistence of a variety of subcultures. One type of pluralism is *cultural pluralism,* in which a group retains values, norms, beliefs, and maybe a language that is somewhat distinct from that of the dominant culture. In both Canada and the United States, for example, many Indian and Inuit peoples retain their traditional language and religious beliefs and values in a society whose dominant group speaks English and practices either Protestantism or Roman Catholicism. *Structural pluralism* exists when minorities maintain groups, organizations, and institutions separate from those of the dominant culture. African Americans, for example, have created their own churches largely because they were not welcome in the churches of the dominant group.

Minority Reaction to Domination

How minority groups respond to domination depends on their numbers and on the power and other resources they have available. Groups without much power may have little choice but *sub-*

mission, where they accept their subordinate status, even if grudgingly, and cooperate or at least acquiesce to the demands placed on them. Slaves in ancient Rome and nineteenth-century Brazil and the United States had little choice but to go along and appear reasonably accepting of their place. To do anything else could have been dangerous because of the enormous disparity in power between slave and slaveowner.

When minorities have more resources, and especially when they have some support and sympathy among significant factions of the dominant group, *social protest* becomes feasible: actions that express disapproval of and attempt to change conventional patterns of dominance and subordination. Such protest could take the form of marches, demonstrations, or civil disobedience that attempts to force authorities to change some policy or practice. The civil rights movement of the 1960s was such a social protest movement in which African Americans and many Anglo supporters attacked entrenched forms of discrimination in the United States.

Separatism is like segregation but with the minority group taking the initiative for creating a separation of dominant and minority groups. It is a common reaction among minorities who have some resources but little support in the dominant group. The nation of Pakistan was created in 1947 by a separatist movement of Muslims who were a small minority in India, which was dominated by a Hindu majority. The Muslim minority had the numbers and the political and military resources to fight successfully for a separate political existence. Other Worlds, Other Ways: French Canada (on pp. 230–231) discusses a present-day separatist movement in Canada.

Infrequently, a minority will go to the point of *rebellion,* attempting to overthrow the political authority of the dominant group. For twenty-five years, the Irish Republican Army has been attempting to reunite Northern Ireland, which is under British control, with the rest of Ireland (Rose, 1990). Irish Catholics are in the minority in Northern Ireland and feel oppressed by the Protestant majority. The Irish Catholics believe at British control of Northern Ireland is a colonial relic that prevents the achievement of the Irish destiny of complete control of the island of Ireland. Bombings and deaths in this long-lasting rebellion have continued into the 1990s.

Switzerland: Cooperation in a Multiethnic Society

Switzerland is often pointed to as a model of effective pluralism because it is made up of three distinct ethnic groups—German, French, and Italian—that work together peacefully and cooperatively. Prior to the nineteenth century, ethnic conflict in Switzerland was constant and often violent (Schmid, 1981; Steiner, 1990). Then, interethnic relations, dominated by German-speaking Swiss, at times verged on civil war. Religious conflict between Catholics and Protestants, often intense and bitter, also contributed to the strife. Ethnic and linguistic equality was imposed on Switzerland by the French, who conquered the country in 1798. Finally, a brief civil war in the 1840s ended with the adoption of a constitution in 1848, which continued the protection of linguistic minorities and created a system of power sharing among ethnic groups that has enabled the Swiss to live in harmony for the last 150 years.

The basic assumption of this power-sharing system is that all three language groups are assured of representation in the government. The Swiss Federal Council, the executive body, includes members from all three ethnic groups, in rough proportions to their numbers in the population. The chairmanship of the council (equivalent to the U.S. presidency) is rotated to a different ethnic group each year, assuring each group a turn. The parliament is elected by proportional representation, with each ethnic group being represented in approximate proportions to its size in the population. Civil service positions and military appointments are also made on the basis of proportional representation. All three languages are considered the national languages of Switzerland. The political system is one of decentralized federalism, with the governments of each canton, or district, having autonomy in the conduct of many of its affairs. Thus, each canton, dominated by a particular ethnic group, controls its own schools and police.

The pluralist Swiss system amounts to what would be called a quota system in the United States. In contrast to Swiss power sharing, the United States and many other nations tend more toward power competition, a system in which each group strives to concentrate as much power in its own hands as it can. Such competition can lead to instability and chaos and often leaves minorities largely disenfranchised and dissatisfied.

OTHER WORLDS, *Other Ways*

FRENCH CANADA: A SEPARATIST MOVEMENT IN A MULTIETHNIC, MULTILINGUAL SOCIETY

In the colonization of North America by Europeans, both the French and the British had a strong presence in what would later become the nation of Canada. Ultimately, Canada became a British colony and a member of the British Commonwealth, but the French remained a strong force, particularly in the province of Quebec, where French culture and language were well entrenched (Balthazar, 1995; See, 1986). When the British North America Act of 1867 established the modern-day Canadian Confederation, it recognized French culture as an integral part of the Canadian nation. For instance, although Canada is mostly English-speaking, the act explicitly protected the use of the French language in the courts and legislature of Quebec and the federal government. So, the dominant English speakers did not use the new confederation to absorb or assimilate the much smaller group of French speakers. It was not an equal relationship, however: The language rights of the English-speaking minority in Quebec were protected, but the French-speaking minorities in the Canadian provinces other than Quebec had no such protection—they could not demand that education or business or government be available to them in their language.

Since confederation, Canada has become a nation dominated by English speakers, although they are a numerical minority in the province of Quebec. Despite this fact, they are a sociological majority in Quebec because they dominate positions of power in education, politics, and business. They maintain this control by virtue of their control over the rest of Canada and their domination of the national government. French Canadians believe, and there is evidence to support them, that they are discriminated against in both Quebec and the rest of Canada. Language has been a focal point for much fury and controversy. English is the official language of Canada, and it is the language spoken in schools, government offices, and businesses. French speakers thus feel automatically discriminated against when they must speak what they see as a foreign language when conducting their daily affairs—even in Quebec, which is predominantly French-speaking.

Fearing that their minority status might lead to a weakening or even disappearance of their ethnic heritage and identity, some French speakers over the years have supported separation from Canada (Dion, 1992). Such separatist sentiments existed as far back as the establishment of the Canadian confederacy, when a faction of the French population called the *Rouges* opposed Quebec's joining the confederation. Until the 1960s, however, such sentiment was not strong. In 1968, the Parti Québecois was created, with the charismatic René Levesque as its leader, and

Swiss pluralism works for a number of reasons. First, since the three ethnic groups are of European heritage, they share a lot of history and culture in common, despite their differences. Second, the three groups have been settled in the region for centuries, and compromises and accommodations have been worked out over the years. Third, the Swiss state has been stable for a number of years, without the political instability that can serve as fertile ground for ethnic conflict. Finally, The Swiss ethnic minorities did not have

to go through a protracted or bitter struggle for their rights that could have left simmering antagonisms. In the light of these reasons, some observers have argued that the Swiss are an exception: The Swiss experience is unique and cannot serve as a model for other societies where conditions make solutions to racial and ethnic conflicts much more difficult. Nevertheless, Jurg Steiner (1990), who has studied the Swiss, says they are not a different or "naturally peaceful" people. Rather, from experience over a long

began demanding a politically autonomous Quebec, although with a strong economic association with Canada. Around 1970, sporadic episodes of violence accompanied these demands, with a number of kidnappings and bombings directed at pressuring the government to make changes (McRae, 1990). In 1976, the Parti Québecois took control of the provincial government and passed some important legislation furthering its aims. For example, it required that all business in the province be conducted in French rather than English. Some businesses left Quebec rather than comply with the law.

By the late 1980s, secessionist sentiment in Quebec was strong and the province had become almost a quasi-state within the confederation of Canada (Dion, 1992). In the late 1980s, an agreement called the Meech Lake Accord was hammered out among the Canadian provinces. It was very favorable toward the independence of Quebec, including such items as the formal recognition of Quebec as a distinct society, a stronger role for Quebec in making appointments to the Supreme Court, and a Quebec veto on constitutional amendments. These were rights no other Canadian province had. Quebec threatened to secede if the accord was not approved. There was strong opposition among English-speaking Canadians to the special treatment of Quebec in the Meech Lake Accord, and the provinces did not ratify the agreement. One of the reasons for failure was that minorities other than French speakers opposed it because it

offered them nothing. Especially in English-speaking provinces, feminists, aboriginal Indians, and various ethnic groups objected that one minority was being selected for special treatment and the others ignored. This controversy documented the extent to which Canada had changed from biculturalism to multiculturalism. French Canadian separatists, however, see the multiculturalism issue as a strategy to dilute and defuse the Quebec question. In 1995, the voters in Quebec very narrowly defeated a referendum that recommended that Quebec secede from Canada.

Serious violence has been avoided thus far in this ethnic dispute in Canada for a number of reasons. One reason is that prosperity and economic growth have persisted in Canada for at least a century, which has diluted support for more extreme measures. A second reason is that Catholics can be found in both English-speaking and French-speaking camps, and this bridge has diffused some of the stereotyping and hostility that might otherwise have led to more intense conflict. A third reason is that a decentralized government has enabled the province of Quebec to gain significant autonomy within the Canadian union, and this autonomy has reduced support for extreme measures. Nevertheless, despite the low level of violence, the Quebec separatist movement of the past thirty years has represented a serious threat to the Canadian confederation, and the situation is very uncertain since the collapse of the Meech Lake Accord.

period of time, they have created a system that reduces conflict between groups and produces greater cooperation, stability, and prosperity. As another expert put it, the lesson to learn from Switzerland is that "successful democratic pluralism depends on minorities' being continually accommodated within the political system" (Schmid, 1981, p. 155).

The Swiss are not without their ethnic conflicts, however, notably over the *Gastarbeiter,* or "foreign workers." Switzerland, like the other industrial

economies of Europe, has attracted poor workers from many eastern European and Third-World countries looking for jobs. These foreign workers are outside the political system and do not have the rights of Swiss citizens. In fact, Switzerland does not consider itself a land of immigrants, as the United States does, and these foreign workers are seen as temporary (even though Switzerland is highly dependent on them and some have been there for a long time). In fact, the Swiss call them *guest workers* rather than *immigrants* to emphasize their temporary connection with Switzerland. These workers have created a number of tensions, one being that they are predominantly Catholic and over time may change the balance of Protestants and Catholics in Switzerland. This possibility is important because the political compromises and accommodations that have made Swiss pluralism possible have been based on the current balance of the two religious groups. Consequently, hostility toward the foreign workers has surfaced, including efforts to restrict their political and social rights and to discourage them from remaining in Switzerland.

Racial and Ethnic Minorities in the United States

You should be able to describe the major racial and ethnic minorities in the United States, discuss their current circumstances and opportunities, explain the variation in achievement found among them, and show how the mass media influence the position of minorities in society.

The picture of prejudice, discrimination, and intergroup relations in the United States is not always a pretty one or one to be proud of. There is not space to focus on all racial and ethnic minorities in the country, so this section will discuss only those that are the largest numerically or that more effectively illustrate sociological approaches to intergroup relations.

The United States is, of course, a land of immigrants. The only difference between groups in this regard is the time of their arrival. Even the group with the deepest roots in American soil, who have called themselves Native Americans or American Indians, are descendants of immigrants who traversed the Bering Straits land bridge from Asia to the Americas tens of thousands of years ago. Beyond immigrant status, however, there is considerable variation in the positions of racial and ethnic groups in the United States. Their treatment today and in the past illustrates how prejudice and discrimination have functioned in U.S. history and illuminates some of the consequences of social stratification discussed in Chapter 6.

African Americans

African Americans comprise the largest nonwhite minority group in the United States, numbering approximately 33 million, or about 12.7 percent of the total population (U.S. Bureau of the Census, 1995). In addition, they are one of the oldest minority groups, with the first Africans arriving from Africa in 1619, not long after the first permanent European settlers in the New World. They are also the only minority group in the United States that was held as slaves. When the British colonized the New World, they followed the practices of the Spanish and Portuguese in bringing black African slaves to work the land (Phillips, 1963; Westermann, 1955). Black Africans were particularly vulnerable to slavery because many of them lived in small, isolated tribes and were unable to protect themselves against more formidable foes. In fact, some of the larger African tribes, such as the Ashanti, actually sold other Africans into slavery (Sowell, 1981).

Technically, all slaves in the United States gained their freedom with the end of the Civil War. However, after a short period during which African Americans exercised a degree of freedom and political control, white southerners began to reassert their dominance when federal troops left the South in 1877. In 1896, the Supreme Court ruled in *Plessy v. Ferguson* that it was constitutional to provide "separate but equal" public facilities for members of different races, and the era of widespread legal segregation began. For six decades, the Plessy case served as the foundation for discrimination against African Americans in schools, housing, and other areas. During this period, a split labor market in black–white relations prevailed (Marks, 1981). Because of deteriorating race relations after the Plessy decision and economic distress in the South, a massive migration of young southern blacks to eastern and midwestern cities began. That was the beginning of large black ghettos in cities such as New York, Detroit, Boston, and Chicago. These concentrations of blacks in cities would later serve as an important mobilizing element in the efforts of African Americans to gain equality.

The 1950s and 1960s were a period of considerable change in the lives of African Americans (Bloom, 1987). In the *Brown v. The Board of Education* decision of 1954, the U.S. Supreme Court ruled that the separate-but-equal doctrine was unconstitutional. The southern states were ordered to integrate their schools "with all deliberate speed," but this process turned out to be rather slow. The civil rights movement emerged, however, and, along with more militant black groups, initiated a drive for more economic and social opportunities for African Americans. Out of the demonstrations, protests, and rioting came the Civil Rights Act of 1964 and the Voting Rights Act of 1965. Later, affirmative-action programs and school busing would be used to provide greater opportunities for blacks in the United States.

The position of African Americans has improved substantially since the 1960s. For example, the number of blacks enrolled in college has increased six times since 1960, whereas enrollment of whites has only tripled; African Americans now constitute 10 percent of all college students, compared to 6 percent in 1960 (U.S. Bureau of the Census, 1995, p. 179). The number of blacks in professional occupations has also increased at a much faster rate than among whites. The percentage of blacks registered to vote has doubled, and the number of blacks holding elected political office has increased by five times.

The current picture, however, is by no means one of unblemished progress, because African Americans still lag behind many other groups by some measures of socioeconomic status (see Table 7.1 and Figure 7.1 [on p. 234]). For example, although the average income of African Americans has climbed in the past thirty years, so has the income of whites, and their relative positions have changed very little. The ratio of black income to white income is virtually the same as it was thirty years ago. Although channels of mobility are open to some African Americans, other blacks are trapped in poverty or in occupations that offer little prestige or hope for advancement. In the mid-1990s, for example, the number of blacks in poverty was actually higher than it had been in 1966, with the poverty rate being three times higher among blacks than among whites (see Chapter 6). This lagging achievement is not due to a lack of aspirations, however, since research shows that African American youth actually have higher educational and occupational aspirations than do white youth (Solorzano, 1991). Somewhere along the way, those high aspirations get sidetracked before becoming reality. The end of this section will explore some reasons for the variations in achievement among racial and ethnic minorities in the United States.

Hispanic Americans

Hispanic Americans, or Latinos, are Americans whose ancestral home is Mexico, Central America, South America, or the Caribbean. They include Mexican Americans (Chicanos), Cubans, and Puerto Ricans. (Some members of this group prefer to be called Hispanic and others Latino; there is no consensus about a proper designation. This

TABLE 7.1   Income of white, black, and Hispanic families, 1960–1993

Year	Median Income			Ratio of Black to White Income	Ratio of Hispanic to White Income
	White	Black	Hispanic		
1960	$ 5,835	$ 3,230	NA*	.55	
1965	7,251	3,993	NA*	.55	
1970	10,236	6,279	NA*	.61	
1975	14,268	8,779	$ 9,551	.61	.67
1980	21,904	12,674	14,716	.58	.67
1985	29,152	16,786	19,027	.58	.65
1993	39,300	21,542	23,654	.55	.60

*Data not available.
Note: From *Statistical Abstract of the United States, 1985* (p. 446) by U.S. Bureau of the Census, 1984, Washington, DC: U.S. Government Printing Office; *Statistical Abstract of the United States, 1995* (p. 474) by U.S. Bureau of the Census, 1995, Washington, DC: U.S. Government Printing Office.

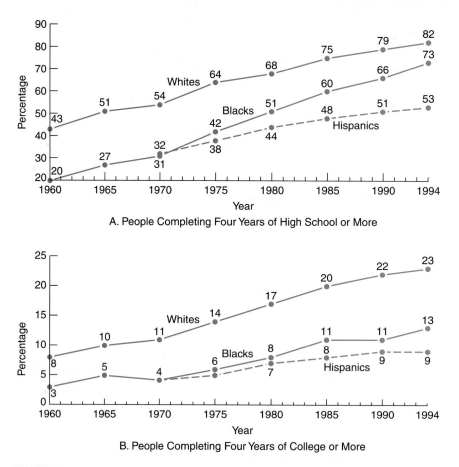

FIGURE 7.1 Educational Attainment, by Race or Ethnicity, Among People Twenty-Five Years Old and Older, 1960–1994 *Note:* From *Statistical Abstract of the United States, 1995* (p. 157) by U.S. Bureau of the Census, 1995, Washington, DC: U.S. Government Printing Office.

text will use Hispanic as the primary designation because it is the term used by the Census Bureau from which much of the data in this chapter was obtained.) In the 1990s there are 27 million Hispanic Americans in the United States, or about 10 percent of the population. There are also an estimated 3 to 6 million Hispanics in the United States illegally.

The largest Hispanic group in the United States, almost two-thirds of the total, is the Mexican Americans (see Figure 7.2). This group has a long history of settlement in the United States (Acuna, 1987; Moore, 1976). In fact, there have been Spanish-speaking communities located throughout what is now the American Southwest since before Mexican independence from Spain in 1821. But as the white population in the Southwest

grew during the 1800s, the economic prospects for these early settlers declined. Light-skinned, pure Spanish settlers who had adopted the white lifestyle were accepted into the white world, but the darker-skinned settlers who maintained their heritage, especially those with some Indian heritage, were viewed as inferiors and bore the brunt of prejudice and discrimination (Vigil, 1980). Following the Mexican Revolution in 1909, hundreds of thousands of Mexican peasants migrated to the Southwest, where there was much demand for inexpensive labor because of expanding agriculture and railroads. The status of these more recent migrants to the United States, however, was low, although perhaps slightly higher than it had been in Mexico. The Depression of the 1930s resulted in a decline in farmwork, driving many Mexican Amer-

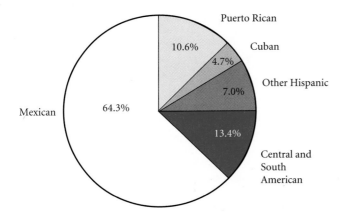

FIGURE 7.2 Percentage Distribution of Hispanic Americans by National Origin, 1993 *Note:* From *Statistical Abstract of the United States, 1995* (p. 51) by U.S. Bureau of the Census, 1995, Washington, DC: U.S. Government Printing Office.

icans into the cities to seek employment or public relief. The first urban barrios, or Spanish-speaking neighborhoods, began to spring up in such cities as Denver, Phoenix, and Los Angeles.

Since World War II, the position of Mexican Americans has changed substantially. First, their numbers have grown steadily because of a continuing stream of migrants from Mexico and a high birthrate among Mexican Americans. By 1980, this group made up almost 20 percent of the California population and had larger concentrations in many urban areas in the Southwest: 62 percent of El Paso residents, for example, were of Hispanic heritage. Second, in part as an outgrowth of the civil rights movement, the Chicano movement gained support in the 1960s in championing the rights of all Hispanics. Cesar Chavez organized the United Farm Workers to fight for better pay and working conditions for Chicano farmworkers, and Reyes Lopez Tijerina started La Alianza Federal de Mercedes to demand the return to Chicanos of land in the Southwest deeded to their ancestors in the Treaty of Guadalupe Hidalgo in 1848.

In the past two decades, Mexican American efforts have focused more on conventional politics and consciousness-raising than on confrontation (Hero, 1992). A number of Chicano organizations, such as the Mexican American Political Alliance (MAPA) in California, were founded in the 1960s and continue to be powerful forces on the political scene, pursuing the interests of Mexican Americans as a group. Consciousness-raising and ethnic awareness have been encouraged by Chicano student organizations in high schools and colleges and by pressures for bilingual education

in communities with large concentrations of Mexican Americans.

Puerto Ricans are the second largest Hispanic group in the United States, comprising 11 percent of all Hispanics. Puerto Ricans were granted U.S. citizenship, as a group, in 1917. A small number of Puerto Ricans immigrated to the mainland United States before World War II, mostly attracted by farm-labor jobs but a few by factory work in the East. Following World War II, this immigration increased dramatically, in large part because of the chronically depressed economy of Puerto Rico. Puerto Ricans have tended to settle in New York City and Chicago (Fitzpatrick, 1987).

Mexican Americans and Puerto Rican Americans today face much the same problems as African Americans: poverty, low educational levels, and poor health in comparison to Anglos (see Table 7.1 and Figures 7.1 and 7.3). For example, two out of five Puerto Rican families in the United States live in poverty, and just 53 percent of Hispanic Americans have completed four years of high school or more, whereas 82 percent of whites have done so. As with African Americans, the incomes of Hispanic families have persistently lagged behind those of white families, remaining at 60 percent of white incomes today, which makes Hispanics worse off now relative to whites than they were twenty years ago.

Hispanics in the United States are a diverse group. In addition to the variation among Hispanic groups already mentioned, for example, Cuban Americans have generally been different from other Hispanics in that they come from more middle-class and affluent origins. Despite their

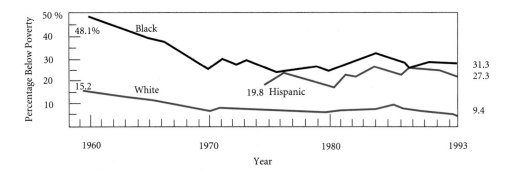

FIGURE 7.3 Percentage of Families in the United States with Incomes Below the Poverty Level, by Race, 1959–1993 *Note:* From *Statistical Abstract of the United States, 1995* (p. 484) by U.S. Bureau of the Census, 1995, Washington, DC: U.S. Government Printing Office.

diversity, some Hispanic groups may be moving toward a more common ethnic identity and consciousness (Totti, 1987). Being of a different color, having a common origin in the "south," speaking related languages, many sharing the experience of discrimination and outsider status—all these characteristics may be forging an ethnic awareness that spans the diversity found in such groups as Mexican Americans and Puerto Ricans. In fact, the term *Latinismo* has been coined to describe a sentimental and ideological identification and loyalty that transcend individual Latino ethnic groups in the United States (Padilla, 1985). This emerging Latino consciousness may be in part political, that is, a realization that advantage can be gained in the struggle for equality and fair treatment by combining forces behind a common symbol. However, Latinismo also represents an identification with and devotion to the collective concerns of peoples in the United States speaking related languages. Groups such as the League of United Latin American Citizens and the Latino Urban Political Association have emerged to represent all Latin ethnic groups, whereas groups such as MAPA and the Puerto Rican Organization for Political Action devote some attention to the concerns of particular nationalities. All of these groups recognize that Hispanics—who may soon be the largest ethnic minority in the United States—can become an effective force for political and social change if they can get beyond their differences and combine their forces.

American Indians

During the fifteenth and sixteenth centuries, there were probably between one million and ten million people living on tribal lands in North America (Snipp, 1989). By the late 1800s, there were only about 250,000. After the founding of the United States, the U.S. Constitution required the federal government to negotiate treaties with these American Indians, but treaties did not prevent whites from robbing Indians of their lands. (Again, there is disagreement about what to call this group. Some members prefer *Native American* to *American Indian;* others insist that only tribal names, such as Comanche, Cree, and Apache, be used because there was much diversity among the native peoples. This text will use American Indian because it is the term used by the Census Bureau from which much of the data in this chapter was obtained.)

In 1824, Congress created the Bureau of Indian Affairs (BIA) as a division of the War Department to seek a military solution to what many Congressmen referred to as the "Indian problem." By 1830, Congress succumbed to pressures for opening up more Indian lands to white settlement and ordered the BIA to relocate all American Indians west of the Mississippi River. It was not until 1924 that Congress passed the Indian Citizenship Act, granting U.S. citizenship to all American Indians. In 1968, Congress enacted the Indian Civil Rights Act, which extended the basic human rights guaranteed by the Bill of Rights to people living on tribal lands. Although this act undoubtedly had many positive benefits, it may have had the negative effect of undermining tribal control and unity among groups that possessed their own judicial systems based on tribal customs (Schaefer, 1993).

By 1995, there were 4.3 million American Indians in the United States (U.S. Bureau of the Census, 1995, p. 14). In 1983, 2.3 percent of U.S.

land (53 million acres) was still being managed by the BIA "on behalf of" the Indians. In 1980, there were 350,000 American Indians, Inuit (Eskimos), and Aleuts living on reservations in the United States (Thornton, 1987). The BIA, now part of the Department of the Interior, has conservation as its prime directive rather than economic development. This deemphasis on economic matters has contributed to the problems of American Indians by making it more difficult for them to improve their economic position (Guillemin, 1980).

American Indians suffer significant social, economic, and health disadvantages in comparison to other ethnic and racial groups (Snipp, 1989; Young, 1994). Nonreservation Indians are somewhat better off than their reservation counterparts, but half of all American Indians live on reservations that are in rural areas. They suffer high levels of unemployment, low levels of income, and poverty rates disproportionate to their numbers in the population. They are also less likely to graduate from high school than people in most other groups. A comprehensive survey in the 1990s of adolescents attending school in reservation communities serviced by the Indian Health Service documented the extensiveness of these problems (Blum, Harmon, Harris, Bergeisen, & Resnick, 1992). When compared with rural white adolescents, the American Indian youth were much more likely to be in poor health, suffer sexual abuse, commit suicide, eat a poor diet, and suffer severe emotional distress.

The 1960s were years when many minority groups began to resist oppression, and American Indians were among them. In 1969, a group of Indians seized Alcatraz Island to call attention to their exploitation. In 1973, members of the American Indian Movement (AIM) staged an armed takeover of Wounded Knee, South Dakota, where whites had killed hundreds of American Indians in the late nineteenth century. These protests may be in part responsible for some recent court decisions ruling that Indian tribes should receive payment for land taken from their ancestors during the nineteenth century. Still, there is a lingering feeling among many American Indians that exploitation continues, albeit in more subtle ways than before (Prucha, 1985).

By the 1990s, the American Indian community in the United States was growing in number and showing renewed pride in its history and culture (Fost, 1991). Although many serious problems persist, a college-educated middle class of American Indians has emerged, and the number of businesses owned by Indians is increasing significantly. Tribes on reservations have been able to exploit gambling and tourism to create jobs, and some have built successful manufacturing businesses. These foundations suggest that a cohesive American Indian culture will grow in the future and may make it possible for more American Indians to succeed on tribal lands.

Asian Americans

Between 1820 and 1970, more than one million legal immigrants from China, Japan, the Philippines, Hong Kong, Korea, and India came to the United States—a mere 3.7 percent of all immigration taking place during that period (Daniels, 1988). The heaviest migration of Chinese to the United States occurred between 1849 and 1882. Although racial prejudices existed toward the Chinese prior to 1849, once their immigration began in large numbers, these sentiments intensified. There was a feeling among many people in the United States that the Chinese would deprive whites of jobs in mining and railroading, another illustration of the split labor market discussed earlier. These feelings culminated in the Chinese Exclusion Act of 1882, which prohibited the entrance of Chinese laborers into the United States for ten years.

Between 1882 and World War II, racist attitudes in the United States characterized the Chinese as a "yellow peril." Many Chinese returned to their own country because of this hostility. Those who remained were forced to move to ghettos called *Chinatowns*. Chinese people were often referred to by the pejorative term *coolies*, and the racism toward Chinese often implied biological differences between Chinese and Anglos. An anthropological study in 1877, for example, concluded, "It is true that ethnologists declare that a brain capacity of less than 85 cubic inches is unfit for free government, which is considerably above that of the coolie as it is below that of the Caucasian" (quoted in Miller, 1969, p. 145).

These anti-Chinese attitudes persisted in the United States until the 1940s. Following Japan's attack on Pearl Harbor, hostilities shifted toward the Japanese, and the Chinese came to be regarded in a more positive way. In 1943, the Chinese remaining

These Japanese Americans are en route to internment in concentration camps during World War II. This internment episode reminds us of the racism and ethnic conflicts that can be found in the history of the United States.

in the United States were granted citizenship. Between 1950 and 1970, Chinese Americans became upwardly mobile, with children of the original immigrants attending colleges and universities and moving into professional and technical positions. Today, the socioeconomic status of Chinese Americans, especially those who have been in the United States for some years, is considerably above the average for Americans as a whole (Barringer, Takeuchi, & Xenos, 1990; Hirschman & Wong, 1986).

The peak period of Japanese immigration to the United States began after the Chinese Exclusion Act, between 1880 and 1924. Unlike the Chinese, Japanese immigrants were permitted to bring their wives with them, which aided in the formation of stable Japanese families, and early relations between white Americans and the Japanese were positive. After Pearl Harbor, Japanese Ameri-

cans were the object of considerable discrimination, being forced to sell their property and being interned in concentration camps (Kitano, 1976; O'Brien & Fugita, 1991). Along with the enslavement of African Americans and the genocidal attacks on American Indians, the imprisonment of Japanese Americans—none of whom had been proven disloyal to the United States—stands as one of the darkest examples of racism in U.S. history.

After their release from the concentration camps after the war, Japanese Americans led successful lives, exceeding many whites in occupational achievements, and most Americans appear to have a high regard for Japanese Americans today (Barringer, Takeuchi, & Xenos, 1990; Ima, 1982). Still, there are occasional flare-ups of the racism that was so prevalent during World War II.

Significant immigration from Asia to the United States has continued in recent decades

(Min, 1994). For example, in the 1970s and 1980s, tens of thousands of refugees entered the United States from Vietnam, Laos, and Cambodia as well as from other parts of Asia. These recent immigrants have mostly followed the route of their predecessors as far as integrating themselves into the United States, taking undesirable jobs that most workers tend to reject, or opening small businesses to make a living. Although there is little widespread discrimination against Asian immigrants, violence does occur. In the 1992 riot in south central Los Angeles, for example, Korean American businesses were apparently targeted for looting and burning by African American and Hispanic American rioters who were angry over what they perceived as mistreatment of blacks and Hispanics by Korean store owners. This riot reflects the economic sources of racial discrimination and conflict discussed earlier. African Americans and Hispanic Americans find themselves in a position of economic subordination to Korean store owners. This subordination has led to stereotyping on both sides, with Koreans accusing blacks and Hispanics of stealing and blacks and Hispanics accusing Koreans of selling poor products at high prices and refusing to hire black or Hispanic employees. Exacerbating this situation is the fact that Koreans have little contact with African Americans and Hispanics outside of this economic (merchant–customer) context.

Today's Immigrants

In 1965, a totally revamped immigration act removed all racial and ethnic quotas for immigrants to the United States. As a consequence of this act and other trends, today's immigrants are quite unlike those of the past (see Figure 7.4). For most of U.S. history, more than three-quarters of the immigrants have been from Europe, with very small proportions coming from Asia or Central and South America. Today, less than 10 percent come from Europe, 38 percent come from Asia, and another 47 percent come from Central and South America.

The data in Figure 7.4 include only people who are legal immigrants to the United States. They do not include tourists, those visiting relatives, and those here on business. Also excluded from those

FIGURE 7.4 Immigrants to the United States, by Country of Last Permanent Residence, 1820–1990 *Note:* From *1984 Statistical Yearbook of the Immigration and Naturalization Service* (pp. 4–5) by U.S. Department of Justice, 1984, Washington, DC: U.S. Government Printing Office; *Statistical Abstract of the United States, 1994* (p. 11) by U.S. Bureau of the Census, 1994, Washington, DC: U.S. Government Printing Office.

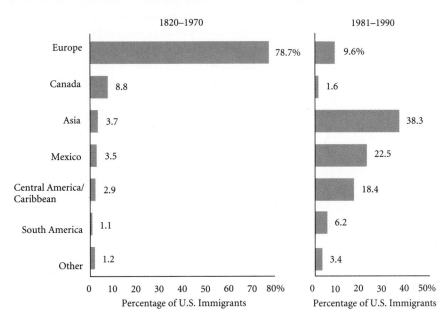

figures are people who enter the United States illegally. It is difficult to know for sure how many undocumented immigrants there are in the United States, but most considered estimates place the number somewhere between two million and four million (Morganthau, 1993). Most are from Central and South America, with about one-half crossing into the United States from Mexico. Most of these undocumented immigrants are economic refugees, fleeing squalor and poverty in their homelands. Some are hoping to remain permanently in the United States, although most plan to stay only for a short period and then return to their homelands. The United States currently has no policy to allow economic refugees to remain here. If caught, they are deported. The reason for this deportation is not so much a lack of sympathy as it is a fear that a policy of allowing undocumented immigrants to stay would open the floodgates to millions of people around the globe who are trying to improve their lives.

The impact of these undocumented immigrants on the United States is complex. On the one hand, they accept jobs that many workers in the United States seem disinclined to do: low-paying, backbreaking farmwork, for example. On the other hand, there is some concern that undocumented immigrants also take some jobs that U.S. citizens may be willing to hold. To protect against this eventuality, hiring undocumented immigrants is now against the law, and employers who do so can be subjected to economic penalties and even imprisonment (Schaefer, 1993). It is hoped that such penalties will help keep undocumented immigrants out of jobs that citizens would like to have. Another concern with undocumented immigrants is the high cost of trying to contain illegal immigration: It is expensive to maintain a border patrol and the investigation section of the Immigration and Naturalization Service.

Achievement and Assimilation Among Immigrant Groups

A recent report by the Census Bureau concludes that immigrants to the United States in recent years have been a varied lot (Bovee, 1993). One-third of recent immigrant families live below the poverty line, but one-quarter of immigrants have a college degree when they arrive here. Many immigrant groups see their incomes rise significantly

above poverty level within a decade of coming to the United States. This variety of experience is documented in the picture just painted of various racial and ethnic minorities in the United States: Some, such as Japanese and Chinese Americans, have become quite successful, whereas others, such as African Americans and Puerto Ricans, still lag behind on most indicators of socioeconomic status. Why the different experiences? The answer is complex. Part of the reason has to do with the cultural background and histories of each group (Sowell, 1996).

The upward mobility of Japanese Americans has a lot to do with their own cultural heritage (Kitano, 1976; Shibutani, 1978). First, the work ethic in Japanese culture is congruent with the values regarding work found in dominant groups in the United States. Japanese culture imbues Japanese Americans with cultural orientations that increase their likelihood of gaining an education or making money in the United States. Second, the Japanese family is highly valued, and family reputation and goals are regarded as more important than individual ones. Individuals gain a sense of self-worth from family membership, and they work hard to avoid bringing shame or disrepute to their family by their own failings. Individual success reflects positively on the family. Third, the Japanese who came to the United States never identified with the lower classes, even when living in poverty. They perceived themselves as successful and respectable, and they passed on middle-class expectations and aspirations to their children. With a cultural heritage like this, young Japanese Americans are fairly well equipped to compete in various economic arenas if given the opportunity to do so.

The Japanese experience suggests, therefore, that "cultural legacy" is the key factor: The values, skills, and traditions that people bring with them play a big part in their success. This cultural heritage has certainly also played a part in the experiences of some recent immigrant groups, such as Koreans, Vietnamese, Arabs, and Cubans. These immigrants often were part of the business and professional classes in their native lands, and this background endowed them with an entrepreneurial spirit, an educational background, or business experience that made it easier for them to do well in the United States. Yet cultural legacy does not always carry the day. For example, in Ireland and other European countries in earlier centuries, Protestants were generally more prosperous than Catholics. Yet Irish Catholic immigrants to the United States have done better than Irish Protestant immigrants (Jencks, 1992).

Although cultural legacy can play an important part, we need to look at other factors as well, some of which may be unique to particular groups. One is the mutual aid organizations that spring up to provide support for some immigrants. They played a role in the success of Irish Catholics as well as some recent immigrants. Koreans, and some other immigrants, for instance, have been able to raise venture capital among friends and family within the ethnic community and sometimes from relatives in their native lands. In some cases, organized "investment clubs" emerge among an ethnic group to provide low-interest loans to start businesses. In other cases, immigrants have ties to the business community in their native lands, which provide them with information and support in starting a new business (Katz & Ryan, 1992). In the case of Cuban immigrants to south Florida in the 1960s and 1970s, some early immigrants were well educated and experienced in business, and they were able to find important positions in banking and commerce. In the name of ethnic solidarity, they then assisted later Cuban immigrants who had less education and fewer resources with which to get a start in business in the United States (Portes & Stepick, 1993).

Some differences between the experience of African Americans and that of other immigrant groups help explain why the black struggle for success has been so difficult (Jencks, 1992). One difference is that, unlike most other immigrants, blacks came involuntarily. European and Asian immigrants saw migration as a new opportunity to be seized and planned to adapt and make the new country their home; those who did not like it or did not do well could return whence they came. Not so for African Americans. Many Africans were forcibly torn from their native lands with little regard for their culture or their heritage and were given no freedom to achieve or develop in the land to which they were brought. Slaves from many different cultural backgrounds were forced together. Slaves were strongly disciplined for showing initiative or independence, and there was often little regard for the integrity of the black family. Whatever entrepreneurial spirit existed in their native cultures was largely destroyed during the slave experience.

A second difference is that African immigrants had, at best, an ambivalence regarding the legitimacy of the social and legal institutions that enslaved them. For many it was outright hostility and resentment. As a consequence, the African American culture that emerged incorporated this resentment and tolerated if not admired resistance to what some perceived as illegitimate social institutions. A third difference is that European immigrant groups, if they shed their ethnic heritage, could become "just plain Americans" and participate in the American success story. Because of visible differences, blacks were never allowed to participate, and so there was less incentive to adopt mainstream culture. Fourth, the mutual supports that some ethnic groups could offer their members have been almost nonexistent among African Americans. Living in poverty in the United States with no link to their native lands meant that there was nowhere to turn for investment loans or other supports.

A final reason for the relatively slow improvement in the circumstances of African Americans is that they still suffer persistent social and economic discrimination. This fact has been further corroborated by a series of reports published in the 1990s showing persisting discrimination against black and Hispanic Americans in jobs and in the rental or purchase of housing (Glass Ceiling Commission, 1995; Munnell, Tootell, Browne, & McEneaney, 1996; Yinger, 1995). When blacks, Hispanics, and whites, all with the same income and educational levels, inquire about renting or buying a house, blacks and Hispanics experience discrimination by being told the house is already rented or sold, being steered to housing in predominantly minority neighborhoods, or being refused a home mortgage loan. This and other research document that African Americans and Hispanic Americans are still not treated equally, nor are their opportunities the same as for white Americans.

So, the factors that lead to success among immigrant groups in the United States are complicated. We cannot assume that, because one group has made it, all have the same opportunities. Their historical experiences and current opportunities are so varied that the outcomes for each group must be considered separately. For African Americans, it has only been in the past few decades that the structures of racial discrimination and oppression have begun to be dismantled, and, as we have seen, discrimination still persists in many forms. As these structures are further dismantled and a supportive cultural environment is allowed to emerge, the achievements of African Americans will likely improve. It will take time to overcome the ghastly legacy of the treatment of African Americans in the United States.

Minorities in the Mass Media

The mass media have come to play an important, although complicated, role in the relationship between majority and minority groups in the United States. The images that the media present of people of various races and ethnic groups can paint a particular group in a positive or negative light. Furthermore, these images, as the interactionist perspective suggests, help to shape people's perceptions and expectations regarding particular groups. After all, the portrayal of an African American or American Indian on television or in a movie is a cultural image that has some societal legitimacy by virtue of having been given space in the mainstream media. So, from the conflict perspective, the media are *contested territory* that groups attempt to influence and control as a part of the struggle over resources in society.

The media are controlled mostly by the dominant racial and ethnic groups in any society, and thus it is their stereotypes of races and ethnic groups that are most likely to find space in the media. This means that, in the United States, whites tend to be disproportionately portrayed in the media and to be placed in the more positive roles—as the good person, the success, the hero, the winner. In fact, until the 1960s at least, movies and television were pretty much a white landscape: Nonwhites appeared only in minor roles, in menial positions, or as criminals or villains. During World War II, for example, films about the war were virulently anti-Japanese and blatantly racist in content, often implying that the Japanese were inherently evil. This is not surprising given the emotions that the war aroused, but it does show in an extreme form the ability of the media to portray the stereotypes of those who control the media.

The images of minorities that the media have presented in the past three decades have certainly improved. As opportunities for minorities in all areas of society have gotten better, more minorities have begun to work in the media industries that produce culture; there are more minority actors, producers, directors, and newscasters. Media stars such as Spike Lee, Geraldo Rivera, Emilio Estevez, Oprah Winfrey, and Bill Cosby have become influential in shaping the presentation of culture through the media. Kevin Costner's movie *Dances with Wolves* turned the traditional stereotyping on its head by presenting European Americans in a substantially negative light while American Indians appear to be the more positive role models. Yet, despite these changes, minorities in general are still underrepresented in the media. In fact, Hispanic Americans may be one of the most underrepresented ethnic groups in the media, seeing its share of characters actually decline since the 1950s (Nieves, 1995). And there are still complaints that Hispanics are more often portrayed as criminals and losers than in more positive roles.

Beyond the issue of the stereotyping of minorities in the media, their underrepresentation is important for other reasons. One is that underrepresentation means that minority actors, directors, camera operators, and other media workers cannot find work in the media industry. For example, the recent movie *The Perez Family* was strongly criticized for casting two Anglos to play the two Cuban lead characters. Difficulty in finding work in the media has been a chronic problem for racial and ethnic minorities. Another reason why the underrepresentation of minorities in the media is cause for concern is that it means fewer minority role models for the young to observe and emulate.

Despite these many negative dimensions to the portrayal of minorities, the impact of the media on people and society is complex. The interactionist perspective makes us aware that people can interpret the same reality in quite different ways, and this is true with the media images. Each person brings his or her own subcultural values, racial or ethnic heritage, personal aspirations, and individual experiences to bear when assessing and interpreting these images. For example, after watching a western film, *The Searchers,* which contained the traditional stereotypes of cowboys and American Indians, Anglos interpreted the film as an affirmation of the values that the European settlers brought to the West and as justifying the imposition of western society on the Indians; they viewed the cowboys as heroes (Shively, 1992). American Indian viewers, on the other hand, thought the film worshiped freedom and autonomy and a regard for the land that are a part of the American Indian heritage. In other words, the lesson that each group learned from the film was quite different; each interpreted the film as, to a degree, consistent with its own needs, circumstances, and heritages.

As the twentieth century comes to a close, the explosion in media, computers, and telecommunications may actually create more opportunities for expression on the part of minorities as more media outlets call for the production of more media products. Since some of these new outlets will be targeted at minority audiences, this expansion will likely create a demand for minority-produced media materials. This will make it more possible for minorities to find media work, contribute to the portrayal of minorities in the media, and make positive minority role models available.

Current Issues in the United States

You should be able to describe the various issues and controversies related to race and ethnic relations in the United States and assess programs intended to improve relations.

At the end of the twentieth century, significant issues remain regarding the relationships between various racial and ethnic groups in the United States. This chapter will close by reviewing a few of them.

Assimilation or Pluralism?

What pattern of minority–majority relations is most desirable in the United States—assimilation, pluralism, or some other pattern? People's response to this question is often colored by a misconception about what has happened historically. The United States is often referred to as a *melting pot* in which the beliefs, values, and lifestyles of many different racial and ethnic groups have been blended together into a unique mix that is called *American.* If this blending had occurred, it would be a form of assimilation in which all groups have changed to some degree in creating an American identity. Actually, the experience of most immigrants has come closer to what Milton Gordon (1964) has called *Anglo conformity:* To

share fully in the American dream, immigrants have been required to renounce their ancestral culture in favor of the beliefs, values, and lifestyle of the dominant white Anglo-Saxon Protestants, WASPs. These WASPs were among the earliest European immigrants to North America. They came from the British Isles and Germany, and they dominated political, economic, and social life in the United States from the sixteenth through the nineteenth centuries. The WASPs were sufficiently fearful of people who immigrated after them—from places such as Ireland, Italy, and Eastern Europe—that they attempted to "Americanize" them rather than let them build their own social institutions and way of life. Many people today still insist on a version of Anglo conformity by arguing that groups such as Hispanics and Asians should learn only English and not be given a bilingual education.

Although Anglo conformity worked for quite a while, it has not persisted. Over time, the original WASP group became such a small minority that it became more difficult for it to force its lifestyle onto others. The outcome, at least to this point, is that the United States remains a highly pluralistic society with many distinct racial and ethnic subcultures. Furthermore, some minorities, especially groups such as blacks and Hispanics, who were never allowed to assimilate by the dominant white groups, prefer it that way.

Whether pluralism is desirable is a matter of considerable controversy (Pettigrew, 1988; Triandis, 1988). Many people argue that extensive pluralism will promote tensions that could flare into conflict in the future, even going so far as separatist movements. They point to the efforts of French Canadians in Quebec to secede from Canada as the kind of discord that pluralism can generate. (See Other Worlds, Other Ways: French Canada in this chapter.) In fact, the Census Bureau reported in 1993 that Spanish rather than English is spoken at home in 7 percent of the families in the United States (Green, 1993). Concern over this possibility has become so strong in some groups that 23 states have now passed laws making English the official language (see Figure 7.5).

Proponents of pluralism, by contrast, contend that racial and ethnic diversity contributes to the richness of U.S. culture and symbolizes the country's roots as a nation open to the oppressed of all

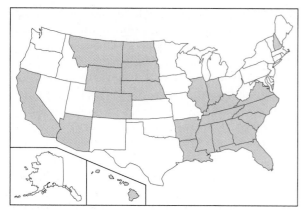

Alabama (1990)
Arizona (1988)
Arkansas (1987)
California (1986)
Colorado (1988)
Florida (1988)
Georgia (1986 & 1996)
Hawaii (1978)
Illinois (1969)
Indiana (1984)
Kentucky (1984)
Louisiana (1811)

Mississippi (1987)
Montana (1995)
Nebraska (1920)
New Hampshire (1995)
North Carolina (1987)
North Dakota (1987)
South Carolina (1987)
South Dakota (1995)
Tennessee (1984)
Virginia (1981 & 1996)
Wyoming (1996)

FIGURE 7.5 States with Official English-Language Laws (and Years Enacted), 1996 *Note: From Facts and Issues, 1996,* Washington, DC: U.S. English Foundation, Inc.

lands. Furthermore, ethnic identity can be a source of pride and positive self-regard for individuals, and speaking in one's native tongue can play an important part in this. Among Latinos, for example, speaking Spanish and having a large and powerful Spanish-language media in the United States are sources of cultural pride and ethnic identity (Totti, 1987).

Race Relations Today: Race or Class?

As discussed earlier, some minority groups, such as blacks, still lag significantly behind other groups on various indicators of socioeconomic status. There is considerable debate over whether this lag is because of racial discrimination or because of the class position held by many blacks, which places them in a weak situation from which to compete for jobs and income.

Sociologist William J. Wilson (1987, 1996) argues that class, rather than race, is the more important factor in determining the social positions of African Americans today. Wilson does not deny that racial antagonism is still with us, or that substantial discrimination against and oppression of blacks not only has clouded U.S. history but also lingers today. But he points out that the real problem today lies in the continuing existence of an underclass of poor, marginally skilled blacks who have little opportunity to obtain the education and skills necessary to succeed in a modern industrial society (see the discussion of poverty in Chapter 6). Such an underclass can also be found among poor whites and among Puerto Ricans and other Hispanic groups (Alex-Assensoh, 1995; Tienda, 1989). Wilson attributes the persistence of this underclass to basic changes in the structure of the U.S. economy, including the relocation of industries away from the communities where many poor people live and a labor market in which people with few job skills or little education are limited to low-paying work with little opportunity for advancement. The primary barrier that this underclass faces, argues Wilson, is the lack of appropriate job-related skills, not racial discrimination. Blacks or Hispanics with job skills or a college education, he argues, will enjoy opportunities and privileges similar to those of their white counterparts in the class hierarchy and will probably not face significant discrimination even if economic conditions deteriorate.

On the other side of this argument are sociologists Joe Feagin and Melvin Sykes (1994), who argue that racial oppression is still a key factor influencing race relations in the United States. They argue that blacks are still oppressed and discriminated against because of their race, although the forms and mechanisms of racial oppression may have changed since the 1950s and 1960s. One difference today is that the overt individual racism of the past has declined considerably, but there is still widespread, institutionalized racism in which such things as residential and school segregation place barriers before the advancement of many blacks but few whites. In addition, many whites find the black urban culture of the 1990s alien and threatening (Jencks, 1992). Consequently, they are less likely to hire blacks, particularly young males. In addition, employers have other motivations for discriminating against blacks in hiring. For example, an employer might believe that a black employee will not attract white customers. In professional sports for many years, owners and managers believed that white fans would not pay to see black players. Today some companies still refuse to hire blacks for highly visible positions, such as receptionist or salesperson, when customers are white.

Feagin and Sykes (1994) interviewed hundreds of middle-class African Americans, who are presumably the ones least affected by race, according to Wilson's argument. Based on these interviews, Feagin and Sykes concluded that "few middle-class African Americans interviewed . . . see the significance of racism in their lives declining" (p. 12). For all these reasons, Feagin and Sykes argue that race still very much determines the position of African Americans as a group.

So, controversy continues over whether the continuing chasm between the achievements of blacks and whites is due predominately to class or to race. Although it may be difficult to resolve the proportionate role of each, it is certain that each plays some part. The issues involved are important, because the contrasting positions on this controversy point to very different policy recommendations for their solutions. The chapter will now consider some of the policies put forth in the past few decades to improve the quality of race relations in the United States.

Advances, Setbacks, and Controversial Policies

Most people would agree that the United States has achieved much over the past few decades in terms of racial and ethnic relations. The collective protest of the civil rights movement forced the nation to confront inequities in the 1950s and 1960s, and a foundation of legislation was established to prevent or punish discrimination on the basis of racial or ethnic identity and to reduce inequities in the stratification system. Surveys by sociologists since the 1960s indicate that people in the United States now show less racial prejudice and are more tolerant of racial diversity than ever before (Steeh & Schuman, 1992). In addition, racial and ethnic minorities are more organized, confident, and optimistic than in the past. Applying Sociology: Combating Prejudice (on pp. 246–247) describes some of the contributions sociologists have made to this improving picture.

Some of the policies that have resulted in advances have been controversial (Bergmann, 1996; Eastland, 1996). Affirmative-action legislation, for

example, was intended to force schools and employers to aggressively seek out minorities when they have vacancies. That policy probably has made it possible for some minorities to overcome persisting discrimination and obtain jobs or entrance into schools that they probably would not have obtained otherwise. Some argue, however, that it has produced reverse discrimination, in which whites lose jobs or positions in school to nonwhites, and the less qualified people are hired over those who are more qualified. What is certainly true is that the policy has produced feelings of frustration, resentment, anger, and cynicism among some whites who feel they are being passed over and are losing out (Bunzel, 1991; Lynch & Beer, 1990). During the 1980s and 1990s, programs to encourage hiring preferences based on racial identity have been scaled back and the courts have weakened the legal foundations that minorities successfully used to bring affirmative-action lawsuits against employers or schools. The overall trend during the 1980s and 1990s has been toward a weakened affirmative-action policy. Yet, the evidence is clear that some minorities do suffer discrimination in the job market, and some form of affirmative action will be needed to deal with it (Jencks, 1992).

Another controversial program has been school busing, which is discussed at greater length in Chapter 12. School busing began in the 1960s, when sociologists published reports documenting the extensive segregation that existed in schools and arguing that the segregation was part of the reason for the poor performance of many African American students. A number of programs were established to provide academic assistance to poor and minority children, including the Head Start program discussed in Chapters 6 and 12. School busing was also initiated to achieve some racial balance in the schools and improve the educational environment for all students. In addition, it was believed that the resulting school integration would bring about reductions in prejudice and discrimination as students of different racial identities met and worked together in school. School busing does seem to have provided modest educational advantages to minority students, and minorities in desegregated schools do show more educational and occupational achievement (Armor, 1995; Entwisle & Alexander, 1994; Longshore & Prager,

APPLYING SOCIOLOGY
Combating Prejudice, Discrimination, and Racial Polarization

During and following World War II, many people, including many sociologists and other social scientists, were horrified by the genocidal attacks on Jews and other groups by Nazis in France, Poland, and other European nations. In part in response to this outrage, applied sociologists have devoted much attention to locating the sources of prejudice and discrimination as well as to developing and evaluating programs to combat them. This applied sociological work has played a key role in developing policies to deal with these problems.

Recently, for example, community leaders and citizens in St. Louis wanted to attack problems of racial isolation and polarization, as well as the lack of educational and occupational opportunities among African Americans in their community (Farley, 1991). They called in sociologists to identify the extent of housing segregation in the community and locate its causes. The sociologists found that one source of segregation was the tendency for some realty companies to steer customers to particular neighborhoods based on the customers' racial identity. This finding was highly controversial because the real estate agents in St. Louis, who were among the community leaders supporting programs to attack racial polarization, felt that they were being unfairly singled out as the source of community segregation. That was not true, since the sociologists involved also identified many other sources of segregation. Despite the debate, the sociological data proved to be convincing because they clearly showed that racial steering did occur. This knowledge translated directly into policies to establish educational and sensitivity programs for real estate agents on multiculturalism and racial diversity.

Sociological research can also be used to document the consequences of racial isolation. In the project in St. Louis, applied sociologists showed that segregation in housing dramatically reduced the occupational opportunities for African Americans, increasing their poverty and other social problems in the St. Louis area. This and other sociological research has also shown that racial isolation produces negative stereotyping, prejudice, and hostility, whereas contact between different racial groups can reduce prejudice (Brewer & Miller, 1988; Miller & Brewer, 1984; Sigelman & Welch, 1993). This knowledge can then be used to develop programs that will encourage people to view members of another racial or ethnic group more positively. One such program was run at a summer camp for children (Clore, Bray, Itkin, & Murphy, 1978). The camp included equal numbers of black and white children, and they came from all levels of the socioeconomic hierarchy. In the camp, all children had the same rights and the same work duties. There was also an equal mix of blacks and whites among the administrators and counselors in the camp, so that the authority structure was not racially biased. In other words, blacks were as likely to exercise power over the children as were whites. During their one-week stay at the camp, children were required to work on cooperative tasks involving group rather than individual goals. By the end of the week, the children who came to the camp with negative attitudes toward members of the other racial group had shifted toward more positive views, suggesting that such intergroup contact can reduce prejudice.

A similar approach was used in Houston in the late 1960s following a series of violent clashes between African American college students and police

1985). It has also reduced levels of racial isolation, which will probably result in less racial tension and stereotyping in the future (Hawley et al., 1983).

Despite its advantages, busing has remained highly controversial and has produced some conflict itself. For example, some argue that busing as caused *white flight,* or whites leaving the cities for the suburbs in order to avoid integrated schools. White flight has occurred, although it cannot be blamed solely on busing. Yet, busing probably

played a part, and white flight has tended to increase segregation in cities and schools (Rivkin, 1994; Smock & Wilson, 1991).

Although there is much in U.S. history to be lamented, people can be proud of the advances in race relations since the 1960s. Yet there are reasons for uncertainty about the future. As noted, some minorities still lag significantly behind Anglos on various indicators of achievement, and sociologists can document blatant discrimination

during which one police officer was killed (Bell, Cleveland, Hanson, & O'Connell, 1969). In this volatile atmosphere, hundreds of police officers and community residents participated in a multicultural awareness program consisting of lectures, discussion, and small-group encounters over a period of weeks. They used role-playing and other group techniques to encourage participants to explore stereotypes, diagnose interracial problems, and cooperatively develop strategies for alleviating those problems. In the process, participants of different racial backgrounds had the opportunity to work together on common problems and get to know one another as individuals rather than as members of a racial category. Just as with the children's camp, this program produced positive changes in the form of less prejudice and more acceptance of people of different racial identities as well as a reduction in the number of complaints filed by citizens against the police.

Applied sociologists and other social scientists can, then, show people how to design such encounters to produce a positive outcome. To be effective, the contact should have the following characteristics:

1. The contact should have high *acquaintance potential,* which means that people have the time and opportunity to get to know one another and to have some personal and intimate associations.
2. The contact should be between people of equal status, rather than between a low-status minority and a higher-status member of the dominant group.
3. The behavior of the minority-group person in the contact should contradict the usual stereotype of members of that group.
4. As a part of the contact, people should work toward cooperative and interdependent goals rather than competitive ones; that is, no one in the group can achieve his or her individual goals unless all the participants work together.
5. The contact situation should have the support of legitimate authorities, such as a school or church, and should involve social norms that dictate friendliness and respect between people.

Many of these features were built into the programs at the children's camp and in Houston. Clearly, though, many of our everyday contacts with members of different races violate these principles, as, for example, when an African American or Hispanic American interacts with an Anglo teacher or social worker. Nonetheless, sociological research and practice have given us the knowledge and the tools to point us in the direction of how to structure situations to reduce racial prejudice and polarization.

When such social programs are established, they should be evaluated to see if they achieve their goals; this evaluation is another common task of applied sociologists (Farley, 1991). In the St. Louis program, for example, sociologists devised a plan for assessing whether different parts of the program achieved their intended goals. Evaluation is a difficult but important task, because it tells whether a particular community-wide effort is just spinning its wheels or maybe making things worse. Sociologists are trained in the research methods and statistical procedures necessary to do such evaluation effectively (Sullivan, 1992).

against many minorities, but especially Hispanic Americans and African Americans, in finding jobs or housing. In addition, although racial violence has been limited of late, periodic outbursts indicate that such conflict is just below the surface. The riot in south central Los Angeles in 1992 was the most recent manifestation of the anger and resentment that can trigger such violence. (The reasons for this outburst are analyzed in detail in Chapter 15.) The same thing happened in Miami in 1989, when a police officer shot and killed a black man on a motorcycle. These violent riots express the anger that many minority youths feel about their position and opportunities in the 1990s. They illustrate the potential for racial conflict that simmers despite the improvements that have been made. The potential for prejudice, discrimination, and racial violence remains strong and can be rekindled if the proper social conditions arise.

Summary

1. A minority group is a group whose members share distinct physical and cultural characteristics, have less access to power and resources than do other groups, and are accorded fewer rights, privileges, and opportunities. The term *minority*, as used by sociologists, relates to a group's position in the stratification system rather than to numerical size.

2. Prejudice and discrimination result from a number of social and psychological causes. Among the social causes are ethnocentrism, competition, socialization, and institutionalized discrimination. Social psychological causes include stereotyping, frustration and aggression, and the authoritarian personality.

3. Discrimination has a number of consequences, including an adverse effect on people's life chances and an increase in tension and hostility in society.

4. The patterns of intergroup relations most commonly found are genocide, segregation, continued subjugation, population transfer, assimilation, and pluralism. The most typical reactions of minorities to domination are submission, social protest, and separatism.

5. Among racial and ethnic groups, African Americans and Hispanic Americans are the largest minorities, and they lag considerably behind other groups in access to education, power, and economically rewarding jobs. One of the most important reasons for this lag is the long history of discrimination and oppression suffered by both groups, making it difficult for them to improve their position in U.S. society.

6. American Indians experience some of the worst conditions of all minority groups in U.S. society. Some Asian Americans, by contrast, have been able to attain a degree of affluence despite the substantial prejudice and discrimination they have experienced.

7. The achievements of immigrant groups in the United States have been highly varied and are affected by the groups' cultural legacy as well as the severity of the oppression and discrimination they experience at the hands of dominant groups. The mass media influence people's perceptions of minority groups as well as serve as a contested territory of cultural resources.

8. Currently in the United States there is controversy over whether minorities should assimilate or whether a high degree of pluralism is acceptable. There is also controversy over whether the continuing gap between black and white achievements is the result of racism or class position. There have been advances and setbacks in race relations in recent decades, and some policies aimed at reducing prejudice and discrimination, such as affirmative action and school busing, have been controversial.

STUDY and Review

Key Terms

assimilation

continued subjugation

discrimination

ethnic group

ethnocentrism

genocide

institutionalized
    discrimination

institutionalized racism

internal colonialism

minority group

pluralism

population transfer

prejudice

race

racism

segregation

split labor market

Multiple-Choice Questions

1. Jewish Americans would most clearly be
    a. a racial group.
    b. an ethnic group.
    c. an authoritarian group.
    d. an example of internal colonialism.
    e. a split labor group.

2. A negative attitude toward certain people based solely on their membership in a particular group is called
    a. prejudice.
    b. discrimination.
    c. a minority group.
    d. pluralism.
    e. segregation.

3. Mary has a negative stereotype toward and dislikes all people from the Middle East, but she does not discriminate against them in hiring for her store because of the laws against it. In Robert Merton's classification, she would be called
   a. an unprejudiced nondiscriminator.
   b. a prejudiced discriminator.
   c. a prejudiced nondiscriminator.
   d. an unprejudiced discriminator.

4. Which of the following is a type of economic exploitation between a dominant group and a minority group?
   a. Ethnocentrism.
   b. Assimilation.
   c. Institutionalized discrimination.
   d. Internal colonialism.
   e. Genocide.

5. The split labor market could be best characterized as
   a. two groups of workers willing to do the same work but for different wages.
   b. a situation in which a dominant group exploits a subordinate group for the benefit of the dominant group.
   c. an unprejudiced person who is a discriminator.
   d. institutionalized discrimination by a dominant group against a minority group.

6. The structural arrangement by which Switzerland has managed to keep peace and cooperation among its three major ethnic groups is called
   a. power sharing.
   b. segregation.
   c. institutionalized discrimination.
   d. population transfer.
   e. assimilation.

7. All of the following are true about Hispanic Americans *except*
   a. they are the second largest minority group discussed in the text.
   b. the largest group among Hispanics is Mexican Americans.
   c. they suffer from low educational levels in comparison to whites.
   d. the gap between Hispanic and white income has narrowed substantially in the past twenty years.

8. According to the text, which of the following elements of Japanese American culture contributed to the success of the Japanese in the United States?
   a. Their Samurai tradition.
   b. Their worship of nobility.
   c. Their work ethic.
   d. Their value of the family.
   e. Both c and d.

9. Over the history of the United States, the experience of most immigrants to this country comes closest to
   a. a melting pot.
   b. continued subjugation.
   c. Anglo conformity.
   d. genocide.
   e. Both a and c.

10. The text concludes which of the following regarding the impact of school busing programs on the performance of minority students?
    a. The amount of white flight from cities is reduced.
    b. Minorities show modest improvements in school performance.
    c. Minorities show dramatic improvements in school performance.
    d. Hostility between minorities and whites increases.

True/False Questions

1. Race and ethnicity are ascribed statuses.

2. From the functionalist perspective, ethnocentrism is always considered to have negative consequences for members of an in-group.

3. According to the conflict perspective, prejudice and discrimination arise when two groups find themselves in competition with one another.

4. The text concludes that racism does lower the self-esteem of minorities in some contexts.

5. African Americans were the only minority group to be enslaved in the United States.

6. Because of casino gambling and other economic enterprises on American Indian reservations, income and educational levels on reservations now approach those for society as a whole.

7. Today, more than one-half of all the immigrants to the United States come from Mexico.

8. The text argues that cultural legacy probably has little to do with how well immigrants to the United States do economically.

9. Contact between different racial and ethnic groups can reduce prejudice if the contact has high acquaintance potential.

10. The text concludes that race is more important than class in determining the social position of African Americans in the United States today.

Fill-In Questions

1. _____ is the view that certain racial or ethnic groups are biologically inferior and can be discriminated against because of this.

2. Fred and Mary believe that their high school is superior to all the other high schools in their district. This is an example of the tendency toward _____.

3. In a split labor market, the group that receives the brunt of the discrimination is the _____.

4. In terms of contributing to prejudice and discrimination, categorization becomes a problem when the categories become _____.

5. _____ occurs when a dominant group moves the members of a minority group, either voluntarily or involuntarily, to a particular geographic area.

6. In contrast to the Swiss political system in which power is shared among various ethnic groups, the United States tends more toward power _____.

7. The ruling in which the U.S. Supreme Court declared the "separate but equal" doctrine to be unconstitutional was _____.

8. U.S. citizenship was granted to all American Indians in the decade of the _____.

9. In recent decades, the largest percentage of immigrants to the United States has come from the geographical region of _____.

10. _____ occurs when white students leave a school district for suburban or private schools in order to avoid school busing or school integration.

Matching Questions

_____ 1. MAPA
_____ 2. apartheid
_____ 3. view that competition causes discrimination
_____ 4. social psychological source of prejudice and discrimination
_____ 5. Ashanti
_____ 6. Cesar Chavez
_____ 7. assimilation
_____ 8. WASPs
_____ 9. Parti Québecois
_____ 10. school busing

A. traditional segregation in South Africa
B. large African tribe
C. a blending of racial and ethnic identities
D. scapegoating
E. Hispanic political group
F. program intended to achieve racial balance in schools
G. Hispanic labor organizer
H. separatism in Canada
I. earliest European immigrants to North America
J. conflict perspective

Essay Questions

1. What is ethnocentrism? What role does it play in prejudice and discrimination?

2. How do competition and socialization influence prejudice and discrimination?

3. According to the text, what detrimental consequences does discrimination have for society?

4. Describe the forms that domination of a minority group by a majority group can take. Give an example of each. How do minority groups respond to this domination?

5. Describe the pattern of intergroup relations that has emerged among the three major ethnic groups in Switzerland. How well does it work? Why?

6. Describe the prejudice and discrimination that Japanese Americans and Chinese Americans experienced after immigrating to this country.

7. In what ways has the experience of African Americans been different from that of other immigrant groups in the United States?

8. What are the characteristics of the contact between racial groups that are most likely to reduce prejudice between the groups?

9. Is the situation of African Americans in the United States today mostly a function of race or class? Make the arguments for both sides of this issue.

10. What does the text conclude regarding what school busing has achieved in the United States?

Answers

Multiple-Choice
1. B; **2.** A; **3.** C; **4.** D; **5.** A; **6.** A; **7.** D; **8.** E;
9. C; **10.** B

True/False
1. T; **2.** F; **3.** T; **4.** T; **5.** T; **6.** F; **7.** F; **8.** F;
9. T; **10.** F

Fill-In
1. racism
2. ethnocentrism
3. lower-priced labor
4. stereotypes
5. population transfer
6. competition
7. *Brown v. The Board of Education*
8. 1920s
9. Asia
10. white flight

Matching
1. E; **2.** A; **3.** J; **4.** D; **5.** B; **6.** G; **7.** C; **8.** I;
9. H; **10.** F

For Further Reading

Carnoy, Martin. (1994). *Faded dreams: The politics and economics of race in America.* New York: Cambridge University Press. This book reports grim findings but a somewhat optimistic assessment of race relations in the United States. Much depends, according to the author, on whether the government will take the initiative to push for more social and economic equality.

Fugita, Stephen S., & O'Brien, David J. (1991). *Japanese American ethnicity: The persistence of community.* Seattle: University of Washington Press. By focusing on the experiences of Japanese Americans, these sociologists investigate the factors that influence whether an immigrant group can maintain a viable community or become completely assimilated by the dominant group.

Massey, Douglas S., & Denton, Nancy A. (1993). *American apartheid: Segregation and the making of the underclass.* Cambridge, MA: Harvard University Press. As the use of *apartheid* in the title implies, these authors see the United States as a rigidly segregated society. They discuss the reasons for this, disputing much of Wilson's argument that racial discrimination is not the major factor affecting the social position of minorities today.

Parrillo, Vincent N. (1996). *Diversity in America.* Thousand Oaks, CA: Pine Forge Press. This is an excellent brief overview of the nature and extent of racial and ethnic diversity in the United States. The author looks at how the pattern of this diversity has changed over time and is careful not to oversimplify the complexity and the richness of the diversity.

Rubin, Lillian B. (1994). *Families on the faultline.* New York: HarperCollins. This book is about white ethnics in the United States, a group sometimes ignored in discussions of race and ethnicity. The author explores how white ethnics are being affected by changes in the world economy, how race has become an issue because of economic competition, and how whites have become more interested in their own ethnicity.

Shorris, Earl. (1992). *Latinos: A biography of the people.* New York: W. W. Norton. This excellent book explores the lives and history of the fastest-growing minority group in the United States, the descendants of the Spanish conquest of the American Indian peoples. Through wonderfully insightful biographical sketches, the author communicates the complex diversity today in the group that is given the single designation of *Latino.*

Stannard, David E. (1992). *American holocaust: Columbus and the conquest of the New World.* New York: Oxford University Press. This book catalogues an "unbroken string of genocidal campaigns" by the Europeans against the tribal peoples of the Americas after Columbus's voyages. The author attempts to explain the brutality and devastation that occurred in terms of European attitudes toward race, religion, war, and conversion.

Takaki, Ronald. (1993). *A different mirror: A history of multicultural America.* Boston: Little, Brown. This is a very readable history of the United States from the perspective of the various immigrant groups that came to these shores. It begins with the Wampanoag Indians of Massachusetts watching the first Europeans arrive and closes with the Los Angeles riots of 1992.

Terkel, Studs. (1992). *Race: How blacks and whites think and feel about the American obsession.* New York: New Press. In this volume you can hear Americans expressing in their own words their opinions about race relations in the United States. There is a range of opinion here to which people are often not exposed.

Tobin, Gary A. (1988). *Jewish perceptions of antisemitism.* New York: Plenum. This book summarizes research on how much anti-Semitism exists in the United States and on Jews' perceptions of their status. It is an excellent analysis of the problems of prejudice and discrimination affecting one of the more successful ethnic groups in the United States.

Zweigenhaft, Richard L., & Domhoff, G. William. (1991). *Blacks in the white establishment? A study of race and class in America.* New Haven: Yale University Press. This is a fascinating follow-up of a 1960s program that sent poor, mostly African American, teens to some of the most elite secondary schools in the nation. The book looks at what happened to them and investigates their socialization to elite power positions and the intertwining of race, class, and education.

CHAPTER

EIGHT *Social Inequality: Gender*

In the early 1600s, the Huron Indians lived in part of what the French explorers of the time called New France—on Georgian Bay north of present-day Toronto in Ontario, Canada (Grant, 1984). Approximately 20,000 in number spread throughout twenty-five villages, the Hurons engaged in slash-and-burn horticulture and were semisedentary. They also traded with various surrounding tribes for subsistence goods as well as luxuries and delicacies. The Hurons were a matrilineal society, meaning that they reckoned kinship and descent through the mother's line (see Chapter 9). The basic social unit for the Hurons was the household, but a number of matrilineally related households formed a longhouse, which was the key unit of production and consumption. Residence in the longhouse was matrilocal, meaning that a married couple lived in the longhouse of the wife's family. Children received their clan membership through their mother, not their father. The members of a longhouse cooperated in horticulture, hunting, and fishing, and the product of their labors was distributed to all members of the longhouse according to certain norms.

By today's standards, Huron women were fairly powerful and independent, and their experience suggests how gender relations are shaped by the social structure, in this case by the matrilineal organization of kinship (Anderson, 1991). Clan leaders were male, but they were appointed by the women in the clan and held their position only as long as clan members thought they were doing an adequate job. The Hurons viewed marriage as a working partnership between a man and a woman rather than as the domination of one person by the other. If anything, given the matrilineal nature of Huron society, men were especially susceptible to the influence of their wife and their mother-in-law, who was the power in the longhouse.

Women held power, in part, because they could expel men from their longhouse. Although marriage was an important institution for the Hurons, they took on partners and divorced them much more casually than people do in the United States, especially before having children. One reason was that, although both men and women made important contributions to subsistence, the kinship structure was such that neither husband nor wife was dependent on the other for necessary foodstuffs. For example, although the men had responsibility for hunting and trading, women were not dependent on their husbands for meat and trade goods because norms called for other men in the women's clan to provide them. Also, since the Hurons were matrilocal, most men lived in their wife's longhouse and were dependent on the wife's family for some food and other daily needs. Actually, men often went back to their mother's longhouse, especially before the couple had a child. This custom gave Huron marriages a seemingly casual air to European explorers. Women's position in Huron society was also strengthened by the fact that men were absent hunting during the summer months, and the women in a longhouse, all of whom were kin and in the same clan, produced almost all food.

The Hurons had rather open attitudes toward sexuality; premarital sex was widespread. In fact, unmarried couples often set up households, and the woman in such a relationship was called *asqua*, or "companion," rather than *atenoha*, or "wife." While in these relationships, each partner might take on other lovers, and these new relationships did not necessarily end if the couple married. The Hurons were also relatively free in expressing their feelings for others and acting on those feelings, a custom that included women reacting against men. Women often disagreed with and disputed the demands of men.

The early 1600s brought French explorers to the New World as a part of the capitalist expansion discussed in Chapters 6 and 7. Responding to growing merchant pressures for new markets and new sources of wealth, the French exploited the Western Hemisphere for fur, fish, agricultural products, and other natural resources. The Hurons came into direct contact with French explorers in 1609 and with French Jesuit missionaries in 1632 (Leacock, 1980). The Jesuits considered the Indians to be pagans who consorted with the devil, and they began what they believed was an apocalyptic battle of good against evil. Because they thought the Hurons' souls were at stake, the Jesuits would go to any lengths to convert the Hurons to Christianity. The Hurons were about to be irrevocably changed.

At the time, many Europeans held the widespread Christian conception that women were bad—evil temptresses, allies of the devil, harbingers of chaos—if they were not controlled. Holding this view, the Jesuits were horrified by what they saw among the Hurons. There was simply too much personal and sexual freedom. The Jesuits viewed the Huron women as wild, ill-mannered, and dangerously lewd because they refused to obey their husbands and fathers and to engage only in discrete, marital sexuality as the Jesuits knew was proper and holy. Some Huron married women even refused to convert to Christianity because it required lifetime fidelity to their husband, which they didn't feel they could promise. All this freedom and independence clashed with the seventeenth-century French view that social order could be based only on power, loyalty, submission, and fear. In the Jesuit idea of society, people submitted to the authority of God, and women submitted to the authority of their husbands—and the Jesuits set about to reproduce this version of reality among the Hurons.

Efforts have been under way around the world these past few decades to reduce the disadvantages suffered by women, and many people may have the overall impression that significant progress is being made. Indeed, there have been many gains. Reality is more complex, however, than first impressions might suggest, and the overall record is spotty. Many statements of fact, if not qualified, are so misleading as almost to constitute myths.

Myth Women have taken their place in the workforce with men, holding more varied jobs and earning higher pay relative to men than ever before.

FACT More women work, but their pay still lags significantly behind that of men doing the same work. This lag is true in virtually all industrial nations, with women in Japan earning only 46 percent of what men do. Also, many low-paying, low-prestige jobs are still female ghettos in the United States; 98 percent of secretaries, 96 percent of receptionists, and 99 percent of dental hygienists were women in the early 1990s.

Myth More women are seeking political office than ever before.

FACT Women, who make up 51 percent of the U.S. population, held 10 percent of the seats in the Senate in 1997 and 11 percent of the seats in the House of Representatives. Women do well in Cuba and Finland, where they hold one-third of the parliamentary seats, but in some African and Arab nations, there are no women in the legislature.

Myth Modernized divorce laws enable women to leave bad marriages and receive alimony and child support from their ex-husbands.

FACT In the United States, women who have children and who divorce suffer a serious decline in their standard of living, whereas men who divorce actually experience an improvement in their standard of living.

Myth By the 1990s, the United States was solidly supportive of equal rights for women.

FACT The Equal Rights Amendment to the Constitution, which would prohibit discrimination on the basis of gender, has yet to be approved.

Myth The courts have ruled that barring women from service and community organizations such as Rotary and the Kiwanis violates antidiscrimination laws. Thus, women now have the same access as men to community and business arenas.

FACT Women have the same access in communities that have antidiscrimination laws. In the thousands of communities where there are no such laws, however, women can be and are excluded from such organizations. In fact, former Presidents Reagan and Bush belong to a very influential social club, the Bohemian Club, which includes many powerful businessmen and politicians but excludes women.

To this end, they preached to the Hurons and coerced them into accepting the Christian view that sexuality outside marriage was evil. They frightened the women into viewing their sexuality as dangerous, something to be controlled. They also encouraged women to accept a subordinate position and submit to the authority of both the church and their husbands. Warfare with the Iroquois and epidemic diseases brought in by the Europeans decimated the Huron population, dropping their numbers by more than half in a few decades. This decline made them much more dependent on the Jesuits and the French. As the Hurons settled around French communities, the longhouse declined as the center of Huron life. Matrilineal control of the longhouse had been the foundation of women's authority and independence among the Hurons, and as the longhouse disappeared, women lost this institutional support. In a relatively short period of time, the French Jesuits, warfare, and disease combined to change the egalitarian gender relations of the Huron into relations of male dominance and female subordination.

A French missionary confronts an Indian council in the seventeenth century. For the Huron Indians of Canada, the influence of French missionaries had profound consequences for gender relations and gender equality.

This brief look at the Hurons suggests some of the variations in gender relations across societies—from relative equality among the Hurons to the substantial inequality among Europeans at the time. It also shows how sociologists look at social and institutional structures, such as family and kinship, to explain gender relations. For sociologists, gender inequality is another dimension of the system of social stratification analyzed in Chapters 6 and 7. Like race and ethnic identity, gender is an ascribed status that can serve as a basis for allocating valued resources and creating social inequality. In fact, in some societies, sexual stratification is so entrenched and irrevocable that it can be considered a form of caste stratification. Gender inequalities are typically justified by **sexism,** *an ideology*

based on the belief that one sex is inherently superior to and should dominate the other sex. This chapter will discuss the reasons why gender inequality occurs, its extent in the United States and around the world, and ways in which it may be changing.

Men and Women in Society

You should be able to describe the extent to which gender differences in behavior are due to biological factors and analyze why gender differences exist according to the three sociological perspectives.

Unlike achieved statuses (such as one's educational level or occupation), there is little, if anything, that people can do to alter their ascribed statuses, such as gender. Gender is also a *master status* because it has considerable social significance in all societies. It is a central determinant of how people view themselves and how others respond to them, and it frequently serves as a basis for social differentiation. In some societies discrimination based on gender is so irrevocable that women have virtually no chance to improve their status. To understand how and why gender shapes the structure of society, it is helpful to understand why gender is an element of social differentiation in societies at all. This chapter will examine four different views on this issue.

The Biological Perspective

One perspective on the role of gender in determining one's position in society is that innate biological differences between men and women shape the contributions each can make to society. One question this raises, of course, is, What precisely are the differences between the sexes? Modern research has documented some distinctions and shown that allegations of other differences are not supported by the available evidence. For example, evidence exists that men are more aggressive and violent and have greater upper-body strength than women. Men also seem to excel in visual-spatial abilities, whereas women do particularly well in verbal skills and creativity. As far as personality characteristics such as sociability, emotionality, dependence, or self-esteem, there is no consistent evidence that the genders differ. Are the differences caused by biology? In only a few realms is there any evidence that they are (Fausto-Sterling, 1992; McCoy, 1985). Higher levels of aggressiveness in males, for example, are common in other species, such as rhesus monkeys, and the trait is almost universal in human cultures. Levels of aggressiveness can also be affected by changes in sex hormones. Thus, there is the suggestion, but by no means conclusive proof, that higher levels of aggressiveness in males are in part biological. In terms of the differences in verbal and spatial-visual ability, some evidence suggests that the brains of males and females are organized differently in this regard. In men, verbal skills are focused on one side of the brain and the spatial-visual skills on the other. In women, each skill can be found on both sides of the brain. This difference in the organization of the brain may account for why women tend to have more verbal skills and men are more adept at spatial-visual tasks. The greater upper-body strength of men is probably attributable to the higher levels of the hormone testosterone among males.

So there undoubtedly are some biological differences between men and women that have implications for social behavior. However, the differences are far fewer and much smaller than was once thought to be the case. Furthermore, the differences appear to relate to general tendencies, such as aggressiveness, rather than to specific social behaviors, such as fighting or playing football. In addition, despite any biological differences, men and women are highly flexible and extremely malleable in terms of what they are capable of doing. Most of our behavior is learned rather than biologically programmed, which means that men can learn to behave in a stereotypically female fashion, and women can learn to behave in ways that we would expect men to behave (Tavris, 1992). Other Worlds, Other Ways: New Guinea (on pp. 258–259) presents some cross-cultural evidence on exactly how variable gender learning can be. A final point is that the differences between men and women refer to average levels of performance, which ignores the significant overlap between the genders. Many women, for example, are more aggressive than some men, and some men are less aggressive than many women. Because of this overlap, gender status alone is a rather

poor basis for establishing social policy or allocating social tasks and rewards.

The Functionalist Perspective

Functionalists argue that some tasks were allocated to men and others to women in preindustrial societies because such arrangements were more convenient and practical (Ford, 1970; Giele, 1978). On the whole, males are physically stronger than women and free of the responsibility of bearing and nursing children. Women, by contrast, were expected to spend much of their adult life either pregnant or rearing their children. In addition, women were a more valuable reproductive resource in that the loss of a woman, as in war, would reduce the reproductive potential of society. The loss of a man, by contrast, could easily be made up for through increased sexual activity on the part of other men. There would be no loss in the overall reproductive potential of society. Given these considerations, functionalists argue, it was more practical in preindustrial societies to assign to men tasks, such as hunting or felling trees, that were physically demanding and might draw them away from home for long periods of time. Men were also assigned the dangerous tasks, such as protecting the group against attack from enemies. Women, who were limited by pregnancy and the need to nurse their young, were considered better suited to such tasks as gathering roots or berries, cooking food, and making pottery. Once these gender-role distinctions had become firmly established as a part of a group's tradition, they were then supported by strong group norms that made these differences independent of their origins. They came to be seen as the natural ways for men and women to behave rather than as practical means of accomplishing societal tasks (Brown, 1970; O'Kelly & Carney, 1986).

Industrialization ushered in a number of significant social changes: the separation of work from family life, smaller families, and a longer life expectancy. As a consequence, women tended to be isolated in the family and given prime responsibility for homemaking and child-rearing duties, whereas men went out and worked. Gender roles became divided on the basis of instrumental and expressive roles (see Chapter 4). *Instrumental tasks* such as hunting, building, or managing a work

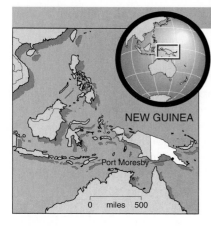

NEW GUINEA

OTHER WORLDS, *Other Ways*

NEW GUINEA: VARIATIONS IN GENDER ROLES IN PREINDUSTRIAL SOCIETIES

New Guinea is a large island in the southwest Pacific Ocean, just north of Australia. It is a part of Melanesia. Three tribes who lived in New Guinea were the Arapesh, the Mundugumor, and the Tchambuli. These peoples had a simple existence, living in thatched houses, cultivating yam gardens, and tending pigs. Margaret Mead (1950) visited them earlier in this century, and her observations there revolutionized our understanding of women and men in society. Many people, both then and today, believe that temperament and personality differences between the genders are stamped in by our biological heritage and that women and men are irrevocably different in terms of the feelings, sentiments, and emotions that come naturally to them. Mead found something remarkably different in New Guinea.

Among the Arapesh, both men and women could be characterized as cooperative, compliant, gentle, and mild mannered. All Arapesh were expected to be unaggressive and responsive to the needs of others rather than self-centered. The men were as nurturing of infants and children as the women were and would rush to soothe an infant who cried. Little boys would treat infant girls like dolls, dressing them with jewelry and bits of clothing. According to Mead, male and female personalities among the Arapesh were not sharply differentiated. To people in the United States, Arapesh men and women would be considered decidedly feminine. The Arapesh did show some gender differentiation, however. The husband–wife relationship was somewhat analogous to the mother–child relationship in that the husband was nurturing of and caring toward his wife but still dominant over her. The wife's role was to display some of the characteristics of a child, being subservient and obedient at some times but mischievous at other times.

The Mundugumor were headhunters and cannibals. Among them, both men and women were equally fierce and aggressive. The women were hot-tempered, hostile, and competitive. Infants who had been abused or abandoned would be ignored by both men and women, and men and women alike would heap ridicule on anyone who was upset by the infant's

team were seen as male tasks, whereas *expressive tasks* such as maintaining harmony and emotional stability were seen as primarily a woman's responsibility. In fact, for men, it became a status symbol to have a wife who did not work. A nonworking wife was taken as an indication of how capable the man was at producing economically and supporting his family. To justify this division of tasks, sexist beliefs emerged that a woman's place was in the home and that women were not biologically equipped for most forms of male work. However, in most preindustrial societies, women were not removed from economically productive roles. Much of what they did, such as gathering roots, tending crops, or herding flocks, contributed significantly to the economic support of the group.

They were by no means limited to child rearing or expressive tasks. Likewise, men were by no means limited to instrumental tasks in preindustrial societies (Murdock, 1934).

From the functionalist perspective, a gender-role division of labor that is no longer consistent with the needs of a particular society could be dysfunctional. To confine women to child rearing or to expressive activities would waste a valuable resource. In industrial societies, families have few children, and they have many supports, such as day care, to help in raising them. So it is no longer necessary for adults—either male or female—to devote their lives to such tasks. It would be better if they used their intellectual, creative, and productive abilities to make additional contributions to

plight or made an attempt to help. Like the Arapesh, the Mundugumor viewed men and women as being alike in terms of temperament and personality. Traits that most societies associated more with women than men—gentleness, warmth, caring—were absent in Mundugumor women. To people in the United States, Mundugumor women and men would seem exaggeratedly masculine. Yet, there was some gender differentiation in behavior: The women were the food providers whereas the men were the headhunters.

The Tchambuli showed yet another variation in gender performance: Women shaved their heads, showed strong and hearty camaraderie with one another, and were aggressive food providers. The men, by contrast, spent their time fixing their hair, gossiping with one another about women, and working on their art carvings and dance steps. Tchambuli women took care of economic matters for the tribe—they were the traders and did the fishing, planting, harvesting, and cooking. Women were considered in their culture to be the more plain-spoken, efficient, impersonal, and practical of the two sexes. The women went about unadorned, whereas the men were highly decorated, concerned about fashions, and vain. In

short, the women were socially dominant, holding the important economic and political roles, whereas the men were socially passive, emotional, and flighty. In other words, Tchambuli gender roles were almost a mirror opposite of the stereotype of male and female roles in the United States. Yet, among the Tchambuli, there were also rituals that portrayed women as inferior to men in terms of how much they knew and their ability to behave morally.

Mead has been criticized for overdrawing the distinctions in gender roles that she found and ignoring the variation in gender performances that are typically displayed in a given society. Yet, her description of these three tribes demonstrates some important points. First, little about gender is irrevocably biological. Human beings are extremely malleable, and each of us is capable of learning a wide range of emotions and behaviors during the socialization process. Second, male dominance is a powerful force in societies. Even among the Tchambuli, where women exhibited dominance in most role performances, symbolic portrayals of male dominance and female subservience were important rituals.

society. Because the birthrate is low and most jobs in industrial societies are not dangerous, there is no need to protect women as a reproductive resource, as was done in the past. In addition, great physical strength is no longer necessary for most jobs in a highly automated, technological society. For all of these reasons, functionalists argue, it is not particularly useful to use gender as a criterion for allocating jobs today. It would be more functional to assign tasks based on individual abilities.

The Conflict Perspective

Many sociologists have questioned whether the fact of a woman having children is the central element in shaping gender roles in society and es-

pecially whether it explains the continued existence of gender stratification. For example, the sociologist Randall Collins (1971) has argued that there is an inherent conflict of interest between men and women and that gender roles can serve as a mechanism by which one group dominates the other. In part, this domination results because males in general are physically stronger than women, which better equips them to use power to their own advantage and gain dominance. But the situation is more complex than this. Through the socialization process, a subtler form of power is exerted and control achieved: people learn to want those things that are in the interests of the dominant group in society. In most societies, women have learned to accept the dominance of males and their own subordinate positions because they believe such dominance is appropriate and even desirable or because they feel they have no other choice.

The economic competition discussed in Chapter 7 also contributes to gender inequality. In simple hunting-and-gathering societies, there is a division of labor based on gender, as we have seen, but there is also considerable equality between men and women. The reason is that women produce as much as and sometimes more than men. Gathering nuts, roots, and berries produces a steady and dependable food supply, whereas the results of hunting can be sporadic. It might be days or weeks before men can fell some game. In the interim, women provide food for the group. In agricultural societies, men tend to dominate economic productivity, in part because their physical strength and freedom from child-bearing duties enable them to engage in extensive, heavy labor that might take them away from home for hours or days at a time. This situation leaves women economically subordinate and unequal. As functionalists point out, this inequality continues into early industrial societies as men work and women stay home. This arrangement benefits men, of course, because they have a corner on the prestigious and powerful positions in society, and most men wish to continue those social practices.

The dominance of men has continued well into the twentieth century in the United States. During World War II, for example, large numbers of women joined the workforce, replacing men serving in the military and showing that women were capable of performing many traditionally male jobs (Van Horn, 1988). Most people assumed that these women were housewives who had no financial need to work but who were doing their part for the war effort and who wanted to return to their traditional roles after the war. In fact, government and industry, through such groups as the Office of War Information and the War Advertising Council, mounted a propaganda effort to encourage the public to believe this. Reality for many of these working women, individually dubbed "Rosie the Riveter," was quite different: Many of them were married and needed those well-paying, previously all-male jobs to support their families. Some were single parents or single women for whom these jobs were their sole source of economic support. Many of these women wanted to continue in these jobs after the war. Despite the fact that these women had shown themselves to be capable of performing well in traditionally male jobs, there was a backlash against them when the war ended and returning servicemen competed with the women for jobs. Many people felt that the women had done their duty and now should return to their homes and families ("where they belonged") and make jobs available for returning servicemen. Public pressure and job discrimination resulted in most of these women leaving the traditionally male jobs (Honey, 1984). From the conflict perspective, then, gender differentiation becomes the battleground for a struggle over scarce resources—in this case, for jobs and prestige. However, this economic competition for jobs—a form of the split labor market discussed in Chapter 7 because women are typically paid less than men—was translated into the sexist ideology that women were incapable of performing the jobs as well as the men.

The Interactionist Perspective

According to the interactionist perspective, human beings relate to one another on the basis of symbols that have social meaning within a given culture or society. Those social meanings are created, communicated, and reinforced as people interact with one another on a daily basis. So we can understand a lot about the creation and maintenance of gender inequality if we watch how men and women interact in various settings. It is through those interactions that the place of men and women in society is defined. Probably the most important symbol system for human beings is language. Interactionists point out that many values, beliefs, and social meanings find expression in different language forms, and an analysis of some of these forms suggests a continuing gender bias in many languages, including English. For example, the gender-specific pronouns *he* and *his* can be used when referring to both men and women, and this convention in English may be a veiled way of maintaining male dominance. Recent investigations suggest that such sexist language is still very much with us and show conclusively that use of the generic *he* does create predominantly male images in people's minds, especially for men (Gastil, 1990; Switzer, 1990). When people read or hear *he*, instead of *she* or *they*,

they think of men, and this tendency can serve as symbolic reinforcement of the exclusion of women from many aspects of society. This linguistic usage, then, may reinforce and help perpetuate sexist thought and action, especially among men, by encouraging a predominantly male imagery when thinking about activities or realms of which both men and women might be a part.

The conversational styles of men and women can also reflect and reinforce gender patterns of dominance and subordination (Spencer & Drass, 1989; Tannen, 1994). Such styles, for example, can have direct implications for gaining and keeping positions of leadership in groups. One investigation focused on the order in which people speak in mixed-sex groups (Aries, 1985). In general, men initiate more conversation and receive more interaction than women. People who initiate the most interaction in groups take up the most time and are considered by others in the group to be leaders. So if women are taught to be submissive or timid around men, they may be less likely or less able to assume leadership in groups. As another example of the effect of conversational style, it is widely believed in the United States that women talk more than men (the stereotype has it that women "chatter on" about frivolous subjects). Yet, many investigations of conversational behavior in mixed groups show that men talk more than women and interrupt while others are talking more than women do. Men also answer questions not addressed to them and continue talking when there is an overlap in conversation. The impact of these different patterns of conversation on gender inequality is quite direct:

> The beliefs that women talk too much and talk about insignificant subjects function to keep women quieter than they might be and to allow men to monopolize social conversations and work groups. The expectation that whatever a woman says is trivial and unimportant creates insecurity, timidity in presenting ideas, and lower feelings of self esteem. . . . The lack of authority attached to female speech patterns lowers a woman's chances for success in many fields and can reinforce the belief that women should stick to the traditional careers of mother and homemaker. (Kirsh, 1983, pp. 74–75)

So it is through interaction patterns such as these that beliefs and practices regarding gender inequality are maintained and reinforced in everyday life. Although the sociological perspectives differ on a number of issues relating to gender stratification, they would all concur with Lenski's view (see Chapter 6) that most societies could function well with must less stratification based on gender than there is, especially industrial societies.

The Socialization of Men and Women

You should be able to describe the role of the family, the schools, and the media in teaching people about gender.

Scientific research has demonstrated that most of our behavior as males and females is not a function of biology but rather of learning. This finding leads to the distinction that sociologists make between *sex* and *gender*. *Male* and *female* are used as sex-related terms—the innate, biological feature of sexual identity. **Sex** refers to *the biological role that each of us plays, such as in reproduction. Masculine* and *feminine,* by contrast, are used as gender-specific terms. **Gender** refers to *learned behavior involving how we are expected to act as males and females in society.* One of the key issues in analyzing gender inequality is how we learn to be masculine and feminine and how this learning contributes to gender differentiation and inequality. This learning occurs in good part through the socialization process, with three major agencies of socialization in industrial societies involved: the family, the schools, and the media.

The Family

Infancy represents the most crucial period for human development because patterns of personality and behavior are established during these years. These early years are also extremely important in the establishment of beliefs about appropriate masculine and feminine behavior. There is a growing body of literature that clearly demonstrates how parents are likely to treat male and female infants and young children in ways consistent with how they view masculinity and femininity. For example, fathers are typically "rougher" with boys and more gentle with girls, and both mothers and fathers tend to speak more softly to girls than to boys (MacDonald & Parke, 1986; Rossi, 1984).

By the age of three, children have acquired a gender identity, which means that they can correctly label themselves as male or female. But at this point, their identity is oversimplified and highly stereotyped. It is also based more on such things as hairstyle or dress than on an accurate awareness of genital differences between the sexes. Once the child's gender identity has been established, he or she then attempts to master the behaviors that are associated with that gender. Behaving "like a boy" or "like a girl" becomes rewarding because it brings approval from adults and peers. Parents still today tend to encourage boys to engage in instrumental play, such as building something, whereas girls are encouraged toward expressive play, such as "dressing up."

Even in childhood, it appears that male activities are valued more than female ones. For example, girls often display a fondness for the higher prestige of the masculine role by becoming tomboys (Burn, O'Neil, & Nederend, 1996; Martin, 1990). Tomboyism is acceptable to a much greater extent than a little boy's being a "sissy." In fact, girls are more prominent in boys' games than boys are in girls' games—testimony to the less negative reactions to tomboys than to "sissies." Other investigators have discovered that boys play more competitive games than girls and that girls typically do not learn how to deal with direct competition (Berliner, 1988; Best, 1983). Children learn from their family experiences what it means to be male and female, and these experiences are extremely strong influences.

Research shows that parents in the 1990s do interact with their children differently from parents of a few decades ago. Parents today are more aware of the negative consequences of gender stereotyping, and they make greater efforts to treat all their offspring alike, regardless of gender. Yet, gender and traditional cultural ways of relating to males and females are powerful forces, and parents still relate to their male and female offspring differently. This is true even of parents who consider themselves egalitarian in terms of gender relations (Weisner, Garnier, & Loucky, 1994).

The Schools

A significant part of the socialization process occurs in the schools. School systems are characteristically staffed in such a way that children's perceptions of masculinity and femininity are reinforced. For example, although most elementary schoolteachers are female, most elementary school principals are male. Thus, from the beginning of school, children see men in positions of authority and dominance over women (Benokraitis & Feagin, 1995; Richmond-Abbott, 1992). In addition, schools and teachers treat children very differently based on their gender, with significant consequences for what children learn about gender (Best, 1983; Thorne, 1993). Investigations have shown that female teachers are more likely to encourage independence and assertion in boys than in girls. Teachers also tend to view girls as less creative than boys, to provide less attention to girls, and to reward female students for conforming and male students for being aggressive. The way teachers do so is quite subtle. Dependence in girls, for example, is encouraged by not sending them off to work on their own, although boys often work alone. As for aggressiveness, boys often have to misbehave to gain their teacher's attention, whereas girls who are quiet and demure are more likely to receive attention from the teacher. So teachers, often without realizing it, reward their students for behaving in a fashion consistent with their own gender-role stereotypes.

Two or more decades ago, the images of males and females presented in school textbooks typically reinforced traditional stereotypes: Males were pictured far more often than females, males were pictured in many occupations and women in few, and female pronouns such as *her* were uncommon. But have there not been changes in this situation in the past twenty years? Not as much as one might think. Things have improved, especially when efforts are made to produce materials that are nonsexist in their presentation. However, stereotyping still persists. Recent studies of children's picture books, for example, find that women are portrayed more frequently than in the past but still less often than men (only one-third of the illustrations are of women), almost no women are portrayed as working outside the home, women are still shown in fewer occupations than men, and women are portrayed as less brave and adventurous and more helpless (Peterson & Lach, 1990; Purcell & Stewart, 1990; Williams, Vernon, Williams, & Malecha, 1987). Furthermore, although men are sometimes portrayed as expressing their emotions, denying one's feelings is still characterized in these books as a normal aspect of maleness.

Even college textbooks are not immune to these influences. Recent studies of the pictorial content of textbooks for college-level psychology and sociology courses found that women are shown less often than men and are portrayed more passively and negatively (Ferree & Hall, 1990; Peterson & Kroner, 1992). For example, the psychology books portray women as the victims of mental disorders and the clients in therapy, whereas men are pictured as the therapists. All these portrayals help to perpetuate the cultural stereotype that men tend to be stronger, more active, and working in the world to solve problems, whereas women are more likely to be weaker, more passive, and focusing their interests around home and family.

Because young schoolchildren are at a formative and impressionable stage in life, the impact that these school experiences have on them is substantial and long-lasting. Evidence shows that sexist treatment in the schools results in lower self-esteem for female grade school and high school students (Martinez & Dukes, 1991; Sadker & Sadker, 1994).

The Media

The media are an extremely important influence on gender-role socialization through their portrayals of men and women. Despite the fact that *Cosmopolitan* magazine is allegedly a publication for "modern women," for example, the cover photographs generally focus on seductive women wearing clothing that is sexually suggestive. In popular romance novels, women are typically portrayed as the victims of male aggression, and this victimization is usually attributed to the nature of their relationship to the aggressors. The impact of these books is significant, because millions of people read them every year. In a recent investigation of newspaper photographs, men appear in the photos far more often than women. Furthermore, men are typically portrayed in professional roles in the photos, whereas women are cast in domestic roles (Luebke, 1989).

Perhaps the most significant media influence on young people is television. It has been estimated that between kindergarten and sixth grade,

children watch from ten to twenty-five hours of television every week. In fact, "children spend more time watching television than they do reading books, listening to the radio, or going to the movies" (Richmond-Abbott, 1992, p. 98). Despite the fact that television has "cleaned up its act" to some extent, this powerful medium still overwhelmingly portrays stereotyped gender roles. Investigations of television programs reveal that many shows present a grossly distorted view of family life, with 75 percent of male roles portrayed in prime time reflecting the images of unmarried men who are "tough" and "cool." Even on public television, there have been strong indicators of gender differentiation—the female puppets on *Sesame Street* have been observed to portray predominantly strident, loudmouthed types. Over the last three decades, only 20 percent of the characters on prime time television shows were female, and most of the women shown were young, unemployed, family-bound, or in comic roles (Richmond-Abbott, 1992). Television and other media in less developed nations around the world also tend to project stereotyped images of women's and men's roles (Mwangi, 1996).

There have, of course, been improvements in the portrayal of women in the movies and on television over the decades. Two of the most popular network shows in the United States in recent years, *Roseanne* and *Murphy Brown,* have featured strong and positive female characters in their starring roles. Yet, a study commissioned by the Screen Actors Guild and released in 1993 found that only one out of three roles in prime time are played by women and that anchors, newsmakers, and authorities on television news shows are overwhelmingly white males. The portrayal of women in children's shows was even more lopsided, according to the report (Gunther, 1993). So, some of the old stereotypes linger, and evidence shows that they affect youngsters' attitudes about these matters. A longitudinal study of gender-role attitudes of teenagers found that watching a lot of television did not make boys more sexist (Morgan, 1972). However, the teenagers who had the least sexist attitudes to begin with—fairly intelligent girls—were most affected by television: Those who watched it a lot developed more sexist attitudes. This again illustrates the subtle ways in which people can develop views of the world that help maintain patterns of dominance and subordination.

The Extent of Gender Inequality in the United States

You should be able to describe the extent to which women and men suffer discrimination in economic and other realms because of their gender.

Although women are a numerical majority in U.S. society, they comprise a minority group, and there are a number of important similarities between women and other minorities (see Chapter 7). Like African Americans, women still have unequal access to valued resources and suffer discrimination on many fronts. Although this chapter will focus primarily on the way in which women suffer from gender inequality, it will also look at some ways in which men have been discriminated against by unreasonable differentiation based on gender.

Economic Discrimination

Women occupy a subordinate position in comparison to men on virtually every dimension of socioeconomic status (SES). The three main dimensions of SES are education, occupation, and income.

Education   Education has long been a key channel of social mobility in the United States, particularly for members of minority groups or others who were disadvantaged. Today, a college education is especially important in gaining prestigious and powerful positions in society, but higher education has never been equally available to all. Until about 1850, women were almost completely excluded from colleges. It was assumed that women needed less education because their careers would be as homemakers and mothers. In fact, in 1873, the U.S. Supreme Court ruled that an Illinois woman could be denied a license to practice law on the grounds that she was female. One Supreme Court justice of the era defended this stance by saying that "the paramount mission and destiny of women are to fill the noble and benign offices of wife and mother. This is the law of the Creator" ("The Brethren's First Sister," 1981, p. 17).

Since 1950, the number of people in the United States twenty-five years of age or older with some college training has quadrupled, and there have been dramatic increases in the proportion of women who pursue some form of advanced education. The percentage of doctoral degrees going to women has grown from 14 percent in 1971 to 37 percent today, and 42 percent of law degrees go to women today, compared with only 5 percent in 1970 (U.S. Bureau of the Census, 1995, pp. 191–192). Still, many more men attain these degrees than do women, and as Figure 8.1 illustrates, the percentage of men who complete college still considerably exceeds that of women. Although women have gained on men in college graduation rates in the past thirty years, a significant gap still exists.

The problems that women face in getting an education, especially in a professional school, can often be subtle and difficult to detect. For example, one study of admission to medical school found that the personal interview part of the admissions process counted more heavily for female than for male applicants (Clayton, Baird, & Levinson, 1984). Furthermore, the women were rated lower on the average on these interviews than were men. This suggests that these interviews, which are subjective assessments by those doing the interviewing, serve as a mechanism to limit women's opportunities to enter medical school. An interesting related issue is that among African Americans, men are slightly worse off in terms of educational achievement than women, suggesting that decades of oppression and racial discrimination have made it especially difficult for black males to be upwardly mobile (see Chapter 7).

Work and the Workplace   Although women constitute 45 percent of the workforce in the United States, they are concentrated at the lower end of the status hierarchy. Table 8.1 (on p. 266) illustrates that women tend to hold jobs such as secretary or receptionist, which provide relatively low income and prestige. The better occupations, such as physician or lawyer, are held primarily by men. Evidence suggests that some of this difference, even in the 1990s, is the result of discrimination in hiring practices. Some employers still prefer to hire men for jobs requiring technical or managerial skills based on the gender-role stereotype that men are more competent at such tasks. This preference is especially true when there is no evidence to suggest superior job performance on the part of either the male or female applicant for a job (Gerdes & Garber, 1983; Zebrowitz, Tenen-

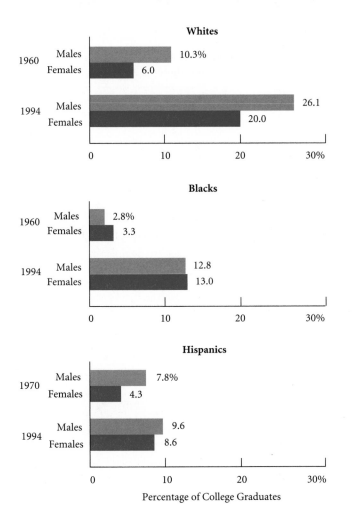

Whites

1960
Males 10.3%
Females 6.0

1994
Males 26.1
Females 20.0

0   10   20   30%

Blacks

1960
Males 2.8%
Females 3.3

1994
Males 12.8
Females 13.0

0   10   20   30%

Hispanics

1970
Males 7.8%
Females 4.3

1994
Males 9.6
Females 8.6

0   10   20   30%

Percentage of College Graduates

FIGURE 8.1 Percentage of People, Twenty-Five Years Old or Older, Completing Four Years or More of College, by Gender and Race, 1960 and 1994 *Note:* From *Statistical Abstract of the United States, 1995* (p. 157) by U.S. Bureau of the Census, 1995, Washington, DC: U.S. Government Printing Office.

baum, & Goldstein, 1991). Table 8.1 illustrates that job opportunities for women have improved since the 1970s, with considerably more women moving into such lucrative jobs as lawyer, physician, or engineer. But the dark side of the issue is that the low-paying and low-prestige jobs are still almost exclusively filled by women. In addition, research shows that women who take traditionally male, blue-collar jobs encounter a hostile climate in terms of how they are treated by their male coworkers and supervisors. These women, as a result are less satisfied with their jobs and experience more stress at work than do women in traditionally female jobs (Mansfield et al., 1991).

Even when educational opportunities are available to women, their chances for success in an occupation are often blocked by obstacles that men usually do not face, such as subtle forms of discrimination in hiring or promotion practices. A 1995 report by a government commission, for example, found evidence that women were discriminated against in promotions to senior management positions in industry (Glass Ceiling Commission, 1995). Although women make up 45 percent of the workforce, they constitute less than 5 percent of senior managers. In addition, the commission found evidence that the disparity was due to discrimination: Male senior managers refused to promote women and other minorities because they viewed such promotions as a direct threat to their own advancement.

Women in the legal profession also experience discrimination. Access to jobs in large law firms is one of the major routes to success in law. Yet, for many years, such firms closed their doors to women. In 1968, one woman lawyer (later to

TABLE 8.1 Employment positions held by women, 1976–1995

Some Jobs Show Changes			Some Jobs Show Little Change		
	Percentage of Jobs Held by Women			Percentage of Jobs Held by Women	
Employment Positions	1976	1995	Employment Positions	1976	1995
Cashiers	87.7%	79.2%	Secretaries	99.0%	98.5%
Food counter clerks	85.5	74.8	Receptionists	96.2	96.5
Food service workers	68.7	58.3	Child-care workers	98.2	96.8
Real estate sales	41.2	50.7	Typists	96.7	94.3
Accountants and auditors	26.9	52.1	Bank tellers	91.9	90.1
Cleaning service workers	33.5	44.9	Bookkeepers	90.0	92.8
Financial managers	24.7	50.3	Health-service workers	86.2	88.2
College and university teachers	31.3	45.2	Hairdressers, cosmetologists	88.0	92.0
Lawyers and judges	9.2	26.2	Librarians	82.4	83.9
Physicians	12.8	24.4	File clerks	85.5	80.2
Police and detectives	3.7	13.5	Schoolteachers (except college and university)	70.9	74.7
Engineers	1.8	8.4	Social workers	61.0	67.9
Fire fighters	0.0	2.7	Construction trades	1.6	2.3

Note: From *Employment and Earnings, 24*(1), pp. 8–9, by U.S. Department of Labor, Bureau of Labor Statistics, 1977; *Employment and Earnings, 43*(1), pp. 171–176, by U.S. Department of Labor, Bureau of Labor Statistics, 1996.

become a federal district judge) was told by a law firm that "we don't hire women; the secretaries might resent it" ("The Brethren's First Sister," 1981, p. 17). There has been an upsurge in the number of women lawyers since 1968—from less than 3 percent of the profession then to 26 percent today. Yet women still make up only a small percentage of the partners in the largest law firms, and recent research shows that, even in the 1990s, female lawyers in the United States get paid less than male lawyers at every level of legal practice, are discriminated against in promotions in large law firms, find it much harder to become partners in large law firms than do men, and are less likely to become law professors than are men (Bernstein, 1996; Spurr, 1990).

Another obstacle that women face in the occupational realm is that they tend to be saddled, more so than men, with familial obligations (Ferree, 1991; Spade & Reese, 1991). Even when both spouses work, and even though men have taken on more responsibilities for these tasks in recent decades, women are still expected to take on more responsibility for raising the children, keeping up the home, and taking care of sick relatives. In fact, research shows that the cost of child care is an important reason why women sometimes quit the jobs they do get (Maume, 1991). Even among college-educated people, it is the rare couple who has a truly symmetrical relationship in which both partners share equally in household and work responsibilities.

Income Classical economic theory claims that wages are determined by the competitive forces of supply and demand. Employers are rational and pay workers what they are worth in terms of the employer's ability to produce goods and services for a price that consumers are willing to pay. In this view, discrimination in pay based on gender or other characteristics is irrational and thus will not persist in the long run. Many economists and much sociological research suggest that this is a simplistic view of the factors that influence the setting of wages (Jacobs & Steinberg, 1990; Peterson, 1990). In addition to being affected by market forces, income levels are also influenced by how much power different groups of workers possess and by cultural stereotypes of what different workers are worth as well as by the traditional levels of pay for different jobs. The effect of these "irrational" factors on women has been that they are paid considerably less than men.

In 1993, the median income for U.S. males working year-round and full-time was $30,407; for females, it was only $21,747 (U.S. Bureau of the Census, 1995). Women's income is about 72 percent of men's income, a figure that has changed only slightly since 1970 (see Table 8.2). Such gender inequality is found in virtually all industrial nations, with women in Australia doing best by earning 79 percent of what men make and in Japan doing worst with 46 percent of men's incomes (Rosenfeld & Kalleberg, 1991). This is a substantial difference. Even if one looks at income levels of male and female workers in the same occupational categories who work year-round and full-time, women earn substantially less than men in every job category (see Table 8.3). Some of these differences in income result from the fact that most men have been working longer than women and thus have gained seniority and salary increases that have boosted their income. However, studies that have taken this fact into account still conclude that women have tended to earn less than men for doing the same job. A recent study by

TABLE 8.2 Ratio of female/male median income, by age, 1970 and 1993, among year-round, full-time civilian workers

Age	1970	1993
All ages	0.59	0.72
15 to 19 years	0.96	
20 to 24 years	0.74	0.95
25 to 34 years	0.65	0.84
35 to 44 years	0.54	0.72
45 to 54 years	0.56	0.62
55 to 64 years	0.60	0.63
65 years and over	0.72	0.67

Note: From *Statistical Abstract of the United States, 1989* (p. 448) by U.S. Bureau of the Census, 1989, Washington, DC: U.S. Government Printing Office; *Statistical Abstract of the United States, 1995* (p. 477) by U.S. Bureau of the Census, 1995, Washington, DC: U.S. Government Printing Office.

TABLE 8.3 Median annual income for year-round full-time workers, by gender and occupational category, 1993

Occupational Group	Male Income	Female Income	Ratio Women/Men
Professional specialty	$45,136	$31,906	.71
Executive, administrative, and managerial	42,722	28,876	.68
Sales	32,327	18,743	.58
Precision production, craft and repair	27,653	21,357	.77
Service workers	20,860	13,126	.63
Technical and related support	35,048	26,324	.75
Administrative support	26,746	20,683	.77
Machine operators, assemblers, and inspectors	23,378	15,379	.66
Transportation and material moving	26,532	19,652	.74

Note: From *Statistical Abstract of the United States, 1995* (p. 435) by U.S. Bureau of the Census, 1995, Washington, DC: U.S. Government Printing Office.

the U.S. Department of Education, for example, looked at the experiences of men and women who graduated from high school in 1972 and thus would be in the middle of their careers at the time of the study (Adelman, 1991). The study found that women on the whole did better in high school and college than men did, they finished college faster, and they had more positive attitudes toward their educational experience. However, by the midpoint in their careers, the women earned less than the men and were more likely to be unemployed. The study looked at comparable men and women, such as those who had no children and had been working equal lengths of time, but still found pay inequities: In only seven of the thirty-three occupations studied did pay equity between men and women occur. The other twenty-six occupations showed men making significantly more than women. No occupation showed women making more than men. Even among men and women in the same age brackets, income differences persist (see Table 8.2). Although the gender difference in income is small among teenagers, differences grow among young adults and become quite large among older adults. It is safe to say then, that not a lot of improvement has occurred, and the prospects for income equality in the near future are not great.

Chapter 6 discussed the issues of the *feminization of poverty*, pointing to the fact that some women are especially vulnerable to falling below the poverty level. By the early 1990s, for example, 10.7 percent of all families in the United States lived below the poverty level, but the rate among female-headed families was 37 percent. And things may actually be getting worse. In 1959, 23 percent of all families living in poverty were headed by women; by 1990, this figure had grown to 53 percent. As Figure 6.5 shows, children living in single-parent, female-headed families are especially likely to be living in poverty. About one out of six women over the age of 65 live below the poverty level—one out of four of those who live alone (U.S. Bureau of the Census, 1993).

Chapter 7 discusses social inequality based on race and ethnicity. People in whom a subordinate racial or ethnic status is combined with a subordinate sexual status are even worse off than women in general (see Figure 8.2). Sixty percent of elderly black women who live alone are living in poverty,

and minority females who work earn less than do their male counterparts or white females (see Figure 8.2). Clearly, minority women in the United States are in a weak and vulnerable position when it comes to competing for economic resources. Even when they have full-time jobs, they tend to be concentrated in those jobs with the lowest income or prestige (Blea, 1991; Higginbotham, 1987).

Discrimination in the Military

Even women who choose the military as a career do not have the same opportunities as men. Although they constitute 11 percent of the armed services, they are currently barred from serving in many combat positions (Spitzer, 1992). In 1993, the Clinton administration opened some, but not all, combat positions to women. This limitation is important because serving in combat positions is one of the best ways to advance one's career in the military. The limitations continue to exist despite the fact that, during the Gulf War of 1991, female soldiers found themselves in combat, performed well by all standards, and were killed in action and taken prisoner by enemy troops. In fact, a poll taken during the Gulf War indicated that half the U.S. public feels that women should have combat assignments if they want them (Fuentes, 1991). The major arguments against women in combat positions, especially ground infantry units, is that they do not have the physical strength or aggressive nature needed for the job, that they would disrupt the cohesiveness and bonding that occurs among men in combat and is important to combat success, and that it violates deep-seated cultural values regarding manhood and womanhood in Western civilization. Supporters of equal opportunities for women argue that women can be trained for the strength and aggressiveness and that they proved themselves in the Gulf War. Furthermore, there is no reason to believe that women could not bond in a military unit as well as men. The major stumbling block, according to this view, is that fighting and military combat are one of the last bastions where men can maintain a separate world into which women are not allowed. Of course, a major factor fueling the movement of women into the military over the past thirty years has been the needs of the military itself, which is ultimately concerned with finding a sufficient

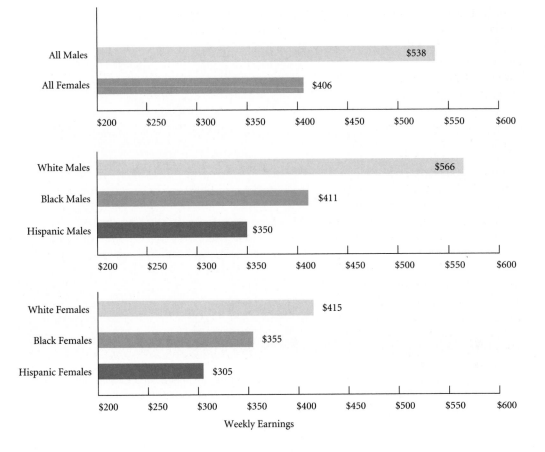

FIGURE 8.2 Median Weekly Earnings of Full-time Workers, by Gender and Race, 1995 *Note:* From *Employment and Earnings, 43*(1), p. 203, by U.S. Department of Labor, Bureau of Labor Statistics, 1996.

number of educated and motivated recruits. Along these lines, three factors are propelling the greater use of women: The all-volunteer military; the increasingly high-tech workplace, which calls for brains and dexterity more than brawn; and the increasing feminization of the workforce. Given these trends, the military may see that it is in its own interests to expand opportunities for women, maybe by opening up more combat positions to them in the future.

Other Types of Discrimination

Discrimination on the basis of gender is not confined to education, occupation, and income. There are various other ways in which women are placed at a disadvantage in the United States. For example, the legal system has built into it a great deal of discrimination against women. In 1990, most states still provided husbands with some loopholes to avoid prosecution for raping their wives (Russell, 1990). In eight states, men cannot be charged with raping their wives as long as they are living together and the wife has not filed for divorce or protection. Twenty-six other states allow charges of marital rape but with exemptions. Depending on the state, for example, a man cannot be charged with raping his wife unless he has kidnapped her or threatened her with a weapon; some of these states do not permit rape charges if the wife is unable to consent to having sex because she is drugged or unconscious. Only sixteen states accord wives the same protection as other women by treating marital rape like any other rape.

This U.S. Army gunner from Michigan is on patrol searching for illegal weapons as part of the Bosnian peacekeeping operation in 1996. Clearly, occupational opportunities for women in the United States are greater than ever.

Women have also experienced discrimination in the realm of retirement income. Retirement plans have traditionally paid women a smaller monthly income than they pay to men with the same accumulated retirement assets. This inequality has been based on the fact that women live longer, on the average, than men. The rationale has been that women will draw the same total assets from their retirement plan as men, but they will draw it out in smaller amounts over a longer period. Women, of course, have complained that this penalizes them for being healthy. They have also argued that there are many other criteria than gender that could be used to determine retirement income, such as genetic susceptibility to heart disease or behavioral factors such as smoking.

Gender Inequality Involving Males

Most discussions of gender inequality focus on women, but men also suffer from unreasonable gender differentiation. Some have even spoken of a *masculine mystique* and the *myth of masculinity*: a set of stereotypes about men, such as their being strong, dominant, tough, unemotional, and so forth (Kimmel, 1996). Socially imposed expectations concerning male behavior can be as limiting for men as the stereotypes involving females have been for women. In terms of professional careers, for example, male secretaries were often regarded as social oddities not long ago. Men who entered such unconventional male roles had to be prepared for incredulous and sometimes even abusive reactions from others. At that time, most men probably did not even consider a profession such as nurse or secretary, even at times when jobs for college graduates in nursing were plentiful and other jobs were scarce. Still, today, very few men go into nursing (see Chapter 10).

The stereotypical male role also limits the opportunities open to men in terms of domestic activities, emotional expression, and relationships with children. Not that many years ago, if a male executive were to ask his employer for paternity leave, his boss would probably have laughed.

Today, leaves of absence for new fathers are becoming more common. At the same time, a form of institutionalized discrimination is still involved, because the man who takes such a leave often loses ground in the competition for advancement and seniority. Although few males identify themselves occupationally as *house husbands,* it is more common than it once was for men to accept equal responsibility with their partners for domestic tasks (Lewis, 1984; McCall, 1988). In fact, despite the cultural assumption that work is the chief activity for men, one investigation found that 90 percent of the male respondents to a survey expressed strong attachments to their roles as husbands and fathers and defined their marital and parental roles as the most important (Cohen, 1987).

Other forms of discrimination against men can be found. For example, some states have laws that make it a punishable offense for men (and presumably other women) to use obscene language in the presence of females. Many insurance companies charge higher automobile insurance premiums to young males because of the higher rate of automobile accidents among that group. Thus, a young man who is a careful driver is penalized by virtue of his gender. Finally, men but not women are required to register for the military draft, and only men could be inducted into the military should the draft itself be reinstated. Women are not required to make any equivalent contribution to national public service. This is true despite the fact that a public opinion poll in the United States during the Gulf War in 1991 showed that half of those surveyed believe that any future draft should include women (Fuentes, 1991).

Gender Stratification in Global Perspective

You should be able to describe the patterns of gender inequality that are found in various nations around the world.

The general patterns of gender inequality found in the United States are reproduced in other societies around the globe, but there are important differences that help us understand some of the intricacies of gender stratification. The overall conclusion, as stated by the Secretary General of the United Nations, is that "the majority [of women] still lag far behind men in power, wealth and opportunity" (United Nations, 1991, p. v). Over the past few decades, a growing number of women have entered the workforce, but in some areas their share of the labor force is still quite small: 17 percent in North Africa and Western Asia and 29 percent in Latin America (in the United States, it is 45 percent). In Algeria, women make up only 9 percent of the workforce and in Egypt only 10 percent. In some areas, like the former Soviet Union and sub-Saharan Africa, women actually lost a little ground since 1970, seeing their share of the labor force decline. Women are also the most affected by economic recession: They are hired later when jobs are expanding and are let go quicker when jobs contract. The women who work generally have the less prestigious and lowest-paying jobs, a situation that cuts across levels of development. In industrialized nations such as Japan and South Korea, women earn about one-half what men do, but this is also true in a less developed nation such as Cyprus. In Iceland, women earn 90 percent of what men do, compared to 72 percent in the United States.

In all parts of the world, the rate of illiteracy is higher among women than men, almost twice as high in Asia. Also, in most places women lag behind men in enrollment in high school and college, although in thirty-three countries more women enroll in higher education than men (including the United States and many nations in Asia, Latin America, and the Caribbean). In addition, around the world, women in educational occupations tend to be in the lower levels teaching primary school rather than the more prestigious and higher-paying postsecondary education.

Worldwide, women are poorly represented in political positions where important decisions are made (United Nations, 1995). Women make up fewer than 10 percent of all members of parliaments or congresses in the world. Women do fairly well in some countries: Finland, Norway, Romania, and Cuba have one-third of their parliamentary seats filled by women. Some African and Arab nations have no women in parliament, and Japan's Diet has less than 2 percent women. The United States does a little better with 10 percent following the upsurge of women elected to Congress in the 1990s, but it still lags significantly behind the more advanced nations.

Increasingly, women have fewer supports to help them take care of their families. In the past few decades, the proportion of births to unmarried women has increased in many nations around the world, and in some cases the increase is dramatic. The proportion has doubled in the United States to 21 percent, but in nations as diverse as Denmark, Norway, and Guam it has increased three or four times. In the Seychelles, French Guiana, and Martinique, two out of every three births are to unmarried women. In addition, many households are headed by women: almost half in nations such as Botswana and Barbados. In the United States 31 percent of households are headed by women, but in Kuwait, Iran, Pakistan, and Burkina Faso it is 7 percent or less. Other Worlds, Other Ways: Mexico (on pp. 274–275) explores in detail the circumstances of poor women in Third-World countries and the institutional forces that shape their lives.

Toward Gender Equality

You should be able to describe the movement for gender equality in the United States and around the world, including what advances and setbacks there have been.

Gender inequality is more widely recognized as unacceptable today than in the past. One of the reasons for this change is that more women around the world are working outside the home or find themselves the sole support of their families. For these women, the kinds of discrimination discussed in this chapter represent a serious problem that could threaten their ability to provide for their families. A second reason for the growth in opposition to gender inequality has been the efforts made by women and men around the world to draw attention to the inequities and to change the social practices that support them. An assessment of the future of gender inequality can begin with a look at the worldwide feminist movement.

Collective Action and the Feminist Movement: A Global Struggle

The **feminist movement**, or **women's movement**, refers to *the collective activities of individuals, groups,*

and organizations whose goal is the fair and equal treatment of women and men around the world. This movement has not been limited to the United States or even to Western democracies. Certainly, the democratic, egalitarian, and individualist ideologies that emerged in Europe and the United States in the seventeenth and eighteenth centuries have been influential in many parts of the world. Many nations, however, have used their own religious beliefs and traditions, combined with ideas from elsewhere, to justify gender equality. The Arab world, for example, was certainly influenced by European belief and example in the 1800s and early 1900s (Barakat, 1993; Hourani, 1991). Yet, there are many in the Arab world who argue that Islamic traditions themselves support the emancipation of women and that the substantial subordination of women in the Arab world is the result of a misinterpretation of the Koran, the Islamic holy book. For instance, one of the pioneers of Arab feminism, Qassem Amin, published a book in 1899 titled *The Liberation of Women* that called for extending to women most of the same rights that men enjoyed. Anticolonialist movements in places such as Palestine, Egypt, and Iraq mobilized women in support of nationalist causes, and this effort produced a variety of women's organizations that have continued the struggle for gender equality (Najjar, 1992). In 1923, Arab feminists convened at a women's conference in Rome, and in 1944 an Arab women's conference held in Cairo called for women to have the same marital rights as men, including the right to initiate divorce. Even such tradition-bound societies as China and Cuba have an active feminist movement, which has at times gained significant support from the Communist government (O'Kelly & Carney, 1986).

Stirrings of feminist activity could also be found in the United States in the 1800s when women such as Susan B. Anthony and Elizabeth Cady Stanton campaigned for women's right to vote. Finally, in 1920, the Nineteenth Amendment to the U.S. Constitution—the Women's Suffrage Amendment—was passed. In the first half of the twentieth century, the nation became involved in two world wars, which took most of the attention away from women's rights for decades. In the late 1940s, fueled by women's work experience during World War II, women renewed the campaign for equal rights, but they were beaten back by the conservative champions of another movement: the "return to normalcy" (Deckhard, 1979). Women were pressured to quit jobs that they held while men had been at war and to return to the home so that the country could resume "normal" operation again.

In 1963, a well-known advocate of women's rights, Betty Friedan, wrote a book titled *The Feminine Mystique.* She took issue with the assumption that women belong in the home, and her argument became the classic indictment of the presumption that women function best as mothers and homemakers. In 1966, Friedan and other feminists organized the National Organization for Women (NOW). At the time, this body of activist women was regarded as radical in mission, but many observers feel that "its style was actually somewhat conservative, and it stressed working through established legislative channels to achieve rights for women" (Richmond-Abbott, 1992, p. 354).

NOW concentrated much of its effort on passage of the Equal Rights Amendment (ERA), a constitutional amendment that would have banned discrimination based on gender. The ERA stated very simply: "Equality of the rights under the law shall not be denied or abridged by the United States or by any State on account of sex." In 1982, the deadline for ratification passed on the ERA because an insufficient number of states were willing to endorse it. The ERA was viewed by many as the Emancipation Proclamation for women. Proponents of the ERA viewed its defeat as a significant setback for the women's rights movement, and it certainly suggests that sentiment still lingers in the United States against complete equality for women. But again, reality is probably more complex than this. Some people opposed the ERA because they believed that existing legislation protected women adequately and that the amendment was redundant, whereas others thought it would produce unisex bathrooms and sanction homosexual marriages. Some women opposed it because they did not want to give up special privileges that they do receive, such as preference in child custody and divorce award cases. So, people opposed the ERA for many reasons, some of them having little to do with resistance to equality for women (Richmond-Abbott, 1992).

In recent decades, feminists in the United States and around the world have created a global network to push for gender equality, of-ten working through international organizations such as the United Nations (UN) or the independent nongovernmental organizations (NGOs) discussed in Chapter 13. The UN formed its Commission on the Status of Women in 1946 to monitor the treatment of women and promote women's rights in all nations (United Nations, 1991). There followed a series of steps to expand the arenas in which nations were to be encouraged to accord equal treatment to women. In 1952, for example, the Convention on the Political Rights of Women established the mandate that all women should have the right to vote, hold office, and exercise public functions. Later conventions extended equal rights to women in marriage and in choosing divorce. The period from 1975 to 1985 was called the United Nations Decade for Women. A Nairobi World Conference on Women in 1985 approved even more stringent and detailed plans for governments to ensure that women have equal rights in education, training, and employment; to attack negative stereotypes and perceptions of women; to encourage men and women to share domestic responsibilities; and to collect statistics to monitor the situation of women. Further steps were made at the UN Conference on Women in Beijing in 1995. Of course, all member nations of the United Nations are not strongly enthusiastic about the advancement of gender equality, but a host of women's NGOs has maintained pressure on the UN to encourage nations on these issues. The outcome of these pressures has been the achievement of important victories in the quest for gender equality in many nations, although much gender inequality still persists on a global scale.

Current Trends in the United States

In the United States, the push for gender equality has been fueled in part by the growing number of women in the workforce and the increasing number of single-parent, female-headed families. These women find gender discrimination to be an unacceptable barrier to their efforts to support their families and achieve other goals. This analysis of gender stratification will close with a brief assessment of prospects for gender equality in the United States in the near future.

Changes in the Law   Over the past thirty years, a significant amount of legislation has been approved

OTHER WORLDS, *Other Ways*

MEXICO: THIRD-WORLD WOMEN AND THE WORLD ECONOMY

The intersection of a number of forces brought many poor Mexican women into the world export economy in the 1960s and 1970s. One force was the so-called Green Revolution of the 1950s and 1960s, which was an effort to increase agricultural production through the use of higher-yielding plant varieties and improved crop management. For many crops in Mexico, it succeeded. The resulting greater potential for profits on the export markets attracted multinational agribusinesses, which expanded production and concentrated land in their hands. This development undermined the traditional peasant economy that had been based on small plots of land farmed by families. It turned many men into day laborers or migratory workers, mostly to the United States where they could earn much more than was possible in the local Mexican economy.

A second force affecting poor Mexican women was the traditional, patriarchal family culture in Mexico. This culture, especially prominent in rural areas, strictly emphasizes subservience and obedience to the father before marriage and the husband after marriage. Marriage, homemaking, and child rearing are the major aspirations and obligations for women. They are not expected or encouraged to achieve high levels of education nor to pursue well-paying or prestigious jobs that men normally hold.

The collision of the forces of world capitalism and traditional gender relations has resulted in the exploitation of poor women in Mexico by multinational corporations. Because of the scarcity of jobs, especially in rural areas, families consent to sending young, unmarried women out to work. Many of these women are still very much under the control of their fathers, who can pressure them to work and support the family. Especially in rural areas, young women are not completely free to leave their family against the dictates of their father because that would reflect negatively on their reputation and might reduce their opportunities to find an acceptable man to marry. So, patriarchy and gender conspire to make these women prisoners of the local economy. To help their families, they look for work as domestics or preferably in the fields or packing plants, which pay better (Arizpe & Aranda, 1981). The women work for very low wages; the work is often insecure because the plants may be closed for months at a time; and they receive few, if any, fringe benefits. The women are willing to work under these conditions because they hope to marry and thus view the work as a temporary interlude. In addition, little other work is available, and they need work desperately to support their families. The multinational corporations even send female recruiters into the community to convince the women that the work is desirable and to assure their families that the women will be safe and protected in the work environment.

Unions have found this female workforce difficult to organize. Part of the reason is that the Mexican

that contributes to the reduction of gender inequality. Legislation prohibits discrimination in loan eligibility based on gender or marital status. Title VII of the 1964 Civil Rights Act makes illegal any gender discrimination in employment practices. Title IX of the Educational Amendments Act specifies that any educational institution discriminating on the basis of gender will be denied federal aid. Other examples of legislation that helps

women are the Displaced Homemaker Act (which assists women who have divorced but have few skills with which to support themselves) and legal provisions for wives who have been abused by their husbands.

In the past decade, a new idea for reducing the economic inequities suffered by women has emerged, called *comparable worth*. The basic idea is that people whose jobs make equivalent demands

government has historically been hostile to unions because multinationals threaten to go elsewhere if they perceive workers to be at all assertive in demanding better wages or working conditions. Some industries, such as growing strawberries, involve very little capital investment, so it is not much of a loss for such a business to close down in Mexico and move to another nation in response to demands for higher wages. However, the women conspire in ensuring their own weakness because their primary goal is marriage and they see the work as temporary and the unions as too much trouble or as costing them money.

Similar gender exploitation occurs in more urban areas, especially along the northern border with the United States. For at least thirty years, the Mexican government has made efforts to attract international export industries to this area (Bustamante, 1983; Fernandez-Kelly, 1983a; Young, 1993). These factories, called *maquiladoras,* import unfinished products, which are then assembled into automobiles, washing machines, or other finished products for export. One of the major attractions for international corporations is a supply of cheap labor, mostly young unmarried women. The income and benefits in these plants vary, but generally they are not sufficient to support a family. Some *maquiladora* women are a part of households with multiple sources of income, and they survive by combining a number of income streams. Other women live in families where a male, such as a father or brother, is unemployed or underemployed, and these women may be the only source of income in the family. As in the agribusiness, women are

sought for *maquiladora* work because, in the eyes of the business managers, they make better workers. These managers told one researcher that women are sought because they are more compliant and docile; they are also more willing to do monotonous, repetitive, and exhausting factory work; all these factors make them difficult for union leaders to organize. Men, by contrast, are seen by these factory managers as poor workers—restless and rebellious and less willing to work at monotonous or difficult jobs or under poor working conditions. This researcher spelled out the implications of this perception:

> The incorporation of women with acute economic needs into the *maquiladora* industry represents . . . the use of the most vulnerable sector of the population to achieve greater productivity and larger profits. The employment of men to perform similar operations would imply higher wages, better working conditions, and more flexible work schedules, all of which would increase labor costs and reduce capitalist gains. (Fernandez-Kelly, 1983b, p. 219)

So, in both rural and urban settings in Third-World nations, international corporations take advantage of patriarchy, traditional gender relations, and the dependency of women in order to maximize profits and exercise control over labor.

on them and that call for similar skills, education, or responsibility should receive roughly similar pay; in other words, "equal pay for comparable worth" (England, 1992). For example, a judge in Seattle ruled in 1983 that the state government was in violation of Title VII of the 1964 Civil Rights Act because it routinely paid jobs performed mostly by women less than those performed mostly by men. His ruling was based in part on a

comparison of state jobs in terms of "worth points," with points given for such things as knowledge and skills required, mental demands, accountability, and working conditions. Since then, twenty-two states have begun to reassess their pay schedules with these ideas in mind. Similarly, in Ontario, which is one of Canada's largest provinces, the Ontario Pay Equity Act, covering 1.7 million workers in public and private settings,

These women work in poor conditions in a cotton mill in China. Poor women in Third-World nations are often exploited because their culture and multinational corporations give them few opportunities other than low-paying, difficult work.

now demands adherence to the principle of comparable worth (Freudenheim, 1989).

It has been a highly controversial development with opponents arguing that it is impossible really to compare the worth of different jobs and that the free market should determine what people are paid. These opponents argue that if women are dissatisfied with low pay in some jobs, they should compete for the higher-paying jobs. Some even suggest that such interference with market mechanisms would disrupt the whole economic system. Supporters argue that women face significant barriers in the competition for jobs and that comparable worth would help overcome generations of discrimination in the way salaries are set. So far, comparable worth has not substantially altered the position of women in society, but it is likely to become a central issue over the next decade (Aldrich & Buchele, 1986; Peterson, 1990).

Changes in the Workplace As the number of women in the workforce has increased and as they have moved into more traditionally male occupations, some new issues have risen to prominence, especially some more subtle and unexpected barriers to advancement that affect women in the 1990s. One study of male and female managers in large business concerns, for example, found that the women promoted to middle-management positions by male supervisors were the less aggressive, less threatening women who did not rock the boat (Harlan & Weiss, 1981). However, these middle-management positions were dead ends for these women because supervisors wanted more aggressive and dynamic people for top positions. This same research also disputed the belief that sexism in the workplace would decline as more women were employed. They found that resistance to women declines at first, but as the proportion of women passes 15 percent, renewed resistance emerges because men feel their opportunities are being reduced as a result of competition with women. Research has also found that when many women are employed in the same job, that job comes to be defined as a woman's job. Once that happens, the job tends to be devalued, with less pay and a smaller budget than when more men held that position (Baron & Newman, 1990; Reskin & Roos, 1990).

Another emerging reality concerning women in executive management positions is that many who occupy these positions are bailing out of the managerial workforce because trying to combine full-time, demanding careers with being wives and mothers has proved too difficult. A recent study showed that the rate of turnover in management positions is nearly three times higher among women than among men, and many women who take maternity leave do not return to work (Schwartz, 1989). In addition, young women appear to be less drawn to high-powered business careers in the 1990s than they were in the 1970s. For example, women today make up a smaller proportion of applicants to graduate programs in business than six years ago (Cowan, 1992). It seems that women today are less willing to make as many compromises in the family area as some young women did a few years ago.

To alleviate this tension between work and child rearing, it has been suggested that corporations offer women two career tracks. One, called *career-primary*, would involve the conventional expectations placed on male employees: career comes first, no time out for personal reasons, and work on nights and weekends if corporate needs demand it. The second track, called *career-and-family* or the *mommy track*, would allow women to pursue careers while also devoting themselves to their families. For example, maternity leave would not be frowned on and excessive demands would not be placed on the women's free time. Critics of such proposals argue that those in the career-and-family track would be discriminated against in any event through smaller pay increases or reduced opportunity for promotion. In fact, research shows that women who interrupt their careers for family reasons, such as raising children, never catch up, in terms of income or promotions, to their female counterparts who stay on the job

(Jacobsen & Levin, 1992). Apparently, their employers think they are not as serious about or as committed to their jobs. So, the career-and-family track would likely produce the same old outcome: women who choose to have children would be discriminated against because they did not follow the male model of career development.

Despite this difficulty we can predict that women will continue to join the workforce in even larger numbers. Substantial improvement is already observable. Nearly one-third of the small businesses in the United States today belong to women, up from 23 percent in the early 1980s. Some labor experts project that this figure may hit 40 percent by the year 2000 (O'Hare & Larson, 1991). Keep in mind that these numbers do not include large corporations, where it is difficult to determine ownership, and that most women's businesses are small. Nonetheless, the growth has been impressive, and credit and capital are now more available to women who wish to start or expand a business. In addition, research shows that college-educated women are becoming much more like their male counterparts in terms of the emphasis they place on work as being essential to a person's life and happiness (Fiorentine, 1988).

As women become more integrated into the workforce, mechanisms are developing to overcome some of the barriers that women have faced in the past. For example, women are excluded from fewer of the social and business networks that can assist one in a career or business. Because of court challenges based on antidiscrimination legislation, women have gained access to some chapters of such organizations as Rotary, the Lions Club, and the Kiwanis where business people often gather. And it makes a big difference to success in business. As one businesswoman put it after she joined Rotary, "Suddenly I was having lunch every week with all the movers and shakers in town. Now they think of me when business opportunities come up" (quoted in Zane, 1991, p. 35). In addition, new networks have emerged to help women. For example, WomenVenture is a nationwide organization that offers seminars and workshops to women on how to start or expand a business, as well as financial backing to 2,500 businesswomen each year. Such organizations and contacts can make the difference between advancement and stagnation in one's business or

Since the Anita Hill–Clarence Thomas episode, the climate in the workplace certainly seems to have changed in relation to how people of different genders treat one another. Both men and women seem more willing to report episodes of sexual harassment and assault. Yet, such disturbing behaviors are still widespread. In fact, in 1992, it came out that a number of women serving in the military in Saudi Arabia and Iraq during the Gulf War were subjected to sexual assault—not by the enemy but by their fellow soldiers. A significant contribution that applied sociologists have made to alleviating this problem is evaluation of its extent and nature. For example, in response to concerns about such problems in the military, Melanie Martindale, working for the Secretary of Defense, conducted a survey on sexual assault and harassment in all branches of the military. Her report, released in 1991, concluded that "the majority of women (64%) and 17 percent of men reported experiencing some form of sexual harassment ranging from jokes to actual assault while on duty" (Martindale, 1991, p. 201). Five percent of women in the military reported that someone raped them or attempted to rape them during the preceding year.

Part of the difficulty with sexual harassment is achieving consensus about what behaviors constitute harassment. Applied sociologists recognize that this difficulty is in part a cultural conflict resting on the fact that men and women tend to attach different meanings to some behaviors. Most men and women agree that demanding sexual favors as a condition of employment or promotion is wrong. However, the Equal Employment Opportunity Commission also defines as harassment behaviors that create a "hostile" environment that makes it more difficult for people to do their job. Thus, repeated sexual advances by a coworker, even if not linked to employment or promotion, could constitute harassment because they are disturbing to the woman and create an environment in which it is difficult for her to work.

This point is where men's and women's perceptions sometimes differ. Many men see such behaviors as relatively harmless and claim they would even be flattered if they were the recipients of such actions by coworkers. Most women, by contrast, find such behaviors insulting, offensive, and even frightening when an economically or socially vulnerable woman sees an implied threat in the advance. Therefore, such behaviors do create a hostile atmosphere in many women's minds. That is why, during the Anita Hill–Clarence Thomas confrontation, we repeatedly heard women exclaim about men: they just don't get it. In other words, men fail to understand why women find such behaviors offensive, demeaning, and maybe even frightening.

With an understanding of social structure, social interaction, and cultural values and norms, applied sociologists can mediate conflicts of this sort, especially when a problem is created or aggravated by a lack of understanding on one side or the other (Miller, 1991). Mediation could be a lengthy process, but it basically involves exercises that give both men and women a better perspective on women's views of these issues. The exercises might be as simple as the

career. The opportunities for advancement for women in the 1990s will undoubtedly improve with the further availability of such supports for women. However, thousands of clubs and organizations still do not admit women because there are no state or local antidiscrimination laws to force them to do so. In fact, as noted earlier, former Presidents Ronald Reagan and George Bush belong to an elite businessmen's social club, the Bohemian Club, which refuses to admit women.

Sexual harassment and assault are serious problems that women face in the workplace, making work for them more difficult and demeaning and in extreme cases impossible. As Applying Sociology: Sexual Assault, Sexual Harassment, and the Empowerment of Women shows, some important strides have been made in overcoming this problem.

The Changing Face of Politics One image from the Anita Hill–Clarence Thomas confrontation in

following short test to help decide whether a remark or a behavior is appropriate (Petrocelli & Repa, 1992):

1. Would you say or do the same thing in front of your spouse?
2. How would you feel if the same remarks or behavior were directed at your mother, sister, wife, or daughter?
3. How would you feel if a man made the same remarks or took the same actions toward you?

If your reaction to any one of these questions is negative, then the remark or behavior might well be seen as inappropriate harassment by a female coworker.

Applied sociologists also recognize that gender socialization can make women vulnerable to assault and exploitation. As Janet Mancini Billson and Estelle Disch (1991, p. 327) put it:

> Women traditionally have been raised to value nurturance, kindness, patience, being "nice," not making waves, being attractive, supportive, caring, understanding, tolerant, and responsible to and for others. This socialization blueprint can make it difficult for women to be confrontive or demanding; to feel comfortable in choosing to take care of self first; or to be honest and forthright.

With this recognition in mind, sociological practitioners work toward the empowerment of women, assisting them in acquiring the personal and social resources that can make them more powerful and less vulnerable in their relations with others. Part of this process involves gaining the educational qualifications and occupational skills that make people less economically dependent on others. Women are less likely to be harassed if they are the boss rather than the subordinate. Another part of this empowerment is for women to learn to view themselves as autonomous, powerful, and directive. In other words, empowerment for women means breaking through the culture of dependency and taking control of their lives.

Finally, sociological consultants work with employers to change the structure of the work environment so that sexual harassment and assault are less likely. Among the structural changes that have proven effective are the following: having a written and publicized policy against such actions, vigorously enforcing the policy, educating employees about what constitutes harassment and how to file a complaint about it, and providing sincere and significant top-management support for the policy (Powell, 1993; Webb, 1991). Such steps should make the workplace of the 1990s a much more hospitable one for women. However, as noted in Chapter 7, discrimination, as well as harassment, tends to rear its head when competition between groups grows fierce. As more women enter the workforce and take jobs traditionally held by men, harassment may emerge as a response to threatened losses. So continued vigilance may be necessary to control this problem.

1991 was unforgettable: A black woman confronting a panel of the all-white, all-male faces of the members of the Senate Judiciary Committee. It brought into stark reality the truth that, although women make up 51 percent of the populace, very few of them are among elected representatives at the national level. Of the 100 senators, the number of women among them fluctuated from a low of none to a high of 2 between 1970 and 1992, rising to 10 in the 1996 election (see Figure 8.3). However, this change hides some dramatic gains that women have made in politics over the past few decades. In 1970, only 25 women ran for seats in the U.S. House of Representatives; by 1992 this had increased six times, to 150 women. Although only 11 percent of the representatives in 1997 were women, that is three times greater than the 3 to 4 percent female representation of the 1970s. Gains have been especially impressive at the state and local levels. Twenty years

FIGURE 8.3 Women in the U.S. Senate and House of Representatives, as a Percentage of Each Body, 1971–1997 *Note:* From *Statistical Abstract of the United States, 1982–1983* (p. 485) by U.S. Bureau of the Census, 1982, Washington, DC: U.S. Government Printing Office; *Statistical Abstract of the United States, 1995* (p. 281) by U.S. Bureau of the Census, 1995, Washington, DC: U.S. Government Printing Office.

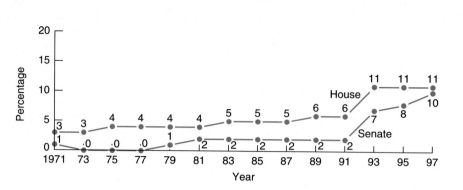

ago, women made up less than 5 percent of all state legislators, compared with 18 percent today. Twenty years ago, a paltry 1 percent of the mayors of cities of more than thirty thousand people in the United States were women; today it is 17 percent. Although women are still far underrepresented in politics, they are beginning to move into more powerful and nationwide political positions. It takes time to get significant numbers of women entrenched in the political system to the point where they can make a run for a Senate seat. We will likely see more of women in politics in the future.

Masculine, Feminine, or Human?

Some of the problems surrounding gender inequality may arise in part because of the oversimplified view that people tend to have of gender, seeing things as either male or female, but not both. In reality, each individual can be seen as a combination of both feminine and masculine characteristics. In fact, masculinity and femininity may not be polar opposites but rather two independent sets of characteristics. So, for example, some very feminine women may have few masculine characteristics, whereas other very feminine women might have many masculine traits. In fact, the word **androgyny** (from the Greek *andro,* "male," and *gyn,* "female") has been coined to describe *a condition where male and female characteristics are not rigidly assigned and there is a blending of the traits, attitudes, and roles of both sexes.* From this perspective, people explore a broad range of gender-

role possibilities and choose emotions and behaviors without regard to gender stereotypes. This perspective does not mean that gender distinctions disappear but that one's biological sex becomes a less rigid determinant of which masculine and feminine traits a particular individual will exhibit. As a result, people can be more flexible in their role-playing and express themselves in a variety of ways other than the traditionally masculine or feminine ways. The trends toward gender equality discussed in this chapter may make more of this flexibility possible in the future. People may be more free to choose roles or tasks at which they are most competent and express emotions or attitudes with which they feel most comfortable—all without regard to whether they will be ridiculed for choosing the "wrong" roles or emotions for their gender.

Summary

1. Gender is an ascribed and a master status. The text examines four different views of gender as an element of social differentiation: the biological perspective along with the three sociological perspectives.

2. *Male* and *female* are sex-related terms; *gender* refers to learned behavior involving how we are expected to act as males and females in society. One of the key issues in analyzing gender inequality is how we learn to be masculine and feminine and how this learning contributes to gender differentiation and inequality. This learning occurs through the socialization process, with three major agencies of socialization being primarily responsible: the family, the schools, and the media.

3. Gender inequality is widespread in the United States. Women occupy a subordinate position in comparison to men on virtually every dimension of socioeconomic status. Discrimination on the basis of gender is not confined to education, occupation, and income. Women also experience unequal treatment in the military and before the courts. Gender inequality also affects men when they are discouraged from pursuing certain kinds of jobs and can be drafted into the military when no equivalent service is asked of women.

4. Women around the globe experience some of the same gender inequalities that women in the United States confront, in such areas as work, education, political participation, and family support. Women in some nations, however, are much better off than women in other nations.

5. Feminist movements can be found in many nations, including the United States, and they have been a significant force in expanding rights and opportunities for women. A global network of such feminist organizations now exists, often working through international organizations such as the United Nations.

6. In the United States, there have been important changes in the law as it relates to gender equality and in the workplace, as more women join the labor force. The presence of women in politics has also increased and will likely continue to do so.

STUDY AND Review

Key Terms

androgyny

feminist movement

gender

sex

sexism

women's movement

Multiple-Choice Questions

1. Regarding biological differences between men and women, the text draws which of the following conclusions?
   a. The differences are actually larger than was once thought.
   b. The differences refer to averages that ignore the significant overlap between the sexes.
   c. Relatively little human behavior is learned through socialization.
   d. There has not been much research on the differences between the sexes.

2. Which of the following conclusions derives from what Margaret Mead found among the three tribes she studied in New Guinea?
   a. Gender-role behavior is produced mostly by biology.
   b. Biological determinism is more powerful than cultural determinism
   c. The media shapes gender-role behavior by providing young boys and girls with models to imitate.
   d. Male dominance is a powerful force in societies.

3. Which of these statements would be most consistent with the conflict perspective?
   a. The gender-role division of labor is most functional when it is consistent with the needs of society.
   b. Gender differentiation is a battleground for the struggle over scarce resources.
   c. Beliefs about gender inequality are maintained and reinforced through patterns of social interaction.
   d. Innate biological differences between men and women shape the contributions each can make to society.

4. Research on conversational styles supports the conclusion that
   a. men talk more than women in mixed-sex conversations.
   b. women talk more than men in mixed-sex conversations.
   c. women interrupt more than men in mixed-sex conversations.
   d. both a and c are supported.
   e. both b and c are supported.

5. Regarding the socialization of children, the text concludes that
   a. boys are more prominent in girl's games than girls are in boy's games.
   b. most elementary school teachers treat boy students and girl students the same.
   c. in childhood, male activities tend to be more valued than female activities.
   d. children's books have eliminated most stereotyped images of the sexes.

6. Among which of the following groups do a higher percentage of women graduate from college in the United States than the percentage among men?
   a. The elderly.
   b. Whites.
   c. Hispanic Americans.
   d. The poor.
   e. African Americans.

7. Classical economic theory claims that wages are determined by
   a. the competitive forces of supply and demand.
   b. how much power different groups of workers possess.
   c. cultural stereotypes of what different groups of workers are worth.
   d. both a and b.
   e. a, b, and c.

8. Which of the following is *not* true regarding the gender inequalities suffered by males in the United States today?
   a. Men but not women must register for the military draft.
   b. More women attend law school than do men.
   c. Men are sometimes charged more for automobile insurance than are women.
   d. Socially imposed expectations limit the freedom of men to choose stereotypically female occupations.

9. Which of the following is true regarding social policy relating to gender equality in the United States today?
   a. Comparable worth has been declared unconstitutional.
   b. The 1964 Civil Rights Act has been repealed.
   c. The Equal Rights Amendment has not been approved.
   d. Men and women have identical opportunities in the military.

10. A situation where male and female characteristics are not rigidly assigned, but instead there is a blending of the traits of both sexes, is called
    a. a master status.
    b. comparable worth.
    c. sexism.
    d. androgyny.
    e. instrumental tasks.

True/False Questions

1. Gender is an ascribed status, but it is not a master status.

2. The text concludes that there are no biological differences between men and women that have any social significance.

3. The functionalist perspective argues that it is more functional in industrial societies to assign tasks to people on the basis of individual abilities rather than ascribed characteristics.

4. Stereotyped views of gender roles have been largely eliminated in children's textbooks but can still be found in college-level textbooks.

5. The group most affected by the portrayal of gender roles on television are teenage boys.

6. There is a higher proportion of college graduates among women today than among men.

7. The percentage of secretaries who are men is virtually unchanged over the past twenty years.

8. One argument that is made for not allowing women into combat units in the military is that their presence would interfere with the male bonding that is important to combat success.

9. The quest for gender equality today is a global movement rather than being limited to western nations or industrial nations.

10. According to the text, androgyny is a thing of the past.

Fill-In Questions

1. _____ is an ideology based on the belief that one gender is superior to and should dominate the other gender.

2. Gender is a(n) _____ because it is a central determinant of how people view themselves and how others respond to them.

3. Building a house or managing the activities of a work team are tasks that sociologists call _____ tasks.

4. The study of the conversational styles of men and women provides evidence for the _____ perspective.

5. The learned behavior involving how we are expected to act as males and females in society is referred to by sociologists as _____ .

6. The three main dimensions of socioeconomic status are education, _____ , and _____ .

7. The employment position that has the highest percentage of jobs held by women is _____ .

8. Two of the forces affecting poor Mexican women, as mentioned in Other Worlds, Other Ways, are _____ and _____ .

9. The idea that people whose jobs make equivalent demands on them should receive roughly similar pay is called _____ .

10. The two career tracks that some have proposed for women to choose between are _____ and _____ .

Matching Questions

_____ 1. longhouse
_____ 2. constitutional amendment banning gender discrimination
_____ 3. Arapesh
_____ 4. maintaining harmony in a family
_____ 5. Rosie the Riveter
_____ 6. Anita Hill
_____ 7. blending of traits of both sexes
_____ 8. WomenVenture
_____ 9. prohibits gender discrimination in education
_____ 10. myth of masculinity

A. ERA
B. expressive task
C. sexual harassment
D. androgyny
E. Huron Indian social unit
F. Title IX of the Educational Amendments Act
G. stereotypes about men
H. New Guinea tribe
I. World War II worker
J. helps women in business

Essay Questions

1. What conclusions does the text draw regarding the impact of biological differences between men and women on social behavior?

2. Describe the gender roles that Margaret Mead found among the three New Guinea tribes that she visited. What important points do we learn from these groups?

3. According to the conflict perspective, what are the reasons for sex stratification in society?

4. What does research show about the impact of gender on conversational styles? What is the importance of these gender differences? How do they relate to the interactionist perspective?

5. Describe the ways in which schools and the media contribute to the problem of gender inequality.

6. Describe the impact of gender and race on people's educational opportunities and accomplishments in the United States.

7. What are the arguments for and against women serving in combat positions in the military?

8. Describe the kinds of gender inequality that confront women in nations around the globe.

9. What are some ways to reduce levels of sexual harassment in the workplace?

10. What changes have occurred in the workplace in the United States in the past thirty years as far as gender inequality is concerned?

Answers

Multiple-Choice

1. B;   **2.** D;   **3.** B;   **4.** A;   **5.** C;   **6.** E;   **7.** A;   **8.** B;
9. C;   **10.** D

True/False

1. F;   **2.** F;   **3.** T;   **4.** F;   **5.** F;   **6.** F;   **7.** T;   **8.** T;
9. T;   **10.** F

Fill-In

1. sexism
2. master status
3. instrumental
4. interactionist
5. gender
6. occupation, income
7. secretaries
8. Green Revolution, patriarchal family, traditional gender roles
9. comparable worth
10. career-primary, career-and-family or mommy track

Matching

1. E;   **2.** A;   **3.** H;   **4.** B;   **5.** I;   **6.** C;   **7.** D;   **8.** J;
9. F;   **10.** G

For Further Reading

Billson, Janet Mancini. (1995). *Keepers of the culture: The power of tradition in women's lives.* New York: Lexington Books. This sociologist interviewed women of many cultures across Canada—Iroquois, Inuit, Jamaican, Ukrainian, and others—who are confronting social change. The book describes the entrenched and pervasive sexism and discrimination that these women face but also explores sources of empowerment for them.

Bonvillain, Nancy. (1995). *Women and men: Cultural constructs of gender.* Englewood Cliffs, NJ: Prentice Hall. This enlightening book explores issues of gender and gender inequality in many cultures around the globe and in societies at many different levels of development, from hunter-gatherers to industrialists. It provides a complete and sophisticated view of gender in society.

Campbell, Anne. (1993). *Men, women, and aggression.* New York: Basic Books. This provocative book takes the position that high levels of aggression in males is not a function of biology but of learning. Men learn while growing up to use aggression as a tool to get their way whereas women don't learn this lesson.

Doyle, James A. (1995). *The male experience* (3rd ed.). Madison, WI: Brown & Benchmark. Whereas most of this chapter has focused on the experience of women, it is important to focus on men's experience also. This book does this in terms of gender socialization, gender inequalities, and historical and cross-cultural comparisons focusing specifically on men.

Faludi, Susan. (1991). *Backlash: The undeclared war against American women.* New York: Crown. This journalist marshals evidence to support the argument that a significant backlash against women's equality has emerged in the United States. She argues that some people, especially men, would like to limit, and maybe even roll back, some of the gains that have been made.

Orenstein, Peggy. (1994). *Schoolgirls: Young women, self-esteem, and the confidence gap.* New York: Doubleday. By looking in depth at the lives of girls at two schools, this book documents the decline in self-esteem and self-confidence that many girls experience as they go through adolescence.

Paludi, Michele A. (Ed.). (1990). *Ivory power: Sexual harassment on campus.* Albany: State University of New York Press. This book documents the extent of sexual harassment of college students and college faculty and discusses why it occurs. It also provides a blueprint for what to do about it.

Reskin, Barbara, & Padavic, Irene. (1994). *Women and men at work.* Thousand Oaks, CA: Pine Forge Press. This book provides a detailed analysis of how men and women fare in the workplace. It is enlightening and includes some material from other cultures and from the minority experience.

Sanday, Peggy Reeve. (1990). *Fraternity gang rape: Sex, brotherhood, and privilege on campus.* New York: New York University Press. Rape may be the ultimate form of control that men exercise over women. This book documents how college women are controlled by it and some of the social and cultural dynamics that encourage gang rape on campus.

Witt, Linda, Paget, Karen M., & Matthews, Glenna. (1994). *Running as a woman: Gender and power in American politics.* New York: Free Press. This book, authored by a political scientist, a historian, and a journalist, is an intriguing look at how women over the years have managed to make inroads into the male-dominated political system. Looking at both the past and the present, it explores strategies, tactics, and possibilities for the future.

Wolf, Naomi. (1991). *The beauty myth: How images of beauty are used against women.* New York: Morrow. This is an intriguing book about how Western culture encourages a conception of beauty that tends to coerce women into doing things that are not in their best interests. It is a thoughtful illustration of how cultures can exercise social control in subtle and often unrecognized ways.

Wood, Julia T. (1994). *Gendered lives: Communication, gender, and culture.* Belmont, CA: Wadsworth. This book provides a comprehensive overview of the multitude of ways that gender pervades our lives and profoundly shapes our thoughts, feelings, and behaviors—often in ways that we are totally unaware of.

PART FOUR

Social Institutions

The chapters in Part Four focus on social institutions—the clusters of statuses, roles, and groups that work together to meet certain needs of society. The particular institutions covered are the family, health care, religion, education, politics, and the economy.

CHAPTER

NINE Family and Human Sexuality

The Trobriand Islands are a part of Melanesia in the South Pacific, near New Guinea. The anthropologist Bronislaw Malinowski (1929) lived there in the early part of the twentieth century and found a family system that was quite different from that in the West. Trobrianders, for example, traced their inheritance through the mother's line rather than the father's (a matrilineal descent system), and a married couple lived with the wife's relatives rather than the husband's (a matrilocal system). Consequently, the role of the Trobriand father was quite different from what people in the United States are used to: The father was neither the primary authority over his children nor their major disciplinarian. Nor was he the major provider of food and other supports to his wife and children. In Trobriand society, the wife's brother performed both of these functions. This convention is very different from families in most Western societies in which paternal authority is usually dominant and the father is at the center of, or at least very important in, his own household. The Trobriand father was almost like a visitor—in some cases, almost a stranger—in his wife's household. The strongest kinship bond in this matrilineal society was that between sister and brother rather than that between husband and wife.

Trobriand sexual practices also were quite different from those in the United States. Premarital sexual intercourse was widely accepted and widely practiced, as is true of many tribal societies, especially in the Pacific. In fact, one anthropological estimate is that well over one-third of human cultures allowed unrestricted premarital sexual activity (Murdock, 1967). For unmarried Trobrianders, sex was common and without guilt. Nevertheless, despite this tolerance, bearing children outside marriage was strongly frowned on, and women who became pregnant were expected to marry. If a woman had a child without marrying, both she and the child were penalized and stigmatized. In fact, births outside marriage were rare among the Trobrianders.

Trobriand sexual and marital practices led Malinowski to argue that the key function of the family as a social institution is to provide children with a socially or legally approved father. In fact, Malinowski's theory was that the family's primary defining element is the legitimation of childbearing. In other words, the relationship between a parent and a child is not merely biological; it is also social and receives recognition or approbation from others depending on how the relationship is established. Marriage was not the social approval of sex between two Trobrianders, since premarital sexuality flourished; rather marriage was the official recognition of and control over childbearing.

Malinowski's theory has been a controversial one in anthropology and sociology. If it is true, what do we make of the many societies in which one-half or more of births are to unmarried mothers? Such birthrates outside marriage are found, for example, in some Caribbean nations as well as

among some groups in the United States today. Clearly, issues of family and human sexuality are more complicated than Malinowski thought.

The example of the Trobriand Islanders, however, makes an important point: Human societies exhibit diverse family forms and sexual practices. In fact, there is some debate over exactly what constitutes a family. Does a family require children, as Malinowski suggests? Must two people be married in order to create a family? Do they even have to be of the opposite sex? Some employers today extend health and life insurance benefits to the unmarried domestic partners of their employees, including gay and lesbian couples. So, what had been defined as "family" benefits in the past are now sometimes extended to those in living arrangements that some would not consider families at all. This situation raises the question of what a family is, and many people have strong feelings about it. In fact, there is a great deal of ethnocentrism surrounding this question, as people claim that their version of the family is the only version possible or permissible. One of the goals of this chapter will be to describe and explain some of the diversity found in family forms.

Trobriand society also illustrates the intimate link between family and human sexuality. Sex and childbearing are related, and family institutions in all societies play a role in regulating both. That is why they are addressed in a single chapter.

Beginning with this chapter, the book returns to a topic introduced in Chapter 2, the importance of social institutions in understanding society. A *social institution* is a persistent and stable cluster of values, statuses, roles, groups, and organizations that function together to meet some basic needs of society that affect its survival. This chapter focuses on the institution of *family*. The following four chapters address *heath-care* institutions (coping with problems of physical and mental health), *religion* (providing answers of ultimate meaning), *education* (learning necessary values and skills), and *politics and the economy* (the production and distribution of goods and services as well as collective power). This list of societal needs, of course, could be much longer, but it will serve as an adequate introduction to the role of social institutions and how they operate. The fact that this book devotes five chapters to the topic demonstrates the central importance of social institutions in the sociological analysis of societies.

Myths FACTS

ABOUT THE FAMILY AND HUMAN SEXUALITY

Myth Unhappy marriages should be maintained when children are involved—"for the sake of the children."

FACT Repeated investigations of divorce and its effects on children have failed to demonstrate the psychological benefits to children of maintaining an unhappy marriage. It may, in fact, be more damaging than divorce itself.

Myth Divorce is a modern phenomenon and was relatively unheard of in premodern societies.

FACT Not only did divorce exist in primitive societies, but it was sometimes easier to obtain and more common than in the United States today.

Myth Teenage pregnancies are on the rise in all modern societies because of the decline in traditional values and the rise in sexual promiscuity.

FACT The United States has many more teenage pregnancies than does any other industrial nation. In societies where effective sex education programs and contraceptives are available to teens, the rate of such pregnancies is two to three times lower than in the United States.

Myth Childbirth outside marriage and declining family sizes are unique to the wealthy industrial nations and come from the affluent lifestyle in those nations.

FACT These trends are found in many nations around the world, including Third-World countries, and are the result of industrialization and modernization rather than affluence.

Family and Kinship in Cross-Cultural Perspective

You should be able to discuss the various social rules that govern practices related to descent, marriage, authority, family size, and mate selection.

The family is the oldest and most fundamental of all social institutions. In fact, the family was at one time the center of the political, economic, educational, and religious activities that will be discussed as separate social institutions in the next four chapters. However, the position of the family in society has changed considerably over time. Some people have even predicted the demise of the family as we know it, pointing to divorce, children born to unmarried women, and premarital sexual activity as evidence. Certainly many controversial issues surround the family in modern society, but before addressing these, we need to know what the family *is* and how it functions in society. The **family** is a *social institution based on kinship that functions to replace members of society and to nurture them.* This seemingly straightforward definition hides considerable complexity and controversy.

Every society has rules or norms that shape family and kin relationships, and the family can take many different forms depending on which particular combination of rules develops in a given society. Once the rules are established, people are socialized to accept their society's form of the family as "natural." In fact, the rules are usually embodied in central cultural values that are internalized, the violation of which is considered unthinkable. Some of the ways these rules can vary are described in this section.

Rules of Descent

All societies have rules of kinship and descent that define the rights of family members and their responsibilities toward one another. These standards establish who is obliged to help in emergencies, who will supervise ceremonies surrounding such events as marriage and death, and who will inherit authority when a powerful family member dies. The term **kin** refers to *people who are related to one another through common ancestry, marriage, or social agreement.* **Consanguineal kin** are *people who are biologically related to one another, such as brothers and sisters or parents and their children.* **Affinal kin** are *people who are related by virtue of a marriage bond, such as husband and wife or parents-in-law.* Many societies also recognize as kin some people who are related neither consanguineally nor affinally. For example, it is common in many societies for a person who is not related to a particular kin group to be placed in the role of guardian of a child and accorded some of the privileges of kinship. In Mexico and other Hispanic cultures, this guardianship takes the form of *compadrazgo,* or "co-parenthood." The co-parent develops close social ties with the family and is viewed as a kind of brother or sister to the parents of the child. He or she would assume child-rearing duties if anything happened to the parents (Slonim, 1991).

Societies differ from one another in terms of whether descent is reckoned through the male or female line. In **patrilineal descent systems,** which are the most common, *descent is determined by the male line, and children belong to the kin group of their father.* In patrilineal societies, a person would not inherit anything from his mother's parents or brothers and sisters because they would be affiliated with another kinship group. In a **matrilineal descent system,** *descent is determined through the female line, and children belong to the kin group of their mother.* In the United States, there is a **bilateral descent system** in which *descent is reckoned more or less equally through both male and female lines.* The boundaries of kin groups in the United States tend to be rather vague, depending on how close one feels to particular consanguineal or affinal kin. In most patrilineal and matrilineal systems, by contrast, membership in kin groups and the resulting social obligations are quite clearly defined.

Rules of Marriage

Every society also has rules that govern who can marry whom. Virtually all societies, for example, have an incest taboo that prohibits marriage or sexual contact between close relatives such as brothers and sisters or parents and their children (Middleton, 1962). In only a few rare instances, such as among the royal families of ancient Egypt and Hawaii, has incest ever been considered socially acceptable. Societies also regulate whom people are permitted to marry beyond their close kin. Some societies, for example, have *rules of* **exogamy,** *which require that people choose a mate outside of their own social group or community.* One benefit of exogamous rules is that alliances can be created between families or villages through intermarriage. At the opposite extreme are *rules of* **endogamy,** *which require marriage within a particular group or community.* In the United States, a form of endogamy has at times been practiced in which marriages across racial lines in particular are discouraged. During the 1950s, for example, more than thirty states prohibited marriage between whites and blacks. In some jurisdictions, laws made it illegal for a white person to marry an American Indian, Chinese, Mexican, Hindu, Melanesian, or Japanese. It wasn't until 1967 that the U.S. Supreme Court ruled the last such miscegenation law unconstitutional (Collins & Coltrane, 1991).

Societies also regulate the number of spouses that a person may have. People in the United States tend to think of **monogamy,** or *marriage between one man and one woman at a time,* as the normal or "civilized" marriage. Yet only about one-quarter of human societies are strictly monogamous (Coult & Habenstein, 1965). In the other societies, **polygamy** is practiced, in which *people can have more than one spouse at a time.* One form of polygamy is **polygyny,** *in which a husband can have more than one wife.* It is a common form of marriage, being the preferred arrangement in parts of Africa, the Middle East, and Asia. Polygyny tends to arise in societies where women are regarded as social or economic assets. Among the Siwai of the South Pacific, for example, status is conferred on men by giving feasts at which roast pig is the main food. Because it is Siwai women who are responsible for cultivating the food to feed pigs, a man with many wives is better equipped to host large feasts (Oliver, 1955). Polygyny is also found in societies where many males are killed in warfare, creating an imbalance in the sex ratio. A second form of polygamy is **polyandry,** *in which a woman can marry more than one man at a time.* Among the Tibetans and the Toda of India, for example, a woman who marries a particular man is considered the wife of all that man's brothers—even brothers who have not yet been born at the time of the marriage (Goldstein, 1971). Among the Toda, fatherhood is not determined by biological paternity; it is conferred on one of the husbands during the wife's seventh month of pregnancy. Polyandry is much less common than polygyny. In societies where female infanticide is practiced, resulting in a shortage of females, polyandry makes it possible for all males to marry.

Rules of Authority

All societies have rules that determine who should wield power and authority in families. In **patriarchal families,** by far the most common, *males are dominant in regulating political and economic decision making.* There is a strong patriarchal trend in families throughout Western civilization, and religious teachings in the Bible and the Koran strongly endorse male dominance. Even today, there are strong patriarchal tendencies in many families in the United States, such as those in the upper classes. Families such as the Kennedys, the Hunts, and the Rockefellers are run largely by males. **Matriarchal families,** *in which women are dominant in power and authority,* are far less common. In fact, some anthropologists argue that no true matriarchies can be found, since even in societies where women gain considerable authority and power, it is shared with men. Among the Huron Indians discussed in the beginning of Chapter 8, and among the Iroquois, for instance, women had the sole authority to appoint men to leadership positions, such as clan leader, but the women could not hold those positions themselves (Farb, 1978).

Although patriarchal trends still exist in modern societies, an **egalitarian family** appears to be emerging *in which husbands and wives share more equally in power and authority.* Especially as women become more economically independent, it is likely that they will continue to gain a more equal say in family matters. Although this egalitarianism may become more common in the future, both patriarchal and matriarchal families will persist in the United States, in some cases because a spouse has left the family, in others because subcultural values dictate that one of these family forms is preferable.

Power and authority relations in families also determine residence patterns. Patriarchal families are also likely to be **patrilocal,** with *the married couple living with or near the husband's family.* Matriarchal families are likely to be **matrilocal,** that is, *living with or near the wife's family.* Although some matrilocal and patrilocal tendencies can be found in the United States, many couples form **neolocal families,** where *residence is separate from the families of either wife or husband.*

Size of Family Unit

Because kin groups can be quite extensive, involving hundreds of people, societies provide rules to regulate which of their members will live and work closely together as a cooperative unit. Thus the size of a typical family unit is normally quite a bit smaller than the kin group. An **extended family** consists of *three or more generations of people who live together or in close proximity and whose lives and livelihoods are closely intertwined* (Nimkoff, 1965). Extended families are often large and usually involve a strong sense of kinship obligation. Family members are expected to help other family members and to remain loyal to the family. Extended families are usually dominated by males, often the eldest male, and tasks are divided along age and sex lines. Extended families are more common in preindustrial than industrial societies for reasons that will be discussed shortly. A **nuclear family** consists of *a married couple and their offspring.* In contrast to extended families, nuclear families are small and less likely to be male dominated.

Families in modern societies are sufficiently complex that many of them cannot be easily classified as either extended or nuclear. Some, for example, can be considered **modified extended families,** *in which elaborate networks of visitation and support remain though each nuclear unit lives separately.* Another type is the **reconstituted family,** or **blended family,** which refers to *a family based on kinship ties that accumulate as a consequence of divorces and remarriages* (Cherlin & Furstenberg, 1994; Chilman, Nunnally, & Cox, 1988). These families involve relationships that are more complex than those of the standard nuclear family. For example, a child may live in a family with a full-blood sibling, a half-blood sibling, and an affinal sibling. The same child may have a "real" father and mother as

This seven-year-old girl and eleven-year-old boy were just married in India. Such arranged marriages can still be found in India and other nations around the world.

well as stepfather or stepmother, and three sets of grandparents. Mothers and fathers may have both biological children and adopted children. Such arrangements, with their attendant complex kinship and legal linkages, can create complications and tensions that are less likely in traditional nuclear or extended-family arrangements (Johnson, Klee, & Schmidt, 1988). For example, in many blended families there is some degree of tension over whether the biological parents should retain the major allegiance of and authority over their children, or whether a stepparent, who has daily control over the child, should predominate.

Mate Selection and Marriage Transactions

Societies also have rules regarding the process of choosing a mate and getting married. For example, the mate selection process can vary from arranged marriages at one extreme to participant-run romances at the other.

In preindustrial societies, in which the extended family and kinship were core social institutions, parents played a key role in deciding when and to whom their children would marry. Because the family in these societies was the major institution performing important societal functions, it is not surprising that marital decisions were not left to whim or fancy. In many of these societies, *arranged marriages* occurred in which parents would select marriage partners for their children, sometimes shortly after their birth. The selection was based on what was considered best for the family, and the prospective marriage partners had little other choice. Such arranged marriages are still common in India and some other societies, and their members generally accept this practice as the wisest way to make marital choices.

A modified form of arranged marriage existed in the preindustrial United States, with young people having some choice in selecting a marriage partner but with parents still retaining substantial control over the ultimate decision. Courtship was common, but it occurred under the ever watchful eyes of parents and other elders in the community. It was a *parent-run* courtship process: Young men and women were allowed to choose from among a pool of partners who were considered acceptable by their parents but were strongly discouraged from going outside that pool (Gordon, 1978a).

In modern industrial societies, the selection of marital partners is based primarily on the individual desires of the prospective mates. Parents can and do play a role in this process, but their influence is typically secondary and often no more important than the suggestions of a close friend. This courtship process, then, is more *participant run,* with romantic love as a primary factor drawing couples toward marriage. One reason for this declining role of parents over the years is that kinship is less important in modern societies, and one's kin, including one's parents, have considerably less stake in who marries whom. A second reason is that children have a greater degree of economic independence from their parents in industrial societies, and parents therefore have less leverage with which to demand a say in the choice of a marriage partner. In the past, parents could withhold economic support from a couple, which usually made it very difficult for them to establish a household. Today, young people are better able to get jobs independently of their families and to support themselves. As the position of the family in society has changed, then, people have gained more freedom of choice regarding a marriage partner.

Families do more than help their offspring choose an acceptable mate. They also sometimes transfer significant amounts of money, goods, or services between the two families involved (Schlegel & Eloul, 1988). The most common of these marriage transactions is called *bridewealth* by anthropologists and involves the bridegroom or his family giving gifts to the bride's family. This custom symbolizes the belief that the bride's family is losing a daughter and should be compensated by the bridegroom's family, which is gaining a daughter. It also demonstrates to the woman's family that the prospective husband has the resources to support a wife and children. Another common form of transfer is *brideservice,* in which the bridegroom offers labor rather than goods to the bride's family. He may work for the bride's father for a time as a means of "buying" the daughter, or in a matrilocal society the bridegroom may move in with and become a working member of his wife's family. Still another form of marriage transaction is the *dowry,* in which the bride's family gives her some money or goods that she and her husband can keep. In a sense, the bride's family "buys" the best husband for their daughter and also makes the dowry available for her economic support. The dowry custom is still practiced in some societies such as India today (see Other Worlds, Other Ways: India on pp. 294–295).

The Family in Society

You should be able to analyze the role of the family in society from both the functionalist and conflict perspectives.

Considerable time has been spent discussing these variations of the family in order to emphasize the point that there is much diversity in the types of families found in human societies. To return to the earlier question of what a family is, we begin to realize that no single form of the family will serve all societies. Compared to other cultures, the family in the United States tends to be monogamous; somewhat patriarchal but leaning toward egalitarian and bilateral arrangements; mostly neolocal, but with pockets of matrilocalism and patrilocalism; and nuclear, but with a good mix of reconstituted and modified extended families. All the qualifications in the previous sentence are indicative of the diversity that exists, which will be elaborated on shortly. First, however, we can better understand why such variation in family types occurs from one culture to another, or from one time to another, if we explore what the sociological perspectives can tell us about the place of the family in society.

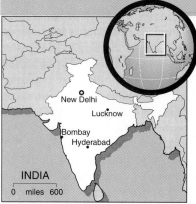

OTHER WORLDS, *Other Ways*

INDIA: DOWRIES AND VIOLENCE AGAINST WOMEN

With almost 900 million people, India is the second largest nation in the world. It has three times more people than the United States on less than one-half of the land mass. India is crowded, relatively poor, and still largely rural. Many Indians are Hindus, and for Hindus, a father has a *dharma,* or "religious duty," to preside over the transfer of authority over his daughter from himself to her husband (Fruzzetti, 1982; Van Willigen & Channa, 1991). Traditionally, this transfer of authority has included a transfer of property from the bride's family to the bridegroom's family, usually in the form of a dowry. In modern India, mate selection is often arranged, especially in rural areas, although not always. Either way, as the possibility of marriage approaches, family representatives may begin to negotiate the dowry and other aspects of the impending marriage. The dowry may consist of both cash and household goods, with the cash going to the bridegroom's father and the household goods going to his family if the couple will live with them or mostly to the couple if they set up an independent household. In fact, some anthropologists believe the dowry may be a way of distributing resources between generations—a kind of inheritance before the parents die—and a way of ensuring that a widow will have support for herself and her children should her husband die. In other words, it transfers resources to the place where a woman will live and bear children (Harrell & Dickey, 1985; Schlegel & Eloul, 1988).

The problem in India is that the operation of the dowry custom sometimes goes awry and has produced disturbing levels of violence against women. Dowries in India today are often open-ended, with a series of exchanges that are not clearly defined ahead of time and persist after the marriage has taken place. The husband or his family may continue making dowry demands on the wife and her family, sometimes long after the marriage ceremony. This practice has resulted in the harassment of women, who are living with their husband's family, and violence against some of them. There are also hundreds, possibly thousands, of dowry deaths each year, sometimes through burning (so common that it has a name in India: *bride-burning*). The women are killed by their husband or his family because they refuse to accede to more dowry demands. Some Indian women commit suicide to relieve their family of the burden of paying a dowry, which can be huge—from one to four times an average worker's annual salary. Other Indian women abort female fetuses for the same reason. To help alleviate these problems, India outlawed dowries in the Dowry Prohibition Act of 1961. By most accounts, the law has been ineffective at stopping either dowries or the problems surrounding them.

If dowries perform important functions for societies, why has the tradition gone so awry in India? Part of the answer has to do with the role of women in economic production and consumption and in the family. For one thing, whether dowry violence occurs

The Functionalist Perspective

Functionalists argue that some form of the family exists in all societies because the family performs certain basic functions that are essential to human survival and the maintenance of society (Eshleman, 1991; Ogburn, 1938). Six major contributions that the family makes to society have been identified.

1. *Regulation of sexual behavior and reproduction.* All societies have rules governing who can engage in sexual activities with whom and under what conditions children should be conceived and born. In most societies, childbearing is limited to marriage and family contexts, which provide a stable setting for having and nurturing children. In this way, the family contributes to the process of replacing people from one generation to the next.

2. *Socialization and education.* All human beings must learn the values, norms, and language of

seems to depend on whether women are seen as a burden or a valuable resource. In parts of India where women are involved in economic production and where the costs (including dowry) of marrying off a daughter are low, dowry violence is low. Where women do not or cannot work and the marriage costs are high, more dowry violence occurs. These same patterns are found not only in different regions in India but also in different castes. Lower-ranking castes place fewer restrictions on women's employment, and there is less reported dowry harassment in those castes.

Another reason for increases in dowry violence is the social and cultural changes that have increased the opportunities for abuses. For one thing, India has been urbanizing, and dowry violence is more common in cities than in rural areas. In villages, caste councils and the two families themselves could regulate the dowry because all parties lived close by and could be watched and pressured so that unreasonable demands were not made. When a couple sets up their own separate residence or moves some distance away to a city, this informal kin and community social control is weakened, and nothing replaces it. The new bride in a city is especially likely to be without familial support and thus vulnerable to victimization.

Social and cultural changes have also pushed up the amount that families demand in a dowry. Since sons are now more likely to move away from their parents, parents expect less overall support from their sons and come to see the dowry as one of the major occasions where they can gain significant material support from their son. Even the bride's family feels some pressure to accept larger dowry demands since a larger dowry is assumed to attract a better-educated and more marketable spouse, who will have greater earning power in the future. This likelihood is especially relevant in the Indian context of inflation, high unemployment, and poverty, which have come with urbanization and modernization.

Merely outlawing dowries in India has not had much of an impact. A more effective attack would institute practices that enhance the economic and social status of women so that large dowries are no longer demanded or dowries are no longer necessary. For example, more extensive employment opportunities could be made available to Indian women, thus making them attractive economic assets even without a dowry. Another possibility would be to change inheritance laws that now favor males. The dowry, after all, is a mechanism for a woman to inherit some of her parents' property before they die. This provision is important because sons often inherit most or all of an estate, leaving daughters with little. A dowry gives the daughter some compensation, but gender-neutral inheritance laws would reduce the need for a dowry. A third change would be to require all marriages to be registered with and licensed by the government, which is currently not true in India. This requirement would make it possible for state control to begin more effectively to replace the control over marriages and dowries once served by family, caste, and community groups in rural areas and small villages.

their culture and develop the skills that are necessary to be useful in society. Parents and other family members usually have primary responsibility for ensuring that children are properly socialized. Thus, as was noted in Chapter 3, the family is the major agency of socialization.

3. *Status conferral.* Families confer on their children a place in society—a position or status relative to other people. By virtue of being born into a particular family, we have certain resources or opportunities available to us. Our racial or ethnic heritage, religion, and social class are determined by the family into which we are born, although some of these characteristics may change later in life.

4. *Economic activity.* The family often serves as the basic unit for economic production, with kinship ties defining who is obliged to work together in order to catch game, grow food, or build shelters.

Family members work together to accomplish the economic tasks necessary for survival. Kinship ties also determine the distribution and consumption of economic goods by establishing who has a right to a share of the goods produced by a family.

5. *Protection.* Families in all societies provide various forms of care and protection to their members, helping them when they are too young, weak, sick, or old to help themselves.

6. *Affection and companionship.* All human beings need love, affection, and psychological support, and for many people these needs are fulfilled by family members. Such support enables us to develop a positive self-concept and sense of self-worth and to dispel loneliness.

All these functions taken together contribute to the continuity of society by ensuring that new members are born and properly socialized.

Although the family often performs these six functions, they can be accomplished in other ways. In fact, the family has been undergoing a major transformation over the past few centuries as a consequence of industrialization, and alternative ways of fulfilling many of these functions are emerging. For example, although most childbearing still occurs in marriages, a growing number of women are having children without marrying. By the 1990s, the U.S. Census Bureau recorded 1.2 million births to unmarried women each year, in comparison to about 400,000 in 1970 (U.S. Bureau of the Census, 1995, p. 77). This increase has occurred in part because women in industrial societies are better able to work and support their children without the assistance of a husband or other relatives. With regard to socialization and education, day-care centers, schools, and colleges are becoming increasingly important in transmitting culture and passing on skills and knowledge. Furthermore, people's positions in industrial societies are determined less by family position and more by their achievements than in the past, although family position does give a person a start in life. In terms of economic activity, most people work outside the home, and the family no longer serves as the center of economic production. Finally, there are hospitals, nursing homes, retirement villages, and many other ways to offer the care and protection that people need.

In other words, the role of the family in performing these functions for society has become less central as other institutional means of accomplishing them have arisen through industrialization. As a consequence, the traditional roles of family and kinship in society have changed, because they are simply not as important as they once were. In the process, the extended family that performed most of these functions in preindustrial societies has become less common. At the same time, the nuclear family has become more prominent because it is better suited to an urbanized industrial society. Industrialism calls for geographic mobility so that workers can go where the jobs are, and the nuclear families with weaker kinship ties make this mobility possible. Industrial societies also emphasize achievement rather than ascription, and these modified kinship relations make it easier for people to be upwardly mobile. Furthermore, large extended families are dysfunctional in urban settings where children are not economic assets. In preindustrial societies, children could work in agricultural settings and therefore contribute economically to the family. Small families are better suited to industrial societies; in fact, the size of the average family in the United States has declined substantially throughout the twentieth century, and people are more likely to be living alone or in nonfamily households (see Figure 9.1).

The part that families play in society, then, has changed with industrialization, and this change has contributed to such things as a rising divorce rate and the emergence of a number of alternatives to traditional family lifestyles. These social developments become a social problem when the changes in the family threaten society with disorganization or instability. One of the key debates regarding family problems centers on whether other institutions can adequately perform the traditional family functions. Can day care, for example, provide the same kind of socialization to cultural values and development of personality that occurs in the traditional family? This issue was analyzed in Applying Sociology: Day Care in Chapter 3. Do divorce and one-parent families result in less effective socialization and more behavior problems for youth when compared with two-parent families? This question will be analyzed later in this chapter. The function of

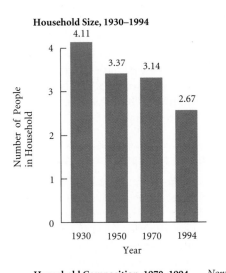

Household Size, 1930–1994

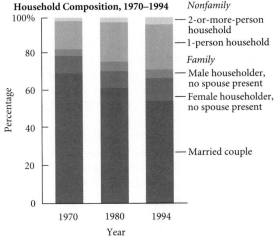

Household Composition, 1970–1994

Nonfamily
— 2-or-more-person household
— 1-person household
Family
— Male householder, no spouse present
— Female householder, no spouse present

— Married couple

FIGURE 9.1 The Average Size and Composition of Households in the United States, 1930–1994
Note: From *Statistical Abstract of the United States, 1982–83* (p. 43) by U.S. Bureau of the Census, 1982, Washington, DC: U.S. Government Printing Office; *Statistical Abstract of the United States, 1995* (p. 58) by U.S. Bureau of the Census, 1995, Washington, DC: U.S. Government Printing Office.

the family that has probably changed least during this process is the provision of affection and companionship, and nuclear families can probably perform this function as well as extended families did. But even this function might be fulfilled in other ways than by the traditional family.

The Conflict Perspective

According to the conflict perspective, the family, along with other social institutions, serves the interests of the dominant groups in society, and there is no reason to assume that a single form of the family would benefit everyone. Rather, the version of the family that is most prominent in society is likely to be the one that is consistent with the values and benefits of the dominant groups. For example, patriarchy is the most common type of authority structure in families, and it serves the interests of men by enabling them to be dominant. In some societies, in fact, women have been so powerless in the family that they were virtual slaves (Chagnon, 1992). In industrial societies, male domination is not this extreme; fewer women today are willing to accept such a subordinate position. In general, women today demand more egalitarian family roles. This change is occurring, however, because women have been accumulating resources that enable them to resist coercion by males. For example, male dominance can be expressed in the form of spouse abuse, which usually involves husbands assaulting their wives. Research indicates that married women with greater economic, social, and educational resources are less likely to be abused and more likely to leave physically abusive husbands (Gelles & Cornell, 1990; Straus, 1991).

The dominant form of the family in society also benefits particular economic interests. For example, the nuclear family serves the interests of capitalist economic institutions because it maximizes the number of consumption-oriented units in society. Each nuclear family buys many consumer items even though some are used only infrequently. Most families, for example, own their own television, stove, food processor, and automobile. A washing machine is used for only a few hours a week, yet most families purchase their own rather than share one with others. In extended or communal families, fewer such consumer goods would be needed because they would be shared, and thus the market for these goods would be smaller, which would hurt the interests of capitalists. Communal families, which are based on the belief in common ownership of at least some material goods, also threaten the basic value of private property on which a capitalist economy rests.

Conflict theorists would also argue that family systems can contribute to the perpetuation of social and economic inequality because inheritance in many societies, especially capitalist ones, is based on kinship. Inheritance makes it possible for a family to accumulate and perpetuate its wealth over generations. Such families as the Carnegies, the Rockefellers, the Astors, the Kennedys, and the Gettys in the United States have amassed enormous fortunes. Anyone who can inherit wealth—of whatever amount—clearly has an advantage over those who come from modest or poor backgrounds. Thus, the family in such societies becomes a vehicle for perpetuating patterns of dominance and subordination.

Conflict theorists argue that the dominant groups protect themselves against threats to their position by teaching people through the schools, the media, and other means that monogamy, nuclear families, family inheritance, and private property are best. Through socialization and education, people internalize these beliefs and they are unlikely, therefore, even to consider other forms of the family, such as communal arrangements. In addition, strong normative pressures motivate people to live in socially acceptable forms of the family. From the conflict perspective, family forms change when new groups acquire the power necessary to gain acceptance for a new form of family. The organization of family life becomes a social problem when groups with the power to make their concerns heard believe that the existing family structure is not serving their interests and they act to change it. The dispute over the proper family form, however, is not couched in the language of personal interests but rather of conflicting values.

Marriage and Divorce in the United States

You should be able to describe the attitudes of people in the United States toward marriage, analyze the extent of divorce and its effects, and assess the family experiences of minorities.

Thus far this chapter has looked at the place of the family as a social institution by considering the many diverse forms of the family and reviewing what the sociological perspectives have to say on this subject. Now it is time to consider the subject in terms of what it means for the United States. First the chapter will look at mate selection practices and attitudes toward marriage; then it will review the extent and consequences of divorce and explore some of the unique family experiences of minorities in the United States.

Choosing a Mate and Attitudes Toward Marriage

It has been noted that the mate selection process in the United States today is participant run, with romantic love playing an important part. Nevertheless, the marriage decision is still strongly influenced by social pressures beyond romantic love. People assess a potential partner's intelligence, education, earning power, and other characteristics. People are likely, for example, to be drawn to each other if they are similar in terms of physical attractiveness. In other words, the marriage choice is in part an *exchange relationship* in which partners assess what they gain from a relationship in comparison to what they have to offer and the alternatives they forgo.

Marriages in the United States also tend to be *homogamous*—people tend to choose partners who have social characteristics similar to their own (Collins & Coltrane, 1991). These characteristics are "social filters" that tend to narrow people's choices among eligible partners. *Age* is a significant filter, with husbands being an average of two and one-half years older than their wives; only 8 percent of married couples have an age difference of larger than ten years, and only 10 percent involve a wife older than her husband (Garrett, 1982). *Religion* is another filter, with Protestants having the highest rates of endogamy, followed by Jews and then Roman Catholics (Kephart & Jedlicka, 1988). *Race* is also a major filter, with only 0.5 percent of all marriages involving black–white couples (U.S. Bureau of the Census, 1995). A final filter is *socioeconomic status,* with people especially likely to choose partners at the same educational and occupational levels as themselves (Kalmijn, 1991). When we see the effect of these filters narrowing people's choices of partners, we can see that mate selection is complex and influenced by many things other than romantic love.

Given the changes in the role of the family in industrial societies, are marriage and family living still popular today? It would seem so: More people in the United States marry than ever before, well over 90 percent. In 1994, 63 percent of all adult men were married, as were 59 percent of all adult women. These figures were higher than they were in 1940 but somewhat lower than at any point since 1950 (see Figure 9.2). Surveys over the past 20 years reveal that both young people and their parents have quite positive attitudes toward marriage and family (Axinn & Thornton, 1996; Martin & Martin, 1984; Moore & Stief, 1991; Thornton, 1989). In a national sample of high school seniors, three-quarters reported that marriage and family life were "extremely

FIGURE 9.2 Marital Status of Adults in the United States, 1940–1994 *Note:* From *Statistical Abstract of the United States, 1982–83* (p. 38) by U.S. Bureau of the Census, 1982, Washington, DC: U.S. Government Printing Office; *Statistical Abstract of the United States* (p. 55) by U.S. Bureau of the Census, 1995, Washington, DC: U.S. Government Printing Office.

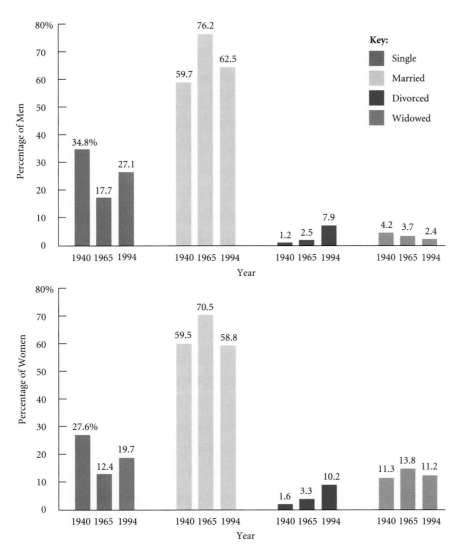

important" to them, and a survey of young adults aged eighteen to twenty-two found that most of them plan to marry before the age of thirty. The vast majority of them also believed that when people marry, it should be "for life." Despite these positive views of marriage, however, the surveys detected some important changes: Compared with attitudes of the 1960s, these young men and women have fewer negative attitudes toward staying single, see fewer advantages in getting married over remaining single, and are not as certain that having children is the best way to go. In fact, the people interviewed seemed reluctant to choose either marriage or being single as the preferred alternative. In short, many view marriage quite positively in the United States today, but alternatives to marriage are also growing in popularity.

These changes in attitudes over the past thirty years suggest that the norms regarding family life in the United States are moving somewhat away from the more traditional and conventional demand that the family consist of a married couple and their children. For some, these changes are one indication that the family is in serious trouble. Some people also view the divorce rate in the United States as an indication of trouble.

Divorce

The Divorce Rate People usually view the widespread incidence and easy availability of divorce as having arisen only recently. In fact, the option for a married couple to dissolve a marriage has existed in many premodern societies. In some hunting-and-gathering bands, for example, a marriage could be easily ended when a couple decided to stop living together, and in horticultural or pastoral societies where some gender equality had developed, divorce could be initiated by women as easily as by men (O'Kelly & Carney, 1986). Nevertheless, to those who believe that marriage should be a lifelong commitment involving a deep emotional sharing between the married couple, today's high divorce rate is viewed as a threat to the family as a social institution.

In calculating the incidence of divorce, most sociologists use a statistic called the **refined divorce rate,** *which is determined by dividing the number of divorces each year by the total number of existing marriages in that year.* This method provides a valid way of comparing the stability of marriages from one year to the next. As Table 9.1 illustrates, the divorce rate has more than doubled since 1940. As a point of comparison, it has been estimated that there were only 1.2 divorces for every one thou-

TABLE 9.1   The rate of marriage and divorce in the United States, 1940–1994

	1940	1945	1950	1955	1960	1965	1970	1975	1980	1985	1990	1994
Marriage rate[a]	82.8	83.6	90.2	80.9	73.5	75	76.5	66.9	61.4	57.5	54.5	51.5
Divorce rate[b]	8.8	14.4	10.3	9.3	9.2	10.6	14.9	20.3	22.6	21.7	20.9	20.5
Remarriage rate[c]						127.8	123.3	117.2	91.3	81.8	76.2	

[a]Marriages per 1,000 unmarried women over 15.

[b]Divorces and annulments per 1,000 married women over 15.

[c]Marriages per 1,000 divorced women over 14.

Note: From "Advance Report of Final Divorce Statistics, 1989 and 1990" by National Center for Health Statistics, 1995, *Monthly Vital Statistics Report, 43* (9), DHHS Publication No. (PHS) 95-1120, Hyattsville, MD: Public Health Service; "Advance Report of Final Marriage Statistics, 1989 and 1990" by National Center for Health Statistics, 1995, *Monthly Vital Statistics Report, 43* (12, Suppl.), DHHS Publication No. (PHS) 95-1120, Hyattsville, MD: Public Health Service; "Annual Summary of Births, Marriages, Divorces, and Deaths: United States, 1994" by National Center for Health Statistics, 1995, *Monthly Vital Statistics Report, 43* (13), DHHS Publication No. (PHS) 96-1120, Hyattsville, MD: Public Health Service.

sand marriages in 1869—reflecting a seventeen-fold increase during the past century (Saxton, 1980, p. 380). Although the trend in divorce rates over the past fifty years has been up, the rate has fluctuated considerably. It rose to 17.9 in 1946, one year after the end of World War II, a rate that is close to the rates found in the past twenty years. Since 1975, the divorce rate has pretty much leveled off.

If we want to know the probability that a given marriage will end in divorce, we need a different statistic. As Figure 9.3 illustrates, the likelihood that a marriage would end in divorce in 1870 was 8 percent. By the 1980s, this figure had risen to more than 50 percent. So though it may be disturbing to many, the statistical likelihood of marriages beginning today ending in divorce is about fifty-fifty. However, those people who divorce are apparently not totally disillusioned with marriage because 75 to 80 percent of them will eventually remarry. But a slightly greater number of these second marriages will end in divorce in compari-son to first marriages (Collins & Coltrane, 1991). This percentage is a little deceiving, however, because it includes a small number of people who divorce and remarry many times. When this group is removed, second marriages are reasonably successful, and many couples in their second marriage report that they are happy.

The divorce rate is but one measure of marital dissolution. Approximately 3 percent of all marriages end in legal separation, where the partners decide to end their relationship but prefer, perhaps for religious reasons, not to divorce. Desertion is another way in which marriages are dissolved, although it is difficult to know the extent of this practice. In any event, we need to be aware that only a portion of all marital dissolutions is reflected in the divorce rate. In fact, given these marital practices, we might refer to the U.S. marriage system as one involving *serial* monogamy rather than monogamy or polygamy. **Serial monogamy** means that *a person is allowed to have more than one spouse, just not at the same time.*

FIGURE 9.3 The Rising Percentage of Marriages Ending in Divorce in the United States, 1867–1985 *Note:* Adapted from *Marriage, Divorce, and Remarriage* by Andrew J. Cherlin, 1992, Cambridge, MA: Harvard University Press. Copyright 1981, 1992 by the President and Fellows of Harvard College. Reprinted by permission.

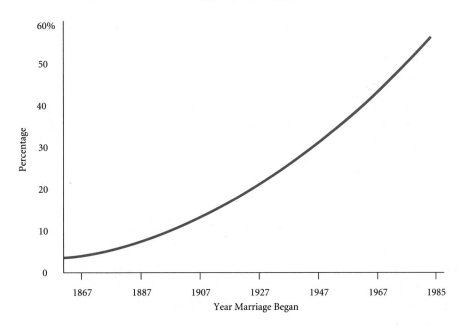

People get divorces for many personal reasons—their spouse has become insensitive, they feel trapped by limited career opportunities, or their sex lives are no longer exciting. Sociologists prefer to focus on the societal conditions that result in a high divorce rate rather than personal reasons for divorce. At least four such societal conditions account for the rising divorce rate over the past century.

First, we have seen that the family performs fewer functions today than in the past, which means there are fewer pressures on couples to stay together if they are unhappy. In the past, the same unhappy couple might have remained married because neither spouse felt he or she could raise the children alone or he or she needed the family for support in old age. Today, single parents are better prepared to raise a child, and most people are supported by retirement plans in their old age. In fact, the high levels of affluence afforded by industrialization have made people less dependent on kinship ties for support, with consequent changes in the family as an institution.

Second, the increasing equality between men and women has created both opportunities and tensions that contribute to the divorce rate (Brehm, 1985). In terms of opportunities, many women today are part of the labor force and thus have the economic ability to support themselves and their children without a husband. This ability reduces the likelihood of women being willing to remain in unsatisfying relationships. In terms of tensions, sexual equality has led to a redefining of the roles in the family, which can cause disagreements and stress that may precipitate divorce. A husband, for example, may feel that his wife should do most of the household chores, whereas she feels these tasks should be divided equally. Such conflicts are especially a problem for women who, after marrying, decide to pursue a career. This life change disrupts an established marital pattern and requires a renegotiation of male and female roles in the family, which is sometimes unsuccessful (Houseknecht, Vaughan, & Macke, 1984).

A third reason for the rising divorce rate is that there is considerably less stigma attached to divorce today than in the past (Thornton, 1985). Divorce in the past was often viewed as a serious failing in a person's life, with divorced people frequently labeled as morally inferior. Females in particular bore the stigma of the divorcee as a "fallen" woman. In precommunist China, for example, the divorce rate was extremely low, but the suicide rate for wives was very high. Wives were guided by a disturbing adage: "Good women should hang themselves; only bad women seek divorce" (Yang, 1965, p. 81). Today, with fifteen million divorced people in the United States, many view divorce as merely another lifestyle choice rather than a reflection of an allegedly weak character.

Finally, as negative attitudes toward divorce have eased, pressures have surfaced to simplify the legal process for obtaining a divorce. These developments have encouraged more people to seek dissolution when they encounter marital difficulties.

Taking all of these factors together, we can make an important overriding observation about the reasons for divorce in the United States: People expect a great deal from the marriage relationship. We allow people to form families partly on the basis of romantic love, which can be fickle and unpredictable. Then we expect those relationships to afford a lifetime of emotional fulfillment, sexual gratification, companionship, and commitment. Is it so surprising, then, that many marriages fail to achieve these ideals? In the past, there were other, more pragmatic pressures for couples to stay together, such as economic constraints, reputation, religious ideals, and maintaining the marriage "for the sake of the children." Today, if the romantic ideal fails, other "barrier strengths" maintaining the marriage are less likely to prevent marital dissolution (Levinger & Moles, 1979).

Who Gets Divorced?   Some couples are at considerably greater risk of getting a divorce than are others (Bahr, 1989). Couples with an increased likelihood of divorcing have the following characteristics:

1. *Social differences between the couple, such as differences in religion, race, social class background, or values.* These differences can place substantial stress on a marriage.

2. *Low socioeconomic standing, such as low income or education.* Unemployment and other stresses that often accompany low social standing probably make it more difficult to achieve a successful marriage.

3. *Young age at marriage.* Very young couples seem especially ill-equipped to make a go of marriage.

4. *Whirlwind romances.* People who have known each other for only a brief period are more likely to choose a partner with whom they will later prove to be incompatible.

The Effects of Divorce   Divorce can be a disruptive and troubling experience, as those who have experienced it will attest. Marital dissolution often precipitates feelings of failure, loneliness, and rejection, along with intense anger and frustration. For many, it represents an assault on their sense of self-worth. Even when a person prefers divorce, an intimate bond is slashed nevertheless, and there is often nothing immediately to take its place. Symptoms of psychological distress, sometimes quite severe, are common among the newly divorced. Divorce is also sometimes associated with increased problems of physical health, with divorced people having more serious illnesses, more chronic disabling conditions, and a higher suicide rate than do single or married people (Kiecolt-Glaser et al., 1987; Verbrugge, 1979).

There has been considerable debate regarding whether the husband or the wife is treated more unfairly in divorce proceedings. Husbands complain about being gouged for alimony or child-support payments, whereas wives protest over allegedly meager or missing payments from husbands. Social scientists have done considerable research on this issue, comparing the experiences of divorced women with those of divorced men and also looking at people's circumstances before and after divorce. The conclusions are remarkably consistent: Women are much more likely than men to suffer economic decline after divorce, and even when men suffer, their economic slide is much less severe and much more short-lived than is that of women (Holden & Smock, 1991; Seltzer, 1994). One reason women end up worse off is that courts typically divide up only tangible property, such as a home, automobile, or belongings. Less tangible but often far more valuable property, such as a professional license that can translate into considerable income throughout a career, is usually not considered a part of the property settlement, and it is the man who is far more likely to possess these less tangible forms of property. There are other reasons for the postdivorce economic decline of women. It is typically the woman who takes custody of children after divorce, and child support awarded by courts is usually meager compared to the father's income; only a minority of fathers comply fully with child-support awards; women earn substantially less than men; and women, having child-rearing responsibilities, suffer barriers in looking for jobs and finding child care.

As far as the children of divorce are concerned, the jury is still out regarding whether they would be better off staying in a conflict-ridden, unhappy home rather than experiencing the divorce of their parents. Divorce is without question difficult for children, and living in a loving home is certainly preferable to experiencing an unhappy home or divorce. We simply lack the research to know all the effects if an unhappy family remains intact.

There are some things that we do know about the effects of divorce on children, however (Furstenberg & Cherlin, 1991; Wallerstein & Blakeslee, 1989). First, the impact on children depends on their age. Children between five and ten, for example, often feel some responsibility for their parents' divorce, and this sense may lead to feelings of guilt and failure. Preteens often express tremendous anger at their parents. Teenagers, by contrast, are often confronted with the matter of parental loyalty, feelings that they must take sides in the conflict and form a coalition with one or the other parent. Furthermore, although adolescents are better able to understand the reasons for divorce, they are often very worried about the effects of separation on their future. A second thing we know about the impact of divorce is that children in divorced homes seem more prone to delinquency (Rankin, 1983; Wells & Rankin, 1991). Third, a common consequence of divorce for both boys and girls is a decline in school performance and a higher high school dropout rate. Finally, research has shown that it is not the fact of the divorce itself that produces all of the negative consequences; the social and emotional conditions that often surround divorce are also a part of the problem (Amato, 1993; Amato & Rezac, 1994; Furstenberg & Teitler, 1994). The poor parenting, conflict between parents, and economic difficulties that often precede or follow divorce contribute to the negative consequences. In addition, divorce may reduce children's access to and ability to use various resources, such as the emotional support and role modeling of both parents.

The impact of divorce on children, however, is not all bad. Research shows that children living in one-parent families sometimes benefit from the experience (Amato, 1987; Goldscheider & Waite, 1991). For example, the single parent sometimes gives his or her teenage offspring more responsibility and a greater role in family decision making. Also, teenage boys in mother-only families tend to take on a considerably greater share of household chores than do boys *or* girls in two-parent homes. In fact, teenage boys living with their mothers develop more egalitarian attitudes toward men's and women's roles, and both boys and girls may become more independent and resourceful. In addition, the experience of divorce is less negative if a child continues to have contact with the parent they no longer live with, especially when the divorced parents have a low-conflict relationship.

In addition to all these impacts of divorce on children, divorce also changes children's attitudes toward family issues: Children whose parents have divorced have more positive attitudes toward premarital sex and cohabitation, express more acceptance of divorce, and have less positive attitudes toward marriage and childbearing (Axinn & Thornton, 1996). So, divorce has widespread and complicated consequences for children and society, and not all of the consequences can be clearly characterized as negative.

The Minority Family Experience

People's family experiences are affected by their position in the social structure. This fact is exemplified in the previous discussion by the analysis of how gender affects divorce outcome and how age and socioeconomic status affect the likelihood of divorce. Minority group status also affects family life, and an overview of the family experiences of a few minorities will round out this discussion of family in the United States.

The African American family today is actually much healthier than many people realize. Recent historical work shows that even during the period of slavery, many slaves lived in stable families and were a part of extensive kinship connections. Research on the black family early in the twentieth century comes to the same conclusion (Engerman, 1977; Gutman, 1976). Research also shows many black families in the past few decades doing well, with an upper class that is wealthy and privileged and very concerned about whom their children will marry (Billingsley, 1992; Zinn & Eitzen, 1990). Middle-class African American families are often dual-income families with good jobs and the resources to send their children to good colleges. In fact, these affluent black families often show more cohesiveness than comparable white families because of the adversity they face as a minority. This sense of adversity can translate into a feeling of embattlement that puts pressure on all family members to achieve—the mother to work and the children to succeed in college (Willie, 1981). Even poorer African American families exhibit significant strengths, such as more effective and extensive use of kinship networks than is found in white families (Jayakody, Chatters, & Taylor, 1993). For example, families headed by black women are more likely to get assistance from relatives, such as a sister or aunt living with them or nearby, than are families headed by white women. In fact, this reliance on a variety of kinship ties in an extended-family network is much closer to what "family" looks like in many other societies; defining the family largely or exclusively in terms of the husband–wife tie, as is done in most white families, is unusual.

Beyond these strengths, the marriage and family experience for African Americans is different in other ways. There are far more black families headed by women—almost 50 percent, compared to about 12 percent among white families. In addition, black women are far less likely to be married and living with a husband. Also, black families are much more likely to be poor, with all the problems poverty can present for a family. It has been popular to attribute the problems of the modern black family to the conditions imposed by slavery—the destruction of African tribal customs, the dispersal of tribal groups, and the disregard for institutions of marriage and family among the slaves. Although there is some truth in this argument, it is probably not a complete explanation of conditions that exist today. Whereas many slaves were treated cruelly, others were not, and there have been strong African families during slavery and since. In addition, the circumstances of the African American family have become noticeably worse since the 1960s (in 1960, only about 20 percent of black families were headed by women). As noted in Chapter 7, the shift in the U.S. economy to a service-oriented, information-based post-

While Hispanic American and African American families confront some problems, families among these groups are stronger and healthier today than many people believe.

industrial economy has meant that people need high levels of skills and education to find good jobs. In addition, jobs have moved away from communities where poor people live. All of this change has meant fewer good jobs that pay enough to support a family in black communities. Furthermore, there is ample evidence that racism and discrimination against African Americans in both employment and housing persists today. They are more likely to be denied good jobs, especially entry-level jobs, because of their race, and are often forced to live in segregated neighborhoods where there are few good jobs (see Chapter 7). As if all that were not enough, the criminal justice system devotes a good portion of its resources toward incarcerating young black males. The War on Drugs of the 1980s and 1990s, for example, has put tens of thousands of young black and Hispanic men in jail. The result for the African American family has been fewer opportunities for black women to find men to marry and less chance for black men to get jobs that would enable them to support a family. Consequently many African American families have adapted to these elements in the social structure by deemphasizing the centrality of the husband–

wife tie and relying on a broader network of kin to fulfill the various functions of the family, such as child rearing. This adaptation is actually common among poor people in many societies.

Hispanic American families show some of the same variations found among African American families, in part because Hispanics also are more likely to be poor than are Anglos. So Hispanics have more female-headed families than Anglos but fewer than African Americans. However, Hispanic American families have some unique qualities (Slonim, 1991; Vega, 1990). Their strong belief in Roman Catholicism along with a strong family orientation in their culture produces a disapproval of divorce. As a consequence, Hispanics are more likely than either Anglos or blacks to be living in a family household and are as likely as Anglos to be in a married-couple household. Hispanics also receive more material and emotional support from an extended kin network. However, this support is less a response to the single-parent problem facing black families than it is a part of a long tradition in Hispanic cultures of family solidarity, which places value on family ties over individual gratification. Nevertheless, there is much variation among Hispanic groups. For example, Cuban Americans are more affluent than many other Hispanic groups and they are more likely to have married-couple households.

Chinese and Japanese cultural values were described in Chapters 2, 3, and 5, and some of that discussion is relevant here because Asian American families bring some distinctive characteristics to U.S. society (Slonim, 1991; Suzuki, 1985). Chinese and Japanese Americans, for example, have retained some of their traditional cultural values such as the importance of the family or collectivity over the individual, self-discipline, social obligation, and respect for the elderly. These values are reflected in families with much stronger and more traditional kinship bonds than are found among other families in the United States. Although they have adopted the nuclear form of the family, there is more support for the elderly in Chinese and Japanese American families, and women are more likely to moderate their achievement aspirations in order to accommodate family demands. Among Asian immigrants from Vietnam and Cambodia in the past few decades, the extended family is often preserved, with many generations living in one home. The circumstances of these immigrants to the United States are explored in Other Worlds, Other Ways: Vietnam (on pp. 308–309). This pattern may change as future generations assimilate into U.S. culture.

Given the rich racial and ethnic diversity that exists in the United States, this discussion could be extended to Arab Americans, Jewish Americans, and many others, but the point has been made that variations in cultural background and position in the social structure produce different family experiences.

Diversity and Change in Sexual Behavior

You should be able to describe the extent of and changes in sexual behavior outside marriage and list some of the reasons for it.

Chapter 5 discussed sexual behavior in the context of deviance and concluded that there are no "natural" or "instinctive" expressions of human sexuality that people engage in largely or completely without learning. While sex is partly biological, it is also strongly shaped and regulated by cultural values and norms, the product of learning in a particular cultural environment. All societies regulate sexuality, although the nature and extent of regulation varies significantly across cultures. One important dimension of that regulation is the extent to which sexual expression is considered appropriate only in the family context. This section will focus on the sexual behaviors most relevant to the family: premarital, extramarital, and gay sexuality.

Premarital Sex

Many Western religions, such as Roman Catholicism, prohibit all sexual activity outside the marital bond. Such a complete prohibition on premarital sex is unusual in human societies. Anthropologists who have looked at many societies, both today and in the past, estimate that only about one-third of human societies require brides to be virgins. More than one-third allow almost completely unrestricted premarital sex (for example, the Trobriand Islanders mentioned in this chapter and the Huron Indians discussed in Chapter 7), and almost another third allow premarital sex with some restrictions, such as avoiding pregnancy (Murdock, 1967).

Today, people in the United States are more divided than in the past over premarital sexuality (Collins & Coltrane, 1991). In the 1960s, only 20 percent believed that premarital sex was acceptable; by the 1990s, about half of the public views it as permissible (Hugick & Leonard, 1991; Tanfer & Cubbins, 1992). Young people are much more likely to approve of premarital sex, as are those who are less religious and who have more egalitarian sex-role attitudes. As in so many other realms, however, attitudes and behavior are sometimes at variance; because people *approve* of a behavior does not mean that they *engage* in it themselves. Information about actual premarital sexual behavior comes from a variety of surveys and interviews. Sexual behavior is a sensitive area, so information about it is not always easy to obtain. Putting together the best information available, we can conclude that sex before marriage, which was once considered taboo in the United States, especially for women, has become routine. Today, 80 to 85 percent of women and 95 percent of men have had sex before marriage. This figure compares with about 50 percent of women and 66 percent of men in the 1920s. So, there has been a gradual increase since that time, but the change is less dramatic than many believe since at least half of all men and women in the 1920s had premarital sexual experience. If there has been a sexual "revolution," it is among women. Whereas the numbers of women having premarital experience gradually increased throughout the century, they did show a leap in the 1960s and 1970s.

In regard to the number of sexual partners, although some popular sports figures in recent years have claimed thousands, that is far from most people's experiences (Tanfer & Cubbins, 1992; Tanfer & Schoorl, 1992). Some research shows that college-educated men have had an average of eight partners during their premarital years, with less educated men having slightly more. A majority of women seem to have no more than a few sexual partners before marriage. It also seems that Acquired Immune Deficiency Syndrome (AIDS) has changed sex for some people, with many claiming they abstain from sex more and have fewer partners than in the past. There has also been a noticeable trend in recent years toward more conservative attitudes toward premarital sex, but it may be that attitudes have changed more in this regard than has behavior (Hugick & Leonard, 1991; Roche & Ramsbey, 1993).

These changes in premarital sexual behavior are often misunderstood and exaggerated. There has been a dramatic change in how publicly people discuss sex and in how openly they recognize the reality of premarital sex. They are also less likely to insist that sex be limited to the marital context. Although changes in actual sexual behavior are real, they have not been as dramatic as many believe, especially when we consider the importance of cohabitation. Among some in the United States today, cohabitation has come to be viewed as a socially acceptable bonding between two people, including sexual exclusivity. In some cases, it even includes childbearing. Cohabitation looks a great deal like what Mali-

nowski, when studying the Trobriand Islanders, called the family. Many cohabitors gain social approval and legitimacy for their union from their friends and families. If we treat cohabitors like married couples and remove their sexual activity from the premarital category, the sexual "revolution" looks even less dramatic. In addition, some experts conclude that the most significant change has been the elimination of the double standard that permitted men to engage in premarital sex ("sow a few wild oats") without sanction but strongly discouraged the same behavior in women (Clement, 1989). Although there are still differences, women's sexual behavior has become much more similar to that of men in the past few decades.

What accounts for the changes in sexual behavior in the twentieth century? One important factor, certainly, is the emergence of easy-to-use, unobtrusive, and reliable contraceptives. They have eased women's fears of pregnancy and widened their options for sexual behavior. A second major factor has been the feminist movement, which emphasized that women should gain control of their lives and be able to make decisions for themselves. It also demanded that women's choices not be limited by sexist or stereotypical views of gender. Without question, many traditional views of women's sexuality were sexist, stereotyped, and wrong. A third factor producing changing sexual practices has been technological developments, such as the automobile, that provide young people with more freedom and the means to escape surveillance by adults.

Despite changes, a double standard still persists in the United States today, especially among adolescents (Turner & Rubinson, 1993). For many male teenagers, sexual conquests remain an important defining experience, and they are expected to "score," or at least boast that they did. Scoring gains approval from one's peers, and the higher score presumably gains more approval. Even the term used (score) implies an aggressive and dominant male activity where the boy bests the girl in some fashion (does the girl lose, in the sense of lose some status, because she is now morally compromised?). For their part, adolescent girls still feel considerable pressures to be

THER WORLDS, *Other Ways*

VIETNAM: FAMILY AND RELIGION AMONG IMMIGRANTS TO THE UNITED STATES

Vietnam is a small nation resting between two giants, China and India (Jamieson, 1993; Karnow, 1981). China occupied Vietnam for hundreds of years, and the struggle for independence against China was critical in shaping Vietnamese nationhood and cultural identity. After achieving independence in 939 A.D., the Vietnamese sharpened their national sentiments and sense of nationhood through periodic clashes with invading armies, especially the Chinese, who persisted in trying to exploit Vietnam. In the 1500s, European explorers, merchants, and missionaries began arriving in Vietnam, and another round of foreign domination began, with the French occupying all of Vietnam by the late 1800s. Both the Chinese and the French were brutal rulers. The Japanese occupied Vietnam during World War II, and the French returned once the Japanese were defeated. The Vietnamese finally defeated the French at Dien Bien Phu in 1954, and Vietnam was divided into North Vietnam, ruled by the communists, and South Vietnam, supported by the United States (Harris et al., 1962). Twenty years later, the North Vietnamese and the Vietcong (communist guerrilla forces) defeated the United States and reunited the two parts of Vietnam.

Vietnam acquired its religious traditions from China—Buddhism, Confucianism, and Taoism (Henkin & Nguyen, 1981; Hickey, 1964). Buddhism and Taoism place great value on humility. They encourage detachment from the material world and view wealth and power as potentially corrupting forces. The way to peace is to reject worldliness and achieve reincarna-tion to a better life by doing good deeds in this life. This point of view can lead to an acceptance of things, both good and bad, that is difficult for Westerners to comprehend. For the Vietnamese, one endures. As noted in the discussion of cultural values in Japan and China, Confucianism places great importance on social obligation and duty to the group, whether it be society, community, or family. It requires each person to give obedience to those in authority over them, whether it be rulers over people, parents over children, or husband over wife. The good society, and the good family, is one in which subordinates faithfully and completely obey the emperor or father.

In the United States, people tend to belong to one religion or another, but the Vietnamese have no difficulty with combining many religious and philosophical systems, including some Western religions, into a coherent belief system that guides their lives. This eclecticism may be a reaction to their historical experience with colonial invaders over the centuries. These religious traditions shape the Vietnamese family, which is large, patriarchal, and extended. A household might contain young children, married sons and their wives, adult daughters who have yet to marry, and assorted other relatives who need support. The emphasis in the family is on collective obligation and decision making; the kind of individualism found in nuclear families in the United States is strongly discouraged. Gender, age, and birth order determine one's position in the family and the rights and obligations one has in relation to others in the family. For example, rights and duties such as supporting older family members, inheriting family property, and working to support the family are rigidly defined by kinship ties.

---

more selective in sexual activities. For them, sex should come after some emotional commitment, such as going steady or becoming engaged. A girl who seeks as many "scores" as the boys do is likely to have a negative reputation in the eyes of her peers—both male and female.

Extramarital Sex

In the United States, with its monogamous form of the family, marriage is defined in terms of sexual exclusivity: Husbands and wives are supposed to have sex only with each other, and there are strong legal and normative pressures toward this end. It

Primary responsibility for the support and moral guidance of the family rests on the oldest male. In traditional Vietnamese families, he will make the major decisions, such as choice of marriage partners or choice of occupations. He also controls family finances, and he decides how much money each family member needs and what purchases to make with the whole family's interests in mind. Although the Vietnamese family is clearly patriarchal, an important tradition of female autonomy has evolved over time. Women play an important role in family finances, although men have the final say. In fact, many Vietnamese women translate their domestic roles into entrepreneurial activities outside the family, such as running a small restaurant. This practice enables them to maintain some independence and autonomy while still supporting a traditional family structure.

After the fall of Saigon and the withdrawal of U.S. forces in 1975, many South Vietnamese emigrated to the United States, large numbers of them settling in California. They brought their religious and family traditions with them, which they used to help them adapt to life in the United States (Gold, 1992; Haines, Rutherford, & Thomas, 1981). In particular, the family, with its emphasis on collective support and goals, has made it possible for them to overcome poverty and other sorts of adversity. The whole extended family might share one apartment or house, and they would have important links to other relatives who did not live with them. Even though other family members might be financially strapped themselves, they would give what assistance they could to others. One Vietnamese woman might employ some aunts or cousins in her restaurant, even though the business was only marginally profitable. Those aunts or cousins, in turn, would work long hours for low wages.

Sometimes, they would keep these jobs, even when better ones came along, because of family obligation. The restaurant owner, in return, would give the workers food or clothing when it was available and let them work flexible hours. If the restaurant was successful, the owner would use some profits to help underwrite a relative's effort to start his or her own restaurant.

Familial obligations, then, are strong and extensive. The restaurant workers receive low wages, but they also know that the owner will do all she can to give family members work and certainly would never hire a nonrelative when kin were available to work. As one Vietnamese in the United States put it:

> We solve problems because the family institution is a bank. If I need money—and my brother and my two sisters are working—I tell them I need to buy a house. I need priority in this case. They say "okay," and they give money to me. And after only two years, I bought a house. . . . Now I help them. They live with me and have no rent (quoted in Gold, 1992, p. 56).

If an elder in the family gets sick, everyone—sons, daughters, and their children—are available to help, and there is less need for expenditures on hospitals, nurses, or nursing homes. The whole extended family combines their resources to buy a small business; then all family members, including children, work there and get support from the business. In fact, these small businesses can be seen as an extension of the practice of women in Vietnam running small enterprises as a part of their domestic duties (Finnan & Cooperstein, 1983). Even refugees without such families in the United States join together to form "families" based on this traditional model.

is almost a property claim that one's spouse is off-limits sexually to anyone else. Reflecting this view, almost all people in the United States believe that extramarital sexual affairs are wrong (Hugick & Leonard, 1991). Despite this disapproval, such affairs are quite common, with about one-third of all married women and two-thirds of all married men having had at least one affair during their lives (Smith, 1990). These figures include, however, the many people who had only one affair during their life and were faithful the rest of the time. In fact, at any given moment, only a small percentage of married people are engaging in extramarital sex (Greeley, 1991). These figures have increased over the last fifty years, but the increase has been larger for women than for men. About half of all women who have affairs have only one, and a lot of this activity occurs when a couple is separated but not legally divorced. So, part of the increase in extramarital affairs is due to the increase in the divorce rate over the past fifty years.

Whether extramarital sex occurs is in part a matter of opportunity. Working women have more such affairs than women who do not work, probably because they have the opportunity to meet more men. However, there is a double standard here, also, in that traditionally wives who have sex with someone other than their husband have met more disapproval than husbands who do the same. In addition, gender affects people's motivation for having an extramarital liaison: Women are more likely to have one for love and men for sex (Glass & Wright, 1992).

Homosexuality

When we look at other cultures, we find many that accept homosexuality as a normal sexual practice, at least for some people and at some points in their lives (Weinrich & Williams, 1990). In the United States, by contrast, a majority believes that homosexual relations between consenting adults should be illegal, a proportion that is significantly higher than it was in the 1970s (Hugick, 1992b). Estimates of the number of adult males in the United States who are predominantly or exclusively gay range from 1 to 5 percent (Billy, Tanfer, Grady, & Keplinger, 1993; Laumann, Gagnon, Michael, & Michaels, 1994; Rogers & Turner, 1991). Lesbians are probably about half as common. In addition, somewhere between 5 and 25 percent of all males have had at least one homosexual encounter. These figures should be viewed with caution, however, because many people undoubtedly refuse to admit to engaging in such behavior when interviewed.

The search for the causes of homosexuality has been very controversial (Hamer & Copeland, 1994). Recent research on twins has provided some evidence of a genetic influence on sexual orientation: Twins who share the same genetic material (monozygotic twins) are much more likely

both to be gay than twins who do not share the exact same genetic material (dizygotic twins) or two adopted brothers who share no genetic material. However, to date, these research efforts have not been able to discover exactly what is inherited. It may be that what is inherited is not sexual orientation directly but rather behaviors that are more likely to be shaped into homosexuality in the proper environment. For example, people may inherit a tendency toward gender nonconformity, such as a tendency for young boys to behave in a stereotypically girlish fashion (be "sissies"). Then the reactions of others to that gender nonconformity may encourage ways of thinking and behaving that come to be defined as "homosexual." So a genetic predisposition may become shaped by social interaction during childhood and the teenage years.

Some psychologists have tried to explain homosexuality as arising from some psychological maladjustment, possibly stemming from a poor parent–child relationship. This explanation has been thoroughly studied over the years, yielding no evidence that homosexuality is linked with psychological problems. Heterosexuals have no fewer psychological problems than do gay men or lesbians, and the latter on the whole are as well adjusted, in both their lives and their sexual orientation, as are the former (Robinson, Skeen, Hobson, & Herrman, 1982; Ross, Paulsen, & Stalstrom, 1988).

Sociologists have recognized that the world does not divide simply into the gay and the straight. Some men and women combine both forms of sexuality in their lives, whereas others are exclusively one or the other. Some married people engage in homosexual affairs while also maintaining active heterosexual activities with their spouse (van der Geest, 1993). So human sexuality is complicated, and a number of social and situational factors shape sexual expression at a given time. In some cases, homosexuality is a matter of experimentation where people are looking for something new, different, or exciting. In others, it is a matter of opportunity, such as in prison when heterosexual partners may not be available. In these cases, the person may not define himself or herself as gay. For some people, however, the process of self-definition through the looking-glass self, as discussed in Chapter 3, comes into play (Troiden,

1989). If people label an individual as gay, that increases the chances that the person will come to accept the label himself or herself. In addition, the labeling by self or others may lead to greater association with others who define themselves as gay. Such association can lead to more opportunities to explore homosexuality. So, the labeling and self-definition processes can precipitate gradual changes in a person's self-concept, along with a growing association with people in the gay community. These changes in turn may help solidify the person's gay self-definition and lifestyle.

There is still a lot that we do not know about sexual orientation. We have no idea whether all, or only some, of homosexuality is biologically linked. There may be many routes—some biological, some situational—to becoming straight or gay. In all likelihood, both biology and social forces will be found to play some part. Despite this uncertainty, we do know that homosexuality is a significant part of the sexuality that people express in society.

In conclusion, changes in attitude and behavior over the past fifty years in the United States have resulted in substantially more sexual activity outside the marriage bond. This activity has direct implications for what constitutes a family in the United States today, which is the next topic.

Diverse Family Lifestyles in Modern Societies

You should be able to describe the diverse family lifestyles that are found in modern societies and explain some of the reasons why they exist.

Earlier, this chapter discussed the diversity of families found around the world and the impact of industrialization on weakening the importance of kinship and encouraging the transition from extended to nuclear families. One consequence of these changes has been an increase in divorce; a second has been a growth in family lifestyles that diverge from the traditional extended or two-parent nuclear family. Some of these lifestyles have arisen as people adapt to the void left by divorce, whereas others are chosen because changes in modern society, including the changes in sexual behaviors just discussed, make them

more attractive, or more necessary, options than in the past (Davidson & Moore, 1992). For example, the greater individualism and egalitarianism of the 1990s has opened up options that fewer people chose in the past. In addition, the changes in sexual behavior have been accompanied by a greater atmosphere of tolerance, which has produced a more varied choice of family lifestyles. There follows a review of some of the major alternatives to the conventional family, with an eye on what future developments are likely.

Dual-Career Families

In the conventional nuclear family in the United States, women either did not work outside the home or held jobs that were considered secondary to those of the husbands. Today, in more than one-half of all two-spouse families, the wife works (see Figure 9.4). In addition, there is an increasing number of **dual-career families** *in which both wives and husbands are committed to career-oriented occupations that offer them fulfillment and opportunities for advancement.* Although it is difficult to estimate the number of dual-career families, census statistics

FIGURE 9.4 Percentage of Married Women in the United States with Spouse Present Who Are Employed, 1940–1994 *Note:* From *Statistical Abstract of the United States, 1978* (p. 404) by U.S. Bureau of the Census, 1978, Washington, DC: U.S. Government Printing Office; *Statistical Abstract of the United States, 1995* (p. 399) by U.S. Bureau of the Census, 1995, Washington, DC: U.S. Government Printing Office.

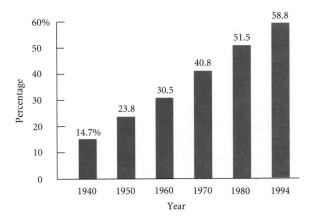

suggest that the number of dual-career couples has grown from 900,000 in 1960 to at least four million today (Barnett & Rivers, 1996).

One of the major tensions that people in dual-career families face is how to resolve disputes over whose career will take precedence. Such conflicts can arise, for example, if either husband or wife wants to move to another city or state in order to advance a career, especially if such a transition would be detrimental to the spouse's career. On a routine basis, there may be disagreement over whose career must suffer in order to raise children or to accomplish household chores. Although these tensions suggest that dual-career marriages are more susceptible to divorce, there is little convincing evidence on this issue so far. Evidence does suggest that women who work out of choice are more satisfied with their marriages than women who work out of a sense of financial obligation, and the men in dual-career families seem to be happy with their marriages (Barnett & Rivers, 1996; Vannoy-Hiller & Philliber, 1989). In addition, dual-career couples are more likely to remain childless, and childless couples tend to have higher levels of marital satisfaction than do couples with children (Houseknecht, 1987). One investigation of dual-career couples working in senior management positions described such marriages as "more equal than others" in that the couples share a more equal partnership, with a more egalitarian decision-making structure, than do couples in more traditional marriages. Furthermore, women in such marriages have greater opportunity to continue to pursue careers, as well as raise their children, in comparison to women in traditional families (Hertz, 1986).

Careers are attractive to both men and women because their work offers financial rewards, status, and excitement. However, the time and commitment devoted to careers compete with the energy people devote to family life, creating tensions in the family. Higher rates of childlessness among dual-career families may be an effort to avoid such competing demands. This solution might create other problems, however. If more people choose careers in the future, it is possible that many will resolve competing demands by choosing not to have children, possibly even choosing not to get married. This situation may

well create a substantial difference in the standard of living between those who devote their energies to careers and those who feel family is important: Careerists will have a substantially more affluent lifestyle, which may make the decision to remain childless appealing to even more people. The outcome, potentially, might be the birth of even fewer children in society. A low birthrate in turn could lead to a number of problems such as an increasingly aged and dependent population that would be difficult and expensive to support (see Chapter 14).

Singlehood

Today, 42 million adults in the United States have never been married. This figure includes slightly more males than females. Many of these people, of course, will eventually marry, but some will choose singlehood over marriage as a lifelong lifestyle. In addition, although the proportion of the population that is single declined between 1940 and 1965, it has increased considerably since then (see Figure 9.2). Added to these never-married people are the many widowed and divorced who, at least temporarily, are single. For example, there are ten million widowed people over sixty-five years of age in the United States, 80 percent of whom are living alone (U.S. Bureau of the Census, 1995, p. 57).

Many people who elect to remain single do so because they believe this lifestyle affords them distinct advantages: freedom from unnecessary commitments, economic independence, opportunities to meet new people and develop new relationships, room for personal growth, or the ability to have a more varied sex life that is free of guilt (Cargan & Melko, 1982; Macklin, 1987). Remaining single does not mean, of course, that there is necessarily a lack of emotional involvement with a partner who is at least semipermanent. Many singles develop intimate relationships, but they refuse to allow these to become permanent bonds based on marital exclusivity. However, as with childlessness among dual-career couples, being single—especially if chosen permanently and in large numbers—may have a long-term effect of lowering the birthrate.

Cohabitation

Cohabitation, or what is commonly called "living together," refers to *relationships in which two people live in the same household and share sexual, emotional, and often economic ties without being legally married.* In 1988, a survey showed that 5 percent of women between the ages of fifteen and forty-four were in a cohabitation relationship, and one-third of all women had cohabited at some point in their lives (London, 1990). Most of the couples involved are young, with 80 percent involving one partner under forty-four years of age. But a substantial number of the couples, approximately 5 percent, involve one partner over sixty-five, and 40 percent of the cohabiting men and 43 percent of the women were previously married (U.S. Bureau of the Census, 1995, p. 55).

People cohabit for many reasons (Cherlin & Furstenberg, 1994; Loomis & Landale, 1994). For some, it is a trial marriage, a time for the couple to get to know each other and determine whether they are compatible before establishing the legal bond. Others view cohabitation as a replacement for marriage, which some women and men see as an unnecessary legal tie. In fact, one group among which cohabitation has increased considerably in the past thirty years is the divorced. People increasingly turn to cohabitation rather than remarriage as a vehicle for establishing an intimate relationship after a failed marriage. These people see cohabitation as being as acceptable as marriage as a context for family-related activities such as having children. Finally, for some elderly couples, for whom marriage means a reduction in Social Security income, cohabitation may be a matter of economic convenience or necessity.

As the number of cohabiting couples has grown, the stigma associated with this lifestyle has declined. Cohabitation is now widely accepted in cities and college communities, and it will probably become even more popular, especially among young and divorced people. As cohabitation has become more common, controversy has arisen about the legal status of the partners in the relationship. Some employers, including some city and county governments, have established domestic partner provisions that accord cohabitants much the same benefits and rights as married couples. This practice has become more common as employers adapt to the kinds of personal arrangements their employees seem to prefer for their personal lives (Wisensale & Heckart, 1993). As a significant number of employees choose not to marry, employers are taking this choice into consideration in their policies. In addition, a number of courts have ruled that the relationship between cohabitants is not unlike that of married couples. For example, cohabitants can make legal arrangements to share their property, and one partner can sue the other for a share of the property and for support payments, or *palimony,* should the relationship dissolve. So, although some people continue to see marriage as the preferable route for organizing one's life, a growing number of people are choosing cohabitation, and the courts are establishing a legal framework that sees cohabitation as being very much like marriage.

Single Parenthood

A rapidly growing alternative to the conventional two-parent nuclear family is one in which there is only one parent. Today, almost 25 percent of all families with children under eighteen years of age are headed by only one parent, mostly by women (U.S. Bureau of the Census, 1995, p. 59). Furthermore, almost one out of every three children lives in a family in which one or both parents are absent (see Figure 9.5 on page 314), and half of all children may spend at least part of their childhood in a single-parent home. Although some families have only one parent because of the death of a spouse, most such situations are the result of divorce. Increasingly, however, children live with parents, usually mothers, who choose not to marry at all. More than three million families are headed by a parent who has never been married. The number of children living with a mother who has never married increased to 9 percent by the mid-1990s. Currently, 30 percent of all births are to unmarried women, in comparison with 4 percent in 1950 (see Figure 9.6 on p. 315). Given these trends in divorce and single motherhood, the proportion of single-parent families is likely to grow considerably in the future. Needless to say, people who view marriage as the only acceptable context for raising children find such developments very disturbing.

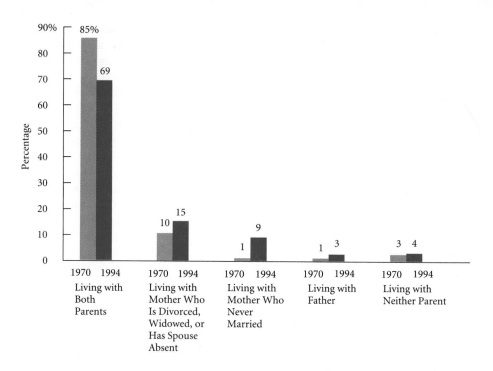

FIGURE 9.5 Living Arrangements of People in the United States Under Eighteen Years of Age, 1970–1994 *Note:* From *Statistical Abstract of the United States, 1995* (p. 66) by U.S. Bureau of the Census, 1995, Washington, DC: U.S. Government Printing Office.

The issue of single parenthood has been controversial because suggestions that children raised by a single parent suffer more problems than children raised by both parents have been strongly attacked for implying that mothers are not adequate parents or that parents should not divorce. These suggestions have been interpreted as limiting women's choices in life, a stance that is not popular in this era of gender equality. Yet, the research on single-parent families does suggest, in a qualified way, that children are often worse off when raised by one parent rather than two, suffering consequences similar to those of children of divorce mentioned earlier. A recent summary of this research concluded as follows:

> Growing up with only one biological parent frequently deprives children of important economic, parental, and community resources, and . . . these deprivations ultimately undermine their chances of future success. . . . While living with just one parent increases the risk of . . . negative outcomes, it is

not the only, or even the major, cause of them. Growing up with a single parent is just one among many factors that put children at risk of failure. (McLanahan & Sandefur, 1994, pp. 2–3)

Not all children in single-parent families will suffer negative consequences, because many factors influence a child's development. Researchers attribute the difficulties of children in single-parent families to three factors: low income, inadequate parental guidance, and less access to community resources. If a single parent can overcome these difficulties, then the children can do quite well. For example, when the decision to have a child is well considered by a woman with the social and economic resources to raise the child adequately, the outcome does not raise serious problems for society, although it might clash with the personal or religious values of some groups.

So, the research does not lead necessarily to the conclusion that divorce or single parenthood is bad. However, single parenthood is especially

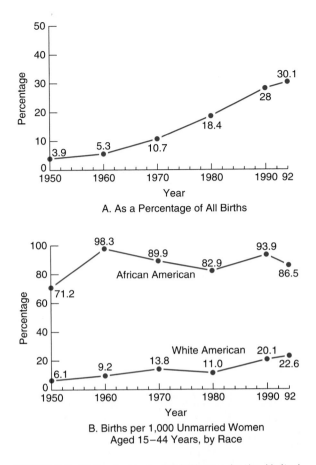

FIGURE 9.6 Births to Unmarried Women in the United States, by Race, 1950–1992 *Note:* From *Statistical Abstract of the United States, 1978* (p. 65) by U.S. Bureau of the Census, 1978, Washington, DC: U.S. Government Printing Office; *Statistical Abstract of the United States, 1995* (p. 77) by U.S. Bureau of the Census, 1995, Washington, DC: U.S. Government Printing Office.

ilies and from families with a history of welfare use (Chase-Lansdale, Brooks-Gunn, & Paikoff, 1991). Although the rate of teenage pregnancy is steady or falling in other industrial nations, it has risen over the last two decades in the United States. Teen pregnancy rates are now two to three times higher in the United States than in most industrial nations, and they are higher in the United States than in *any* other industrial nation (Moore & Stief, 1991). When single parents are unprepared for parenthood, society often ends up assuming some of the responsibility for the care and keeping of their children, and problems such as poverty, child abuse, and delinquency are often exacerbated.

The increase in single-parent families may be changing kinship in the United States toward a more *matrilineal* system. Anthropologists argue that the family in the United States has a somewhat matrilineal focus to begin with, in that mothers tend to be more prominent in kinship affairs and play a more central role in kinship matters (Johnson, Klee, & Schmidt, 1988). Men's role in the family system tends to be more peripheral and unstable. When the family is under stress, for example, it is more often the women who take control of the family. Men are considerably less likely to have custody of their children, and men are much more likely than women to be homeless or live in a nonfamily household. Furthermore, after divorce, children perceive their fathers as more socially and emotionally distant and less available to them. Postdivorce children also turn to their mothers for help much more than to their fathers. If divorce and single parenthood become more common, this matrilineal cast to kinship in the United States may become more prominent.

Gay Families

Gay and lesbian couples sometimes form units that, from a sociological perspective, resemble families because the units perform many of the functions that families perform in society, as described earlier in this chapter. These relationships are often monogamous, the norm for families in U.S. culture, with some degree of permanence and an emphasis on sexual exclusivity (Berger, 1990; Lewin, 1993). In fact, lesbians value monogamy in a relationship and are about as possessive of their partners as are men and women in

widespread among groups who are more likely to lack the financial resources to support the child, such as minorities and teenagers (Luker, 1996; Zill & Nord, 1994). For example, more than half of all births to African American and Puerto Rican American women are to unmarried women, and both of these groups have some of the highest rates of poverty in the United States (see Figure 9.6). For teenagers, in particular, becoming a mother is a difficult burden: They often lack the maturity and economic resources for good child rearing, and the burden often severely limits their educational and employment opportunities. This fact is especially true for teenagers from poor fam-

heterosexual marriages. A smaller percentage of gay men put as much value on sexual exclusivity in a relationship. Gay and lesbian couples sometimes have children from previous marriages or they adopt or conceive through artificial insemination. Children in gay or lesbian families are much less common than in heterosexual families because the courts have been reluctant to give custody to an openly gay parent, and adoption agencies have viewed gay homes as inappropriate for child placement. Estimates are that one-third of lesbians are mothers and between one-quarter and one-half of gay men are fathers, although many do not have custody of their offspring (Green & Bozett, 1991). Thus the socialization and education functions of the family are performed by some gay couples,

and research gives no evidence that the children are compromised in any significant way by being raised by a gay parent (Golombok & Tasker, 1995; Patterson, 1992).

Gay couples also often form an economic unit through the common ownership of property, such as a home, and the combining of financial resources. The courts have yet to give legal sanction to these economic ties, but some corporations are beginning to do so by extending benefits and rights to the unmarried domestic partners of their employees, whether they be a heterosexual couple or a gay couple. As evidence that the relationship is reasonably permanent, some employers look for signs of economic interdependence, such as joint bank accounts or co-owned property. Finally,

This gay marriage ceremony is being performed in Michigan in 1996. Although the idea of gay families is still controversial, sociologists recognize that gay men and lesbians often form same-sex relationships that have many of the sociological attributes normally associated with traditional families.

many gay couples provide the protection and the personal gratification that are among the functions of the units typically called families.

So, many gay men and lesbians form relationships that have many of the sociological attributes normally associated with families. To be sure, gay couples face significant stressors, especially when they perform parenting roles (Levy, 1992). They may suffer discrimination in both occupation and housing. They are also likely to be labeled deviant by many and cast into a marginal role. One way in which society marginalizes gays is by denying official legitimation to their bond in the form of marriage ceremonies or licenses that signify societal approval. Some gay couples have ceremonies to mark their commitment to each other; these rituals perform the same functions of public affirmation and legitimation that marriage ceremonies do. In Denmark, same-sex couples were given the right to marry in a registry bureau in 1989. In the United States, however, many people are still opposed to offering such societal approval to gay couples. Groups such as the Gay and Lesbian Parents Coalition International have formed to assist gay parents with these problems.

A Global Perspective

Some of the trends in family life found in the United States are also occurring in other nations (Bruce, Lloyd, & Leonard, 1995; United Nations, 1991). In the past few decades, for example, the percentage of births to unmarried women has increased in most nations, in some cases dramatically. The proportion has doubled in the United States to 30 percent, but in nations as diverse as Denmark, Norway, and Guam it has increased 300 to 400 percent. In the Seychelles, French Guiana, and Martinique, two out of every three births are to unmarried women. In addition, many households are headed by women: almost 50 percent in nations like Botswana and Barbados, 31 percent in the United States. Household size has also been decreasing in every part of the world, suggesting that the family is becoming a smaller kinship unit. The birthrate in most societies around the world has been declining, and the divorce rate has been increasing. All these trends suggest the extent to which the form of the family is shaped by the needs of society. Earlier, this chapter pointed out that industrial societies generally tend to weaken kinship and family structures, in part because the family in such societies performs fewer functions and is thus less important. Industrial societies tend to encourage nuclear families and to be more permissive of divorce. Such societies also sometimes split families up as some members must migrate looking for work. In addition, greater gender equality and higher levels of education for women offer them more opportunities in terms of supporting their families. The result, in most nations, is that the family has declined in both size and significance, and women have fewer supports with which to take care of themselves and their families. It is a worldwide trend—a by-product of industrialization—although the pace and extent of the developments vary from one society to another.

Violence in the Family

You should be able to describe the nature and extent of violence in the family and the social conditions that produce it.

The family is usually viewed as a place where love and affection abound, but one research team concluded that there is a darker side to family life: "Violence between family members is probably as common as love" (Straus, Gelles, & Steinmetz, 1980, p. 13). National surveys have concluded that one-sixth of married people in the United States have engaged in at least one act of violence against their spouse each year, although these figures probably underestimate the total amount of violence between husbands and wives because people are often reluctant to admit such goings-on in their families (Gelles & Cornell, 1990). More than 50 percent of married couples have had violent exchanges with each other at some point during their marriages. Of course, some of the violence reported includes pushes or shoves where no serious physical harm comes to the victims. Even so, it is obvious that a serious problem exists. Of the 51 million married couples in the United States, at least 6 percent experience conjugal violence involving kicking, biting, punching, or even more severe forms of violence (Straus,

1991). Violence of this sort also occurs among dating couples and cohabitants. Estimates are that one out of five college couples experiences kicking, biting, slapping, or more serious violence while courting (Murphy, 1988).

How are we to explain this high level of marital violence? One reason for it is that the use of violence to settle disputes is widely accepted in the United States, especially among males. Traditional norms in many U.S. subcultures support male domination in marriage. In fact, men with traditional, or nonegalitarian, views toward gender-role relationships are more likely to approve of using violence against a spouse and are more likely to have actually used severe violence against their spouse. A second reason is poverty: Serious violence within families is disproportionately a problem of the poor and economically disadvantaged. Families with low educational and occupational attainment are especially at risk of spouse abuse. A third reason contributing to marital violence is gender inequality (Crossman, Stith, & Bender, 1990; Kalmuss & Straus, 1982; Straus, 1991). Wife beating is much more likely to occur in families where power over decision making is concentrated in the husband's hands—the rate is approximately twenty times that found in families where egalitarian decision making is accepted. When women have more social and economic resources, such as a job with which to support themselves, they are less likely to be abused and more likely to leave an abusive husband. A final reason contributing to marital violence is social isolation: When a spouse has few contacts with people other than her husband, she is less likely to define the abuse as unjustified and to seek assistance (Stets, 1991).

Child abuse is also widespread in families in the United States, with 60 percent of couples acknowledging at least one violent act against a child. One investigation reported that more than one out of every one hundred children under the age of eighteen are the victims of serious abuse or neglect every year (Straus & Gelles, 1986; U.S. Advisory Board, 1995). As with spouse abuse, child abuse is concentrated not only among low-income families but also among the extremely poor (Gelles, 1992; Pelton, 1978). For these families, economic hardships interact with immedi-

ate situational stresses—disputes between parents, a burdensome number of children, a child who creates problems for parents—to bring about incidents of child abuse. Poor, young parents and poor, single mothers are especially at risk of using the most abusive forms of violence against their children. Child abuse is also a behavior pattern that is passed on from generation to generation in some families. For example, a review of studies on child abuse found that although around 3 percent of parents abuse their children, that rate is 30 percent or more among parents who were themselves abused as children (Gelles & Conte, 1990).

The elderly also experience abuse in families, with thirty-two out of every one thousand older people suffering some type of abuse, well over half of it physical violence (Pillemer & Finkelhor, 1988). Older men are more likely to be victims of abuse than are older women, and women are more likely to abuse their elder husbands than men are to abuse their elder wives. However, women suffer more injuries and emotional distress when they are abused than do men. Also, those who live alone or who are not married are less likely to suffer abuse than those who are married or live with others, and those who live with a spouse and an offspring are especially at risk of suffering abuse. One conclusion from these findings is that abuse of the elderly is in part a matter of opportunity: Those who live alone or with fewer people are less likely to be abused because there are fewer people around to abuse them. This fact is probably part of the reason why men suffer more abuse than women: Because women live longer than men, older women are more likely to be living alone than are older men.

To some extent, abuse of the elderly reflects one of the weaknesses of the modern nuclear family: It lacks the extensive support network and additional helping hands that are available in the extended family or even the modified extended family. As has been noted, people often expect each person in the nuclear family to be a breadwinner, a companion, and so on. When society burdens one person with a wide range of difficult tasks, including taking care of a child or an impaired older parent, the stresses will sometimes accumulate to the point where abuse is likely. Recent research, however, points to a different relationship between dependency and abuse: Abuse is more likely to occur when the caregiver is dependent on the elderly person under his or her care. Such abuse is especially likely when the caregiver is financially dependent on the elderly person under his or her charge, is personally or emotionally troubled, or abuses alcohol or drugs (Greenberg, McKibben, & Raymond, 1990; Pillemer & Finkelhor, 1989). In these situations, caregivers may be responding to their feelings of powerlessness in the relationship and resorting to one of the few power resources they have available: force and violence.

Thus, research on abuse of the elderly provides further evidence for the part that inequitable distributions of power and resources play in family violence. Those who are dependent—whether they be children or frail elderly—are at risk of suffering violence at the hands of others. Those with access to economic and social resources, such as wives with careers or the elderly who can live on their own, are better equipped to avoid violence. And those who feel helpless and powerless—such as poor, single mothers or caregivers who are dependent on their elderly charges—may lash out in violence as a reaction to their circumstances.

Family, Sexuality, and the Mass Media

You should be able to describe and explain how the mass media have affected the family and sexuality in modern societies.

This chapter has explored a number of social forces that have produced dramatic changes in family life and human sexuality, especially the role of industrialization. The modern mass media, especially now that they are establishing a global reach, have been a significant part of this impact in the last half of the twentieth century. As Chapter 3 points out, the media are one of the most important agencies of socialization. In fact, the media, and especially television, have probably come to rival the family as the most significant socializer of children in the United States and other nations where the media are pervasive. In most human societies through history, parents and families have been the dominant forces in children's lives and have largely controlled the transmission of values and norms having to do with religion, sexuality, and other matters. Now, through the compelling vehicle of television, advertisers, producers, and media corporate executives have the attention of children with limited interference from their parents. Some people have argued that this produces a further erosion of the importance of family and kinship in society as family and parents become less central in the transmission of cultural values and norms. For young children, television has become an electronic nanny, relieving parents of some of the difficulty and drudgery of overseeing the activities of children but also becoming a powerful and competing influence in the children's lives.

Whereas many people, especially parents, bemoan this intrusion of the media into traditional family realms, sociologists and other social scientists have attempted to assess scientifically the extent and consequences of the intrusion. The research to date is equivocal in its condemnation of this new role for the media. Some negative consequences can be found. For example, Chapters 3 and 12 discuss the research showing that viewing violence in the media increases the likelihood that children will resort to violence in real life. What is unclear, however, is whether, in the absence of television, families would do a better job of socialization. In addition, those chapters also describe some positive functions of the media, such as providing a wide range of role models and educational programs to the young.

In addition to the role of agent of socialization, the mass media also function to shape people's beliefs and values regarding what the family is like in society or what it should be like. Studies of the content of television shows over the decades document changing portrayals of the family. The portrayals mirror actual family forms in some respects but seriously distort them in others (Huston et al., 1992; Murray, 1993). Through the 1950s, families on television always had two parents, and either they had two or three children or they were a recently married couple who had yet to begin having children. Popular examples of this were *Father Knows Best, Ozzie and Harriet,* and *I Love Lucy.* Although media executives claimed to be merely describing what most families then were like, this chapter has shown that at that time family violence was widespread, extramarital sex was not uncommon, and divorce did occur. Yet, television did not portray these social realities. Their absence from television helped to foster the belief that the happy, nuclear family with an average of two children was the norm. Television also tended to portray more middle-class and affluent families than existed in reality and to ignore working-class families or to portray them in a more negative light.

In the 1960s and 1970s, television began to portray more single-parent families; however, most of these families were headed by men even though in reality most single-parent families were headed by women. These early portrayals of single-parent families stood out in another regard: The family resulted from a parental death rather than divorce, even though divorce, then and now, is the far more common cause for a family to have only one parent. Despite the appearance of single-parent families on television during these decades, most family portrayals were still of traditional families, often presented in an almost idyllic version, such as on *The Waltons* and *Little House on the Prairie.* Working-class families also made more of an appearance in this period, such as the Bunker family in *All in the Family,* but they were typically presented in a negative, although humorous, light (for example, the character of the lovable but bumbling and racist Archie Bunker).

By the 1980s and 1990s, the portrayal of families on television has become more realistically diverse, with more single-parent, female-headed families portrayed. However, the ratio of male to female single-parent families is still much more heavily skewed toward the male end than is the case among actual families. In addition, television still downplays some of the serious problems that confront modern families, such as poverty, access to child care, family conflict and violence, and unemployment.

Another dimension of family life portrayed on television is the kinds of social relationships that exist among parents and children. Although there are exceptions, television portrays mostly affluent, competent, and successful families in which individual family members get along with one another reasonably well (although some superficial conflict does occur). The family members portrayed are far more intelligent, clever, and humorous than is true of the average person. To the extent that real parents and children use the portrayal on television as a model and source of norms for family life and interaction, their own families may come up woefully short in the comparison.

These portrayals of family and sexuality are important because research documents that young viewers' beliefs and values regarding family life and sexuality are affected by what they see on television (Dorr, Kovaric, & Doubleday, 1990). They tend to see the traditional nuclear family as the norm, despite the enormous diversity that actually exists. To the extent that these images are a distortion of reality, young people's efforts to organize their own personal lives will be based on a distortion of what is possible. The effect of television portrayals of families has probably been to support the status quo and to ignore or disparage any changes in family form that may have been occurring at a given time.

The Future of the Family

You should be able to discuss what is in store for the family as a social institution in modern societies.

Most sociologists today are confident that the family as a social institution will survive in modern societies such as the United States. To be sure, the family is changing, and it confronts some serious problems, such as a high divorce rate and too much family violence. As noted, however, the family unit performs important functions for society, and some type of family will persist for that reason. The real issue is not whether the family will survive but what form it will take. What seems to be emerging in modern

APPLYING SOCIOLOGY
Family Disintegration: Is It Real and What Should Be Done About It?

Over the past few decades, there have been optimists and pessimists among sociologists in regard to the future of the family in advanced industrial nations such as the United States. On the one hand, the optimists, such as Judith Stacey (1990) and Arlene Skolnick (1991), point to the strengths and the adaptability of the contemporary family and argue that there is really nothing to worry about. The high divorce rate is normal, they argue, and the alternative lifestyles that are emerging, such as single-parent or gay families, are adaptations that will make the family a more flexible institution in a highly diverse world. On the other hand, the pessimists are deeply concerned about the disintegration of the family and how it seems to be fueling some of the most urgent social problems. For example, David Popenoe (1993), who heads a national organization of experts called the Council on Families in America, points to evidence that he thinks demonstrates how crime, drug abuse, and many other serious social problems stem in part from the collapse of the well-functioning, two-parent family over the past three decades.

One of the major roles of applied sociologists in this debate has been to conduct research that will help answer key questions such as, Are single-parent families one of the significant causes of crime and drug problems? Are other factors, such as poverty, the real culprits? What social conditions produce such a high rate of single parenthood? And, finally, what social policies could help reduce the number of single-parent families or break the link between single parenthood and social pathology? All these questions need to be answered if we are to launch effective social policies to attack these social ills.

In fact, a number of these questions have been addressed in this or other chapters. For example, some of the social conditions that produce single parenthood (such as high divorce rates, changing sexual norms, and discrimination against minority males in jobs and housing) have been noted. It has also been shown that poverty tends to be an important factor in linking single parenthood and social pathology. So, applied sociological work in this area recognizes the complexity of social conditions that produce social pathology. Sociologists, for example, have tested a variety of ways of intervening in family violence to see which approaches most effectively reduce it (see Applying Sociology: How to Stop Men from Battering Women in Chapter 5). They have also provided support for family education and counseling that will help people make better marital choices and overcome the difficulties and conflicts that inevitably surface in any marriage. Sociologists have also done research on day care (see Applying Sociology: Day Care in Chapter 3) to find the most effective assistance for parents in two-parent, single-parent, and gay families as they struggle with the dual demands of work and child rearing. In all these ways, applied sociologists help individuals and society adapt as the family changes in response to social conditions in an advanced industrial society.

One thing to notice is that sociology focuses on *structural* considerations, as emphasized in Chapter 1: how social pathology arises from certain characteristics of the social structure and how social policy needs to focus on changing those structures (Sullivan, 1997). Clinical sociologists, psychologists, and other counselors also build on this information by working with troubled families in an effort to alleviate distress and mediate conflict (Hurvitz & Straus, 1991; Roberts, 1991). Sociology comes into play here because the troubles families confront are rooted in their social circumstances or in the weak or shattered social structures that surround them. Sociologists can help people identify inconsistencies or inadequacies in the role structure that might create difficulties in maintaining a marriage, or they might help individuals become aware of competing values that may lead teenagers to become pregnant. Sociologists and family counselors can then work with people to develop the strengths in their marriage and family relationships. Thus sociological knowledge about the place of the family in society, how it is changing, and how the family relates to other social groups and institutions can serve as a foundation for family counseling.

industrial societies is a **pluralistic family system** in which *a number of different types of family exist side by side, each having an attraction for some people.* So, in the United States today, some people live in extended families, some in blended families, and still others in same-sex families. Given the vast diversity in the culture and the changing role of the family, such pluralistic family arrangements are probably more adaptive. They permit people of many occupations, religions, ethnic groups, and lifestyles to find a form of the family that best fits their values and needs. Whereas some people are tolerant of this diversity, others find some alternatives to be morally unacceptable, and this conflict will probably persist in the future. Such conflict will be especially salient in the public policy arena where groups do battle to gain acceptability for their values or ways of life. For example, some have opposed public support for sex education for teenagers on the grounds that it promotes premarital sex and pregnancy outside marriage. Others have opposed treating gay couples as married couples, as some employers have done, for purposes of allocating employee benefits. The outcome of this conflict will determine which forms of the family are acceptable at any given moment, and that will likely change from time to time.

Some people have expressed alarm at the rise in the divorce rate during the twentieth century, predicting the demise of the family as we know it. Actually, the divorce rate has been fairly stable for the past twenty years. It may have stopped increasing because the marriage rate has declined by about one-third over the past thirty years (see Table 9.1). It may also be, however, that the divorce rate has risen as high as it is likely to go in response to changing social conditions brought about by industrialization. Nevertheless, there is no reason to believe that the divorce rate will decline significantly in the future. The current divorce rate in the United States may well be one that is commensurate with social conditions and the position of the family in a mature industrial society. In fact, many of the trends we have observed in the United States—toward smaller families, more divorce, and less respect for elders—can be found occurring to a degree in more traditional societies such as China and Mexico as they industrialize and modernize (Kosberg, 1992).

Still, the state of the modern family has been the focus of intense debate, and applied sociologists have devoted considerable attention to figuring out what its future is, as Applying Sociology: Family Disintegration (on page 321) suggests.

Summary

1. The family is a social institution based on kinship that functions to replace members of society and to nurture them. All societies have rules and norms that shape family and kin relationships; therefore, the family can take a variety of forms.

2. In the United States today, the family tends to be monogamous, egalitarian, bilateral, neolocal, and nuclear. Many American families, however, diverge somewhat from this pattern.

3. The functionalist perspective posits that some form of the family has existed in all societies because the family performs certain basic functions that are essential to human survival and the maintenance of society. The conflict perspective sees the family as serving the interests of the dominant groups in society.

4. Mate selection in the United States is an exchange relationship and tends to be homogamous. Also, the attitudes of people in the United States toward marriage and the family remain quite positive although there have been changes in attitudes in the past thirty years.

5. The divorce rate has been steadily rising in the United States, which may be attributed to the fact that people expect a great deal from the marriage relationship. Some couples are at considerably greater risk of divorcing than are others. Divorce has consequences in terms of people's health and the reactions of children. The family experiences of racial and ethnic minorities in the United States tend to be different from white family experiences.

6. The amount of sexual behavior occurring outside of the family context has been increasing in the United States, a trend that has implications for what constitutes the American concept of a family.

7. Many different family lifestyles have emerged over the past few decades in the United States. Many consider these lifestyles to be another dimension of the problems surrounding the family today. Among them are dual-career families, singlehood, cohabitation, single parenthood, and gay families. Some of the developments found in U.S. families can also be found in families in other nations.

8. Violence among family members is common in the United States, occurring chiefly between married couples or directed at dependent children or the elderly.

9. The mass media have come to rival the family as a socializer of children. Portrayals in the mass media do not simply mirror what occurs in reality; they also function to shape people's beliefs and values regarding family and human sexuality.

10. Most sociologists are confident that the family will survive as a social institution but that family relationships will be pluralistic in the future, with different forms of family existing side by side, each having an attraction for some segment of the populace.

STUDY Review

Key Terms

affinal kin

bilateral descent system

blended family

cohabitation

consanguineal kin

dual-career family

egalitarian family

endogamy

exogamy

extended family

family

kin

matriarchal family

matrilineal descent system

matrilocal family

modified extended family

monogamy

neolocal family

nuclear family

patriarchal family

patrilineal descent system

patrilocal family

pluralistic family system

polyandry

polygamy

polygyny

reconstituted family

refined divorce rate

serial monogamy

Multiple-Choice Questions

1. The mate selection process in modern industrial societies is most likely to involve
   a. arranged marriages.
   b. parent-run courtship.
   c. participant-run courtship.
   d. brideservice.

2. Which of the following perspectives would argue that family institutions exist in society because families make important contributions to human survival and the maintenance of society?
   a. The functionalist perspective.
   b. The conflict perspective.
   c. The interactionist perspective.
   d. The extended-family perspective.

3. By the early 1990s, the most common household in the United States had which of the following compositions?
   a. Male head of household, no spouse present.
   b. Female head of household, no spouse present.
   c. One person.
   d. A married couple.
   e. Two or more unrelated people.

4. Which of the following statements is true regarding the marital status of people in the United States today as compared to fifty years ago?
   a. A substantially smaller percentage of people are married today.
   b. A substantially larger percentage of people are divorced today.
   c. A substantially larger percentage of people are single today.
   d. A substantially larger percentage of people are widowed today.

5. The likelihood in the United States today that a marriage will end in divorce is closest to which of the following figures?
   a. 15 percent.
   b. 30 percent.
   c. 50 percent.
   d. 70 percent.
   e. 85 percent.

6. All of the following were identified as placing a couple at a higher risk of divorce *except*
   a. social differences between the couple.
   b. high socioeconomic standing.
   c. young age at marriage.
   d. whirlwind romances.

7. Which of the following statements is true regarding extramarital sexual affairs in the United States?
   a. Men are more likely to have such affairs than are women.
   b. Women are more likely to have such affairs than are men.
   c. Men and women are equally likely to have such affairs.
   d. The proportion of married people who have such affairs has declined over the past fifty years.

8. Over the past fifty years, the percentage of married women who work outside the home has
   a. declined steadily.
   b. increased steadily.
   c. increased until 1970 and then declined.
   d. increased until 1970 and then leveled off.
   e. remained level until 1970 and then increased.

9. Given the research findings on spouse abuse, which of the following women would most likely be at risk of being abused by a spouse?
   a. A woman whose spouse has traditional, nonegalitarian views toward gender-role relationships.
   b. A woman with high levels of education and other economic resources.
   c. A woman with an elaborate social network of friends and relatives.
   d. A woman who shares power over decision making equally with her husband.

10. Based on research on family violence, the text concludes that which of the following is a key element of the abuse of spouses, children, and the elderly?
    a. The high divorce rate.
    b. The growth in extended families.
    c. The inequitable distribution of power and resources in the family.
    d. A resurgence in patriarchy.

True/False Questions

1. The United States today has a bilateral descent system.

2. The matriarchal family appears to be emerging in modern industrial nations.

3. Extended families are more functional in industrial societies than are nuclear families.

4. Young people in the United States today, when compared to their parents, have fewer negative attitudes toward staying single.

5. Even though it is difficult for parents to remain together in a conflict-ridden marriage, research shows that children are almost always better off when such parents stay together rather than divorce.

6. There is a higher divorce rate in Hispanic American families than in Anglo families.

7. More adults are single (never married) today than was the case fifty years ago.

8. Looking at the trends in divorce and single motherhood, the text predicts that the proportion of single-parent families will decline in the future.

9. While the proportion of births to unmarried women has been increasing in the United States, it has been declining in most nations around the world.

10. Levels of child abuse are higher among the poor than they are among the affluent.

Fill-In Questions

1. In terms of residence patterns, patriarchal families are also likely to be _____ families.

2. The _____ family is one in which elaborate networks of visitation and support are found among extended relatives but each nuclear unit lives separately.

3. A(n) _____ family is one based on kinship ties that accumulate as a consequence of divorces and remarriages.

4. When marital partners are chosen primarily on the basis of the individual desires of the prospective mates, this is called a(n) _____ courtship process.

5. Marriage transactions involve an exchange of money, goods, or services between the families of the marrying couple; two forms of such transactions are _____ and _____ .

6. A homogamous marriage system is one in which people choose marriage partners who _____ .

7. A marriage system that allows people to have more than one spouse, but not at the same time, is called _____ .

8. The most common arrangement for children and teenagers in the United States today is to be living with _____ .

9. Two factors that account for the increasing frequency of premarital sexual activity in the United States in the twentieth century are _____ and _____ .

10. According to the text, the family organization that seems to be developing in modern industrial societies is the _____ family system.

Matching Questions

_____ 1. patriarchy
_____ 2. parent-run
_____ 3. more than one spouse at a time
_____ 4. status conferral
_____ 5. palimony
_____ 6. nuclear family
_____ 7. norms prohibiting interracial marriage
_____ 8. a woman marrying more than one man at a time
_____ 9. double standard
_____ 10. cohabitation

A. polygamy
B. cohabitant support payments
C. endogamy
D. courtship in preindustrial United States
E. trial marriage
F. function of the family
G. married couple and children
H. sexual norms
I. male domination
J. polyandry

Essay Questions

1. Describe the various rules of descent and rules of authority that are found in family systems in various cultures.

2. What is a dowry? What is the status of dowries in India? What problems have they created and why?

3. Compare and contrast the functionalist and conflict perspectives on the family. Be sure to address what functions the family performs.

4. How have attitudes toward marriage and having children changed over the past fifty years in the United States?

5. Describe the four social conditions discussed in the text that account for the rising divorce rate over the past century in the United States.

6. What are the social characteristics of couples who are at the greatest risk of experiencing a divorce?

7. Describe the family experiences of African Americans, Hispanic Americans, and Asian Americans. Show how their experiences are similar to and different from those of white Americans.

8. How and why have patterns of premarital sex and extramarital sex changed in the United States during the twentieth century?

9. Describe the trends in cohabitation and single parenthood in the United States in the past few decades. What problems have these trends created?

10. What are the social conditions that increase the likelihood of violence in a family?

11. According to the text, what is the likely future of the family in modern industrial societies? Is the family disintegrating? Argue both sides of this issue.

Answers

Multiple-Choice
1. C; **2.** A; **3.** D; **4.** B; **5.** C; **6.** B; **7.** A; **8.** B;
9. A; **10.** C

True/False
1. T; **2.** F; **3.** F; **4.** T; **5.** F; **6.** F; **7.** F; **8.** F;
9. F; **10.** T

Fill-In
1. patrilocal
2. modified extended
3. reconstituted, blended
4. participant-run
5. bridewealth, brideservice, dowry
6. have social characteristics similar to their own
7. serial monogamy
8. both parents
9. reliable contraceptives, feminist movement, technological developments that free the young
10. pluralistic

Matching
1. I; **2.** D; **3.** A; **4.** F; **5.** B; **6.** G; **7.** C; **8.** J;
9. H; **10.** E

For Further Reading

Berger, Brigitte, & Berger, Peter L. (1983). *The war over the family: Capturing the middle ground.* New York: Anchor Press/Doubleday. In this controversial book, two well-known sociologists argue that the traditional nuclear family should be embraced as a repository of important personal values and social virtues. It is a spirited defense of the embattled nuclear family.

Coontz, Stephanie. (1992). *The way we never were: American families and the nostalgia trap.* New York: BasicBooks. This enlightening book by a historian debunks the many myths that people hold regarding in how much better shape the institution of the family was in the United States in earlier times.

Fisher, Helen E. (1992). *Anatomy of love: The natural history of monogamy, adultery, and divorce.* New York: W. W. Norton. This is an interesting review of some of the things we know about various forms of sexual behavior. The author makes some cross-cultural comparisons but also considers the evidence regarding whether some sexual behavior involves biological programming.

Hill, Robert B., et al. (1993). *Research on the African-American family: A holistic approach.* Westport, CT: Auburn House. This is a comprehensive review of the current research on the strengths and weaknesses of the African American family in the United States today. It gives a thorough review of the social conditions in the African American community and society at large that have shaped the African American family.

Kitson, Gay C. (1992). *Portrait of divorce.* New York: Guilford Press. This book summarizes research on divorce and the divorce process. It looks at the reasons that people divorce, how divorce affects children, and ways that divorce might be prevented.

Moen, Phyllis. (1989). *Working parents: Transformations in gender roles and public policies in Sweden.* Madison: University of Wisconsin Press. This book explores some innovative social policies in Sweden that encourage women to have children and continue working. Some of the policies might be useful to consider for the United States.

Morgan, Leslie A. (1991). *After marriage ends: Economic consequences for midlife women.* Newbury Park, CA: Sage. This book analyzes the social and demographic differences between women who divorce and those who stay married and looks at the economic consequences for the women who divorce.

Moynihan, Daniel Patrick. (1985). *Family and nation: The Godkin lectures, Harvard University.* San Diego: Harcourt Brace Jovanovich. The author of this important statement is a sociologist-politician who argues that poverty among children is exacerbated by the disintegration of the traditional family structure and the growth of single-parent families. Moynihan's social policy recommendations are definitely controversial.

Pirog-Good, Maureen A., & Stets, Jan E. (Eds.). (1989). *Violence in dating relationships.* New York: Praeger. Because dating typically precedes family formation and because violence while dating may presage violence after marriage, violence between dating partners is a useful topic to understand in the analysis of family problems. This book presents research on the correlates and consequences of both physical and sexual abuse.

Sanday, Peggy Reeves. (1996). *A woman scorned: Acquaintance rape on trial.* New York: Doubleday. This anthropologist looks at rape and acquaintance rape as a cultural practice. She views rape and other sorts of violence between men and women not as a biological inevitability but as an outgrowth of cultural attitudes toward men, women, and sex in Western cultures.

Stacey, Judith. (1996). *In the name of the family: Rethinking family values in the postmodern age.* Boston: Beacon Press. Based on interviews with single mothers and working-class families, this sociologist paints a positive picture of the family, documenting its strengths and its more egalitarian division of labor when compared to the past.

CHAPTER TEN

Health and Health-Care Institutions

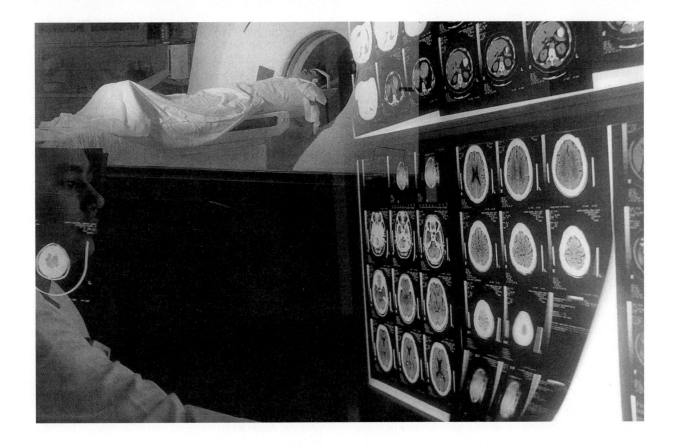

In the late Middle Ages, around 1200 to 1400, Europe was still a largely feudal society where serfs worked the fields under the tutelage of the nobility. Most people lived in rural areas, but trade and commerce were expanding, both within Europe and with the Middle East and Far East. Much of this economic activity was centered in cities, where merchants from the surrounding countryside met with traders who had transported goods from a far distance. Medieval cities were small by today's standards but growing in size and becoming increasingly crowded and unsanitary. These conditions set the stage for a terrible pandemic that afflicted the Continent and England and illustrates the many social implications of health and illness.

In one of the earliest episodes of the pandemic, a trading ship from Genoa landed in Sicily with sailors dead and dying at their oars (Tuchman, 1978). They were foul-smelling and in great pain, with terrible black growths in their armpits and groins. From such beginnings the bubonic plague, or Black Death, swept through Europe in the mid-1300s. It was by far the worst epidemic experienced in human history. Estimates are that one-quarter of the population of Europe and the Middle East died in the decade beginning in 1348; England and Italy may have lost as much as one-half their populations. Possibly as many as nine out of ten Londoners died (Paul, 1966).

Bubonic plague is a bacterial disease that is normally found in field rodents, such as ground squirrels, chipmunks, and rats (Hirst, 1953). Fleas that bite these rodents can also contract the plague bacillus. Rat and flea bites spread the disease to humans. When humans are infected, they experience fever, pain, and swollen lymph nodes in the groin and armpit (called *buboes*, hence the name of the disease). If not treated with antibiotics, most infected people die within a few days as infection of the bloodstream produces heart failure. If the plague infects the lungs, the disease becomes highly communicable because the bacillus is spread to others through coughing.

The reason for this pandemic of bubonic plague had as much to do with social developments as with biological ones. After all, the plague bacillus is a constant presence in the rodent population, but social developments increased the chances of its transmission into human environments. One such development was the growing medieval cities, which concentrated more people together and also made an attractive environment for black rats. Most rodents avoid human contact as much as they can, but the black rat is an indoor animal. The thatch and wattle-and-daub houses of Europe in the 1300s offered easy entry and a good hiding place for these rats. In addition, people stored food in their houses rather than in separate buildings, and the practice of the time was to throw garbage into the streets. The food in the houses and the streets filled with filth attracted more rats. All these social developments brought rats and fleas into closer contact with people. On top of that, medical knowledge was lacking in medieval Europe, and no one realized how the disease was spread. Pests and vermin were such a constant part of life of the times that no one suspected their role in disease.

Another social development was the growth in trade and commerce, which meant that more people were traveling around the Continent and over to England, as well as traveling overland and by ship from Russia and the Middle East. Infected rats, fleas, and humans spread the disease as they traveled. Medical researchers speculate that the plague entered Europe with travelers from southern Russia or China.

People responded to the plague with a variety of social behaviors that had implications for the spread of the disease and for other social institutions. Many fled the plague-ravaged cities for the countryside, not realizing that they often carried the disease with them. Social factors influenced who could take flight, since it was the rich who had country estates to flee to; meanwhile, as one historian put it, "the urban poor died in their burrows" (Tuchman, 1978, p. 98). Frightened populations seized on outlandish explanations—that the plague was a punishment from God for sins, or that European Jews had poisoned the water and caused the plague. The latter rumor caused the persecution and slaughter of many Jews. The Roman Catholic Church lost influence and authority because it could do nothing to stop the terrible scourge. People took their religious fervor to one of the many new sects that emerged, and the plague may have helped set the stage for the Protestant Reformation a century and a half later when papal authority was effectively challenged. The plague may also have contributed to the disintegration of feudalism and the manorial system because it produced a labor shortage that drove up wages and made it easier for serfs to leave a lord's estate and find wage work in towns and cities.

Thus the bubonic plague illustrates how health and illness are not merely individual concerns or biological matters but have important social dimensions. Social factors influence whether people become ill, and cultural values and social structure influence how people respond to illness. Societies create health-care institutions to cope with illness and cultural beliefs about what causes disease and how to treat it. There is also a social structure of healing roles to assist people who are sick, and illnesses affect how other social institutions, such as religion or the family, operate. This chapter will review these social dimensions of health, illness, and health-care institutions. Along the way, it will also assess the status of the health-care system in the United States.

Myths & FACTS

ABOUT HEALTH AND HEALTH-CARE INSTITUTIONS

Myth The poor in the United States receive shoddy health care, finding it difficult to see a doctor or gain admission to a hospital.

FACT Some poor people are quite a bit more likely than the affluent to see a doctor or be hospitalized. Government health insurance for the poor has given some of them far more access to health care than ever before, although it may be of lower quality than the care available to more affluent people.

Myth Women are healthier than men (or vice versa).

FACT Reality is complicated on this question. Men have higher mortality rates, but women are more likely to have acute, nonlife-threatening illnesses. Men, by contrast, tend to have higher rates of serious, chronic illnesses. So the facts on gender and health depend on how one measures health.

Myth Thanks to modern science, people today have a healthy diet and can look forward to a long life.

FACT People in most hunting-and-gathering societies probably had healthier diets than most people in the United States have today. They ate a wide range of fruits, nuts, grains, and other plant foods and relied on meat relatively little. Hunters and gatherers could, if they survived infancy and childhood, look forward to a relatively long life. However, the hunters and gatherers still died at a younger age than most people today, and the quality of their life in terms of their health status was not nearly as good.

Myth By the end of the twentieth century, modern medicine has triumphed by becoming so effective against disease that people around the world are coming to rely on it exclusively.

FACT Modern medicine has become effective, and most people do use it, but people are unwilling to put all their eggs in one basket when confronting something as frightening and unpredictable as disease or injury. People continue to rely on alternative healing practices in addition to modern medicine when they believe these approaches may be helpful.

Sociological Perspectives on Health, Illness, and Health Care

You should be able to analyze health, illness, and health-care institutions from the three theoretical perspectives and show how social and political factors influence what conditions are defined as illnesses.

The three theoretical perspectives—functionalist, conflict, and interactionist—provide an introduction to the sociological analysis of health, illness, and health-care institutions.

The Functionalist Perspective

From the functionalist perspective, illness has more to do with how well people can function in society than with their biological condition. Disease threatens the social order because those who are ill may be unable to make necessary contributions to society. Sick people may not be able to raise food, build houses, drive trucks, or rear children as they are expected to. This inability makes them burdensome and nonproductive; to use a concept from Chapter 5, it also makes them *deviant,* since they will not be behaving in ways society expects of them. In extreme cases, such deviance could threaten the survival of society if widespread disease produced social disorder. That happened among the Huron Indians, discussed in the beginning of Chapter 8, when French explorers brought diseases that devastated their populations.

Given these consequences, the sociologist Talcott Parsons (1951) argued that society needs mechanisms for returning people to their nonde-viant roles. Ostracizing or imprisoning them, which are common responses to other deviant be-haviors, is ineffective. Instead, society must help these deviants to become "normal" again. So, we call these people *ill* and place them in the **sick role,** which carries *a set of expectations intended to guide the behavior of people who are ill.* The normative expectations of the sick role are designed to facil-itate people's return to health. For example, peo-ple occupying the sick role are excused from their normal role obligations to the extent that the ill-ness calls for. This allowance provides people with rest that will facilitate the healing process. Sick people can also claim assistance and sympathy from others because such help can also advance the healing process. In addition, the sick role car-ries certain obligations: People are expected to seek competent care and cooperate with those try-ing to heal them. These obligations are also in-tended to speed people's return to health.

The function of health-care institutions, then, is to return people to normal social functioning. All the parts of the health-care system function to achieve that goal. Doctors, nurses, pharmaceutical companies, and hospitals each play a part in the process. To work effectively, the different parts of the health-care system need to be well integrated. Doctors diagnose illness, nurses assist doctors in bringing about a cure, and pharmaceutical com-panies provide the drugs that enable doctors and nurses to do their jobs. Each position in the social structure of health care has certain responsibili-ties. Doctors diagnose illness, but they don't man-ufacture drugs; likewise, nurses assist doctors in carrying out treatments, but they don't prescribe drugs. If the system works reasonably well, people will receive the help they need to regain health, if that is possible given the level of medical knowl-edge of the society. However, the system does not always work as smoothly as just described because social conditions can interfere.

For example, health care in the United States is operated largely as a profit-making institution, as is the rest of the economy (see Chapter 13). Because large sums of money can be made from medical services and products, there is consider-able abuse in these areas, such as unnecessary surgeries and the overutilization of drugs. In addition, people who are unable to pay for ser-vices often do not receive adequate medical care.

The point is that, in some situations, the profit-making dimension of the health-care system is not well integrated with, and may work against, the goal of achieving the highest possible level of health.

The Conflict Perspective

Health and health care are highly valued in all so-cieties, and they are also scarce resources. Interest groups compete with one another to gain what they feel is their fair share of those resources, as they do with other scarce resources. Staying healthy depends on having access to adequate food, satisfactory employment conditions, clean water, and good health care. Generally, as will be shown, people with higher social and economic standing in a society have greater access to these resources, and they are generally healthier than the less affluent. For example, high infant mortal-ity among the poor is not surprising, from the con-flict perspective, because the poor are less able to afford nutritious food, sanitary living conditions, access to prenatal care, and the other things that reduce infant mortality.

In addition to the issue of whether groups re-ceive services is the problem of how much those services will cost—in both monetary and non-monetary terms—and who benefits most from health-care treatment. In this context, the health-care system is an arena for competition among a variety of groups: health-care consumers, doctors, nurses, hospital administrators, medical techni-cians, pharmaceutical companies, and a host of others. People must pay, in some fashion, for health-care goods and services, and many people make a living through providing those goods and services. Naturally, what benefits one group, such as low health-care costs for the consumer, may work to the disadvantage of other groups, such as doctors and nurses. Beyond money, prestige and power are also involved in the health-care delivery process.

The inequitable distribution of money, pres-tige, and power in the health-care system may be viewed as a problem by those groups who feel they are receiving less than their fair share of resources. From the conflict perspective, however, there is no state of the system that is preferred or necessarily beneficial to all. If some group gains additional benefits, other groups must lose something. What determines who gains and who loses is the exercise of power. Groups have various power strategies available to them. Nurses and doctors, for example, can go on strike or in other ways withhold their services in order to force concessions from competing groups. Recently, many doctors began refusing to provide obstetrical services because of the substantial increase in malpractice insurance for that specialty. Another power strategy is to influence Congress and state legislatures to approve legislation that benefits particular groups. In fact, many interest groups in the health field have formed political action committees to collect contributions and press their interests. The American Medical Association (AMA) and other physicians' groups have been very effective at lobbying over the years, partly because of the substantial economic resources of their constituents. For example, the AMA has, to date, successfully fought all efforts to establish a national health-insurance program.

The Interactionist Perspective

The interactionist perspective emphasizes that health care is provided in a variety of medical encounters where people come together in face-to-face interaction (Waitzkin, 1991). In these encounters, doctors, nurses, and patients exchange symbols and social meanings as they perform their social roles. The symbols and meanings communicate information not only about disease and treatment but also much more than that—about social standing, valued statuses, and a variety of other things. For example, the fact that many patients wait long periods of time to see doctors but doctors rarely wait for patients who are late communicates who has more power and importance in the relationship. When patients are fed or taken to the X-ray lab when the hospital wishes rather than when the patients would prefer, it is clear that patients have less control over events than does the hospital bureaucracy. When nurses address doctors with the honorific title *Doctor* and their surname while many doctors call nurses by their first names, the stratification hierarchy of the hospital is reproduced and reaffirmed. In all these ways, daily encounters in health settings communicate something about social standing,

power, and worth, and tend to reflect those same elements in the larger society.

Illnesses themselves have social meaning and may imply something about the patient. Some illnesses such as cancer are frightening because of the pain and death that they imply. For a young man, a knee injury may be a badge of courage and prowess in athletic competition. Some health conditions may imply a socially devalued or stigmatized status, such as venereal disease for a prostitute or hepatitis for an intravenous drug user. In some societies, illness was considered to be retribution from God, and thus the sick were considered sinners. Some cultures considered the mentally ill to be possessed by the devil. In short, diseases are interpreted to mean something about the person who has them, and sometimes this meaning includes stigmatization and devaluation.

The three sociological perspectives identify social mechanisms that influence how people with illnesses are treated by others. This treatment can have important—in some cases, life-and-death—consequences for people who become ill. Such was the case with Acquired Immune Deficiency Syndrome (AIDS), which emerged in the United States in the 1970s, and the sociological lessons to be learned from the history of this disease make it worth an extended analysis.

Politics, Stigma, and the AIDS Epidemic

Understanding diseases such as the bubonic plague and AIDS involves a complex intertwining of biology with political, social, and cultural considerations. As the interactionist perspective suggests, health, illness, and disease are given meaning by people in a particular social and cultural environment, and how we treat those who are ill is a function of these meanings. The impact of social and cultural forces on the treatment of the ill is especially evident in seriously threatening diseases (Sigerist, 1977). Among the Kubu people of Sumatra, for example, serious diseases that produced high fevers were viewed as extremely threatening. In fact, they so frightened the Kubu that the sick person was shunned—isolated completely—as if he or she were dead. The ancient Babylonians had a different view of disease: It was punishment for sin and wickedness—it was believed that people who suffered pain and

Human response to disease is shaped in part by the social meanings that are imparted to the disease and its victims. Significant political and social pressure has been required to overcome resistance from many directions to providing support and research for AIDS.

discomfort were paying for their sins. Because of the spiritually unclean nature of sick people, they were marked by the Babylonians with a stigma. They were not physically shunned, but they were socially isolated until they had made some atonement for their sins. More recently, and continuing into the twentieth century, a disease such as leprosy has provoked reactions of both stigmatization and shunning or isolation.

We might be tempted to think that by the end of the twentieth century, our reactions to disease have become more rational and scientific than those of the Kubu or the ancient Babylonians. Yet social life is complex, and people's reactions to disease are no exception. In the case of AIDS, many social and cultural factors came together to produce a significant delay in

the attack on the disease in the United States (Burkett, 1996; Shilts, 1987).

Despite the growing scientific evidence in the early 1980s about the mode of transmission of AIDS and the ominous realization about its potentially monstrous dimensions, tragedy was heaped on tragedy when research and policy development were delayed as the disease spread. The reasons for this delay were complicated, but some of them are strikingly similar to the reactions to disease among the Kubu and ancient Babylonians. First of all, stigmatization of the supposedly unclean or morally suspect patient clearly played a role: The disease was linked with homosexuality and illegal drug use. Many people in positions of political and economic power in the United States either thought that these were powerless groups whose problems need not be seriously attended to or that they were disreputable groups whose lifestyle ought to be discouraged if not eradicated. In fact, some fundamentalist religious leaders declared that AIDS was punishment for the sins of homosexuals—not a far cry from the ancient Babylonian belief about disease. One conservative newspaper columnist wrote: "The poor homosexuals—they have declared war upon nature, and now nature is exacting an awful retribution" (quoted in Shilts, 1987, p. 311). Some people believed that these groups were sufficiently unrespectable that they were getting what they deserved, and the government need not respond too quickly to the growing epidemic.

A second reason for the delayed response to AIDS was the Reagan administration policy of smaller government involvement and greater austerity in social and health programs. The first AIDS victim in the United States appeared in 1980, and the Reagan administration entered office in 1981. The competition for government funds in the early 1980s was fierce, and AIDS researchers typically lost out.

A third reason for the delay had to do with urban politics. New York City had the largest number of AIDS cases in the country, yet New York Mayor Edward Koch refused to do anything about it for a number of years, apparently because of the belief that support for gay causes would link him with the gay rights movement and hurt his chances for reelection.

Fourth, the politics of gay communities figured into the delay. There were intense conflicts among gays over how, or whether, to respond to the AIDS epidemic. Some gays proposed closing gay bathhouses on the grounds that these places, where unprotected sex and multiple sexual partners were common, helped spread the disease. The owners of the baths objected strenuously, as did many gays who felt that such a move would be an attack on their sexual freedom and an attempt to restrict the open expression of their sexual orientation. As a consequence, the gay community found itself divided and unable to launch a united campaign for more research and programs on AIDS.

The overall consequence of these political and social factors was that AIDS research and programs were delayed significantly and the disease gained a substantial foothold. Had the government acted as quickly and aggressively as it has with other diseases (such as Legionnaire's Disease in the 1970s), the spread of AIDS would have been much less substantial. Once the cause of the disease and the mode of transmission were established, steps were taken to control it. The gay community, in particular, has emphasized health education, the practice of safe sex, and a change in sexual lifestyles as ways of preventing the spread of the disease. And this effort has resulted in dramatic declines in risky sexual behavior among some gay men, although unsafe sexual and drug use practices remain unacceptably high (Kolata, 1995; Lemp et al., 1994). Among intravenous drug users, their sexual partners, and their babies, incidence of the disease continues to grow.

Even if the disease were to stop spreading entirely, it is still a huge health problem. AIDS is now the leading cause of death among young adults. More than 200,000 people in the United States have AIDS, and close to one million are infected with the human immunodeficiency virus (HIV) that causes the disease; forty thousand new infections occur each year (Kolata, 1995; Rosenberg, 1995). This will translate into massive health-care costs as these people develop full-blown AIDS. Currently in the United States, three-quarters of the people newly infected with HIV are drug addicts, either heroin addicts who share infected needles or crack addicts who have unprotected sex with multiple partners. Heterosexual transmission of AIDS is growing, with about a quarter of the new infections so transmitted; another quarter of new infections are among gay men. Worldwide, however, 60 percent of HIV infection results from heterosexual intercourse.

AIDS is a huge epidemic by any standards, and its magnitude has been exacerbated by the complex social and political forces that influenced society's response to the disease. The reaction to AIDS brings home to us how much people in the United States are like the Kubu, the Babylonians, and all other human groups. Human response to disease is shaped not only by the biomedical nature of disease but also by the social meanings we impart to disease and its victims. By understanding this fact, we are better able to shape a more rational health policy that can effectively attack disease and protect health.

Health, Illness, and Society

You should be able to describe how levels of so-cietal development and a person's social posi-tion influence health and illness.

Social epidemiology is *the branch of sociology that studies how social factors influence the distribution and spread of disease in a group.* Epidemiologists have learned that which diseases afflict people depends very much on the kind of society they live in and their position in the social structure. This chapter will look first at how the diseases that are likely to kill or disable people have changed over time as societies have changed from hunting-and-gathering societies to agricultural and then in-dustrial societies.

Health and Societal Development

Most diseases can be classified as acute or chronic. **Acute diseases** are *those with a fairly quick, and some-times dramatic and incapacitating, onset from which a person either dies or recovers.* They are often caused by an organism or parasite that infects or invades the body and disrupts its functioning, such as with influenza, tuberculosis, and gastroenteritis. **Chronic diseases,** such as heart disease and can-cer, *progress over a long period of time and often exist long before they are detected.* Early symptoms of these diseases are often absent or easily ignored. They are usually caused by a mixture of biological, so-cial, and environmental factors.

In preindustrial societies, infectious and para-sitic diseases posed some of the more serious health threats (Black, 1978; Dunn, 1978). Diseases such as influenza, diphtheria, and typhoid could strike quickly and were highly contagious and often fatal, especially among infants, the weak, and the elderly. Accidents such as drowning and burns also took their toll, as did cannibalism, in-fanticide, and human sacrifice. All these threats added up to a life expectancy in preindustrial so-cieties that was rather short by today's standards, probably around twenty-five to thirty-five years. However, this short life expectancy was the result in good part of high rates of infant and childhood mortality; if one survived the illnesses of infancy and childhood, one had a reasonable chance to live much longer.

Anthropologists estimate that a hunter-gatherer who survived to age fifteen could antici-pate an average life expectancy of fifty-five years (Antonovsky, 1972; Konner, 1987). In fact, the hunter-gatherer lifestyle was basically healthy, with a good diet including a wide variety of healthy foods. People had little contact with other groups, so the transmission of diseases was reduced. When agricultural societies emerged, people's lifestyles changed and so did the threats to their health. Agriculturalists typically depended on a smaller number of crops for most of their diet and were thus more vulnerable to failures in the food sup-ply. So, starvation and malnutrition, which are in-frequent among hunter-gatherers, became a more serious threat. In addition, agriculturalists usually engage in extensive trading with other groups, a practice that set the stage for the spread of infec-tious and parasitic diseases.

With the emergence of industrial societies, there has been a dramatic increase in life ex-pectancy, to around seventy-five years in the United States today (U.S. Bureau of the Census, 1995). The death rate has also changed apprecia-bly, dropping from 17 deaths per 1,000 people in the United States in 1900 to just over 8 deaths today (see Figure 10.1). The declining death rate and increasing life expectancy can be attributed in good part to two related factors: declines in in-fant and childhood mortality and changes in lifestyle.

Infant mortality today is less than one-sixth of what it was a century ago. So a newborn infant today has a far better chance of surviving than did infants in earlier times and consequently has a bet-ter chance of living into old age. For those who survive through childhood, however, industrial-ization has led to considerably smaller increases in longevity over that of their preindustrial counter-parts. A study in Massachusetts, for example, re-vealed that the life expectancy of fifteen-year-olds in 1869 was only five years less than that of fifteen-year-olds a century later (Vinovskis, 1978). Fur-thermore, there was virtually no increase in the life expectancy of thirty-year-olds between 1869 and 1969. Another study showed that people born in the United States in 1980 can expect to live twenty-four years longer than those born in 1900. Someone who was twenty years old in 1980, how-ever, could expect to live only about twelve years

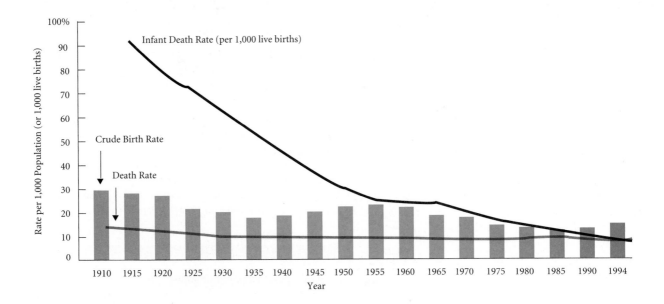

FIGURE 10.1 Birth and Death Rates in the United States, 1910–1994 *Note:* From *Statistical Abstract of the United States, 1982–83* (p. 60) by U.S. Bureau of the Census, 1982, Washington, DC: U.S. Government Printing Office; *Statistical Abstract of the United States, 1992* (p. 64) by U.S. Bureau of the Census, 1992, Washington, DC: U.S. Government Printing Office; "Births, Marriages, Divorces, and Deaths for January 1995" by National Center for Health Statistics, 1995, *Monthly Vital Statistics Report, 44*(1), DHHS Publication No. (PHS) 95–1120, Hyattsville, MD: Public Health Service.

longer than a twenty-year-old could in 1900 (National Center for Health Statistics, 1984). These figures illustrate that a major benefit of industrialization in terms of health and longevity is that we have a much greater chance of living through infancy and childhood. Industrialization provides less benefit in terms of longevity once we reach adulthood.

The second key factor in increasing longevity has been changes in people's lifestyles. In fact, such change has probably been at least as important as treatment offered by modern medicine (McKeown, Brown, & Record, 1972; McKeown, Record, & Turner, 1975). Industrialization has made available better diets, improved sanitation, better sewage disposal, and cleaner water. Consequently, people are exposed to fewer infectious and parasitic diseases and are better able to resist those to which they are exposed. The death rate for scarlet fever, for example, had dropped to practically zero by the 1940s, when effective medical treatment for it first became available (McKinlay & McKinlay, 1977).

Despite declining mortality rates and increasing longevity, we must all die someday, and the diseases we die of today are different from those of the past. In 1900 in the United States, the top three killers were acute infectious diseases, which accounted for more than twice the number of deaths that heart disease and cerebrovascular disease did (see Figure 10.2). Today, four of the five leading causes of death are chronic diseases, the fifth being accidents. So acute infectious diseases have become relatively unimportant in terms of mortality, and chronic diseases confront society with a different set of problems than did the acute ones in an earlier era (Mumford, 1983). Chronic diseases develop over a long period of time, may go unnoticed until extensive damage has occurred, and are often associated with people's lifestyles. Effective treatment of such diseases calls for continual rather than intermittent health care and may require that people change their lifestyles. Furthermore, the most effective and least expensive way of dealing with most chronic diseases is probably **preventive medicine,** *changes in*

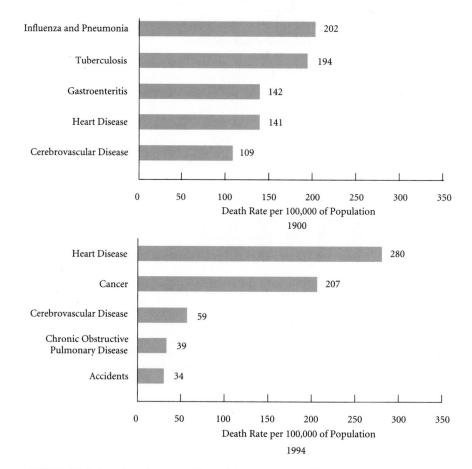

FIGURE 10.2 Leading Causes of Death in the United States, 1900 and 1994
Note: From *Vital Statistics Rates in the United States, 1900–1940* (pp. 210–215) by U.S. Bureau of the Census, 1943, Washington, DC: U.S. Government Printing Office; "Births, Marriages, Divorces, and Deaths for January 1995" by National Center for Health Statistics, 1995, *Monthly Vital Statistics Report, 44*(1), DHHS Publication No. (PHS) 95–1120, Hyattsville, MD: Public Health Service.

lifestyle or other steps that help avoid the occurrence of disease (McKinlay, 1986). Yet modern medicine is not organized around prevention but rather toward **curative** or **crisis medicine:** *treating people's illness after they become ill.* Modern medicine arose early in the twentieth century when acute infectious diseases were the major health problems, and medical education trained doctors with a crisis orientation. This approach is effective with such infectious diseases as influenza, pneumonia, or diphtheria, in which medical measures introduced after a person becomes ill can often return the person to complete health. With chronic diseases, however, much damage has already been done—and often cannot be reversed—by the time symptoms manifest themselves and medical intervention occurs. A person who suffers a heart attack, for example, may already have severe blockage of coronary arteries, and the damage typically cannot be completely undone with such modern medical measures as angioplasty or coronary artery bypass surgery. To date in the United States, preventive medicine has had a considerably lower priority—in terms of research and program funding, the construction of medical facilities, and the allocation of health-care personnel—than has crisis-oriented medicine. In fact, Joseph Califano argues that the crisis orientation in the United States has led to a sick-care system rather than a health-care system:

> We have been paying for a sick-care system. Fundamentally, we've provided too many financial incentives for doctors to treat us when we are sick rather than teach us how to stay well, to send us to the hospital rather than keep us out of it. (Califano, 1986, p. 186)

So we have come to depend on medical practitioners intervening after we have become sick and returning us to health. Some have argued that this dependence has become pathological because it blinds people to the part that they can play in maintaining and protecting their own health (Illich, 1976). Believing that miracle medicine can save them under virtually any circumstances, people may continue to smoke, overeat, and eat foods high in cholesterol. Too late they find out that medicine may be able to help them but it often cannot save them. People suffering with emphysema from smoking all their lives can gain some extra years of life from oxygen tanks and respirators, but there is no way that the damage to their lungs can be undone. People want to believe in the myth of miracle medicine, and medicine itself often helps to perpetuate it.

So one of the major problem areas in the health-care system in the United States today is that the health-care organization has not adapted to the changing nature of the diseases we face. Another problem is that, although death rates are down and life expectancy is up, people in the United States are not so well-off when compared with some other countries. For example, the life expectancy of women in fifteen other nations exceeds that of women in the United States, whereas men in the United States have shorter life spans than their counterparts in twenty other nations (see Figure 10.3 on p. 340). Men in Cuba and Costa Rica and women in Spain and Greece live longer than men and women in the United States. Likewise, the United States has a higher infant mortality rate than seventeen other nations (see Figure 10.4 on p. 341). In fact, infant mortality rates in the United States are almost *twice* as high as in Japan. Part of the reason the health status of the population is this low is that certain social and cultural factors have a detrimental impact on the health of many people.

Health and Social Position

Within any given society, social and cultural factors influence who is in greatest danger of becoming ill and dying. Four major sociocultural factors will be considered. Socioeconomic status, gender, and lifestyle have a similar impact on health in societies around the world. The fourth factor, race, is discussed because of the dramatic impact it has on morbidity and mortality in the United States.

Socioeconomic Status *Socioeconomic status* (SES) refers to people's position in society as measured by their income, educational attainment, and occupational status. The effect of SES on health is very clear: Those who are lower on such things as income, educational achievement, and occupational status generally have higher disease rates and death rates than do their more affluent counterparts (Aday, 1993; Williams & Collins, 1995). With few exceptions, the incidence of diseases such as cancer, heart disease, diabetes, high blood pressure, arthritis is higher among those in the lower SES ranges. Infant mortality is also substantially greater among children born into low SES families. One of the major reasons for the substandard health status of the poor is that they live in situations that substantially increase their general susceptibility to disease. They live under less sanitary conditions, have less nutritious diets, and are less likely to take preventive health actions such as obtaining routine physical examinations. Regarding infant mortality, poor women are less likely to have prenatal checkups and more likely to have poor diets that result in infants with low birth weights. These things contribute to infant mortality. Furthermore, despite the considerable advances brought about by Medicare and Medicaid, many poor people are not covered by these programs, and some health care still depends on out-of-pocket costs, which the poor usually cannot afford. Finally, the medical care that the poor do receive is likely to be of lower quality. They are more likely to be treated in a hospital outpatient clinic or emergency room where continuity of care, follow-up treatment, and patient education are less common than in a physician's office. And even when the poor have the same health insurance as the more affluent, such as Medicare, the poor do not receive the same level of health

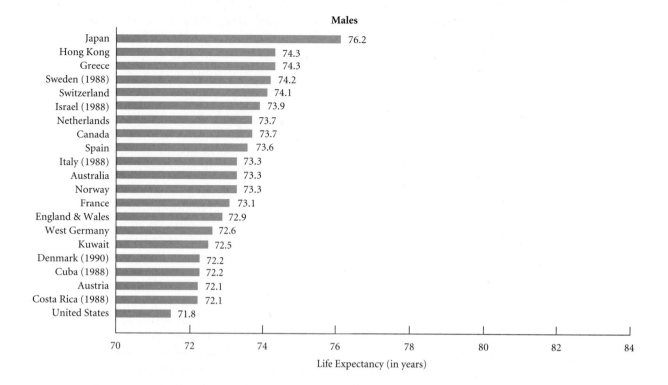

Males

Country	Life Expectancy
Japan	76.2
Hong Kong	74.3
Greece	74.3
Sweden (1988)	74.2
Switzerland	74.1
Israel (1988)	73.9
Netherlands	73.7
Canada	73.7
Spain	73.6
Italy (1988)	73.3
Australia	73.3
Norway	73.3
France	73.1
England & Wales	72.9
West Germany	72.6
Kuwait	72.5
Denmark (1990)	72.2
Cuba (1988)	72.2
Austria	72.1
Costa Rica (1988)	72.1
United States	71.8

Life Expectancy (in years)

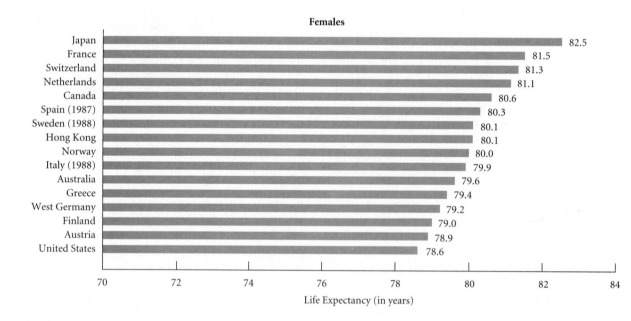

Females

Country	Life Expectancy
Japan	82.5
France	81.5
Switzerland	81.3
Netherlands	81.1
Canada	80.6
Spain (1987)	80.3
Sweden (1988)	80.1
Hong Kong	80.1
Norway	80.0
Italy (1988)	79.9
Australia	79.6
Greece	79.4
West Germany	79.2
Finland	79.0
Austria	78.9
United States	78.6

Life Expectancy (in years)

FIGURE 10.3 Life Expectancy at Birth in the Countries with the Highest Life Expectancies, by Sex (for 1989 unless other year mentioned) *Note*: From *Health, United States, 1992* (pp. 42–43) by National Center for Health Statistics, 1993, DHHS Publication No. (PHS) 93–1232, Hyattsville, MD: Public Health Service.

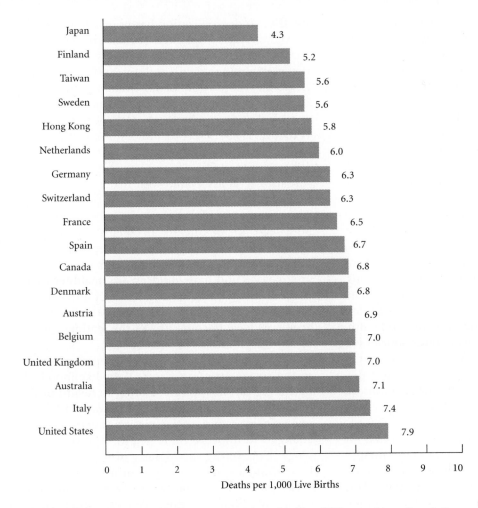

FIGURE 10.4 Infant Mortality Rates, Countries with Five Million or More Population, 1995 *Note:* From *Statistical Abstract of the United States, 1995* (pp. 849–850) by U.S. Bureau of the Census, 1995, Washington, DC: U.S. Government Printing Office.

care: Poor people receive fewer preventive services, such as influenza immunizations, and less adequate care for chronic diseases (Gornick et al., 1996).

Gender Women appear to be healthier than men, especially if we consider longevity as the key measure of health. The life expectancy of women today is seven years greater than that of men, compared with only three years more at the turn of the century (Figure 10.3; National Center for Health Statistics, 1984). Women also have lower rates of most serious chronic illnesses. What accounts for these differences? First, women may be biologically more capable of survival than are men (Wal-

dron, 1986). Males have higher death rates than females at every age, including deaths of fetuses. This fact suggests that women may have some sort of biological advantage in comparison with men, but the explanation is more complex than that. Higher mortality among males is also due to traditional gender-role definitions that encourage males to be aggressive and to seek more stressful and dangerous occupations where they might, for example, come into contact with industrial carcinogens. In addition, the lifestyles of men in the United States have traditionally been less healthy than those of women. For example, men drink more alcohol and smoke more tobacco. One health researcher concluded that "cigarette smoking is the primary cause of men's excess lung cancer and emphysema mortality. . . . The total pathological effect of smoking . . . makes a major contribution to the sex differential in total death rates" (Waldron, 1986). Although the gap between men and women in smoking and drinking has narrowed, it is still there. Finally, cultural definitions of women as the "weaker sex" may lead women to respond more quickly to symptoms and to seek medical care earlier in an illness episode. If so, this treatment may enhance the likelihood of effective medical intervention for women.

Race Most studies of the relationship between health status and race have involved comparisons between African Americans and white Americans. All these studies reach distressingly similar conclusions: African Americans in the United States are at a serious disadvantage when it comes to health, having considerably higher death rates, shorter life expectancies, and more serious life-threatening health conditions such as hypertension and diabetes than do whites (Manton, Patrick, & Johnson, 1987; Williams & Collins, 1995). One major reason for this difference, of course, is that race is associated with SES, with blacks being lower in SES on the average than whites (Keil, Sutherland, Knapp, & Tyroler, 1992). Yet even when researchers control for SES, some racial difference persists. This difference is probably accounted for by the unique social position of African Americans in the United States: The combination of years of racial oppression, poverty, and physically demanding occupations probably works to generate more stress in the lives of blacks than in other racial groups at the same SES level. This stress, in turn, produces greater susceptibility to disease. Minorities other than blacks also suffer substantial health problems. American Indians, especially those on reservations, have disproportionately high mortality rates from such things as accidents, alcoholism, and suicide, because of long-standing problems of poverty and unemployment (Young, 1994). Some of the impact of race on health has to do with discrimination: Research shows that, even when African Americans have the same level of health insurance as whites, they receive fewer and less adequate health-care services, and this undoubtedly contributes to their overall higher levels of illness and death (Gornick et al.,1996).

Lifestyle Industrialization has unquestionably improved people's lives, but it has also created health hazards, largely unknown in preindustrial societies, that contribute to death and misery. For example, a substantial portion of all human cancers are caused in part by environmental conditions, such as air pollution or chemicals in the water and soil (Proctor, 1995). Occupational stress is linked to heart disease and hypertension (Schnall & Kern, 1986; Thoits, 1995). Unemployment, or even the threat of it, is associated with many physical and mental disorders (Kessler, House, & Turner, 1987). The use of alcohol, tobacco, and other drugs can also cause serious health problems. There even appears to be an association between health and the quality of a person's family life: People who are married and have children are healthier than people who are single or have no children (Verbrugge, 1983). Finally, as Figure 10.2 illustrates, accidents have become one of the leading causes of mortality in modern society.

Thus, in many complex ways people's position in the social structure affects their likelihood of becoming ill. Any overall solution to health problems must take into account the ways in which people's lives and social circumstances can be changed to improve their health. Applying Sociology: Uncovering the Mystery of AIDS describes how applied sociologists use information about social position and lifestyle to help discover the causes of diseases. Other Worlds, Other Ways: Zaire (on pp. 344–345) explores this problem regarding the spread of AIDS in an African nation.

Health-Care Systems in Cross-Cultural Perspective

You should be able to describe the health-care beliefs and practices of personalistic, naturalistic, and scientific health-care systems as well as those of Chinese and holistic medicine.

Human beings have come up with a variety of explanations for what causes disease and how to cure it. In fact, because disease is complicated, unpredictable, and frightening, societies often have a number of disease theories in order to increase their chance of finding a cure. This chapter will review some of these beliefs and take a

APPLYING SOCIOLOGY
Uncovering the Mystery of AIDS

In the early 1980s, doctors in New York were surprised when some young men began showing up in their offices with diseases such as *pneumocystis carinii* pneumonia and Kaposi's sarcoma, a rare form of skin cancer. Both these diseases are rare in healthy young people. Adding to these physicians' surprise was the fact that many of these men were friends or had mutual friends. Sociologists, physicians, and other scientists at the Centers for Disease Control (CDC) in Atlanta were informed about these puzzling occurrences and began to look into a single possible cause. A first step in understanding a new disease is often to focus on the social characteristics and lifestyles of people who contract it to see if some clues might be found regarding mode of transmission or potential causes. Scientists at the CDC did this with these mysterious early cases. They noticed something distinctive about the patients: They were either gay males or intravenous drug users. Participating in this study was William Darrow, a research sociologist at the CDC with expertise in sexually transmitted diseases and the gay community. At the time, there was great controversy and confusion about the new disease. Many thought it was relatively unimportant, whereas others thought it might be linked to inhalants that some gays used at the time to enhance sexual pleasure. Darrow, looking at the social characteristics and lifestyle patterns of the early victims, was alarmed and concluded: "It looks more like a sexually transmitted disease than syphilis" (Shilts, 1987, p. 87).

In the first half of the 1980s, Darrow and other CDC scientists attempted to gather evidence showing that AIDS was sexually transmitted. If they could show that, they could make some recommendations about curing, or at least controlling the spread of, AIDS. As an important step in establishing that the disease was sexually transmitted, they needed to compare the sexual activities of gay men with the disease to those of gay men without it (Jaffe et al., 1983). They asked health departments, private clinics, and private physicians to provide names of gay men who would be willing to participate in the study. They also asked each AIDS victim to provide the name of a gay male friend who had not been his sexual partner. All these men were interviewed extensively about their lives and sexual behavior. In this pioneering study Darrow and his colleagues found a link between sexual activities and AIDS: AIDS victims, compared to those free of the disease, were more likely to engage in what is now called unsafe sex, they had many more sexual partners, and they were more likely to find sex partners in gay bathhouses. In a later study of AIDS among prostitutes, they used a similar sampling procedure: recruiting prostitutes from among women in prison, from venereal disease clinics, and from methadone maintenance clinics. In these studies, they found that the prostitutes at greatest risk of contracting AIDS were those who were also intravenous drug users and whose partners never used condoms (Darrow et al., 1987).

From research such as this, Darrow and other scientists fighting the AIDS battle were able to determine that AIDS was transmitted through contact with bodily fluids such as blood or semen. Once this fact was established, they could make some critical public health recommendations aimed at controlling the spread of AIDS: Test the blood supply for antibodies to the AIDS virus, educate people about safe sex, and close or closely regulate gay bathhouses and other settings conducive to multiple sex partners. Darrow's involvement in this research illustrates one of the contributions of applied sociologists to the health field: conducting research to discover the causes of illnesses and assisting policy makers to develop effective public health programs to attack diseases.

---

look at some of the health-care systems in which they are found in order to gain a sense of the variety that exists.

Personalistic Health-Care Systems

Small hunting-and-gathering bands often had animistic religions, meaning that they believed souls or spirits lived in the world and did good or bad things to people (see Chapter 11). Hunters and gatherers applied this animistic conception to disease and concluded that disease was an unnatural condition sometimes caused by spirit intrusion, that is, invasion by an outside force such as a spirit, agent, or ancestor's soul that still roamed the world. These are called *personalistic* health-care

OTHER WORLDS, *Other Ways*

ZAIRE: THE SPREAD OF AIDS IN A THIRD-WORLD NATION

Zaire is a nation of thirty-seven million people in central Africa. Sixty-two percent of its population lives in rural areas (United Nations, 1991; U.S. Bureau of the Census, 1995). A relatively poor nation, Zaire trails many Western nations in health statistics. The crude death rate stands at 16 per thousand, compared to 8.5 in the United States, and the infant mortality rate is 108 per thousand compared to 10 in the United States. The life expectancy in Zaire is twenty-eight years shorter than in the United States. Zaire also stands out in another respect—a very high rate of infection with the AIDS virus. In the urban areas, 6 to 8 percent of all people are infected with the AIDS virus, and in the rural areas 3 to 4 percent (Schear, 1992).

Zaire's heavy burden of AIDS infection is reflected in many other African nations (Lear, 1996). Overall estimates are that 1 in 40 Africans is infected with the virus, including 750,000 children. A million Africans have already died of AIDS. The AIDS epidemic in Africa is different from that in the United States in two important ways. First, almost all transmission of the virus is through heterosexual relations,

with only a small fraction through homosexual contact. Second, women make up half of the AIDS cases in Africa but only a small percentage in the United States.

The reasons for the pattern of the AIDS epidemic in Zaire have to do with social and economic life in that nation and many other parts of Africa (Packard & Epstein, 1992; Schear, 1992). Especially in rural areas, impoverished families have few opportunities for earning money. Even small landholders find it difficult to survive on the land and must look for non-agricultural income. As a consequence, many African men migrate long distances from their family, for months at a time, to find work. Especially in rural areas, families send their members, both men and women, to seek employment in urban areas or on plantations and large agricultural projects. Other men make a living by driving long-haul truck routes. This pattern has created a class of men and women who work in urban and industrial settings but who cannot afford to support their families there and so are separated from them for long periods. For such men and women, this life encourages the use of multiple sexual partners. Women who cannot find other employment often turn to full-time or part-time prostitution. Some African men who work far from their families maintain a relationship, and may even set up households, with second wives. Other men engage prostitutes when

systems because of the belief that disease is caused by the active, purposeful intervention of a sensate being (Foster & Anderson, 1978). In some cases, the evil agent was believed to be directed by a human being, such as a witch or a sorcerer. In some societies, even accidents were viewed this way: Falling from a coconut palm could be caused by witchcraft performed on a person by someone else (Harley, 1941). Another cause of disease, in the view of hunter-gatherers,

was improper behavior on the part of the patient, a breach of taboo, which displeased a spirit or ancestor.

Some personalistic beliefs can be found in folk medicine in many places today. For example, voodoo, which is practiced in some Caribbean countries and places that have many immigrants from the Caribbean, such as Florida, is founded on belief in the supernatural and witchcraft. Voodoo *root doctors* are believed by their followers

they are away from home. These social practices result in multiple sexual partners, which increases the likelihood of transmission of the disease. It also produces a high prevalence of other sexually transmitted diseases, which cause lesions that make the transfer of the AIDS virus easier. The spread of AIDS in Zaire and other parts of Africa, then, is assisted by the impoverishment and disruption of families.

Another factor contributing to the spread of AIDS is that many African men refuse to use condoms. Prostitutes are powerless to force such safe sex practices on their customers because the easy availability of prostitutes puts the customer in a more advantageous position. Wives who are in a subordinate position and burdened with children also may not be in a position to make such demands.

The consequences of the AIDS epidemic in Africa could be dramatic. The economies of Zaire and other nations could suffer a severe blow as the death toll increases. In the cities of Zaire and other central African countries, thousands in the professional elite groups have died in their prime. Some cash crops have remained unharvested because of the death toll among young agricultural workers. The same situation is occurring in mining, and Zaire's share of world copper production may dwindle in the coming years. Pessimistic estimates are that one-quarter of the workers in Africa will fall ill with AIDS or die within the next

fifteen years. The health-care systems in Zaire and other African countries are not up to such a burden. They have far fewer doctors, nurses, and hospital beds than Western nations, and their fragile budget cannot afford the costly medication that can ease the symptoms of AIDS but not cure the disease. In some cities, most of the hospital beds are already filled with patients with AIDS. AIDS will prove to be a terrible economic burden for economies that are already fragile.

One way to limit the spread of AIDS in Zaire is to reduce the migratory labor and prostitution that play such a key part. Such a change is unlikely in the near future, however, because there are not enough well-paying jobs near people's families so that they don't need to migrate looking for work. As long as these economic conditions exist, thousands of men will be migratory laborers and thousands of women will be forced into prostitution to support their families. Another approach is to encourage safe sex practices, especially the use of condoms. Governments have tried public education programs to change people's behavior, but without much success. In Zaire, however, entrepreneurs selling condoms for profit have experienced a tenfold increase in condom sales from 1989 to 1993.

to be able to cast spells on people that can make them sick or cure them of illness. (Voodoo is discussed at greater length in Chapter 11.)

Healers in these personalistic systems are *shamans,* a combination of doctor and religious leader, or *diviners,* people knowledgeable about the spirit world. The healers address both the immediate physical problem, such as a broken leg or nausea, and the question of what has caused it. If they decide that the cause is spirit intrusion, then they might suggest a remedy to expel the spirit, such as inducing vomiting or bloodletting. If they decide the cause is breach of taboo, they might serve as a counselor, assisting the patient in making a confession and atoning for sins. The healers deal not only with all kinds of disease but also with misfortunes such as the loss of a relative or disappointment in love. In their healing capacity they can serve as agents of social control by defining illness as a sign that people have not been behaving properly. Their medical recommendation might be for people to behave according to the accepted moral code of their society in order to cure or prevent disease.

Naturalistic Health-Care Systems

In the preindustrial, agricultural societies of China, Greece, and India, health-care systems developed that relied much more heavily on natural forces as explanations of illness. Unlike personalistic medicine, *naturalistic* medicine considers disease as largely the result of the impersonal working of forces in nature or the body. Supernatural beings or spiritual forces can influence how or when these natural processes work, but disease is basically a natural process that human beings can understand and influence. In such belief systems, the body is seen as made up of a number of elements; health results when these elements are all in the proper balance, or equilibrium. Disease occurs when the elements fall out of balance. Depending on the health system, the elements in the body might be heat and cold, humors (fluids), or something else. The elements can fall out of balance because of excessive heat or cold in the person's environment, a poor diet, or excessive emotion. In Greek humoral pathology, for example, which can be traced back to the sixth century B.C., there were four humors: blood, phlegm, black bile, and yellow bile. The proper balance of these kept a person healthy.

The healers in naturalistic health-care systems are physicians or herbalists who are trained in the remedies that can restore the body's equilibrium. Unlike the personalistic systems in which the healers are also religious figures, in naturalistic systems they are skilled practitioners who learn their art through training and apprenticeship. The focus of treatment is to restore the proper balance through changes in diet or by bleeding and purgings. Surgery is not common, although occasionally it is resorted to as a way to restore equilibrium.

Scientific Health-Care Systems

Scientific health-care systems view disease as a natural process caused by specific biological factors responsible for each disease (Salmon, 1984). Medical knowledge is based on scientific research rather than religious tradition, as in personalistic systems. Unlike naturalistic medicine, scientific medicine admits of no spiritual or supernatural role in the disease process. Disease is caused by natural, biological forces, and social and emotional forces are seen as secondary or unimportant.

Healers in scientific medicine are extensively trained physicians with a thorough knowledge of anatomy, physiology, and biology. The physician has responsibility for diagnosis and cure, and the patient is in a relatively passive role. Physicians may use invasive, or heroic, drug and surgical interventions, such as chemotherapy or open heart surgery. Physicians also centralize their healing activities in hospitals or medical centers where patients come to them rather than the other way around. Scientific medicine has risen to its greatest prominence in Europe and the United States in the past two centuries, although it is found in all nations of the world today.

Chinese Medicine

Present-day Chinese medicine is a good example of a medical system that has incorporated a lot of scientific medicine while retaining many traditional Chinese beliefs about health and disease. Traditional Chinese medicine is a naturalistic system concerned with the balance of two basic elements or forces, the *yin* and the *yang*. In Chinese philosophy, the yin and the yang are the primordial elements from which the universe evolved, and these two forces lie behind all natural phenomena, including the human body (Chow, 1984; Ergil, 1996). They are seen as complementing dualities, such as right and left, heaven and earth, good and bad, male and female. Yang is heat and can cause fever, whereas yin is cold and causes chills. So, some diseases are yang diseases and others are yin diseases, but yin and yang constitute a single entity in an individual, and the proper balance of each is essential to health. Thus harmony is equated with health and disruption with illness. Another important concept is the notion of *chi*, or vital energy, that flows through the body.

Healers in China have a number of procedures to influence the balance of the yin and the yang. One is acupuncture, in which fine needles are inserted into the body at key points to influence the flow of *chi* in the body. Another is

China has incorporated much scientific medicine into its health-care system while retaining many traditional Chinese beliefs about health and disease. Chinese Americans and others in the United States also use many traditional Chinese remedies.

acupressure, which uses fingertips on the same points to apply pressure. A third procedure is moxibustion, in which sticks made of rolled leaves are burned over points of the body for varying periods of time. The heat produced is thought to influence the flow of *chi.*

In modern China, scientific medicine and traditional Chinese medicine are used together to diagnose and treat disease. This combination is also favored by many Chinese Americans (and many others), who use acupuncture and herbal medicine alongside the medicines and surgeries offered by scientific medicine. Chinese medicine is but one illustration of the variety of healing practices used in the United States to supplement scientific medicine.

Holistic Medicine

Nonscientific healing systems treat the whole person in the sense that they focus on the psychological, social, and spiritual needs of the individual as well as the physical complaints. In naturalistic systems like the Chinese one, for example, it is assumed that a person's emotional state both affects and is affected by disease, so a healer might spend some time assessing the person's frame of mind and choose a remedy in part to produce a particular emotional outcome. Personalistic healers often come to a patient's home and include the whole family in healing rituals as a way of providing social support for the patient. Scientific medicine moved away from that practice by defining illness purely in biological terms. It assumes that emotions or spiritual condition is secondary or possibly irrelevant. Diagnosis and treatment can be accomplished by isolating the individual and treating the problem as purely biological.

In response to the impersonality of scientific medicine, many doctors, nurses, and patients have been drawn to *holistic medicine,* an effort to provide for the whole needs of sick people by using not only scientific medicine but also any other alternative healing systems that devote attention to people's emotional, social, and spiritual needs (Gordon, 1984; Micozzi, 1996). Holistic healing assumes that a person constitutes a single biological, psychological, and social unity and that disease can be effectively treated only if all three aspects are considered. In holistic medicine, the unique needs of each individual are addressed, and there is an emphasis on educating the patient in order to encourage people to take care of themselves rather than become overly dependent on scientific healers. Holistic healing does not shy away from using healing techniques that have not been accepted by scientific medicine. It might use chiropractic, homeopathy, naturopathy, spiritual healing, herbal therapy, or a range of other interventions that scientific medicine believes to have little therapeutic value. Many people use scientific medicine along with one or more of these other approaches when they become ill. One estimate in the early 1990s is that one out of every three people in the United States uses healers in these alternative areas during a year, and it tends to be the better educated and those with higher incomes who go to them (Eisenberg et al., 1993). With something as unpredictable and potentially threatening as disease, people are inclined to use whatever is available rather than rely solely on one approach.

Having noted the variety of health-care systems in the world and the fact that people frequently use more than one, this chapter will now focus on the social structure of health care as it relates to scientific medicine.

The Social Structure of Health Care

You should be able to describe the social factors influencing whether people seek health care, the various healing roles in the health-care system, and the consequences of the corporatization of health care.

In Chapter 2, *social structure* is defined as the organized patterns of interaction that exist in a group or society. Health-care institutions also have a social structure, involving identifiable and predictable ways that patients, nurses, doctors, and people in other healing roles interact with one another.

Seeking Health Care

One of the key roles in the social structure of health care is, of course, that of the person who is sick. The sick role has already been discussed along with some of the expectations associated with it. Recognizing that one is sick and seeking health care is a complicated process. The person must decide whether some physical or mental symptoms or distress is due to an illness and not just some temporary condition. If the person decides he or she has an illness that needs attention, then the person must decide whether self-medication is appropriate or whether a professional healer is called for. If a professional is needed, then the question is whether to choose a doctor, chiropractor, herbalist, or some other kind of healer.

Sociologists have done much research on the factors involved in these decisions (Andersen, 1995; Kaplan, 1989). One of the major factors is, understandably, the severity of the symptoms. With severe symptoms, such as traumatic injury or a serious heart attack, virtually everyone defines himself or herself as ill and seeks treatment from professional healers. Most illness, however, involves less severe and more ambiguous symptoms, and even serious illness like heart disease often first appears with mild and ambiguous symptoms. It is in these circumstances that social and cultural factors play a greater role. One of the strongest social influences on how we seek health care is SES (Dutton, 1986). People of higher SES are quicker to define symptoms as illness and to seek professional care. People of lower SES are more inclined to ignore minor symptoms or to define them as a part of the natural aging process. Part of the reason for this difference is financial: People of higher SES can better afford medical care. But more than finances are involved, since at each income level, people with more education tend to seek care more quickly than those with less education. Levels of knowledge also play a part; lower-class people tend to know less about the causes and meanings of various symptoms and be more frightened of possible medical treatments.

Before the introduction of Medicare and Medicaid in the 1960s, the poor went to the doctor less and were admitted to the hospital less than the nonpoor. This fact is especially surprising since the poor have more illnesses than the nonpoor and thus a greater need for medical services. These two programs, however, went a long way toward rectifying the disparity, and the poor now use health services more than the nonpoor. Nevertheless, given the greater need for services among the poor, they actually use services less relative to their need than do the nonpoor. In addition, they are more likely to visit a public clinic, public hospital, or emergency room where the service is likely to be less complete and less personal and involve considerably longer delays in receiving care.

Gender also influences whether one seeks help; women are more likely to seek medical attention than are men. The reason is partly that women have a higher rate of illness than men do. Also, because of gender-role socialization, women seem more inclined than men to seek assistance when they feel ill. Men are more inclined to ignore illness or attempt to take care of problems themselves.

Race and ethnicity also influence how people respond to symptoms (Kurtz & Chalfant, 1991). Mexican Americans and Asian Americans, especially recent immigrants, are more likely to rely on friends, relatives, or folk healers rather than go to a physician or a hospital. This preference is sometimes due to unfamiliarity with, or a distrust of, what seem like distant and impersonal medical institutions. It is also due to the greater availability of folk healers. In some Mexican American communities, for example, *curanderas* are available with many healing techniques familiar to people in the community. Likewise, in Chinese American communities, there are herbal shops and healers practiced in such ancient Chinese techniques as acupuncture and moxibustion. The underutilization of doctors and hospitals is also due to lack of availability. African Americans and Hispanic Americans are much less likely to have health insurance that would help pay for visits to a doctor or hospital.

So, one key element of the social structure of health care is sick people themselves—how they define themselves as sick, how they act on that definition, and what role they adopt. The social structure of health care also includes the various healing roles. Some of the healing roles in other cultures were discussed earlier in the chapter. Because of limited space, this discussion will focus on the major healers in scientific health-care systems such as that of the United States: physicians and nurses.

The Medical Profession

At the top of the hierarchy of healers in scientific medicine, of course, are physicians, scientifically trained practitioners who have primary responsibility for diagnosing and treating disease. Physicians have gained this position in part because of their effectiveness at curing disease and alleviating suffering. Equally important, however, is the fact that they have been politically active in seeking societal legitimation for their position as preeminent healers. In the United States, the establishment of the American Medical Association in 1847 marked the beginning of the effort to convince state legislatures to accord physicians a virtual legal monopoly over the practice of medicine.

Medicine today is considered a *profession,* an occupation that involves extensive training and in which members have exclusive control over a specified area of practice. Professionals also control entrance into the profession, set standards for performance, and exercise autonomy over the flow of their work (Freidson, 1970). As professionals, physicians receive considerably more income, prestige, and power than people in most other occupations. Chapter 6 noted that physicians rank high in the prestige hierarchy in the United States. In addition, they earn on the average approximately $175,000 a year, five times that of the average household income (U.S. Bureau of the Census, 1995). In part because of their high income and prestige, physicians possess considerable political power.

A significant trend in medicine over the past four decades has been the increasing specialization of physicians. General practitioners (GPs) in office-based practice declined from 22 percent of all physicians in the United States in 1965 to 14 percent today (U.S. Bureau of the Census, 1995). Specialization, of course, is one way for physicians to cope with a field of knowledge that has become increasingly complex and technologically sophisticated. In addition, there is an economic incentive: Specialization is much more lucrative than general practice. In fact, a recent specialty, called *family practice,* has emerged to perform many of the primary-care functions originally performed by GPs. The role of the family practitioner is to serve as the physician of first contact, provide basic medical care, and refer the patient to appropriate specialists. They are called *family* physicians because of the recognition that the family plays an important role in motivating people to stay healthy, in detecting illness, and in providing early treatment. Thus the family unit, rather than the individual, is viewed as the focus of health-care efforts.

Along with a dominant position in society, physicians are also dominant in the social structure of health care. For example, they have much more control over the medical encounter than do patients. The discussion of the interactionist perspective noted that physicians can be late for appointments whereas most patients do not have that leeway. Doctors also have societal authority to decide who is sick by diagnosing and treating disease. They are given this authority because of their expert knowledge of disease and medicine. Yet, in this process, doctors are also influenced by cultural beliefs and the social characteristics of patients. For example, some physicians believe the cultural stereotype that women complain excessively and therefore may take the symptoms of women less seriously. Research shows that when women complain of chest pains, physicians are much more likely to dismiss the complaint as due to psychological distress than if male patients complain (Tobin et al., 1987). When men complain about symptoms that prevent them from going to work, doctors intervene with medications; when women complain about psychological distress because of problems in the home, doctors tend to respond with sympathy but little aggressive intervention. In fact, overall, patients tend to interact in a passive fashion with their physicians, especially women patients. In regard to SES and gender, most patients are below their physicians in the social structure, which makes them less willing to be confrontative or assertive in the medical encounter (Waitzkin, 1991).

The practice of medicine has changed significantly in the past few decades (Hafferty & Light, 1995). Previously, most physicians were solo practitioners who worked independently out of their own offices. Such practices are much less common today. Now, many physicians band together with other physicians into some kind of professional and financial association. A group of physicians may share office space and equipment, for example, thus reducing costs and giving them more free time, since they can share the burden of work and cover for one another on nights and weekends. Another development is for physicians to become salaried employees, working for a group practice, a hospital, or a health maintenance organization. This opportunity is attractive, especially for young physicians, because it avoids the expense of setting up a practice. However, such arrangements mean a change in the practice of medicine because these employees, more than half of all physicians today, lose some of their autonomy. They are less able to decide which patients to see or how many to see, and they may lose some control over what diagnoses to make and treatments to recommend. Their employers can take an intense interest in their practice, especially in these days of concern about rising health-care costs, and may pressure physicians to make medical decisions that keep costs down and profits up.

The Nursing Profession

Nurses constitute the second most important group of healers in the social structure of scientific health care. During the nineteenth century, nurses had responsibility for hygiene and sanitation in hospitals and for maintaining discipline on wards. They were not considered to be assisting in the treatment process. With the proliferation of technology and specialization, nurses gradually came to be viewed as *ancillary* to medicine, with physicians assigning to them many routine chores, such as taking blood pressures. By the first few decades of the twentieth century, nurses had become defined as technical assistants to physicians, and the structure of domination among health-care providers had become solidified, with nurses subordinate to physicians (Bellaby & Oribabor, 1980).

This subordinate position of nursing in the health-care hierarchy has proved highly resistant to change, despite efforts by nursing leaders to emphasize the nurse–physician relationship as one of equals. Nurses have little control over their working conditions and little say in medical decision making. In addition, they are paid substantially less than physicians, with an average salary of $35,000 per year for a full-time registered nurse, and nurses share in little of doctors' prestige. Their subordinate position continues despite the fact that nurses today are highly trained and have considerable responsibility, dealing many times with life-and-death issues. In fact, much more of the health care of people who are hospitalized is provided by nurses than by doctors. One reason for

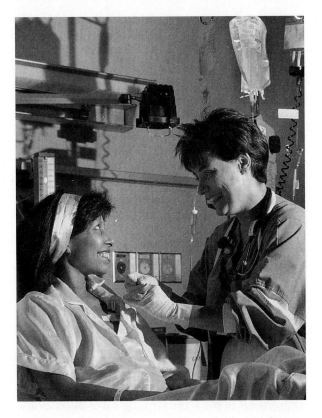

Nurses, nurse practitioners, and physicians' assistants provide much of the patient care today that physicians provided in earlier decades.

the subordinate position of nursing is that many physicians have strongly opposed upgrading it because they view an autonomous nurse as a person practicing medicine and thus a threat to their monopoly. In addition, nursing is an overwhelmingly female occupation, and nurses face the same obstacles to change that other women have faced in a society that is male dominated. Physicians, who are largely male, have tended to assume that employees who are mostly women need not be taken seriously or accorded respect and authority.

New Health-Care Practitioners

Until recently, there has been a shortage of physicians in the United States, especially in rural and inner-city areas. To alleviate this problem, the government has supported the development of physi-

cian extenders, practitioners trained to perform some of the simple and routine health-care tasks traditionally accomplished by physicians. Nurse practitioners (NPs), for example, are registered nurses with advanced training that in some cases includes a master's degree in nursing. Physician's assistants (PAs) have some medical training and can work only under the supervision of a physician. NPs and PAs do such things as conduct routine physical examinations or provide simple emergency and prenatal care. They normally work under the guidance of a physician and may serve as the patient's initial contact with the health-care system. In these ways, NPs and PAs provide medical doctors with more time to make complex diagnostic and treatment decisions. Studies show that NPs and PAs can do the things they are trained for as well as physicians can, and they can do it at substantially less cost (Robyn & Hadley, 1980).

Other alternatives exist to highly trained, specialized, and expensive physicians in the delivery of health-care services. Midwives, for example, deliver babies in many rural areas as safely as do physicians in hospitals, especially when life-saving technology is not immediately needed during the delivery (Durand, 1992). In fact, physicians tend to make more life-saving interventions that are not necessary, a tendency that actually increases the risk to the mother and infant. Health policy makers had hoped that alternative healers, such as midwives and NPs, would produce less reliance on traditionally trained physicians and thus make health care more accessible and less expensive. This substitution may not be happening, however, to the extent that it could. One reason is that some doctors are reluctant to accept these personnel, believing that only physicians are competent to provide key medical services. In addition, a surplus of physicians is now emerging, at least in some specialties. Consequently, physicians may come to see these other providers as competition for a shrinking health-care dollar. So the situation remains unsettled.

Hospitals and the Corporatization of Health Care

The earliest hospitals in history were traveling military hospitals to serve the soldiers of the Roman

Empire. Later, hospitals were places where the poor went to die. They served less of a medical function and more of a social-control function. People who could afford their own physicians avoided hospitals because hospitals could do little for them. With little specialized medical knowledge and only rudimentary medical equipment, there was little benefit to treating patients in hospitals rather than doctors' offices or patients' homes. As a result of the development of modern medical knowledge and technologically sophisticated equipment over the past 150 years, hospitals made the transition into modern medical centers for the effective practice of medicine. The social organization of these hospitals constitutes yet another dimension of the social structure of modern health-care systems.

Early in the twentieth century, most hospitals were nonprofit facilities run either by a religious order or charitable organization or by a city or county government. Their primary motivation was patient care, and they were highly accountable to their patients and the community they served. The people who ran the hospitals typically lived in the community they served, and the community had a variety of mechanisms for influencing hospital decisions and the allocation of resources. In the last few decades, a different type of hospital has become more significant: the *proprietary hospital,* an investor-owned, profit-making corporation. These hospitals are primarily motivated by maintaining and increasing profits, and as they become more widespread, the U.S. health-care system may change significantly. Consider the following examples:

1. A young woman was admitted to a for-profit hospital in Tennessee with a life-threatening irregular heartbeat. When the hospital learned that her health insurance covered only 80 percent of her hospitalization and that, being of modest means, she would be hard-pressed to pay the remaining 20 percent, it recommended she be transferred to a nearby university hospital. When that hospital had no room for her, the for-profit hospital discharged her with medications to take at home—a move that independent medical experts called "totally inappropriate" for "a patient who is a candidate for sudden death" (Lindorff, 1992, p. 16).

2. One hospital sent some of its physicians a memo informing them that their position at the hospital would be terminated if they did not admit more patients. It also kept a physician profile showing how many patients each one admitted, how long the patients stayed, and whether they payed their bills. Physicians who admitted the "wrong" kind of patient—the really sick, the elderly, the expensive, or the ones whose bills were not paid fully by someone—found they lost their privileges at the hospital.

3. Some hospitals refuse to treat ailments that are expensive and unprofitable. Many have closed their emergency rooms because these attract people of modest means who do not have health insurance and cannot pay their bills.

The hospitals involved in these practices are privately owned and intended to make a profit for their investors, just like a car dealership, a bakery, or a tavern. In other words, health-care institutions are a part of the U.S. capitalist economic system described in Chapter 13. This situation is not new. After all, physicians have been business entrepreneurs in the United States since the nation's founding, pharmaceutical companies have always tried to make a profit selling people drugs, and there have always been privately owned hospitals. What is different today are the size and scope of the privatization and corporatization of health care in the United States. One in four acute-care hospitals is now investor owned. In these corporate settings, control and authority over medical decisions and issues are gradually shifting from the hands of patients, physicians, and community leaders to corporate headquarters and medical industry entrepreneurs, and the primary motivation of these corporations is to increase corporate profits. The public sector of community and nonprofit hospitals is being forced to adopt some of the same strategies or be run out of business.

The corporate takeover of hospitals began with the emergence of Medicare and Medicaid, which meant huge profits could be made treating the recipients of these programs. By the 1980s, in the Wall Street world of medicine, patients were known as *revenue bodies,* hospitals were *profit centers,* and the goal was to maximize the return on each admission. What has emerged is a rather chilling trend: "Charging every penny that can be charged for patient care, and avoiding as much as possible the treatment of patients unable to pay. It also means marketing, or offering paying patients what they *think* they need, while eliminating services a community might *really* need but which aren't profitable" (Lindorff, 1992, p. 18). So young professionals with good health insurance get valet parking and luxurious birthing rooms, but poor pregnant women, even when they have Medicaid, find that they are not welcome. And the professionals have to travel farther to find a community hospital that offers emergency services when they have an accident.

There are, of course, benefits to this privatization. Especially for those with good health insurance or the wealthy who can afford to pay on their own, medicine in the United States provides some excellent services. As will be described in Chapter 13, capitalism is based on the assumption that competition and profit seeking will work in the interests of the consumer by providing the widest range of goods and services at the lowest price. These incentives should, in theory, encourage private health-care businesses to provide high-quality, inexpensive health care.

However, it does not seem to work out that way (Lindorff, 1992). In areas where many hospitals compete with one another for patients, both for-profit and nonprofit hospitals charge about the same for various procedures; when there is no competition, for-profits actually charge more for services than do the nonprofits. It seems that, in a noncompetitive environment, the temptation to raise charges, and thus increase profits, is too great to resist. The overall lower costs of nonprofit hospitals are especially surprising because they do not dump expensive services such as obstetrics in the way that the for-profits have.

The privatization and corporatization of health care also mean that those who cannot afford health care—the poor who do not qualify for Medicaid and those who do not have health insurance on the job—do not have access to the health services they need. Even those with Medicaid find that they have limited access to the system because corporate hospitals and doctors prefer to serve those whose insurance will pay higher fees for services than will Medicaid. In addition, expensive medicine, such as obstetrics and emergency medicine, gets dumped onto pub-

licly owned hospitals, which further taxes their ability to provide quality care to their patients. And some question whether profit seeking by doctors and hospitals always works in the best interests of the patient. As one health economist put it: "The real threat to health care is when the doctors' and the hospitals' interests become aligned against the interests of the patient. It's possible that the corporations could usurp the physicians' power" to act as an advocate for the patients (quoted in Lindorff, 1992, p. 86).

Dr. Arnold S. Relman (1980), editor of the prestigious *New England Journal of Medicine*, calls this a **medical-industrial complex:** *a coincidence of interests between physicians and other health-care providers and the industries producing health-care goods and services, with both parties profiting from the increased use of these commodities while the health-care consumer pays enormous costs for inadequate care.* This arrangement is analogous to the military-industrial complex discussed in Chapter 13. It can lead to a conflict of interest because many of the businesses are owned by doctors or employ doctors. Like other enterprises, these businesses stand to increase their profits by "selling" as much of their commodity as they can, just as a person who sells cars profits by increasing sales. This situation raises the question of whether health-care decisions are motivated by the health needs of the consumer or by the profit needs of the medical-industrial complex.

Looking at these problems with the privatized health-care system, some critics have argued that they arise, in part, because health care is different from other segments of the economy; it has elements that make it less subject to the laws of competition and the marketplace:

1. Ninety percent of the U.S. populace is covered by some form of third-party insurance, which means that they do not have to pay for many health-care goods and services out of their pockets. Because they do not pay directly, they have less incentive to shop around for the best buy.

2. In most economic situations, consumers decide how many goods or what kinds of services they will purchase. Health-care consumers, however, are heavily dependent on their doctors—the very ones who benefit economically from the provision of services—for expert advice on what they need. It is the physician who recommends that we have surgery, for example, and few health-care consumers have the expertise to ignore that advice.

3. Many practices common in other realms are not available in medicine. Consumers cannot, for example, test a health-care service before purchasing or obtain a money-back guarantee to protect against faulty procedures.

Many critics regard the profit-making nature of the health-care system as a major factor leading people in the United States to pay more for lower-quality health care than they should (Mumford, 1983).

There is contentious debate about what, if anything, to do about all these problems. Relman has urged the AMA to discourage physicians from commercially exploiting health care by being financially involved in health-care businesses. Other critics, such as Ivan Illich (1976) and Robert Sherrill (1995), believe that the capitalist nature of the health-care system is the fundamental problem. For these radical critics, only a complete restructuring of the system can prevent widespread abuses and exploitation. Some of these critics call for much more government involvement in protecting health-care consumers, controls over excess profit making in health care, and possibly even a socialized health-care system. Current social policy tends to support the profit-oriented nature of the system, but change could occur in the future.

Issues in Health Care in the United States

You should be able to discuss and evaluate the issues of rising health-care costs, adequate access to health care, the quality of medical services, and gender inequality in health care.

The previous section noted that people who can obtain access to health care in the United States often receive very good treatment. Yet, some people do not have that access, and other problems exist in the health-care system. This section will review some of the major problems that concern people today before turning to what might be done about them.

Rising Health-Care Costs

For most of the twentieth century, the rise in the cost of health care has been remarkably rapid and consistent. In 1970, it cost about $74 to stay in a major hospital for one day. By 1993, the average cost of a one-day hospital stay had risen to an astounding $881 (U.S. Bureau of the Census, 1995, p. 127). Per capita expenditures for health care have increased over fortyfold since 1950 (see Table 10.1). People now pay $3,607 each year for health-care goods and services for each man, woman, and child in the United States—more than $14,000 a year for a family of four. Inflation accounts for some of this increase, but inflation during the same period increased overall prices only about six times. What accounts for the skyrocketing growth in health-care costs? There are a number of factors (McCue, 1989).

First and probably most important is the fact that there has been a growing demand for health-care services, and a basic economic principle is that increasing demand for something tends to push up prices. The U.S. population is larger, more affluent, and older, and these factors tend to increase the demand for a finite amount of health-care goods and services. Affluent people can afford more and better health care, and they are more knowledgeable about what services are available. Older people have more health problems and require more health-care services. These services are also more widely available today because there are more physicians and more hospital services in suburbs and small towns.

Second, and probably equally important, is the availability of diagnostic and treatment procedures that were unheard of five, ten, or twenty years ago. These procedures can be very costly. Premature babies who would have died two decades ago are now saved in expensive, neonatal intensive care units (but at a high cost: from $200,000 to $1 million for an infant who weighs only one pound at birth). Laser surgery, CAT scanners, cobalt treatment, ultrasound, coronary bypass operations, angioplasty procedures, magnetic resonance imaging—these and many other procedures did not exist several years ago. Some think that heart transplants will be routine in the not too distant future, and they now can cost more than $300,000 apiece.

TABLE 10.1 National health expenditures in the United States, 1940–1994, expressed in percentages

	1940	1950	1960	1970	1980	1994
Percentage of GNP	4.0%	4.6%	5.2%	7.2%	9.1%	13.8%
Per capita expenditures	$29	$78	$142	$334	$1,054	$3,607
Percentage spent for:						
hospital care	25.0%	30.7%	32.9%	37.4%	41.0%	36.4%
physicians' services	24.4%	22.4%	21.6%	19.4%	18.9%	19.4%
dentists' services	10.4%	7.8%	7.5%	6.5%	6.2%	4.3%
other professional services	4.5%	3.2%	3.3%	2.0%	2.3%	6.0%
drugs and sundries	16.0%	13.7%	13.9%	10.3%	7.6%	8.4%
eyeglasses and appliances	4.6%	3.9%	2.9%	2.6%	2.0%	1.4%
nursing-home care	.7%	1.5%	1.9%	5.5%	8.2%	7.9%
other health services	2.4%	3.3%	4.0%	3.2%	2.4%	2.1%
expense for prepayment and administration	4.1%	3.6%	3.9%	3.6%	3.7%	5.3%
government public health activities	4.0%	2.9%	1.6%	2.1%	2.9%	2.8%
research and medical facilities construction	3.5%	7.0%	6.6%	7.4%	4.8%	3.1%

Note: From "National Health Expenditures, Fiscal Year 1977" by Robert M. Gibson and Charles R. Fisher, 1978, *Social Security Bulletin, 41,* p. 15; "National Health Expenditure Projections, 1994–2005" by Sally T. Burner and Daniel R. Waldo, 1995, *Health Care Financing Review, 16,* pp. 221–236.

Third, health care is a labor-intensive industry—it requires many people to act as providers—and the cost of health care rises quickly when health-care providers lobby for higher salaries. Nurses, nurses' aides, medical technologists, and many others think they have been underpaid in the past and are demanding salaries they believe to be commensurate with their training and responsibilities. In addition, although physicians' incomes have dropped slightly in the mid-1990s, their incomes previously rose at a much faster rate than the incomes of most workers: Surgeons' and radiologists' incomes nearly doubled during the 1980s, whereas full-time workers' incomes went up by 40 percent and full-time female workers' by only 12 percent (Anstett, 1992). Also, savings through automation are not as easy to achieve in the health field as in other industries. Advances in health technology often involve completely new procedures, which call for new technicians, instead of replacing something that had been done less efficiently by older technology. Thus improvements in health technology often result in the need for more, not fewer, workers.

Fourth, economic competition and the check on costs that it can afford are weaker in the health field than in other economic areas. Consequently, physicians and hospitals can raise costs with less concern about market considerations. As is discussed in Chapter 13, free competition is a key element in a capitalist economy, ensuring the lowest prices and the highest-quality goods and services. The ways in which the health field diverges from the ideal of free competition were discussed in the preceding section.

Fifth, there is a tendency to overutilize health-care services and even to perform completely unnecessary diagnostic and treatment procedures.

One reason for this is the way people pay for health care, which leaves both the physician and the patient with little reason to show restraint in the use of services. A very common mode of paying for health care, especially prior to the 1990s, has been through **third-party medicine,** in which *the patient pays premiums into a fund and the doctor or hospital is paid from this fund for each treatment provided the patient.* The first two parties in the transaction, of course, are the patient and the doctor or hospital. The third party might be a private health insurance company or a government program such as Medicare or Medicaid.

The basic flaw in such payment schemes is that the party paying the bill—the third-party source of funds—does not participate in the decision about how much or what kinds of services to provide. Patients have already paid their premiums and do not have to pay more as additional services are rendered, and physicians and hospitals benefit financially when more services are provided. The result is too many and sometimes completely unnecessary medical procedures being done. In 1992, for example, *Consumer Reports* published a study concluding that as much as 20 percent of all surgeries and medical services provided in the United States were unnecessary, costing health-care consumers $130 billion each year (Anstett, 1992). This problem is especially serious with very profitable procedures, such as coronary artery bypass surgery, 30 percent of which may be unnecessary, and cesarean births, 50 percent of which may be unnecessary (Barron, 1989).

Finally, there are a number of other reasons for increasing costs. The number of malpractice suits and the size of the financial judgments against physicians in these litigations have increased. Consequently, malpractice premiums for physicians rose by 18 percent per year in the 1980s, with some specialties seeing much greater increases (Brostoff, 1992). This rise in costs is then passed on to the health-care consumer. In addition, as mentioned earlier, crisis medicine tends to be more expensive in the long run than preventive medicine, but the health-care system still tends to emphasize the former. Also, many powerful interest groups benefit from rising costs: physicians, hospital administrators, the pharmaceutical industry, and so on. Health-care consumers benefit most from controlling costs, but they have yet to organize into a powerful lobby group.

Access to Medical Services

Many people in the United States do not have easy access to medical care (Wolfe, 1994). Because health care is a commodity sold in the marketplace, those who can afford to pay receive medical services, whereas those who cannot are left to fend for themselves. The high cost of health care means that only the wealthiest can afford to pay out of their own pockets for medical services. Most people rely on health insurance, either purchased by themselves or provided by an employer. The poor and less well-to-do, who cannot find a job or whose employer does not provide health insurance, are out in the cold (Seccombe & Amey, 1995). This situation has been eased somewhat with the introduction of programs of publicly financed health insurance such as Medicaid. Since these programs became available in the 1960s, the health-care utilization rates among the poor have increased considerably. In a comparison of people with equivalent health status, however, the poor still have considerably less access to health care than do the nonpoor. In addition, fewer than one-half of the poor are eligible for Medicaid (Howell, 1988; Newacheck, 1988). As a consequence, one-third of the poorest people under the age of sixty-five have no health-insurance coverage; for them, access to medical care is quite limited. In addition to the poor, there are others who find themselves without health insurance: laid-off employees; people who retire before they are eligible for Medicare; young people who are too old for coverage under their parents' health-insurance plan; and widows, widowers, and divorced people who had depended on their spouses' health insurance. Altogether thirty-nine million people, or 15 percent of the populace, are without health insurance (U.S. Bureau of the Census, 1995, p. 118).

One critic of the health-care delivery system argues that the United States has a four-tier health-care system (Steinberg, 1985). The top tier consists of people with full health-insurance coverage or some other means to pay for necessary care. They have complete access to excellent health care. Below them are those with limited health-insurance coverage, who do not have complete access but do have their essential health needs taken care of. The third tier consists of those on Medicaid, who have access to the health-care system if they can find someone to offer treatment or nursing homes that will admit them. Some Medicaid recipients find it difficult to locate physicians who will treat them. At the bottom of the system are the uninsured for whom access to health care is practically nonexistent.

Quality of Medical Services

Rising costs and the intense competition among hospitals may be affecting the quality of health care in the United States. To keep costs down and profits up, hospitals have cut back on services to patients (Gordon, 1995). For example, the number of registered nurses has been cut significantly, and their work has been taken over by lower-paid but less highly trained nursing assistants and technicians. Registered nurses are also given responsibility for supervising these less trained workers, further taking away from nurses' direct contact with patients. The Health Care Financing Administration has cited these and other cutbacks as among the reasons for a decline in services to the point of increased injury and suffering to patients in some hospitals.

Cutbacks such as these, along with the highly bureaucratic organization of the health-care system, can result in highly impersonal and even dehumanizing health-care services. The standardization of health care can benefit the health-care system because it is less expensive. Yet it can lead patients to feel dissatisfied, lonely, and frightened. However, if people receive expert medical treatment, does it matter if they are emotionally dissatisfied by the experience? Much evidence indicates that it does (DiMatteo & DiNicola, 1982; Mumford, Schlesinger, & Glass, 1982). Studies of the placebo effect document that what people think and feel about their treatment—their faith that they will be cured—affects the likelihood of a recovery. Other research shows that patients who receive group or emotional support from friends or health-care providers recover more quickly from illness, injury, or surgery. In addition, research indicates that people who are emotionally satisfied with their treatment by a hospital or doctor are more likely to follow medical advice. So, how the health-care system treats people does matter: People who are dehumanized are less likely to respond to treatment and less likely to do what their doctors recommend.

Gender Inequality in Health Care

Gender inequality pervades the health-care system in the United States, with widespread ramifications. First, the health-care industry is male dominated, with men holding most of the prestigious, well-paying, and powerful positions (see Figure 10.5). Men make up 76 percent of today's physicians, for example, whereas 93 percent of the registered nurses are women. Almost all dentists are men, whereas practically all dental assistants and dental hygienists are women. Clearly, the health-care system involves men in positions of authority telling women what to do. This was not always the case. In the nineteenth century, women, working as midwives or other types of healers, provided much of the medical care for families. As more medical schools developed in the late 1800s, women were excluded from most of them. By the turn of the century, legislation banned the "practice of medicine" by anyone not trained in a state-approved medical school. The result: Women were effectively banned from the practice of medicine. During the first half of the twentieth century, medical schools admitted few, if any, women. Even through the 1960s, medical and dental education were male preserves: Although a few women were admitted, they often met with hostility or demeaning jokes, making the difficult trek through school even tougher. It was not really until the late 1970s that medical and dental education began to open up to women. Today more than one-third of both medical and dental students nationwide are women (see Figure 10.6 on p. 359). There has been less change, however, in the sparse numbers of men in nursing schools.

One reason for concern about male dominance in the health field is that it has severely restricted women's access to lucrative and prestigious occupations. These issues of economic discrimination are discussed in more detail in Chapter 8. Another reason for concern is that male dominance may have had a detrimental effect on the health and health care of women (Scully, 1994). Male physicians over the years held the same stereotypes about women that other men in the United States did, and these influenced what physicians defined as illness and what treatments they made available. For example, one stereotype viewed menstruation as unclean or abnormal, and physicians contributed to this view by

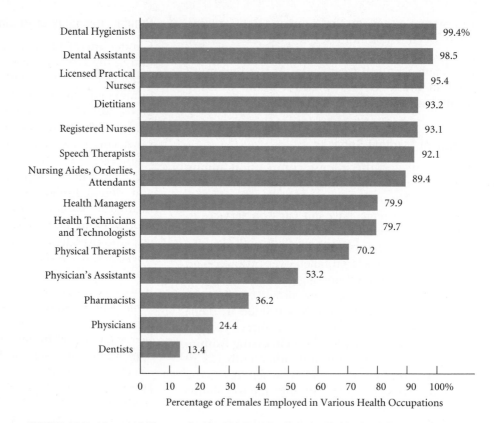

FIGURE 10.5 Men and Women in Health Occupations in the United States, 1995
Note: From *Employment and Earnings: Vol. 3, No.1* (pp. 171–176) by U.S. Department of Labor, Bureau of Labor Statistics, 1996.

"medicalizing" menstruation, defining it as a medical condition or weakness calling for some intervention. In the nineteenth century and well into the twentieth, menstruation has been viewed as a pathological condition sometimes having serious consequences and influencing women's ability to think and make decisions. In fact, the reputed ill effects of women's reproductive biology have been an important staple in a sexist ideology justifying the inequitable treatment of women. From the late 1800s until recently, the process of childbirth has been viewed as a medical procedure rather than the profoundly natural and personal event that it really is. Women were routinely given powerful anesthetics that prevented them from experiencing the birth of their children. Then they might not even be permitted to see their infants for a few days after birth, a practice that interfered with the bonding that occurs between mothers and babies. More recently, the number of cesarean births has grown from 5 percent to almost 25 percent of all

births, giving the United States the highest rate of such births (U.S. Bureau of the Census, 1995). Some cesareans, of course, are medically justified, but there is much suspicion that some are performed for the convenience of medical personnel, to protect against malpractice suits, or because doctors and hospitals are reimbursed more for surgical births. In any event, the mother loses control of the birth process when it becomes overly medicalized. Over the years, then, male dominance in medicine has meant that men have been the "authorities" telling women about their own bodies, and what the men told the women sometimes did more to bolster inaccurate stereotypes or line the pockets of physicians than to benefit the health of women.

The medical procedure that is among those most likely to be performed unnecessarily—hysterectomy—affects only women. A conservative estimate is that one-third of all hysterectomies over the years were probably medically unjustified

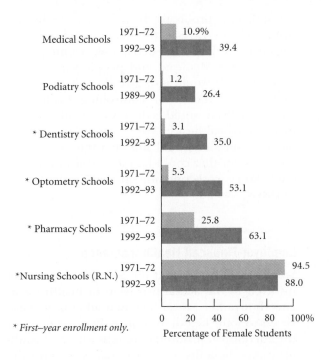

Medical Schools	1971–72	10.9%
	1992–93	39.4
Podiatry Schools	1971–72	1.2
	1989–90	26.4
* Dentistry Schools	1971–72	3.1
	1992–93	35.0
* Optometry Schools	1971–72	5.3
	1992–93	53.1
* Pharmacy Schools	1971–72	25.8
	1992–93	63.1
*Nursing Schools (R.N.)	1971–72	94.5
	1992–93	88.0

0 20 40 60 80 100%

* First–year enrollment only.

Percentage of Female Students

FIGURE 10.6 Enrollment of Women in Schools for Health Occupations, United States, Academic Years 1971–1993 *Note*: From *Health, United States, 1990* (p. 172) by National Center for Health Statistics, 1991, DHHS Publication No. (PHS) 91–1232, Hyattsville, MD: Public Health Service; *Health, United States, 1994* (p. 210) by National Center for Health Statistics, 1995, DHHS Publication No. (PHS) 95–1232, Hyattsville, MD: Public Health Service.

(Stroman, 1979). Some observers have questioned whether a medical profession dominated by women would have routinely performed such surgeries. In addition, feminists argue that medical research has been dominated by the sexist assumption that it is the woman's responsibility to orchestrate birth-control efforts. Consequently, most birth-control research has been focused on female contraceptive devices rather than effective procedures for male contraception.

Financing Health Care in the United States

You should be able to analyze the various alternative ways of financing health care in the United States and discuss whether health care is a privilege or a right.

One approach to alleviating some of the problems discussed in the preceding section is to find a better way of financing health care in the United States. Such financing has been a highly controversial issue, and this section will review some of the major proposals for change.

Publicly Funded Health Insurance

One approach to increasing people's access to health care is through publicly funded health insurance. Two government programs that have probably had the most profound effects on health-care delivery in the United States are Medicare and Medicaid, both established in 1965. These programs are based on the assumption that all citizens have a right to medical treatment irrespective of their financial circumstances. **Medicare** is *government health insurance for those over sixty-five years of age.* The program pays some of the costs for hospitalization, nursing-home care, and some home health care. For a monthly fee, the elderly can also purchase medical insurance from Medicare that will cover other services such as doctors' fees and outpatient services. **Medicaid** is *a joint federal–state program to provide medical care for low-income people of any age.*

These two programs have gone a long way toward reducing the differences in the use of health care between the affluent and the poor. Unlike in the past, the poor today visit doctors and enter hospitals more frequently than the well-to-do. To that extent, these two programs have achieved one of their major goals, which was to make health care available to all citizens regardless of financial circumstances. But these plans are not without their problems. First, they are very expensive and growing more so. Both traditionally have involved third-party payment arrangements and suffered from the same cost problems of all such fee schemes. A second problem, especially with Medicaid, has been fraud, committed by both recipients and providers of health care. Some physicians have provided unneeded treatments, and some medical laboratories have routinely charged for tests never performed (Jesilow, Pontell, & Geis, 1993).

A number of efforts have been made to control the skyrocketing costs of Medicaid and Medicare. Some states have developed *preferred provider* programs for Medicaid in which a hospital or a group of doctors agrees to provide all health-care services to Medicaid recipients in a particular geographic area, receiving, in return, one annual, lump-sum payment. This arrangement encourages the providers to prevent costs from exceeding the annual amount that they are paid because they will not receive any additional payments and are contractually required to provide services. For Medicare, the federal government instituted a new payment mechanism in the early 1980s called diagnostically related groupings (DRGs). This strategy involves placing each hospitalization episode into one of about 450 diagnostic groupings. Then all treatments in a single grouping receive the same reimbursement, whether any particular case actually costs more or less. If a case costs more to treat, the hospital must make up the difference; if it costs less, the hospital keeps the surplus. The purpose is to offer doctors and hospitals a financial incentive for keeping an eye on lowering costs.

Medicare and Medicaid amount to government health insurance for the poor and the elderly. Some have proposed that these benefits be extended as a right to all citizens through **national health insurance:** *government health insurance covering all citizens* (Intriligator, 1993). Great Britain had such a program as early as 1911. In fact, the United States is alone among the industrial nations in not providing some form of national health insurance or health service (Lindorff, 1992). National health insurance would alleviate a number of problems. It would ensure health-insurance coverage to the many people who do not currently have any, such as low-income people ineligible for Medicaid and people who are between jobs. It would also give the government a more direct means of controlling health-care costs. Finally, it would reduce the likelihood of a two-tiered health-care system. However, national health insurance would still be a third-party payment system that could be costly if it did not include some cost-containment mechanisms, such as DRGs.

Employer-Financed Health Insurance

Some would prefer that the government not get involved in the actual provision of health insurance but rather just ensure that all citizens have access to some health insurance. Because many of the currently uninsured have jobs with no health-insurance benefits, one proposal is to have the government require that all employers provide comprehensive health insurance for their employees. For employers who are too small to afford such insurance, the government could pay the insurance premiums. The Clinton administration proposed such a program in 1994, called *managed competition,* but it gained insufficient support to win approval (Skocpol, 1996). Such a program would be expensive, of course, and it would put a burden on small businesses. In addition, the consumer would pay for it through higher prices for goods and services. Yet it would provide many more people with access to health care. It is also more acceptable to many than programs such as national health insurance because it accomplishes the goal with minimal government involvement. In 1996, President Clinton signed into law legislation that makes it easier for workers to leave an employer and retain their health insurance for a period of time or be covered for preexisting conditions under a new employer's health insurance. This was a relatively minor change because it did not cover all workers, but the legislation did alleviate what had been a serious problem—workers losing health coverage, especially for preexisting conditions, when they change or quit jobs.

Health Maintenance Organizations and Managed Care

In discussing Medicaid, preferred provider programs were mentioned. When these kinds of arrangements emerged many decades ago, they were called *health maintenance organizations* (HMOs), and they represented an alternative to traditional health insurance for financing health care. A **health maintenance organization** is *an organization that agrees to provide for all of a person's health-care needs for a fixed premium.* Whereas health insurance is third-party medicine involving a separate payment for each service rendered, HMOs receive a set fee and agree to take care of all of a person's health needs for that fee. In so doing, the HMO assumes a financial risk that the services they give patients might cost more than the premiums the HMO takes in. If this happens, the HMO loses money, so the HMO has an incentive to control costs that the physician or patient in third-party medicine does not have.

In the last decade, a number of trends discussed in this chapter—the corporatization of health care, increased competition in the health-care field, and rising costs—have led to the emergence of what is now called **managed care:** *health care that is organized like an HMO, with networks of hospitals and doctors who provide for all the health-care needs for large groups of people and who charge a flat fee or limit the fees that they charge* (Eckholm, 1994; Miller & Luft, 1994). HMOs are a form of managed care. Some HMOs and managed-care systems own their own hospitals and employ health-care providers, including physicians. People in managed-care arrangements typically have a limited choice of doctors to select from, and the managed-care system exercises tight control over medical treatments and therefore costs. Two-thirds of the people who work at medium and large companies in the United States today are enrolled in managed-care health systems rather than traditional health insurance. Whereas most HMOs used to be not-for-profit organizations, today most HMOs and managed-care systems are for-profit. Insurance companies, traditional HMOs, and hospitals have taken the lead in developing managed-care plans and offering them to employers, usually at a lower price than that of traditional health insurance. Many recipients of Medicare and Medicaid are now in managed-care systems.

One of the motivations for developing HMOs and managed-care systems has been cost containment, and studies of HMOs indicate that they are less expensive than traditional health insurance and provide equivalent levels and quality of services (Brown, Clement, Hill, Retchin, & Bergeron, 1993; Greenfield, Rogers, Mangotich, Carney, & Tarlov, 1995). They have lower hospitalization rates and do fewer unnecessary surgeries. These benefits may derive from the HMO's mode of financing, which gives the HMO an incentive to economize, or from their greater use of preventive health care. However, it may also be that, in the past when these studies were done, healthier people joined HMOs and this accounted for their lower costs. The managed-care systems of today have not yet been extensively studied in terms of these outcomes.

Despite the benefits, recent trends in managed care have been criticized on a number of grounds. For one thing, managed care does nothing to help those without health insurance. Second, the oversight of medical decisions common in managed care threatens the independence and autonomy of medical practitioners. This is true in part because, in some communities, managed care enrolls so many people that insufficient business is left for physicians who are not part of the managed-care system. To make a living, doctors have little choice but to sign on with the managed-care system for whatever pay and working conditions it dictates. In fact, physicians' incomes have stopped rising and may even be falling because of the cost controls of managed care (Freudenheim, 1995). A third criticism of managed-care systems is that they aggressively compete for contracts, offering employers low premiums and then pressuring doctors to limit medical procedures and hospitals to cut staff and procedures in order to come in under cost and make a profit. Patients may suffer from this practice if needed health-care services are not provided (Ware, Bayliss, Rogers, Kosinski, & Tarlov, 1996).

A final criticism of managed care is that it represents a dramatic shift in control over medical

OTHER WORLDS, *Other Ways*

CANADA AND SWEDEN: PAYING FOR HEALTH CARE IN OTHER NATIONS

Earlier in this chapter, two rather disturbing facts emerged. One is that the United States does not come off very well in international comparisons of health status. For example, in comparison to most other industrial nations, people in the United States live shorter lives and lose more infants to death. The second disturbing fact is that people in the United States pay more for health care than do people in these other nations. Why do consumers in these other nations pay less and receive more? Some critics attribute this difference to the largely unregulated, laissez-faire nature of the U.S. health-care system, which leaves many people with limited or no access to health care.

In Sweden, France, Australia, Germany, Canada, and many other nations, health services are paid for with money collected by the government (Cockerham, 1995). This arrangement is similar to Medicare and Medicaid in the United States. Employers and employees pay taxes that are placed in a fund from which medical bills are paid. Canada, for example, provided hospital insurance for its citizens beginning in 1961

and physician's care insurance starting in 1971 (Bennett & Adams, 1993). The entire population is covered, and 95 percent of hospital and physician costs are paid by federal or provincial taxes. The system does not pay for some amenities, such as private hospital rooms or cosmetic surgery. Everything else is covered, and Canadians rarely even see a hospital bill. Patients can choose their own physicians, and physicians are private, self-employed practitioners, not government employees. Hospitals operate on a budget that is set largely by provincial governments. Thus Canada has an essentially private health-care system that is paid for almost entirely by public money.

One way in which the costs of such universal coverage can be paid for is by keeping the price of health care down. For example, in Canada, the government sets all doctor and hospital fees, and physicians cannot charge more for services than the insurance will pay. Canadian physicians do not earn the lucrative incomes that their U.S. counterparts do, although physicians are still among the highest-paid professional groups in Canada. However, Canadian doctors do not have to worry about billing patients, preparing insurance forms, or writing off bad debts. Another way Canada pays for its system is through progressive taxes, or tax rates that increase with income. This arrangement makes for a larger kitty from which to

decisions, from the hands of many dispersed doctors and local hospitals to the directors of these huge corporate empires. And these health empires have been merging at a rapid rate, with the result being that the system is moving toward an oligopoly (see Chapter 13). There is little evidence at this point that health-care consumers benefit from these mergers through better care or lower costs (Feldman, Wholey, & Christianson, 1996). So, the kind of health care that more and more people in the United States receive today is determined by a contract negotiated between their employer and a national (or global) corporate health-care giant. At this point, it is unclear what all the benefits and disadvantages of managed care are and whether

the former outweigh the latter. For the moment, because of the stress on privatization in the United States, managed care is at the center of the social-policy stage, and other alternatives such as national health insurance are not much discussed.

Health Care: A Privilege or a Right?

The debate over how to finance health care has to do, in part, with whether people consider health care to be a privilege or a right. Some people see access to health care as a privilege of those who can afford to pay for it. This view is consistent with the capitalist and market foundations of the U.S. economy; health care is an economic service, and

pay for health care. In the United States, health-insurance premiums tend to be the same, irrespective of people's income.

Of course, it is not possible to spend less on health care and cover more people, as the Canadians do, without some costs. One cost is that there are sometimes waits for hospital beds and some types of surgical procedures, especially nonemergency surgeries. In addition, some state-of-the-art technology, such as magnetic resonance imaging, is not as widely available as in the United States. Yet another cost is the higher taxes to pay for the universal, government-provided coverage.

These costs, however, do not seem too painful because Canadians still live longer and have less infant mortality than do people in the United States. In addition, one should look at health-care financing programs in terms of *who* bears the costs, since someone must bear the costs of any program. Currently, in the United States, those who benefit the most are the affluent; those fortunate enough to have good, employer-provided health insurance; and the elderly with Medicare. A shift to a Canadian-style system would mean redirecting some of the benefits from those groups to the poor, the unemployed, the underemployed, and other marginal groups. It comes down to *how* health care will be rationed, not whether it will

be rationed. Will some poor and unemployed be denied basic health care, such as prenatal care or frequent doctor visits for sick people? Or will some of the affluent be denied rapid access to elective surgeries or exotic technologies, such as coronary bypass surgery for elderly patients?

Sweden has a truly socialized health-care system, with the government nationalizing most health-care facilities and employing health-care workers. Health services are free to any who need them, and little money changes hands between patient and health-care providers. Taxes support the health-care system, and Sweden does have high taxes, in part to support the health-care system. However, the Swedes are also among the healthiest people in the world. They live two years longer than people in the United States and have lower infant mortality. Sweden is an interesting contrast with both Canada and the United States in that it runs a generally effective, socialized system of health care in a capitalist country. Canada and Sweden suggest some of the ways in which health care can be made more available to all citizens, recognizing that there are advantages and disadvantages to each approach.

it can be most efficiently produced and distributed through competition in the marketplace. The opposite view is that society needs to ensure that people are healthy so that they can work and accomplish other tasks essential to the maintenance of society. Therefore, high-quality health care should be a fundamental right of all citizens. Most industrial nations today have taken the latter view, but there is still controversy regarding this issue in the United States, and many citizens have little or no access to health care. Other Worlds, Other Ways: Canada and Sweden discusses the means of financing health care in these two countries, nations where health care is considered a right of all citizens.

Summary

1. From the functionalist perspective, illness threatens the survival of society because sick people cannot accomplish essential tasks. The health-care system becomes a problem when it fails to return sick people to normal social functioning.

2. From the conflict perspective, health and health care are scarce resources over which interest groups compete. The inequitable distribution of these resources reflects the overall inequitable distribution of resources in society. This inequality becomes a problem when some group thinks that it is not receiving its fair share of these resources.

3. The interactionist perspective recognizes that illnesses involve a network of social meanings and social expectations. In medical encounters, people exchange meanings about social standing, power, and worth in the medical setting as well as society as a whole.

4. AIDS in the United States illustrates that cultures stigmatize illnesses and that such stigmatization can influence how people who are sick are treated.

5. Social epidemiologists have researched how the kinds of diseases that affect us depend on the level of societal development and on our position in society.

6. Diseases can be classified as acute or chronic, with the former contributing more to the death rate in preindustrial societies. In industrial societies, the death rate drops substantially and life expectancy increases, largely because of declines in infant and childhood mortality and changes in lifestyle. The four major sociocultural factors that affect health and illness are socioeconomic status, gender, race, and lifestyle.

7. A wide variety of health-care systems can be found cross-culturally that differ in terms of what are seen as causes of diseases and what treatments are effective. Three types of such systems are the personalistic, the naturalistic, and the scientific. Chinese medicine combines both naturalistic and scientific medicine.

8. Health-care institutions have a social structure that involves organized patterns of interaction between people who are sick and people in various healing roles. A variety of sociocultural factors influence whether people define themselves as sick, whether they seek care from a healer, and from which healer they seek care.

9. Two key healer roles in scientific medicine are physicians and nurses, with the former having considerably more authority, status, and power than the latter. In modern societies, much of health-care delivery occurs in hospitals, which have become highly bureaucratic and are increasingly likely to be investor-owned corporations.

10. A number of problems are associated with health and illness in the United States: Health-care costs have been rising rapidly; some people do not have access to the health services that they need; some of the health services that people receive are impersonal, dehumanizing, and unpleasant; substantial gender inequality exists in the health-care field.

11. A central issue in deciding how to attack problems in health care is whether access to health care should be every citizen's right or whether it is a privilege of those who can afford to pay for it. Problems have been attacked through publicly funded health insurance, employer-financed health insurance, and the emergence of health maintenance organizations and managed-care arrangements.

STUDY AND Review

Key Terms

acute disease

chronic disease

crisis medicine

curative medicine

health maintenance organization

managed care

Medicaid

medical-industrial complex

Medicare

national health insurance

preventive medicine

sick role

social epidemiology

third-party medicine

Multiple-Choice Questions

1. The concept of the sick role is associated most clearly with which of the following perspectives?
   a. The functionalist perspective.
   b. The conflict perspective.
   c. The managed-care perspective.
   d. The deinstitutionalization perspective.

2. Which of the following statements would be most consistent with the interactionist perspective on health-care institutions?
   a. Health and health care are scarce resources, and interest groups compete with one another to gain a share of them.
   b. Disease is a threat to the social order because those who are ill are less able to make useful contributions to society.
   c. People attach social meanings to various illnesses and the meanings may imply something about the worth of the person who is ill.
   d. The health-care system involves an inequitable distribution of money, prestige, power, and other resources.

3. The most common cause of death in the United States today is
   a. acute disease.
   b. cancer.
   c. pneumonia.
   d. heart disease.
   e. cerebrovascular disease.

4. Which of the following statements is true regarding the impact of social factors on health?
   a. Men live longer than women.
   b. The poor have higher death rates than do the affluent.
   c. Among African Americans and white Americans in the same social class, no differences in disease or death rates exist.
   d. All of the above are true.
   e. Both b and c are true.

5. Which of the following statements is true regarding Chinese medicine today?
   a. It incorporates both scientific medicine and traditional Chinese beliefs about disease.
   b. It is an example of a personalistic health-care system.
   c. It has ignored scientific medicine.
   d. Both a and b are true.

6. The social structure of health care would include all of the following except
   a. physicians.
   b. nurses.
   c. nurse practitioners.
   d. patients.
   e. none of the above groups is excepted.

7. Which of the following are factors that have contributed to rising health-care costs in the United States?
   a. A growing demand for health-care services.
   b. The growth of new diagnostic and treatment procedures.
   c. Weak economic competition in the health-care field.
   d. All of the above.
   e. Both b and c.

8. Concern over male dominance in the health field has been raised for all of the following reasons *except*
   a. it restricts women's access to lucrative occupations.
   b. it may have had a detrimental effect on the health care received by women.
   c. it contributes to the problem of the medical-industrial complex.
   d. it may lead to unnecessary treatments for women's health problems.

9. Which type of health-care financing arrangement pays for all of a person's health-care needs for a fixed premium each month or year?
   a. The medical-industrial complex.
   b. National health insurance.
   c. Third-party medicine.
   d. Socialized medicine.
   e. Health maintenance organizations.

10. Which of the following was *not* cited as a disadvantage in the Canadian health-care system in comparison with that of the United States?
    a. Canadians pay higher taxes.
    b. Canadian patients sometimes wait for hospital beds.
    c. Some advanced technology is not as widely available in Canada.
    d. Health-care costs are higher in Canada.

True/False Questions

1. Worldwide, more than one-half of all new HIV infections result from male homosexual contact.

2. The transition from preindustrial to industrial societies has been associated with a shift from chronic diseases to acute diseases as the most serious health threat.

3. Because modern medicine arose when acute infectious diseases were the major health threats, medical education evolved to train doctors with a crisis orientation.

4. The United States has one of the lowest infant mortality rates in the world—only two nations have lower rates.

5. Holistic medicine largely ignores scientific medicine and relies heavily on Chinese medicine.

6. The trend in medicine today is for fewer physicians to be salaried employees and for more to go into solo practice.

7. The text takes the stance that no groups in the United States benefit from the corporatization of health care.

8. National health expenditures in the United States today constitute a larger percentage of the gross national product than was the case fifty years ago.

9. Third-party medicine, unless controlled, tends to lead to an overutilization of health-care services.

10. According to the text, the health-care system in Canada is an example of a truly socialized health-care system.

Fill-In Questions

1. The _____ refers to the set of expectations intended to guide the behavior of people who are ill.

2. The branch of sociology that studies how social factors influence the distribution and spread of disease is _____.

3. The kinds of diseases that pose the most serious health threats to preindustrial societies are _____.

4. Changes in lifestyle or other steps that help avoid the occurrence of disease are called _____ medicine.

5. The healers in personalistic health-care systems are called _____ and _____.

6. Two procedures used in Chinese medicine to balance the yin and the yang are _____ and _____.

7. In the United States, two relatively new healing roles that are classified as physician extenders are _____ and _____.

8. The _____ is the phenomenon in the health-care field that is analogous to the military-industrial complex.

9. When a patient pays premiums to a fund and then the hospital or doctor is paid from this fund for each treatment provided the patient, this is a system of _____ medicine.

10. Medicare and Medicaid amount to _____ for the elderly and the poor.

Matching Questions

_____ 1. heart disease
_____ 2. crisis medicine
_____ 3. third party in health financing
_____ 4. illness as deviance
_____ 5. Greek humoral pathology
_____ 6. voodoo
_____ 7. medical specialty
_____ 8. proprietary hospital
_____ 9. Sweden
_____ 10. Medicare

A. naturalistic health-care system
B. health-insurance company
C. profit-making corporation
D. personalistic health-care system
E. functionalist perspective
F. socialized health care
G. family practice
H. diagnostically related groupings
I. chronic disease
J. curative medicine

Essay Questions

1. Compare and contrast the functionalist, conflict, and interactionist perspectives on health and health care.

2. How does the health status of people differ in preindustrial and industrial societies? What produces these differences?

3. How do socioeconomic status, gender, and race affect people's likelihood of getting sick or dying? Why do these factors have that impact?

4. Using the examples of both the United States and Zaire, what are the social, political, and economic factors that have contributed to the spread of AIDS in those two societies?

5. Compare and contrast personalistic, naturalistic, and scientific health-care systems in terms of their beliefs about disease and their healing practices.

6. Describe the social structure of health care in the United States, including a discussion of the social roles involved and social expectations for the behavior of people within those roles.

7. What is meant by the privatization and corporatization of health care in the United States? What are the benefits and disadvantages of this trend?

8. Explain why health-care costs have been rising in the United States over the past fifty years.

9. How much gender inequality exists in the health-care system in the United States? Why is it considered a problem?

10. Describe the different methods for financing health care in the United States. What are their advantages and disadvantages?

Answers

Multiple-Choice
1. A; **2.** C; **3.** D; **4.** B; **5.** A; **6.** E; **7.** D; **8.** C; **9.** E; **10.** D

True/False
1. F; **2.** F; **3.** T; **4.** F; **5.** F; **6.** F; **7.** F; **8.** T; **9.** T; **10.** F

Fill-In
1. sick role
2. social epidemiology
3. acute disease, infectious and parasitic disease
4. preventive
5. shamans, diviners
6. acupuncture, acupressure, moxibustion
7. nurse practitioners, physician's assistants
8. medical-industrial complex
9. third-party
10. government health insurance

Matching
1. I; **2.** J; **3.** B; **4.** E; **5.** A; **6.** D; **7.** G; **8.** C; **9.** F; **10.** H

For Further Reading

Braithewaite, Ronald L., & Taylor, Sandra E. (Eds.). (1992). *Health issues in the black community.* San Francisco: Jossey-Bass. This comprehensive book of readings covers many of the health issues that confront the African American community in the United States and makes recommendations for improvement.

Corea, Gena. (1992). *The invisible epidemic: The story of women and AIDS.* New York: HarperCollins. This disturbing book documents how gender influences the provision of health care and the medical paternalism that pervades the U.S. health-care system. It reports how medicine underreports and misdiagnoses AIDS in women, with tragic results.

Frohock, Fred M. (1992). *Healing powers: Alternative medicine, spiritual communities, and the state.* Chicago: University of Chicago Press. This book covers an important topic that could be only briefly mentioned in the chapter: holistic health, alternatives to scientific medicine, and religious and spiritual healing.

Isaac, Rael Jean, & Armat, Virginia C. (1990). *Madness in the streets: How psychiatry and the law abandoned the mentally ill.* New York: Free Press. In this book, a sociologist and a journalist combine forces to provide a history of the deinstitutionalization of the mentally ill and a strong criticism of the policy on the grounds that it really means doing little for the mentally ill.

Mirowsky, John, & Ross, Catherine E. (1989). *Social causes of psychological distress.* New York: Aldine de Gruyter. These authors present convincing evidence to show that mental illness, especially depression and anxiety, is profoundly influenced by some very important social conditions.

Navarro, Vicente. (1986). *Crisis, health, and medicine: A social critique.* New York: Tavistock. This is a sophisticated and fundamental criticism of the U.S. health-care system that sees the profit orientation as one of the key problems.

Rushing, William A. (1995). *The AIDS epidemic: Social problems of an infectious disease.* Boulder, CO: Westview Press. This is a recent and comprehensive assessment of AIDS, including social factors in the spread of the disease as well as how society has reacted to it.

Starr, Paul. (1982). *The social transformation of American medicine.* New York: Basic Books. Starr gives an insightful analysis of the changes in the power and authority of the medical profession over the past two centuries. This is not an easy book, but it is one well worth spending time with.

Starr, Paul, & Zelman, Walter. (1992). *The logic of health-care reform.* Knoxville, TN: Grand Rounds Press/Whittle Direct Books. Starr is a sociologist, and both authors were members of President Clinton's health-care team. They propose using global budgeting and managed competition to reform the health-care system.

Wolinsky, Howard, & Brune, Tom. (1994). *The serpent on the staff: The unhealthy politics of the American Medical Association.* New York: Putnam. Whereas the authors do show a clear bias against the AMA, they also make many important points and provide useful information about the role of that organization in shaping health-care policy in the United States.

ELEVEN *Religion*

West Africa contains such present-day nations as Nigeria, Benin, and the Ivory Coast. In precolonial Africa, the religion of many peoples in this area was called *Vodu,* the Dahomean word for "deity" or "spirit." *Vodu* was a highly structured religious and magical system that was integrated into all parts of West African life (Mulira, 1990). It was based on the idea that a Supreme Being, or Creator, was at the top of a hierarchy of deities, and the lesser deities served as intermediaries between people and the Supreme Being. Families, clans, and villages had their own deities, who protected people and justified all aspects of social life. The deities legitimized who held power in a village, who headed a family, or who worked in a particular occupation. *Vodu* also included a host of priests, priestesses, apprentices, and others who served the deities and carried out sacred rituals.

Another powerful force in *Vodu* were witches, people who were feared because they were believed to have supernatural powers. They were considered highly destructive and had no positive role in society. Among many African groups, witches were postmenopausal women. They were believed to have the power to change people into animals and to gain control over people's actions and make them do as the witches pleased. All illnesses that could not be cured by herbalists, or root doctors, were believed to be the work of witches.

In the territory of the Yoruba tribe (present-day Nigeria), the people called their deities *orisha* (Brandon, 1990). In the Yoruba religion, each deity had a name and a personality. In ceremonies of spirit possession, it was believed that a deity would take control of a person and send him or her into a trance. The Yoruba also believed in reincarnation and, along with other West African tribes, used dance as a way to worship. Another form of worship was animal sacrifice.

Columbus first made landfall in the Western Hemisphere in 1492, and as noted in Chapter 7, the Portuguese made first contact in Brazil in 1500. These arrivals were the beginning of a massive expansion and colonization of the New World, fueled by capitalism's demand for economic growth. It was not long before African slaves were brought to the New World as a part of this colonization. The first African slaves arrived in the West Indies in 1504 and in the Jamestown colony (present-day Virginia) in 1619. Many of these slaves were from West Africa around present-day Benin and Nigeria, and they brought their native *Vodu* religion with them. In the New World, however, the religion changed some and so did the name. The religion now exists in two forms: *Voodoo* and *Santería* (Olmos & Paravisini-Gebert, 1997).

Voodoo first entered what is now the United States in the 1600s, probably in the New Orleans area, since many slaves there had come from Caribbean islands where voodoo was widely practiced. Voodoo today represents one clear survival of African culture in the New World. It adapted to its new surroundings. For example, the names of the *Vodu* deities were often changed to those of Roman Catholic saints, and the African concepts of good and evil were sometimes recast as the Christian heaven and hell. Slave owners sometimes suppressed voodoo because in the Caribbean and Brazil it had provided the organizational focus for slave revolts. Nevertheless, voodoo remains today a viable religious system with a pantheon of gods who are responsible for the physical and social order. It gives meaning and purpose to the lives of those who believe in it. Those unfamiliar with voodoo tend to see it as a magical system of spells and trances, but these practices, although important, are not its essence.

Santería is also an outgrowth of African tribal religion, and it combined elements of Roman Catholicism into a new folk religion among the slaves in the Caribbean. It emerged in Cuba during the period of slavery. *Santería* means "worship of the saints," and, like followers of voodoo, believers in *Santería* used the names of Roman Catholic saints for their deities. In fact, some followers used the Yoruba word for their deities (*orisha*) and the Spanish word for saint (*santos*) interchangeably. Today, there are an estimated seventy thousand followers of *Santería* in the Miami area and one million in the United States (Rohter, 1993). The city of Miami outlawed animal sacrifice as a way of discouraging *Santería*, but the Supreme Court ruled unanimously in 1993 that the ordinance was unconstitutional and that First Amendment freedoms extend to Afro-Caribbean religious rituals just as they do to Judeo-Christian ones.

Santería and voodoo illustrate a number of points that this chapter will elaborate on. One is the importance and pervasiveness of religion, which archaeological and other evidence suggests is found in one form or another in all human societies. The earliest evidence of religious rituals can be found in the burial practices of early human groups who populated Europe and Southwest Asia more than thirty thousand years ago. These Paleolithic peoples buried their dead by laying them out carefully in pits dug into the floors of caves. They also placed tools, parts of animals, and other objects in the graves along with the bodies. Although no written record remains to confirm that these practices were religious, they strongly suggest that these early humans believed in a life after death or a spirit that would survive death.

Santería and voodoo also illustrate the diffusion of religions around the world, as human beings engage in commerce or war, or in other ways intermingle with those from other cultures. The result is that, except for simple and isolated

Myths & FACTS

ABOUT RELIGION

Myth Religions appeared among human beings only with the rise of the great agricultural civilizations of the past ten thousand years. Earlier human groups were pagans.

FACT Evidence of religious rituals can be found among the artifacts of human groups at least thirty thousand years ago. In fact, historically, religion can be found in virtually all human societies.

Myth The European colonists who settled in North America in the 1500s and 1600s were escaping religious persecution. Therefore, they placed freedom of religion at the center of the new societies they created.

FACT Actually many of the colonies, even at the time of the Declaration of Independence in 1776, were intolerant of religious diversity and sometimes even established their own official state religions. However, complex social and historical forces, to be discussed in this chapter, led to the guarantee of religious freedom in the Constitution of the United States.

Myth New religious sects tend to come and go in the United States, with most of them lasting less than a decade and having little permanent impact on the religious scene.

FACT Although some new religions do not last long, most survive and become a continuing part of the religious environment in their communities.

Myth Until recent times, most nations were united behind one religion, such as Roman Catholicism in Spain, the Anglican Church in England, or Confucianism in China.

FACT Actually, religious history is much more complicated. Through trade and war, people have spread their religions around the globe for many centuries. So, Islam has been in China for more than one thousand years, and Roman Catholicism was spread around the globe beginning with the European colonial expansion five hundred years ago.

---

societies, religious practices tend to be diverse, with many different religions found in most societies today. To provide a better appreciation for this diversity, the following analysis of religion as a social institution includes a review of the major religions of the world. As a scientific discipline, sociology does not assess the truth or falsity of these religious beliefs. As pointed out in Chapter 1, such questions are matters of tradition, faith, or revelation. Some or all of the religious beliefs in the world may be true, but such verity cannot be settled through scientific observation. Sociology studies religion as a social institution that performs some functions for society, is transmitted to the next generation through the socialization process, and is influenced by the social and cultural context in which it exists. These are some of the topics to be covered in this chapter.

What Is Religion?

You should be able to define religion and describe the major forms it can take.

When most people think about religion, they refer to their own spiritual preference, which for many people in the United States follows Judeo-Christian traditions. Yet there is tremendous variety in both religions and their expression. Sociologists have been careful to avoid a narrow definition of religion that could reflect ethnocentric biases about what religions *should* be like. Emile Durkheim (1915/1965), a pioneer in the sociological study of religion, argued that the distinctive feature of religion is that it views the world as divided into things that are considered sacred and things that are regarded as profane. The **sacred** are *those things that are awesome, mysterious, extraordinary, or absolute and transcend everyday experience.* Such phenomena demand respect and reverence. The **profane** is *the world of the ordinary and routine,* which can be easily comprehended. Objects become sacred or profane when they are so defined by a particular group. Such definition is what makes possible a wide variety of religions: virtually anything can be defined as sacred.

Using Durkheim's distinction, then, we can define **religion** as *a collectively held set of symbols and rituals that express a basic understanding of the world, especially its sacred dimension, and address the ultimate concerns of the meaning of human existence* (Geertz, 1966). We can illustrate this definition by discussing several varieties of religion that can be found in the world.

Animism is *the belief that souls, spirits, or spiritual beings inhabit the world and play a significant role, for good or ill, in human affairs.* The people of Melanesia, for example, believed in *mana*—a power or spirit that could inhabit people, places, or things. Regardless of whether one had experienced extraordinarily good luck or calamitous misfortune, mana might be at work (Codrington, 1965).

A variant on animism is **totemism,** in which *a plant, animal, or object is considered to have some sacred power or spirit.* In totemistic religions, a family or village might believe that it has a special relationship with the totem object, which is considered both supernatural and ancestrally related to that family or village. Aboriginal groups in Australia, for example, had a complex totemistic religion in which each person had his or her own individual totem object as well as shared a different totem object with all others of the same gender and another based on the kinship group. Totems were believed to provide assistance in hunting and gathering and offer protection against disease. Totems could also punish people who had violated important social norms. Animism and totemism tend to be associated with simpler societies, such as those of hunter-gatherers and some horticulturalists, and some sociologists believe that totemism is one of the earliest forms of religion to emerge among human groups.

Theistic religions *posit the existence of one or more gods not of human origin that are believed to play a role in the creation and maintenance of the universe and take an interest in human affairs.* The Dahomeans of western Africa, for example, believed in a large number of gods, each being held responsible for the creation of a certain part of nature (Wallace, 1966). Dahomean gods went to war, participated in sexual activities, conducted business, and were prone to creating a degree of mischief. The Dahomean's religion was **polytheistic,** involving *a belief in many gods.* **Monotheistic religions** are based on *a belief in one supreme god that is ultimately responsible for the universe.* The three great religions that emerged in the Middle East—Judaism, Christianity, and Islam—are monotheistic, worshiping Yahweh, God, and Allah, respectively. In addition to the single supreme god, monotheistic religions often include supernatural beings or spirits, such as angels or devils, who are subordinate and possess considerably fewer powers.

Religions of the way are *religions that posit no deity, but rather center on immutable and life-guiding truths that reveal the proper way to achieve fulfillment.* Such religions as early Buddhism, early Confucianism, and philosophical Taoism, for example, do not have gods that are responsible for creating the world and telling people how to run their lives. Rather, these religions spell out an ethical way to live that provides ultimate personal harmony with the universe. Religions of the way consider their noble truths and ideals to be sacred, transcending everyday experience and inspiring awe and reverence.

A Global Perspective: Religions of the World

You should be able to describe the basic beliefs, teachings, and holy figures of the six major religions in the world and discuss their similarities and differences.

This book has emphasized that the belief systems of human beings are highly diverse. This diversity is reflected in the religions of various cultures. Most people around the world claim adherence to a religion, of which there are literally thousands (see Table 11.1). There is no possible way to discuss all of them here, but it is useful to provide an overview of the religions with the most adherents and those that have been especially influential in the United States (H. Smith, 1991).

TABLE 11.1 Religious population of the world, by region, 1994 (in thousands, except percent)

Religion	Total	Percent Distribution	Africa	Asia	Latin America	Northern America	Europe	Eurasia[1]	Oceania
Total population	5,661,525	100.0	722,814	3,345,498	474,240	288,788	514,655	287,164	28,366
Christians	1,901,148	33.6	351,682	304,887	442,140	247,293	422,159	109,747	23,240
Roman Catholics	1,058,069	18.7	132,102	132,053	411,514	100,386	267,972	5,615	8,427
Protestants	391,143	6.9	93,865	87,051	17,513	99,652	75,441	9,903	7,718
Orthodox	174,184	3.1	30,685	3,904	1,789	6,217	36,869	94,129	591
Anglicans	78,038	1.4	28,873	755	1,319	7,593	33,625	1	5,872
Other Christians	199,707	3.5	66,158	81,125	10,004	33,445	8,252	100	623
Muslims	1,033,453	18.3	293,993	675,297	1,395	5,500	13,194	43,967	107
Nonreligious[2]	923,104	16.3	2,936	733,740	19,327	22,910	58,199	82,236	3,756
Hindus	764,000	13.5	1,608	759,059	912	1,315	725	2	379
Buddhists	338,621	6.0	23	336,755	559	578	279	401	26
Atheists	239,111	4.2	344	167,739	3,329	1,367	16,362	49,407	563
Chinese folk-religionists[3]	149,336	2.6	14	149,037	76	126	61	1	21
New-religionists[4]	128,975	2.3	23	126,869	548	1,473	51	1	10
Tribal religionists	99,150	1.8	69,872	28,197	967	42	1	—	71
Sikhs	20,204	0.4	29	19,557	8	363	237	1	9
Jews	13,451	0.2	128	4,289	458	5,907	1,761	813	95
Shamanists	11,010	0.2	1	10,754	1	1	2	250	1
Confucians	6,334	0.1	1	6,300	2	26	2	2	1
Baha'is	5,835	0.1	1,631	2,817	827	379	93	7	81
Jains	3,987	0.1	57	3,906	4	4	15	—	1
Shintoists	3,387	0.1	—	3,383	1	1	1	—	1
Other religionists	20,419	0.4	472	12,912	3,686	1,503	1,513	329	4

— Represents zero.

[1] Source's term for the former Soviet Union.

[2] People professing no religion, nonbelievers, agnostics, freethinkers, and dereligionized secularists indifferent to all religion.

[3] Followers of traditional Chinese religion (local deities, ancestor veneration, Confucian ethics, Taoism, etc.).

[4] Followers of Asiatic 20th-century New Religions, New Religious movements, radical new crisis religions, and non-Christian syncretistic mass religions.

Note: Reprinted with permission from *Britannica Book of the Year*, 1994. Copyright Encyclopaedia Britannica, Inc.

Judaism

The two religions that have played the greatest part in the development of Western Europe and the United States, of course, are Judaism and Christianity. The older of the two religions, Judaism, emerged in Mesopotamia, in the Middle East, about four thousand years ago. It is based on the Hebrew Bible, which is the Old Testament of the Christian Bible. The Torah, or first five books of the Hebrew Bible, is believed by Jews to contain God's will or law. Among other things, the Torah describes the lives of early Israelites, such as Abraham and Moses, as they migrated to Canaan (Palestine), were enslaved in Egypt, wandered the desert after gaining their freedom, and received the Ten Commandments from God at Mount Sinai. Additional aspects of the Jewish belief system are contained in the Talmud, a body of interpretation and scholarly teaching. Judaism was one of the first clearly monotheistic religions in the world, with the Hebrew Bible clearly stating that there is only one God. Judaism professes that ancient Israelites and modern Jews are a chosen people having a special relationship with God and a special obligation to bring God's word to other people through their example. Abraham is believed to have made a covenant with God that established the special position of Jews and also gave them a homeland that would be theirs and their descendants' forever. God leads the chosen people by speaking through the prophets. Jews believe that the Messiah will one day appear and bring redemption and God's rule to the world. Judaism emphasizes the importance of the family and of doing good deeds and that the human condition can be improved.

There is some diversity in present-day Judaism; there are three main branches in the United States. *Orthodox Judaism* follows strictly the divine books and the laws as promulgated by Moses. Orthodox believers follow dietary laws (certain foods are designated *kosher*), observe the traditional Sabbath by abstaining from work and travel, and segregate men and women during religious services. *Reform Judaism* attempts to adjust to present-day conditions by allowing Jews to modify some rituals and practices to take into account new social and cultural developments. While retaining the basic ethical principles of Judaism, for example, Reform Judaism allows for the modification of the dietary rules or use of a language other than Hebrew in services. *Conservative Judaism* falls in between the two, with a strong emphasis on retaining Jewish traditions and following most of the observances provided for in the Torah but also allowing some compromise with modernity.

Christianity

The foundation of Christianity is the belief that Jesus was the Christ, meaning the anointed one or the Messiah looked for by the Jews. Christianity emerged about two thousand years ago as a result of a schism with Judaism over this belief. Christians follow Christ's teachings as found in the New Testament of the Bible. Like Jews, Christians are monotheistic, but they traditionally interpret monotheism as a Holy Trinity of three people who are three aspects of a unity: God the Father; Jesus—or God's Word made flesh; and the Holy Spirit, the universal presence of God.

Christianity has also diversified over the centuries. After Christ's death and believed resurrection in Jerusalem, Christianity spread through Europe and the Middle East as the Roman Empire expanded. After the Roman Empire collapsed in the West and was succeeded by the Byzantine Empire in the East in the fifth and sixth centuries, Christianity gradually split into two main bodies. The Latin church in the West was headed by the bishop of Rome, or Pope. The Byzantine church in the East—later called Orthodox—was under the authority of the emperor in Constantinople. In Europe in the sixteenth century, groups of Christian reformers in the West, who came to be known as Protestants, rejected papal authority, left the Church—the remains of which became the Roman Catholic Church—and established separate Christian denominations. Today, Roman Catholics are united under the authority of the Pope, there are many Protestant and other denominations, and there are many Orthodox churches and other Eastern churches associated with various national or ethnic groups. About 56 percent of the world's Christians are Roman Catholics, 25 percent are Protestant, and the remainder are Eastern Orthodox or belong to other small churches.

Islam

Islam, a more recent religion than Judaism or Christianity, was founded by the prophet Muhammad in the seventh century when he received the Koran (Islamic hold scriptures) from Allah (God). Islam is a monotheistic religion, whose followers (Muslims) believe that Muhammad is the final holy prophet in a line that traces back to Jesus, Moses, and Abraham. In fact, some Muslims believe that Muhammad was merely clarifying Abraham's teachings and correcting errors that Moses and Jesus had made.

Islam is Arabic for "submission" or "surrender," and it implies a total commitment in faith and obedience to the one God, Allah. Muslims surrender to the will of an awesome God whose righteousness and mercy permeate the universe. Muhammad, who was born in Mecca (in present-day Saudi Arabia) is considered a great prophet, but he is a man and is not worshiped as Christ is in Christianity; only Allah is worshiped. The Koran is a set of rules for conduct that relate to family and other realms of life. The family as characterized in the Koran is patriarchal, polygamous, and patrilineal (see Chapter 9), although most Muslims today do not practice polygamy. By most interpretations of the Koran, women are considered subordinate to men. However, some today argue that this view is a misinterpretation of the Koran, and as noted in Chapter 8, there are believers in gender equality and a feminist movement in Islamic nations. Muslims worship Allah through prayer five times a day while facing Mecca, by giving alms to the poor, and by making a pilgrimage to Mecca at least once during their lifetime. Islam prohibits eating pork, drinking alcohol, and engaging in usury (lending money at excessively high interest rates).

Islam has no central authority, such as the Pope in Roman Catholicism, so there are many variants on Islam around the world. The two main divisions in Islam are the Sunni and the Shi'ite. This schism occurred after Muhammad's death when a struggle ensued over who would be Muhammad's successor. The Sunni believed that the successor should be chosen by the elders in the Islamic community from among the men in Muhammad's tribe. They also believed that proper Islamic practice required a return to the original teachings of the Koran. So, the Sunni are more conservative in the sense of demanding a more strict adherence to the fundamentals of the Koran. Regarding successorship, the Shi'ites believe that there is a line of twelve pure and sinless *imams,* or religious leaders, who are the only proper inheritors of Muhammad's authority and of understanding of the Koran. The Shi'ites believe these *imams* receive divine inspiration when reading and interpreting the Koran so that new revelations are possible. Shi'ites also insist on a return to Islamic fundamentals, but they tend to choose more selectively from the teachings of the Koran.

Hinduism

Hinduism developed in India some 3,500 years ago. Its beliefs and practices are contained in its holy books, the Vedas and the Upanishads. Unlike the Bible and the Koran, which are considered to be the inspired words of God, these books consist of ritual hymns and the moral lessons of great teachers. Hinduism is really a large array of sects rather than a single religious organization with a clearcut hierarchy. Over thousands of years, Hinduism evolved by incorporating many different Indian tribal beliefs and foreign beliefs, and much of this diversity still persists. On the popular level Hindus believe in many gods, a slightly different pantheon for each village or family, who act much like human beings, doing both good and evil in the world. They worship these gods in order to have bountiful crops, ward off disease, or have sons. On a more sophisticated level, Hindus may devote themselves to worship of one supreme God or to meditating on the Absolute.

Central to Hinduism is a belief in an ideal way of life, embodied in the concepts of *dharma,* or order, and *karma,* or personal destiny. Hindus believe that there is a natural order to the cosmos that governs both nature and social life. The good person strives to understand that order and live according to its rules. *Karma* involves understanding one's personal place in this order and living in harmony with it. For Hindus, the key to life is to perform properly the duties of one's position as defined by caste, community, and gender. Thus Hinduism is at the basis of the caste system in

India, described in Chapter 6, because people should obey the rules of the caste into which they are born.

Another important concept in Hinduism is the transmigration of souls, according to which a person's soul is born again in another form after the earthly body dies. One is reincarnated as a higher or lower being depending on whether a person behaved in harmony with the cosmos in the previous life. So, for Hindus, it is important to live in accordance with one's position in life because doing so influences what happens in the next life. If the person continues to live in harmony with the cosmos, he or she will eventually be freed from earthly existence, never to be reincarnated again. Then they will have achieved *nirvana*. In this life, people can work toward it by practicing the disciplines of Yoga, adhering to Vedic scriptures, or following a renowned guru, or teacher.

Buddhism

Buddhism was founded about 2,500 years ago in northern India by Siddhartha Gautama, who is known as the Buddha, or Enlightened One. The Buddha claimed to have attained enlightenment through meditation, and he attracted monks and nuns who carry on his teachings. Buddhism has many similarities with Hinduism, which should not be surprising since they developed in close proximity. In addition, Gautama was the son of an upper-caste Hindu ruling family in northern India, and Buddhism was a reaction against some Hindu traditions of the time. Like Hinduism, the Buddha preached that the goal of religious practice and moral behavior was nirvana, a state of enlightenment, and that people would go through a cycle of lives before achieving nirvana. In nirvana, people are released from the earthly cycle of suffering and rebirth. The basic principles of Buddhism are found in the Four Noble Truths: Earthly life involves suffering; suffering is caused by desire and self-centeredness; selfish desire can be overcome; it can be overcome through proper moral action supported by meditation. Thus, Buddhism is based on ethical practices as well as disciplined behavior.

Buddhism eventually spread through much of Asia, where it remains popular today. The Buddhist faithful consist of monks, nuns, and laypeople. Like Christianity, Buddhism developed a diversity of groups around the world. The majority recognize many Buddhist divinities. Most monks live in monastic communities supported by laypeople, where their days are filled with meditation, study, preaching, and going into the outside world to beg for food. Sometimes a Buddhist monk will develop a reputation for holiness so that his monastery becomes a holy shrine that attracts pilgrims who come to pray. Some monasteries have gathered a huge following in this fashion. Among laypeople, Buddhism is often practiced along with some other religion, such as Shinto in Japan. This plurality of religious practice is sometimes difficult for people in the West to understand because we think of people as belonging to only one religion. But it is not unusual in the East.

Confucianism

Confucianism was founded by Confucius, a Chinese teacher and scholar who lived about the same time as the Buddha. The followers of Confucius wrote down his teachings, and these writings, the *Analects,* form the basis of Confucianism. Confucius lived in a time of social upheaval and large-scale corruption that caused widespread oppression and misery in China. Unlike Buddha, who focused on withdrawal from the world to achieve personal salvation, Confucius gave practical advice aimed at achieving social harmony in the world. Confucianism is a moral system that stresses social order, harmony, peace, and justice. These are to be achieved by changing individual behavior. Proper behavior includes the individual's duty to obey the elders in the family and the ruler of the state. The moral person strives for *jen,* or sympathy and respect for others, loyalty to others, and avoiding self-interestedness. The way family members treat one another, in terms of respect, support, and loyalty, should serve as the model for society.

At its inception, Confucianism was more a philosophy and ethical system than a religion because it had no conception of supernatural deities or a reality different from physical and social reality. Confucius did believe, however, that there was a moral force in the world that was like a divine order, and that morality was a form of spirituality. In addition, people incorporated local gods into Confucianism, and eventually some believers came to view Confucius himself as a deity. Confucianism has influenced not only China but also Korea, Vietnam, and Japan. Many people who are Taoists (Taoism is an ancient Chinese religion), Buddhists, or even Christians also abide by Confucian ideals, so the impact of Confucianism has been widespread.

Diffusion of Religion

Although each religion emerged in a particular geographic place and is most strongly identified with particular areas, the striking aspect of the major religions is their massive diffusion around the world. All the religions that have been discussed are practiced by at least a few people on all the world's continents. Islam was spread in Asia by traders and soldiers from its inception. Christianity and Judaism spread from the Middle East into Europe as the Roman Empire expanded and then were spread around the world beginning in the fifteenth century with the European colonial expansion. Chapter 7, for example, described how the Spanish and Portuguese brought Christianity to the tribal peoples of Brazil in 1500; Chapter 8 related that the French brought Christianity to the tribes of North America in the 1600s. These instances illustrate how religion is often an important part of cultural conquest. Since cultural norms and values are embodied in and legitimated by native religions, the destruction of these religions or their adaptation to the ways of the dominant group is an important part of changing a people's way of life.

The twentieth century has been witness to further diffusion of religion around the globe. Christian missionaries from the United States and Europe have traveled to Asia, Africa, and South America looking for converts. Mormons have mounted an especially extensive missionary effort. Following World War II, Western Europe opened its doors to foreign workers as a way of rebuilding its labor force, a policy that brought in Buddhists, Hindus, and Muslims from many nations. In the 1960s and then again in 1990, the United States changed its immigration laws so that more people from the Middle East and the Far East could enter. The result has been an influx of Buddhists, Hindus, and Muslims—and even some Taoists and Shintoists.

So, the world today is characterized by the diffusion of religions, which means that in most places people have many choices. Later this chapter will discuss some of the consequences of this diffusion in the United States.

Sociological Approaches to the Study of Religion

You should be able to describe the approaches of Durkheim, Marx, and Weber concerning the role of religion in society.

Because religion is virtually universal in human societies, a major thrust of the sociological investigation of religion has been to decipher the part that religions play in society. This chapter will look at the work of the three sociologists—Durkheim, Marx, and Weber—who established the central issues in this area. Each man's work offers an insightful perspective that furthers our understanding of religion, and each isolates important elements of the role of religion in society.

Durkheim: A Functionalist Perspective

Emile Durkheim's (1915/1965) perspective on religion is rather startling for many people. Durkheim concluded that when people worship deities or spirits, they are in reality worshiping their own society. He reached this conclusion by first assuming, as do all sociologists, that society has an enormous impact on people. During our relatively short lives, society provides us with many things that we had no part in creating: language, tools, norms, values, a name, kinship, and so on. It is these provisions made available by society that enable us to make our journey through life. Without society and the things it provides, we would not survive. Yet society is intangible and impossible to see. This truth, argued Durkheim, leads people to believe that invisible forces in the world provide for us, guide us, and in some cases, hinder our progress. Not recognizing that society itself is this invisible force, people imagine a sacred world to which they accord the respect and awe that such powerful forces appear to warrant.

Durkheim's analysis of the origins of religion as being misplaced reverence for the powers of society is penetrating indeed, although many sociologists today question whether it is an accurate account of the origins of all religions (Mol, 1979). Nonetheless, Durkheim focused our concern on the functions that religion performs for society. Today we recognize that religion performs a number of social functions.

First, religion enhances social solidarity by establishing and reinforcing fundamental cultural values. Religious rituals are very important in this regard, because they provide a context for the public and communal expression of faith in values and traditions. By coming together periodically for public rituals, people can maintain a sense of common identity and shared purpose. The result is what Durkheim called a *moral community*: a group bound together by their religion-based values and identity.

Second, religion offers a sacred legitimation of values and social practices whose desirability may not be directly observable or verifiable. There is much that is unknown and unknowable in the world, and society must socialize people to behave in appropriate ways. Conformity to the social structure becomes not merely a practical matter but something required by powerful, awesome, and otherworldly forces.

Third, religion provides meaning for people's lives and purpose to their existence. Religion proposes answers to such questions as "Why am I here?" and "Why must I suffer and eventually die?" In answer to these questions, most religions posit some sort of afterlife as the ultimate goal of earthly existence, which offers consolation in the face of uncertainty, grief, and loss.

Finally, religion functions to support and interpret important life events and transitions. From birth to death, we experience many rites of passage that document our having moved into new positions in the social structure. Marriage ceremonies, bar and bat mitzvahs, and last rites—each places an event within a larger sacred context and provides guidance for how individuals should behave. In other words, when events are important to society, people are rarely left to experience and interpret them without careful guidance.

Durkheim's functional perspective on religion is insightful, but it is not the whole picture. Other dynamics are at work that suggest a different side to religion.

Marx: A Conflict Perspective

The conflict perspective on religion emerged in good part from the work of Karl Marx (1848/1964), who argued that religion can serve as a mechanism for perpetuating patterns of dominance and subordination. To understand how religion can play this role, it is helpful to use the concept of *alienation,* which refers to feelings of separation, isolation, and powerlessness. Marx insisted that people could become alienated from their religion just as they sometimes can from their work. People become alienated from religion by viewing it as something separate from and independent of human beings—they fail to recognize that religions are human creations. Instead, they come to believe that spirits, totems, or deities—rather than human beings—control the social world. It is the gods, people believe, that ordain what political, economic, and familial institutions should be like, and human beings are powerless to change these social arrangements.

Once this alienation occurs, it protects the status quo because people feel helpless in the face of the powerful spiritual forces that presumably have shaped society. In addition, Marx argued, it would seem arrogant for human beings to change what they believe some deity has ordained. In this fashion, groups benefiting from existing social arrangements find their positions protected by the force of religion. In India, for example, the Hindu religion justifies an elaborate caste system in which some people are born into high positions whereas others are relegated at birth to a highly stigmatized out-caste position (see Chapter 6). The Hindu belief in reincarnation encourages people to accept their fate rather than attempt to change society. Elements of Christianity and Judaism also persuade their followers to accept an inequitable distribution of resources. Christianity teaches, for example, that the meek shall inherit the earth and that important human rewards are to be found in the afterlife. These teachings suggest that people should concern themselves with spiritual issues and the afterlife rather than trying to acquire more political power and economic rewards in the here-and-now. Such an ideology can direct one's attention away from earthly inequalities and encourage an acquiescence to the status quo. Gender inequalities have also been perpetuated by positing that male domination is in the divine order. In Roman Catholicism, for instance, only males can be priests, one of the more prestigious and powerful positions in the church. Orthodox Jewish men chant a prayer praising the virtues of manhood:

> Blessed art thou, O lord our God, King of the Universe that I was not born a gentile.
>
> Blessed art thou . . . that I was not born a slave.
>
> Blessed art thou . . . that I was not born a woman.

Given its role in society, Marx called religion *the opiate of the people* because, in his judgment, it dulled their discontents and misdirected their energies. He thought that religion encouraged *false class consciousness* by discouraging people from discovering those beliefs and practices that were in their own class interests, namely for the oppressed to rise up and struggle for a greater share of societal resources.

Weber: Religion and Social Change

Although Durkheim's and Marx's views are quite different, they both characterized religion as a rather conservative force that perpetuates existing social arrangements. In contrast, Max Weber (1905/1958) suggested that religious beliefs could promote social change. Weber came to this conclusion because he observed a link between the emergence of capitalism in Europe and the beliefs of certain Protestant groups. He noticed that capitalism first arose in the West rather than the East and that it tended to emerge in Protestant European countries rather than in Roman Catholic ones. To explain this link, Weber focused on the development of some religious doctrines during the Protestant Reformation, a sixteenth-century religious movement that was an attempt to reform the Catholic Church. One such doctrine was Calvinism, based on the teachings of the sixteenth-century French theologian John Calvin. *Calvinism* is an extremely ascetic form of Protestantism that emphasizes self-denial, self-mortification, and austerity as means of salvation. Calvinists also believe that the sole reason people are alive is to glorify God through hard work and an ascetic life.

Another traditional element of Calvinism is *predestination,* the belief that a person's salvation has been determined by God before he or she is born, and nothing a person does on earth can change that outcome. This doctrine, needless to say, created enormous anxiety regarding whether a person is among the saved or the damned, and led people to search for some worldly sign of their fate. This worldly sign was tied to another important idea that emerged from the Protestant Reformation, a new version of "the calling." Prior to the sixteenth century, Christians had viewed a person's calling in a religious sense: people did God's work by becoming monks or nuns. Beginning with Martin Luther, however, a new concept of the calling emerged: People's duty on earth was to develop to their fullest whatever talents God gave them. Thus one could have a calling to be a merchant, a politician, or a laborer. According to Weber, this doctrine provided a moral justification for worldly pursuits, including economic activity. Calvinists came to believe that economic success meant that God looked favorably on a person, and it could be taken as a sign of salvation. Furthermore, hard work, an ascetic and strictly disciplined life, and deferred gratification increased a person's chances for economic success.

Weber used the term **Protestant ethic** to refer to *the belief that an ascetic life of strict discipline and hard work that results in economic success is a sign of one's worth or that one is among the elect who will go to heaven.* Weber's thesis was that this ascetic Protestantism played an important role in the emergence of capitalism. It encouraged such behavior as hard work, frugality, saving, and reinvestment of earnings, which represent the core of capitalism. These activities were consistent with the profit-seeking economic behavior encouraged by capitalists. The basic principles of the Protestant ethic are summarized in Figure 11.1.

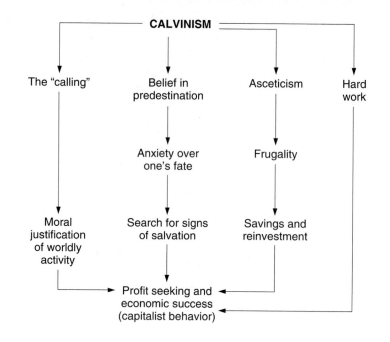

CALVINISM

The "calling" → Moral justification of worldly activity

Belief in predestination → Anxiety over one's fate → Search for signs of salvation

Asceticism → Frugality → Savings and reinvestment

Hard work

Profit seeking and economic success (capitalist behavior)

FIGURE 11.1 The Relationship Between the Protestant Ethic and Capitalism

Weber's hypothesis linking Protestantism and capitalism has caused great controversy. A major criticism of his conclusion is that economic change had begun in Europe prior to the Protestant Reformation and that this economic activity resulted in religious changes, rather than the reverse (Robertson, 1933; Samuelsson, 1961). Another criticism is that many Catholics were merchants and entrepreneurs in the early development of capitalism. However, Weber never claimed that Protestantism *caused* capitalism to come into being. Rather, he argued that the kernel of both the religious creed and the economic activity already existed, and there was an *elective affinity* between them. Because each was supportive of the other, people tended to link them in such a way that they became mutually reinforcing (Winter, 1977). Weber recognized that social change results from the confluence of many factors. His argument was the Calvinism was one among numerous forces in Europe following the Protestant Reformation that contributed to the emergence of capitalism. Other Worlds, Other Ways: China and Lebanon (on pp. 382–383) suggests some other ways in which religion can be a part of the process of social change.

The Organization of Religion

You should be able to list the basic characteristics of churches, ecclesia, denominations, sects, and cults.

Just as religions vary greatly in terms of what their members define as sacred, so there is also great variation in the ways that religions are organized. The earliest religions, for example, had no formal religious organization, no church, and no specialized clergy (Bellah, 1964). Rather, ceremonies were informal, and each person might play many different roles in these rituals over time. More modern societies, however, have specialized religious organizations, and a priesthood emerges in the form of a full-time, professional religious class. In describing religion in modern societies, sociologists distinguish among a number of different levels of organization (Chalfant, Beckley, & Palmer, 1994; Stark & Bainbridge, 1979).

A **church** is *a religious organization that is recognized and socially accepted, tolerates other religions, and lives in harmony with the larger society.* In some societies, a church is what is called an **ecclesia,** *an official state religion.* Although other religions may not be forbidden, the ecclesia is given a special place in social life. It is believed to embody important cultural values, and the religious leaders may be consulted regarding political and economic decisions. The state often provides financial support for the ecclesia, which also supervises the education of the young. Prior to the Protestant Reformation, the Roman Catholic Church was an ecclesia in most European countries and still is in Spain today. The Anglican Church in England and the Islamic religion in Iran are other examples of ecclesia.

In the United States, there is no ecclesia. Rather, churches take the form of **denominations:** *organized churches that have no official sanction from the state.* Sociologists use the term *denomination* differently from its common everyday use, where it usually refers to one of the many denominations of Protestantism. For sociologists, *denomination* means any church that is established and socially accepted but is not a state-sanctioned church. As sociologists use the term, denominations in the United States today would include the various Protestant groups, such as Methodists and Presbyterians, as well as Roman Catholicism, Islam, and Judaism. The last three religions are well established but with no official state sanction, hence not *ecclesia.* (The terms *church* and *denomination* are sometimes used interchangeably when discussing religious organization in societies like the United States that have no ecclesia.)

Sects are *smaller, less formally organized religious groups whose members reject some elements of the larger society and that exist in some degree of tension with society and the secular world.* In some cases, sects have broken away from an existing church. The Catholic Charismatic Renewal, for example, has separated itself to some degree from the Roman Catholic Church. The Branch Davidians were in part an offshoot of the Seventh-Day Adventists. In other cases, a sect may be a totally new development, possibly imported from another society. The Buddhist Church in America and the Krishna Consciousness group are illustrations. Joining sects can involve an intense conversion process, sometimes including withdrawal from previous commitments and relationships.

The distinction between churches and sects is one of degree. At one extreme are "pure" churches that possess all of the characteristics listed in Table 11.2, and at the other extreme are "pure" sects with all of the opposite characteristics. Many religious organizations fall somewhere in be-

TABLE 11.2 Characteristics of churches and sects

Churches tend to	Sects tend to
• Be inclusive, in that their standards for membership are less rigorous	• Be exclusive, in that they do not allow commitment to or membership in other religious groups
• Accept and be willing to work with other religious groups	• View themselves as a fellowship of the elect who alone hold the real truth
• Tolerate some diversity of belief and controversy over principles	• Emphasize purity of doctrine and traditional ethical principles
• Have a professional, full-time clergy with educational credentials and formal ordination ceremonies	• Emphasize lay participation in rituals and decision making, even though they may have some professionally trained clergy
• Gain most new members because they are born to current members of the church	• Gain many new members by conversion
• Give more weight to rewards in this world	• Emphasize otherworldly issues such as salvation and deliverance from hell
• Emphasize formal religious expression with less congregational participation	• Encourage spontaneous and emotional forms of religious expression
• Tolerate other religious groups and endorse the existing social order	• Be in protest against other religious groups or elements of the secular world

OTHER WORLDS, *Other Ways*

CHINA AND LEBANON: REVOLUTIONARY ISLAM AND POLITICAL CHANGE

Kashgar is a city of more than 100,000 people in the Xinjiang autonomous region in the far west of China, bordering on Tibet, Pakistan, and nations that were part of the former Soviet Union. Much of the area is remote desert and mountains, and many people there are nomads, who herd their flocks from horseback. In Kashgar, many men carry jeweled knives and the women wear veils; camels and donkeys are a common mode of transport seen on the streets. In 1993, a bomb destroyed much of the Oasis Hotel on the central square of Kashgar and killed three people. Although the bombers were never found, authorities assume that they were Islamic separatists intent on making Xinjiang an independent Muslim state (Kristof, 1993b).

Although Westerners associate China more with Confucianism or Buddhism, Islam has a long history in China (Gladney, 1991). Beginning in the seventh century, Arab, Persian, and Mongolian Muslim merchants, militia, and officials settled along the coasts of China. These Muslims settlers tended to live in tightly knit enclaves that zealously protected their culture and identity from defilement by the dominant ethnic group, the Han Chinese. Approximately twenty million Muslims live in China today, with heavy concentrations in the northwest and in the Xinjiang region.

Chinese troops crushed a small armed Muslim rebellion in Baren, Xinjiang, in 1990, allegedly precipitated by the efforts of the authorities to close mosques and stop the construction of new mosques and Islamic schools. In response, residents attacked the troops, and twenty-two people were killed before the rebellion was squashed. The continuing presence of troops and roadblocks in the region attests to the authorities' belief that significant rebellious sentiment persists. Most Chinese in Xinjiang are Muslims, and many view the Chinese troops as an invading army. There are also ethnic differences, because most Xinjiang Muslims are Uighurs, Kazaks, and Uzbeks, whereas the majority ethnic group in China is Han. Some ethnic groups, such as the Uigurs, even speak their own language. The Islamic separatists hope to establish an independent nation named Eastern Turkestan, suggesting the region's historical links with the Turkic peoples of central and western Asia rather than with the rest of China. In fact, the Xinjiang Mus-

---

tween. Some sects are referred to as **cults:** *small, loosely organized groups that are typically held together by a charismatic figure. Charisma* refers to that powerful, but often elusive, personal quality that provides one person with great influence over others. The Branch Davidians are an example of a cult. Their leader, David Koresh, exercised considerable charismatic influence over the members of the group until his death.

Sects and cults sometimes emerge when church members, dissatisfied with the traditionalism or lack of emotional involvement found in their church, break away and join or form a new religion that offers these characteristics. Over time, these sects may become more like churches as their members grow older and become more affluent and conservative. In addition, second-generation sect members are less likely to have the emotional commitment or to have experienced the dissatisfaction that the original sect followers had. Thus a cycle can occur from church to sect and back again. Not all sects, however, can be traced to dissatisfied church members. Many sects, such as the Unification Church, are imported from another society and attract people because of their novelty. Furthermore, not all sects are destined to become churches. Some sects have existed for decades, and a few for centuries (Wilson, 1982).

Other Worlds, Other Ways: Comanches and Northern Paiutes (on pp. 384–385) discusses the

lims have been inspired of late by Muslim successes in those regions: Muslims threw the Soviet army out of Afghanistan in the 1980s, and with the collapse of the Soviet Union in the early 1990s, Muslim states were established in Kazakhstan, Krygystan, and Tajikistan—all bordering Xinjiang. The Muslim separatists of Xinjiang believe it is now their turn. The Chinese authorities have generally allowed the Muslims religious freedom, but they have also demanded strict political allegiance. Any *mullah,* or Islamic religious leader, who criticizes the government may be arrested, and many mosques were closed after the rebellion in Baren.

The Muslim separatist movement in China is an outgrowth of the fact that Islam is a broadly encompassing religious belief system that is meant to apply to all aspects of life and that denies any separation between personal life, religious life, and political life. In fact, a basic precept of Islamic faith is that "Islam is religion and state." This precept has made Islam into a powerful revolutionary force to overthrow non-Muslim rulers in many nations and establish *shari'a,* or "Islamic law," as the political and moral code of society. Although the revolutionary movement in China is still small and not well known outside Xinjiang, Islamic revolutionary groups in Lebanon have received international attention (Deeb, 1992). The Lebanese *Hizballah* ("Party of God") was founded in 1982 by Muhammad Hussain Fadlallah, a Shi'ite mullah. Hizballah believes that all Muslims have a religious obligation to fight against "heretical," or non-Islamic, governments, such as the one in Lebanon, and against nonbelievers in Islam. The goal is to establish an Islamic state governed by *shari'a,* which would apply to all people, non-Islamic as well as Islamic. Fadlallah believes that if one accepts the Islamic code, then all non-Muslims are devils or infidels and are dangerous. He divides political parties and politicians into two simple groups: the hizballah, or the "Party of God," to which all believers in Islam belong, and the Party of the Devil, to which everyone else belongs. So, the Islamic political revolution is a strongly religious crusade at the same time that it focuses on political change.

Not all Muslims take as extreme a position as Hizballah in Lebanon, but the examples of Lebanon and China suggest one of the ways in which religious beliefs can affect and change other institutions in society. They also illustrate the diversity of religions found in most societies today.

emergence of some religious movements among American Indians that resemble sects. These movements developed as the onslaught of European civilization continued to erode the Indians' traditional territory and way of life. It illustrates another way in which religion plays a part in social and cultural change: helping people adapt to change, rather than being the force for change as with revolutionary Islam. The United States today provides a virtual supermarket of churches, sects, and cults—reflecting the same diversity that is found in the religions around the world. The remainder of this chapter will investigate the diverse religious beliefs, practices, and organizations in the United States.

Religion in the United States

You should be able to discuss religiosity and its correlates, describe the effect of socioeconomic status and politics on religion, and analyze trends in secularization and religious pluralism in the United States.

In the past few decades, the debate over the extent and strength of religion in the United States has been intense and controversial. In the 1960s, the "God is dead" debate raged over whether people still believed in religion at all. By the 1990s, one theologian blamed the following list of social ills on the decline of religion and the

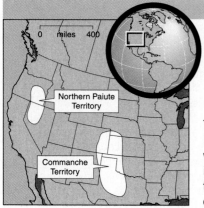

Northern Paiute
Territory

Commanche
Territory

0   miles   400

OTHER WORLDS, *Other Ways*

COMANCHES AND NORTHERN PAIUTES: PEYOTE AND GHOST DANCE MOVEMENTS AS RESPONSES TO CULTURAL CHANGE

The Comanche Indians, who were discussed in the opening to Chapter 2, exemplify the shattering effect of the invasion of Euro-Americans and the creation of the reservation system. The Comanches, who roamed the southern Great Plains in small bands chasing buffalo, were used to living in small groups and moving around frequently. By the 1860s, the buffalo herds had been largely destroyed, and the Comanches had been forced into geographically limited reservations. There was no longer reason or opportunity for them to roam and hunt. For them, "being Comanche" was no longer possible. The world as they knew it—small bands roaming the plains and gathering in larger divisional meetings with other Comanches—no longer existed.

With the loss of their way of life and their culture torn asunder, sometimes in one generation, the Comanches and other tribal peoples experienced a wrenching dislocation. Chapter 7 observed that these conditions resulted in a precipitous decline in the American Indian population, in fact their near extinction. Under conditions such as these where substantial social change is occurring, religion can offer people an explanation of their sufferings and sorrows that provides some hope for the future. Yet established religions often fail in this regard because they are linked to the way of life that is either gone or undergoing change. So new religious expressions develop that gain popularity because they offer people a way out of their misery and degradation. That happened to the American Indians. One new religious development

was the emergence of a peyote cult (La Barre, 1964; Lanternari, 1963). Although peyote (a drug derived from cactus) was well integrated into the cultures of ancient Mexico before the advent of the Europeans, it did not appear in the United States until after 1850. It was probably first picked up by Comanche or Apache raiding parties in northern Mexico.

Common to all Indian users of peyote was the belief that it constituted a sacrament enabling its user to absorb some of the powers of the Great Spirit and that it was a vehicle for learning the will of the Great Spirit. Indians believed that the Great Spirit made peyote available to ease their pain and suffering. While under the influence of peyote, people were to examine their lives to see if they had violated certain cultural norms, such as caring for one's family, self-reliance, and the avoidance of alcohol. In this way, peyote helped its users to find the "road to good."

As the use of peyote spread, each tribe adapted it to fit its own cultural beliefs. The Comanches had known about peyote for some time and used it for medicinal purposes, but prior to being forced onto reservations, they had not had public peyote ceremonies. On the reservation, however, they began public rituals involving peyote that seemed to replace the divisional gatherings of old. The divisional gatherings had been a time for thousands of Comanches, who had been traveling around hunting in much smaller divisions, to gather together, renew friendships, perform familiar rituals, and share their common heritage and identity as Comanches. On the reservation, however, the divisional gatherings no longer seemed needed, since the Comanches now lived fairly close together, and consequently these gatherings fell into disuse. In addition, the European settlers and military were afraid large gatherings of Comanches might lead to an attack and therefore discouraged them. The peyote rituals came to serve the old functions of the divisional gatherings. At the peyote rituals, Comanches would participate in the various cultural practices that had once been the focus of the small bands and divisional gatherings. Thus the peyote cult provided some American Indians with a coherent set of cultural guidelines to follow and a sacred legitimation for them. In this way, it helped them cope with the disintegration of their traditional culture.

Other religious movements sprang from the same soil of cultural collapse, such as the Ghost Dance movements of 1870 and 1890 (Thornton, 1987). Both originated among the Northern Paiutes of western Nevada. The 1870 movement spread only into Oregon and California, but the 1890 movement spread to American Indian tribes throughout the Rocky Mountain and midwestern regions. Central to the Ghost Dance movements was the belief that all whites would be destroyed (some said by fire, others by being swallowed by the earth), that dead Indians would be returned to life, and that all Indians would live on in an earthly paradise filled with game (especially buffalo) and other elements of Indian culture. The central ritual of the Ghost Dance was a ceremony in which individuals clasped hands and moved in a circle while chanting prayers.

The link between cultural collapse and the rise of new religious expressions among American Indians was studied by the sociologist Michael Carroll (1975). In particular, he found a close association between the decline in the buffalo herd and the spread of the 1890 Ghost Dance movement to new tribes: Those tribes that had most recently experienced the loss of the buffalo were the most likely to adopt the Ghost Dance. Carroll attributes this acceptance to *relative deprivation:* the perception of how deprived one's situation is, especially compared to the past or to others' situation. Those who had more recently experienced the loss of the buffalo herd felt more deprived because their immediate past had been much better. Thus they needed the solace of ecstatic religious involvement more than those who had had time to forget or to adapt to existing, even if less desirable, social conditions.

Remnants of both the peyote cult and the Ghost Dance persist today. The peyote cult coalesced into a group called the Native American Church, which continues to use peyote as a part of its rituals. The Ghost Dance continues as the Bole-Maru cult among some American Indians (Thornton, 1987). Yet these religious expressions are largely things of the past. They declined in part because fearful whites and the U.S. government worked to suppress the religions that they believed could only cause trouble among the Indians. Also, conditions changed as some American Indians assimilated into European society and the religious groups did not seem to work.

The peyote cult and the Ghost Dance movements illustrate the sociological truism that when people are frightened, vulnerable, or in crisis, a certain number will turn to religion as a means of coping. However, neither movement halted the destruction of American Indian culture. They may have provided individuals with a sense of peace or personal efficacy, but the European culture still persevered. This example raises once again the issue of the role of religion in society. In this case, as the conflict perspective would suggest, religion seemed to serve more as a means of deflecting the activities of the powerless into channels that could serve as little threat to the powerful.

rise of secularism: "a startling increase in promiscuity, divorce, and abortion; the widespread acceptance in the media of pornography and of homosexuality; and a tolerance of deviant behavior from impiety to the use of drugs" (Dougherty, 1990, p. 113). At the same time, Fundamentalism and television evangelists seem to be more popular than ever. Are people in the United States less—or more—religious today than in the past? This depends in part on how one defines *religious*. **Religiosity** refers to *the degree of commitment to religion*. Sociologists measure religiosity by looking at people's religious preferences; their membership in churches, temples, or synagogues; and the actual religious practices in which they engage.

Extent of Religiosity

If we look at religious preferences, then people in the United States are quite religious. In 1993, 91 percent of adult Americans expressed a preference for some religious group (see Figure 11.2). The majority chose a Protestant denomination and another one-quarter chose the Roman Catholic Church. If we look at church membership to assess religiosity, however, the picture changes a little, with only 65 percent of people in the United States claiming membership in a church, temple, or synagogue. This figure suggests that many people express their religiosity in ways other than joining a church.

Church membership in the United States tends to be associated with certain characteristics (Chalfant, Beckley, & Palmer, 1994). For example, married people are more likely to be members than singles, and the elderly have considerably higher membership rates than the young. Furthermore, Jews have considerably lower membership rates than do Catholics or Protestants. These differences suggest that religious membership is more than simply an expression of faith in a particular set of beliefs. It is also a social act that entwines people in a network of relationships and serves a variety of functions. For example, for some married people, church membership serves as a means of providing religious training for children (Hoge & Carroll, 1978). For elderly people, the church may serve as a focal point for leisure activities and the development of friendships.

Although religious preferences are extensive in the United States, religious practice suggests that people have become *less* religious since the

FIGURE 11.2 Religious Preference in the United States, 1957–1993 *Note:* From *Statistical Abstract of the United States, 1993* (p. 67) by U.S. Bureau of the Census, 1993, Washington, DC: U.S. Government Printing Office; *Statistical Abstract of the United States, 1995* (p. 68) by U.S. Bureau of the Census, 1995, Washington, DC: U.S. Government Printing Office.

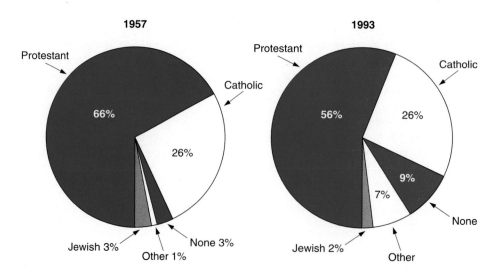

1960s. In terms of church or synagogue attendance, there has been a noticeable, although not dramatic, decline from close to 50 percent attending once a week or more often in the 1950s to near 40 percent today (Saad, 1996). Since the mid-1970s, this decline has leveled off. Among Catholics, however, the decline has been dramatic, from more than 70 percent in the 1950s to close to 50 percent today. Furthermore, levels of church attendance may actually be substantially lower than this, since these statistics are based on surveys that ask people to report whether they go to church or synagogue. There is strong evidence that many people tell surveyers that they attend church—probably because that seems like the socially acceptable thing to report—even when they do not attend as often as they claim (Hadaway, Marler, & Chaves, 1993).

However, compared to people in other countries, people in the United States are far more religious. When religiosity is measured by attendance at a church or synagogue at least two or three times a month, 44 percent in the United States do so, as compared to 17 percent in Britain, 15 percent in West Germany, and 11 percent in Norway. People in the United States are also more likely to believe in God and in a life after death than people in many other nations (see Figure 11.3 on p. 388). If religiosity is measured by the importance attached to religion, religiosity in the United States is considerably above that of other industrial nations and is matched only by people living in Latin America, Africa, and Asia. Thus, although there have been important changes in religious behavior in the past few decades, the overall interest in religious practices is still quite high in the United States in comparison to that of other nations.

Socioeconomic Status and Politics

People's religiosity, especially church membership and religious practice, is linked to their social position. Consistent relationships exist between socioeconomic status (SES) and religion in the United States (Davis & Smith, 1994; Greeley, 1989; Roof & McKinney, 1987). Figure 11.4 (on p. 389) compares the income and educational achievements of many religious groups in the United States. Jews consistently rank among the highest of all religious groups on the three dimensions of SES—education, occupation, and income. Catholics stand at about the average in terms of educational achievement and occupational attainment. Episcopalians and Presbyterians rank high on education and occupation and are nearly equal to Jews. Methodists are lower on these dimensions but above Catholics. Lutherans and Baptists rank relatively low on most SES dimensions.

As has been noted, Marx viewed religion as a tool for appeasing the poor by convincing them to accept their disadvantaged plight. This view might lead us to expect that the poor would be more heavily involved in religious activity as they attempt to smooth the rough edges of their lives. In actuality, the reverse is true: people who are low in SES are less likely to be involved in religious activities (Gaede, 1977; Stark, 1972). Members of the middle and upper classes are more likely to participate in public religious rituals, join church organizations, and be knowledgeable about religious beliefs in general. These types of activities tend to confirm the respectability and success of the affluent. The poor, by contrast, are more likely to undergo intense religious experiences, to be strongly committed to their religious beliefs, and to feel that their own religion is the only means of salvation. These religious beliefs and activities may better meet the needs of the poor in terms of warding off feelings of failure, powerlessness, and isolation.

In addition to the links with SES, religion is also associated with politics. It is not clear whether religious people are more or less politically conservative than nonreligious people. What is clear, however, is that Jews are the most likely to be Democrats, followed closely by Catholics, and Protestants are more likely to be Republicans (Davis & Smith, 1994). These differences are even more marked if we look only at Protestant denominations without a large black membership. Such findings are understandable when we recognize that historically, the Republicans have been the party of the privileged, and Protestants—at least the white congregations—are among the more privileged groups in the United States. Catholics and Jews have a more recent immigrant heritage and experienced prejudice and discrimination at the hands of the Protestant majority when they

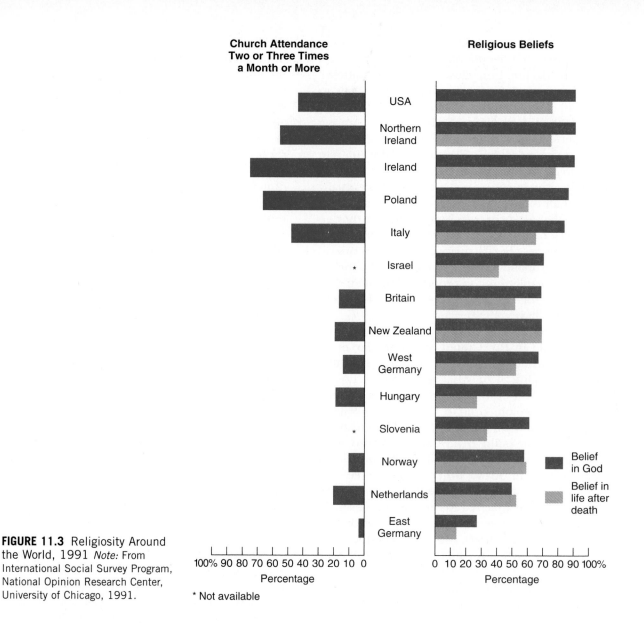

Church Attendance Two or Three Times a Month or More

Religious Beliefs

USA
Northern Ireland
Ireland
Poland
Italy
Israel *
Britain
New Zealand
West Germany
Hungary
Slovenia *
Norway
Netherlands
East Germany

Belief in God

Belief in life after death

FIGURE 11.3 Religiosity Around the World, 1991 *Note:* From International Social Survey Program, National Opinion Research Center, University of Chicago, 1991.

100% 90 80 70 60 50 40 30 20 10 0
Percentage

* Not available

0 10 20 30 40 50 60 70 80 90 100%
Percentage

first arrived in the United States. Having neither wealth nor status, they tended to turn to the Democrats, who have historically been the party of working people and the underdog.

Secularization

Although many in the United States consider themselves religious, the trend over the past few centuries has been for people to relegate religion to a narrower sphere in their lives. These trends are broadly characterized as **secularization:** *the process through which the influence of religion is removed from many institutions in society and dispersed into private and personal realms* (Carter, 1993; Luckmann, 1967). One manifestation of this is shown in Figure 11.5 (on p. 390) : In the 1980s and 1990s, a substantially smaller percentage of people in the United States would agree that religion is very important in their lives than was the case in the 1950s.

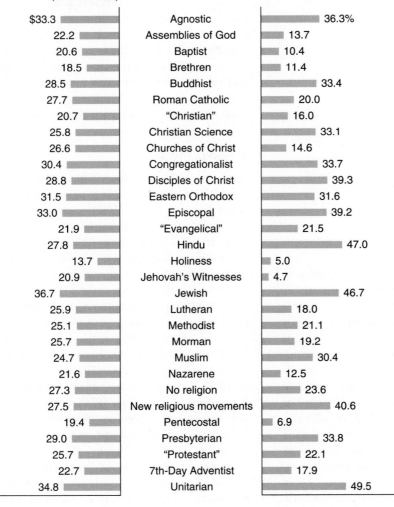

Income		Education
Median Annual Household Income (in thousands)		College Graduates (percent)
$33.3	Agnostic	36.3%
22.2	Assemblies of God	13.7
20.6	Baptist	10.4
18.5	Brethren	11.4
28.5	Buddhist	33.4
27.7	Roman Catholic	20.0
20.7	"Christian"	16.0
25.8	Christian Science	33.1
26.6	Churches of Christ	14.6
30.4	Congregationalist	33.7
28.8	Disciples of Christ	39.3
31.5	Eastern Orthodox	31.6
33.0	Episcopal	39.2
21.9	"Evangelical"	21.5
27.8	Hindu	47.0
13.7	Holiness	5.0
20.9	Jehovah's Witnesses	4.7
36.7	Jewish	46.7
25.9	Lutheran	18.0
25.1	Methodist	21.1
25.7	Morman	19.2
24.7	Muslim	30.4
21.6	Nazarene	12.5
27.3	No religion	23.6
27.5	New religious movements	40.6
19.4	Pentecostal	6.9
29.0	Presbyterian	33.8
25.7	"Protestant"	22.1
22.7	7th-Day Adventist	17.9
34.8	Unitarian	49.5

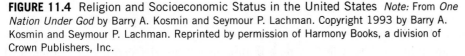

FIGURE 11.4 Religion and Socioeconomic Status in the United States *Note:* From *One Nation Under God* by Barry A. Kosmin and Seymour P. Lachman. Copyright 1993 by Barry A. Kosmin and Seymour P. Lachman. Reprinted by permission of Harmony Books, a division of Crown Publishers, Inc.

Secularization does not mean religion is disappearing but rather that it is practiced mostly at special times and places. At work, at play, or while shopping, for example, people's behavior is shaped mostly by nonreligious considerations, although religious beliefs may play a part in moral decisions or how people relate to others. The beginning of secularization can be traced back hundreds of years and can be attributed in good part to the emergence of highly differentiated societies with an elaborate division of labor. As this differentiation occurred, the various institutions in society came to serve special and limited functions. Distinct political, economic, and religious

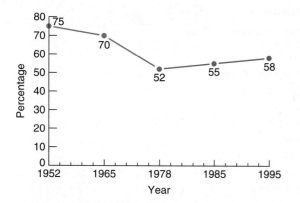

FIGURE 11.5 Percentage of People in the United States Who State That Religion Is Very Important in Their Lives, 1952–1995 *Note:* From "America's Religious Commitment Affirmed," January 1996, *The Gallup Poll Monthly*, p. 22.

institutions emerged, and the influence of religion was increasingly limited to narrower realms.

The growth of science and technology in the past few centuries has also played an important role in the declining influence of religion. One of the functions of religion is that it provides meaning to a mysterious world, but science uses observational techniques in order to understand the world, thus rendering it less mysterious. Instead of using religion to understand disease or to raise bountiful crops, we more frequently turn to science and the technology that science has made available. Although science may not provide answers to questions of ultimate meaning, it does narrow the spheres of life where we may feel the need to turn to religion.

Despite the process of secularization, most sociologists agree that religion, in one form or another, will continue to play an important part in society. For one thing, people still face personal problems and seek answers to questions of ultimate meaning. Conventional churches will satisfy this need for some people, and others will turn to more personal and private belief systems such as meditation, yoga, or scientology. In addition, even in a secularized society, religion contributes to social solidarity and cohesion, which Durkheim argued is one of the central functions of religion in society. Robert Bellah (1988), for example, has argued that there is a *civil religion* in the United

States that serves precisely this function. This **civil religion** is *a set of beliefs and rituals that exists outside any organized church and sanctifies a particular nation and its way of life*. It contains a set of symbols toward which people can express agreement and gain a sense of common heritage and unity. Civil religion in the United States rests on a set of general dogmas: beliefs in some deity, in a higher law, and in life after death. It also includes a belief in the sacredness of the United States and in the reward of virtue and the punishment of evil.

Religious Pluralism

Many of the European colonists who came to the New World were escaping religious persecution (Littell, 1962; Marty, 1984). After arriving, they often recreated communities of religious intolerance. In some cases they maintained what was in effect an ecclesia or official state religion. The Puritans established a theocracy in Massachusetts that mixed religious law and secular law, and the Church of England became the official religion of the Virginia, Carolina, and Georgia colonies. At the time of the Declaration of Independence in 1776, nine of the thirteen colonies had officially established religions. Gradually, however, these religious monopolies began to break down under the weight of a number of social forces. One was the increasing religious diversity that resulted from wave after wave of new immigrants that arrived in the United States. The early immigrants came to constitute a small proportion of the population and found it difficult to maintain their monopoly over what was considered acceptable religious practice. Every colony had a growing number of religious dissenters. Because of this religious diversity, and because the values of the new nation emphasized freedom of choice and individual responsibility, the Constitution of the United States, ratified in 1789, was quickly amended to guarantee freedom of religion and the separation of church and state.

The result today in the United States is considerable religious pluralism (Roof, 1993). Although Roman Catholicism, Protestantism, and Judaism are the three major religious groups and dominate in numbers, there is much diversity within each in terms of theology and social practice. In addition, there are many groups that fall

The religious scene in the United States today is characterized by considerable religious diversity. This girl lights the seventh and final candle of Kwanzaa, which some African Americans practice as a religious ceremony that is linked to their own African heritage.

outside these three. As Figure 11.2 shows, the three major religious groups in the United States have declined in the past thirty years, while the percentage of the populace that claims a religious preference other than one of these has increased significantly. The major elements of this diversity and the constantly changing scene of religion in the United States will be described in the rest of this chapter.

The Ecumenical Movement The term *ecumenism* refers to efforts at bringing harmony to the various religions and denominations by emphasizing the similarities of their doctrines and establishing cooperative interdenominational work. The ecumenical movement gained strength in the 1960s and 1970s in response to declining church memberships and contributions. Some religious leaders believed that a cooperative effort among religions would more effectively stem the decline

than would competition for new members. The ecumenical movement has resulted in some cooperative efforts, such as the integration of social services provided by different agencies and occasionally the merging of different denominations. Most of this ecumenism, however, has involved mainline Protestant denominations whose doctrines are not too dissimilar and whose members have similar social backgrounds. Such large Protestant denominations as the Southern Baptist Convention, the Churches of Christ, and the Lutheran Church (Missouri Synod) have largely rejected ecumenism because of doctrinal differences. In fact, this attempt to bring denominations together has created further divisions between those churches who join the movement and those who do not. This ecumenical conflict also represents in part a class conflict, with the ecumenical supporters consisting of mainline, more affluent Protestant denominations, and the opponents tending to be less affluent, evangelical groups (Chalfant, Beckley, & Palmer, 1994). The ecumenical movement has also been associated with political liberalism and social activism, which causes further division in the more conservative Protestant denominations.

Fundamentalism and Evangelicalism In the past few decades, there has been an upsurge in conservative Protestantism, including fundamentalism and evangelicalism. These terms are often misused and sometimes used interchangeably. *Fundamentalists* believe in a literal interpretation of the Bible and a return to the teachings of the Bible as a foundation for Christian faith. *Evangelicals* emphasize a personal commitment to Jesus Christ and the subjective experience of personal salvation, or being *born again*. Evangelicalism involves an intense commitment to one's church and beliefs and an effort to seek new converts through *testifying* to one's beliefs. Although some evangelicals are fundamentalists, not all of them are.

Since the 1980s, evangelicals and fundamentalists have become heavily involved in political and social issues. Many political candidates have emphasized their evangelical backgrounds, including Presidents Carter, Clinton, Ford, and Reagan. In 1988, the fundamentalist Reverend Pat Robertson was a serious candidate for the Republican nomination for the presidency. Many political candidates have run on platforms emphasizing the traditional morality of these groups, and lobbying efforts have been made to outlaw abortion, allow prayer in the schools, block passage of the Equal Rights Amendment, and oppose civil rights for homosexuals. Organizations such as the Moral Majority, the Roundtable, and Christian Voice have backed that conservative agenda. In fact, critics have charged that some actions of these evangelical groups threaten existing religious pluralism because the groups are attempting to legislate a particular set of religious beliefs, thus blurring the separation between church and state.

Mass Media and the Televangelists The use of the mass media to distribute religious messages is nothing new. After all, the Roman Catholic bishop Fulton J. Sheen began broadcasting radio sermons in 1928 and later moved to television. In the past three decades, however, television evangelism has boomed with the emergence of *televangelists,* preachers who send their message to millions of homes and raise millions of dollars to support their evangelical ministry and to finance conservative political lobbying and campaigns. Pat Robertson, Jimmy Swaggart, and Jim Bakker, for example, became well known in the 1980s and at their height had celebrity status. Toward the end of the 1980s, however, televangelists saw their viewers and their revenues tumble precipitously (Hadden, 1993). One reason for this was the highly publicized financial and sexual scandals that rocked a couple of the ministries. Another reason was that the market for TV ministries had become saturated—there were just too many religious broadcasters for the potential audience. Yet a third reason for the decline was that some preachers, especially Jerry Falwell and Pat Robertson, deeply involved their ministries in political campaigns, and it appears that many Americans do not like to see their religious leaders too active in politics. So, for a time in the late 1980s, the viewers and the revenues dwindled. Television ministries are resilient, however, and are making a comeback in the 1990s. The number of religious television stations continues to grow, and the increasing number of channels on cable television has allowed for the expansion of religious programming. One cable channel is a collective effort of mainline Protestant, Jewish, Roman Catholic, and Eastern Orthodox groups. So, television ministries will remain a fairly secure feature of religious life in the United States.

Televangelists represent something new in religious pluralism because they openly compete with one another and with conventional religious denominations for adherents, often ignoring denominational lines. According to one person who has researched these ministries: "Televangelists know how to reach the individual Christian, offering hope and love to ameliorate fear and anxiety and, perhaps more importantly, offering membership into their television communities as a means of acknowledging the viewers' importance to them" (Frankl, 1987, p. 148). Without ever stepping into a church building or meeting face to face with a minister, people join a church and "attend" religious services. For the televangelist, people are consumers shopping for some religious experience. Denominational doctrines and boundaries are less important than effective media presentations that can convince the television audience to join and send an offering to support the ministry.

People who watch televangelists tend to be female, older, with lower income and education, and from southern or midwestern states (Clymer, 1987; Horsfield, 1984). These characteristics point to one source of support for televangelists: part of their appeal is to people experiencing some social isolation or those suffering from economic deprivation.

Whereas televangelists use the mass media to spread their religious message and draw adherents, the media also has a different, and sometimes unwanted impact on religion: Media coverage of religious groups, and especially sects and cults, is a powerful influence in shaping how the public perceives them. In the 1980s, for example, many dramatic stories appeared in the media about satanic cults. Many of them included stories of the "satanic ritual abuse" of children. Beyond the worship of Satan, these cults were said to engage in such things as drinking blood and cannibalism. The image presented was of a large, growing movement that posed a serious threat to established religions and especially to children and youth. The vast majority of the reports turned out to be false or highly exaggerated, but the media—less concerned about weighing evidence than profiting from sensational stories—contributed to a definition of reality regarding religious activity in the United States.

Another example of this has to do with *Santería,* discussed in the opening section of this chapter. What draws the media's attention to this group is again the sensational aspects of their religious practice, such as the ritual sacrifice of chickens and goats. Rarely does the media explain clearly and completely the doctrines of the group and connect the ritual practices with these doctrines. The impression the media presents is of an extreme, primitive, and possibly cruel group. So whereas the televangelists use the media to spread their word and attract followers, the media can also make it more difficult for small, obscure religious groups with little access to resources to gain a hearing in the religious supermarket of the United States today.

Growth in Islam   Of the world's religions discussed earlier in this chapter, Judaism and Christianity clearly have the most members and longest tradition in the United States. Nevertheless, Islam has shown remarkable growth, especially since the 1960s (Bernstein, 1993). There are approximately four million Muslims in the United States, and if present trends in birth rates and immigration patterns persist, Muslims will outnumber the six million Jews early in the twenty-first century. In the mid-1990s there were more than 1,100 mosques in the United States, 80 percent of which were founded since the mid-1980s.

Some African slaves brought to North America during the colonial period were probably Muslim, and small numbers of Muslims came to the United States in the late 1800s and early 1900s. Developments in the 1960s, however, set the stage for the recent upsurge in Islam in the United States. One development was new laws that permitted more immigration from Muslim nations in the Middle East and Asia. The second development was the conversion of African Americans to Islam, inspired partly by Elijah Muhammad, founder of the Nation of Islam, and Malcolm X. Since Islam is a traditional religion in parts of Africa, it was attractive to African Americans as a link to their homeland. Islam also offered an identity that they believed was stripped from them during slavery and a coherent symbol and belief system that was independent of the dominant white culture. Possibly as many as one-quarter of Muslims in the United States are black.

Most Muslims in the United States have assimilated to a significant degree, adopting lifestyles similar to those of non-Muslim Americans. However, as noted, Islamic beliefs include social prescriptions that diverge from other trends in the United States. For example, Islam emphasizes a sexual modesty and conservatism that, as noted in Chapter 9, is less widely held today by many people in the United States than in the past. Islam also requires clear distinctions in gender roles, with women having primary responsibility for home and family, which Chapter 8 noted many women in the United States find too limiting. Thus there is tension between some traditional Islamic beliefs and the customs of many Americans. But some Christian and Jewish groups hold equally conservative normative strictures, so Islam is not unique in that regard. Despite any distinctiveness that might cause tension, the Muslim community in the United States today is flourishing, with its own schools, social clubs, marriage services, magazines, and bookstores. Muslims will continue to be a significant part of the religious mosaic in the United States.

New Religious Movements   The number of new religious groups in the United States has continued to grow over the past few decades (Robbins, 1988). Some of them are offshoots of the mainline religions, such as the Children of God and Jews for Jesus; others are extensions of traditional religions in other cultures, such as the Krishna Consciousness movement and the cult of Bhagwan Shree Rajneesh, which are of Hindu origin. Still

others are a hybrid, such as the Reverend Sun Myung Moon's Unification Church.

There are a number of misconceptions about these new religions (Melton, 1993). One is that most of them are a byproduct of the counterculture of the 1960s. Some of them did emerge in the 1960s, but that was the result of changes in the laws in 1965 that resulted in a large influx of immigrants from Asia. Some of these immigrants established Hindu or Buddhist temples in their new home, and some U.S.–born young people were drawn to these exotic new religions. Buddhism had already begun to make an impact in the United States in the 1950s, as soldiers who experienced life in Japan following World War II returned with new ideas about religion. Furthermore, more unconventional religions emerged in the 1970s and 1980s than in the

The religious pluralism of the United States is reflected in this Buddhist wedding ceremony in Massachusetts. Immigration has contributed to the growth of religions such as Islam, Buddhism, and Hinduism in the United States in recent decades.

1960s. All these facts suggest that the 1960s were not terribly special, as far as these unconventional religions are concerned; rather, the emergence of these new religions is the result in part of the increasing multicultural nature of the U.S. populace.

A second misconception regarding these religions is that many of them are ephemeral and short-lived, with no significant, lasting impact on U.S. culture. Whereas that is true of a few, most of these groups survive and become a continuing part of the religious environment in their communities. A few even prosper. After all, the Mormons were an unconventional offshoot at their inception in the early 1800s, and they have become a well established and highly influential member of the social, political, and religious communities of the United States.

There are many reasons why people join these new religions. First of all, like the fundamentalists and evangelicals, the new religions can offer support and sustenance for people suffering from social isolation or economic deprivation. Their intense commitment and bonds of community are often more appealing to people than the more formal and staid approaches of the mainline religions. Second, the growing bureaucracy and impersonality of modern society leaves many people feeling alienated, and the trend toward secularization has left many people with feelings of uncertainty about moral and personal values. Sects and cults offer an escape from that alienation and uncertainty. They offer an exhilarating feeling of becoming a new person, taking control of one's life, and experiencing deep involvement with accepting, like-minded people. Third, sects and cults offer support to people experiencing the uncertainties often associated with transitions in the life cycle, such as young people coming to adulthood and separating from their family or a person who has just dropped out of college or lost a job. Finally, joining religious movements is one way that people use to adapt to the disruption that often accompanies social change.

These, then, are the structural sources of the development of new religions in the United States: social isolation, economic deprivation, bureaucracy, secularization, and life cycle transitions. Because these conditions are permanent features of modern society, new religious movements are likely to have a continuing appeal.

Applying Sociology: Identifying Extremism in Religious Cults (on pp. 396–397) looks at how sociological research can offer a more complete and balanced view of these new religious groups to counter the more stereotyped and hysterical view sometimes held by the public. This diversity of religious expression in the United States suggests that the country may experience a reorientation of religious life away from an exclusively Western Judeo-Christian focus.

Summary

1. As an empirical discipline, sociology cannot assess the truth or falsity of religious beliefs. Rather, sociologists study religions as social institutions that function in the social world, are transmitted through the socialization process, and are influenced by the social and cultural context in which they exist.

2. Religions distinguish between the sacred and the profane. Religion as an institution is a collectively held set of symbols and rituals that express a basic understanding of the world, especially its sacred dimension, and address the ultimate concerns of the meaning of human existence.

3. Religions come in many forms, such as animism, theism, and religions of the way. And there is great diversity in the religions around the world. There has been much diffusion of religions around the world as human societies interact with one another through trade or war.

4. Religions serve a number of important functions. They enhance social solidarity by reinforcing cultural values. They also give a sacred legitimation to cultural values and practices, provide meaning for human lives, and assist people in understanding life events.

5. Religions can serve as mechanisms of oppression whereby the powerful protect their position by convincing subordinate groups that the existing distribution of resources is ordained by some deity. This is possible because people become alienated from religion, forgetting that it is a human creation.

APPLYING SOCIOLOGY
Identifying Extremism in Religious Cults

In 1978, news began to leak out of Guyana, a small country in South America, about a shocking murder-suicide in a religious cult that had migrated there from the United States. The People's Temple, headed by the Reverend Jim Jones, had developed an isolated community in the steamy rain forest of Guyana. Jones himself was both charismatic and tyrannical in the control he exercised over the members of the cult. He demanded complete allegiance from his followers. His control was so complete that he had been able to convince many of them to move from the relative comfort of California to the deep rain forest of Guyana. In the end, apparently paranoid that outsiders threatened his control, he orchestrated a nightmarish death episode in which cyanide poison was squirted down the throats of infants and children, adults voluntarily drank poisoned Koolaid, and resisters were shot to death. More than nine hundred followers, including Jones himself, died on that day (Wooden, 1981).

Fifteen years later, David Koresh, another charismatic leader, headed a religious cult called the Branch Davidians. He gathered his followers in a heavily armed compound called Ranch Apocalypse, outside Waco, Texas. When agents of the Bureau of Alcohol, Tobacco, and Firearms tried to enter in a search for illegal weapons, cult members killed four and wounded sixteen of them in a hail of gunfire. The agents retreated, and a fifty-one-day standoff began. Koresh claimed to be Jesus Christ and refused to negotiate with the authorities. In the end they attacked the compound, which immediately caught fire and burned to the ground, killing the sixty adults and twenty-six children and teenagers inside. Authorities maintain that Koresh or his followers deliberately set the fire rather than lose control of the group (Gibbs, 1993).

The public sometimes finds it hard to fathom such groups, especially to understand why people would submit to such seeming madmen. Sociologists have studied hundreds upon hundreds of such groups over the decades and have learned quite a bit about them. They have found that the People's Temple and the Branch Davidians are the exception in the sense that very few such groups go to such bizarre extremes. In fact, most religious sects and cults are fairly respectable, have a positive impact on their members' lives, and probably make a positive contribution to society by encouraging their members to work hard and avoid drugs and crime. By looking at the ways people are attracted to these unconventional religions, we can also catch a glimpse of what can go wrong and produce a Jim Jones or David Koresh.

People become involved in such unconventional religions for a variety of reasons (Richardson, 1978; Robbins, 1988). First of all, people who are attracted to these groups tend to be those who, possibly because of early socialization, view the world in a religious light and define problems and their solutions in terms of religious forces. Second, people are attracted to these groups because they are experiencing some personal troubles or difficulties or a life transition that has left them temporarily adrift from social ties. All people, of course, experience troubles and transitions, but for some the accompanying pain or self-doubt is so enormous that they are desperate to find a solution to their problems—or avoid them by immersion in some ecstatic experience.

Sociologists have also learned that a key step in the conversion process is when people come to believe that a particular religious group can offer them solace, and this belief is where a group's recruitment efforts are directed. Their members are sent to beaches, college communities, or other places where those whose lives are in transition are likely to congregate. Since young people are the category most likely to have lives in some turmoil, many of these recruitment efforts are directed at them.

The popular image is that people are "programmed" or "brainwashed" when they join these groups. An "anticult" or "deprogramming" movement has emerged to fight against such unconventional religions. Sociological research suggests, however, that although these groups certainly influence their members, the influence is limited. In fact, most people leave these groups after a year or two (Levine, 1986). People entered and left both the People's Temple and the Branch Davidians almost until the end. For many, the groups are temporary retreats where they can find support, think through their problems, and decide what their next steps in life will be. Eventually, they return to a more conventional life, although their moral and spiritual lives are likely to remain permanently affected by their experiences.

Why the tragic end for the People's Temple and the Branch Davidians? Sociological research points to some of the differences between these and other cults and the things to watch for. One is that the cults came under the sway of a charismatic, highly manipulative, and ultimately psychologically unstable leader. Some of the people attracted to such groups are lonely, isolated, and desperate for some certainty in their lives, which makes them especially vulnerable to such exploitation. In most such groups, the leaders do not take exploitative advantage of the situation; Jones and Koresh did. A second difference is that the leaders went to extremes to isolate their followers from contact with or influence by others. Jones physically isolated them in the rain forests of Guyana; the Branch Davidians were required to surrender all their money and belongings to Koresh, effectively isolating them from any resources that might have enhanced their personal independence. A third difference is the belief in an apocalyptic confrontation with the larger society. Both Jones and Koresh had the paranoid view that society was out to destroy them. Koresh had stockpiled hundreds of rifles, machine guns, and hand grenades at Ranch Apocalypse.

Although most religious sects and cults are reasonably benign, people should be wary of a group that exhibits these characteristics.

Like the Hare Krishnas pictured here, most nonconventional religions are relatively benign, teaching their followers to lead law-abiding and productive lives. Sometimes, however, such groups can go terribly awry, as the Branch Davidian sect did in Texas.

6. Religion can play a part in social change. The Protestant ethic, for example, played a role in bringing about capitalism in Europe, and Islam today is a force promoting political change in a number of places around the world.

7. Some religions have very informal organizations, with little specialization of religious roles. Most modern religions, however, are highly specialized and have a full-time clergy. In the United States, most religions are either churches or sects.

8. People in the United States tend to be a fairly religious people, especially in comparison to most other nations. People's religiosity is affected by their socioeconomic status. Religion, in turn, has an effect on political party preferences.

9. Secularization has occurred because societies have become highly differentiated and because science has dispelled some of the mysteries in life.

10. The United States is characterized by religious pluralism. Recent developments in this area have been the ecumenical movement, fundamentalism, the use of the mass media to transmit religious messages, and the growth of Islam. In addition, many new religious sects have emerged in the past few decades.

STUDY AND Review

Key Terms

animism	Protestant ethic
church	religion
civil religion	religions of the way
cults	religiosity
denomination	sacred
ecclesia	sects
monotheistic religions	secularization
polytheistic religions	theistic religions
profane	totemism

Multiple-Choice Questions

1. Judaism, Christianity, and Islam are considered to be
   a. polytheistic religions.
   b. monotheistic religions.
   c. religions of the way.
   d. animistic religions.
   e. both b and c.

2. Which of the following religions is based on the belief that Jesus was the Christ or the Messiah?
   a. Christianity.
   b. Judaism.
   c. Hinduism.
   d. Both a and b.
   e. Both a and c.

3. Which of the following religions is based on the belief in the transmigration of souls?
   a. Christianity.
   b. Judaism.
   c. Islam.
   d. Hinduism.
   e. Confucianism.

4. All of the following were identified by Emile Durkheim as functions performed by religion *except*
   a. it enhances social solidarity.
   b. it encourages individualistic behavior.
   c. it offers sacred legitimation of values.
   d. it provides meaning for people's lives.
   e. all of the above were identified by Durkheim.

5. According to the conflict perspective, people tend to become alienated from religion. One consequence of this alienation is
   a. people drift away from religion.
   b. the status quo is protected.
   c. people's false class consciousness is reduced.
   d. religion no longer serves as the opiate Marx described.

6. In looking at the link between the emergence of capitalism and certain religious beliefs, Max Weber focused on which religious doctrine?
   a. Hinduism.
   b. Judaism.
   c. Calvinism.
   d. Animism.
   e. Taoism.

7. In comparison to churches, sects tend to
   a. gain new members through birth to current members.
   b. tolerate other religious groups.
   c. be exclusive in their membership practices.
   d. have a professional, full-time clergy.
   e. tolerate diversity of beliefs.

8. The largest proportion of people in the United States state a preference for which of the following religions?
   a. Protestantism.
   b. Catholicism.
   c. Judaism.
   d. Islam.
   e. A majority state a preference for no religion.

9. Which of the following statements is true regarding the link between religion and politics?
   a. Religious people are more politically conservative than are nonreligious people.
   b. Nonreligious people are more politically conservative than are religious people.
   c. Jews are more likely to be Democrats than are Protestants.
   d. Protestants are more likely to be Democrats than are Catholics.

10. The ecumenical movement in the United States emphasizes
    a. the literal interpretation of the Bible.
    b. a personal commitment to Jesus Christ and being born again.
    c. the use of television to distribute religious messages.
    d. harmony between and the similarities among the various religions and denominations.

True/False Questions

1. Voodoo and *Santería* in the Caribbean and the Americas are outgrowths of African tribal religions.

2. Totemism is a variant on animism.

3. Hinduism is older than Christianity and Islam.

4. The founder of Confucianism is Siddhartha Gautama, who is known as the Enlightened One.

5. When Karl Marx referred to religion as "the opiate of the people," he meant that religion helped to reduce their feelings of alienation.

6. In his studies on religion, Max Weber found that it was difficult for people to follow the Protestant ethic and engage in capitalist activity at the same time.

7. The Hizballah in Lebanon is a religious group that hopes to bring about political changes.

8. Religious cults are small, loosely organized sects that are often held together by a charismatic figure.

9. Before the American Revolution in 1776, none of the colonies in the New World had official state religions or ecclesia.

10. Islam had no adherents in the United States until the 1970s when immigration from the Middle East to the United States began.

Fill-In Questions

1. Emile Durkheim argued that the distinctive feature of religion is that it views the world as divided into two realms, the _____ and the _____ .

2. Polytheistic religions involve a belief in _____ .

3. The branch of Judaism that follows strictly the divine books and the laws as promulgated by Moses is _____ .

4. The basic principles of Buddhism are stated in the _____ .

5. When Karl Marx said that people become alienated from religion, he meant that they _____ .

6. Max Weber argued that there was an _____ between Protestantism and capitalism.

7. _____ is an official state religion.

8. The peyote and Ghost Dance movements among American Indians arose as a response to _____ .

9. _____ is the process through which the influence of religion is removed from many institutions in society and dispersed into private and personal realms.

10. Those who believe in a literal interpretation of the Bible and the use of biblical teachings as a foundation of faith are called _____ .

Matching Questions

_____ 1. Calvinism
_____ 2. *dharma* and *karma*
_____ 3. evangelicalism
_____ 4. denomination
_____ 5. Branch Davidians
_____ 6. degree of commitment to religion
_____ 7. civil religion
_____ 8. Jerry Falwell and Pat Robertson
_____ 9. *Vodu*
_____ 10. Islam

A. cult
B. sanctifies a nation and way of life
C. "the calling"
D. Hinduism
E. born again
F. televangelists
G. West African religion
H. established and socially accepted church
I. Koran
J. religiosity

Essay Questions

1. How would a sociologist define religion? Describe the major forms that religion can take.

2. When and how did Judaism, Christianity, and Islam emerge? Describe the basic beliefs of each religion.

3. When and how did Hinduism, Buddhism, and Confucianism emerge? Describe the basic beliefs of each religion.

4. Compare and contrast the functionalist and conflict perspectives on religion. Show clearly how they differ from one another.

5. According to Max Weber, what is the relationship between Protestantism and capitalism? Describe all the elements of that relationship.

6. In a number of places in the chapter, the role of religion in the process of political and social change is discussed. Review the examples discussed in the chapter, and describe what they tell us about how religion affects social change.

7. Define and describe the different levels of religious organization that sociologists use in describing religion in modern societies. Give an example of each.

8. What is the extent of religiosity in the United States? How does the United States compare with other nations?

9. What is the relationship between socioeconomic status and politics in the United States?

10. What reasons were given in the text for why new religions emerge in the United States?

Answers

Multiple-Choice
1. B; 2. A; 3. D; 4. B; 5. B; 6. C; 7. C;
8. A; 9. C; 10. D

True/False
1. T; 2. T; 3. T; 4. F; 5. F; 6. F; 7. T;
8. T; 9. F; 10. F

Fill-In
1. sacred, profane
2. many gods
3. orthodox Judaism
4. Four Noble Truths
5. view religion as something separate and independent of human beings
6. elective affinity
7. an ecclesia
8. cultural change or cultural dislocation or cultural collapse
9. secularization
10. fundamentalists

Matching
1. C; 2. D; 3. E; 4. H; 5. A; 6. J; 7. B;
8. F; 9. G; 10. I

For Further Reading

Berger, Peter L. (1967). *The sacred canopy: Elements of a sociological theory of religion.* Garden City, NY: Doubleday. This is a classic introduction to the sociological study of religion.

Haddad, Yvonne Yazbeck, & Lummis, Adair T. (1987). *Islamic values in the United States: A comparative study.* New York: Oxford University Press. The authors provide a detailed analysis of the adaptations made by Muslim immigrants to the United States.

Hammond, Philip E. (1992). *Religion and personal autonomy: The third disestablishment in America.* Columbia: University of South Carolina Press. This sociologist makes a compelling argument that religion in the United States has changed over the years: It has become more personal, less communal, and less involving. He draws out the historical implications of this change.

Lawless, Elaine J. (1988). *God's peculiar people: Women's voices and folk tradition in a pentecostal church.* Lexington: University Press of Kentucky. This book explores the role that women play in many religions, even when they are barred from formal roles of preacher or minister.

Lewis, James R., & Melton, J. Gordon (Eds.). (1992). *Perspectives on the new age.* Albany: State University of New York Press. This is an interesting book of readings on such new age spiritual practices as channeling and witchcraft. The book assesses whether they should be considered religions and looks at the response to them of some older religions.

McGuire, Meredith B. (1992). *Religion: The social context* (3rd ed.). Belmont, CA: Wadsworth. This readable and thorough review of the field of the sociology of religion shows in detail how religion affects societies and individuals.

Nielson, Niels C., Jr., et al. (1993). *Religions of the world* (3rd ed.). New York: St. Martin's Press. This book provides a comprehensive, yet readable survey of the religions of the world—their beliefs and practices and the issues important to them. It firmly grounds religions in their social and cultural context.

Richardson, James T., Best, Joel, & Bromley, David G. (Eds.). (1991). *The satanism scare.* New York: Aldine de Gruyter. This is an excellent investigation of satanism and satanic cult activity in the United States. The authors provide a realistic description and assessment of the phenomenon as well as an insightful discussion of why it has aroused so much hysteria. It is a good case study of competition among religious communities.

Stark, Rodney, & Bainbridge, William Sims. (1985). *The future of religion: Secularization, revival, and cult formation.* Berkeley: University of California Press. This is a thought-provoking analysis of the impact of secularization on religion in the modern era.

Wilcox, Clyde. (1992). *God's warriors: The Christian right in twentieth-century America.* Baltimore: Johns Hopkins University Press. This is an excellent analysis of the Christian Anticommunism Crusade of the 1960s, Jerry Falwell's Moral Majority of the 1980s, and Pat Robertson's 1988 presidential campaign. The author looks at the depth and scope of support for these groups and their impact on American politics.

CHAPTER TWELVE

Education and the Mass Media

The Jesuits are a Roman Catholic religious order founded in 1539 by a Spaniard, Ignatius Loyola. In their early years they were a militant monastic order that stressed education and were considered an intellectual and moral elite among Catholics. Emerging in the midst of the Protestant Reformation, the Jesuits were founded to bring people back to the Catholic faith and were staunch defenders of papal authority. They organized themselves along military lines and undertook to spread Catholicism across international boundaries.

Fourteen years after their founding, the Jesuits arrived in Brazil, suffused with zeal and dedication to convert the indigenous tribal peoples, whom they, like all Europeans, called *heathens* (Hemming, 1978). The Jesuits and the Indians got along fairly well. The Jesuits were free of the intense material greed that fueled virtually all of the behavior of the Portuguese colonists, and the Indians found they could trust the priests. In addition, the Jesuits provided some protection against Portuguese excesses. In fact, the Jesuits set up mission villages, called *aldeias* in Portuguese, to which many Indians fled when defeated by the Portuguese in colonial wars.

In the *aldeias,* the Jesuits set up schools for the Indians. The Jesuits concentrated their educational efforts mostly on the young. Adults were more resistant to missionary schooling because the Jesuits were asking them to give up some long-held traditional practices, such as polygyny and cannibalism. Children were more impressionable. In the schools, the young were taught Christianity, of course, but they learned much more than that. As one Jesuit wrote from Bahia state in Brazil in 1558: "Their children are instructed; the innocent ones about to die are all baptised; they are forgetting their customs and exchanging them for good ones" (quoted in Hemming, 1978, p. 101). In other words, the schools aspired to replace traditional ways with the more "civilized" ways of sixteenth-century Europeans. The children learned not only to read and write but also to sing songs and play musical instruments from Europe. Girls were instructed in how to weave cloth so that they could cover themselves rather than go naked as was their custom before the Portuguese came. The missionaries believed that the children could then make further inroads on the Indian way of life by teaching their parents. Some Indian children even used their European education as an excuse to dominate and patronize their parents. The children were beginning to accept the European view that Indian ways were heathen and backward. The children were discouraged from learning tribal ways, such as animistic religions or the skills of hunters and warriors. As a consequence, according to one historian, the children "would also become accomplices in the emasculation of tribal culture" (Hemming, 1978, p. 111). Not only was the education given the Indians devoid of tribal skills, but also it neglected to train the children in the skills and orientations that would make them competitive in the much harsher colonial world dominated by the Portuguese.

Education is *the systematic, formal process through which specialized teachers transmit skills, knowledge, and values to students.* In the long run, the education that the Jesuits provided to the Indians of Brazil helped to solidify colonial domination by encouraging young Indians to accept European religious and political authority and to reject tribal sources of wisdom, tradition, and authority. The schools also helped to reproduce a stratification system based on European dominance and Indian subordination by making sure the Indians did not receive skills that would give them an equal advantage with the Europeans in colonial trade. The experience of the Brazilian Indians begins to shed light on some of the complex ways in which education as a social institution contributes to the maintenance of society. The following analysis of education begins with a discussion of the emergence of education as a separate social institution.

A Global Perspective on Education

You should be able to describe how education differs in preindustrial and industrial societies and how colonization and modernization have changed education.

Informal Education

In traditional Yoruk society in Turkey, many of the women were highly skilled basket makers who produced sophisticated baskets that were both functional and beautiful. Yet they received no formal training and only small amounts of informal instruction in basket making. Rather, during their childhood, Yoruk girls would watch their mothers, aunts, and older sisters weave baskets and would become skilled weavers themselves merely by observation (O'Neale, 1932). In many preindustrial societies, such as the Yoruk, it is difficult to distinguish education from the general process of socialization (see Chapter 3). The reason is that specialized educational institutions had not yet emerged. Instead, education took place during informal, daily interactions with family members and others. There were no special buildings called schools and no specialized roles for teachers or students. In fact, anyone could serve as a teacher if children learned from that person by watching him or her plow the fields, bake bread, or weave baskets, and practically all adults served, at one time or another, as teachers of children.

Myths & FACTS

ABOUT EDUCATION AND THE MASS MEDIA

Myth When British and Portuguese explorers after Columbus found new lands, they set up schools to teach the natives skills that would help them survive better.

FACT These explorers typically considered the indigenous inhabitants to be uncivilized and believed that the only way they could become civilized was to learn European ways. The primary result of European schooling of the inhabitants was to protect the interests of the Europeans and in many cases to destroy the inhabitants' culture.

Myth The primary purpose of education is to teach the young reading, writing, and other skills that are essential for them to make a contribution to society.

FACT Although education does this task, it also performs an array of other functions, some not widely recognized. For example, it instills patriotism and other attitudes that encourage students to accept the social order, and it is a sorting mechanism that enables some people to obtain rewarding positions in society while others receive more lowly positions.

Myth People need more education today than in former times because today's jobs are more complicated and the technology more sophisticated, requiring more extensive training.

FACT This belief is partly true, but reality is more complicated. Only part of the increase in educational requirements for jobs in the twentieth century can be accounted for by actual increases in the training essential to do the jobs. Educational levels for jobs have risen in part because some groups benefit from this "credentials race."

Myth Entertaining television shows and movies that contain violence, such as *Terminator* or *Lethal Weapon,* do not harm young people who watch them as long as the shows are clearly fictional and fanciful.

FACT Overwhelming research evidence concludes that young children, especially males, who watch violent television shows or movies are more likely to behave aggressively or violently themselves.

In agricultural societies, some specialized educational institutions began to emerge, but they were much more limited than they are today (Fagerlind & Saha, 1989). As much as five thousand years ago, for example, scribes in Mesopotamia and Egypt received institutionalized training in the art of writing. In larger agricultural societies, such as ancient China and Greece, a wealthy elite emerged that could afford to withdraw their children from work and send them to school or hire teachers to educate them at home. Confucius, the founder of one of the world's religious systems discussed in Chapter 11, was a teacher in ancient China. Education for the elite, however, had more to do with philosophical, religious, or moral training for society's future ruling class than with practical skills such as those of a carpenter or doctor. Such education of an elite was in marked contrast to the informal education through socialization or apprenticeship that the masses of people experienced.

Colonization and Education

Long before there was much formal schooling, cultural interchange occurred between societies that came together in war or through economic exchange. In these encounters, ideas, art works, and tools were exchanged and often reshaped to fit the new culture. These cultural items then influenced what people learned through general acculturation and whatever formal schooling there was. For example, Europeans entered the Middle East in the twelfth and thirteenth centuries as part of the Crusades, religious wars to capture the Holy Land from the Muslims, and they brought back to

Europe Arabic mathematics and medicine, which then became a part of Western civilization and education.

From the fifteenth to the nineteenth centuries, Western European nations explored and colonized much of Africa, parts of Asia, and all of the Western Hemisphere. In most places, the imperial nations viewed the indigenous cultures in the lands they colonized as uncivilized and inferior to European culture. The Europeans usually attempted to replace tribal religions, political systems, and economic arrangements with new ones based on European models. In some places, such as North and South America, this policy meant the virtual destruction of tribal cultures either through neglect or active intent. In India, which had a large and ancient civilization before the British came, including the two great religions of Hinduism and Buddhism, the British did not destroy the culture, but they did choose to live apart from it. They created a system of education in English for the elite in India.

In the eyes of these colonizers, the indigenous peoples could become civilized or developed only by adopting European culture, language, and education. To that end, the colonizers imposed Western models of education. In some cases, as with the Jesuits in South America and Canada (see the discussion of the Hurons in Chapter 8), Christian churches ran mission schools where Indians were taught Christianity and encouraged to drop their "pagan" religion. They were also taught Western political and economic concepts as well as Western ideas about family and gender roles. In other cases, such as in India, the colonizing nations established specialized training schools where a small indigenous elite was taught to run the government and businesses. Needless to say, the political and economic ideologies that they learned in those schools tended to be those that supported the interests of the colonizing nations and helped maintain the status quo.

In the midst of and supported by the bounty of this colonization, the European nations began to industrialize in the 1700s (Gutek, 1993). With industrialization, education came to stress training in scientific and technical knowledge and processes that were needed to operate industrial technology. To be sure, some informal education still occurs in industrial societies, as when a young girl learns how to do carpentry by watching her father build kitchen cabinets. Industrial societies, however, have occasioned a massive shift to specialized educational institutions with educational specialists doing the teaching.

Modernization and Education

With the expansion of industrial capitalism in the nineteenth and twentieth centuries, the industrial nations needed raw materials such as oil from many nations around the world. In addition, they turned to the less developed nations as sources of labor and as receptive markets for their products. According to world-system theory, these needs produced an intense interest on the part of industrial nations regarding social and economic developments in the less developed nations of the world (Feinberg & Avakov, 1991; Najafizadeh & Mennerick, 1990). The Western nations believed that economic underdevelopment and illiteracy would cause social instability, which in turn would threaten the economic environment in these nations. To maintain a receptive economic environment, the industrial nations have encouraged the modernization of the "backward" social, economic, and educational institutions of the less developed nations. **Modernization** refers to *the social and economic changes that accompany the transition to an industrial economy.* The traditional economy of subsistence, labor-intensive farming with little surplus for sale or investment, is seen as backward. It needs to be replaced with an industrial economy based on mass production, specialization, and surplus for investment. Civilization came to be defined in terms of an industrialized and urbanized society. The success of modernization efforts was defined in mostly economic terms, as increases in the gross national product. So governments and experts in the industrial nations provided the resources and expertise to achieve modernization to the governments and experts of the less developed nations.

Two of the major barriers to modernization were believed to be inefficient traditional institutions, such as the schools, and cultural behavior patterns that inhibited productivity, such as a lack of initiative and a heavy reliance on kinship. So

A Christian missionary works with tribal peoples in China. When colonial nations bring education to the peoples of other lands, they often make irrevocable changes in the traditional way of life.

the modernization effort focused on establishing modern educational programs that would produce productive and efficient managers and workers and that would change traditional values and behaviors. To those ends, the modernizing schools trained people in literacy skills, technology, and the engineering and managerial specializations that are needed in such an economy. The schools also taught new attitudes of efficiency, productivity, and obedience that would produce good industrial workers. The schools and the growing national communications media also offered new sources of authority to replace clan elders or village authorities. Traditional education, often done by elders, was much more informal and accomplished on the job. Modernizing education is much more formal and competitive, especially at the secondary and postsecondary levels.

As nations modernize, then, they establish centralized, state-run, mass educational institutions. One of the goals of these schools is *nation building*, or encouraging citizens to shift their allegiance to the nation-state. In traditional societies, people feel more of a connection to a tribe, a clan, a caste, or a village than they do to the nation as a whole, since the nation is often the creation of Western colonizing efforts rather than indigenous. These varying sources of loyalty weaken the central authority of the state. As part of the modernization effort, loyalty needs to be shifted to the national government so that it can maintain social control and political stability.

Schools play a role in this process through courses in civic education and national history, involving praise of national heroes and emphasis on national symbols. A standardized curriculum with mass-produced textbooks contributes to this effort. The result is more cultural homogeneity and the erosion of local customs and traditions.

Nations around the world vary in how modernized they have become. One indication of this variation is levels of illiteracy, which can vary substantially, even in the same region of the world, as Figure 12.1 shows. Critics argue, however, that modernization is not simply a matter of improving "backward" nations; it is also a part of the world system of capitalist development (see Chapter 6). Modernization is in part a neocolonial Westernization of these societies to make them receptive areas for investment by multinational, mostly Western, corporations and local elite (Fagerlind & Saha, 1989).

Although modernization brings some benefits, such as economic growth and a reduction in illiteracy, these benefits are not universally distributed to all groups in society. For example, the rates of illiteracy reported in Figure 12.1 hide considerable gender disparity that results because women are far less likely to have literacy skills than are men in many nations. In addition, modernization can become a virtual cultural assault on traditional values and institutions, such as religion and the family, and a promotion of Western social and political values. With the changes have come some severely negative consequences, such as the disintegration of family life and increases in violent crime and drug and alcohol abuse.

Another negative, and largely unexpected, consequence is that modernization may actually *reduce* women's chances for educational advancement. Recent research shows that increasing multinational investment in Third-World nations

FIGURE 12.1 Illiteracy Rates in Selected Nations for People Aged 15 Years Old and Older for Various Years, 1980–1992 *Note:* From *Statistical Yearbook, 1993,* 40th ed. (pp. 83–88) by United Nations, 1995, New York: United Nations.

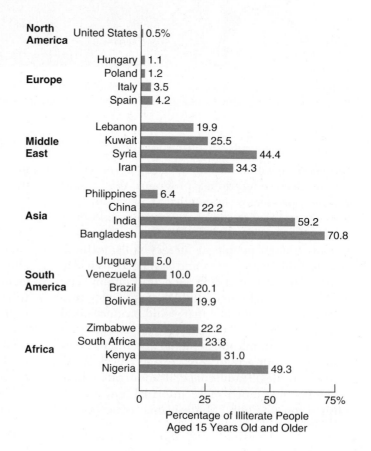

actually slows the entry of women into higher education (Clark, 1992). The reason may be that this sort of economic development creates low-paying jobs that attract women, who are then more likely to have children rather than pursue higher education. Elites may in fact encourage women to have more children in order to maintain a supply of cheap labor, which is what attracted international investment in the first place. Critics charge that these changes in the world system occur because they benefit the dominant nations, and educational systems play a key role in this process.

This overview of education around the globe suggests that educational institutions play a much more complex role in society than just educating the young. Other Worlds, Other Ways: Nigeria (on pp. 410–411) describes how modernized education affected one African nation. The three theoretical perspectives offer some additional insight into the place of educational institutions in society and the consequences they have for groups in various positions in the social structure.

Sociological Perspectives on Education

You should be able to analyze educational institutions using the three sociological perspectives, including an assessment of the functions of education, credentialism, the hidden curriculum, and labeling.

The Functionalist Perspective

From the functionalist perspective, education performs a number of important services that contribute to the operation and maintenance of society (Feinberg & Soltis, 1992).

The Transmission of Culture and Skills Schools supplement the family by passing on to youngsters important elements of their culture, particularly the values, norms, and skills that they will need to function in society. These include not only learning how to read and write but also learning a society's history and values. Through reading about the life of Abraham Lincoln, for example, children come to believe that even people from humble backgrounds can succeed in the United States. In grade school, proper interpersonal behavior is taught to children when they are graded on cooperation, deportment, and personal habits. Brazilian Indian schoolchildren in the 1500s learned from the Jesuits that tribal ways were "heathen" and European ways were "civilized." Schoolchildren also learn about patriotism through history and rituals such as reciting the Pledge of Allegiance. In addition, whether one wants to be a carpenter, lawyer, doctor, or welder, much of the training necessary to perform jobs will be learned in either an academic or vocational school. In transmitting culture, schools provide stability to existing social arrangements. Sometimes, however, the elements of culture intended for transmission to the young can be controversial. The contemporary debate in the United States over school prayer, for example, illustrates how groups can disagree over what elements of culture schools should teach.

Custody of the Young In addition to socialization, schools serve the latent function of providing custodial care for children and young people. Prior to industrialization, children were at home much of the time, and adults were usually around, either members of the extended family or parents working the family farm or business. Today, however, parents are usually away from home during the day, typically at work, and other adults are often not available. Thus schools have come to serve as a kind of extended day care that begins at about age four or five and does not usually end until at least age sixteen. Until recently, even universities served in place of parents. Although off-campus living, coed dormitories, and unrestricted privileges are commonplace today, the lives of college students a few decades ago were much more restricted. Young women in particular were affected, often being required to be in the residence halls, without male companionship, by a specified time of the evening.

A Social Network for the Young Schools are settings in which young people of about the same age can come together, develop friendships, and participate in group activities. Because children and adolescents in industrial societies are largely barred from the adult work world, schools enable them to develop a peer culture in which they can gain status by being popular, dressing fashionably, or excelling in sports. This youth culture has values that

OTHER WORLDS, *Other Ways*

NIGERIA: EDUCATION AND NATION BUILDING IN A TRIBAL SOCIETY

NIGERIA

Lagos

0   miles   1000

Nigeria is the most populous nation in Africa, with 123 million people. It is a fairly poor nation with a high rate of population growth. Nigeria was one of the African nations colonized during the period of European expansion beginning in the 1500s. At the time of colonization, the area called Nigeria today was inhabited by two major ethnic groups: the Islamic Yorubas in the north and the animistic Ibos in the south. Even though the Yorubas, the Ibos, and the other, smaller tribes in this region had no shared identity or common purpose, the British organized the area into a single administrative colonial region.

Education in precolonial Nigeria was organized on a kinship and tribal basis (Kurian, 1988). The skills and knowledge that people needed to make a contribution to society were passed on informally by village elders by example and through an extensive oral tradition. The only formal schools were Koranic schools among the Yoruba to teach Islamic traditions and

practices. After colonization, the British introduced British-style formal education, but it was made available only on a limited basis. Nigerians in the military and civil service were given an education so that they could assist the British administrators and military to rule Nigeria. These educated Nigerians tended to develop into an elite. Missionaries set up some primary schools, but these were not widely available and tended to focus on religious education. They also tended to stress British cultural values rather than African values.

By the early twentieth century, the British colonial administration had established an educational structure in Nigeria, chiefly in urban areas, based on these government and missionary schools. Still, most Nigerians, especially in rural areas, were taught through informal education or in the Yoruba Koranic schools. In the 1920s, a university and some postsecondary training colleges were established, as the British began to create a system of higher education for the elite in Nigeria.

The British school system in Nigeria reflected the values behind schooling in Britain (Gutek, 1993). The educational ideal was the widely educated person

are distinct from and may even clash with the values of the wider culture. (You may recall the discussion of argot in teen subcultures in Chapter 2.) Young people, for example, may value different music, freer expressions of sexuality, and different styles of clothing from the preferences of their parents. Among their peers, these values are supported and reinforced.

Innovation and Change Educational institutions not only transmit knowledge to the young but also create new knowledge or modify existing knowledge. This process, in turn, can result in new technologies or social practices. Many advances in the field of medicine, for example, have resulted from research conducted at universities in such fields as

biochemistry and genetics. Beyond the production of new knowledge, educational institutions function to encourage innovation and change by serving as an open forum for the exchange of ideas and viewpoints. Colleges and universities in particular encourage students to question and doubt as a means of better understanding human values and social arrangements. In addition, young college students, free from parental surveillance, have a chance to experiment with lifestyles that their parents might not approve of.

Sorting and Social Mobility Schools are one of the major mechanisms for sorting people into various occupational and social roles. Most jobs call for some minimal educational attainment. Likewise,

rather than the technically trained one. The educated person was supposed to be learned in the classics, history, literature, and languages rather than trained for some specific occupation. Thus the educational system worked against vocational and technical training even though Nigeria was economically underdeveloped. Nigeria became an independent nation in 1960, but it was an artificial creation that satisfied British colonial needs more than the desires of the various tribes, ethnic groups, and religions that lived in the region. As a result, Nigeria experienced a severe civil war in the 1960s and some political instability since then. The number of schools declined and school attendance dropped.

A difficult educational problem for independent Nigeria has been to develop a single, national language (Ikejiani, 1964). A common language can help a nation develop a sense of identity and shared history as well as communicate a shared value system. Nigeria has more than four hundred languages and dialects. To choose the language of a particular tribe or ethnic group is resisted by other tribes and ethnic groups who fear that domination by the chosen group would follow. English has been used to link various

groups within Nigeria, but it is a colonially imposed language and associated with the Nigerian elite and is thus less acceptable to the masses of people. Since the ethnic groups of Nigeria are regionally based, groups can continue using their own language in the schools rather than be forced to adopt a common language. So the schools in Nigeria have had difficulty in promoting allegiance to the nation over allegiance to the tribe. Most Nigerians still identify with their tribe or ethnic group first. Since a common language seems unlikely to develop, educators have proposed a three-language approach in which children would learn the three major Nigerian languages: Ibo, Yoruba, and Hausa.

Nigerian education confronts a number of other problems. It has produced a group of college-educated people who cannot find employment in Nigeria and may serve as a source of significant social discontent. Education is also much more available in urban areas than in rural ones, which means that urban youth have more social and economic opportunities. Finally, gender affects education in Nigeria, with males being significantly more likely to attend school (United Nations, 1991).

to move up the educational ladder, one must successfully complete all of the rungs below. At each step, some people are sorted out, while others seek higher educational degrees. Schools, then, are societal screening mechanisms. Schools also enable people from different social backgrounds to become upwardly mobile if they can obtain the requisite educational degrees. In fact, free public education in the United States was designed as a means of enabling immigrants to become integrated into U.S. society and to advance in the social hierarchy.

Today, it is virtually impossible to attain high-status positions without considerable education, and increasingly, graduate or professional degrees are required. As Figure 12.2 (on p. 412) demon-

strates, a strong association exists between people's level of education and their ability to obtain jobs that pay a high income—getting more education enhances the ability to support a family. From the functionalist perspective, this is beneficial because society gains when people pursue the higher levels of education called for by today's important occupations; individuals also benefit because they reap rewards by doing things that benefit society (recall the discussion of the functionalist perspective on stratification in Chapter 6).

The Conflict Perspective

Although the functionalist view emphasizes the contribution of educational institutions to the

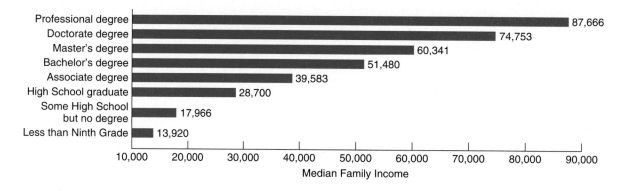

FIGURE 12.2 Median Income of Family Based on Educational Attainment of the Head of the Household, United States, 1993 *Note:* From *Statistical Abstract of the United States, 1995* (p. 470) by U.S. Bureau of the Census, 1995, Washington, DC: U.S. Government Printing Office.

maintenance of the whole system, the conflict view stresses the fact that education can be a mechanism that powerful groups use to limit the opportunities of the less powerful in society (Hurn, 1992). Here is how such limitation can happen.

Promoting Existing Political and Economic Arrangements According to Marxian conflict theorists, schools in practically all societies tend to promote the existing political and economic structures, which in turn serve the interests of the more powerful groups (Apple, 1982; Carnoy & Levin, 1985). In the United States schools promote the ideology of capitalism—the value of the private ownership of goods, private enterprise, and profit making—and two-party democracy. Although other economic and political arrangements may be discussed, especially at the college level, the overwhelming message is that capitalism and democracy are the preferred systems, verging almost on the sacred.

At a more subtle level, schools support existing economic and social arrangements by teaching a **hidden curriculum,** *the training of students in values and norms that help to perpetuate the existing system of stratification.* The hidden curriculum exists side by side with the formal curriculum of reading, mathematics, and science. For example, students are trained to be submissive and cooperative in bureaucratic and authoritarian settings. After all, beginning in kindergarten, at least in public schools, children learn to be compliant and cooperative

and to adapt to the schedule of the schools as established by educational authorities. School begins and ends when the authorities say it will, and topics change with a set rhythm that may be totally unrelated to the needs and moods of many of the children. "Good" students sit quietly at their desks, raise their hands and wait to be given permission before speaking, and address teachers and school administrators with respect and deference. Grades reward students who fit best in this system and punish those who create problems by being disruptive. In short, the hidden curriculum produces a cooperative and compliant labor force for work in the corporations and bureaucracies of a capitalist economy. Such behavior helps to maintain a system in which the powerful retain and expand their wealth and authority, although many workers experience alienation and frustration in their jobs.

The Credentials Race For much of the twentieth century, there has been a credentials race in the United States (Collins, 1979). In 1940, less than 25 percent of adults in the United States had graduated from high school, in comparison with more than 80 percent today (see Figure 12.3). The number of college degrees conferred rose from fewer than 500,000 in 1950 to more than one million per year today, and the number of doctorates from 6,000 to more than 40,000. Functionalists would argue that this "credentialing" of U.S. society reflects the higher level of skill and education

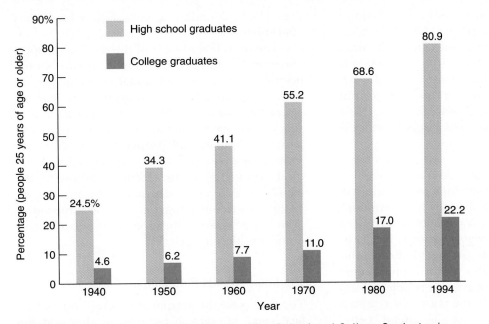

FIGURE 12.3 Percentage of Adults Who Are High School and College Graduates in the United States, 1940–1994 *Note:* From *Statistical Abstract of the United States, 1982–1983* (p. 143) by U.S. Bureau of the Census, 1982, Washington, DC: U.S. Government Printing Office; *Statistical Abstract of the United States, 1995* (p. 157) by U.S. Bureau of the Census, 1995, Washington, DC: U.S. Government Printing Office.

needed for occupations today. Yet, considerable evidence exists that the minimum educational requirements for many jobs today are higher than are actually necessary to do the job (Newman et al., 1978; Rodriguez, 1978). In fact, it has been estimated that only about 15 percent of the increase in educational requirements for jobs during the twentieth century can be accounted for by *actual* increases in skills and expertise needed to perform these tasks (Berg & Gorelick, 1970; Collins, 1979). Furthermore, studies of insurance sellers and clerks show that better educated people in these jobs are not necessarily better or more productive workers than their less educated counterparts (Berg, 1975). Other studies show that although educational credentials are important in getting people jobs in organizations, they do not have much impact on whether these people are promoted (Bills, 1988).

Why, then, is there such a race for higher credentials? Conflict theorists argue that some groups have a vested interest in placing greater emphasis on the importance on educational degrees. For example, raising the educational thres-

hold for particular jobs is an easy out for harried personnel managers who can use educational degrees as a simple sifting device in selecting employees. In addition, educational institutions have a vested interest in this degree inflation because it generates a greater demand for their educational services. In fact, schools help to create this situation by producing more people with degrees than are needed. Students may not need the degrees to *do* the job, but they need the degrees to *get* the job. Most important, however, degree inflation serves as a way of maintaining the privileges of some while controlling the aspirations of others. By elevating degree requirements for particular jobs, people who have earned the degrees, or who are in a position to obtain them, protect their own positions and those of their offspring by restricting competition. Fifty years ago, it was the affluent who were likely to have a high school diploma and thus had access to the better jobs that required a high school education. Today, with high school education increasingly common, the college or graduate degree represents the minimum requirement for better jobs. The less affluent and minority group members have more difficulty obtaining those degrees and thus getting the jobs that require them. Furthermore, argue conflict theorists, because the inequities result from differences in educational levels, they have legitimacy in the eyes of people who believe that educational opportunities are open to everyone (Bowles & Gintis, 1976). But are there equal educational opportunities in the United States?

Education and Social Inequality   As was explained in Chapter 6, educational attainment in industrial nations is the most critical factor in determining upward social mobility, especially intergenerational mobility. Yet although education makes social mobility possible, according to the conflict perspective, education also makes it much more likely that the offspring of affluent people will succeed than the offspring of the poor. The reason is that affluent youngsters usually attend better schools in which the staff and resources are of higher quality and the atmosphere is more encouraging of academic achievement. In addition, the families of affluent youngsters are supportive of educational accomplishments and are better able to pay for tutors or tuition for private schools and college. Without such advantages, less affluent children are more likely to experience failure in school. And failure leads to reduced willingness to put forth the necessary effort to succeed, which increases the likelihood of further failures.

The sociologist James Coleman and his associates (1966), in a report now popularly known as the Coleman Report, documented how these factors affected African Americans in the 1960s. Coleman found that racial segregation in U.S. public schools was extensive. He also discovered that African American students performed more poorly than other racial or ethnic groups. These black students, Coleman and his coauthors argued, suffered from poor facilities and teachers and from school and home environments that provided little motivation to the students to excel. The study also showed that black students who attended desegregated schools with a better motivational atmosphere showed improved academic performance. The motivational atmosphere in the school basically had to do with the proportion of lower-class to middle-class pupils. Blacks attending schools with a middle-class atmosphere did better than blacks attending schools with a lower-class atmosphere.

The overall argument of the conflict perspective, then, is that powerful forces in educational institutions work toward **social reproduction,** or *passing social and economic inequalities on from one generation to the next and thus perpetuating the existing stratification system.* Just as well-to-do parents can pass their money and property on to their offspring, they also pass along their social and cultural advantages in the form of access to the education that will assist their offspring. Figure 12.2 points to one impact of this social reproduction: the effect of education on a person's economic position in society.

The Interactionist Perspective

The interactionist perspective focuses on face-to-face social interaction between teacher and student in the classroom. It recognizes that social expectations and social meanings are a part of that interaction and play a powerful role in what students learn and accomplish in school as well as how they feel about themselves.

Labeling and Ability Grouping   Students in school are subjected to constant evaluation between the ages of five and eighteen, because the purpose of schooling, in addition to transmitting skills, is to judge how well students have learned and, by implication, how competent and intelligent they have become. A great deal is at stake for students because their grades and their teachers' written reports about them become an official record—a publicly stamped label—that follows them throughout their lives. According to the interactionist perspective, this labeling can have serious consequences for students (Wilkinson & Marrett, 1985). Chapter 5 noted that labeling a person as a deviant can serve as a self-fulfilling prophecy when people begin to conform to the expectations of the labels attached to them. Likewise, a similar process can occur in the classroom when teachers label students as bright or dull. Once students are so labeled, teachers may treat them a little differently, possibly giving the students who are labeled bright a little more encouragement and assistance. In addition, the students labeled dull may assume that there is some truth in the label and may not try very hard. The result of both the students' and the teachers' reactions may be reinforcement of the label (Dusek, 1985).

Another practice common in elementary and secondary schools that has important effects on students is tracking (Hallinan, 1996; Jones, Vanfossen, & Ensminger, 1995). *Tracking*, or *ability grouping*, refers to clustering people together into classes or tracks within classes that contain students of comparable abilities or students with similar educational goals (academic versus nonacademic tracks). Tracking is done on the assumption that students will be better able to learn if they are in a classroom with others who have equal ability. The danger in tracking, however, is that the track becomes a label that creates expectations on the part of both the teacher and the students regarding how well individual students will perform. Teachers may tend to encourage performances that are consistent with the track a student is in, and students assume that being placed in a track indicates the performance level of which they are capable (Oakes, 1985). Because of these problems, some schools have discarded formalized ability grouping.

Education in the United States

You should be able to discuss the emergence of educational institutions in the United States, analyze schools as bureaucracies, evaluate how effective schools are, and describe what reforms have been instituted.

Educational institutions in the United States are as formalized and specialized as those of any other nation. They are also an outgrowth of the country's particular historical and cultural development. This chapter will briefly review that history before moving on to some current controversies and debates about how well U.S. schools work.

A Historical View

During the colonial period, education in the United States was mostly informal, with children learning what they needed to know from family and friends. In fact, the primary purpose of schooling then was to further one's religious training (Mayer, 1961). Literacy was valued because it enabled people to read the Bible, but most of what the average person needed to know in order to make a living was learned from parents and other relatives while growing up. Schools and colleges existed, but extensive formal education was limited to a small elite. It was not until 1864 that the first state compulsory school attendance law was enacted. In 1900, only 6 percent of the seventeen-year-olds in the United States had graduated from high school. With little paperwork and few specialized occupations, a lack of education in a preindustrial United States was not a great hindrance for most people.

As the nation began to industrialize, education underwent drastic changes, and an educational revolution began in the 1870s (Hurn, 1992; Trow, 1961). Increased specialization created thousands of new occupations and generated tremendous amounts of new information. It became more and more necessary for all people to receive a substantial amount of education in order to earn a living in the new industrial nation. The growth of science led to the creation of more technical knowledge, and the expanding size of bureaucratic organizations called for more managers and supervisors to coordinate the activities of other employees. Information became more important in large enterprises with highly specialized workforces, and white-collar workers possessing a mastery of literacy skills controlled this information. The number of white-collar workers in the United States doubled between 1950 and 1975, and the number of technical and professional occupations grew at a rate much faster than the expansion of the workforce as a whole.

Basic educational skills such as the ability to read and write are no longer a privilege of the elite. They have become essential to maintaining even the simplest lifestyle. Consider the things one might do in a normal day that call for such skills: read street signs, textbooks, or cooking instructions on a frozen dinner; write a note to a friend; fill out a job application; or sign one's name on a check.

Schools as Bureaucracies

It has been many years since students in the United States attended one-room schoolhouses where young people of varying ages were clustered

This classroom in New York in the late 1800s illustrates the growth in mass education in industrial nations. In the United States, mass education provided people with literacy skills they needed in order to work in an industrial economy and helped to "Americanize" the children of immigrants.

together with one teacher to learn the three R's. Much has changed since those days, as the educational system has become more complex and increasingly graded by age. Knowledge has become highly specialized, and students, especially at the college level, are expected to choose a distinct body of knowledge (their academic major) around which to organize their career plans in the work world.

Chapter 4 described the bureaucratic organization of universities in some detail. Most primary and secondary schools are also rigidly bureaucratic—some would say even more so than many universities—and the consequences continue to be the source of considerable debate. School officials maintain that bureaucracy is necessary in

order to deal with the sheer volume of students and the ever-expanding curriculum. On a more subtle level, Talcott Parsons (1959) argued that the bureaucratic nature of schools is beneficial in modern societies because it socializes children into the impersonal, competitive adult world with its emphasis on secondary relationships (see Chapter 3). In schools, children learn something that they typically do not learn in families: bureaucratic schedules operate independently of people's needs and desires. In this way, people learn what to expect in the business and government bureaucracies in which they will probably work as adults.

Critics observe that there is a conflict of interest between the needs of the educational system to process large numbers of students and the individual student's need to be treated as a person rather than a number on a computer printout (Apple, 1982; Giroux, 1985). These observers charge that bureaucratic schools are a classic example of *goal displacement,* where teachers and administrators devote more effort to maintaining the existing system and preserving their jobs than to the traditional goals of the educational process. In addition, modern bureaucratic educational systems tend to stifle creativity, originality, and independent thinking (Katz, 1987). Lesson plans, hall monitors, and rigid class periods promote inflexibility and dependence rather than curiosity and a desire to think independently. By contrast, some critics dispute both the positive and negative views of modern education by calling attention to the rather loosely structured nature of U.S. educational systems, where rules are precariously negotiated by various participants (such as teachers, administrators, and parent groups), with the end result being chaos rather than the kind of efficient organization usually associated with well-functioning bureaucratic institutions (Tyler, 1985).

The controversy over bureaucracy in the school system will very likely continue. Chapter 4 noted that bureaucracy has its benefits and that modern societies tend toward bureaucratic organization. Certainly, as with automobile assembly lines, school bureaucracies can process larger numbers of students than can other forms of organization. Nevertheless, many people question whether large-scale processing equates with good education, and schools have received severe criticism regarding their effectiveness.

Effectiveness of the Educational System

Since the 1970s, serious criticism has been directed at the U.S. educational system. Some critics argue that the schools promote social inequality in the ways suggested by the conflict perspective. Other critics maintain that freedom and anarchy reign in the schools, leading to a decline in national morality. Probably the largest group of critics are concerned over whether students are developing adequate competence in the basic skills they will need to make a contribution to society and help the United States retain a competitive edge in the world. In 1986, for example, Secretary of Education William J. Bennett

released a report on elementary and secondary education in the United States, indicating that many schools—particularly in grades four through twelve—are failing to teach complicated subject matter to students, with the result that U.S. youth are ill-prepared to take on a variety of job responsibilities that are vital to the well-being of the entire nation. In the same year, the Carnegie Forum on Education and the Economy (1986) released a report indicating that the schools, as currently configured and administrated, are failing to prepare students adequately for work-related positions in an increasingly technological society. Performance on standardized tests, such as the Scholastic Aptitude Test (SAT), has fallen substantially since the 1960s, although verbal SAT scores have been steady and math scores have risen some since 1980 (Arenson, 1996). A study by the National Center for Improving Science Education, funded by the National Science Foundation and released in 1996, concluded that high school students in Europe and Japan take more demanding science courses than do U.S. students and they do better in those more difficult courses than U.S. students do in the easier courses they take ("Study Finds . . . ," 1996). U.S. students also do more poorly on science and mathematics tests than do students in many other nations (see Figure 12.4). Most studies on this topic conclude that students in the United States display a disturbing lack of knowledge about science, geography, history, and government; many students, for example, cannot locate Greece on a map or state when Abraham Lincoln was President (Finn, 1989).

Yet, controversy rages over whether and in what realms U.S. schools are failing. Psychologist David Berliner and sociologist Bruce Biddle (1995) argue that much of the criticism is based on a misunderstanding of the data, or in some cases a deliberate attempt to ignore the facts in order to trash the schools. They argue, for example, that SAT scores are no longer falling, that school spending has gone up because we ask so much of the schools in terms of special education programs, and that many standardized tests, such as the SAT, are poor measures of educational quality and achievement. The schools may not be getting any better, Berliner and Biddle argue, but they probably haven't been getting any worse either.

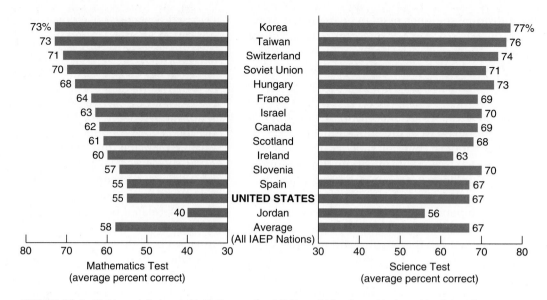

FIGURE 12.4 Math and Science Test Scores for 13-Year-Olds, from Nations Participating in the International Assessment of Educational Progress (IAEP), 1991 *Note:* From *Digest of Education Statistics: 1995* (pp. 432, 435) by U.S. Department of Education, National Center for Education Statistics, 1995, Washington, DC: U.S. Government Printing Office.

An issue about which most researchers will agree is that, although some students attend good schools and get an excellent education, other students are definitely failed by the educational system. Students who are especially likely to be failed by the schools are those from low-income families, those whose parents have low educational attainment, those from single-parent families, and those who cannot speak English well (Peng & Lee, 1992). The result is an unacceptably high school dropout rate in the United States, with African American and Hispanic American students especially hurt (see Figure 12.5). A number of reforms in education in the United States have been proposed to help alleviate some of these inadequacies.

Reforms and Trends

Educators and laypeople alike seem to be constantly tinkering with the U.S. educational system, and there are many ideas for reforms to make it more effective. This section will explore the major innovations, with an eye on evidence regarding their effectiveness.

Magnet Schools, Charter Schools, and Choice Some educators and politicians have suggested that education is like any other consumer market and that schools should compete for students in the same way that other businesses compete for customers—in free and open competition. If schools had to attract students by convincing them and their parents that they had the best education to offer, then the schools would be motivated to

FIGURE 12.5 High School Dropouts in the United States, 14 to 24 Years Old, by Race and Ethnic Origin, 1993 *Note:* From *Statistical Abstract of the United States, 1995* (p. 174) by U.S. Bureau of the Census, 1995, Washington, DC: U.S. Government Printing Office.

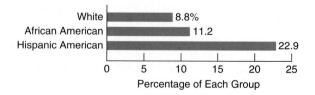

provide the best product: superior teachers, excellent resources, and solid programs. In a competitive market, if schools had a mediocre curriculum or lackluster faculty, their enrollments would decline, and they would either close their doors or improve. This reform is sometimes called parental choice; private schools in the United States already operate in such an environment (Coleman, 1992). One way of implementing choice in the public schools would be to permit students to attend any school they please, whether it be in their district or elsewhere in the state. This policy is already being followed in some school districts, where *magnet schools* offer special programs in particular areas, such as computer applications or performing arts. One of the original reasons for magnet schools was to increase racial integration in the schools, but it also has the effect of increasing choice.

A more recent variation on the choice issue is the charter schools that have been established in a number of states (Finn, 1996). Charter schools are basically schools that operate autonomously with a charter directly from the state instead of being under local school district control. They receive state funding but are free from many school district rules and have more freedom than mainstream schools in budgeting, hiring, and curriculum decisions. Charter schools have been set up with diverse goals: to establish back-to-basics education, to focus on environmental education, or to emphasize learning by doing.

Some critics have proposed extending the idea of choice to all of education by having the government give parents a voucher worth enough to pay for a child's education at any public school. Parents would then send their child to the school of their choice, paying for it with the voucher money. Some supporters of voucher plans even propose that parents be able to use the vouchers at private religious schools as partial payment of their tuition, although this may violate the constitutional separation of church and state.

There is both strong support for and opposition to choice, charter schools, and vouchers (Astin, 1992; Smith & Meier, 1995). Proponents argue that these educational innovations offer students more choices, and the competition among schools will enhance the quality. In addition, charter schools encourage parents to become active in their children's school and are more responsive to the needs of the community. Critics of these innovations, however, argue that they may promote more segregation and divisiveness because some parents, both white and nonwhite, would likely choose their children's school on the basis of its racial or ethnic composition. A second criticism is that parents may not always be in the best position to assess the quality of schools. As in other arenas of open competition, desperate schools might sometimes resort to exaggeration, trickery, or downright fraud in their efforts to attract students, and the educations of some children would likely suffer. A third criticism is that some families would be forced to use schools near their homes, especially the poor without access to transportation. These schools would have meager resources and be poorly run because they could not attract students from other communities, but they would survive by getting enough students from poor families in the neighborhood to keep their doors open.

Because many schools and children would probably benefit from a choice system, it has retained strong support among the public. In fact, more than twenty states have adopted plans that let students go to schools outside their local school district, although some states have limitations such as setting aside a certain number of spots in a school for children in that district. Milwaukee schools have even experimented with a voucher plan that allows some inner-city youth to spend state money to attend private schools chosen by their parents. In 1993, however, voters in California rejected a choice plan that would have allowed parents to use their vouchers in private schools.

Back to Basics Social science research shows that students in Roman Catholic schools perform better than children in public schools, even when racial and social-class differences between the schools are taken into account (Bryk, Lee, & Holland, 1993; Coleman, Hoffer, & Kilgore, 1982; Marsh, 1991). One reason for this is that Catholic schools place more emphasis on a strong core curriculum and require students to take more academically demanding course work. Thus, students in Catholic schools are likely to take more academic basics, such as science, math, and history, and fewer nonacademic courses, such as auto mechanics or physical education. Another reason for the better performance in Catholic schools is that they have more effective discipline, with more emphasis on obedience and respect for authority. This emphasis creates a climate that enables teachers to do their job with less disruption or fear of danger and encourages students to learn.

Many educational reformers and parents have pushed for such a back to basics approach, with an emphasis on the traditional core curriculum and a return to strong discipline. Many schools have adopted some of these changes, reducing elective courses, having more required courses, and in some cases establishing strict dress codes with punishments for violation. Some states have established standardized examinations that students must pass before receiving a high school diploma.

Compensatory Education   Virtually all criticism of education in the United States recommends devoting more resources to the education of low-income children. Since the Coleman Report in the 1960s, research has documented that some children come to school educationally handicapped because their home environment does not provide them with the support and assistance that would make learning more effective. In Chapter 6, Applying Sociology: Creating and Evaluating Programs That Assist the Poor discussed the Head Start program, a preschool program to help poor children prepare for school. Head Start children are taught reading and language skills that most preschool children learn at home from their parents. Research over the years has provided strong evidence that Head Start gives poor children some significant advantages. Head Start children, when compared to other poor children, are less likely to be assigned to special education classes or to be kept back a grade in school, and they do better on mathematics achievement tests and show more improvement in IQ scores. Head Start children are also less likely to repeat a grade, get in trouble with the law, or become teenage mothers. In addition, they have a better family life and more positive self-concepts. Finally, as young adults, Head Start children are more likely to go to college and hold a steady skilled job. With benefits such as these, Head Start children should be better equipped to support themselves and their families as adults.

Despite its clear benefits to society, Head Start provides services to only some low-income children. Many educational reformers argue that the benefits of extending such compensatory education programs to all low-income children would be enormous.

School Integration   In part because of the Coleman Report's conclusions about the negative effect of school segregation on student performance, efforts at school integration, sometimes by busing students from one school to another, have been made since the 1960s. Such integration, it was believed, would improve the performance of minority students as well as reduce prejudice and discrimination in the long run.

Busing and integration have been highly controversial policies. Have they worked? In terms of school achievement, some studies have found improvements with integration and others have not (Armor, 1989; Crain & Mahard, 1983; Longshore & Prager, 1985; Rist, 1979).

Overall, integration has probably made modest improvements in school achievement by African American students, especially when students are integrated in the early grades. The reason that the impact has not been more uniformly positive is because so many other factors—socioeconomic status, family background, racial tensions in the schools, and the manner in which integration is accomplished—also influence achievement. However, there are signs that school integration may be producing benefits beyond its impact on school achievement. Research in the early 1980s suggested that school integration has helped to reduce racial isolation in the United States and that this will reduce racial tensions and stereotyping in the future (Hawley et al., 1983). Furthermore, recent research suggests that the experience in desegregated schools has an impact on blacks later in life: They are more likely to attend predominantly white colleges, socialize with whites outside of school, and live in integrated neighborhoods as adults (Braddock, 1985; Braddock, Crain, & McPartland, 1984). In addition, concerns about integration and busing have led to creative developments in schools designed to attract both white and minority students such as the magnet schools discussed earlier. So it may be that the impact of school integration will be more subtle and will surface only after integration has been a reality for a long period, possibly decades. Rather than a dramatic increase in school performance, we may see a gradual easing of racial tensions as young people of different racial background mingle in the schools, or an improvement in the schools as they strive to attract an acceptable racial mix among their students.

Nevertheless, despite efforts to integrate the schools, the Harvard Project on School Desegregation reported in 1993 that the schools have become more segregated by race than they were in the 1970s ("Race Still Divides Schools," 1993). This situation results largely from segregated housing patterns. A few schools have even been segregated on purpose in order to support the special educational needs of minorities. Special schools have been designed for African American males in Detroit, Hasidic Jewish children in New York, and gay adolescents in New York (Chira, 1993). The idea behind such segregated schools is that they provide a better learning environment for minorities with special problems or who confront substantial hostility from other students. In addition, specially designed programs can be provided to enhance learning and self-esteem. So, the educational system in the United States continues to struggle with the issue of whether, or under what conditions, integration is a desirable educational goal.

Upgrading Schools and Teachers In 1996, the National Commission on Teaching and America's Future published a report that concluded that many teachers in U.S. schools have not been adequately trained in teaching skills or in the subjects that they teach (Applebome, 1996). Some teachers have neither a college major nor a minor in the main subjects they teach. Given circumstances such as these, most critics of the U.S. educational system recommend devoting more resources to schooling so that teachers have the skills, services, staff, and up-to-date technology they need to be effective. Many critics also argue that society needs to rethink how it prepares and motivates teachers. Teachers should have salaries and opportunities that will make teaching competitive with other professional occupations so that the

best people are drawn to teaching. Higher salaries would help, but teachers' pay could also be linked to merit. For example, schools might have a merit hierarchy, with master teachers receiving higher pay and having some responsibility for assisting other teachers to develop their skills and test innovative teaching techniques. In addition, teachers might be subject to standardized testing on a periodic basis in order to assess their continuing competence. Just as many other professions require graduate or professional degrees, some critics suggest that a bachelor's degree be required as a prerequisite for the professional study of teaching and that the minimum degree for being certified as a teacher be a master's degree.

There is, needless to say, much controversy over which of these reforms are most important or will be most effective. This is not surprising given the highly pluralistic nature of society in the United States. The country has many religious, racial, ethnic, and subcultural groups, each expecting the schools to promote, or at least not oppose, its values and lifestyle. Thus the schools become a forum in which conflicts over cultural diversity are debated. Nonetheless, schools need to adapt to changing conditions, especially to the need for new and complex skills that are called for in an increasingly competitive global economy. Applying Sociology: Evaluating Educational Innovations (on p. 422) points to some of the contributions that sociologists make to educational reforms.

Higher Education

There are more than thirteen million men and women enrolled in more than three thousand institutions of higher education in the United States, including one thousand two-year community colleges and in excess of two thousand four-year colleges and universities. There are also nearly eight thousand noncollegiate postsecondary schools, including technical institutes, business schools, hospital-affiliated nursing schools, and other vocational training institutions (U.S. Bureau of the Census, 1995).

Just as U.S. elementary and secondary schools have been criticized, so have colleges and universities. In the 1980s, for example, philosopher Allan Bloom (1987) published a scathing critique

One of the major activities of sociologists in the educational realm is the development and evaluation of innovative educational programs for schools. Those who fund education—private foundations, the government, and private citizens—want solid evidence that their money is providing some positive benefit to students. Earlier this chapter discussed the work of sociologist James Coleman in assessing the impact of segregated schools on student achievement. Because of this applied sociological research, new educational policies were developed that focused on desegregating schools and providing compensatory education. Since then, applied sociologists have continued to monitor whether such policies are having positive outcomes, and the results of some of this work were reported in this chapter.

I was personally involved in a recent evaluation of an educational innovation. The new program combined the resources of the department of social services with those of a community mental health center to provide cooperative educational and social services to grade school children. The three state government agencies funding this program insisted that the continuation of the funding depended on the unequivocal demonstration that the children and the schools involved experienced some positive benefits. To begin the research, we used the results of prior research on child development and school performance to determine what specific outcomes this social service program would be likely to have. Once the outcomes were determined, we set about measuring them by surveying teachers, parents, and students and looking for indicators of student performance in the school records. We surveyed both schools with the innovative program and schools with a more traditional approach.

By almost all measures, the program proved to be a success. For example, the provision of the services resulted in better school performance on the part of the children and less disruptive behavior in the classroom. In addition, in the schools with the program, parents were more involved in school affairs, and much prior educational research shows that such parental involvement results in better student performance. The final step in this applied research project was to present the results to the heads of the state agencies that funded the program; this evidence, along with other input, convinced them to keep supporting the program.

Applied sociologists work not only on problems confronting students but also those confronting teachers and school administrators. Schools, after all, are organizations, and the teachers and administrators are influenced by how well or poorly those organizations work. Sociologists with expertise in organizations and organizational behavior can conduct an organizational diagnosis, discussed in Chapter 4, which uses sociological theories and research to assess how well organizations operate and how their performance can be improved (Harrison, 1991). In some schools, the role structure for teachers may be ambiguous or contradictory, and this role strain can cause difficulties for teachers. For example, teachers may be placed under competing and contradictory demands, as school boards demand one thing, parents demand another, and students insist on yet a third approach. The teachers' ability to navigate this confusing terrain depends on whether they have clear authority in their classrooms and whether they have consistent direction from principals and other school administrators. In fact, much sociological research shows that teacher performance improves when they have strong leadership in a principal and when the school is organized like a community, with supportive relationships among teachers and a sense of shared values and mission (Lee, Dedrick, & Smith, 1991).

Applied sociologists, then, analyze the role structure and organizational authority in schools and make recommendations for change to enhance teaching effectiveness. Of course, some of these educational problems are not easily resolved because schools are subject to inherently conflicting demands. In these cases, clinical sociologists and other counselors work with teachers on ways to prevent the organizational problems from creating personal stress or depression (Saunders, 1991).

to the effect that college education has become heavily oriented toward narrowly focused, vocationally directed education in fields such as accounting, nursing, and social work. The curriculum has become directed by the students' demands that their education lead to a job and financial success upon graduation. The result is a curriculum that downplays or completely ignores areas of literature, philosophy, and the humanities that, Bloom argues, contain the central beliefs and values of western civilization. Furthermore, Bloom contends, the student, feminist, and Black Power movements of the 1960s and 1970s have led to the emergence of a cultural relativism in college curricula that views all values and cultures as equal and demands little of students in terms of moral decision making or critical thinking. Finally, according to Bloom, efforts to introduce multiculturalism in the curriculum have resulted in the displacement of what he regards as more valuable teachings of the Western heritage. As a consequence of these trends, college students today have a limited appreciation for the roots of the culture of the Western world and the United States.

A very different perspective on higher education was presented by historian Lawrence Levine (1996) in the 1990s. Levine, for example, praises the trend toward multiculturalism as an inevitable and essential response to the racial, ethnic, and cultural diversity that is increasingly characteristic of the United States. Colleges must adapt to these changes. Furthermore, Levine sees a curriculum narrowly focused on Western classics as overly restrictive; students are exposed only to the thoughts of white males of Western European origin and learn little of the literature and art of women or of peoples in Asia, Africa, and the Americas. Instead, colleges should explore the widest range of cultural values and lifestyles in order to most completely enhance an understanding of the human condition. However, Levine is critical of some dimensions of higher education today, especially the tendency for courses to be isolated from one another rather than forming an integrated whole throughout the student's education. He also argues that university faculty tend to become isolated into their own separate, heavily jargonistic disciplines and to give too much weight to research productivity rather than

teaching skills in making promotion and tenure decisions.

Other criticisms of today's colleges and universities have surfaced. For example, in 1994, Ernest L. Boyer, president of the Carnegie Foundation for the Advancement of Teaching, criticized colleges and universities in the United States on quite different grounds, arguing that "higher education's historic commitment to service [to society] seems to have diminished" (p. A48). He challenged higher education to put more emphasis on the practical and to tie research to practice in a way that helps people solve problems and improves the human condition.

Whereas some of these criticisms of higher education are at variance with one another, the recommendations they make for improvement are not necessarily contradictory. Among the improvements suggested by various critics are the following:

1. Colleges and universities must seek greater continuity with public schools in terms of requirements so that entering freshmen will have the necessary academic skills to be successful.

2. Colleges and universities should evaluate their curricula in order to ensure that students' education is not too narrow and vocationally oriented.

3. There is far too much emphasis on conformity and too little attention paid to fostering creativity in our college classrooms.

4. Faculty and administrators must concentrate on cooperating with each other in governing colleges and universities, including efforts to involve students in campus governance.

5. All too frequently, colleges and universities are isolated from the society at large, thus producing situations in which both the people who teach and the people who (supposedly) learn are severely limited in terms of how much they know about the real world. Colleges should communicate knowledge and apply it to people's everyday lives.

To appreciate educational institutions in the United States more fully, it is helpful to compare them with those in another advanced industrial nation. Other Worlds, Other Ways: Japan points to some ways in which Japanese education differs from education in the United States.

Nagano
Tokyo
JAPAN
Yokohama
0   miles   200

OTHER WORLDS, *Other Ways*

JAPAN: VARIATIONS IN EDUCATIONAL INSTITUTIONS IN INDUSTRIAL SOCIETIES

When Japan was defeated in World War II, the United States and its allies imposed demands on their foe that were to change the structure of Japanese society significantly. The changes basically pushed Japan toward a more democratic and egalitarian state in which the hereditary monarchy had less control than formerly over government and society. Included among the changes were giving workers the right to organize and extending complete civil rights to women. In education, the U.S. Occupation sought to eliminate the militarism and extreme nationalism that existed in the schools prior to the war. This involved the dismissal of teachers and administrators who held such views and revising textbooks. The Occupation also gave the Japanese educational system the same basic structure that education has in the United States: six years of elementary school and three years each of junior high school and high school, followed by four years of college.

Japanese education, however, has some features that are quite different from education in the United States (Gutek, 1993; Kumagai, 1996). One is that the central government through the Ministry of Education, controls Japanese educational policy, curriculum design, and even textbook selection. By contrast, the United States decentralizes these matters to the level of state or local school boards. Decentralization provides parents with more control over educational institutions, but it also makes for significant disparities in the resources available to students in schools and in the achievement levels of schools.

Another difference is that Japan treats teachers much better than the United States does. Japanese teachers have a strong national union that assists them with both salary negotiations and having an input into educational policy. They also receive the equivalent of tenure when they are hired, with the assurance of a lifelong job as long as they do not seriously violate expected conduct. Teachers in the United States must earn tenure over a period of three to five years, and they then can be terminated if

student enrollments decline. In addition, Japanese teachers are paid better than engineers and some business people, and they are held in high esteem by their fellow citizens (Hayakawa, 1986).

One of the most striking differences between Japanese and U.S. education is the nature of the transitions from one school level to another (Feinberg, 1993; Kumagai, 1996). During the last year in junior high school, Japanese students take a high school entrance examination, which is the key determinant of placement in high school. Students can take the exam for any public, academic high school in their district, but if they flunk the exam, they will probably have to attend a lower-prestige private school or public, vocational high school. The high school entrance exam is so important to Japanese teenagers that a whole industry of private tutors, "cram schools," and magazines and materials has emerged to help them choose the right school and pass the exam.

Entrance into the government-run national universities and the higher-prestige private universities is also determined almost entirely by an entrance examination. Students are allowed to take the exam for only two universities during a given year. Once accepted to a university, students are admitted to a particular department, or major. If they wish to change departments, they must seek entrance to the university again since each department sets the score on the exam that will be needed for admission to the department.

Because of the stakes involved in the examinations at the end of junior high and high school, Japanese students tend to be much more serious and to study much harder than do students in the United States. Junior high and high school curricula in Japan are also more advanced in science, mathematics, and foreign languages. In some areas, Japanese high school graduates probably have the same knowledge level as college graduates in the United States. The intense pace does not continue at the college level, however, as students seem to ease up after their hard charge through the lower levels. One educational expert concluded: "The Japanese university is notorious as the weakest link in its educational system in terms of the development of academic skills" (Feinberg, 1993, p. 198).

Education, Communication, and the Mass Media

You should be able to discuss the mass media in terms of when it emerged; how it affects people, schools, and society; who controls it; and whether it constitutes neocolonization.

This chapter has stated that educational institutions attempt to influence people to adopt new values and acquire new skills. Education is not alone in this effort. Chapter 3 noted that whereas the family is the primary agency of socialization, the mass media are also influential in this regard. The mass media also affect education: Modern mass media have become an important adjunct in the schools' efforts to influence people, while at the same time the media compete with the schools for people's time and attention. The media have become highly controversial because of their power and pervasiveness and because they bring both advantages and disadvantages. This analysis of educational institutions will close with an assessment of the communications and media industries.

Emergence of the Mass Media

The mass media consist of print media, such as books, magazines, and newspapers, and electronic media in the form of television and radio. The print media were the earliest forms of mass media, and their growth depended on a literate population. In any society where most of the population is illiterate, the reach of the print media will be limited. There were high rates of illiteracy in the United States before the twentieth century, a situation that is still true in Third-World nations, where 30 percent of the people are illiterate (see Figure 12.1). In fact, mass education and the print media tend to expand together, with the former providing a large populace with the skills necessary for the expansion of the latter.

In the fifteenth century, Johannes Gutenberg invented a printing press that used movable type, an invention that opened the door to printing large quantities of text. Single sheets of information and small pamphlets were printed in the eighteenth century. Eventually, the newspaper emerged, which is printed on a regular basis and contains a wide range of information aimed at a whole community. As more people learned to read and newspapers became more widely available, they became a significant source of communication and influence. There were news articles about political and economic events of the day, of course, but there were also advertisements in which business people tried to sell products to consumers. Thus the print media significantly expanded the network of social influence that surrounded people.

In the twentieth century, the print media have continued to grow and become more technologically sophisticated, but the real revolution has been the electronic media: radio, telephones, television, and computers. All these devices are, of course, products of the twentieth century. In the United States telephones were fairly widely available before World War II and are virtually universal today, but that is not true in many parts of the world. Whereas the United States today has almost one telephone for each person, such nations as China, Myanmar (Burma), and Bangladesh have less than one instrument for each hundred citizens. Radios were also widely available before World War II, but there is still a substantial disparity in numbers of radios between the European nations and the Third-World nations, as Table 12.1 indicates.

Although television was invented before World War II, its mass distribution did not begin until the 1950s, and its growth has been phenomenal. As Figure 3.3 shows, virtually every home in the United States has at least one television, and more than half the households have cable television and VCRs, which are indicators of more extensive and sophisticated use of the medium. Figure 12.6 (on p. 427) shows the contrasting patterns in television and newspaper usage since 1970—a growth in the number of televisions coinciding with a decline in the per capita circulation of daily newspapers. In short, people are watching television more and reading the newspaper, and probably other printed media, less, a trend that is disturbing to some observers. As with the other mass media, the disparity in the distribution of televisions around the globe is substantial (see Table 12.1). The United States has far more televisions available to its citizens than does any other nation—eight televisions for every ten

TABLE 12.1 Newspapers, televisions, and radios, in selected nations, per 1,000 people, 1993

Nation	Newspapers[a]	Televisions	Radios
United States	236	816	2120
Europe			
Finland	512	504	996
France	205	412	890
Italy (1989)	106	429	802
U.K. (1988)	383	435	1146
Middle East			
Iran	20	63	230
Kuwait	248	346	408
Lebanon	185	346	887
Syria	22	62	257
Asia			
Bangladesh	6	6	47
China	43	38	184
India	31	40	80
Japan	577	618	911
Latin America			
Brazil	55	209	390
Mexico	116	150	255
Nicaragua	23	67	261
Venezuela	205	163	443
Africa			
Kenya	14	11	87
Nigeria	18	38	196
South Africa	32	101	314
Zimbabwe	19	27	86

[a]Number of printed copies of newspapers circulated per issue, 1992.

Note. From *Statistical Yearbook, 1995* by United Nations Educational, Scientific, and Cultural Organization, 1995, Paris: UNESCO.

people. By contrast, Bangladesh and Kenya have eleven or fewer televisions for every one thousand people. Media experts expect, however, that the twenty-first century will be witness to the expansion of the mass media to these other nations. Not all nations will be flooded with media to the extent that the United States and Canada are, but the media will become a more routine cultural presence in the daily lives of most people.

Effects of the Mass Media

As the mass media have become a pervasive cultural force, concern has grown about their effects on people's lives. Researchers have been investigating this issue, and some of the findings of this research are presented in this and other chapters in this book. Some have concluded that the mass media have helped to create a complex **popular culture,** or *products and activities designed*

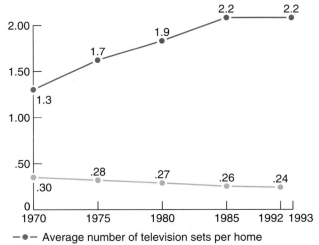

— ● — Average number of television sets per home
— ● — Number of newspapers in daily circulation, per capita

FIGURE 12.6 Changes in Television and Newspaper Use in the United States, 1970–1993 *Note:* From *Statistical Yearbook* by United Nations Educational, Scientific, and Cultural Organization, 1989, 1994, 1995, Paris: UNESCO; *Statistical Abstract of the United States, 1995,* by U.S. Bureau of the Census, 1995, Washington, DC: U.S. Government Printing Office.

for mass consumption and used for leisure or entertainment (Brummett, 1991). The media are a part of the popular culture in that the two most common leisure-time activities in the United States are watching television and reading the newspaper. The media also help disseminate information and trends that are a part of the popular culture. Through the media, people can be in touch with popular music, professional sports, mud wrestling, and religious services. In a postindustrial economy such as that of the United States, people have free time to devote to these activities and the economic resources to consume the products of popular culture. Sociologists point to the fact that the mass media are not merely vehicles to communicate information; they are also an industry that employs many people and manipulates people's needs and desires through advertising. The explosion of the media is in part a consequence of the expansive nature of a capitalist economy looking for new products to sell and new markets to attract. The intersection of people's desire to be fashionable and to be entertained with capitalism's need to find new markets and enhance profits has made the mass media a major industry in the United States and other affluent nations. When surplus income becomes more available in less developed nations, the mass media are likely to expand there also.

Much of the research on the effects of the mass media has focused on television, because of its pervasiveness, and on the industrial nations where it has been widely available for some time. One focus of concern has been on whether the portrayal of violence on television can cause people to be more violent in real life. There seems little doubt at this point that television does contribute to the levels of violence in society (Felson, 1996; Huston et al., 1992; Van Evra, 1990). Most research over the past forty years has concluded that when children and youth watch violence on television, they are more likely to act aggressively or violently themselves, especially in situations that are conducive to violence. The impact is greater for males than for females and for children who are more aggressive to begin with (Josephson, 1987). Children between the ages of eight and twelve seem to be especially vulnerable to the effects of watching violence on television.

Television encourages people toward violence in three ways. First, action dramas can be arousing to viewers and may stimulate them in the direction of physical activity and release. This effect is probably of short duration, from hours to days. Second, television provides viewers with legitimizing models for violence in much the same way that parents or peers can serve as models. In fact, it

Most sociological research over the decades concludes that watching violence on television increases the likelihood that children will behave aggressively or violently, especially children between the ages of eight and twelve.

is difficult to watch television without being exposed to models of violence. Thus, children learn the potential for acting violently in particular situations, and the amount of such violence on television has not declined in the past few decades and may have actually increased. Also, the violence seen on television has some unreal or surrealistic qualities. People bleed little, and the actual pain and agony resulting from a violent attack are rarely portrayed. The consequences of violence often seem antiseptic and rather unimportant. Third, television conveys attitudes and values, and it can teach children to view violence or antisocial behavior as a desirable or "manly" way to behave.

In addition to violence, concern about the effect of watching television has focused on the educational skills and aptitudes of children and youth. A study of three communities in Canada both before and after they had access to television

found that children's reading skills declined after the introduction of television, a detrimental effect inasmuch as reading seems to be more beneficial to children's aptitude and achievement than watching television (Gaddy, 1986; Williams, 1986). Also, overall, watching television has more negative effects than positive ones on children's creativity, especially their verbal skills (Singer, 1993). Yet, most research fails to show that watching more television has a directly negative effect on achievement or aptitude (although, if watching television takes the place of reading, the decline in reading can negatively affect achievement) (Gortmaker, Salter, Walker, & Dietz, 1990). So, the effect of television on children and youth in these areas is complex—it may provide both benefits and disadvantages.

One of the most pervasive effects of the media may be not the direct content of the programming but the more subtle and indirect support that it gives to cultural beliefs and stereotypes (Signorielli, 1993). Chapter 8 notes that schoolbooks still portray women less frequently overall and also less frequently in jobs outside the home. This practice carries over into newspapers; men appear in newspaper photographs far more often than women, and men are typically photographed doing professional activities whereas women are shown in domestic roles.

Another series of studies found that newspaper and magazine photographs present men's and women's bodies differently: Pictures of men tend to feature the face more prominently, whereas picture of women show more of the body and treat the face as a less prominent feature (Archer, Iritiani, Kimes, & Barrios, 1983; Nigro, Hill, & Gelbein, 1988). The researchers labeled this gender differentiation *face-ism,* and they studied its impact by having people look at pictures of the same individual that varied only in terms of facial prominence. For the photo where the face was more prominent, the individual was rated as more intelligent, more ambitious, and physically better looking. Thus the extent of face-ism in the photograph influences people's judgments of the person portrayed. When women's faces are less prominently displayed, the stereotype that women are less intelligent, ambitious, and capable may be further perpetuated. The researchers concluded that face-ism may reinforce another cultural stereotype, "that essential aspects of personal identity are thought to be centered in different anatomic locations in men and women. Men are represented by their heads and faces; women are represented using more of their bodies" (Archer et al., 1983, p. 733).

As for television, two of the most popular network shows in recent years, *Roseanne* and *Murphy Brown,* have featured strong and positive female characters in their starring roles. Yet, a study commissioned by the Screen Actors Guild and released in 1993 found that only one out of three roles in prime time are played by women and that anchors, newsmakers, and authorities on television news shows are overwhelmingly white males (Gunther, 1993). The portrayal of women in children's shows was even more lopsided, according to the report. It is clear that some of the old stereotypes linger, and evidence shows that they affect youngsters' attitudes. A longitudinal study of gender-role attitudes of teenagers found that watching a lot of television did not make boys more sexist (Morgan, 1972). However, teenagers who had the least sexist attitudes—fairly intelligent girls—were most affected by television: Those who watched it a lot developed more sexist attitudes.

So, the media's greatest impact may be in perpetuating stereotypes that work to the benefit of some groups but to the disadvantage of others. The mass media are also in a position to have great influence in setting the societal agenda—the issues that the public discusses and considers important. National magazines, big-city newspapers, and television networks have this influence because they can reach such large numbers of people. On such topics as what causes crime and whether feminism is losing support, individuals may have strong opinions but relatively little direct knowledge to support them. Those who control the media can communicate their ideas on these topics to millions of people, a capability that affords them enormous influence in defining what topics people will consider important and what solutions to problems will be considered practical.

Much of the impact of the mass media discussed thus far is negative, but an important positive impact should be mentioned: The media considerably expand the channels of communication available to people. Especially with cable television, fiber optics, and electronic networks such as the Internet (see Chapter 4), the number of outlets and vehicles for communication are becoming truly astounding. There are channels devoted to religious programming, MTV offering popular music, community channels that offer community groups a means of getting their message out to a larger audience, and home shopping channels. Of course, whether people benefit from this explosion of possibilities depends on who controls these opportunities.

Control of the Mass Media

If all groups had access to the media to present their views, or if television and print journalists worked independently of powerful groups in society, then the media might provide a truly democratic experience. In fact, the press and television do expose various acts of corruption, often motivating different levels of government to prosecute the offenders. Yet the media are themselves private companies and usually corporate in structure. They pursue greater profits and larger amounts of power in the same fashion as other corporations discussed in Chapter 13. And as has occurred in other corporate sectors, there has been concentration of power among the media:

> Sooner or later a handful of corporations [will] control most of what the average American reads, sees, and hears . . . the same few corporations will control all the important mass media not just in the United States but globally. Nevertheless, there is close to total silence in the mainstream news on the social consequences of this concentration. It is a silence that extends to the news and commentary in major newspapers, magazines, and broadcast news operations. The public learns only of the stock market transactions, the building of dazzling empires, and the personalities of the corporate leaders. (Bagdikian, 1990, p. x)

All newspapers in the United States were once local affairs—small businesses whose main concerns focused on the town or county in which their readers lived (Demers, 1996). To be sure, newspaper owners, executives, and editors were often heavily involved in local issues, such as who was elected mayor or which new employers moved to town, but their influence only rarely extended beyond the local region.

Today, the press is big—and concentrated—business. The sociologist Peter Dreier (1982) found that the twenty-five largest newspaper companies accounted for 53 percent of the daily newspapers sold in the United States. In fact, many newspapers have achieved legal monopolies as cities both small and large have become one-newspaper towns. In addition, the parent corporations of newspapers have influence that stretches far beyond the local level. The newspaper companies are linked to other corporate members of the economic elite through the membership of newspaper executives on the boards of business corporations, banks, and financial institutions. The Dow Jones Company, for example, which publishes the *Wall Street Journal,* had twenty-four such linkages with the 1,300 largest corporations listed by *Fortune* magazine. The Times Mirror Company, publisher of the *Los Angeles Times,* also

had twenty-four such linkages. Newspaper executives are also involved in the revolving door through which members of the economic elite serve for a time in high-level government positions and then return to their corporate jobs. At the time of Dreier's research, thirty-six executives from the twenty-four largest newspaper companies had been or were then serving in one of these government positions.

What is the impact of this concentration on the role of the media in society? The simple conclusion is that the media are mere apologists for the power elite and corporate capitalism. Much research shows, however, that the impact is much more subtle (Demers, 1996; Dreier, 1982). As newspaper companies become larger, form monopolies, and establish links with the power elite, Dreier found, they often develop a viewpoint that has been labeled *corporate liberalism,* which tends to look positively on unions, social welfare programs, and government regulation. However, it is not a socialist position, as discussed in Chapter 13, because corporate liberalism retains the belief that a corporate economy based on private enterprise is the most efficient economic system. In this view, government programs and regulations are intended to protect people against the few weaknesses or excesses that can be found in capitalism. In fact, newspapers and other media following this corporate liberal ideology may sometimes be critical of big government and corporate capitalism, but this criticism stems not from an opposition to capitalism but from a desire to promote responsible capitalism. One latent function of such criticism is to protect capitalism from challenges and discourage interest in more radical changes that would significantly threaten corporate control by the power elite. One researcher concludes that "the corporate newspaper should be seen as a social institution that *promotes controlled social change*—change that at times accommodates the needs and interests of challenging groups but that usually does not dramatically alter the power of dominant groups" (Demers, 1996, p. 319).

Looking at not only newspapers but the media in general, much has occurred in the past two decades. In particular, control over the media has become much more concentrated and global in scope. By the 1990s, more than 70 percent of the daily newspapers in the United States were owned by outside corporations, and fourteen of these corporations had most of the business. Despite the existence of more than 25,000 media outlets in the United States, a mere "*twenty-three corporations* [italics added] control most of the business in daily newspapers, magazines, television, books, and motion pictures" (Bagdikian, 1990, p. 4). As the twentieth century draws to a close, a race is emerging with a few mega-corporations trying to control the print and electronic media around the globe. One of the more ambitious efforts has been that of the Australian Rupert Murdoch and his News Corporation. The Corporation owns, in whole or in part, the Fox TV network with 158 affiliate stations in the United States; a number of publishing companies, including HarperCollins and Basic Books; Star TV of Hong Kong, which beams its programs through satellite to thirty-nine countries from the Middle East to Asia; the 20th Century Fox movie studio; British Sky Broadcasting, a satellite television service for Britain and Europe; and many newspapers and magazines around the world. Other giant corporations are working hard to compete with Murdoch, and the concentration of media resources he has managed to achieve may be a portent of the future.

Executives in these corporate media empires, of course, insist that such concentration will *improve* the media. In fact, David Demers's (1996) research on concentration in the newspaper industry argues that such concentration will enable diversity in newspaper content to survive in a highly competitive media environment.

Other observers are more pessimistic regarding the effect of concentration in the media. Reviewing all of these trends, Edward Herman (1993) concludes that, on the important issues, the media "serve mainly as a supportive arm of the state and dominant elites, focusing heavily on themes serviceable to them, and debating and exposing within accepted frames of reference (p. 25)."

Applied social researchers such as Peter Dreier and Ben Bagdikian agree in their concern that concentrated power over public information is inherently antidemocratic:

> When the central interests of the controlling corporations are at stake, mainstream American news becomes heavily weighted by whatever serves the economic and political interests of the corporations that own the media. The voice of the giants becomes ever more loud and drowns out with greater success the small media voices of dissent. Now that media owners are so large that they are part of the highest levels of the world economy, the news and other public information become heavily weighted in favor of all corporate values. (Bagdikian, 1990, pp. x–xi)

The additionally disturbing aspect of such a trend is that, as the dissenting voices are silenced, people become less and less aware that they are being presented with a distorted view because they have fewer guideposts with which to measure the accuracy or completeness of what they see, read, and hear.

Education and the Electronic Classroom

Traditionally, the television, like movies, has been seen as separate from education, if not antithetical to it in the sense that it competes for students' time and attention. This situation is rapidly changing as technological developments have created some possibilities for the educational use of the electronic media. One of the most striking developments was the marketing in the 1980s of a news show with advertisements for use in high school classrooms. A company called Whittle Communications provided computer and television equipment to high schools free of charge with the agreement that students would be required to watch their twelve-minute news summary and accompanying advertisements each day. This offer is, to date, one of the most significant intrusions of mass media into the classroom. Many teachers and parents were concerned because it seemed to turn control of the curriculum over to a private corporation whose primary concern was profit making. It also introduced commercialism into the educational system by requiring students to watch advertisements. Many school systems went along with the offer, however, because the temptation of the computer equipment was too great to resist.

Some educators fear that more such intrusion is yet to come: The electronic media will enter the schools as a way of manipulating values and consumer behavior. Then, those who control the media will have direct access with their messages to students when they are very open to persuasion. Teachers and parents will lose more control over the education of children especially when, as in the Whittle experience, teachers do not have the freedom to reject the technology. In addition, television and videotapes are such a powerfully appealing medium that the desires and admonitions of parents and teachers are likely to appear pale by comparison.

On the positive side, the electronic media are likely to produce some significant educational innovations. The emerging technologies of video, computers, compact disks, and the Internet will make available to students multimedia educational materials that combine print, images, and sound into a sophisticated presentation. The *Encyclopedia Britannica* is now available on a single compact disk, which means that students with a computer and CD-ROM player at their desk can do a substantial amount of research very easily. Such technology will afford teachers many more effective teaching tools to use in the classroom.

The emerging technology of fiber optic cables, which greatly expands the amount of information that can be carried through cable, will also open many new possibilities. For example, it will expand the opportunities for interactive learning through television. Traditional television is one-way communication: A signal comes into a home but nothing goes out. With interactive communication, the signal goes both ways: A teacher can send a signal into a home, and a student can respond to the teacher. This *interactive learning through video* is called **distance education.** It is currently in use at some universities; a professor lectures before a camera, and the lecture is transmitted instantly to a number of classrooms many miles away. There is also a camera in those remote classrooms so the students can ask questions and get immediate feedback from the professor. It is just like being in the same classroom except that teacher and students might be five hundred or more miles apart. The time may come when much of education occurs in this fashion, and the notion that all students must gather together in a classroom to be taught may become obsolete. Teachers can also prepare lessons and store them on disk or tape to be retrieved by students when

they are ready. In all likelihood, some learning will still occur in traditional schools, but the emerging technology will introduce more flexibility and innovation into the educational system.

Students' ability to benefit from these educational innovations will depend on whether they can tap into the *information superhighway*. Students whose parents cannot afford a home wired with fiber optic cable, for example, may find themselves at an educational disadvantage when it comes to using what the new technology has to offer. Unless programs are instituted to assure some equity in access to this technology, children in poor families or disadvantaged schools will find themselves further behind others, and the gap between the haves and the have-nots may become even wider.

The Global Mass Media: Neocolonization?

The United States clearly dominates the global mass media (Turow, 1992). For example, three-quarters of the broadcast and basic cable television revenues and four-fifths of pay television revenues around the world are generated by mass media materials produced in the United States. Worldwide, more than half of all films rented to theaters or purchased for home video viewing are U.S. products. This overwhelming U.S. presence has produced opposition in many nations that see it as **cultural colonialism,** *a cultural assault that, if not diminished, will change values, norms, and ways of life.* Indeed, the cultural penetration of the world by U.S. media can be likened to the geographical penetration of other continents by European explorers in earlier centuries. Just as the Jesuits brought their schools to the South American Indians, modern media magnates send television serials such as *Dallas* or movies such as *Terminator* to nations around the world. The result, many fear, will be the same: Irreversible change in the recipients' cultural values and the ultimate destruction of traditional ways of life. As U.S. values regarding work, gender relations, religion, violence, and many other things become pervasive, the result could be the transformation of nations into capitalist economies and consumer marketplaces for the products of Western popular culture. Such a transformation would be a further expansion of world capitalism with its emphasis on market forces, profit making, surplus accumulation, and economic growth.

By the end of the twentieth century, the U.S. media are receiving some fairly stiff competition from the Japanese and European media. Such competition simply means that wealthy industrial nations of the world dominate the media market and are thus in a strong position to communicate their views on capitalism, privatization, commercialization, and civilization. In fact, the United States and other Western nations have worked through the United Nations to encourage freedom of the media in all nations because their well-developed media industry will dominate any open market. Many nations oppose this freedom because they want their indigenous media to have a chance to develop and to preserve aspects of their traditional way of life. Even the notion that the media should be free of government control is a Western cultural value that not all nations around the world agree with. Many nations view the media as a tool of nation building, to be used by the government to encourage patriotism and desired values and behavior.

Summary

1. Education is the systematic, formal process through which specialized teachers transmit skills, knowledge, and values to students. In pre-industrial societies, much of education was informal, being a part of the general process of socialization.

2. Colonizing nations have used education to change the cultural values and social practices of the peoples they colonize. In the twentieth century, education has also been a key vehicle of modernization, although critics argue that modernization is in part neocolonial Westernization of these societies to make them receptive to investment.

3. From the functionalist perspective, education is a social institution that serves a number of important functions, including the transmission of culture, training people for important positions, providing custodial care and a social network for the young, encouraging innovation and social change, sorting people into positions, and enabling social mobility.

4. From the conflict perspective, education is a mechanism for maintaining the existing class structure and protecting the interests of dominant groups. This end is accomplished by requiring educational achievements in order to get jobs. Such requirements effectively discriminate against people of lower socioeconomic status because they are less able to acquire the necessary education.

5. The interactionist perspective recognizes that social expectations and social meanings are a part of the interaction between teachers and students. Practices such as grading and tracking students can result in social labels that might produce a self-fulfilling prophecy.

6. Formal education in the United States emerged as religious training and as a way to Americanize immigrants. Mass education developed in the twentieth century because industrialization required a more literate and skilled workforce.

7. Education in the United States occurs in schools that are highly bureaucratic, which has sparked debate over whether bureaucracies are efficient ways to teach or merely stifle creativity. There has also been severe criticism of U.S. schools in regard to how effectively they teach the young. A number of reforms have been proposed that would improve schools: parental choice, back to basics curricula, compensatory education, school integration, and upgrading schools and teachers.

8. The mass media play a key role in educating the young, influencing people, and shaping society. The media affect a number of realms of life: They produce popular culture, they can induce people toward violent behavior, and they give subtle and indirect support for existing cultural beliefs and stereotypes.

9. The mass media are increasingly concentrated into the hands of a few large corporations; this concentration may have detrimental affects on the free flow of information and ideas. Some argue that Western control of the media around the world has produced cultural colonialism.

STUDY AND Review

Key Terms

cultural colonialism

distance education

education

hidden curriculum

modernization

popular culture

social reproduction

Multiple-Choice Questions

1. When specialized educational institutions emerged in agricultural societies, they were most often intended for
   a. training of the lower classes in practical skills.
   b. religious and moral training of the elite.
   c. a supplement to informal education at home.
   d. training for the middle class in management skills.

2. Through courses in civic education and national history, schools in traditional societies play a role in
   a. nation building.
   b. informal education.
   c. distance education.
   d. popular culture.

3. The concept of a hidden curriculum in schools is most clearly associated with which perspective?
   a. The functionalist perspective.
   b. The conflict perspective.
   c. The interactionist perspective.
   d. The modernization perspective.

4. Which of the following is true in regard to the credentials race in the United States?
   a. The educational requirements for most jobs today are lower than they need to be.
   b. The educational credentials required for jobs have been going down in the past few decades.
   c. The educational requirements for many jobs today are higher than they need to be.
   d. The race ended a couple of decades ago.

5. During the colonial period in the United States, the primary purpose of schooling was to
   a. encourage social mobility.
   b. discourage social mobility.
   c. incorporate the American Indians into the colonies.
   d. further religious training.

6. Magnet schools are
   a. schools that centralize all the educational functions in a school district.
   b. the schools that attract the largest number of students in a school district.
   c. schools that offer special programs in particular subject areas to attract students.
   d. schools that have reduced the extent of bureaucracy in their organization.

7. Research on education has shown that
   a. students in Roman Catholic schools perform better than students in public schools.
   b. students in public schools perform better than students in Catholic schools.
   c. students in U.S. schools do better in math and science than students in most other industrial nations.
   d. more highly bureaucratic schools encourage more creativity among their students than less bureaucratic schools.

8. As the number of televisions in homes in the United States has grown,
   a. the number of newspapers in circulation has also grown.
   b. the number of newspapers in circulation has declined.
   c. the literacy rate has declined.
   d. popular culture has declined.
   e. both b and c have occurred.

9. The group that is most likely to be influenced toward violence by watching violence on television is
   a. older adults.
   b. teens between 15 and 18 years of age.
   c. children between 8 and 12 years of age.
   d. children under 5 years of age.

10. The elite newspapers in the United States criticize government and corporations because
    a. the newspapers oppose capitalism.
    b. the newspapers are trying to deflect attention from their own inadequacies.
    c. the newspapers favor socialism.
    d. the newspapers favor responsible capitalism.

True/False Questions

1. Specialized educational institutions first emerged in hunting- and-gathering societies.

2. Even after formal educational institutions have emerged, such as in industrial societies, informal education still occurs.

3. In the twentieth century, the Western industrial nations have discouraged more traditional societies from going through the process of modernization.

4. Precolonial Nigeria had no formal schools.

5. The danger of tracking in schools is that the track can become a label that creates expectations for how teachers and students should behave.

6. Among those students who are especially at risk for failure in schools in the United States are those whose parents have low educational attainment.

7. Overall, integration of schools in the United States has probably resulted in modest improvements in school achievement by African American students.

8. The reach of the print media will be more expansive in societies with a lower rate of literacy.

9. In Japan, the central government controls educational policy and curriculum design.

10. Traditional societies in the twentieth century are no longer threatened by cultural colonialism.

Fill-In Questions

1. The social and economic changes that accompany the transition to an industrial economy are called _____ .

2. The term *nation building* refers to _____ .

3. The term _____ refers to the training of students in values and norms that help to perpetuate the existing system of stratification.

4. Powerful forces in educational institutions work toward _____ , or passing social and economic inequalities on from one generation to the next.

5. According to the interactionist perspective, the grades and other reports that schools accumulate about a student become a _____ .

6. When teachers and administrators in schools devote more attention to maintaining the educational system than to the traditional educational goals, they are engaging in _____ .

7. School reform that is based on the notion that schools should compete for students in an open marketplace is called _____ .

8. The _____ approach to education emphasizes the traditional core curriculum and a return to strong discipline.

9. _____ refers to the products and activities designed for mass consumption and used for leisure or entertainment.

10. The overwhelming U.S. presence in the production and distribution of films and videos around the globe has produced opposition in many nations because it may lead to _____ .

Matching Questions

_____ 1. function of education
_____ 2. Ibo
_____ 3. social reproduction
_____ 4. tracking
_____ 5. magnet schools
_____ 6. compensatory education
_____ 7. mass media
_____ 8. corporate liberalism
_____ 9. distance education
_____ 10. modernization

A. parental choice
B. Head Start
C. custody of the young
D. source of popular culture
E. Nigerian language
F. viewpoint of elite newspapers
G. conflict perspective
H. interactive learning through video
I. ability grouping
J. transition to industrial economy

Essay Questions

1. How did the Western European nations use educational institutions as they explored and colonized many nations around the world between the fifteenth and the nineteenth centuries?

2. What role has education played in the processes of modernization and nation building?

3. What functions does education perform that contribute to the operation and maintenance of society?

4. According to the conflict perspective, in what ways does education work as a mechanism to limit the opportunities of the less powerful in society?

5. What contribution does the interactionist perspective make to our understanding of education as a social process?

6. Discuss criticisms of the educational system in the United States. Include in your answer an assessment of schools as bureaucracies and of the effectiveness of schools.

7. What reforms are being implemented, or might be implemented, in schools in the United States to overcome some of the problems discussed in the text?

8. How is education in Japan similar to education in the United States? How do they differ?

9. Describe the emergence of the mass media and some of the effects that it has had on society.

10. Both historically and today, who controls the mass media in the United States? What are the advantages and disadvantages of the kinds of control that exist today?

Answers

Multiple-Choice
1. B; 2. A; 3. B; 4. C; 5. D; 6. C; 7. A; 8. B; 9. C; 10. D

True/False
1. F; 2. T; 3. F; 4. F; 5. T; 6. T; 7. T; 8. F; 9. T; 10. F

Fill-In
1. modernization
2. encouraging citizens' to shift their allegiance to the nation-state
3. hidden curriculum
4. social reproduction
5. publicly stamped label
6. goal displacement
7. parental choice
8. back to basics
9. popular culture
10. cultural colonialism

Matching
1. C; 2. E; 3. G; 4. I; 5. A; 6. B; 7. D; 8. F; 9. H; 10. J

For Further Reading

Ballantine, Jeanne. (1993). *The sociology of education: A systematic analysis* (3rd ed.). Englewood Cliffs, NJ: Prentice-Hall. This comprehensive textbook on the sociology of education provides a complete overview of the topics, theories, and research that sociologists focus on in the institution of education.

Berger, Arthur Asa, (Ed.). (1986). *Television in society.* New Brunswick, NJ: Transaction Books. These essays provide an overview of the sociological analysis of television in society. They focus on such things as what values are communicated through the television, whether television encourages violence, and concentration of control over television.

Carnoy, Martin, & Samoff, Joel. (1990). *Education and social transition in the Third World.* Princeton, NJ: Princeton University Press. This volume explores the issue of educational change in Third-World nations, especially the extent to which traditional values are preserved or threatened by proposed changes.

Cookson, Peter W., & Persell, Caroline Hodges. (1985). *Preparing for power: America's elite boarding schools.* New York: Basic Books. Based on in-depth interviews at elite boarding schools, these sociologists document how the schools prepare the offspring of the powerful to take over positions of power in American society.

Gans, Herbert J. (1979). *Deciding what's news.* New York: Pantheon. This is an excellent sociological study of the agenda-setting function of the mass media. The author explores how the news that we see on television is processed by the media.

Hurn, Christopher. (1978). *The limits and possibilities of schooling: An introduction to the sociology of education.* Boston: Allyn & Bacon. Although some specific issues have changed since this book was written, it still stands as a basic introduction to how sociologists study the institution of education.

Mazzocco, Dennis W. (1994). *Networks of power: Corporate TV's threat to democracy.* Boston, MA: South End Press. This thought-provoking book describes the extent to which the media, and television in particular, are now concentrated in the hands of a few powerful corporate giants and the consequences this may have for democratic institutions.

Mitroff, Ian I., & Bennis, Warren. (1989). *The unreality industry: The deliberate manufacturing of falsehood and what it is doing to our lives.* New York: Oxford University Press. This is a hard-hitting critique of the mass media on the grounds that they invent realities and then encourage people to believe the inventions are true. The authors explore some of the dangerous effects of this behavior.

Zweigenhaft, Richard L., & Domhoff, G. William. (1991). *Blacks in the white establishment? A study of race and class in America.* New Haven, CT: Yale University Press. This is a fascinating follow-up on a 1960s program that sent poor, mostly African American teenagers to some of the most elite secondary schools in the nation. The book looks at what happened to them, as well as investigates the socialization to elite power positions and the intertwining of racial identity, class, and education.

CHAPTER THIRTEEN *Political and Economic Institutions*

Before the British colonized parts of Africa, the Tiv were a small tribe in West Africa, not far from the Yoruba discussed in Chapter 12 (Bohannon & Bohannon, 1953). The Tiv had a subsistence economy, producing only enough food and other goods for the needs of their tribe. They did not increase production in order to have a surplus to sell or trade to another tribe. Even though each Tiv family worked their own plot of land, the food produced was considered to be the property of the tribe as a whole rather than the grower. If another family's crop was too small and they needed some extra food, other Tiv families would give it to them, expecting nothing immediate in return but confident that the needy family would come to their assistance at some future time of need.

The Tiv family did not own the plot they worked. The land belonged to the whole tribe, and each family was assigned a plot to work for a period of time. When the soil was exhausted, the plot would be left idle for a while, and the family would be assigned a new plot. The Tiv would actively debate which gardens should be idle each season and where the dispossessed families should start a new garden. The Tiv would have been aghast at the thought of buying and selling land for money. They had a currency, which they used to buy some ceremonial items, but they did not think of purchasing food or land with it because these belonged to the tribe as a whole. The land was considered a resource for the whole tribe to nurture and to use; it was unimaginable to them that it could be a commodity to be bought and sold.

An economy with some similarities to that of the Tiv existed in New England around the time of the American Revolution in 1776 (Szatmary, 1980). It was a subsistence economy in which yeoman farmers grew just enough food to feed their families. They also produced most of the other things they needed, such as clothing. Some manufactured items, such as glass or gunpowder, had to be bought, and the farmers grew a small surplus of food to barter for these goods. However, they grew much less on their farms than they were capable of. In fact, they typically cultivated only a small portion of their land—as little as 5 or 10 percent, in some cases—because that was sufficient to supply home needs and a small surplus to trade. They increased the amount of land under cultivation only out of necessity, usually because their family had grown larger.

The choice of crops of these New England yeoman farmers also arose from their subsistence approach. One major crop was Indian corn, which had little market value and tended to deplete the soil more quickly than crops like hemp or flax for which there was a brisk market. Indian corn was grown because it provided sustenance for both humans and animals on the farm. They also grew small amounts of many crops rather than large amounts of those few crops that had the highest market value; that is, they grew what their forefathers had grown and what would provide the most variety for their families. These subsistence practices stemmed in part from a strong sense of independence. To survive by one's own efforts was seen as indicative of such independence. Independence, however, did not mean competitiveness. These farmers engaged in elaborate cooperative, community-oriented exchanges with other farmers, especially during the busy harvest season. Neighbors would exchange labor, tools, and animals with one another. Like the Tiv,

they saw themselves as involved in a communal activity rather than in economic competition with other farmers.

To understand present-day U.S. culture, it is sometimes helpful to look at different cultures. The Tiv and the New England yeoman farmers had an economy largely devoid of some characteristics of modern economies: competition, private property (the Tiv), profit seeking, accumulation of surplus, commercialism, and economic expansion. People often view their own way of life as the natural way to live, seeing competition, for example, or profit seeking as the natural way for human beings to behave. Yet, the Tiv and the New England farmers indicate that such ways are not natural but rather are cultural products—ways of life that people learn as members of a particular culture. As this chapter begins, it is wise to keep in mind that present-day economic and political institutions are also cultural products, outgrowths of centuries-long historical trends.

The term **economics** refers to *the processes through which goods and services are produced and distributed in societies.* Economic systems are closely linked to political systems. **Politics** refers to *the use of power to determine whose values will predominate, how rewards and resources will be allocated, and the manner in which conflicting interests in society will be resolved* (Segal, 1974). Both these institutions center on the same key social process in society: the exercise of power in the allocation of scarce resources. In fact, a classic description of politics could aptly be applied to *both* political and economic institutions: They determine "who gets what, when, and how" (Lasswell, 1936). In a small society like that of the Tiv, the two institutions almost blend into one, with the same village leaders playing a part in both realms. In all societies, political decisions influence economic policies and practices, and economic conditions affect what happens in the political realm.

A major bone of contention among social scientists has involved which of these institutions predominates in the exercise of power. Because politicians pass legislation that establishes national economic policy, one might conclude that politics is the main engine allocating resources in society. Yet Frederick Engels (1888/1969) once referred to *economic relations* as "the decisive element" in society while characterizing the political order as "subordinate." This chapter will address this issue,

Myths & FACTS

Myth U.S. citizens are a politically active people, with most of them participating in the democratic process.

FACT Actually, most people in the United States are politically acquiescent. Barely one-half of U.S. citizens vote in presidential elections and fewer still in other elections. Most other industrial democracies have much higher rates of political participation among their citizens.

Myth States and governments work, especially in democracies, to protect all citizens equally.

FACT In all societies, states and governments come to be dominated by particular groups with special interests. Those groups tend to rule in ways that protect and benefit their own interests, although they may believe that they are ruling in the interests of all the people.

Myth The U.S. economy represents a pure form of capitalism.

FACT There are no pure forms of capitalism in the world today. Even in the United States, the government is involved in controlling and regulating the economy in many different ways.

Myth The people who hold stock in a corporation own the corporation and can control the policies of the corporation.

FACT In reality, a corporate board of directors and the professional managers they hire run the daily affairs of the corporation. The vast majority of the stockholders own such a small share of the company that they do not have the time, the expertise, or the inclination to pay much attention to how the corporation is run. In addition, stockholder meetings are held very infrequently, and thus stockholders have few opportunities for input.

Myth For capitalist economies to be efficient and successful, there should be an atmosphere of freewheeling competition among entrepreneurs, with the government staying out of the picture.

FACT Although freewheeling competition has advantages at times, the Japanese economy has been quite strong even though the Japanese see competition as potentially dangerous and disruptive. In fact, the Japanese government works closely with business and industry to keep competition under control.

---

although not with the goal of resolving it. Rather, the chapter will focus on the role of each institution and the way the institutions work together in exercising power and allocating resources.

Politics, Power, and Authority

You should be able to define power and the different types of authority and explain the differences between state and government.

Power is *the ability of one group to realize its will, even in the face of resistance from other groups* (Weber, 1919/1958). Power can arise from many sources: the strength of numbers, efficient organization, access to wealth or status, or control of political and economic institutions. Whatever its source, power

enables its possessor to compel others to act in a particular fashion. However, all power is not alike. In some cases, groups have power because they can threaten to use force should others not comply. The U.S. Congress, for example, has the power to require young men to register to be drafted into the military, even though many of them would prefer not to register. Congress's power in this area rests on its ability to levy fines and prison sentences on those who refuse to register.

However, such explicit coercion, although important, is a costly way to exercise power because it ties up resources such as the money necessary to staff police forces and build prisons, and it generates resentment among the governed. For this reason, rulers attempt to make their exercise of power *legitimate*. **Legitimacy** is *"the capacity of the system to engender and maintain the belief that the* existing . . . institutions are the most appropriate ones for the society" (Lipset, 1959, p. 64). *Legitimate power,* or what sociologists call **authority,** is *obeyed because people believe it is right and proper that they obey.* Some young people register for the draft, for example, because they believe the government should have the power to create a military force to control internal disorder or protect against external threat. They may still prefer not to enter the military, but they accept the government's right to require them to serve society in this fashion.

Most people in the United States view the existing political and economic arrangements as reasonably legitimate, and this acceptance has been an important source of stability for U.S. society. However, the degree of legitimacy accorded to institutions varies from time to time and group to group in the United States. The anti-war movement of the 1960s and the militia movement of the 1990s are symptomatic that the accordance of legitimacy to political institutions is not universal. Chapter 7 notes that some African Americans, reacting to the enslavement of their ancestors and their own experiences with discrimination, feel some ambivalence toward the legitimacy of U.S. political institutions. Finally, a survey in 1994 found that 41 percent of the people expressed "very little" confidence in the U.S. Congress; likewise, 34 percent had little confidence in the federal government, 39 percent had little confidence in political parties, and 22 percent had little confidence in large corporations (U.S. Bureau of the Census, 1995, p. 288). So, political and economic institutions in the United States have not won the complete support of all citizens.

Types of Authority

Political and economic institutions can rest on one, two, or all three of the following types of authority (Weber, 1925/1947).

Traditional authority is based on historical custom and loyalty to established ways of doing things. Perhaps the best political example is found in societies that have hereditary rule. In such cases, the seat of political power rests with a group leader or chief. In tribal societies, for example, when the ruler dies, leadership is passed to his eldest son, and all of the accumulated power then devolves on that individual. In such societies, the norms surrounding who has authority are often considered sacred. Such traditional leaders not only have great power but also command reverence and sentimental respect from group members.

Charismatic authority is based on the presumed special and extraordinary powers or qualities of some individual. The emphasis here is on the *perception* of unique qualities, whether or not the person actually possesses them. Adolf Hitler and Mao Zedong exemplify charismatic leaders who exercised tremendous political authority in their respective countries, Germany and China. Charismatic authority also exists in democratic societies, and political leaders such as John F. Kennedy, Martin Luther King, Jr., Ronald Reagan, and Jesse Jackson have been acknowledged as having considerable charisma, although their appeal is not universal. Charismatic authority, however, is the most unstable type of authority, because the leader may die or because of illness or injury be unable to remain charismatic. If that happens, the leader's authority may disappear unless it is preserved in traditions or transformed into the third type of authority.

Legal-rational authority depends on laws and rules that define who possesses what type of power over whom. For example, the President of the United States has a great deal of authority, including the ability to recommend that the country go to war, but the President must gain the approval of Congress in order to declare war. Executive privilege gives the President a measure of power that few other political figures in the United States possess. Despite this considerable authority, if Presidents exceed the established boundaries of this privilege, they can be impeached. Because their office is based on legal-rational authority, Presidents cannot pass it on to their offspring. In addition, the rights and obligations of the office remain with the office when a particular President, no matter how charismatic, leaves. This rule affords institutions based on legal-rational authority a high degree of stability.

Authority, of course, can derive from more than one of these sources. The U.S. presidency, for example, gains much of its legitimation from legal-rational authority. However, the Constitution is now two centuries old, and this time span has accorded it a degree of traditional authority as well. So, the powers of the presidency, as defined in the Constitution, have also gained legitimation through custom. In addition, some Presidents, such as Ronald Reagan, have used their charisma to gain some support for their presidential actions.

State and Government

Although political authority today rests in specialized offices such as the presidency, that has not always been the case. The emergence of the state as the seat of political authority is linked to societal evolution.

Formal political institutions do not exist in hunting-and-gathering societies. Rather, decisions are made collectively, and somewhat democratically, based on the mutual welfare of the group (see Chapter 2). In horticultural and pastoral societies, separate political leadership emerges in the form of a chieftainship whose authority is passed on through inheritance. However, it is not until agricultural societies arise that the state appears. The **state** is *a political institution with legitimate control over the use of force within a particular territory* (Weber, 1925/1947). The reasons for the emergence of the state as the supreme political authority are complex (Service, 1975; Thomas & Meyer, 1984). In general, however, a social hierarchy emerged in agricultural societies that enabled some people to accumulate and control a considerable amount of resources. Control was also extended over a considerable amount of territory. Higher population density, elaborate irrigation systems, the development of trade networks, and increased specialization— these and other factors called for both more centralized and more assured control over a given geographic territory, and the state emerged as the social institution to perform this function. In industrial societies, with larger populations and even greater wealth, the state becomes even more essential to controlling and organizing social and economic life. Increasing levels of military competition in agricultural societies also produced a need for more centralized coordination and control.

The **government** can be defined as *the operation of the state by a particular group of people who have the authority to make decisions and supervise the allocation of resources.* Today, the legitimacy of the state is usually not questioned. Few people doubt that a single political authority should have the power to rule over a particular geographic territory. However, people do often question whether a certain government— meaning the group of people currently in power— should have the legitimate right to rule.

Sociological Perspectives on Political and Economic Institutions

You should be able to describe the insights of the functionalist and conflict perspectives regarding political and economic institutions.

Before describing the different types of political and economic systems that are found in societies, it is helpful to assess these institutions from both the functionalist and conflict perspectives.

The Functionalist Perspective

From the functionalist perspective, economic institutions accomplish an important task—they produce and distribute the goods and services that are essential to the survival of society. Economic systems provide all the food, clothing, and other material things that people need. Some economic systems do this better than others. Political institutions, such as states and governments, also perform important functions that are beneficial to the societies in which they emerge. First, the state provides a framework in which rules and norms of conduct are created, stability is encouraged, and social order is enhanced. In less complex societies, decision making is based on consensus, and norms are enforced through informal sanctions. More complex societies have far too many people with differing interests for such techniques to be effective. The citizenry grants the state and governmental institutions the authority to make policy choices and to create laws that are binding on everyone. In addition, people recognize the government's authority to apply sanctions against those who disobey established rules and regulations.

A second function of the state is to establish a setting in which individuals and groups can bargain with one another to resolve conflicts. Thus the government makes rules and then serves as a kind of mediator between different parties or interest groups in society, and it also has the power to render decisions that tell each party what it may and may not do. In performing this function, government helps society direct itself and look ahead to the future.

Third, the state has considerable responsibility for maintaining a stable economy. It does so by ensuring that social conditions are conducive to the smooth operation of the economy. Governments, for example, often build railroads and highways to ensure transportation of economic goods. Political policies are also used to control inflation and employment. And the government subsidizes the training of people in certain fields to ensure an adequate supply of labor.

Finally, the state protects society from external threats. A society's government also assists in relationships with other countries. This assistance is sometimes diplomatic, as when the United States acts as mediator for crises in the Middle East, and sometimes economic, as when the United States sends foreign aid to other nations as a way of maintaining friendly relations.

The function of political and economic institutions, then, is to make organized social life possible in societies that are large and complex. Without these institutions, according to the functionalist perspective, life would be chaotic and virtually impossible.

The Conflict Perspective

Unlike the functionalists, who argue that political and economic institutions emerge out of societal need, conflict theorists maintain that these structures are ultimately designed to benefit dominant groups. The French philosopher Jean Jacques Rousseau (1762/1950), writing during the 1700s, provided an early, conflict-oriented explanation of how state and government were born: "The first man who, having enclosed a piece of ground, bethought himself of saying, 'This is mine,' and found people simple enough to believe him, was the real founder of civil society." In other words, the state is merely a *social contract* that is designed to maintain order. But, Rousseau argued, not all citizens benefit equally from this contract; rather, the wealthy gain the most advantage from protecting the status quo.

More recently, Karl Marx (1848/1964) argued that economic institutions play a key role in shaping all other institutions. In his view, political institutions, including the state, are created by members of the ruling class in society to protect their economic position. Marx declared, "The history of all hitherto existing societies is the history of class struggle." This class struggle involves two groups, one of which dominates and the other of which is exploited. Political, religious, educational, and other institutions are designed to pro-

tect the privileged position of the ruling class by maintaining existing economic institutions.

There is undoubtedly much truth to Marx's argument that the state serves the interests of the powerful. However, we also need to recognize that political and economic institutions are necessary at the same time for other reasons, in particular to fulfill the functions pointed out in the discussion of the functionalist approach. Without some central authority, large and complex societies could not survive. Once these social institutions come into existence to serve these functions, however, they become a prize that benefits any group that can gain control of them. In fact, a major issue that sociologists research is the extent to which political and economic institutions in a particular society serve the interests of a small group of people or provide benefits to many groups, both powerful and otherwise. This question will be addressed shortly with regard to U.S. society. First, however, it is necessary to compare some of the different types of political and economic institutions that can be found in various societies.

Types of Government

You should be able to explain the different forms of government and discuss the prerequisites for democracy and the factors influencing political participation in democratic societies.

Governments in modern societies can take a number of different forms. One simple way to distinguish among them is to separate nondemocratic governments, especially oligarchy and totalitarianism, from democratic ones.

Oligarchy and Totalitarianism

In his discussion of the "iron law of oligarchy," Robert Michels (1915/1966) argued that whenever groups reach a size where consensus-oriented decision making is no longer workable, oligarchy is likely to develop. **Oligarchy,** as noted in Chapter 4, means *rule by a small number of people in which other group members take little part in making decisions.* Power becomes concentrated in the hands of what Michels referred to as *expert leaders.* There are several reasons why oligarchies emerge. First, oligarchy provides a predictable and efficient system of leadership, which could become unruly if too many people were involved. Second, many people are apathetic. They are not really concerned about who rules them and have no particular motivation to take power themselves. Third, most people have neither the time nor the resources to work toward gaining political control. Given these tendencies, it is not surprising that oligarchy is a common form of government. As will be shown, there are even those who argue that the United States is in reality governed by a relatively small, elite group of political and economic leaders who are largely impervious to the wishes of the majority.

A special form of oligarchy is **totalitarianism.** In this type of government, *all the familiar social institutions, such as the economy, education, and to some extent the family and religion, are under total state control.* Citizens are expected to pay allegiance to only one political regime, which dominates every aspect of social life. Some totalitarian regimes are *dictatorships,* in which a single individual is at the pinnacle of power. The classic example of this type of regime in recent times was Adolf Hitler's Nazi Germany.

Democracy

An absolutely pure democracy has never really existed, for in such a government, every citizen would be able to participate in *every* decision relevant to society. Not only would such a situation be unwieldly, but also people would have time for little else in their lives. The governments that come closest to this democratic ideal are probably those of the early Greek city-states. In fact, the term *democracy* is derived from a Greek term that implies "the people rule." But even there, certain categories of people did not participate in the governmental process, including women and slaves. Taking these practical realities into account, Seymour Martin Lipset (1959) has defined **democracy** as "*a political system which supplies regular constitutional opportunities for changing the governing officials, and a social mechanism which permits the largest possible part of the population to influence major decisions by choosing among contenders for political office*" (p. 27).

In a democracy, political authority is created by the consent of the governed, and this consent serves as a source of legitimacy for the government. Democracies are usually *representative* governments in which citizens choose the rulers through a competitive election process. These representatives need to be sensitive to citizen sentiment, for if they do not represent their constituencies, they will probably fail to be reelected. Certain guaranteed rights, such as freedom of speech, are provided to every citizen in a democracy. Such public liberties are spelled out in documents such as the U.S. Bill of Rights and cannot be arbitrarily removed by the government. Certainly, the rights of some people are violated in a democracy, but checks and balances ensure that these violations are minimized. If people believe that their freedom of speech has been violated, for example, they can file suit against the government.

Social Conditions for Democracy   Democratic governments do not thrive everywhere. In fact, stable, long-term democracies are relatively rare, being limited largely to advanced industrial societies. Why is this true? There appear to be certain social conditions important to the survival of democracies (Lipset, 1959; Neubauer, 1967; Segal, 1974). First, democracy is closely associated with economic development—more developed economies are more likely to have stable democratic governments. The reason for this connection is probably that developed societies have a well-educated citizenry whose members want to participate in the political process. Such societies also have an entrenched middle class with a stake in maintaining the social order.

Second, stable democracies usually have a system of checks and balances, which keeps the state open to criticism and suggestions for improvements. For example, in the United States, both the President and the Congress have veto power over each other, which ultimately leads to political issues being examined and exposed to considerable scrutiny. Another example is the fact that democratic governments remain open to criticism by the press.

Third, stable democracies are more likely to emerge in societies where people have loyalties to many different groups rather than societies in which there are major social cleavages. These many loyalties prevent society from becoming polarized into a few homogeneous, hostile groups. People may side with a particular group on some issues but oppose that same group on other issues. For example, in the United States, many affluent and well-educated people have favored environmental legislation that was opposed by other affluent, well-educated people in the business community. At the same time, many working class and poor people have sided with the business people in opposing environmental legislation that they viewed as a threat to their jobs.

Fourth, stable democracies are likely to exist when the citizenry is well informed about political practices, and where people share common values about the legitimacy of the governmental system. For example, in the United States, groups tend to believe that their interests will not be ignored even if their political representatives have lost an election. When people know what is going on within their government, a general feeling of trust is promoted. By the same token, when the public learns that their supposedly democratic government is denying them access to information, they may come to distrust government, and the legitimacy accorded it may decline.

Finally, stable democracies are more likely to exist when economic and social systems are viewed as effective. Effectiveness enhances the legitimacy accorded to the political system. When high rates of inflation, high unemployment, or other threatening disruptions exist, people are more likely to question whether the existing political institutions are proper and appropriate.

Political Participation in Democracies Citizens of the United States have a democratic right to participate in the political process, but how many take advantage of that right? In reality, a relatively small number do. Despite the central importance of voting to a democracy, the rate at which people in the United States vote is low and has been declining. As Figure 13.1 shows, in the presidential elections from 1976 (Carter versus Ford) to 1996 (Clinton versus Dole), only slightly more than half the people of voting age voted. The turnout in 1988 (Bush versus Dukakis) and 1996 were the lowest in more than fifty years, although the rate improved a little in 1992.

In years when there is no presidential election, the picture is even more disturbing, as Figure 13.2 shows. In the last two decades of off-year elections for the House of Representatives, only about one-third of the people of voting age voted; since 1934, no off-year election has produced more than a 45

FIGURE 13.1 Participation in U.S. Presidential Elections, 1932–1996 *Note:* From *Statistical Abstract of the United States, 1995* (p. 290) by U.S. Bureau of the Census, 1995, Washington, DC: U.S. Government Printing Office.

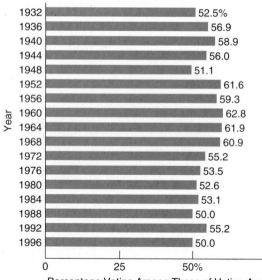

FIGURE 13.2 Participation in Elections to the U.S. House of Representatives in Years with No Presidential Election, 1934–1994 *Note:* From *Statistical Abstract of the United States, 1995* (p. 290) by U.S. Bureau of the Census, 1995, Washington, DC: U.S. Government Printing Office.

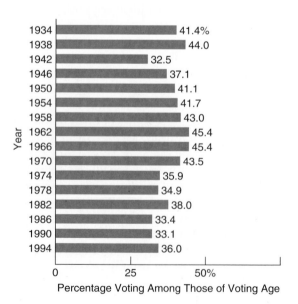

percent voter turnout. Still fewer people vote in most state and local elections. Moreover, there has been a steady decline in voter participation since the 1960s. In fact, the United States ranks last in voter turnout among the world's major democracies, where 70 to 80 percent of the eligible voters participate in national elections (Piven & Cloward, 1988; Teixeira, 1992).

Why do so few people in the United States exercise their democratic right to vote? One factor is electoral barriers that discourage people from voting. For example, voter registration laws in many states are quite restrictive, requiring people to register long before election day. In addition, people often have to travel long distances to the registration office and wait in line for long periods of time. Some other democracies have automatic registration systems; Canada sends registration officials door to door to make sure everyone is registered to vote. According to the political scientist Steven Rosenstone, "Modified registration laws would increase overall voter turnout by about 9 percent. . . . Blacks, Hispanics, and the poor would benefit the most from the changes" ("U-M Political Scientist," 1988, p. 8). Beyond these registration barriers, voter turnout is low because many people fail to see any major differences between candidates or political parties and thus see no point in voting. In addition, many people lack a sense of political efficacy: the feeling that their actions, including voting, have an impact on what politicians or the government actually does.

Who votes and who does not in the United States? Generally, the well-to-do are most likely to vote, and the dispossessed are least likely to do so (Wolfinger & Rosenstone, 1980). Voting rates increase among those with higher incomes, higher levels of education, and more prestigious occupations. The reason is that these people probably think they have more of a stake in who wins an election. They also probably think that their voting will make a difference and thus is worth the time and effort. In addition, the better educated and more affluent are more likely to be informed about the issues in a campaign (see Figure 13.3).

Voting rates also increase as people get older. Considerably less than one-half of the people under twenty-five who are eligible to vote actually do so in presidential elections. Many young people do not feel strong ties to a community, in part

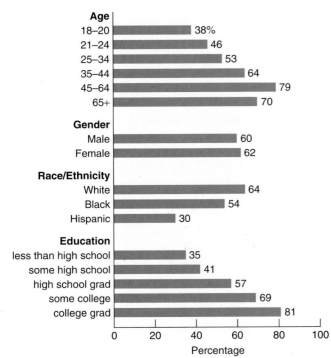

FIGURE 13.3 Percentage of Registered Voters in the United States Who Reported That They Actually Voted, 1992, by Age, Gender, Race/Ethnicity, and Education *Note: From Statistical Abstract of the United States, 1995* (p. 289) by U.S. Bureau of the Census, 1995, Washington, DC: U.S. Government Printing Office.

because they have yet to establish families and careers. They may not feel that expressing their preferences through voting is necessary or will gain them anything. As marital and occupational ties are established, people tend to feel more of a stake in their community, and voting rates increase. Political party preference is also affected by social factors, as mentioned in Chapter 11. Those who vote Republican are likely to be affluent, Protestant, and rural, whereas Democratic voters are more likely to be working class, Catholic, and urban. There are certainly exceptions to this likelihood, but these relationships point to the fact that the Republicans tend to be the party of the privileged, whereas the Democrats represent the "common people."

Gender also influences political participation (U.S. Bureau of the Census, 1995). Women are slightly more likely to register to vote and to vote than men are. In addition, research documents the existence of a gender gap in voting behavior, with women favoring Democratic candidates and men favoring Republican candidates. Women are more likely to identify themselves as Democrats than men are, and in presidential elections more women vote for the Democratic nominees than men do. In 1992 just before the election, for example, 48 percent of the female voters, compared to only 39 percent of male voters, expressed a preference for Bill Clinton (Hugick, 1992a). This gender gap is probably attributable to the fact that the Democratic party has traditionally been more supportive of issues that directly affect women, such as the right to an abortion and equal employment and educational opportunities for women.

Types of Economic Systems

You should be able to describe the basic principles of capitalist, socialist, and mixed economies.

To survive, every society must ensure that food, clothing, shelter, and other materials are produced and distributed to the members of society who need them. The rules and social practices that govern this production and distribution make up the economic institutions of a society. Economic institutions can take many different forms. For example, in some societies such as the

Tiv, discussed earlier, every member has a right to a share of societal resources, including food, shelter, and clothing. Everyone is expected to work, and those who do not may be ridiculed and even ostracized. In turn, anyone who produces a surplus of food or anything else is under strong normative pressure to share it with others. No money changes hands, and the idea of paying for food and shelter would not occur to anyone. This form of reciprocal exchange is quite different from the economies of modern nations. Most nations today have a *market economy,* which is based on the exchange of money for goods and services in the marketplace. People sell their labor for a certain amount of money, and then the money is used to purchase goods and services. Although modern economies share this market foundation, they differ from one another in significant ways. This chapter will look at three main types of modern economic systems: capitalism, socialism, and mixed economies.

Capitalism

Capitalism contains three features that, taken together, distinguish it from other economic systems: *the means of economic production and distribution are privately held, the profit motive is the primary force guiding people's economic behavior, and there is free competition among both producers and consumers of goods* (Gottlieb, 1988). The proponents of capitalism argue that these features provide for consumer control over the quantity, quality, and price of goods. In its pure form, capitalism works like this. Seeking profits is, in a sense, merely unleashing personal greed. But that is quite appropriate, argue proponents of capitalism, because the possibility of profit gives capitalists the motivation to provide more and better goods and services. If a demand exists for some product, someone will come along and provide it if he or she can profit from doing so. Furthermore, the profit motive encourages innovation and creativity because entrepreneurs will look for novel goods and services—some that the consumer has not even thought of—that they can sell for a profit. Capitalists must be constantly on the lookout for new products lest someone else beat them to the punch and corner a market. Thus, from this profit-seeking motive, consumers benefit from having more and better goods available. Open competition among capitalists also benefits consumers by enabling them to choose among a number of items, comparing price against quality. If the quality of products is too low or the price too high, people will not buy them and the capitalists will be out of business unless they change. Adam Smith referred to the conjunction of profit seeking with competition as the *invisible hand* of market forces that would ensure that the supply of goods is roughly equivalent to the demand for them and that the public has available the goods that it can afford with the highest quality possible.

The role of government in this process, argue those who favor pure capitalism, should be to stand aside and let market forces operate unhindered. The government is necessary to maintain public order and protect against foreign threats, but any effort by the government to regulate the market is regarded as disastrous. Government regulation of prices or wages, for example, would interfere with both the profit motive and the competitive element and thus reduce the incentive to develop new and better products. In short, government policy under capitalism should be one of laissez-faire: The government should leave the market alone.

There are no pure forms of capitalism in the world today. Even in the United States, the government has always been involved to a degree in controlling and regulating the economy. Toward the end of the nineteenth century, for example, the freewheeling economic environment was highly aggressive, with small competitors being eliminated by ever larger ones. Huge monopolies resulted in which one company dominated a given product field. Through legislation such as the Sherman Antitrust Act of 1890 and the Clayton Act of 1914, the government controlled the ability of companies to monopolize a market and ensured that there would be some competition.

The government has also worked to protect people against some of the ravages of open-ended competition. For example, the government provides price supports for many agricultural products, because otherwise a bountiful crop would bring intense competition among farmers, who might be forced to lower their prices below the point at which they could make a profit. The government also legislates minimum wages, establishes unemployment insurance, and arbitrates labor disputes. **Welfare capitalism** is the term for *economies* such as the United States *that combine a strongly competitive market and private property with some government regulation for the public good.*

Despite this government involvement in economic activity, the U.S. economy is one of the most capitalistic in the world. There is strong resistance to government interference in the economy and little support for government ownership of utilities, railroads, or other industries that are often government-owned in other capitalist societies. All capitalist economies are not identical, however, and Other Worlds, Other Ways: Japan (on pp. 450-451) points out how even competition, which is at the center of capitalism, can have different meanings in different capitalist economies.

Socialism

Socialism refers to *economies in which the means of production and distribution are collectively held so that the goods and services that people need are provided and equitably distributed.* In capitalism, production is based on *economic demand:* goods and services are provided if people can afford them. With socialism, production is based on *human need:* Goods and services are produced because people need them, irrespective of whether they can afford them (Harrington, 1989). Pure socialist economies reject the profit motive, recognizing that one person's profit is another's loss. In addition, socialists argue, the profit motive provides a built-in incentive for one person to exploit another, for example, by keeping wages low in order to increase profits. In fact, socialism emerged as a coherent ideology during the early stages of industrialization when workers' wages were exceedingly low, often barely enough to survive. People worked long hours under dangerous conditions with little hope of improving their lot. Although conditions in today's capitalist societies have improved, socialists still argue that capitalism sets one person in competition with another—either capitalist against capitalist or capitalist against consumer—and the inevitable outcome is a highly unjust and inequitable distribution of resources.

In socialist economies, the primary motivation for economic activity is to achieve collective goals, such as a higher standard of living for all citizens. To do so, the economy is highly centralized, with national authorities making decisions for the whole nation about what to produce and how to distribute these products. Because profit

OTHER WORLDS, *Other Ways*

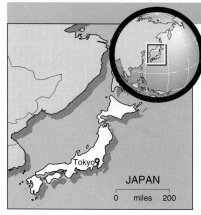

JAPAN: DIVERGENT CULTURAL CONCEPTIONS OF ECONOMIC ACTIVITY

This book has emphasized repeatedly that people tend to view their own perspective on things as the natural way to see things. A degree of ethnocentrism is involved here in that we accept our view as the only correct one. Ethnocentrism can lead to misunderstandings in international political and economic relations since different cultures attach various meanings to notions of appropriate economic markets and social welfare (Lanciaux, 1991). In the United States, the belief is widespread that competition in the marketplace and the individual pursuit of self-interest will produce the greatest good to the greatest number, and thus the markets will maximize social welfare. This belief is almost gospel with many people in the 1990s, and they also assume that other cultures with market economies have adopted these beliefs.

One need not look far, however, to see that nations with strong market economies can have quite different cultural belief systems. Probably the best example is Japan, which has one of the strongest market economies in the world. Yet, some Japanese cultural views on economic activities are in stark contrast to views commonly held in the United States (Fallows, 1994; Prestowitz, 1989). One of the sharpest differences has to do with competition. The United States sees competition in all its forms as good and assumes that unfettered competition is the major fuel that produces the benefits of capitalism. Chapters 3 and 4 noted that the Japanese place high value in *omoiyari,* or "harmony," in personal relationships, a value that produces some ambivalence toward competition. Although the Japanese recognize that competition can be beneficial, they believe it can also be dangerous and disruptive to social and economic stability. So, both in personal relationships and in national economic activities, the Japanese control competition. This distrust of competition has led Japanese industry to develop *keiretsu,* which are groups of businesses that agree to buy and sell goods to one another on a continuing basis without using competition to find the lowest bidder. The Japanese government encourages such cooperation as a way of protecting stable intercorporate relations. Instead of encouraging vigorous competition that would drive weaker companies out of business, the government encourages businesses to divide up markets so that all firms have a better chance to survive. *Keiretsu* relationships are personal and reciprocal, and they reduce costs and risks while enhancing communication and

and consumer demands are not key elements in these decisions, the decisions can presumably be made with the collective interests of society as a whole in mind. If national leaders decide that the country should strengthen its industrial base, for example, then heavy machinery and equipment will be produced, which might result in fewer consumer items, such as clothing or radios, being available. Because collective goals rather than profit govern production, unprofitable businesses might be kept running or prices for products kept lower than production costs in order to ensure their distribution.

As with capitalism, pure socialism is rare. Most socialist economies do allow for the private ownership of some goods, such as personal or household items. In addition, some people are allowed to engage in capitalist activity. In China, for example, farmers are allowed to sell some of their produce in a competitive marketplace. China is also experimenting with programs in some industries in which consumer demand, rather than central authorities, determines how much is produced. In these programs, factory managers can, within limits, manipulate wages and other costs in order to break even or make a profit. Most means

trust among industries (Harrison, 1994; Lincoln, Gerlach, & Ahmadjian, 1996). The government also assists struggling businesses so that they have a better chance to survive. Cooperation among business, workers, and government is extensive, harmonious, and of long standing in Japan; in the United States, business and labor see themselves as competitors, and government is mostly out of the picture.

The economist Lester Thurow (1992) argues that the unbridled emphasis on individualism, dog-eat-dog competition, and laissez-faire government in the United States is quite at variance with what is found in Japan:

> America and Britain trumpet individualistic values: the brilliant entrepreneur, Nobel Prize winners, large wage differentials, individual responsibility for skills, . . . profit maximization, and hostile mergers and takeovers—their hero is the Lone Ranger. In contrast, Germany and Japan trumpet communitarian values: business groups, social responsibility for skills, teamwork, firm loyalty, industry strategies, and active industrial policies that promote growth. (p. 32)

In Japan, the group, community, or business firm is much more at the center of identity and the focus of loyalty. The business offers lifetime employment, and employees respond with intense devotion to the company. Whereas a U.S. business would expect its employees to quit and go to another job that offers more money, Japanese firms still refer to such behavior as *treason*.

Thurow concludes that the United States could learn some important lessons from Japan and other capitalist market economies around the world:

1. The government should invest heavily in the economic infrastructure, such as roads, airports, and other facilities that businesses need to be competitive.
2. The government should provide capital and protection to some new industries that show promise and nurture them until they are better able to compete.
3. Industry should view labor as an essential resource to be nurtured rather than an adversary to be wary of; industry and government should fund job training and education so that the U.S. workforce is competitive.
4. People in the United States should drop their reverence for unfettered competition; as with so many aspects of social reality, competition can be both beneficial and harmful, and people need to recognize and encourage the beneficial aspects while protecting against negative consequences.

of economic production, however, are still collectively rather than privately owned.

At this point, a word needs to be said about communism, a term that is routinely misused in the United States. *Communism* is the term Karl Marx used to describe the utopian end stage of the struggle over capitalism. In a communist society, all goods would be communally owned; people would not work for wages but rather would give according to their abilities; and there would be no scarcity of goods and services, allowing people to receive whatever they needed. In addition, the state would become less important and its role would dwindle. According to these criteria, there are no communist societies in the world today. Nations that are commonly referred to as communist are actually socialist.

Mixed Economies

The economies discussed thus far tend toward pure capitalism or pure socialism, although each includes some elements of the other. Another type of economy, found in Sweden, Denmark, and a number of other Western European nations, is the **mixed** or **democratic socialist economy,** *in* *which there are strong elements of both capitalism and socialism* (Brus & Laski, 1989). In mixed economies, most industry is privately owned and oriented toward profit making. In addition, despite considerable government regulation, there is a competitive market economy, and consumer demand determines much of what is produced. However, in mixed economies, many important industries, such as banks, railroads, the communications industry, the media, and hospitals, are state owned. Mixed economies provide for strong regulation of the private sector by the state. High taxes and an elaborate welfare system are established in hopes of achieving the national goal of a fair and equitable distribution of resources. Through such mechanisms, proponents of mixed economies hope to avoid the extensive social inequality that can accompany capitalism and the economic inefficiency that sometimes afflicts socialist economies.

With this background on the various types of political and economic institutions found in societies, attention can now turn to sociological research on the workings of these institutions in modern societies. The first topic will be the distribution of political and economic power in the United States and whether such power is controlled by a small, oligarchical group.

Who Rules in the United States?

You should be able to explain the power elite and pluralist perspectives on power in the United States and assess the evidence for each one.

Analysis of the issue of who rules in the United States makes it abundantly clear that political and economic institutions are intertwined as sources of power and authority. Review of the two major models of power, the power elite model and the pluralist model, follow.

The Power Elite Model

In the 1950s, the sociologist C. Wright Mills (1956) proposed what has come to be called the **power elite model** to explain the exercise of power in the United States. Deriving his approach from the conflict perspective, Mills argued that *a small group of very powerful people make just about all the important decisions in the United States.* This power elite consists of the people who hold the top positions in the government, the economic realm, and the military. Included in this group are the President and the cabinet, the executives who run the large corporations, and the generals and admirals who run the Pentagon. According to Mills, the government, corporations, and the military dominate people's lives today, and it is from controlling them that power is derived. Other theorists argue that the power elite also includes the major media corporations that control publications such as *Time* and *Newsweek*, the major foundations (such as the Ford and Lilly foundations), and the presidents and trustees of the major private universities (such as Harvard and Yale) (Dye, 1995).

The people who make up the power elite, according to Mills, share certain social characteristics that set them apart from others in the United States. For example, they tend to come from affluent families that have been wealthy for at least two generations, families whose wealth in most cases far exceeds what the average person can ever expect to have. The elite is almost exclusively made up of white males whose parents were born in the United States. They come largely from urban areas and have attended the more prestigious colleges and universities, such as Princeton, Yale, Stanford, Dartmouth, and Harvard. Furthermore, their offspring attend the same private schools and universities, where social contacts are forged that will later prove beneficial in establishing their own positions among the elite. When these young members of the power elite graduate, their careers and lifestyles will be similar and will crisscross throughout their lifetime. Finally, the informal social ties of power elite, such as what parties they attend or where they go for vacation, tend to reinforce their dominant positions. The Bohemian Grove, for example, is a vacation retreat in California, but it is also a place where the powerful can develop or nurture acquaintances that will later prove helpful in landing a contract or passing a piece of legislation.

According to Mills, the power elite is a cohesive group, and the interests of its various members in the government, corporate, and military sectors tend to coincide. Below the elite, there is a middle level of diverse interest groups that includes most members of Congress, professional organizations, many lobbyists, and most unions. Members of these groups participate in making decisions about issues of secondary importance that have little effect on the elite. At the bottom is the great mass of citizens who have virtually no power because they do not belong to organizations that wield power. They may vote, but Mills viewed this privilege as meaningless because most elected officials are only in middle-level positions, whereas real decision-making power rests with the elite. In addition, the power elite is highly influential in determining which candidates the political parties will place before the electorate.

The Pluralist Model

Some sociologists argue that Mills's view is distorted and overly conspiratorial because there is actually little concentration of power and coincidence of interests among the elite (Kornhauser, 1966). Instead, the **pluralist model** views power as *pluralistic, or spread over a large number of groups with divergent values, interests, and goals.* According to David Riesman (1961), society contains veto groups with the ability to block decisions that might adversely affect their positions. For example, labor unions can exert considerable influence on issues affecting their members, such as raising unemployment benefits or minimum wage laws. Similarly, farmers may fight to stop the lowering of price supports for farm products. To be sure, pluralists recognize that some groups have far more power and other resources than do other groups, and there is considerable inequity in society. However, they argue that there is no single, cohesive, dominant elite, and power is not centralized in the hands of a few.

Below the elite, according to the pluralists, is the unorganized, but not entirely powerless, public (Rose, 1967). With the vote, the public can exercise some constraint over the behavior of those in power. In addition, the public has other ways to exert influence. Cesar Chavez, for example, harnessed this power in the 1960s in his attempt to improve the plight of migrant farm workers. He organized a consumer boycott of the lettuce and grapes grown by those farm owners who refused to negotiate with the farm workers. This boycott was effective, and the sales of lettuce and grapes dwindled. In part because of this effort, the farmers ultimately negotiated. The environmental movement has also used its ability to organize large numbers of people for public protest as a tool in struggling against corporate power. Especially in the areas of air pollution and the use of pesticides,

these groups have organized seemingly powerless people to shape public policy successfully (Hoberg, 1992). Given these examples, pluralists dispute the power elite view and argue that the mass of the citizenry can effectively exert an influence, even against what seem to be formidable corporate foes.

Assessment of the Models

What is one to conclude regarding who rules in the United States? Clearly, the realities of holding power in this society are more complex than either the power elite or the pluralist models alone suggest. For example, the political scientist Thomas R. Dye (1995) reviewed the corporate and governmental sectors in the United States and located approximately seven thousand positions in corporations, the government, and the military that direct most of the nation's economic and social policy. According to Dye, this very small group of people represent Mills's power elite. The sociologist G. William Domhoff (1967/1983) went a step further by studying the social backgrounds of the people who occupy these elite positions. He discovered that members of the upper class participate in an elaborate network of informal social contacts, just as Mills suggested. However, Domhoff did not find the cohesiveness or coincidence of interests among these people that Mills implied. Nevertheless, there are significant linkages and influence peddling among the various sectors of the power elite. Members of the corporate elite, for example, make sizable contributions to both the Republican and Democratic parties in hopes of influencing the decisions of the President, congressional representatives, and other politicians. In fact, some would argue that, because of political contributions, corporate lobbying, and other forms of influence, the corporate elite exercises overwhelming control over politicians, government regulatory agencies, and government bureaucrats who are supposed to be controlling the corporations and protecting the rights and interests of the average person. In this view, the average citizen has little influence and is largely at the mercy of corporate goals (Greider, 1992).

Research on the power elite has also focused on links between business and the military. In his final speech before leaving office in 1961, former President Dwight D. Eisenhower, himself a five-star general during World War II, warned of the dangers posed by a **military-industrial complex,** referring to *the relationship between the military that wants to purchase weapons and the corporations that produce the weapons.* Both the military and the corporations benefit from a large military budget and from policies favoring military solutions to international problems. The potential danger of a powerful military-industrial complex is that defense decisions and the development of weapons systems may be influenced by what is beneficial to the military and defense industries rather than by what is necessary for national security. One way in which the coincidence of interests among members of the military-industrial complex might occur is if there were a periodic interchange of top-level personnel between the military and defense industries. And, as Mills and others have shown, such interchanges do tend to occur. During a three-year period in the 1970s, for example, more than two thousand high-ranking defense department officials left their government jobs and accepted positions with corporate defense contractors (Edwards, 1977). A more recent study by the government found that six thousand of the thirty thousand people with the rank of army major or higher who left the Pentagon in 1983 and 1984 worked for companies doing business with the Pentagon. Many worked on the same military projects in private industry that they had worked on at the Pentagon (Cushman, 1986). When corporations hire former government officials, they hope that their contacts and knowledge of government and the policy process will work to the benefit of the corporation.

Although there clearly are important links between the military and corporations suggesting a military-industrial complex, the picture is considerably more complicated. Many corporations actually oppose increases in defense spending, fearing that these will adversely affect the economy and result in higher taxes. One study, for example, found active opposition to increases in defense spending between 1948 and 1953—a period including the Korean War—among executives of some of the largest business, industrial, and financial corporations in the country, even among some firms with defense contracts (Lo, 1982). So the military-industrial complex, although important, does not exist in a vacuum. There are other powerful groups, even among the

power elite, with competing interests, and there are less powerful groups that still wield considerable power, especially on domestic issues.

In short, both the power elite and pluralist models offer significant insight into the question of who rules the United States. As the power elite model suggests, a relatively small number of people hold enormous power. They control much of foreign policy and make decisions that shape the direction of economic development. This ruling group, although possibly not conspiratorial or completely cohesive, ranks far above most other citizens in political, economic, and social clout. Yet as the pluralist position suggests, many groups that are not a part of this elite can occasionally wield power, especially on domestic social policy and local and regional issues. This is the realm in which many of the battles over solutions to social problems addressed by sociologists are likely to be fought. And most people in the United States have an opportunity to play a part in these less powerful, but still quite important, groups.

The U.S. Economy: Concentration and Change

You should be able to describe recent trends in the U.S. economy and discuss the problems they have created.

Capitalism in the United States has undergone considerable change in the past two centuries. This chapter will focus on three central issues: the rise of corporations, the changing labor force, and the globalization of the labor force.

The Corporate Economy

Capitalism in the United States once consisted of small, local businesses and many competitors. Consequently, power in the economic sector was decentralized, diffused, and limited to local or regional levels. It was almost impossible for businesses to accumulate substantial power at the national level. Today, the economy is very different: it is highly centralized and international in scope, and a small number of people can gain enormous control over wealth and power.

Corporate Growth and Concentration Capitalism in the United States is no longer based on the individual ownership of businesses. Rather, the dominant form of business today is the **corporation,** *a business enterprise that is owned by stockholders, most of whom are not involved in running the daily affairs of the business.* Three key characteristics distinguish corporations from individually owned businesses. First, corporations have access to a much broader source of capital than do individuals because the former can sell stock to thousands of stockholders. Second, stockholders, who own the corporation, have only a limited liability should the corporation be sued or go bankrupt. Stockholders lose only the funds they have invested. Third, the ownership of corporations is separate from the control of its policies and daily affairs. The stockholders own a part of the corporation, but most stockholders are not involved in the actual running of the company. It is run by professional managers who are ultimately appointed by a board of directors that is elected by stockholders. These managers typically own little or no stock in the company. Legally, the stockholders run the corporation, but for all practical purposes the board and the managers do. Most shareholders own only a small number of shares in the company, and they have neither the time, the expertise, nor the inclination to pay much attention to how the company is run. The board and the managers are in a position to make recommendations that most shareholders will accept with little thought. So the board and corporate managers control the corporation without being substantial owners of it. Unlike in individually owned businesses, the ownership of corporations is easily transferable, and should a major stockholder die, the corporation continues to function as usual. Because of these characteristics, the corporate economic structure is extremely attractive to investors. Large amounts of capital can be accumulated with minimum risk to individuals.

Because of the advantages that stem from corporate organization, corporations now dominate the economy, with a relatively small number of corporations accounting for most business activity. There are more than three million corporations in the United States, but most are small and have a minor impact on society. Economic resources, and thus influence and power, tend to be concentrated in the larger corporations. For example, the largest two hundred corporations employ 80 percent of all people who work for corporations. Of all the assets held by industrial corporations in the United States, 75 percent of those assets are held by the largest one hundred of those corporations (U.S. Bureau of the Census, 1995, p. 563). As these large corporations have come to dominate the economy, it has become possible for some to control substantial segments of economic life to the point of restricting competition in the marketplace.

One form of restrictive growth is called a *monopoly*—the control of a product or service by one company. For example, in the early 1990s, Nintendo controlled about 80 percent of the $5 billion video-game market in the United States. Related to the monopoly is the *oligopoly,* in which a few corporations control a market. Some sectors of the U.S. economy are highly oligopolistic, in some cases approaching a monopoly. In the cigarette industry, for example, the four largest corporations control close to 90 percent of production. In a 1980s court case, the American Telephone and Telegraph Company was forced to divest those companies that were providing local telephone service. The government has also filed suit against IBM and the four largest producers of breakfast cereals for monopolizing their markets. Chapter 12 discusses the emergence of media oligopolies on a global scale in the past few decades.

Another form of corporate growth representing a concentration of economic power is the *conglomerate,* which is a corporation that owns other companies in fields quite different from that of the parent company. For example, through mergers in the 1990s, Time Warner became the owner of many cable television franchises and channels (including HBO, Cinemax, CNN, and TBS Superstation), many book publishers (including Time-Life Books, Warner Books, and the Book-of-the-Month Club), Warner Brothers Movie Studios, at least twenty-five magazines (including *Time, People,* and *Sports Illustrated*), the Atlanta Braves, the Atlanta Hawks, and numerous other corporations. In fact, some corporations are in good part holding companies whose major purpose is to coordinate the activities and profits of all the corporations they own. Conglomerates are advantageous in that they provide stability through diversity: Losses in one industry can be counterbalanced by the parent company through profits made in an unrelated business.

Multinational and Global Corporations As corporations have grown over the decades, the larger ones have extended their activities into a number of different countries (Barnet & Cavanaugh, 1994). By the 1970s, *multinational corporations* had emerged, which made a large commitment of resources to international business and engaged in manufacturing, production, and sales in a number of countries. These overseas corporate activities tended to involve separate operations in the various countries, often tailored to local social and economic conditions. By the 1990s, *global corporations* had become the prominent actors on the world scene: A few hundred corporations whose economic activities span the globe, using modern financial, industrial, and telecommunications technology to mount a worldwide, integrated system of production and distribution. Corporations have gone multinational, and then global, because enormous profits can be made with such an organization. There are lucrative markets for their goods outside the United States. In addition, the cost of labor, land, and taxes is considerably lower in places such as Mexico, Taiwan, and Korea than in the United States. In 1988, 8 percent of all money spent for plants and equipment by corporations headquartered in the United States was spent outside the country; this percentage has been growing steadily for a number of years (Uchitelle, 1989). This fact reflects the extent to which U.S. corporations now participate in a global economy, in which national boundaries have become less important as determinants of or restraints on economic competition. As a result, labor and capital in the United States must compete with labor and capital in many countries around the world.

The concentration of economic power and the growth of global corporations raises the question of whether corporations pursue goals that are broadly beneficial to society or goals that enhance the narrow interests of particular groups. Large corporations control such vast resources that their activities shape in substantial ways the lives of average people in the United States. With their primary goal being to make and increase profits and to ensure corporate growth, corporations may not necessarily act in the best interests of other groups

or society as a whole. For example, when a corporation decides to relocate outside a central city area to reduce its taxes, the city loses jobs and tax revenue; these losses can bring about increases in unemployment and poverty in the city. This issue has become especially poignant in the last few decades. In fact, a major element of the recession in the early 1980s and the weak economy of the early 1990s was the flight of U.S. jobs overseas. Such job movement illustrates one of the major problems created by multinational and global corporations: Because their primary intent is to maximize profits, their actions can run counter to national political and economic goals. For example, the president of NCR Corporation, when asked about the competitiveness of the United States, responded, "I don't think about it at all. We at NCR think of ourselves as a globally competitive company that happens to be headquartered in the United States" (quoted in Uchitelle, 1989, p. 13). The chairman of President Reagan's Council of Economic Advisors, reacting to comments such as these, saw a "growing tension between the global nature of American business and the goals of the territorial United States" (quoted in Uchitelle, 1989, p. 13). However, others argue that at least some of this drain of U.S. productive dollars is offset by foreign corporations that pump money into their U.S. operations, which creates jobs here.

The Changing Labor Force

Although conglomerates and multinationals, along with capitalists and entrepreneurs, play important roles in creating and running large business concerns, they are far overshadowed in number by the masses of working people who staff these organizations. And workers have made significant efforts to concentrate economic power in their own hands. The rudiments of labor organizing can be traced to the colonial period in the United States, when impressment, or enforced labor, led to rioting among sailors and longshoremen. It was not until the late nineteenth century, however, and the emergence of business firms employing thousands of workers, that the labor movement emerged as a significant political force in the U.S. economy. Capitalists, pursuing the profit motive, were inclined to pay workers as little as possible. The capitalists could do so more easily because large numbers of people had immigrated to the United States in the late 1800s, creating a labor surplus in some industries. In response, working people organized to pursue their own interests. Capitalists staunchly opposed the labor movement, believing that higher wages would generate laziness among workers and threaten the American way of life.

The owners' resistance and the workers' determination made U.S. labor history one of the bloodiest and most violent of any industrial nation. In Lattimer, Pennsylvania, in 1897, for example, thirteen striking coal miners were shot to death and another thirty-nine were wounded by a sheriff's posse who stopped their march. In 1913, seventy-four people, including eleven children and two women, were killed in a clash between National Guard troops and strikers in Colorado (Novak, 1978; Taft & Ross, 1969). There were hundreds of other such incidents. However, the workers eventually prevailed, and by the 1930s legislation gave them the right to organize and to bargain collectively with employers.

The number of workers belonging to labor unions continued to grow, reaching more than 22 million in the 1970s. With the right to strike firmly established for most workers, unions have been in a strong position to gain even higher wages and larger fringe benefit packages for their members. In recent decades, public employees such as teach-

ers and fire fighters have proved to be a significant source of recruitment to the ranks of unionization, despite the fact that it is illegal in many states for public employees to strike. In fact, some teachers have been fired for joining illegal strikes.

Although unions have gained considerable power in the United States, their future is somewhat uncertain. Union membership as a proportion of the workforce has been declining since the 1950s and is presently at its lowest point since 1940 (see Figure 13.4). The number of people belonging to unions has declined to fewer than 17 million. The primary reason is that occupations traditionally unionized—blue-collar industrial jobs—have been declining in numbers whereas the number of white-collar employees, who have traditionally not unionized, is growing. In fact, sometimes the United States is called a postindustrial society because a shrinking proportion of the workforce labors in industrial occupations. Because of automation, robotization, and other technology, fewer workers are needed to make the products necessary for the U.S. lifestyle (see Chapter 15). The largest growth in the workforce has been in white-collar jobs such as sales, management, teaching, or clerical work (see Figure 13.5). A second reason for the decline in unions is that many corporations over the past four decades have relocated in states having weak

FIGURE 13.4 Union Membership in the United States as a Percentage of Total People Employed, 1950–1995 Note: From *Statistical Abstract of the United States, 1984* (p. 439) by U.S. Bureau of the Census, 1983, Washington, DC: U.S. Government Printing Office; *Employment and Earnings* by U.S. Department of Labor, Bureau of Labor Statistics, various years.

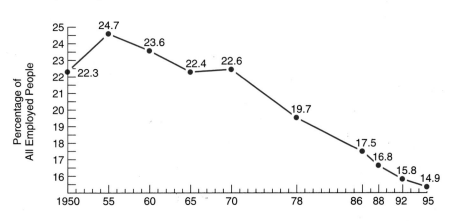

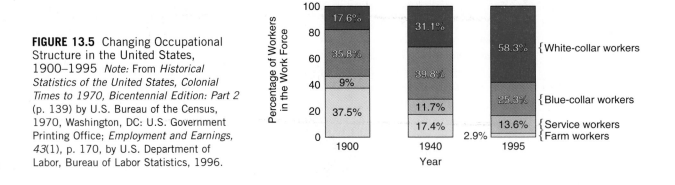

FIGURE 13.5 Changing Occupational Structure in the United States, 1900–1995 *Note:* From *Historical Statistics of the United States, Colonial Times to 1970, Bicentennial Edition: Part 2* (p. 139) by U.S. Bureau of the Census, 1970, Washington, DC: U.S. Government Printing Office; *Employment and Earnings, 43*(1), p. 170, by U.S. Department of Labor, Bureau of Labor Statistics, 1996.

union organizations or have moved overseas where unions are either weak or nonexistent. This latter trend reflects the maturing of a global economy, and its effect on workers will be so substantial in the foreseeable future that an extended discussion of it is appropriate.

Global Competition: Worker Dislocation and Unemployment

Over the past forty years, the percentage of people in the United States who are unemployed has been gradually increasing. In the 1950s, the unemployment rate rarely crept above 5 percent, whereas in the 1980s and 1990s it has not fallen below 5 percent. Further, these official unemployment statistics do not include people who are unemployed but have quit looking for a job—so-called discouraged workers. They also do not include those who are underemployed, working part-time, or working at a temporary job that does not pay enough to support a family. When these people are counted, the unemployment problem in the United States is even more grave than the official statistics suggest. Teenagers, African Americans, and other minorities are most heavily affected by this problem.

One of the reasons for this persistent unemployment in the United States is the trends in the world economic system described in Chapter 6 and elsewhere in this chapter. Factories in the United States have closed and moved overseas or contracted with manufacturers in other countries. Countries in Latin America and Asia have been especially receptive to U.S. businesses. The minimum wage in the United States is more than six dollars per hour, and well-paid workers on automobile assembly lines can earn $24 per hour.

By contrast, global sportswear companies headquartered in the United States pay young girls and women in Indonesia *$1.35 per day* to assemble sports shoes for export to the United States (Barnet & Cavanagh, 1994). Hundreds of U.S. companies have left the United States and opened up shop in *maquiladoras* factories in Mexico that take advantage of cheap labor, weak unions, and lax environmental regulations to assemble products and export them to the United States. Many thousands of U.S. jobs have been lost to these *maquiladoras*, which offer the best of both worlds to U.S. companies—cheap labor and easy access to U.S. markets to sell their products (see Other Worlds, Other Ways: Mexico in Chapter 8).

Workers who lose their jobs to such foreign competition, sometimes called *displaced workers,* numbered more than five million between 1987 and 1994 (Aronowitz & DiFazio, 1994; U.S. Bureau of the Census, 1995, p. 419). These workers are often well educated and highly skilled, and belong to groups with traditionally low levels of unemployment. These factors have led some to assume that these same unemployed people would quickly find jobs comparable to the ones they had lost. Research investigations show otherwise, however, suggesting that these unemployed are clear victims of the world economic system (Devins, 1986; Zippay, 1991). Some of these displaced workers never return to the labor force. Those who do find themselves unemployed for some time—one and a half years, on average—almost all experience a permanent decline in family income because of their job loss. Many are forced to accept irregular work at low-paying jobs with few fringe benefits. In addition, African Americans and Hispanic Americans are hit much harder by job displacement than are whites: These groups are more likely to

These women are working in a *maquiladora* in Mexico. Such factories often drain jobs out of the United States and exploit workers in Mexico through low wages, long hours, and poor working conditions.

be displaced, are jobless for longer, and are much less likely to be reemployed (Boisjoly & Duncan, 1994; Kletzer, 1991).

One disturbing trend during recent economic downturns has been a shift in the characteristics of the long-term unemployed in the United States; they are considerably more likely to be between the ages of 30 and 55 than in the past (Ilg, 1994). These workers are in the middle of their working lives and often have considerable work experience and skills. Still, they find themselves out of work and facing substantial difficulties finding another job. In the past, these long-term unemployed were more likely to be younger people who had fewer job skills and less experience. This trend shows that today's unemployment problem is due more to the unavailability of jobs than to a dearth of job skills among those seeking work.

Whereas world competition is probably the major factor in the growth in unemployment in the United States, other factors contribute. There has been considerable growth in the teenage labor market, and the number of women joining the workforce has grown over the decades. In addition, automation has replaced human workers with machines.

Unemployment, as tragic as it may be, is not the only consequence of competition between workers in the United States and overseas. It also means that the jobs available to workers in the United States may not pay as well as they did in the past. In fact, by 1990, more full-time workers had low-paying jobs than in earlier decades (U.S. Bureau of the Census, 1992). In 1964, 24 percent of full-time workers had poverty-level incomes. By 1979, this figure had dropped to 12 percent. However, it climbed steadily through the 1980s until, by 1990, 18 percent of full-time workers had incomes that would not bring their families out of poverty. Apparently, although new jobs were created during the 1980s, the jobs tended to be at the low end of the pay scale. So, even when the economy provides work, that work is less likely to pay enough to support a family. Lower pay does not mean, however, that these workers are living in poverty; instead, it means that someone else in the family, such as a spouse, has to work in order to bring the family's income above the poverty level.

With advanced industrial capitalism and a global economy, then, the situation of workers has changed, and the relative power of workers and employers seems to have shifted toward the latter (Harrison, 1994). Although labor unions still provide some workers with important protections against low wages or job loss, unions have become a less effective counterbalance to the substantial power of corporations.

Whereas predicting the ultimate outcome of these changes is difficult, a number of trends are emerging that may influence labor relations of the future. One is that labor unions may globalize by encouraging union organizing among workers overseas. Unions in the United States, for example, are helping workers organize unions in Mexico, South Africa, and other nations. If pay and working conditions in these other nations rise, then those workers will pose less of a threat to the jobs of workers in the United States (Cavanagh & Broad, 1996).

A second trend has been for workers to protect their interests through *worker empowerment*—workers gaining management authority and control. In some cases, empowerment has involved workers gaining partial ownership in a company and having a stake in how it is run and in the consequences of their own work performance. Today, ten thousand U.S. firms with eleven million employees have some form of employee ownership (Tseo & Ramos, 1995). In other cases, worker empowerment has involved changes in the structure of companies so that employees have more of a say in company decision making, more opportunities for advancement, and increased access to powerful people and resources in the organization. Whatever form it takes, worker empowerment has focused on reducing the sense of powerlessness and lack of control that many workers experience. And research shows that worker participation and employee ownership can increase a company's productivity (Blinder, 1990; Rosen & Youngs, 1991).

Although these trends would provide some protections for workers, employees may still be vulnerable without some fundamental changes in economic institutions. True protection of workers would occur, some argue, only if the United States and other nations developed more of a mixed economy, with the government taking more control of some economic realms in order to pursue collective goals. Proponents of an extreme power elite position would argue that inequality and exploitation are inherent elements of capitalism because capitalism is ultimately fueled by personal greed and acquisition. As such, capitalism can only work to benefit the powerful. Some form of a mixed economy would balance the avarice inherent in capitalism by injecting an element of the public good into economic activities and decisions. Others, including some pluralists, would argue that capitalism can benefit most citizens through the checks and balances of competing interest groups. This is not to say that capitalism can achieve equality or that everyone will benefit. But if the government encourages the development of diverse interest groups, large numbers of citizens will be able to pursue their goals. Applying Sociology: Assisting Workers points to the contributions of some applied sociologists who have played a part in this process of change in the workplace.

The Global Economic System

You should be able to discuss the extent of and reasons for economic concentration and inequality among the nations of the world, what problems this creates, and what forms of resistance have emerged.

Concentration and Inequality

Some of the trends found in the U.S. economy are reproduced on a global scale. In particular, the trends show a pattern of concentration of wealth and resources in the hands of a few nations—the highly industrialized, capitalist nations of North America, Europe, and Asia, which now dominate the world economy. Figure 13.6 (on p. 462) suggests the extent of that domination by showing that most of the largest corporations in the world are headquartered in a small number of nations. The United States, Japan, and six European nations account for 450 of the largest 491 corporations. Further, 60 percent of those 491 corporations are found in only *two* of the world's more than two hundred nations: the United States and Japan. So, when we talk of global corporations dominating

Chapter 1 mentioned that sociology has long focused its attention on social reform, or making improvements in people's lives. In the realm of political and economic institutions, reform has meant focusing on issues of work and the workplace. One key issue is the plight of displaced workers—people who lose their jobs when plants are shut down or move to other states or nations. As nations become more interdependent in a capitalist world system, this problem becomes chronic. In the late 1980s, for example, an automobile assembly plant in Wisconsin shut down; five thousand people lost their jobs. Community groups formed to assist in rebuilding the economic base of the community after the plant left. A part of this effort was to provide programs to assist the laid-off workers in rebuilding their lives. To help them, accurate information was needed on the consequences of the plant shut down and the progress of the workers toward reintegration into the workforce. The groups were particularly interested in the role played by education and retraining in people's finding jobs. The community hired a group of researchers, including sociologists, to collect this data (Greider, Denise-Neinhaus, & Statham, 1992).

The researchers began by reviewing the existing research on the experiences of displaced workers. Then they conducted surveys of a sample of the workers displaced by the Wisconsin closing at three different points in time to assess their progress back into the workforce. One thing the researchers found was that job training was detrimental in the short term but beneficial in the long term: workers who received job training after plant closing had higher rates of unemployment after one year but lower rates after two years. The type of job training received was also important; workers receiving company training did better than those receiving union training. One important use of this research was to provide objective, unbiased information to local news media, public officials, and labor leaders about how the workers were doing. The research results were also used by local technical colleges in planning new job-training programs and by government agencies in seeking state and federal funds for job training.

Applied sociologists have also worked with labor unions on ways to improve labor contracts and to provide better conditions in the workplace (Shostak, 1992). For example, sociologists have conducted surveys on working conditions, morale of workers, worker health and safety issues, and other topics about which unions need information to protect their workers. Sociologists also provide information about future trends in the workplace that union leaders need to know about. Sociologists can detect trends in permanent joblessness, the growth in part-time workers, and the use of more contract workers. All these factors influence the environment in which workers of the future will be seeking and trying to keep jobs.

Applied sociologists focus on additional workplace issues that have been highlighted in other chapters. Chapters 2 and 12 discussed role strain in work settings and how that can affect people's performance. Chapter 8 analyzed sexual harassment at work and showed how sociologists work to reduce it. In all these ways, applied sociologists use their theories and research to create better and more equitable work environments.

---

world trade, we really mean that a relatively few nations of the world dominate that trade.

Another way to look at the economic circumstances of the world is by comparing the economic resources that people have available to spend. The gross national product (GNP) represents the total output of goods and services in a nation. It is sometimes taken as a rough measure of the wealth of a nation. The GNP in the United States is much larger than that of most other nations because there is a much larger populace. A more useful comparison is how much GNP per person is available, and Figure 13.7 (on p. 462) shows the enormous disparities in the world. The United States, the other industrialized nations, and some of the oil-producing nations of the Middle East do very well while most other nations lag far behind. (See also Figure 6.2.)

Many reasons can be found for these disparities, but the three chief explanations are circumstances, cultural theory, and world-system theory. Some of the differences are the result of

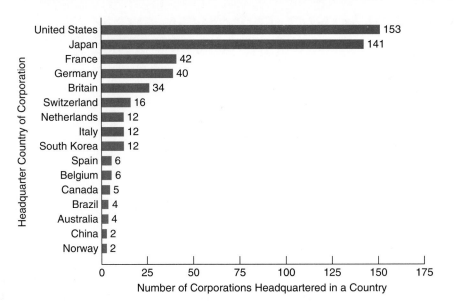

FIGURE 13.6 Nations in Which the 491 Largest Corporations are Headquartered, 1995 *Note:* From *Fortune,* August 5, 1996, pp. F1–F10.

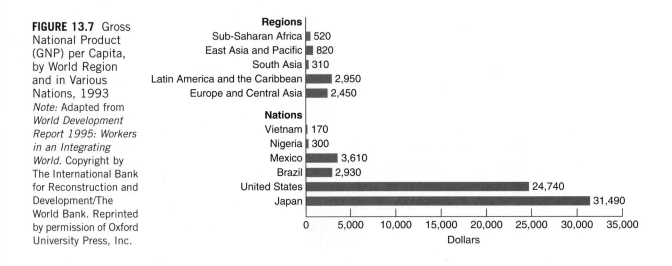

FIGURE 13.7 Gross National Product (GNP) per Capita, by World Region and in Various Nations, 1993 *Note:* Adapted from *World Development Report 1995: Workers in an Integrating World.* Copyright by The International Bank for Reconstruction and Development/The World Bank. Reprinted by permission of Oxford University Press, Inc.

a particular country's geographic or historical circumstances. Saudi Arabia, Kuwait, and the United Arab Emirates, for example, do quite well because they have large reserves of oil to tap as a source of wealth. The United States is fortunate to have much highly arable land. Some of the nations of sub-Saharan Africa have parched land with unpredictable rainfall and often long periods of drought. In short, some nations are more blessed with good resources, and they tend to be among the "have" nations.

The second explanation, cultural theory, argues that some cultural traditions encourage ways of thinking and behaving that are more conducive to producing wealth and economic growth. Chapter 11 addressed this issue in discussing how the Protestant ethic encouraged people to work hard, be frugal, save, and reinvest. Max Weber used this cultural orientation to help account for the rise of capitalism in Europe. More recently, analysts have suggested that Confucian traditions in such countries as South Korea, Hong Kong, Singapore, Japan, and Taiwan may have a similar outcome (Harrison, 1992). Confucianism places high value on attaining an education as a route toward the highest form of service to society—governing for social reform and advancement (see Chapter 11). In ancient China, Confucian education emphasized merit in the educational process, so that those with the greatest skills and highest virtues would become the governors of society. In these Asian countries, educational administrators and teachers are held in high regard. This combination of education and merit means that social mobility is a part of social and economic life in these nations. Thus, their cultural orientation encourages people to work hard and achieve, behaviors that in turn will increase the likelihood of national economic growth and development.

The third explanation of these worldwide economic disparities focuses on the centuries-long historical process discussed in Chapter 6 as the capitalist world system. *World-system theory* focuses on the expansive nature of capitalism and its emphasis on market forces, profit making, and surplus accumulation. Capitalism's drive to find new markets creates a pressure to seek out new territories in which to invest. Today, corporations' search for new markets has created a global economy with an international stratification system. According to world-system theory, a hierarchy of nations has emerged, divided roughly into *core nations* (capitalist, technologically advanced nations searching for opportunities to expand investment) and *peripheral nations* (less developed nations that provide cheap labor, produce food, and serve as a source of raw materials). There are also *semi-peripheral nations* that are large or have some special resources and therefore fall in between; they are less dependent on the core nations and sometimes act as core nations themselves (Apter, 1986; Chase-Dunn & Grimes, 1995; Chirot, 1986). Figure 6.2 identified the core nations of the world as the high-income economies, the semi-peripheral nations are the middle-income economies, and the peripheral nations are the low-income economies.

In this international stratification system, the core nations dominate and exploit the peripheral nations. The key to the system is trade, with some nations exporting goods while others serve primarily as a labor pool and a source of natural resources. Some world-system theorists argue that the nature of capitalism is such that it creates social inequalities through its tendency to distribute resources unequally. This inequality exists within nations, which have both rich and poor people, and at the international level, where the policies of core nations help keep peripheral nations less developed. The core nations extract natural resources and cheap labor from the peripheral nations in order to produce manufactured goods that are then exported for profit. Through political, economic, and sometimes military intervention, the core nations encourage the emergence of political and economic elites in the peripheral nations who will assist in the economic expansion of the core.

This economic expansion is also assisted by some global financial institutions that have emerged during the twentieth century (George & Sabelli, 1994; Rich, 1994). Among such institutions are the International Bank for Reconstruction and Development (or World Bank) and the International Monetary Fund (IMF). These global financial institutions lend money, guarantee private investments, help stabilize prices and currencies, and encourage private investment in development. They receive funding from their member nations (most nations belong), but their decision making and voting power tends to be dominated by the wealthy industrial nations of Europe and North America. In short, they function much like a central bank for the world, lending money and expertise to support economic development in developing nations. However, the support is not free: They demand that nations organize their economies in ways that support corporate growth. Often this means reducing domestic spending on things like schools, health, and social services. It can also require that nations stress export industries rather than production for domestic consumption.

The global concentration of power has also been enhanced by global trade agreements that encourage free trade among nations and discourage hindrances to trade, such as tariffs or restrictive labor policies. The most recent such agreements are the North American Free Trade Agreement (NAFTA) of 1994 and the World Trade Organization (WTO) of 1995. This global free-for-all in trade benefits the large, established corporations because they have the resources with which to compete in this environment. Small or new corporations, or noncorporate forms of organization, are no match for these established concentrations of power.

Global corporations and their supporting organizations generally subscribe to the ideology that levels of world prosperity are unlimited, that such prosperity can extend to all people, and that economic development and capitalist expansion, largely unfettered by government intervention, is the best means to achieve such global prosperity. In fact, many supporters of these organizations claim that they will eventually eradicate poverty around the world. To support such economic development, world economies have become organized around market-oriented production and continual mass consumption. This has been called the *commodification of the globe,* a system in which everything is a commodity to be sold and market value determines all (Rich, 1994, p. 6). In such a global economic environment, political boundaries and national allegiances are becoming less important determinants of economic activity. Other World, Other Ways: Nicaragua (on pp. 466–467) looks at how the workings of the world economic system affected the historical development and economic circumstances of the peoples of Nicaragua.

Unemployment, Dislocation, and Resistance

On a global scale, there is considerable controversy over whether the policies of organizations such as the World Bank or the IMF benefit all, or even most, citizens of the nations in which they operate (George & Sabelli, 1994; Rich, 1994). Although many people do benefit, the policies have also meant drastic reductions in wages for some; lowered expenditures for health, education, and other social services; and devastating degradation of the environment. A United Nations report published in 1994 characterized the current employment situation around the world as "the worst global employment crisis since the Great Depression of the 1930s" (Hartman, 1994, p. 5A). Around the world, 120 million people are officially registered as unemployed—a figure that everyone agrees is conservative—and at least another 700 million are underemployed, which means that they do not earn enough to support themselves and their families.

As with unemployment in the United States, the world situation is due in part to the nature of the global economy that is emerging as industrialism and capitalism advance around the world. This world economy is characterized by a relative dearth of entry-level jobs that pay a decent wage. There is also a shortage of jobs for people with low levels of education or few skills. The modern workplace is increasingly a high-technology environment, calling for considerable education and training. Those who, because of poverty or lack of access, do not receive such training and education find few places where they can earn a living wage. These trends have resulted in a polarization of the world's work-

These demonstrators are protesting against the practices of global financial institutions, such as the World Bank. The protestors claim that these organizations displace people from their homes and cause environmental degradation in places such as the Chiapas region of Mexico.

force: An increasing chasm between high-wage and low-wage workers. This means that people who get good jobs do fairly well for themselves and their families, but those without the necessary education and skills live increasingly marginal and precarious lives. Added to this is the increasing use of a geographically mobile labor force—immigrants, both legal and illegal, who are forced to travel to where the jobs (typically low-paying) are. It doesn't matter whether it is Mexican peasants traveling to the United States, Palestinians going to Kuwait, or Turks going to Germany. Corporations depend on this flexible, low-paid pool of labor to help keep costs down and profits up.

In addition to fostering unemployment, the global economy has displaced tens of thousands of poor people from their homes to make way for dams, logging activities, or large-scale agricultural and industrial developments. Often, these people must resettle in less desirable areas. Some critics dispute whether organizations such as the World Bank and the IMF have been successful in their stated goals of promoting development through large loans to governments. Critics of these organizations argue that their practices have dislocated people, exacerbated economic inequality and ethnic tensions, and promoted environmental degradation while benefiting corporations, the elite, and a small segment of the workforce.

The globalization of corporate control in the past century has also created new or enhanced threats to democratic practices and institutions around the world. These large corporations are sometimes wealthier than the nations in which they operate, giving the corporations enormous power from which to demand that a country adopt policies that are beneficial to the corporation. In fact, governments in smaller nations may deliberately avoid political and economic policies inconsistent with the goals of the corporations. In these ways, social policies in some nations, even in the United States, may result not from the democratic wishes of the populace but from implied or explicit demands from powerful corporations. Corporations may intervene in the democratic process of a nation by supplying campaign funds to particular political candidates, or in a few cases by attempting to overthrow elected officials (Barnet & Cavanagh, 1994).

Global financial institutions, such as the IMF and the World Bank, also intervene in the democratic process of some nations. Because these world institutions often operate in secret, ordinary citizens and their governments may have little knowledge of or input into what these organizations do. Dispensing large amounts of money and making policies at the international level, these organizations have become almost quasi-governments themselves, whose policies affect people's lives around the world. For example, as a condition of supporting a nation, these organizations often require the establishment of an administrative structure within the government, partly under World Bank or IMF control, that may circumvent or ignore the policies of elected or appointed officials.

Corporations and their world financial institutions are private or semi-private organizations and as such are largely beyond democratic control. The result is that the important economic and political decisions that shape the lives and opportunities of people around the world are in the hands of these powerful private and semi-private entities. Their decisions often change traditional cultures and ways of life as they push social and political changes that further economic development.

On a global scale, people have organized to fight against the actions of governments, corporations, and international financial organizations. The term *nongovernmental organizations* (NGOs) is now used to refer to grass-roots citizen organizations that have emerged to fight the intrusive and destructive policies of governments or groups like the World Bank and the IMF (Rich, 1994). These NGOs use whatever resources they have available, including education, boycotts, and demonstrations, in order to stop or change activities with detrimental social or environmental consequences. The NGOs are usually small and focus on specific problems that a village or a people confront. International networks of NGOs have emerged to provide mutual help through the exchange of information, resources, and personnel. These NGOs have had some success in alleviating the negative impact of the actions of corporations and of organizations such as the World Bank and the IMF.

OTHER WORLDS, *Other Ways*

NICARAGUA: POLITICAL AND ECONOMIC CHANGE IN A PERIPHERAL NATION

Nicaragua is a Central American nation of about four million people, the largest nation in the region. It is rich in natural resources, with much open land and soil and a climate that will support a variety of agricultural products. It also has reserves of timber, silver, and gold, as well as coastlines along both the Pacific Ocean and the Caribbean Sea for shipping. Yet, Nicaragua is a poor nation, with a GNP of less than $1,000 per person (compared to more than 20,000 in the United States). Over the years, the Nicaraguan economic elites have focused their attention on international trade, viewing poor Nicaraguans as a cheap labor supply to be exploited. In the past few decades, Nicaragua has gone through considerable political instability and has experienced significant changes in its social, economic, and political structures. Like El Salvador, discussed in Chapter 6, Nicaragua provides a good illustration of some of the political and economic processes discussed in this chapter.

Nicaragua's problems began with the Spanish conquest in the sixteenth century (Newson, 1987). Before the arrival of the Spanish, the indigenous peoples had an advanced agrarian society that supported them quite well. The *conquistadores* took control and demanded payment in gold from the Indians. They also took Indians for the slave trade and introduced disease for which the Indians had no immunity. Within a matter of decades, the Spanish devastated the Nicaraguan economy and society. The agricultural base of the region was nearly destroyed, and disease and a lack of food produced a high death rate. The Spanish elite accumulated wealth from mining gold and exporting timber, cattle, and some crops to other

Spanish colonies. They used the Indians as cheap labor and denied their traditional rights to the land.

With the collapse of Spanish colonial rule in the early 1800s, Nicaragua began to resurrect an internally focused economy that provided more food and other goods to Nicaraguans. A part of this economy involved Indians reclaiming land that was theirs by tradition. Between cattle ranching and peasant farming, the economy of Nicaragua was fairly self-sufficient.

This self-sufficiency ended when the coffee boom hit Central America in the late 1800s (Walker, 1991). Since the elite needed much fertile land to expand coffee production for export, they manipulated the government to pass legislation saying that any land not owned by legal title belonged to the government and could be sold to the highest bidder. Since many Indians were squatters on their land without such title, they were dispossessed and the coffee barons expanded. In addition, these new landless peasants provided a large, unskilled workforce that the coffee growers needed during the few months of harvest season each year.

The peasants revolted over this shabby treatment in the War of the Communeros, but they lost. With no other way to survive, many Nicaraguans who had once been self-sufficient peasant farmers became a rural laboring class dependent on the coffee plantations. This new coffee economy depended on a greater investment in machinery and labor, and so it became dominated by big business, large landholders, and foreigners. Some small peasant farming persisted, along with some cattle ranching, but the Nicaraguan economy had become heavily dependent on one export product.

The profits of coffee production went to the elite and foreigners, while average Nicaraguans were exploited through low wages and few opportunities for improvement. Nicaragua became a nation with a large mass of people living at a desperate subsistence level and a tiny middle and upper class to whom most resources and profits flowed. The country was also drawn into and became dependent on the capitalist world system. According to one expert on Nicaragua, the nation had become a classic example of world-system dependency: "a special situation in which the economy of a weak country is externally oriented and the government is controlled by national and/or international elites . . . that benefit from this economic relationship" (Walker, 1991, p. 3).

The United States has a long history of involvement in Nicaragua. U.S. troops occupied it from 1927 to 1933, fighting a peasant rebellion led by Augusto Sandino. During its occupation, the United States established and trained the Nicaraguan National Guard. Unable to defeat Sandino, the United States worked out a compromise and withdrew in 1933. Within a few years, the leader of the National Guard, Anastasio Somoza Garcia, arranged to have Sandino killed, overthrew the president of Nicaragua, and arranged for his own election as president. Somoza or one of his sons ruled Nicaragua from 1936 to 1979 (Walker, 1991).

Nicaragua eventually became less dependent on coffee but remained dependent on export. When the world price of cotton increased in the 1950s, for example, cattle ranches and peasant farms were converted to cotton production, resulting in more landless peasants and less agricultural production for domestic consumption. This "development" and "progress" tended to benefit the small elite. For much of the twentieth century, the Somoza family controlled the government and the National Guard and used them to suppress any dissent or rebellion. The elite supported the Somoza family rule since it provided the political and social stability that permitted them to run their

profitable export activities. Political institutions under the Somozas appeared democratic, with elections, constitutionally guaranteed human rights, and a bicameral legislature. In reality, the Somozas were complete dictators, supported by the National Guard. The elections, for example, were a sham, controlled by the Somozas through press censorship, ballot-box stuffing, and multiple voting by their supporters. Other political parties existed, but they had virtually no chance of gaining control of the government through elections. Workers and peasants had no channels of influence to the Somoza government.

The 1970s were a decade of decline for the Somoza regime. It began with a devastating earthquake that killed ten thousand Nicaraguans, but the Somoza family responded by ruthlessly exploiting the tragedy for their own economic benefit. This and other events intensified opposition to the regime, even among the Nicaraguan elite, who resented the way the Somoza family shamelessly took personal advantage of every economic sector in the nation and excluded the elite from even a small role in politics. The Somozas also came under international pressure. President Carter and Amnesty International wanted the Somozas to reduce the political repression and torture by which they maintained their grip on power. The International Monetary Fund wanted Nicaragua to institute economic reforms that would enable its economy to modernize. This decline in support led to the success of a popular revolt, and the Somoza government was overthrown by the Sandinist Front of National Liberation (FSLN) in 1979. Nicaragua is still struggling, however, since the successful revolution was followed by a decade of civil war that further devastated the Nicaraguan economy. In the civil war, the United States supported the counterrevolutionary contras against the ruling FSLN.

Politics, the Economy, and the Mass Media

You should be able to discuss the influence of the mass media in the political and economic realms.

The interactionist perspective stresses how people's definitions of situations serve as a mechanism of social control, shaping their thoughts, desires, and behaviors. In the modern world, the mass communications media play a central role in shaping definitions of political and economic reality.

Politics, Persuasion, and Propaganda

Politics, especially in democracies, is the domain of persuasion and influence. Politicians use the resources available to them to gain the support of other politicians, elites, and the citizenry in advancing a particular political agenda that encompasses, among other things, a particular set of values. At the same time, the elites and ordinary citizens make efforts to control and manipulate the actions of politicians. The power elite, pluralist, and world-system theories all agree that the ability to persuade and influence is not equally distributed among all groups in society. A corporate executive with the formal authority and power to decide where plants will be located or which employees will be retained generally has much more ability to influence than does the average citizen without such formal authority or informal power. Access to and control over the mass media has today become a key determinant of a group's ability to persuade or influence.

A naive view of the media in this process is that they serve as a passive mechanism of communication, enabling each side in the process of political persuasion to communicate with the other and to learn what the other is thinking and doing. In reality, the modern mass media have become one of the most powerful forces shaping and controlling the persuasive process. The media play this role by being used by others as well as by being an independent institutional force in society that pursues its own goals.

A good example of the role of the media in this political process can be found in the Persian Gulf War of 1991 (Hallin, 1991; Mowlana, Gerbner, & Schiller, 1992). This brief war against Iraq involved a multinational force of United Nations members but was largely organized and directed by the United States. As a means of controlling potential opposition to the war, political and military leaders decided to strictly control the media's access to information and to the war zone. The policy was to keep the media as far away from the war zone as possible and to place maximum restrictions on their activities. A great deal of information about the war came from political and military press briefings; staged news events such as political speeches; and tapes, graphics, and interviews supplied to the press by the military or government. This meant that the information and images that the media had available were mostly those approved by military and political leaders and those that placed the war in the most positive light.

The outcome was remarkable: For people in the United States watching the war on television, it appeared to be an astonishingly "clean" war, devoid of the bloodshed, terror, pain, and horror that normally accompany war. Almost no one reported from or sent images back directly from the field of battle. People did not see the suffering and death that accompanies war. The images available to the media also stressed the role of technology in the form of smart bombs and laser-guided missiles. Battles appeared to be fought by experts and technicians; people saw fuzzy but dramatic pictures taken from planes of buildings blowing up, and organized charts and maps at press briefings showing the progress of the war. The networks hired their own military commentators, usually retired military or Defense Department officials who claimed the status of independent experts. Even the images of soldiers going into battle stressed the mastery of technology: They were the pilots of highly sophisticated jet fighters or the monitors of sophisticated radar in AWACS surveillance planes. The image presented was of businesslike and professional experts doing their job.

So, without question, politicians and military leaders exploited the media to persuade the public in the United States to support the war and military solutions to international conflicts. Yet, the media also constitute an independent institutional force in society with its own agenda. After all, the media could have chosen not to broadcast any images rather than give the one-sided portrayal that was available to them. However, sociologist David Altheide (1993) points out that, in the modern mass media, "marketing logic, or what the audi-

The mass media projects powerful images that can encourage people to support war efforts, as occurred during the Persian Gulf War, or to oppose war efforts, as occurred during the Vietnam War.

ence approves of or 'buys,' informs message selection or production" (p. 54). A primary motivation of the media, even in the news divisions, is an economic one: to increase audience share, which enhances advertising revenues. In this view, the media were not exploited, but were co-conspirators: They willingly worked with political and military leaders to present a certain image of the war because the media elite believed it would be the most marketable image (MacArthur, 1992).

The media experience during the Gulf War was quite different from what occurred during the Vietnam War when reporters, photographers, and television crews were given fairly free rein to go where they wished. They could ride helicopters into battle and join soldiers on dangerous patrols. The more realistic, and certainly more sobering, media portrayal of that war undoubtedly helped to turn some public opinion against the war. In fact, the tight controls of the media in the Gulf War were clearly a reaction on the part of the government to what was seen as a loss in the battle to influence the public during the Vietnam War.

Persuasive efforts can sometimes become **propaganda:** *the deliberate spread of one-sided information or ideas with the intent of helping or harming particular people, groups, institutions, or societies.* Other terms sometimes used in this context are *misinformation, disinformation,* or *censorship.* All point to one-sided efforts to persuade. Certainly, propaganda can be spread in ways other than through the media, but the modern media are especially powerful and pervasive in this realm. The images provided by television, video, and computer-generated imaging are so compelling that their ability to persuade and shape people's visions of reality are difficult to resist. Even when people are clearly aware that the media can mislead them, the images are often so dramatic and enticing that they are irresistible. Modern media technology has provided those who can control the technology with powerful tools to spread propaganda to other groups.

So the media are not solely the coercive mechanism of one group. Rather, they can be thought of as contested territory that is battled over by various groups. But at the same time, the political and economic elites clearly have more opportunities and resources with which to shape media images than does the average person.

Advertising

In the economic realm, one form of persuasion is advertising, and we have just noted its role in determining media content: Media elites manipulate media content in order to increase viewers and thus advertising revenues. This suggests that the viewer is doing the persuading, but a powerful persuasive effort goes in the other direction, with economic interests expending enormous advertising efforts and resources to convince the public to purchase goods. In fact, modern capitalist economies, which are based on economic growth through the mass production of goods and services, can be sustained only through the mass consumption of all that is produced. So advertising, which is the primary vehicle for persuading people to purchase those goods and services, is an essential element to maintaining modern economies. As an economic activity, advertising is enormous and worldwide. In the United States alone, advertising in the mid-1990s produced revenues of $24 billion, a 60 percent increase since the mid-1980s (U.S. Bureau of the Census, 1995, p. 796).

Although advertising has been around in one form or another for eons, mass advertising became possible only with the advent of mass communications media, beginning with the invention of the printing press (see Chapter 12). In modern times, newspapers, magazines, radios, and eventually television have served as vehicles for advertising.

While most people complain about the intrusiveness or the insipidness of advertising, sociologists search for its social importance. Chapter 1 discusses the concepts of manifest and latent functions. Certainly the manifest function of advertising is to serve as a vehicle of communication whereby consumers learn what goods and services are available and economic interests try to influence people's economic behavior. However, sociologists are never content to focus only on the manifest functions of an activity or institution since most also serve some latent functions. One of the latent functions of advertising, as with other uses of the media, is to provide support, often subtle and indirect, for cultural values, beliefs, and stereotypes. At a basic level, the pervasiveness of advertising itself is an affirmation of and legitimation for capitalism, consumerism, and economic growth. It is an embodiment of the commodification of the world, discussed in Chapter 2, in which the social worth of an object or activity is determined by its economic worth in the marketplace. Through advertising, people come to believe that their social worth as human beings is embodied in their ability to purchase the trendiest (and often most expensive) sneakers or sunglasses. Also, the images portrayed in advertising may support the values of patriotism, gender equality, and racial equality, or gender and racial inequality. In other words, beyond the information about a product contained in an advertisement, there are messages about what is good and proper that may have nothing to do with the product itself but that do influence people's definitions of reality.

Summary

1. Economics involves the processes through which goods and services are produced and distributed. Politics is the use of power to determine whose values will predominate, how rewards and resources will be allocated, and the manner in which conflicting interests will be resolved.

2. Legitimacy is the capacity of the system to engender and maintain the belief that the existing institutions are the most appropriate ones for the society. Legitimate power is what sociologists call authority.

3. There are three types of authority: traditional, charismatic, and legal-rational.

4. The state is a political institution with legitimate control over the use of force within a particular territory. Government involves the operation of the state by a particular group of people who have the authority to make decisions and supervise the allocation of resources.

5. According to the functionalist perspective, political and economic institutions perform certain functions that are beneficial to the societies in which they emerge, and these functions make organized social life possible. Conflict theorists

maintain that political and economic institutions emerge as a consequence of the efforts of dominant groups in society, which these structures are ultimately designed to benefit.

6. There are many different types of governments, including oligarchy, totalitarianism, and democracy.

7. There are several different types of economic systems, including capitalism, which involves private ownership of property, the profit motive, and free competition between producers and consumers of goods; socialism, which involves collectively held means of production and distribution; and mixed economies, which have strong elements of both capitalism and socialism.

8. There are two basic models of political power in the United States. The power elite model, which is based on the conflict perspective, maintains that a small group of very powerful people, drawn from the economic sector, politics, and the military, make all the important decisions in the United States. The pluralist model maintains that power is spread over a large number of groups with divergent values, interests, and goals. In truth, the distribution of power in the United States probably lies somewhere between these two extremes.

9. The U.S. economy has undergone considerable change. The dominant form of business organization is now the corporation, a business enterprise that is owned by stockholders who may not be involved in running the daily affairs of the business. Another development has been the emergence of powerful labor unions. However, in an advanced industrial economy, labor unions find some of their power dwindling as blue-collar workers come to constitute a smaller proportion of the workforce and the labor force becomes global.

10. The global economy seems to reproduce some of the characteristics of the U.S. economy, especially the concentration of wealth and economic resources in the hands of a few nations. Three explanations for this situation are circumstances, cultural theory, and world-system theory. This global economic concentration and inequality produce a variety of problems in various nations and generate organized resistance.

11. The mass media are a key resource that groups can use in an effort to influence political and economic life. While the media are contested territory, with numerous groups attempting to use and control them, elite groups are generally more successful at gaining such control.

STUDY and Review

Key Terms

authority

capitalism

corporation

democracy

democratic socialist economy

economics

government

legitimacy

military-industrial complex

mixed economy

oligarchy

pluralist model

politics

power

power elite model

propaganda

socialism

state

totalitarianism

welfare capitalism

Multiple-Choice Questions

1. Both political and economic institutions center on the same key social process, namely
   a. the exercise of power in the allocation of scarce resources.
   b. the transition from socialist to capitalist economies.
   c. the emergence of market economies in advanced industrial societies.
   d. the globalization of labor.

2. Traditional authority is best defined as based on
   a. the extraordinary powers or qualities of some individual.
   b. laws and rules that define who can do what.
   c. power elite position.
   d. loyalty to established ways of doing things.

3. Which of the following is true regarding voting behavior in the United States?
   a. Older people are more likely to vote than are younger people.
   b. Those with low incomes are more likely to vote than are those with high incomes.
   c. Men are more likely to vote than are women.
   d. People in the United States vote at higher rates than do people in the other major democracies of the world.

4. According to proponents of a pure capitalist economy, the government should do all of the following *except*
   a. maintain public order.
   b. protect against foreign threats.
   c. regulate prices and wages.
   d. government should do all of these.
   e. government should do none of these.

5. As used by Karl Marx, the term *communism* refers to
   a. socialist economies in advanced industrial societies.
   b. the utopian end stage of the struggle against capitalism.
   c. oligarchical political structures as exist in Russia and China.
   d. the process of bringing corporations under state ownership and control.

6. Which of the following statements is consistent with the power elite model of power distribution in the United States?
   a. A small group of powerful people make most important decisions.
   b. Power is spread over a large number of groups.
   c. There is no significant military-industrial complex in the United States.
   d. There is no cohesive elite with power centralized in its hands in the United States.
   e. The unorganized public can exercise constraint over those in power through use of the vote.

7. If the ABC Corporation controlled 96 percent of the sales for breakfast cereal in the United States, the corporation would be called a (an)
   a. oligopoly.
   b. conglomerate.
   c. monopoly.
   d. oligarchy.

8. Which of the following is *not* one of the reasons for the decline in the proportion of workers in the United States who are unionized?

   a. Traditionally unionized occupations have declined in number.
   b. Multinational corporations have declined in significance.
   c. Corporations have relocated to states with weak union organizations.
   d. The number of white-collar occupations has been growing.

9. Which of the following is true regarding changes in the occupational structure in the United States since 1900?
   a. The proportion of farm workers has increased.
   b. The proportion of blue-collar workers has increased.
   c. The proportion of service workers has declined.
   d. The proportion of white-collar workers has increased.

10. The problem of unemployment in the United States has grown worse over the decades because
   a. there is increased competition from foreign workers.
   b. the proportion of blue-collar jobs has grown and the proportion of white-collar jobs has declined.
   c. the number of women entering the workforce has declined.
   d. U.S. corporations have avoided competing in global markets.

True/False Questions

1. Politics refers to the processes through which goods and services are produced and distributed in society.

2. Today in the United States, the legitimacy of the state is usually not questioned, but people sometimes do question the legitimacy of particular governments.

3. Totalitarianism is a special form of oligarchy.

4. The primary motivation for economic activities in socialist economies is to earn a profit.

5. In assessing the power elite model, the text concludes that a small group of people in the United States do hold enormous power, control foreign policy, and shape the direction of economic development.

6. In the United States, union members as a proportion of the workforce have been declining since the 1950s.

7. Worker displacement has affected white workers more severely than black workers in the 1980s and 1990s.

8. In the last few decades in the United States, the relative power of workers and employers seems to have shifted toward employers and away from workers.

9. More than half of the world's largest 491 corporations are headquartered in Asia.

10. In the international stratification system, according to world-system theory, the peripheral nations dominate and exploit the core nations.

Fill-In Questions

1. Authority is referred to by sociologists as _____ power.

2. The three types of authority found in political and economic institutions are _____ , _____ , and _____ .

3. A political institution with legitimate control over the use of force within a particular territory is called _____ .

4. In capitalist economic systems, _____ is the primary motive guiding people's economic behavior.

5. Economic systems in which there are strong elements of both capitalism and socialism are called _____ .

6. A sociologist named _____ originally proposed what has come to be called the power elite model of the exercise of power in the United States.

7. A _____ is a corporation that owns other companies in economic spheres quite different from that of the parent company.

8. _____ are workers who have lost their jobs because manufacturing plants in the United States have moved to other countries.

9. According to world-system theory, the three types of nations that make up the world economic system are _____ , _____ , and _____ .

10. The text uses the term _____ to describe the mass media as something that many groups battle to control.

Matching Questions

_____ 1. capitalism
_____ 2. power elite model
_____ 3. *maquiladoras*
_____ 4. Sweden and Denmark
_____ 5. Robert Michels
_____ 6. Dwight D. Eisenhower
_____ 7. Martin Luther King, Jr. and Ronald Reagan
_____ 8. totalitarian regime
_____ 9. business groups in Japan
_____ 10. gender gap

A. factories in Mexico producing goods for export to the United States
B. conflict perspective
C. warned of the danger of the military-industrial complex
D. charisma
E. economic production and distribution privately held
F. dictatorship
G. iron law of oligarchy
H. *keiretsu*
I. mixed economies
J. pattern of voting behavior in U.S.

Essay Questions

1. Define and give examples of the various types of authority on which political and economic institutions can rest. Distinguish between the concepts of *state* and *government*.

2. Compare and contrast what the functionalist and conflict perspectives have to say about political and economic institutions.

3. What is a democracy? What social conditions seem to be important to the survival and long-term stability of democratic political institutions?

4. Define *capitalism, socialism,* and *mixed economies.* Show how each economic system differs from the others in terms of organization and motivation for economic activity.

5. Compare the U.S. economy with the economy of Japan, especially in terms of how each defines and orients toward the competitive nature of capitalism.

6. Assess how well the power elite and pluralist models describe the exercise of power in the United States. What evidence is presented on this issue in the text?

7. What is a corporation? What are the benefits and disadvantages of corporate organization?

8. How is the labor force in the United States changing? Why are these changes occurring? Include in your answer a discussion of displaced workers.

9. Describe the concentration of economic resources at a global level. How does world-system theory explain this concentration?

10. Describe the political and economic changes that have occurred in Nicaragua historically and in the present. Relate the changes to the world economic system.

Answers

Multiple-Choice
1. A; 2. D; 3. A; 4. C; 5. B; 6. A; 7. C;
8. B; 9. D; 10. A

True/False
1. F; 2. T; 3. T; 4. F; 5. T; 6. T; 7. F;
8. T; 9. F; 10. F

Fill-In
1. legitimate
2. traditional, charismatic, and legal-rational
3. a state
4. profit-making
5. mixed economies, democratic socialist economies
6. C. Wright Mills
7. conglomerate
8. displaced workers
9. core, peripheral, semi-peripheral
10. contested territory

Matching
1. E; 2. B; 3. A; 4. I; 5. G; 6. C; 7. D;
8. F; 9. H; 10. J

For Further Reading

Brecher, Jeremy, & Costello, Tim. (1994). *Global village or global pillage: Economic reconstruction from the bottom up.* Boston: South End Press. These authors have many constructive suggestions for how to alleviate the more damaging consequences of the actions of global corporations and institutions. But, they argue, labor, nongovernmental, and other grass-roots organizations will have to make a concerted, global effort or the corporations and their supporting governments will gain the upper hand.

Domhoff, G. William. (1996). *State autonomy or class dominance? Case studies on policy making in America.* New York: Aldine de Gruyter. This is a contemporary case study analysis from the power elite perspective. It focuses on the relative importance of political and economic realms in the exercise of power in the United States. The author concludes that power is concentrated more in the hands of corporate chiefs than in the hands of political leaders.

Fallows, James. (1996). *Breaking the news: How the media undermine American democracy.* New York: Pantheon. This readable book by a well-known journalist analyzes the role of the media in democratic societies, showing how the media in the United States has sometimes performed that role well and at other times poorly.

Heilbroner, Robert. (1993). *21st century capitalism.* New York: W. W. Norton. These brief but thoughtful essays explore what capitalism, which seems destined to be the dominant economic system of the next century, could be like in the future. The author argues that both capitalism and socialism contain strengths that should be incorporated into a twenty-first century capitalism.

Malinowski, Bronislaw. (1922). *Argonauts of the Western Pacific.* London: Routledge & Kegan Paul. This classic anthropological work describes a primitive nonmarket economy, showing how economic arrangements can differ from modern ones.

Mander, Jerry, & Goldsmith, Edward (Eds.). (1996). *The case against the global economy.* San Francisco: Sierra Club Books. The authors of articles in this book document the many negative consequences of the growing global economy, spell out the forces that drive it, and suggest alternatives that stress local development.

McCartney, Laton. (1988). *Friends in high places: The Bechtel story: The most secret corporation and how it engineered the world.* New York: Simon & Schuster. This is a book about a large and powerful U.S. corporation whose top executives shuttled between business and government service in the 1980s. It is an excellent case study of how the military-industrial complex works.

Rifkin, Jeremy. (1994). *The end of work: The decline of the global labor force and the dawn of the post-market era.* New York: Putnam. This is a more pessimistic view of future changes in the world economy. This author sees automation and other changes in technology dislodging millions of workers from their jobs around the world.

Rothschild, Joyce, & Whitt, J. Allen. (1986). *The cooperative workplace: Potentials and dilemmas of organizational democracy and participation.* New York: Cambridge University Press. This book suggests some alternate ways of organizing the workplace in which workers can participate in collective and democratic decision making.

Shostak, Arthur B. (1991). *Robust unionism: Innovations in the labor movement.* Ithaca, NY: Cornell University, ILR Press. This applied sociologist has worked with the labor movement in the United States for many years, and here he suggests some changes in unions that would make them more effective supports for working people in the changing economy of the 1990s.

PART FIVE

Human Ecology and Social Change

The chapters in Part Five focus on the processes of social change and the consequences of that change. In particular, they address issues of population growth and distribution, urbanization, collective efforts by people to bring about or resist change, and theories of social change.

CHAPTER FOURTEEN Human Ecology: Population and Community

A number of chapters have highlighted different non-European peoples of the Americas. Chapter 2 discussed the Comanches of the Great Plains in North America, Chapter 4 the Yanomamos of Brazil. Other chapters looked at the Natchez, the Hurons, and the tribal peoples of Brazil. One notable fact about all the groups mentioned is that they lived in small villages and survived by a combination of hunting, horticulturalism, and pastoralism. This survey could leave the impression that these tribal peoples of the Americas never organized large civilizations with great cities at their center, such as was common in Europe and Asia. This impression would be quite wrong.

The Aztecs emerged as a distinct hunting society in Mexico in the twelfth century (Farb, 1978). They were few in number and had a difficult time securing a spot in central Mexico, which was crowded with various other tribes. Eventually, they settled in a large plain filled with lakes and surrounded by mountains, the area where Mexico City later emerged. By the early 1400s, the Aztecs had multiplied, successfully battled many rival tribes, and emerged as the mightiest state in Mexico. By terror and by diplomacy, they forced the other peoples of central Mexico to accept their dominion over the region and created a vast agricultural civilization. By the time the Spanish and Portuguese explorers were beginning to head for the Americas in the late 1400s, the Aztecs ruled over much of what today is the nation of Mexico, with a population of possibly six million people.

At the center of their domain, on the site of modern-day Mexico City, they began building a grand city in the mid-1300s. This city, Tenochtitlán, was called by one anthropologist "one of the most magnificent cities ever erected on any continent" (Farb, 1978, p. 157). Built on an island in a chain of lakes, it was easily defensible from attack and centrally located for controlling trade with many surrounding groups. At the center of the city stood the remarkable Great Temple, which was dedicated by the sacrifice of twenty thousand captives. The Aztecs established schools and encouraged people in the crafts and literature. When the Spanish arrived, the Aztecs were ruled by a king named Moctezuma, and they had achieved a high and sophisticated culture.

Tenochtitlán was, by all accounts, magnificent (Hardoy, 1975). Estimates of its size range from 100,000 to 300,000 residents—a good-sized city even by today's standards. It was surrounded by snow-covered peaks and cultivated mountain slopes. Rising majestically above the calm turquoise of the lakes on which it was built and the green of the trees planted in groves around it, it appeared to be part city and part floating garden. The Aztecs built aqueducts across the lakes to carry water and causeways for people to walk to the mainland, where they worked plots of land. Dozens of temples rose above the skyline, which was dominated by the Great Temple. There were broad plazas and exotic gardens, and ornate palaces dotted the city. Bernal Díaz, a Spanish conquistador who first gazed on Tenochtitlán in 1519, described it this way:

> It was like the enchantments they tell of in the legend of Amadis, on account of the great towers and [temples] and buildings rising from the water, and all built of masonry. And some of our soldiers even asked whether the things that we saw were not a dream. . . . I do not know how to describe it. . . .

> Some of the soldiers among us who had been in many parts of the world, in Constantinople, and all over Italy, and in Rome, said that so large a marketplace and so full of people and so well regulated and arranged, they had never beheld before. (Díaz, 1638/1956, pp. 218–219)

Tenochtitlán was not the only pre-Columbian city in the Americas. Seven hundred years earlier the Mayans, at the height of their rule of the same region, built the city of Teotihuacán about forty miles north of Mexico City. Farther south the Incas solidified their control over territory covering modern-day Ecuador, Peru, and Bolivia and ruled from the Peruvian city of Cuzco. So, in the Americas, as in other parts of the world, empires arose through diplomacy and military might, and cities emerged because they served as centers of trade and culture and because they could centralize military authority.

This chapter is about *human ecology,* the size and distribution of human populations, including the growth of cities. The term *ecology* is connected in most people's minds with the biological world of plants and animals and their relationships to their environment. Over the past few decades, ecology has become a popular topic primarily because of the growing concern with environmental pollution and degradation. We should remember that human beings are one of the many animals studied by ecologists. Sociologists use the term **human ecology** to refer to *the study of human populations and communities, including their distribution across and impact on the physical environment they inhabit.* This chapter will review the basics in the field of human ecology: the growth of human populations, their geographic distribution, and the emergence of communities and cities.

The Study of Human Populations

You should be able to describe the three demographic variables and current trends in the age and sex structure of the United States.

There are many things about each of our lives that we generally consider to be very personal, such as whether we marry, how often and with whom we have sexual relations, whether we use contraceptives, and how many children (if any) we plan to

Myths & FACTS

ABOUT POPULATION AND COMMUNITY

Myth The most important factor in controlling world population growth is technology: Modern contraceptive technology is essential if people are to control their fertility.

FACT The most crucial ingredient in world population growth is human values and desires. Effective contraceptive procedures have been available for some time, but as long as people place a high value on having many children, world population will continue to grow.

Myth The United States achieved Zero Population Growth (ZPG) when the birthrate dropped below replacement level during the 1970s.

FACT Although the U.S. birthrate has been dropping steadily and has remained below replacement level for some time, this rate will have to continue for another generation (about seventy years) before the country reaches ZPG.

Myth Latin America's cities have grown rapidly in recent decades because young people prefer not to live on farms or in rural communities, and they migrate to the cities.

FACT Although preference for urban life certainly plays a part in this migration, other complex social processes are at work. For example, international corporations often purchase large amounts of farmland to grow export products, and this practice throws peasants off the land. These landless peasants often have nowhere else to go but the cities.

Myth In the teeming slums of Third-World cities in Latin America, family disintegration is a major problem, which exacerbates other problems such as drug use and crime.

FACT Although families have their problems in the cities, families often remain together, and kinship helps to define important networks of reciprocal exchange through which people with few material resources help one another survive. Each family in a network contributes what it is able and receives on the basis of what other families have. In these ways, families persist and display innovative responses to adversity.

---

have. There are, however, social scientists, called *demographers,* who are acutely interested in these matters because they help shape the population of the United States and the world. **Demography** is *the study of the size, composition, and distribution of human populations and how these factors change over time.* Each of us participates in at least two demographic acts that affect human populations—we are born and we will eventually die. Many of us also engage in other demographic acts, such as having children. All of these individual decisions and activities combine into an enormous wave of actions that make the world population what it is today.

Elements of Demographic Change

The term **population** refers to *the total number of people inhabiting a particular geographic area at a spec-*

ified time. The three basic elements that shape the size, composition, and distribution of human populations are fertility, mortality, and migration.

Fertility **Fertility** refers to *the actual number of children born.* It is distinguished from **fecundity,** or *the biological maximum number of children that could be born.* Because women rarely have the maximum number of children of which they are capable, the fertility of a society is normally quite a bit lower than its fecundity. The simplest measure of fertility is the *crude birthrate,* the number of live births occurring in a particular population during a given year for each one thousand people in that population. Figure 10.1 (on p. 337) shows the crude birthrate in the United States between 1910 and 1994. This method of calculating fertility is crude because it ignores the age and sex structure of populations. A more refined measure is the *general fertility rate,* the number of live births per year for each one thousand women of childbearing age, generally considered to be between fifteen and forty-four. This general fertility rate provides a more accurate view of how fertile a society is because it is calculated using only women who are in the age bracket where they might have children. As can be seen in Figure 10.1, the crude birthrate in the United States dropped to a fairly low level in the 1930s, below nineteen births per one thousand people. This decline was undoubtedly related to the Great Depression, when many people could not afford to have children. By 1940, however, the birthrate was on the rise. The late 1940s was the period of the post-war *baby boom* when couples who had postponed having children during World War II established their families. By the mid-1950s, the birthrate peaked, and after 1957 another decline began. This decline continued fairly steadily until the mid-1970s, when the birthrate reached an all-time low of less than fifteen per one thousand people. Since then, the crude birthrate has stayed at that low level, with slight increases in some years.

Demographers also use another measure of fertility called the *total fertility rate,* which is the average number of children a woman will have in her lifetime, based on current birthrates. With today's birthrates, for example, women average about 2 children in contrast to 3.5 children in the early 1960s (U.S. Bureau of the Census, 1995, p. 76). For other purposes, demographers use *age-specific birthrates,* which calculate the number of births among women in a particular age category. In fact, a slight increase in the birthrate since 1980 can be attributed in part to the number of women who had delayed having children and then decided in their thirties to have at least one child. Some demographers have even referred to this increase as a *baby boomlet,* because the number of births to women between thirty and thirty-nine years of age more than doubled.

Mortality **Mortality** refers to *the number of deaths that occur in a particular population.* As with fertility, mortality in a society can be described in a number of ways. The *crude death rate* refers to the total number of deaths for every 1,000 people (see Figure 10.1 on p. 337). As noted in Chapter 10, the crude death rate in the United States has declined substantially over the past century, from 17 per 1,000 in 1900 to about 8.7 today. However, as Figure 10.1 illustrates, there has been relatively little change in the past two decades. The crude death rate, although useful for some purposes, is necessarily limited because certain social factors place some people at much greater risk of death than others. The very young and the old, for example, have much higher death rates than other age groups. Thus, *sex-* or *age-specific death rates* are often used to measure the number of people in an age or sex grouping who have died for each 1,000 people in that category. In fact, deaths among infants under one year of age have shown the greatest declines of all age groups, dropping from about 100 per 1,000 births in 1915 to 8.5 today. Finally, *life expectancy* refers to the number of years, on the average, that people can expect to live. People in the United States have experienced a substantial increase in life expectancy during this century, as Table 14.1 illustrates. As can be seen, the life expectancy of women has increased more than that of men. The difference in

TABLE 14.1 Expectation of life at birth in the United States, 1920–1995

Year	Male	Female	Total
1920	53.6	54.6	54.1
1930	58.1	61.6	59.7
1940	60.8	65.2	62.9
1950	65.6	71.1	68.2
1960	66.6	73.1	69.7
1970	67.1	74.7	70.8
1980	70.0	77.5	73.7
1990	71.8	78.8	75.4
1995*	72.8	79.7	76.3

*Projection.

Note: From *Statistical Abstract of the United States, 1978* (p. 69) by U.S. Bureau of the Census, 1978, Washington, DC: U.S. Government Printing Office; *Statistical Abstract of the United States, 1995* (p. 86) by U.S. Bureau of the Census, Washington, DC: U.S. Government Printing Office.

life expectancy between the sexes was only one year in 1920, and it is seven years today. Some of the reasons for this difference are discussed in Chapter 10.

When we combine the results of the crude birthrate and the crude death rate, we derive an indication of the growth of a population, and the difference between these two figures is referred to as the *rate of natural increase*. For example, in 1990, the crude birthrate of the United States was 14.9 and the crude death rate was 8.7, yielding a rate of natural increase of 0.62 percent.

Migration   On the most general level **migration** refers to *a permanent change of residence*. The term *immigration* refers to movement *into* a particular country, whereas *emigration* involves moving *out*. In analyzing migration, demographers look for *push* and *pull* factors. Sometimes, people are pushed out of one country because of poor economic times, unstable political conditions, and the like. Many Southeast Asians migrated to the United States in the 1970s and 1980s, for example, because of the unpredictable political situation in that part of the world. In other cases, there is a pull or attraction that leads people to migrate to a particular place. Many Europeans migrated to the United States in the belief that they would have better economic and social opportunities.

Emigration from the United States has been very low, but immigration has been a significant factor in U.S. population growth. All people in the United States are immigrants or the descendants of immigrants. Even recently, immigrants have made a significant impact on the populace. During the 1980s, for example, more than five million people immigrated to the United States. Although that is less than 2 percent of the current population, most of these people were young, with 26 percent being under sixteen years of age and another 59 percent between sixteen and forty-four. Many will eventually bear children, thus adding further to the population growth. The composition of these immigrant groups has also changed (see Figure 7.3 on p. 236). Although in the past most came from Europe, the largest group today comes from Asia.

Migration is also an important variable in the population within a particular nation. For example, the population density of the Southern and Western states in the United States has risen dramatically in recent decades because of in-migration from other states. Likewise, the number of people living in some other states has declined because of out-migration. Since 1980, North Dakota and Iowa have experienced a net decline in population, and some states, such as New York and Pennsylvania, have shown almost no increase (U.S. Bureau of the Census, 1995, p. 28). All other states showed some increase. In the 1990 Census, California, Texas, and Florida accounted for more than half of the United States' population growth during the 1980s. These three states together have a 1990 population of nearly sixty million, which is almost as many people who lived in the entire nation in 1890. The Northeast grew less than 3 percent and the Midwest only 1.5 percent during the 1980s, whereas the South gained 16 percent and the West 21 percent. The population stagnation in some regions can contribute to high rates of unemployment and fewer job opportunities in the states showing little growth. These socioeconomic factors then have a further effect on migration patterns. People have moved out of some states and into others in search of employment or more lucrative career opportunities.

Population Composition: Age and Sex Structure

Fertility, mortality, and migration affect not only the size of a population but also its composition. Every population has a wide variety of demographic characteristics, such as sex and age. Demographers use the term *sex ratio* to describe the number of males per 100 females in a given population. If an equal number of males and females exists, the sex ratio is 100. Today, the sex ratio in the United States is 95.3, meaning there are 95.3 men for every 100 women (U.S. Bureau of the Census, 1995, p. 16). This figure varies according to age, however. There are approximately 106 males born for every 100 females. At sixty-five years of age, the ratio drops to around 67, which reflects a higher death rate for males. The sex ratio also varies from one time period to another. It was 106 in 1910, showing a surplus of men over women. The sex ratio also varies according to race and ethnicity. Among whites in the United States, it is 95.5, and it is 90.1 among African Americans and 99.5 among Hispanic Americans.

Changes in the composition of a population can have important social ramifications. An unbalanced sex ratio, for example, can affect people's opportunities to marry or have children. Changes in the age composition also have consequences. An aging populace means that there are fewer workers in proportion to retired people. This imbalance creates problems when it comes to supporting retired citizens in the fashion to which they have become accustomed. It has also meant that there are fewer young people enrolled in school, which has resulted in school closings and reduced job opportunities for teachers. During the 1980s, the same problem also began to affect the nation's colleges.

World Population Growth

You should be able to describe current patterns of population growth in the world and explain why such growth is often difficult to control.

Most of human history has passed on an earth that was only sparsely populated. It has been estimated, for example, that there were fewer people on the Earth seven thousand years ago than there are in larger cities such as New York or Tokyo today. At the time of Christ, approximately two thousand years ago, there were probably not many more people alive than currently live in the United States. In Figure 14.1, it can readily be seen that, prior to 1750, world population was small and growth was slow. After 1750, world population began to increase at a more rapid rate, and it continues to grow even more rapidly today. Only in the last two centuries has world population exceeded 1 billion. Currently, world population is about 5.8 billion (see Figure 14.2). Current projections are that the world population could *double* again by the middle of the next century or just beyond. Demographers caution, however, that such long-range projections are speculative because levels of birthrate and death rate are likely to shift in the interim in ways that are difficult to predict. The largest nation in the world today is China, with 1.2 billion people. The United States is the third largest nation, with a population of 260 million, behind China and India.

The primary reason for the low rate of population growth in the world prior to 1750 was the relatively high death rate in practically every society. For example, until 1600, the average life expectancy in European countries was little more than thirty-five years, in comparison to more than seventy years in industrial societies today. One important factor in the high death rate at that time was the extremely high infant mortality rate. In some societies, as many as 50 percent of the infants born would die within their first year of life (Antonovsky, 1972). The two most important variables producing these high death rates were disease and famine. In fact, disease has accounted for more deaths in the Western world than any other factor throughout history. Before the modern era, knowledge and technology related to medicine, sanitation, and agriculture were not sufficiently advanced to lower the death rate and thus increase life expectancy. Although famine is something with which most people in the United States are unfamiliar, at times it has led to astonishingly high death rates. For example, a severe famine in China in 1877 and 1878 was responsible for the deaths of between nine and thirteen million people (Petersen, 1975). The modern-day effects of famine may be observed in Somalia, where, despite the world's ability to produce food, many people have died of starvation in recent years.

The Demographic Transition

One of the earliest attempts to understand population growth began two centuries ago, at the beginning of the Industrial Revolution in Europe, when the English clergyman Thomas Robert Malthus (1798/1960) published his *Essay on the Principle of Population*. Malthus argued that an immutable passion exists between the sexes that leads to reproduction, and that societies have a limited ability to produce food. The consequence of these facts, he believed, is that the human population tends to grow at a faster rate than does the ability to produce food. If these tendencies continue unchecked, then populations will eventually grow larger than the food supply can support. Malthus believed that human beings could intercede in this process and control population

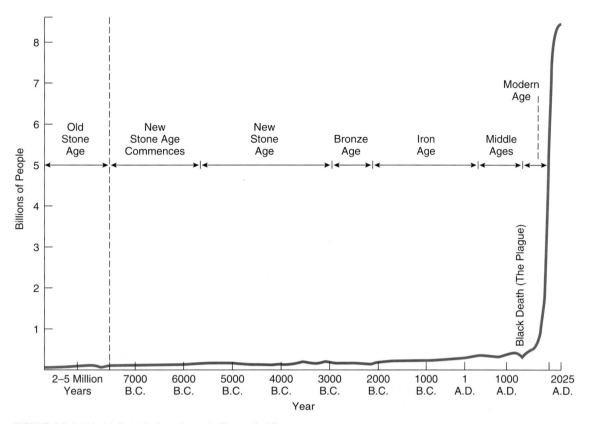

FIGURE 14.1 World Population Growth Through History *Note:* From *World Population: Fundamentals of Growth* (3rd ed.) by Population Reference Bureau, 1995.

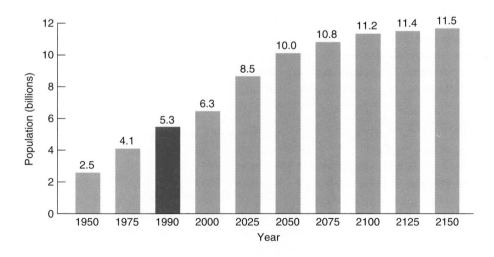

FIGURE 14.2 World Population, 1950–2150 *Note:* From *Long-range World Population Projections: Two Centuries of Population Growth, 1950–2150* (pp. 18–24) by United Nations, 1992, Sales No. E. 92. XIII. 3.

growth by postponing marriage or remaining celibate, but he was pessimistic about whether human intervention would completely save the day. He thought populations would continue to grow, ultimately being checked by deaths due to starvation, disease, and war.

Malthus's view of population growth is basically functionalist, because he viewed population size and food supplies as two parts of a system that should be balanced. If either part changes, it will affect the other. Karl Marx disputed Malthus's position and took a more conflict-oriented approach toward population problems. He argued that there are powerful groups, the capitalists, who benefit from restrictions in the food supply. Because capitalism is based on profit making, food and other goods are not produced unless people are willing to pay a profitable price for them. And less food may be produced than people actually need so that the low supply of food will increase the price. With an economy based on producing food for human *need* rather than profit, Marx argued, technology could be harnessed to produce a sufficient amount of food for a growing population. (The foundations of capitalist and socialist economies are discussed in Chapter 13.)

Both the Malthusian and Marxian views of population problems have adherents today, and both views are applicable to some elements of the problem of population growth. Rather than debate which approach is more accurate, modern demographers have attempted to understand what underlies the rapid world population growth of the past few centuries. Underlying this growth is a process referred to as the **demographic transition,** *the changing patterns of birthrates and death rates brought about by industrialization* (Kammeyer & Ginn, 1986). The reasons for this transition are complex. It is useful to divide the demographic transition into four stages (see Figure 14.3).

The *preindustrial stage* is characterized by high birthrates and death rates, resulting in a population that grows slowly, if at all. Throughout much of human history, societies have been in this preindustrial stage.

For most Western nations, including the United States, the preindustrial stage existed until the onset of industrialization between 1750 and 1850, when the *transitional,* or *early industrial, stage* began. This stage is characterized by continuing high birthrates but declining death rates. The falling death rates occur because of improvements in lifestyle resulting from industrial development (see Chapter 10). More and better food was available, for example, which helped people resist infectious diseases and reduced infant mortality. In addition, improvements in transportation, communication, and sanitation contributed to a lowering of the death rate. Cultural values, however, still encouraged people to have large families, so the birthrate stayed high. The *gap between the high birthrates and low death rates*—commonly called a **demographic gap**—resulted in explosive population growth during the early industrial period. The death rate was too low to keep population size stable when the birthrate remained high.

The third stage, called the *industrial stage,* is characterized by a continued decline in the death rate and a declining birthrate. During this stage medicine became more effective in controlling acute and chronic diseases and thus contributed to additional declines in the death rate. In addition, industrial technology eventually made it possible for people to lead cleaner and healthier lives. The decline in the birthrate was a response to the impact of industrialization on cultural values regarding childbearing. Urbanization and increasing education, for example, led couples to desire smaller families than in the past.

The *postindustrial stage* of the demographic transition, which some demographers prefer to consider a continuation of the industrial stage, is characterized by low birthrates and low death rates, once again a roughly stable population with little growth. The industrialized nations, such as the United States, Japan, and some European countries, may be currently entering this stage, although how low their birthrates and death rates will go and for how long are matters of some speculation.

The Extent of Overpopulation

The fully industrialized nations in the world today, including the United States, have experienced the demographic transition and now exhibit relatively low birthrates and death rates. If these low rates continue, then the populations of these countries will eventually stabilize, with little if any subsequent growth. However, many nations in the world

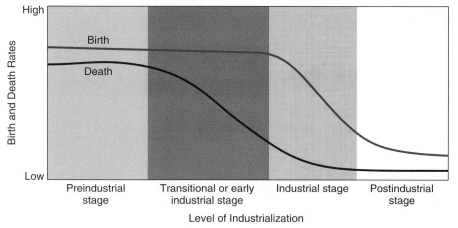

FIGURE 14.3 The Demographic Transition

High

Birth and Death Rates

Birth

Death

Low

Preindustrial stage

Transitional or early industrial stage

Industrial stage

Postindustrial stage

Level of Industrialization

are considerably less industrialized and have not yet gone through this transition in birthrates and death rates; they are where today's world population problem can be most clearly located. In these nations, the death rate has dropped considerably, owing in large part to the introduction of modern medicine, sanitation, and public health efforts. Insecticides, better transportation, and improved agricultural practices, for example, have made more and better food available. The impact of these changes on mortality has frequently been dramatic. In Sri Lanka between 1945 and 1949, the crude death rate declined from twenty-two deaths per one thousand people to twelve per one thousand; in 1947 alone, the life expectancy rose from forty-three to fifty-two.

Although the developing nations of the world have not gone through the demographic transition, many of them have experienced a significant decline in their fertility. Nations such as Peru and Mexico, for example, will have seen their total fertility rate decline from more than six children per woman in the 1970s to fewer than three by the year 2000 (Robey, Rutstein, & Morris, 1993; U.S. Bureau of the Census, 1995). However, these lower fertility rates are still quite high and contribute significantly to world population growth. When these high birthrates are combined with the substantial declines in the death rate that have occurred, the result is a continuing and large demographic gap. Ghana and Cambodia, for example, are projected to have rates of natural in-

crease of more than 3 percent in the 1990s. This increase compares with the U.S. rate of natural increase of 0.62.

When today's industrialized nations went through the demographic transition, their death rates declined slowly over many decades, so population growth was gradual, allowing cultural values regarding childbearing and family size to change, yielding smaller families. The developing nations of today, however, have seen their death rates drop rapidly, and cultural values do not change that quickly. The cultural values in developing nations are changing—women in these nations desire smaller families and are increasing their use of contraceptives. However, behavior has not changed sufficiently to come anywhere near eliminating the demographic gap that represents world population growth. Thus the developing regions of the world are expected to grow at an annual rate of 2 percent during the 1990s, as compared with 0.5 percent in the fully industrialized nations. Figure 14.4 shows the impact of these differing rates of natural increase: Europe and North America, where most of the industrial nations are, will contain a dwindling proportion of the world's population, whereas Africa and Latin America, containing mostly developing nations, will see its proportion of the world's population grow significantly.

The impact of these changes can be better understood if we examine the number of years required for the world's population to double in

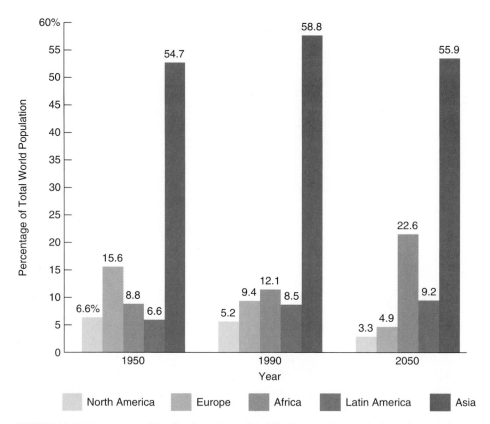

FIGURE 14.4 Percentage Distribution of the World's Population in Various Geographic Areas, 1950–2050 *Note:* From *Long-range World Population Projections: Two Centuries of Population Growth, 1950–2150* (pp. 18–24) by United Nations, 1992, Sales No. E. 92. XIII. 3.

size. Demographers refer to this figure as the *doubling time*. From the beginning of the Christian era, it took 1,650 years for the population to double. By comparison, if current rates of world population growth continue, only forty years will pass until world population again doubles its size.

Will the developing nations of the world today lower their birthrates before world population grows disastrously out of control? It must be kept in mind that the demographic transition is a description of a long historical trend found in some nations, all of which have experienced occasional changes in birthrates or death rates that go against this trend. We do not know if the developing nations of today will follow the same path (Organski, Kugler, Johnson, & Cohen, 1984). One thing is clear, however. In a preindustrial era, population growth, or the lack of it, was

determined primarily by a high death rate, over which people had little control. Today, growth is determined to a large extent by factors, especially fertility, over which people do have some control. Thus, the attention of those concerned about overpopulation today has been focused on issues of fertility control.

The Consequences of Overpopulation

One important consequence of population growth is *crowding*. Studies of animals have shown that extreme crowding can have considerable negative consequences, including elevated aggression levels and erratic behavior. Animal studies, however, are only suggestive of how crowding may affect human beings, because people's reactions would depend on people's past experiences and expectations. In addition, it is possible to design living quarters and work areas in which *density* is high but people do not have the *impression* of being crowded, so potentially negative effects could be avoided. The psychologist Jonathan Freedman (1975) has argued that crowding *by itself* does not have negative consequences. Rather, crowding is usually associated with other social conditions such as poverty that produce increases in crime or aggression (Ehrlich & Ehrlich, 1990; Liddell & Kruger, 1987). Thus there is considerable controversy over the impact of crowding. Yet if world population doubles in the next forty years and doubles again after that, we will experience serious overcrowding. The deleterious impact of this dramatic growth will be difficult to alleviate.

Another consequence of population growth is the potential for *food shortages.* Especially in developing nations, it is difficult to increase agricultural production enough to keep up with population growth. As a consequence, millions of people die each year from starvation and malnutrition. It is a poignant commentary on Marx's view of population problems that farmers in the United States are sometimes paid to keep some of their cropland out of production while other people in the world do not have enough food to eat.

Still another consequence of population growth is the growing *depletion of the world's natural resources.* There is considerable debate over precisely how serious this problem is. One research group estimated, for example, that world petroleum resources would be exhausted in fifty years and natural gas in thirty-eight years (Meadows, Meadows, Randers, & Behrens, 1972). Yet new finds of such resources have led others to call such pessimistic estimates unrealistic. For example, a report to the President on the state of the world in the year 2000, titled *The Global 2000 Report* (Teich, 1986), concludes that most minerals can be maintained at desirable levels through discoveries and judicious investment. Although there may be problems in petroleum production, the report sees plenty of time to shift to other energy resources or reduce consumption. In either case, the world's resources are finite, and as developing nations become more affluent, they will place increasing strain on the supply of resources. One of

the world's natural resources is *living space.* Wars have been fought over the need for more land. Population growth in the future could result in other wars over land space or other dwindling natural resources (Homer-Dixon, 1993).

Controlling Population Growth

Given the problems of overpopulation, intense efforts have been directed toward controlling population growth through the only reasonable means that we have—reducing fertility.

Family Planning   Some modern population control efforts have focused on encouraging people to decide consciously how many children they want, with the hope that they will choose to have smaller families. Such family-planning programs encourage couples to have children when and if offspring are desired. Experience with such programs has shown that, when women realize they have a choice of whether to have children, they most often choose to have fewer children than they would have had otherwise. Still, people who desire children will have them, and people's desires arise out of socialization into a particular set of cultural values. Other Worlds, Other Ways: China describes the experiences of one developing nation's efforts to control population growth in a cultural context that was not supportive of these efforts.

Research on the effectiveness of family-planning services generally shows that they increase contraceptive use, reduce fertility, and result in smaller families (Jacobson, 1988; Mauldin, 1975; Robey, Rutstein, & Morris, 1993). However, the provision of such services is not a total answer to the world's population problem. In many countries with active family-planning efforts, such as China, South Korea, and Costa Rica, social and economic changes—to be discussed in a moment—probably account for much of the lowering of fertility. In other countries, such as Kenya, India, and the Dominican Republic, family-planning programs have had little observable effect. Why? As noted earlier, values are a critical element in reducing fertility—people must want to have fewer children before family-planning efforts will work. In many countries, however,

0   miles   2000

CHINA
Beijing
Shanghai
Guangdong

OTHER WORLDS, *Other Ways*

CHINA: POPULATION POLICY—BIG PROBLEMS, DRACONIAN SOLUTIONS

China has a tremendous problem on its hands. It has a land area about the same as the United States but more than four times as many people. Whereas the United States has a population of 270 million, China has 1.2 billion people—22 percent of the world's people with only 7 percent of the earth's arable land (U.S. Bureau of the Census, 1995, pp. 845–847). To make matters worse, China's population is growing more than twice as fast: It has an annual growth rate of 1.4 compared to 0.62 in the United States. In 1991, the average Chinese woman had 2.3 children, compared to 1.8 in the United States; in the mid-1990s, the crude birth rate was 18 births per 1,000 people compared to 14 per 1,000 in the United States. Yet another problem is that China's population is much younger than the U.S. population, which means a larger proportion of the Chinese are still planning to have children. Therefore, even if China brought its birthrate down to U.S. levels, China's population would still grow much faster than the U.S. population. Experts expect China's population to peak at 1.9 billion by the middle of next century.

Such population growth puts an enormous strain on China's environment in terms of whether it can produce sufficient food for that many people and ab-sorb the pollutants generated. Rapid population growth also hinders economic development since whatever economic growth occurs is absorbed supporting the growing population instead of being available for investment in new industries or machinery. For these reasons, the Chinese authorities have been deeply concerned for decades about controlling population growth.

By the end of the 1970s, Chinese authorities were sufficiently concerned to institute a one-child family program for all couples who did not already have more than one child. Incentives were created for families that achieved the goal, such as granting a government stipend to one-child families until the youngster is fourteen years old; there were also penalties for families with more than two children, including salary deductions and tax surcharges. Even more controversial was the use of government-employed family-planning workers to consult with, and in some cases cajole, couples about their sexual behavior and use of contraceptives.

Through the 1980s, the birthrate in China came down, but not nearly as quickly as the authorities had hoped. By the late 1980s, it began to look as if the Chinese would not reach the targets they had set. For example, the crude birthrate had dropped from twenty-five per one thousand in 1980 to only twenty-two by 1990—not much improvement to show for the program. Alarmed authorities, pushing for a renewed effort to achieve the goals, introduced a responsibility

women have large numbers of children because they have been taught to want them, and cultural values are supportive of large families. In addition, in some societies, large families are a central support when people are sick, out of work, or face other misfortunes. In short, children take the place of old-age or unemployment insurance. In such settings, family planning will probably have only a marginal effect.

Economic Development   Certain social and economic changes probably account for more of the decline in fertility than family planning. These changes are generally called *economic development* (Bouvier, 1984). Developing nations that are actively involved in programs to control population growth have placed a major emphasis on economic development. Although these countries recognize the need for family planning, they argue that no

system in which district and township officials would be held personally responsible if the people under their jurisdiction did not achieve the goals (Kristof, 1993a). These officials could lose bonuses or be fined or dismissed. Another part of the program was compulsory, organized sterilizations, in which family-planning cadres would descend on a village and take all women who already had a child to a clinic to be fitted with an intrauterine device or sterilized. A third part of the program focused on women who become pregnant without authorization, using strong social pressure on them to have an abortion. Out of fear that they would not achieve their goals, some overly zealous local officials got carried away, forcing some women to have abortions and smashing the huts of a few women who had unauthorized births (WuDunn, 1993).

This draconian program had an effect. The birthrate dropped significantly in 1992, with the average Chinese woman having 1.9 children—about the same as in the United States. In addition, the number of sterilizations went way up and very few children born were third or subsequent births. However, these successes have not been without costs. A major cost is that female infanticides have increased. The Chinese, especially in rural areas, want sons so they can extend the male line into the future, some even feeling they have dishonored their ancestors if they fail to do so. Female infanticide allows them to try again for a male child when the government is strongly urging a one-child family. Reports of increases in drownings and other murders of female infants emerged in the 1980s. In some cases, apparently, Chinese midwives, following instructions from the parents, keep a bucket of water handy during delivery; if the child born is female, she is drowned immediately and reported as a stillborn (Kristof, 1993a). Information on the sex ratio in China supports the idea that some female infanticide is occurring. Biologically in human populations, about ninety-four females are born for every hundred males. In recent years in China, as few as eighty-five to eighty-nine females were reported born for each hundred males. Some of these figures involve families just not reporting a female birth to authorities so they can try again to have a male. But part of the situation is undoubtedly due to infanticide. If China's sex ratio is this skewed, then a few decades down the road Chinese men may have difficulty finding wives.

The experience of China highlights the importance of cultural values in influencing people's behavior. Even when the government provides benefits for those who lower their fertility and penalties for those who do not cooperate, people will continue to reproduce if they value children. When government intervention goes contrary to people's deeply held values, it is not likely to be very effective, short of strongly repressive and authoritarian measures. Even these measures may not remain effective for long.

program of population control can be completely effective unless it is part of a more general program of economic development. A number of changes that accompany economic development—especially urbanization, increasing levels of education, and a rising standard of living—lead people to view large families as less desirable. In urban settings and since the passage of child labor laws in the United States, there is no longer a distinct economic advantage to having many children. In fact, in urban, industrial societies, large families lead to crowded housing and a drain on family finances. Furthermore, when women receive more education, they usually want to pursue a career or develop talents other than domestic ones, and large families make this effort more difficult. Finally, economic development affords people a more affluent lifestyle, and large families are expensive. Many couples decide to spend their resources on consumer goods or leisure activities rather than raise a large family. Even with economic development, most people want to become parents, but they are more likely to opt for a smaller number of children. And as small families become common, they are viewed increasingly as normal, and people feel social pressures not to have large families.

Recent research suggests, however, that economic development may not be as critical to reducing fertility as once thought (Robey, Rutstein, & Morris, 1993). Many of today's developing nations have reduced their fertility significantly even though they have not experienced significant economic development. In fact, some nations have experienced declining fertility even though their economic circumstances have become worse. It appears that some of the elements originally linked with economic development, such as urbanization, also influence fertility in the absence of economic development: Even in less developed nations, people in cities have fewer children because there are fewer advantages to having children in such settings. In addition, the mass media have contributed to the spread of information about contraception and to the propagation of values regarding small families in less developed nations, and this has helped bring down fertility levels. What is uncertain at this point is whether fertility levels can be brought down to the level in industrial nations without significant economic development.

The Status of Women   Another important element in controlling population growth is the status of women. The United Nations has for decades vigorously promoted programs to improve women's lives by providing them with opportunities in education, employment, and political participation, as well as support in their domestic and maternal roles (see Chapter 8). Research conducted by the United Nations has shown consistently that educational attainment and labor force participation of women are particularly important elements in a population policy: Educated women who work outside the home have fewer children than do less educated women who are not part of the labor force (Repetto, 1994).

Research conducted in the United States also shows that better educated women who have careers, or at least are a part of the labor force, desire smaller families and are more sensitive to the overall issue of population growth (Houseknecht, 1987; Thompson, 1980). So, programs intended to advance sexual equality around the world will likely have a positive impact on controlling population growth.

Communities and Urbanization

You should be able to trace the pattern of urbanization and suburbanization in the United States and Third-World cities and describe what is distinct about postindustrial cities.

This chapter has discussed some of the major elements of human ecology—the size and composition of human populations. In the context of migration, it mentioned the geographical distribution of people. The remainder of this chapter will discuss the topic of population distribution in more detail, especially the emergence of communities and urbanization in human societies. A community is more than a gathering of people in a geographic location. A **community** consists of *a group of people who share a common territory and a sense of identity or belonging, and who interact with one another* (Poplin, 1979).

The Emergence of Cities

The earliest human communities were small hunting-and-gathering bands, usually consisting of between forty and one hundred people. These bands were usually nomadic, roaming the land in search of food and game, and all the people knew one another well. Then, about fifteen thousand years ago, small fishing villages began to appear around the Baltic Sea, surviving off the plentiful fish. Approximately ten thousand years ago, people discovered how to cultivate plants and domesticate animals. These skills afforded them greater control over their food supply and permitted a growing surplus of food. The result was the emergence of agricultural villages, and later cities, in fertile river valleys around the world. A **city** is *a* relatively large, permanent community of people who rely on surrounding agricultural communities for their food supply. As a consequence of developing agriculture, then, human communities grew enormously in size. The biblical city of Ur, for example, located at the juncture of the Tigris and Euphrates rivers, had 24,000 people (Hawley, 1971). At the height of the Roman Empire, Rome is estimated to have had as many as one million residents, and the Aztec city of Tenochtitlán, as noted earlier, may have contained a few hundred thousand inhabitants. Prior to the Industrial Revolution, however, only a few cities had as many as 100,000 people.

Industrialization ushered in ever-increasing urbanization, with cities growing far larger than their preindustrial predecessors. By the mid-twentieth century, cities such as New York, Paris, and Tokyo had many millions of inhabitants. Two hundred years ago, only 5 percent of all people in the United States lived in urban areas, in contrast to 77 percent today (see Figure 14.5). The New York metropolitan area has more than eighteen million people, and Mexico City—site of ancient Tenochtitlán—has more than twenty million. Why has this extensive urbanization occurred? One of the main reasons is that most economic activity in industrial societies is nonagricultural, and such activity benefits from being concentrated geographically. With industry and jobs located in cities, people are drawn to the cities to find work. So *community* for most people in the United States today means a city, whether it be large or small.

Suburbanization

Equally as important as the growth of cities has been the growth of **suburbs,** *less densely populated areas, primarily residential in nature, on the outskirts of a city.* Mass suburbanization is a relatively recent

FIGURE 14.5 Percentage of Urban Population in the United States, 1790–1990
Note: From *Statistical Abstracts of the United States, 1991* (pp. 17, 27) by U.S. Bureau of the Census, 1991, Washington, DC: U.S. Government Printing Office.

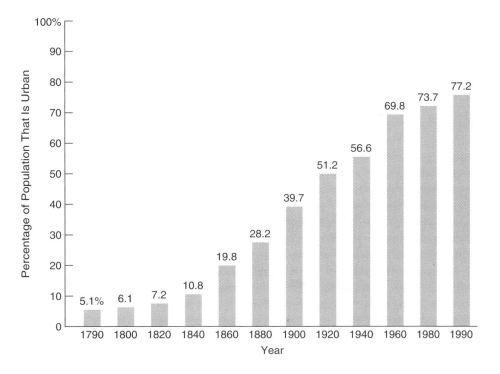

Government policies that assisted people in purchasing new homes in the suburbs rather than existing housing in the city encouraged the suburbanization of cities such as Los Angeles. Severe air pollution was one of the eventual results.

development. In the United States, it arose out of a complex set of social factors (Banfield, 1990). One factor was the economic and technological developments that made it possible for people to live far from where they worked. Early in the twentieth century, most people were limited in where they could live by the need to find transportation to work. This need meant that most had to live in the cities, near where the jobs were. Because there were relatively few automobiles and highways, people walked or used public transportation to go to work and shopping. This situation encouraged the concentration of population, and central cities served as the commercial and cultural core of urban areas. By the 1940s and 1950s, the increasing affluence of many people, along with the automobile, made it feasible for them to live farther from work and opened up suburban life to the middle class.

In addition to these economic developments, government policy contributed to suburbanization. For example, the federal government paid 80 percent of the cost of developing the interstate highway system. With cars and high-speed highways, people can now live far from where they work and shop. In sprawling cities such as Los Angeles, for example, it is common to live fifty or more miles from where one works. The policies of the Federal Housing Administration (FHA) and the Veterans Administration (VA) also encouraged the development of suburbs (Bullock, Anderson, & Brady, 1983). Beginning in the 1930s, the FHA and the VA made available federally guaranteed mortgage loans for the purchase of new homes. Because land outside the cities was both inexpensive and available, that was where much of the construction took place. The FHA and VA did not provide loans to purchase existing homes or build apartments, policies that would have encouraged people to continue living in the cities. Other social policies have contributed to suburban development, such as a low tax on gasoline, which removes an economic incentive for people to live in more centralized communities, and a tax deduction for the interest on a home mortgage and property taxes. By contrast, most European nations have taxed gasoline heavily and have devoted more resources to maintaining public transportation than to building highways. The European policies have focused more on population concentration as a way to preserve open space. So, encouraged by all of these policies, the flight of people from cities was in full swing, and especially in the early years, it was the more affluent city dwellers who moved to the suburbs. It should be kept in mind that this suburbanization occurred not simply because people wanted to move to the suburbs. It also depended on the development of new transportation technologies and on federal social policy on taxes, housing, and transportation. That these developments had such wide-ranging affects should not be surprising given the functionalist point about the interdependence among the different elements of social systems. The manifest function of the social policies was to stimulate economic development. Their latent function was to encourage decentralization of urban areas and to bring about the eventual decline of many cities. Clearly, all the ramifications of these policies were not considered when they were established.

These same developments eventually made it possible for businesses and factories also to move outside cities. Businesses were originally located in cities because workers lived there and transportation was available to ship their products. By the 1950s, cities no longer possessed those exclusive attractions. A labor force and highways were available in the suburbs. In addition, suburban land was typically less expensive, taxes were lower, and affluent suburbs could afford to offer tax breaks to industries to relocate. Suburban shopping malls were situated next to freeways and equipped with huge parking lots. The malls were clean, spacious, and keyed to an affluent lifestyle. They drew consumer dollars out of the city as urban stores established suburban outlets. Increasing crowding and congestion in cities, along with the growth of numerous other problems, also made the suburbs popular as a "rural refuge." In their early development, suburbs were not economically self-supporting, since many residents made their livelihood in the cities. By the 1970s, however, 75 percent of all suburban residents both lived and worked in the suburbs and only about 25 percent commuted to the central city to work. Today, the United States is a nation of suburbanites, with 60 percent of its metropolitan population living in the suburbs. And it is the suburbs, rather than the central cities, that have shown the most significant population growth over the past two decades.

The Postindustrial City

Although many people and some jobs have left the city, other jobs have remained. Many cities have retained or increased jobs in the financial service industries, those related to the functioning of corporate headquarters, telecommunications and publishing, and those involving nonprofit and governmental activities (Heenan, 1991). This is true of some large cities such as New York, Chicago, Houston, and Atlanta, and some smaller cities, such as Memphis, Des Moines, Madison (Wisconsin), and Ann Arbor (Michigan). In other words, the changes in cities reflect the changes in the economy discussed in Chapter 13: The stagnation in the manufacturing sector and the growth of the service sector.

Recent technological developments, however, may reduce the need for corporations or service industries to concentrate their workers in one locale. Computers, microwave transmission, fax machines, and communications satellites make it possible for people to communicate over long distances instantly, effortlessly, and relatively inexpensively. Overnight parcel delivery is available almost everywhere today, and information can be sent rapidly over the telephone lines from one computer to another. Teleconferencing means that even meetings can be held when those "present" are separated by long distances. (Closely related is the concept of distance education, discussed in Chapter 12.)

There will still be some need for centralization. Top corporate executives will need close contact with attorneys, investment counselors, management-consulting firms, and advertising executives. But many other jobs can be decentralized. For example, Eastern Airlines moved its reservation centers to Charlotte, North Carolina, and Woodbridge, New Jersey, and Exxon moved its corporate headquarters to Irving, Texas (Kindel, 1990). It will take some years to see the effects of new technological developments, but they well may encourage further decentralization of urban areas.

A Global Perspective on Urbanization

Growth and Overurbanization As Figure 14.6 illustrates, nations vary tremendously in how much of their population lives in cities. At one extreme is Rwanda with only 6 percent of its population in

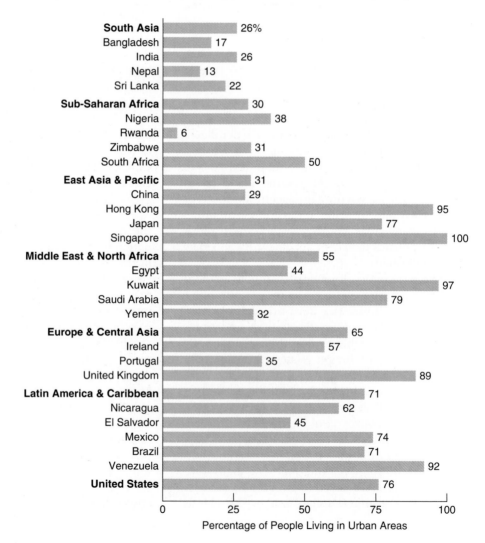

FIGURE 14.6 Worldwide Levels of Urbanization, 1993 *Note:* Adapted from *World Development Report 1995.* Copyright 1995 by The International Bank for Reconstruction and Development/The World Bank. Reprinted by permission of Oxford University Press, Inc.

urban areas; at the other is the city-nation of Singapore with all its citizens living within the urban shadow of its sole city, Singapore. Whereas overall levels of urbanization in Asia and Africa are significantly lower than in Europe or the Americas, many cities in those regions are growing rapidly. In addition, many cities in Latin America have experienced explosive growth in the past four decades. Both Mexico City and São Paulo, Brazil, for example, grew from approximately 3 million people to 24 million since 1950. By contrast, Los Angeles, one of the fastest-growing cities in the United States, grew from 2 million to 3.5 million during the same period.

The preceding description of the process of urbanization focused mostly on the experiences of industrial nations such as the United States. Urbanization in the developing nations of the world has been influenced by different social and economic forces. Nevertheless, a few generalizations can be made (Kasarda & Crenshaw, 1991). One is that the industrialized nations tend to have higher rates of urbanization than the less industrialized nations. This difference is explained by the fact that, as in the United States, urbanization develops with and is supportive of industrialization.

A second generalization is that the rapidly growing cities in many Third-World nations today are facing more adverse conditions than did the cities of Europe and North America that matured during the nineteenth and early twentieth centuries. For one thing, today's Third-World cities are growing much more rapidly and thus experiencing the problems of crowding, crime, and pollution to a much higher degree. In addition, they

This photo of Rio de Janeiro, Brazil, shows poor children in a *favela,* or slum, while considerable wealth exists a short distance away. Rio and other Latin American cities have grown very rapidly and do not have sufficient jobs and housing for their people.

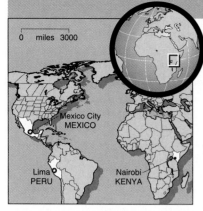

THER WORLDS, *Other Ways*

PERU, KENYA, MEXICO: THE SOCIAL ORGANIZATION OF THIRD-WORLD SLUMS

Mexico, along with many other Third-World nations, has been undergoing rapid urbanization, which has put a strain on the ability of its cities to house and employ all the people living there. In the mid-1960s, half of Mexico's population lived in rural areas; today only one-quarter does (World Bank, 1995). This rural-to-urban migration is typically the result of push-pull factors. People are pushed out of the rural environment because of a lack of jobs or land on which to make a living; they are pulled toward cities by the belief, or hope, that they will have better opportunities there. The result is often massive crowding and poverty in squatter settlements or shanty towns. What is remarkable about these settlements, however, is not just the poverty but the creativity, initiative, and persistence with which the inhabitants adapt to and attempt to overcome the almost insurmountable adversity they face.

The *barriadas* of Lima, Peru, for example, have shown phenomenal growth (Stokes, 1995). These substandard and often illegal neighborhoods arise on the periphery of the city, sometimes created by people who simply occupy a piece of vacant, inhospitable land. One settlement, which climbs the sides of a valley surrounding Lima, was described thus:

> The highest houses, erected by the most recent arrivals, are no more than boxes made of six bamboo mats—four for the walls, one for the roof and one for the floor. These are slung on a framework of wooden supports to make a single room, no more than eight feet square, that must accommodate anything up to eight or ten people. (Harrison, 1983, p. 104)

Although it is hard to imagine such a dwelling as a step up, for some it represents an improvement. Most residents of *barriadas* are recent arrivals from rural areas, but many have moved out from the packed, filthy slums of central Lima. "Their move to the squatter areas is a refusal to pay any more rent—an act of self-liberation" (Harrison, 1983, p. 104). When resources become available, residents of the *barriadas* improve their homes, replacing the straw walls with wood and the straw roof with plastic sheeting. The squatters in Lima often join together in political movements that pressure politicians to provide them with sewage, water, or other urban amenities (Castells, 1988). The existence of these squatter areas is due in part to institutional permissiveness: Political and bureaucratic authorities simply ignore them, at least for a period of time. The land, being on the outskirts of the city, is without great economic value. As the city grows around the *barriadas,* however, property values rise and open the way for profitable housing construction. When that happens, the squatters are in danger of being expelled and having their homes destroyed.

The picture that emerges in Lima and other Third-World cities is of poor people struggling with great tenacity to improve their lives. A similar picture appears in Nairobi, the capital of Kenya (Nelson, 1988). Less than one-quarter of Kenya's population

face much more severe economic competition from the advanced industrial nations with their already modernized cities and substantial economic resources. When the cities of the United States and Europe were developing, they were the advanced cities of their time and thus were attractive to investors and credit markets. Today's developing cities struggle to compete with already mature adversaries in other nations.

A third generalization is that urbanization in the Third World has been driven as much, or possibly more, by the pressures of the capitalist

lives in urban areas, but growth in those areas has been fast. As in Lima, the squatter settlements in Nairobi grow on the periphery of the city and are largely unplanned and uncontrolled. In Nairobi, more women than men live in these settlements, and most of the women are heads of their own households. They show remarkable ingenuity in supporting themselves. Most residents cannot find jobs in what economists call the formal economic sector, the large-scale, capital-intensive, wage-earning part of the economy, where a person formally applies for a job, has a steady place and hours of work and decent pay, and works at the same job for a period of time. Therefore, they turn to the informal economy, sometimes called street occupations or the unorganized sector. These are jobs one does in the street, if one is willing to do them. They are generally low-paying, low-prestige jobs. The women in Nairobi's squatter settlements tend toward certain kinds of street occupations. One, of course, is prostitution; another is selling food and beer and child-care services. Men engage in a much wider range of street occupations: casual wage work, driving illegal taxis, delivery services, street sweeping, and bicycle repair, as well as criminal activities such as theft and fencing stolen goods. Both men and women shift from one occupation to another, depending on which seems to offer them the most money on a given day. Unable to find jobs in the formal sector, they do what they can to get by.

The final notable fact about these squatter towns in Third-World cities is the creative development of networks of exchange that provide people with some economic security when they are chronically under-employed or unemployed. In squatter settlements in Mexico City, for example, the basic unit of social organization is the nuclear family, but each nuclear family develops an elaborate exchange network with other families, often relatives, but not always (Lomnitz, 1988). Sometimes a family, especially a young couple, will temporarily move in with relatives, but couples prefer to live on their own if they can. More often a group of families will inhabit a compound, each family in its own residence but sharing a common outdoor area for cooking, washing, and playing. In this case, geographic proximity helps to define the social network: each family is a separate economic unit, but all families in the compound provide reciprocal assistance to one another. In other cases, one family will develop reciprocal ties with a family in another compound because they are related through blood or marriage.

These social networks engage in daily, or almost daily, exchanges of goods and services, enabling each impoverished family to tap into a resource base that is substantially larger than its own. The families in a network might pool money for rent or entertainment, use common cooking facilities, help one another on construction projects, or share a television or latrine. Each family contributes what it is able and receives on the basis of what it needs and what resources the network has. Through such networks, the poor in these squatter communities display an innovative response to adversity: With few resources available to each family, they maximize the resource base through social arrangements based on communal sharing.

world system as it has been by internal pressures toward industrialization. For example, Other Worlds, Other Ways: Nicaragua in Chapter 13 noted that international investors bought large tracts of land in Nicaragua to grow coffee and cotton for export. This practice forced Nicaraguan peasant farmers off the land and fueled population growth in the cities. In other places, capital-intensive foreign investment in manufacturing for export products has stimulated booming growth in small and medium-size cities, as happened in Mexico with the *maquiladoras* along the U.S. border, as described in Chapters 2 and 8. These plants sprouted in cities such as Juarez and Matamoros, manufacturing goods for export and drawing in thousands of people from surrounding rural areas. So, some of the pressures toward urbanization in these developing nations are external, controlled by international elites rather than national leaders.

A final generalization, which really stems from the previous one, is that some cities in developing nations have experienced *overurbanization,* having populations larger than the city can house, employ, and adequately take care of (Smith, 1991a). When foreigners invest in agriculture for export and retard industrial development, people are pushed off the land, but there are insufficient jobs and housing for them in the cities. When there are too many people in the cities for the available resources, the result is squatter slums. Other Worlds, Other Ways: Peru, Kenya, Mexico (on pp. 496–497) describes how people adapt to city life under these conditions.

Global Cities   World urbanization is not characterized solely by the growth of more and larger urban centers around the world; in addition, some cities are performing some new functions in the world economy (Sassen, 1991; Smith & Timberlake, 1993). The term **global cities** has been given to *cities in a postindustrial society that serve as centers of commerce, finance, and political and economic decision making for the global economic system.* It is in these urban centers that economic and political leaders coordinate the activities of global corporations. The design and marketing of products as well as financial activities, accounting, and advertising are performed in these global centers. However, in a postindustrial city, the actual production and manufacturing of goods is often done elsewhere. These cities are also often the centers of cultural production and distribution through the mass media. It is in these cities that the organization and design of movies, television shows, and news production occur. The emergence of these global cities has rested on the revolutions in computers and telecommunications of the past few decades; these advances have meant that geographic distance is no longer a hindrance to communication and control. So, these cities serve not only as the economic centers of their particular region of the world but also as the centers of coordination and control of global economic production and market distribution. In the United States, New York and Los Angeles would certainly be considered global cities; likewise, London, Tokyo, and Hong Kong would be given this designation.

Global cities, like other cities around the world, attract the poor and those dislocated by economic development. As a consequence, global cities often exhibit vast disparities in wealth, with the richest beneficiaries of the global economy living alongside the desperately poor. For example, Los Angeles, as the center of global media production, is home to some fantastically wealthy media stars and moguls; yet in 1995, seventy immigrants from Thailand, mostly women, were found in a prison-like garment factory in the Los Angeles area where they worked and lived in virtual slavery. The women had migrated from desperate poverty in Thailand in hopes of improving their circumstances; once in the United States, they found themselves toiling long hours for low wages under conditions that violated health and safety laws, and prevented from leaving the factory at any time. So, increasingly these global cities are characterized by powerful and highly profitable global corporations coexisting with masses of poor people and low-wage workers. In fact, as is pointed out in Chapter 13, it is often the actions of the corporations, at least in part, that have created the circumstances of those urban poor. Some of the largest clothing manufacturers in the United States bought their clothing stock from the factories that enslaved the Thai women just mentioned, and some of the toniest department and clothing stores in U.S. global cities sold products from the factories to their wealthy customers.

Urbanism as a Way of Life

You should be able to discuss the different perspectives on the nature and quality of urban life.

Sociologists have made numerous efforts to characterize the impact of city life on people and their relationships with one another. All these characterizations focus, in some way, on whether city life involves any sense of community. Three approaches are particularly useful in understanding urban life: The view that cities produce a peculiar urban consciousness, the view that people in cities can have a sense of community, and the view that subcultures play a key role in shaping life in cities.

Urban Consciousness

The observations of Ferdinand Tönnies (1887/1963) and others lead to the conclusion that urbanization results in more secondary group relations in people's lives and fewer primary group ties (see Chapters 2 and 4). It is the extension of secondary group ties that lends city life its impersonal character, the feeling that most people care little about anyone else as a person. This impersonality can lead to feelings of alienation from others. People who have many secondary ties and few primary ones might even feel a desperate sense of isolation. Based on the work of Tönnies and others, Louis Wirth (1938) and other urban sociologists at the University of Chicago championed the viewpoint that city life shapes city dwellers by creating an urban consciousness, a distinctive way of thinking about and a unique awareness of their surroundings. Three elements of city life play a role here: Large numbers of people, high density, and heterogeneity. People protect themselves from the large numbers and the density by interacting with one another in highly impersonal ways, and their lives become segmented, with only specialized roles being relevant in particular settings. Social relations are also highly depersonalized, with kinship bonds weakening and community identity fading. Given the thousands of people and dozens of settings that urban dwellers might face each day, it is not surprising that they respond with impersonality and emotional distance. To devote time and energy to all these people would be draining and impractical. In this mass of humanity, individuals can feel quite insignificant, knowing little about and having few contacts with most people around them. What knowledge one has of other people is often very superficial. Furthermore, relationships that do develop are most often secondary and

based on rational calculation of self-interest rather than affection. This calculation can lead city dwellers to feel preyed on by others. What emerges is a distinctive urban consciousness: People are reserved in social relationships, rational, and self-interested.

The heterogeneity of cities also has important effects on the urban consciousness. Neighborhoods are often highly segregated along racial, ethnic, religious, or socioeconomic lines. Yet it is difficult to avoid mingling with many different kinds of people at work, while shopping, or while traveling from place to place. These people not only may be different but also may be viewed as potentially dangerous or threatening. A mentally disturbed person shouting obscenities in the street or some tough-looking teenagers can be frightening and can motivate people to take a cold and aloof attitude toward those around them. Again, a distinctive urban consciousness emerges that says it is probably best to ignore much of what goes on around you lest it bring you trouble. This diversity leads to a greater tolerance of different lifestyles, but often the tolerance is not based on acceptance but on resignation. City dwellers typically have little choice but to mingle with people very different from themselves, no matter how they feel about it.

Urban Communities

The dreary picture of urban life painted by Wirth and others of the early Chicago school may have been due in part to the fact that many of these sociologists were first-generation urbanites themselves, having grown up in small towns or rural villages, and the negative aspects of urbanism deeply impressed them. It may also have resulted from the fact that the Chicago of the 1920s and 1930s that they studied was undergoing a period of considerable growth, in-migration, and social disorder. More recent perspectives on urban life have focused more on the positive elements of urbanism.

In contrast to Tönnies, Wirth, and others, Herbert Gans (1962/1972) argues that cities do retain a sense of community in neighborhoods where people identify with and have a sense of positive regard for one another. In fact, contrary to what Wirth proposed, research shows that family ties remain as strong in urban areas as in rural areas (Wilson, 1993). In some places, strong ethnic or racial bonds may lend a considerable degree of cohesiveness to a neighborhood. In Hispanic communities, for example, ethnic identity may be reflected in stores and restaurants catering to Hispanic tastes or in the routine use of Spanish in shops. There may also be organizations of Hispanic students or business people that emphasize the common heritage and interests of the people in the community. In addition, even in neighborhoods with a number of ethnic or racial groups, ethnic group boundaries often serve as symbols of solidarity and regulate patterns of interaction, with people having close ties to members of their own racial or ethnic group and maintaining distance from others (Suttles, 1968). Furthermore, communities in cities are not limited to particular neighborhoods but may be based on common interests or leisure activities.

Gans's argument, then, is that urban life does not have a uniform impact on people, although the tendencies described by Wirth can certainly be found. Rather, there are many lifestyles in cities, and the impact of the city on particular people depends on the groups to which they belong. Thus social characteristics such as age, education, or racial and ethnic group membership are critical factors affecting people's adaptations to city life.

Urban Subcultures

Claude Fischer (1975) attempted to synthesize Wirth's and Gans's positions. Fischer recognized that the social characteristics considered important by Gans—race, sex, age, income level, and so on—play significant roles in shaping the variety of lifestyles that emerge in cities. Yet he argued that the variables considered central by Wirth—size, density, and heterogeneity—are also important, lending an intensity to the impact of subcultural group membership that is usually absent in small towns and rural areas. One reason for this greater intensity is that there are enough people with particular characteristics in cities that they will learn about one another, establish meeting places such as bars or parks, develop specialized activities, and

thus form a subculture (see Chapter 2). Research supports Fischer's basic idea that nontraditional or unconventional subcultures are more likely to emerge and thrive in urban areas (Jang & Alba, 1992). In nonurban areas, such subcultures are considerably less likely to form because there will be fewer people with similar characteristics, and the chance of their forming a subculture is considerably reduced. In addition, because city dwellers are unlikely to know most people they come in contact with each day, they rely on characteristics such as social class, age, or ethnicity to decide whether they have anything in common with a person, how to relate to the person, or whether the person represents a threat. Because these subcultural characteristics are so important in social contacts, urbanites become more skilled at picking up cues, such as styles of dress, that signify subcultural membership, and this skill is often considered sophistication by both urbanites and nonurbanites alike. In short, according to Fischer, urban life is different because it tends to magnify the importance of subcultural differences between people. Within this context, though, many urbanites maintain rich and complex networks of social relationships. Fischer's conclusion is that community size by itself does not lead to alienation or other negative consequences.

Urban Life: An Assessment

It should be clear by now that the impact of urban life cannot be characterized simply as good or bad. Reality is more complex than that. Impersonality, isolation, and anonymity do exist in cities—especially among those with few economic or social resources or no subcultural ties—but there are also many communities and subcultures in cities that are rich sources of personal relationships and identity. Cities also offer leisure, cultural, and economic resources that are usually not available in rural areas. There are, for example, baseball, football, and hockey games; opera and ballet; museums; large shopping centers; and restaurants with many cuisines. In addition, the anonymity of cities can be a source of freedom from the curious eyes of one's neighbors. People are freer to pursue lifestyles that might be frowned on in smaller towns. Finally, cities offer a wider ranger of occupational opportunities than are found in small communities. This dimension of city life can be especially important to couples pursuing dual careers (see Chapter 9). In small towns with fewer job opportunities, many such couples would either have to break up or settle for only one partner pursuing a career.

Urban Ecology

You should be able to describe the processes of urban change and the three theories of urban structure.

Urban ecology is *the study of the distribution of people and families within urban centers and how cities relate to the surrounding environment.* One of the major concerns of urban ecologists has been to understand how cities change over time and what urban patterns emerge.

Urban Processes

Cities are like elaborately embroidered quilts, with each part having a distinctive character and all parts together forming a unique but recognizable pattern. This pattern changes continually as the character of neighborhoods changes. Urban ecologists have identified three core processes that describe how cities change: *segregation, invasion,* and *succession.*

Segregation refers to *the isolation of certain activities or people in particular areas of a city,* which occurs for a number of reasons. In some cases, one particular use is incompatible with another. Industrial and residential uses tend to be segregated from one another, for example, because people generally prefer that their homes not be located near factories. Segregation can also occur because it is beneficial to a particular activity. Commercial establishments, for example, are often concentrated in particular areas so that shoppers can have ready access to many different business establishments. A shop that is isolated from other retail stores may not survive because shoppers are less likely to drop in and browse. Shopping malls are based on the notions of segregation and concentration. Finally, segregation occurs because people

with particular characteristics or lifestyles either prefer to live in a particular neighborhood or are forced to. Italians, Poles, or gays in the United States, for example, may want to live with others like themselves, and African Americans have often been barred from living in white neighborhoods.

Invasion *occurs when new people or activities move into an already established area.* Invasion can be motivated by many factors. An area with a growing population may cease to meet people's needs and force them to disperse into new areas. Economic decisions can also cause invasion. A business, for instance, may decide to relocate in a residential area because the land is cheaper, the taxes lower, or the clientele closer at hand. Political decisions can also play a role in invasion. In Detroit in the early 1980s, for example, the city government helped General Motors build a new factory in a previously residential area in order to promote economic growth, a move that angered the residents of the area because many were forced to move.

If the invasion of an area is large enough, the previous residents or users may leave, and the new residents may come to dominate the area. This transition is called **succession.** One of the most noticeable examples of invasion and succession has been the changing racial composition of neighborhoods in many cities during the twentieth century. As African Americans migrated from the South to the cities of the Northeast, Midwest, and West, scarce housing forced them to begin to invade previously all-white neighborhoods, although often not without considerable tension and violence. As the African American population in the neighborhood grew, many whites left until eventually the area became predominantly black. In cities such as Los Angeles and San Francisco, a similar invasion and succession process occurred as the Hispanic population grew. Succession is not inevitable, however. In some communities, groups have formed to convince whites to remain in a racially mixed neighborhood, and most cities today possess some such areas.

Urban Structures

The urban processes of segregation, invasion, and succession are continual, resulting in constantly

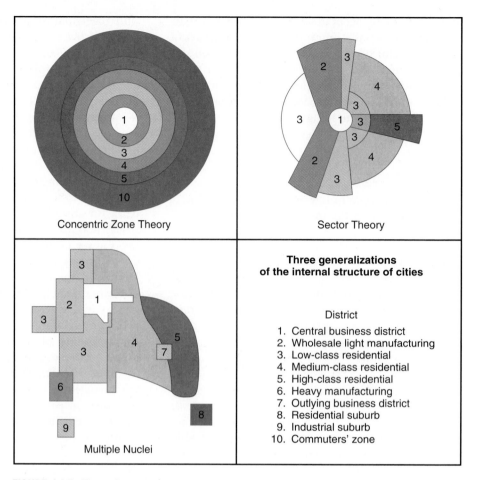

Concentric Zone Theory

Sector Theory

**Three generalizations
of the internal structure of cities**

District

1. Central business district
2. Wholesale light manufacturing
3. Low-class residential
4. Medium-class residential
5. High-class residential
6. Heavy manufacturing
7. Outlying business district
8. Residential suburb
9. Industrial suburb
10. Commuters' zone

Multiple Nuclei

FIGURE 14.7 Three Descriptions of the Internal Structure of Cities *Note:* From "The Nature of Cities" by Chauncy D. Harris and Edward L. Ullman, *The Annals of the American Academy of Political and Social Science, 242.* Copyright 1945 by The American Academy of Political and Social Science.

changing patterns in the urban quilt. At any given point, the outcome of these processes is that a city has a particular structure, in terms of the patterns of use throughout its neighborhoods. In most cases, this urban structure reflects some combination of three patterns: *concentric zones, sectors,* and *multiple nuclei.*

Early in the twentieth century, sociologists Robert Park, Ernest Burgess, and Roderick McKenzie (1925) detected certain patterns in the way that Chicago was evolving. From their observations, they formulated the **concentric-zone theory** of urban growth. What they observed was essentially *a succession of zones, each having a particular purpose or use, that radiated out from the center of*

the city in a pattern of concentric circles (see Figure 14.7). A critical factor determining the use to which a neighborhood was put was its distance from the center of the city. The central business district, for example, contained the major commercial, social, and civic activities—the stores, office buildings, banks, theaters, and so on. This location facilitated transportation to work and other activities, especially prior to the widespread availability of the automobile. The zone in transition surrounding the business district was an area of deteriorating residences with businesses and light manufacturing beginning to invade. It was also characterized by higher rates of crime than the zones farther out. The next zone, of low-class residential housing, contained inexpensive housing that was superior to that available in the transition zone but still within easy access to the places of work in the central business district. Beyond it were the zones of better residences, containing well-to-do single-family dwellings and apartment buildings. Outside the city limits was the commuter's zone, which contained housing for the relatively affluent. People in this zone could afford to take the train or own an automobile to get to work.

The concentric-zone theory suggests a direct link between socioeconomic status and place of residence. This theory is most accurate in describing cities such as New York and Chicago that developed during the nineteenth and early twentieth centuries when public transportation was commonly used and automobiles were either nonexistent or very expensive. It was the affluent who could afford the transportation that enabled them to live far from their workplace in the central business district.

To explain how urban growth can differ from a simple concentric approach, Homer Hoyt (1939) developed **sector theory,** which argues that *some cities grow in the form of sectors, or slices of land use, that extend outward from the center of the city toward the periphery, much like slices of a pie.* The city is still seen as roughly circular, growing out from the center toward the periphery. However, expansion of various types of land use does not occur evenly around the center; rather, it extends out along main lines of transportation (by road, rail, or river) or in directions that offer the least resistance. Thus transportation routes and geographic factors, rather than distance from the center of the city, shape urban development. For example, an industrial area that began on the southern side of the city would continue to develop in a southerly direction along a major highway or some other transportation artery.

Some cities do not fit either the concentric-zone theory or the sector theory. To describe the development of these cities, Chauncy Harris and Edward Ullman (1945) have advanced the **multiple-nuclei theory,** which holds that *cities develop a number of different areas, or nuclei, that are devoted to particular uses.* A city may begin with a single nucleus—a retail district, for example, or the port facilities of a transportation hub. Over time, other nuclei develop as the city experiences migration or specialization. The rise of separate districts is due to a number of factors. First, some uses require special facilities and resources, and urban nuclei will arise where appropriate facilities are available. Water transportation, for instance, requires access to a river or bay, and manufacturing requires large blocks of land on which to build factories. Second, some activities benefit from concentration. For example, retail districts concentrate businesses to attract large numbers of customers. Third, the history and traditions of a particular area in a city can shape it use. The Boston Common, for example, and New York's Central Park are prime pieces of property in or adjacent to business areas, yet sentiment in both cities would strongly oppose any commercial development in the parks. Thus Harris and Ullman argue that growth will be influenced by numerous factors, and larger cities will have more numerous and specialized nuclei.

Cities grow and change in complex ways, and each of these approaches to urban development offers important insights into the process of urban change. As cities in the United States have evolved, they have come to face serious problems, some of which are discussed in the next section.

The Future of Cities in the United States

You should be able to discuss the major problems faced by cities in the United States and some of the policies that have been devised to resolve these difficulties.

Problems such as crime, poverty, unemployment, and deteriorating housing can be found in both urban and rural areas, but the magnitude of these problems is generally much more evident in cities. It is the central city in a metropolitan area that suffers most severely from these problems, although some suburban communities in recent years have found themselves beset with similar difficulties. Many problems that have an impact on urban areas have been discussed elsewhere in this book, for example in Chapters 5, 6, and 7. An element common to many of these problems is economic decline.

Economic Decline

One of the premier problems that many U.S. cities confront is that they are in a state of economic decline. Indeed, since the 1970s, a number of cities, especially in the Northeast and Midwest, have been on the brink of financial collapse. In 1975, New York City was unable to pay its bills, banks refused to give any assistance, and only a complicated bailout from the federal government saved it from financial disaster. In 1978, Cleveland became the first U.S. city since the Depression of the 1930s actually to go into financial default. During the recession of the early 1980s, Boston and Detroit were so short of funds that their governments had to consider not paying for essential city services such as fire and police protection. In the early 1990s, New York City was again in fiscal crisis, cutting services and raising local taxes (Caraley, 1992).

One major cause of these financial problems has been the flight of people and jobs from many cities since World War II. Of the twenty largest cities in 1990, nine have lost population since 1950. Of the twenty largest in 1950, eighteen have lost people. And population growth has been much slower in the central cities than elsewhere. As is pointed out in Chapter 13, the centralization of economic organization in the United States has meant that a relatively small number of corporations account for an increasingly large share of economic activity. When one of these large business enterprises leaves a city, the departure has a ripple effect as smaller companies that support it also move. As businesses and affluent residents left the cities, the tax rolls declined. The poor and elderly who remained paid fewer taxes and used more city services than did the well-to-do who left. As a result, many cities have faced severe financial crises over the past few decades, and these economic difficulties contributed to all the other problems of the cities.

Government Programs and Urban Renewal

Until the 1980s, urban policy in the United States was based on the assumption that the federal government was in the best position to fund programs to attack urban problems. Cities and states have fewer funds for such efforts and more incentives to underfund such programs. In the last twenty years, however, urban policy has changed dramatically, with a decided shift in the opposite direction—toward less federal government involvement (Caraley, 1992). The Reagan and Bush administrations argued that a strong and healthy economy is a far more promising approach to solving urban problems than direct federal intervention. From their perspective, the key role of the federal government in solving urban problems is to keep the economy healthy, not to intervene with federal programs and funding. States and cities should be allowed to choose which services they need and want.

The result of this shift has been a catastrophic decline in federal support for cities. Federal programs have been turned over to the states and cities, and the states and cities—in poor financial shape themselves—have drastically cut or eliminated the programs. Federal aid has dropped from 22 percent of large cities' general expenditures in 1980 to 6 percent today, but aid given by state governments has not increased to take up the slack.

Despite this shift toward a laissez-faire policy, some significant federal urban programs persist. The many federal programs that provide direct funds or services to the poor are a significant form of assistance to urban areas. These programs include Medicaid, Social Security, welfare, housing assistance, and food stamps. All these programs are key resources used by cities to alleviate the problems their citizens face. The Housing Act of 1949 initiated a program of *urban renewal,* which has been a prominent approach to urban problems over the years (Hawley, 1971). The major purpose of urban renewal has been to rebuild blighted areas of cities, to provide low-cost housing for urban poor, and to stimulate private investment in the inner city through the physical redevelopment of deteriorated areas. Government funds were used to acquire and clear land and to relocate people who lost their dwellings on account of this program. Urban renewal was also supposed to attract private investors.

After many years of operation, urban policy makers recognized that urban renewal had probably not produced its intended benefits. Rather

The theory behind urban renewal policies was that demolishing old buildings, as is being done here in Detroit, would make way for new development. The policy did not work as well as its advocates thought it would.

than try to renovate existing buildings, planners typically had them torn down, in part because they believed that destroying dilapidated buildings was an essential first step in solving the problems of crime and poverty. Often these buildings were replaced with luxury apartments or office buildings that were more profitable to private-sector developers. The poor, who had originally occupied a neighborhood, were driven into other neighborhoods, which then often began to deteriorate. The original neighborhood entered a chain of invasion, and then succession, from a working-class area to a slum. Because of these problems, urban renewal

funds declined over the years, and in the 1980s the programs were combined into the Community Development Block Grant (CDBG) program (Wong & Peterson, 1986). The CDBG program has goals similar to those of urban renewal, but it gives local officials a larger role in developing urban renewal projects and greater flexibility in how federal funds are used. The CDBG program shifted from an emphasis on providing direct assistance to low-income residents to a focus on economic development.

These and other federal programs have channeled significant resources to cities with serious problems. However, the hands-off posture in the United States' urban policy in recent years has meant fewer funds than in the past. Many urban policy makers argue that federal assistance for urban problems is still appropriate because the cities, for the most part, did not create the problems that now ravage them: poverty, drug addiction, homelessness, AIDS, and so on. It is the cities that suffer from these problems most seriously, and these policy makers argue that society as a whole has a responsibility to assist cities with them.

Private Investment

Despite the prominent role of the federal government in attacking urban problems over the years, there has been a trend since the 1970s to turn to private investment as a means of improving the conditions of cities. A major thrust of these efforts is to use private funds to develop shopping centers in cities that can compete with suburban shopping malls and to construct housing that can draw people away from suburban tract homes. In this way, it is hoped, people—and financial resources—can be attracted back into the city. The idea is that if cities can be made into enjoyable places to live and work, then decentralization might be slowed or halted and the financial problems that are at the core of so many urban difficulties alleviated. Many cities now boast such developments: Water Tower mall in Chicago, Union Station in Cincinnati, Quincy Market in Boston, Renaissance Center in Detroit, and Pier 39 in San Francisco to name a few. Although some of these developments used federal funds, private financing has been central to their completion.

Another approach to encouraging private development in cities through minimal government action is variously called *enterprise zones, urban free-enterprise zones,* or *empowerment zones* (Lehman, 1994). The basic idea is to designate a neighborhood as an enterprise zone based on high levels of unemployment or poverty and little economic development. Businesses locating in such zones would be taxed at a lower rate than in other areas of the city and would be subject to less stringent regulation than businesses outside the zone. To receive these benefits, the businesses might be required to have a certain proportion of zone residents among their employees. This approach is based on the assumption that the tax and regulatory system stifle initiative and self-improvement. Remove these inhibitors, proponents argue, and new businesses will arise to take advantage of the opportunities for economic development that exist even in blighted neighborhoods. These new ventures will then help rebuild the neighborhood economy, providing jobs that will improve the general economic conditions in the city. Seventy such empowerment zones were established in the United States in the 1990s.

Gentrification

Another development in resettling cities in the last few decades has been dubbed **gentrification:** *The return of relatively affluent households to marginal neighborhoods where run-down housing is being rehabilitated or new housing constructed* (Beauregard, 1990; Kerstein, 1990). Gentrification is a complicated process that occurs in different ways in different cities. In some cases, it is encouraged by the policies of local, state, or federal governments; in others, it is driven by the actions of private developers looking for a profitable business deal. In some places, private–public partnerships have been the catalyst. Gentrification is more likely to occur in neighborhoods with good-quality housing stock of some historical value and where there is no organized group in the community that resists it. Gentrification is also fueled by the decisions of affluent families who may find suburban life too expensive or who do not feel the need for large houses because they have smaller families than their parents had. For others, especially professional couples with fairly substantial incomes, the city affords easy access to restaurants, cultural events, and the like. For dual-career couples, who are far more common today than in the 1950s when suburbanization surged, the city offers access to many desirable jobs for both partners.

Gentrification has been hailed as the beginning of the rebirth of urban areas in the United States. Although it will probably help to stem the flow of economic resources out of the city, the numbers involved are difficult to calculate but are probably somewhat small. Nevertheless, it should contribute to increasing the tax base of the city, restoring neighborhoods through the rehabilitation of housing, and enhancing neighborhood businesses. Some urban planners argue that these renovated neighborhoods will serve as a magnet that will attract more affluent people into the city.

However, not all the effects of gentrification are beneficial. As affluent people move into and renovate neighborhoods, the value of property increases and both rent and property taxes escalate. As a result, the people who lived in the neighborhood prior to gentrification—often the poor, the elderly, and minorities—can no longer afford it and are forced to move, sometimes from homes they have occupied for decades. The only housing these people can afford may be more dilapidated than their previous residence.

Regional Planning and Cooperation

Many cities have recognized that some urban problems can be solved only if regional planning and cooperation can be achieved. After all, the geographic boundaries of cities were established many years ago, and today they are rather arbitrary designations. Some have proposed a metropolitan government that would have political jurisdiction over a city and its suburbs and would consolidate all government services. Such an overarching political structure is probably not feasible in most cases. One problem is deciding where one city and its suburbs ends and another begins. In addition, few cities or suburbs would be willing to accede to such a centralized authority. They prefer to retain political power and patronage in their own hands.

On a smaller scale, however, cooperation between political entities in metropolitan areas has been established over specific issues. Issues such as transportation and water pollution affect the whole metropolitan region and can benefit from regional decision making. In some cases, the courts have even ruled that school segregation is a regional problem and called for transfers of students between city and suburban schools. Cleveland has made major strides in regional cooperation, with the city and suburbs sharing responsibility for big infrastructure projects such as roads and transportation. It also has a payroll tax on all people who work in Cleveland, including those who live in suburbs. This tax is a major infusion of funds for the city. It has been controversial, but many suburban residents accept some responsibility for helping alleviate the problems of the city because they gain benefits from the city. As the president of the Greater Cleveland Growth Organization put it: "Cleveland is the downtown shopping center for this area. It is where entertainment is. Sports. Where all our major corporations are. We recognize that if downtown is not clean, safe and active, then the entire region will start falling apart" (quoted in Barrett & Greene, 1991, p. 34).

In developing and evaluating plans and policies to alleviate problems in cities in the United States and around the world, it is important to recognize that urban conditions are shaped by macrosociological conditions, such as industrialization, modernization, and the world economic system. As these conditions change, cities are affected. Urban sociologists continue to accumulate knowledge about how these structures affect life for people in cities, some of which has been presented in this chapter. Applying Sociology: The Fear of Crime (on pp. 508–509) gives a concrete example of how sociologists can contribute to making city life better.

Summary

1. Human ecology and demography study the growth and distribution of populations through the investigation of fertility, mortality, the rate of natural increase, and migration.

2. There are different ways of looking at population growth. The theory of the demographic transition is concerned with changing patterns of birth and death rates brought about by industrialization. The demographic gap is the gap between high birthrates and low death rates, which during the early industrial period in different societies' development resulted in explosive population growth.

3. Populations that have experienced the demographic transition have low birthrates and low death rates, resulting in stable population size, but other developing countries are still growing at rapid rates. Some of the consequences of overpopulation

One area in which applied sociologists have been very active is in urban policy and planning, using sociological theories and research to design cities and social institutions that make urban life safer, more enjoyable, and more fulfilling. Urban crime is one of the more difficult problems such sociologists have attacked.

> When one out of every three American households is directly victimized each year, it isn't long before everyone has either been a victim himself or had someone very close to him victimized. The problem is not just what crime does to people's lives; it is also what the fear of crime does to our society. (*"Images of Fear,"* 1985, p. 44)

In December of 1984, a seemingly mild-mannered man named Bernhard Goetz made national news when he shot four teenagers in a New York City subway car. Allegedly, Goetz did so because the young men were trying to rob him under the threat of deadly force. Further investigation of the incident revealed some contrasting elements. The teenage perpetrators, although perhaps intending to intimidate Goetz, were armed only with a small screwdriver. In addition, not only was Goetz carrying a .38 revolver, but also he had recently acquired several handguns—apparently because of his rising fear of being a crime victim.

The Goetz episode brings home once again, as if we needed further proof, the extent to which the quality of life in cities is lowered by crime, fear, and the restrictions that city residents impose on their daily routines as a consequence. Chapter 5, for example, noted that the crime most feared by women who live in cities is rape (Gordon & Riger, 1989). That fear directly affects their daily lives as they avoid going out alone, avoid going to certain neighborhoods, and in-

stall security devices in their houses or apartments. The other crimes women fear most are robbery and burglary. Another study found that one-half of the women in large cities felt that it was unsafe to be out in their neighborhood after dark (Davis & Smith, 1994). Fear of crime is common among older people, especially women. Studies indicate that people are more likely to take precautions against crime if they have been victims themselves or if they are more fearful of crime (Conklin, 1976; Miethe, 1995). Rather than focus on how these individual characteristics influence taking precautions, however, some research has considered the role of social and physical characteristics of the environment.

One such approach has been to focus on community organization as an important ingredient in urban residents' fear of crime. Barbara Kail and Paula Kleinman (1985) have conducted a series of investigations in different ethnic communities to assess the complex relationship between urban residents' reactions to the fear of crime and their degree of integration into the communities in which they live. These researchers found that the existence of formally organized local community associations can diminish fear and self-imposed limitations on activities. One example of such an association is the Basic Car Plan in Los Angeles, in which neighborhood residents can meet the police officers who are regularly assigned to their area. In the absence of such formal efforts, some urban dwellers develop informal techniques for dealing with fear and victimization. For example, such techniques might include casual gatherings designed to air mutual concerns about crime and discuss possible strategies for protection. At least one investigation has determined that urban residents who are more integrated into the social fabric of a neighborhood—the

are crowding, food shortages, and depletion of the world's natural resources. Family planning, economic development, and improving the status of women are among the programs that have been employed in dealing with overpopulation.

4. A community is a group of people who share a common territory and a sense of identity or

belonging, and who interact with one another. In industrial societies, cities have grown through a process of urbanization and suburbanization, and a *postindustrial city* may be emerging that is less centralized than industrial cities.

5. Cities in developing nations have had different experiences, especially in terms of confronting

ones active in formal and informal community organizations—are less fearful of crime (Hunter & Baumer, 1982).

Previous investigations have shown that when individuals take precautions to deal with their fear of crime this behavior may only deflect crime rather than reduce it: The criminal merely victimizes someone else. Furthermore, these individual efforts may actually inhibit the community's response to the crime problem (Dubow & Emmons, 1981). More recent research, such as that of Kail and Kleinman, suggests that if existing formal organizations can be strengthened, then fear of crime will be reduced, which also reduces the extent to which individuals place restrictions on their behavior. Thus, community organization appears to be a key ingredient in elevating the quality of life by reducing people's fear of crime (Bennett, 1995).

Based on years of study of crime in cities, sociologists and urban planners have come to recognize the role that architecture and urban design play in crime. They have developed a new approach that has come to be called the *defensible space* strategy because it focuses on changes in the physical environment that make it easier for neighborhoods and communities to defend themselves against crime (Cisneros, 1995; Crowe, 1991; Newman, 1972). This approach is based on the recognition that many criminals are, to a degree, rational; they calculate how they can obtain the greatest gain for the least risk. As the likelihood of getting caught increases, criminals either commit crimes somewhere else or avoid committing crimes. In addition, many neighborhoods and buildings in cities are designed in such a way that they discourage social interaction and social participation on the part of residents. They isolate people from one another, which tends to increase the opportunities for criminals to

operate unobserved. So, the defensible space strategy designs locations so as to impress on intruders the recognition that they are likely to be observed, be identified, and have difficulty escaping if they commit a crime. With such ideas in mind, sociologists and urban planners suggest a few design considerations that would make crime less likely:

1. Buildings should have only a small number of units sharing the same entryway off the street. In this way, residents know who lives there, who has a right to be there, and who is a stranger.
2. Windows, lighting, entryways, and paths should be designed so that there is continuous surveillance by the residents. This arrangement reduces the number of isolated spots where crime can occur unobserved.
3. Lobbies should be designed not merely as an entryway to the building but as a social center where people congregate. This might be done by having newsstands or recreation items in or near the lobby.
4. Buildings should be low-rise with fewer residents to reduce feelings of anonymity, isolation, and lack of identity with the building. Research shows that the crime rate is higher in taller and more populous buildings.
5. Neighborhoods should be designed as small mini-neighborhoods, with no through streets and a limited number of entryways. In this way, the neighbors know who belongs there and who is an intruder, and criminals will fear being trapped in a neighborhood that has only one exit.

more adverse conditions and being more affected by the capitalist world system.

6. For many people in the United States, urbanism has become a way of life, and for some, an urban consciousness has developed. The study of urban living has been approached from different perspectives, including Gans's urban communi-

ties strategy and Fischer's urban subcultures approach.

7. Urban ecology is the study of the distribution of people and facilities within urban centers and how cities relate to the surrounding social environment. Urban change involves such processes as segregation, invasion, and succession. There are different ways of approaching the study of urban growth, including the concentric-zone theory, the sector theory, and the multiple-nuclei theory.

8. Cities in the United States have numerous problems, notably economic decline and crime.

Urban revitalization programs such as urban renewal and gentrification have been devised to deal with these problems. Urban planning has also used private investment, enterprise zones, and regional cooperation and planning to alleviate the problems of cities.

STUDY and Review

Key Terms

city

community

concentric-zone theory

demographic gap

demographic transition

demography

fecundity

fertility

gentrification

global cities

human ecology

invasion

migration

mortality

multiple-nuclei theory

population

sector theory

segregation

suburbs

succession

urban ecology

Multiple-Choice Questions

1. In regard to life expectancy in the United States,
   a. men live longer than women.
   b. the life expectancy of men and women is the same.
   c. the life expectancy of men has been declining in the past few decades.
   d. the gap between the life expectancy of men and women is larger today than seventy years ago.

2. The United States is currently entering which stage of the demographic transition?
   a. The preindustrial stage.
   b. The transitional stage.
   c. The early industrial stage.
   d. The industrial stage.
   e. The postindustrial stage.

3. Which region of the world will see its proportion of the world population grow most significantly in the next fifty years?
   a. Africa.
   b. Asia.
   c. North America.
   d. Europe.
   e. The Caribbean.

4. The social and economic changes that probably account for more of the decline in fertility than family planning in nations today are called
   a. urban homesteading.
   b. fecundity.
   c. demography.
   d. economic development.
   e. gentrification.

5. Programs to promote gender equality around the world will probably have which effect?
   a. A positive impact on controlling world population growth.
   b. A negative impact on controlling world population growth.
   c. Little impact on world population growth.
   d. A reduction in fecundity.

6. According to the text, agricultural villages and then cities emerged in human history because of
   a. industrialization.
   b. capitalism.
   c. the cultivation of plants and domestication of animals.
   d. technological developments in transportation.

7. In comparison to cities in industrial nations, cities in Third-World nations
   a. have experienced underurbanization.
   b. face more adverse conditions than did cities emerging in Europe and North America a century ago.
   c. have been ignored by the capitalist world economic system.
   d. have been growing at a slower pace.

8. According to the sector theory of urban growth, urban development is shaped most importantly by
   a. distance from the center of a city.
   b. transportation routes and geographic factors.
   c. the capitalist world economic system.
   d. the number of specialized nuclei that develop.

9. One major cause of the financial problems in cities in the United States has been
   a. the growing demographic gap in cities.
   b. the flight of people and jobs from cities.
   c. the overpopulation of cities.
   d. the gentrification of cities.

10. To reduce fear of crime and enhance social participation among urban residents, urban planners recommend
    a. constructing low-rise buildings.
    b. not building lobbies of buildings as social centers.
    c. having as many units as possible sharing the same entryway off the street.
    d. constructing high-rise buildings.

True/False Questions

1. The fertility of a society is usually at about the same level as its fecundity.

2. The two largest nations in the world in terms of population are China and the United States.

3. When the demographic gap gets narrower, societies experience greater population growth.

4. The current estimated doubling time for the world's population is approximately forty years.

5. Cities are communities, but communities are not necessarily cities.

6. In the 1930s and 1940s, the U.S. government, in order to promote racially integrated communities, promoted policies that discouraged people from moving to the suburbs.

7. According to Louis Wirth, the urban consciousness that city dwellers often develop involves a reserve in social relationships and a focus on rational self-interest.

8. The changing racial composition of neighborhoods in many cities in the United States provides an example of the urban processes of invasion and succession.

9. The urban renewal program continues to be the major federal program providing support for urban areas in the United States.

10. The poor in cities in the United States are the major beneficiaries of the process of gentrification.

Fill-In Questions

1. The difference between the crude birthrate and the crude death rate is referred to as the _____ .

2. The two types of migration discussed in the text are _____ and _____ .

3. The _____ stage of the demographic transition is characterized by high birthrates and high death rates.

4. Two of the consequences of overpopulation that are discussed in the text are _____ and _____ .

5. China's one-child family program for reducing population growth appears to have resulted in an increase in _____ .

6. In understanding how living in cities affects people, Claude Fischer stressed the importance of _____ .

7. The study of the distribution of people and families within urban areas is called _____ .

8. The theory of urban structures that argues that the critical factor in urban usage is the distance of a neighborhood from the center of the city is called _____ .

9. Areas of a city where new businesses are given tax breaks or are subject to less stringent regulation are called _____ .

10. _____ refers to the return of relatively affluent households to marginal neighborhoods where run-down housing is rehabilitated.

Matching Questions

_____ 1. process of urban change
_____ 2. number of deaths in a population
_____ 3. emigration
_____ 4. China
_____ 5. functionalist approach to population dynamics
_____ 6. conflict approach to population dynamics
_____ 7. transitional stage of demographic transition
_____ 8. Louis Wirth
_____ 9. family planning
_____ 10. urban renewal

A. world's largest nation
B. succession
C. Karl Marx
D. population control program
E. urban consciousness
F. moving out of a particular country
G. government urban program
H. mortality
I. Thomas Robert Malthus
J. early industrial stage of demographic transition

Essay Questions

1. Define the field of demography. What are the elements of demographic change? How have they been changing in the United States during the twentieth century?

2. What is the demographic transition? Describe the stages of the demographic transition, discussing what happens at each one.

3. What consequences of world population growth does the text discuss? Summarize the impacts of those consequences.

4. What efforts does the text discuss for controlling world population growth? Describe each one and assess its effectiveness.

5. Describe the growth of cities and suburbs in human societies. What policies of the federal government contributed to the growth of the suburbs in the United States? How are the postindustrial cities different from cities in an industrial era?

6. Using Peru, Kenya, and Mexico as examples, describe the social organization of Third-World slums, especially in terms of people's ability to adapt to adversity.

7. Describe the three perspectives that the text presented on the nature and quality of urban life.

8. Describe the three core processes that urban ecologists use in describing how cities change over time. Summarize the three theories that predict the urban structures that result from these processes of change.

9. What factors have produced the economic decline of cities in the United States?

10. What programs and trends, both public and private, can be currently identified as affecting urban problems in the United States?

Answers

Multiple-Choice
1. D;   2. E;   3. A;   4. D;   5. A;   6. C;   7. B;   8. B;   9. B;   10. A

True/False
1. F;   2. F;   3. F;   4. T;   5. T;   6. F;   7. T;   8. T;   9. F;   10. F

Fill-In
1. rate of natural increase
2. immigration, emigration
3. preindustrial
4. crowding, food shortages, depletion of natural resources
5. female infanticide
6. urban subcultures
7. urban ecology
8. concentric-zone theory
9. urban free enterprise zones, empowerment zones
10. gentrification

Matching
1. B;   2. H;   3. F;   4. A;   5. I;   6. C;   7. J;   8. E;   9. D;   10. G

For Further Reading

Ehrlich, Paul R., & Ehrlich, Anne H. (1990). *The population explosion*. New York: Simon & Schuster. This book, by well-known ecologists, summarizes the consequences of continued population growth for the world and argues strongly that such growth must be controlled.

Gans, Herbert J. (1991). *People, plans, and policies: Essays on poverty, racism, and other national urban problems*. New York: Columbia University Press. This is an excellent set of essays by a well-respected specialist in urban affairs. The issues discussed range from problems of architecture to poverty and the underclass.

Garreau, Joel. (1991). *Edge city: Life on the new frontier.* New York: Doubleday. *Edge city* is the author's name for those suburbs that have grown large enough to be considered self-sufficient. He provides an interesting perspective on that part of urban life where many people live, suggesting that edge cities reflect such U.S. values as individualism and homesteading.

Kasarda, John D., & Parnell, Allan M. (Eds.). (1993). *Third World cities: Problems, policies, and prospects*. Newbury Park, CA: Sage. These two sociologists have brought together some of the most recent research being done on the problems confronting cities in Third-World nations. This volume views the problems of cities from a global perspective.

Meadows, Donella H., Meadows, Dennis L., & Randers, Jorgen. (1992). *Beyond the limits: Confronting global collapse, envisioning a sustainable future.* Post Mills, VT: Chelsea Green Publishing Co. This is a recent assessment by three of the same scientists who conducted the study for the Club of Rome twenty years ago. Their conclusions are a little more optimistic now, but only assuming that there are changes in both lifestyle and technology.

Portes, Alejandro, & Stepick, Alex. (1993). *City on the edge: The transformation of Miami*. Berkeley: University of California Press. This is an excellent analysis of the development of Miami as its Cuban population has grown. It is a complex story that ties in urban development, ethnicity, and socioeconomic status.

Sale, Kirkpatrick. (1980). *Human scale*. New York: Coward, McCann, & Geohegan. Assessing huge urban developments, Sale contends that going beyond "human scale" causes impersonality and a number of other problems. He argues for small-scale developments in urban planning.

Sowell, Thomas. (1996). *Migrations and cultures: A world view.* New York: BasicBooks. This book explores the experiences of a number of groups (Germans, Japanese, Italians, Chinese, Jews, and Indians) as they migrated to many nations around the world. The author explores the reasons why some immigrants do well in their adopted lands whereas others do not.

CHAPTER FIFTEEN

Collective Behavior, Social Change, and Modernization

Because life always demands that we make decisions before we have all the knowledge we would like, before, that is, we quite know what we are doing, history always includes tragedy. The shock of flowing blood is often required of human beings before they can recognize where they are heading. The guns of Lattimer may be seen as a lesson in the tragic sense of life. (Novak, 1978, p. xviii)

In the sweltering August heat of eastern Pennsylvania in 1897, miners in the anthracite coal fields walked off their jobs. It was a clumsy, haphazard, and disorganized strike. The miners were not unionized—they were simply fed up with low wages and dangerous working conditions. There was little safety equipment in the mines, and cuts, bruises, broken bones, and disfigurement were common. In 1894 alone, 446 men were killed in coal-mining accidents in eastern Pennsylvania.

On top of this volatile situation, intense ethnic hostilities existed among the coal miners. Groups that had migrated to the United States decades earlier—the Welsh, Irish, and Germans—considered themselves "true Americans" and were repelled by the onslaught of more recent immigrants from Italy and Eastern Europe. These "new" immigrants spoke little English, but they worked very hard and saved their money hoping to return to the "old country"—Poland, Hungary, Slovakia, the Ukraine—or bring their families to the United States.

The strike limped along for a few weeks, with initiative fluctuating from the hands of mine owners to the hands of the strikers. Finally, on the hot afternoon of September 10, the strikers confronted a posse in the small, depressing mining town of Lattimer, near Hazleton, Pennsylvania. The sound of gunfire roared across the fields and forests. Nineteen miners—with rich ethnic names such as Broztowski, Chrzeszeski, Rekewicz, and Ziominski—fell mortally wounded. Another thirty-nine were injured (Novak, 1978).

Fifteen years later in Colorado, eight thousand miners went on strike when the Colorado Fuel and Iron Company refused to recognize the right of the United Mine Workers of America to unionize (Taft & Ross, 1969). The strikers moved their families out of company-owned houses and into a tent city at Ludlow. National Guard troops were called in. On April 20, 1914, the troops attacked the tent colony. Five men and a boy were killed by the machine-gun crossfire. Still unsatisfied, the militia burned the tent colony. This holocaust, which has since come to be known as the Ludlow Massacre, resulted in the suffocation deaths of two women and eleven children. The surviving strikers and their families dispersed into the countryside, and for ten days there were sporadic clashes between the strikers and the militia. By the time the strike had ended, the death toll had risen to seventy-four.

Lattimer and Ludlow are hardly household words today. Yet these two incidents—by themselves seemingly minor events in the sweep of history—were critical parts of a profound revolution that changed the nature of human societies. Those events in the hot, dusty summer of Pennsylvania and the chilly spring of Colorado were links in the vast process of social change that we call the Industrial Revolution. As has been described in Chapters 9 through 13, industrialization led to dramatic changes in all social institu-

tions, including the family, religion, education, politics, and the economy. In the process of industrialization, new power and authority relations were forged between workers and industrial managers. Clashes such as those at Lattimer and Ludlow were examples of the mechanisms through which these social changes were made. One wonders whether the miners in Lattimer and Ludlow were ever able to gain some perspective on their actions. Did they (or the mine owners) recognize the small but significant part that their actions played in one of the vastest transformations in human history? In all likelihood, their goals were more modest—to end this strike, to gain a little more compensation, and to introduce a few safety devices into the mines. Yet their actions played a part, however small, in modernizing the United States.

Social change is the topic of this chapter. First it will discuss what sociologists call collective behavior and social movements, which can play an important part in the process of change, and then it will analyze the major theories of social change.

The Nature of Collective Behavior

You should be able to discuss the various forms of collective behavior and the conditions necessary for their development.

The working people of Lattimer and Ludlow took matters into their own hands. The conventional ways of doing things—looking for a better job or asking their boss for higher wages—seemed unlikely to resolve their plight, so they engaged in what sociologists call **collective behavior:** *relatively unstructured and spontaneous actions that arise in situations where more conventional behavior seems inappropriate or ineffective* (Goode, 1992; Lofland, 1981). Collective behavior is less enduring than institutionalized behavior based on established social norms, roles, and relationships. In fact, in collective behavior, people's actions often do not appear to be guided by the usual norms governing human conduct. Rather, new and temporary norms emerge as accepted standards. Collective behavior covers a broad range of activities: a rioting mob, a crowd panic, fads and fashions,

Myth In the race riots that have occurred in U.S. cities over the past thirty years the rioters have come from the ranks of the criminals, the unemployed, and the poor.

FACT Although such people certainly played a part, the people arrested for rioting have also included educated, employed, and seemingly law-abiding citizens who were reacting against what they saw as the injustices of racial discrimination and oppression.

Myth When people are pushed to the limit in terms of deprivation or oppression, they become susceptible to the appeals of revolutionary demagogues.

FACT The origins of revolution are often found in relative rather than absolute deprivation. Severely deprived people tend to respond with apathy or acquiescence. On the contrary, people with some hope that their lives will get better, but who see that hope threatened, are more likely to join a revolution.

Myth Now that we have moved into a postindustrial era, automation and computerization will usher in a life of leisure and material comfort for people in the United States.

FACT There is little consensus about what technological developments such as automation and computerization will hold for the future. Some argue that there will be fewer jobs and that many of them will be tedious and low-paying with few prospects for advancement. There may be intense competition for the limited number of good jobs, and those who get them will live comfortably while the less fortunate will scrape by.

Myth Modernization is a worldwide trend that will result in the less developed nations achieving the economic productivity and standard of living of the United States, Japan, and other fully industrialized nations.

FACT This could happen, but reality may be more complex. The developing nations today face much more adverse conditions in their struggle to industrialize than their predecessors did. In addition, there may be economic and social processes at work that will keep the global system stratified into the well-off industrial nations and the less-well-to-do Third-World nations.

---

responses to disaster, a mass migration, the spread of a rumor, or the actions of an audience at a soccer match.

Although collective behavior contrasts sharply with the more institutionalized forms of behavior, the difference is actually a matter of degree. That is, completely institutionalized behavior lies at one end of a continuum and totally spontaneous, unorganized behavior at the other extreme (see Figure 15.1 on p. 518). For example, the inauguration of a President falls at the institutionalized end of the scale: It is a rigid, predictable, ritualized performance with little opportunity for spontaneity or creativity. At the other end of the scale, some mass panics involve practically no structure

or coordination of behavior. In between those two extremes, we can identify some race riots in which people coordinate their behavior in order to loot stores or attack the police. Protest demonstrations exhibit still more structure, including extensive planning, leadership, monitors, and the like.

The Preconditions of Collective Behavior

Understanding collective behavior is a substantial task in view of its spontaneous nature and the many forms that it can take. What, after all, do a panic, a riot, and a fad have in common? The sociologist Neil Smelser (1963) has provided us with

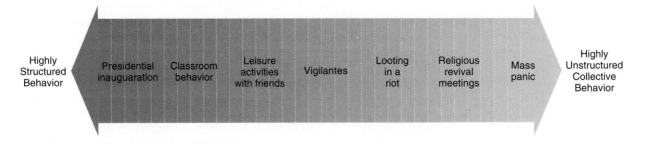

FIGURE 15.1 The Continuum of Institutionalized and Collective Behavior

a comprehensive approach to this problem. He argues that, whatever form collective behavior takes, it involves people's efforts to cope with stressful and uncertain social conditions. Smelser suggests that the following six preconditions must all exist for collective behavior to occur:

1. *Structural conduciveness* refers to the social conditions that make it *possible* for a particular kind of collective behavior to occur. A panic, for example, could not occur if people were standing in an open field where there was no possibility of their being trapped. Likewise, a race riot would be impossible in a community where there was only one racial group.

2. *Structural strain* refers to ambiguities, discrepancies, threats, or conflicts in people's lives that place strain on them and generate frustration or anger. This strain can take many forms: poverty, unemployment, racial or sexual discrimination, or any situation in which people's expectations are unfulfilled. College students, for example, experience structural strain when their educational accomplishments do not lead to the jobs they expect to obtain.

3. *Generalized belief* refers to the ideas that people have about the source of the strain they are experiencing and about what can be done to alleviate it. These ideas are not necessarily accurate—they are people's *definition of the situation,* and people act on the basis of these judgments. People on the extreme edge of the Patriot movement in the United States, for example, believe in white supremacy and espouse virulent forms of anti-Semitic and anti-African American bigotry. Groups such as Posse Comitatus and American Christian

Patriots attribute problems such as crime and unemployment to the power of Jews and racial minorities. Such a generalized belief has motivated some extreme members of the Patriot movement to espouse, and even carry out, acts of violence against members of minorities in order to advance their goal of white supremacy (Dees, 1996).

4. *Precipitating factors* are incidents that make strain or frustration immediate and intense and that serve as a trigger or a catalyst to collective outbursts. In the 1980 riot in the predominantly African American Liberty City area of Miami, for example, the catalyst was the acquittal of four white police officers in the beating death five months earlier of an African American insurance agent. This acquittal infuriated the African American community because it seemed like yet another instance of whites going unpunished for perpetrating violence against African Americans. Eight white people and nine blacks died before the violence finally subsided.

5. *Mobilization* occurs when people are brought into action and their behaviors are directed toward some specific goals. Such direction might involve, for example, someone standing on a car exhorting a crowd to attack the police or loot a store. Mobilization might also take the form of someone throwing the first rock, thereby serving as a model for others. In other words, mobilization can be spontaneous and unstructured, or it can involve highly structured leadership.

6. *Social control* refers to any mechanisms that prevent, interrupt, or slow down the emergence of collective behavior. It could take the form of police actions to control a crowd, negotiations to stop a riot, or pulling the plug on a loudspeaker

A man searches through the remains of the tent city in Ludlow, Colorado after the militia had attacked and burned it in 1914. This tragedy gives stark testimony to the passions that can surround collective behavior and social change.

to prevent a leader from mobilizing a group. Social control can intervene in any of the other five preconditions. Weak or ineffective social control is necessary for collective behavior to occur.

Smelser's approach to collective behavior is useful because it is sufficiently general to be applicable to all forms of collective behavior. To understand whether collective behavior will occur in a particular situation or what form it will take, we need to assess the character of the six preconditions in that situation. As this chapter discusses some different types of collective behavior, readers should keep Smelser's approach in mind.

Applying Sociology: The Los Angeles Riot (on pp. 520–522) discusses sociological research on riots and applies it to the riot in south central Los Angeles in 1992. The role of Smelser's pre-

conditions can be seen in that riot and also the role that sociological research can play in helping people figure out how to prevent such ghastly events from happening again. Riots actually contain within them a number of types of collective behavior, such as rumors and crowd behavior. This chapter will explore more of the process of collective behavior by analyzing three types of such behavior: rumors, mass behavior, and crowd behavior.

Rumors

Rumors are *unauthenticated messages, although they are not necessarily false* (Rosnow & Fine, 1976). Rumor is a form of collective behavior, and it also plays an important role in many other forms of collective behavior, such as mass hysteria and riots.

APPLYING SOCIOLOGY

The Los Angeles Riot: Failing to Act on What We Know

The images of the riot in south central Los Angeles in 1992 were very disturbing: panoramic views of the towers of smoke from many buildings burning at once, looters emerging from stores with their arms laden with stolen goods, store owners shooting their guns at crowds to keep them at bay, innocent bystanders savagely beaten and helpless. By the time it was over, fifty-three people had died, and there was $1 billion in property damage. Especially disturbing was the realization that we had seen it all before: in Miami in the 1980s and in many U.S. cities in the 1960s. Most people are familiar with the immediate precipitant of the Los Angeles riot (Dentler, 1992). Four police officers were on trial for the beating of the African American motorist Rodney King. The beating was videotaped and had been widely shown on television. King was beaten repeatedly and over a prolonged period of time by a number of officers, even when King seemed helpless on the ground. The acquittal of the officers, Smelser's precipitating factor, sparked the riot. The acquittal was seen by African Americans in Los Angeles as convincing proof that the police were free to assault blacks at will and that the criminal justice system would provide blacks with no legal recourse against such violence. This was their generalized belief. Other recent events in Los Angeles provided fuel for such beliefs: African American men were routinely arrested and mistreated by the police, and a store owner who shot and killed a sixteen-year-old African American girl was convicted of a minor charge and spent no time in jail.

There is much still to be learned about the Los Angeles riot, but what is already disturbingly clear is that we have failed to apply what we have learned from earlier riots. Riots in the 1960s and the 1980s have been studied extensively by sociologists and other social scientists. These riots essentially served as field experiments in which researchers could compare cities that experienced riots with those that did not. Researchers also compared people who joined in the riots with those who lived in the riot community but did not participate (McPhail, 1971; Olzak & Shanahan, 1996; Porter & Dunn, 1984; Spilerman, 1976). From this research, sociologists and policy makers learned a great deal about why riots happen. Unfortunately, society has not responded by changing the conditions that produce such riots. What are those conditions?

One thing we learned is that such riots start when a highly volatile event, such as the acquittal of the police officers, enrages an aggrieved group. The same thing happened in Miami in 1980. The immediate cause of that riot was the acquittal of four Miami police officers in a murder trial for the death of an African American insurance agent, Arthur McDuffie. The acquittal infuriated African Americans in Miami just as the acquittal was to enrage blacks in Los Angeles a decade later. The climate was also the same: There had been police killings and assaults of blacks in Florida to fuel beliefs about police racism and disregard for African Americans. Despite these lessons, authorities in Los Angeles apparently did not take seriously enough the potential threat posed as the trial of the officers came to an end.

In addition to discovering the immediate causes of riots, the research on earlier riots also tells us about the structural strain that can play a part. Here, too, we see how thoroughly we have failed to apply lessons from the past. It is almost a cliché to say that economic deprivation and racial discrimination lay at the root of the riots of the 1960s. Clearly, people who are well-off economically are disinclined to take to the streets, even if provoked. But people who are severely oppressed are also unlikely to engage in such activism. Their feelings of helplessness are more likely to result in resignation or withdrawal. Instead of the total underdog, it is people who have hopes for improvement in their lives but see those hopes threatened who are most inclined to respond to deprivation and oppression through rioting. In other words, it is *relative deprivation* that often underlies collective violence.

Research on the 1960s riots documented this truth in several ways. It was not cities where blacks were worst off that experienced riots. Rather, it was cities where blacks had made considerable improvements such that there were small gaps between the incomes of blacks and whites. It was also blacks in the middle levels of educational ranks who rioted, not those with the least education. Such advances in income and education had led people to hope for further improvement and led to deeply felt frustration when the improvements were not forthcoming.

Firefighters pour water on a store set on fire during a riot in St. Petersburg, Florida, in 1996. This disturbance documents that the social conditions for such outbursts still exist in the United States.

Likewise, research on the 1980 Miami riot showed that "rioters by no means came exclusively from the ranks of the poor or unemployed or the criminal classes. Many held jobs, were normally law-abiding and did not otherwise fit the stereotypical image of a 'rioter'" (Porter & Dunn, 1984, p. 183). Criminals or the unemployed may have played a part in starting the riot, but seemingly respectable African Americans provided the numbers that kept it going and contributed to heightening the levels of emotion and destruction. What evidence we have at this point from Los Angeles suggests the same thing: Many looters and arrestees worked or were in school. In addition, economic competition plays an important part.

Recent research shows that riots are more likely to occur in cities where job opportunities for African Americans have contracted and where immigration has created tight labor markets (Olzak & Shanahan, 1996). The combination of relative deprivation along with stiff competition for jobs makes cities especially susceptible to unrest.

Beyond gaining knowledge about relative deprivation, we learned from earlier riots of a number of other factors that contribute to the likelihood of a riot occurring. These factors suggest that riots occur when members of minority groups feel left out of society, isolated from sources of political and economic power, ignored by the powers that be, and victimized by the

(continued)

social order that is supposed to serve and protect them. When there are few channels for resolving grievances or when the system appears unresponsive to expressions of discontent, people are more willing to turn to collective violence. In earlier riots, isolation from the political system was evidenced by such things as few or no African American police officers in a city. Presumably, a city sensitive to the needs of blacks would hire black police officers, and such officers would be more responsive to the needs and problems of the black community. In these earlier riots, cities with fewer black police officers were more likely to experience a riot. Likewise, cities with few African American store owners and those where officials were elected on a citywide rather than district basis (making it more difficult for blacks, who are typically a numerical minority in a city but a majority in some districts, to gain office) had more riots.

Once again, Los Angeles in 1992 fit the profile for a riot-prone city fairly well. The city did have a black mayor, but blacks were underrepresented at all levels of the police force. It also had a relatively small number of black store owners and professionals, espe-

cially in south central Los Angeles, where the riot occurred. In addition, competition for jobs was stiff, and many of the store owners in south central Los Angeles were Asian Americans who seemed to be doing fairly well even though they had immigrated to the United States only recently. Their apparent success contributed to the feelings of resentment and isolation in the African American community. Overall, the poverty, unemployment, and segregation in their community left these blacks feeling effectively disenfranchised.

We learned a great deal about collective violence from the research conducted in earlier decades. Our failure to apply that research by making changes in social policy is one of the reasons for the disastrous riot in Los Angeles in 1992. Social policies could have been established that would have improved the economic circumstances of African Americans and reduced feelings of isolation and disenfranchisement. Many of these policies are discussed in Chapters 6 and 7, and need not be repeated here. What does need reiteration is that, if society does nothing, it will probably have more such riots in the future.

Although people often discount the importance of rumors (as in "It's *only* a rumor"), rumors are important mechanisms of communication in many different situations. For example, in ambiguous settings where something unusual or startling has occurred, rumors may be the only source of information that people have. In addition, in stressful or anxious situations, people may pass on and accept rumors as a way of alleviating their anxiety (Rosnow, 1991). This was shown to be the case in the study of the willingness of college students to accept and pass on rumors about AIDS: Students experiencing the most anxiety and uncertainty were most willing to believe and transmit misconceptions about AIDS, regardless of whether they had confidence in the truth of the rumors they were passing on (Kimmel & Keefer, 1991).

Tamotsu Shibutani (1966) has referred to rumors as *collective transactions* to emphasize their

role as group efforts to develop a shared definition of some situation. "Rumor develops as [people] caught together in an ambiguous situation attempt to construct a meaningful interpretation of it by pooling their intellectual resources" (p. 164). Shibutani's approach to understanding rumor focuses on the concerns of the interactionist perspective regarding the importance of social meanings and their emergence from social interaction. Thus the rumor process is an interchange between people in which new bits of information are weighed and assessed against what is already known or suspected.

Although rumors are often distorted as they are exchanged, that does not always happen. There are situations in which people take a *critical set* toward rumors, which means that because of their own knowledge or the characteristics of the situation, people are skeptical about rumors and better able to assess their accuracy (Buckner, 1965). In other situations, however, people have an *uncritical set* and are likely to pass on an untruth or distort a rumor. Another factor that is likely to affect the distortion of a rumor is the group context in which it spreads. If it is spread serially from one person who knows the rumor to another person unfamiliar with it, then distortion is likely to occur because there are few checks on any person distorting it in the process of passing it on. If a rumor comes to a whole group, however, the resulting interchange and feedback will reduce the likelihood of distortion.

When rumor distortion does occur, it can happen in three different ways. First, as a rumor is retold, a process of *leveling* occurs in which the rumor is shortened and made more concise by eliminating some details. Second, through a process called *sharpening*, people give selective emphasis to some parts of a rumor, reporting some details and ignoring others. Finally, through what is called *assimilation,* elements of the rumor are changed, so that the overall rumor is consistent and fits in with prejudices or preconceptions of those transmitting the rumor (Koenig, 1985).

Although many rumor situations are characterized by ambiguity or anxiety, people pass on rumors for many reasons. In some cases, they may simply be bored and have nothing better to do. In other cases, individuals may feel that they will gain something from telling others about a rumor.

> One can readily visualize rumormongering as a transaction in which someone passes a rumor for something in return—another rumor, clarifying information, status, power, control, money, or some other resource. When information is scarce, the rumormonger can exact a high price for his tales. When the market for rumors expands, the number of rumors will proliferate. (Rosnow & Fine, 1976, p. 77)

This element in the rumor process can be a significant motivation to pass on rumors—even rumors whose authenticity one might doubt.

Mass Behavior

Mass behavior is *collective behavior in which the actions of people are not coordinated, people have little or no contact with one another, and yet there is still some uniformity of behavior and a general awareness of the* *others in the group*. Three types of mass behavior will be discussed: panic, mass hysteria, and fads and fashions.

Panic   On a cold and snowy winter evening in 1913, the Italian Hall in Calumet, Michigan, was gaily decorated for a Christmas party intended to bring some joy into the lives of children whose fathers, copper miners, had been on strike for many months. As the children celebrated, someone shouted "fire." The frightened children rushed for the exits. In a horrifyingly brief period of time, seventy-four people were dead, mostly children. They were crushed to death by the sheer weight of their own small bodies as they rushed to the exits of the building but the exit doors would not open. There was no fire (Thurner, 1984).

The Italian Hall disaster is a classic case of a **panic,** *an uncoordinated, mass attempt to avoid some immediate, perceived threat*. Panic behavior is sometimes referred to as irrational, but such statements are based on a misunderstanding of panic by people who observe it only from a distance. For people in the situation, mass behavior at the time seems rational, logical, and understandable. In a panic situation, people have relatively little information on which to base their decisions (e.g., the shouted word "fire" and the immediate reactions of others). In addition, there is a sense of urgency—if there is a fire, we must act quickly to save ourselves. This lack of information coupled with the sense of urgency leads people to be very suggestible. If the behavior of others—for example, their tentative movements toward exits—hints that the danger is real, people are likely to accept the suggestion and follow suit.

Although there was no actual fire in the Italian Hall in Calumet, all too often there is real danger, and with horrifying results: 600 people died in the Iroquois Theater fire in 1903; the Coconut Grove Night Club fire in Boston in 1942 resulted in 488 deaths; the Beverly Hills Supper Club fire in Kentucky in 1977 claimed 164 lives. Some of these lives probably would have been saved if there had not been mass panic. But how can panic be avoided in such situations? Studies indicate that people are much more likely to survive such disasters when they are familiar with emergency exits from buildings (Abe, 1976). Thus fire drills, when possible, can build in behavior patterns for people to rely on in panic situations. People are also more likely to survive when they engage in familiar and habitual behavior, such as moving to a known part of buildings. Finally, the survivors are those who act cautiously and avoid following in the footsteps of large numbers of people.

Mass Hysteria   In 1938, Orson Welles performed a radio dramatization of H. G. Wells's science fiction novel *The War of the Worlds,* about an invasion of the Earth by creatures from Mars. Welles's hour-long performance was cast as a musical show that was repeatedly interrupted by live "newscasts" of the invasion. As the show progressed, the newscasts reported that U.S. cities were being attacked and destroyed and their residents killed by the "invaders." If one listens to recordings of the broadcast today, it is obvious that it is a fictional account. The events recounted, for example, span many days but the show itself is only an hour long. In addition, the "newscasters" appear to be everywhere: in cities, in farmhouses, even riding with pilots in airplanes attacking the Martians. Yet, despite its clearly fictional nature, a survey found that a quarter of the listeners believed the broadcast was authentic. Many of these people were frightened by the broadcast, and some actually panicked and fled their homes out of fear. Others telephoned relatives or prayed as a means of consolation (Cantril, 1940).

The reaction to this radio broadcast is an example of **mass hysteria:** *an emotionally charged reaction by a large number of people to some anxiety-producing event.* Mass hysteria is similar to panic but spread over a larger area and a longer time period. Despite the name of *mass* hysteria, recent research has shown that most of these episodes are less widespread than the term implies (Marx & McAdam, 1994). Only a small number of the listeners to Welles's broadcast took any substantial action. Nonetheless, how could a reaction such as this happen? One reason was that radio was still a relatively new phenomenon in 1938, and people were not as sophisticated regarding the broadcast medium as they are today. People were just beginning to get much of their daily news from the radio, and interruptions of programs for news—the format used in Welles's program—were quite common. Furthermore, relatively little was known about other planets, and many people assumed that there might be life forms on them. The famous Martian "canals" had been observed, and there was speculation that they might have been constructed by "Martians." Adding to this credulity was the fact that science fiction had only recently acquired a mass audience by 1938. Given all these elements, the stage was set for a mass hysterical reaction to Welles's broadcast. Such a response to the same stimuli would be unlikely today because the preconditions that existed then have changed. This is not to say that people are less susceptible to mass hysteria today—only that the precipitating conditions are likely to be different.

Fads and Fashions   A **fad** is *a short-lived behavior engaged in by a large number of people; it is not part of a longer trend.* The list of fads in recent U.S. history is almost endless: meditation, jogging, hot tubs, roller blading, bungee jumping, break dancing, and so on. Not everyone, of course, participates in every fad. People are attracted to particular fads for a variety of reasons. In some cases, a fad is a means of asserting one's identity and feeling part of a group. In the 1970s, for example, the use of cocaine was a fad in some social circles—an emblem of wealth and status. It was a way for the user to say, "I am modern, I am with it." In the 1960s, marijuana was the drug that set one apart from one's more conservative and less adventuresome contemporaries. Today, some fads are to avoid drugs, drink fruit juice, and pump iron to improve one's body.

Where fads often carry slightly negative connotations—as in the pejorative term *faddist—fashions* tend to be more socially acceptable. **Fashion** refers to *behavior that is a part of the continuous process of establishing currently acceptable modes of dress, appearance, or behavior.* Fashions are much like fads although more continuous: There is always something that is considered in style and other things that are considered outmoded. Because of the part they play in establishing normative behavior, fashions can be found in all societies (Kroeber, 1919). Both fads and fashions are considered collective behavior because they are relatively unstructured and spontaneous, with their precise content emerging from the interactions of many people.

Crowds

The most thoroughly investigated form of collective behavior is probably the *crowd*. A **crowd** is *a temporary grouping of people who are in fairly close physical proximity to one another and whose attentions are focused on some common object or event.* Crowds include such things as a mob of looters roaming the streets, a pack of celebrants enjoying their home team's World Series victory, and a hostile group confronting a police squadron.

Characteristics of Crowds   Despite the considerable variety among crowds, they all share certain characteristics (Blumer, 1951; Goode, 1992):

1. *Uncertainty.* Crowds involve a degree of ambiguity or uncertainty: People are not sure what others will do or how they themselves ought to behave. This is even true among spectators at a sporting event. Although most will watch the game with a degree of decorum, some might shout obscenities, while others might throw objects onto the playing field; a fistfight might even break out between two excited spectators. Professional hockey matches in North America are notorious for this uncertainty regarding the behavior of both spectators and players. In fact, uncertainty is one element of sporting events that makes them so exciting to watch.

2. *Suggestibility.* Because of the lack of structure in crowds, people need to look for guidance for their behavior in places other than the preexisting normative structure. This need makes crowd members much more open and sensitive to the suggestion of others in the crowd than they might normally be. This suggestibility, however, is not totally uncritical. People take suggestions only if the suggestions are consistent with the prevailing mood and conception of appropriate behavior in the crowd.

3. *Anonymity.* Surrounded by a mass of other people, individuals in crowds often feel that they are unrecognized and thus anonymous. They believe they will go unnoticed and so will not be held responsible for their actions. People might shout, throw rocks, or set fire to buildings if their feelings of anonymity offer a sense of protection.

4. *Permissiveness.* The atmosphere of a crowd tends to encourage a broadening of the limits of acceptable behavior, and people are likely to express attitudes or engage in actions that they would refuse to do under other conditions. Permissiveness should not, however, be confused with a total *lack* of limits. In crowds, normative limitations may be extended considerably, but they are never eliminated. In the riot in Los Angeles in 1992, for example, rioters did not loot all businesses—they tended to attack Korean-owned and white-owned shops and spare those owned by African Americans or Latinos.

5. *Emotional Arousal.* Heightened emotional arousal results from the rapid communication that occurs between crowd members. In crowds, a person is bombarded with stimuli: sounds, shouts, large numbers of people, and movement. These stimuli tend to increase one's awareness of others and easily translate into a heightening of one's own emotional arousal.

Types of Crowds   Although crowds have much in common, there are also differences among crowds, especially in terms of goals and the amount of coordination of behavior among members. Using these criteria, we can distinguish among four types of crowds (Blumer, 1951; Goode, 1992).

A **casual crowd** is *a temporary grouping in which there is little structure and the members do not engage in any distinct, coordinated crowd actions.* Crowd members are passive, and there is little sense of crowd unity or involvement. Casual crowds, such as people watching firefighters control a blaze, are very unstable, and people enter and leave them easily. Despite their temporary and unstable nature, casual crowds are important because they can serve as a nucleus for other types of crowds.

Conventional crowds are *one of the more "regularized" forms of crowds because they are planned and socially sanctioned gatherings that are relatively structured.* Audiences at a sporting event, a religious rally, or a rock concert are examples of conventional crowds. Although such gatherings are planned and sanctioned, they nonetheless exhibit the characteristics—uncertainty, suggestibility, permissiveness, and emotional arousal—found in other crowds. At a rock concert, for example, there is often an air of expectancy—almost an electricity—about how things will turn out. How

TABLE 15.1 Types of collective behavior

		Acting Crowds	Expressive Crowds	Mass Behavior
Dominant emotion	Fear	Disaster teams Vigilante groups	Salem witch hunt	Rumors following Three Mile Island disaster Panic
	Hostility	Looters Prison riots	Burning buildings during race riots	Mass rioting
	Joy		Religious revival meeting Concert audience Dancing mania Mardi Gras carnival	Fads and fashions

Note: Adapted from "Collective Behavior: The Elementary Forms" by John Lofland, 1981, in Morris Rosenberg and Ralph H. Turner (Eds.), *Social Psychology: Sociological Perspectives,* New York: Basic Books.

will the audience behave? Will there be any untoward events? Might things even get totally out of control?

An **acting crowd** is *one in which attention and activity are directed toward some goal or objective.* Rioting mobs, looters, and protest demonstrators are examples of acting crowds. Acting crowds are often the most violent and destructive type of crowd, but they are also among the most significant crowds in terms of social change.

Expressive crowds are *crowds that focus on the expression of emotions and the personal gratification of their members.* Their goal is to change the mood, feelings, or behavior of those participating in the crowd. Expressive crowds are often more highly charged with emotion and more frenzied in behavior than are other crowds. For example, when victory was declared over Germany and Japan at the end of World War II, people in cities such as New York and San Francisco poured into the streets to celebrate, forming expressive crowds. There was much drinking, revelry, and dancing in the streets. Women hugged and kissed soldiers and sailors who were total strangers

to them. Behavior that was normally inhibited became common.

John Lofland (1981) has also classified crowds according to the dominant emotion of their members: fear, hostility, or joy. Combining this dimension with the distinction between acting and expressive crowds and mass behavior, six types of collective behavior emerge (see Table 15.1). A particular crowd might fall into more than one category, if, for example, crowd members were expressing both fear and hostility. This classification nonetheless illustrates the wide-ranging forms of collective behavior.

Behavior in Crowds   One of the major concerns in the sociological study of crowds has been to discover the factors that shape the behavior of people in crowds (McPhail, 1991). In the past few decades, our understanding of crowd behavior has been revised substantially. We now recognize that people in crowds are not necessarily behaving irrationally, nor do all members of a crowd feel and behave in the same fashion. To understand crowd behavior more fully, it is useful to review the four major processes that shape human behavior in crowds: contagion, convergence, emergent norms, and decision making. Much of what is discussed here involves Smelser's precondition of mobilization, because it involves the face-to-face social interaction that influences whether people will participate in a crowd action. Even if structural strain, a generalized belief, and a precipitating factor are present, people are not likely to become part of a crowd unless they are mobilized.

Contagion refers to the rapid spread of feelings, attitudes, and behaviors through a crowd. A phenomenon called circular reaction plays an important part in contagion (Blumer, 1951). *Circular reaction* refers to a process of "interstimulation" in which person A's response reflects, possibly to a heightened degree, the emotions that person B has just expressed and then serves as a stimulus for further reaction on the part of person B. Thus A and B repeatedly stimulate each other, thereby increasing their respective intensity and emotion. Person B, for example, shouts, "Let's attack the police." Person A quickly agrees, and this agreement serves as further impetus for B to proceed. The process involves quick reactions without the assessment and consideration that usually occur in less emotionally volatile settings. Another important factor affecting contagion is *milling:* random, erratic, fluctuating behavior. People in crowds are constantly walking around, talking, looking, moving, or shouting. In terms of the contagion process, milling makes people more sensitive to and responsive to the behavior of others in the crowd. When there is great, agitated movement, we tend to direct our attention toward it. By restricting our focus of attention to the crowd actions, we become more aware of the feelings and attitudes of the crowd members and are more likely to be influenced by them.

A second process affecting crowd behavior is *convergence:* People are drawn together in part because they share common qualities, predispositions, or interests (Milgram & Toch, 1968). The nature of these predispositions and interests can be highly variable. Sigmund Freud argued, for example, that crowd members are responding to similar unconscious motives, including a desire to return to infancy and an identification with the leaders of the crowd. Other convergence theorists

have focused on such things as frustration and strain as the common predisposition that underlies crowd behavior. The psychologists John Dollard and his colleagues (1939) along with Leonard Berkowitz (1971) have argued that increasing frustration leads to an enhanced tendency toward aggression and that aggression can readily take the form of rioting and other types of crowd behavior. Certainly, for example, the ghetto riots of the 1960s and the riots in Miami and Los Angeles in the 1980s and 1990s involved people who were reacting to common experiences of discrimination and oppression. We need to be careful, however, and recognize that not all crowd members act on the same motivations. Although some rioters may be responding to discrimination and oppression, others act out of the possibility of personal gain or are in search of a little excitement.

In addition to contagion and convergence, crowd behavior is often influenced by a third process: normative prescriptions and proscriptions, called *emergent norms,* not unlike those that guide behavior in other settings (Turner, 1964). In crowd settings, a new social structure comprised of new norms and social roles emerges to shape and constrain behavior. This new normative structure is unique to the situation in which it evolves, and it changes or disappears as the situation changes. Social pressure develops that encourages crowd members to behave in conformity to the emerging norms—or at least not to violate them. People become aware of the emergent norms by observing what others in the crowd say and do. In a riot, for example, seeing others looting stores—especially if the looters appear otherwise respectable—suggests that some people view looting as appropriate in this situation. And we know from considerable research that people in ambiguous or emotional situations tend to adopt the standards and judgments of those around them. This tendency can give the emergent norms considerable power over people's behavior.

A fourth process affecting crowd behavior is *collective decision making* in which crowd members calculate the benefits and costs of particular actions and choose those with the most desirable outcomes (Berk, 1974). The benefits of participating in a riot, say, might include the ability to vent one's anger or the opportunity to acquire some goods by looting a store. The costs would include the chance of being injured or arrested. If others join the rioting, then the costs are lowered because each person is less likely to be picked out of a large crowd by the police. In fact, there may be a threshold for participating in riot actions, such as a minimum number of people a person would have to see join in before that person would do so (Granovetter, 1978). Thus people in crowds assess alternatives in much the same fashion as people do in more institutionalized settings. However, given the highly emotional and volatile nature of many crowd settings, the decision making occurs much more quickly and with less consideration than in other situations.

To understand crowd behavior, then, we need to consider all four processes of contagion, convergence, emergent norms, and decision making.

Other factors contribute to crowd situations, such as Smelser's conduciveness, which was discussed earlier. In addition, if people are to participate in crowd actions, they need to learn, possibly through radio or television, that the crowd exists. After all, despite the existence of factors such as conduciveness and strain, a crowd will not develop unless sufficient people assemble at a common site and direct their attention to some common event. So an important factor in crowd development is the communication process that makes such assembling likely (McPhail & Wohlstein; Sullivan, 1977). Thus, crowds are very complex phenomena. The major elements involved are summarized in Figure 15.2. Other Worlds, Other Ways: Britain describes how some forms of collective behavior emerge in Britain, but not in the United States, because of social conditions particular to Britain.

FIGURE 15.2 A Sociological Explanation of Crowd Behavior

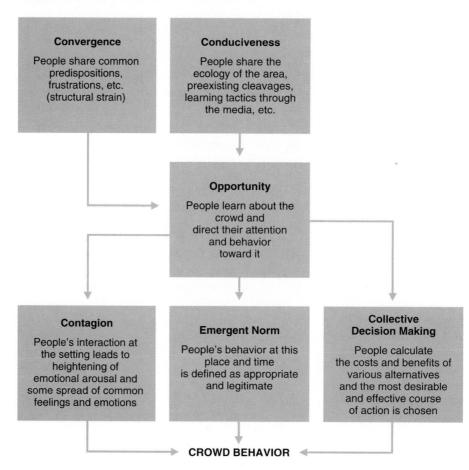

OTHER WORLDS, *Other Ways*

BRITAIN: THE CAUSES OF VIOLENCE AMONG SPORTS FANS

On October 11, 1977, the Rangers of Glasgow, Scotland, were playing the Aston Villa, a team from Birmingham, England, in an exhibition soccer game. Exhibition games are supposed to be friendly—they are not included in a team's season record—but this game had to be stopped in less than an hour. Shouting Ranger supporters stormed onto the field when Aston Villa took a 2–0 lead. Police had to be called in with dogs to break up the fighting on the field. Cans and bottles were hurled at the fans of both teams, and ambulances carried away twenty injured people. Nineteen people were arrested. In 1986 and again in 1988, British soccer fans turned violent when their teams played on the Continent. In one incident, a number of people were killed when a wall collapsed on some fans.

Such violence among fans at soccer games is commonplace in Britain. Fans not only fight police, referees, and one another during games but also roam the streets after games, breaking windows and looting. Violence has also been associated with professional sports such as hockey in the United States.

In outbursts of fan violence, conventional crowds become acting mobs. Why does this happen? Many say that it is inherent in contact sports such as hockey, soccer, and football—they encourage violence because they are violent sports in which physical contact is common. But such violence does not occur at all matches, nor is it common in every country. According to the sociologist Alan Roadburg (1980), fan violence, like other forms of collective behavior, is the result of a particular combination of social circumstances. The conditions surrounding British soccer matches, he says, are especially conducive to violence and are unlikely to be found in the United States.

One factor that distinguishes British from North American soccer games is the stadiums in which the matches are held. In England, stadiums tend to be older, and they are located in the centers of cities where little parking is available. Thus people must either walk or take the train to the stadium. As thousands of people converge on the stadium together, excitement can build to a high pitch. In the United States, stadiums tend to be newer, and they are generally reached by car. In the isolation of private automobiles, intense feelings of crowd involvement are less likely to build up.

British stadiums are also much more crowded than those in North America, and they are constructed in such a way that they encourage milling and circular reactions. They include an area called the *terrace,* where as many as 70 percent of the spectators stand rather than sit. There are considerable movement and congestion on the terraces, which heighten the crowd's emotional arousal. As one observer described it, "the senses of triumph and dejection experienced [in the terraces] are never quite matched in any seated section of a football ground" (quoted in Roadburg, 1980, p. 269). In North American soccer games, all of the spectators are normally seated, and the kind of contagion that occurs in the terraces is less likely.

Finally, the nature of the fans who attend soccer games and their loyalty to their teams are different in Britain and the United States. In the latter, soccer is a family spectator sport, and women and children make up a sizable proportion of the audience. In Britain, few women and children attend. Another factor is that soccer is the primary sports interest for many fans in Britain, especially among the working class that makes up most of the audience. In the United States, fans' loyalties are extended to teams in several different sports. Furthermore, many British fans have played soccer themselves, which makes them feel more personally involved in the game than do those who were introduced to the sport just a decade ago, as in the United States. Together, these factors make British fans intensely loyal to their teams—indeed, they view them almost as extensions of themselves. The defeat or humiliation of a team is taken very seriously. Referees, police, the opposing team's fans, and even shops in an opposing team's community may be attacked as symbols of the opposing team. Given the different circumstances surrounding the game in the United States, however, the violence associated with soccer in England is unlikely to follow the sport across the Atlantic.

Social Movements

You should be able to describe what social movements are and trace their development.

A **social movement** is "*a conscious, collective organized attempt to bring about or resist large-scale change . . . by noninstitutionalized means*" (Wilson, 1973, p. 8). Examples of social movements are the French Revolution, the American Revolution, the feminist movement, the labor movement, the environmental movement, the gay liberation movement, and the Unification Church. In their early stages, social movements are like other forms of collective behavior, rather unorganized and spontaneous. In fact, social movements sometimes grow out of dissatisfaction that first makes itself felt through other forms of collective behavior such as crowds or riots. Over time, however, social movements develop more organization, possibly including a formal leadership and decision-making apparatus, rules and regulations, established meeting times, and the like. Some social movements even go through a process of *institutionalization* whereby they become a formal and accepted part of society. For example, when the Mormons (Latter-Day Saints) emerged in the early 1800s, they were an unconventional social movement that was the target of considerable hostility and vituperation. Today, the Mormon Church is an accepted and respectable institution in the United States.

The Development of Social Movements

Smelser's preconditions for collective behavior provide a useful scheme for understanding the way social movements develop. Three of the preconditions will be emphasized: structural strain, generalized belief, and mobilization. In terms of structural strain, social movements tend to arise in situations in which there is some oppression, deprivation, frustration, or contradiction (Wood & Jackson, 1982). The social movement constitutes people's effort to rectify the undesirable social conditions. And the deprivation that produces social movements tends to be relative rather than absolute. *Relative deprivation* occurs when people believe that their situation is worse than it should be when compared to the situations of others. Some people in the United States, for example, might feel deprived if there were no meat or poultry available in the stores because they have become used to these foods as a matter of course. Many people in Bangladesh, by contrast, view those foods as a luxury rather than a necessity. Thus social conditions that would constitute sufficient strain to produce a social movement in one setting would not necessarily do so in another.

A special set of circumstances that can produce relative deprivation is called the *phenomenon of rising expectations*. This phrase refers to a situation in which people have been experiencing some improvements in their lives and come to expect further improvements in the future. This phenomenon is an element of James C. Davies's (1962) J-curve theory of revolutions. This theory posits that support for a social movement or revolution is greatest when a long period of improving conditions, accompanied by expectations that improvement will continue, is followed by a halt or reversal in improvements. It is called the J-curve because the line tracing these economic conditions (see Figure 15.3) looks like an inverted J. As the gap between what people expect and what they actually receive widens, it reaches a point at which these circumstances seem intolerable. The people may still be fairly well-off compared to earlier years or compared to the circumstances of others, but they are comparing their present circumstances to where they expected to be, not to where they were previously or where others are. At this point, says Davies, people are in a revolutionary state of mind in that they would be receptive to joining a social movement should the opportunity arise.

The historian Crane Brinton (1965) argues that the American Revolution of 1776 illustrates the effect of rising expectations on the propensity to revolt. In the half-century before the Revolution, the colonies were growing and prosperous. The balance of trade was improving, and the colonists had gained increasing political independence from England. What, then, triggered the Revolution? England engaged in a few actions that, although posing no major threat to existing economic conditions, cast doubt on whether opportunities would continue to expand in the future. For example, England incorporated some of the lands west of the Allegheny Mountains into

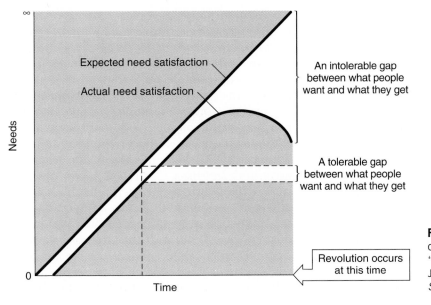

FIGURE 15.3 The J-Curve Theory of Revolutions *Note:* Reprinted from "Toward a Theory of Revolution" by James C. Davies, 1962, *American Sociological Review, 27,* p. 6.

Canada. American land speculators, including George Washington, had been hoping to expand their economic fortunes westward, and their hopes were thus threatened. Other British actions limited the rights of colonists to levy their own taxes and tightened the money supply to the colonies. It was these threats to the continuing growth in prosperity in the colonies, rather than extremes in poverty or political oppression, that generated support for the Revolution. (Applying Sociology: The Los Angeles Riot, in Chapter 14, discusses relative deprivation in the context of race riots, a form of crowd behavior rather than a more permanent and enduring social movement.)

Relative deprivation and a threat to rising expectations, although essential in the emergence of social movements, are not sufficient. In addition, people need to develop a *generalized belief* in the form of shared targets of hostility who are held responsible for hardship, suffering, and oppression. People begin to express their concerns and anger, and a sense of identity and common fate emerges. Possibly with the help of political leaders or intellectuals, people refine their concerns and identify those people or social conditions responsible. They also set forth a vision of the future, portraying the changes that are possible or likely if a certain course of action is followed.

Finally, if a sustained social movement is to emerge, there must be a *mobilization of resources* toward that end (Pichardo, 1988; Zald, 1992). Leaders must be found, money must be collected, and ways of exercising power must be located. In addition, organization, administration, procedures, and strategies must evolve. If the organization fails to accomplish these things, its survival is threatened. The movement may divide into a number of weak and powerless factions, or its lack of success in accomplishing goals may drive members away. Many incipient social movements—even when the strain was substantial and the generalized belief existed—have floundered because the essential mix of resources was not mobilized.

Social Change

You should be able to explain the four different theoretical perspectives on social change.

With an understanding of collective behavior and social movements, one can look back on incidents such as Lattimer and Ludlow with a better sense of why those men and women did what they did and the part that their actions played in changing the United States.

Social change refers to *relatively long-term and permanent alterations in the components of culture, social structure, and social behavior.* These alterations can include changes in cultural values, norms, and roles, as well as changes in social institutions such as the family, religion, or education (see Chapter 2). This book has discussed many illustrations of social change. At this point a more general understanding of the process of social change is needed.

Theories of Change

Sociologists, anthropologists, and historians have all developed theories of social change. Their investigations have addressed the issue of whether there is any pattern or purpose to the seeming kaleidoscope of change that we observe over the span of human history. Although there is some overlap among the various theories, we can classify them into four distinct groups: evolutionary, functionalist, conflict, and cyclical theories. Each theory makes a unique contribution to the understanding of social change (Lauer, 1991; Vago, 1988).

Evolutionary Theories Evolutionary theories have had many proponents in both Europe and the United States over the past two centuries (Durkheim, 1893/1947; Morgan, 1877; Parsons, 1951). These theories are based on the assumption that change is natural and that human societies move through a set of predictable, cumulative stages. Much of the evidence for evolutionary theories of change derives from historical and anthropological studies showing that some small and simple societies have become large and complex. This development convinced many observers that such a transition was natural. The approach of early evolutionists was called *unilinear evolution* because all societies were assumed to develop along a single sequence of stages involving "progress." Lewis Henry Morgan (1877), for example, reasoned that "primitive" societies became more "advanced," evolving from savagery to a barbaric state and ultimately to civilization. The transition from one stage to another occurs because of some major invention such as the making of fire, the development of the bow and arrow, or the harnessing of fossil fuels.

As more anthropological and historical evidence accumulated during the twentieth century, social scientists began to recognize some basic flaws in unilinear theories of evolution. First of all, they were too simple. All societies did not move through the same stages, and some skipped stages by moving from very simple starting points to merging with complex industrial societies. In addition, the early unilinear theories were very ethnocentric, as Morgan's use of the terms *savagery* and *barbarism* illustrates. These observers viewed their own society as preferable and the others as less desirable. It was assumed not only that all societies *would* become like Western industrial society, but also that they *should* do so. They also tended to emphasize one aspect of change, namely technological and economic development, as the key criterion of evolution.

More recently, some sociologists and anthropologists have argued for a *multilinear theory* of evolutionary change (Lenski, Lenski, & Nolan, 1991; Steward, 1955). According to this approach, there is a *tendency* for societies to evolve toward greater complexity and adaptability, although evolution may not be universal. Furthermore, because each society begins from a different starting point and encounters different experiences along the way, the outcome of the evolutionary process is unlikely to be uniform. Rather, it occurs along a number of different paths, and change is no longer equated with progress as it was with many unilinear theorists. There may even be periodic or short-term reversals in the trend. Nevertheless, multilinear evolutionists argue that, over the long run, there is a general direction to social change: from small, simple societies to large, complex ones.

Functionalist Theories Functionalist theories of society place considerable emphasis on factors that contribute to social order and stability. Most functionalists, however, also recognize the importance of social change. Robert Nisbet (1969), for example, argues that "the fundamental assumption of the functionalist is . . . that . . . there are sources of change within social systems, more or less natural sources, and that from these there flow patterns of change that are as congruent to the social system as growth is within the living organism" (p. 235).

Functionalists argue that social systems are never fully or completely integrated. There are always strains, contradictions, and inconsistencies. For example, educational institutions are intended to train people to fill occupational roles in the economic sector, yet today many college graduates cannot find jobs that use their college training. Going to college generates expectations on the part of individuals regarding the jobs they will probably hold. For many, these expectations go unfulfilled, a situation of inconsistency that causes one of the strains in contemporary U.S. society. Social change results when the system attempts to adjust to the strains. Minor amounts of malintegration are not terribly disruptive and would probably lead to little, if any, social change. As malintegration increases, however, there is more of a tendency for the system to respond.

Another aspect of the functionalist theory of social change is structural differentiation, or the increasing specialization of roles. Differentiation can arise because of population growth, technological developments, or other factors. For example, as noted in Chapter 9, the many functions that were once performed by the family are now differentiated and performed by other institutions, such as schools, churches, or businesses. When structural differentiation occurs, other parts of society must change in order to be integrated with the newly emerged structures. In this fashion, functionalists view societies as constantly adapting and evolving as new situations arise. Many functionalists argue that the pattern of this evolution is generally toward more complex and differentiated social structures.

Despite the part accorded to social change by functionalists, the functional approach has still been criticized for deemphasizing change, especially rapid and substantial change. By suggesting that social change normally involves slow and incremental adjustments, functionalists seem to imply that existing social arrangements are the most desirable and that disruptive social change is unusual or abnormal.

Conflict Theories The conflict view of social change was discussed in Karl Marx's analysis of social stratification described in Chapter 6. Marx characterized society as involving a constant struggle between social classes over scarce resources. The more dominant classes use their resources to coerce and exploit those below them. In some societies, it is the peasants who are dominated by a nobility or landed aristocracy; in other societies, it is the workers who are controlled by factory owners, or it may be a racial or ethnic minority that is subordinated to a dominant racial group. In the long run, however, subordinate groups will push for changes in the distribution of resources. It might take some leadership to get them moving, or it might require the mobilization of some new resources, as discussed earlier regarding the development of social movements. But when the opportunity arises, said Marx, they will push, and the ultimate outcome will be changes in the distribution of resources in society.

Ralf Dahrendorf (1959) criticized Marx on the grounds that Marx had overemphasized the role of economic processes in social change. Dahrendorf argued that we should look more broadly at *authority,* the legitimate power to enforce the norms of a group. For example, parents have authority over their children, teachers over students, and correctional officers over prison inmates. There is typically an unequal distribution of authority, and those with authority find it in their own interests to maintain and protect the status quo, whereas those without authority find that some form of change would be more beneficial to them. Thus for Dahrendorf, like Marx, there is an inherent tendency toward change in society, and the change will occur if the right opportunities arise.

Both Marx and Dahrendorf tend to emphasize the importance of impersonal social forces, and especially economic forces, in social change and to downplay the role of other factors. More recent conflict approaches to understanding social movements and social change have departed from this view by recognizing the part of factors other than economic change and class conflict (Buechler, 1995). Such theorists as Herbert Marcuse and Jurgen Habermas, for example, argue that people's ideas, awareness, and identity can be important and thus education and consciousness-raising can serve as catalysts for social change. Other research documents that social movements that are focused around issues of ethnicity, gender, or religion can be important sources of social change. Conflict over ideas, beliefs, values, or ways of life can be as important as conflicts over economic or political resources and power. Furthermore, all these factors can serve as catalysts for social change even when the economic or social conditions seen as important by Marx do not exist. According to these new approaches to social movements and social change, then, society is characterized by conflict and struggle, but social change is not solely, or in some cases even primarily, the result of impersonal structural forces; other noneconomic and nonstructural factors can play an important role. Actually, Marx in some of his writings conceded some of these other factors, but they were always subsidiary to the forces of economics.

Cyclical Theories   The notion that life is a cycle is a familiar one; we can see it as people age and die or the seasons change. There have also been cyclical theories to explain how societies change. Cyclical theory "essentially argues that all man's experience has happened before—a kind of sense of *déjà vu* on the grand scale, the disturbing sensation that we have been along this way before. . . . [The theory] does not deny change, but it does deny that it is leading anywhere over the long term" (Moore, 1974, p. 44). It can be seen that cyclical theories clearly contrast with evolutionary theories. The best-known cyclical theory in sociology was developed by Pitirim Sorokin (1937), although he never called his theory cyclical.

Sorokin maintained that societies are made up of three primary orientations: the *ideational,* the *sensate,* and the *idealistic.* The ideational system emphasizes faith, spiritual matters, religion, and feelings; the sensate emphasizes sense experiences and tends to be rational, scientific, and materialistic; the idealistic orientation is a combination of the other two, emphasizing human creativity and rationality. Sorokin conceived of societal change as a fluctuation over long historical periods from an emphasis on an ideational orientation through the idealistic to a sensate emphasis, and then back to ideational.

Another cyclical theory of societal change was developed in the early twentieth century by the German historian Oswald Spengler, who argued that societies age like people: They are born, grow to a mature state or *golden age,* and then decline and die. There are, of course, societies that appear to fit the descriptions of change offered by a Sorokin or a Spengler. The Roman Empire, for example, had a golden age and then declined. It also seemed to make the transition from an ideational orientation to an idealistic and then a sensate one. Some have argued that Western civilization is also in a sensate period with a heavy emphasis on materialism and science, and that it is in its decline.

Although it is difficult to discount cyclical theories completely, social scientists and historians have been hesitant to adopt them for one primary reason: It is difficult to prove that a particular theme dominates a given era. One can always find historical proof to document the existence of other themes at the same time. If the contemporary United States, for example, is interpreted as a sensate culture, how does one account for the emergence of fundamentalist Christians, the Moral Majority, and other devoutly religious groups? In other words, depending on where we wish to direct our attention, we can find proof for the existence of all three of Sorokin's cultural trends during a given era. Which trend is dominant becomes a matter of interpretation over which historians will naturally disagree. It is equally difficult to define what constitutes the maturity of a civilization. For these reasons, sociologists have not found cyclical theories of social change to be particularly useful in understanding human history.

The Future: Global Modernization?

You should be able to discuss the different positions on modernization and the development of a postindustrial society in the United States and the less developed nations of the world for the foreseeable future.

The concept of modernization was introduced in Chapter 12, but it warrants reemphasis here because it has become one of the more profound influences on human societies. **Modernization** refers to *the economic, social, and cultural changes that occur when a preindustrial society makes the transition to an advanced industrial society.* Many nations in the world today, including the United States, Japan, and the other industrial nations, have modernized, and many others are moving in that direction. These issues have been discussed at a number of points in this book, but it is worth returning to that discussion to see what the future might hold.

Modernization in the Less Developed Nations

Many proponents of the evolutionary theories of social change assume that the experience of the advanced industrial nations will be reproduced by the less developed nations of the world today. That is, those nations are destined to change in the direction of the same high levels of industrialization, urbanization, education, income, and lifestyles that now characterize the developed nations. Presumably, these nations will experience improvements in health care, housing, and nutrition and will become consumer societies with a wide array of goods and services available and a generally affluent citizenry to purchase them. In other words, the world will move toward global modernization: The twin engines of capitalism and industrialism will propel all nations into a materially comfortable future.

Certainly, many nations around the world are moving toward modernization. Levels of urbanization, education, literacy, and standard of living are rising in many places. It may be overly optimistic, however, to conclude that all nations can or should strive for the standards of the currently industrialized nations. One reason why the experiences of today's less developed nations may be different is that most currently industrialized nations modernized under different and much more favorable circumstances. They had a long time to industrialize and no already-industrialized nations to compete for resources and markets. They also had a much more abundant supply of natural resources to support industrialization. The United States, for example, had an ample supply of fertile land, coal, and iron ore and access to cheap foreign oil and other resources.

The currently industrialized nations of the West were also assisted in their industrialization and modernization by centuries of ruthless exploitation of weaker nations and peoples. England, the United States, and others used slavery and colonization in India, the Americas, and many other places around the world as vehicles of economic development. In the Americas, European imperial nations drove the Indians from their land and if necessary exterminated them in the name of cultural and economic development. This plunder of land, resources, and peoples added immeasurably to the economic wealth and development of many currently industrialized nations.

Because of the political, military, and cultural climate in the world in the late twentieth century, most developing nations today do not have access to the same forms of exploitation to assist them in modernizing. They also have access to fewer resources in general, so they must compete for them with other nations in overseas markets at great expense. Many of these nations have had to go heavily into debt by borrowing from the already-industrial nations in order to purchase these materials. Recent research shows that the burden of these debts has had severely negative consequences for Third-World nations. El Salvador and Venezuela, as noted in Chapter 6, have had to cut back on social services in recent decades in order to pay off these mounting debts. Such cutbacks have resulted in higher infant mortality, reduced childhood immunization, less adequate nutrition for children, and lower economic growth (Bradshaw, Noonan, Gash, & Sershen, 1993). These are burdens that the currently industrialized nations did not have to face as they industrialized.

World-system theorists argue that we need to look at the entire capitalist world system to grasp the circumstances of the developing nations today (Chase-Dunn & Grimes, 1995). They would agree that the experience of today's developing nations will be different, but they attribute this difference to their dependency on the industrial nations. The currently industrial nations have been core, or dominant, nations for centuries, and in fact it was their exploitation of the other nations that helped support their industrialization. As noted in Chapter 13, the corporate might in the world resides in a small number of core nations. These corporations invest in other nations and create jobs for some workers, but they also exploit their natural resources and siphon off profits and wealth to the core nations.

The debts mentioned a moment ago contribute to the transfer of wealth from periphery to core nations. The banks of industrial nations earn interest on those debts, interest which comes out of the gross national product of the periphery

The material products of the industrial nations can be found in profusion around the globe. What is unclear is whether worldwide modernization will produce convergence, with the modernizing nations becoming much like those that are already developed, or divergence, with persisting differences in lifestyles and standards of living.

nations. The agricultural and industrial development in which the core nations invest also tends to be land-intensive and capital-intensive, which means that it produces relatively few jobs while removing land from the control of peasants who once lived from it. Although some people in the Third World benefit from these practices, the outcome for many is fewer jobs, low-paying jobs, and inadequate housing in crowded cities.

Modernization brings with it many positive things, such as a higher standard of living, but it is not solely an economic process. It also changes cultural norms, values, and institutions. In the currently industrialized nations, for example, modernization has produced weaker kinship ties,

a more fragile family, and gender equality. As has been noted throughout this book, many of the less developed nations are more traditional cultures that place great value on strong kinship ties, large families, and in some cases male dominance, or patriarchy. Not all peoples view cultural change as a result of modernization positively. As more nations modernize, we may learn whether the economic dimensions of modernization can be achieved without all the social and cultural changes that accompanied the process in the West. It may be that unique social and cultural forces will produce a number of versions of modernization.

There is no consensus, then, about what the future holds for the Third-World nations

(Robertson, 1992). Some see *convergence,* with these countries becoming very much like the already-developed nations. Others predict *divergence,* with the developing nations having different experiences, retaining unique social and cultural elements, and possibly remaining subordinate to the core nations in the world stratification system. Other Worlds, Other Ways: Russia (on pp. 538–539) analyzes these issues as they apply to the recent breakup of the Soviet Union and the current status of Russia.

Change, Modernization, and the Mass Media

The process of modernization has been occurring in different nations around the world for a number of centuries, as Chapter 12 points out. In the twentieth century, the mass media have come to play a powerful role in the modernization process, although it is difficult to predict their ultimate impact since the technology is still evolving. One approach to these issues, called *development communication,* is based on the assumption that the widespread dissemination of the various forms of media, such as television and newspapers, is a significant force in both economic and social modernization in a society. In this view, the media help to promote a shift from authoritarian to more democratic forms of politics and organizational life and from traditional to more modern and egalitarian cultural forms (Schiller, 1989; Sussman & Lent, 1991; West & Fair, 1993).

In terms of economic development, the mass media are the modern equivalent of the highways of an earlier era: They provide the infrastructure

Modern mass media and communications technologies are at the center of the process of modernization today. However, the role of the media in the process is neither simple nor clear-cut.

SOVIET UNION

0   miles   1600

RUSSIA

OTHER WORLDS, *Other Ways*

RUSSIA: COLLECTIVE BEHAVIOR, SOCIAL CHANGE, AND MODERNIZATION

The world has seen some remarkable changes since 1989. The collapse of the Soviet Union and the disintegration of the Berlin Wall are two of the most profound changes of the twentieth century. I was born at about the end of World War II, which marked the beginning of the Cold War. I did not imagine that the Cold War would end during my lifetime, but it has, and the modern history of Russia can tell us much about collective behavior, social change, and modernization.

The Russian Revolution of 1917 marked the rise of the communists to power in Russia (Skocpol, 1986). Previously the Russian Empire had been a feudal society, with a technologically backward and unproductive agricultural economy. Other European nations such as Britain and France had modernized before Russia, which left Russia in a very weak position from which to compete in world markets. It was vulnerable to fiscal crises and popular protest from the mass of peasants. Early in the twentieth century, the confluence of these factors created a highly revolutionary situation in Russia. A revolution was attempted in 1905, without success, and after Russia was further weakened by fighting in World War I, a number of revolutionary groups combined to overthrow the Tsar. Among these revolutionary groups, the Bolsheviks, or communists, ultimately prevailed.

With the communists in power, a period of authoritarian and despotic rule began in the Union of Soviet Socialist Republics (USSR), as the country was called. Under Josef Stalin, for example, there were death squads and purges and concentration camps in Siberia. In addition, the Communist Party attempted to put into action Karl Marx's utopian ideas about

society. To that end, they declared all free markets, competition, and private industry to be tools of exploitation and thus to be eliminated. Instead, they developed a highly centralized economy of collective farms and factories that were state controlled and run. Decisions about production and distribution were determined by collective goals rather than market demand. After overthrowing the highly oppressive and unjust tsarist regime, the new Soviet rulers believed that markets would simply reproduce a new stratification system in which owners of factories and land would dominate and oppress workers and peasants.

World War II was the event that produced the real conflict between the Soviet Union and the West. The Soviet Union and the United States were allies against Germany in the war, but the Soviet Union suffered terribly from it. Germany occupied large parts of the country west of the Ural Mountains. Although the United States lost only 300,000 people in the war, mostly military personnel, the Soviet Union is estimated to have lost twenty million as a result of military action, starvation, and disease. In part to protect itself from such invasion in the future, the Soviet Union created a barrier around itself after the war. In some cases, it absorbed nations into itself, for example, Latvia, Lithuania, and Estonia. In other cases, it installed communist governments in the nations of Eastern Europe and left Soviet troops to ensure that governments not friendly to the Soviets did not emerge. Thus the era of the Cold War between the East and the West began; it dominated world politics and economics for the next forty-five years.

Then in the 1980s, a revolution began that was less violent than the one in 1917 but no less important (Dunlop, 1993). Beginning with Mikhail Gorbachev's policy of *glasnost* (openness), the totalitarian communist hold over the Soviet Union began to disintegrate. In 1990 and 1991, dictatorships in East Germany, Hungary, Poland, Romania, and Czechoslovakia were overthrown, some through violent revolution. The wall separating East Berlin and West Berlin was torn down. All the nations of Eastern Europe and the Soviet Union began introducing market forces into their economies—some gradually, others rapidly. In 1991, Gorbachev officially resigned as president of the USSR, and the Soviet Union ceased to exist. A new entity called the Commonwealth of Independent States (CIS) was established; the largest state in the CIS was Russia, led by Boris Yeltsin. Not only were the Eastern European nations freed of Soviet domination, but numerous areas that had been a part of the Soviet Union declared their independence.

What brought about this revolution? There were a number of important forces at work (Goldman, 1991; Sedaitis & Butterfield, 1991). One is that the Soviet economic system was notoriously inefficient. For example, many stores sold only one type of product such as bread or meat, which meant that people had to spend much time shopping. In many stores, a customer would go to one counter to learn if, say, a pound of tea was available and be given a ticket to take to the cashier; after paying the cashier, the customer would then go to a third clerk to pick up the tea. The system employed lots of people, but it was costly and inefficient. You can well imagine that Soviet products were not very competitive on world markets. As the decades wore on, the Soviet economy remained in the doldrums, battling against these inefficiencies and becoming more depressed. The inefficiencies remained as a permanent impediment to further modernization, and the resultant economic difficulties weakened the authority of communist rule. As noted in Chapter 13, political leaders need to be seen as effective by those they rule if they are to maintain their hold on power.

Another factor contributing to this revolution was the burdensome cost to the Soviet Union of maintaining the Cold War and its empire. Of course, the Cold War was a burden for the United States too, but the U.S. economy was much stronger and far more advanced than the Soviet economy. The Cold War drained Soviet resources that could have been used to develop the agricultural and industrial infrastructure of the nation.

Yet another factor playing a part in the downfall of the Soviet Union was growing nationalist sentiment among many peoples under Soviet domination. People in Latvia, Byelorussia, Uzbekistan, and many other areas never perceived themselves as "Russian" despite intense "Russification" campaigns by the Moscow government over the years. These republics wanted independence and their historical national identity. In fact, the Baltic republic of Lithuania may have served as the final straw in the collapse of the Soviet Union when it declared its independence in 1990. Other republics soon followed.

The experience of Russia in 1917 and 1990 illustrates that the process of modernization cannot be understood only in terms of processes internal to a nation. It is also a process that involves contact and competition with other nations. Both then and now, Russia confronted some of the same pressures that other less developed nations have faced—an expanding capitalist world system. Competition with the core nations left Russia weakened in terms of its economic and technological position. The Russian experience also illustrates how collective behavior—in the form of public protest or revolution—plays a part in the process of social change. It remains to be seen whether Russia in the future will achieve the same levels of modernization as the other industrial nations (convergence) or whether its own political, cultural, economic, and geographic circumstances will result in a different line of development (divergence).

for development. In terms of political and cultural development, the flow of messages in the media can help to promote the diffusion and adoption of modern ideas in developing nations. In addition, the media make available a wide range of ideas that compete with more traditional and entrenched beliefs and values. People come under the influence of many more sources of information, and competing political parties can challenge existing structures and authorities. The collapse of the Soviet Union, described in the Other Worlds, Other Ways section, provides some evidence for this. The collapse was helped by the growth in televisions and VCRs that challenged the government monopoly over information and spread radical new ideas among the people of the Soviet Union and Eastern Europe.

This development communication stance has been a controversial approach to the role of the media in the process of modernization. Many critics argue that it is either wrong or vastly oversimplified. One criticism has been that the spread of the media is not always associated with social modernization in the form of democratic and egalitarian social, political, and economic structures. Some nations, such as Singapore and South Korea, have at times had extensive modern media organizations along with highly authoritarian political structures and political repression. In these and other situations, the role of the media seems to involve primarily a top-to-bottom flow of information and influence (Bourgault, 1995). In other words, the media serve primarily as a tool for the national and international political and economic elites to impose change on a nation. The media are a mechanism through which social planners and development agencies impose modernization, along with its attendant changes in cultures and values, on a people. Such organizations as the World Bank and the International Monetary Fund, discussed in Chapter 13, have often been criticized for approaching modernization and the adoption of capitalist economic forms in this fashion. Such an approach assumes that experts, elites, and outsiders can come up with solutions to whatever problems confront a Third-World people. This one-sided view regarding modernization often produces development that is at best lopsided, benefiting mostly the affluent, Westernized groups in society and leaving significant dislocation and poverty for others.

An alternate view of the modernization process is that it is, or should be, shaped by the cultural values and traditions of the people of a nation or region. In this view, the role of the media in modernization focuses on the possibilities the media afford for empowerment (Bourgault, 1995). The media can serve as a vehicle for indigenous, grassroots involvement in economic, political, and cultural development. The nongovernmental organizations (NGOs) that are discussed in Chapters 8 and 13 can use the media to communicate, coordinate, and disseminate ideas; for these organizations, the media are a powerful tool in working against the dominance of oligarchical governments and corporations. NGOs can use modern communications technology, such as computers, satellites, and data banks, to tie together small, previously isolated groups that may have some interests in common and raise funds to support their cause. At the local level, villagers use newsletters, radio shows, and locally produced television shows to bolster their own cultural values and encourage what they define as positive behavior. This has occurred in Africa, for example, where villagers have produced and distributed radio and television shows that present their vision of cultural values and societal organization and enable them to make connections with other villagers in Africa or elsewhere.

So, modern mass media and communications technology are clearly at the center of the process of modernization today. However, the role of the media is neither simple nor clear-cut. The media can assist movement toward more democratic and egalitarian social structures, but they can also support more authoritarian and oligarchical goals when controlled by the political and economic elite. Furthermore, whereas the elites and corporations exert significant control over the media, as other chapters in this book have pointed out, the media are also contested territory that is used by many groups to advance their goals. Whether the emerging technologies of the Internet and satellite communications will provide more pressures toward democratization is a question that only future research can answer.

The United States: A Postindustrial Future?

Some sociologists suggest that the United States is becoming a **postindustrial society,** *one that is dominated by a highly technological form of production and that devotes greater resources to providing services than to industrial production* (Bell, 1973; Hage & Powers, 1992). There is still some debate over what a postindustrial society will be like. Social scientists who consider themselves futurists attempt to predict developments based on contemporary trends. This discussion illustrates some of the projections that they have made and about which there is some consensus.

The economy of a postindustrial society will probably be quite different, reflecting trends already underway. Although industrial societies emphasize the extraction of natural resources and the manufacturing of goods, there will in the future be a shift: Most workers will manage other workers, process information, or provide services to other people. As noted in Chapter 13, an ever-growing proportion of the workforce is in white-collar and service occupations, and in the future there will probably be even fewer industrial workers. In this kind of economy, access to information and the possession of a specialized knowledge will come to play a greater role in determining a person's position in society. Daniel Bell (1973) coined the term *knowledge class* to refer to people such as teachers, computer programmers, and engineers whose basic stock-in-trade is the knowledge and intellectual skills they have acquired.

Many futurists believe that postindustrial society will be a high-technology society, with computers and advances in electronic engineering opening up vast possibilities for both affluence and leisure. *Automation,* the use of machines to operate the manufacturing process, will free people from many of the laborious and boring jobs and make it possible to produce vast quantities of products inexpensively. Many industries already use robots extensively. In a few cases, factories are run almost entirely by robots, with only a few technicians to ensure that nothing goes awry.

A postindustrial society will also involve a greater extension of secondary groups into people's lives (see Chapter 4). This extension has already occurred through the removal of many activities such as education from the family context. With the recent emergence of day-care centers, even the socialization of the very young sometimes occurs in a secondary context.

Despite the optimistic tone of some futurists, dark clouds are on the horizon. Some people argue that changes in the workforce will actually increase unemployment and poverty. With automation, for example, there may be fewer jobs for people to do. In addition, many people in the rapidly expanding service and white-collar sectors receive low pay, such as maids, bank tellers, waitresses, and clerks. Thus there may be intense competition for the better jobs, and those who get them will live comfortably while others will continue to live a considerably less affluent life.

Others argue that an increasingly sophisticated technology poses many serious problems. First of all, the United States continues to require a vast supply of energy and raw materials, and at least one research group predicted that the supply would begin to fail in the not-too-distant future, with the possible collapse of industrial society within a century (see Chapter 14). Ironically, a computer model enabled them to make these predictions. Other people have pointed to nuclear weapons as a serious threat to the continuation of the U.S. way of life. With the proliferation of such weapons, some forecasters believe it is only a matter of time until a nuclear war is fought, with calamitous results. Another unsettling development made possible by high technology is that computer files, microscopic listening devices, and instantaneous communication make it possible to maintain a degree of surveillance over people's lives that was unheard of a few decades ago. All the credit card transactions people make or the checks they write, for example, can be stored in a computer, ready for instantaneous retrieval to document where the people were, what they bought, and how much they spent during a given period. So, although a postindustrial society will have many benefits, the social processes analyzed in this book—including conflict, exploitation, and oppression—will by no means be eliminated.

The Globalization of Labor

Just as the circumstances of the Third-World nations can be fully understood only in a global context, the future of the United States is also affected by worldwide trends. Chapter 13 pointed out that the global concentration of power has been enhanced by global trade agreements that encourage free trade among nations and discourage hindrances to trade, such as tariffs or restrictive labor policies. The most recent such trade agreements are the North American Free Trade Agreement (NAFTA) of 1994 and the World Trade Organization (WTO) of 1995. These treaties promote a global free-for-all in trade that benefits large, established corporations because they have the resources with which to compete in this environment. The treaties point to an important world trend: the globalization of labor as labor markets become world phenomena rather than simply national. Such globalization has occurred for centuries, as this book has illustrated at many points (for example, the Europeans' use of indigenous people's labor in the Americas). But today it is much more extensive. More than in the past, corporations roam the globe looking for cheap sources of labor. As a result, every worker is potentially competing with the cheapest workers in the world. Nations often use tariffs against imported goods as a way to protect their own industries and workers. Workers in the United States have definitely benefited from this protectionist policy in the past and are among the best paid in the world. In the case of NAFTA, many fear that elimination of tariffs will mean job migration to Mexico where wages are lower, and that this competition will lower the wages of U.S. workers. Only time will tell if these predictions are correct.

One of the challenges confronting the discipline of sociology is to understand societies and social change in sufficient detail that sociologists can make predictions about the future with some accuracy. There are, of course, always uncertainties because unknown events that have not yet happened will influence future outcomes. This discussion of modernization, a postindustrial United States, and the changes in Russia reflects the current state of knowledge: Some things we can understand and predict fairly well, but for others we have to wait and see how events play out. Either way, sociologists make available what they know to planners and policy makers who make decisions about the political, economic, and social future of the United States and other nations around the globe.

Summary

1. Collective behavior is less enduring than institutionalized behavior and plays an important part in social change. Actually, there is a continuum of behavior that ranges from the highly structured at one end to the very unstructured at the other.

2. Smelser argues that collective behavior arises when the following six preconditions for collective behavior exist: structural conduciveness, structural strain, a generalized belief, precipitating factors, mobilization, and the failure of social control.

3. Rumors are unauthenticated messages. They are forms of collective behavior themselves, in addition to serving as a form of communication in other types of collective behavior. Rumors are collective transactions in which a group attempts to develop a shared definition of some situation. Rumors can be distorted through leveling, sharpening, and assimilation.

4. Mass behavior is collective behavior in which the actions of people are not coordinated, people have little or no contact with one another, and yet there is still some uniformity of behavior. The major types are panic, mass hysteria, fad, and fashion.

5. A crowd is a temporary grouping of people who are in fairly close physical proximity to one another and whose attentions are focused on some common object or event. Crowds are characterized by uncertainty, suggestibility of crowd members, anonymity, permissiveness, and emotional arousal. There are casual, conventional, acting, and expressive crowds.

6. Four major processes shape behavior in crowds: contagion, convergence, emergent norms, and collective decision making.

7. A social movement is a conscious, collective, organized attempt to bring about or resist social change through noninstitutionalized means. Social movements emerge as ways for people to cope with some deprivation or frustration. Relative deprivation and the phenomenon of rising expectations play an important role here. If social movements are to emerge, there must also be a mobilization of the necessary resources.

8. There are four major theories of social change. Evolutionary theories are based on the assumption that change is natural and societies evolve through a set of predictable, cumulative changes. Functional theories argue that social change is necessary as societies adapt to strains, inconsistencies, or a lack of integration in the social structure. Conflict theories posit that change results when oppressed groups rearrange the patterns of dominance and subordination in society. Cyclical theories are based on the assumption that change occurs in repetitive cycles over long periods of time.

9. Modernization is a worldwide trend in social change today, but there is debate as to whether the fate of the developing nations will be convergence or divergence. Some argue that developing nations will not achieve the same level of industrialization as the currently industrialized nations. The United States may be moving toward a postindustrial society, which could have both positive and negative consequences.

STUDY and Review

Key Terms

acting crowd	mass behavior
casual crowd	mass hysteria
collective behavior	modernization
conventional crowd	panic
crowd	postindustrial society
expressive crowd	rumors
fad	social change
fashion	social movement

Multiple-Choice Questions

1. Which of the following would involve the most highly institutionalized behavior?
   a. Mass panic.
   b. Looting in a riot.
   c. A baseball game.
   d. A political protest demonstration.
   e. The ceremony inaugurating a monarch.

2. Someone standing on a car exhorting a crowd to attack the police most clearly exemplifies which precondition of collective behavior?
   a. Structural conduciveness.
   b. Structural strain.
   c. Mobilization.
   d. Generalized belief.

3. In studies of urban riots in the United States over the last three decades, which of the following conclusions were drawn?
   a. Absolute deprivation rather than relative deprivation is the cause of collective violence.
   b. Participants in the riots were mostly criminals and unemployed people.
   c. Relative deprivation rather than absolute deprivation is the cause of collective violence.
   d. The cities that experienced riots were the ones in which African Americans had been most successful at gaining political office.

4. Which of the following are types of mass behavior?
   a. Panic.
   b. Fads.
   c. Rioting crowd.
   d. All of the above.
   e. a and b.

5. A (an) _____ crowd is one in which attention and activity are directed toward some goal or objective.
   a. acting
   b. conventional
   c. casual
   d. expressive
   e. mass

6. When social movements go through the process of institutionalization, they
   a. cease to exist as a part of society.
   b. become a formal and accepted part of society.
   c. become a part of the process of collective behavior.
   d. become more susceptible to rumors.

7. The J-curve theory of revolutions explains the emergence of social movements as being related to
   a. absolute deprivation.
   b. an evolutionary theory of change.
   c. mass behavior.
   d. the phenomenon of rising expectations.

8. Which of the following statements would be most consistent with the multilinear theory of evolutionary change?
   a. There is a tendency for societies to evolve toward greater complexity and adaptability.
   b. In the long run, subordinate groups in society will push for changes in the distribution of resources, producing change.
   c. Change occurs because social systems are never fully or completely integrated.
   d. There are cycles of change in societies, but they do not lead anywhere over the long term.

9. Which of the following is a criticism of cyclical theories of social change?
   a. It is difficult to prove that a particular theme dominates a given era.
   b. They tend to deemphasize change, especially rapid and substantial change.
   c. It has not been proven that societies tend to progress.
   d. They tend to overemphasize the extent of change.

10. Which of the following trends would be *least* indicative of a transition toward a postindustrial society?
    a. Greater devotion of resources to providing services.
    b. A growing emphasis on the manufacture of goods and industrial production.
    c. Greater emphasis on processing information.
    d. Growing white-collar and service occupations.

True/False Questions

1. In most cases, collective behavior is less enduring than is institutionalized behavior.

2. The acquittal of four police officers in the beating of an African American was the precipitating event of the riot in south central Los Angeles in 1992.

3. People who take a more critical set toward rumors will be more likely to pass on untruths or distort rumors.

4. Fads are more continuous than are fashions.

5. A process called *circular reaction* can play an important part in the spread of feelings and behaviors through a crowd.

6. In Britain, women and children make up a sizable proportion of the audience at soccer games, whereas in North America the soccer audiences are mostly men.

7. The American Revolution of 1776 was triggered more by absolute deprivation than by relative deprivation.

8. One of the flaws of unilinear theories of societal evolution is that they are too simple.

9. Most social scientists agree that the modernization of nations in the future will follow the path of divergence rather than convergence.

10. A postindustrial society will see a greater extension of secondary groups into people's lives.

Fill-In Questions

1. _____ is the precondition of collective behavior that refers to the ideas that people have about the source of the strain they are experiencing.

2. Rumors are best referred to as _____.

3. Tamotsu Shibutani has referred to rumors as _____ to emphasize their role as group efforts to develop a shared definition of some situation.

4. Three ways in which rumor distortion can occur are _____, _____, and _____.

5. A _____ is an emotionally charged reaction by a large number of people to some anxiety-producing event.

6. Three of the characteristics that all crowds share are _____, _____, and _____.

7. The three dominant emotions found among members of a crowd are _____, _____, and _____.

8. Two ways in which contagion, or the rapid spread of feelings and behavior through a crowd, can occur are through _____ and _____.

9. Relatively long-term and permanent alterations in the components of culture, social structure, and social behavior are called _____.

10. According to Pitirim Sorokin's cyclical theory of social change, societies are made up of three primary orientations: _____, _____, and _____.

Matching Questions

_____ 1. Lattimer and Ludlow
_____ 2. Neil Smelser
_____ 3. panic
_____ 4. expressive crowd
_____ 5. James C. Davies
_____ 6. Ralf Dahrendorf
_____ 7. Oswald Spengler
_____ 8. *glasnost*
_____ 9. patterns of modernization
_____ 10. definition of the situation

    A. preconditions of collective behavior
    B. cyclical theory of social change
    C. labor clashes
    D. Russian reform
    E. J-curve theory of revolution
    F. convergence and divergence
    G. mass behavior
    H. conflict theory of social change
    I. religious revival meeting
    J. generalized belief

Essay Questions

1. Define and give an example of all of the preconditions for collective behavior.

2. What are the social conditions that helped produce urban riots in the United States, such as the south central Los Angeles riot in 1992?

3. Describe and give an example of the characteristics that all crowds share.

4. Define the different types of crowds and give an example of each.

5. Compare and contrast the contagion, convergence, emergent norms, and collective decision-making approaches to understanding people's behavior in crowds.

6. Using the comparison of soccer in Britain and North America as an example, what are the social conditions that increase the likelihood of violence among fans at sporting events?

7. Describe the J-curve theory of revolutions. Relate it to the American Revolution of 1776.

8. Compare and contrast the four theories of social change presented in the text.

9. What is the process of modernization? What does modernization hold in the future for the less developed nations of the world as well as for the United States?

10. Describe how the processes of collective behavior and modernization have played a part in transforming Russia and the former Soviet Union.

Answers

Multiple-Choice
1. E; 2. C; 3. C; 4. E; 5. A; 6. B; 7. D; 8. A;
9. A; 10. B

True/False
1. T; 2. T; 3. F; 4. F; 5. T; 6. F; 7. F; 8. T;
9. F; 10. T

Fill-In

1. generalized belief
2. unauthenticated messages
3. collective transactions
4. leveling, sharpening, assimilation
5. mass hysteria
6. uncertainty, suggestibility, anonymity, permissiveness, emotional arousal
7. fear, hostility, joy
8. circular reaction, milling
9. social change
10. ideational, idealistic, sensate

Matching

1. C; **2.** A; **3.** G; **4.** I; **5.** E; **6.** H; **7.** B; **8.** D; **9.** F; **10.** J

For Further Reading

Chirot, Daniel. (1994). *How societies change.* Thousand Oaks, CA: Pine Forge Press. This book stresses the evolutionary approach to social change and provides an excellent synopsis of how societies have changed since early human societies.

Curtis, Russell L., & Aguirre, Benigno, E. (Eds.). (1993). *Collective behavior and social movements.* Boston: Allyn & Bacon. This book of readings provides a good exposure to the interesting topics covered in the sociological study of collective behavior and social movements.

Lofland, John. (1996). *Social movement organizations: Guide to research on insurgent realities.* Hawthorne, NY: Aldine de Gruyter. This book provides a comprehensive summary of what sociologists have learned about how the organization of social movements influences how such movements develop and what they accomplish. The book focuses on the causes of social movements, why people join them, what strategies they use, and what their consequences are.

McAdam, Douglas. (1990). *Freedom summer.* New York: Oxford University Press. This is an excellent book about U.S. young people who went to the South in the 1960s to join protest movements against racial discrimination and segregation. The book shows how this experience with collective behavior affected them for the rest of their lives.

Postman, Neil. (1992). *Technopoly: The surrender of culture to technology.* New York: Knopf. This book contains a strong and controversial criticism of what technology is doing to modern society. The author especially focuses on how technology can change cultural values and even demean the importance we place on human beings.

Rifkin, Jeremy. (1991). *Biosphere politics: A new consciousness for a new century.* New York: Crown. The author argues that our uses of science and technology have gotten out of hand and threaten our way of life because they have divorced human life itself from the natural world. He proposes a new and certainly controversial consciousness regarding how human beings should relate to their world.

Stern, Kenneth S. (1991). *A force upon the plain: The American militia movement and the politics of hate.* New York: Simon & Schuster. The author, an expert on hate groups, provides a detailed analysis of the most significant revolutionary groups in the United States today—right-wing hate groups committed to white supremacy and the overthrow of the government. This analysis provides good examples of the structural strain and resource mobilization that underlie social movements.

Teich, Albert H. (Ed.). (1993). *Technology and the future* (6th ed.). New York: St. Martin's Press. The articles that make up this book focus on the role of technology in social change.

Thornton, Russell. (1986). *We shall live again: The 1870 and 1890 ghost dance movements as demographic revitalization.* New York: Cambridge University Press. In this short but interesting book, the author produces data to show which Indian tribes and which individuals were attracted to the Ghost Dance movements (see Chapter 11).

West, Guida, & Blumberg, Rhoda L. (Eds.). (1990). *Women and social protest.* New York: Oxford University Press. This book of readings investigates women's involvement in collective behavior and social movements of various sorts in a number of countries.

APPENDIX
Sociology on the Internet

The last few decades have ushered in some remarkable changes in human societies, although we cannot be sure as yet of the exact sociological ramifications of all the changes. The changes are a product of advanced computer technology and global communications systems, and they involve the ability to exchange massive amounts of information almost instantaneously on a global scale. Sociologists have begun to study the social implications of these technological advances, and some of this research is reported in this text (for example, in Chapters 4 and 12). The purpose of this Appendix is to describe some ways in which sociologists use this global computer network in their work and to point the student to some sources of sociological information on this network.

This global communications system is called the *Internet,* or simply the *Net.* It will become an increasingly important source of communication and information exchange, although at the moment, because it is so new, it can seem a little chaotic and disorganized at times. The Internet can be accessed in a number of ways, but the ways most useful for materials related to sociology are electronic mail (E-mail), the World Wide Web (WWW or the Web), discussion lists, and usenet groups. This Appendix will explain some of the basics on using the Internet and provide some exercises to help you do so. However, keep a couple of things in mind. First, addresses and procedures on the Internet change frequently, so addresses that work as I write this Appendix may have changed by the time you try them. Second, in part because of the first point, be ready to explore and innovate. If an address or procedure described in this Appendix doesn't work, use some of the other tools described to search out the desired information or site. Use what is described in this Appendix as a platform from which to find other sources of information related to sociology and other ways to use the Internet. A final point is that I will assume that you know how to operate in a Windows environment and how to access the Internet through your university computer or a commercial computer service. For good introductions to using the Internet, see McLaren (1996) and Poindexter (1996).

The Basics

One of the most widespread uses of the Net is for E-mail, which involves typing a message on a screen and sending it electronically. Many universities provide their students with an E-mail address, or you can get an E-mail address by subscribing to a commercial service such as America Online or Compuserve. You will have to contact the computer center on your campus or one of the commercial services to learn exactly how to get your Internet address and how to send E-mail.

WWW is a program that allows access to the Internet for a variety of uses. For example, the Web can be used to access the home pages or other locations that are made available by individuals and organizations. Many of these locations are called *http* sites, which stands for *Hypertext Transfer Protocol*. Hypertext involves the linking of many documents together, so that clicking on a word or symbol (called a *button*) in one document will transfer you to other documents on a similar topic. Buttons are usually set apart on the screen in a different color from the rest of the text. If you move the arrow/cursor on the screen to a button and the arrow/cursor becomes a little fist pointing a finger, this means that this button is a link to other sites; clicking on it will move you to those other sites.

A few basic commands need to be described. I will use a Web browser called Netscape Navigator because it is widely used and is the one that I have available. At the top of the screen is a menu bar with commands such as File and Edit. Below that is a toolbar with commands such as Back and Forward. Just below the toolbar is the location block where you can type in Internet addresses and hit Enter to go to that site. Below the location block are directory buttons, with commands such as Net Search and Newsgroups. One handy command is the Back button on the toolbar. By clicking on that button, you go back to the previous site that you had visited. This is useful while surfing the net because sometimes you go down a path that proves unproductive or uninteresting; you can backtrack to the point where you had diverged down that path by hitting the Back button the requisite number of times.

Browsing through the Web is often done with what are called *search engines*. Search engines allow you to enter key words in a search box, and then the computer program searches for all materials in its database that contain those key words. Browsing is also done through *subject guides,* which are like the table of contents to a book: You are presented with a list of topics that can be clicked on to produce a list of topics or actual web sites on those topics. Some search vehicles use both search engines and subject guides. The addresses of some of the more common search vehicles are as follows:

http://altavista.digital.com

http://www.yahoo.com

http://www.lycos.com

The search vehicle is activated by typing its address in the location block. In some computer facilities, you can also activate a search vehicle by clicking the Net Search button on the Directory line. In addition, some universities and commercial outfits will let you select among search vehicles at their home page. It is often a good idea to use more than one search vehicle in a search, since each of them uses different criteria and procedures and each will come up with somewhat different materials.

Chapter 1: General Issues

Discussion lists are groups that you can join in which you receive all messages that are sent to the group. In addition, any message you send to the group is distributed to all group members. Discussion lists are usually focused on a particular topic, such as investment advice, model airplanes, or Jungian psychology. A discussion list relevant to sociology is the TEACHSOC list, whose members focus on issues related to the teaching of sociology in colleges and universities. Many members are college and university professors of sociology, but graduate and undergraduate students in sociology also belong and contribute. To join the list, you would send an E-mail message to LISTSERV@MAPLE.LEMOYNE.EDU and put in the message "SUBSCRIBE TEACHSOC Your Name".

A general Internet address that has links to many resources related to sociology is

http://socsci.colorado.edu/SOC/links.html

Be aware that some Internet addresses are *case sensitive,* meaning that it matters if a letter is typed in lower- or uppercase (capital) letters. So, always use the case indicated in the address in order to be careful. This Internet location is a page maintained by the Department of Sociology at the University of Colorado. At that address, you will find a list of subjects available, such as Resources for Sociology Graduate Students, Sociology Departments on the WWW, Professional Organizations in Sociology, General Sociology Resources, and a host of particular topic listings (Criminology Resources, Demography Resources, Family Resources, and so on). Click on Sociology Departments on the WWW and see if your university department is listed there. Explore some of the other topics.

Two other good addresses for beginning to learn more about sociology are as follows:

http://diogenes.baylor.edu/WWWproviders/

Larry_Ridener/DSS/DEADSOC.HTML

http://diogenes.baylor.edu/WWWproviders/

Larry_Ridener/DSS/INDEX.HTML

The first address takes you to a page called The Dead Sociologists Society, which has all kinds of links to other lists relating to sociology. The second is The Dead Sociologists Index, and it lists twelve sociologists who are now deceased but were very important in the development of sociology. Some of them you have learned about in this text (such as Marx, Durkheim, and Weber). Under each sociologist are listed two topics (The Person and The Work) and a number of subtopics. Click on the subtopics to learn more about the person or his work. For example, click on Marx and then Class Theory to learn more about Marx's basic conflict theory and theory of social class. Under the second address, you can also locate a course syllabus for a course in sociological theory by clicking on the phrase Social Theory Syllabus.

This will give you an idea of what the content of some upper-division sociology courses are like.

Dial into the search vehicle called Yahoo (see address listed earlier) and begin by selecting Social Science and then Sociology. At this point, you still have many choices. Start by selecting Organizations and then you will have choices of going to the home pages of many sociological organizations in the United States (both regional and national), Canada, New Zealand, and other countries. Start by choosing American Sociological Association. The American Sociological Association (ASA) is the main national organization for the discipline of sociology. At this location, you can learn more about sociology and about the services provided to sociologists by their national organization. You can find out about the ASA's publications and how to order them (at this time, a summary of the ASA's Report on Violence is displayed); you can also learn about the ASA's Code of Ethics, browse the employment bulletin to see the kinds of occupations that sociologists seek, and learn about the annual meeting that the ASA holds each year. If you go back to the Organizations page and select Courses, you can learn about various college courses in sociology. Currently, if you select San Diego State University-SO 101, you will get to the home page of a sociologist at that university and can peruse his syllabus and other materials for his introductory sociology class. What are the differences between his course and the course that you are taking? Search for some other courses and syllabi and make similar comparisons.

One way to find many locations relating to sociology is by activating the Altavista search engine (see address listed earlier). Type sociology in the box and click Submit. It will locate hundreds of home pages related to sociology, usually displaying them in groups of ten or twenty, starting with those most closely relevant to the key word you have typed. Once you have looked at the first group, you can move to another group by finding the group of numbers starting with "1" and clicking on an additional number. A new list of sites will be displayed. By exploring these sites, you can find home pages on college programs in sociology (both graduate and undergraduate), research institutes, papers addressing sociological topics that someone has posted to the Net, a new publication called the Electronic Journal of Sociology, and many other things.

A final site that is of general interest is this:

http://cti.itc.virginia.edu/~jkh8x/soc257/adrian.html

This site contains a document called Informal Guide to Research on the World Wide Web, which a sociologist prepared for students to use. You will find some helpful suggestions on browsing the Web.

Chapter 2

One of the wondrous things about the Internet is that it offers an opportunity to explore the cultures of the world with a few keystrokes. Chapter 2 discusses the cultural diversity in the world, and this exercise moves you toward exploring this diversity on the Internet. There are almost an infinite number of routes that can be taken; I will describe one route to illustrate how this can be done. Dial into the Altavista search engine. In the search box, type "culture and asia." (Of course, you would not include the quotation marks.) The operator *and* in the entry tells Altavista to include sites on the Internet that include *both* keywords. This provided me with many thousands of entries, one of which was RPL: Asia Pacific Culture. This led to, among other things, the Culture Page of the Chinese Internet Directory. After clicking on that, I selected the English language (if you speak a Chinese dialect, you can pick one of those), and then, in order, I selected English Index, Culture, Customs, and Traditional Customs. At this last stop, you can explore Chinese customs that surround particular areas of life such as weddings or clothing. Locate information that relates to Chinese cultural values, norms, roles, and social institutions, as discussed in Chapter 2. How does what you find here point to differences from mainstream U.S. culture?

If you choose a search vehicle other than Altavista, you will get somewhat different results, but you can still make the same kind of exploration, searching for different cultural ways and trying to describe and understand them. Each student in your class should try going down a different cultural path. Also, where my search ended (at Traditional Customs) could be the beginning of a more detailed search: Use the Back button to return to any of the preceding levels and make some different choices to go down an alternate path.

Chapter 3

You can go to the Dead Sociologist's Index described earlier and explore the discussion of Cooley and Mead. Their theories of socialization and social interaction are more detailed than there was space to discuss in Chapter 3. Report to the class on what you have learned that supplements the material presented in this chapter.

Many areas of socialization are not discussed in this chapter. You can use the Internet to explore these areas. Using the Altavista search vehicle, type "socialization" into the search field. This will produce thousands of sites, many of them irrelevant to our topic (such as Puppy Socialization). However, you will also find many relevant topics, such as sites on the political socialization of children and on home schooling. Neither of these topics is discussed in the text, but each is a part of the overall process of socialization. Report to the class on what additional subareas of socialization you found. You could do the same thing with the Yahoo search vehicle by clicking on Society at the main Yahoo menu and then searching for "socialization."

Another topic to search for is socialization practices in other cultures. Either in Altavista or in Yahoo (under Society), search for "children and Samoa" or "children and Asia" or any other nation or region. Report to the class on what you learn about socialization and the place and treatment of children in these cultures.

Chapter 4

Begin by going to the Dead Sociologists Index described earlier. Review what Max Weber had to say about bureaucracy. What do you learn here that was not covered in the text discussion of bureaucracy?

The textbook discusses a number of different types of formal organizations, such as coercive and commonweal (see Table 4.1). You can use a search vehicle on the Internet to find examples of these types of organizations and learn about their structure and membership. In the search box, type two key words, such as "organization" and "commonweal." You can begin to describe these organizations in terms of what goals they pursue, how they get their members, and how large and bureaucratic they are.

Chapter 5

This exercise will send you to a home page that contains the results of a nationwide survey that is conducted in the United States each year. Called the General Social Survey, it is conducted by the National Opinion Research Center at the University of Chicago. Begun in 1972, the survey is based on a large sample of adults and is considered to be one of the most scientifically sound sources of data about social issues available. You can get access to the results of these surveys by going to

http://www.icpsr.umich.edu

Once there, click on Contents, then General Social Survey Site, and then GSS Search Engine. Now you are ready to look for questions that were asked in the survey that are relevant to a topic of interest to you. One approach is to enter your own key words on a topic. Another approach is to click on the Subject Index button, and it will list all the topics covered in the surveys. To see how it works, scroll down the list and click on the subject Capital Punishment. This displays a list of abbreviated names, each identifying a question that was asked relating to the subject of capital punishment. Click on CAPPUN. This will provide you with people's responses to the question of whether they favor or oppose capital punishment. How much support is there for capital punishment in the United States? How has that support changed over the past two decades? Go back to the Subject Index and scroll through it for other topics related to crime, punishment, or the criminal justice system. Explore these areas and provide a summary of what can be learned about these topics from the data available in the General Social Survey.

Chapter 6

The U.S. Census Bureau provides enormous amounts of information about stratification and economic inequality in the United States. Start by going the Bureau's home page:

http://www.census.gov

You will find a button that says Current Economic Indicators. Click on it, and then in succession click on About People: Income and Income Inequality. Then you will have a series of tables to select from, or Middle Class Highlights. Exploring these sites will provide you with much detailed data on income distribution and inequality in the United States, in some cases going back fifty years. How much income inequality is there? Are the disparities getting wider? How does this information supplement (and support or contradict) the figures presented in the text? Explore around this overall Census Bureau site. Can you find information on poverty, unemployment, or homelessness that will provide additional insight into the U.S. stratification system?

Explore the issues of stratification and inequality in other cultures. Select one of the search vehicles and enter some key words that include a particular nation or region that you are interested in, such as "stratification and Russia," "class and Africa," or "inequality and Brazil." Report what you find to the class.

Chapter 7

The Internet is an excellent place to search for materials on minority groups and to explore some of the sociological dimensions of minority group status. A good way to begin is by dialing into the Yahoo search engine. Click on Society and Culture and then Minorities. Now you are ready to have Yahoo search for materials on various minority groups. There is a box where you can type various key words for Yahoo to search on. You should try to locate materials on minority groups that are not covered in the book or are only briefly covered. Remember that minority status need not be based only on race or ethnicity. Be creative. As an example, type in "vietnamese" and click Search. You will get numerous options, one of which is Business and Economy: Organizations: Cultural: Vietnamese: Vietnamese Students Association. Clicking on this option results in a list of universities. Click on Michigan State University, and you can learn about the Michigan State University Vietnamese Student Association. Through exploring this and other sites, what have you learned about primary group relationships, formal organizations, and subcultures among the minority groups you have explored?

Chapter 8

A good way to learn about policies and practices related to sexual harassment is to conduct an Internet search for sites related to this topic. To do this, you should activate a search vehicle (see earlier explanation) and type "sexual harassment" in the search box. Click the Search button, and a large array of sites will be displayed in groups of ten, with those fitting your search dimensions most closely displayed first. You can then click on the sites you wish to visit. Some of the most relevant sites I found from the search vehicle I used were SASH (Sociologists Against Sexual Harassment, a professional organization of sociologists whose research and social policy development focus on issues of sexual harassment) and the sexual harassment policies of a variety of universities and private companies. See if your university policy is displayed. What issues do these policies commonly address? Do other universities address issues that do not appear in your university's sexual harassment policy? From all the sites you visit in this search, describe the social network of groups and organizations that have emerged to deal with the issue of sexual harassment. Are they all working for common goals, or do some of the groups come into competition and conflict with one another?

Chapter 9

The following address provides information relating to fathers in modern society:

http://www.xs4all.nl/~sheldon/fathlink.html

It provides links to information on fathering, divorce, health, and child abuse. It also shows how to subscribe to two discussion lists related to being a father: FATHER-L (focusing on the role and importance of fathers in their children's lives) and SINGLE-FATHER (focusing on issues relating to fathers raising their children alone). Explore this location and its various linked sites and describe what it says about the structure and role of the family in modern societies. From what you see here, is the family healthy or disintegrating?

Using the Yahoo search vehicle, click on Society and Culture and then Lesbians, Gays, and Bisexuals. You will then have many options to choose among, such as African Americans, Asians, Organizations, Relationships, Military, and Sports. If you click on Organizations, you will have choices like Politics and Civil Rights and Youth. Explore these various areas and identify all the social mechanisms (groups and organizations) that gays use to support their lifestyle and to adapt to their position in society.

Chapter 10

There are innumerable sources of information about health issues worldwide available on the Internet. Begin by going to the University of Colorado site we used previously:

http://socsci.colorado.edu/SOC/links.html

From this page, select Subjects: Demography, then WWW Virtual Library: Demographic and Population Studies, and then World Health Organization. This gets you to the home page of the World Health Organization (WHO), a global organization that conducts research on and runs programs promoting world health. You could have gotten to this site directly through this address:

http://www.who.ch

However, I sent you through the University of Colorado link because you can use that link to explore many other sociological topics related to health and other issues. (This also illustrates the point that you can get to most Internet sites through a variety of paths because of the complex web of interlinkages that make up the Net.) From the WHO home page, select World Health Report, then World Health Report 1996, and then 50 Facts of Health. At this point, there are numerous topics to choose from: Birth, Life expectancy, Death, Child health, and so on. Explore these various topics with an eye on identifying information about the rates of disease and death in various nations and regions and the impact of social and cultural factors on health and illness.

Chapter 11

Religion is so pervasive and so important to people that it is almost too easy to find sites related to religion on the Internet. One approach is to use the Yahoo search vehicle and click on Society and Culture and then Religion. This opens up a large menu of choices that can be explored. Virtually any topic discussed in Chapter 11 can be found here. Another approach is to use a search vehicle to find material on specific religions. If you search for "Unification Church," for example, you will find a host of sites devoted not only to that particular religious group but also to many sects, cults, and other non-mainstream religions. You can address issues of whether the groups are large or small, growing or declining; you can also try to determine who is attracted to the various groups. From the information you gather, does each group appear to be closer to a church or a sect? Another approach is to search for particular religions: Enter "Buddhism," "Taoism," or the names of other religions into a search and see what you come up with. Can you describe the organizational structures of these religions? In what parts of the United States or the world are they most popular? Another interesting direction is to search for "electronic church." This can help you assess further the role of the mass media in modern religions. From what you learn about

electronic churches, can you say anything about the social organization of religions in modern societies?

Chapter 12

The U.S. Department of Education makes available numerous publications on the Internet and can be a good source of information about educational data, trends, and policies. Dial in to their home page with this address:

http://www.ed.gov/pubs

Once there, click on Education Statistics, which will lead you to the publications page of the National Center for Education Statistics. At this point, you are free to explore. As a start, click Student Outcomes, and you will get a list of publications reporting research on how quickly college students advance through their education and how well they do in school. Click on one publication: Descriptive Summary of 1989–90 Beginning Postsecondary Students: 5 Years Later. This is a report of research on how rapidly students from different kinds of colleges and universities progress through their education and when their education ends. Summarize the results. How does this report relate to some of the educational issues discussed in Chapter 12? Explore this site by moving backward and then clicking down other paths. What other material can you uncover that relates to issues of this chapter?

Chapter 13

A number of chapters in this book have suggested that the Internet might serve as a vehicle of empowerment by enabling dispersed populations to communicate and organize electronically. Along these lines, the Internet makes possible more direct, immediate, and interactive contact between citizens and government. Both houses of the U.S. Congress have web sites at these addresses:

http://www.senate.gov

http://www.house.gov

Dialing into the Senate web site will give you such options as Senators with E-Mail Addresses; Directory of Senators by Name; Senate Leadership; Senate Legislative Action; and Full Listing of Committee Assignments. By clicking on the appropriate button, you can find out a senator's E-mail address and committee assignments. Senate Legislative Action will give you a Daily Digest option with a record of Senate and House activities for the previous day. Browse through the activities of the previous day and find a topic that relates to issues discussed in this text. E-mail your senators with your thoughts on the topic. Do the same thing with your representative. The House web site has an interesting option called Empowering the Citizen. Explore it. Report to your class any reactions that you get from your senators or representative. Together with other students in the class, explore both of these web sites with an eye on how they can be used as tools of citizen influence and empowerment.

Chapter 13 discussed issues of whether legitimacy is accorded to political and economic institutions. This topic can be explored with the General Social Survey, discussed in relation to Chapter 5 earlier in this Appendix. Follow the same steps described there until you have the list of subjects displayed, and then click on the subject Confidence. Then click on CONFED, and you will be given the results of the question that asked people how much confidence they had in the executive branch of the federal government. Clicking on CONLEGIS and CONBUS will display the results of questions about people's confidence in the legislative branch of government and the business community, respectively. The results for many different years are displayed separately so you can look at changes over time. With these results, you can answer the following questions: How confident are people in the executive branch? In whom do people have the least confidence: the executive branch, the legislative branch, or the business community? Has confidence in these three institutions been increasing or decreasing over time? Search for other topics of interest to your class either by using the key word search or by clicking on the appropriate subject heading.

Chapter 14

It is now possible to retrieve data from the Census over the Internet. To do so, go to the University of Colorado site described in this Appendix in the section on Chapter 1. Select Subjects: Demography. One of the options that is then available is 1990 Census Data Lookup. This will give you many options for tapping into Census data and publications. Explore this site by selecting STF3A, and then selecting Go To Level State—Place. This will enable you to select which state you want data on. Highlight your state in the window and select Submit. A similar screen will give you an option to Retrieve area you've selected; this is where you can choose your own town and select Submit. In the next window, choose Tables and then Submit. This brings you to the final window where you select the actual variables about which you want to see statistics. You can choose, for example, to see Race by gender by Hispanic origin, and this will break down the population figures on your particular area by these three variables. Scroll through and select other variables for analysis. However, be forewarned: You are dealing with so much data here that your search is likely to be a little slow at times. Present the results of what you found about your local community to the class.

Chapter 15

The Internet can be a useful tool for discovering the social movement organizations that have arisen to deal with various issues and problems in the world. The reason for this is that these organizations often make themselves prominently visible on the Internet as a mechanism for attracting new members and support. Using a search vehicle, enter key words, such as "feminism" and "organization" or "environment" and "organization." There are many particular problem areas that could be searched. Another approach is to search for "NGO." Nongovernmental organizations are often social movements themselves or are parts of larger social movements. With the material that you find in these searches, describe the

Denominations Organized churches whose members live in harmony with society but have no official relationship with the state; denominations often have a sizable membership.

Dependent variable Variable that is affected or changed over time by some other variable.

Deviance Behaviors or characteristics that violate important group norms and as a consequence meet with social disapproval.

Differential association theory View that deviant behavior is learned in interaction with other people in a process of communication and that this learning occurs for the most part within intimate primary groups such as families and friendship groups.

Discrimination Unequal treatment of people because they are members of a particular group.

Distance education Interactive learning through video.

Dual-career family Family in which both the wife and the husband are committed to occupations that offer them fulfillment and opportunities for advancement.

Ecclesia Sociological term for religion officially sanctioned by the state.

Economics Processes through which goods and services are produced and distributed.

Education Systematic, formal process through which specialized teachers transmit skills, knowledge, and values to students.

Egalitarian family Family in which husband and wife share somewhat equally in power and authority.

Endogamy Rule requiring marriage within a particular group or community.

Estate system of stratification A stratification system in which social position is strongly influenced by heredity, but unlike in the caste system, land ownership or political and military power can also be important.

Ethnic group People who share a common historical and cultural heritage and sense of group identity and belongingness.

Ethnocentrism Tendency to view one's own culture as the best and only proper way to live and to compare other cultures to one's own as the standard.

Exogamy Rule requiring people to choose a mate outside their own social group or community.

Experiment Controlled method of observation in which independent variables are manipulated to ascertain their influence on dependent variables.

Expressive crowd Crowd that focuses on the expression of emotions and the personal gratification of its members.

Expressive roles *See* Socioemotional roles.

Extended family Family of three or more generations of people who live together or in close proximity.

Fad Behavior engaged in by a large number of people for a short time; fads are not part of longer trends.

Family Social institution based on kinship that derives from common ancestry, marriage, or social agreement; it functions to replace and nurture members of society.

Fashions Currently acceptable modes of dress, appearance, or behavior.

Fecundity Biological maximum number of children that could be born in a group or society.

Feminist movement Collective activities of individuals, groups, or organizations whose goal is the fair and equal treatment of women and men around the world.

Fertility Actual number of children born in a group or society.

Folkways Norms such as handshaking that are customary, popular, and widely performed but not required.

Formal organizations Large, special-purpose organizations explicitly established to achieve specific goals.

Functionalist perspective Theoretical view based on the notion that a society is a system made up of a number of interrelated and interdependent elements, each of which performs a function that contributes to the operation of the whole.

Gemeinschaft Type of society in which social life is governed by personal, informal considerations, with tradition and custom prevailing.

Gender Learned behavior involving how we are expected to behave as males and females in society.

Generalized other Organized attitudes, rules, and judgments of an entire group.

Genocide Pattern of intergroup relations in which a dominant group attempts to exterminate a minority group.

Gentrification Return of affluent households to urban neighborhoods where run-down housing is being rehabilitated or new housing constructed.

Gesellschaft Type of society characterized by specialization, individualism, rationality, and impersonality.

Global cities Cities in a postindustrial society that serve as centers of commerce, finance, and political and economic decision making for the global economic system.

Government Operation of the state by a particular group of people who have the authority to make decisions and supervise the allocation of resources.

Group Collection of people who have an awareness that they share something in common and who interact with one another on the basis of interrelated statuses and roles.

Group cohesion Degree to which groups stick together and members feel committed to one another and attracted to the group.

Group polarization Tendency for decisions that evolve from group participation to be more extreme than those made by individuals.

Groupthink Tendency in highly cohesive groups to encourage unanimity of opinion and consensus at the expense of critical abilities and the realistic appraisal of alternatives.

Health maintenance organization Organization that agrees to provide for all of a person's health-care needs for a fixed periodic premium.

Hidden curriculum Training of students in school in the values and norms that help to perpetuate the existing system of stratification.

Human ecology Study of human populations and communities, including their distribution across and impact on the physical environment they inhabit.

Hypothesis Tentative statement that can be tested regarding relationships between two or more variables.

Ideal culture Culture that people claim to accept or wish existed.

Impression management Effort to control the meanings that others attach to our performance or to a situation.

Independent variable Variable that brings about changes in other variables.

In-group Group that one feels positively toward and identifies with, and that produces a "we" feeling.

Institutionalized discrimination Inequitable treatment of a group resulting from practices or policies that are incorporated into social, political, or economic institutions, and that operate independently from the prejudices of individuals.

Institutionalized racism *See* Institutionalized discrimination.

Instrumental roles *See* Task roles.

Interactionist perspective Theoretical view that focuses on everyday social interaction between people rather than on larger societal structures such as politics or education. It emphasizes the importance of the subjective interpretation of reality.

Internal colonialism Situation in which a subordinate group provides cheap labor that benefits the dominant group; the subordinate group is then further exploited by having to purchase expensive goods and services from the dominant group.

Internalization Process of incorporating beliefs, values, and norms into our personal codes of conduct to the point that they seem to come from inside us instead of being dictated from the outside.

Invasion Urban process in which new people or activities move into an already established area of a city.

Kin People who are related to one another through common ancestry, marriage, or social agreement.

Labeling theory Theory of deviance suggesting that whether others label or define a person as deviant is a critical determinant in the development of a pattern of deviant behavior.

Laws Rules that have been formally codified and enacted by a political authority. Laws often reflect mores.

Leadership Exercise of influence over a group such that the group's behavior is directed toward particular outcomes or goals.

Legitimacy Capacity of a social system or institution to engender and maintain the belief that the existing institutions are the most appropriate ones for a society.

Life cycle Succession of statuses and roles that people in a particular society experience in a fairly predictable pattern as they grow older.

Life span *See* Life cycle.

Looking-glass self Process through which we develop a self-concept based on the reactions of other people to ourselves and our behavior.

Managed care Networks of hospitals and doctors, organized like health maintenance organizations, that provide for all the health-care needs for large groups of people and that charge a flat fee or limit the fees they will charge.

Mass behavior Collective behavior in which the actions of people are not coordinated and people have little or no contact with one another, and yet there is still some uniformity of behavior and general awareness of the others in the group.

Mass hysteria Emotionally charged reaction to an anxiety-producing event by a large number of people.

Mass media Channels of communication in modern societies that can reach large numbers of people, sometimes instantaneously.

Master status Status central to people's views of themselves and to how others respond to them.

Material culture All of the physical objects, or artifacts, made or used by a people.

Matriarchal family Family in which women are dominant in power and authority.

Matrilineal descent system System in which descent is determined through the female line, and children belong to the kin group of their mother.

Matrilocal family Family system in which a couple lives with or near the wife's family.

Medicaid Joint federal–state program to provide medical care for low-income people of any age.

Medical-industrial complex Coincidence of interests between physicians and other health-care providers and the industries producing health-care goods and services, with both parties profiting from the increased use of these commodities.

Medicare Government health insurance for those over sixty-five years of age.

Migration Permanent change of residence.

Military-industrial complex Relationship between the military, which needs to purchase weapons, and the corporations that produce the weapons.

Minority group Group whose members share distinct physical and cultural characteristics; who are denied access to power and resources available to other groups; and who are accorded fewer rights, privileges, and opportunities.

Mixed economy Economy in which there are strong elements of both capitalism and socialism.

Modernization Economic, social, and cultural changes that occur when a preindustrial society makes the transition to an advanced industrial society.

Modified extended family Family that retains elaborate networks of visitation and support even though each nuclear unit lives separately.

Monogamy Marriage between one man and one woman at a time.

Monotheistic religions Religions based on a belief in one supreme God who is ultimately responsible for the universe.

Mores Norms that are mandatory and that invoke strong feelings of right and wrong; their violation usually results in punishment.

Mortality Number of deaths that occur in a particular population.

Multiple-nuclei theory Theory that cities develop a number of different areas, or nuclei, that are devoted to particular uses.

National health insurance Government health insurance covering all citizens.

Neolocal family Family system in which a couple resides separately from the families of either wife or husband.

Nonmaterial culture All of the parts of culture that have no physical existence, such as language, ideas, knowledge, and behaviors.

Norms Expectations or rules of conduct that guide people's behavior.

Nuclear family Family that consists of a married couple and their offspring.

Observational techniques Direct observation of behavior by sociologists, by either seeing or hearing what people do.

Oligarchy Concentration of power in the hands of a few people at the top of an organization.

Open stratification systems Stratification systems having ranks with less well-defined boundaries that may be crossed more readily.

Out-group Group to which one does not belong and toward which one feels neutral or hostile. We view out-groups as "they" who are different from and less desirable than ourselves.

Panic Uncoordinated mass attempt to avoid some immediate perceived threat.

Participant observation Research design in which researchers involve themselves in the daily round of activities of the group being studied and observe group members in their natural environment.

Parties Social strata resulting from differences in power.

Patriarchal family Family in which the males are dominant in making political and economic decisions and women and children are subordinate.

Patrilineal descent system System in which descent is determined by the male line and children belong to the kin group of their father.

Patrilocal family Family system in which the married couple lives with or near the husband's family.

Personality Constellation of attitudes, needs, traits, feelings, and behavior patterns that are relatively stable throughout life.

Pluralism Existence of a number of racial and ethnic groups living side by side, each retaining a distinct identity and lifestyle while still participating in some aspects of the larger culture.

Pluralistic family system Family system in which a number of different types of family exist side by side, each having an attraction for some people.

Pluralist model View that power in U.S. society is spread over a number of groups rather than concentrated in a single group.

Politics Use of power to determine whose values will predominate, how rewards and resources will be allocated, and how conflicting interests will be resolved.

Polyandry Form of polygamy in which a woman can marry more than one man at a time.

Polygamy Form of marriage in which people can have more than one spouse at a time.

Polygyny Form of polygamy in which a man can marry more than one woman at a time.

Polytheistic religions Religions that posit a belief in the existence of a number of gods.

Popular culture Products and activities designed for mass consumption and used for leisure or entertainment.

Population Total number of people inhabiting a particular geographic area at a specified time.

Population transfer Pattern of intergroup relations in which the dominant group moves a minority, either voluntarily or involuntarily, to a particular geographic area.

Postindustrial society Societies that are dominated by a highly technological form of production and devote more attention to service industries, information production, and economic consumption than they do to industrial production.

Power Ability of one group to realize its will even in the face of resistance from other groups.

Power elite model View of power distribution in the United States that characterizes society as having an extremely unequal power structure with a small group of people making all important decisions.

Prejudice Irrational attitude toward certain people based solely on their membership in a particular group.

Prestige Social esteem or honor that is accorded to particular people by others; for Weber, a key dimension of the stratification system.

Preventive medicine Making changes in lifestyle or taking other steps that help avoid the occurrence of disease.

Primary deviance Violation of social norms in which the violator is not caught or is excused rather than labeled as a deviant.

Primary group Small group in which relations between members are personal, intimate, and nonspecialized.

Primary socialization Process that transforms infants into truly social human beings by teaching them basic values, skills, and language.

Profane World of ordinary and routine things that can be easily comprehended, as distinct from sacred.

Protestant ethic Belief that an ascetic life of strict discipline and hard work that results in economic success is a sign of one's worth or that one is among the elect who will go to heaven.

Race Group of people who are believed to be a biological group sharing genetically transmitted traits that are defined as important.

Racism View that certain ethnic or racial groups are biologically inferior to other groups and the practices of domination and exploitation that result from such a view.

Real culture Actual behavior of people in relation to the beliefs, values, and norms of their culture.

Reconstituted family Family based on kinship ties that accumulate as a consequence of divorces and remarriages.

Reference group Group that people use as a standard in evaluating or understanding themselves, their attitudes, and their behavior.

Refined divorce rate Measure of the divorce rate that involves dividing the number of divorces each year by the total number of existing marriages in the year.

Relationship-oriented roles *See* Socioemotional roles.

Religion Collectively held set of symbols, rituals, and beliefs that expresses a basic understanding of the world, especially its sacred dimension, and addresses the ultimate concerns of the meaning of human existence.

Religions of the way Religions based not on the existence of deities but on immutable truths in the minds of believers that reveal the proper way to achieve fulfillment.

Religiosity Importance or degree of commitment accorded religion by a person.

Research methods Detailed plan that specifies how observations will be made in order to test hypotheses.

Resocialization Learning of new sets of values, beliefs, and behaviors that are different from those previously held.

Role conflict Situation in which two or more roles a person must play are incompatible or inconsistent.

Roles Behaviors expected of people who occupy particular statuses.

Role set All the roles that are associated with a particular social status.

Role strain Situation in which people have difficulty performing a role.

Role-taking Rehearsing in imagination how others perceive things and how they are likely to behave.

Rumors Unauthenticated messages that may be true or false.

Sacred Ideas or objects viewed as awesome, mysterious, extraordinary, or absolute that transcend everyday experience.

Sanctions Rewards or punishments people receive for conforming to or violating norms.

Science Method of obtaining objective and systematic knowledge of the world through observation.

Secondary deviance Deviant behavior that a person adopts in response to the reaction of others to that person's primary deviance.

Secondary group Group characterized by limited face-to-face contact, task-oriented and impersonal relationships, and specialized and limited ties.

Sector theory View that cities grow in sectors, slices of land use that extend outward from the center of the city toward the periphery much like slices of a pie.

Sects Religious bodies that are less formally organized than churches, whose members reject some elements of the larger society, and that exist in some degree of tension with society.

Secularization Process through which the influence of religion is removed from many institutions in society and dispersed into private and personal realms.

Segregation Urban process in which certain activities or people are isolated in particular areas of cities; also, a pattern of intergroup relations in which the social lives of dominant and minority groups are kept separate.

Self-concept Conception that we have of who we are—our unique characteristics and attributes—as well as about our nature and worth as human beings.

Serial monogamy Marriage practice in which people are allowed to have more than one spouse, but not at the same time.

Sex Biological role that each of us plays, such as in reproduction or nursing.

Sexism Belief that one sex is superior to and should dominate the other sex.

Sick role Set of expectations intended to guide the behavior of people who are ill.

Significant others Specific people, such as a parent or sibling, whose opinions children care about.

Significant symbol Symbol based on shared meanings that people understand and recognize in the same way.

Social change Relatively long-term and permanent alterations in the components of culture, social structure, and social behavior.

Social class Social stratum based on wealth or economic position; people in the same social class share similar life chances or opportunities.

Social control Social mechanisms used to encourage people to conform to the norms of society.

Social epidemiology Branch of sociology that deals with how social factors influence the distribution of disease within a population.

Social institution Relatively stable cluster of statuses, roles, and groups that work together to fulfill some needs that all societies must satisfy.

Socialism Economic system in which the means of production and distribution are collectively held so that the goods and services that people need are produced and equitably distributed.

Socialization Process by which people develop their personal identities and learn the ways of a particular group or society.

Social mobility Movement of people from one social position to another in the stratification hierarchy.

Social movement Conscious, collective, organized attempt to bring about or resist large-scale social change through noninstitutionalized means.

Social reproduction Passing on social and economic inequalities from one generation to the next and thus perpetuating the existing stratification system.

Social stratification Ranking of people into a hierarchy in which the resources considered valuable by society are unequally distributed.

Social structure Organized patterns of social interaction and social relationships that exist in a group or society.

Society Group of people who are relatively self-sufficient and who share a common territory and culture.

Sociobiology Field based on the idea that the genetic makeup of humans and other animals plays a powerful role in shaping their social behavior.

Socioeconomic status (SES) A person's social location on the basis of three dimensions of stratification: wealth, power, and prestige.

Socioemotional roles Roles in which leaders work to produce harmony, enjoyment, relaxation, and high morale among group members.

Sociological imagination Ability to understand the relationship between what is happening in people's personal lives and the social forces that surround them.

Sociological perspective View that emphasizes the powerful role that group membership and social forces play in shaping human behavior.

Sociology Scientific study of society and human social behavior.

Split labor market Competitive situation in which two groups of workers are willing to do the same work but for different wages.

State Political institution with legitimate control over the use of force within a particular territory.

Status Designated position in a group or society.

Status group People who occupy similar prestige levels and thus share a common lifestyle.

Status inconsistency   Situation in which a person ranks high on one dimension of stratification but low on another.

Subculture   Group within a culture that has some values, beliefs, and norms that are different from those of the larger culture.

Suburbs   Less densely populated areas, primarily residential, on the outskirts of a city.

Succession   Urban process in which previous residents or users of a neighborhood leave and new residents come to predominate.

Survey   Research design in which data are collected from a large group of people by asking them questions about their behavior or attitudes.

Task roles   Actions of leaders that move a group toward achieving its goals.

Theistic religion   Religion that posits the existence of one or more gods, not of human origin, that are believed to play a role in the creation and maintenance of the universe and take an interest in human affairs.

Theoretical perspective   Set of fundamental assumptions about the nature and operation of society that serves as a source of more specific theories.

Theory   Set of statements that explains the relationship among phenomena.

Third-party medicine   Medical payment system in which the patient pays premiums into a fund and the doctor or hospital is paid from this fund for each treatment provided to the patient.

Total institutions   Organizations that tightly regiment the lives of their members or inmates, who are isolated from the rest of society for part of their lives.

Totalitarianism   Type of government in which all the familiar social institutions, such as the economy, education, and to some extent the family and religion, are under total state control.

Totemism   Belief system in which a plant, animal, or object is considered to have some sacred power or spirit.

Urban ecology   Study of the distributions of people and facilities within urban centers and how cities relate to the surrounding environment.

Values   Conceptions of what is right and desirable that serve as criteria for choosing goals or behaviors.

Variable   Property or characteristic that can take differing values.

Wealth   Person's total economic assets; for Weber, one important dimension of the stratification system.

Welfare capitalism   Economies that combine a strongly competitive market and private property with some government regulation for the public good.

Women's movement   *See* Feminist movement.

World-system theory   Proposition that the world's nations have become increasingly interdependent, both economically and politically, and are now linked in a worldwide stratification system, with some nations having more power and resources than other nations.

Bibliography

Abadinsky, H. (1994). *Organized crime* (4th ed.). Chicago: Nelson-Hall.

Abe, K. (1976). The behavior of survivors and victims in a Japanese nightclub fire: A descriptive research note. *Mass Emergencies, 1,* 119–124.

Acuna, R. (1987). *Occupied America: A history of Chicanos* (3rd ed.). New York: Harper & Row.

Adam, H., & Moodley, K. (1986). *South Africa without apartheid: Dismantling racial domination.* Berkeley: University of California Press.

Aday, L. A. (1993). *At risk in America: The health and health care needs of vulnerable populations in the United States.* San Francisco: Jossey-Bass.

Adelman, C. (1991). *Women at thirtysomething: Paradoxes of attainment.* Washington, DC: U.S. Department of Education.

Agnew, R. (1991). A longitudinal test of social control theory and delinquency. *Journal of Research in Crime and Delinquency, 28,* 126–156.

Alba, R. D. (1995). Assimilation's quiet tide. *Public Interest, 119,* 3–18.

Aldrich, M., & Buchele, R. (1986). *The economics of comparable worth.* Cambridge, MA: Balinger.

Alex-Assensoh, Y. (1995). Myths about race and the underclass: Concentrated poverty and "underclass" behaviors. *Urban Affairs Review, 31,* 3–19.

Allan, E. A., & Steffensmeier, D. J. (1989). Youth underemployment and property crime: Differential effects of job availability and job quality on juvenile and young adult arrest rates. *American Sociological Review, 54,* 107–123.

Altheide, D. L. (1993). Electronic media and state control: The case of Azscam. *Sociological Quarterly, 34,* 53–69.

Alwin, D. F., Cohen, R. L., & Newcomb, T. M. (1991). *Political attitudes over the life span: The Bennington women after fifty years.* Madison: University of Wisconsin Press.

Amato, P. R. (1987). Family processes in one-parent, stepparent, and intact families: The child's point of view. *Journal of Marriage and the Family, 49,* 327–337.

Amato, P. R. (1993). Children's adjustment to divorce: Theories, hypotheses, and empirical support. *Journal of Marriage and the Family, 55,* 23–38.

Amato, P. R., & Rezac, S. J. (1994). Contact with nonresident parents, interparental conflict, and children's behavior. *Journal of Family Issues, 15,* 191–207.

Andersen, R. M. (1995). Revisiting the behavioral model and access to medical care: Does it matter? *Journal of Health and Social Behavior, 36,* 1–10.

Andersen, R., & Anderson, O. W. (1979). Trends in the use of health services. In H. E. Freeman, S. Levine, & L. G. Reeder (Eds.), *Handbook of medical sociology* (3rd ed.). Englewood Cliffs, NJ: Prentice-Hall.

Anderson, K. (1991). *Chain her by one foot: The subjugation of women in seventeenth century New France.* New York: Routledge.

Anstett, P. (1992, June 23). U.S. consumers pay for health care ills. *Detroit Free Press,* p. 1.

Antonovsky, A. (1972). Social class, life expectancy, and overall mortality. In E. G. Jaco (Ed.), *Patients, physicians, and illness* (2nd ed.). New York: Free Press.

Apple, M. W. (1982). *Education and power.* London: Routledge & Kegan Paul.

Applebome, P. (1996, September 13). Report on training of teachers gives the nation a dismal grade. *New York Times,* p. A1.

Apter, D. E. (1986). *Rethinking development, modernization, dependency, and post-modern politics.* Beverly Hills, CA: Sage Publications.

Archer, D., Iritiani, B., Kimes, D. D., & Barrios, M. (1983). Face-ism: Five studies of sex differences in facial prominence. *Journal of Personality and Social Psychology, 45,* 725–735.

Ardrey, R. (1967). *The territorial imperative.* New York: Atheneum.

Arenson, K. W. (1996, August 23). Tougher courses paying off in higher S.A.T. scores, College Board says. *New York Times,* p. A11.

Argyris, C. (1964). *Integrating the individual and the organization.* New York: Wiley & Sons.

Aries, E. (1985). Male-female interpersonal styles in all-male, all-female, and mixed groups. In A. G. Sargent (Ed.), *Beyond sex roles* (2nd ed.). St. Paul, MN: West.

Ariès, P. (1962). *Centuries of childhood* (R. Baldick, Trans.). New York: Random House.

Arizpe, L., & Aranda, J. (1981). The comparative advantages of women's disadvantages: Women workers in the strawberry export agribusiness in Mexico. *Signs, 7,* 453–473.

Armor, D. J. (1989). After busing: Education and choice. *Public Interest, 95,* 24–37.

Armor, D. J. (1995). *Forced justice: School desegregation and the law.* New York: Oxford University Press.

Aronowitz, S., & DiFazio, W. (1994). *The jobless future: Sci-tech and the dogma of work.* Minneapolis: University of Minnesota Press.

Ashton, H. (1967). *The Basuto* (2nd ed.). London: Oxford University Press.

Astin, A. W. (1992). Educational "Choice": Its appeal may be illusory. *Sociology of Education, 65,* 255–260.

Axinn, W. G., & Thornton, A. (1996). The influence of parents' marital dissolutions on children's attitudes toward family formation. *Demography, 33,* 66–81.

Bagdikian, B. H. (1990). *The media monopoly* (3rd ed.). Boston: Beacon Press.

Bahr, S. J. (1989). *Family interaction.* New York: Macmillan.

Baker, T. L., & Velez, W. (1996). Access to and opportunity in postsecondary education in the United States: A review. *Sociology of Education* [Special issue], 82–101.

Bales, R. F. (1953). The equilibrium problem in small groups. In T. Parsons, R. F. Bales, & E. A. Shils (Eds.), *Working papers in the theory of action.* Glencoe, IL: Free Press.

Ball-Rokeach, S. J. (1973). From pervasive ambiguity to a definition of the situation. *Sociometry, 36,* 378–389.

Baloyra, E. A. (1982). *El Salvador in transition.* Chapel Hill: University of North Carolina Press.

Balthazar, L. (1995). Quebec and the ideal of federalism. *Annals of the American Academy of Political and Social Science, 538,* 40–53.

Banfield, E. C. (1990). *The unheavenly city revisited.* Prospect Heights, IL: Waveland Press.

Barakat, H. (1993). *The Arab world: Society, culture, and state.* Berkeley: University of California Press.

Barnet, R. J., & Cavanagh, J. (1994). *Global dreams: Imperial corporations and the new world order.* New York: Simon & Schuster.

Barnett, R. C., & Rivers, C. (1996). *She works/he works: How two-income families are happier, healthier, and better off.* San Francisco: HarperSanFrancisco.

Barnlund, D. C. (1989). *Communicative styles of Japanese and Americans: Images and realities.* Belmont, CA: Wadsworth.

Baron, J. M., & Newman, A. E. (1990). For what it's worth: Organizations, occupations, and the value of work done by women and nonwhites. *American Sociological Review, 55,* 155–175.

Baron, R. A., & Richardson, D. R. (1994). *Human aggression* (2nd ed.). New York: Plenum.

Barrett, K., & Greene, R. (1991, February 19). American cities: A special report. *Financial World*, pp. 20–37.

Barringer, H. R., Takeuchi, D. T., & Xenos, P. (1990). Education, occupational prestige, and income of Asian Americans. *Sociology of Education, 63*, 27–43.

Barron, J. (1989, April 16). Unnecessary surgery. *New York Times Magazine*, Part 2, pp. 44–46.

Bartos, O. J. (1996). Postmodernism, postindustrialism, and the future. *The Sociological Quarterly, 37*, 307–325.

Basow, S. A. (1992). *Gender: Stereotypes and roles* (2nd ed.). Pacific Grove, CA: Brooks/Cole.

Beauregard, R. A. (1990). Trajectories of neighborhood change: The case of gentrification. *Environment and Planning, 22*, 855–874.

Bell, D. (1973). *The coming of post-industrial society*. New York: Basic Books.

Bell, R. L., Cleveland, S. E., Hanson, P. G., & O'Connell, W. E. (1969). Small group dialogue and discussion: An approach to police–community relationships. *Journal of Criminal Law, Criminology, and Police Science, 60*, 242–246.

Bellaby, P., & Oribabor, P. (1980). The history of the present—contradiction and struggle in nursing. In C. Davies (Ed.), *Rewriting nursing history*. Totowa, NJ: Barnes & Noble.

Bellah, R. N. (1964). Religious evolution. *American Sociological Review, 29*, 358–374.

Bellah, R. N. (1988). Civil religion in America. *Daedalus, 117*, 97–118.

Bellah, R. N., Madsen, R., Sullivan, W. M., Swidler, A., & Tipton, S. M. (1985). *Habits of the heart: Individualism and commitment in American life*. Berkeley: University of California Press.

Beniger, J. R. (1993). The control revolution. In A. H. Teich (Ed.), *Technology and the future* (6th ed.). New York: St. Martin's Press.

Bennett, A., & Adams, O. (1993). *Looking north for health: What we can learn from Canada's health care system*. San Francisco: Jossey-Bass.

Bennett, S. F. (1995). Community organizations and crime. *Annals of the American Academy of Political and Social Science, 539*, 72–84.

Bennett, W. J. (1986). *First lessons: A report on elementary education in America*. Washington, DC: U.S. Government Printing Office.

Benokraitis, N. V., & Feagin, J. R. (1995). *Modern sexism: Blatant, subtle, and covert discrimination* (2nd ed.). Englewood Cliffs, NJ: Prentice-Hall.

Berg, B. L. (1994). *Qualitative research methods for the social sciences* (2nd ed.). Boston: Allyn & Bacon.

Berg, I. (1975). Rich man's qualifications for poor man's jobs. In I. L. Horowitz & C. Nanry (Eds.), *Sociological realities II*. New York: Harper & Row.

Berg, I., & Gorelick, S. (1970). *Education and jobs: The great training robbery*. New York: Praeger.

Berger, P. L. (1963). *Invitation to sociology: A humanistic perspective*. Garden City, NY: Anchor Press.

Berger, R. M. (1990). Men together: Understanding the gay couple. *Journal of Homosexuality, 19*, 31–49.

Bergmann, B. R. (1996). *In defense of affirmative action*. New York: BasicBooks.

Berk, R. A. (1974). *Collective behavior*. Dubuque, IA: W. C. Brown.

Berkowitz, L. (1971). The study of urban violence: Some implications of laboratory studies of frustration and aggression. In J. C. Davies (Ed.), *When men revolt and why*. New York: Free Press.

Berliner, D. (1988). Math teaching may favor boys over girls. *Education Digest, 53*, 29.

Berliner, D. C., & Biddle, B. J. (1995). *The manufactured crisis: Myths, fraud, and the attack on America's public schools*. Reading, MA: Addison-Wesley.

Bernstein, N. (1996, January 8). Equal opportunity recedes for most female lawyers. *New York Times*, p. A12.

Bernstein, R. (1993, May 2). A growing Islamic presence: Balancing sacred and secular. *New York Times*, p. 1.

Berreman, G. D. (1987). Caste in India and the United States. In C. S. Heller (Ed.), *Structured social inequality: A reader in comparative social stratification* (2nd ed.). New York: Macmillan

Besharov, D. J. (1992). A new start for head start. *American Enterprise, 3,* 52–57.

Best, R. (1983). *We've all got scars: What boys and girls learn in elementary school.* Bloomington: Indiana University Press.

Betz, M., Davis, K., & Miller, P. (1978). Scarcity, income advantage, and mobility: More evidence on the functional theory of stratification. *Sociological Quarterly, 19,* 399–413.

Biblarz, T. J., & Raftery, A. E. (1993). The effects of family disruption on social mobility. *American Sociological Review, 58,* 97–109.

Biddle, B. J., & Thomas, E. J. (1966). *Role theory: Concepts and research.* New York: Wiley & Sons.

Bieber, I., et al. (1962). *Homosexuality.* New York: Basic Books.

Billingsley, A. (1992). *Climbing Jacob's ladder: The enduring legacy of African-American families.* New York: Simon & Schuster.

Bills, D. B. (1988). Educational credentials and promotions: Does schooling do more than get you in the door? *Sociology of Education, 61,* 52–60.

Billson, J. M., & Disch, E. (1991). Empowering women: A clinical sociology model for working with women in groups. In H. M. Rebach & J. G. Bruhn (Eds.), *Handbook of clinical sociology.* New York: Plenum Press.

Billy, J. O. G., Tanfer, K., Grady, W. R., & Keplinger, D. H. (1993). The sexual behavior of men in the United States. *Family Planning Perspectives, 25,* 52–60.

Black, D. (1993). *The social structure of right and wrong.* San Diego: Academic Press.

Black, F. L. (1978). Infectious diseases in primitive societies. In M. H. Logan & E. E. Hunt, Jr. (Eds.), *Health and the human condition.* North Scituate, MA: Duxbury Press.

Blalock, H. M., Jr. (1982). *Race and ethnic relations.* Englewood Cliffs, NJ: Prentice-Hall.

Blasi, J. (1986). *The communal experience of the kibbutz.* New Brunswick, NJ: Transaction Books.

Blau, P. M., & Duncan, O. D. (1967). *The American occupational structure.* New York: Wiley & Sons.

Blea, I. I. (1991). *La chicana and the intersection of race, class, and gender.* New York: Praeger.

Blinder, A. S. (Ed.). (1990). *Paying for productivity: A look at the evidence.* Washington, DC: Brookings Institution.

Bloom, A. (1987). *The closing of the American mind.* New York: Simon & Schuster.

Bloom, J. (1987). *Class, race, and the civil rights movement.* Bloomington: Indiana University Press.

Blum, R. W., Harmon, B., Harris, L., Bergeisen, L., & Resnick, M. D. (1992). American Indian-Alaska native youth health. *Journal of the American Medical Association, 267,* 1637–1644.

Blumer, H. (1951). Collective behavior. In A. M. Lee (Ed.), *New outline of the principles of sociology.* New York: Barnes & Noble Books.

Blumer, H. (1962). Society as symbolic interaction. In A. M. Rose (Ed.), *Human behavior and social processes.* Boston: Houghton Mifflin.

Blumstein, P., & Schwartz, P. (1983). *American couples.* New York: Morrow.

Bodley, J. H. (1994). *Cultural anthropology: Tribes, states, and the global system.* Mountain View, CA: Mayfield.

Bohannon, L., & Bohannon, P. (1953). *The Tiv of Central Nigeria.* London: International African Institute.

Boisjoly, J., & Duncan, G. J. (1994, June). Job losses among Hispanics in the recent recession. *Monthly Labor Review,* pp. 16–23.

Bonacich, E. (1972). A theory of ethnic antagonism: The split-labor market. *American Sociological Review, 37,* 547–559.

Boswell, T. E. (1986). A split labor market analysis of discrimination against Chinese immigrants, 1850–1882. *American Sociological Review, 51,* 352–371.

Bourgault, L. M. (1995). *Mass media in Sub-Saharan Africa.* Bloomington: Indiana University Press.

Bouvier, L. F. (1984). Planet Earth 1984–2034: A demographic vision. *Population Bulletin, 39*(1).

Bovee, T. (1993, September 23). Many immigrants start slow, but then get ahead, census finds. *Detroit Free Press,* p. 5A.

Bowles, S., & Gintis, H. (1976). *Schooling in capitalist America.* New York: Basic Books.

Boyer, E. L. (1994, March 9). Creating the new American college. *The Chronicle of Higher Education*, p. A48.

Braddock, J. H. (1985). School desegregation and black assimilation. *Journal of Social Issues, 41,* 9–22.

Braddock, J. H., Crain, R. L., & McPartland, J. M. (1984). A long-term view of desegregation: Some recent studies of graduates as adults. *Phi Delta Kappan, 66,* 259–264.

Bradshaw, Y. W., Noonan, R., Gash, L., & Sershen, C. B. (1993). Borrowing against the future: Children and Third World indebtedness. *Social Forces, 71,* 629–656.

Brandon, G. (1990). Sacrificial practices in Santeria, an African-Cuban religion in the United States. In J. E. Holloway (Ed.), *Africanisms in American culture.* Bloomington: Indiana University Press.

Branegan, J. (1993, January 18). Is Singapore a model for the West? *Time,* pp. 36–37.

Braun, D. (1991). *The rich get richer: The rise of income inequality in the United States and the world.* Chicago: Nelson-Hall.

Brehm, S. S. (1985). *Intimate relationships.* New York: Random House.

The brethren's first sister. (1981, July 20). *Time,* pp. 8–19.

Brewer, M. B., & Miller, N. (1988). Contact and cooperation: When do they work? In P. A. Katz & D. A. Taylor (Eds.), *Eliminating racism: Profiles in controversy.* New York: Plenum Press.

Brinton, C. (1965). *The anatomy of revolution* (rev. ed.). New York: Vintage.

Broch, H. B. (1990). *Growing up agreeably: Bonerate childhood observed.* Honolulu: University of Hawaii Press.

Brostoff, S. (1992). Medical malpractice claims fuel health care cost boom. *National Underwriter, 96,* 2.

Brown, J. K. (1969). Female initiation rites: A review of the current literature. In D. Rogers (Ed.), *Issues in adolescent psychology.* New York: Appleton-Century-Crofts.

Brown, J. (1970). A note on the division of labor by sex. *American Anthropologist, 72,* 1073–1078.

Brown, R. S., Clement, D. G., Hill, J. W., Retchin, S. M., & Bergeron, J. W. (1993). Do health maintenance organizations work for Medicare? *Health Care Financing Review, 15,* 7–23.

Brownmiller, S. (1975). *Against our will: Men, women and rape.* New York: Simon & Schuster.

Bruce, J., Lloyd, C. B., & Leonard, A. (1995). *Families in focus.* New York: Population Council.

Brummett, B. (1991). *Rhetorical dimensions of popular culture.* Tuscaloosa: University of Alabama Press.

Brus, W., & Laski, K. (1989). *From Marx to the market: Socialism in search of an economic system.* Oxford: Clarendon Press.

Brydon, L., & Chant, S. (1989). *Women in the Third World: Gender issues in rural and urban areas.* New Brunswick, NJ: Rutgers University Press.

Bryk, A. S., Lee, V. E., & Holland, P. B. (1993). *Catholic schools and the common good.* Cambridge, MA: Harvard University Press.

Buckner, H. T. (1965). A theory of rumor transmission. *Public Opinion Quarterly, 29,* 54–70.

Buechler, S. M. (1995). New social movement theories. *The Sociological Quarterly, 36,* 441–464.

Bullock, C. S., III, Anderson, J. E., & Brady, D. W. (1983). *Public policy in the eighties.* Monterey, CA: Brooks-Cole.

Bullough, V. L. (1976). *Sexual variance in society and history.* New York: Wiley & Sons.

Bunzel, J. H. (1991). Black and white at Stanford. *Public Interest, 105,* 61–77.

Burkett, E. (1996). *The gravest show on Earth: America in the age of AIDS.* New York: Houghton Mifflin.

Burks, A. (1984). *Japan: Profile of a post industrial power.* Boulder, CO: Westview Press.

Burn, S. M., O'Neil, A. K., & Nederend, S. (1996). Childhood tomboyism and adult androgyny. *Sex Roles, 34,* 419–428.

Bustamante, J. A. (1983). *Maquiladoras:* A new face of international capitalism on Mexico's northern frontier. In J. Nash & M. P. Fernandez-Kelly (Eds.), *Women, men, and the international division of labor.* Albany: State University of New York Press.

Calem, R. E. (1993, April 18). Working at home, for better or worse. *New York Times,* Sec. 3, pp. 1, 6.

Califano, J. A., Jr. (1986). *America's health care revolution: Who lives? Who dies? Who pays?* New York: Random House.

Cantril, H. (1940). *The invasion from Mars.* Princeton, NJ: Princeton University Press.

Caraley, D. (1992). Washington abandons the cities. *Political Science Quarterly, 107,* 1–30.

Carey, A. (1967). The Hawthorne studies: A radical criticism. *American Sociological Review, 32,* 403–416.

Cargan, L., & Melko, M. (1982). *Singles: Myths and realities.* Beverly Hills, CA: Sage Publications.

Caringella-Macdonald, S. (1990). State crises and the crackdown on crime under Reagan. *Contemporary Crises, 14,* 91–118.

Carnegie Forum on Education and the Economy. (1986). *A nation prepared: Teachers for the 21st century.* New York: Carnegie Corporation.

Carnoy, M., & Levin, H. M. (1985). *Schooling and work in the democratic state.* Stanford, CA: Stanford University Press.

Carroll, M. P. (1975). Revitalization movements and social structure: Some quantitative tests. *American Sociological Review, 40,* 389–401.

Carter, S. L. (1993). *The culture of disbelief: How American law and politics trivialize religious devotion.* New York: Basic Books.

Castells, M. (1988). Squatters and the state in Latin America. In J. Gugler (Ed.), *The urbanization of the Third World.* New York: Oxford University Press.

Caughy, M. O., DiPietro, J. A., & Strobino, D. M. (1994). Day-care participation as a protective factor in the cognitive development of low-income children. *Child Development, 65,* 457–471.

Cavanagh, J., & Broad, R. (1996, March 18). Global reach: Workers fight the multinationals. *The Nation,* pp. 21–24.

Cavender, G. (1991). Alternative theory: Labeling and critical perspectives. In J. F. Sheley (Ed.), *Criminology: A contemporary handbook.* Belmont, CA: Wadsworth.

Chagnon, N. A. (1992). *Yanomamo* (4th ed.). Fort Worth, TX: Harcourt Brace Jovanovich.

Chalfant, H. P., Beckley, R. E., & Palmer, C. E. (1994). *Religion in contemporary society* (3rd ed.). Itasca, IL: Peacock.

Chambliss, W. J. (1975). Toward a political economy of crime. *Theory and Society, 2,* 149–170.

Chambliss, W. J. (1991). Biology and crime. In J. F. Sheley (Ed.), *Criminology: A contemporary handbook.* Belmont, CA: Wadsworth.

Champion, D. J. (1975). *The sociology of organizations.* New York: McGraw-Hill.

Chase-Dunn, C., & Grimes, P. (1995). World-systems analysis. *Annual Review of Sociology, 21,* 387–417.

Chase-Lansdale, P. L., Brooks-Gunn, J., & Paikoff, R. L. (1991). Research and programs for adolescent mothers: Missing links and future promises. *Family Relations, 40,* 396–403.

Cherlin, A. J., & Furstenberg, F. F., Jr. (1994). Stepfamilies in the United States: A reconsideration. In J. Hagen & K. S. Cook (Eds.), *Annual review of sociology: Vol. 20.* Palo Alto, CA: Annual Reviews Inc.

Chilman, C., Nunnally, E. W., & Cox, F. M. (Eds.). (1988). *Variant family forms.* Beverly Hills, CA: Sage Publications.

Chira, S. (1993, July 11). Rethinking deliberately segregated schools. *New York Times,* Sec. 4, p. 20.

Chirot, D. (1986). *Social change in the modern era.* San Diego: Harcourt Brace Jovanovich.

Chow, E. P. Y. (1984). Traditional Chinese medicine: A holistic system. In J. W. Salmon (Ed.), *Alternative medicines: Popular and policy perspectives.* New York: Tavistock.

Church, N. (1991). The effects of social change on clinical practice. In H. M. Rebach & J. G. Bruhn (Eds.), *Handbook of clinical sociology.* New York: Plenum.

Cisneros, H. G. (1995). *Defensible space: Deterring crime and building community.* Washington, DC: U.S. Department of Housing & Urban Development.

Clancy, P. M. (1986). The acquisition of communicative style in Japanese. In B. B. Schieffelin

& E. Ochs (Eds.), *Language socialization across cultures*. Cambridge: Cambridge University Press.

Clark, R. (1992). Multinational corporate investment and women's participation in higher education in noncore nations. *Sociology of Education, 65*, 37–47.

Clarke-Stewart, A. (1993). *Daycare* (rev. ed.). Cambridge, MA: Harvard University Press.

Clayton, O., Jr., Baird, A. C., & Levinson, R. M. (1984). Subjective decision making in medical school admissions: Potentials for discrimination. *Sex Roles, 10*(7/8), 527–532.

Clement, U. (1989). Profile analysis as a method of comparing intergenerational differences in sexual behavior. *Archives of Sexual Behavior, 18*, 229–237.

Clore, G. L., Bray, R. M., Itkin, S. M., & Murphy, P. (1978). Interracial attitudes and behavior at a summer camp. *Journal of Personality and Social Psychology, 36*, 107–116.

Clymer, A. (1987, March 31). Survey finds many skeptics among evangelists' viewers. *New York Times*, p. 1.

Cockerham, W. C. (1995). *Medical sociology* (6th ed.). Englewood Cliffs, NJ: Prentice-Hall.

Cockerham, W. C. (1996). *Sociology of mental disorder* (4th ed.). Englewood Cliffs, NJ: Prentice-Hall.

Codrington, R. H. (1965). Mana. In W. A. Lessa & E. Z. Vogt (Eds.), *Reader in comparative religion* (2nd ed.). New York: Harper & Row.

Cohen, L. E., & Felson, M. (1979). Social change and crime rate trends. *American Sociological Review, 44*, 588–609.

Cohen, L. E., Felson, M., & Land, K. C. (1980). Property crime rates in the United States: A macrodynamic analysis, 1947–1977; with ex ante forecasts for the mid-1980's. *American Journal of Sociology, 86*, 90–118.

Cohen, T. F. (1987). Remaking men: Men's experiences becoming and being husbands and fathers and their implications for reconceptualizing men's lives. *Journal of Family Issues, 8*(1), 57–77.

Coleman, J. S. (1992). Some points on choice in education. *Sociology of Education, 65*, 260–262.

Coleman, J. S., Campbell, J. E., Hobson, L., McPartland, J., Mood, A., Weinfield, F., & York, R. (1966). *Equality of educational opportunity*. Washington, DC: U.S. Government Printing Office.

Coleman, J. S., Hoffer, T., & Kilgore, S. (1982). *Public and private high schools: An analysis of high schools and beyond*. Washington, DC: National Council for Education Statistics.

Coleman, J. W. (1989). *The criminal elite: The sociology of white collar crime* (2nd ed.). New York: St. Martin's Press.

Collins, R. (1971). A conflict theory of sexual stratification. *Social Problems, 19*, 3–21.

Collins, R. (1975). *Conflict sociology: Toward an explanatory science*. New York: Academic Press.

Collins, R. (1979). *The credential society*. New York: Academic Press.

Collins, R. (1989). Sociology: Proscience or antiscience. *American Sociological Review, 54*, 124–139.

Collins, R., & Coltrane, S. (1991). *Sociology of marriage and the family* (3rd ed.). Chicago: Nelson-Hall.

Colvin, M. (1991). Crime and social reproduction: A response to the call for 'outrageous' proposals. *Crime and Delinquency, 73*, 436–448.

Conklin, J. G. (1976). Robbery, the elderly and fear: An urban problem in search of a solution. In J. Goldsmith and S. S. Goldsmith (Eds.), *Crime and the Elderly*. Lexington, MA: Lexington Books.

Cooley, C. H. (1902). *Human nature and the social order*. New York: Scribner's.

Coser, L. A. (1956). *The functions of social conflict*. Glencoe, IL: Free Press.

Côté, J. E., & Allahar, A. L. (1996). *Generation on hold: Coming of age in the late twentieth century*. New York: New York University Press.

Coult, A. D., & Habenstein, R. W. (1965). *Cross tabulations of Murdock's "world ethnographic sample."* Columbia: University of Missouri Press.

Cowan, A. L. (1992, September 27). For women, fewer M.B.A.'s. *New York Times*, Sec. 3, p. 4.

Crain, R. L., & Mahard, R. E. (1983). The effect of research methodology on desegregation-achievement studies. *American Journal of Sociology, 88,* 839–854.

Cromwell, P. F., Marks, A., Olson, J. N., & Avary, D. W. (1991). Group effects on decision-making by burglars. *Psychological Reports, 69,* 579–588.

Crossman, R. K., Stith, S. M., & Bender, M. M. (1990). Sex role egalitarianism and marital violence. *Sex Roles, 22*(5/6), 293–304.

Crowe, T. D. (1991). *Crime prevention through environmental design.* Boston: Butterworth-Heinemann.

Crystal, S., Shea, D., & Krishnaswami, S. (1992). Educational attainment, occupational history, and stratification: Determinants of later-life economic outcomes. *Journal of Gerontology, 47,* S213–S221.

Cuklanz, L. M. (1996). *Rape on trial: How the mass media construct legal reform and social change.* Philadelphia: University of Pennsylvania Press.

Cullen, F. T., Link, B. G., & Polanzi, C. W. (1982). The seriousness of crime revisited: Have attitudes toward white-collar crime changed? *Criminology, 20,* 83–102.

Cullen, J. B., & Novick, S. M. (1979). The Davis-Moore theory of stratification: A further examination and extension. *American Journal of Sociology, 84,* 1414–1437.

Curran, D. J., & Cook, S. (1993). Growing fears, rising crime: Juveniles and China's justice system. *Crime and Delinquency, 39,* 296–315.

Currie, E. (1985). *Confronting crime: An American challenge.* New York: Pantheon Books.

Curtiss, S. (1977). *Genie: A psycholinguistic study of a modern-day "wild child."* New York: Academic Press.

Cushman, J. H., Jr. (1986, August 31). Pentagon-to-contractor job shift is profiled. *New York Times,* p. 37.

Dahrendorf, R. (1959). *Class and class conflict in industrial society.* Stanford, CA: Stanford University Press.

Dalton, G. (1972). Peasantries in anthropology and history. *Current Anthropologist, 13,* 385–416.

Daniels, R. (1988). *Asian America: Chinese and Japanese in the United States since 1850.* Seattle: University of Washington Press.

Danziger, S., & Gottschalk, P. (Eds.). (1993). *Uneven tides: Rising inequality in America.* New York: Russell Sage Foundation.

Darrow, W. W., et al. (1987). *Multicenter study of human immunodeficiency virus antibody in U.S. prostitutes.* Paper presented at the Third International Conference on AIDS, Washington, DC.

Davenport, W. H. (1977). Sex in cross-cultural perspective. In F. A. Beach (Ed.), *Human sexuality in four perspectives.* Baltimore: Johns Hopkins University Press.

Davidson, J. K., Sr., & Moore, N. B. (1992). *Marriage and family.* Dubuque, IA: William C. Brown.

Davies, J. C. (1962). Toward a theory of revolution. *American Sociological Review, 27,* 5–19.

Davis, J. A., & Smith, T. W. (1994). *General social surveys, 1994.* Chicago: National Opinion Research Center, producer; Storrs: University of Connecticut, Roper Center for Public Opinion Research, distributor.

Davis, K. (1940). Extreme social isolation of a child. *American Journal of Sociology, 45,* 554–564.

Davis, K. (1947). Final note on a case of extreme isolation. *American Journal of Sociology, 52,* 432–437.

Davis, K., & Moore, W. (1945). Some principles of stratification. *American Sociological Review, 10,* 242–249.

Day, R. A., & Day, J. V. (1977). A review of the current state of negotiated order theory: An appreciation and a critique. *Sociological Quarterly, 18,* 126–142.

DeBose, C. E. (1992). Codeswitching: Black English and standard English in the African-American linguistic repertoire. *Journal of Multilingual and Multicultural Development, 13*(1-2), 157–167.

Deckhard, B. (1979). *The women's movement.* New York: Harper & Row.

Deeb, M. (1992). Militant Islam and the politics of redemption. *Annals of the American Academy of Political and Social Science, 524,* 52–65.

Deegan, M. J. (1988). *Jane Addams and the men of the Chicago school.* New Brunswick, NJ: Transaction Books.

Dees, M. (1996). *Gathering storm: America's militia threat.* New York: HarperCollins.

Delattre, E. J. (1990). New faces of organized crime. *American Enterprise, 1,* 38–45.

Demers, D. P. (1996). *The menace of the corporate newspaper: Fact or fiction?* Ames, IA: Iowa State University Press.

Demo, D. H., & Hughes, M. (1990). Socialization and racial identity among black Americans. *Social Psychology Quarterly, 53,* 364–374.

Dentler, R. A. (1992). The Los Angeles riots of spring 1992: Events, causes, and future policy. *Sociological Practice Review, 3,* 229–244.

Devine, J. A., Plunkett, M., & Wright, J. D. (1992). The chronicity of poverty: Evidence from the PSID, 1967–1987. *Social Forces, 70,* 787–812.

Devine, J. A., Sheley, J. F., & Smith, M. D. (1988). Macroeconomic and social-control policy influences on crime rate changes, 1948–1985. *American Sociological Review, 53,* 407–420.

Devine, J. A., & Wright, J. D. (1993). *The greatest of evils: Urban poverty and the American underclass.* Hawthorne, NY: Aldine de Gruyter.

Devins, R. M. (1986). Displaced workers: One year later. *Monthly Labor Review, 109,* 40–43.

Díaz, B. (1956). *The discovery and conquest of Mexico.* New York: Farrar, Straus, & Cudahy. (Original work published 1638)

DiMatteo, M. R., & DiNicola, D. D. (1982). *Achieving patient compliance: The psychology of the medical practitioner's role.* New York: Pergamon Press.

Dion, S. (1992). Explaining Quebec nationalism. In R. K. Weaver (Ed.), *The collapse of Canada?* Washington, DC: Brookings Institution.

DiPrete, T. A. (1993). Industrial restructuring and the mobility response of American workers in the 1980s. *American Sociological Review, 58,* 74–96.

Dollard, J., Miller, N. E., Doob, L. W., Mowrer, O. H., & Seers, R. R. (1939). *Frustration and aggression.* New Haven: Yale University Press.

Domhoff, G. W. (1967). *Who rules America?* Englewood Cliffs, NJ: Prentice-Hall.

Domhoff, G. W. (1983). *Who rules America now?* Englewood Cliffs, NJ: Prentice-Hall.

Doob, C. B. (1993). *Racism: An American cauldron.* New York: HarperCollins.

Dorr, A., Kovaric, P., & Doubleday, C. (1990). Age and content influences on children's perceptions of the realism of television families. *Journal of Broadcasting and Electronic Media, 34,* 377–397.

Dougherty, J. P. (1990). What was religion: The demise of a prodigious power. *Modern Age, 33,* 113–121.

Dreier, P. (1982). The position of the press in the U.S. power structure. *Social Problems, 29,* 298–310.

Dubow, F., & Emmons, D. (1981). The community hypothesis. In D. A. Lewis (Ed.), *Reactions to crime.* Beverly Hills, CA: Sage Publications.

Duke, J. T. (1976). *Conflict and power in social life.* Provo, UT: Brigham Young University Press.

Dunford, F., Huizinga, D., & Elliott, D. (1989). *The Omaha domestic violence police experiment.* Washington, DC: National Institute of Justice.

Dunlop, J. B. (1993). *The rise of Russia and the fall of the Soviet empire.* Princeton, NJ: Princeton University Press.

Dunn, F. L. (1978). Epidemiological factors: Health and disease in hunter-gatherers. In M. H. Logan & E. E. Hunt, Jr. (Eds.), *Health and the human condition.* North Scituate, MA: Duxbury Press.

Dunphy, D. C. (1972). *The primary group: A handbook for analysis and field research.* New York: Appleton-Century-Crofts.

Durand, A. M. (1992). The safety of home birth: The farm study. *American Journal of Public Health, 82,* 450–453.

Durkheim, E. (1947). *The division of labor in society* (G. Simpson, Trans.). New York: Free Press. (Original work published 1893)

Durkheim, E. (1965). *The elementary forms of religious life.* (J. W. Swain, Trans.). New York: Free Press. (Original work published 1915)

Dusek, J. B. (Ed.). (1985). *Teacher expectancies.* Hillsdale, NJ: Erlbaum.

Dutton, D. B. (1986). Social class, health and illness. In L. H. Aiken & D. Mechanic (Eds.), *Applications of social science to clinical medicine and health policy.* New Brunswick, NJ: Rutgers University Press.

Dye, T. R. (1995). *Who's running America: The Clinton years* (6th ed.). Englewood Cliffs, NJ: Prentice-Hall.

Eagly, A. H. (1983). Gender and social influence: A social psychological analysis. *American Psychologist, 38,* 971–981.

Earley, P. C. (1989). Social loafing and collectivism: A comparison of the United States and the People's Republic of China. *Administrative Science Quarterly, 34,* 565–581.

Early, J. D., & Peters, J. F. (1990). *The population dynamics of the Mucajai Yanomama.* San Diego: Academic Press.

Eastland, T. (1996). *Ending affirmative action: The case for colorblind justice.* New York: BasicBooks.

Easterlin, R. A., & Crimmins, E. M. (1991). Private materialism, personal self-fulfillment, family life, and public interest: The nature, effects, and causes of recent changes in the values of American youth. *Public Opinion Quarterly, 55,* 499–533.

Ebel, R. H. (1982). Political instability in Central America. *Current History, 81,* 56–59.

Eckholm, E. (1994, December 18). While Congress remains silent, health care transforms itself. *New York Times,* p. A1.

Edwards, M. (1977, March 15). Golden threads to the Pentagon. *Nation,* pp. 306–308.

Edwards, W. F., & Winford, D. (Eds.). (1991). *Verb phrase patterns in black English and Creole.* Detroit: Wayne State University Press.

Ehrlich, P. R., & Ehrlich, A. H. (1990). *The population explosion.* New York: Simon & Schuster.

Eisenberg, D. M., Kessler, R. C., Foster, C., Norlock, F. E., Calkins, D. R., & Delbanco, T. L. (1993). Unconventional medicine in the United States: Prevalence, costs, and patterns of use. *New England Journal of Medicine, 328,* 246–252.

Ellis, G. J., & Petersen, L. R. (1992). Socialization values and parental control techniques: A cross-cultural analysis of child-rearing. *Journal of Comparative Family Studies, 23,* 39–54.

Engels, F. (1969). Ludwig Feuerbach and the end of classical German philosophy. In *Karl Marx and Frederick Engels: Selected works.* New York: International. (Original work published 1888)

Engerman, S. L. (1977). Black fertility and family structure in the United States: 1880–1940. *Journal of Family History, 2.*

England, P. (1992). *Comparable worth: Theories and Evidence.* New York: Aldine de Gruyter.

Entwisle, D. R., & Alexander, K. L. (1994). Winter setback: The racial composition of schools and learning to read. *American Sociological Review, 59,* 446–460.

Ergil, K. V. (1996). China's traditional medicine. In M. S. Micozzi (Ed.), *Fundamentals of complementary and alternative medicine.* New York: Churchill Livingstone.

Erikson, E. H. (1950). *Childhood and society.* New York: Norton.

Erikson, E. H. (1982). *The life cycle completed: A review.* New York: Norton.

Erikson, K. T. (1966). *Wayward puritans.* New York: Wiley & Sons.

Eshleman, J. R. (1991). *The family: An introduction* (6th ed.). Boston: Allyn & Bacon.

Etzioni, A. (1991). *A responsive society: Collected essays on guiding deliberate social change.* San Francisco: Jossey-Bass.

Evans, E. D., Rutberg, J., Sather, C., & Turner, C. (1991). Context analysis of contemporary teen magazines for adolescent females. *Youth and Society, 23,* 99–120.

Fagerlind, I., & Saha, L. J. (1989). *Education and national development: A comparative perspective* (2nd ed.). Oxford: Pergamon Press.

Fairbanks, J. K. (1989). *The great Chinese revolution: 1800–1985.* New York: Harper & Row.

Fallows, J. (1994). *Looking at the sun: The rise of the new East Asian economic and political system.* New York: Pantheon.

Farb, P. (1978). *Man's rise to civilization: The cultural ascent of the Indians of North America* (2nd ed.). New York: E. P. Dutton.

Faris, J. H. (1977). An alternative perspective to Savage and Gabriel. *Armed Forces & Society, 3,* 457–462.

Farley, J. E. (1991). Combatting racial polarization: A sociologist's contribution. *Sociological Practice Review, 2,* 287–297.

Farrag, A. (1971). Social control among the Mzabite women of Beni-Isguen. *Middle Eastern Studies, 7,* 317–327.

Fausto-Sterling, A. (1992). *Myths of gender: Biological theories about women and men.* New York: BasicBooks.

Fay, B. (1987). *Critical social science: Liberation and its limits.* Ithaca, NY: Cornell University Press.

Feagin, J. R., & Sykes, M. P. (1994). *Living with racism: The black middle-class experience.* Boston: Beacon Press.

Featherman, D. L., & Hauser, R. M. (1978). *Opportunity and change.* New York: Academic Press.

Federal Bureau of Investigation. (1995). *Uniform crime reports: Crime in the United States, 1994.* Washington, DC: U.S. Government Printing Office.

Fein, M. (1990). *Role change: A resocialization perspective.* New York: Praeger.

Feinberg, R. E., & Avakov, R. M. (1991). *U.S. and Soviet aid to developing countries.* New Brunswick, NJ: Transaction Books.

Feinberg, W. (1993). *Japan and the pursuit of a new American identity: Work and education in a multicultural age.* New York: Routledge.

Feinberg, W., & Soltis, J. F. (1992). *School and society* (2nd ed.). New York: Columbia University, Teachers College Press.

Feldman, R., Wholey, D., & Christianson, J. (1996). Effect of mergers on health maintenance organization premiums. *Health Care Financing Review, 17,* 171–190.

Felson, R. B. (1996). Mass media effects on violent behavior. In J. Hagan & K. S. Cook (Eds.), *Annual review of sociology: Vol. 22.* Palo Alto, CA: Annual Reviews Inc.

Fernald, A., & Morikawa, H. (1993). Common themes and cultural variations in Japanese and American mothers' speech to infants. *Child Development, 64,* 637–656.

Fernandez-Kelly, M. P. (1983a). *For we are sold, I and my people: Women and industry in Mexico's frontier.* Albany: State University of New York Press.

Fernandez-Kelly, M. P. (1983b). Mexican border industrialization, female labor force participation, and migration. In J. Nash & M. P. Fernandez-Kelly (Eds.), *Women, men, and the international division of labor.* Albany: State University of New York Press.

Ferree, M. M. (1991). The gender division of labor in two-earner marriages: Dimensions of variability and change. *Journal of Family Issues, 12,* 158–180.

Ferree, M. M., & Hall, E. J. (1990). Visual images of American society: Gender and race in introductory sociology textbooks. *Gender and Society, 4,* 500–533.

Fiedler, F. E. (1967). *A theory of leadership effectiveness.* New York: McGraw-Hill.

Fiedler, F. E. (1981). Leadership effectiveness. *American Behavioral Scientist, 24,* 619–632.

Fijnaut, C. (1990). Organized crime: A comparison between the United States of America and Western Europe. *British Journal of Criminology, 30,* 321–340.

Fine, G. A. (1984). Negotiated orders and organizational cultures. *Annual Review of Sociology, 10,* 239–262.

Fine, G. A., & Kleinman, S. (1979). Rethinking subculture: An interactionist analysis. *American Journal of Sociology, 85,* 1–20.

Finn, C. E., Jr. (1989). A nation still at risk. *Commentary, 87,* 17–23.

Finn, C. E., Jr. (1996, August 24). Teachers vs. education. *New York Times,* p. 19.

Finnan, C. R., & Cooperstein, R. (1983). *Southeast Asian refugee resettlement at the local level.* Menlo Park, CA: SRI International.

Fiorentine, R. (1988). Increasing similarities in the values and life plans of male and female college students? Evidence and implications. *Sex Roles, 18,* 143–158.

Fischer, C. (1975). Toward a subcultural theory of urbanism. *American Journal of Sociology, 80,* 1319–1341.

Fishbein, D. H. (1990). Biological perspectives in criminology. *Criminology, 28,* 27–66.

Fishman, M. (1978). Crime waves as ideology. *Social Problems, 25,* 531–543.

Fitzpatrick, J. P. (1987). *Puerto Rican Americans: The meaning of migration to the mainland* (2nd ed.). Englewood Cliffs, NJ: Prentice-Hall.

Flacks, R. (1971). *Youth and social change.* Chicago: Markham.

Foner, A., & Kertzer, D. (1978). Transitions over the life course: Lessons from age-set societies. *American Journal of Sociology, 83,* 1081–1104.

Ford, C. S. (1970). Some primitive societies. In G. H. Seward & R. C. Williamson (Eds.), *Sex roles in society.* New York: Random House.

Fost, D. (1991, December). American Indians in the 1990s. *American Demographics,* pp. 26–34.

Foster, G. M., & Anderson, B. G. (1978). *Medical Anthropology.* New York: Wiley & Sons.

Foster, M. W. (1991). *Being Comanche: A social history of an American Indian community.* Tucson: University of Arizona Press.

Fowler-Salamini, H., & Vaughan, M. K. (Eds.). (1994). *Women of the Mexican countryside, 1850–1990.* Tucson: University of Arizona Press.

Fox, T. G., & Miller, S. M. (1965). Intercountry variations: Occupational stratification and mobility. *Studies in Comparative International Development, 1,* 3–10.

Fraiberg, S. (1977). *Every child's birthright.* New York: Basic Books.

Frankl, R. (1987). *Televangelism: The marketing of popular religion.* Carbondale: Southern Illinois University Press.

Freedman, J. L. (1975). *Crowding and behavior.* San Francisco: Freeman.

Freeman, D. (1983). *Margaret Mead and Samoa: The making and unmaking of an anthropological myth.* Cambridge: Harvard University Press.

Freeman, R. B., & Holzer, H. J. (Eds.). (1986). *The black youth employment crisis.* Chicago: University of Chicago Press.

Freidson, E. (1970). *The profession of medicine.* New York: Dodd, Mead.

Freudenheim, M. (1989, July 30). Ontario pay equity law has employers scrambling. *Detroit Free Press,* Sec. C, p. 1.

Freudenheim, M. (1995, November 17). Doctors' incomes fall as managed care grows. *New York Times,* p. 1.

Freund, P., & McGuire, M. (1995). *Health, illness, and the social body.* Englewood Cliffs, NJ: Prentice-Hall.

Fritz, J. M. (1991). The contributions of clinical sociology in health care settings. *Sociological Practice, 9,* 15–29.

Fruzzetti, L. M. (1982). *The gift of a virgin: Women, marriage, and ritual in a Bengali society.* New Brunswick, NJ: Rutgers University Press.

Fuentes, A. (1991, October 28). Women warriors: Equality, yes—militarism, no. *Nation,* pp. 516–519.

Funk, R. B., & Willits, F. K. (1987). College attendance and attitude change: 1970–1981. *Sociology of Education, 60,* 224–231.

Furstenberg, F. F., & Cherlin, A. J. (1991). *Divided families: What happens to children when parents part.* Cambridge: Harvard University Press.

Furstenberg, F. F., Jr., & Teitler, J. O. (1994). Reconsidering the effects of marital disruption: What happens to children in early adulthood? *Journal of Family Issues, 15,* 173–190.

Gaddy, G. D. (1986). Television's impact on high school achievement. *Public Opinion Quarterly, 50,* 340–359.

Gaede, S. (1977). Religious participation, socioeconomic status, and belief-orthodoxy. *Journal for the Scientific Study of Religion, 16,* 245–253.

Gage, M. G., & Christensen, D. H. (1991). Parental role socialization and the transition to parenthood. *Family Relations, 40,* 332–337.

Gallagher, T. J., Johnson, E. O., Van Valey, T. L., & Malaret, D. R. (1992). *Job-seeking and academic success among sociologists: The effects of departmental prestige and gender.* Paper presented at the annual meeting of the American Sociological Association, Pittsburgh.

Gans, H. J. (1962). *The urban villagers.* New York: Free Press.

Gans, H. J. (1972). Urbanism and suburbanism as ways of life: A re-evaluation of definitions. In J. J. Palen & K. Flaming (Eds.), *Urban America.* New York: Holt.

Garrett, W. R. (1982). *Seasons of marriage and family life.* New York: Holt.

Gastil, J. (1990). Generic pronouns and sexist language: The oxymoronic character of masculine generics. *Sex Roles, 23*(11/12), 629–643.

Geertz, C. (1966). Religion as a cultural system. In M. Banton (Ed.), *Anthropological approaches to the study of religion.* New York: Praeger.

Geertz, C. (1973). *The interpretation of cultures.* New York: Basic Books.

Gelles, R. J. (1992). Poverty and violence toward children. *American Behavioral Scientist, 35,* 258–274.

Gelles, R. J., & Conte, J. R. (1990). Domestic violence and sexual abuse of children: A review of research in the eighties. *Journal of Marriage and the Family, 52,* 1045–1058.

Gelles, R. J., & Cornell, C. P. (1990). *Intimate violence in families* (2nd ed.). Newbury Park, CA: Sage Publications.

George, S., & Sabelli, F. (1994). *Faith and credit: The World Bank's secular empire.* Boulder, CO: Westview Press.

Gerdes, E. P., & Garber, D. M. (1983). Sex bias in hiring: Effects of job demands and applicant competence. *Sex Roles, 9*(3), 307–319.

Gibbs, N. (1993, May 3). Oh, my god, they're killing themselves. *Time,* pp. 26–43.

Giele, J. Z. (1978). *Women and the future.* New York: Free Press.

Gilbert, D. A., & Kahl, J. A. (1993). *The American class structure* (4th ed.). Belmont, CA: Wadsworth.

Gilder, G. (1993, September 11). The death of telephony. *The Economist,* pp. 75–78.

Gilligan, C. (1983, May). *Challenging existing theories: Conclusions.* Paper presented at the Eighth Annual Conference for Helpers of Adults, University of Maryland, College Park.

Gillmor, D., & Doig, S. K. (1992, January). Segregation forever? *American Demographics,* pp. 48–51.

Giroux, H. A. (1985). Theories of reproduction and resistance in the new sociology of education: A critical analysis. *Harvard Educational Review, 53*(3), 257–293.

Gladney, D. C. (1991). *Muslim Chinese: Ethnic nationalism in the People's Republic.* Cambridge: Harvard University, Council on East Asian Studies, & Harvard University Press.

The Glass Ceiling Commission. (1995). *Good for business: Making full use of the nation's human capital, a fact-finding report of the federal Glass Ceiling Commission.* Washington, DC: U.S. Government Printing Office.

Glass, S. P., & Wright, T. L. (1992). Justifications for extramarital relationships: The association between attitudes, behavior, and gender. *Journal of Sex Research, 29,* 361–387.

Goduka, I. N. (1990). Ethics and politics of field research in South Africa. *Social Problems, 37,* 329–340.

Goff, C., & Nason-Clark, N. (1989). The seriousness of crime in Fredericton, New Brunswick: Perceptions toward white-collar crime. *Canadian Journal of Criminology, 31*(1), 19–34.

Goffman, E. (1959). *The presentation of self in everyday life.* New York: Doubleday.

Goffman, E. (1961). *Asylums: Essays on the social situation of mental patients and other inmates.* Chicago: Aldine Press.

Goffman, E. (1963). *Stigma: Notes on the management of spoiled identity.* Englewood Cliffs, NJ: Prentice-Hall.

Gold, S. J. (1992). *Refugee communities: A comparative field study.* Newbury Park, CA: Sage Publications.

Goldman, M. (1991). *What went wrong with perestroika.* New York: Norton.

Goldman, P., & Van Houten, D. R. (1977). Managerial strategies and the worker: A Marxist analysis of bureaucracy. *Sociological Quarterly, 18,* 108–125.

Goldscheider, F. K., & Waite, L. J. (1991). *New families, no families? The transformation of the American home.* Berkeley: University of California Press.

Goldstein, M. C. (1971). Stratification, polyandry, and family structure in Central Tibet. *Southwest Journal of Anthropology, 27,* 65–74.

Golombok, S., & Tasker, F. (1996). Do parents influence the sexual orientation of their children? Findings from a longitudinal study of lesbian families. *Developmental Psychology, 32,* 3–11.

Goode, E. (1992). *Collective behavior.* Fort Worth, TX: Harcourt Brace Jovanovich.

Goode, W. J. (1960). A theory of role strain. *American Sociological Review, 25,* 483–495.

Goodman, M. E. (1967). *The individual and culture.* Homewood, IL: Dorsey.

Gordon, J. S. (1984). Holistic health centers in the United States. In J. W. Salmon (Ed.), *Alternative medicines: Popular and policy perspectives.* New York: Tavistock.

Gordon, M. (1978). *The American family: Past, present, and future.* New York: Random House.

Gordon, M. M. (1964). *Assimilation in American life.* New York: Oxford University Press.

Gordon, M. M. (1978). *Human nature, class, and ethnicity.* New York: Oxford University Press.

Gordon, M. M. (1988). *The scope of sociology.* New York: Oxford University Press.

Gordon, M. T., & Riger, S. (1989). *The female fear.* New York: Free Press.

Gordon, S. (1995, February 13). Cutbacks on caregivers: Is there a nurse in the house. *The Nation,* pp. 199–202.

Gornick, M. E., Eggers, P. W., Reilly, T. W., Mentnech, R. M., Fitterman, L. K., Kucken, L. E., & Vladeck, B. C. (1996). Effects of race and income on mortality and use of services among Medicare beneficiaries. *New England Journal of Medicine, 335,* 791–799.

Gortmaker, S. L., Salter, C. A., Walker, D. K., & Dietz, W. H., Jr. (1990). The impact of television viewing on mental aptitude and achievement: A longitudinal study. *Public Opinion Quarterly, 54,* 594–604.

Gottfredson, M. R., & Hirschi, T. (1990). *A general theory of crime.* Stanford, CA: Stanford University Press.

Gottlieb, M. (1988). *Comparative economic systems: Preindustrial and modern case studies.* Ames: Iowa State University Press.

Gouldner, A. W. (1976). The dark side of the dialectic: Toward a new objectivity. *Sociological Inquiry, 46,* 3–16.

Granovetter, M. (1978). Threshold models of collective behavior. *American Journal of Sociology, 83,* 1420–1443.

Grant, J. W. (1984). *Moon of wintertime: Missionaries and the Indians of Canada in encounter since 1534.* Toronto: University of Toronto Press.

Grant, P. R. (1991). Ethnocentrism between groups of unequal power under threat in intergroup competition. *Journal of Social Psychology, 13,* 21–28.

Greeley, A. M. (1989). *Religious change in America.* Cambridge, MA: Harvard University Press.

Greeley, A. M. (1991). *Faithful attraction.* New York: Tor Books.

Green, C. (1993, April 28). Now heard in more homes: *?Como esta? Detroit Free Press,* p. 5.

Green, G. D., & Bozett, F. W. (1991). Lesbian mothers and gay fathers. In J. C. Gonsiorek & J. D. Weinrich (Eds.), *Homosexuality: Research implications for public policy.* Newbury Park, CA: Sage Publications.

Greenberg, J. R., McKibben, M., & Raymond, J. A. (1990). Dependent adult children and elder abuse. *Journal of Elder Abuse and Neglect, 2*(1/2), 73–86.

Greenfield, S., Rogers, W., Mangotich, M., Carney, M. F., & Tarlov, A. R. (1995). Outcomes of patients with hypertension and non-insulin dependent diabetes mellitus treated by different systems and specialties: Results from the medical outcomes study. *Journal of the American Medical Association, 274,* 1436–1444.

Gregg, S. A. (Ed.). (1991). *Between bands and states.* Carbondale: Southern Illinois University, Center for Archaeological Investigations.

Greider, P., Jr., Denise-Neinhaus, S., & Statham, A. (1992). Education and training as facilitating reemployment after a plant shutdown. *Sociological Practice Review, 3,* 220–228.

Greider, W. (1992). *Who will tell the people: The betrayal of American democracy.* New York: Simon & Schuster.

Gross, E., & Etzioni, A. (1985). *Organizations in society.* Englewood Cliffs, NJ: Prentice-Hall.

Gross, G. R., Cross, T. M., & Smith, J. E. (1991). *The Michigan corrections officers' stress survey: Organizational versus individual stressors.* Paper presented at the annual meeting of the Academy of Criminal Justice Sciences, Nashville, TN.

Gumperz, J. J., & Levinson, S. C. (1991). Rethinking linguistic relativity. *Current Anthropology, 32,* 613–623.

Gunther, M. (1993, June 16). Women, minorities get short end on small screen, study says. *Detroit Free Press,* pp. 1C, 3C.

Gurman, E. B., & Long, K. (1992). Gender orientation and emergent leader behavior. *Sex Roles, 27,* 391–400.

Gutek, G. L. (1993). *American education in a global society.* New York: Longman.

Gutman, B. (1976). *The black family in slavery and freedom: 1750–1925.* New York: Pantheon.

Haas, J. E., & Drabek, T. E. (1973). *Complex organizations: A sociological perspective.* New York: Macmillan.

Hadaway, C. K., Marler, P. L., & Chaves, M. (1993). What the polls don't show: A closer look at U.S. church attendance. *American Sociological Review, 58,* 741–752.

Hadden, J. K. (1993). The rise and fall of American televangelism. *Annals of the American Academy of Political and Social Science, 527,* 113–130.

Hafferty, F. W., & Light, D. W. (1995). Professional dynamics and the changing nature of medical work. *Journal of Health and Social Behavior* [Special issue], 132–153.

Hage, J., & Powers, C. H. (1992). *Post-industrial lives: Roles and relationships in the 21st century.* Newbury Park, CA: Sage Publications.

Haines, D., Rutherford, D., & Thomas, P. (1981). Family and community among Vietnamese refugees. *International Migration Review, 15,* 310–319.

Hall, E. T. (1966). *The hidden dimension.* Garden City, NY: Doubleday.

Hallin, D. (1991). TV's clean little war. *The Bulletin of Atomic Scientists, 47,* 17–19.

Hallinan, M. T. (1996). Track mobility in secondary school. *Social Forces, 74,* 983–1002.

Halloran, R. (1969). *Japan: Images and realities.* New York: Knopf.

Hamer, D., & Copeland, P. (1994). *The science of desire: The search for the gay gene and the biology of behavior.* New York: Simon & Schuster.

Harding, S. (1986). *The science question in feminism.* Ithaca, NY: Cornell University Press.

Hardoy, J. E. (Ed.). (1975). *Urbanization in Latin America.* Garden City, NY: Anchor Press.

Hare, A. P. (1976). *Handbook of small group research* (2nd ed.). New York: Free Press.

Harlan, A., & Weiss, C. (1981). *Final report from "moving up: Women in managerial careers"* (Working Paper No. 86). Wellesley, MA: Wellesley College, Center for Research on Women.

Harley, G. W. (1941). *Native African medicine: With special reference to its practice in the Mano tribe of Liberia.* Cambridge: Harvard University Press.

Harrell, S., & Dickey, S. A. (1985). Dowry systems in complex societies. *Ethnology, 24,* 105–120.

Harrington, M. (1989). *Socialism: Past and future.* New York: Arcade Publishing.

Harris, C. D., & Ullman, E. L. (1945). The nature of cities. *Annals of the American Academy of Political and Social Science, 242,* 7–17.

Harris, G. L., et al. (1962). *U.S. Army handbook for Vietnam.* Washington, DC: U.S. Government Printing Office.

Harris, M. (1977). *Cannibals and kings: The origins of cultures.* New York: Random House.

Harrison, B. (1994). *Lean and mean: The changing landscape of corporate power in the age of flexibility.* New York: BasicBooks.

Harrison, L. E. (1992). *Who prospers? How cultural values shape economic and political success.* New York: Basic Books.

Harrison, M. I. (1991). Invitation to organizational diagnosis. *Sociological Practice Review, 2,* 169–179.

Harrison, P. (1983). *The Third World tomorrow: A report from the battlefront in the war against poverty* (2nd ed.). New York: Pilgrim Press.

Harrison, W. D. (1980). Role strain and burnout in child-protective service workers. *Social Service Review, 54,* 31–44.

Hartman, C. (1994, March 7). UN group describes unemployment crisis. *Detroit Free Press,* p. 5A.

Hauser, R. M., & Featherman, D. L. (1973). Trends in the occupational mobility of U.S. men, 1962–1970. *American Sociological Review, 38,* 302–310.

Hawley, A. H. (1971). *Urban society: An ecological approach.* New York: Ronald Press.

Hawley, W. D., et al. (1983). *Strategies for effective desegregation.* Lexington, MA: Lexington Books.

Hayakawa, M. (1986). *The quality and socioeconomic status of teachers in Japan: Final report.* Aichi, Japan: Japanese National Institute of Education.

Headley, B. D. (1991). Race, class, and powerlessness in world economy. *Black Scholar, 21,* 14–21.

Heenan, D. A. (1991). *The new corporate frontier: The big move to small town, U.S.A.* New York: McGraw-Hill.

Hegstrom, J. L., & Griffith, W. I. (1992). Dominance, sex, and leader emergence. *Sex Roles, 27,* 209–220.

Heimer, K., & Matsueda, R. L. (1994). Role-taking, role commitment, and delinquency: A theory of differential social control. *American Sociological Review, 59,* 365–390.

Hemming, J. (1978). *Red gold: The conquest of the Brazilian Indians.* Cambridge: Harvard University Press.

Hemming, J. (1987). *Amazon frontier: The defeat of the Brazilian Indians.* London: Macmillan.

Hendry, J. (1995). *Understanding Japanese society* (2nd ed.). London: Routledge.

Henkin, A. B., & Nguyen, L. T. (1981). *Between two cultures: The Vietnamese in America.* Saratoga, CA: Century Twenty One Publishing.

Herman, E. S. (1993). The media's role in U.S. foreign policy. *Journal of International Affairs, 47,* 23–45.

Hero, R. E. (1992). *Latinos and the U.S. political system.* Philadelphia: Temple University Press.

Hersch, S. M. (1970). *My Lai 4.* New York: Random House.

Hertz, R. (1986). *More equal than others: Women and men in dual-career marriages.* Berkeley: University of California Press.

Hewitt, J. P. (1994). *Self and society: A symbolic interactionist social psychology* (6th ed.). Boston: Allyn & Bacon.

Heydebrand, W. (1977). Organizational contradictions in public bureaucracies: Toward a Marxian theory of organizations. *Sociological Quarterly, 18,* 83–107.

Hickey, G. C. (1964). *Village in Vietnam.* New Haven: Yale University Press.

Higginbotham, E. (1987). Employment for professional black women in the twentieth century. In C. Bose & G. Spitze (Eds.), *Ingredients for women's employment policy.* Albany: State University of New York Press.

Hirschel, J., Hutchison, I., III, & Dean, C. (1992). The failure of arrest to deter spouse abuse. *Journal of Research in Crime and Delinquency, 29,* 7–33.

Hirschi, T. (1969). *Causes of delinquency.* Berkeley: University of California Press.

Hirschman, C., & Wong, M. G. (1986). The extraordinary educational achievement of Asian-Americans: A search for historical evidence and explanations. *Social Forces, 65,* 1–27.

Hirst, L. F. (1953). *The conquest of plague: A study of the evolution of epidemiology.* Oxford: Clarendon Press.

Hoberg, G. (1992). *Pluralism by design: Environmental policy and the American regulatory state.* New York: Praeger.

Hoebel, E. A. (1972). *Anthropology: The study of man* (4th ed.). New York: McGraw-Hill.

Hoecker-Drysdale, S. (1992). *Harriet Martineau: First woman sociologist.* Oxford: Berg.

Hoffman, C., Lau, I., & Johnson, D. R. (1986). The linguistic relativity of person cognition: An English-Chinese comparison. *Journal of Personality and Social Psychology, 51,* 1097–1105.

Hofstede, G. (1980). *Culture's consequences: International differences in work related values.* Beverly Hills, CA: Sage Publications.

Hoge, D. R., & Carroll, J. W. (1978). Determinants of commitment and participation in suburban protestant churches. *Journal for the Scientific Study of Religion, 17,* 107–127.

Holden, K. C., & Smock, P. J. (1991). The economic costs of marital dissolution: Why do women bear a disproportionate cost? In W. R. Scott & J. Blake (Eds.), *Annual review of sociology: Vol. 17.* Palo Alto, CA: Annual Reviews.

Hollander, E. P. (1985). Leadership and power. In G. Lindzey & E. Aronson (Eds.), *Handbook of social psychology: Vol. 2.* New York: Random House.

Homer-Dixon, T. (1993, January 31). Destruction and death. *New York Times,* Sec. 4, p. 17.

Honey, M. (1984). *Creating Rosie the Riveter: Class, gender, and propaganda.* Amherst: University of Massachusetts Press.

Hong, L. K. (1978). Risky shift and cautious shift: Some direct evidence on the culture-value theory. *Social Psychology, 41,* 342–346.

Honig, A. S., & Park, K. J. (1993). Effects of day care on preschool sex-role development. *American Journal of Orthopsychiatry, 63,* 481–486.

Hornung, C. A., McCullough, B. C., & Sugimoto, T. (1981). Status relationships in marriage: Risk factors in spouse abuse. *Journal of Marriage and the Family, 43,* 675–692.

Horowitz, R. (1987). Community tolerance of gang violence. *Social Problems, 34,* 437–450.

Horsfield, P. G. (1984). *Religious television: The American experience.* New York: Longman.

Hostetler, J. A. (1993). *Amish society* (4th ed.). Baltimore: Johns Hopkins University Press.

Hourani, A. (1991). *A history of the Arab peoples.* Cambridge: Harvard University Press, Belknap Press.

Houseknecht, S. (1987). Voluntary childlessness. In M. B. Sussman & S. K. Steinmetz (Eds.), *Handbook of marriage and the family.* New York: Plenum Press.

Houseknecht, S. K., Vaughan, S., & Macke, A. S. (1984). Marital disruption among professional women: The timing of career and family events. *Social Problems, 31,* 273–284.

Hout, M. (1988). More universalism, less structural mobility: The American occupational structure in the 1980s. *American Journal of Sociology, 93,* 1358–1400.

Howell, E. M. (1988). Low-income persons' access to health care: NMCUES Medicaid data. *Public Health Reports, 103,* 507–514.

Hoyt, H. (1939). *The structure and growth of residential neighborhoods in American cities.* Washington, DC: U.S. Government Printing Office.

Hudson, F. M. (1991). *The adult years: Mastering the art of self-renewal.* San Francisco: Jossey-Bass.

Hugick, L. (1992a, November). 1992 presidential campaign: November. *Gallup Poll Monthly,* pp. 2–10.

Hugick, L. (1992b, June). Public opinion divided on gay rights. *Gallup Poll Monthly,* p. 3.

Hugick, L., & Leonard, J. (1991, October). Sex in America. *Gallup Poll Monthly,* pp. 60–73.

Humphreys, L. (1970). *Tearoom trade.* Chicago: Aldine Publishing.

Hunter, A., & Baumer, T. L. (1982). Street traffic, social integration, and fear of crime. *Sociological Inquiry, 52,* 122–131.

Hurn, C. J. (1992). *The limits and possibilities of schooling* (3rd ed.). Boston: Allyn & Bacon.

Hurst, C. E. (1992). *Social inequality: Forms, causes, and consequences.* Boston: Allyn & Bacon.

Hurvitz, N., & Straus, R. A. (1991). *Marriage and family therapy: A sociocognitive approach.* New York: Haworth Press.

Huston, A. C., et al. (1992). *Big world, small screen: The role of television in American society.* Lincoln: University of Nebraska Press.

Ikejiani, O. (Ed.). (1964). *Nigerian education.* Bristol, England: Longman of Nigeria.

Ilg, R. E. (1994, June). Long-term unemployment in recent recessions. *Monthly Labor Review,* pp. 12–15.

Illich, I. (1976). *Medical nemesis.* New York: Bantam Books.

Ima, K. (1982). Japanese Americans: The making of "good people." In A. G. Dworkin & R. J. Dworkin (Eds.), *The minority report* (2nd ed.). New York: Holt.

Images of fear: On the perception and reality of crime. (1985, May). *Harper's Magazine,* pp. 39–48.

Intriligator, M. D. (1993). A way to achieve national health insurance in the United States: The Medicare expansion proposal. *American Behavioral Scientist, 36,* 709–723.

Ispa, J. M., Thornburg, K. R., & Gray, M. M. (1990). Relations between early childhood care arrangements and college students' psychosocial development and academic performance. *Adolescence, 25,* 529–542.

Iutcovitch, J. M., & Iutcovitch, M. (1987). *The sociologist as consultant.* New York: Praeger.

Jacobs, J. A., & Steinberg, R. J. (1990). Compensating differentials and the male-female wage gap: Evidence from the New York State comparable worth study. *Social Forces, 69,* 439–468.

Jacobsen, J. P., & Levin, L. M. (1992). *The effects of intermittent labor force attachment on female earnings.* Paper presented at the meetings of the American Economic Association, New Orleans.

Jacobson, J. (1988). Planning the global family. In L. R. Brown et al. (Eds.), *State of the world 1988: A worldwatch report on progress toward a sustainable society.* New York: Norton.

Jaffe, H. W., et al. (1983). National case-control study of Kaposi's sarcoma and *pneumocystis carinii* pneumonia in homosexual men: 1. Epidemiological results. *Annals of Internal Medicine, 99,* 145–151.

James, J. (1977). Prostitutes and prostitution. In E. Sagarin & F. Montanino (Eds.), *Deviants: Voluntary actors in a hostile world.* Morristown, NJ: General Learning Press.

Jamieson, N. L. (1993). *Understanding Vietnam.* Berkeley: University of California Press.

Jang, S. J., & Alba, R. D. (1992). Urbanism and nontraditional opinion: A test of Fischer's subcultural theory. *Social Science Quarterly, 73,* 596–609.

Janis, I. L. (1982). *Victims of groupthink* (2nd ed.). Boston: Houghton Mifflin.

Jayakody, R., Chatters, L. M., & Taylor, R. J. (1993). Family support to single and married African American mothers: The provision of financial, emotional, and child care assistance. *Journal of Marriage and the Family, 55,* 261–276.

Jeffrey, C. R. (1967). *Criminal responsibility and mental disease.* Springfield, IL: Chas. C Thomas.

Jeffrey, P. (1993). Targeted for death: Brazil's street children. *Christian Century, 110,* 52–55.

Jencks, C. (1992). *Rethinking social policy: Race, poverty, and the underclass.* Cambridge: Harvard University Press.

Jencks, C., Smith, M., Acland, H., Bane, M. J., Cohen, D., Gintis, H., Heyns, B., & Michelson, S. (1972). *Inequality: A reassessment of the effect of family and schooling in America.* New York: Basic Books.

Jesilow, P., Pontell, H. N., & Geis, G. (1993). *Prescription for profit: How doctors defraud Medicaid.* Berkeley: University of California Press.

Johnson, A. W., & Earle, T. (1987). *The evolution of human societies: From foraging group to agrarian state.* Stanford, CA: Stanford University Press.

Johnson, C. L., Klee, L., & Schmidt, C. (1988). Conceptions of parentage and kinship among children of divorce. *American Anthropologist, 90,* 136–144.

Johnston, L. D., O'Malley, P. M., & Bachman, J. G. (1996). *National survey results on drug use from the monitoring the future study, 1975–1994: Vol. II. College students and young adults* (NIH Pub. No. 96-4027). Rockville, MD: National Institute on Drug Abuse.

Jones, E. E., Farina, A., Hastorf, A. H., Markus, H., Miller, D. T., & Scott, R. A. (1984). *Social stigma: The psychology of marked relationships.* New York: Freeman.

Jones, J. D., Vanfossen, B. E., & Ensminger, M. E. (1995). Individual and organizational predictors of high school track placement. *Sociology of Education, 68,* 287–300.

Jones, S. R. G. (1990). Worker interdependence and output: The Hawthorne studies reevaluated. *American Sociological Review, 55,* 176–190.

Josephson, W. L. (1987). Television violence and children's aggression: Testing the priming, social script, and disinhibition predictions. *Journal of Personality and Social Psychology, 53*(5), 882–890.

Joyner, C. (1978). Crabgrass and bureaucrats. *The Midwest Quarterly, 20,* 18–31.

Kagan, J., Kearsley, R. B., & Zelazo, P. R. (1978). *Infancy: Its place in human development.* Cambridge, MA: Harvard University Press.

Kahn, A. J., & Kamerman, S. B. (1987). *Child care: Facing the hard choices.* Dover, MA: Auburn House.

Kail, B. L., & Kleinman, P. H. (1985). Fear, crime, community organization, and limitations on daily routines. *Urban Affairs Quarterly, 20*(3), 400–408.

Kalinich, D. B., & Pitcher, T. (1987). *Surviving in corrections: A guide for corrections professionals* (2nd ed.). Springfield, IL: Chas. C Thomas.

Kalmijn, M. (1991). Status homogamy in the United States. *American Journal of Sociology, 97,* 496–523.

Kalmuss, S., & Straus, M. A. (1982). Wife's marital dependency and wife abuse. *Journal of Marriage and the Family, 44,* 277–286.

Kammeyer, K. C. W., & Ginn, H. (1986). *An Introduction to population.* Chicago: Dorsey.

Kanter, R. M. (1989). *When giants learn to dance.* New York: Simon & Schuster.

Kanter, R. M. (1993). *Men and women of the corporation.* New York: BasicBooks.

Kaplan, H. B. (1989). Health, disease, and the social structure. In H. P. Freeman & S. Levine (Eds.), *Handbook of medical sociology* (4th ed.). Englewood Cliffs, NJ: Prentice-Hall.

Karnow, S. (1981). *Vietnam: A history.* New York: Penguin Books.

Karp, D. A., & Yoels, W. C. (1979). *Symbols, selves, and society: Understanding interaction.* New York: Lippincott/Harper & Row.

Kasarda, J. D., & Crenshaw, E. M. (1991). Third World urbanization: Dimensions, theories, and determinants. In W. R. Scott & J. Blake (Eds.), *Annual review of sociology: Vol. 17.* Palo Alto, CA: Annual Reviews.

Katz, D., & Ryan, R. A. (1992, May 10). Symbols of success, targets of rage. *Detroit News,* Sec. B, p. 1.

Katz, M. B. (1987). *Reconstructing American education.* Cambridge, MA: Harvard University Press.

Kaufman, D. R., & Richardson, B. L. (1982). *Achievement and women: Challenging the assumptions.* New York: Free Press.

Keil, J. E., Sutherland, S. E., Knapp, R. G., & Tyroler, H. A. (1992). Does equal socioeconomic status in black and white men mean equal risk of mortality? *American Journal of Public Health, 82,* 1133–1136.

Kelling, G. W. (1975). *Language: Mirror, tool, and weapon.* Chicago: Nelson-Hall.

Kennedy, L. W. (1990). *On the borders of crime: Conflict management and criminology.* New York: Longman.

Kephart, W. M., & Jedlicka, D. (1988). *The family, society, and the individual* (6th ed.). New York: Harper & Row.

Kephart, W. M., & Zellner, W. W. (1994). *Extraordinary groups: An examination of unconventional life-styles* (5th ed.). New York: St. Martin's Press.

Kerbo, H. R., & McKinstry, J. A. (1995). *Who rules Japan? The inner circles of economic and political power.* Westport, CT: Praeger.

Kerstein, R. (1990). Stage models of gentrification: An examination. *Urban Affairs Quarterly, 25,* 620–639.

Kersten, J. (1993). Street youths, *bosozoku,* and *yakuza:* Subculture formation and societal reactions in Japan. *Crime and Delinquency, 39,* 277–295.

Kessler, R. C., House, J. S., & Turner, J. B. (1987). Unemployment and health in a community sample. *Journal of Health and Social Behavior, 28,* 51–59.

Kett, J. F. (1977). *Rites of passage: Adolescents in America, 1970 to the present.* New York: Basic Books.

Kiecolt-Glaser, J. K., et al. (1987). Marital quality, marital disruption, and immune function. *Psychosomatic Medicine, 49,* 13–34.

Kimmel, A. J., & Keefer, R. (1991). Psychological correlates of the transmission and acceptance of rumors about AIDS. *Journal of Applied Social Psychology, 21,* 1608–1628.

Kimmel, M. (1996). *Manhood in America: A cultural history.* New York: Free Press.

Kindel, S. (1990, September 4). The life and death of cities. *Financial World,* pp. 28–30.

Kirsh, B. (1983). Sex roles and language use: Implications for mental health. In V. Franks & E. D. Rothblum (Eds.), *The stereotyping of women: Its effects on mental health.* New York: Springer.

Kitano, H. H. L. (1976). *Japanese Americans* (2nd ed.). Englewood Cliffs, NJ: Prentice-Hall.

Kletzer, L. G. (1991). Job displacement, 1979–86: How blacks fared relative to whites. *Monthly Labor Review, 114,* 17–25.

Knottnerus, J. D. (1987). Status attainment research and its image of society. *American Sociological Review, 52,* 113–121.

Koenig, F. (1985). *Rumor in the marketplace: The social psychology of commercial hearsay.* Dover, MA: Auburn House.

Koentjaraningrat. (1988). The Indonesian mentality and development. *Sojourn, 3*(2), 107–133.

Kogan, N., & Wallach, M. A. (1964). *Risk-taking: A study in cognition and personality.* New York: Holt.

Kohlberg, L. (1981). *The philosophy of moral development.* New York: Harper & Row.

Kohn, M. L., & Slomczynski, K. M. (1990). *Social structure and self-direction: A comparative analysis of the United States and Poland.* Cambridge, MA: Basil Blackwell.

Kolata, G. (1995, February 28). New picture of who will get AIDS is crammed with addicts. *New York Times,* p. B6.

Konner, M. (1987, December 27). Childbearing and age. *New York Times Magazine,* pp. 22–23.

Kornhauser, W. (1966). "Power elite" or "veto groups." In R. Bendix & S. M. Lipset (Eds.), *Class, status, and power* (2nd ed.). New York: Free Press.

Kosberg, J. I. (Ed.). (1992). *Family care of the elderly: Social and cultural changes.* Newbury Park, CA: Sage Publications.

Krantz, D. S., Grunberg, N. E., & Baum, A. (1985). Health psychology. *Annual Review of Psychology, 36,* 349–384.

Kressel, N. J. (1996). *Mass hate: The global rise of genocide and terror.* New York: Plenum.

Kristof, N. D. (1993a, April 25). China's crackdown on births: A stunning and harsh success. *New York Times,* p. 1.

Kristof, N. D. (1993b, August 14). A Muslim region is tugging at the ties that bind China. *New York Times,* p. 1.

Kroeber, A. L. (1919). On the principle of order in civilization as exemplified by changes of fashion. *American Anthropologist, 21,* 235–263.

Kroeber, A. L., & Kluckhohn, C. (1952). *Culture: A critical review of concepts and definitions.* New York: Random House.

Krymkowski, D. H., & Krauze, T. K. (1992). Occupational mobility in the year 2000: Projections for American men and women. *Social Forces, 71,* 145–157.

Kumagai, F. (1996). *Unmasking Japan today: The impact of traditional values on modern Japanese society.* Westport, CT: Praeger.

Kuper, H. (1963). *A South African kingdom: The Swazi.* New York: Holt.

Kurian, G. T. (1988). Nigeria. In G. T. Kurian (Ed.), *World education encyclopedia.* New York: Facts on File.

Kurtz, R. A., & Chalfant, H. P. (1991). *The sociology of medicine and illness* (2nd ed.). Boston: Allyn & Bacon.

La Barre, W. (1964). *The peyote cult* (enlarged ed.). New York: Schocken.

Lafree, G., Drass, K. A., & O'Day, P. (1992). Race and crime in postwar America: Determinants of African-American and white rates, 1957–1988. *Criminology, 30,* 157–185.

Lanciaux, B. (1991). Ethnocentrism in U.S./Japanese trade policy negotiations. *Journal of Economic Issues, 25,* 569–580.

Lanternari, V. (1963). *The religions of the oppressed.* New York: Mentor.

Larson, C. J. (1995). Theory and applied sociology. *Journal of Applied Sociology, 12*(2), 13–29.

Lasswell, H. D. (1936). *Politics: Who gets what, when, and how.* New York: McGraw-Hill.

Latane, B., Williams, K. D., & Harkins, S. (1979). Many hands make light the work: The causes and consequences of social loafing. *Journal of Personality and Social Psychology, 37,* 822–832.

Lauer, R. H. (1991). *Perspectives on social change* (4th ed.). Boston: Allyn & Bacon.

Laumann, E. O., Gagnon, J. H., Michael, R. T., & Michaels, S. (1994). *The social organization of sexuality: Sexual practices in the United States.* Chicago: University of Chicago Press.

Lazarsfeld, P. F., & Reitz, J. G. (1989). History of applied sociology. *Sociological Practice, 7,* 43–52.

Leacock, E. (1980). Montagnais women and the Jesuit programme for colonization. In M. Etienne & E. Leacock (Eds.), *Women and colonization.* New York: Praeger.

Lear, D. (1996). Women and AIDS in Africa: A critical review. In J. Subedi & E. B. Gallagher (Eds.), *Society, health, and disease: Transcultural perspectives.* Upper Saddle River, NJ: Prentice-Hall.

Leavitt, G. C. (1992). General evolution and Durkheim's hypothesis of crime frequency: A cross-cultural test. *Sociological Quarterly, 33,* 241–263.

Lee, V. E., Brooks-Gunn, J., Schnur, E., & Liaw, F-R. (1990). Are Head Start effects sustained? A longitudinal follow-up comparison of disadvantaged children attending Head Start, no preschool, and other preschool programs. *Child Development, 61,* 495–507.

Lee, V. E., Dedrick, R. F., & Smith, J. B. (1991). The effect of the social organization of schools on teachers' efficacy and satisfaction. *Sociology of Education, 64,* 190–208.

Lehman, J. S. (1994). Updating urban policy. In S. H. Danziger, G. D. Sandefur, & D. H. Weinberg (Eds.), *Confronting poverty: Prescriptions for change.* New York & Cambridge, MA: Russell Sage Foundation & Harvard University Press.

Lemp, G. F., Hirozawa, A. M., Givertz, D., Nieri, G. N., Anderson, L., Lindegren, M. L., Janssen, R. S., & Katz, M. (1994). Seroprevalence of HIV and risk behaviors among young homosexual and bisexual men: The San Francisco/Berkeley young men's survey. *Journal of the American Medical Association, 272,* 449–454.

Lenski, G. (1966). *Power and privilege: A theory of social stratification.* New York: McGraw-Hill.

Lenski, G., Lenski, J., & Nolan, P. (1991). *Human societies: An introduction to macrosociology* (6th ed.). New York: McGraw-Hill.

Lerner, W. D., & Raczynski, J. M. (1988). The economic shaping of substance abuse. In B. A. Ray (Ed.), *Learning factors in substance abuse* (NIDA Research Monograph 84, DHHS Pub. No. (ADM) 88-1576). Rockville, MD: National Institute on Drug Abuse.

Levin, J., & McDevitt, J. (1993). *Hate crimes: The rising tide of bigotry and bloodshed.* New York: Plenum Press.

Levin, J., & Levin, W. C. (1994). *The functions of discrimination and prejudice* (2nd ed.). New York: Harper & Row.

Levine, L. (1996). *The opening of the American mind.* Boston: Beacon Press.

LeVine, R. A. (1969). Culture, personality, and socialization: An evolutionary view. In D. A. Goslin (Ed.), *Handbook of socialization theory and research.* Chicago: Rand McNally.

LeVine, S. (1993). *Dolor y alegria: Women and social change in urban Mexico.* Madison: University of Wisconsin Press.

Levine, S. (1986). *Radical departures: Desperate detours to growing up.* San Diego: Harcourt Brace Jovanovich.

Levinger, G., & Moles, O. C. (Eds.). (1979). *Divorce and separation: Context, causes and consequences.* New York: Basic Books.

Levinson, D. J. (1978). *The seasons of a man's life.* New York: Knopf.

Levinson, D. J. (1996). *The seasons of a woman's life.* New York: Alfred A. Knopf.

Levy, E. F. (1992). Strengthening the coping resources of lesbian families. *Families in Society, 73,* 23–31.

Lewin, E. (1993). *Lesbian mothers: Accounts of gender in American culture.* Ithaca, NY: Cornell University Press.

Lewin, K., Lippitt, R., & White, R. K. (1939). Patterns of aggressive behavior in experimentally created "social climates." *Journal of Social Psychology, 10,* 271–299.

Lewis, R. A. (1984). Some changes in men's values, meanings, roles, and attitudes toward marriage and family in the U.S.A. In *Social change and family policies: Part 1.* Melbourne: Australian Institute of Family Studies.

Li, D. J. (1978). *The ageless Chinese*. New York: Scribner's.

Li, V. H. (1977). Law and penology: Systems of reform and correction. In A. A. Wilson, S. L. Greenblatt, & R. W. Wilson (Eds.), *Deviance and social control in Chinese society*. New York: Praeger.

Liddell, C., & Kruger, P. (1987). Activity and social behavior in a South African township nursery: Some effects of crowding. *Merrill-Palmer Quarterly, 33*(2), 195–211.

Light, W. J. H. (1986). *Psychodynamics of alcoholism: A current synthesis*. Springfield, IL: Charles C Thomas.

Likert, R. (1967). *The human organization*. New York: McGraw-Hill.

Lincoln, J. R., Gerlach, M. L., & Ahmadjian, C. L. (1996). *Keiretsu* networks and corporate performance in Japan. *American Sociological Review, 61*, 67–88.

Lindesmith, A. R., Strauss, A. L., & Denzin, N. K. (1991). *Social psychology* (7th ed.). Englewood Cliffs, NJ: Prentice-Hall.

Lindorff, D. (1992). *Marketplace medicine: The rise of the for-profit hospital chains*. New York: Bantam Books.

Lindsey, L. L. (1997). *Gender roles: A sociological perspective* (3rd ed.). Upper Saddle River, NJ: Prentice-Hall.

Lipset, S. M. (1959). *Political man: The social bases of politics*. Garden City, NY: Anchor.

Lipset, S. M., & Bendix, R. (1959). *Social mobility in industrial society*. Berkeley: University of California Press.

Littell, F. (1962). *From state to church pluralism: A Protestant interpretation of religion in American history*. Chicago: Aldine Publishing Co.

Little, R. W. (1970). Buddy relations and combat performance. In O. S. Grusky & G. A. Miller (Eds.), *The sociology of organizations*. New York: Free Press.

Litwak, E. (1961). Models of bureaucracy which permit conflict. *American Journal of Sociology, 67*, 177–184.

Lo, C. Y. H. (1982). Theories of the state and business opposition to increased military spending. *Social Problems, 29*, 424–438.

Lofland, J. 1981. Collective behavior: The elementary forms. In M. Rosenberg & R. H. Turner (Eds.), *Social psychology: Sociological perspectives*. New York: Basic Books.

Lofland, J., & Lofland, L. H. (1995). *Analyzing social settings* (3rd ed.). Belmont, CA: Wadsworth.

Lombroso, C. (1911). *Crime: Its causes and remedies*. Boston: Little, Brown.

Lomnitz, L. (1988). The social and economic organization of a Mexican shanty town. In J. Gugler (Ed.), *The urbanization of the Third World*. New York: Oxford University Press.

London, K. A. (1990). Cohabitation, marriage, marital dissolution, and remarriage: United States, 1988. *Advance data from vital and health statistics* (No. 194). Hyattsville, MD: National Center for Health Statistics.

Longshore, D., & Prager, J. (1985). The impact of school desegregation: A situational analysis. *Annual Review of Sociology, 11*, 75–91.

Loomis, L. S., & Landale, N. S. (1994). Nonmarital cohabitation and childbearing among black and white American women. *Journal of Marriage and the Family, 56*, 949–962.

Lubman, S. B. (1969). Form and function in the Chinese criminal process. *Columbia Law Review, 69*, 535–575.

Luckmann, T. (1967). *The invisible religion*. New York: Macmillan.

Lucy, J. A., & Shweder, R. A. (1979). Whorf and his critics: Linguistic and nonlinguistic influences on color memory. *American Anthropologist, 81*, 581–615.

Luebke, B. F. (1989). Out of focus: Images of women and men in newspaper photographs. *Sex Roles, 20*(3/4), 121–133.

Luker, K. (1996). *Dubious conceptions: The politics of teenage pregnancy*. Cambridge, MA: Harvard University Press.

Lynch, F. R., & Beer, W. R. (1990). You ain't the right color, pal: White resentment of affirmative action. *Policy Review, 51*, 64–67.

Lyson, T. A., & Squires, G. D. (1993). The "lost generation" of sociologists. *Footnotes, 21*, 4–5.

MacArthur, J. R. (1992). *Second front: Censorship and propaganda in the Gulf War.* New York: Hill & Wang.

MacDonald, K., & Parke, R. (1986). Parent-child physical play: The effects of sex and age of children and parents. *Sex Roles, 15,* 367–378.

Mackie, D., & Cooper, J. (1984). Attitude polarization: Effects of group membership. *Journal of Personality and Social Psychology, 46,* 575–585.

Macklin, E. (1987). Non-traditional family forms. In M. Sussman & S. Steinmetz (Eds.), *Handbook of marriage and the family.* New York: Plenum Press.

MacLeod, J. (1987). *Ain't no makin' it: Leveled aspirations in a low income neighborhood.* Boulder, CO: Westview Press.

Maddison, A., et al. (1992). *The political economy of poverty, equity, and growth: Brazil and Mexico.* New York: Oxford University Press & World Bank.

Mageo, J. M. (1991). Samoan moral discourse and the *Loto. American Anthropologist, 93,* 405–420.

Maguire, K., & Flanagan, T. J. (Eds.). (1991). *Sourcebook of criminal justice statistics: 1990.* Washington, DC: U.S. Department of Justice, Bureau of Justice Statistics.

Malinowski, B. (1929). *The sexual life of savages in North-Western Melanesia.* New York: Harcourt.

Malinowski, B. (1954). *Magic, science, and religion and other essays.* New York: Anchor Press.

Malthus, T. R. (1960). *On population.* (G. Himmelfarb, Ed.). New York: Modern Library. (Original work published 1798)

Mansfield, P. K., Koch, P. B., Henderson, J., Vicary, J. R., Cohn, M., & Young, E. W. (1991). The job climate for women in traditionally male blue-collar occupations. *Sex Roles, 25*(1/2), 63–79.

Manton, K. G., Patrick, C. H., & Johnson, K. (1987). Health differentials between blacks and whites: Recent trends in mortality and morbidity. *Milbank Quarterly, 65* (Suppl. 1), 129–199.

Marden, C. F., Meyer, G., & Engel, M. H. (1992). *Minorities in American society* (6th ed.). New York: HarperCollins.

Marks, C. (1981). Split-labor markets and black-white relations, 1865–1920. *Phylon, 42,* 293–308.

Marks, C. (1991). The urban underclass. *Annual Review of Sociology, 17,* 445–466.

Marsh, H. W. (1991). Public, Catholic single-sex, and Catholic coeducational high schools: Their effects on achievement, affect, and behaviors. *American Journal of Education, 99,* 320–356.

Marshall, D. S. (1974). Too much sex in Mangaia. In E. Goode & R. Troiden (Eds.), *Sexual deviance and sexual deviants.* New York: Morrow.

Martin, C. L. (1990). Attitudes and expectations about children with nontraditional and traditional gender roles. *Sex Roles, 22*(3-4), 151–165.

Martin, D., & Martin, M. (1984). Selected attitudes toward marriage and family life among college students. *Family Relations, 33,* 293–300.

Martindale, M. (1991). Sexual harassment in the military: 1988. *Sociological Practice Review, 2,* 200–216.

Martinez, R., & Dukes, R. L. (1991). Ethnic and gender differences in self esteem. *Youth and Society, 22,* 318–338.

Marty, M. (1984). *Pilgrims in their own land: 500 years of religion in America.* Boston: Little, Brown.

Marx, G. T., & McAdam, D. (1994). *Collective behavior and social movements: Process and structure.* Englewood Cliffs, NJ: Prentice-Hall.

Marx, K. (1964). *Selected writings in sociology and social philosophy.* (T. B. Bottomore & M. Rubel, Eds.). Baltimore: Penguin. (Original work published 1848)

Marx, K. (1967). *Das kapital.* New York: International. (Original work published 1867–1895)

Maryanski, A., & Turner, J. H. (1992). *The social cage: Human nature and the evolution of society.* Stanford, CA: Stanford University Press.

Massey, D. S. (1987). Understanding Mexican migration to the United States. *American Journal of Sociology, 92,* 1372–1403.

Massey, D. S. (1990). American apartheid: Segregation and the making of the underclass. *American Journal of Sociology, 96,* 329–357.

Massey, D. S., & Denton, N. A. (1992). Residential segregation of Asian-origin groups in U.S. metropolitan areas. *Sociology and Social Research, 76,* 170–177.

Matras, J. (1984). *Social inequality, stratification, and mobility* (2nd ed.). Englewood Cliffs, NJ: Prentice-Hall.

Matsueda, R. L. (1992). Reflected appraisals, parental labeling, and delinquency: Specifying a symbolic interactionist theory. *American Journal of Sociology, 97,* 1577–1611.

Mauldin, W. P. (1975). Assessment of national family planning programs in developing countries. *Studies in Family Planning, 6,* 30–36.

Maume, D. J., Jr. (1991). Child-care expenditures and women's employment turnover. *Social Forces, 70,* 495–508.

Mayer, M. (1961). *The schools.* New York: Harper & Brothers.

Mayo, E. (1933). *The human problems of an industrial civilization.* New York: Macmillan.

McCall, R. B. (1988). Real men do change diapers. *Parents, 63,* 202.

McClendon, M. J. (1976). The occupational status attainment process in males and females. *American Sociological Review, 41,* 52–64.

McCoy, N. L. (1985). Innate factors in sex differences. In A. G. Sergent (Ed.), *Beyond sex roles* (2nd ed.). St. Paul, MN: West Publishing.

McCue, J. D. (1989). *The medical cost-containment crisis: Fears, opinions, and facts.* Ann Arbor, MI: Health Administration Press.

McKeown, T., Brown, R. G., & Record, R. G. (1972). An interpretation of the modern rise of population in Europe. *Population Studies, 26,* 345–382.

McKeown, T., Record, R. G., & Turner, R. D. (1975). An interpretation of the decline of mortality in England and Wales during the twentieth century. *Population Studies, 29,* 391–422.

McKinlay, J. B. (1986). A case for refocusing upstream: The political economy of illness. In P. Conrad & R. Kern (Eds.), *The sociology of health and illness: Critical perspectives* (2nd ed.). New York: St. Martin's Press.

McKinlay, J. B., & McKinlay, S. M. (1977). The questionable contribution of medical measures to the decline of mortality in the United States in the twentieth century. *Milbank Memorial Fund Quarterly/Health and Society, 55,* 405–428.

McLanahan, S., & Sandefur, G. (1994). *Growing up with a single parent: What hurts, what helps.* Cambridge, MA: Harvard University Press.

McLaren, B. J. (1996). *Understanding and using the Internet.* Minneapolis/St. Paul: West.

McPhail, C. (1971). Civil disorder participation: A critical examination of recent research. *American Sociological Review, 36,* 1058–1073.

McPhail, C. (1991). *The myth of the madding crowd.* New York: Aldine de Gruyter.

McPhail, C., & Wohlstein, R. T. (1983). Individual and collective behaviors within gatherings, demonstrations, and riots. *American Review of Sociology, 9,* 579–600.

McPherson, J. M., Popielarz, P. A., & Drobnic, S. (1992). Social networks and organizational dynamics. *American Sociological Review, 57,* 153–170.

McRae, K. D. (1990). Canada: Reflections on two conflicts. In J. V. Montville (Ed.), *Conflict and peacemaking in multiethnic societies.* Lexington, MA: Lexington Books.

Mead, G. H. (1934). *Mind, self, and society.* (C. W. Morris, Ed.). Chicago: University of Chicago Press.

Mead, M. (1950). *Sex and temperament in three primitive societies.* New York: Mentor.

Mead, M. (1961). *Coming of age in Samoa: A psychological study of primitive youth for Western civilization.* New York: Morrow Quill.

Meadows, D. H., Meadows, D. L., Randers, J., & Behrens, W. W. III. (1972). *The limits to growth.* New York: New American Library.

Melton, J. G. (1993). Another look at new religions. *Annals of the American Academy of Political and Social Science, 527,* 97–112.

Mencken, H. L. (1957). *The American language* (4th ed.). New York: Knopf.

Merton, R. K. (1949). Discrimination and the American creed. In R. M. MacIver (Ed.), *Discrimination and national welfare.* New York: Harper & Brothers.

Merton, R. K. (1968). *Social theory and social structure* (2nd ed.). New York: Free Press.

Michels, R. (1966). *Political parties.* New York: Free Press. (Original work published 1915)

Micozzi, M. S. (Ed.). (1996). *Fundamentals of complementary and alternative medicine.* New York: Churchill Livingstone.

Middleton, R. (1962). Brother-sister and father-daughter marriage in ancient Egypt. *American Sociological Review, 27,* 603–611.

Middleton, R. (1976). Regional differences in prejudice. *American Sociological Review, 41,* 94–117.

Miethe, T. D. (1995). Fear and withdrawal from urban life. *Annals of the American Academy of Political and Social Science, 539,* 14–27.

Milgram, S. (1973). *Obedience to authority: An experimental view.* New York: Harper & Row.

Milgram, S., & Toch, H. (1968). Collective behavior: Crowds and social movements. In G. Lindzey & E. Aronson (Eds.), *The handbook of social psychology: Vol. 4* (2nd ed.). Reading, MA: Addison Wesley.

Miller, A. D., & Ohlin, L. E. (1985). *Delinquency and community: Creating opportunities and controls.* Beverly Hills, CA: Sage Publications.

Miller, G. A. (1963). *Language and communication.* New York: McGraw-Hill.

Miller, J. S. (1991). Clinical sociology and mediation. In H. M. Rebach & J. G. Bruhn (Eds.), *Handbook of clinical sociology.* New York: Plenum Press.

Miller, N., & Brewer, M. (1984). *Groups in contact: The psychology of desegregation.* Orlando, FL: Academic Press.

Miller, R. H., & Luft, H. S. (1994). Managed care plans: Characteristics, growth and premium performance. In G. S. Omenn (Ed.), *Annual review of public health, Vol. 15.* Palo Alto, CA: Annual Reviews Inc.

Miller, S. C. (1969). *The unwelcome immigrant.* Berkeley: University of California Press.

Mills, C. W. (1956). *The power elite.* New York: Oxford University Press.

Mills, C. W. (1959). *The sociological imagination.* New York: Oxford University Press.

Milne, R. S., & Mauzy, D, K. (1990). *Singapore: The legacy of Lee Kuan Yew.* Boulder, CO: Westview Press.

Min, P. G. (Ed.). (1994). *Asian Americans: Contemporary trends and issues.* Thousand Oaks, CA: Sage.

Mirowsky, J., & Ross, C. E. (1989). *Social causes of psychological distress.* New York: Aldine de Gruyter.

Mol, H. (1979). The origin and function of religion: A critique of, and alternative to, Durkheim's interpretation of the religions of Australian aborigines. *Journal for the Scientific Study of Religion, 18,* 379–389.

Monaghan, P. (1993). Sociologist is jailed for refusing to testify about research subject. *Chronicle of Higher Education, 39,* 10.

Montgomery, T. S. (1982). *Revolution in El Salvador: Origins and evolution.* Boulder, CO: Westview Press.

Monti, D. J. (1991). The practice of gang research. *Sociological Practice Review, 2,* 29–39.

Moore, J. W. (1976). *Mexican Americans.* Englewood Cliffs, NJ: Prentice-Hall.

Moore, K. A., & Stief, T. M. (1991). Changes in marriage and fertility behavior: Behavior versus attitudes in young adults. *Youth and Society, 22,* 362–386.

Moore, W. E. (1974). *Social change* (2nd ed.). Englewood Cliffs, NJ: Prentice-Hall.

Moorhead, G., Ference, R., & Neck, C. P. (1991). Group decision fiascoes continue: Space shuttle Challenger and a revised groupthink framework. *Human Relations, 44,* 539–550.

Morgan, E. (1972). *The descent of women.* New York: Stein & Day.

Morgan, L. H. (1877). *Ancient society.* Chicago: H. Kerr.

Morganthau, T. (1993, August 9). America: Still a melting pot? *Newsweek,* pp. 16–23.

Moskos, C. C. (1970). *The American enlisted man.* New York: Russell Sage Foundation.

Mott, F. L. (1991). Developmental effects of infant care: The mediating role of gender and health. *Journal of Social Issues, 47*(2), 139–158.

Mowlana, H., Gerbner, G., & Schiller, H. I. (Eds.). (1992). *Triumph of the image: The media's war in the Persian Gulf—A global perspective.* Boulder, CO: Westview Press.

Mulira, J. G. (1990). The case of voodoo in New Orleans. In J. E. Holloway (Ed.), *Africanisms in American culture.* Bloomington: Indiana University Press.

Mumford, E. (1983). *Medical sociology: Patients, providers, and policies.* New York: Random House.

Mumford, E., Schlesinger, H. G., & Glass, G. V. (1982). The effects of psychological intervention on recovery from surgery and heart attacks: An analysis of the literature. *The American Journal of Public Health, 72,* 141–151.

Munnell, A. H., Tootell, G. M. B., Browne, L. E., & McEneaney, J. (1996). Mortgage lending in Boston: Interpreting HMDA data. *The American Economic Review, 28,* 25–53.

Murdock, G. P. (1934). *Our primitive contemporaries.* New York: Macmillan.

Murdock, G. P. (1967). *World ethnographic atlas.* Pittsburgh: University of Pittsburgh Press.

Murphy, J. E. (1988). Date abuse and forced intercourse among college students. In G. T. Hotaling, D. Finkelhor, J. T. Kirkpatrick, & M. A. Straus (Eds.), *Family abuse and its consequences: New directions in research.* Newbury Park, CA: Sage Publications.

Murphy, R. F. (1968). Social distance and the veil. In M. H. Fried (Ed.), *Readings in anthropology: Cultural anthropology* (2nd ed.). New York: Thomas Y. Crowell.

Murray, J. P. (1993). The developing child in a multimedia society. In G. L. Berry & J. K. Asamen (Eds.), *Children and television: Images in a changing sociocultural world.* Newbury Park, CA: Sage.

Mwangi, M. W. (1996). Gender roles portrayed in Kenyan television commercials. *Sex Roles, 34,* 205–214.

Myers, D. G., & Lamm, H. (1976). The group polarization phenomenon. *Psychological Bulletin, 83,* 602–627.

Najafizadeh, M., & Mennerick, L. A. (1990). Educational ideologies and technical development in the Third World. In M. Mtewa (Ed.), *International science and technology.* New York: St. Martin's Press.

Najjar, O. A. (1992). Between nationalism and feminism: The Palestinian answer. In J. M. Bystydzienski (Ed.), *Women transforming politics: Worldwide strategies for empowerment.* Bloomington: Indiana University Press.

National Center for Educational Statistics. (1993). *Digest of educational statistics, 1993.* Washington, DC: U.S. Government Printing Office.

National Center for Health Statistics. (1984). *Vital statistics of the United States, 1980: Vol. 2, Sec. 6. Life tables* (DHHS Publication No. (PHS) 84-1104). Washington, DC: U.S. Government Printing Office.

Neckerman, K. M., & Kirschenman, J. (1991). Hiring strategies, racial bias, and inner-city workers. *Social Problems, 38,* 433–447.

Nelson, N. (1988). How women and men get by: The sexual division of labour in a Nairobi squatter settlement. In J. Gugler (Ed.), *The urbanization of the Third World.* New York: Oxford University Press.

Nettler, G. (1974). *Explaining crime.* New York: McGraw-Hill.

Neubauer, D. E. (1967). Some conditions of democracy. *American Political Science Review, 61,* 1002–1009.

Neugarten, B. L., & Datan, N. (1973). Sociological perspectives on the life cycle. In P. B. Baltes & K. W. Schaie (Eds.), *Lifespan development psychology: Personality and socialization.* New York: Academic Press.

Newacheck, P. W. (1988). Access to ambulatory care for poor persons. *Health Services Research, 23,* 401–419.

Newcomb, T. M. (1943). *Personality and social change.* New York: Dryden Press.

Newcomb, T. M. (1958). Attitude development as a function of reference groups: The Bennington study. In E. E. Maccoby, T. M. Newcomb, & E. L. Hartley (Eds.), *Readings in social psychology* (3rd ed.). New York: Holt.

Newman, D., Amidei, N. J., Carter, B. L., Day, D., Kruvant, W. J., & Russell, J. L. (1978). *Protest, politics, and prosperity: Black Americans and white institutions, 1940–1975.* New York: Pantheon.

Newman, K. S. (1993). *Declining fortunes: The withering of the American dream.* New York: Basic Books.

Newman, O. (1972). *Defensible space.* New York: Macmillan.

Newson, L. A. (1987). *Indian survival in colonial Nicaragua.* Norman: University of Oklahoma Press.

Nielson, F. (1994). Sociobiology and sociology. *Annual Review of Sociology, 20,* 267–303.

Nieves, S. (1995). Puerto Ricans: The incredible shrinking image. *Critica: A Journal of Puerto Rican Policy and Politics, 13,* 1, 6–7.

Nigro, G. W., Hill, D. E., & Gelbein, M. E. (1988). Changes in the facial prominence of women and men over the last decade. *Psychology of Women Quarterly, 12,* 225–235.

Nimkoff, M. F. (Ed.). (1965). *Comparative family systems.* Boston: Houghton Mifflin.

Nisbet, R. A. (1969). *Social change and history.* New York: Oxford University Press.

North, L. (1986). Bitter grounds: Roots of revolt in El Salvador. In J. A. Goldstone (Ed.), *Revolutions: Theoretical, comparative, and historical studies.* San Diego: Harcourt Brace Jovanovich.

Novak, M. (1978). *The guns of Lattimer: The true story of a massacre and a trial, August 1897–March 1898.* New York: Basic Books.

Oakes, J. (1985). *Keeping track: How schools structure inequality.* New Haven, CT: Yale University Press.

O'Brien, D. J., & Fugita, S. S. (1991). *The Japanese American experience.* Bloomington: Indiana University Press.

Ogburn, W. F. (1938). The changing family. *Family, 19,* 139–143.

O'Hare, W., & Larson, J. (1991). Women in business: Where, what, and why. *American Demographics, 13,* 34–38.

O'Kelly, C. S., & Carney, L. S. (1986). *Women and men in society: Cross-cultural perspectives on gender stratification.* Belmont, CA: Wadsworth.

Oliver, D. (1955). *A Solomon Island society.* Cambridge, MA: Harvard University Press.

Oliver, M. I., & Shapiro, T. M. (1990). Wealth of a nation: A reassessment of asset inequality in America shows at least one third of households are asset-poor. *American Journal of Economics and Sociology, 49,* 129–151.

Oliver, S. C. (1968). Ecology and cultural continuity as contributing factors in the social organization of the Plains Indians. In Y. A. Cohen (Ed.), *Man in adaptation: The cultural present.* Chicago: Aldine-Atherton.

Olmos, M. F., & Paravisini-Gebert, L. (Eds.). (1997). *Sacred possessions: Vodou, santeria, obeah, and the Caribbean.* New Brunswick, NJ: Rutgers University Press.

Olsen, M. E. (1978). *The process of social organization: Power in social systems* (2nd ed.). New York: Holt.

Olzak, S. (1992). *The dynamics of ethnic competition and conflict.* Stanford, CA: Stanford University Press.

Olzak, S., & Shanahan, S. (1996). Deprivation and race riots: An extension of Spilerman's analysis. *Social Forces, 74,* 931–961.

O'Neale, L. M. (1932). *Yurok-Karok: Basket weavers.* Berkeley: University of California Press.

Orcutt, J. D., & Turner, J. B. (1993). Shocking numbers and graphic accounts: Quantified images of drug problems in the print media. *Social Problems, 40,* 190–206.

Organski, A. F. K., Kugler, J., Johnson, J. T., & Cohen, Y. (1984). *Births, deaths, and taxes: The demographic and political transitions.* Chicago: University of Chicago Press.

Ozaki, R. (1978). *The Japanese: A cultural portrait.* Tokyo: Tuttle.

Packard, R. M., & Epstein, P. (1992). Medical research on AIDS in Africa: A historical perspective. In E. Fee & D. M. Fox (Eds.), *AIDS: The making of a chronic disease.* Berkeley: University of California Press.

Padilla, F. M. (1985). *Latino ethnic consciousness: The case of Mexican Americans and Puerto Ricans in Chicago.* Notre Dame, IN: University of Notre Dame Press.

Pallas, A. M., Entwisle, D. R., Alexander, K. L., & Weinstein, P. (1990). Social structure and the development of self-esteem in young children. *Social Psychology Quarterly, 53,* 302–315.

Park, R. E., Burgess, E. W., & McKenzie, R. D. (1925). *The city*. Chicago: University of Chicago Press.

Parker, F. L., Piotrkowski, C. S., & Peay, L. (1987). Head start as a social support for mothers: The psychological benefits of involvement. *American Journal of Orthopsychiatry, 57*(2), 220–225.

Parkinson, C. N. (1962). *Parkinson's law* (2nd ed.). Boston: Houghton Mifflin.

Parsons, T. (1951). *The social system*. New York: Free Press.

Parsons, T. (1956). Suggestions for a sociological approach to the theory of organizations. *Administrative Science Quarterly, 1*, 63–85.

Parsons, T. (1959). The school class as a social system. *Harvard Educational Review, 29*, 297–318.

Parsons, T. (1971). *The system of modern societies*. Englewood Cliffs, NJ: Prentice-Hall.

Parsons, T., & White, W. (1964). The link between character and society. In T. Parsons (Ed.), *Social structure and personality*. New York: Free Press.

Pate, A. M., & Hamilton, E. E. (1992). Formal and informal deterrents to domestic violence: The Dade County spouse assault experiment. *American Sociological Review, 57*, 691–697.

Patterson, C. J. (1992). Children of lesbian and gay parents. *Child Development, 63*, 1025–1042.

Paul, J. R. (1966). *Clinical epidemiology*. Chicago: University of Chicago Press.

Pelton, L. (1978). The myth of classlessness in child abuse cases. *American Journal of Orthopsychiatry, 48*, 569–579.

Peng, S. S., & Lee, R. M. (1992). *Measuring student at-riskness by demographic characteristics*. Paper presented at the annual meeting of the American Educational Research Association, San Francisco.

Pessen, E. (1971). The egalitarian myth and the American social reality: Wealth, mobility, and equality in the "era of the common man." *American Historical Review, 76*, 989–1034.

Peter, L. J., & Hull, J. (1969). *The Peter principle*. New York: Morrow.

Petersen, W. (1975). *Population* (3rd ed.). New York: Macmillan.

Peterson, J. (1990). The challenge of comparable worth: An institutionalist view. *Journal of Economic Issues, 24*, 605–612.

Peterson, S. B., & Kroner, T. (1992). Gender biases in textbooks for introductory psychology and human development. *Psychology of Women Quarterly, 16*, 17–36.

Peterson, S. B., & Lach, M. A. (1990). Gender stereotypes in children's books: Their prevalence and influence on cognitive and affective development. *Gender and Education, 2*(2), 185–197.

Petrocelli, W., & Repa, B. K. (1992). *Sexual harassment on the job*. Berkeley, CA: Nolo Press.

Pettigrew, T. F. (1988). Integration and pluralism. In P. A. Katz & D. A. Taylor (Eds.), *Eliminating racism: Profiles in controversy*. New York: Plenum.

Phillips, G. M., & Wood, J. T. (Eds.). (1984). *Emergent issues in human decision making*. Carbondale: Southern Illinois University Press.

Phillips, U. B. (1963). *Life and labor in the old South*. Boston: Little, Brown.

Pichardo, N. A. (1988). Resource mobilization: An analysis of conflicting theoretical variations. *Sociological Quarterly, 29*, 97–110.

Pillemer, K., & Finkelhor, D. (1988). The prevalence of elder abuse: A random sample survey. *Gerontologist, 28*(1), 51–57.

Pillemer, K., & Finkelhor, D. (1989). Causes of elder abuse: Caregiver stress versus problem relatives. *American Journal of Orthopsychiatry, 59*, 179–187.

Piven, F. F., & Cloward, R. A. (1988). *Why Americans don't vote*. New York: Pantheon.

Platt, A. M. (1991). *E. Franklin Frazier reconsidered*. New Brunswick, NJ: Rutgers University Press.

Plog, F., & Bates, D. G. (1980). *Cultural anthropology* (2nd ed.). New York: Knopf.

Poindexter, S. E. (1996). *The Internet using Netscape navigator software*. Cambridge, MA: Course Technology.

Popenoe, D. (1993, April 14). Scholars should worry about the disintegration of the American family. *Chronicle of Higher Education,* Sec. A, p. 48.

Poplin, D. E. (1979). *Communities: A survey of theories and methods of research.* New York: Macmillan.

Porter, B., & Dunn, M. (1984). *The Miami riot of 1980: Crossing the bounds.* Lexington, MA: Lexington Books.

Portes, A., & Stepick, A. (1993). *City on the edge: The transformation of Miami.* Berkeley: University of California Press.

Pospisil, L. J. (1958). *Kapauku Papuans and their law.* New Haven, CT: Yale University Publications in Anthropology.

Pospisil, L. J. (1963). *The Kapauku Papuans of New Guinea.* New York: Holt.

Powell, G. N. (1993). *Women and men in management.* Newbury Park, CA: Sage Publications.

Prestowitz, C. (1989). *Trading places: How we are giving our future to Japan and how to reclaim it.* New York: Basic Books.

Proctor, R. N. (1995). *Cancer wars: How politics shapes what we know and don't know about cancer.* New York: Basic Books.

Prucha, F. P. (1985). *The Indians in American society: From the Revolutionary War to the present.* Berkeley: University of California Press.

Purcell, P., & Stewart, L. (1990). Dick and Jane in 1989. *Sex Roles, 22*(3-4), 177–185.

Putnam, R. D. (1996, Winter). The strange disappearance of civic America. *The American Prospect,* pp. 34–48.

Quinney, R. (1974). *Critique of legal order: Crime control in capitalist society.* Boston: Little, Brown.

Rabin, A. I., & Beit-Hallahmi, B. (1982). *Twenty years later: Kibbutz children grown up.* New York: Springer.

Race still divides schools, study shows. (1993, December 14). *Detroit Free Press,* p. 5.

Rankin, J. H. (1983). The family context of delinquency. *Social Problems, 30,* 466–479.

Real, M. R. (1977). *Mass-mediated culture.* Englewood Cliffs, NJ: Prentice-Hall.

Rebach, H. M. (1991). Intervention in clinical sociology. In H. M. Rebach & J. G. Bruhn (Eds.), *Handbook of clinical sociology.* New York: Plenum Press.

Rebach, H. M., & Bruhn, J. G. (1991). Clinical sociology: Defining the field. In H. M. Rebach & J. G. Bruhn (Eds.), *Handbook of clinical sociology.* New York: Plenum Press.

Reiman, J. (1996). *. . . And the poor get prison: Economic bias in American criminal justice.* Boston: Allyn & Bacon.

Reischauer, E. O. (1988). *The Japanese today.* Cambridge, MA: Harvard University Press.

Relman, A. S. (1980). The new medical-industrial complex. *New England Journal of Medicine, 303,* 963–970.

Repetto, R. (1994). *The 'second India' revisited.* Washington, DC: World Resources Institute.

Reskin, B. F., & Roos, P. A. (1990). *Job queues, gender queues: Explaining women's inroads into male occupations.* Philadelphia: Temple University Press.

Rice, B. (1982). The Hawthorne defect: Persistence of a flawed theory. *Psychology Today, 16,* 71–74.

Rich, B. (1994). *Mortgaging the Earth: The World Bank, environmental impoverishment, and the crisis of development.* Boston: Beacon Press.

Richardson, J. T. (Ed.). (1978). *Conversion careers: In and out of the new religions.* Beverly Hills, CA: Sage Publications.

Richmond-Abbott, M. (1992). *Masculine and feminine: Gender roles over the life cycle* (2nd ed.). New York: McGraw-Hill.

Riding, A. (1989). *Distant neighbors: A portrait of the Mexicans.* New York: Vintage Books.

Riesman, D. (1961). *The lonely crowd.* New Haven, CT: Yale University Press.

Rist, R. C. (1979). *Desegregated schools: Appraisals of an American experiment.* New York: Academic Press.

Ritchie, J., & Ritchie, J. (1989). Socialization and character development. In A. Howard & R. Borofsky (Eds.), *Developments in Polynesian ethnology.* Honolulu: University Press of Hawaii.

Rivkin, S. G. (1994). Residential segregation and school integration. *Sociology of Education, 67,* 279–292.

Roadburg, A. (1980). Factors precipitating fan violence: A comparison of professional soccer in Britain and North America. *British Journal of Sociology, 31,* 265–276.

Robbins, T. (1988). *Cults, converts and charisma: The sociology of new religious movements.* Newbury Park, CA: Sage Publications.

Roberts, L. W. (1991). Clinical sociology with individuals and families. In H. M. Rebach & J. G. Bruhn (Eds.), *Handbook of clinical sociology.* New York: Plenum Press.

Robertson, H. M. (1933). *Aspects of the rise of economic individualism.* London: Cambridge University Press.

Robertson, R. (1992). *Globalization: Social theory and global culture.* London: Sage Publications.

Robey, B., Rutstein, S. O., & Morris, L. (1993). The fertility decline in developing countries. *Scientific American, 269,* 60–67.

Robinson, B. E., Skeen, P., Hobson, C. F., & Herrman, M. (1982). Gay men's and women's perceptions of early family life and their relationships with parents. *Family Relations, 31,* 79–83.

Robyn, D. L., & Hadley, J. (1980). New health occupations: Nurse practitioners and physicians' assistants. In J. Feder, J. Holahan, & T. Marmor (Eds.), *National health insurance: Conflicting goals and policy choices.* Washington, DC: Urban Institute.

Roche, J. P., & Ramsbey, T. W. (1993). Premarital sexuality: A five-year follow-up study of attitudes and behavior by dating stage. *Adolescence, 28,* 67–80.

Rodriguez, O. (1978). Occupational shifts and educational upgrading in the American labor force between 1950 and 1970. *Sociology of Education, 51,* 55–67.

Roethlisberger, F. J., & Dickson, W. J. (1939). *Management and the worker.* Cambridge, MA: Harvard University Press.

Rogers, S. M., & Turner, C. F. (1991). Male-male sexual contact in the U.S.A.: Findings from five sample surveys, 1970–1990. *Journal of Sex Research, 28,* 491–519.

Rohter, L. (1993, June 13). Santeria faithful hail court ruling. *New York Times,* p. 16.

Roof, W. C. (1993). *A generation of seekers: The spiritual journeys of the baby boom generation.* San Francisco: HarperSanFrancisco.

Roof, W. C., & McKinney, W. (1987). *American mainline religion: Its changing shape and future.* New Brunswick, NJ: Rutgers University Press.

Rose, A. M. (1967). *The power structure: Political process in American society.* New York: Oxford University Press.

Rose, R. (1990). Northern Ireland: The irreducible conflict. In J. V. Montville (Ed.), *Conflict and peacemaking in multiethnic societies.* Lexington, MA: Lexington Books.

Rosen, C., & Youngs, K. M. (Eds.). (1991). *Understanding employee ownership.* Ithaca, NY: ILR Press.

Rosenberg, M., & Pearlin, L. I. (1978). Social class and self-esteem among children and adults. *American Journal of Sociology, 84*(1), 53–77.

Rosenberg, P. S. (1995). Scope of the AIDS epidemic in the United States. *Science, 270,* 1372–1375.

Rosenfeld, R. A., & Kalleberg, A. L. (1991). Gender inequality in the labor market: A cross-national perspective. *Acta Sociologica, 34,* 207–225.

Rosenhan, D. L. (1973). On being sane in insane places. *Science, 179,* 250–258.

Rosnow, R. L. (1991). Inside rumor: A personal journey. *American Psychologist, 46,* 484–496.

Rosnow, R. L., & Fine, G. A. (1976). *Rumor and gossip.* New York: Elsevier.

Ross, C. E., & Mirowsky, J. (1988). Child care and emotional adjustment to wives' employment. *Journal of Health and Social Behavior, 29,* 127–138.

Ross, M. W., Paulsen, J. A., & Stalstrom, O. W. (1988). Homosexuality and mental health: A cross-cultural review. *Journal of Homosexuality, 15,* 131–152.

Rossi, A. (1984). Gender and parenthood. *American Sociological Review, 49,* 1–19.

Rossi, P. H., Berk, R. A., & Lenihan, K. J. (1980). *Money, work, and crime: Experimental evidence.* New York: Academic Press.

Rossides, D. W. (1990). *Social stratification: The American class system in comparative perspective.* Englewood Cliffs, NJ: Prentice Hall.

Rousseau, J. J. (1950). *The social contract.* New York: Dutton. (Original work published 1762)

Ruggles, P. (1990). *Drawing the line: Alternative poverty measures and their implications for public policy.* Washington, DC: Urban Institute Press.

Russell, D. E. H. (1990). *Rape in marriage.* Bloomington: Indiana University Press.

Saad, L. (1996, January). American's religious commitment affirmed. *The Gallup Poll Monthly,* pp. 21–23.

Sacco, V. F. (1995). Media constructions of crime. *Annals of the American Academy of Political and Social Science, 539,* 141–154.

Sadker, M., & Sadker, D. (1994). *Failing at fairness: How America's schools cheat girls.* New York: Charles Scribner's.

Salmon, J. W. (1984). Introduction. In J. W. Salmon (Ed.), *Alternative medicines: Popular and policy perspectives.* New York: Tavistock.

Samuelsson, K. (1961). *Religion and economic action: A critique of Max Weber* (E. G. French, Trans.). New York: Harper Torchbooks.

Sanders, W. B. (1974). *The sociologist as detective: An introduction to research methods.* New York: Praeger.

Santino, U. (1988). The financial mafia: The illegal accumulation of wealth and the financial-industrial complex. *Contemporary Crises, 12,* 203–243.

Sapir, E. (1929). The status of linguistics as a science. *Language, 5,* 207–214.

Sapp, S. G., Harrod, W. J., & Zhao, L. J. (1996). Leadership emergence in task groups with egalitarian gender-role expectations. *Sex Roles, 34,* 65–80.

Sassen, S. (1991). *The global city: New York, London, Tokyo.* Princeton, NJ: Princeton University Press.

Saunders, B. (1991). Clinical educational sociology: Interventions for school staff. In H. M. Rebach & J. G. Bruhn (Eds.), *Handbook of clinical sociology.* New York: Plenum Press.

Savin-Williams, R. C. (1990). *Gay and lesbian youth: Expressions of identity.* New York: Hemisphere Publishing.

Saxton, L. (1980). *The individual, marriage, and the family* (4th ed.). Belmont, CA: Wadsworth.

Schaefer, R. T. (1993). *Racial and ethnic groups* (5th ed.). New York: HarperCollins.

Schear, S. (1992). AIDS in Africa. *Dissent, 39,* 397–398.

Scheff, T. (1984). *Being mentally ill* (2nd ed.). New York: Aldine Publishing Co.

Schiller, H. (1989). *The corporate takeover of public expression.* New York: Oxford University Press.

Schlegel, A., & Eloul, R. (1988). Marriage transactions: Labor, property, status. *American Anthropologist, 90,* 291–309.

Schlossberg, N. K. (1985). The adult experience. In A. G. Sargent (Ed.), *Beyond sex roles* (2nd ed.). St. Paul, MN: West Publishing Co.

Schmid, C. L. (1981). *Conflict and consensus in Switzerland.* Berkeley: University of California Press.

Schnall, P. L., & Kern, R. (1986). Hypertension in American society: An introduction to historical materialist epidemiology. In P. Conrad & R. Kern (Eds.), *The sociology of health and illness* (2nd ed.). New York: St. Martin's Press.

Shusky, E. L., & Culbert, T. P. (1967). *Introducing culture.* Englewood Cliffs, NJ: Prentice-Hall.

Schwartz, F. N. (1989). Management women and the new facts of life. *Harvard Business Review, 67,* 65–76.

Scully, D. (1994). *Men who control women's health: The miseducation of obstetrician-gynecologists.* New York: Teachers College Press.

Seccombe, K., & Amey, C. (1995). Playing by the rules and losing: Health insurance and the working poor. *Journal of Health and Social Behavior, 36,* 168–181.

Sedaitis, J. B., & Butterfield, J. (Eds.). (1991). *Perestroika from below: Social movements in the Soviet Union.* Boulder, CO: Westview Press.

See, K. O. (1986). *First world nationalisms: Class and ethnic politics in Northern Ireland and Quebec.* Chicago: University of Chicago Press.

Segal, D. R. (1974). *Society and politics.* Glenview, IL: Scott, Foresman.

Segal, D. R., Schubert, J. D., & Li, X. (1991). Establishing unit cohesion in the U.S. Army: A half-century of applied research. *Sociological Practice Review, 2,* 9–14.

Seltzer, J. A. (1994). Consequences of marriage dissolution for children. In J. Hagan & K. S. Cook (Eds.), *Annual review of sociology: Vol. 20.* Palo Alto, CA: Annual Reviews Inc.

Serrin, W. (1989). The myth of the 'new work': A great American job machine? *Nation, 249,* 269–272.

Service, E. R. (1975). *Origins of the state and civilization.* New York: Norton.

Sewell, W. H. (1971). Inequality of opportunity for higher education. *American Sociological Review, 36,* 793–808.

Shaw, M. E. (1976). *Group dynamics* (2nd ed.). New York: McGraw-Hill.

Shaw, M. E., & Costanzo, P. R. (1982). *Theories of social psychology* (2nd ed.). New York: McGraw-Hill.

Sherif, M. (1936). *The psychology of social norms.* New York: Harper & Brothers.

Sherman, L. W., & Berk, R. A. (1984). The specific deterrent effects of arrest for domestic violence. *American Sociological Review, 49,* 261–271.

Sherrill, R. (1995, January 9/16). Dangerous to your health: The madness of the market. *The Nation,* p. 45–72.

Shibutani, T. (1966). *Improvised news: A sociological study of rumor.* Indianapolis: Bobbs-Merrill.

Shibutani, T. (1978). *The derelicts of Company K.* Berkeley: University of California Press.

Shils, E. A., & Janowitz, M. (1948). Cohesion and disintegration in the Wehrmacht in World War II. *Public Opinion Quarterly, 12,* 280–315.

Shilts, R. (1987). *And the band played on: Politics, people, and the AIDS epidemic.* New York: St. Martin's Press.

Shively, J. (1992). Cowboys and Indians: Perceptions of western films among American Indians and Anglos. *American Sociological Review, 57,* 725–734.

Shostak, A. (1992). Applied sociology and the labor movement: On bargaining mutual gains. *Journal of Applied Sociology, 9,* 11–28.

Shupe, A. D., Jr., & Bromley, D. G. (1980). Walking a tightrope: Dilemmas of participant observation of groups in conflict. *Qualitative Sociology, 2,* 3–21.

Sigelman, L., Bledsoe, T., Welch, S., & Combs, M. W. (1996). Making contact? Black-white social interaction in an urban setting. *American Journal of Sociology, 101,* 1306–1332.

Sigelman, L., & Welch, S. (1993). The contact hypothesis revisited: Black-white interaction and positive racial attitudes. *Social Forces, 71,* 781–795.

Sigerist, H. E. (1977). The special position of the sick. In D. Landy (Ed.), *Culture, disease, and healing: Studies in medical anthropology.* New York: Macmillan.

Signorielli, N. (1993). Television, the portrayal of women, and children's attitudes. In G. L. Berry & J. K. Asamen (Eds.), *Children and television: Images in a changing sociocultural world.* Newbury Park, CA: Sage Publications.

Silverstein, K. (1993, June 28). The miracle runs out in Venezuela. *Nation,* pp. 904–906.

Simmons, J. L. (1969). *Deviants.* Berkeley, CA: Glendessary.

Simons, R. L., & Gray, P. A. (1989). Perceived blocked opportunity as an explanation of delinquency among lower-class black males: A research note. *Journal of Research in Crime and Delinquency, 26,* 90–101.

Simpson, G. E., & Yinger, J. M. (1985). *Racial and cultural minorities: An analysis of prejudice and discrimination* (5th ed.). New York: Plenum Press.

Simpson, J. C. (1995). Pluralism: The evolution of a nebulous concept. *American Behavioral Scientist, 38,* 459–477.

Sims, R. R. (1992). Linking groupthink to unethical behavior in organizations. *Journal of Business Ethics, 11,* 651–662.

Singer, D. G. (1993). Creativity of children in a television world. In G. L. Berry & J. K. Asamen (Eds.), *Children and television: Images in a changing sociocultural world.* Newbury Park, CA: Sage Publications.

Skocpol, T. (1986). France, Russia, China: A structural analysis of social revolutions. In J. A. Goldstone (Ed.), *Revolutions: Theoretical, comparative, and historical studies.* San Diego: Harcourt Brace Jovanovich.

Skocpol, T. (1996). *Boomerang: Clinton's health security effort and the turn against government in U.S. politics.* New York: W. W. Norton.

Skolnick, A. (1991). *Embattled paradise: The American family in an age of uncertainty.* New York: Basic Books.

Slonim, M. B. (1991). *Children, culture, and ethnicity: Evaluating and understanding the impact.* New York: Garland.

Smelser, N. J. (1963). *Theory of collective behavior.* Glencoe, IL: Free Press.

Smith, D. A. (1991). Method and theory in comparative urban studies. *International Journal of Comparative Sociology, 32,* 39–58.

Smith, D. A., & Timberlake, M. (1993). World cities: A political economy/global network approach. In R. Hutchison (Ed.), *Research in urban sociology, Vol. 3.* Greenwich, CN: JAI Press.

Smith, H. (1991). *The world's religions.* San Francisco: HarperSanFrancisco.

Smith, K. B. (1981). Class structure and intergenerational mobility from a Marxian perspective. *Sociological Quarterly, 22,* 385–401.

Smith, K. B., & Meier, K. J. (1995). *The case against school choice: Politics, markets, and fools.* Armonk NY: M. E. Sharpe.

Smith, K. B., & Stone, L. H. (1989). Rags, riches, and bootstraps: Beliefs about the causes of wealth and poverty. *Sociological Quarterly, 30*(1), 93–107.

Smith, T. W. (1990). *Adult sexual behavior in 1989.* Paper presented at the American Association for the Advancement of Science.

Smitherman, G. (1986). *Talkin and testifyin: The language of black America.* Detroit: Wayne State University Press.

Smock, P. J., & Wilson, F. D. (1991). Desegregation and the stability of white enrollments: A school-level analysis. *Sociology of Education, 64,* 278–292.

Smole, W. J. (1976). *The Yanoama Indians: A cultural geography.* Austin: University of Texas Press.

Snipp, C. M. (1989). *American Indians: The first of this land.* New York: Russell Sage Foundation.

Solorzano, D. G. (1991). Mobility aspirations among racial minorities, controlling for SES. *Sociology and Social Research, 75,* 182–188.

Sorokin, P. A. (1937). *Social and cultural dynamics.* New York: American Book.

Soule, S. A. (1992). Populism and black lynching in Georgia, 1890–1900. *Social Forces, 71,* 431–449.

Sowell, T. (1981). *Ethnic America: A history.* New York: Basic Books.

Sowell, T. (1996). *Migrations and cultures: A world view.* New York: BasicBooks.

Spade, J. Z., & Reese, C. A. (1991). We've come a long way, maybe: College students' plans for work and family. *Sex Roles, 24*(5-6), 309–321.

Speicher, B. L., & McMahon, S. M. (1992). Some African-American perspectives on black English vernacular. *Language in Society, 21,* 383–407.

Spencer, J. W., & Drass, K. A. (1989). The transformation of gender into conversational advantage: A symbolic interactionist approach. *Sociological Quarterly, 30,* 363–383.

Spilerman, S. (1976). Structural characteristics of cities and the severity of racial disorders. *American Sociological Review, 41,* 771–793.

Spitzer, K. (1992, July 5). Group may give women a fighting chance at combat. *Detroit News and Free Press,* p. 2.

Spurr, S. J. (1990). Sex discrimination in the legal profession: A study of promotion. *Industrial and Labor Relations Review, 43,* 406–417.

Stacey, J. (1990). *Brave new families: Stories of domestic upheaval in late twentieth century America.* New York: Basic Books.

Stamps, P. L., & Piedmonte, E. B. (1986). *Nurses and work satisfaction.* Ann Arbor, MI: Health Administration Press.

Stanko, E. A. (1995). Women, crime, and fear. *Annals of the American Academy of Political and Social Science, 539,* 46–58.

Stark, R. (1972). The economics of piety: Religious commitment and social class. In G. Thielbar & A. Feldman (Eds.), *Issues in Social Inequality.* Boston: Little, Brown.

Stark, R., & Bainbridge, W. S. (1979). Of churches, sects, and cults: Preliminary concepts for a theory of religious movements. *Journal for the Scientific Study of Religion, 18,* 117–131.

Steeh, C., & Schuman, H. (1992). Young white adults: Did racial attitudes change in the 1980s? *American Journal of Sociology, 98,* 340–367.

Steinberg, J. (1985). Letter from the editor, *Health/PAC Bulletin, 16,* 3.

Steiner, J. (1990). Power-sharing: Another Swiss "export product"? In J. V. Montville (Ed.), *Conflict and peacemaking in multiethnic societies.* Lexington, MA: Lexington Books.

Stets, J. E. (1991). Cohabiting and marital aggression: The role of social isolation. *Journal of Marriage and the Family, 53,* 669–680.

Stevenson, R. W. (1993, September 19). Racial tensions in London as neo-Nazi wins election. *New York Times,* p. 8.

Steward, J. H. (1955). *Theory of culture change.* Urbana: University of Illinois Press.

Stewart, J. B. (1991). *Den of thieves.* New York: Simon & Schuster.

Stokes, S. C. (1995). *Cultures in conflict: Social movements and the state in Peru.* Berkeley: University of California Press.

Stouffer, S. A., et al. (1949). *The American soldier: Combat and its aftermath.* Princeton, NJ: Princeton University Press.

Straus, M. A. (1991). Physical violence in American families: Incidence rates, causes, and trends. In D. D. Knudsen & J. L. Miller (Eds.), *Abused and battered: Social and legal responses to family violence.* New York: Aldine de Gruyter.

Straus, M., & Gelles, R. J. (1986). Societal change and change in family violence from 1975 to 1985 as revealed by two national surveys. *Journal of Marriage and the Family, 48,* 465–479.

Straus, M. A., Gelles, R. J., & Steinmetz, S. K. (1980). *Behind closed doors: A study of family violence in America.* Garden City, NY: Anchor Press.

Strauss, A., Fagerhaugh, S., Suczek, B., & Wiener, C. (1985). *The social organization of medical work.* Chicago: University of Chicago Press.

Stroman, D. F. (1979). *The quick knife: Unnecessary surgery U.S.A.* Port Washington, NY: Kennikat Press.

Stryker, S. (1990). Symbolic interactionism: Themes and variations. In M. Rosenberg & R. H. Turner (Eds.), *Social psychology: Sociological perspectives.* New Brunswick, NJ: Transaction Books.

Study finds U.S. students lag foreigners. (1996, March 24). *New York Times,* p. 18.

Sullivan, T. J. (1977). The "Critical Mass" in crowd behavior: Crowd size, contagion and the evolution of riots. *Humboldt Journal of Social Relations, 4,* 46–59.

Sullivan, T. J. (1992). *Applied sociology: Research and critical thinking.* New York: Macmillan.

Sullivan, T. J. (1997). *Introduction to social problems* (4th ed.). Boston: Allyn & Bacon.

Sumner, W. G. (1906). *Folkways.* Boston: Ginn.

Sussman, G., & Lent, J. A. (1991). *Transnational communications: Wiring the Third World.* Newbury Park, CA: Sage.

Sutherland, E. H. (1949). *White collar crime.* New York: Dryden Press.

Sutherland, E. H., & Cressey, D. R. (1978). *Criminology* (10th ed.). Philadelphia: Lippincott.

Suttles, G. D. (1968). *The social order of the slum.* Chicago: University of Chicago Press.

Suzuki, B. H. (1985). Asian-American families. In J. M. Henslin (Ed.), *Marriage and Family in a Changing Society* (2nd ed.). New York: Free Press.

Swanton, J. R. (1911). Indian tribes of the lower Mississippi valley and adjacent coast of the Gulf of Mexico. *Bureau of American Ethnology Bulletin.*

Switzer, J. Y. (1990). The impact of generic word choices: An empirical investigation of age- and sex-related differences. *Sex Roles, 22,* 69–82.

Sykes, G. M., & Cullen, F. T. (1992). *Criminology* (2nd ed.). Forth Worth, TX: Harcourt Brace Jovanovich.

Szatmary, D. P. (1980). *Shays' rebellion: The making of an agrarian insurrection.* Amherst: University of Massachusetts Press.

Taft, P., & Ross, P. (1969). American labor violence: Its causes, character, and outcome. In H. D. Graham & T. R. Gurr (Eds.), *Violence in America*. New York: Bantam Books.

Tanfer, K., & Cubbins, L. A. (1992). Coital frequency among single women: Normative constraints and situational opportunities. *Journal of Sex Research, 29,* 221–250.

Tanfer, K., & Schoorl, J. J. (1992). Premarital sexual careers and partner change. *Archives of Sexual Behavior, 21,* 41–68.

Tannen, D. (1994). *Gender and discourse.* New York: Oxford University Press.

Tavris, C. (1992). *The mismeasure of woman.* New York: Simon & Schuster.

Taylor, C. S. (1993). *Girls, gangs, women and drugs.* East Lansing: Michigan State University Press.

Teich, A. H. (Ed.). (1986). *Technology and the future* (4th ed.). New York: St. Martin's Press.

Teixeira, R. A. (1992). *The disappearing American voter.* Washington, DC: Brookings Institution.

Tepperman, L. (1975). *Social mobility in Canada.* Toronto: McGraw-Hill Ryerson.

Thio, A. (1994). *Deviant behavior* (4th ed.). New York: Harper & Row.

Thoits, P. A. (1995). Stress, coping, and social support processes: Where are we? What next? *Journal of Health and Social Behavior* [Special issue], 53–79.

Thomas, G. M., & Meyer, J. W. (1984). The Expansion of the state. *Annual Review of Sociology, 10,* 461–482.

Thomas, W. I., & Thomas, D. S. (1928). *The child in America.* New York: Knopf.

Thompson, K. S. (1980). A comparison of black and white adolescents' attitudes about having children. *Journal of Marriage and the Family, 42,* 133–140.

Thorne, B. (1993). *Gender play: Girls and boys in school.* New Brunswick, NJ: Rutgers University Press.

Thornton, A. (1985). Changing attitudes toward separation and divorce: Causes and consequences. *American Journal of Sociology, 90,* 856–872.

Thornton, A. (1989). Changing attitudes toward family issues in the United States. *Journal of Marriage and the Family, 51,* 873–893.

Thornton, R. (1987). *American Indian holocaust and survival: A population history since 1492.* Norman: University of Oklahoma Press.

Thornton, R. Y., & Endo, K. (1992). *Preventing crime in America and Japan: A comparative study.* Armonk, NY: M. E. Sharpe.

Thurman, M. D. (1982). A new interpretation of Comanche social organization. *Current Anthropology, 23,* 578–579.

Thurner, A. W. (1984). *Rebels on the range: The Michigan copper miners' strike of 1913–1914.* Lake Linden, MI: Forster.

Thurow, L. (1992). *Head to head: The coming economic battle among Japan, Europe, and America.* New York: Morrow.

Tienda, M. (1989). Puerto Ricans and the underclass debate. *Annals of the American Academy of Political and Social Science, 501,* 105–119.

Tinbergen, N. (1955). The curious behavior of the Stickleback. In *Twentieth century bestiary.* New York: Simon & Schuster.

Tjosvold, D., Andrews, I. R., & Struthers, J. T. (1992). Leadership influence: Goal interdependence and power. *Journal of Social Psychology, 132,* 39–50.

Tobin, J. N., et al. (1987). Sex bias in considering coronary bypass surgery. *Annals of Internal Medicine, 107,* 19–25.

Tönnies, F. (1963). *Community and society.* East Lansing: Michigan State University Press. (Original work published 1887)

Totti, X. F. (1987). The making of a Latino ethnic identity. *Dissent, 34,* 537–543.

Treiman, D. J., & Terrell, K. (1975). The process of status attainment in the United States and Great Britain. *American Journal of Sociology, 81,* 563–583.

Triandis, H. C. (1988). The future of pluralism revisited. In P. A. Katz & D. A. Taylor (Eds.), *Eliminating racism: Profiles in controversy.* New York: Plenum Press.

Troiden, R. R. (1989). The formation of homosexual identities. *Journal of Homosexuality, 17,* 43–73.

Trow, M. (1961). The second transformation of American secondary education. *International Journal of Comparative Sociology, 2*, 144–166.

Tseo, G. K. Y., & Ramos, E. L. (1995). Employee empowerment: Solution to a burgeoning crisis? *Challenge, 38*, 25–31.

Tuchman, B. W. (1978). *A distant mirror: The calamitous 14th century*. New York: Random House.

Tumin, M. M. (1953). Some principles of stratification: A critical review. *American Sociological Review, 18*, 387–394.

Turnbull, C. M. (1961). *The forest people*. New York: Simon & Schuster.

Turner, J., & Maryanski, A. (1979). *Functionalism*. Menlo Park, CA: Benjamin/Cummings.

Turner, J. S., & Rubinson, L. (1993). *Contemporary human sexuality*. Englewood Cliffs, NJ: Prentice-Hall.

Turner, M. E., Pratkanis, A. R., Probasco, P., & Leve, C. (1992). Threat, cohesion, and group effectiveness: Testing a social identity maintainance perspective on groupthink. *Journal of Personality and Social Psychology, 63*, 781–796.

Turner, R. H. (1964). Collective behavior. In R. E. L. Faris (Ed.), *Handbook of modern sociology*. Chicago: Rand McNally.

Turow, J. (1992). *Media systems in society*. New York: Longman.

Tyler, W. B. (1985). The organizational structure of the school. *Annual Review of Sociology, 11*, 49–73.

Tylor, S. E. B. (1958). *Primitive culture: Vol. 1*. New York: Harper Torchbooks. (Original work published 1871)

Uchitelle, L. (1989, March 26). Trade barriers and dollar swings raise appeal of factories abroad. *New York Times*, pp. 1, 13.

U-M political scientist faults voter registration laws for low turnout. (1988, March 16). *Detroit Free Press*, p. 8.

United Nations. (1991). *The world's women, 1970–1990: Trends and statistics*. (United Nations Publication No. E. 90.XVII. 3). New York: United Nations.

United Nations. (1995). *Human development report*. New York: Oxford University Press.

U.S. Advisory Board on Child Abuse and Neglect, U.S. Department of Health and Human Services. (1995). *A nation's shame: Fatal child abuse and neglect in the United States*. Washington, DC: U.S. Government Printing Office.

U.S. Bureau of the Census (1992). *Workers with low earnings: 1964 to 1990* (Current Population Reports, Series P-60, No. 178). Washington, DC: U.S. Government Printing Office.

U.S. Bureau of the Census (1993). *Poverty in the United States, 1992* (Current Population Reports, Series P-60, No. 185). Washington, DC: U.S. Government Printing Office.

U.S. Bureau of the Census (1995). *Statistical abstract of the United States, 1995*. Washington, DC: U.S. Government Printing Office.

U.S. Bureau of the Census. (1996). *Statistical abstract of the United States, 1996*. Washington, DC: U.S. Government Printing Office.

Vago, S. (1980). *Social change* (2nd ed.). New Brunswick, NJ: Prentice Hall.

Van der Dennen, J., & Falger, V. (Eds.). (1990). *Sociobiology and conflict: Evolutionary perspectives on competition, cooperation, violence, and warfare*. London: Chapman & Hall.

Van der Geest, H. (1993). Homosexuality and marriage. *Journal of Homosexuality, 24*, 115–123.

Van Evra, J. (1990). *Television and child development*. Hillsdale, NJ: Lawrence Erlbaum Associates.

Van Gennep, A. (1960). *The rites of passage*. Chicago: University of Chicago Press.

Van Horn, S. H. (1988). *Women, work, and fertility, 1900–1986*. New York: New York University Press.

Vanneman, R., & Cannon. L. W. (1987). *The American perception of class*. Philadelphia: Temple University Press.

Vannoy-Hiller, D., & Philliber, W. W. (1989). *Equal partners: Successful women in marriage*. Newbury Park, CA: Sage Publications.

Van Willigen, J., & Channa, V. C. (1991). Law, custom, and crimes against women: The problem of dowry death in India. *Human Organization, 50*, 369–377.

Veblen, T. (1912). *The theory of the leisure class*. New York: Macmillan.

Vega, W. A. (1990). Hispanic families in the 1980s: A decade of research. *Journal of Marriage and the Family, 52*, 1015–1024.

Verbrugge, L. M. (1979). Marital status and health. *Journal of Marriage and the Family, 41*, 267–285.

Verbrugge, L. M. (1983). Multiple roles and physical health of women and men. *Journal of Health and Social Behavior, 24*, 16–30.

Veum, J. R., & Gleason, P. M. (1991). Child care: Arrangements and costs. *Monthly Labor Review, 114*, 10–17.

Vigil, J. D. (1980). *From Indians to Chicanos: A sociocultural history.* St. Louis: C. V. Mosby.

Vinovskis, M. A. (1978). Angel's heads and weeping willows: Death in early America. In M. Gordon (Ed.), *The American family in social-historical perspective.* New York: Random House.

Volti, R. (1988). *Society and technological change.* New York: St. Martin's Press.

Waitzkin, H. (1991). *The politics of medical encounters: How patients and doctors deal with social problems.* New Haven, CT: Yale University Press.

Waldman, P. (1987, July 24). Motivate or alienate? Firms hire gurus to change their "cultures." *Wall Street Journal*, p. 1.

Waldron, I. (1986). Why do women live longer than men? In P. Conrad & R. Kern (Eds.), *The sociology of health and illness: Critical perspectives* (2nd ed.). New York: St. Martin's Press.

Walker, T. A. (1991). *Nicaragua: The land of Sandino.* Boulder, CO: Westview Press.

Wallace, A. F. C. (1966). *Religion: An anthropological view.* New York: Random House.

Wallace, E., & Hoebel, E. A. (1952). *The Comanches: Lords of the southern plains.* Norman: University of Oklahoma Press.

Wallerstein, I. (1979). *The capitalist world-economy.* New York: Cambridge University Press.

Wallerstein, I. (1984). *The politics of the world-economy: The states, the movements, and the civilizations.* London: Cambridge University Press.

Wallerstein, J. S., & Blakeslee, S. (1989). *Second chances: Men, women, and children a decade after divorce.* New York: Ticknor & Fields.

Wanner, R. A., & Lewis, L. S. (1978). The functional theory of stratification: A test of some structural hypotheses. *Sociological Quarterly, 19*, 414–428.

Ware, J. E., Jr., Bayliss, M. S., Rogers, W. H., Kosinski, M., & Tarlov, A. R. (1996). Differences in 4-year health outcomes for elderly and poor, chronically ill patients treated in HMO and fee-for-service systems. *Journal of the American Medical Association, 276*, 1039–1047.

Wasik, B. H., Ramey, C. T., Bryant, D. M., & Sparling, J. J. (1990). A longitudinal study of two early intervention strategies: Project CARE. *Child Development, 61*, 1682–1696.

Watson, W., Michaelsen, L. K., & Sharp, W. (1991). Member competence, group interaction, and group decision making: A longitudinal study. *Journal of Applied Psychology, 76*, 803–809.

Webb, S. L. (1991). *Step forward: Sexual harassment in the workplace.* New York: Mastermedia.

Weber, M. (1947). *Theory of social and economic organization* (A. M. Henderson & T. Parsons, Trans.). New York: Free Press (Original work published 1925)

Weber, M. (1958). *The Protestant ethic and the spirit of capitalism* (Talcott Parsons, Trans.). New York: Scribner's. (Original work published 1905)

Weber, M. (1958). *From Max Weber: Essays in sociology* (H. H. Gerth & C. Wright Mills, Eds., Trans.). New York: Oxford University Press. (Original work published 1919)

Weinrich, J. D., & Williams, W. L. (1990). Strange customs, familiar lives: Homosexualities in other cultures. In J. C. Gonsiorek & J. D. Weinrich (Eds.), *Homosexuality: Research implications for public policy.* Newbury Park, CA: Sage Publications.

Weisner, T. S., Garnier, H., & Loucky, J. (1994). Domestic tasks, gender egalitarian values, and children's gender typing in conventional and nonconventional families. *Sex Roles, 30*, 23–54.

Welles, C. (1988, February 22). What led Beech Nut down the road to disgrace. *Business Week*, pp. 124–128.

Wellman, B., Salaff, J., Dimitrova, D., Garton, L., Gulia, M., & Haythornthwaite, C. (1996). Computer networks as social networks: Collaborative work, telework, and virtual community. In J. Hagan & K. S. Cook (Eds.), *Annual review of sociology, Vol. 22*. Palo Alto, CA: Annual Reviews Inc.

Wells, L. E., & Rankin, J. H. (1991). Families and delinquency: A meta-analysis of the impact of broken homes. *Social Problems, 38,* 71–93.

West, H. G., & Fair, J. E. (1993). Development communication and popular resistance in Africa: An examination of the struggle over tradition and modernity through media. *African Studies Review, 36*(1): 91–114.

Westermann, W. L. (1955). *The slave systems of Greek and Roman antiquity*. Philadelphia: American Philosophical Society.

Wheaton, E. (1987). *Codename GREENKIL: The 1979 Greensboro killings*. Athens: University of Georgia Press.

Whitbourne, S. K., Zuschlag, M. K., Elliot, L. B., & Waterman, A. S. (1992). Psychosocial development in adulthood: A 22-year sequential study. *Journal of Personality and Social Psychology, 63,* 260–271.

Whitcomb, G. R., & Williams, E. G. (1978). Leadership and productivity in planning organizations: A case study. *Administration in Social Work, 2,* 85–94.

White, D. R., Murdock, G. P., & Scaglion, R. (1971). Natchez class and rank reconsidered. *Ethnology, 10,* 369–388.

White, R. K., & Lippitt, R. O. (1960). *Autocracy and democracy*. New York: Harper & Brothers.

White, S. (1989). Backchannels across cultures: A study of Americans and Japanese. *Language in Society, 18,* 59–76.

Whorf, B. (1956). *Language, thought, and reality*. New York: Wiley & Sons.

Whyte, W. F. (1965). *Street corner society*. Chicago: University of Chicago Press.

Widdicombe, S., & Wooffitt, R. (1995). *The language of youth subcultures: Social identity in action*. New York: Harvester Wheatsheaf.

Wilkinson, B. (1988). Social engineering in Singapore. *Journal of Contemporary Asia, 18,* 165–188.

Wilkinson, L. C., & Marrett, C. B. (Eds.). (1985). *Gender influences in classroom interaction*. Orlando, FL: Academic Press.

Williams D. R., & Collins, C. (1995). U.S. socioeconomic and racial differences in health: Patterns and explanations. *Annual Review of Sociology, 21,* 349–386.

Williams, D. R., Takeuchi, D. T. & Adair, R. K. (1992). Socioeconomic status and psychiatric disorder among blacks and whites. *Social Forces, 71,* 179–194.

Williams, J. A., Jr., Vernon, J. A., Williams, M. C., & Malecha, K. (1987). Sex role socialization in picture books: An update. *Social Science Quarterly, 68,* 148–156.

Williams, R., Jr. (1970). *American society: A sociological interpretation*. New York: Knopf.

Williams, S., & Taormina, R. J. (1992). Group polarization in business decisions in Singapore. *Journal of Social Psychology, 132,* 265–267.

Williams, T. M. (Ed.). (1986). *The impact of television: A natural experiment in three communities*. Orlando, FL: Academic Press.

Willie, C. V. (1981). *A new look at black families*. Bayside, NY: General Hall.

Wilson, B. (1982). *Religion in sociological perspective*. Oxford: Oxford University Press.

Wilson, J. (1973). *Introduction to social movements*. New York: Basic Books.

Wilson, K. L., & Zurcher, L. A. (1976). Status inconsistency and participation in social movements: An application of Goodman's hierarchical model. *Sociological Quarterly, 17,* 520–533.

Wilson, R. W. (1977). Perceptions of group structure and leadership position as an aspect of deviance and social control. In A. A. Wilson, S. L. Greenblatt, & R. W. Wilson (Eds.), *Deviance and social control in Chinese society*. New York: Praeger.

Wilson, T. C. (1993). Urbanism and kinship bonds: A test of four generalizations. *Social Forces, 71,* 703–712.

Wilson, W. J. (1987). *The truly disadvantaged: The inner city, the underclass, and public policy*. Chicago: University of Chicago Press.

Wilson, W. J. (1996). *When work disappears: The world of the new urban poor*. New York: Alfred A. Knopf.

Wiltfang, G. L., & Scarbecz, M. (1990). Social class and adolescents' self esteem: Another look. *Social Psychology Quarterly, 53,* 174–183.

Winter, J. A. (1977). *Continuities in the sociology of religion.* New York: Harper & Row.

Wirth, L. (1938). Urbanism as a way of life. *American Journal of Sociology, 44,* 8–20.

Wisensale, S. K., & Heckart, K. E. (1993). Domestic partners: A concept paper and policy discussion. *Family Relations, 42,* 199–204.

Witkin, G. (1991, August 19). The men who created crack. *U.S. News and World Report,* pp. 44–53.

Wolf, E. R. (1969). *Peasant wars of the twentieth century.* New York: Harper & Row.

Wolfe, A. (1993). *The human difference: Animals, computers, and the necessity of social science.* Berkeley: University of California Press.

Wolfe, B. L. (1994). Reform of health care for the nonelderly poor. In S. H. Danziger, G. D. Sandefur, & D. H. Weinberg (Eds.), *Confronting poverty: Prescriptions for change.* New York & Cambridge, MA: Russell Sage Foundation & Harvard University Press.

Wolff, E. N. (1995). *Top heavy: A study of the increasing inequality of wealth in America.* New York: Twentieth Century Fund.

Wolfinger, R. E., & Rosenstone, S. J. (1980). *Who votes?* New Haven, CT: Yale University Press.

Wong, K. K., & Peterson, P. E. (1986). Urban response to federal program flexibility: Politics of community development block grant. *Urban Affairs Quarterly, 21,* 293–310.

Wong, S-K. (1990). Understanding cross-national variations in occupational mobility. *American Sociological Review, 55,* 560–573.

Wood, J. L., & Jackson, M. (1982). *Social movements: Development, participation and dynamics.* Belmont, CA: Wadsworth.

Wooden, K. (1981). *The children of Jonestown.* New York: McGraw-Hill.

Worchel, S., & Shackelford, S. L. (1991). Groups under stress: The influence of group structure and environment on process and performance. *Personality and Social Psychology Bulletin, 17,* 640–647.

World Bank. (1995). *World development report 1995: Workers in an integrated world.* New York: Oxford University Press.

Wright, E. O., & Martin, B. (1987). The transformation of American class structure. *American Journal of Sociology, 93,* 1–29.

WuDunn, S. (1993, April 25). Births punished by fine, beating, or ruined home. *New York Times,* p. 6.

Yang, C. K. (1965). *Chinese Communist society: The family and the village.* Cambridge, MA: MIT Press.

Yinger, J. (1995). *Closed doors, opportunities lost: The continuing costs of housing discrimination.* New York: Russell Sage Foundation.

Yoder, J. D. (1991). Rethinking tokenism: Looking beyond the numbers. *Gender & Society, 5,* 178–192.

Young, G. (1993). Gender inequality and industrial development: The household connection. *Journal of Comparative Family Studies, 24,* 1–20.

Young, T. K. (1994). *The health of Native Americans: Toward a biocultural epidemiology.* New York: Oxford University Press.

Youniss, J. (1985). *Adolescent relations with mothers, fathers, and friends.* Chicago: University of Chicago Press.

Zablocki, B. D., & Kanter, R. M. (1976). The differentiation of life-styles. In A. Inkeles (Ed.), *Annual review of sociology: Vol. 2.* Palo Alto, CA: Annual Reviews.

Zald, M. N. (1992). Looking back to look forward: Reflections on the past and future of the resource mobilization research program. In A. D. Morris & C. M. Mueller (Eds.), *Frontiers in social movement theory.* New Haven, CT: Yale University Press.

Zand, D. E. (1974). Collateral organization: A new change strategy. *Journal of Applied Behavioral Analysis, 10,* 63–89.

Zane, J. P. (1991, December 8). In some cities, women still battle barriers to membership in all-male clubs. *New York Times,* p. 35.

Zawitz, M. W., et al. (1988). *Report of the nation on crime and justice* (2nd ed.). Washington, DC: U.S. Department of Justice, Bureau of Justice Statistics.

Zebrowitz, L. A., Tenenbaum, D. R., & Goldstein, L. H. (1991). The impact of job applicants' facial maturity, gender, and academic achievement on hiring recommendations. *Journal of Applied Social Psychology, 21,* 525–548.

Zey-Ferrell, M. (1981). Criticisms of the dominant perspective on organizations. *Sociological Quarterly, 22,* 181–205.

Zigler, E., & Muenchow, S. (1992). *Head start: The inside story of America's most successful educational experiment.* New York: Basic Books.

Zill N., & Nord, C. W. (1994). *Running in place: How American families are faring in a changing economy and an individualistic society.* Washington, DC: Child Trends, Inc.

Zimbardo, P. G. (1973). A field experiment in auto shaping. In C. Ward (Ed.), *Vandalism.* New York: Van Nostrand Reinhold.

Zinn, M. B., & Eitzen, D. S. (1990). *Diversity in families* (2nd ed.). New York: HarperCollins.

Zippay, A. (1991). *From middle income to poor: Downward mobility among displaced steelworkers.* New York: Praeger.

Photo Credits

Name Index

Davenport, W. H., 153
Davidson, J. K., Sr., 311
Davies, J. C., 530, 531
Davis, J. A., 185, 195, 387, 508
Davis, K., 80, 188, 189, 190, 193
Day, J. V., 131
Day, R. A., 131
Dean, C., 159
DeBose, C. E., 51
Deckhard, B., 273
Dedrick, R. F., 422
Deeb, M-J., 383
Deegan, M. J., 29
Dees, M., 518
Delattre, E. J., 157
Demers, D. P., 430, 431
Demo, D. H., 92
DeMott, B., 215
Denise-Neinhaus, S., 461
Dentler, R. A., 520
Denton, N. A., 227, 251
Denzin, N. K., 49, 83
Devine, J. A., 148, 199, 204
Devins, R. M., 458
DeVita, P. R., 73
Diaz, B., 478
Dickey, S. A., 294
Dickson, W. J., 26, 127
Dietz, W. H., Jr., 428
DiFazio, W., 458
DiMatteo, M. R., 357
DiNicola, D. D., 357
Dion, S., 230, 231
DiPietro, J. A., 89
DiPrete, T. A., 209
Disch, E., 279
Doig, S. K., 227
Dollard, J., 527
Domhoff, G. W., 251, 437, 453, 474
Doob, C. B., 223
Dorr, A., 320
Doubleday, C., 320
Dougherty, J. P., 386
Doyle, J. A., 284
Drabek, T. E., 120, 126
Drass, K. A., 148, 261
Dreier, P., 430, 431
Drobnic, S., 116
Du Bois, W. E. B., 29
Duke, J. T., 16
Dukes, R. L., 224, 263
Duncan, G. J., 459
Duncan, O. D., 209
Dunford, F., 159
Dunlop, J. B., 538
Dunn, F. L., 336
Dunn, M., 520, 521
Dunphy, D. C., 110
Durand, A. M., 351
Durkheim, E., 147, 371, 372, 377, 378, 379, 532, 549
Dusek, J. B., 415
Dutton, D. B., 348
Dye, T. R., 452, 453
Dynes, R. R., 36

Eagly, A. H., 118
Earle, T., 63

Earley, P. C., 133
Early, J. D., 108
Easterlin, R. A., 24, 48
Eastland, T., 245
Ebel, R. H., 188
Eckholm, E., 361
Edwards, M., 454
Edwards, W. F., 51
Ehrlich, A. H., 487, 513
Ehrlich, P. R., 487, 513
Eisenberg, D. M., 348
Eisenhower, D. D., 453
Eitzen, D. S., 177, 304
Elkin, F., 104
Elliot, L. B., 86
Elliott, D., 159
Ellis, G. J., 86
Eloul, R., 293, 294
Emmons, R. J., 509
Endo, K., 171
Engel, M. H., 220
Engels, F., 440
Engerman, S. L., 304
England, P., 275
Ensminger, M. E., 415
Entwisle, D. R., 224, 245
Epstein, P., 344
Ergil, K. V., 346
Erikson, E. H., 84, 85, 86, 94, 98
Erikson, K. T., 161, 177
Eshleman, J. R., 294
Estevez, E., 242
Etzioni, A., 4, 5, 73, 122, 124
Evans, E. D., 69

Fadlallah, M. H., 383
Fagerhaugh, S., 131
Fagerlind, I., 405, 408
Fair, J. E., 537
Fairbanks, J. K., 165
Falger, V., 79
Fallows, J., 450, 474
Faludi, S., 284
Falwell, J., 392
Farb, P., 182, 226, 291, 477, 478
Faris, J. H., 121
Farley, J. E., 246, 247
Farrag, A., 163
Fausto-Sterling, A., 257
Fay, Brian, 27
Feagin, J. R., 244, 245, 262
Featherman, D. L., 208, 209
Fein, M., 96, 104
Feinberg, R. E., 406
Feinberg, W., 409, 424
Feldman, R., 362
Felson, M., 149
Felson, R. B., 427
Ference, R., 120
Fernald, A., 94
Fernandez-Kelly, M. P., 55, 275
Ferree, M. M., 263, 266
Fiedler, F. E., 116, 117
Fijnaut, C., 158
Fine, G. A., 56, 73, 131, 519, 523
Finkelhor, D., 318, 319
Finn, C. E., Jr., 417, 419
Finnan, C. R., 309

Fiorentine, R., 277
Fischer, C., 500
Fishbein, D. H., 146
Fisher, C. R., 355
Fisher, H. E., 326
Fishman, M., 173
Fitzpatrick, J. P., 235
Flacks, R., 99
Flanagan, T. J., 166
Fost, D., 237
Foster, G. M., 344
Foster, M. W., 39
Fowler-Salamini, H., 54
Fox, T. G., 208
Fraiberg, S., 88
Frankel, L., 36
Frankl, R., 392
Frazier, E. F., 29
Freedman, J. L., 487
Freeman, D., 76
Freeman, H. E., 36
Freeman, R. B., 202
Freidson, E., 349
Freud, S., 91, 527
Freudenheim, M., 276, 361
Freund, P., 210
Friedan, B., 273
Friedman, L. M., 177
Fritz, J. M., 32
Frohock, F. M., 367
Fruzzetti, L. M., 294
Fuentes, A., 268, 271
Fugita, S. S., 238, 251
Funk, R. B., 114
Furstenberg, F. F., Jr., 291, 303, 304, 313

Gaddy, G. D., 428
Gaede, S., 387
Gage, M. G., 93
Gagnon, J. H., 310
Gallagher, T. J., 97
Gans, H. J., 215, 436, 499, 500, 513
Garber, D. M., 264
Garnier, H., 262
Garreau, J., 513
Garrett, W. R., 298
Gash, L., 535
Gastil, R. D., 260
Gautama, S., 376
Geertz, C., 42, 372
Geis, G., 360
Gelbein, M. E., 429
Gelles, R. J., 297, 317, 318
George, S., 463, 464
Gerbner, G., 468
Gerdes, E. P., 264
Gerlach, M. L., 451
Giacolone, R. A., 73
Gibbs, N., 396
Gibson, R. M., 355
Giele, J. Z., 257
Gilbert, D. A., 195
Gilder, G., 137
Gilligan, C., 97, 105
Gillmor, D., 227
Ginn, H., 484
Gintis, H., 414
Giroux, H. A., 417
Gladney, D. C., 382
Glantz, K., 141

Glass, G. V., 357
Glass, S. P., 310
Gleason, P. M., 88
Goduka, I. N., 30, 31
Goetz, B., 508
Goff, C., 159
Goffman, E., 61, 73, 99, 141, 146
Gold, S. J., 309
Goldman, M., 539
Goldman, P., 130
Goldscheider, F. K., 304
Goldsmith, E., 474
Goldstein, L. H., 265
Goldstein, M. C., 291
Golombok, S., 316
Goode, E., 516, 525
Goode, W. J., 62
Goodman, M. E., 43
Gorbachev, M., 538, 539
Gordon, A. J., 141
Gordon, J. S., 347
Gordon, M., 293
Gordon, M. M., 27, 228, 243
Gordon, M. T., 508
Gordon, S., 357
Gorelick, S., 413
Gornick, M. E., 340, 342
Gortmaker, S. L., 428
Gottfredson, M. R., 146
Gottlieb, M., 448
Gottschalk, P., 199
Gouldner, A. W., 27
Grady, W. R., 310
Granovetter, M., 528
Grant, J. W., 253
Grant, P. R., 56
Grasmick, H. G., 177
Gray, M. M., 89
Gray, P. A., 148
Greeley, A. M., 310, 387
Green, C., 243
Green, G. D., 316
Greenberg, J. R., 319
Greene, R., 507
Greenfield, S., 361
Gregg, S. A., 63
Greider, P., Jr., 461
Greider, W., 453
Griffith, W. I., 118
Grimes, P., 192, 463, 535
Gross, E., 124
Gross, G. R., 65
Grunberg, N. E., 62
Guillemin, J., 237
Gumperz, J. J., 50
Gunther, M., 263, 429
Gurman, E. B., 118
Gutek, G. L., 406, 410, 424
Gutenberg, J., 425
Gutman, B., 304

Haas, J. E., 120, 126
Habenstein, R. W., 290
Habermas, J., 533
Hadaway, C. K., 387
Haddad, Y. Y., 401
Hadden, J. K., 392
Hadley, J., 351
Hafferty, F. W., 350
Hage, J., 541
Haines, D., 309

Hall, E. T., 48
Hall, E. J., 263
Hallin, D., 468
Hallinan, M. T., 415
Halloran, R., 111
Hamer, D., 310
Hamilton, E. E., 159
Hammer, T. J., 105
Hammond, P. E., 401
Handel, G., 104
Hanson, P. G., 247
Harding, S., 27
Hardoy, J. E., 478
Hare, A. P., 114
Harkins, S., 132
Harlan, A., 276
Harley, G. W., 344
Harmon, B., 237
Harrell, S., 294
Harrington, M., 449
Harris, C. D., 502, 503
Harris, G. L., 308
Harris, L., 237
Harris, M., 73, 145
Harrison, B., 451, 460
Harrison, L. E., 463
Harrison, M. I., 126, 422
Harrison, P., 496
Harrison, W. D., 65
Harrod, W. J., 118
Hartman, C., 464
Hauser, R. M., 208, 209
Hawley, A. H., 491, 504
Hawley, W. D., 246, 420
Hayakawa, M., 424
Headley, B. D., 150
Heckart, K. E., 313
Heenan, D. A., 493
Hegstrom, J. L., 118
Heilbroner, R., 474
Heimer, K., 151
Hemming, J., 218, 403, 404
Hendry, J., 171
Henkin, A. B., 308
Herman, E. S., 431
Herrman, M., 310
Hersch, S. M., 119
Hertz, R., 312
Hewitt, J. P., 17
Heydebrand, W., 130
Hickey, G. C., 308
Higginbotham, E., 268
Hill, A., 278
Hill, D. E., 429
Hill, J. W., 361
Hill, R. B., 326
Hirschel, J., 159
Hirschi, T., 13, 146, 147
Hirschman, C., 238
Hirst, L. F., 330
Hitler, A., 442, 445
Hoberg, G., 453
Hobson, C. F., 310
Hoebel, E. A., 39, 72
Hoecker-Drysdale, S., 29
Hoffer, T., 419
Hoffman, C., 50
Hofstede, G., 132, 133
Hoge, D. R., 386
Holden, K. C., 303
Holland, P. B., 419
Hollander, E. P., 116
Holzer, H. J., 202
Homer-Dixon, T., 487

Subject Index

Generalized other, 83–84
Generational mobility, 208
Genocide, 218–219, 225–226
Gentrification, 506–507
Germany, 226–227, 445
Geronticide, 145
Gesellschaft, 66-67, 110
Ghost Dance Movement, 384–385
Global perspective, 6–9
    on cities, 494–498
    on corporations, 456, 460–462, 464–465
    on crime, 170–172
    on economic concentration and
        inequality, 191–193, 456, 458–467
    on the economy, 191–193, 439–440,
        458–467
    on education, 404–409, 417–418
    on the family, 308–309, 317
    on the feminist movement, 272–273
    on gender stratification, 271–273,
        274–275, 408–409
    on health and health care, 339–348,
        362–363
    on the mass media, 19–20, 425–426, 432–433
    on population growth, 482–490
    on postindustrial society, 67, 541–542
    on poverty, 201–202
    on religion, 369–377
    on social stratification, 188–189,
        192–194, 196–197, 274–275
    on work and labor, 458–460, 541–542
Government, 443–449. See also Democracy;
    Oligarchy; Totalitarianism
Group polarization, 118–119
Groups, 62–63, 110
    boundary maintenance in, 112–113
    conformity in, 115–116, 119–120, 128
    decision making in, 118–119
    experimental and control, 24–25
    functions of, 110–114
    gender and, 117–118
    leadership in, 115–118
    mass media and, 135–137
    types of, 110–114
Groupthink, 119–120, 126
Gulf War. See Persian Gulf War

Hawthorne effect, 26–27
Head Start, 207, 420
Healers, 345–347, 349–351
Health
    divorce and, 303
    gender and, 64–65, 340–342
    global perspective on, 342–348, 362–363
    lifestyle and, 336–339, 342, 343
    race and, 235, 237, 342
    social structure and, 62, 64–65, 339–342
    societal development and, 330, 336–339
    socioeconomic status and, 210–211, 348
    sociological perspectives on, 331–333
Health care
    access to, 356–357
    corporatization of, 351–354, 361–362
    cost of, 354–356, 361
    cross-cultural perspective on, 342–348
    financing, 359–363
    gender in, 349–350, 357–359
    minorities and, 349
    quality of, 339, 357
    right vs. privilege, 362–363
    seeking, 211, 348–349
    social structure of, 348–354
    socioeconomic status and, 339
    sociological perspectives on, 331–333

Health insurance, 359–363
Health maintenance organizations (HMOs),
    361–362
Heredity and the environment, 78–80
Hidden curriculum, 412
Hinduism, 186, 229, 294, 375–378
Hispanic Americans, 22, 233–236. See also
    Minority groups
    discrimination against, 241–242
    education and, 418
    family and, 305–306
    health and, 349
    poverty and, 235–236
Hizballah (Party of God), 383
Holistic medicine, 347–348
Homicide, 156, 170–171
Homogamy, 298–300
Homosexuality, 23–24, 316
    AIDS and, 334–335, 343
    attitudes toward, 310–311
    causes of, 310–311
    discrimination against, 311, 316
    incidence of, 310–311
Hopi Indians, 50
Horizontal mobility, 207–208
Horticultural societies, 63–65, 108–109,
    110, 191
Hospitals, 351–354
Human ecology, 478
Human relations approach, 125–128,
    130–131
Hunting and gathering societies, 63, 99,
    108–109, 110, 191, 260, 336, 343–344
Huron Indians, 253–256, 291
Hypotheses, 13–14
Hysterectomies, 358–359

Ideal type, 122
Illiteracy, 271, 406, 408, 425
Illness. See Disease; Health; Mental illness
Imitation, 83
Immigrants, 240–242, 308–309
Immigration, 237–242, 481
Immigration and Naturalization Service, 240
Impression management, 61–62
Incas, 478
Incest, 290
Income
    distribution of, 199–202
    education and, 411–412
    gender and, 266–269
    by race and ethnicity, 233, 236–237
    religion and, 389
Independent variable, 13–14, 24–26
India, 186–187, 229, 294–295, 378, 406
Indian Citizenship Act, 236
Indian Civil Rights Act, 236
Indians. See also American Indians
    of Brazil, 217–219, 403–404
    of Canada, 253–256
    of Mexico, 477–478
Individualism, 4–5, 40–41, 43–44, 67, 69, 91,
    132–133, 171, 451
Industrialization
    cities and, 491–492
    crime and, 147
    education and, 406–409, 415–416
    the family and, 296, 316–317
    gender and, 257–259, 408–409
    health and, 336–339, 342
    preindustrialized society compared
        with, 66–67
    social change and, 535–536
    socialization and, 99

social stratification and, 191–192, 209, 516
    social structure and, 110
Inequality. See Social inequality
Infanticide, 291, 489
Infant mortality, 336–339, 341, 482
Informal structure of organizations,
    127–129, 131
Informed consent, 28, 30–31
In-group, 112–113
Innovation, 52–53, 148–149
Instincts, 78–79
Institutionalization of social movements, 530
Institutionalized behavior, 517–518
Institutionalized discrimination, 223, 224
Institutionalized racism, 223
Instrumental roles. See Task roles
Integration, 245–246, 420–421
Interactionist perspective, 14, 17–19, 21
    on crime and deviance, 150–152, 169
    on education, 414–415
    on gender, 260–261
    on groups and organizations, 111, 131
    on health and health care, 333
    on mass media, 20, 169, 242, 468
    on political and economic institutions,
        468–470
    on socialization, 81–86, 94–95
Interest groups, 17
Intergenerational mobility, 208
Internal colonialism, 223
Internalization, 49
International Monetary Fund (IMF), 197,
    463–465, 467, 540
Internet, 52, 135–137, 432, 547–555
Interviews, 23–24
Intragenerational mobility, 208
Inuit, 50, 145, 228
Invasion, 501
Ireland, 229
Irish Republican Army, 229
Iron law of oligarchy, 132–133
Iroquois Indians, 291
Islam, 272, 375, 381–383, 393–394
Isolation, 80–81
Israel, 90–91

Japan
    child rearing in, 94–95
    competition in, 450–451
    crime in, 170–172
    education in, 424
    family in, 171–172, 240
    friendship in, 111
    religion in, 171
    values in, 45–46, 450–451
Japanese Americans, 238, 240, 306. See also
    Minority groups
Jesuit missionaries, 218–219, 254–255,
    403–404
Judaism, 374, 377, 379, 387
Juvenile delinquency. See Delinquency

Kaingang Indians of Brazil, 218
Kapauku Papuans of New Guinea, 52, 163
Kayapo Indians of Brazil, 218
Keiretsu, 450–451
Kenya, 496–497
Kibbutz, 90–91
Kinship, 288–290. See also Family
Koran, 272
Korean War, 121, 128
Krishna Consciousness, 381
Kubu of Sumatra, 333–335

Third-World nations *(cont.)*
  modernization in, 535–539
  poverty in, 274–275, 496–497
  slums in, 496–497
  stratification in, 196–197, 274–275
  women in, 54–55, 274–275, 497
Tibet, 290
Tiv of Africa, 439–440
Toda of India, 290
Total institutions, 99–100
Totalitarianism, 444–445
Totemism, 372
Tracking, 415
Tradition, 10–11, 45
Traditional authority, 442
Treaty of Guadalupe Hidalgo, 235
Trobriand Islanders, 56, 287–288
Truk Islands, 153
Tuareg of Saharan Africa, 6

Underclass, 204–205, 244
Unemployment, 226–227, 237, 342,
  458–459, 464–465
Unification Church, 382
Unions, labor, 456–458, 460
United Farm Workers, 235
United Nations Commission on
  Women, 273
Universities and colleges, 23–24, 44,
  113–114, 264–265, 421, 423
Urban ecology, 501–503
Urban-free enterprise zones, 506
Urbanism, perspectives on, 498–500.
  See also Cities
Urbanization, 295–296, 490–498.
  See also Cities
Urban planning, 507–509
Urban problems. *See* Cities
Urban processes, 501
Urban renewal, 504–505
Urban structures, 501–503
Urban subcultures, 500

Values
  Amish, 47
  Chinese, 132–133, 144, 306, 450–451, 489
  Japanese, 45–46, 94–95, 306

  in organizations, 132–133
  population and, 487–488, 489
  Samoan, 75–77
  in scientific research, 12, 27
  United States mainstream, 43–45, 144
  of university students, 23–24
Variables, 13–14, 24–26
Venezuela, 196–197
Verification of theories, 14
Vertical mobility, 207–208. *See also*
  Social mobility
Veterans Administration, 492–493
Vietcong, 119, 121, 308
Vietnamese, 308–309
Vietnam War, 119, 121, 469
Violence, 156–157
  ethnic, 226–227
  in the family, 317–319
  labor and, 515–516
  mass media and, 90–91, 427–428
  sources of, 520–521
  sports and, 529
  women and, 158–159, 294–295, 297, 489
Violent crime. *See* Crime
Voodoo, 344–345, 369–371
Voting, 446–448, 453
Voting Rights Act of 1965, 233
Vouchers, for school choice, 419

War, 119, 121. *See also* Violence
War on drugs, 305
WASPs, 243
Wealth, 183–184
Welfare, 10
White-collar crime, 158–161
White flight, 246
Women. *See also* Gender; Gender inequality
  abuse of, 158–159, 294–295, 297,
    317–319, 489
  adult life stages of, 97
  in business, 129–130, 276–278
  divorce and, 303
  education and, 264–265, 271
  employment of, 97, 260, 264–267, 271,
    276–278, 294–295, 311, 408–409
  empowerment of, 278–279
  in the family, 97, 314–316

  in female-headed families, 200–201,
    203, 272
  in health care, 340–342, 349–350, 357–359
  income and, 266–269
  in industrial societies, 257–259
  mass media and, 20, 263, 429
  in the military, 268–269
  in organizations, 129–130
  politics and, 271, 278–280
  poverty and, 200–201, 203, 268
  in preindustrial societies, 52,
    253–256, 257
  rape and, 156–157, 166
  religion and, 379
  retirement and, 270
  role strain and, 64–65
  sexuality and, 254–256
  in Third-World nations, 54–55, 274–275,
    489–490, 497
Women's Movement. *See* Feminist movement
Work. *See also* Employment
  education and, 412–414
  ethic, 44, 240
  in postindustrial societies, 134–135,
    457–458, 464–465
  women and, 264–267, 271, 276–279,
    408–409
Worker dislocation, 458–460
World Bank, 196–197, 463–465, 540
World-system theory, 192–194, 196–197,
    227, 406, 461–464, 466–467, 496–498,
    535–536
World Trade Organization (WTO),
    463–464, 542
World War II, 121, 238, 242, 538
World Wide Web (WWW), 135–136

Yakuza, 172
Yanomamo, 107–111, 219
Yoruba of Nigeria, 370, 410–411
Yoruk society, 404
Youth, 69, 156, 224, 409–410
Yugoslavia, 226–227

Zaire, 43, 344–345
Zuni Indians, 50